HALSBURY'S
Laws of England

FIFTH EDITION
2014

Volume 41

This is volume 41 of the Fifth Edition of Halsbury's Laws of England, containing the third part of the title EMPLOYMENT.

The title EMPLOYMENT replaces the EMPLOYMENT title contained in volumes 39 (2009), 40 (2009), 41 (2009).

Volumes 39 (2009), 40 (2009), 41 (2009) may now be archived.

For a full list of volumes comprised in a current set of Halsbury's Laws of England please see overleaf.

Fifth Edition volumes:

1 (2008), 2 (2008), 3 (2011), 4 (2011), 5 (2013), 6 (2011), 7 (2008), 8 (2010), 9 (2012), 10 (2012), 11 (2009), 12 (2009), 13 (2009), 14 (2009), 15 (2009), 16 (2011), 17 (2011), 18 (2009), 19 (2011), 20 (2014), 21 (2011), 22 (2012), 23 (2013), 24 (2010), 25 (2010), 26 (2010), 27 (2010), 28 (2010), 30 (2012), 31 (2012), 32 (2012), 33 (2013), 34 (2011), 35 (2011), 36 (2011), 37 (2013), 38 (2013), 38A (2013), 39 (2014), 40 (2014), 41 (2014), 41A (2014), 42 (2011), 43 (2011), 44 (2011), 45 (2010), 46 (2010), 47 (2014), 47A (2014), 48 (2008), 49 (2008), 50 (2008), 51 (2013), 52 (2014), 53 (2014), 54 (2008), 55 (2012), 56 (2011), 57 (2012), 58 (2014), 58A (2014), 59 (2014), 59A (2014), 60 (2011), 61 (2010), 62 (2012), 63 (2012), 64 (2012), 65 (2008), 66 (2009), 67 (2008), 68 (2008), 69 (2009), 70 (2012), 71 (2013), 72 (2009), 73 (2009), 74 (2011), 75 (2013), 76 (2013), 77 (2010), 78 (2010), 79 (2014), 80 (2013), 81 (2010), 82 (2010), 83 (2010), 84 (2013), 84A (2013), 85 (2012), 86 (2013), 87 (2012), 88 (2012), 88A (2013), 89 (2011), 90 (2011), 91 (2012), 92 (2010), 93 (2008), 94 (2008), 95 (2013), 96 (2012), 97 (2010), 97A (2014), 98 (2013), 99 (2012), 100 (2009), 101 (2009), 102 (2010), 103 (2010), 104 (2014)

Fourth Edition volumes (bold figures represent reissues):

12(1)

Additional Materials:

Sentencing and Disposition of Offenders (*Release and Recall of Prisoners*) containing vol **92** (2010) paras 761–820; *Tort* (*Conversion and Wrongful Interference with Goods*) containing vol **45**(2) (Reissue) paras 542–686

Fourth and Fifth Edition volumes:

2014 Consolidated Index (A–E), 2014 Consolidated Index (F–O), 2014 Consolidated Index (P–Z), 2015 Consolidated Table of Statutes, 2015 Consolidated Table of Statutory Instruments, etc, 2014 Consolidated Table of Cases (A–G), 2014 Consolidated Table of Cases (H–Q), 2014 Consolidated Table of Cases (R–Z, ECJ Cases)

Updating and ancillary materials:

2014 Annual Cumulative Supplement; Monthly Current Service; Annual Abridgments 1974–2013

November 2014

HALSBURY'S
Laws of England

Volume 41

2014

 LexisNexis®

Members of the LexisNexis Group worldwide

United Kingdom	LexisNexis, a Division of Reed Elsevier (UK) Ltd, Lexis House, 30 Farringdon Street, LONDON, EC4A 4HH, and 9–10, St Andrew Square, EDINBURGH, EH2 2AF
Australia	LexisNexis Butterworths, Chatswood, New South Wales
Austria	LexisNexis Verlag ARD Orac GmbH & Co KG, Vienna
Benelux	LexisNexis Benelux, Amsterdam
Canada	LexisNexis Canada, Markham, Ontario
China	LexisNexis China, Beijing and Shanghai
France	LexisNexis SA, Paris
Germany	LexisNexis GmbH, Dusseldorf
Hong Kong	LexisNexis Hong Kong, Hong Kong
India	LexisNexis India, New Delhi
Italy	Giuffrè Editore, Milan
Japan	LexisNexis Japan, Tokyo
Malaysia	Malayan Law Journal Sdn Bhd, Kuala Lumpur
New Zealand	LexisNexis NZ Ltd, Wellington
Singapore	LexisNexis Singapore, Singapore
South Africa	LexisNexis Butterworths, Durban
USA	LexisNexis, Dayton, Ohio

FIRST EDITION	*Published in 31 volumes between 1907 and 1917*
SECOND EDITION	*Published in 37 volumes between 1931 and 1942*
THIRD EDITION	*Published in 43 volumes between 1952 and 1964*
FOURTH EDITION	*Published in 56 volumes between 1973 and 1987, with reissues between 1988 and 2008*
FIFTH EDITION	*Published between 2008 and 2014, with reissues from 2014*

A CIP Catalogue record for this book is available from the British Library.

ISBN 13 (complete set, standard binding): 9781405734394

ISBN 13: 9781405790260

ISBN 978-1-4057-9026-0

9 781405 790260

Typeset by Letterpart Limited, Caterham on the Hill, Surrey CR3 5XL
Printed and bound by CPI Group (UK) Ltd, Croydon, CR0 4YY
Visit LexisNexis at www.lexisnexis.co.uk

EMPLOYMENT

Consultant Editor
IAN SMITH, LLB, MA,
of Gray's Inn, Barrister;
Emeritus Professor of Employment Law,
School of Law, University of East Anglia

The law stated in this volume is in general that in force on 1 October 2014, although subsequent changes have been included wherever possible.

Any future updating material will be found in the Current Service and annual Cumulative Supplement to Halsbury's Laws of England.

Editors of this Volume

MARTIN COOK, BA

CAROL MARSH, LLB, MA

MOHINI TULLOCH, LLM

AMANDA WRIGHT, LLB

Commissioning Editor

CLAIRE TURPIN, LLB, MSc

Indexer

JAMES A. WARD, BA, LLB,
a Solicitor of the Senior Courts of England and Wales

Managing Editor

HELEN HALVEY, LLB

TABLE OF CONTENTS

HOW TO USE HALSBURY'S LAWS OF ENGLAND

Volumes

Each text volume of Halsbury's Laws of England contains the law on the titles contained in it as at a date stated at the front of the volume (the operative date).

Information contained in Halsbury's Laws of England may be accessed in several ways.

First, by using the tables of contents.

Each volume contains both a general Table of Contents, and a specific Table of Contents for each title contained in it. From these tables you will be directed to the relevant part of the work.

Readers should note that the current arrangement of titles can be found in the Current Service.

Secondly, by using tables of statutes, statutory instruments, cases or other materials.

If you know the name of the Act, statutory instrument or case with which your research is concerned, you should consult the Consolidated Tables of statutes, cases and so on (published as separate volumes) which will direct you to the relevant volume and paragraph. The Consolidated Tables will indicate if the volume referred to is a Fifth Edition volume.

(Each individual text volume also includes tables of those materials used as authority in that volume.)

Thirdly, by using the indexes.

If you are uncertain of the general subject area of your research, you should go to the Consolidated Index (published as separate volumes) for reference to the relevant volume(s) and paragraph(s). The Consolidated Index will indicate if the volume referred to is a Fifth Edition volume.

(Each individual text volume also includes an index to the material contained therein.)

Additional Materials

The reorganisation of the title scheme of Halsbury's Laws for the Fifth Edition means that from time to time Fourth Edition volumes will be *partially* replaced by Fifth Edition volumes.

In certain instances an Additional Materials softbound book will be issued, in which will be reproduced material which has not yet been replaced by a Fifth Edition title. This will enable users to remove specific Fourth Edition volumes from the shelf and save valuable space pending the replacement of that material in the Fifth Edition. These softbound books are supplied to volumes subscribers free of charge. They continue to form part of the set of Halsbury's Laws Fourth Edition Reissue, and will be updated by the annual Cumulative Supplement and monthly Noter-Up in the usual way.

Updating publications

The text volumes of Halsbury's Laws should be used in conjunction with the annual Cumulative Supplement and the monthly Noter-Up.

The annual Cumulative Supplement

The Supplement gives details of all changes between the operative date of the text volume and the operative date of the Supplement. It is arranged in the same volume, title and paragraph order as the text volumes. Developments affecting particular points of law are noted to the relevant paragraph(s) of the text volumes. As from the commencement of the Fifth Edition, the Supplement will clearly distinguish between Fourth and Fifth Edition titles.

For narrative treatment of material noted in the Cumulative Supplement, go to the Annual Abridgment volume for the relevant year.

Destination Tables

In certain titles in the annual *Cumulative Supplement*, reference is made to Destination Tables showing the destination of consolidated legislation. Those Destination Tables are to be found either at the end of the titles within the annual *Cumulative Supplement*, or in a separate *Destination Tables* booklet provided from time to time with the *Cumulative Supplement*.

The Noter-Up

The Noter-Up is contained in the Current Service Noter-Up booklet, issued monthly and noting changes since the publication of the annual Cumulative Supplement. Also arranged in the same volume, title and paragraph order as the text volumes, the Noter-Up follows the style of the Cumulative Supplement. As from the commencement of the Fifth Edition, the Noter-Up will clearly distinguish between Fourth and Fifth Edition titles.

For narrative treatment of material noted in the Noter-Up, go to the relevant Monthly Review.

REFERENCES AND ABBREVIATIONS

ACT	Australian Capital Territory
A-G	Attorney General
Admin	Administrative Court
Admlty	Admiralty Court
Adv-Gen	Advocate General
affd	affirmed
affg	affirming
Alta	Alberta
App	Appendix
art	article
Aust	Australia
B	Baron
BC	British Columbia
C	Command Paper (of a series published before 1900)
c	chapter number of an Act
CA	Court of Appeal
CAC	Central Arbitration Committee
CA in Ch	Court of Appeal in Chancery
CB	Chief Baron
CCA	Court of Criminal Appeal
CCR	County Court Rules 1981 (as subsequently amended)
CCR	Court for Crown Cases Reserved
C-MAC	Courts-Martial Appeal Court
CO	Crown Office
COD	Crown Office Digest
CPR	Civil Procedure Rules
Can	Canada
Cd	Command Paper (of the series published 1900–18)
Cf	compare
Ch	Chancery Division
ch	chapter
cl	clause
Cm	Command Paper (of the series published 1986 to date)

Cmd	Command Paper (of the series published 1919–56)
Cmnd	Command Paper (of the series published 1956–86)
Comm	Commercial Court
Comr......................................	Commissioner
Court Forms (2nd Edn).........	Atkin's Encyclopaedia of Court Forms in Civil Proceedings, 2nd Edn. See note 2 post.
CrimPR	Criminal Procedure Rules
DC..	Divisional Court
DPP	Director of Public Prosecutions
EAT	Employment Appeal Tribunal
EC..	European Community
ECJ...	Court of Justice of the European Community
EComHR...............................	European Commission of Human Rights
ECSC......................................	European Coal and Steel Community
ECtHR Rules of Court...........	Rules of Court of the European Court of Human Rights
EEC..	European Economic Community
EFTA	European Free Trade Association
EWCA Civ	Official neutral citation for judgments of the Court of Appeal (Civil Division)
EWCA Crim...........................	Official neutral citation for judgments of the Court of Appeal (Criminal Division)
EWHC...................................	Official neutral citation for judgments of the High Court
Edn..	Edition
Euratom	European Atomic Energy Community
Ex Ch	Court of Exchequer Chamber
ex p	ex parte
Fam	Family Division
Fed	Federal
Forms & Precedents (5th Edn)......................................	Encyclopaedia of Forms and Precedents other than Court Forms, 5th Edn. See note 2 post.
GLC	Greater London Council
HC	High Court
HC	House of Commons
HK	Hong Kong
HL..	House of Lords
IAT	Immigration Appeal Tribunal
ILM..	International Legal Materials
INLR	Immigration and Nationality Law Reports
IRC..	Inland Revenue Commissioners
Ind..	India

Int Rels	International Relations
Ir	Ireland
J	Justice
JA	Judge of Appeal
Kan	Kansas
LA	Lord Advocate
LC	Lord Chancellor
LCC	London County Council
LCJ	Lord Chief Justice
LJ	Lord Justice of Appeal
LoN	League of Nations
MR	Master of the Rolls
Man	Manitoba
n	note
NB	New Brunswick
NI	Northern Ireland
NS	Nova Scotia
NSW	New South Wales
NY	New York
NZ	New Zealand
OHIM	Office for Harmonisation in the Internal Market
OJ	The Official Journal of the European Community published by the Office for Official Publications of the European Community
Ont	Ontario
P	President
PC	Judicial Committee of the Privy Council
PEI	Prince Edward Island
Pat	Patents Court
q	question
QB	Queen's Bench Division
QBD	Queen's Bench Division of the High Court
Qld	Queensland
Que	Quebec
r	rule
RDC	Rural District Council
RPC	Restrictive Practices Court
RSC	Rules of the Supreme Court 1965 (as subsequently amended)
reg	regulation
Res	Resolution
revsd	reversed

Rly...	Railway
s...	section
SA..	South Africa
S Aust....................................	South Australia
SC..	Supreme Court
SI...	Statutory Instruments published by authority
SR & O..................................	Statutory Rules and Orders published by authority
SR & O Rev 1904	Revised Edition comprising all Public and General Statutory Rules and Orders in force on 31 December 1903
SR & O Rev 1948	Revised Edition comprising all Public and General Statutory Rules and Orders and Statutory Instruments in force on 31 December 1948
SRNI	Statutory Rules of Northern Ireland
STI..	Simon's Tax Intelligence (1973–1995); Simon's Weekly Tax Intelligence (1996-current)
Sask	Saskatchewan
Sch..	Schedule
Sess...	Session
Sing	Singapore
TCC	Technology and Construction Court
TS...	Treaty Series
Tanz..	Tanzania
Tas..	Tasmania
UDC..	Urban District Council
UKHL......................................	Official neutral citation for judgments of the House of Lords
UKPC	Official neutral citation for judgments of the Privy Council
UN	United Nations
V-C..	Vice-Chancellor
Vict...	Victoria
W Aust....................................	Western Australia
Zimb	Zimbabwe

NOTE 1. A general list of the abbreviations of law reports and other sources used in this work can be found at the beginning of the Consolidated Table of Cases.

NOTE 2. Where references are made to other publications, the volume number precedes and the page number follows the name of the publication; eg the reference '12 Forms & Precedents (5th Edn) 44' refers to volume 12 of the Encyclopaedia of Forms and Precedents, page 44.

NOTE 3. An English statute is cited by short title or, where there is no short title, by regnal year and chapter number together with the name by which it is commonly known or a description of its subject matter and date. In the case of a foreign statute, the mode of citation generally follows the style of citation in use in the country concerned with the addition, where necessary, of the name of the country in parentheses.

NOTE 4. A statutory instrument is cited by short title, if any, followed by the year and number, or, if unnumbered, the date.

TABLE OF STATUTES

TABLE OF STATUTORY INSTRUMENTS

TABLE OF CIVIL PROCEDURE

Civil Procedure Rules 1998, SI 1998/3132 (CPR)

Practice Directions

TABLE OF EUROPEAN UNION LEGISLATION

TABLE OF
NON-STATUTORY MATERIAL

TABLE OF CASES

PARA

PARA

PARA
Z

Decisions of the European Court of Justice are listed below numerically. These decisions
are also included in the preceding alphabetical list.

EMPLOYMENT

VOLUME 39

5. TERMINATION OF EMPLOYMENT

(1) IN GENERAL

722. Termination of employment; in general. Employment may in general be terminated at common law either by dismissal or by resignation. If it is terminated by dismissal, that dismissal may at common law be either lawful or wrongful[1]; and a dismissal, whether lawful or wrongful, may be challenged as being unfair by statute[2]. Resignation may be either with or without notice[3], but in either event it usually means that the employee gives up his statutory rights[4], unless the employee can claim either:

(1)   that on the facts there was no true resignation[5]; or

(2)   that the employer's conduct was such that the employee was entitled to leave, and claim to have been constructively dismissed[6].

In addition to resignation, statutory rights may also be lost by the operation of other, less typical, forms of termination at common law without the existence of a dismissal, namely:

(a)   termination by expiry[7];

(b)   the dissolution of the employing enterprise[8];

(c)   frustration of the contract[9];

(d)   termination by mutual consent[10];

(e)   death of a party[11]; or

(f)   termination in some other way by operation of law[12].

1   As to the meaning of 'wrongful dismissal' see PARA 825.

2   As to unfair dismissal see PARA 755 et seq.

3   An employee is justified in terminating his employment without notice where his employer has fundamentally broken the contract, or where he reasonably anticipates danger to his life or personal injury: *Limland v Stephens* (1801) 3 Esp 269; *Priestley v Fowler* (1837) 3 M & W 1; *Turner v Mason* (1845) 14 M & W 112; *Donovan v Invicta Airways Ltd* [1970] 1 Lloyd's Rep 486, CA. As to enforcement by the employer of the employee's obligation to give notice see PARA 734.

4   Ie especially to claim unfair dismissal (see PARA 762) or a redundancy payment (see PARA 835), both of which are dependent on there being a 'dismissal'.

5   This may be the case where there has been a pressurised resignation ('resign or be dismissed'): *East Sussex County Council v Walker* (1972) 7 ITR 280, NIRC; *Allders International Ltd v Parkins* [1981] IRLR 68, EAT. It is a question of fact for the tribunal or court to decide who was really responsible for the termination: *Martin v Glynwed Distribution Ltd* [1983] ICR 511, [1983] IRLR 198, CA; *Caledonian Mining Co Ltd v Bassett* [1987] ICR 425, [1987] IRLR 165, EAT.

6   See PARA 763.

7   See PARA 725.

8   See PARAS 726, 727.

9   See PARAS 728, 729.

10   See PARAS 730, 731.

11   See PARA 732.

12   See e g *Tarnesby v Kensington and Chelsea and Westminster Area Health Authority (Teaching)* [1981] ICR 615, [1981] IRLR 369, HL (loss of registration as a medical practitioner meant that the employee was by law no longer permitted to hold his appointment, and so his contract of employment was automatically terminated).

723. Duration of employment. In the absence of any express stipulation as to duration or expiry[1], every contract of employment[2] is treated as determinable by reasonable notice[3] or, if greater, the statutory minimum[4] period of notice[5].

1   As to termination by expiry see PARA 725.

2   As to the meaning of 'contract of employment' see PARA 2.

3 This is the basic common law term implied in the absence of an express term on notice: see PARA 733. Where such a term exists, it is one of the terms of employment which must be contained in the written statement of terms and conditions which is to be given to an employee under the Employment Rights Act 1996 s 1(4)(e): see PARA 119.

4 See the Employment Rights Act 1996 s 86; and PARA 736.

5 The ancient rule was that a general hiring, ie the taking on of an employee without limit of time, was for a year, whether the contract was oral or in writing, and whether or not it was a renewal of a previous contract: see Co Litt 42b; 1 Bl Com (14th Edn) 425; *R v St Peter's, Dorchester* (1763) Burr SC 513; *R v Elslack Inhabitants* (1785) 4 Doug KB 211; *R v Macclesfield Inhabitants* (1789) 3 Term Rep 76; *R v Long Whatton Inhabitants* (1793) 5 Term Rep 447; *R v Hales Inhabitants* (1794) 5 Term Rep 668; *R v Worfield Inhabitants* (1794) 5 Term Rep 506; *Huttman v Boulnois* (1826) 2 C & P 510; *Beeston v Collyer* (1827) 4 Bing 309; *R v St Andrew, Pershore* (1828) 8 B & C 679; *Fawcett v Cash* (1834) 5 B & Ad 904; *Bayley v Rimmell* (1836) 1 M & W 506; *Buckingham v Surrey and Hants Canal Co* (1882) 46 LT 885, DC; *Cayme v Allan, Jones & Co* (1919) 35 TLR 453, DC. However, this rule has no place in modern employment law and there is now no such presumption: *Richardson v Koefod* [1969] 3 All ER 1264, [1969] 1 WLR 1812, CA.

724. Character references; in general. There is no general obligation, either at common law or by virtue of any statutory provision[1], on an employer to give a character reference to a former employee on the termination of the employment[2]. If the employer does give a reference and it is negligently written, a recipient who suffers damage because of it may be able to sue the employer for negligent misstatement on ordinary principles[3]; and an employer, when writing a reference, also owes a duty of care to the former employee, who may sue if he suffers loss through a negligently written reference upon which a third party relies[4].

Where employment is offered to a person 'subject to satisfactory references', that is likely to be construed as meaning satisfactory subjectively to the employer, not as imposing an obligation to employ if the references are satisfactory in an objective sense[5].

1 There is a statutory obligation to give a qualifying employee a statement of reasons for dismissal (see the Employment Rights Act 1996 s 92; and PARA 755) but this falls far short of a right to a reference.

2 *Carrol v Bird* (1800) 3 Esp 201. There is no implied term in modern employment law that the employer will give a reference (*Lawton v BOC Transhield Ltd* [1987] ICR 7, [1987] IRLR 404); sed quaere whether in certain specific circumstances, where references are particularly essential, there might be such an implication (*Spring v Guardian Assurance plc* [1994] 3 All ER 129 at 178–179, [1994] ICR 596 at 647, HL, per Lord Woolf). A refusal to give a reference for discriminatory reasons (eg because the employee has brought discrimination proceedings against the employer) may itself constitute unlawful discrimination: Case C-185/97 *Coote v Granada Hospitality Ltd* [1998] ECR I-5199, [1999] ICR 100, ECJ; applied in *Coote v Granada Hospitality Ltd (No 2)* [1999] ICR 942, [1999] IRLR 452, EAT. See also *Chief Constable of West Yorkshire Police v Khan* [2001] UKHL 48, [2001] 4 All ER 834, [2001] 1 WLR 1947 (references not provided so as to preserve employer's position in pending proceedings for racial discrimination).

3 Ie under the rule in *Hedley Byrne & Co Ltd v Heller & Partners Ltd* [1964] AC 465, [1963] 2 All ER 575, HL: see NEGLIGENCE vol 78 (2010) PARA 14. The defendant in *Hedley Byrne & Co Ltd v Heller & Partners Ltd* escaped liability because of a disclaimer clause, but it has since been held that such a clause is subject to the test of reasonableness in the Unfair Contract Terms Act 1977 s 2(2): see *Smith v Eric S Bush (a firm), Harris v Wyre Forest District Council* [1990] 1 AC 831, [1989] 2 All ER 514, HL; and CONTRACT vol 22 (2012) PARA 410. See also NEGLIGENCE vol 78 (2010) PARA 74. If the reference is given fraudulently, the employer may be liable to the recipient for the tort of deceit: *Foster v Charles* (1830) 6 Bing 396 (affd 7 Bing 105); *Wilkin v Reed* (1854) 15 CB 192.

4 *Spring v Guardian Assurance plc* [1994] 3 All ER 129, [1994] ICR 596, HL; and see *Lawton v BOC Transhield Ltd* [1987] 2 All ER 608, [1987] ICR 7 (where the principle was accepted but the claim failed on the facts). Where the employer does give a reference, it must be true, accurate and fair, though it does not necessarily have to be full and comprehensive: *Bartholomew v London Borough of Hackney* [1999] IRLR 246, CA; applied in *Kidd v Axa Equity and Law*

Life Assurance Society plc [2000] IRLR 301. Statements unfavourable to the employee should be confined to those matters into which the employer has made reasonable investigation (by analogy with the approach to dismissal on grounds of misconduct: see PARA 703) and which he has reasonable grounds for believing to be true: *Cox v Sun Alliance Life Ltd* [2001] EWCA Civ 649, [2001] IRLR 448. Failure to give a reference that is reasonable and fair (even if strictly accurate) may breach the implied term of trust and respect (see PARA 48), justifying the employee in leaving and claiming constructive dismissal: *TSB Bank plc v Harris* [2000] IRLR 157, EAT. As to the position where a reference is allegedly libellous see DEFAMATION vol 32 (2012) PARA 614. As to whether a statement which has the effect of preventing its subject from being employed in a particular occupation or profession under the rules of the relevant regulatory body can engage the Convention for the Protection of Human Rights and Fundamental Freedoms (Rome, 25 March 1957; TS 1 (1973); Cmnd 5179), First Protocol (1952), art 1 (right to the peaceful enjoyment of possessions) (see RIGHTS AND FREEDOMS vol 88A (2013) PARA 534 et seq) see *Legal and General Assurance Ltd v Kirk* [2001] EWCA Civ 1803, [2002] IRLR 124 (right to trade as a company representative not a 'possession' for these purposes). An employer may be liable in respect of statements made about an employee or former employee in contexts other than giving a reference: see *McKie v Swindon College* [2011] EWHC 469 (QB), [2011] IRLR 575 (former employer liable for negligent misstatements made to current employer about former employee). See also *Jackson v Liverpool City Council* [2011] EWCA Civ 1068, [2011] IRLR 1009 (reference indicating that there were uninvestigated complaints about employee was lawful).

5   *Wishart v National Association of Citizens Advice Bureaux Ltd* [1990] ICR 794, [1990] IRLR 393, CA, at 801 and 395 per Mustill LJ, and at 805 and 397 per Ralph Gibson LJ. On general principle, the obligation of one or both parties might be made subject to a condition that it is to be immediately binding but that, if certain facts are ascertained to exist, or upon the occurrence or non-occurrence of some further event, then either the contract is to cease to bind or one or both parties are to have the right to avoid the contract or bring it to an end: see *Ryan v Blackburn with Darwen Borough Council* [2004] All ER (D) 12 (Oct), EAT (applicant was offered, and he accepted, a temporary teaching post but he had full rights as a teacher only for as long as the Criminal Records Bureau did not report unsatisfactorily), applying *Total Gas Marketing Ltd v Arco British Ltd* [1998] 2 Lloyd's Rep 209, HL. See CONTRACT vol 22 (2012) PARA 531.

(2) TERMINATION WITHOUT DISMISSAL

(i) In general

725. Termination by expiry. As the ordinary law of contract is applicable to contracts of employment[1], the parties who enter the contract may also stipulate how it is to end. Thus certain untypical contracts of employment may be worded or otherwise constructed in such a way that the contract terminates by expiry or performance, in which case, unless statute intervenes[2], there is no dismissal. Such contracts may fall into the following categories:

(1)   a contract may be stated to last for a set period of time, in which case it is considered to be a fixed-term contract and at the end of the relevant period it terminates by expiry[3];

(2)   a contract may be to perform a particular task or amount of work, in which case it expires by performance on the completion of that task or work[4];

(3)   a contract may be expressed to be subject to a particular contingency such as the continuance of outside funding for the post, in which case the contract may terminate on the happening or otherwise of that contingency[5].

The potential disadvantage to the employee of there being no dismissal by the employer is removed in the two principal areas of unfair dismissal law and redundancy rights because, for those purposes, the non-renewal of a limited-term contract is deemed to be a dismissal[6]; moreover, termination is subject to the employees being treated fairly in relation to comparable permanent employees[7].

A genuinely fixed-term contract does not lose that character if it contains a clause allowing termination by notice, before the expiry of the fixed term[8].

1   See PARA 1.
2   See notes 6–7.
3   A contract is not for a fixed term if it fixes merely the minimum duration: *Fuller-Shapcott v Chilton Electric Ltd* (1970) 5 ITR 186; *Weston v University College, Swansea* [1975] IRLR 102. As to the fair treatment of employees on fixed-term contracts see PARA 84 et seq.
4   See *Wiltshire County Council v National Association of Teachers in Further and Higher Education* [1980] ICR 455 at 460, [1980] IRLR 198 at 200, CA, per Lord Denning MR (examples of 'purpose contracts' would be: (1) a seaman engaged for the uncertain duration of a voyage (cf *Hellyer Bros Ltd v McLeod, Boston Deep Sea Fisheries Ltd v Wilson* [1987] 1 WLR 728, [1987] ICR 526, CA); and (2) someone engaged to cut down a certain number of trees). See also *Ironmonger v Movefield Ltd (t/a Deering Appointments)* [1988] IRLR 461, EAT.
5   *Brown v Knowsley Borough Council* [1986] IRLR 102, EAT.
6   See the Employment Rights Act 1996 s 95(1)(b) (cited at PARA 762), s 136(1)(b) (cited at PARA 864).
7   See the Fixed-term Employees (Prevention of Less Favourable Treatment) Regulations 2002, SI 2002/2034; and PARA 85 et seq.
8   *Dixon v BBC* [1979] QB 546, [1979] ICR 281, CA, disapproving on this point *BBC v Ioannou* [1975] QB 781, [1975] ICR 267, CA; *Ramsay v WB Anderson & Sons Ltd* [1974] IRLR 164. The position is the same under the Fixed-term Employees (Prevention of Less Favourable Treatment) Regulations 2002, SI 2002/2034 (see PARA 85 et seq): *Allen v National Australia Group Europe Ltd* [2004] IRLR 847, EAT (Sc).

726.   Dissolution of a partnership.   Whether a change in the composition of the partnership employing the employee affects the contract of employment depends on the express or implied intention of that contract[1]. The death of one of the partners terminates the contract if that contract is sufficiently related to the personal conduct of the deceased partner[2], but not if the actual composition of the partnership is not of such importance[3]. A change of partners may or may not operate as a wrongful dismissal, depending on the circumstances and the intent of the contract, but a major change entailing the dissolution of the partnership normally so operates[4]. If, however, the employee continues to work for the newly constituted firm, that may constitute a waiver of his common law rights[5]; and, in such a case, the employee's continuity of employment is expressly preserved by statute[6].

1   *Briggs v Oates* [1991] 1 All ER 407 at 414, [1990] ICR 473 at 481 per Scott J.
2   *Tasker v Shepherd* (1861) 6 H & N 575; *Hoey v Macewan and Auld* (1867) 5 M 814, Ct of Sess; *Harvey v Tivoli (Manchester) Ltd* (1907) 23 TLR 592; *Tunstall v Condon* [1980] ICR 786, EAT.
3   *Phillips v Alhambra Palace Co* [1901] 1 KB 59.
4   *Brace v Calder* [1895] 2 QB 253, CA; *Dobbin v Foster* (1844) 1 Car & Kir 323; *Hobson v Cowley* (1858) 27 LJ Ex 205; *Tunstall v Condon* [1980] ICR 786, EAT; *Briggs v Oates* [1990] ICR 473 at 481, [1990] IRLR 472 at 476. 'A contract to serve four employers cannot without express language be construed as a contract to serve two of them': *Brace v Calder* above at 263 per Rigby LJ; applied by Scott J in *Briggs v Oates* above. The practical importance of a finding of wrongful dismissal is that it releases the employee from a restraint of trade clause (as in *Briggs v Oates*).
5   *Hobson v Cowley* (1858) 27 LJ Ex 205.
6   See the Employment Rights Act 1996 s 218(5); and PARA 135.

727.   Insolvency of employer.   The appointment of a receiver by the court automatically terminates all contracts of employment between a company and its employees[1]. It is immaterial that the receiver continues to carry on the business temporarily since he does not do so as an agent for the company; and employees who continue to work for him do so under new contracts of employment entered into with him[2].

The appointment out of court of a receiver and manager to act as agent of the company[3] does not, however, operate to terminate existing contracts of employment unless:

(1)   the appointment is accompanied by a sale of the business of the company; or

(2)   simultaneously with, or very soon after, the appointment, the receiver enters into a new agreement with a particular employee which is inconsistent with a continuation of his previous contract of service; or

(3)   the continuation of a particular employee's employment is inconsistent with the role and functions of the receiver and manager[4].

If, however, the receiver is acting as agent for the debenture holders, it is apprehended that the appointment will terminate the company's contracts of employment[5].

If a receiver appointed out of court closes the company's business down, all outstanding contracts of employment are thereby terminated[6]. If, however, the receiver sells the whole or part of the company's business undertaking carried on in the United Kingdom as a going concern, the rights, powers, obligations and liabilities of the company towards persons employed in the undertaking or the part of an undertaking which is sold are transferred to the purchaser; and the employee's rights against the purchaser are the same as if the company and the purchaser were the same person[7]. An employee may nevertheless terminate his employment without notice if a substantial change is made in his working conditions, or if the change in the identity of his employer is significant and, in the circumstances, detrimental to him[8].

A resolution for the voluntary winding up of a company automatically operates as a notice of dismissal of the employees, if it involves a termination of the employees' employment by the company[9]; and the making of a compulsory winding-up order operates to terminate all contracts of employment between the company and its employees[10].

The bankruptcy of an employer does not automatically terminate contracts of employment between the bankrupt and his employees[11]. Where, however, a bankruptcy order is made in respect of an individual to whom another individual was an apprentice or articled clerk at the time when the petition on which the order was made was presented, and the bankrupt or the apprentice or clerk gives notice to the trustee terminating the apprenticeship or articles, the indenture of apprenticeship or, as the case may be, the articles of agreement are discharged with effect from the commencement of the bankruptcy[12].

1   As to the priority in corporate and individual insolvency of an employee's unpaid remuneration see PARA 627; and as to an employee's rights on an employer's insolvency see PARA 628. As to the meanings of 'employee' and 'contract of employment' see PARA 2.

2   *Reid v Explosives Co Ltd* (1887) 19 QBD 264, CA. The exception to the general rule has been attributed to the personal nature of contracts of employment: see *Midland Counties District Bank Ltd v Attwood* [1905] 1 Ch 357 at 362 per Warrington J.

3   An administrative receiver is deemed to be the company's agent, unless and until the company goes into liquidation; and he is personally liable on any contract entered into by him in the carrying out of his functions, except in so far as the contract otherwise provides, and, to the extent of any qualifying liability, on any contract of employment adopted by him in the carrying out of those functions: see the Insolvency Act 1986 s 44(1)(a), (b); and COMPANY AND PARTNERSHIP INSOLVENCY vol 16 (2011) PARA 351.

4   *Griffiths v Secretary of State for Social Services* [1974] QB 468, [1973] 3 All ER 1184; *Re Foster Clark Ltd's Indenture Trusts, Loveland v Horscroft* [1966] 1 All ER 43, [1966] 1 WLR 125; *Re Mack Trucks (Britain) Ltd* [1967] 1 All ER 977, [1967] 1 WLR 780. Quaere the position where a receiver, appointed out of court, merely continues the employment of the company's employees during his receivership, without making a new contract: see *Re Mack Trucks (Britain) Ltd* at 983 and 787 per Pennycuick J. As to the meaning of 'contract of service' see PARA 1 note 1.

5   There is no clear judicial authority, but *Hopley-Dodd v Highfield Motors (Derby) Ltd* (1969) 4 ITR 289 is sometimes cited as authority for this proposition.

6   *Re General Rolling Stock Co, Chapman's Case* (1866) LR 1 Eq 346; *Measures Bros Ltd v Measures* [1910] 2 Ch 248, CA.

7   See the Transfer of Undertakings (Protection of Employment) Regulations) 2006, SI 2006/246; and PARA 137 et seq.

8   See the Transfer of Undertakings (Protection of Employment) Regulations) 2006, SI 2006/246, reg 4; and PARA 139.

9   *Reigate v Union Manufacturing Co (Ramsbottom) Ltd* [1918] 1 KB 592 at 606, CA, per Scrutton LJ; *Fowler v Commercial Timber Co Ltd* [1930] 2 KB 1 at 5, CA, per Scrutton LJ; *Deaway Trading Ltd v Calverley* [1973] 3 All ER 776, [1973] ICR 546, NIRC; *Fox Bros (Clothes) Ltd v Bryant* [1979] ICR 64, [1978] IRLR 485, EAT. As to the voluntary winding up of a company see COMPANY AND PARTNERSHIP INSOLVENCY vol 17 (2011) PARA 898 et seq.

10   *Re Foster Clark Ltd's Indenture Trusts, Loveland v Horscroft* [1966] 1 All ER 43, [1966] 1 WLR 125; *Re Mack Trucks (Britain) Ltd* [1967] 1 All ER 977, [1967] 1 WLR 780. As to the winding up of a company by the court see COMPANY AND PARTNERSHIP INSOLVENCY vol 16 (2011) PARA 386 et seq.

11   *Thomas v Williams* (1834) 1 Ad & El 685 (employer's bankruptcy held to be no answer to an action for wages which became due after the bankruptcy). See also note 1.

12   See the Insolvency Act 1986 s 348; and BANKRUPTCY AND INDIVIDUAL INSOLVENCY vol 5 (2013) PARA 720. As to termination of apprenticeship agreements see PARA 749 et seq.

(ii) Frustration

728. In general. A contract is frustrated where without default of either party a contractual obligation has become incapable of being performed because the circumstances in which performance is called for would render it a thing radically different from that which was undertaken by the contract[1]. The doctrine of frustration may apply to a contract of employment which is affected by sufficiently drastic external factors[2], with the effects that:

(1)   the contract terminates automatically, without the need for any action by the employer[3];

(2)   there is no right to any back pay from the date of frustration to any later date[4]; and

(3)   the fact that termination is by operation of law means that there is no dismissal, which in turn means that the employee cannot claim unfair dismissal or a redundancy payment[5].

It was suggested that the doctrine of frustration should not be applied to contracts of employment which may be terminated in any event by relatively short notice[6]. The orthodox approach that the doctrine can apply has, however, been reasserted[7] although there are clear indications that it should not be found readily by an employment tribunal because of its adverse effects on employment rights[8].

The frustrating event must, under the normal law of contract, be the fault of neither party[9]; but, in the context of alleged frustration of a contract of employment through the imprisonment of the employee[10], it has been held that it is only the party seeking to rely on frustration who must not be at fault[11].

1   *Davis Contractors Ltd v Fareham UDC* [1956] AC 696, [1956] 2 All ER 145, HL; and see CONTRACT vol 22 (2012) PARA 468 et seq.

2   Certain older cases concerned being called up or interned in times of war: *Horlock v Beal* [1916] 1 AC 486, HL; *Marshall v Glanvill* [1917] 2 KB 87; *Unger v Preston Corpn* [1942] 1 All ER 200; *Morgan v Manser* [1948] 1 KB 184, [1947] 2 All ER 666; cf *Nordman v Rayner and Sturges* (1916) 33 TLR 87. It is not enough, however, if the contract is still capable of performance, even though subject to a previously unforeseen risk: *Converform (Darwen) Ltd v Bell* [1981] IRLR 195, EAT.

3   *Marshall v Harland & Wolff Ltd* [1972] 2 All ER 715 at 719, [1972] ICR 101 at 106, NIRC, per Sir John Donaldson P (disapproving dicta to the contrary in *Thomas v John Drake & Co Ltd* (1971) 6 ITR 146). There is no requirement on the employer to give notice (or to pay in lieu of notice) if the contract is frustrated: *GF Sharp & Co Ltd v McMillan* [1998] IRLR 632, EAT. It is not necessary in principle to be able to fix an exact date of termination by frustration, though in the context of a statutory action it may be necessary: *Williams v Watsons Luxury Coaches Ltd* [1990] ICR 536, [1990] IRLR 164, EAT. See *Four Seasons Healthcare Ltd v Maughan* [2005] IRLR 324, EAT (where employee found to be unfit to work at a hospital pursuant to statute, frustration could not be backdated to when initial allegation against him was made).

4   *Unger v Preston Corpn* [1942] 1 All ER 200. Wages due up to the date of frustration may be recovered under the Law Reform (Frustrated Contracts) Act 1943 ss 1(3), 2(4): see CONTRACT vol 22 (2012) PARAS 486–487.

5   If, however, the frustrating event relates to the employer, including his death, and the contract thereby terminates by operation of law, the employee's redundancy rights are preserved: see the Employment Rights Act 1996 s 136(5); and PARA 867.

6   *Harman v Flexible Lamps Ltd* [1980] IRLR 418, EAT (sickness); and see *Norris v Southampton City Council* [1982] ICR 177, [1982] IRLR 141, EAT (imprisonment constituted repudiatory conduct by employee, not frustration).

7   *Notcutt v Universal Equipment Co (London) Ltd* [1986] 3 All ER 582, [1986] ICR 414, CA (sickness); *FC Shepherd & Co Ltd v Jerrom* [1987] QB 301, [1986] ICR 802, CA (imprisonment).

8   *Notcutt v Universal Equipment Co (London) Ltd* [1986] 3 All ER 582 at 586, [1986] ICR 414 at 420, CA, per Dillon LJ; *FC Shepherd & Co Ltd v Jerrom* [1987] QB 301 at 329, [1986] ICR 802 at 823, CA, per Mustill LJ (in the context of a particularly exhaustive dismissal procedure); *Williams v Watsons Luxury Coaches Ltd* [1990] ICR 536 at 541, [1990] IRLR 164 at 167, EAT, per Wood P (particularly where questions of redundancy or disability arise). In the case of a disabled person, before the doctrine of frustration can apply, an employment appeal tribunal has to consider, over and above other factors identified in the relevant authorities, the additional factor of whether the employer is in breach of a duty to make reasonable adjustments: *Warner v Armfield Retail & Leisure Ltd* [2014] ICR 239, [2013] All ER (D) 260 (Oct), EAT.

9   See e g *Davis Contractors Ltd v Fareham UDC* [1956] AC 696, [1967] 2 All ER 145, HL; *Paal Wilson & Co A/S v Partenreederei Hannah Blumenthal* [1983] 1 AC 854, [1983] 1 All ER 34, HL. See also CONTRACT vol 22 (2012) PARA 470.

10   See PARA 729.

11   *FC Shepherd & Co Ltd v Jerrom* [1987] QB 301 at 319, [1986] 3 All ER 589 at 597, CA, per Lawton LJ, and at 325 and 601 per Mustill LJ. Alternatively, it may be argued that it was not the commission of the offence, but rather the sentence of the court, that was the frustrating event: see *Hare v Murphy Bros Ltd* [1974] 3 All ER 940 at 942, [1974] ICR 603 at 607, CA, per Lord Denning MR; *FC Shepherd & Co Ltd v Jerrom* at 336 and 608 per Balcombe LJ.

729. Frustration through illness or imprisonment. It is clear that a contract of employment may be frustrated through a serious illness or accident befalling the employee[1], though it may be a difficult question of fact and degree as to whether the circumstances are sufficiently serious to warrant such a drastic finding by a tribunal or court[2]. By way of guidance, case law has suggested the following factors for consideration[3]:

(1)   the terms of the contract, including any provisions as to sick pay[4];

(2)   how long the employment was likely to last in the absence of sickness, a temporary or specific hiring being more likely to be frustrated;

(3)   the nature of the employment, in particular whether the employee was in a key post which had to be filled permanently if his absence was prolonged[5], or whether it could be held open for a considerable time[6];

(4)   the nature of the illness or injury, how long it has continued and the prospects for recovery;

(5)   the period of past employment, a longstanding relationship being less easily destroyed;

(6)   the risk to the employer of acquiring obligations in respect of redundancy payments or compensation for unfair dismissal to a replacement employee;

(7)   whether wages have continued to be paid;

(8)   the acts and statements of the employer in relation to the employment, including the dismissal of, or failure to dismiss, the employee[7];

(9)   whether in all the circumstances a reasonable employer could be expected to wait any longer[8].

The other principal ground of frustration in the case law is the imprisonment of the employee[9]; and this may frustrate the contract of employment and is not to be countered with the argument that it was self-induced[10]. There are no fixed rules as to when imprisonment will have this effect; it remains a question of fact requiring consideration of all the circumstances of the employment and the sentence[11].

1   *Notcutt v Universal Equipment Co Ltd* [1986] 3 All ER 582, [1986] ICR 414, CA (disapproving *Harman v Flexible Lamps Ltd* [1980] IRLR 418, EAT); and see PARA 728.

2   Cf *Poussard v Spiers and Pond* (1876) 1 QBD 410; *Bettini v Gye* (1876) 1 QBD 183. See also *Condor v Barron Knights Ltd* [1966] 1 WLR 87. The fact that the contract becomes subject to a previously unforeseen risk of disabling illness is not sufficient: *Converform (Darwen) Ltd v Bell* [1981] IRLR 195, EAT. Teachers who lack the physical or mental capacity to fulfil employment obligations may be dismissed if they refuse to resign on that account: see EDUCATION vol 36 (2011) PARA 924.

3   The factors listed in heads (1)–(5) in the text were set out in the leading case of *Marshall v Harland & Wolff Ltd* [1972] 2 All ER 715 at 718–719, [1972] 1 WLR 899 at 903–904, NIRC, per Sir John Donaldson P; and those in heads (6)–(9) in the text were added in *Egg Stores (Stamford Hill) Ltd v Leibovici* [1977] ICR 260 at 265, [1976] IRLR 376 at 378, EAT, per Phillips J, when considering, in particular, the application of the doctrine of frustration to contracts terminable on relatively short notice.

4   Where the contract of employment specifically envisages the sort of incapacity in question, eg by the incorporation of a generous permanent health insurance scheme to cover long-term incapacity, that may mean that such incapacity does not frustrate the contract because it is not an unforeseen event: *Villella v MFI Furniture Centres Ltd* [1999] IRLR 468. As to the payment of wages during sickness see PARA 27; and as to statutory sick pay see PARA 558 et seq.

5   *Hebden v Forsey & Son* [1973] ICR 607, [1973] IRLR 344, NIRC.

6   *Maxwell v Walter Howard Designs Ltd* [1975] IRLR 77.

7   *Hart v AR Marshall & Sons (Bulwell) Ltd* [1977] ICR 539, [1977] IRLR 51, EAT.

8   If the contract was not frustrated, the employee may seek to bring proceedings for unfair dismissal. As to dismissal for incapability on the grounds of ill health see PARA 775. The factors applying to frustration and those applying to unfair dismissal through illness are theoretically separate (*Tan v Berry Bros & Rudd Ltd* [1974] ICR 586, [1974] IRLR 244, NIRC); but, if the further factors in heads (6)–(9) in the text are acted on (particularly the factor in head (9) in the text, with its reference to the reasonableness of the employer's reaction), the two tests are arguably similar: see *Egg Stores (Stamford Hill) Ltd v Leibovici* [1977] ICR 260 at 265, [1976] IRLR 376 at 378, EAT, per Phillips J.

9   In this context, even if the contract is not frustrated, a dismissal because of an immediate term of imprisonment of any significant length passed on the employee is likely to be fair, as being for 'some other substantial reason' under the Employment Rights Act 1996 s 98(1)(b), (4) (see PARA 766 et seq): *Kingston v British Railways Board* [1984] ICR 781, [1984] IRLR 146, CA.

10   *FC Shepherd & Co Ltd v Jerrom* [1987] QB 301, [1986] ICR 802, CA (disapproving *Norris v Southampton City Council* [1982] ICR 177, [1982] IRLR 141, EAT); and see PARA 728.

11   See *Chakki v United Yeast Co Ltd* [1982] 2 All ER 446, [1982] ICR 140, EAT, where it was said that the question is to be determined by considering: (1) when it was commercially necessary for the employer to make a decision about the employee's future; (2) what a reasonable employer would consider to be the likely length of the employee's absence over the next few months; and

(3) whether, in the light of the employee's likely absence, it was reasonable to engage a permanent rather than a temporary replacement (the employee was sentenced to 11 months' imprisonment at the beginning of his annual holiday, but only spent one day in prison before being released on bail pending his appeal, which resulted a month later in the sentence being varied to probation; no frustration); but cf *Harrington v Kent County Council* [1980] IRLR 353, EAT (employee given an immediate sentence of 12 months' imprisonment; contract held to have been frustrated, even though it was known to the employers that the employee was appealing, his appeal being successful three months later). See also *Four Seasons Healthcare Ltd v Maughan* [2005] IRLR 324, EAT (imposition of bail conditions which prevented employee from entering the premises of his employer did not frustrate the contract).

(iii) Mutual Consent

730. In general. As a matter of ordinary contract law, the parties to a contract of employment, having made it, are equally capable of agreeing to terminate it[1]. This may, however, materially prejudice an employee's statutory rights[2] because, if an employment terminates by mutual consent, there is no dismissal as required in order to bring claims for unfair dismissal or a redundancy payment[3]. Mutual termination should not be found readily; genuine cases may arise[4], but normally it does not occur[5]. Mutual termination may, however, properly apply where the employee agrees, without compulsion, to accept voluntary early retirement, offered by the employer on terms more generous than under the ordinary redundancy payments scheme and where it is understood that the normal statutory rights are not to apply in addition[6].

1   *SW Strange Ltd v Mann* [1965] 1 All ER 1069, [1965] 1 WLR 629 (termination of one contract by mutual agreement, followed by creation of a separate contract without the restraint of trade clause in contention). As to discharge by subsequent agreement see CONTRACT vol 22 (2012) PARA 576.
2   The position is similar to that of frustration of contract, ie a normal principle of contract law having unfortunate results if applied strictly to cases concerning an employee's statutory rights: see PARA 728.
3   As to the meaning of 'dismissal' in the context of unfair dismissal see PARA 762; and as to the meaning of 'dismissal' in the context of redundancy law see PARA 864.
4   See eg *SW Strange Ltd v Mann* [1965] 1 All ER 1069, [1965] 1 WLR 629; *Lipton Ltd v Marlborough* [1979] IRLR 179, EAT (agreement for employment to cease immediately, to avoid a contractual restriction on the employee requiring six months' notice and a restraint of trade clause).
5   See *McAlwane v Boughton Estates Ltd* [1973] 2 All ER 299, [1973] ICR 470, NIRC; *Lees v Arthur Greaves (Lees) Ltd* [1974] 2 All ER 393, [1974] ICR 501, CA (both cases where an employee already under notice from the employer requested to leave earlier, eg to take other employment; the employer argued that this was mutual termination, replacing the original dismissal by notice, but this argument was disapproved, the proper interpretation being merely an agreed variation of the notice period). See also *Glacier Metal Co Ltd v Dyer* [1974] 3 All ER 21, [1974] IRLR 189, NIRC; *Glencross v Dymoke* [1979] ICR 536, EAT. Where an employee has agreed to accept the loss of his post under the terms of a compromise agreement [now settlement agreement], which provided for postponement of the date on which the employee's employment would cease, and the compromise agreement [now settlement agreement] is then found to be void (see PARA 151), what results is not an agreed termination of the old contract, but a repudiated contract: *Eastbourne Borough Council v Foster* [2001] EWCA Civ 1091, [2002] ICR 234 (the continued existence of a de facto relationship of employment entitled the employee to reasonable notice and, in contract, to claim for work actually performed, while in restitution he was both obliged to return the sums received under the void compromise agreement [now settlement agreement], and at the same time entitled to a defence of change of position).
    If an employee is induced, by a fraudulent misrepresentation made by a representative of the employer, to agree to resign or leave voluntarily, it is at least arguable that it was the employer who had really terminated the employment contract: *Post Office v Sanhotra* [2000] ICR 866, EAT (employee ignorant of fact that employers had not given him a good reference). See also *White v Bristol Rugby Ltd* [2002] IRLR 204 (employee sought to 'opt out' of his contract

before joining club but the contract's terms excluded oral representations upon which he wanted to rely; contract could not be terminated by employee unilaterally refusing to serve his employer).

6   *Birch v University of Liverpool* [1985] ICR 470, [1985] IRLR 165, CA; and see *Scott v Coalite Fuels and Chemicals Ltd* [1988] ICR 355, [1988] IRLR 131, EAT (mutual termination applied, even where the employee was already under notice of dismissal for redundancy); *Logan Salton v Durham County Council* [1989] IRLR 99, EAT (employee agreed to terminate his employment on agreed terms rather than go through with a disciplinary hearing to consider his dismissal; such an agreement was said to be consistent with good industrial relations and not to fall foul of the Employment Rights Act 1996 s 203 (restrictions on contracting out) (see PARA 150). The fact that an employee in an ordinary redundancy case volunteers to be made redundant does not, however, mean that there is no dismissal, and thus he may claim a redundancy payment in the ordinary way: *Burton, Allton & Johnson Ltd v Peck* [1975] ICR 193, [1975] IRLR 87; *Morley v CT Morley Ltd* [1985] ICR 499, EAT (cited in PARA 864 note 4). The exception in *Birch v University of Liverpool* is unlikely to apply if there is any element of compulsion or pressure by the employer. As to the analogous area of pressurised resignations see PARA 722 note 5. See also *Lassman v De Vere University Arms Hotel* [2003] ICR 44, EAT (employee accepted what amounted to dismissal by reason of redundancy, having rejected other options which amounted to unilateral variation of the contract; no consensual termination of employment).

731.   Agreement for automatic termination.   An agreement for the automatic termination of a contract of employment in certain circumstances[1] is void[2] because it purports to exclude or limit the operation of the statutory provision giving an employee the right to claim unfair dismissal[3].

1   See eg *British Leyland (UK) Ltd v Ashraf* [1978] ICR 979, [1978] IRLR 330, EAT, (distinguished in *Midlands Electric Manufacturing Co Ltd v Kanji* [1980] IRLR 185, EAT, and *Tracey v Zest Equipment Co Ltd* [1982] ICR 481, [1982] IRLR 268, EAT; disapproved in *Igbo v Johnson, Matthey Chemicals Ltd* [1986] ICR 505, [1986] IRLR 215, CA).
2   Ie under the Employment Rights Act 1996 s 203 (restrictions on contracting out): see PARA 150.
3   *Igbo v Johnson, Matthey Chemicals Ltd* [1986] ICR 505, [1986] IRLR 215, CA (disapproving *British Leyland (UK) Ltd v Ashraf* [1978] ICR 979, [1978] IRLR 330, EAT).

(iv) Death of Employer or Employee

732.   In general.   A contract of employment is discharged by the death of either the employee[1] or the employer[2]. This relatively simple common law position is, however, of diminished practical importance due to the existence of special statutory rules covering the effect of death in the three most important areas, namely, unfair dismissal[3], redundancy rights[4], and continuity of employment[5].

1   *Stubbs v Holywell Rly Co* (1867) LR 2 Exch 311.
2   *Farrow v Wilson* (1869) LR 4 CP 744; *Graves v Cohen* (1929) 46 TLR 121.
3   See the Employment Rights Act 1996 Pt X (ss 94–134A); and PARA 757 et seq.
4   See the Employment Rights Act 1996 ss 174–176; and PARAS 889, 890.
5   See the Employment Rights Act 1996 s 218(4); and PARA 135.

(3) DISMISSAL ON NOTICE

(i) The Doctrine of Notice

733.   Notice at common law.   In the absence of an express stipulation[1] or customary arrangement[2] as to notice, a contract of employment is terminable at common law by reasonable notice[3]. The question as to what is a reasonable period of notice is one of fact, depending on all the circumstances of the case and the nature of the employment[4], and an implied term of reasonable notice may be greater than the statutory minimum applicable to all employees[5].

In the absence of any stipulation to the contrary, there is no obligation for notice to be given in writing[6]; but notice must be unambiguous[7] and must, in the case of notice given by an employer, be given directly to the employee[8]. It is normally lawful for an employer to give the employee wages in lieu of notice[9], on the basis that:

(1)   in most contracts the employer's obligation is to pay wages, not to provide work[10]; and

(2)   in any event, even if such a dismissal was wrongful, a payment of wages in lieu usually has the character of damages for such wrongful termination[11] and normally compensates the employee in full[12].

The general rule is that, once notice has been given effectively by either party, it may not be withdrawn unilaterally; and thus withdrawal of notice may be by mutual consent only[13].

1   If, as is usually the case, there is an express term in a contract of employment as to notice, on either side or both sides, it is one of the matters which must be included in the written statement of terms and conditions of employment: see the Employment Rights Act 1996 s 1(4)(e); and PARA 119. A contract may, unusually, specifically limit the grounds on which notice may be given: *McClelland v Northern Ireland General Health Services Board* [1957] 2 All ER 129, [1957] 1 WLR 594, HL. Further, there may exceptionally be cases where the court or tribunal will imply a limitation on the right to terminate by notice, where to do so would deprive the employee of some other valuable benefit meant to be given under the contract: *Aspden v Webbs Poultry and Meat Group (Holdings) Ltd* [1996] IRLR 521 (breach of contract to terminate by notice in order to deprive employee of rights under a permanent health insurance scheme); *Adin v Sedco Forex International Resources* Ltd [1997] IRLR 280, Ct of Sess. See the support for this development in *Brompton v AOC International Ltd and Unum Ltd* [1997] IRLR 639 at 643, CA, per Staughton LJ (obiter); but c f the qualification in *Hill v General Accident Fire and Life Assurance Corpn plc* [1998] IRLR 641, Ct of Sess, that the employer must still be able to dismiss for misconduct or redundancy. See also *Jenvey v Australian Broadcasting Corpn* [2002] EWHC 927 (QB), [2003] ICR 79, [2002] IRLR 520 (term implied into a contract of employment so that an employer could not lawfully exclude or limit an employee's right to contractual benefits which accrued by reason of redundancy by dismissing him for a reason other than redundancy, notwithstanding a decision to make him redundant). A mere statement that employment is 'permanent', 'permanent and pensionable' or some other such formulation will not, however, be taken literally and the contract will still be considered terminable by notice: *McClelland v Northern Ireland General Health Services Board* above; and see *Clark v Independent Broadcasting Corpn* [1974] 2 NZLR 587. If, however, a term in the contract is to remove the normal right to notice (or pay in lieu), it must do so unambiguously: *T & K Home Improvements Ltd v Skilton* [2000] IRLR 595, CA (clause permitting employer to dismiss 'with immediate effect' in case of failure to achieve performance targets held not to deny the employee payment in lieu of notice). As to the meaning of 'contract of employment' see PARA 2; and as to fixed-term contracts with or without notice provisions see PARA 725.

2   *George v Davies* [1911] 2 KB 445, DC.

3   *Richardson v Koefod* [1969] 3 All ER 1264, [1969] 1 WLR 1812, CA (cited in PARA 723 note 5); *James v Thomas H Kent & Co Ltd* [1951] 1 KB 551, [1950] 2 All ER 1099, CA. Any express term purporting to deny the employee the normal right to notice must be clear and unambiguous: *T & K Home Improvements Ltd v Skilton* [2000] IRLR 595, CA.

4   For an example of the process of quantifying notice see *Hill v CA Parsons & Co Ltd* [1972] Ch 305, [1971] 3 All ER 1345, CA.

5   Ie under the Employment Rights Act 1996 s 86: see PARAS 735, 736.

6   *Latchford Premier Cinema Ltd v Ennion* [1931] 2 Ch 409.

7   In particular, this means that a mere indication of future dismissal (particularly of impending redundancies) is not in itself notice of dismissal: *Morton Sundour Fabrics Ltd v Shaw* (1966) 2 ITR 84; *Pritchard-Rhodes Ltd v Boon and Milton* [1979] IRLR 19, EAT; *International Computers Ltd v Kennedy* [1981] IRLR 28, EAT; *Doble v Firestone Tyre and Rubber Co Ltd* [1981] IRLR 300, EAT; *Haseltine Lake & Co v Dowler* [1981] ICR 222, [1981] IRLR 25, EAT. This is particularly important in the law relating to redundancy in the context of the giving of counter-notice by an employee: see PARA 866.

8   It is not, therefore, enough for notice to be given to the employee's trade union: *Morris v CH Bailey Ltd* [1969] 2 Lloyd's Rep 215, CA. When notice is sent by post, it is effective only when

it is communicated to the employee, not when it is posted: *Brown v Southall and Knight* [1980] ICR 617, [1980] IRLR 130, EAT; *Hindle Gears Ltd v McGinty* [1985] ICR 111, [1984] IRLR 477, EAT (both cases of summary dismissal, but the same principle should apply to dismissal by notice). When notice is given orally, it is construed as exclusive of the day on which it is given: *West v Kneels Ltd* [1987] ICR 146, [1986] IRLR 430, EAT.

9   *Konski v Peet* [1915] 1 Ch 530.

10 See PARA 30. For the potentially wider approach under which employees may all have a legitimate interest in actually performing their work see, however, *William Hill Organisation Ltd v Tucker* [1999] ICR 291, [1998] IRLR 313, CA; in such a case, to be lawful a payment in lieu would need to be covered by an express provision in the contract.

11 *Dixon v Stenor Ltd* [1973] ICR 157, [1973] IRLR 28, NIRC; *Delaney v Staples (t/a De Montfort Recruitment)* [1992] 1 AC 687, [1992] ICR 483, HL (because a unilateral payment of wages in lieu is damages for wrongful dismissal, it is not 'wages' for the purposes of the Employment Rights Act 1996 Pt II (ss 13–27) (see PARA 254 et seq) and so a failure to make such a payment, e g where the employer purports to dismiss for cause without notice, is not an unlawful deduction under s 13 if there is no prior written agreement: see PARA 255). As to the categorisation of different forms of payments in lieu see *Delaney v Staples (t/a De Montfort Recruitment)* at 692 and 488–489 per Lord Browne-Wilkinson. The general rule that dismissal with wages in lieu is a wrongful dismissal with damages does not apply if the contract itself specifically gives the employer the right to terminate with either notice or payment in lieu: *Rex Stewart Jeffries Parker Ginsberg Ltd v Parker* [1988] IRLR 483, CA; *Delaney v Staples (t/a De Montfort Recruitment)* above. If the right to notice is waived (see PARA 735), termination of the contract without notice is not a breach and no damages are due: see *Trotter v Forth Ports Authority* [1991] IRLR 419, Ct of Sess.

12 There may, however, be other, collateral, matters depending on the technical nature of the dismissal, in particular whether a restraint of trade clause in the contract is invalidated, which it is if the dismissal is wrongful, but not if it is lawful under the contract, as in *Rex Stewart Jeffries Parker Ginsberg Ltd v Parker* [1988] IRLR 483, CA. Further, if there is a contractual entitlement to payment in lieu: (1) any moneys not paid under it can be recovered as a debt under the contract with no obligation on the employee to mitigate loss (*Abrahams v Performing Right Society* [1995] ICR 1028, [1995] IRLR 486, CA; *Gregory v Wallace* [1998] IRLR 387, CA); and (2) amounts paid under the contractual clause are subject to income tax (*EMI Group Electronics Ltd v Coldicott (Inspector of Taxes)* [1999] STC 803, [1999] IRLR 630, CA). However, if the contract merely enables the employer to make a payment in lieu, he has a choice whether or not to make such a payment and any claim by the employee is a claim for damages, against which the consequences of mitigation fall to be offset: *Cerberus Software Ltd v Rowley* [2001] EWCA Civ 78, [2001] ICR 376, [2001] IRLR 160.

The normal contractual rule of termination of contract applies in the employment context (including cases of wrongful dismissal: see PARA 825 et seq), ie that a party's repudiation terminated a contract of employment only if and when the other party elected to accept the repudiation (ie the 'elective' theory of termination of contract is adopted in preference to the 'automatic theory': that repudiation of a contract of employment by the employer which took the form of an express and immediate dismissal automatically terminated the contract): *Geys v Société Générale, London Branch* [2012] UKSC 63, [2013] 1 AC 523, [2013] 1 All ER 1061, [2013] ICR 117, [2013] IRLR 122. If an employer wished to exercise a contractual right to dismiss an employee by making a payment in lieu of notice, it had to notify the employee in clear and unambiguous terms that such a payment had been made and that it had been made in the exercise of that right; if a payment in lieu of notice were made direct to an employee's bank account, the bank would not without more be the employee's agent for the receipt of notification of what the payment was for: *Geys v Société Générale, London Branch* (a term should be implied as a necessary incident of the employment relationship that the parties would notify each other in 'clear and unambiguous terms' when a right to terminate the contract was exercised, and that the party exercising the right would specify how and when the right was intended to operate; there was no conflict between an explicit contractual term allowing termination on three months' notice and an employee handbook provision allowing for immediate termination with payment in lieu of notice).

13 *Riordan v War Office* [1959] 3 All ER 552, [1959] 1 WLR 1046 (affd [1960] 3 All ER 774n, [1961] 1 WLR 210, CA); *Harris and Russell Ltd v Slingsby* [1973] 3 All ER 31, [1973] ICR 454, NIRC. There are, however, cases in the law of unfair dismissal suggesting that a hot-headed resignation or dismissal followed swiftly by repentance and withdrawal of notice should be considered realistically, to see whether the original resignation or dismissal was unequivocal: *Sothern v Franks Charlesly & Co* [1981] IRLR 278, CA; *Barclay v City of Glasgow District Council* [1983] IRLR 313, EAT; *Martin v Yeoman Aggregates Ltd* [1983] ICR 314, [1983]

IRLR 49, EAT; *Sovereign House Security Services Ltd v Savage* [1989] IRLR 115, CA; but see also *Ali v Birmingham City Council* [2008] All ER (D) 260 (Oct), EAT (where the employee's resignation was reaffirmed by him several times on the same day and then withdrawn four days later it was decided that the resignation remained effective and termination proceeded). Where an employee's resignation is prima facie unambiguous, an employer is entitled to accept it at face value unless there are special circumstances, perhaps due to a conflict of personalities or individual characteristics, in which case he should allow a reasonable time for investigation: *Kwik-Fit (GB) Ltd v Lineham* [1992] ICR 183, [1992] IRLR 156, EAT (unfair dismissal case). A unilateral withdrawal by an employer from a notice of dismissal because of a mistaken expectation that an employee would accept proposed self-employment terms does not fall within the special circumstances exception: *Willoughby v CF Capital plc* [2011] EWCA Civ 1115, [2012] ICR 1038, [2011] IRLR 985 (notice was unambiguous and it terminated her employment just as the employer had intended; once given, the employer could not unilaterally withdraw it).

734. Employer's right to enforce notice. If an employee leaves employment without giving the notice required of him under his contract of employment, that is a breach of contract for which the employer may sue the employee[1]. In most cases such a cause of action is technical only and hardly worth pursuing[2]. Seeking to enforce notice may, however, be of incidental importance where the employee, possibly in a sensitive position, is contractually obliged to give a long period of notice and the employer wishes to ensure that the employee does not go to work for a competitor during that period[3]. In such a case the employer may claim not to accept the employee's breach of contract and may seek an injunction restraining the employee from working for a competitor, either on the basis of an express or implied duty of good faith[4] or of a clause in the contract[5] specifically permitting the employer to insist that the employee waits out the period of notice, not actually working for the employer, but not free to start working for someone else[6]. The practical remedy to enforce this aspect of a notice requirement is an injunction, which is a discretionary remedy; provided that the employer continues to pay the employee the remuneration due under the contract during the notice period, he may apply for such an injunction but its granting is not automatic and, in exercising its discretion, the court may take into account the need of the employer for protection, questions of confidential information, possible detriment to both parties and the nature of the employment that the employee wishes to take up[7].

If an employee leaves without giving due notice under the contract, the employer may lawfully retain, as liquidated damages, any wages due to the employee at the time of his breach of contract only if there is a contractual term to that effect[8]; moreover, any attempt to retain some or all of such wages already earned without a written term to that effect in the contract, a written notification of a term to that effect or the employee's prior written agreement or consent is likely to be an unlawful deduction, recoverable by the employee[9] under the Employment Rights Act 1996[10].

1   *Huttman v Boulnois* (1826) 2 C & P 510.
2   Ie particularly as a court will not normally specifically enforce a contract of employment to the extent of actually requiring an employee to work: see PARA 826. See also the Trade Union and Labour Relations (Consolidation) Act 1992 s 236 (no court may, whether by way of: (1) an order for specific performance of a contract of employment; or (2) an injunction restraining a breach or threatened breach of such a contract, compel an employee to do any work or attend at any place for the doing of any work); and PARA 1348.
3   This indirect way of protecting trade secrets and customer connections may, in particular circumstances, be of more practical use to an employer than the more traditional means of a restraint of trade clause in the contract of employment: see PARA 19. There is no objection in principle to the use of both a restraint clause and a clause such as this: *Crédit Suisse Asset Management Ltd v Armstrong* [1996] ICR 882, [1996] IRLR 450, CA.

4 *Evening Standard Co Ltd v Henderson* [1987] ICR 588, [1987] IRLR 64, CA. However, for the more restrictive approach, that an implied restriction can only apply if there is no interest of the employee in actually performing his work, but only in being paid, see *William Hill Organisation Ltd v Tucker* [1999] ICR 291, [1998] IRLR 313, CA (injunction refused on that basis, in the absence of an express restriction). The implied restriction can only apply where the contract remains in force: *JA Mont (UK) Ltd v Mills* [1993] IRLR 172, CA.

5 Such a clause is generally known as a 'garden leave clause'. Such an express clause is necessary in a case where the employee can show an interest in actually performing his work, not just in receiving pay: *William Hill Organisation Ltd v Tucker* [1999] ICR 291, [1998] IRLR 313, CA.

6 See *Provident Financial Group plc v Hayward* [1989] 3 All ER 298, [1989] ICR 160, CA; *Euro Brokers Ltd v Rabey* [1995] IRLR 206 (six month 'garden leave clause' enforced).

7 *Provident Financial Group plc v Hayward* [1989] 3 All ER 298, [1989] ICR 160, CA. In such a case the court has the power, if necessary, to narrow the scope of the contractual obligation if it is too wide as drafted: *Provident Financial Group plc v Hayward*; *GFI Group Inc v Eaglestone* [1994] IRLR 119. Cf the position in a case of a formal restraint of trade clause where the court will normally only approve or disapprove the clause as it stands, and not modify it: see *JA Mont (UK) Ltd v Mills* [1993] IRLR 172, CA; and COMPETITION vol 18 (2009) PARA 377 et seq.

8 The employee's right to payment is not affected by his subsequent breach: *Parkin v South Hetton Coal Co* (1907) 24 TLR 193, CA; *Button v Thompson* (1869) LR 4 CP 330; *Warburton v Heyworth* (1880) 6 QBD 1, CA; *Margerison v Bertwistle* (1872) 36 JP 100; *George v Davies* [1911] 2 KB 445, DC. This principle applies even where the employee is summarily dismissed for misconduct: *Boston Deep Sea Fishing and Ice Co v Ansell* (1888) 39 ChD 339, CA; *Healey v SA Française Rubastic* [1917] 1 KB 946. Quaere, however, whether a court might now permit an employer to claim an equitable set-off; and see, in the different context of a breach of contract by the employee during employment, *Sim v Rotherham Metropolitan Borough Council* [1987] Ch 216, [1986] ICR 897 (cited in PARA 29 note 5). Even if this were allowed, the employer would still be faced with the difficulty presented by the Employment Rights Act 1996 Pt II (ss 13–27) (unlawful deductions from wages) (see PARA 254 et seq): see note 10.

It was established principle that an employer could defend a claim for damages for wrongful dismissal by using at trial, in its defence of justification, evidence of misconduct by the employee that had not been known to the employer at the time of dismissal. However, having chosen to exercise its contractual power to terminate the contract without notice, but with pay in lieu, the defendant company had not been entitled to resile from the contractual consequences of its choice by later following the different common law route of accepting repudiation by relying, after the termination event, on an earlier act of misconduct by the claimant of which it had been unaware at the relevant date: *Cavenagh v William Evans Ltd* [2012] EWCA Civ 697, [2013] 1 WLR 238, [2012] ICR 1231, [2012] IRLR 679.

9 Ie under the Employment Rights Act 1996 Pt II.

10 Although this point was not directly before the Court of Appeal in *Delaney v Staples (t/a De Montfort Recruitment)* [1991] 2 QB 47, [1991] ICR 331, CA (affd on other grounds [1992] 1 AC 687, [1992] ICR 483, HL), it is submitted that it follows from the reasoning in relation to the claim for outstanding commission and holiday pay (the employee has already earned the sum due during the course of employment and so it is 'wages' within the Employment Rights Act 1996 s 27 (see PARA 254); it is then declared by s 13(3) (see PARA 255) that any payment of an amount less than the total amount properly payable to the worker is to be treated as a 'deduction', and thus subject to the rules on prior written agreement in s 13(1) (see PARA 255)). See also *Chiltern House Ltd v Chambers* [1990] IRLR 88, EAT; *New Centurion Trust v Welch* [1990] ICR 383, [1990] IRLR 123, EAT.

(ii) Minimum Notice Periods

735. In general. Although the length of notice to be given by each party to a contract of employment is primarily a matter for that contract[1], any such contractual provision, express or implied, is subject to statutory minimum periods of notice which override any inconsistent contractual terms[2]. These statutory minima apply, with certain exceptions[3], to any employee[4]; and they operate, if necessary, by amending by statute the relevant notice term of the employee's contract[5] and so any complaint by the employee that he has not been given the statutory minimum notice remains essentially a contractual claim, not a special statutory claim[6].

The existence of the statutory minimum periods of notice does not affect any right of either party to a contract of employment[7] to treat the contract as terminable without notice by reason of the conduct of the other party[8]; nor do the statutory provisions setting out the statutory minimum periods of notice[9] prevent either party from waiving his right to notice on any occasion or from accepting a payment in lieu of notice[10].

For certain statutory purposes in the context of unfair dismissal law and redundancy law, the date of a dismissal may be notionally extended by the length of the statutory minimum notice period where the employer has not given such notice[11].

1   See PARA 733.
2   See the Employment Rights Act 1996 s 86; and PARA 736.
3   As to excluded categories of employment see PARAS 166–168. The Employment Rights Act 1996 Pt IX (ss 86–93), except s 92 (see PARA 755) and s 93 (see PARA 756), does not apply to Crown employment: see s 191(1), (2)(d); and PARA 163.
4   Ie subject to his meeting the qualifying conditions: see PARAS 736, 737. As to the meaning of 'employee' see PARA 2. As to statutory contracts see PARA 736 note 2.
5   See the Employment Rights Act 1996 s 86(3); and PARA 736.

6   *Westwood v Secretary of State for Employment* [1985] AC 20, [1985] ICR 209, HL (approving *Secretary of State for Employment v Wilson* [1978] 3 All ER 137, [1978] ICR 200, EAT).
7   As to the meaning of 'contract of employment' see PARA 2.

8   Employment Rights Act 1996 s 86(6). If an employer wishes to rely on s 86(6) and its retention of the power of summary dismissal for gross misconduct, it is not sufficient merely to label the dismissal as having been for gross misconduct, but rather the employer must be able to substantiate his allegations: *Lanton Leisure Ltd v White and Gibson* [1987] IRLR 119, EAT. See also *R (on the application of West Midlands Fire and Rescue Authority) v First Secretary of State in the Office of the Deputy Prime Minister* [2008] EWHC 1458 (Admin), [2008] All ER (D) 389 (Jul) (application for judicial review, of Secretary of State's finding that the employee fire officer's conduct in preparation for a national strike did not amount to gross misconduct, dismissed as the Secretary of State had been entitled to conclude that the sanction of summary dismissal was inappropriate). Where the employee leaves in response to the employer's conduct, that may constitute a constructive dismissal for the purposes of unfair dismissal law and redundancy law: see PARAS 763, 864.
9   Ie the Employment Rights Act 1996 s 86: see PARA 736.
10 Employment Rights Act 1996 s 86(3). As to payment of wages in lieu of notice see PARA 733. If the right to notice is waived, the right to payment in lieu is also impliedly waived: *Trotter v Forth Ports Authority* [1991] IRLR 419, Ct of Sess; *Baldwin v British Coal Corpn* [1995] IRLR 139.
11 See the Employment Rights Act 1996 s 97(2)–(5) (cited in PARA 764), s 145(5), (6) (cited in PARA 871 note 20).

736.   Statutory minimum periods of notice.   The notice required to be given by an employer[1] to terminate the contract of employment[2] of a person who has been continuously employed[3] for one month[4] or more is not less than:

(1)   one week's[5] notice if his period of continuous employment is less than two years[6];

(2)   one week's notice for each year of continuous employment if his period of continuous employment is two years or more but less than 12 years; and

(3)   12 weeks' notice if his period of continuous employment is 12 years or more[7].

The notice required to be given by an employee[8] who has been continuously employed for one month or more to terminate his contract of employment is not less than one week[9].

Any provision for shorter notice in any contract of employment with a person who has been continuously employed for one month or more has effect subject to the provisions described above[10].

Any contract of employment of a person who has been continuously employed for three months or more which is a contract for a term certain of one month or less has effect as if it were for an indefinite period and, accordingly, the statutory minimum periods of notice apply to the contract[11].

1 As to the meaning of 'employer' see PARA 2.
2 As to the meaning of 'contract of employment' see PARA 2.
  The Employment Rights Act 1996 ss 86–91 (see also PARA 737 et seq) apply in relation to a contract all or any of the terms of which are terms which take effect by virtue of any provision contained in or having effect under an Act of Parliament, whether public or local, as they apply in relation to any other contract; and, for these purposes, the reference to an Act of Parliament includes, subject to any express provision to the contrary, an Act passed after the Employment Rights Act 1996: s 91(6).
3 As to continuity of employment see PARA 130 et seq.
  It was said in *Hambling v Marsden Builders Ltd* (1966) 1 ITR 494 that the relevant period of employment was to be calculated to the date of expiry of the notice, not to the date at which notice was given; sed quaere.
4 As to the meaning of 'month' for these purposes see PARA 130 note 11.
5 The definition of 'week' given by the Employment Rights Act 1996 s 235(1) (see PARA 126 note 13) does not apply for these purposes (see s 235(1)), but the expression has not been defined otherwise.
6 As to the meaning of 'year' for these purposes see PARA 130 note 11.
7 Employment Rights Act 1996 s 86(1). This requirement does not survive if the contract is frustrated: *GF Sharp & Co Ltd v McMillan* [1998] IRLR 632, EAT. As to the modification of the Employment Rights Act 1996 s 86(1) in relation to National Health Service employees see PARA 326 note 13.
8 As to the meaning of 'employee' see PARA 2; and as to excluded classes of employment see PARAS 166–168.
9 Employment Rights Act 1996 s 86(2). As to the modification of s 86(2) in relation to National Health Service employees see PARA 326 note 13.
10 Employment Rights Act 1996 s 86(3). The right of waiver is not, however, affected: see PARA 735. As to the modification of s 86(3) in relation to National Health Service employees see PARA 326 note 13.
11 Employment Rights Act 1996 s 86(4). Section 86(4) has been used to prevent an employer from avoiding liability for statutory sick pay by putting the employee on to 'daily contracts' (over a period of nine months): *Brown v Chief Adjudication Officer* [1997] ICR 266, [1997] IRLR 110, CA. As to the modification of the Employment Rights Act 1996 s 86(4) in relation to National Health Service employees see PARA 326 note 13. As to the fair treatment of employees on fixed-term contracts see PARA 84 et seq.

(iii) Rights and Liabilities during Notice Period

737. Rights of employee in period of notice. If:

(1) an employer[1] gives notice to terminate the contract of employment[2] of a person who has been continuously employed[3] for one month[4] or more[5]; or

(2) an employee[6] who has been continuously employed for one month or more gives notice to terminate his contract of employment[7],

the statutory provisions relating to periods of notice[8] have effect as respects the liability of the employer for the required[9] period of notice[10].

These provisions do not, however, apply in relation to a notice given by the employer or the employee if the notice to be given by the employer to terminate the contract must be at least one week[11] more than the required[12] notice[13].

If an employer fails to give the required notice[14], the rights conferred by the statutory provisions relating to periods of notice[15] must be taken into account in assessing his liability for breach of the contract[16].

1   As to the meaning of 'employer' see PARA 2.
2   As to the meaning of 'contract of employment' see PARA 2; and as to statutory contracts see PARA 736 note 2.
3   As to continuity of employment see PARA 130 et seq.
4   As to the meaning of 'month' for these purposes see PARA 130 note 11.
5   Employment Rights Act 1996 s 87(1).
6   As to the meaning of 'employee' see PARA 2.
7   Employment Rights Act 1996 s 87(2).
8   Ie the Employment Rights Act 1996 ss 88–91: see PARA 738 et seq.
9   Ie required, in a case falling within head (1) in the text, by the Employment Rights Act 1996 s 86(1) (see PARA 736) or, in a case falling within head (2) in the text, by s 86(2) (see PARA 736).
10 Employment Rights Act 1996 s 87(1), (2). This applies where notice is given; but, if notice is not given, the employee must sue under his contract, with the possible help of s 91(5) (see the text and notes 14–16). In either event, there is no special statutory claim before a tribunal and so the employee must sue in contract in the ordinary courts. As to the jurisdiction of the civil courts in employment cases generally see PARA 1436.
11 As to the meaning of 'week' for these purposes see PARA 126 note 13.
12 Ie the notice required by the Employment Rights Act 1996 s 86(1): see PARA 736.
13 Employment Rights Act 1996 s 87(4).
14 See note 10.
15 Ie the rights given by the Employment Rights Act 1996 ss 87–90: see also PARA 738 et seq.
16 Employment Rights Act 1996 s 91(5). Where the employer is insolvent, amounts payable under s 86(1) or (2) are guaranteed by the Secretary of State and payable out of the National Insurance Fund: see s 184(1)(b); and PARA 628. Even where these statutory provisions are invoked, the employee's rights remain essentially contractual not statutory, and thus e g the employee is under a duty to mitigate his loss (see PARA 831): *Westwood v Secretary of State for Employment* [1985] AC 20, [1985] ICR 209, HL.

738.   Employments for which there are normal working hours.   If an employee[1] has normal working hours[2] under the contract of employment[3] in force during the period of notice[4], and if during any part of those normal working hours the employee is:

(1)   ready and willing to work but no work is provided for him by his employer[5];

(2)   incapable of work because of sickness or injury;

(3)   absent from work wholly or partly because of pregnancy or childbirth[6] or on adoption leave[7], parental leave[8] or ordinary or additional paternity leave[9]; or

(4)   absent from work in accordance with the terms of his employment relating to holidays,

the employer is liable to pay the employee for the part of normal working hours covered by heads (1) to (4) above a sum not less than the amount of remuneration for that part of normal working hours calculated at the average hourly rate of remuneration produced by dividing a week's pay[10] by the number of normal working hours[11].

Any payments made to the employee by his employer in respect of the relevant part of the period of notice, whether by way of sick pay, statutory sick pay[12], maternity pay, statutory maternity pay[13], paternity pay, ordinary statutory paternity pay, additional statutory paternity pay[14], adoption pay, statutory adoption pay[15], holiday pay or otherwise, go towards meeting the employer's liability under these provisions[16].

Where notice was given by the employee, the employer's liability under these provisions does not arise unless and until the employee leaves the service of the employer in pursuance of the notice[17].

1 As to the meaning of 'employee' see PARA 2.
2 As to the calculation of normal working hours see PARA 142.
3 As to the meaning of 'contract of employment' see PARA 2; and as to statutory contracts see PARA 736 note 2.

4 For these purposes, 'period of notice' means: (1) where notice is given by an employer, the period of notice required by the Employment Rights Act 1996 s 86(1) (see PARA 736); and (2) where notice is given by an employee, the period of notice required by s 86(2) (see PARA 736): s 87(3). As to the meaning of 'employer' see PARA 2.

5 Taking other work during the notice period (when not required to work by the employer) is not a breach of contract at common law and so the employee remains entitled to this notice payment: *Hutchings v Coinseed Ltd* [1998] IRLR 190, CA.

6 As to the meaning of 'childbirth' see PARA 356 note 4.
7 As to adoption leave see PARA 377 et seq.
8 As to parental leave see PARA 390 et seq.

9 'Ordinary or additional paternity leave' means leave under the Employment Rights Act 1996 ss 80A–80B (see PARAS 368, 369): s 235(1) (definition substituted by the Work and Families Act 2006 Sch 1 para 43). See also note 11.

10 As to the calculation of a week's pay see PARA 143; and as to the calculation date see PARA 146.

11 Employment Rights Act 1996 s 88(1) (amended by the Employment Relations Act 1999 Sch 4 Pt III paras 5, 10; the Employment Act 2002 Sch 7 paras 24, 29(1), (2); and the Work and Families Act 2006 Sch 1 para 39(1), (2)). As from a day to be appointed, in head (3) in the text: (1) a reference to 'shared parental leave' is added after the reference to 'adoption leave'; (2) the reference to 'ordinary or additional paternity leave' is replaced by a reference to 'paternity leave': Employment Rights Act 1996 s 88(1) (as so amended; and prospectively amended by the Children and Families Act 2014 Sch 7 para 37). At the date at which this volume states the law, that day had been appointed as 1 December 2014 for the purposes of head (1) above: see the Children and Families Act 2014 (Commencement No 3, Transitional Provisions and Savings) Order 2014, SI 2014/1640, art 5(1), (2)(l). For the purposes of head (2) above, 5 April 2015 has been appointed: see the Children and Families Act 2014 (Commencement No 3, Transitional Provisions and Savings) Order 2014, SI 2014/1640, art 7(r). As from a day to be appointed, 'paternity leave' means leave under the Employment Rights Act 1996 s 80A (see PARA 368) or s 80B (see PARA 369): see s 235(1) (definition prospectively substituted by the Children and Families Act 2014 Sch 7 para 42). At the date at which this volume states the law, that day had been appointed as 5 April 2015: see the Children and Families Act 2014 (Commencement No 3, Transitional Provisions and Savings) Order 2014, SI 2014/1640, art 7(u). See also note 9. 'Shared parental leave' means leave under the Employment Rights Act 1996 s 75E (see PARA 398) or s 75G (see PARA 399): see s 235(1) (definition added by the Children and Families Act 2014 Sch 7 para 42).

12 As to statutory sick pay see PARA 558 et seq.
13 As to statutory maternity pay see PARA 401 et seq.
14 As to statutory paternity pay see PARA 443 et seq.
15 As to statutory adoption pay see PARA 488 et seq.

16 Employment Rights Act 1996 s 88(2) (amended by the Employment Act 2002 Sch 7 paras 24, 29(1), (3); and the Work and Families Act 2006 Sch 1 para 39(1), (2)). As from a day to be appointed, in the Employment Rights Act 1996 s 88(2) (see also the text and notes 12–15): (1) the reference to 'shared parental pay, statutory shared parental pay' is added after the reference to 'statutory adoption pay'; and (2) the reference to 'ordinary statutory paternity pay, additional statutory paternity pay' is replaced by a reference to 'statutory paternity pay': see s 88(2) (as so amended; and prospectively amended by the Children and Families Act 2014 Sch 7 para 37). At the date at which this volume states the law, that day had been appointed as 1 December 2014 for the purposes of head (1) above: see the Children and Families Act 2014 (Commencement No 3, Transitional Provisions and Savings) Order 2014, SI 2014/1640, art 5(1), (2)(l). For the purposes of head (2) above, 5 April 2015 has been appointed: see the Children and Families Act 2014 (Commencement No 3, Transitional Provisions and Savings) Order 2014, SI 2014/1640, art 7(r).

17 Employment Rights Act 1996 s 88(3).

739. Employments for which there are no normal working hours. If an employee[1] does not have normal working hours[2] under the contract of employment[3] in force in the period of notice[4], the employer[5] is liable to pay the employee for each week[6] of the period of notice a sum not less than a week's pay[7]. This liability of the employer is conditional on the employee being ready and willing to do work of a reasonable nature and amount to earn a week's pay[8]; but this condition does not apply in respect of any period during which the employee is:

(1)   incapable of work because of sickness or injury;

(2)   absent from work wholly or partly because of pregnancy or childbirth[9] or on adoption leave[10], parental leave[11] or ordinary or additional paternity leave[12]; or

(3)   absent from work in accordance with the terms of his employment relating to holidays[13],

and any payment made to an employee by his employer in respect of such a period, whether by way of sick pay, statutory sick pay[14], maternity pay, statutory maternity pay[15], paternity pay, ordinary statutory paternity pay, additional statutory paternity pay[16], adoption pay, statutory adoption pay[17], holiday pay or otherwise, is to be taken into account for these purposes as if it were remuneration paid by the employer in respect of that period[18].

Where the notice was given by the employee, the employer's liability under these provisions does not arise unless and until the employee leaves the service of the employer in pursuance of the notice[19].

1   As to the meaning of 'employee' see PARA 2; and as to excluded classes of employment see PARAS 166–168.
2   As to the calculation of normal working hours see PARA 142.
3   As to the meaning of 'contract of employment' see PARA 2; and as to statutory contracts see PARA 736 note 2.
4   As to the meaning of 'period of notice' see PARA 738 note 4.
5   As to the meaning of 'employer' see PARA 2.
6   As to the meaning of 'week' for these purposes see PARA 126 note 13.
7   Employment Rights Act 1996 s 89(1). As to the calculation of a week's pay see PARA 143; and as to the calculation date see PARA 146.
8   Employment Rights Act 1996 s 89(2).
9   As to the meaning of 'childbirth' see PARA 356 note 4.
10   As to adoption leave see PARA 377 et seq.
11   As to parental leave see PARA 390 et seq.
12   As to the meaning of 'ordinary or additional paternity leave' see PARA 738 note 9. See note 13.
13   Employment Rights Act 1996 s 89(3) (amended by the Employment Relations Act 1999 Sch 4 Pt III paras 5, 11; the Employment Act 2002 Sch 7 paras 24, 30(1), (2) and the Work and Families Act 2006 Sch 1 para 40(1), (2)). As from a day to be appointed, in head (3) in the text: (1) the reference to 'shared parental leave' is added after the reference to 'adoption leave'; (2) the reference to 'ordinary or additional paternity leave' is replaced by a reference to 'paternity leave': Employment Rights Act 1996 s 89(3) (as so amended; and prospectively amended by the Children and Families Act 2014 Sch 7 para 38). At the date at which this volume states the law, that day had been appointed as 1 December 2014 for the purposes of head (1) above: see the Children and Families Act 2014 (Commencement No 3, Transitional Provisions and Savings) Order 2014, SI 2014/1640, art 5(1), (2)(m). For the purposes of head (2) above, 5 April 2015 has been appointed: see the Children and Families Act 2014 (Commencement No 3, Transitional Provisions and Savings) Order 2014, SI 2014/1640, art 7(s). As to the meaning of 'shared parental leave' and 'paternity leave' see PARA 738 note 11.
14   As to statutory sick pay see PARA 558 et seq.
15   As to statutory maternity pay see PARA 401 et seq.
16   As to statutory paternity pay see PARA 443 et seq.
17   As to statutory adoption pay see PARA 488 et seq.
18   Employment Rights Act 1996 s 89(4) (amended by the Employment Act 2002 Sch 7 paras 24, 30(1), (3); and the Work and Families Act 2006 Sch 1 para 40(1), (3)). As from a day to be

appointed, in the Employment Rights Act 1996 s 89(4) (see also the text and notes 14–17): (1) the reference to 'shared parental pay, statutory shared parental pay' is added after the reference to 'statutory adoption pay'; and (2) the reference to 'ordinary statutory paternity pay, additional statutory paternity pay' is replaced by a reference to 'statutory paternity pay': see s 89(4) (as so amended; and prospectively amended by the Children and Families Act 2014 Sch 7 para 38). At the date at which this volume states the law, that day had been appointed as 1 December 2014 for the purposes of head (1) above: see the Children and Families Act 2014 (Commencement No 3, Transitional Provisions and Savings) Order 2014, SI 2014/1640, art 5(1), (2)(m). For the purposes of head (2) above, 5 April 2015 has been appointed: see the Children and Families Act 2014 (Commencement No 3, Transitional Provisions and Savings) Order 2014, SI 2014/1640, art 7(s).

19 Employment Rights Act 1996 s 89(5).

740.   Allowances for incapacity benefit, contributory employment and support allowance and industrial injury benefit.   Where the arrangements in force relating to the employment[1] are such that:

(1)   payments by way of sick pay are made by the employer[2] to employees[3] to whom the arrangements apply, in cases where any such employees are incapable of work because of sickness or injury; and

(2)   in calculating any payment so made to any such employee, an amount representing, or treated as representing, short-term incapacity benefit[4], contributory employment and support allowance[5] or industrial injury benefit[6] is taken into account, whether by way of deduction or by way of calculating the payment as a supplement to that amount,

then, if:

(a)   during any part of the period of notice[7] the employee is incapable of work because of sickness or injury;

(b)   one or more payments by way of sick pay are made to him by the employer in respect of that part of the period of notice; and

(c)   in calculating any such payment, such an amount as is referred to in head (2) above is taken into account,

the amount so taken into account is to be treated[8] as having been paid by the employer to the employee by way of sick pay in respect of that part of that period, and is to go towards meeting the liability[9] of the employer during the period of notice[10].

1   As to the meaning of 'employment' see PARA 2.
2   As to the meaning of 'employer' see PARA 2.
3   As to the meaning of 'employee' see PARA 2; and as to excluded classes of employment see PARAS 166–168.
4   Although the employee is not entitled to claim unemployment benefit for the period in respect of which future wage loss compensation is granted, there is no such bar on receiving incapacity benefit under the Social Security (Incapacity for Work) (General) Regulations 1995, SI 1995/311; as that benefit is not necessarily based on inability to work, its receipt by the dismissed employee does not per se disqualify him from an award for future loss—it remains a question of fact whether the employee could have worked during the period of any such award: *Sheffield Forgemasters International Ltd v Fox* [2009] ICR 333, [2009] IRLR 192, EAT. As to the right to short-term incapacity benefit see the Social Security Contributions and Benefits Act 1992 s 30A; and WELFARE BENEFITS AND STATE PENSIONS vol 104 (2014) PARA 472. In fact most employees, even those under notice, now receive state benefit during sickness through their employer as statutory sick pay (see PARA 558 et seq) and this is taken into account in the Employment Rights Act 1996 s 88(2) (see PARA 738) and s 89(4) (see PARA 739).
5   As to the right to contributory employment and support allowance see WELFARE BENEFITS AND STATE PENSIONS vol 104 (2014) PARA 252.
6   As to the right to industrial injury benefit see the Social Security Contributions and Benefits Act 1992 s 94; and WELFARE BENEFITS AND STATE PENSIONS vol 104 (2014) PARA 175. See also note 4.
7   As to the meaning of 'period of notice' see PARA 738 note 4.

8   Ie for the purposes of the Employment Rights Act 1996 s 88 (see PARA 738) or s 89 (see PARA 739).
9   Ie under the Employment Rights Act 1996 s 88 (see PARA 738) or s 89 (see PARA 739).
10   Employment Rights Act 1996 s 90(1), (2) (s 90(1) amended by SI 2008/1879).

741. Employer not liable to make payments in certain circumstances. An employer[1] is not liable[2] to make any payment in respect of a period during which an employee[3] is absent from work[4] with the employer's leave granted at the employee's request[5]. Nor is any payment due[6] in consequence of a notice to terminate a contract given by the employee if, after the notice is given and on or before the termination of the contract, the employee takes part in a strike[7] of employees of the employer[8].

1   As to the meaning of 'employer' see PARA 2.
2   Ie under the Employment Rights Act 1996 s 88 (see PARA 738) or s 89 (see PARA 739).
3   As to the meaning of 'employee' see PARA 2; and as to excluded classes of employment see PARAS 166–168.
4   Ie including any period of time taken off in accordance with the Employment Rights Act 1996 Pt VI (ss 50–63C) (see PARA 326 et seq) or the Trade Union and Labour Relations (Consolidation) Act 1992 s 168 or s 170 (time off for trade union duties and activities) (see PARAS 1065, 1066).
5   Employment Rights Act 1996 s 91(1).
6   See note 2.
7   As to the meaning of 'strike' see PARA 134 note 4.
8   Employment Rights Act 1996 s 91(2).

742. Termination of employment during period of notice. If during the period of notice[1]:

(1)   the employer[2] breaks the contract of employment[3], payments received[4] in respect of the part of the period after the breach go towards mitigating the damages recoverable by the employee[5] for loss of earnings in that part of the period of notice[6];

(2)   the employee breaks the contract and the employer rightfully treats the breach as terminating the contract[7], no payment is due to the employee[8] in respect of the part of the period of notice falling after the termination of the contract[9].

1   As to the meaning of 'period of notice' see PARA 738 note 4.
2   As to the meaning of 'employer' see PARA 2.
3   As to the meaning of 'contract of employment' see PARA 2; and as to statutory contracts see PARA 736 note 2.
4   Ie under the Employment Rights Act 1996 s 88 (see PARA 738) or s 89 (see PARA 739).
5   As to the meaning of 'employee' see PARA 2; and as to excluded classes of employment see PARAS 166–168.
6   Employment Rights Act 1996 s 91(3). This emphasises the overall contractual (rather than statutory) nature of the employee's remedies in this area: see PARA 737 note 10.
7   As to lawful summary dismissal see PARA 743.
8   See note 4.
9   Employment Rights Act 1996 s 91(4).

(4) SUMMARY DISMISSAL

743. Employer's right of summary dismissal. An employer has a common law right to dismiss an employee without notice on the grounds of the employee's gross misconduct, and such a dismissal is not wrongful[1]. Originally this right was explained as a legal incident of the status of master and servant but, in line with the modern contractual analysis of the employment relationship[2], it is now explained in contractual terms, as the acceptance by the employer of a repudiation of the contract by the employee[3]. Alternatively, gross misconduct justifying summary dismissal may be seen as conduct so undermining the trust and confidence[4] which is inherent in the particular contract of employment that the employer should no longer be required to retain the employee in his employment[5].

The power of summary dismissal is not removed or directly altered by the modern employment protection legislation, either as to minimum periods of notice[6] or as to the statutory claim for unfair dismissal[7]. For the purposes of a claim for unfair dismissal, the factor of summary dismissal can be considered only in the context of whether or not it was reasonable to dismiss at all; if the decision was reasonable, the dismissal may not be unfair but may nevertheless be wrongful if the misconduct was not actually gross and no notice was given[8].

1   *Callo v Brouncker* (1831) 4 C & P 518. As to gross misconduct see PARA 743. As to wrongful dismissal see PARA 825 et seq.
2   See PARA 1.
3   *Boston Deep Sea Fishing and Ice Co v Ansell* (1888) 39 ChD 339, CA; *Laws v London Chronicle (Indicator Newspapers) Ltd* [1959] 2 All ER 285, [1959] 1 WLR 698, CA; *Denmark Productions Ltd v Boscobel Productions Ltd* [1969] 1 QB 699, [1968] 3 All ER 513, CA; *Pepper v Webb* [1969] 2 All ER 216, [1969] 1 WLR 514, CA. *Boston Deep Sea Fishing and Ice Co v Ansell* above was applied in *Lakshmi v Mid-Cheshire Hospitals NHS Trust* [2008] EWHC 878 (QB), [2008] IRLR 956, [2008] All ER (D) 353 (Apr).
4   As to the implied term of trust and confidence see PARA 48.
5   *Neary v Dean of Westminster* [1999] IRLR 288 at 291 per Lord Jauncey of Tullichettle.
6   See the Employment Rights Act 1996 s 86; and PARAS 735, 736.
7   See PARA 755 et seq. The continued existence and availability of the power to dismiss summarily is referred to in the ACAS Code of Practice 1: Disciplinary and Grievance Procedures (2009): see PARA 707. As to the ACAS Code of Practice 1: Disciplinary and Grievance Procedures see PARA 701 et seq and as to ACAS Codes of Practice generally see PARAS 1223–1224. See also the non-statutory guide: Discipline and Grievances at work: The ACAS guide (September 2014), in particular Appendix 2. As to Discipline and Grievances at work: The ACAS guide (September 2014) see PARA 701.
8   *Treganowen v Robert Knee & Co Ltd* [1975] ICR 405, [1975] IRLR 247; *BSC Sports and Social Club v Morgan* [1987] IRLR 391, EAT. As to the possible significance of the dismissal being summary as one of the circumstances to be considered in assessing fairness under the Employment Rights Act 1996 s 98(4) (see PARA 765) see *Eastland Homes Partnership Ltd v Cunningham* (2014) UKEAT/0272/13/MC; and PARA 776 note 6.
    The fact that a dismissal without notice is warranted does not mean that the employer need not apply normal disciplinary procedures applying to that employment. The ACAS Code of Practice 1: Disciplinary and Grievance Procedures (2009) states a fair disciplinary process should always be followed, before dismissing for gross misconduct: see PARA 701. See also Discipline and Grievances at work: The ACAS guide (September 2014), p 32. See note 7.

744. Factors giving rise to summary dismissal. When summary dismissal was viewed as a right inherent in the status of master and servant[1], the courts sought to isolate and categorise the various forms of misconduct by the employee that justified such action by the employer[2]. However, now that summary dismissal is explained in contractual terms, the question is whether the misconduct was sufficiently grave to amount to a repudiation by the employee of the contract of employment[3], either as to the whole contract or as to a particular part of it of fundamental importance[4]; this is a question of fact in any particular case[5], depending on the circumstances of the case, the nature of the employment and, possibly, the terms of the particular contract in question[6], and previous case law is of limited precedent value, particularly as attitudes to certain forms of misconduct may change over time[7].

It is now common for employees to be subject to written disciplinary procedures[8] which often expressly state the employer's power of summary dismissal and indicate what may constitute gross misconduct warranting such dismissal[9]. Such a clause normally covers certain immutable areas which would warrant summary dismissal in almost any employment[10], but may also be used by an employer to specify, in addition, conduct which will not be tolerated in the particular circumstances of that employment. While most such clauses are not exhaustive and thus do not restrict the employer's ability to dismiss summarily, there may be cases where, as a matter of construction of the contract, the particular clause does limit the employer's right, either as to the substantive grounds on which he may exercise it[11] or as to the procedure which he must adopt in order to exercise it[12]. The fact that particular conduct is expressly stated to constitute gross misconduct and to warrant summary dismissal does not mean that a dismissal on that ground is automatically fair under statute, since disciplinary rules cannot oust the jurisdiction of an employment tribunal to look into the overall merits, substantive and procedural, of a dismissal[13], though such express coverage, made known to the employee and consistently acted on by the employer, could be important evidence in an unfair dismissal case[14].

There is no common law right for an employee to be given reasons for his dismissal by his employer; but an employee who has been continuously employed for not less than one year as at the effective date of termination of his contract[15] has a statutory right to be provided by the employer, on request, within 14 days of that request, with a written statement giving particulars of the reasons for his dismissal[16].

1   See PARA 743.
2   The judgment of Parke B in *Callo v Brouncker* (1831) 4 C & P 518, referring to moral misconduct (pecuniary or otherwise), wilful disobedience or habitual neglect, was treated as laying down set rules on summary dismissal. There is also a large body of old, sometimes very old, case law which established that an employee could be summarily dismissed if:
    (1)   he wilfully disobeyed the lawful and reasonable instructions of his employer and the disobedience was so grave that it went to the root of the contract of employment (*Spain v Arnott* (1817) 2 Stark 256; *Callo v Brouncker*; *Turner v Mason* (1845) 14 M & W 112; *Acklam v Sentinel Insurance Co Ltd* [1959] 2 Lloyd's Rep 683 at 689 per Salmon J (it was necessary to show either that an order of vital importance was disobeyed or that an order of not so great importance was persistently neglected); and see *Jacquot v Bourra* (1839) 7 Dowl 348; *Beale v Great Western Rly Co* (1901) 17 TLR 450, DC; *Lilley v Elwin* (1848) 11 QB 742; *Renno v Bennett* (1842) 3 QB 768; *Churchward v Chambers* (1860) 2 F & F 229; *Parkin v South Hetton Coal Co* (1907) 98 LT 162, 24 TLR 193, CA; *Smith v Thompson* (1849) 8 CB 44; *Walters v Hughes* (1913) 48 L Jo 340; *Pepper v Webb* [1969] 2 All ER 216, [1969] 1 WLR 514, CA; and head (2) below), although an employee was not bound to obey instructions to do something not properly appertaining to the character or capacity in which he was engaged (*Price v Mouat* (1862) 11 CBNS 508) or which involved a reasonable apprehension of danger to the employee's life or person (*Turner v Mason* above at 118 per Alderson and Rolfe BB; and see *Bouzourou v Ottoman Bank* [1930] AC 271, PC; *Ottoman Bank v Chakarian* [1930] AC 277, PC; *McDonald v Moller Line (UK) Ltd* [1953] 2 Lloyd's Rep 662) or to accept an order to connive at the falsification of his employer's records (*Morrish v Henlys (Folkestone) Ltd* [1973] 2 All ER 137, [1973] ICR 482, NIRC);
    (2)   he was guilty of misconduct inconsistent with his proper discharge of the duties for which he was engaged, e g fraud or dishonesty in connection with his employer's business (*Brown v Croft* (1828) 6 C & P 16n; *Cunningham v Fonblanque* (1833) 6 C & P 44 at 49 per Parke J; *Phillips v Foxall* (1872) LR 7 QB 666 at 680 per Blackburn J; and see *Willets v Green* (1850) 3 Car & Kir 59) or conduct so insulting and insubordinate as to be incompatible with the continuance of the relationship of employer and employee (*Edwards v Levy* (1860) 2 F & F 94 at 95 per Hill J (where it was pointed out that a single instance of insolence in the case of an employee in such a

position as that of a newspaper critic would hardly justify dismissal); and see *Wilson v Racher* [1974] ICR 428, CA (one instance of bad language did not justify dismissal); *Shaw v Chairitie* (1850) 3 Car & Kir 21; *Pepper v Webb* above (a minor act of insubordination might be the 'last straw' justifying dismissal)), there being no fixed rule of law defining the degree of misconduct which would justify dismissal (*Clouston & Co Ltd v Corry* [1906] AC 122 at 129, PC; and see *Laws v London Chronicle (Indicator Newspapers) Ltd* [1959] 2 All ER 285 at 287, [1959] 1 WLR 698 at 700, CA, per Lord Evershed MR (the conduct complained of had to be such that the employee disregarded the essential conditions of his contract); *Healey v SA Française Rubastic* [1917] 1 KB 946 at 947 per Avory J; *Ramsden v David Sharratt & Sons Ltd* (1930) 35 Com Cas 314 at 319, HL, per Lord Warrington of Clyffe; *Bell v Lever Bros Ltd* [1932] AC 161, HL (apart from concealment amounting to fraud, an employee was under no duty to disclose his misconduct to his employer)), or an offence outside his employment of such a character as to make it unsafe for the employer to retain him (*Pearce v Foster* (1886) 17 QBD 536 at 539–540, CA, per Lord Esher; and see *R v Brampton Inhabitants* (1777) Cald Mag Cas 11; *R v Welford Inhabitants* (1778) Cald Mag Cas 57; *Atkin v Acton* (1830) 4 C & P 208; *Connors v Justice* (1862) 13 ICLR 451 (cases involving immoral conduct));

(3) he was habitually neglectful in respect of the duties for which he was engaged (*Callo v Brouncker* above at 519 per Parke J; *Cunningham v Fonblanque* above at 49 per Parke J; *Lomax v Arding* (1855) 10 Exch 734 at 736 per Pollock CB; *Edwards v Levy* (1860) 2 F & F 94 at 95 per Hill J; and see *Robinson v Hindman* (1800) 3 Esp 235 per Lord Kenyon) but not if there was only an isolated instance of neglect (*Edwards v Levy* above at 95 per Hill J; and see *Fillieul v Armstrong* (1837) 7 Ad & El 577; *Gould v Webb* (1855) 4 E & B 933), unless attended by serious consequences (*Edwards v Levy* above; *Baster v London and County Printing Works* [1899] 1 QB 901 at 903, DC, per Darling J; and see *Jupiter General Insurance Co Ltd v Shroff* [1937] 3 All ER 67, PC (where it was pointed out that the test had to vary with the nature of the employment and the nature of the responsibility of the task carried out by the employee));

(4) notwithstanding his being a skilled employee and thus there being on his part an implied warranty that he was reasonably competent for the work which he was employed to undertake, he proved to be incompetent (*Harmer v Cornelius* (1858) 5 CBNS 236 at 246 per Willes J; *Cuckson v Stones* (1858) 1 E & E 248 at 257 per Lord Campbell CJ; *Searle v Ridley* (1873) 28 LT 411);

(5) he was permanently incapable of work due to illness (*Cuckson v Stones* above at 257 per Lord Campbell CJ; *Jackson v Union Marine Insurance Co Ltd* (1874) LR 10 CP 125 at 145 per Bramwell B) or temporarily incapable of work due to illness if the resulting incapacity went to the root of the matter and frustrated the object of the engagement (*Jackson v Union Marine Insurance Co Ltd*; *Poussard v Spiers and Pond* (1876) 1 QBD 410), but not otherwise (*Bettini v Gye* (1876) 1 QBD 183; *Warburton v Co-operative Wholesale Society Ltd* [1917] 1 KB 663, CA (applied more recently in *Kaur v British Library* [2008] All ER (D) 22 (Sep), EAT); and see *Loates v Maple* (1903) 88 LT 288 (jockey engaged for three flat-racing seasons; incapacitated for two months of one season); *Storey v Fulham Steel Works Co* (1907) 24 TLR 89, CA (agreement to employ plaintiff as works manager for five years; employers not justified in purporting to terminate agreement at a time when the employee had been ill for some months, but the agreement had more than two years to run, and there was no reason to think that the employee would not recover));

(6) his conduct was incompatible with the faithful discharge of his duty to his employer, eg where, unknown to his employer, he entered into transactions whereby his personal interests conflicted with his duty as an employee in his particular capacity (*Pearce v Foster* above; and see *Ridgway v Hungerford Market Co* (1835) 3 Ad & El 171; *Sinclair v Neighbour* [1967] 2 QB 279, [1966] 3 All ER 988, CA), or if he took a secret commission (*Boston Deep Sea Fishing and Ice Co v Ansell* (1888) 39 ChD 339, CA; *Swale v Ipswich Tannery Ltd* (1906) 11 Com Cas 88), even though it was an isolated act (*Boston Deep Sea Fishing and Ice Co v Ansell* above), unless he was able to discharge the burden which lay on him of proving that there was nothing improper in the transaction in question (*Federal Supply and Cold Storage Co of South Africa v Angehrn and Piel* (1910) 80 LJPC 1; and see *Sinclair v Neighbour* above (there need be no dishonesty)) or he claimed to be a partner (*Amor v Fearon* (1839) 9 Ad & El 548) or his conduct had been such that it would be injurious to the employer's business to

retain him (*Lacy v Osbaldiston* (1837) 8 C & P 80; *Nichol v Martyn* (1799) 2 Esp 732 per Lord Kenyon CJ; and see *East Anglian Rlys Co v Lythgoe* (1851) 10 CB 726). The cases cited in heads (1)–(6) above should be approached with caution and are now not always likely to be followed.

3   Generally speaking, gross misconduct justifying dismissal must amount to a repudiation of the contract of employment by the employee, and this generally required either wilful and deliberate contravention of an essential term of the contract or gross negligence: *Sandwell & West Birmingham Hospitals NHS Trust v Westwood* (2009) UKEAT/0032/09 (gross misconduct was not a reasonable characterisation by the employer of the nurse's conduct in this case: two things need to be distinguished: (1) the conduct alleged must be capable of amounting to gross misconduct; (2) the employer must have a reasonable belief that the employee has committed such misconduct; but the character of the misconduct should not be determined solely by, or confined to, the employer's own analysis, subject only to reasonableness: the question as to what is gross misconduct must be a mixed question of law and fact and that will be so when the question falls to be considered in the context of the reasonableness of the sanction in unfair dismissal or in the context of breach of contract).

     Sandwell & West Birmingham Hospitals NHS Trust v Westwood was cited in *Knight v Robert Bates Wrekin Landscapes Ltd* [2014] All ER (D) 262 (Feb), EAT, a case where the reasons for dismissal were characterised as theft and removing goods from the site amounting to a breach of security rules, although the misconduct was minor and/or inadvertent. The case proceeded with general principles of contractual interpretation in mind: the general understanding of employer and employee is that, absent gross misconduct or gross negligence, an employee will be entitled to notice and, in that light, the clause in the contract of employment that set out circumstances in which the employment might be terminated without notice or payment in lieu of notice (including if the employee commits any breach of the employer's or customer's security rules) could not be applied to any breach, however minor or inadvertent: it applies to a breach which is serious and wilful or grossly negligent, applying normal principles of employment law.

     It is important that an employer cannot simply characterise something as gross misconduct and rely upon having a reasonable belief that it was gross misconduct and then seek the conclusion that the dismissal must be within the band of reasonable responses because summary dismissal, irrespective of mitigation, is a reasonable response to gross misconduct; if the employer chooses the route of gross misconduct, it must be prepared to justify that: *Eastland Homes Partnership Ltd v Cunningham* (2014) UKEAT/0272/13/MC.

4   See PARA 743. See also *Freeth v Burr* (1874) LR 9 CP 208; applied in *General Billposting Co Ltd v Atkinson* [1909] AC 118, HL. See also *McCormack v Hamilton Academical Football Club Ltd* [2011] CSIH 68, [2012] IRLR 108, IH (summary dismissal has to be regarded as an exceptional remedy, warranted only where an employee's conduct amounted to a repudiation of the fundamental terms of the contract and made the continuance of the contract of service impossible, calling for substantial justification and swift action; it will not readily be sustained for misconduct which only peripherally affects the performance of core duties under the relevant employment contract, and summary dismissal having the appearance of an afterthought will stand little chance of being upheld). See note 3.

5   *Clouston & Co Ltd v Corry* [1906] AC 122, PC; *Jupiter General Insurance Co Ltd v Shroff* [1937] 3 All ER 67, PC; *Neary v Dean of Westminster* [1999] IRLR 288.

6   *Re Rubel Bronze and Metal Co Ltd and Vos* [1918] 1 KB 315. If an employee is to be summarily dismissed for breach of an express or implicit term of the contract of employment, it may be necessary for a court to decide first on the interpretation of that term to determine whether the employee was indeed in breach of it.

7   *Wilson v Racher* [1974] ICR 428, [1974] IRLR 114, CA. This is analogous to the position in the law of negligence where it is stressed that the question whether a defendant is in breach of a duty of care is one of fact on which previously decided cases will have little bearing: see e g *Qualcast (Wolverhampton) Ltd v Haynes* [1959] AC 743, [1959] 2 All ER 38, HL; *Worsfold v Howe* [1980] 1 All ER 1028, [1980] 1 WLR 1175, CA.

8   These may be either directly contained in the contract of employment or exist separately (e g in a company handbook) and be incorporated into the contract by reference. Where there is a disciplinary procedure, the written statement of terms and conditions of employment must contain a note specifying it: see the Employment Rights Act 1996 s 3(1); and PARA 120.

9   Employers should inform employees of the likely consequences of breaking disciplinary rules and, in particular, they should list examples of acts of gross misconduct that may warrant summary dismissal: see the ACAS Code of Practice 1: Disciplinary and Grievance Procedures (2009) para 23; Discipline and Grievances at work: The ACAS guide (September 2014), p 31; and PARA 707. As to the ACAS Code of Practice 1: Disciplinary and Grievance Procedures

(2009) see PARA 701 et seq and as to ACAS Codes of Practice generally see PARAS 1223–1224. See also PARA 702. A clause permitting summary dismissal must be clear and unambiguous: *T & K Home Improvements Ltd v Skilton* [2000] IRLR 595, CA (clause stating that failure to meet targets would lead to 'instant' dismissal held not strong enough to merit summary dismissal).

10 The ACAS advisory handbook, Discipline and grievances at work (2009), provides practical advice and guidance in disciplinary matters, including guidance relating to summary dismissal. As to the status of the advisory handbook see PARA 701. See also *Procter v British Gypsum Ltd* [1992] IRLR 7, EAT. See also PARA 702. Employers should give all employees a clear indication of the type of misconduct which, in the light of the requirements of the employer's business, will warrant dismissal without the normal period of notice or pay in lieu of notice. So far as possible the types of offences which fall into this category of 'gross misconduct' should be clearly specified in the rules, although such a list cannot normally be exhaustive: Discipline and Grievances at work: The ACAS guide (September 2014), p 31. If an employer considers an employee guilty of gross misconduct and thus liable for summary dismissal, it is still important to follow a fair procedure as for any other disciplinary offence. This will include establishing the facts of the case before taking any action, holding a meeting with the employee and allowing the employee the right of appeal. It should be made clear to the employee that dismissal is a possibility: see p 32.

11 *Dietmann v Brent London Borough Council* [1988] ICR 842, sub nom *Dietman v Brent London Borough Council* [1988] IRLR 299, CA; and see PARA 699.

12 *Jones v Lee* [1980] ICR 310, [1980] IRLR 67, CA.

13 *Laws Stores Ltd v Oliphant* [1978] IRLR 251, EAT; *Taylor v Parsons, Peebles NEI Bruce Peebles Ltd* [1981] IRLR 119, EAT; *Ladbroke Racing Ltd v Arnott* [1983] IRLR 154, Ct of Sess. See also *Coxon v Rank Xerox UK Ltd* [2003] ICR 628, EAT (whole process defective where major international company gave employee short notice of unparticularised allegations described as 'gross misconduct' and 'breach of trust').

14 As to unfair dismissal and misconduct generally see PARAS 776–779.

15 As to the effective date of termination in a case of summary dismissal see the Employment Rights Act 1996 s 97(1)(b); and PARA 764.

16 See the Employment Rights Act 1996 s 92; and PARA 755.

745. Grounds for dismissal discovered subsequently. The common law rule relating to wrongful dismissal[1] is that, provided good cause for dismissal in fact existed, it is immaterial whether or not it was known to the employer at the time of dismissal[2]. A summary dismissal can, therefore, be justified by facts only ascertained by the employer subsequent to the dismissal, and on grounds differing from those alleged at the time[3]. This may be contrasted with the rule in the statutory claim for unfair dismissal, in which a tribunal must look at the facts actually known to and actuating the employer at the time of dismissal[4], so that after-acquired evidence cannot make a dismissal fair[5].

1 See PARA 825.

2 *Boston Deep Sea Fishing and Ice Co v Ansell* (1888) 39 ChD 339, CA; *Willets v Green* (1850) 3 Car & Kir 59; *Spotswood v Barrow* (1850) 5 Exch 110; *Cyril Leonard & Co v Simo Securities Trust Ltd* [1971] 3 All ER 1313 at 1320–1321, [1972] 1 WLR 80 at 85–86, CA, per Russell LJ. *Boston Deep Sea Fishing and Ice Co v Ansell* above was applied in *Lakshmi v Mid-Cheshire Hospitals NHS Trust* [2008] EWHC 878 (QB), [2008] IRLR 956, [2008] All ER (D) 353 (Apr).

3 *Boston Deep Sea Fishing and Ice Co v Ansell* (1888) 39 ChD 339, CA; *Ridgway v Hungerford Market Co* (1835) 3 Ad & El 171; *Baillie v Kell* (1838) 4 Bing NC 638. See also note 2.

4 *W Devis & Sons Ltd v Atkins* [1977] AC 931, [1977] ICR 662, HL. Further evidence uncovered by an internal appeal procedure subsequent to the dismissal may be taken into consideration: *West Midlands Co-operative Society Ltd v Tipton* [1986] AC 536, [1986] ICR 192, HL; and see PARA 770.

5 It may, however, be relevant when assessing compensation: see PARA 821. See also *Orr v Milton Keynes Council* [2011] EWCA Civ 62, [2011] 4 All ER 1256, [2011] IRLR 317, [2011] ICR 704 (it was inherent in *W Devis & Sons Ltd v Atkins* [1977] AC 931, [1977] ICR 662, [1977] 3 All ER 40, HL, that an employer's decision might turn out to be open to criticism with hindsight, but that could not affect the result).

746. Condonation. Given the contractual analysis applied to summary dismissal[1], an employer faced with a repudiatory breach of the contract of employment has the choice whether to accept the repudiation and dismiss or to affirm the contract; thus an employer who, with full knowledge of the employee's misconduct, elects to continue him in his service cannot subsequently dismiss him for the offence which he has condoned[2].

1 See PARA 743.
2 *Horton v McMurtry* (1860) 5 H & N 667; *Phillips v Foxall* (1872) LR 7 QB 666; *Beattie v Parmenter* (1889) 5 TLR 396, CA; *Federal Supply and Cold Storage Co of South Africa v Angehrn and Piel* (1910) 80 LJPC 1, PC. A modern example in an analogous context is *Bond v CAV Ltd, Neads v CAV Ltd* [1983] IRLR 360 (employer did not insist on the use by employees of machinery which was the subject of a dispute; he was held to have waived the employees' breach of contract, thus losing any right to make deductions from wages).

(5) ENFORCEMENT AND TERMINATION OF APPRENTICESHIP

(i) Enforcement of Apprenticeship Agreement

747. Breach by apprentice. At common law, where an apprentice is guilty of a breach of contract contained in an apprenticeship agreement[1], the master is entitled to sue the party to the agreement who has bound himself as surety for the good behaviour of the apprentice[2], and to recover damages for the loss of his services[3], up to the time of the claim brought, but not for the loss of his services during the remainder of the term for which the apprentice is bound[4]. If the apprentice absents himself from work for a long (but not a trifling) period[5], or repudiates the contract on attaining his majority[6], the surety is liable.

The apprentice himself, if he is of full age[7], may be sued for any portion of his premium agreed to be paid which may remain unpaid, notwithstanding that he was a minor at the time when the agreement to pay it was made[8].

The court will not order specific performance of an apprenticeship agreement[9] nor, during the currency of the agreement, grant an injunction against a breach[10].

1 As to excuses for the non-performance of the apprenticeship agreement see PARA 748. As to the position of apprentices and youth trainees at common law see also PARAS 112, 128–129, 748, 749–754. As to the statutory law on apprenticeships see EDUCATION vol 35 (2011) PARA 682 et seq.
2 *Russell v Shinn* (1861) 2 F & F 395. As to the surety's liability if the minor avoids the agreement on attaining the age of 18 see PARA 749. A covenant by a person who has bound himself as surety may be released by a change in the master's circumstances: *Ellen v Topp* (1851) 6 Exch 424; and see PARAS 751–753.
3 *Russell v Shinn* (1861) 2 F & F 395; *Lewis v Peachey* (1862) 1 H & C 518.
4 *Lewis v Peachey* (1862) 1 H & C 518.
5 *Wright v Gihon* (1829) 3 C & P 583. The fact that the master has taken no steps to find the apprentice may be urged in mitigation of damages: *Russell v Shinn* (1861) 2 F & F 395.
6 *Cuming v Hill* (1819) 3 B & Ald 59.
7 As to the position when he is a minor see PARA 128.
8 *Walter v Everard* [1891] 2 QB 369, CA. A master is also entitled to any money which the apprentice may earn, during the unexpired term, after leaving him: *Meriton v Hornsby* (1747) 1 Ves Sen 48; *Hill v Allen* (1748) 1 Ves Sen 83.
9 See *Webb v England* (1860) 29 Beav 44; and SPECIFIC PERFORMANCE vol 95 (2013) PARA 307.
10 Thus an injunction cannot be obtained by the father of an apprentice who is a minor to restrain the master from pursuing his remedies at law if the minor defaults (*Argles v Heaseman* (1739) 1 Atk 518); nor against the minor to restrain a breach by him of the apprenticeship agreement during its currency (*De Francesco v Barnum* (1889) 43 ChD 165). It is otherwise in the case of acts or omissions after the apprenticeship has ceased: *Gadd v Thompson* [1911] 1 KB 304, DC.

If a contract is on the whole for the benefit of the apprentice, the court may enforce a restrictive covenant after the termination of the apprenticeship: see *Gadd v Thompson*. See also CIVIL PROCEDURE vol 11 (2009) PARA 461. As to covenants in restraint of trade see PARA 19; and COMPETITION vol 18 (2009) PARA 377 et seq.

748. Excuses for apprentice's non-performance of agreement. It is an implied term in an apprenticeship agreement that the fulfilment of the covenant to serve is to depend on the continued capacity of the apprentice to perform his part of the agreement; and, accordingly, non-performance of the agreement is excused when due to incapacity caused by illness, even though the covenant to serve is absolute and unconditional[1]. Temporary illness does not, however, discharge the agreement[2].

An apprentice is justified in quitting his master's service if he has reasonable grounds for fearing that he will suffer physical harm if he were to remain[3].

An apprentice cannot be required by his master to serve outside the United Kingdom, save in the case of a master whose business normally takes him abroad[4].

1 *Boast v Firth* (1868) LR 4 CP 1; cf *R v Hales-Owen Inhabitants* (1718) 1 Stra 99. As to the position of apprentices and youth trainees at common law see also PARAS 112, 128–129, 747, 749–754. As to the statutory law on apprenticeships see EDUCATION vol 35 (2011) PARA 682 et seq.
2 See *Patten v Wood* (1887) 51 JP 549, DC (where an apprentice was held entitled, during temporary illness, to the wages covenanted to be paid in the apprenticeship agreement).
3 *Halliwell v Counsell* (1878) 38 LT 176. Formerly the master had the right to administer moderate chastisement (*Gylbert v Fletcher* (1629) Cro Car 179; *Penn v Ward* (1835) 2 Cr M & R 338), but any attempt to exercise that right would now invite a claim for assault (*R v Josephson* (1914) 110 LT 512).
4 *Coventry v Woodhall* (1615) Hob 134.

(ii) Termination of Apprenticeship Agreement

749. Minor's power to dissolve apprenticeship agreement. A minor cannot dissolve his apprenticeship agreement unless it is clearly shown to be for his benefit to be released; and, in general, it is not for his benefit[1].

Such an agreement is, however, voidable at the option of the apprentice on his attaining the age of 18[2], but the election to avoid must be made within a reasonable time after his reaching that age[3]; and it is not enough to justify the master in treating such a voidable agreement as avoided that the apprentice has been guilty of a simple act of misconduct or done something forbidden by the apprenticeship agreement, such as running away or otherwise absenting himself[4]. Avoidance by the apprentice of his agreement on reaching the age of 18 is no defence in a claim for breach of an absolute covenant by another person that the apprenticeship is to be for a period extending beyond that time[5].

1 *R v Great Wigston, Leicester, Inhabitants* (1824) 3 B & C 484; *R v Austrey Inhabitants* (1758) Burr SC 441; *Waterman v Fryer* [1922] 1 KB 499; cf *R v Mountsorrel Inhabitants* (1815) 3 M & S 497 (where, the master having absconded so that the apprentice could no longer derive instruction or support from him, the court thought it better that the apprenticeship agreement should be dissolved than that the apprentice should remain unemployed and uninstructed); and see *Slade v Metrodent Ltd* [1953] 2 QB 112, [1953] 2 All ER 336 (minor bound by arbitration clause if contract as a whole is for his benefit). When a minor, having no power to dissolve his apprenticeship, purports to bind himself to a second master, the second binding is invalid: *R v Great Wigston, Leicester, Inhabitants* above. In *Richardson v Colne Fishery Co* (1897) 77 LT 501, the fact that the apprentice had, during the apprenticeship period, been in employment other than that of his master did not prevent its being held that he had served his master 'duly and truly', such employment being with his master's consent. As to the position of apprentices

and youth trainees at common law see also PARAS 112, 128–129, 747–748, 750–754. As to the statutory law on apprenticeships see EDUCATION vol 35 (2011) PARA 682 et seq.

2   *Ex p Davis* (1794) 5 Term Rep 715 at 716 per Lord Kenyon. As to the age of majority being 18 years see the Family Law Reform Act 1969 s 1(1), (2); and CHILDREN AND YOUNG PERSONS vol 9 (2012) PARA 1.

3   *Wray v West* (1866) 15 LT 180. What is a reasonable time is a question of fact in each case: *Wray v West.*

4   *Gray v Cookson* (1812) 16 East 13; *Smedley v Gooden* (1814) 3 M & S 189; *Coghlan v Callaghan* (1857) 7 ICLR 291. As to the effect on an apprenticeship agreement of misconduct by the apprentice see PARA 754.

5   *Cuming v Hill* (1819) 3 B & Ald 59.

750.   Termination of apprenticeship agreement by mutual consent.   All the original parties to an apprenticeship agreement may validly agree to terminate the agreement, even though the apprentice is still a minor[1]. The parties concerned having consented to the termination of the apprenticeship, its formal dissolution may be effected by a cancellation of the agreement[2], by its destruction[3] or by the mutual surrender of the parts of the agreement[4].

If an agreement for the determination of an apprenticeship agreement is entered into between the master and the apprentice under which payment is made by the apprentice in consideration of the waiver by the master of his rights during the unexpired portion of the term, so that in a claim on the covenants in the apprenticeship agreement the apprentice could plead accord and satisfaction[5], the agreement will be regarded, from the time of such payment, as no longer existing, although in fact neither given up nor cancelled[6].

An apprentice is entitled to the same minimum period of notice as an employee[7].

1   *R v Weddington Inhabitants* (1774) Burr SC 766; *R v Spawnton Inhabitants* (1775) Burr SC 801. As to the position of apprentices and youth trainees at common law see also PARAS 112, 128–129, 747–748, 749, 751–754. As to the statutory law on apprenticeships see EDUCATION vol 35 (2011) PARA 682 et seq.

2   *R v Titchfield Inhabitants* (1763) Burr SC 511.

3   *R v Weddington Inhabitants* (1774) Burr SC 766; *R v Spawnton Inhabitants* (1775) Burr SC 801.

4   *R v St Mary Kallendar, Winchester, Inhabitants* (1748) Burr SC 274; *R v Titchfield Inhabitants* (1763) Burr SC 511; *R v Notton Inhabitants* (1768) Burr SC 629.

5   As to accord and satisfaction see CONTRACT vol 22 (2012) PARA 605 et seq.

6   *R v Harberton Inhabitants* (1786) 1 Term Rep 139; *R v Devonshire Justices* (1777) Cald Mag Cas 32; cf *R v Warden Inhabitants* (1828) 2 Man & Ry KB 24.

7   See the Employment Rights Act 1996 s 86; and PARA 736. Where the apprenticeship agreement provides that the apprentice might be transferred to another master to complete his apprenticeship, the two masters are nevertheless separate employers for the purposes of determining continuous employment under Pt XIV Ch I (ss 210–219) (see also PARA 130 et seq): *Lee v Barry High Ltd* [1970] 3 All ER 1040, [1970] 1 WLR 1549, CA. As to redundancy payments see PARA 835 et seq.

751.   Death of master or apprentice.   An apprenticeship agreement is determined by the death of the master[1]. Thus in the absence of a special covenant to the contrary[2], the apprentice is not bound to serve the master's personal representatives[3], nor are the personal representatives under any obligation to keep and maintain the apprentice[4].

The permanent illness or death of the apprentice also determines the apprenticeship agreement[5], but his marriage does not[6].

1   *R v Chirk* (1774) Burr SC 782; *Whincup v Hughes* (1871) LR 6 CP 78; and see *R v Peck* (1698) 1 Salk 66 per Holt CJ (where it was said that by the custom of London the executor should put the apprentice to another master of the same trade). As to the position of apprentices and youth

trainees at common law see also PARAS 112, 128–129, 747–748, 749–750, 752–754. As to the statutory law on apprenticeships see EDUCATION vol 35 (2011) PARA 682 et seq.

2   See *Cooper v Simmons* (1862) 7 H & N 707 (where such a covenant was held, in the case of a minor, not to be disadvantageous, and was, therefore, enforced).
3   *Baxter v Burfield* (1747) 2 Stra 1266.
4   *R v Prat* (1692) 12 Mod Rep 27; *R v Peck* (1698) 1 Salk 66. See note 1; and WILLS AND INTESTACY vol 103 (2010) PARA 1215.
5   *Boast v Firth* (1868) LR 4 CP 1; and see PARA 748.
6   *R v Tardebigg Inhabitants* (1753) Say 100.

752.   Bankruptcy of master.   Where a bankruptcy order is made in respect of an individual to whom another individual was an apprentice at the time when the petition on which the order was made was presented, and the bankrupt or the apprentice gives notice to the trustee terminating the apprenticeship, the indenture of apprenticeship is discharged with effect from the commencement of the bankruptcy[1].

1   See the Insolvency Act 1986 s 348 (effect of bankruptcy on apprenticeships etc); PARA 628 note 21; and BANKRUPTCY AND INDIVIDUAL INSOLVENCY vol 5 (2013) PARA 720. As to the position of apprentices and youth trainees at common law see also PARAS 112, 128–129, 747–748, 749–751, 753–754. As to the statutory law on apprenticeships see EDUCATION vol 35 (2011) PARA 682 et seq.

753.   Change in composition of firm or in master's business.   If a person is apprenticed to a firm, the dissolution of the partnership by the death[1] or retirement[2] of one of the partners normally terminates the apprenticeship. An apprentice to a firm is discharged if the firm divides itself into two or more new firms, neither of which carries on in its entirety the business to which the apprentice was bound[3]. The same result follows if the master changes his trade or business or relinquishes one department or branch of it[4]. This is not so if the business is simply diminished in extent, provided that the master remains able to carry out his covenant to teach the apprentice[5].

1   *R v St Martin's, Exeter, Inhabitants* (1835) 2 Ad & El 655.
2   *Brook v Dawson* (1869) 20 LT 611; *Couchman v Sillar* (1870) 22 LT 480; and see *Lloyd v Blackburn* (1842) 9 M & W 363 at 364 per Lord Abinger CB; *Popham v Jones* (1853) 13 CB 225. The dissolution of the partnership may be a breach of the covenants in the apprenticeship agreement: see *Titmus and Titmus v Rose and Watts* [1940] 1 All ER 599.
3   *Eaton v Western* (1882) 9 QBD 636, CA (where the apprentice was bound to an engineering firm at Lambeth which split into two firms, one carrying on the manufacturing part of the business at Derby, and the other the repairing and agency part at Lambeth; as neither carried on the business in its entirety, it was held that the apprentice was no longer bound, and that the apprentice and his father were entitled to damages for breach of covenant against the partners). As to the position of apprentices and youth trainees at common law see also PARAS 112, 128–129, 747–748, 749–752, 754. As to the statutory law on apprenticeships see EDUCATION vol 35 (2011) PARA 682 et seq.
4   *Ellen v Topp* (1851) 6 Exch 424 (where the apprentice was to be taught the business of an auctioneer, appraiser and corn factor, but after a time the master ceased to act as a corn factor).
5   *Batty v Monks* (1865) 12 LT 832 (where the fact that the master discontinued making up prescriptions for other medical men and confined himself to making up his own did not disqualify him for teaching the apprentice 'the art and mystery of an apothecary').

754.   Misconduct by apprentice.   Unless there is a covenant[1] or a custom[2] to the contrary, misconduct on the part of the apprentice does not entitle the master to terminate the apprenticeship agreement[3]. Thus the master is not justified in dismissing the apprentice merely for neglect[4], disobedience to orders[5], absence[5], or for intoxication[6], but must depend for his remedy on the covenants in the agreement[7]. If, however, he is sued on the covenant to teach and maintain the apprentice, it is a good answer that the apprentice was a habitual thief[8], or that he absented himself or by other wilful acts prevented the master from carrying out the covenant[9].

1   See e g *Westwick v Theodor* (1875) LR 10 QB 224; *Maw v Jones* (1890) 25 QBD 107.
2   *Woodroffe v Farnham* (1693) 2 Vern 291 (custom of London that apprentice could be dismissed for frequent gaming).
3   *Wise v Wilson* (1845) 1 Car & Kir 662 at 669 per Lord Denman CJ; *Westwick v Theodor* (1875) LR 10 QB 224 at 226 per Blackburn J; and see *Phillips v Clift* (1859) 4 H & N 168 at 173–174 per Watson B; *Waterman v Fryer* [1922] 1 KB 499. As to damages for breach of contract see PARA 828 et seq. As to the position of apprentices and youth trainees at common law see also PARAS 112, 128–129, 747–748, 749–753. As to the statutory law on apprenticeships see EDUCATION vol 35 (2011) PARA 682 et seq.
4   *Therman v Abell* (1688) 2 Vern 64 (where the master was ordered by the court to refund part of the premium and to deliver up the indentures).
5   *Winstone v Linn* (1823) 1 B & C 460.
6   *Wise v Wilson* (1845) 1 Car & Kir 662.
7   *Winstone v Linn* (1823) 1 B & C 460 at 467 per Bayley J.
8   *Cox v Mathews* (1861) 2 F & F 397; approved and followed in *Learoyd v Brook* [1891] 1 QB 431; cf *Phillips v Clift* (1859) 4 H & N 168 (where general dishonesty was alleged but not a criminal taking, and the master was held not to be justified in dissolving the apprenticeship agreement); *Addams v Carter* (1862) 6 LT 130; *Waterman v Fryer* [1922] 1 KB 499. In *Wise v Wilson* (1845) 1 Car & Kir 662, the master, an apothecary, was held justified in dismissing his pupil and assistant for drunkenness on the ground that such conduct was dangerous to patients for whom the pupil and assistant had to make up medicines, and was consequently injurious to the business; but the pupil and assistant was not regarded exactly as an apprentice, but as a person somewhere between an employee and an apprentice.
9   *Hughes v Humphreys* (1827) 6 B & C 680; *Winstone v Linn* (1823) 1 B & C 460 at 467 per Bayley J; *Raymond v Minton* (1866) LR 1 Exch 244, explained in *Learoyd v Brook* [1891] 1 QB 431 at 433 per AL Smith J.

6. UNFAIR DISMISSAL AND WRONGFUL DISMISSAL

(1) EMPLOYEE'S RIGHTS IN RELATION TO UNFAIR DISMISSAL

(i) Right to Written Statement

755. Written statement of reasons for dismissal. An employee[1] is entitled:

(1) if he is given by his employer[2] notice of termination of his contract of employment[3];

(2) if his contract of employment is terminated by his employer without notice[4]; or

(3) if, where he is employed under a limited-term contract[5], the contract terminates by virtue of the limiting event without being renewed[6] under the same contract[7],

to be provided by his employer with a written statement giving particulars of the reasons for his dismissal[8]. An employee is entitled to such a written statement only if he makes a request for one[9]; and such a statement must be provided within 14 days of that request[10]. Nor is an employee so entitled to a written statement unless on the effective date of termination[11] he has been, or will have been, continuously employed[12] for a period of not less than two years[13] ending with that date[14].

An employee is, however, entitled to a written statement without having to request it and irrespective of whether the employee has been continuously employed for any period if the employee is dismissed:

(a) at any time while the employee is pregnant or after childbirth[15] in circumstances in which ordinary[16] or additional[17] maternity leave period ends by reason of the dismissal[18]; or

(b) while absent from work during an ordinary[19] or additional[20] adoption leave period in circumstances in which that period ends by reason of the dismissal[21].

A written statement provided in this way is admissible in evidence in any proceedings[22].

1 As to the meaning of 'employee' see PARA 2.
2 As to the meaning of 'employer' see PARA 2.
3 Employment Rights Act 1996 s 92(1)(a). See also note 8. As to the meaning of 'contract of employment' see PARA 2.
4 Employment Rights Act 1996 s 92(1)(b). See also note 8. As to notice see PARA 733 et seq; and as to dismissal without notice see PARA 743 et seq.
5 For these purposes, a contract of employment is a 'limited-term contract' if:
    (1) the employment under the contract is not intended to be permanent (Employment Rights Act 1996 s 235(2A)(a) (s 235(2A), (2B) added by SI 2002/2034)); and
    (2) provision is accordingly made in the contract for it to terminate by virtue of a limiting event (Employment Rights Act 1996 s 235(2A)(b) (as so added)).
    'Limiting event', in relation to a contract of employment, means:
    (a) in the case of a contract for a fixed term, the expiry of the term (s 235(2B)(a) (as so added));
    (b) in the case of a contract made in contemplation of the performance of a specific task, the performance of the task (s 235(2B)(b) (as so added)); and
    (c) in the case of a contract which provides for its termination on the occurrence of an event (or the failure of an event to occur), the occurrence of the event (or the failure of the event to occur) (s 235(2B)(c) (as so added)).

6   For these purposes, except in so far as the context otherwise requires, 'renewal' includes extension; and any reference to renewing a contract or a fixed term is to be construed accordingly: see the Employment Rights Act 1996 s 235(1).

7   Employment Rights Act 1996 s 92(1)(c) (substituted by SI 2002/2034). See also note 8.

       In relation to government training schemes, agency workers or apprentices, head (3) in the text applies where the employee is employed under a contract for a fixed term and that term expires without being renewed under the same contract: Employment Rights Act 1996 s 92(1)(c); and see the Fixed-term Employees (Prevention of Less Favourable Treatment) Regulations 2002, SI 2002/2034, regs 18–20 (excluded classes of person under fixed-term work regulations); and PARA 94.

8   See the Employment Rights Act 1996 s 92(1). The written statement may refer to other documentation already given, provided that copies of that documentation are enclosed: *Gilham v Kent County Council* [1985] ICR 227, sub nom *Kent County Council v Gilham* [1985] IRLR 16, CA, distinguishing *Horsley Smith and Sherry Ltd v Dutton* [1977] ICR 594, [1977] IRLR 172, EAT.

       As to the remedy of an employee for infringement of the right conferred by the Employment Rights Act 1996 s 92 see s 93; and PARA 756. In addition, this right does not apply to a share fisherman (see s 199(2); and PARA 167) or to a police officer (see s 200(1); and PARA 168), and may also be lost for some other reason than statutory exclusion, in particular because the contract of employment is illegal (see PARA 18) or has terminated for some reason other than dismissal (see PARA 725 et seq). As to the modification of s 92 in relation to governing bodies of schools having a right to a delegated budget, acting in the exercise of their employment powers, see EDUCATION vol 35 (2011) PARA 355 et seq.

9   It is not sufficient that the employer voluntarily gives a statement of reasons, without request, which the employee then seeks to challenge; there must be a request by the employee: *Catherine Haigh Harlequin Hair Design v Seed* [1990] IRLR 175, EAT.

10   Employment Rights Act 1996 s 92(2) (amended by the Employment Act 2002 Sch 7 paras 24, 31). The provision made by the Employment Rights Act 1996 s 92(2) is subject to s 92(4), (4A) (see the text and notes 15–21): see s 92(2) (as so amended). See *Keen v Dymo Ltd* [1977] IRLR 118 (failure to comply with the employee's request within the 14-day period amounts to an unreasonable refusal to comply with that request); but see PARA 756 note 6.

11   For these purposes, the 'effective date of termination' means:

    (1)   in relation to an employee whose contract of employment is terminated by notice, the date on which the notice expires (Employment Rights Act 1996 s 92(6)(a));

    (2)   in relation to an employee whose contract of employment is terminated without notice, the date on which the termination takes effect (s 92(6)(b)); and

    (3)   in relation to an employee who is employed under a limited-term contract which terminates by virtue of the limiting event without being renewed under the same contract, the date on which the termination takes effect (s 92(6)(c) (substituted by the Employment Relations Act 2004 Sch 1 para 28)).

    Where, however:

    (a)   the contract of employment is terminated by the employer (Employment Rights Act 1996 s 92(7)(a)); and

    (b)   the notice required by s 86 (see PARA 736) to be given by an employer would, if duly given on the material date, expire on a date later than the effective date of termination (as defined by s 92(6)) (s 92(7)(b)),

the later date is the effective date of termination (see s 92(7)). For the purpose of head (b) above, 'material date' means the date when notice of termination was given by the employer or, where no notice was given, the date when the contract of employment was terminated by the employer: see s 92(8).

12   As to continuity of employment see PARA 130 et seq.

13   As to the meaning of 'year' for these purposes see PARA 130 note 11.

14   Employment Rights Act 1996 s 92(3) (amended by the Employment Act 2002 Sch 7 paras 24, 31; and SI 2012/989). The provision made by the Employment Rights Act 1996 s 92(3) is subject to s 92(4), (4A) (see the text and notes 15–21) (see s 92(3) (as so amended)); and has effect (as so amended) in any case where the period of continuous employment begins on or after 6 April 2012 (see the Unfair Dismissal and Statement of Reasons for Dismissal (Variation of Qualifying Period) Order 2012, SI 2012/989, arts 1, 4). As to the modification of the Employment Rights Act 1996 s 92(3) in relation to National Health Service employees see PARA 326 note 13. See also note 8.

15   As to the meaning of 'childbirth' see PARA 356 note 4.

16   As to ordinary maternity leave see PARA 356 et seq.

17   As to additional maternity leave see PARA 356 et seq.

18 See the Employment Rights Act 1996 s 92(4) (amended by the Employment Relations Act 1999 Sch 4 Pt III paras 5, 12). See also note 8.
19 As to ordinary adoption leave see PARA 356 et seq.
20 As to additional adoption leave see PARA 379 et seq.
21 Employment Rights Act 1996 s 92(4A) (added by the Employment Act 2002 Sch 7 paras 24, 31). See also note 8.
22 Employment Rights Act 1996 s 92(5). See also note 8. An employer is not estopped by what he puts in the written statement, but in practice establishing a different reason later may be difficult: see *Abernethy v Mott, Hay and Anderson* [1974] ICR 323, [1974] IRLR 213, CA.

756. Complaint to employment tribunal: statement of reasons for dismissal not provided or are inadequate or untrue. A complaint may be presented to an employment tribunal[1] by an employee[2] on the ground[3]:

(1)   that the employer[4] unreasonably failed[5] to provide a written statement of reasons for dismissal[6]; or

(2)   that the particulars of reasons given in purported compliance with the statutory requirement to provide such a statement[7] are inadequate or untrue[8].

An employment tribunal must not consider such a complaint relating to the reasons for a dismissal, however, unless it is presented to the tribunal at such a time that the tribunal would[9] consider a complaint of unfair dismissal in respect of that dismissal presented at the same time[10].

Where an employment tribunal finds such a complaint well-founded[11]: (a) it may make a declaration as to what it finds the employer's reasons were for dismissing the employee[12]; and (b) it must make an award that the employer pay to the employee a sum equal to the amount of two weeks' pay[13].

1   As to employment tribunals see PARA 1399 et seq; and as to the procedure on a complaint to an employment tribunal see PARA 1453 et seq.
2   As to the meaning of 'employee' see PARA 2.
3   See the Employment Rights Act 1996 s 93(1) (s 93(1)–(3) amended by the Employment Rights (Dispute Resolution) Act 1998 s 1(2)(a)). This right does not apply to a share fisherman (see the Employment Rights Act 1996 s 199(2); and PARA 167) or to a police officer (see s 200(1); and PARA 168), and may also be lost for some other reason than statutory exclusion, in particular because the contract of employment is illegal (see PARA 18) or has terminated for some reason other than dismissal (see PARA 725 et seq). As to the modification of s 93 in relation to governing bodies of schools having a right to a delegated budget, acting in the exercise of their employment powers, see EDUCATION vol 35 (2011) PARA 355 et seq.
      The remedy of an employee for infringement of the right conferred by s 92 (see PARA 755) is by way of complaint to an employment tribunal and not otherwise: see s 205(1); and PARA 1406. There is a requirement also for early ACAS conciliation to be tried in order to promote a settlement before tribunal proceedings are instituted on a complaint under the Employment Rights Act 1996 s 93: see the Employment Tribunals Act 1996 s 18(1)(b); and PARA 152 note 1. As to the constitution and powers of ACAS see PARA 1213 et seq.
4   As to the meaning of 'employer' see PARA 2.
5   Ie under the Employment Rights Act 1996 s 92: see PARA 755.
6   Employment Rights Act 1996 s 93(1)(a).
      Under the Employment Protection (Consolidation) Act 1978 s 53(4) (repealed) a complaint could be presented on the ground that the employer had unreasonably refused to provide a written statement. That right was amended by the Trade Union Reform and Employment Rights Act 1993 s 49(2), Sch 8 para 11 (repealed) to apply more broadly to where the employer 'failed' to give such a statement; and previous case law on the meaning of refusal is now inapplicable. Even if there has been a positive refusal, the employee's right will be infringed only if that refusal was unreasonable: *Daynecourt Insurance Brokers Ltd v Iles* [1978] IRLR 335, EAT. If the employer fails to provide a proper statement by simply referring instead to earlier conversations or letters (see PARA 755 note 10), that failure may not be unreasonable in the circumstances (*Marchant v Earley Town Council* [1979] ICR 891, [1979] IRLR 311, EAT); but it is not enough for the employer to rely on an answer given to a tribunal in response to the employee's complaint of unfair dismissal (*Rowan v Machinery Installations (South Wales) Ltd* as reported

in [1981] ICR 386, [1981] IRLR 122, EAT). If the employer fails to provide a statement because he believes that the employee was not dismissed, that may be a defence, provided that the belief was honestly and reasonably held: *Brown v Stuart Scott & Co* [1981] ICR 166, EAT; *Broomsgrove v Eagle Alexander Ltd* [1981] IRLR 127, EAT.

7   Ie under the Employment Rights Act 1996 s 92: see PARA 755.
8   Employment Rights Act 1996 s 93(1)(b). When deciding whether a written statement is untrue, the tribunal is restricted to deciding whether the employer has truthfully stated the reason for which he dismissed; this is not the stage at which to consider whether that reason itself was true (in the sense of justified by the facts): *Harvard Securities plc v Younghusband* [1990] IRLR 17, EAT.
9   Ie in accordance with the Employment Rights Act 1996 s 111: see PARA 804.
10 Employment Rights Act 1996 s 93(3) (as amended: see note 3).
11 See the Employment Rights Act 1996 s 93(2) (as amended: see note 3).
12 Employment Rights Act 1996 s 93(2)(a).
13 Employment Rights Act 1996 s 93(2)(b). As to the calculation of a week's pay see PARA 143 et seq.

(ii) Right Not to be Unfairly Dismissed

A. IN GENERAL

757. Employee's right not to be unfairly dismissed. An employee[1] has a statutory right not to be unfairly dismissed[2] by his employer[3]. The remedy of an employee for infringement of this right is by way of complaint to an employment tribunal and not otherwise[4].

Where a teacher in a foundation, voluntary aided or foundation special school[5] is dismissed by the governing body of the school[6] in pursuance of a requirement of the local authority under the Education Act 2002[7], the statutory provisions relating to unfair dismissal[8] have effect in relation to the dismissal as if[9]: (1) the local authority had at all material times been the teacher's employer[10]; (2) the local authority had dismissed him[11]; and (3) the reason or principal reason for which it did so had been the reason or principal reason for which it required his dismissal[12].

1   As to the meaning of 'employee' see PARA 2.
2   As to the meaning of 'dismissal' see PARA 762. The statutory action for unfair dismissal and the longstanding common law claim for wrongful dismissal (see PARA 825 et seq) must not be confused: the existence of the statutory action does not affect, still less abrogate, the common law claim, which continues to exist independently, either in addition to the statutory action or applying in cases where the statutory action for some reason is inapplicable: *Treganowan v Robert Knee & Co Ltd* [1975] ICR 405, [1975] IRLR 247; *BSC Sports and Social Club v Morgan* [1987] IRLR 391, EAT. See also note 3.
3   Employment Rights Act 1996 s 94(1). As to the meaning of 'employer' see PARA 2. The provision made by s 94(1) has effect subject to the provisions of ss 95–134A (see also PARA 758 et seq), particularly s 108 (qualifying period of employment: see PARA 758), and s 110 (dismissal procedures agreements: see PARA 759), and subject to the provisions of the Trade Union and Labour Relations (Consolidation) Act 1992, particularly ss 237–239 (dismissal for taking part in industrial action: see PARAS 1350–1352): Employment Rights Act 1996 s 94(2). In addition, this right does not apply to a share fisherman (see s 199(2); and PARA 167) or to a police officer (see s 200(1); and PARA 168), and may also be lost for some other reason than statutory exclusion, in particular because the contract of employment is illegal (see PARA 18) or has terminated for some reason other than dismissal (see PARA 725 et seq). As to the modification of Pt X (ss 94–134A) (unfair dismissal: see also PARA 758 et seq) in relation to persons holding ecclesiastical office under common tenure see the Ecclesiastical Offices (Terms of Service) Regulations 2009, SI 2009/2108, reg 33; and ECCLESIASTICAL LAW vol 34 (2011) PARA 407.
4   See the Employment Rights Act 1996 s 205(1); and PARA 1406. As to the right to present a complaint of unfair dismissal before an employment tribunal see PARA 804; and as to procedure before an employment tribunal see PARA 1453 et seq. As to the tradition of the Employment Appeal Tribunal in unfair dismissal cases see *Baker Perkins Ltd v Melone* [2009] All ER (D) 202

(Jan), EAT (the Appeal Tribunal does not normally alter a view as to fairness or unfairness of a dismissal unless there were sufficiently clear facts apparent that would enable it to say that the employment tribunal on the facts found by them had come to the wrong decision). See also *Small v London Ambulance Service NHS Trust* [2009] EWCA Civ 220, [2009] IRLR 563 (in an unfair dismissal case the tribunal should have confined its consideration to facts relating to the employer's handling of the employee's dismissal rather than introducing its own findings of fact about the employee's conduct, including aspects that had been disputed at the internal disciplinary hearing: in the circumstances this amounted to the tribunal substituting itself and its findings for the employer's and not keeping the issues and facts separate; it was not the tribunal's role to conduct a rehearing of the facts forming the basis of the employer's decision to dismiss).

The Employment Rights Act 1996 s 94(1) (see the text and notes 1–3) can apply to an employee who sometimes works outside the United Kingdom but, for the tribunal to exercise jurisdiction, he must establish the 'necessary link' with the United Kingdom (for instance, where his absences from the United Kingdom are short, or by demonstrating that he falls within a category of worker that is recognised for these purposes, eg: (1) peripatetic workers (and eg airline pilots) based in Great Britain, for whom a 'base' test remains the best solution; (2) certain ex-patriate employees posted abroad by a British employer for the purpose of a business carried on in Great Britain (e g a foreign correspondent on assignment for a British newspaper); or (3) certain ex-patriate employees of a British employer operating within what amounts to an extra-territorial British enclave in a foreign country): *Lawson v Serco Ltd, Botham v Ministry of Defence, Crofts v Veta Ltd* [2006] UKHL 3, [2006] 1 All ER 823, [2006] IRLR 289 (the concept of employment in Great Britain may not be easy to apply to peripatetic employees but the common sense of treating the base of a peripatetic employee, for the purposes of the statute, as his place of employment, remains valid). In a standard case, ie one dependent on whether the employee is working in Great Britain at the time when he is dismissed, the starting point is the *Lawson v Serco* test but the tribunal must make a 'broad factual enquiry' to meet the different circumstances existing for a particular category of employee: *YKK Europe Ltd v Heneghan* [2010] ICR 611, [2010] IRLR 563, EAT (employee working abroad returned to the United Kingdom on garden leave before dismissal, and was not working at the date of dismissal). In peripatetic cases too, the tribunal is required to consider the factual circumstances which indicate how the contract was being operated at the date of dismissal: *Hunt v United Airlines Ltd* [2008] ICR 934, [2008] All ER (D) 35 (Apr), EAT (where the employee was not actually working at the date of dismissal, the employment tribunal had to look more broadly at the facts in evaluating where the relevant base was rather than simply asking where the employee was working at the date of dismissal; in this case, a US flight attendant had not been based in London when illness intervened to prevent her planned transfer from France to Heathrow and the tribunal therefore lacked jurisdiction to hear her claim for unfair dismissal); and see *Diggins v Condor Marine Crewing Services Ltd* [2009] EWCA Civ 1133, [2010] ICR 213, [2010] IRLR 119 (*Lawson v Serco Ltd* principles could apply to those working on board ships where the specific rules in relation to UK-registered ships set out in the Employment Rights Act 1996 s 199(7) (see PARA 167) did not apply; ship's officer sailing from Portsmouth to the Channel Islands found to be a peripatetic employee based in Great Britain because he had no connection himself with Guernsey, where his employer company was based, and even less with the Bahamas, where the ship was registered). Accordingly, jurisdiction remains a question of applying *Lawson v Serco Ltd* but the threefold classification of the circumstances in which a 'foreign' dismissal can be litigated before a tribunal is not exhaustive and there can be a further residual category, applying where, on the facts, there is a sufficiently close connection with the legal system in Great Britain: *Duncombe v Secretary of State for Children, Schools and Families (No 2)* [2011] UKSC 36, [2011] 4 All ER 1020, [2011] ICR 1312, [2011] IRLR 840 (teachers employed by the Secretary of State to work in European Schools set up to provide a distinctively European education principally for the children of officials and employees of the European Union did not fall within specific examples given in *Lawson v Serco Ltd* but employment in an 'international enclave' with no particular connection with any other legal system had such an overwhelmingly closer connection with Britain and with British employment law than with any other system of law that it was right to conclude that Parliament had intended that the employees should enjoy protection from unfair dismissal); and see *Ministry of Defence v Wallis* [2011] EWCA Civ 231, [2011] ICR 617, [2011] All ER (D) 97 (Mar) (dependants of public servants posted abroad worked for the Ministry of Defence wholly outside Great Britain in the British Section of International Schools under contracts governed by English law; their employment had such clear, firm, sound connections with Britain or England that it was appropriate that each should have the protection of English unfair dismissal law). It seems that the question whether, on given facts, a case falls within the scope of the Employment Rights

Act 1996 s 94(1) is a question of law, but that the open-ended language of s 94(1) leaves room for some exceptions to the general rule where the connections both with Great Britain and with British employment law are sufficiently strong to show that that could be justified; however, it would always be a question of fact and degree as to whether the connection was sufficiently strong to overcome the general rule that the place of employment was decisive: *Ravat v Halliburton Manufacturing and Services Ltd* [2012] UKSC 1, [2012] 2 All ER 905, [2012] ICR 389, [2012] IRLR 315 (employee lived in Great Britain, but worked 28 days in Libya followed by 28 days off at home on a 'commuter or rotational basis' and did not fit into any of the permissible examples in *Lawson v Serco Ltd*: proper law of the employment contract can be a relevant factor, as could (on the facts here) the reassurance given to the claimant by the company that he would continue to come under British law, and whilst neither being British nor working for a British company would establish jurisdiction, that meant that they were not sufficient, but they could still be relevant). The starting point in applying the substantial connection test is that the statute will have no application to work outside the United Kingdom, and Parliament would not have intended that unless there were a sufficiently strong connection, where 'sufficiently' has to be understood as 'sufficient to displace that which would otherwise be the position': *Powell v OMV Exploration & Production Ltd* [2014] ICR 63, [2014] IRLR 80, EAT (applying *Lawson v Serco Ltd* principles to employee working as an international commuter, his employment had insufficient connection with Great Britain to establish jurisdiction over his unfair dismissal claim; he habitually worked in Dubai not Great Britain (a question of fact), and was required to sue his employer in the state of its domicile, Austria). The object of the exercise, however, is not to make a comparative analysis in order to decide which system of law is more or less favourable to the employee, but rather simply to decide whether an employee is able to except himself from the general rule in relation to expatriate employees by demonstrating that he has sufficiently strong connections with Great Britain and British employment law: *CreditSights Ltd v Dhunna* [2014] EWCA Civ 1238, [2014] All ER (D) 140 (Sep) (it cannot realistically have been Parliament's intention that the 'general rule' in relation to expatriate employees should be regarded as ousted in any case in which the local employment law is less favourable to the employee than British employment law).

Since the coming into force of the Equality Act 2010, the principles set out in *Lawson v Serco Ltd* apply equally to claims under that Act. As to the consideration of jurisdiction in discrimination cases see *Williams v University of Nottingham* [2007] IRLR 660, EAT (tribunal had no jurisdiction to hear claim by employee employed outside Great Britain, whose employment was not for the purposes of a business carried out at an establishment in Great Britain); *British Airways plc v Mak* [2011] EWCA Civ 184, [2011] ICR 735 (proportion of working time spent within Great Britain of cabin crew, who lived in Hong Kong and worked on flights between Hong Kong and London, was not so small as to be *de minimis*, and there was therefore jurisdiction to hear their claims of race and age discrimination); and DISCRIMINATION vol 33 (2013) PARA 7.

5   As to the meanings of 'foundation school', 'voluntary aided school' and 'foundation special school' see EDUCATION vol 35 (2011) PARAS 106, 108.

6   As to the governing bodies of maintained schools see EDUCATION vol 35 (2011) PARA 226 et seq. As to the modification of the Employment Rights Act 1996 Pt X (see also PARA 758 et seq) in relation to governing bodies of schools having a right to a delegated budget, acting in the exercise of their employment powers, see EDUCATION vol 35 (2011) PARA 355 et seq.

7   Ie under the Education Act 2002 s 36(7), Sch 2 para 7: see EDUCATION vol 35 (2011) PARA 353. For these purposes, 'local authority' has the meaning given by Education Act 1996 s 579(1) (see EDUCATION vol 35 (2011) PARA 24): see the Employment Rights Act 1996 s 134(3) (added by SI 2010/1158).

8   Ie the Employment Rights Act 1996 Pt X: see also PARA 758 et seq.

9   See the Employment Rights Act 1996 s 134(1) (amended by the School Standards and Framework Act 1998 Sch 30 para 55; the Education Act 2002 Sch 21 para 30; and by SI 2010/1158).

For the purposes of a complaint under the Employment Rights Act 1996 s 111 (see PARA 804) as it has effect by virtue of s 134(1):

(1)   the provisions of s 117(4) (see PARA 813) apply as if for the words 'not practicable to comply' there were substituted the words 'not practicable for the local authority to permit compliance' (s 134(2)(a) (s 134(2)(a), (b) amended by SI 2010/1158)); and

(2)   the provisions of the Employment Rights Act 1996 s 123(5) (see PARA 818) apply as if any reference to the employer were a reference to the local authority (s 134(2)(b) (as so amended)).

See also note 4.

10 Employment Rights Act 1996 s 134(1)(a) (s 134(1)(a), (b) amended by SI 2010/1158).

11 Employment Rights Act 1996 s 134(1)(b) (as amended: see note 10).
12 Employment Rights Act 1996 s 134(1)(c).

B. EXCLUDED CLASSES OF EMPLOYMENT

758. Qualifying period. The statutory right not to be unfairly dismissed[1] does not apply to the dismissal[2] of an employee[3] unless he has been continuously employed[4] for a period of not less than two years[5] ending with the effective date of termination[6]. However, if an employee is dismissed by reason of any specified medical requirement or recommendation[7], this exclusion has effect, in relation to that dismissal, as if for the words 'two years' there were substituted the words 'one month'[8]; and the exclusion does not apply at all:

(1) if one of a number of specified provisions[9] relating to particular forms of dismissal is applicable[10]; or

(2) if the reason (or, if more than one, the principal reason) for the dismissal is, or relates to, the employee's political opinions or affiliation[11]; or

(3) where the reason or principal reason for the dismissal (or selection for redundancy) is related to the employee's union membership or activities[12]; or

(4) if the reason (or, if more than one, the principal reason) for the dismissal is, or is connected with, the employee's membership of a reserve force (as defined in the Armed Forces Act 2006)[13].

1 Ie the provision made by the Employment Rights Act 1996 s 94: see PARA 757. As to the modification of Pt X (ss 94–134A) (unfair dismissal: see also PARAS 757, 759 et seq) in relation to governing bodies of schools having a right to a delegated budget, acting in the exercise of their employment powers, see EDUCATION vol 35 (2011) PARA 355 et seq; and as to the modification of Pt X in relation to persons holding ecclesiastical office under common tenure see the Ecclesiastical Offices (Terms of Service) Regulations 2009, SI 2009/2108, reg 33; and ECCLESIASTICAL LAW vol 34 (2011) PARA 407.

2 As to the meaning of 'dismissal' see PARA 762.

3 As to the meaning of 'employee' see PARA 2.

4 As to continuity of employment see PARA 130 et seq. See also PARA 764 note 17.

5 As to the meaning of 'year' for these purposes see PARA 130 note 11.

6 Employment Rights Act 1996 s 108(1) (s 108(1), (2) amended by SI 2012/989). As to the meaning of 'effective date of termination' see PARA 764. A challenge to a claim of unfair dismissal on the ground that the qualifying period has not been served should be made in good time by the employer: *Leicester University Students' Union v Mahomed* [1995] ICR 270, [1995] IRLR 292, EAT. See also *M & P Steelcraft v Ellis* [2008] ICR 578, [2008] IRLR 355, EAT (requisite period had not been established due to claimant having been a prisoner with a resettlement unit during first part of time with employer only becoming an employee after his release). As to the modification of the Employment Rights Act 1996 s 108(1) (2) in relation to National Health Service employees see PARA 326 note 13.

The qualifying period of two years, having been raised to that length with effect from 1 June 1985 by the Unfair Dismissal (Variation of Qualifying Period) Order 1985, SI 1985/782, art 3(1), was challenged on the ground that a two-year qualifying period disproportionately affected female employees without justification, but eventually the House of Lords, applying Case C–167/97 *R v Secretary of State for Employment, ex p Seymour-Smith* [1999] 2 AC 554, [1999] All ER (EC) 97, ECJ, held that unlawful indirect discrimination was not established: *R v Secretary of State for Employment, ex p Seymour-Smith (No 2)* [2000] ICR 244, [2000] IRLR 263, HL. However, with effect from 1 June 1999, the Unfair Dismissal and Statement of Reasons for Dismissal (Variation of Qualifying Period) Order 1999, SI 1999/1436, came into force (see art 1(1)), lowering the period to one year, before that period was restored to two years again by the Unfair Dismissal and Statement of Reasons for Dismissal (Variation of Qualifying Period) Order 2012, SI 2012/989, which came into force on 6 April 2012 (see art 1).

7 Ie any such requirement or recommendation as is referred to in the Employment Rights Act 1996 s 64(2): see PARA 596.

8 Employment Rights Act 1996 s 108(2) (as amended: see note 6). As to the meaning of 'month' for these purposes see PARA 130 note 11. See also note 6.

9 The provisions specified are:
(1) the Employment Rights Act 1996 s 98B(1), read with s 98B(2) (jury service: see PARA 785) (s 108(3)(aa) (added by the Employment Relations Act 2004 s 40(6)));
(2) the Employment Rights Act 1996 s 99(1) (leave for family reasons: see PARA 784), read with any regulations made thereunder (s 108(3)(b) (substituted by the Employment Relations Act 2004 s 57(1), Sch 1 para 32));
(3) the Employment Rights Act 1996 s 100(1), read with s 100(2), (3) (health and safety cases: see PARA 786) (s 108(3)(c));
(4) s 101(1), read with s 101(2) or s 101(3) (shop workers and betting workers who refuse Sunday work: see PARA 787) (s 108(3)(d));
(5) s 101A (working time cases: see PARA 788) (s 108(3)(dd) (added by SI 1998/1833));
(6) the Employment Rights Act 1996 s 102 (trustees of occupational pension schemes: see PARA 790) (s 108(3)(e));
(7) s 103 (employee representatives: see PARA 791) (s 108(3)(f));
(8) s 103A (protected disclosure: see PARA 792) (s 108(3)(ff) (added by the Public Interest Disclosure Act 1998 ss 7(1), 18(2)));
(9) the Employment Rights Act 1996 s 104(1), read with s 104(2), (3) (assertion of statutory right: see PARA 793) (s 108(3)(g) amended, s 108(3)(gg) added, by the National Minimum Wage Act 1998 ss 25, 53, Sch 3);
(10) the Employment Rights Act 1996 s 104A(1), read with s 104A(2) (national minimum wage: see PARA 794) (s 108(3)(gg) (as so added; amended by the Tax Credits Act 1999 Sch 3 para 3(3), Sch 6));
(11) the Employment Rights Act 1996 s 104B(1), read with s 104B(2) (tax credit: see PARA 795) (s 108(3)(gh) (added by the Tax Credits Act 1999 Sch 3 para 3(3), Sch 6; amended by SI 1999/3323));
(12) the Employment Rights Act 1996 s 104C (flexible working cases: see PARA 796) (s 108(3)(gi) (added by the Employment Relations Act 2004 s 41(5)));
(13) the Employment Rights Act 1996 s 104D(1), read with s 104D(2) (pension enrolment: see PARA 797) (s 108(3)(gj) (added by the Pensions Act 2008 s 57(1), (5)));
(14) the Employment Rights Act 1996 s 104E (applications for employer support for employee study and training: see PARA 798) (s 108(3)(gk) (added by the Apprenticeships, Skills, Children and Learning Act 2009 Sch 1 paras 1, 4));
(15) the Employment Rights Act 1996 s 104F(1), read with s 104F(2) (blacklists: see PARA 799) (s 108(3)(gl) (added by SI 2010/493));
(16) the Employment Rights Act 1996 s 104G (employee shareholder status: see PARA 800) (s 108(3)(gm) (added by the Growth and Infrastructure Act 2013 s 31(5)));
(17) the Employment Rights Act 1996 s 105 (redundancy: see PARA 781) (s 108(h) (amended by SI 1999/3323; SI 2000/1551));
(18) the Transnational Information and Consultation of Employees Regulations 1999, SI 1999/3323, reg 28(3) or (6), read with reg 28(4), (7) (see PARA 1277) (Employment Rights Act 1996 s 108(3)(hh) (added by SI 1999/3323; amended by SI 2000/1551; SI 2002/2034));
(19) the Part-time Workers (Prevention of Less Favourable Treatment) Regulations 2000, SI 2000/1551, reg 7(1) (see PARA 78) (Employment Rights Act 1996 s 108(3)(i) (added by SI 2000/1551; amended by SI 2002/2326));
(20) the Fixed-term Employees (Prevention of Less Favourable Treatment) Regulations 2002, SI 2002/2034, reg 6(1) (see PARA 89) (Employment Rights Act 1996 s 108(3)(j) (added by SI 2002/2034; amended by SI 2004/3426));
(21) the European Public Limited-Liability Company Regulations 2004, SI 2004/2326, reg 42(3) or (6) (revoked: see now the European Public Limited-Liability Company (Employee Involvement) (Great Britain) Regulations 2009, SI 2009/2401, reg 29(3) or (6); and PARA 1333) (Employment Rights Act 1996 s 108(3)(k) (added by SI 2004/2326; amended by SI 2006/349));
(22) the Information and Consultation of Employees Regulations 2004, SI 2004/3426, reg 30(3) or (6), read with reg 30(4), (7) (see PARA 1312) (Employment Rights Act 1996 s 108(3)(l) (added by SI 2004/3426; amended by SI 2006/1031));
(23) the Occupational and Personal Pension Schemes (Consultation by Employers and Miscellaneous Amendment) Regulations 2006, SI 2006/349, Schedule para 5(3) or 5(5) (see **PERSONAL AND OCCUPATIONAL PENSIONS** vol 80 (2013) PARA 486) (Employment Rights Act 1996 s 108(3)(m) (added by SI 2006/349; amended by SI 2006/2059));

(24) the European Cooperative Society (Involvement of Employees) Regulations 2006, SI 2006/2059, reg 31(3) or 31(6) (see PARA 1338) (Employment Rights Act 1996 s 108(3)(o) (added by SI 2006/2059));

(25) the Companies (Cross-Border Mergers) Regulations 2007, SI 2007/2974, reg 46 or reg 47 (see COMPANIES vol 15 (2009) PARA 1451) (Employment Rights Act 1996 s 108(3)(p) (added by SI 2007/2974; amended by SI 2010/93));

(26) the European Public Limited-Liability Company (Employee Involvement) (Great Britain) Regulations 2009, SI 2009/2401, reg 29(1)(a), (b) (see COMPANIES vol 14 (2009) PARA 5) (Employment Rights Act 1996 s 108(3)(q) (added by SI 2009/2401)); or

(27) the Agency Workers Regulations 2010, SI 2010/93, reg 17(1) (dismissal for applying agency worker regulations: see PARA 103) (Employment Rights Act 1996 s 108(3)(r) (added by SI 2010/93)).

As from a day to be appointed under the Education and Skills Act 2008 s 173(4), the Employment Rights Act 1996 s 101B (participation in education or training: see PARA 789) is also specified for these purposes: see s 108(3)(de) (prospectively added by the Education and Skills Act 2008 s 39(1), (4)). However, at the date at which this volume states the law, no such day had been appointed.

10 See the Employment Rights Act 1996 s 108(3). Where an applicant lacks the qualifying period but seeks to use one of these exceptions, the burden of proving the reason or principal reason is on him: *Smith v Hayle Town Council* [1978] ICR 996, [1978] IRLR 413, CA; *Maund v Penwith District Council* [1984] ICR 143, [1984] IRLR 24, CA.

11 Employment Rights Act 1996 s 108(4) (added by the Enterprise and Regulatory Reform Act 2013 s 13). This amendment to the Employment Rights Act 1996 s 108 was made in response to Application 47335/06 *Redfearn v United Kingdom* [2013] IRLR 51, 33 BHRC 713, ECtHR (legal system which allowed dismissal from employment solely on account of an employee's membership of a political party carried with it the potential for abuse and was a breach of the right to freedom of association; employee's dismissal on basis of election as local councillor for the BNP unlawful).

12 See the Trade Union and Labour Relations (Consolidation) Act 1992 s 154; and PARA 1056.

13 Employment Rights Act 1996 s 108(5) (added by the Defence Reform Act 2014 s 48(1), (2)). The amendment made by s 48(2) applies only where, in relation to the employee, the effective date of termination (as defined in the Employment Rights Act 1996 s 97: see PARA 764) falls on or after the day on which the Defence Reform Act 2014 s 48 comes into force (ie on or after 1 October 2014: see the Defence Reform Act 2014 (Commencement No. 2) Order 2014, SI 2014/2370, art 4): Defence Reform Act 2014 s 48(4). As to the meaning of 'reserve force' see the Armed Forces Act 2006 s 374; and ARMED FORCES vol 3 (2011) PARA 470 (definition applied by the Employment Rights Act 1996 s 108(5) (as so added)).

759.   Dismissal procedures agreements. Where a dismissal procedures agreement[1] is designated by an order[2] which is for the time being in force, the provisions of that agreement relating to dismissal[3] have effect in substitution for any rights under the statutory protection from unfair dismissal[4]; and, accordingly, that statutory protection does not apply to the dismissal of an employee[5] from any employment[6] if it is employment to which, and he is an employee to whom, those provisions of the agreement apply[7]. If, however, the agreement includes provision that it does not apply to dismissals of particular descriptions, this exclusion does not apply to a dismissal of any such description[8].

1 As to the meaning of 'dismissal procedures agreement' see PARA 150 note 9.

2 Ie under the Employment Rights Act 1996 s 110(3): see PARA 760. As to the modification of Pt X (ss 94–134A) (unfair dismissal: see also PARAS 757 et seq, 760 et seq) in relation to governing bodies of schools having a right to a delegated budget, acting in the exercise of their employment powers, see EDUCATION vol 35 (2011) PARA 355 et seq; and as to the modification of Pt X in relation to persons holding ecclesiastical office under common tenure see the Ecclesiastical Offices (Terms of Service) Regulations 2009, SI 2009/2108, reg 33; and ECCLESIASTICAL LAW vol 34 (2011) PARA 407.

3 As to the meaning of 'dismissal' see PARA 762.

4 Ie the Employment Rights Act 1996 s 94: see PARA 757.

5 As to the meaning of 'employee' see PARA 2.

6 As to the meaning of 'employment' see PARA 2.

7   See the Employment Rights Act 1996 s 110(1). Where an award is made under a designated
    dismissal procedures agreement, it may be enforced, in England and Wales, by leave of the
    County Court, in the same manner as a judgment of the court to the same effect and, where
    leave is given, judgment may be entered in terms of the award: see s 110(6)(a) (added by the
    Employment Rights (Dispute Resolution) Act 1998 s 12(3), (5); amended by the Crime and
    Courts Act 2013 s 17(5), Sch 9 Pt 3 para 52(1)(b), (2)). As to the meanings of 'England' and
    'Wales' see PARA 2 note 12.
8   Employment Rights Act 1996 s 110(2) (substituted by the Employment Rights (Dispute
    Resolution) Act 1998 s 12(1), (5)).

760.   Form, content and revocation of a dismissal procedures agreement.   An
order designating a dismissal procedures agreement[1] may be made by the
Secretary of State[2], on an application being made to him jointly by all the parties
to the agreement, if he is satisfied that:

(1)   every trade union[3] which is a party to the agreement is an independent
      trade union[4];

(2)   the agreement provides for procedures to be followed in cases where an
      employee[5] claims that he has been, or is in the course of being, unfairly
      dismissed[6];

(3)   those procedures are available without discrimination to all employees
      falling within any description to which the agreement applies[7];

(4)   the remedies provided by the agreement in respect of unfair dismissal
      are on the whole as beneficial as, but not necessarily identical with,
      those provided in respect of unfair dismissal by the statutory
      provisions[8];

(5)   the agreement includes provision either for arbitration in every case[9], or
      for:

      (a)   arbitration where, by reason of equality of votes or for any other
            reason, a decision under the agreement cannot otherwise be
            reached[10]; and

      (b)   a right to submit to arbitration any question of law arising out of
            such a decision[11]; and

(6)   the provisions of the agreement are such that it can be determined with
      reasonable certainty whether a particular employee is one to whom the
      agreement applies[12].

If, at any time when such an order is in force in respect of a dismissal
procedures agreement, the Secretary of State is satisfied, whether on an
application made to him by any of the parties to the agreement or otherwise,
that:

(i)   it is the desire of all the parties to the dismissal procedures agreement
      that the order should be revoked[13]; or

(ii) the agreement no longer fulfils all the conditions specified in heads (1)
      to (6) above[14],

he must revoke the order by a further such order[15].

1   Ie for the purposes of the Employment Rights Act 1996 s 110: see also PARA 759. As to the
    meaning of 'dismissal procedures agreement' see PARA 150 note 9.
2   As to the Secretary of State see PARA 5 note 21. As to the making of orders under the
    Employment Rights Act 1996 generally see PARA 162. At the date at which this volume states
    the law, no such order had been made.
       As from a day to be appointed under the Employment Act 2002 s 55(2), the Secretary of
    State may by order amend the Employment Rights Act 1996 s 110(3) (see heads (1) to (6) in the
    text) so as to add to the conditions specified therein such conditions as he may specify in the
    order: s 110(3A) (prospectively added by the Employment Act 2002 s 44). However, at the date
    at which this volume states the law, no such day had been appointed.

3 As to the meaning of 'trade union' see PARA 150 note 9.
4 Employment Rights Act 1996 s 110(3)(a). As to the meaning of 'independent trade union' see PARA 150 note 9.
5 As to the meaning of 'employee' see PARA 2.
6 Employment Rights Act 1996 s 110(3)(b). As to unfair dismissal see PARA 762 et seq.
7 Employment Rights Act 1996 s 110(3)(c).
8 Employment Rights Act 1996 s 110(3)(d). The provisions referred to in the text are those of Pt X (ss 94–134A) (unfair dismissal: see also PARAS 757 et seq, 761 et seq). As to the modification of Pt X in relation to governing bodies of schools having a right to a delegated budget, acting in the exercise of their employment powers, see EDUCATION vol 35 (2011) PARA 355 et seq; and as to the modification of Pt X in relation to persons holding ecclesiastical office under common tenure see the Ecclesiastical Offices (Terms of Service) Regulations 2009, SI 2009/2108, reg 33; and ECCLESIASTICAL LAW vol 34 (2011) PARA 407.
9 See the Employment Rights Act 1996 s 110(3)(e) (substituted by the Employment Rights (Dispute Resolution) Act 1998 s 12(2), (5)).
10 Employment Rights Act 1996 s 110(3)(e)(i) (as substituted: see note 9).
11 Employment Rights Act 1996 s 110(3)(e)(ii) (as substituted: see note 9).
12 Employment Rights Act 1996 s 110(3)(f).
13 Employment Rights Act 1996 s 110(4)(a).
14 Employment Rights Act 1996 s 110(4)(b).
15 See the Employment Rights Act 1996 s 110(4). The transitional provisions which may be made in an order under s 110(4) include, in particular, provisions directing that:
  (1) an employee: (a) is not to be excluded from his rights under s 94 (see PARA 757) where the effective date of termination falls within a transitional period which ends with the date on which the order takes effect and which is specified in the order; and (b) is to have an extended time for presenting a complaint under s 111 (see PARA 804) in respect of a dismissal where the effective date of termination falls within that period (see s 110(5)(a)); and
  (2) where the effective date of termination falls within such a transitional period, an employment tribunal is, in determining any complaint of unfair dismissal presented by an employee to whom the dismissal procedures agreement applies, to have regard to such considerations as may be specified in the order, in addition to those specified in Pt X (see also PARAS 757 et seq, 761 et seq) and the Employment Tribunals Act 1996 s 10(4), (5) (see PARA 1448) (Employment Rights Act 1996 s 110(5)(b) (amended by the Employment Rights (Dispute Resolution) Act 1998 s 1(2)(a), (c))).
As to the meaning of 'effective date of termination' see PARA 764.

(iii) Death of Employer or Employee

761. Death of employer or employee. Where the employer[1] or the employee[2] dies, certain of the statutory provisions relating to unfair dismissal have effect subject to modifications[3].

Where an employer has given notice to an employee to terminate his contract of employment[4], and where, before that termination the employee or the employer dies[5], the statutory unfair dismissal provisions[6] apply as if the contract had been duly terminated by the employer by notice expiring on the date of the death[7].

1 As to the meaning of 'employer' see PARA 2.
2 As to the meaning of 'employee' see PARA 2.
3 For the specified modifications see the text and notes 4–7; and PARAS 764 note 17, 811 note 7, 812 note 5, 813 note 9.
4 Employment Rights Act 1996 s 133(1)(a). As to the meaning of 'contract of employment' see PARA 2.
5 Employment Rights Act 1996 s 133(1)(b).
6 Ie the Employment Rights Act 1996 Pt X (ss 94–134A) (unfair dismissal: see also PARAS 757 et seq, 762 et seq). As to the modification of Pt X (ss 94–134A) in relation to governing bodies of schools having a right to a delegated budget, acting in the exercise of their employment powers, see EDUCATION vol 35 (2011) PARA 355 et seq; and as to the modification of Pt X in relation to

persons holding ecclesiastical office under common tenure see the Ecclesiastical Offices (Terms of Service) Regulations 2009, SI 2009/2108, reg 33; and ECCLESIASTICAL LAW vol 34 (2011) PARA 407.

7   See the Employment Rights Act 1996 s 133(1). Where:
    (1)   an employee's contract of employment has been terminated (s 133(2)(a));
    (2)   by virtue of s 97(2) or (4) (see PARA 764), a date later than the effective date of termination as defined in s 97(1) (see PARA 764) is to be treated for certain purposes as the effective date of termination (s 133(2)(b)); and
    (3)   the employer or the employee dies before that date (s 133(2)(c)),
    s 97(2) or (4) applies as if the notice referred to therein as required by s 86 (see PARA 736) expired on the date of the death (see s 133(2)).

(2) MEANING OF 'UNFAIR DISMISSAL'

(i) Dismissal; Effective Date of Termination

762.   Meaning of 'dismissal'.   An employee[1] is dismissed[2] by his employer[3] if, and only if[4]:

(1)   the contract under which he is employed is terminated by the employer, whether with or without notice[5]; or

(2)   he is employed under a limited-term contract[6], and that contract terminates by virtue of the limiting event[7] without being renewed[8] under the same contract[9]; or

(3)   the employee terminates the contract under which he is employed, with or without notice, in circumstances in which he is entitled to terminate it without notice by reason of the employer's conduct[10].

Where:

(a)   an employer gives notice to an employee to terminate his contract of employment[11]; and

(b)   at a time within the period of that notice, the employee gives notice to the employer to terminate the contract of employment on a date earlier than the date on which the employer's notice is due to expire[12],

the employee is to be taken[13] to be dismissed by his employer; and the reason for the dismissal is to be taken to be the reason for which the employer's notice is given[14].

There can be no claim for unfair dismissal if on the facts of the case the employee terminated the employment by resigning (unless it is a case of constructive dismissal[15], or of the employee being forced to resign under the threat of dismissal or some other pressure[16]), or if the employment ended in law in some other way, for example by expiry or performance[17], by mutual consent[18], by frustration[19] or by the operation of some other rule of law[20].

1   As to the meaning of 'employee' see PARA 2.
2   Ie for the purposes of the Employment Rights Act 1996 Pt X (ss 94–134A) (unfair dismissal: see also PARAS 757 et seq, 763 et seq). As to the modification of Pt X in relation to governing bodies of schools having a right to a delegated budget, acting in the exercise of their employment powers, see EDUCATION vol 35 (2011) PARA 355 et seq; and as to the modification of Pt X in relation to persons holding ecclesiastical office under common tenure see the Ecclesiastical Offices (Terms of Service) Regulations 2009, SI 2009/2108, reg 33; and ECCLESIASTICAL LAW vol 34 (2011) PARA 407.
3   As to the meaning of 'employer' see PARA 2.
4   See the Employment Rights Act 1996 s 95(1) (amended by the Employment Relations Act 2004 Sch 1 para 29, Sch 2). The Employment Rights Act 1996 s 95(1) is subject to s 95(2) (see the text and notes 11–14): see s 95(1) (as so amended). See also note 2.
5   Employment Rights Act 1996 s 95(1)(a). See also note 2.

In the case of both dismissal and resignation, a tribunal may need to look at the realities of the situation to decide on the legal outcome, certainly where the words used by the party in question were ambiguous, and possibly even where the words themselves appear unambiguous: *Sovereign House Security Services Ltd v Savage* [1989] IRLR 115, CA; *BG Gale Ltd v Gilbert* [1978] ICR 1149, [1978] IRLR 453, EAT; *Sothern v Franks Charlesly & Co* [1981] IRLR 278, CA; *J and J Stern v Simpson* [1983] IRLR 52, EAT; *Barclay v City of Glasgow District Council* [1983] IRLR 313, EAT; *Kwik-Fit (GB) Ltd v Lineham* [1992] ICR 183, [1992] IRLR 156, EAT. The onus is normally on the employer to ensure communication of the fact and date of dismissal, since the doctrine of constructive notice will not apply (eg to the sending of a letter and when the employee should have received it): *Widdicombe v Longcombe Software Ltd* [1998] ICR 710, EAT. See also *Zulhayir v JJ Food Service Ltd* [2011] All ER (D) 137 (Sep), EAT (termination cannot be implied; no effective steps had been taken until solicitors' letter prompted employee's claim).

A radical change of terms of employment, insisted on unilaterally by the employer, may be considered an ordinary dismissal by the employer under the Employment Rights Act 1996 s 95(1)(a) (ie without invoking the law on constructive dismissal (see PARA 763)), allowing the employee to claim unfair dismissal even if still employed by that employer under the new contract: *Hogg v Dover College* [1990] ICR 39, EAT; *Alcan Extrusions v Yates* [1996] IRLR 327, EAT. See also *Darby v Law Society of England and Wales* (2008) 152 Sol Jo (no 37) 29, [2008] All ER (D) 129 (Aug), EAT (on the true construction of correspondence relating to possible new packages sent by the employer to employees, employees had been given notice of termination of then-current contracts of employment, which were terminated, and thus as a matter of law the employees had been dismissed); cf *Saminaden v Barnet, Enfield and Haringey NHS Trust* [2008] All ER (D) 286 (Nov), EAT (employee had written letter to employer saying that he was working in the demoted position under protest and would be presenting a grievance about the downgrading).

Although at common law, once notice has been given it cannot be unilaterally withdrawn (see PARA 733), it is possible that an employer may be able to take back clear words of dismissal spoken in the heat of the moment: *Martin v Yeoman Aggregates Ltd* [1983] ICR 314, [1983] IRLR 49, EAT. Often described as an 'exception' to the withdrawal rule, this qualification is more in the nature of a 'cautionary reminder' because it affords the giver of the notice the opportunity to satisfy the recipient that he never intended to give it in the first place (that, in effect, his mind was not in tune with his words): *Willoughby v CF Capital plc* [2011] EWCA Civ 1115, [2012] ICR 1038, [2011] IRLR 985 (employer could not unilaterally withdraw from notice of dismissal on basis of mistaken expectation that employee would accept proposed transfer to self-employment). See also *Ali v Birmingham City Council* [2008] All ER (D) 260 (Oct), EAT (where the employee's resignation was reaffirmed by him several times on the same day, but then withdrawn four days later, it was decided that the resignation remained effective and termination proceeded).

In the orthodox contractual analysis, the circumstance given at head (1) in the text occurs in a misconduct case where the employee is guilty of a repudiatory breach of contract, which the employer accepts by dismissing him (see PARA 743): *Pendlebury v Christian Schools North West Ltd* [1985] ICR 174, EAT. However, it is not possible for an employer to argue that misconduct by the employee was so serious that it terminated the contract automatically, without the need for a dismissal; such ideas of 'self-dismissal' have been disapproved and so in such a case it is still necessary for the employer to take steps to dismiss: *London Transport Executive v Clarke* [1981] ICR 355, [1981] IRLR 166, CA (disapproving previous findings of 'self-dismissal' in *Gannon v JC Firth Ltd* [1976] IRLR 415, EAT; *Smith v Avana Bakeries Ltd* [1979] IRLR 423, EAT; *Kallinos v London Electric Wire* [1980] IRLR 11, EAT). See also PARA 826 note 4.

Moreover, any attempt by the employer to provide in advance for such an argument, by getting the employee to agree that, if a certain event occurs (eg not returning from leave of absence on time), his contract will end automatically or he will be deemed to have dismissed himself, is likely to be void under the Employment Rights Act 1996 s 203 (restrictions on contracting out: see PARA 150): *Igbo v Johnson, Matthey Chemicals Ltd* [1986] ICR 505, [1986] IRLR 215, CA (disapproving *British Leyland (UK) Ltd v Ashraf* [1978] ICR 979, [1978] IRLR 330, EAT); and see PARA 731.

6   As to the meaning of 'limited-term contract' see PARA 755 note 5.
7   As to the meaning of 'limiting event' see PARA 755 note 5.
8   As to the meaning of 'renewal' see PARA 755 note 6.
9   Employment Rights Act 1996 s 95(1)(b) (substituted by SI 2002/2034). See note 2. See also PARA 766.

In relation to government training schemes, agency workers or apprentices, head (2) in the text applies where the employee is employed under a contract for a fixed term and that term expires without being renewed under the same contract: Employment Rights Act 1996 s 95(1)(b); and see the Fixed-term Employees (Prevention of Less Favourable Treatment) Regulations 2002, SI 2002/2034, regs 18–20 (excluded classes of person under fixed-term work regulations); and PARA 94.

10 Employment Rights Act 1996 s 95(1)(c). See note 2. Dismissal in the circumstances specified in s 95(1)(c) is referred to as 'constructive dismissal': see PARA 763. See *Roberts v Gregorek (t/a Anglers Paradise)* [2008] All ER (D) 37 (May), EAT (no fundamental breach of employment contract entitling the employee to maintain that her trust and confidence in her employer had been irrevocably damaged; and no constructive dismissal as the employer was not aware of the employee's concerns about the removal of certain nesting for birds at the employer's establishment).

11 Employment Rights Act 1996 s 95(2)(a). See note 2. As to the meaning of 'contract of employment' see PARA 2.

12 Employment Rights Act 1996 s 95(2)(b). See note 2.

13 See note 2.

14 See the Employment Rights Act 1996 s 95(2). See note 2. See also *Thompson v GEC Avionics Ltd* [1991] IRLR 488, EAT. There is no particular form or length required for the counter-notice: *Ready Case Ltd v Jackson* [1981] IRLR 312, EAT. Lodging an application for unfair dismissal before the expiry of the employer's notice will not, however, be construed as counter-notice: *Cardinal Vaughan Memorial School Governors v Alie* [1987] ICR 406, EAT. On general principles, an agreement between the parties, at the instigation of either, to terminate before the expiry of an existing notice is likely to be construed merely as varying that notice, not as termination of the contract by mutual agreement: *McAlwane v Boughton Estates Ltd* [1973] 2 All ER 299, [1973] ICR 470, NIRC; *Lees v Arthur Greaves (Lees) Ltd* [1974] 2 All ER 393, [1974] ICR 501, CA; *Glacier Metal Co Ltd v Dyer* [1974] 3 All ER 21, [1974] IRLR 189, NIRC; *Springbank Sand and Gravel Co Ltd v Craig* [1974] ICR 7, [1973] IRLR 278, NIRC. Where, however, the employer dismisses the employee before expiry of the employee's notice, that will be a dismissal on ordinary grounds: *British Midland Airways Ltd v Lewis* [1978] ICR 782, EAT (criticised in *Marshall (Cambridge) Ltd v Hamblin* [1994] ICR 362, [1994] IRLR 260, EAT; sed quaere). As to where there was disagreement between the employee and employer about whether there had been dismissal or termination of contract by mutual consent and its importance in the context of overlap with other proceedings in regard to loss of bonuses see *GFI Holdings Ltd v Camm* [2008] All ER (D) 74 (Sep), EAT. As to the equivalent, but differently drafted and more restrictive, provision in redundancy law see PARA 866.

15 See PARA 763.

16 In a 'resign or be dismissed' case a tribunal may decide that the employee was in fact dismissed: *Martin v Glynwed Distribution Ltd* [1983] ICR 511, [1983] IRLR 198, CA (no dismissal on the facts); *East Sussex County Council v Walker* (1972) 7 ITR 280, NIRC. The tribunal may also so decide with other forms of pressure, such as threatening to call the police (*Allders International Ltd v Parkins* [1981] IRLR 68, EAT) or where the employee is inveigled into resigning by the employer (*Caledonian Mining Co Ltd v Bassett* [1987] ICR 425, [1987] IRLR 165, EAT (decided under what is now the Employment Rights Act 1996 s 136(1)(a): see PARA 864)). An agreed resignation on acceptable terms does not constitute dismissal, even if there is a threat of termination in the background: *Sheffield v Oxford Controls Co Ltd* [1979] ICR 396, [1979] IRLR 133, EAT; *Staffordshire County Council v Donovan* [1981] IRLR 108, EAT; *Logan Salton v Durham County Council* [1989] IRLR 99, EAT. However, where an employee negotiates satisfactory severance terms during the course of a meeting in which his dismissal is raised without warning, this does not allow the employer to claim that proper negotiation and discussion had led to resignation at the election of the employee: see *Sandhu v Jan de Rijk Transport Ltd* [2007] EWCA Civ 430, [2007] ICR 1137, [2007] IRLR 519 (ultimately the question is: '*who really ended it?*'). A hot-headed resignation which is accepted at face value by the employer may also amount to dismissal: see the cases cited in PARA 733 note 13.

17 See PARA 725.

18 See PARAS 730, 731.

19 See PARAS 728, 729.

20 See PARA 726 (dissolution of a partnership), PARA 727 (insolvency of employer), PARA 732 (death of employer or employee).

763.   Constructive dismissal.   An employee[1] who terminates the contract of employment[2], with or without notice, may still claim to have been dismissed[3] if the circumstances are such that he is entitled[4] to terminate it without notice by reason of the employer's[5] conduct ('constructive dismissal')[6].

The employee must leave in response to the breach of contract[7]. While, as a matter of fact, the employee may usually be expected to indicate that he is treating the contract as repudiated[8], there is no rule of law that the employee must always inform the employer of the true reason for leaving[9]. Delay in so doing may amount to waiver of the breach and affirmation of the contract[10], though this will depend on the facts of the case, and a realistic approach must be taken, so that it may be reasonable for the employee to work on for a period under protest[11], especially if trying to resolve matters without leaving[12] or seeking other work before leaving[13].

Whether there has been a repudiatory breach by the employer entitling the employee to leave is essentially a question of fact for a tribunal in the circumstances of the individual case; an appellate court will rarely interfere with the tribunal's decision on the point[14] and reported cases should not be regarded as precedents. Among the types of breach of contract by the employer that may support a finding of constructive dismissal[15] are:

(1)   a failure to pay wages[16] or unilateral decision to cut pay[17];
(2)   demotion or other change in status[18];
(3)   a change of job content not permitted or envisaged by the contract[19];
(4)   undermining a senior employee's position[20];
(5)   change of the place of work, or breach of a mobility clause, whether express or implied[21];
(6)   unilateral change of hours[22];
(7)   failure to ensure the employee's safety[23];
(8)   breach of the term of trust and respect[24];
(9)   failure to follow a contractually binding disciplinary procedure[25];
(10)   imposition of a disciplinary measure in a disproportionate manner[26];
(11)   failure to provide a reasonably suitable working environment[27];
(12)   failure to deal with grievances properly and timeously[28].

A constructive dismissal is not automatically unfair; and, therefore, once it has been established as a dismissal, the tribunal must proceed to apply the normal tests of fairness[29]. If a constructive dismissal is found to be unfair, there may still be a finding of contributory fault on the part of the employee[30].

1   As to the meaning of 'employee' see PARA 2.
2   As to the meaning of 'contract of employment' see PARA 2.
3   As to the meaning of 'dismissal' see PARA 762.
4   For these purposes, 'entitled' means contractually entitled, so that an employee seeking to rely on constructive dismissal must show that the employer was guilty of a repudiatory breach of contract, not simply of unreasonable conduct: *Western Excavating (ECC) Ltd v Sharp* [1978] QB 761, [1978] ICR 221, CA. The trigger for a decision to accept a repudiatory breach of contract need not itself have been the subject of a grievance raised by an employee: *Morton v Thornton Print Ltd* [2008] All ER (D) 30 (Sep), EAT. The breach may be of an implied term, not just an express term, but there must be such a breach and so eg a change to a discretionary 'works rule' (see PARA 116) may be insufficient: *Dryden v Greater Glasgow Health Board* [1992] IRLR 469, EAT (no implied right to smoke, so introduction of a no-smoking policy did not found constructive dismissal). Reasonableness or otherwise of the employer's conduct may be evidence, but the test remains contractual: *Courtaulds Northern Spinning Ltd v Sibson* [1988] ICR 451, [1988] IRLR 305, CA; *Brown v Merchant Ferries Ltd* [1998] IRLR 682, NI CA. The possible rigour of this rule has, however, been lessened by the development of the implied term of trust and respect (see PARA 48) with the result that behaviour sufficiently unreasonable to be in breach of that term may be relied on in that way. Certain (or possibly all)

express terms giving rights to employers may in effect be required to be exercised reasonably (see PARA 113), particularly if the term of trust and respect may be relied on and argued to be an overriding term, as in *United Bank Ltd v Akhtar* [1989] IRLR 507, EAT. See also *White v Reflecting Roadstuds Ltd* [1991] ICR 733, [1991] IRLR 331, EAT (doubting any general requirement of reasonableness but affirming the importance of this term). It has been held that express disciplinary powers must be exercised by an employer reasonably and proportionately (see PARA 699) which could be of considerable significance where an employer imposes a particular penalty and the employee leaves in consequence. As to the burden of proof see PARA 769.

It was held that there can be a constructive dismissal where the employer threatens unilateral changes, but by lawful means (the giving of full notice to determine the existing contract): *Greenaway Harrison Ltd v Wiles* [1994] IRLR 380, EAT. Although this was explained in terms of the policy behind the Employment Rights Act 1996 s 95(1)(c) (see PARA 762), it appears to be out of line with the normal approach of requiring contractual breach by the employer: see e g *Marshall (Cambridge) Ltd v Hamblin* [1994] ICR 362, [1994] IRLR 260, EAT (no constructive dismissal where wages in lieu were given under a term in the contract, even though the employee sustained financial loss); *Dryden v Greater Glasgow Health Board.*

5   As to the meaning of 'employer' see PARA 2. Action by a superior, e g a supervisor or foreman, constitutes the employer's conduct, provided that the superior was acting in the course of his employment, even if that superior does not have the power to dismiss: *Hilton International Hotels (UK) Ltd v Protopapa* [1990] IRLR 316, EAT. Likewise, there could still be a constructive dismissal even though the relevant resolution by the employing body turned out to be invalid: *Warnes v Trustees of Cheriton Oddfellows Social Club* [1993] IRLR 58, EAT.

6   See the Employment Rights Act 1996 s 95(1)(c); and PARA 762. Where the employer's repudiatory conduct is only anticipatory, it may be withdrawn before the employee accepts it, without there being a constructive dismissal: *Norwest Holst Group Administration Ltd v Harrison* [1985] ICR 668, sub nom *Harrison v Norwest Holst Group Administration Ltd* [1985] IRLR 240, CA. See also *Roberts v Gregorek (t/a Anglers Paradise)* [2008] All ER (D) 37 (May), EAT; and PARAS 762, 764. However, once an employer is in repudiatory breach of the employee's contract, he cannot avoid a constructive dismissal by a unilateral offer to make amends: the employee may choose to accept an apology or offer to put matters right, but he also retains the right to continue to act on the breach and still leave and claim constructive dismissal: *Bournemouth University Higher Education Corpn v Buckland* [2010] EWCA Civ 121, [2011] QB 323, [2010] 4 All ER 186 (in employment law there is no room for the doctrine that a fundamental breach, if curable and if cured, takes away the innocent party's option of acceptance; to introduce that concept could only be on grounds that were capable of extension to other contracts). *Bournemouth University Higher Education Corpn v Buckland* applies where the employer has committed a repudiatory breach, but there is a fundamental distinction, which it is perhaps more easy to recognise than to define, between there being a fundamental breach of contract that an apology by an employer cannot cure and there being action by an employer that can prevent a breach of contract taking place: *Assamoi v Spirit Pub Company (Services) Ltd (formerly known as Punch Pub Co Ltd)* [2012] All ER (D) 17 (Sep), EAT (the whole object of a grievance procedure and a disciplinary procedure is that an employee has the opportunity to articulate his concerns about the behaviour of management and to defend himself against allegations that in some way he is unfit to remain in the employment of the employer).

The test for breach of a fundamental term for these purposes is objective and is not to be judged by a 'range of reasonable responses' test (which, accordingly, applies only to the overall question of fairness, not to the question of whether there has been a dismissal: see PARA 767): *Bournemouth University Higher Education Corpn v Buckland* (in determining whether or not the employer is in fundamental breach of the implied term of trust and confidence the unvarnished test in *Malik v Bank of Credit and Commerce International SA (in liquidation), Mahmud v Bank of Credit and Commerce International SA (in liquidation)* [1998] AC 20, [1997] 3 All ER 1, HL (see PARA 48 note 3) is still to be applied; any other approach would be contrary to the basic authority of *Western Excavating (ECC) Ltd v Sharp* [1978] QB 761, [1978] ICR 221, CA (see note 4)). This is consistent with *Triggs v GAB Robins (UK) Ltd* [2007] 3 All ER 590, [2007] ICR 1424, [2007] IRLR 857, EAT ('range of reasonable responses test' had no application where employer's conduct of a grievance procedure was the 'final straw' relied upon); and settles the doubt raised by the application of a 'range of reasonable responses' test to the question of dismissal in *Dutton & Clark Ltd v Daly* [1985] ICR 780, [1985] IRLR 363, EAT; and *Abbey National plc v Fairbrother* [2007] IRLR 320, EAT (applied in *Claridge v Daler Rowney Ltd* [2008] ICR 1267, [2008] IRLR 672, EAT).

7   *Gaelic Oil Co Ltd v Hamilton* [1977] IRLR 27, EAT; *Logabax Ltd v Titherley* [1977] ICR 369,
    [1977] IRLR 97, EAT; *Walker v Josiah Wedgwood & Sons Ltd* [1978] ICR 744, [1978] IRLR
    105, EAT.
8   *Hunt v British Railways Board* [1979] IRLR 379, EAT. A contract may generally be repudiated
    by the action of the employer even if he is not intending to repudiate it (*Post Office v Roberts*
    [1980] IRLR 347, EAT; *Millbrook Furnishing Industries Ltd v McIntosh* [1981] IRLR
    309, EAT), although it has been held that an employer does not repudiate the contract merely by
    insisting on what he genuinely believes to be the proper construction of it (eg as to whether
    something is or is not payable), even if that opinion is incorrect (see *Frank Wright & Co*
    (Holdings) Ltd v Punch [1980] IRLR 217, EAT). This possible exception was treated with
    caution in *Financial Techniques (Planning Services) Ltd v Hughes* [1981] IRLR 32, CA, *BBC v*
    Beckett [1983] IRLR 43, EAT, and *Brown v JBD Engineering Ltd* [1993] IRLR 568, EAT, but
    was mentioned with approval (albeit without reference to authority) in *Bridgen v Lancashire*
    County Council [1987] IRLR 58 at 60, CA, per Sir John Donaldson MR (obiter). An
    employment tribunal is not invariably required to ascertain the real point in time in which the
    employee had to make a decision whether to resign; the true position is that it is a question of
    fact in each case whether there had been affirmation of the contract of employment and that
    affirmation would be regarded as having occurred if there had been a sufficient delay after the
    employer had made his final decision sufficiently clear: *Simms v Sainsbury Supermarkets Ltd*
    [2005] All ER (D) 144 (Mar), EAT. An act of acceptance of a repudiation does not have to be in
    any particular form: *Potter v RJ Temple plc (in liquidation)* (2004) Times, 11 February, [2003]
    All ER (D) 327 (Dec), EAT (communication of acceptance by fax). However, a breach of
    contract cannot be relied on to support a case of repudiation once the contract has been
    affirmed in the knowledge of that breach: *Cook v MSHK Ltd* [2009] EWCA Civ 624 at [60],
    [2009] IRLR 838 at [60].
9   *Weathersfield Ltd v Sargent* [1999] ICR 425, sub nom *Weathersfield Ltd (t/a Van and Truck*
    Rentals) v Sargent [1999] IRLR 94, CA (disapproving *Holland v Glendale Industries Ltd* [1998]
    ICR 493, EAT).
10 The fact of giving notice does not by itself constitute affirmation because the Employment
    Rights Act 1996 s 95(1)(c) (see PARA 762) anticipates the point by stating that the employee may
    terminate 'with or without notice': *Cockram v Air Products plc* [2014] IRLR 672, EAT. Where
    the employee gives notice in excess of the notice required by his contract, he is offering
    additional performance of the contract to that which is required by it, and that additional
    performance may be consistent only with affirmation of the contract, but it is a question of fact
    and degree whether in such circumstances his conduct is properly to be regarded as affirmation
    of the contract: *Cockram v Air Products plc*. See also *Chindove v William Morrisons*
    Supermarket plc [2014] All ER (D) 121 (Aug), EAT (affirmation remains an open question of
    fact and depends upon the context and not upon any strict time test; where an employee is sick
    and not working, it could not be assumed that he was honouring his contract and continuing to
    do so in a way which was inconsistent with his deciding to leave).
    Past waived breaches may, however, be used in evidence of a later allegation of breach of the
    term of trust and respect (see *Lewis v Motorworld Garages Ltd* [1986] ICR 157, [1985] IRLR
    465, CA; and PARA 48); and, where the breach is of a continuing nature, the employee may
    choose to respond to a later breach, even if he has waived earlier ones (*Reid v Camphill*
    Engravers [1990] ICR 435, [1990] IRLR 268, EAT). See also *Da'Bell v NSPCC* [2010] IRLR
    19, EAT (delay in handing in letter of resignation regarding a single breach that had occurred
    months before indicated either affirmation or a detachment from reasoning of breach of
    contract; employee's claim for constructive unfair dismissal necessarily failed).
11 *Bashir v Brillo Manufacturing Co* [1979] IRLR 295, EAT; *Sheet Metal Components Ltd v*
    Plumridge [1974] ICR 373, [1974] IRLR 86, NIRC. The employee may have a reasonable
    period to decide how to respond to the employer's conduct: *Air Canada v Lee* [1978] ICR 1202,
    [1978] IRLR 392, EAT; *Bliss v South East Thames Regional Health Authority* [1987] ICR 700,
    [1985] IRLR 308, CA (an application of the same principle to a common law claim); *GW*
    Stephens & Son v Fish [1989] ICR 324, EAT. See also *Hogg v Dover College* [1990] ICR
    39, EAT (employee held to have been constructively dismissed from his senior post, even though
    he continued to work in the junior capacity that was offered to him instead); *Saminaden v*
    Barnet, Enfield and Haringey NHS Trust [2008] All ER (D) 286 (Nov), EAT (employee who
    wrote a letter, when ordered to present himself for duties in a demoted job, letting his employers
    know that he would do so only under protest and that he would be presenting a grievance about
    the attempted downgrading, could not be said to have given any agreement to the downgrading,
    still less written agreement to it). Where an employee continues in employment after any breach
    by her employer that consists of a requirement to do work outside the scope of the original
    employment contract, this does not constitute acceptance of the new conditions or agreement,

either expressly or impliedly, to vary the scope of her contract, and where the original contractual job continues to exist and to be capable of performance by the employee, the employee can continue to perform; it is the employer who in such circumstances has to decide what stance to take: *Adamas Ltd v Chung* [2011] UKPC 32, [2011] IRLR 1014.

12 *WE Cox Toner (International) Ltd v Crook* [1981] ICR 823, [1981] IRLR 443, EAT; *Post Office v Roberts* [1980] IRLR 347, EAT. See, however, *Henry v London General Transport Services Ltd* [2002] EWCA Civ 488, [2002] ICR 910, [2002] IRLR 472 (employees continued to work under new conditions for two months before instituting proceedings; difficult to conclude other than that new terms had been accepted), applying *WE Cox Toner (International) Ltd v Crook.*

13 *Waltons and Morse v Dorrington* [1997] IRLR 488, EAT; *Jones v F Sirl & Son (Furnishers) Ltd* [1997] IRLR 493, EAT. Causation must still be shown, and as a matter of fact the longer the delay and the more importance the search for other work takes on, the more difficult it may be to show the continuing causal link between the employer's conduct and the employee's leaving.

14 *Pedersen v Camden London Borough Council* [1981] ICR 674n, [1981] IRLR 173, CA; *Woods v WM Car Services (Peterborough) Ltd* [1982] ICR 693, [1982] IRLR 413, CA; and see PARA 1429.

15 Heads (1)–(12) in the text do not, however, constitute an exhaustive list. See *Webster v Woodhouse School* [2009] EWCA Civ 91, [2009] ICR 818, [2009] IRLR 568 (where an employee of a school as head of care was successful in a constructive dismissal claim on the facts alleging that the employer had effectively instructed him to dismiss a disabled person that the employee had recruited for a probationary period prompting his (ie the employee's) resignation).

16 *Stokes v Hampstead Wine Co Ltd* [1979] IRLR 298, EAT. Failure to give an annual pay rise or other bonus could be constructive dismissal if there was a contractual entitlement to it (*Pepper and Hope Ltd v Daish* [1980] IRLR 13, EAT); but such a contractual entitlement is unlikely to be inferred (*Murco Petroleum Ltd v Forge* [1987] ICR 282, [1987] IRLR 50, EAT, applying *FC Gardner Ltd v Beresford* [1978] IRLR 63, EAT). Failure to pay wages on the due date may not necessarily amount to constructive dismissal (*Adams v Charles Zub Associates Ltd* [1978] IRLR 551, EAT); but any deliberate refusal to pay an element of remuneration is likely to be construed as striking at the heart of the contract and so as giving rise to constructive dismissal (*Cantor Fitzgerald International v Callaghan* [1999] 2 All ER 411, [1999] ICR 639, CA). See also *Judge v Crown Leisure Ltd* [2005] EWCA Civ 571, [2005] IRLR 823 (promise at Christmas party to increase wages not contractually binding).

17 *Industrial Rubber Products v Gillon* [1977] IRLR 389, EAT; *High v British Railways Board* [1979] IRLR 52, EAT (no dismissal on the facts); *Gillies v Richard Daniels & Co Ltd* [1979] IRLR 457, EAT (whether a unilateral reduction in pay or fringe benefits is sufficiently material to constitute constructive dismissal is a matter of fact and degree); *Lewis v Motorworld Garages Ltd* [1986] ICR 157, [1985] IRLR 465, CA. Payment of less than the statutory minimum under a wages order (now mostly obsolete: see PARA 26) may entitle the employee to leave: *Reid v Camphill Engravers* [1990] ICR 435, [1990] IRLR 268, EAT. A change in the payment system reducing remuneration but permitted by the contract may not, however, be found to be constructive dismissal: *Spafax Ltd v Harrison, Spafax Ltd v Taylor* [1980] IRLR 442, CA (common law claim); *White v Reflecting Roadstuds Ltd* [1991] ICR 733, [1991] IRLR 331, EAT.

18 *Coleman v S and W Baldwin* [1977] IRLR 342, EAT; *Bashir v Brillo Manufacturing Co* [1979] IRLR 295, EAT. See also note 11. It is otherwise where the demotion is justified under the firm's disciplinary procedure: *Phillips v Glendale Cabinet Co Ltd* [1977] IRLR 307, EAT.

19 *Pedersen v Camden London Borough Council* [1981] ICR 674n, [1981] IRLR 173, CA; *Seligman and Latz Ltd v McHugh* [1979] IRLR 130, EAT; *Ford v Milthorn Toleman Ltd* [1980] IRLR 30, CA; *McNeill v Charles Crimin (Electrical Contractors) Ltd* [1984] IRLR 179, EAT; *Hogg v Dover College* [1990] ICR 39, EAT; *Josiah Mason College v Parsons* [2005] All ER (D) 22 (Apr), EAT (teacher employed to teach specific subjects could not be required to teach a different subject, even with consultation). It is otherwise if the change in duties is within the contract: *Peter Carnie & Son Ltd v Paton* [1979] IRLR 260, EAT. For these purposes, it is open to an employment tribunal to determine the employee's duties under his contract: *Hilton v Shiner Ltd (Builders Merchants)* [2001] IRLR 727, EAT (change of job content evident from facts despite no written job description). Whether a temporary change in duties or demotion, especially if the pay remains the same, entitles the employee to leave depends on the circumstances: *McNeill v Charles Crimin (Electrical Contractors) Ltd*; *Millbrook Furnishing Industries Ltd v McIntosh* [1981] IRLR 309, EAT. See also *Land Securities Trillium Ltd v Thornley* [2005] IRLR 765, EAT; *Luke v Stoke-on-Trent City Council* [2007] EWCA Civ 761, [2007] ICR 1678, [2007] IRLR 777. See also note 11.

20 *Wetherall (Bond St W1) Ltd v Lynn* [1978] ICR 205, [1977] IRLR 333, EAT; *Associated Tyre Specialists (Eastern) Ltd v Waterhouse* [1977] ICR 218, [1976] IRLR 386, EAT; *Wadham Stringer Commercials (London) Ltd and Wadham Stringer Vehicles Ltd v Brown* [1983] IRLR 46, EAT.

21 *O'Brien v Associated Fire Alarms Ltd* [1969] 1 All ER 93, [1968] 1 WLR 1916, CA; *Hawker Siddeley Power Engineering Ltd v Rump* [1979] IRLR 425, EAT. It is otherwise where there are no grounds on the facts for inferring any geographical limitation into the contract: *Express Lift Co Ltd v Bowles* [1977] ICR 474, [1977] IRLR 99, EAT; *Little v Charterhouse Magna Assurance Co Ltd* [1980] IRLR 19, EAT. A mobility clause may be implied, probably covering reasonable travelling distance and/or on reasonable notice: *Courtaulds Northern Spinning Ltd v Sibson* [1988] ICR 451, [1988] IRLR 305, CA; *Prestwick Circuits Ltd v McAndrew* [1990] IRLR 191, Ct of Sess. Even an express mobility clause may be expected to be exercised reasonably, or at least not in such a way as to breach the implied term of trust and respect: *United Bank Ltd v Akhtar* [1989] IRLR 507, EAT; but cf *Rank Xerox Ltd v Churchill* [1988] IRLR 280, EAT; *White v Reflecting Roadstuds Ltd* [1991] ICR 733, [1991] IRLR 331, EAT. See also *Home Office v Evans* [2007] EWCA Civ 1089, [2008] ICR 302, [2008] IRLR 59.

22 *Derby City Council v Marshall* [1979] ICR 731, [1979] IRLR 261, EAT; *Simmonds v Dowty Seals Ltd* [1978] IRLR 211, EAT. It is otherwise where the employer has the contractual right to vary: *Dal v Orr* [1980] IRLR 413, EAT. A lay-off without contractual authority, express or implied, eg from custom and practice in the industry, may entitle the employee to leave: *D & J McKenzie Ltd v Smith* [1976] IRLR 345, Ct of Sess; *Waine v R Oliver (Plant Hire) Ltd* [1977] IRLR 434, EAT; *Kenneth MacRae & Co Ltd v Dawson* [1984] IRLR 5, EAT.

23 *Graham Oxley Tool Steels Ltd v Firth* [1980] IRLR 135, EAT; *Dutton & Clark Ltd v Daly* [1985] ICR 780, [1985] IRLR 363, EAT (but cf the reservations about the correctness of the general approach in this case in note 6); *Keys v Shoefayre Ltd* [1978] IRLR 476, EAT; cf *Wilkins v Cantrell and Cochrane (GB) Ltd* [1978] IRLR 483, EAT. Failure to investigate safety complaints may found constructive dismissal (*British Aircraft Corpn v Austin* [1978] IRLR 332, EAT); likewise with failure to take seriously a complaint of sexual harassment (*Bracebridge Engineering Ltd v Darby* [1990] IRLR 3, EAT).

24 See PARA 48. See eg *Varma v North Cheshire Hospital NHS Trust* (2008) 103 BMLR 117, [2008] All ER (D) (Jul), EAT (pre-registration house officer who resigned after being suspended and told of disciplinary hearings due to his unusual behaviour unsuccessfully claimed constructive dismissal due to his employer's breach of the implied term of trust and confidence; and in the circumstances the employer's selection of the wrong disciplinary process not crucial).

25 *Post Office v Strange* [1981] IRLR 515, EAT. See also *Tolson v Governing Body of Mixenden Community School* [2003] IRLR 842, EAT (when determining an issue as to constructive dismissal, the conduct to be considered is that of the employer, so an alleged failure by the employee regarding following or not following a grievance procedure cannot be relevant). See also *Varma v North Cheshire Hospital NHS Trust* (2008) 103 BMLR 117, [2008] All ER (D) (Jul), EAT; and note 24.

26 *BBC v Beckett* [1983] IRLR 43, EAT; *Cawley v South Wales Electricity Board* [1985] IRLR 89, EAT.

27 *Waltons and Morse v Dorrington* [1997] IRLR 488, EAT. See also *Bunning v GT Bunning & Sons Ltd* [2004] All ER (D) 214 (Nov), EAT (pregnant employee objected to continuing work as welder fitter).

28 *WA Goold (Pearmak) Ltd v McConnell* [1995] IRLR 516, EAT.

29 *Savoia v Chiltern Herb Farms Ltd* [1982] IRLR 166, CA. Often the factors applying to whether the employee was constructively dismissed will be the same as those applying to whether the dismissal was fair and, therefore, in practice a constructive dismissal will often be unfair (*Cawley v South Wales Electricity Board* [1985] IRLR 89, EAT); but this is not necessarily so, and in a relevant case the tribunal must consider both matters (*Stephenson & Co (Oxford) Ltd v Austin* [1990] ICR 609, EAT).

30 *Garner v Grange Furnishing Ltd* [1977] IRLR 206, EAT; *Associated Tyre Specialists (Eastern) Ltd v Waterhouse* [1977] ICR 218, [1976] IRLR 386, EAT; and see *Frith Accountants v Law* [2014] IRLR 510, [2014] ICR 805, EAT (tribunal had been entitled to reach the conclusion that there had been no causal contribution with regard to the compensatory award under the Employment Rights Act 1996 s 123(6) (see PARA 821) but the reasoning on causation did not apply in respect of the basic award under s 122(2) (see PARA 821)). As to the effect of contributory fault generally on the amount of compensation awarded for dismissal see PARA 821.

A finding of contributory fault in a constructive dismissal case may be made without the need for exceptional circumstances: *Morrison v Amalgamated Transport and General Workers' Union* [1989] IRLR 361, NI CA; *Polentarutti v Autokraft Ltd* [1991] ICR 757, [1991] IRLR

457, EAT. As to mitigation in constructive dismissal cases see particularly *Stuart Peters Ltd v Bell* [2009] EWCA Civ 938, [2010] 1 All ER 775, [2009] ICR 453; and PARAS 819 note 5, 822 note 3.

764.   The effective date of termination.   For the purposes of the law of unfair dismissal[1], the 'effective date of termination' means[2]:

(1)   in relation to an employee whose contract of employment is terminated by notice[3], whether given by his employer[4] or by the employee, the date on which that notice expires[5];

(2)   in relation to an employee whose contract of employment is terminated without notice, the date on which the termination takes effect[6]; and

(3)   in relation to an employee who is employed under a limited-term contract[7] which terminates by virtue of the limiting event[8] without being renewed[9] under the same contract, the date on which the termination takes effect[10].

Where the contract of employment is terminated by the employer[11], and where the notice required[12] to be given by an employer would, if duly given on the material date[13], expire on a date later than the effective date of termination[14], the later date is, for the purposes of the qualifying period of employment[15] and for the purposes of the basic award of compensation[16], the effective date of termination in relation to the dismissal[17].

Where:

(a)   the contract of employment is terminated by the employee[18];

(b)   the material date[19] does not fall during a period of notice given by the employer to terminate that contract[20]; and

(c)   had the contract been terminated not by the employee but by notice given on the material date by the employer, that notice would have been required[21] to expire on a date later than the effective date of termination[22],

then, for the purposes of the qualifying period of employment[23], and for the purposes of the basic award of compensation[24], the later date is the effective date of termination in relation to the dismissal[25].

1   Ie the Employment Rights Act 1996 Pt X (ss 94–134A) (unfair dismissal: see also PARAS 757 et seq, 765 et seq). As to the modification of Pt X in relation to governing bodies of schools having a right to a delegated budget, acting in the exercise of their employment powers, see EDUCATION vol 35 (2011) PARA 355 et seq; and as to the modification of Pt X in relation to persons holding ecclesiastical office under common tenure see the Ecclesiastical Offices (Terms of Service) Regulations 2009, SI 2009/2108, reg 33; and ECCLESIASTICAL LAW vol 34 (2011) PARA 407.

2   See the Employment Rights Act 1996 s 97(1). The provision so made is subject to s 97(2)–(5) (see the text and notes 11–25): see s 97(1). See also note 1. The effective date of termination is a statutory construct which depends on what has happened between the parties over time and not on what they may agree to treat as having happened: *Fitzgerald v University of Kent at Canterbury* [2004] EWCA Civ 143, [2004] ICR 737, [2004] IRLR 300 (consensual arrangement to antedate termination of employment ineffective; agreement caught in any event by the restriction on contracting-out in the Employment Rights Act 1996 s 203 (see PARA 150)). The fixing of the effective date of termination is generally a matter of applying the statutory wording, so that extrinsic matters such as receipt of a form P45 are irrelevant: *Newham London Borough v Ward* [1985] IRLR 509, CA. The date is not delayed by the fact that the employee has pursued an internal appeal against his dismissal (*J Sainsbury Ltd v Savage* [1981] ICR 1, [1980] IRLR 109, CA), unless the firm's procedure operates by merely suspending the contract pending the hearing (*Hassan v Odeon Cinemas Ltd* [1998] ICR 127, EAT; *Drage v Governors of Greenford High School* [2000] ICR 899, [2000] IRLR 314, CA); similarly, if the employer dismisses instantly, in breach of a contractually binding procedure, that does not affect the effective date of termination (*Batchelor v British Railways Board* [1987] IRLR 136, CA).

     The Employment Rights Act 1996 s 97(1) does not specify the effective date of termination in a constructive dismissal case (although there is a statutory extension for certain purposes) and so it is necessary in each case to consider the facts and apply the ordinary rules in s 97(1): *BMK Ltd v Logue* [1993] ICR 601, sub nom *BMK Ltd and BMK Holdings Ltd v Logue* [1993] IRLR 477, EAT. If the employee leaves immediately, that is his effective date of termination (see eg *Western Excavating (ECC) Ltd v Sharp* [1978] QB 761, [1978] ICR 221, CA), but in a more complicated case the tribunal may have to consider when the employee accepted the employer's repudiation (*GW Stephens & Son v Fish* [1989] ICR 324, EAT) and may apply a stated date given by the employee when resigning (*Crank v HM Stationery Office* [1985] ICR 1, EAT). The employee must communicate the intent to terminate if there is to be a constructive dismissal, which is not to be dated to an earlier stage when he simply decided to leave: *Edwards v Surrey Police* [1999] IRLR 456, EAT.

3 As to the meanings of 'employee' and 'contract of employment' see PARA 2.
4 As to the meaning of 'employer' see PARA 2.
5 Employment Rights Act 1996 s 97(1)(a). See note 1. Where notice is given orally on a day when work is performed, the notice period runs from the following day: *West v Kneels Ltd* [1987] ICR 146, [1986] IRLR 430, EAT. The same rule applies to written notice, unless the contract of employment indicates otherwise: *Wang v University of Keele* [2011] IRLR 542, EAT.

Where dismissal is by the giving of wages in lieu, the effective date of termination depends on how the dismissal is construed: (1) if it is meant to be a dismissal with notice, but with the employee not required actually to work out the notice, the date is the date of the expiry of the notice; (2) if it is meant to be an instant dismissal, but with payment for what should have been the notice period (as, in effect, damages for wrongful dismissal: *Dixon v Stenor Ltd* [1973] ICR 157, [1973] IRLR 28, NIRC), the date is the date the employment terminates: *Adams v GKN Sankey Ltd* [1980] IRLR 416, EAT; *Leech v Preston Borough Council* [1985] ICR 192, [1985] IRLR 337, EAT. Any ambiguity, especially in a letter of dismissal, should be resolved in the employee's favour: *Chapman v Letheby and Christopher Ltd* [1981] IRLR 440, EAT. In many cases the (simpler) result will be that the effective date of termination is when the employment actually ends, not the end of the notional notice period: see eg *Dedman v British Building and Engineering Appliances Ltd* [1974] 1 All ER 520, [1974] ICR 53, CA; and *Robert Cort & Son Ltd v Charman* [1981] ICR 816, [1981] IRLR 437, EAT (approved in *Radecki v Kirklees Metropolitan Borough Council* [2009] EWCA Civ 298, [2009] ICR 1244, [2009] IRLR 555 (council's communication that employee was being taken off the payroll did not amount to an express statement that he was being dismissed, but it nonetheless unequivocally conveyed that his employment was being terminated)).

6 Employment Rights Act 1996 s 97(1)(b). See note 1.

Where the employee is summarily dismissed, the effective date of termination is the date of that summary dismissal even if: (1) that dismissal is wrongful; (2) it is effected while the employee was already under ordinary notice from the employer; and/or (3) the effect of the summary dismissal is to bring forward the effective date of termination, so that the employee lacks the continuous employment necessary in order to claim unfair dismissal: *Stapp v Shaftesbury Society* [1982] IRLR 326, CA. The 'automatic dismissal theory' applies (in contradistinction to the 'elective theory' which holds for common law claims for wrongful dismissal: see PARA 826 note 4) so that the employee cannot seek to delay the effective date of termination by arguing that he did not accept the employer's repudiation of the contract by wrongfully dismissing him: *Robert Cort & Son Ltd v Charman* [1981] ICR 816, [1981] IRLR 437, EAT (applied in *Duniec v Travis Perkins Trading Co Ltd* [2014] All ER (D) 136 (Aug), EAT).

Ultimately, the burden is on the employer to ensure communication of the fact and date of dismissal: *Widdicombe v Longcombe Software Ltd* [1998] ICR 710, EAT. In applying the statutory framework to the facts of a case, however, the tribunal needs to be mindful, as a question of fact, of the human dimension in considering what is or is not reasonable to expect of someone facing the prospect of dismissal from employment, and the legal test is to be applied subjectively to the employee, in his or her particular circumstances: *GISDA Cyf v Barratt* [2010] UKSC 41, [2010] 4 All ER 851, [2010] IRLR 1073, [2010] ICR 1475. Being a statutory construct (see note 2), designed to hold the balance between employer and employee, the Employment Rights Act 1996 s 97(1) is not to be interpreted following the route of conventional contract law: *GISDA Cyf v Barratt*. Where dismissal is effected by letter, the contract of employment does not terminate until the employee reads the letter of termination or has a reasonable opportunity to do so: *Brown v Southall & Knight* [1980] ICR 617, [1980] IRLR 130, EAT (termination does not date from the time when he might reasonably have been expected to receive the notice, eg by letter sent in the ordinary post). Actual receipt is required, there being no place for a doctrine of constructive notice, except perhaps where the employee deliberately refuses to accept or read the letter: *McMaster v Manchester Airport plc* [1998] IRLR 112, EAT. *Brown v Southall & Knight* and *McMaster v Manchester Airport plc* were both approved in *GISDA Cyf v Barratt*. The principle does not operate, however, so as to exclude communication of the employee's dismissal to a third party (eg an instructed solicitor) rather than by a direct route to the employee: *Robinson v Dr Bowskill and Fairhill Medical Practice* [2014] ICR D7, [2013] All ER (D) 351 (Nov), EAT (employee acquired knowledge of her dismissal at the time when she was told by her solicitor, who had received notice by email from the employer the day before, rather than when the employee read the formal letter of dismissal from her employer, which was received the day after). See also *Potter v RJ Temple plc (in liquidation)* (2004) Times, 11 February, [2003] All ER (D) 327 (Dec), EAT (employee's acceptance by fax of employer's repudiatory breach was effective from the date on which the fax was received).

Very exceptionally, it may be necessary to put a precise time on the effectiveness of a summary dismissal: see *Octavius Atkinson & Sons Ltd v Morris* [1989] ICR 431, [1989] IRLR 158, CA (dismissal took effect from the moment the employee was dismissed without notice at lunchtime and was not rendered unfair by employer's failure to offer alternative employment which became available only in the afternoon, despite the employee being paid for travelling time to cover his 100 mile journey home at the end of the working day).

7 As to the meaning of 'limited-term contract' see PARA 755 note 5.

8 As to the meaning of 'limiting event' see PARA 755 note 5.

9 As to the meaning of 'renewal' see PARA 755 note 6.

10 Employment Rights Act 1996 s 97(1)(c) (substituted by SI 2002/2034). See note 1. As to the expiry of a limited-term contract as a head of dismissal see PARA 762; and as to internal appeals see PARA 708.

In relation to government training schemes, agency workers or apprentices, head (3) in the text provides that, in relation to an employee who is employed under a contract for a fixed term, which expires without being renewed under the same contract, the 'effective date of termination' means the date on which the term expires: Employment Rights Act 1996 s 97(1)(c); and see the Fixed-term Employees (Prevention of Less Favourable Treatment) Regulations 2002, SI 2002/2034, regs 18–20 (excluded classes of person under fixed-term work regulations); and PARA 94.

11 Employment Rights Act 1996 s 97(2)(a). See note 1.

12 Ie by the Employment Rights Act 1996 s 86: see PARA 736. In the context of the equivalent provision in redundancy law (see s 145(5); and PARA 871 note 20) it has been held that the fact that the employee waived his notice (ie under s 86(3): see PARA 736) does not affect the statutory extension of the effective date of termination, since s 145(5) only adopts the notice 'required' by s 86(1) and so is unaffected by any waiver under s 86(3): *Secretary of State for Employment v Staffordshire County Council, Secretary of State for Employment v Cameron Iron Works* [1989] ICR 664, [1989] IRLR 117, CA. *Quaere* whether this casts doubt on the decision in *Lanton Leisure Ltd v White and Gibson* [1987] IRLR 119, EAT, that, where there was no right to minimum notice under what is now the Employment Rights Act 1996 s 86(1) because the employee was summarily dismissed for gross misconduct (see s 86(6)), the extension in s 97(2) may not apply.

13 For these purposes, 'material date' means: (1) the date when notice of termination was given by the employer (Employment Rights Act 1996 s 97(3)(a)); or (2) where no notice was given, the date when the contract of employment was terminated by the employer (s 97(3)(b)).

14 Employment Rights Act 1996 s 97(2)(b). The text refers to the effective date of termination as defined by s 97(1) (see the text and notes 1–10): see s 97(2)(b). See also note 1.

15 Ie for the purposes of the Employment Rights Act 1996 s 108(1): see PARA 758.

16 Ie for the purposes of the Employment Rights Act 1996 s 119(1): see PARA 815. The date mentioned in the text also applies for the purposes of s 227(3) (repealed): see s 97(2).

17 Employment Rights Act 1996 s 97(2). See note 1. The extension is only for the period of the statutory minimum notice, not for any longer period of contractual notice: *Fox Maintenance Ltd v Jackson* [1978] ICR 110, [1977] IRLR 306, EAT. It is not open to the courts, through the machinery of an award of damages for wrongful dismissal (see PARA 825 et seq), to circumvent the deliberate legislative decision embodied in the Employment Rights Act 1996 s 97(2), which postpones the effective date of termination until the end of the statutory notice period only: *Harper v Virgin Net Ltd* [2004] EWCA Civ 271, [2005] ICR 921, [2004] IRLR 390 (contractual notice period exceeded statutory notice period).

Where, in the case of an employee, a date later than the date which would be the effective date of termination, by virtue of the Employment Rights Act 1996 s 97(1) (see heads (1)–(3) in the text), is treated for certain purposes as the effective date of termination by virtue of s 97(2) or (4), the period of the interval between the two dates counts as a period of employment in ascertaining for the purposes of s 108(1) (see PARA 758) or s 119(1) (see PARA 815) the period for which the employee has been continuously employed: s 213(1). See also *Cookson and Zinn Ltd v Morgan* [1979] ICR 425, EAT.

As to the effective date of termination when the employer or the employee dies before the date which is deemed by virtue of the Employment Rights Act 1996 s 97(2) or (4) see s 133(2); and PARA 761 note 7.

18 Employment Rights Act 1996 s 97(4)(a). See note 1.
19 For these purposes, 'material date' means: (1) the date when notice of termination was given by the employee (Employment Rights Act 1996 s 97(5)(a)); or (2) where no notice was given, the date when the contract of employment was terminated by the employee (s 97(5)(b)).
20 Employment Rights Act 1996 s 97(4)(b). See note 1.
21 See note 12.
22 Employment Rights Act 1996 s 97(4)(c). The text refers to the effective date of termination as defined by s 97(1) (see the text and notes 1–10): see s 97(4)(c). See also note 1.
23 See note 15.
24 See note 16.
25 Employment Rights Act 1996 s 97(4). See note 1.

(ii) Unfairness

765. Fairness of dismissal. In determining[1] whether the dismissal[2] of an employee[3] is fair or unfair, it is for the employer[4] to show[5]:

(1) the reason, or, if more than one, the principal reason, for the dismissal[6]; and

(2) that it is either a reason which[7]:
  (a) related to the capability[8] or qualifications[9] of the employee for performing work of the kind which he was employed by the employer to do[10];
  (b) related to the conduct of the employee[11];
  (c) was that the employee was redundant[12]; or
  (d) was that the employee could not continue to work in the position[13] which he held without contravention, either on his part or on that of his employer, of a duty or restriction imposed by or under an enactment[14],

  or is some other substantial reason[15] of a kind such as to justify the dismissal of an employee holding the position which that employee held[16].

Where the employer has fulfilled the requirements of heads (1) and (2) above, then[17] the determination of the question whether the dismissal is fair or unfair, having regard to the reason shown by the employer[18]:

(i) depends on whether in the circumstances, including the size and administrative resources of the employer's undertaking[19], the employer acted reasonably or unreasonably[20] in treating it as a sufficient reason for dismissing the employee[21]; and

(ii) must be determined in accordance with equity and the substantial merits of the case[22].

It is absolutely fundamental that an employment tribunal hearing a claim for unfair dismissal should set out clearly the terms of the statutory provisions above which apply to the case, or at least offer a distillation of the questions that any relevant provision requires it to decide; and it should then show, in its judgment, that it has decided those questions, what answers it gives to them, and what are the reasons for those answers[23].

1 Ie for the purposes of the Employment Rights Act 1996 Pt X (ss 94–134A) (unfair dismissal: see also PARAS 757 et seq, 766 et seq). As to the modification of Pt X (ss 94–134A) in relation to

governing bodies of schools having a right to a delegated budget, acting in the exercise of their employment powers, see EDUCATION vol 35 (2011) PARA 355 et seq; and as to the modification of Pt X in relation to persons holding ecclesiastical office under common tenure see the Ecclesiastical Offices (Terms of Service) Regulations 2009, SI 2009/2108, reg 33; and ECCLESIASTICAL LAW vol 34 (2011) PARA 407.

2 As to the meaning of 'dismissal' see PARA 762.

3 As to the meaning of 'employee' see PARA 2.

4 As to the meaning of 'employer' see PARA 2.

5 See the Employment Rights Act 1996 s 98(1).

6 Employment Rights Act 1996 s 98(1)(a).

7 Ie a reason falling within the Employment Rights Act 1996 s 98(2) (see heads (a) to (d) in the text): see s 98(1)(b).

8 As to the meaning of 'capability' see PARA 773.

9 As to the meaning of 'qualifications' see PARA 773.

10 Employment Rights Act 1996 s 98(2)(a). See PARAS 773–775.

11 Employment Rights Act 1996 s 98(2)(b). See PARAS 776–779.

12 Employment Rights Act 1996 s 98(2)(c). See PARAS 780–782.

13 For these purposes, except in so far as the context otherwise requires, 'position', in relation to an employee, means the following matters taken as a whole: (1) his status as an employee; (2) the nature of his work; and (3) his terms and conditions of employment: see the Employment Rights Act 1996 s 235(1).

14 Employment Rights Act 1996 s 98(2)(d). See PARA 783.

15 See PARA 766.

16 Employment Rights Act 1996 s 98(1)(b). In addition to the general categories mentioned in the text, there are special provisions relating to dismissals involving part-time workers (see PARA 78) and fixed-term workers (see PARA 89); to dismissals resulting from exercising the right to be accompanied at a disciplinary or grievance hearing (see PARA 721); to dismissals resulting from taking leave for family reasons (see PARA 784); to dismissals which fall under various headings of special or automatically unfair reasons (see PARAS 785–801); to dismissals on the transfer of an undertaking (see PARA 803); and to dismissals relating to trade union membership or non-membership (see PARA 1056) and to industrial action (see PARA 1351). As to procedural fairness see PARA 768.

17 Ie subject to the Employment Rights Act 1996 ss 98A–107 (s 98A repealed) (see PARAS 768, 784 et seq) and the Trade Union and Labour Relations (Consolidation) Act 1992 ss 152–153, 238, 238A (dismissal on ground of trade union membership or activities or in connection with industrial action) (see PARAS 1056, 1351–1352): Employment Rights Act 1996 s 98(6) (amended by the Employment Relations Act 1999 Sch 4 Pt III paras 5, 15(b); the Employment Act 2002 Sch 7 paras 24, 32; and the Employment Relations Act 2004 Sch 1 para 30). See note 20.

18 See the Employment Rights Act 1996 s 98(4) (amended by SI 2006/1031; SI 2011/1069). See note 20. An employment tribunal must test both procedural and substantive elements to decide on the merits of a dismissal: the Employment Rights Act 1996 s 98 applies to the substantial merits of the case (see PARA 767); and s 98A (repealed) embodies a test of procedural fairness (see PARA 768). The 'band of reasonable responses' test (see PARA 767) ought to be applied to both procedural and substantive elements: *Whitbread plc (t/a Whitbread Medway Inns) v Hall* [2001] EWCA Civ 268, [2001] ICR 699, [2001] IRLR 275. See also *Lawton v British Association for Service to the Elderly* [2008] All ER (D) 11 (Sep), EAT; *Rice v Countrywide Estate Agents* [2009] All ER (D) 223 (Feb), EAT. If an employer takes action against an employee which amounts to a dismissal, and does so without having considered the legal consequences, or does so on a mistaken view of what those consequences would be, the dismissal may nonetheless be held to be fair; but the fact that the employer took the action in such circumstances will not ipso facto make the dismissal fair: *Docherty v SW Global Resourcing Ltd* [2013] CSIH 72, [2013] IRLR 874, IH (tribunal, when considering the fairness question overall, had failed properly to consider whether the company's ignorance of the law had been excusable and, if it had been, whether that had been a decisive consideration or one outweighed by other factors).

19 It is likely that this requirement, which was originally introduced by the Employment Act 1980 s 6 (repealed), merely made express what was already the existing practice of tribunals (see *Tiptools Ltd v Curtis* [1973] IRLR 276, NIRC; *MacKellar v Bolton* [1979] IRLR 59, EAT; *Royal Naval School v Hughes* [1979] IRLR 383, EAT (obiter); *Bevan Harris Ltd (t/a Clyde Leather Co) v Gair* [1981] IRLR 520, EAT; *Brandon and Goold v Murphy Bros* [1983] IRLR 54, EAT) and is only a factor to be considered. It does not necessarily justify departure from basic procedural requirements: *Henderson v Granville Tours Ltd* [1982] IRLR 494, EAT (no excuse for failure properly to investigate a complaint made against the employee). See also

Amara v Central and North West London Mental Health NHS Trust [2008] All ER (D) 320 (May), EAT (investigation by employer so unreasonable that it had not, by the objective standards of reasonable employer, amounted to a reasonable investigation).

20 An employer would not be acting reasonably in dismissing an employee for a reason which constitutes an unjustified interference with the employee's rights under the Convention for the Protection of Human Rights and Fundamental Freedoms (Rome, 25 March 1957; TS 1 (1973); Cmnd 5179) and the Human Rights Act 1998 (see RIGHTS AND FREEDOMS vol 88A (2013) PARAS 14, 88): *X v Y* [2004] EWCA Civ 662, [2004] ICR 1634, [2004] IRLR 625 (affg [2003] ICR 1138, [2003] IRLR 561, EAT) (employer treated employee's caution for sex offence as evidence of gross misconduct; employee's wish to keep the matter private did not engage the Convention right to respect for his private and family life). This consideration applies whether or not the employer is a public authority because, by a necessary process of interpretation (see the Human Rights Act 1998 s 3; and RIGHTS AND FREEDOMS vol 88A (2013) PARA 16), Convention rights are blended with the law on unfair dismissal in the Employment Rights Act 1996, albeit without creating new private law causes of action against private sector employers: *X v Y*. As to guidance offered to employment tribunals in assessing the relevance of points raised under the Human Rights Act 1998 in unfair dismissal cases between private litigants see *X v Y* at [63] per Mummery LJ. At least in cases where a public authority is involved, the words 'reasonably or unreasonably' in the Employment Rights Act 1996 s 98(4), (6) (see also the text and notes 17–19, 21–22) should be interpreted as including 'having regard to the applicant's Convention rights': *Pay v Lancashire Probation Service* [2004] ICR 187, [2004] IRLR 129, EAT (employee who engaged in publicly-advertised bondage, domination and sado-masochism activities in his spare time was dismissed fairly; the publicity attached to his activities defeated the claim based on respect for his private life; the public authority's competing need to protect its reputation and maintain public confidence justified any interference with his right to freedom of expression; the employee subsequently failed in an application to the European Court of Human Rights: *Pay v United Kingdom* [2009] IRLR 139, ECtHR). See further PARAS 776, 778.

21 Employment Rights Act 1996 s 98(4)(a). See note 20.

22 Employment Rights Act 1996 s 98(4)(b). See note 20.

23 *Tansell v Henley College Coventry* [2013] IRLR 174, EAT. An employment tribunal dismissing an unfair dismissal claim does not discharge its statutory responsibility to give reasons unless it states: (1) that it is satisfied that the employer has proved a reason for the dismissal in accordance with the Employment Rights Act 1996 s 98(1) (see the text and notes 1–16); (2) what that reason is; and (3) that the reason is one of those provided for by the statute (ie is among those listed in s 98(2) (see heads (a) to (d) in the text)): *Tansell v Henley College Coventry* (in an employment tribunal judgment rejecting a claim for unfair dismissal, the finding by the employment tribunal as to the 'reason' for dismissal should virtually leap from the page, such is its significance).

766. Dismissal for 'some other substantial reason'. Dismissal for 'some other substantial reason'[1] is a wide, residual category; it is not to be construed *eiusdem generis* with the other reasons for dismissal[2] that are listed in the statute[3]; and an employer may seek to rely on it where he believed he had a fair reason to dismiss which did not fall within those other reasons[4]. Thus, except in the cases where a dismissal is deemed by statute[5] to be for 'some other substantial reason', this question is one for the employment tribunal to decide on the facts of the case[6], and it is not possible to give an exhaustive list of matters which may come within this category[7].

1 See the Employment Rights Act 1996 s 98(1)(b); and PARA 765.

2 See the Employment Rights Act 1996 s 98(2); and PARA 765.

3 *RS Components Ltd v Irwin* [1974] 1 All ER 41, [1973] ICR 535, NIRC.

4 *Harper v National Coal Board* [1980] IRLR 260, EAT; *Gilham v Kent County Council (No 2)* [1985] ICR 233, sub nom *Kent County Council v Gilham* [1985] IRLR 18, CA. A mistaken belief that the employee has resigned may be a substantial reason for insisting that the employment terminates: *Ely v YKK Fasteners (UK) Ltd* [1994] ICR 164, [1993] IRLR 500, CA. Even if a reason is 'substantial', the tribunal must still go on to decide on overall fairness; thus the first stage of the inquiry is whether the reason is one which could justify the dismissal of the employee, and the second stage of the inquiry is whether on the facts of the case it was fair to dismiss the employee in question: see *Dobie v Burns International Security Services (UK) Ltd*

[1984] 3 All ER 333, [1984] ICR 812, CA. *Dobie v Burns International Security Services (UK) Ltd* was applied in *Cafagna v ISS Mediclean Ltd* [2009] All ER (D) 233 (Jan), EAT.

5 See eg the Employment Rights Act 1996 s 106(1) (dismissal of replacement where employee returns from leave for family reasons or replacement where suspension of employee on medical grounds comes to an end: see PARA 801); the Transfer of Undertakings (Protection of Employment) Regulations 2006, SI 2006/246, reg 7(2) (dismissal consequent on a transfer of an undertaking for an 'economic, technical or organisational reason entailing changes in the workforce': see PARA 803). In each case, an employment tribunal must still proceed to consider whether the dismissal was fair in the circumstances under the Employment Rights Act 1996 s 98(4): see PARAS 765, 767.

6 *Priddle v Dibble* [1978] 1 All ER 1058, [1978] ICR 149, EAT.

7 The most important and widespread application of this category has been to cases of changing business needs or reorganisations: see PARA 802. The range of miscellaneous applications has covered:

(1)   employer's mistaken belief that he had other fair grounds (*Bouchaala v Trusthouse Forte Hotels Ltd* [1980] ICR 721, [1980] IRLR 382, EAT (approved in *Klusova v Hounslow London Borough Council* [2007] EWCA Civ 1127, [2008] ICR 396, [2007] All ER (D) 105 (Nov)); *Taylor v Co-operative Retail Services Ltd* [1981] ICR 172, [1981] IRLR 1, EAT (affd [1982] ICR 600, [1982] IRLR 354, CA); *Leyland Vehicles Ltd v Jones* [1981] ICR 428, [1981] IRLR 269, EAT);

(2)   personality clashes (*Treganowan v Robert Knee & Co Ltd* [1975] ICR 405, [1975] IRLR 247; *Turner v Vestric Ltd* [1980] ICR 528, [1981] IRLR 23, EAT; and see *Huggins v Micrel Semiconductor (UK) Ltd* [2004] All ER (D) 07 (Sep), EAT (Sc) (breakdown of trust and confidence in the relationship between employee and employer which had been caused or contributed to by the employee's conduct));

(3)   dismissal at the behest of an important customer (*Scott Packing and Warehousing Ltd v Paterson* [1978] IRLR 166, EAT; *Dobie v Burns International Security Services (UK) Ltd* [1984] 3 All ER 333, [1984] ICR 812, CA; cf *Grootcon (UK) Ltd v Keld* [1984] IRLR 302, EAT);

(4)   various forms of temporary or fixed-term engagements (*Terry v East Sussex County Council* [1976] ICR 536, [1976] IRLR 332, EAT (approved in *Fay v North Yorkshire County Council* [1986] ICR 133, sub nom *North Yorkshire County Council v Fay* [1985] IRLR 247, CA); *Beard v St Joseph's School Governors* [1978] ICR 1234, [1979] IRLR 144, EAT);

(5)   imprisonment (*Kingston v British Railways Board* [1984] ICR 781, [1984] IRLR 146, CA);

(6)   dismissal of spouse in 'husband and wife team' (*Kelman v Oram* [1983] IRLR 432, EAT; but cf *Wadley v Eager Electricals Ltd* [1986] IRLR 93, EAT);

(7)   dismissal to make way for owner's son (*Priddle v Dibble* [1978] 1 All ER 1058, [1978] ICR 149, EAT);

(8)   foreign government's policy (*East African Airways Corpn v Foote* [1977] ICR 776, EAT);

(9)   domestic government's pay policy (*Industrial Rubber Products v Gillon* [1977] IRLR 389, 13 ITR 100, EAT);

(10)   dismissal of chief executive after corporate take-over (*Cobley v Forward Technology Industries plc* [2003] EWCA Civ 646, [2003] ICR 1050, [2003] IRLR 706); and

(11)   difficult personality of the employee causing problems for the employer's undertaking (*Perkin v St George's Healthcare NHS Trust* [2005] EWCA Civ 1174, [2006] ICR 617, [2005] IRLR 934).

Where an employee is dismissed at the behest of a third party who may have acted unfairly, however, the dismissal is fair only if the employer has done everything that he reasonably can to avoid or mitigate the injustice: *Henderson v Connect (South Tyneside) Ltd* [2010] IRLR 466, EAT.

An employee's dismissal for refusing contractual variation to work on Sundays due to his religious beliefs has been held to be fair for 'some other substantial reason' and not in breach of the European Convention on Human Rights art 9 (see RIGHTS AND FREEDOMS vol 88A (2013) PARA 368 et seq): *Copsey v WBB Devon Clays Ltd* [2005] EWCA Civ 932, [2005] ICR 1789, [2005] IRLR 811 (employee refused alternative work options offered by employer to accommodate employee's request not to work on Sundays). Although sexual orientation used to be cited as falling under the 'some other substantial reason' category (*Boychuk v HJ Symons Holdings Ltd* [1977] IRLR 395, EAT; *Saunders v Scottish National Camps Association Ltd* [1980] IRLR 174, EAT (affd [1981] IRLR 277, Ct of Sess); *Wiseman v Salford City Council* [1981] IRLR 202, EAT), this is now one of the 'protected characteristics' defined under the

Equality Act 2010 which makes it unlawful to discriminate against, harass, or victimise a person at work or in employment services (as well as in other contexts) on that ground unless the exceptions provided for apply: see DISCRIMINATION vol 33 (2013) PARA 1 et seq. Furthermore, by a necessary process of interpretation (see the Human Rights Act 1998 s 3; and RIGHTS AND FREEDOMS vol 88A (2013) PARA 16), an employee's rights under the Convention for the Protection of Human Rights and Fundamental Freedoms (Rome, 25 March 1957; TS 1 (1973); Cmnd 5179) and the Human Rights Act 1998 (see RIGHTS AND FREEDOMS vol 88A (2013) PARAS 14, 88) are blended with the law on unfair dismissal in the Employment Rights Act 1996: *X v Y* [2004] EWCA Civ 662, [2004] IRLR 625 (affg [2003] ICR 1138, [2003] IRLR 561, EAT) (a person's sexual orientation per se does not warrant a fair dismissal; sexual offences may continue to do so as they are not a purely private matter). See also Application 28274/08 *Heinisch v Germany* [2011] IRLR 922, ECtHR (freedom of expression infringed where nursing home worker dismissed after making criminal complaint and disseminating information about standard of care).

767.   Whether employer acted reasonably; the range of reasonable responses.
Whether an employer[1] acted reasonably or unreasonably in treating a reason[2] as a sufficient reason for dismissing an employee[3] must be determined in accordance with equity[4] and the substantial merits of the case[5]. The key consideration for an employment tribunal is, therefore, the reasonableness or otherwise of the employer's conduct, not the injustice to the employee[6].

In adjudicating on the reasonableness of the employer's conduct, an employment tribunal must not simply substitute its own views for those of the employer and decide whether it would have dismissed on those facts; it must make a wider inquiry, to determine whether a reasonable employer could have decided to dismiss on those facts[7]. The basis of this approach (the 'range of reasonable responses test') is that in many cases there is a band of reasonable responses to the employee's conduct within which one employer might reasonably take one view and another quite reasonably take another; the function of a tribunal as an industrial jury is to determine whether in the particular circumstances of each case the decision to dismiss the employee fell within the band of reasonable responses which a reasonable employer might have adopted[8]. If the dismissal falls within the band, the dismissal is fair; but, if the dismissal falls outside the band, it is unfair[9].

1   As to the meaning of 'employer' see PARA 2.
2   Ie a reason falling within the Employment Rights Act 1996 s 98(2) (see PARA 765) or some other substantial reason (see PARA 766).
3   As to the meaning of 'employee' see PARA 2.
4   'This does not mean that the principles of 'equity' as contrasted with the 'common law' are applicable as such, but rather that in considering whether the employer acted reasonably or unreasonably the tribunal should adopt a broad approach of common sense and common fairness, eschewing all legal or other technicality': *Earl v Slater and Wheeler (Airlyne) Ltd* [1973] 1 All ER 145 at 150, [1972] ICR 508 at 513, NIRC, per Sir John Donaldson P. See also *Wailes Dove Bitumastic Ltd v Woolcocks* [1977] ICR 817 at 820, EAT, per Kilner Brown J (concept of fairness in all the circumstances means that both sides in any situation ought to be looked at by the employment tribunal with sympathetic understanding). It is a general equitable concept that fairness is achieved by treating like cases alike; thus if the employee was dismissed, when others previously guilty of similar misconduct had only been disciplined, that may point to unfairness: *Post Office v Fennell* [1981] IRLR 221, CA; *Eagle Star Insurance Co Ltd v Hayward* [1981] ICR 860, EAT. See also *Cain v Leeds Western Health Authority* [1990] ICR 585, [1990] IRLR 168, EAT (no answer to complaint of inconsistent treatment that different managers had taken the comparable decisions whether to dismiss); *Procter v British Gypsum Ltd* [1992] IRLR 7, EAT (employer should seek to discover how previous like cases had been treated). It is, however, arguable that:
    (1)   this wide 'equitable' jurisdiction is given in order that each case may be judged flexibly on its own particular merits (see *Taylor v Parsons Peebles NEI Bruce Peebles Ltd* [1981] IRLR 119, EAT; *Paul v East Surrey District Health Authority* [1995] IRLR 305, CA);

(2)   in many instances previous cases will not be truly comparable and that a 'tariff' approach is not appropriate for industrial misconduct (see *Hadjioannou v Coral Casinos Ltd* [1981] IRLR 352, EAT; *Securicor Ltd v Smith* [1989] IRLR 356, CA; cf *Hillcrest Care Ltd v Morrison* [2004] All ER (D) 220 (Oct), EAT (failure of tribunal to consider whether a contemporaneous case was truly comparable to that of the employee made its decision legally flawed)); and

(3)   particularly in misconduct cases, factors in mitigation in the individual case (such as length of service) may well assume major importance (*Harrow London Borough v Cunningham* [1996] IRLR 256, EAT; and see PARA 777).

See also *Moult v East Sussex County Council* [2008] All ER (D) 100 (Jun), EAT; *Ashraf v Metropolitan Police Authority* [2008] All ER (D) 301 (Nov), EAT.

5   See the Employment Rights Act 1996 s 98(4); and PARA 765.

6   *Polkey v AE Dayton Services Ltd* [1988] AC 344, [1988] ICR 142, HL (approving *Sillifant v Powell Duffryn Timber Ltd* [1983] IRLR 91, EAT; and overruling *British Labour Pump Co Ltd v Byrne* [1979] ICR 347, [1979] IRLR 94, EAT, and all cases supporting it).

Whilst injustice, or lack of it, to the employee may not affect the issue of whether the dismissal was fair or not, it is highly relevant to the question of the appropriate remedy and, in particular, what, if any, compensation should be awarded: see PARA 818. Note also that the effect of *British Labour Pump Co Ltd v Byrne* was restored partially by the Employment Rights Act 1996 s 98A (repealed) in the context of procedural fairness, because, if an employer can show that a failure in any element of his own disciplinary and dismissal procedures which goes beyond the minimum statutory requirement would have made no difference to the decision to dismiss, that will not of itself cause the dismissal to be unfair: see PARA 768. The ACAS Code of Practice 1: Disciplinary and Grievance Procedures offers advice on what constitutes reasonable behaviour when dealing with disciplinary and grievance issues: see PARA 700 et seq. As to ACAS Codes of Practice generally see PARAS 1223–1224.

In the context of constructive dismissal see in particular *Abbey National plc v Fairbrother* [2007] IRLR 320, [2007] All ER (D) 24 (Jan); *Claridge v Daler Rowney Ltd* [2008] ICR 1267, [2008] IRLR 672, EAT; and PARA 763.

7   *Post Office v Foley, HSBC Bank plc (formerly Midland Bank plc) v Madden* [2001] 1 All ER 550, [2000] ICR 1283, CA, applying *Iceland Frozen Foods Ltd v Jones* [1983] ICR 17, [1982] IRLR 439; *NC Watling & Co Ltd v Richardson* [1978] ICR 1049, [1978] IRLR 255, EAT; *Rolls Royce Ltd v Walpole* [1980] IRLR 343, EAT; *British Leyland (UK) Ltd v Swift* [1981] IRLR 91, CA; *Gair v Bevan Harris Ltd* [1983] IRLR 368, Ct of Sess; *Securicor Ltd v Smith* [1989] IRLR 356, CA; *British Gas plc v McCarrick* [1991] IRLR 305, CA. In *Vickers Ltd v Smith* [1977] IRLR 11, EAT, this test was expressed particularly strongly, as meaning that a dismissal can be unfair only if the decision to dismiss is perverse; but later cases have held that this extreme position is incorrect: see *Iceland Frozen Foods Ltd v Jones*; *Rentokil Ltd v Mackin* [1989] IRLR 286, EAT. As to the dangers of slipping into a 'substitution mindset' see *London Ambulance Services NHS Trust v Small* [2009] EWCA Civ 220, [2009] IRLR 563; applied in *Kuehne and Nagel Ltd v Cosgrove* [2014] All ER (D) 33 (May), EAT (tribunal must consider: (1) the question of the employer's belief, an essentially subjective test, which did not require the belief itself to be reasonable but simply required the respondent to demonstrate that that was the belief that it had had in mind that had led it to dismiss, and (2) the question of fairness, ie whether the employer had had reasonable grounds for that belief). See also *Fuller v Brent LBC* [2011] EWCA Civ 267, [2011] ICR 806, [2011] IRLR 414; and *Tayeh v Barchester Healthcare Ltd* [2013] EWCA Civ 29, [2013] IRLR 387, 131 BMLR 85, [2013] ICR D23 (falsification of BHL's written records was a serious matter capable of meriting dismissal but it had been an error of approach for the tribunal to have reviewed the panel's decision by its own mistaken assessment that such falsification was an offence of a less serious character than others listed in the company handbook)

Where a case concerns the credibility of a witness against the employee, the proper approach is for the tribunal to decide whether it was reasonable for the employer to have believed the witness, not whether the tribunal itself believes his evidence: *Linfood Cash and Carry Ltd v Thomson* [1989] ICR 518, [1989] IRLR 235, EAT; *British Gas plc v McCarrick*. See *Rhondaa Cynon Taff Borough Council v Close* [2008] IRLR 868, [2008] All ER (D) 278 (Jun), EAT (in an employer's investigation of an employee care worker and the death of a patient the employer's decision to rely on police witness statements was in the circumstances not outside the band of reasonable responses). See also *Taylor v OCS Group Ltd* [2006] EWCA Civ 702, [2006] ICR 1602, [2006] IRLR 613; *Mainwaring v Corus UK Ltd* [2007] All ER (D) 08 (Oct), EAT; *Celebi v Compass Group UK and Ireland Ltd (t/a Scolarest)* [2009] All ER (D) 172 (Jan), EAT; *Small v London Ambulance Service NHS Trust* [2009] EWCA Civ 220, [2009] IRLR 563.

8   *Iceland Frozen Foods Ltd v Jones* [1983] ICR 17 at 24–25, [1982] IRLR 439 at 442 per
    Browne-Wilkinson P. This remains probably the best summary of the hitherto accepted
    approach for a tribunal. As to the 'range of reasonable responses test' see also PARA 763 note 6.
    The range of reasonable responses test was directly attacked as an unnecessary and undesirable
    gloss on the wording of the statute by Morison P in *Haddon v Van den Bergh Foods Ltd* [1999]
    ICR 1150, [1999] IRLR 672, EAT (and see the support given by the Scottish Employment
    Appeal Tribunal in *Wilson v Ethicon Ltd* [2000] IRLR 4, EAT), but the Employment Appeal
    Tribunal under Lindsay P subsequently held that, as a matter of precedent, it had not been open
    to the court in *Haddon v Van den Bergh Foods Ltd* to disapprove such a well-accepted test
    (*Midland Bank plc v Madden* [2000] 2 All ER 741, [2000] IRLR 288, EAT) and the
    Employment Appeal Tribunal under Judge Peter Clark held that, in determining the question of
    reasonableness, the Employment Appeal Tribunal and employment tribunals are bound to
    follow and apply the propositions set out in *Iceland Frozen Foods Ltd v Jones* (*Beedell v West
    Ferry Printers Ltd* [2000] IRLR 650, EAT). In *Post Office v Foley, HSBC Bank plc (formerly
    Midland Bank plc) v Madden* [2001] 1 All ER 550, [2000] ICR 1283, CA (approving *Beedell v
    West Ferry Printers Ltd*; and disapproving *Haddon v Van den Bergh Foods Ltd*), the Court of
    Appeal reaffirmed that the test expounded by Browne-Wilkinson P in *Iceland Frozen Foods Ltd
    v Jones* at 24–25 and 442 remains binding; the 'range of reasonable responses' approach does
    not become one of perversity, nor is it rendered unhelpful, by the fact that there may be extremes
    and that dismissal is the ultimate sanction; and any suggestion that a tribunal is free to substitute
    its own judgment for that of the employer is an impermissible departure from the established
    test.
        The 'band of reasonable responses' test provides a sufficiently robust, flexible and objective
    analysis of all aspects of the decision to dismiss to provide guarantee for an employee's right to
    respect for his private and family life under the Convention for the Protection of Human Rights
    and Fundamental Freedoms (Rome, 25 March 1957; TS 1 (1973); Cmnd 5179) art 8, and the
    Human Rights Act 1998 (see RIGHTS AND FREEDOMS vol 88A (2013) PARA 317 et seq): *Turner
    v East Midlands Trains Ltd* [2012] EWCA Civ 1470, [2013] 3 All ER 375, [2013] IRLR 107,
    [2013] ICR 525.
9   See note 8.

768. Procedural fairness in relation to dismissal generally. With effect from
6 April 2009[1], any failure by an employer[2] to follow a procedure in relation to
the dismissal[3] of an employee[4] is no longer regarded[5] as by itself making the
employer's action unreasonable if he shows that he would have decided to
dismiss the employee if he had followed the procedure[6]. However, the statutory
test of fairness that must be applied to any case of dismissal[7] includes the concept
of procedural fairness so that a dismissal may be unfair because an unfair
procedure was adopted (even where the employer otherwise had a sound
substantive reason for the dismissal)[8]. There is no longer a statutory obligation
imposed on an employer to have a formal disciplinary procedure[9], but the
adoption of such a procedure is recommended; it should be set down in writing,
be specific and clear and, when applied, it will be judged against the standards of
fairness, effectiveness, and consistency[10]. Although the rules of natural justice do
not apply directly to form an independent ground on which a decision to dismiss
may be attacked, a breach may be an important matter when an employment
tribunal is considering the overall fairness of a dismissal[11].

A breach in procedure is merely one of the factors to be taken into account[12],
but the House of Lords in 1988[13] placed emphasis on procedural fairness so that
it is likely that a breach of procedure will make a dismissal unfair[14]; and the
previous rule that, if the breach of procedure in fact made no difference[14], then
the actual dismissal could be held to have been fair[16] was disapproved[17].
Ultimately, however, the overall fairness of the dismissal, including any
procedural matters, remains a question of fact for the employment tribunal[18].

1   The Employment Rights Act 1996 s 98A (added by the Employment Act 2002 s 34(1), (2)),
    which provided for unfair dismissal on the basis of an employer's failure to complete statutory
    dismissal and disciplinary procedures satisfactorily, was repealed by the Employment Act 2008

ss 2, 20, Schedule Pt 1 with effect from 6 April 2009, but with savings for the purpose of ongoing cases. As to transitional provisions in regard to the repeal of the Employment Rights Act 1996 s 98A by the Employment Act 2008 see the Employment Act 2008 (Commencement No 1, Transitional Provisions and Savings) Order 2008, SI 2008/3232, art 3, Schedule; and PARAS 698–700. With the repeal of the statutory dismissal and disciplinary procedures in April 2009, the law reverts to the position it had reached before the statutory procedures were introduced in 2004: see PARA 700 et seq.

2   As to the meaning of 'employer' see PARA 2.
3   As to the meaning of 'dismissal' see PARA 762.
4   As to the meaning of 'employee' see PARA 2.
5   Ie for the purposes of the Employment Rights Act 1996 s 98(4)(a): see PARA 765.
6   See the Employment Rights Act 1996 s 98A(2) (repealed). To the extent that it still applies (see note 1), s 98A(2) adopts a rule established initially in *British Labour Pump Co Ltd v Byrne* [1979] ICR 347, [1979] IRLR 94, EAT, which had been approved in *W & J Wass Ltd v Binns* [1982] ICR 486, [1982] IRLR 283, CA, and relied on and applied frequently, but which had been overruled (together with all cases supporting or applying it) in *Polkey v AE Dayton Services Ltd* [1988] AC 344, [1988] ICR 142, HL. See note 14. In *Software 2000 Ltd v Andrews* [2007] ICR 825, [2007] IRLR 568, EAT, the effect of the Employment Rights Act 1996 s 98A(2) was summarised as being that:
   (1)   if fair procedures are applied and complied with, the employer satisfies the test required by s 98A(2), and the dismissal is then fair by virtue of s 98A(2), the onus being firmly on the employer to establish that, on the balance of probabilities, the dismissal would have occurred when it did in any event; but
   (2)   if the chance of dismissal is considered to be less than 50% on the balance of probabilities, the response should be to adjust compensation accordingly.
However, since the repeal of s 98A(2), consideration of whether an employee would or would not have been dismissed in any event was to be based on a percentage representing the chance that the employee would still have lost his employment had a correct procedure been followed, and not on the balance of probabilities; the position is again that chance of dismissal now runs across the whole spectrum from 0% to 100%, as assessed by the tribunal (the 'spectrum approach'). The correct way to apply *Polkey v AE Dayton Services Ltd*, therefore, is to assess a percentage likelihood of dismissal having happened anyway, and to apply that as the reduction: *Ministry of Justice v Parry* [2013] ICR 311, EAT (the tribunal had adopted the wrong test, a '51% likely' test, to the reduction, according to which anything less than 50% leads to no reduction, and anything more than 50% leads to a 100% reduction, based on a 'yes/no' distinction, ie dismissal or not); and see *Hill v Governing Body of Great Tey Primary School* [2013] IRLR 274, EAT (tribunal's conclusion is expressed as a certainty, tending to suggest that a percentage chance approach was not being adopted; an assessment made in accordance with *Polkey v AE Dayton Services Ltd* is predictive: could the employer fairly have dismissed and, if so, what were the chances that the employer would have done so? It requires an assessment of chance, which depends upon all the facts, best assessed by the primary fact finder); *Audsley v Riverside Industrial Equipment Ltd* [2014] All ER (D) 109 (Apr), EAT (tribunal had either applied the wrong test or had reached a perverse decision in refusing to consider any reduction under *Polkey v AE Dayton Services Ltd* at all, especially set against its finding that the employee had been 50% at fault; the language used ('*what would have happened?*') was that of probability and not chance, whereas *Polkey v AE Dayton Services Ltd* was all about chance); *Howie v Kidron House* [2014] All ER (D) 116 (Apr), EAT (tribunal had erred in law by applying too high a test and had not considered whether or not there had been a chance, on the evidence, that the employee would have been dismissed, fairly, in any event). See also notes 14, 17.

7   Ie in the Employment Rights Act 1996 s 98(4): see PARA 765.
8   *Earl v Slater and Wheeler (Airlyne) Ltd* [1973] 1 All ER 145, [1972] ICR 508, NIRC; approved in *W Devis & Sons Ltd v Atkins* [1977] AC 931, [1977] ICR 662, HL. It is axiomatic, however, that an employer cannot rely on applying his own disciplinary policy to argue that a dismissal was fair where the policy itself is inherently unfair: see eg *John Lewis plc v Coyne* [2001] IRLR 139, EAT (employer's reliance on policy that automatic dismissal follows a finding of dishonesty, exactingly defined, made the procedure adopted unfair). See also *Crawford v Suffolk Mental Health Partnership NHS Trust* [2012] EWCA Civ 138, [2012] IRLR 402 (procedural defects found in employers disciplinary proceedings).
9   Where such a procedure exists, the employer must include a note to that effect, giving specified information, in the written statement of terms and conditions which he is obliged to give to all his employees: see the Employment Rights Act 1996 s 3; and PARA 120. The fact that an employer's disciplinary procedure has contractual effect is not determinative in an unfair

dismissal case, when all the circumstances still have to be considered: *Westminster City Council v Cabaj* [1996] ICR 960, [1996] IRLR 399, CA.

10 See ACAS Code of Practice 1: Disciplinary and Grievance Procedures (2009); Discipline and Grievances at work: The ACAS guide (September 2014); and PARA 698 et seq.

11 *Slater v Leicestershire Health Authority* [1989] IRLR 16 at 19, CA per Parker LJ; and see *Haddow v ILEA* [1979] ICR 202, EAT; *Alidair Ltd v Taylor* [1978] ICR 445, sub nom *Taylor v Alidair Ltd* [1978] IRLR 82, CA; *Campion v Hamworthy Engineering Ltd* [1987] ICR 966, CA. The rules of natural justice must be applied to the context of industrial relations and dismissal realistically and with common sense, bearing in mind that an employing organisation cannot operate necessarily in as detached a manner as a court of law: see eg *Rowe v Radio Rentals Ltd* [1982] IRLR 177, EAT; *R v Chief Constable of South Wales, ex p Thornhill* [1987] IRLR 313, CA (a civil action); *Ulsterbus Ltd v Henderson* [1989] IRLR 251, NI CA; *Slater v Leicestershire Health Authority*; cf *Moyes v Hylton Castle Working Men's Social Club and Institute Ltd* [1986] IRLR 482, EAT (a more serious approach to natural justice).

There is, however, no rule of law preventing an employer from dismissing an employee following a second set of disciplinary proceedings based on the same facts as earlier disciplinary proceedings but, in assessing the fairness of the dismissal, the court must take the earlier disciplinary proceedings into account: *Sarkar v West London Mental Health NHS Trust* [2010] EWCA Civ 289, [2010] IRLR 508 (in applying the range of reasonable responses test, tribunal was entitled to attach weight to employer's inconsistency in dealing with the same matters firstly by dealing with them under a procedure that could not result in his dismissal, then, following the breakdown of negotiations, by charging the employee with gross misconduct and dismissing him); *Christou v Haringey London Borough* [2013] EWCA Civ 178, [2014] QB 131, [2014] 1 All ER 135, [2013] ICR 1007, [2013] IRLR 379 (while the factual substratum of the complaints against the claimants had been the same, the first disciplinary process had focused on procedural errors and the second on substantive errors of judgment and breaches of the child protection plan; the view of the tribunal as to the justification for reopening the case, namely that the allegations of misconduct were very serious because they involved a risk to a member of the public and that new managers were entitled to take a different view about the gravity of the claimants' conduct, was a proper and sufficient basis for its conclusion that the dismissals were fair, notwithstanding the double jeopardy principle).

12 *Hollister v National Farmers Union* [1979] ICR 542, [1979] IRLR 238, CA; and see *Bailey v BP Oil (Kent Refinery) Ltd* [1980] ICR 642, [1980] IRLR 287, CA; *Kingston v British Railways Board* [1984] ICR 781, [1984] IRLR 146, CA.

13 Ie in *Polkey v AE Dayton Services Ltd* [1988] AC 344, [1988] ICR 142, HL: see notes 6, 14, 17.

14 *Polkey v AE Dayton Services Ltd* [1988] AC 344, [1988] ICR 142, HL. For subsequent cases applying the approach in *Polkey v AE Dayton Services Ltd* prior to 2004 see eg *Hooper v British Railways Board* [1988] IRLR 517, CA; *McLaren v National Coal Board* [1988] ICR 370, [1988] IRLR 215, CA; *Whitbread & Co plc v Mills* [1988] ICR 776, [1988] IRLR 501, EAT; *Spink v Express Foods Group Ltd* [1990] IRLR 320, EAT; *Stoker v Lancashire County Council* [1992] IRLR 75, CA. See further note 6. Procedural lapse does not mean that a dismissal is automatically unfair: see *Polkey v AE Dayton Services Ltd* at 364 and at 163 per Lord Bridge of Harwich (the test of reasonableness may be satisfied if the employer acted reasonably at the time of dismissal in taking the view that in the exceptional circumstances of the particular case the procedural steps normally appropriate would have been futile). Even this exception was later construed narrowly, as applying principally to the facts of *Polkey v AE Dayton Services Ltd* itself (a redundancy dismissal with no consultation because of immediate financial crisis) in *Spink v Express Foods Group Ltd*, although a wider approach was subsequently taken in *Duffy v Yeomans & Partners Ltd* [1995] ICR 1, [1994] IRLR 642, CA by reliance on the speech of Lord Mackay of Clashfern LC in *Polkey v AE Dayton Services Ltd* to the effect that it may be enough that the employer could have taken that view. See also *McLaren v National Coal Board* at 377 and at 218 per Sir John Donaldson MR (unfair to dismiss without a hearing, even at the height of the miners' strike; 'no amount of industrial warfare, and no amount of heat, can of itself justify failing to give an employee an opportunity of giving an explanation of his conduct ... You have the position that acceptable reasons for dismissing may change in a varying industrial situation, but the standards of fairness never change. They are immutable but are applied in a different situation'). It used to be thought that a failure to follow a fair procedure when taking the initial decision to dismiss could be rectified by a full and proper hearing on an internal appeal but that has been disapproved as a rule of law and the proper test is now whether the appeal was conducted in a fair and open-minded way: see PARA 708.

15 Ie where the employer could show that the employee would still have been dismissed even if a proper procedure had been adopted, and that that dismissal would have been reasonable.

16 Ie the rule in *British Labour Pump Co Ltd v Byrne* [1979] ICR 347, [1979] IRLR 94, EAT; approved in *W & J Wass Ltd v Binns* [1982] ICR 486, [1982] IRLR 283, CA, and relied on and applied frequently until *Polkey v AE Dayton Services Ltd* [1988] AC 344, [1988] ICR 142, HL (see note 17).

17 *British Labour Pump Co Ltd v Byrne* [1979] ICR 347, [1979] IRLR 94, EAT was overruled by the House of Lords in *Polkey v AE Dayton Services Ltd* [1988] AC 344, [1988] ICR 142, HL with all cases supporting or applying it (it had already been strongly criticised in *Sillifant v Powell Duffryn Timber Ltd* [1983] IRLR 91, EAT by Browne-Wilkinson P, whose judgment was adopted by Lord Mackay of Clashfern LC in *Polkey v AE Dayton Services Ltd*). It was accepted, however, in *Polkey v AE Dayton Services Ltd* that the question whether the employee had suffered any loss or injustice may well be relevant at the later stages of assessing compensation; thus, if the employee would in fact have been dismissed shortly anyway, had a fair procedure been adopted, that may well limit the amount awarded: see *Mining Supplies (Longwall) Ltd v Baker* [1988] ICR 676, [1988] IRLR 417, EAT; *Tele-Trading Ltd v Jenkins* [1990] IRLR 430, CA; cf *Devonshire v Trico-Folberth Ltd* [1989] ICR 747, sub nom *Trico-Folberth Ltd v Devonshire* [1989] IRLR 396, CA (insufficient that the employer could have dismissed on a fair ground when in fact he had decided not to). See further note 6.

18 Cf the facts and decision in *Dillett v National Coal Board* [1988] ICR 218, CA and *McLaren v National Coal Board* [1988] ICR 370, [1988] IRLR 215, CA (cited in note 14). See also *Jafri v Lincoln College* [2014] EWCA Civ 449, [2014] All ER (D) 146 (Apr) (assertion of single point that employer should have pursued the disciplinary process to a conclusion might have been grounds for the case to have been remitted to the tribunal for further evidence to be taken but it could not be said that a reasonable tribunal had been bound to take that argument on board for itself).

769.   Burden of proof on employer who has dismissed employee.   Once the fact of dismissal[1] has been either proved[2] or accepted, the burden of proof is on the employer[3] to show:

(1)   what was the reason, or, if there was more than one, the principal reason, for the dismissal[4]; and

(2)   that it was one of the reasons listed under statute[5], or was some other substantial reason[6] of a kind such as to justify the dismissal of an employee[7] holding the position which that employee held[8].

If the employer produces evidence seeking to establish one reason and the employee considers that that was not the true reason, there is an evidential burden on the employee to produce some evidence to cast doubt on that reason; but, once this is discharged, the persuasive burden remains on the employer[9]. The only exception is where the employee lacks the normal two-year qualifying period[10] and seeks to show that, contrary to the employer's case, the real reason for dismissal falls within one of the exceptional cases where no qualifying period is required[11], in which case the burden of proving the real reason is on the employee[12].

The burden of proof on the overall question of whether the employer acted reasonably in treating the reason as a sufficient reason for dismissing the employee[13] is now made deliberately neutral[14].

If, in an exceptional case, an employment tribunal is genuinely unable to decide where the truth lies on a particular point, it is entitled to decide the matter by reference to the burden of proof[15].

1 As to the meaning of 'dismissal' see PARA 762.

2 If the employer disputes that the employee was dismissed (either actually or constructively: see PARA 763), the burden of proving dismissal is on the employee: *Morris v London Iron and Steel Co Ltd* [1988] QB 493, [1987] ICR 855, CA.

3 As to the meaning of 'employer' see PARA 2.

4 See the Employment Rights Act 1996 s 98(1)(a); and PARA 765. If an employer seeks to rely on more than one reason, he must either establish them all or show that the dismissal was fair solely on those that he can establish: *Smith v Glasgow City District Council* [1987] ICR 796, [1987] IRLR 326, HL. The employer must argue grounds to be relied on specifically: see

Murphy v Epsom College [1985] ICR 80, [1984] IRLR 271, CA. A reason is the 'set of facts known to the employer or, it may be, of beliefs held by him which cause him to dismiss the employee': *Abernethy v Mott Hay and Anderson* [1974] ICR 323 at 330, [1974] IRLR 213 at 215, CA, per Cairns LJ; approved in *W Devis & Sons Ltd v Atkins* [1977] AC 931, [1977] ICR 662, HL. This has two particular effects:

    (1)   it is not necessarily fatal if the employer has put the wrong 'label' on his reason for dismissing (*Hannan v TNT-IPEC (UK) Ltd* [1986] IRLR 165, EAT);

    (2)   in most cases it is enough for the employer to show, subjectively, that he believed in the existence of the reason, especially in misconduct or incapability cases (see PARAS 773–775), though this does not apply in redundancy or statutory restriction cases where the employer must show that the facts relied on actually existed (see *Elliott v University Computing Co (Great Britain) Ltd* [1977] ICR 147, EAT; *Bouchaala v Trusthouse Forte Hotels Ltd* [1980] ICR 721, [1980] IRLR 382, EAT).

An erroneous belief may still constitute 'some other substantial reason' (see PARA 766).

    In a case of dismissal by notice, it may be necessary to consider the reason in relation both to when notice was given and when it expired: *Parkinson v March Consulting Ltd* [1998] ICR 276, [1997] IRLR 308, CA; *West Kent College v Richardson* [1999] ICR 511, EAT. Thus facts arising during the notice period may be relevant: *Stacey v Babcock Power* [1986] ICR 221, sub nom *Stacey v Babcock Power (Construction Division)* [1986] IRLR 3, EAT (work becoming available when employee was under notice for redundancy); *Alboni v Ind Coope Retail Ltd* [1998] IRLR 131, CA (fair consideration given to alternatives proposed by employee under notice); *White v South London Transport Ltd* [1998] ICR 293, EAT (report from company doctor during notice period relevant to an illness dismissal).

5   Ie a reason falling within the Employment Rights Act 1996 s 98(1)(b), (2): see PARA 765.

6   Ie falling otherwise within the Employment Rights Act 1996 s 98(1)(b): see PARAS 765, 766.

7   As to the meaning of 'employee' see PARA 2.

8   See the Employment Rights Act 1996 s 98(1)(b); and PARA 765. If the employer fails to establish the reason on which he relies, the finding of the employment tribunal should be unfair dismissal: see *Timex Corpn v Thomson* [1981] IRLR 522, EAT; *Earl v Slater and Wheeler (Airlyne) Ltd* [1973] 1 All ER 145, [1972] ICR 508, NIRC; *Green v Southampton Corpn* [1973] ICR 153, NIRC; *Babar Indian Restaurant v Rawat* [1985] IRLR 57, EAT. It is an error of law for a tribunal simply to consider whether there was a dismissible offence without first having been satisfied by the employer as to the reason for dismissal: *Adams v Derby City Council* [1985] IRLR 163, EAT. Any reply to a request for written reasons for dismissal may be given in evidence: see PARA 755.

9   *Maund v Penwith District Council* [1984] ICR 143, [1984] IRLR 24, CA. See also *Kuzel v Roche Products Ltd* [2008] EWCA Civ 380, [2008] ICR 799, [2008] IRLR 530, where whistleblowing was alleged as the reason for dismissal (the court said that when an employee positively asserts that there was a different and inadmissible reason for his dismissal, he must produce some evidence supporting the positive case, such as making protected disclosures but this does not mean that, in order to succeed in an unfair dismissal claim, the employee has to discharge the burden of proving that the dismissal was for that different reason; rather it is sufficient for the employee to challenge the evidence produced by the employer to show the reason advanced by him for the dismissal and to produce some evidence of a different reason).

10   See PARA 758.

11   Ie the cases set out in the Employment Rights Act 1996 s 108(3): see PARA 758.

12   *Smith v Hayle Town Council* [1978] ICR 996, [1978] IRLR 413, CA. If the employee does have the necessary qualifying period, the burden remains on the employer in the normal way: *Shannon v Michelin (Belfast) Ltd* [1981] IRLR 505, NI CA.

13   See the Employment Rights Act 1996 s 98(4); and PARA 765.

14   Before the Employment Protection (Consolidation) Act 1978 s 57(3) (repealed) (from which the Employment Rights Act 1996 s 98(4) derives) was amended by the Employment Act 1980 s 6 (repealed), the burden of proof was on the employer on this question too; the amendment restored the position to what it was under the Industrial Relations Act 1971 s 24(6) (repealed), when the law of unfair dismissal was first enacted: see *Earl v Slater and Wheeler (Airlyne) Ltd* [1973] 1 All ER 145, [1972] ICR 508, NIRC. In practice, it may be that the amendment had little significance, since the primary burden of adducing the facts and the true reason remains on the employer, and matters relevant to that will also be relevant to the application of the Employment Rights Act 1996 s 98(4): see *Smith v Glasgow City District Council* [1987] ICR 796, [1987] IRLR 326, HL. Any formal reference by a tribunal to a burden of proof being on the employer under the Employment Rights Act 1996 s 98(4) is, however, likely to be held to be an error of law: *Post Office (Counters) Ltd v Heavey* [1990] ICR 1, [1989] IRLR 513, EAT.

15 *Morris v London Iron and Steel Co Ltd* [1988] QB 493, [1987] ICR 855, CA. This is subject to
    the caveat that such recourse to the burden of proof should not be made simply as an easy or
    convenient way for the tribunal to make up its mind: *Morris v London Iron and Steel Co Ltd.*

770.   Grounds discovered subsequently; internal appeal procedures. It is a
central principle of unfair dismissal law that the fairness of a dismissal should be
determined on the facts as known to the employer at the date of dismissal[1]. In
contrast to the common law on wrongful dismissal[2], an employer cannot rely on
subsequently discovered facts, especially misconduct by the employee, to justify a
dismissal that was unfair on the facts known at the time[3]. Where, however, a
disciplinary procedure operates by effecting the dismissal, but subject to a right
of appeal[4], the internal appeal is an integral part of the dismissal procedure, so
that matters coming to light on the appeal may be considered when deciding on
fairness[5]. This is subject to the limitations that: (1) information coming to light
at the appeal cannot be used to establish a new ground for dismissal, other than
that relied on by the employer[6]; and (2) fresh evidence arising after the
determination of the internal appeal remains irrelevant to the question of
fairness[7].

1   *W Devis & Sons Ltd v Atkins* [1977] AC 931, [1977] ICR 662, HL; reaffirmed in *Polkey v AE
    Dayton Services Ltd* [1988] AC 344, [1988] ICR 142, HL (where the rule in *British Labour
    Pump Co Ltd v Byrne* [1979] ICR 347, [1979] IRLR 94, EAT was disapproved, partly on the
    grounds that it offended this principle). The relevant time for consideration of the facts is the
    date when the dismissal takes effect, so that matters occurring after notice has been given, but
    before it expires, may be taken into account: see *Williamson v Alcan (UK) Ltd* [1978] ICR 104,
    [1977] IRLR 303, EAT; *Stacey v Babcock Power Ltd* [1986] ICR 221, [1986] IRLR 3, EAT;
    Alboni v Ind Coope Retail Ltd [1998] IRLR 131, CA; *White v South London Transport Ltd*
    [1998] ICR 293, EAT.
2   See *Boston Deep Sea Fishing and Ice Co v Ansell* (1888) 39 ChD 339, CA; and PARA 745.
3   The fact that the employee was guilty of serious, though undiscovered, misconduct may,
    however, be taken into consideration by an employment tribunal when deciding on remedies; in
    particular, it may have a major impact on compensation, in an extreme case leading to a nil
    award: see PARA 821. See also *Polkey v AE Dayton Services Ltd* [1988] AC 344, [1988] ICR
    142, HL. When *W Devis & Sons Ltd v Atkins* [1977] AC 931, [1977] ICR 662, HL (cited in
    note 1) was decided, there was a minimum basic award figure which had to be awarded, but this
    was abolished by the Employment Act 1980 (repealed) so that contributory fault can cover any
    action of the employee prior to the dismissal, even if unknown to the employer: see PARA 821. In
    relation to compensation generally see *Tele-Trading Ltd v Jenkins* [1990] IRLR 430, CA.
4   An employee whose appeal is turned down will be considered dismissed as from the original
    date of dismissal, not as from the (later) date of the unsuccessful appeal: *J Sainsbury Ltd v
    Savage* [1981] ICR 1, [1980] IRLR 109, CA; approved in *West Midlands Co-operative
    Society Ltd v Tipton* [1986] AC 536, [1986] ICR 192, HL. This point is of significance when
    applying the three-month limit for bringing an unfair dismissal claim: see PARA 804. It also has
    the corollary that if the appeal succeeds the employee is reinstated with retrospective effect: *West
    Midlands Co-operative Society Ltd v Tipton*. However, it is possible for the outcome of an
    internal appeal process to vary an employee's effective date of termination (see PARA 764)
    deliberately as part of its decision, so that this becomes the effective date of termination for
    statutory purposes: see *Hawes & Curtis Ltd v Arfan* [2012] ICR 1244, EAT. *Hawes &
    Curtis Ltd v Arfan* was distinguished in *Rabess v London Fire and Emergency Planning
    Authority* [2014] All ER (D) 188 (Sep), EAT (decision on appeal did nothing to alter the date of
    dismissal, despite recognition that employee would have been entitled to notice and payment in
    lieu of notice). See also PARA 708.
5   *West Midlands Co-operative Society Ltd v Tipton* [1986] AC 536, [1986] ICR 192, HL
    (approving *Rank Xerox (UK) Ltd v Goodchild* [1979] IRLR 185, EAT; *National Heart and
    Chest Hospitals Board of Governors v Nambiar* [1981] ICR 441, [1981] IRLR 196, EAT;
    Sillifant v Powell Duffryn Timber Ltd [1983] IRLR 91, EAT; *Greenall Whitley plc v Carr* [1985]
    ICR 451, [1985] IRLR 289, EAT); *McLaren v National Coal Board* [1987] ICR 410, EAT (affd
    [1988] ICR 370, [1988] IRLR 215, CA). Denial of a right to an internal appeal may itself be
    taken into account and may make the dismissal unfair: *West Midlands Co-operative Society Ltd
    v Tipton.*

6   *Monie v Coral Racing Ltd* [1981] ICR 109, [1980] IRLR 464, CA.
7   *Greenall Whitley plc v Carr* [1985] ICR 451, [1985] IRLR 289, EAT.

771.   Pressure on employer to dismiss unfairly.   In determining[1] any question:

(1)   as to the reason, or principal reason, for which an employee[2] was dismissed[3];

(2)   whether the reason, or principal reason, for which an employee was dismissed was one of the reasons allowed for[4] under statute[5]; or

(3)   whether an employer[6] acted reasonably in treating the reason, or principal reason, for which an employee was dismissed as a sufficient reason for dismissing him[7],

no account is to be taken of any pressure which, by calling, organising, procuring or financing a strike or other industrial action[8], or threatening to do so, was exercised on the employer to dismiss the employee[9]; and any such question must be determined as if no such pressure had been exercised[10].

1   Ie for the purposes of the Employment Rights Act 1996 Pt X (ss 94–134A) (unfair dismissal: see also PARAS 757 et seq, 772 et seq). As to the modification of Pt X in relation to governing bodies of schools having a right to a delegated budget, acting in the exercise of their employment powers, see EDUCATION vol 35 (2011) PARA 355 et seq; and as to the modification of Pt X in relation to persons holding ecclesiastical office under common tenure see the Ecclesiastical Offices (Terms of Service) Regulations 2009, SI 2009/2108, reg 33; and ECCLESIASTICAL LAW vol 34 (2011) PARA 407.
2   As to the meaning of 'employee' see PARA 2.
3   Employment Rights Act 1996 s 107(1)(a). As to the meaning of 'dismissal' see PARA 762.
4   Ie a reason fulfilling the requirement of the Employment Rights Act 1996 s 98(1)(b), (2): see PARA 765.
5   Employment Rights Act 1996 s 107(1)(b).
6   As to the meaning of 'employer' see PARA 2.
7   Employment Rights Act 1996 s 107(1)(c). See PARA 767.
8   There is no statutory definition of 'strike or other industrial action' for these purposes.
9   See the Employment Rights Act 1996 s 107(2). The pressure need not be explicitly aimed at the dismissal of the employee: *Ford Motor Co Ltd v Hudson* [1978] ICR 482, [1978] IRLR 66, EAT.
10 See the Employment Rights Act 1996 s 107(2). If no other reason can be shown, the dismissal is unfair: *Hazells Offset Ltd v Luckett* [1977] IRLR 430, EAT. The Employment Rights Act 1996 s 107 does not apply to a share fisherman (see s 199(2); and PARA 167) or to a police officer (see s 200(1); and PARA 168).
    The Employment Protection (Consolidation) Act 1978 s 63 (repealed) (from which the Employment Rights Act 1996 s 107 derives) used to be significant under the old law on the closed shop, but since the repeal by the Employment Act 1988 of the legal protection given to closed shop dismissals, it is of less importance; indeed, even if an employer dismisses because of trade union pressure and that dismissal is unfair, with or without the application of the Employment Rights Act 1996 s 107, the trade union may be ordered to pay some or all of the compensation awarded (see the Trade Union and Labour Relations (Consolidation) Act 1992 s 160; and PARA 1062).

(iii)   Particular Cases of Unfairness

A.   IN GENERAL

772.   Difficulty of establishing general principles in cases of unfair dismissal. In a complaint of unfair dismissal[1], most questions to be resolved by the employment tribunal are questions of fact for that tribunal; and where in similar cases two different tribunals come to different conclusions, those different conclusions must both be upheld as correct unless either tribunal has erred in law[2]. It is thus difficult to establish general principles which will apply in particular cases[3]. Even where the higher courts have laid down guidelines for tribunals hearing complaints of unfair dismissal[4], these guidelines have never been intended to be rules of law, and failure to adopt one is not of itself an appealable error of law[5].

1 Ie under the Employment Rights Act 1996 s 111: see PARA 804.
2 *Naylor v Orton & Smith Ltd* [1983] ICR 665 at 673, [1983] IRLR 233 at 237, EAT, per Browne-Wilkinson P. The point at issue in the case was the meaning of 'strike or other industrial action' in what is now the Trade Union and Labour Relations (Consolidation) Act 1992 s 238 (see PARA 1351); and this has been held to be a question of fact: see *Coates v Modern Methods and Materials Ltd* [1983] QB 192, [1982] ICR 763, CA ('taking part in a strike').
3 Disparity of tribunal decisions on ostensibly similar facts is an inherent feature of the tribunal system: *Gilham v Kent County Council (No 2)* [1985] ICR 233, sub nom *Kent County Council v Gilham* [1985] IRLR 18, CA. See also *Kidd v DRG (UK) Ltd* [1985] ICR 405 at 417, [1985] IRLR 190 at 196, EAT, per Waite P (a case on sex discrimination). Cf *McLaren v National Coal Board* [1988] ICR 370, [1988] IRLR 215, CA (dismissal without a proper hearing during the dislocation of the miners' strike held to be unfair); *Dillett v National Coal Board* [1988] ICR 218, CA (similar dismissal held not to be unfair).
4 As to guideline decisions and precedents in tribunal proceedings generally see PARA 1445.
5 *Jowett v Earl of Bradford (No 2)* [1978] ICR 431 at 436, sub nom *Earl of Bradford v Jowett* [1978] IRLR 16 at 18, EAT, per Bristow J; *Rolls Royce Motors Ltd v Dewhurst* [1985] ICR 869, [1985] IRLR 184, EAT. Ironically, the only certain grounds of perversity would be if a tribunal held that it was legally bound to apply an earlier authority, rather than the general test contained in the relevant statutory provision: *Rolls Royce Motors Ltd v Dewhurst*.

B. CAPABILITY OR QUALIFICATIONS

773. Fairness of dismissal for reason related to employee's capability or qualifications. A dismissal[1] is not unfair if it is shown by the employer[2] to have been imposed for a reason related to the capability or qualifications of the employee[3] for performing work of the kind which he was employed to do by the employer, and if it was reasonable in the circumstances[4]. For these purposes, in relation to an employee:

(1) 'capability' means capability assessed by reference to skill, aptitude, health or any other physical or mental quality[5]; and the question for a tribunal is not whether incapability has actually been proved, but whether the employer reasonably believed the employee to be incapable[6];

(2) 'qualifications' means any degree, diploma or other academic, technical or professional qualification relevant to the position[7] which the employee held[8]; and this may include a driving licence[9] or relate to aptitude tests set by the employer[10].

1 As to the meaning of 'dismissal' see PARA 762.
2 As to the meaning of 'employer' see PARA 2.
3 As to the meaning of 'employee' see PARA 2.
4 See the Employment Rights Act 1996 s 98(2)(a), (4); and PARA 765.
5 Employment Rights Act 1996 s 98(3)(a). In *Wilson v Post Office* [2000] IRLR 834, CA, it was suggested that a poor attendance record, although possibly caused by ill-health, should be dealt with as 'some other substantial reason' under the Employment Rights Act 1996 s 98(1)(b) (see PARA 765) rather than under s 98(2)(a), (3)(a). If an employee is capable of the work but unwilling to do it, that is more properly dealt with as a case of misconduct, amenable to disciplinary warnings: *Sutton and Gates (Luton) Ltd v Boxall* [1979] ICR 67, [1978] IRLR 486, EAT. Where an employee is so incompetent that a warning is unlikely to result in an improvement in his work, no warning is necessary: *Littlewoods Organisation Ltd v Egenti* [1976] ICR 516, [1976] IRLR 334, EAT.
6 *Alidair Ltd v Taylor* [1978] ICR 445, sub nom *Taylor v Alidair Ltd* [1978] IRLR 82, CA. In determining that question, the tribunal may consider evidence of incompetence from the opinions of the employee's superiors (*Cook v Thomas Linnell & Sons Ltd* [1977] ICR 770, [1977] IRLR 132, EAT) or from complaints from customers (*AJ Dunning & Sons*

(Shopfitters) Ltd v Jacomb [1973] ICR 448, [1973] IRLR 206, NIRC). Where a customer insists on the employee's dismissal and puts commercial pressure on the employer to dismiss him, that may constitute 'some other substantial reason': see PARA 766. Objective evidence may be expected, to substantiate such opinion, and the employee may seek to rebut the allegations of incapability: see eg *Fletcher v Photo Precision* [1973] IRLR 80; *Raynor v Remploy Ltd* [1973] IRLR 3; *Castledine v Rothwell Engineering Ltd* [1973] IRLR 99. The employee's attitude, eg inflexibility or lack of adaptability, may amount to incapability: *Abernethy v Mott, Hay and Anderson* [1974] ICR 323, [1974] IRLR 213, CA; *Lewis Shops Group v Wiggins* [1973] ICR 335, [1973] IRLR 205, NIRC. A series of relatively minor incidents may add up to a reasonable belief in incapability: *Miller v Graham's Executors* [1978] IRLR 309, EAT.

7 As to the meaning of 'position' see PARA 765 note 13.

8 Employment Rights Act 1996 s 98(3)(b). Whatever is claimed to be a qualification must be substantially concerned with the employee's aptitude or ability: *Blue Star Ship Management Ltd v Williams* [1978] ICR 770, [1979] IRLR 16, EAT.

9 *Tayside Regional Council v McIntosh* [1982] IRLR 272, EAT.

10 *Blackman v Post Office* [1974] ICR 151, [1974] IRLR 46, NIRC.

774. Procedural fairness in cases of incapability.

Whether a dismissal on the grounds of incapability is fair may depend on the procedure adopted by the employer to deal with the problem[1]. The giving of warnings is appropriate to incapability cases[2], as well as misconduct cases, though the emphasis is more on giving a reasonable opportunity to improve than in an ordinary disciplinary case[3]. Other relevant factors may be: (1) proper appraisal of the employee's performance[4] and discussion of the results with him[5]; (2) whether proper instruction and support were given[6]; (3) what training was given[7]; (4) whether consideration was given to alternative work[8].

1 Disciplinary situations include misconduct and/or poor performance. If employers have a separate capability procedure they may prefer to address performance issues under this procedure: see ACAS Code of Practice 1: Disciplinary and Grievance Procedures (2009) para 1; and PARA 702. As to rules and performance standards generally see Discipline and Grievances at work: The ACAS guide (September 2014), pp 11–12, Appendix 4 (dealing with absence). As to the status of the ACAS guidance see PARA 701; and as to ACAS Codes of Practice generally see PARAS 1223–1224.

2 *Winterhalter Gastronom Ltd v Webb* [1973] ICR 245, [1973] IRLR 120, NIRC.

3 See *Mansfield Hosiery Mills Ltd v Bromley* [1977] IRLR 301, EAT; *Winterhalter Gastronom Ltd v Webb* [1973] ICR 245, [1973] IRLR 120, NIRC. For guidance on handling cases of unsatisfactory performance see Discipline and Grievances at work: The ACAS guide (September 2014), which suggests that a 'quiet word' is often all that is required to improve an employee's conduct or performance, particularly in small firms, backed up by additional training, coaching and advice, where necessary, but that if informal action does not bring about an improvement, or the misconduct or unsatisfactory performance is considered too serious to be classed as minor, employers should provide employees with a clear signal of their dissatisfaction by taking formal action: see p 10 ('Resolve discipline issues informally').

4 *Post Office v Mughal* [1977] ICR 763, [1977] IRLR 178, EAT. That case concerned a probationer, and the need to assess and instruct such an employee has been recognised as a particular requirement: see *White v London Transport Executive* [1982] QB 489, [1981] IRLR 261, EAT; *ILEA v Lloyd* [1981] IRLR 394, CA.

5 *Cook v Thomas Linnell & Sons Ltd* [1977] ICR 770, [1977] IRLR 132, EAT.

6 While there is no implied term that an employer will provide support, assistance, guidance and training (*White v London Transport Executive* [1982] QB 489, [1981] IRLR 261, EAT (no constructive dismissal through lack of training)), lack of it may be a factor to be taken into account (see eg *Davison v Kent Meters Ltd* [1975] IRLR 145). Lack of support may be relevant, as it may be in a constructive dismissal case: see PARA 763. See note 1.

7 Adequate training may be particularly important where the employee is promoted to a new job requiring new skills: see eg *Burrows v Ace Caravan Co (Hull) Ltd* [1972] IRLR 4; *Welsh v Associated Steels and Tools Co Ltd* [1973] IRLR 111. Refusal to undergo training may count against the employee: *Coward v John Menzies (Holdings) Ltd* [1977] IRLR 428, EAT.

8 Although this is no general requirement in a simple incapability case (*Bevan Harris Ltd (t/a Clyde Leather Co) v Gair* [1981] IRLR 520, EAT), it may be a factor, especially in a case where the employee has been promoted but fails to cope with the new duties (*Draper v Kraft*

Foods Ltd [1973] IRLR 328; *Kendrick v Concrete Pumping Ltd* [1975] IRLR 83; cf *White v London Transport Executive* [1982] QB 489, [1981] IRLR 261, EAT).

775. Dismissal for ill health. Incapability because of severe ill health[1] may frustrate the contract of employment[2], but short of that it is possible for a dismissal on grounds of ill health to be fair, provided that a proper procedure is adopted[3]:

(1)   the sick employee should be consulted and the matter discussed with him to discover the true medical position[4];

(2)   the employer must in many cases seek a reliable medical opinion[5], either from the employee's own doctor or from another doctor or specialist[6]; there may be a term in the contract of employment requiring the employee to undergo medical examination, but, if there is not, the employer cannot lawfully insist on it[7] and so must proceed on the facts as known to him if the employee refuses;

(3)   in the light of heads (1) and (2) above, a decision must be taken whether to dismiss and that remains a managerial decision, not a medical one; the basic question to be determined when assessing the fairness of a decision to dismiss is whether, in all the circumstances, the employer can be expected to wait any longer and, if so, how much longer[8], which must be considered in the light of:

(a)   the medical evidence as to the nature of the illness and the likely length of the absence[9];

(b)   the urgency of the need to replace the employee[10];

(c)   the employee's length of service[11]; and

(d)   whether there is a possibility of alternative employment[12].

A sick pay term in the contract is not a relevant factor, since it is not necessarily fair to dismiss when contractual sick pay runs out, and not necessarily unfair to dismiss before that[13].

Persistent intermittent absences for ill health may justify dismissal; and, unless there is a particular underlying medical cause, such cases are dealt with primarily as disciplinary matters of absenteeism, particularly where the individual instances are minor and not medically verifiable[14]. An employer is entitled to look behind a doctor's certificate or a self-certificate if he suspects that the employee is not actually ill, misuse of such a certificate being a disciplinary offence[15].

1   A distinction should be made between absence on grounds of illness or injury and absence for no good reason which may call for disciplinary action. As to the ACAS guidance to be followed where the employee is absent because of illness or injury see Discipline and Grievances at work: The ACAS guide (September 2014), Appendix 4 (dealing with absence). As to the status of the ACAS guidance see PARA 701; and as to ACAS Codes of Practice generally see PARAS 1223–1224.

2   See PARA 729.

3   Such a dismissal may be fair even if it is the work itself that is causing the illness (*Glitz v Watford Electric Co Ltd* [1979] IRLR 89, EAT), though not if the employer has failed to take all reasonable steps to eliminate the problem (*Jagdeo v Smiths Industries Ltd* [1982] ICR 47, EAT; and see *Piggott Bros & Co Ltd v Jackson* [1992] ICR 85, [1991] IRLR 309, CA). There is no general principle that a work-related injury or illness must be treated more leniently by the employer: *London Fire and Civil Defence Authority v Betty* [1994] IRLR 384, EAT; but see *Edwards v Governors of Hanson School* [2001] IRLR 733, EAT (allegations that an employer is responsible for the illness of an employee which led to dismissal should be considered when assessing whether a compensatory award for unfair dismissal is just and equitable). If the employee's state of health makes him a danger to other employees, that is a factor in the employer's favour: *Harper v National Coal Board* [1980] IRLR 260, EAT; *Converform (Darwen) Ltd v Bell* [1981] IRLR 195, EAT. The particular nature of the employment may make

good health essential (*Taylorplan Catering (Scotland) Ltd v McInally* [1980] IRLR 53, EAT); this is amenable to being expressly included in the contract of employment (*Leonard v Fergus & Haynes Civil Engineering Ltd* [1979] IRLR 235, Ct of Sess). As to the possible duty in law imposed on an employer to dismiss an employee for his own good so as to protect him from physical danger caused by ill health see *Coxall v Goodyear Great Britain Ltd* [2002] EWCA Civ 1010, [2003] 1 WLR 536, [2003] ICR 152; and PARA 33. Where the employment is the cause of the illness, it may be incumbent on the employer to make greater efforts to find the employee alternative employment or tolerate a longer period of absence: *McAdie v Royal Bank of Scotland* [2007] EWCA Civ 806, [2008] ICR 1087, [2007] IRLR 895.

4   *East Lindsey District Council v Daubney* [1977] ICR 566, [1977] IRLR 181, EAT; reaffirmed in *A Links & Co Ltd v Rose* [1991] IRLR 353, Ct of Sess. The onus is primarily on the employer to seek out information, not on the employee to volunteer it: *Mitchell v Arkwood Plastics (Engineering) Ltd* [1993] ICR 471, EAT. An ordinary warning is not appropriate: *Spencer v Paragon Wallpapers Ltd* [1977] ICR 301, [1976] IRLR 373, EAT. Insufficient consultation may thus make a dismissal unfair (*Owen v Funditor Ltd* [1976] ICR 350; *Townson v Northgate Group Ltd* [1981] IRLR 382, EAT); but consultation may be dispensed with if, on the facts, representations by the employee could have no effect (*Walton v TAC Construction Materials Ltd* [1981] IRLR 357, EAT), though any argument as to whether lack of consultation made any difference must be considered in the light of *Polkey v AE Dayton Services Ltd* [1988] AC 344, [1988], ICR 142, HL (cited in PARA 767).

5   *Patterson v Messrs Bracketts* [1977] IRLR 137, EAT. In some circumstances, a second opinion, or the opinion of a specialist, may be appropriate: *Crampton v Dacorum Motors Ltd* [1975] IRLR 168. The chosen medical practitioner must be supplied with accurate information: see *Ford Motor Co Ltd v Nawaz* [1987] ICR 434, [1987] IRLR 163, EAT.

6   If a report is requested from the employee's own doctor, the procedure laid down in the Access to Medical Reports Act 1988 must be satisfied: see ss 3–7; and MEDICAL PROFESSIONS vol 74 (2011) PARA 41 et seq. *Quaere* whether the right of access under s 1 applies if a report is sought from the company doctor (especially if that doctor has treated the employee in the past).

7   *Bliss v South East Thames Regional Health Authority* [1987] ICR 700, [1985] IRLR 308, CA.

8   *Spencer v Paragon Wallpapers Ltd* [1977] ICR 301, [1976] IRLR 373, EAT.

9   *Luckings v May & Baker Ltd* [1974] IRLR 151, NIRC; *Liverpool Area Health Authority (Teaching) Central and Southern District v Edwards* [1977] IRLR 471, EAT. Where there is an enhanced pension on retirement through ill-health, the employee's right to the benefit of ill-health retirement should also be considered: *Haigh v First West Yorkshire Ltd(t/a First Leeds)* [2008] IRLR 182, [2008] All ER (D) 207 (Jan), EAT.

10 See *Tan v Berry Bros & Rudd Ltd* [1974] ICR 586, [1974] IRLR 244, NIRC; *Spencer v Paragon Wallpapers Ltd* [1977] ICR 301, [1976] IRLR 373, EAT. In some types of business the need for healthy employees may be particularly important: see note 3. The employer may also need to consider the effect of the employee's absence through sickness on other employees, e g where they work as a team: *Ali v Tillotsons Containers Ltd* [1975] IRLR 272; *Pascoe v Hallen and Medway* [1975] IRLR 116. See also *Haigh v First West Yorkshire Ltd (t/a First Leeds)* [2008] IRLR 182, [2008] All ER (D) 207 (Jan), EAT; and note 9.

11 While length of service will often be relevant in misconduct cases (see PARAS 776–779), in cases involving dismissal on the ground of ill-health its relevance is not quite so clear cut; the critical question in every case is whether the length of the employee's service, and the manner in which they worked during that period, yields inferences that indicate that the employee is likely to return to work as soon as they can: *BS v Dundee City Council* [2013] CSIH 91, [2014] IRLR 131.

12 Although there is no positive obligation to find alternative employment or create a new job (*Shook v Ealing London Borough Council* [1986] ICR 314, [1986] IRLR 46, EAT), this may be a factor to be taken into consideration if reasonable to do so in the circumstances (*Merseyside and North Wales Electricity Board v Taylor* [1975] ICR 185, [1975] IRLR 60; *Taylorplan Catering (Scotland) Ltd v McInally* [1980] IRLR 53, EAT; *Garricks (Caterers) Ltd v Nolan* [1980] IRLR 259, EAT). See also *Haigh v First West Yorkshire Ltd (t/a First Leeds)* [2008] IRLR 182, [2008] All ER (D) 207 (Jan), EAT; and note 9.

13 *Smiths Industries Aerospace and Defence Systems Ltd v Brookes* [1986] IRLR 434, EAT; *Coulson v Felixstowe Dock and Rly Co* [1975] IRLR 11; *Hardwick v Leeds Area Health Authority* [1975] IRLR 319. As to the payment of wages during sickness see PARA 27; and as to statutory sick pay see PARA 558 et seq. Dismissal for the purpose of avoiding statutory sick pay is ineffective for that purpose: see PARA 561.

14 *International Sports Co Ltd v Thomson* [1980] IRLR 340, EAT; *Rolls Royce Ltd v Walpole* [1980] IRLR 343, EAT; *Lynock v Cereal Packaging Ltd* [1988] ICR 670, [1988] IRLR 510, EAT.

15 *Hutchinson v Enfield Rolling Mills Ltd* [1981] IRLR 318, EAT. See also *Taylor v Merseyrail Electrics 2002 Ltd* [2007] All ER (D) 44 (Nov), EAT (in the absence of contradictory medical evidence an employer could not go behind what appeared on the face of a medical certificate).

C. CONDUCT

776.   Fairness of dismissal for reason related to employee's conduct.   A dismissal[1] is not unfair if it is shown by the employer[2] to have been imposed for a reason related to the conduct[3] of the employee[4] and if it was reasonable in the circumstances[5]. At common law, an employee may be summarily dismissed for gross misconduct[6] and for any other reason by notice[7]; whilst there may in practice be considerable concurrence in many cases between the common law and the statutory law of unfair dismissal, and both may have to be developed to deal with modern forms of misconduct[8], unfair dismissal is not tied to common law contract-based concepts, and looks at the substance and fairness of the dismissal[9].

Where the misconduct in question is blatant or obvious, the question is whether dismissal was a fair sanction[10]. In many cases, however, the misconduct is not obvious, and thus a primary question arises as to whether the misconduct has been proved as against that employee[11]. It is well established that in a case of suspected misconduct the test of fairness is not whether the employer has proved the employee guilty, and still less whether he has done so beyond reasonable doubt, but rather whether the employer genuinely believed on reasonable grounds in the employee's guilt[12]. This involves a threefold test:

(1)   the employer must establish that he genuinely did believe the employee guilty of the misconduct[13];

(2)   that belief must have been formed on reasonable grounds[14]; and

(3)   the employer must have investigated the matter reasonably[15].

If, after all reasonable investigation, the employer can determine only that one of two or more employees must be guilty, it may be fair to dismiss both or all of them if there are pressing business reasons for doing so[16].

In deciding whether a dismissal for misconduct was unfair, the fact that the employee was in breach of company rules or procedures may be important evidence[17]. Similarly, breach of a lawful order[18] may be significant, though this may require an inquiry into what the employer was and was not contractually able to order[19]. Beyond that, it is impossible to categorise all cases in which an employer may or may not dismiss fairly, since each case will depend on its own facts[20]. The following disciplinary offences have tended to occur in the reported cases: fighting[21]; drunkenness[22]; insubordination or abusive behaviour[23]; theft or dishonesty[24]; clocking offences[25]; refusal to perform normal duties[26]; unauthorised absence[27]; working for a competitor[28]; wilfully inadequate performance[29]; and computer misuse[30].

1   As to the meaning of 'dismissal' see PARA 762.
2   As to the meaning of 'employer' see PARA 2.
3   'Conduct' means action which in some way reflects on the relationship of employer-employee: *Thomson v Alloa Motor Co Ltd* [1983] IRLR 403, EAT. See also *Bowater v Northwest London Hospitals NHS Trust* [2011] EWCA Civ 63, [2011] IRLR 331, 118 BMLR 163 (majority of the tribunal had been entitled to find that summary dismissal was outside the range of reasonable responses to the employee's conduct, which could have been described as lewd but would have been considered by a large proportion of the population to be merely humorous); and see *Haslem v GM Packaging (UK) Ltd* [2014] All ER (D) 209 (Feb), EAT (wrong to focus solely on the sexual activity as the principal reason for dismissal rather than the whole of the conduct leading to dismissal).

4   As to the meaning of 'employee' see PARA 2.
5   See the Employment Rights Act 1996 s 98(1)(b), (2)(b), (4); and PARA 765.
6   See PARA 743. See also ACAS Code of Practice 1: Disciplinary and Grievance Procedures (2009)
    paras 22–23; and PARA 707. As to the status of the ACAS guidance see PARA 701; and as to
    ACAS Codes of Practice generally see PARAS 1223–1224.
        If the employer's view that the misconduct is serious enough to be characterised as gross
    misconduct is objectively justifiable (as opposed to subjectively: see *Sandwell & West
    Birmingham Hospitals NHS Trust v Westwood* (2009) UKEAT/0032/09; and PARA 744) then
    summary dismissal on that ground should be considered as one of the circumstances, along with
    everything else that is relevant under the Employment Rights Act 1996 s 98(4) (see PARA 765),
    against which to judge the reasonableness or unreasonableness of treating the conduct as a
    sufficient reason for dismissal: see *Eastland Homes Partnership Ltd v Cunningham* (2014)
    UKEAT/0272/13/MC; and PARA 744. See also *Brezan v Zimmer Ltd* [2009] All ER (D) 17
    (Oct), EAT (only conclusion to which the tribunal could properly have come was that the
    employer's belief that there had been gross misconduct fell within the range of reasonable
    responses); *Brito-Babapulle v Ealing Hospital NHS Trust* [2013] IRLR 854, EAT (although
    claiming sick pay whilst working elsewhere is in general regarded very seriously by employers,
    that is not to say that dismissal is an inevitable conclusion; a logical jump from gross
    misconduct to the proposition that dismissal must then inevitably fall within the range of
    reasonable responses gives no room for considering whether, though the misconduct is gross and
    dismissal almost inevitable, mitigating factors may be such that dismissal is not reasonable).
7   See PARA 733.
8   See eg *Denco Ltd v Joinson* [1992] 1 All ER 463, [1991] ICR 172, EAT (computer misuse
    merits summary dismissal, which is most likely to be fair). Disciplinary situations may arise
    from cases of misconduct and/or poor performance. As to guidance and rules relating to
    performance standards generally see Discipline and Grievances at work: The ACAS guide
    (September 2014), pp 11–12, Appendix 4 (dealing with absence). As to gross misconduct
    specifically see pp 31–32.
9   See PARAS 743, 757 note 2. This distinction was reaffirmed in *Farrant v Woodroffe School*
    [1998] ICR 184, [1998] IRLR 176, EAT (mistaken belief that employee's conduct constituted a
    breach of contract).
10 See PARA 777.
11 This is particularly important where the employee is accused of a criminal offence: see further
    PARA 778.
12 *British Home Stores Ltd v Burchell* [1980] ICR 303n, [1978] IRLR 379, EAT (approved in *W
    Weddel & Co Ltd v Tepper* [1980] ICR 286, [1980] IRLR 96, CA; doubted in *Anandarajah v
    Lord Chancellor's Department* [1984] IRLR 131, EAT; reaffirmed in *ILEA v Gravett* [1988]
    IRLR 497, EAT; *Whitbread & Co plc v Mills* [1988] ICR 776, [1988] IRLR 501, EAT; *Louies v
    Coventry Hood and Seating Co Ltd* [1990] ICR 54, [1990] IRLR 324, EAT; *Scottish Midland
    Co-operative Society Ltd v Cullion* [1991] IRLR 261, Ct of Sess); *Midland Bank plc v Madden*
    [2000] 2 All ER 741, EAT; revsd sub nom *Post Office v Foley, HSBC Bank plc (formerly
    Midland Bank plc) v Madden* [2001] 1 All ER 550, [2000] ICR 1283, CA (the employer is the
    proper person to conduct the investigation into the alleged misconduct; the tribunal's function is
    to decide whether that investigation was reasonable in the circumstances and whether the
    decision to dismiss, in the light of the results of that investigation, was a reasonable response).
    Post Office v Foley, HSBC Bank plc (formerly Midland Bank plc) v Madden was applied in
    Celebi v Compass Group UK and Ireland Ltd (t/a Scolarest) [2009] All ER (D) 172 (Jan), EAT.
    For the purposes of the test in *British Home Stores Ltd v Burchell*, the answer to the question:
    '*whose knowledge or state of mind was intended to count as the knowledge or state of mind of
    the employer?*' will be: '*the person who was deputed to carry out the employer's functions under
    the Employment Rights Act 1996 s 98*' (see PARA 765): *Orr v Milton Keynes Council* [2011]
    EWCA Civ 62, [2011] 4 All ER 1256, [2011] ICR 704, [2011] IRLR 317 (an organisation has
    to deal with disciplinary matters through managers below what would normally be 'guiding
    minds' level).
        Although itself concerned with suspected dishonesty, *British Home Stores Ltd v Burchell*
    applies to other forms of misconduct: *Distillers Co (Bottling Services) Ltd v Gardner* [1982]
    IRLR 47, EAT. However, whilst being of great practical importance, the principles in *British
    Home Stores Ltd v Burchell* are not to be applied over-rigidly (especially in cases with little
    conflict on the facts): *Boys and Girls Welfare Society v McDonald* [1996] IRLR 129, EAT. These
    principles, and their application to the test of fairness under the Employment Rights Act 1996
    s 98(4) (see PARAS 765, 767), were strongly reaffirmed in *Post Office v Foley, HSBC Bank plc
    (formerly Midland Bank plc) v Madden*, disapproving criticisms made in *Midland Bank plc v
    Madden* [2000] IRLR 288, EAT. It has since been suggested that, in cases involving misconduct,

the rules on unfair dismissal clarified by the Court of Appeal in _Post Office v Foley, HSBC Bank plc (formerly Midland Bank plc) v Madden_ may need to be considered in the light of an employee's rights under the Convention for the Protection of Human Rights and Fundamental Freedoms (Rome, 25 March 1957; TS 1 (1973); Cmnd 5179) and the Human Rights Act 1998 (see RIGHTS AND FREEDOMS vol 88A (2013) PARAS 14, 88): _Pay v Lancashire Probation Service_ [2004] ICR 187 at 198, [2004] IRLR 129 at 134, EAT, per McMullen J. See also _Perkin v St George's Healthcare NHS Trust_ [2005] EWCA Civ 1174, [2006] ICR 617, [2005] IRLR 934 (an important (and first) case on dismissal due to awkward personality, which, even if it produces no actual misconduct, can constitute 'some other substantial reason' (see the Employment Rights Act 1996 s 98(1)(b); and PARA 765) if it has a serious effect on the employer's business). See also _Steele v William Hill Organisation Ltd_ [2008] All ER (D) 80 (Aug), EAT; _Rees v Makro Self Service Wholesalers_ [2008] All ER (D) 96 (Aug), EAT; _Tombling v West Coast Trains Ltd (t/a Virgin Trains)_ [2009] All ER (D) 57 (Apr), EAT.

13 It is implicit in _British Home Stores Ltd v Burchell_ [1980] ICR 303n, [1978] IRLR 379, EAT, that the employer's initial suspicion may be turned by reasonable investigation into the necessary positive belief. See also _Perkin v St George's Healthcare NHS Trust_ [2005] EWCA Civ 1174, [2006] ICR 617, [2005] IRLR 934; and note 12.

14 This usually means that the belief is supported by objective evidence: see _Morley's of Brixton Ltd v Minott_ [1982] ICR 444, [1982] IRLR 270, EAT. Matters coming to light after the time of dismissal do not affect this question: _W Devis & Sons Ltd v Atkins_ [1977] AC 931, [1977] ICR 662, HL; _Ferodo Ltd v Barnes_ [1976] ICR 439, [1976] IRLR 302, EAT. It may be necessary on the facts to investigate the background, not just the actual misdeed: _Chamberlain Vinyl Products Ltd v Patel_ [1996] ICR 113, EAT (proved abusiveness may have been due to an underlying psychiatric cause).

15 Complaints against the employee should be investigated properly: _Henderson v Granville Tours Ltd_ [1982] IRLR 494, EAT. The depth of investigation depends on the circumstances of the case and how strong the initial suspicion is (_ILEA v Gravett_ [1988] IRLR 497, EAT); difficult surrounding circumstances will not normally justify a lack of investigation (_McLaren v National Coal Board_ [1988] ICR 370, [1988] IRLR 215, CA; c f _Dillett v National Coal Board_ [1988] ICR 218, CA). In determining whether an employer has carried out such investigation as was reasonable in all the circumstances, the relevant circumstances include the gravity of the charges and their potential effect upon the employee's reputation, employment and prospects of future employment: _A v B_ [2003] IRLR 405, EAT. The reasonableness of an investigation also necessarily involves a consideration of any delays; in certain circumstances, a delay in the conduct of the investigation might of itself render an otherwise fair dismissal unfair: _Marley Homecare Ltd v Dutton_ [1981] IRLR 380, EAT; _Royal Society for the Prevention of Cruelty to Animals v Cruden_ [1986] ICR 205, [1986] IRLR 83, EAT; _A v B_. In deciding whether the sufficiency of an investigation into misconduct was adequate, the tribunal necessarily had to examine and consider the nature and extent of the investigations carried out by the employer and the content and reliability of what those investigations revealed before it could reach a view on whether a reasonable employer would have regarded the investigatory process as sufficient in matters such as extent and reliability or as calling for further steps: _Sneddon v Carr-Gomm Scotland Ltd_ [2012] CSIH 28, [2012] IRLR 820, IH (without further more detailed inquiry, there had been insufficient grounds for believing that care worker had been guilty of alleged misconduct). An employer to whom a third party discloses information or makes allegations should assess for itself, as far as practicable, the reliability of what it has been told, checking the integrity of the informant body and the safeguards within its internal processes concerning the accuracy of the information supplied: _Leach v Office of Communications_ [2012] EWCA Civ 959, [2012] ICR 1269, [2012] IRLR 839 (case involving allegations of child abuse in Cambodian courts and press). The anonymity of those who have made allegations against the employee does not necessarily prejudice a fair hearing where the investigating officer can be cross-examined in detail as to the nature and extent of the investigation and as to why he accepted or rejected evidence: _Asda Stores Ltd v Thompson_ [2002] IRLR 245, EAT. As to hearings see PARAS 703 et seq, 777; and as to investigation see also PARA 703.

The 'range of reasonable responses' test (see PARA 767) may apply as much to the reasonableness of an investigation as to the reasonableness of a decision to dismiss: _J Sainsbury plc v Hitt_ [2002] EWCA Civ 1588, [2003] ICR 111, [2003] IRLR 23. _J Sainsbury plc v Hitt_ was applied in _Celebi v Compass Group UK and Ireland Ltd (t/a Scolarest)_ [2009] All ER (D) 172 (Jan), EAT. An investigation may also be required to satisfy a test of proportionality if any aspect of it breaches an employee's right to respect for his private and family life under the Convention for the Protection of Human Rights and Fundamental Freedoms (Rome, 25 March 1957; TS 1 (1973); Cmnd 5179) ('ECHR') art 8(1) and the Human Rights Act 1998 (see RIGHTS AND FREEDOMS vol 88A (2013) PARA 317 et seq): _McGowan v_

Scottish Water [2005] IRLR 167, EAT (Sc) (employers' use of covert video surveillance was proportionate as it went to the heart of the investigation into their suspicions that an employee was falsifying his time sheets); and see *City and County of Swansea v Gayle* [2013] IRLR 768, EAT (employment tribunal cannot adjudicate upon any freestanding claim of a breach of ECHR art 8; the reasonableness of the investigation must be seen within the context of the 'range of reasonable responses' test).

16 *Monie v Coral Racing Ltd* [1981] ICR 109, [1980] IRLR 464, CA; *Parr v Whitbread & Co plc* [1990] ICR 427, [1990] IRLR 39, EAT. The position of each employee must be considered separately: *Gibson v British Transport Docks Board* [1982] IRLR 228, EAT.

17 *Hadjioannou v Coral Casinos Ltd* [1981] IRLR 352, EAT; *McPhie and McDermott v Wimpey Waste Management Ltd* [1981] IRLR 316, EAT; *Marley Homecare Ltd v Dutton* [1981] IRLR 380, EAT. In this context, a relatively clear disciplinary rule should not be interpreted legalistically: *British Railways Board v Jackson* [1994] IRLR 235, CA. Breach of a clear rule will not per se make the dismissal fair, and the tribunal retains its discretion to review the dismissal as a whole: see PARA 744. The fact that the employee was clearly on notice of the results of particular misconduct may, however, be important, as may lack of such a clear warning in the terms of employment: *Distillers Co (Bottling Services) Ltd v Gardner* [1982] IRLR 47, EAT; *Trusthouse Forte (Catering) Ltd v Adonis* [1984] IRLR 382, EAT. Some forms of misconduct are so grave that it matters little whether they are spelled out in the employer's disciplinary rules: *Ulsterbus Ltd v Henderson* [1989] IRLR 251, NI CA. As to disciplinary powers and procedures generally see PARA 698 et seq.

18 An employee may refuse an unlawful order and, in some circumstances, a dangerous one: see PARA 31. See also *Piggott Bros & Co Ltd v Jackson* [1992] ICR 85, [1991] IRLR 309, CA (employees dismissed after refusing to work with materials which in the past had adversely affected their health; the employment tribunal's decision that the dismissals were unfair on the facts could not be characterised as perverse).

19 *Redbridge London Borough Council v Fishman* [1978] ICR 569, [1978] IRLR 69, EAT; *Cole v Midland Display Ltd* [1973] IRLR 62, NIRC; *Simmonds v Dowty Seals Ltd* [1978] IRLR 211, EAT. However, there is not necessarily a complete correlation between contractual power and fairness of the dismissal, since in exceptional cases it may be fair to dismiss an employee for refusing an order contrary to his contract (*Brandon and Goold v Murphy Bros* [1983] IRLR 54, EAT) or contrary to a health and safety requirement (*Lindsay v Dunlop Ltd* [1980] IRLR 93, EAT) or to agree to a contractual change (*Farrant v Woodroffe School* [1998] ICR 184, [1998] IRLR 176, EAT) or, conversely, unfair to dismiss for breach of an order within the contract, if the employee was for some reason acting reasonably in refusing it (*Union of Construction, Allied Trades and Technicians v Brain* [1981] ICR 542, [1981] IRLR 224, CA).

20 See PARA 772.

21 See *Dacres v Walls Meat Co Ltd* [1976] ICR 44, [1976] IRLR 20, EAT; *Stevenson v Golden Wonder Ltd* [1977] IRLR 474, EAT; *CA Parsons & Co Ltd v McLoughlin* [1978] IRLR 65, EAT; *Taylor v Parsons Peebles NEI Bruce Peebles Ltd* [1981] IRLR 119, EAT; *Gibson v British Transport Docks Board* [1982] IRLR 228, EAT; *Procter v British Gypsum Ltd* [1992] IRLR 7, EAT.

22 See *Dairy Produce Packers Ltd v Beverstock* [1981] IRLR 265, EAT. See also *O'Flynn v Airlinks The Airport Coach Co Ltd* [2002] All ER (D) 05 (Jul), EAT (employee failed random drug and alcohol test).

23 See *Retarded Children's Aid Society Ltd v Day* [1978] 1 WLR 763, [1978] IRLR 128, CA; *Shortland v Chantrill* [1975] IRLR 208 (dismissal unfair on the facts); *Wood v Kettering Co-operative Chemists Ltd* [1978] IRLR 438, EAT.

24 See *Budgen & Co v Thomas* [1976] ICR 344, [1976] IRLR 174, EAT (dismissal unfair on the facts); *Trust Houses Forte Hotels Ltd v Murphy* [1977] IRLR 186, EAT; *Docherty v Reddy* [1977] ICR 365, EAT; *British Leyland (UK) Ltd v Swift* [1981] IRLR 91, CA; *Morley's of Brixton v Minott* [1982] ICR 444, [1982] IRLR 270, EAT; *University College at Buckingham v Phillips* [1982] ICR 318, EAT; *Maintenance Co Ltd v Dormer* [1982] IRLR 491, EAT; *Sillifant v Powell Duffryn Timber Ltd* [1983] IRLR 91, EAT; *Linfood Cash and Carry Ltd v Thomson* [1989] ICR 518, [1989] IRLR 235, EAT (dismissal unfair on the facts); *Post Office (Counters) Ltd v Heavey* [1990] ICR 1, [1989] IRLR 513, EAT. In determining whether an employee has been dishonest, it has been suggested that the employer should apply the test laid down in *R v Ghosh* [1982] QB 1053, [1982] 2 All ER 689, CA (see CRIMINAL LAW vol 25 (2010) PARA 279): *John Lewis plc v Coyne* [2001] IRLR 139, EAT. As to theft from customers see *Rentokil Ltd v Mackin* [1989] IRLR 286, EAT.

25 *Dalton v Burton's Gold Medal Biscuits Ltd* [1974] IRLR 45, NIRC; *Meridian Ltd v Gomersall* [1977] ICR 597, [1977] IRLR 425, EAT; *Stewart v Western SMT Co Ltd* [1978] IRLR 553, EAT; *Elliott Bros (London) Ltd v Colverd* [1979] IRLR 92, EAT.

26 *UBAF Bank Ltd v Davis* [1978] IRLR 442, EAT; *Martin v Solus Schall* [1979] IRLR 7, EAT;
    W & J Wass Ltd v Binns [1982] ICR 486, [1982] IRLR 283, CA; *Brandon and Goold v Murphy
    Bros* [1983] IRLR 54, EAT.
27 *Rasool v Hepworth Pipe Co Ltd* [1980] ICR 494, sub nom *Rasool v Hepworth Pipe Co Ltd
    (No 2)* [1980] IRLR 137, EAT; *London Transport Executive v Clarke* [1981] ICR 355, [1981]
    IRLR 166, CA; *Hutchinson v Enfield Rolling Mills Ltd* [1981] IRLR 318, EAT; *Tracey v Zest
    Equipment Co Ltd* [1982] ICR 481, [1982] IRLR 268, EAT; *Murray Mackinnon v Forno* [1983]
    IRLR 7, EAT (dismissal unfair on the facts); *Lynock v Cereal Packaging Ltd* [1988] ICR 670,
    [1988] IRLR 510, EAT; *Williams v Cheshire Fire and Rescue Service* [2008] All ER (D) 296
    (Jul), EAT. As to guidance on dealing with absence see Discipline and Grievances at work: The
    ACAS guide (September 2014), pp 11–12, Appendix 4 (dealing with absence); and note 8.
28 *Golden Cross Hire Co Ltd v Lovell* [1979] IRLR 267, EAT. However, detriment to the employer
    needs to be shown (*Nova Plastics Ltd v Froggatt* [1982] IRLR 146, EAT) and it may not be
    enough that the employee is seeking work with a competitor (*Harris and Russell Ltd v Slingsby*
    [1973] 3 All ER 31, [1973] ICR 454, NIRC) or intending to leave to set up a competing business
    (*Laughton v Bapp Industrial Supplies Ltd* [1986] ICR 634, [1986] IRLR 245, EAT); c f where
    the employee actually seeks to obtain orders in competition with the employer in preparation for
    leaving (*Adamson v B & L Cleaning Services Ltd* [1995] IRLR 193, EAT). Even if the employer
    dismisses the employee unfairly under the Employment Rights Act 1996 s 98 (see PARA 765), the
    employer can still take advantage of a restraint of trade clause: see *Lonmar Global Risks Ltd
    (formerly SBJ Global Risks Ltd) v West* [2010] EWHC 2878 (QB), [2011] IRLR 138; and PARA
    19. As to restraint of trade clauses and 'garden leave clauses' see PARA 19; and as to the implied
    duty of fidelity see PARAS 67–71.
29 *MacKellar v Bolton* [1979] IRLR 59, EAT. If not wilful, inadequacy lies more under the heading
    of incapability: see PARA 773.
30 *Denco Ltd v Joinson* [1992] 1 All ER 463, [1991] ICR 172, EAT. See also *Thomas v Hillingdon
    London Borough Council* (2002) Times, 4 October, [2002] All ER (D) 202 (Sep), EAT
    (accessing pornography on office computer during working hours amounted to gross
    misconduct).

777. Procedural fairness in cases of misconduct. Misconduct is the area to
which disciplinary procedures have most obvious relevance[1]. Procedural fairness
is, therefore, of particular significance[2] and, except in a case of gross misconduct
where summary dismissal is warranted[3], the application of a system of warnings
is particularly appropriate[4]. There is, however, no longer a statutory procedure
which is required to conform to minimum standards where its application could
lead to dismissal[5]; the current approach to disciplinary and grievance procedures
is one that involves less emphasis on mechanics and statutory requirements and
more emphasis on flexibility and non-statutory and non-mandatory guidance[6].
Where the employer is investigating a serious allegation of misconduct, especially
of a criminal nature, it may be appropriate to suspend the employee with pay for
a short period while the investigation is undertaken[7].
   Once fair procedures have been applied and followed, the employer must
decide whether dismissal is a fair sanction, taking into account all the
circumstances including any matters in mitigation, particularly the employee's
length of service[8]. When deciding on whether a dismissal was fair, a tribunal in a
misconduct case may be faced with a difficult balance between certainty of
treatment and flexibility of treatment[9], and in this area it is particularly
important that the tribunal does not simply substitute its own view for that of
the employer, but rather applies the correct 'range of reasonable responses' test[10].
Special consideration should be given to the way in which disciplinary
procedures operate in the case of trade union officials, since disciplinary action
against a trade union official can lead to a serious dispute if it is seen as an attack
on the union's functions[11]. However, normal disciplinary standards apply to their
conduct as employees[12], and where disciplinary action is being considered
against an employee who is a trade union representative the normal disciplinary
procedure should be followed, although it might be advisable, depending on the

circumstances, to discuss the matter at an early stage with an official employed by the union, after obtaining the employee's agreement[13].

1   Disciplinary situations may arise from cases of misconduct and/or poor performance. As to guidance and rules relating to performance standards generally see Discipline and Grievances at work: The ACAS guide (September 2014), pp 11–12, Appendix 4 (dealing with absence). As to the status of the ACAS guidance see PARA 701; and as to ACAS Codes of Practice generally see PARAS 1223–1224.

2   See PARA 768.

3   See PARAS 743–746.

4   The law on warnings in misconduct cases has been summarised in *Wincanton Group plc v Stone* [2013] IRLR 178, EAT. Although an employer should not normally dismiss in reliance on an expired warning for misconduct, that expired warning may be relevant in other ways, eg in deciding whether there are mitigating factors: *Webb v Airbus UK Ltd* [2008] EWCA Civ 49, [2008] ICR 561, [2008] IRLR 309. See also *Davies v Sandwell MBC* [2013] EWCA Civ 135, [2013] IRLR 374 (final warning properly taken into account by employer in dismissing employee, provided that the warning was issued in good faith, that there were at least prima facie grounds for imposing it and that it was not manifestly inappropriate to issue it); *Santos v Disotto Food Ltd* [2014] All ER (D) 139 (Apr), EAT (in finding that the employee had been dismissed for misconduct, not for lack of capability, and that the misconduct had been so slight a matter that no reasonable employer could have reasonably contemplated dismissing an employee because of that matter, tribunal had minimised importance of earlier warnings given to employee and taken a view that was unreasonably dismissive of the employer's own view of the history). There may be cases, however, where on the facts a warning would be otiose: see PARA 707.

5   See PARAS 698, 768. A failure to follow the statutory dismissal, disciplinary and grievance procedures, where they applied, could have had a number of legal implications for the parties: see PARAS 698.

6   See PARA 700 et seq. A failure to follow any part of the recommended guidance does not, in itself, render a person or organisation liable to proceedings: see PARA 701.

7   See Discipline and Grievances at work: The ACAS guide (September 2014), pp 17–18. In cases where a period of suspension with pay is considered necessary, this period should be as brief as possible, should be kept under review and it should be made clear that this suspension is not considered a disciplinary action: see ACAS Code of Practice 1: Disciplinary and Grievance Procedures (2009) para 8; and PARA 703.

8   *Johnson Matthey Metals Ltd v Harding* [1978] IRLR 248, EAT; *Trusthouse Forte (Catering) Ltd v Adonis* [1984] IRLR 382, EAT. In a case of gross misconduct, length of service may, however, become immaterial: *AEI Cables Ltd v McLay* [1980] IRLR 84, Ct of Sess; and see *British Leyland (UK) Ltd v Swift* [1981] IRLR 91, CA.

9   See PARA 767 note 4.

10   See PARA 767. For an example see *Rentokil Ltd v Mackin* [1989] IRLR 286, EAT; *Small v London Ambulance Service NHS Trust* [2009] EWCA Civ 220, [2009] All ER (D) 179 (Mar).

11   See ACAS Code of Practice 1: Disciplinary and Grievance Procedures (2009) para 29; and PARA 709. See also Discipline and Grievances at work: The ACAS guide (September 2014), pp 19, 35; and see note 7.

12   *Fowler v Cammell Laird (Shipbuilders) Ltd* [1973] IRLR 72.

13   See ACAS Code of Practice 1: Disciplinary and Grievance Procedures (2009) para 29; and PARA 709. See also Discipline and Grievances at work: The ACAS guide (September 2014), pp 19, 35; and see *Donnelly v London Brick Co Ltd* [1974] IRLR 331. See also note 7.

778.   Bearing of criminal offences on decision to dismiss.   An employee should not be dismissed or otherwise disciplined solely because he or she has been charged with or convicted of a criminal offence; the question to be asked in such cases is whether the employee's conduct or conviction merits action because of its employment implications[1].

Where the alleged misconduct concerns a criminal offence committed at work (often, but not necessarily, theft), the onus remains on the employer to conduct reasonable investigations and to make the decision whether to dismiss[2]. Since the test is whether the employer had a genuine and reasonable belief in guilt[3], not whether he has conclusively proved the employee to be guilty, the fact that the employee has subsequently been acquitted of the criminal charge is not relevant[4]. Where the misconduct is the subject of police inquiries and possible charges, it is still proper for the employer to make his own inquiries of the employee or his lawyers[5]; the employee should be given an opportunity to make his case in the internal proceedings[6], but failure to do so does not preclude the employer from proceeding with a potentially fair dismissal if the facts as known to him warrant it, even where the employee's silence is due to impending criminal proceedings[7]. Information provided by the police from their investigations may be taken into consideration by the employer when deciding whether to dismiss[8]; but the police should not be involved in the conducting of internal disciplinary procedures[9].

Criminal offences outside employment should not be considered as automatic reasons for dismissal[10]; the main consideration should be whether the offence is one that makes the individual unsuitable for his type of work[11]. An employee should not be dismissed solely because a charge against him is pending or because he is absent through having been remanded in custody[12].

1   See Discipline and Grievances at work: The ACAS guide (September 2014), pp 35–36. As to the status of the ACAS guidance see PARA 701; and as to ACAS Codes of Practice generally see PARAS 1223–1224. As to spent convictions see PARA 779. See also the text and notes 10–12.
    Nevertheless, a failure by an employee to inform his employer of criminal charges against him, even if subsequently dropped, may constitute an abuse of trust sufficiently serious to justify summary dismissal: *Leach v Office of Communications* [2012] EWCA Civ 959, [2012] ICR 1269, [2012] IRLR 839 (employee had concealed from his employer the fact that his case involving allegations of child abuse had been in the Cambodian courts and press, and had lied to his employer about the reason why he was unable to start work on the appointed date). See also note 11.
2   As to the general approach to investigation see PARA 776. There is no single, overall principle here, but rather a spectrum of possibilities; in practice, most cases will still require employer investigation, even if the police are involved (*Lovie Ltd v Anderson* [1999] IRLR 164, EAT); and serious allegations of criminal misbehaviour require nothing less than an even-handed approach by employers to the investigation, especially where, as is frequently the situation, the employee is denied the opportunity of being able to contact potentially relevant witnesses by reason of his suspension (*A v B* [2003] IRLR 405, EAT). Where the police are called in they should not be asked to conduct any investigation on behalf of the employer, nor should they be present at any meeting or disciplinary meeting: see Discipline and Grievances at work: The ACAS guide (September 2014), p 36.
3   *British Home Stores Ltd v Burchell* [1980] ICR 303n, [1978] IRLR 379, EAT; and see PARA 776.
4   *Da Costa v Optolis* [1977] IRLR 178, EAT; *Harris (Ipswich) Ltd v Harrison* [1978] ICR 1256, [1978] IRLR 382, EAT; *Dhaliwal v British Airways Board, British Airways Board v Day* [1985] ICR 513, EAT (police statements ruled inadmissible by a criminal court properly relied on by employer when deciding whether to dismiss).
    Equally, it is not sufficient to defer the decision, in order to dismiss automatically, if the employee is later convicted of the offence by a court: *McLaren v National Coal Board* [1988] ICR 370, [1988] IRLR 215, CA. Where the employee's conduct requires prompt attention, the employer need not await the outcome of the prosecution before taking fair and reasonable action either: see Discipline and Grievances at work: The ACAS guide (September 2014), p 36.
5   *Harris (Ipswich) Ltd v Harrison* [1978] ICR 1256, [1978] IRLR 382, EAT, not following *Carr v Alexander Russell Ltd* [1979] ICR 469n, [1976] IRLR 220, EAT (a Scottish decision which was followed in *Conway v Matthew Wright & Nephew Ltd* [1977] IRLR 89, EAT, and *Parker v Clifford Dunn Ltd* [1979] ICR 463, [1979] IRLR 56, EAT); and see *Tesco Group of Companies (Holdings) Ltd v Hill* [1977] IRLR 63, EAT. Where, however, an employee is convicted of a criminal offence at work after changing his plea to 'guilty', it is perverse to suggest that a reasonable employer would have made inquiries of the employee's legal adviser regarding the circumstances in which the plea was changed: *British Gas plc v McCarrick* [1991] IRLR 305, CA.
6   *Ladbroke Racing Ltd v Mason* [1978] ICR 49, EAT.
7   *Harris v Courage (Eastern) Ltd* [1981] ICR 496, [1981] IRLR 153, EAT.
    Where an employee, charged with or convicted of a criminal offence, refuses or is unable to cooperate with the employer's disciplinary investigations and proceedings, this should not deter

an employer from taking action; the employee should be advised in writing that unless further information is provided, a disciplinary decision will be taken on the basis of the information available and could result in dismissal: see Discipline and Grievances at work: The ACAS guide (September 2014), p 36.

8 *Carr v Alexander Russell Ltd* [1979] ICR 469n, [1976] IRLR 220, EAT; *Parker v Clifford Dunn Ltd* [1979] ICR 463, [1979] IRLR 56, EAT; *Rhondda Cynon Taf County Borough Council v Close* [2008] IRLR 868, EAT.

9 *Read v Phoenix Preservation Ltd* [1985] ICR 164, [1985] IRLR 93, EAT. See also note 2.

10 If the employee is imprisoned, that may on the facts frustrate the contract: see PARA 729.

11 The 'range of reasonable responses' test (see PARA 767) is particularly important in this context, especially where the employer claims to be taking into consideration the potential reaction of customers or clients (see also PARA 766 note 7). Where an employee has been found guilty of, or has pleaded guilty to, a criminal offence outside work, it will normally be reasonable for the employer to rely on that for reasonable belief in guilt; the question then becomes the reasonableness of the decision to dismiss in the light of that: *P v Nottinghamshire County Council* [1992] ICR 706, [1992] IRLR 362, CA; *Secretary of State for Scotland v Campbell* [1992] IRLR 263, EAT. This may particularly be the case where the employee, in a position of trust at work, is convicted of an offence of dishonesty outside work: *Moore v C & A Modes* [1981] IRLR 71, EAT. Sexual offences committed outside employment have fallen into this category on the basis that, depending on the nature of the employment, they may cause an employee to be viewed as a potential risk, especially where children are involved: *Nottinghamshire County Council v Bowly* [1978] IRLR 252, EAT; *Wiseman v Salford City Council* [1981] IRLR 202, EAT (in both cases, employees cautioned for gross indecency following incidents outside work). However, it has been suggested that these cases require re-examination in the light of an employee's rights under the Convention for the Protection of Human Rights and Fundamental Freedoms (Rome, 25 March 1957; TS 1 (1973); Cmnd 5179) and the Human Rights Act 1998 (see RIGHTS AND FREEDOMS vol 88A (2013) PARAS 14, 88): *Pay v Lancashire Probation Service* [2004] ICR 187 at 198, [2004] IRLR 129 at 134, EAT, per McMullen J. Notwithstanding this, sexual offences may still be relevant on other grounds: see eg *X v Y* [2004] EWCA Civ 662, [2004] ICR 1634, [2004] IRLR 625 (employee dismissed for gross misconduct on the basis that he had committed a significant criminal offence which he had deliberately decided not to disclose); and *Leach v Office of Communications* [2012] EWCA Civ 959, [2012] ICR 1269, [2012] IRLR 839 (cited in note 1). As to drug offences see *Norfolk County Council v Bernard* [1979] IRLR 220, EAT (teacher's dismissal for possession of cannabis unfair); *Mathewson v RB Wilson Dental Laboratory Ltd* [1988] IRLR 512, EAT (dental technician's dismissal for possession of cannabis fair).

An employee who has been charged with, or convicted of, a criminal offence may become unacceptable to colleagues, resulting in workforce pressure to dismiss and threats of industrial action: see Discipline and Grievances at work: The ACAS guide (September 2014), pp 36–37. Employers should bear in mind that they may have to justify the reasonableness of any decision to dismiss and that an employment tribunal will ignore threats of, and actual industrial action when determining the fairness of a decision: see the Employment Rights Act 1996 s 107; and PARA 771.

12 See *Securicor Guarding Ltd v R* [1994] IRLR 633, EAT (employee should not be dismissed solely because a criminal charge is pending).

Where the nature of the alleged offence may not justify disciplinary action, eg off-duty conduct which has no bearing on employment, but the employee may not be available for work because he or she is in custody or on remand, employers should decide whether, in the light of the needs of the organisation, the employee's job can be held open; where a criminal conviction leads, eg to the loss of a licence, so that continued employment in a particular job would be illegal, employers should consider whether alternative work is appropriate and available: see Discipline and Grievances at work: The ACAS guide (September 2014), p 36.

779. Rehabilitation of Offenders Act 1974. In normal circumstances a dismissal for obtaining employment by concealing a previous conviction is fair[1]. Some convictions may, however, become spent under the Rehabilitation of Offenders Act 1974[2]; and where that is the case:

(1) where a question seeking information with respect to a person's previous convictions, cautions, offences, conduct or circumstances is put to an individual, the question is to be treated as not relating to spent convictions or spent cautions or to any circumstances ancillary to spent

convictions or spent cautions and he is not to be subjected to any liability or otherwise prejudiced in law by reason of any failure to acknowledge or disclose a spent convictions or spent caution or any circumstances ancillary to a spent convictions or spent caution in his answer to the question[3];

(2)   a conviction or caution which has become spent or any circumstances ancillary thereto, or any failure to disclose a spent conviction or caution or any such circumstances, is or are not a proper ground for dismissing or excluding a person from any office, profession, occupation or employment, or for prejudicing him in any occupation or employment[4].

There are exclusions from heads (1) and (2) above in respect of certain specified professions, employments, offices or occupations[5].

There is, however, no express statutory provision that a dismissal for failure to disclose a spent conviction is unfair[6].

1   *Torr v British Railways Board* [1977] ICR 785, [1977] IRLR 184, EAT. As to criminal offences committed, or alleged to have been committed, by an employee while with his current employer see PARA 778.

2   See SENTENCING AND DISPOSITION OF OFFENDERS vol 92 (2010) PARA 660 et seq.

3   See the Rehabilitation of Offenders Act 1974 s 4(2); and SENTENCING AND DISPOSITION OF OFFENDERS vol 92 (2010) PARA 664. As to the circumstances in which s 4(2) does not apply see SENTENCING AND DISPOSITION OF OFFENDERS vol 92 (2010) PARA 664.

4   See the Rehabilitation of Offenders Act 1974 s 4(3)(b); and SENTENCING AND DISPOSITION OF OFFENDERS vol 92 (2010) PARA 666. As to the exceptions see SENTENCING AND DISPOSITION OF OFFENDERS vol 92 (2010) PARA 685 et seq.

5   As to excepted professions etc see SENTENCING AND DISPOSITION OF OFFENDERS vol 92 (2010) PARA 687 et seq.

6   A finding of unfairness by a tribunal in such circumstances was, however, upheld in *Property Guards Ltd v Taylor and Kershaw* [1982] IRLR 175, EAT (the statutory provisions cannot be 'disapplied' by the employer arguing that the employee was in a position of special trust and so should have revealed even a spent conviction; the only persons in such a category are those expressly covered by the statutory exceptions (see heads (1) and (2) in the text)). See also *Hendry v Scottish Liberal Club* [1977] IRLR 5 (spent conviction for possession of cannabis not a proper ground for dismissal). *Quaere* whether there is ever a positive duty on the employee to disclose his own previous misconduct: see PARA 67.

D. REDUNDANCY

780. Fairness of dismissal for reason related to employee's redundancy. A dismissal[1] is not unfair if it is shown by the employer[2] to have been imposed for the reason that the employee[3] was redundant and if it was reasonable in the circumstances[4]. The receipt of a redundancy payment[5] does not preclude the employee from also claiming that his dismissal was unfair[6], though in such a claim the statutory presumption of redundancy[7] does not apply[8].

The decision whether to make redundancies lies with the employer, and that aspect cannot be challenged by the employee in an unfair dismissal claim[9]. However, the procedure and effects of a redundancy can be challenged as unfair by a dismissed employee:

(1)   if he was selected for dismissal for a specified reason relating to trade union membership[10] or in specified circumstances[11];

(2)   if the redundancy was badly handled and, therefore, unfair[12] on general principles[13];

(3)   if the redundancy was discriminatory[14], especially in relation to the criteria used to determine who was selected for dismissal[15].

1   As to the meaning of 'dismissal' see PARA 762.

2   As to the meaning of 'employer' see PARA 2.
3   As to the meaning of 'employee' see PARA 2.
4   See the Employment Rights Act 1996 s 98(1)(b), (2)(c), (4); and PARA 765.
5   As to the meaning of 'redundancy payment' see PARA 836.
6   *Clarkson International Tools Ltd v Short* [1973] ICR 191, [1973] IRLR 90, NIRC; *Hinckley and Bosworth Borough Council v Ainscough* [1979] ICR 590, [1979] IRLR 224, EAT. A tribunal should, however, be wary of a claim for unfair dismissal that is merely a way of 'topping up' a redundancy payment with the extra compensation for unfair dismissal: *Clarkson International Tools Ltd v Short*; *Lifeguard Assurance Ltd v Zadrozny* [1977] IRLR 56, EAT; *British United Shoe Machinery Co Ltd v Clarke* [1978] ICR 70, [1977] IRLR 297, EAT.
7   Ie made for the purposes of a reference to an employment tribunal, by virtue of the Employment Rights Act 1996 s 163(2): see PARA 886.
8   *Midland Foot Comfort Centre Ltd v Richmond* [1973] 2 All ER 294, sub nom *Midland Foot Comfort Centre v Moppett* [1973] ICR 219, NIRC.
9   *Moon v Homeworthy Furniture (Northern) Ltd* [1977] ICR 117, [1976] IRLR 298, EAT; *James W Cook & Co (Wivenhoe) Ltd v Tipper* [1990] ICR 716, [1990] IRLR 386, CA. A tribunal may, however, require to be satisfied, at the least, that the employer's decision was genuine, which may mean adducing some evidence of objective need: *Ladbroke Courage Holidays Ltd v Asten* [1981] IRLR 59, EAT; *Orr v Vaughan* [1981] IRLR 63, EAT. The employee may seek to show that the redundancy was a sham; and for the possibility of an extension of the time limit in order to do so see *Churchill v Yeates & Sons Ltd* [1983] ICR 380, [1983] IRLR 187, EAT; *Machine Tool Industry Research Association v Simpson* [1988] ICR 558, [1988] IRLR 212, CA. Because a tribunal is not entitled to substitute its own view of what should have happened had an employer acted fairly (see PARA 767), it has to consider whether employees might have been dismissed fairly and, if it found that there had been a chance that they would have been dismissed, then, applying the principle in *Polkey v AE Dayton Services Ltd* [1988] AC 344, [1988] ICR 142, HL (see PARA 768), it was required to fix a percentage and to apply a reduction: *Wincanton Group Ltd v Cort* [2014] All ER (D) 163 (Apr), EAT (tribunal had not found that the redundancy exercise had been in any way a sham, or that there had been an ulterior motive, or that the employer had deliberately set out to dismiss either or both of the employee; while it had been for the tribunal to check that the criteria for selection given in evidence by the employer had been cogent and could be described as fair, it had not been for them to go further and to decide that a different selection could have been made). Even if a business reorganisation does not involve redundancy, a dismissal pursuant to it may still be fair, as being for 'some other substantial reason': see PARA 802.
10 Ie a reason specified in the Trade Union and Labour Relations (Consolidation) Act 1992 s 153: see PARA 1056.
11 Ie specified in the Employment Rights Act 1996 s 105: see PARA 781.
12 Ie under the Employment Rights Act 1996 s 98(4): see PARA 765.
13 *Bessenden Properties Ltd v Corness* [1977] ICR 821n, [1974] IRLR 338, CA. See further PARA 782.
14 There is no provision in the Employment Rights Act 1996 Pt X (ss 94–134A) (unfair dismissal: see also PARAS 757 et seq, 781 et seq) specifically stating that a discriminatory redundancy is unfair, but it is submitted that it could be so on general principles: see further DISCRIMINATION vol 33 (2013) PARA 1 et seq. See also PARA 608. As to the modification of Pt X in relation to governing bodies of schools having a right to a delegated budget, acting in the exercise of their employment powers, see EDUCATION vol 35 (2011) PARA 355 et seq; and as to the modification of Pt X in relation to persons holding ecclesiastical office under common tenure see the Ecclesiastical Offices (Terms of Service) Regulations 2009, SI 2009/2108, reg 33; and ECCLESIASTICAL LAW vol 34 (2011) PARA 407.
15 *Clarke v Eley (IMI) Kynoch Ltd, Eley (IMI) Kynoch Ltd v Powell* [1983] ICR 165, [1982] IRLR 482, EAT (the selection of part-timers first was held to be unlawful indirect sex discrimination, even though jointly agreed with the trade union and, under the unfair dismissal rules alone, probably fair); but cf the decision to the contrary on the same issue in *Kidd v DRG Ltd (UK)* [1985] ICR 405, [1985] IRLR 190, EAT; and see *Bascetta v Abbey National plc* [2009] All ER (D) 153 (Mar), EAT (employee selected for redundancy who brought a claim alleging unfair dismissal and victimisation was unsuccessful on appeal by the employer as the tribunal had based its decision on an issue which had not been raised explicitly by the employee). See also note 9. Selection on the basis, often adopted, of last-in-first-out ('LIFO') may not constitute unlawful sex discrimination: see *Clarke v Eley (IMI) Kynoch Ltd, Eley (IMI) Kynoch Ltd v Powell* at 175 and 487, obiter, per Browne-Wilkinson P. Moreover, it has also been held that the use of LIFO as one of several criteria does not constitute age discrimination: *Rolls Royce plc v UNITE the Union* [2009] EWCA Civ 387, [2010] 1 WLR 318, [2010] ICR 1, [2009] IRLR 576

(principle may be applied to serve legitimate aims such as rewarding loyalty and maintaining a stable workforce). The use of LIFO alone would now have to be considered and justified under the Equality Act 2010: see further DISCRIMINATION vol 33 (2013) PARA 1 et seq.

781.   Redundancy dismissals unfair by statute.   An employee[1] who is dismissed[2] is to be regarded[3] as unfairly dismissed if:

(1)   the reason (or, if more than one, the principal reason) for the dismissal is that the employee was redundant[4];

(2)   it is shown that the circumstances constituting the redundancy applied equally to one or more other employees in the same undertaking[5] who held positions[6] similar to that held by the employee and who have not been dismissed by the employer[7]; and

(3)   it is shown that any of heads (a) to (z) below applies[8], namely:

(a)   if the reason (or, if more than one, the principal reason) for which the employee was selected for dismissal was one of those[9] applicable to jury service cases[10];

(b)   if the reason (or, if more than one, the principal reason) for which the employee was selected for dismissal was one of those[11] applicable to health and safety cases[12];

(c)   if either: (i) the employee was a protected shop worker[13] or an opted-out shop worker[14], or a protected betting worker[15] or an opted-out betting worker[16], and the reason (or, if more than one, the principal reason) for which the employee was selected for dismissal was one applicable[17] to refusal to do Sunday work[18]; or (ii) the employee was a shop worker or a betting worker and the reason (or, if more than one, the principal reason) for which the employee was selected for dismissal was one applicable[19] to refusal to do Sunday work[20];

(d)   if the reason (or, if more than one, the principal reason) for which the employee was selected for dismissal was one of those applicable[21] to working time cases[22];

(e)   as from a day to be appointed[23], if the reason (or, if more than one, the principal reason) for which the employee was selected for dismissal was one applicable[24] to an employee's participation in education or training[25];

(f)   if the reason (or, if more than one, the principal reason) for which the employee was selected for dismissal was one of those applicable[26] to acting as trustee of an occupational pension scheme[27];

(g)   if the reason (or, if more than one, the principal reason) for which the employee was selected for dismissal was one of those applicable[28] to acting, or seeking election, as an employee representative[29];

(h)   if the reason (or, if more than one, the principal reason) for which the employee was selected for dismissal was one of those applicable[30] to making a protected disclosure[31];

(i)   if the reason (or, if more than one, the principal reason) for which the employee was selected for dismissal was one of those applicable[32] to asserting a statutory right[33];

(j)   if the reason (or, if more than one, the principal reason) for which the employee was selected for dismissal was one of those applicable[34] to national minimum wage cases[35];

(k)   if the reason (or, if more than one, the principal reason) for which the employee was selected for dismissal was one of those applicable[36] to tax credit cases[37];

(l)   if the reason (or, if more than one, the principal reason) for which the employee was selected for dismissal was one of those applicable[38] to flexible working cases[39];

(m) if the reason (or, if more than one, the principal reason) for which the employee was selected for dismissal was one of those applicable[40] to applications for employer support for employee study and training[41];

(n)   if the reason (or, if more than one, the principal reason) for which the employee was selected for dismissal was one of those applicable[42] to participating in protected industrial action[43];

(o)   if the reason (or, if more than one, the principal reason) for which the employee was selected for dismissal was one of those applicable[44] to exercising functions or rights in relation to a European Works Council[45];

(p)   if the reason (or, if more than one, the principal reason) for which the employee was selected for dismissal was one of those applicable[46] in relation to part-time workers[47];

(q)   if the reason (or, if more than one, the principal reason) for which the employee was selected for dismissal was one of those applicable[48] in relation to fixed-term employees[49];

(r)   if the reason (or, if more than one, the principal reason) for which the employee of a European public limited-liability company was selected for dismissal was one of those applicable[50] to acting, or seeking election, as a member of a special negotiating body or of a representative body, as an information and consultation representative, or as an employee member in a supervisory or administrative organ[51];

(s)   if the reason (or, if more than one, the principal reason) for which the employee was selected for dismissal was one of those applicable[52] in relation to information and consultation representatives[53];

(t)   if the reason (or, if more than one, the principal reason) for which the employee was selected for dismissal was one of those applicable[54] in relation to his functions or activities as a representative consulted about an occupational or personal pension scheme[55];

(u)   if the reason (or, if more than one, the principal reason) for which the employee was selected for dismissal was one of those applicable[56] in relation to the involvement of employees in a European Co-operative Society[57];

(v)   if the reason (or, if more than one, the principal reason) for which the employee was selected for dismissal was one of those applicable[58] in relation to pension enrolment[59];

(w) if the reason (or, if more than one, the principal reason) for which the employee was selected for dismissal was one of those applicable[60] in relation to cross-border mergers[61];

(x)   if the reason (or, if more than one, the principal reason) for which the employee was selected for dismissal was one applicable[62] in relation to involvement of employees in a European Public Limited-Liability Company[63];

(y)   if the reason (or, if more than one, the principal reason) for which the employee was selected for dismissal related to a prohibited list and the required condition[64] was met[65];

(z)   if the reason (or, if more than one, the principal reason) for which an agency worker who is an employee was selected for dismissal was one of those applicable[66] in relation to agency workers[67].

1   As to the meaning of 'employee' see PARA 2.
2   As to the meaning of 'dismissal' see PARA 762.
3   Ie for the purposes of the Employment Rights Act 1996 Pt X (ss 94–134A) (unfair dismissal: see also PARAS 757 et seq, 782 et seq). As to the modification of Pt X in relation to governing bodies of schools having a right to a delegated budget, acting in the exercise of their employment powers, see EDUCATION vol 35 (2011) PARA 355 et seq; and as to the modification of Pt X in relation to persons holding ecclesiastical office under common tenure see the Ecclesiastical Offices (Terms of Service) Regulations 2009, SI 2009/2108, reg 33; and ECCLESIASTICAL LAW vol 34 (2011) PARA 407. Where a dismissal is unfair under the Employment Rights Act 1996 s 105, the qualifying period for unfair dismissal does not apply: see s 108(3)(h); and PARA 758 note 9. For the purposes of s 36(2)(b) (employment as a shop worker or a betting worker: see PARA 321) or s 41(1)(b) (opted-out shop worker or betting worker: see PARA 323), the appropriate date in relation to s 105 is the effective date of termination: s 105(8). As to the meaning of 'effective date of termination' see PARA 764.
4   Employment Rights Act 1996 s 105(1)(a). For the purposes of Pt X, 'redundancy case' means a case where s 105(1)(a) and s 105(1)(b) (see head (2) in the text) are satisfied: see s 105(9). As to the meaning of 'redundancy' see PARA 870.
5   There is no statutory definition of 'undertaking' for these purposes. Common organisational factors may be important: *Gargrave v Hotel and Catering Industry Training Board* [1974] IRLR 85, NIRC; *Oxley v Tarmac Roadstone Holdings Ltd* [1975] IRLR 100; *Kapur v Shields* [1976] 1 All ER 873, [1976] ICR 26; *Bray v Tarmac Construction Ltd* [1976] IRLR 86.
6   As to the meaning of 'position' see PARA 765 note 13. A similar job title does not necessarily mean similar positions: *Simpson v Roneo Ltd* [1972] IRLR 5. Different classes of employee may occupy different positions: *Powers and Villiers v A Clarke & Co (Smethwick) Ltd* [1981] IRLR 483, EAT.
7   Employment Rights Act 1996 s 105(1)(b). See note 4. As to the meaning of 'employer' see PARA 2.
8   See the Employment Rights Act 1996 s 105(1)(c) (substituted by SI 2006/2059; and amended by SI 2007/2974; SI 2010/93). In addition to the specific provisions cited in heads (a) to (z) in the text, dismissal for redundancy is also unfair where the reason for selection relates to union membership or activities (see the Trade Union and Labour Relations (Consolidation) Act 1992 s 153; and PARA 1056), or relates to actions taken in respect of the statutory recognition procedure (see s 70A, Sch A1 para 162; and PARA 1171).
9   Ie the reasons specified in the Employment Rights Act 1996 s 98B(1) (unless the case is one to which s 98B(2) applies): see PARA 785.
10 Employment Rights Act 1996 s 105(2A) (added by the Employment Relations Act 2004 s 40(5)).
11 Ie the reasons specified in the Employment Rights Act 1996 s 100(1), read with s 100(2), (3): see PARA 786.
12 Employment Rights Act 1996 s 105(3). Where s 105(3) applies, there is no statutory limit on the compensatory award: see s 124(1A); and PARA 823 note 6.
13 As to the meaning of 'protected shop worker' see PARA 321; and as to the meaning of 'shop worker' see PARA 321 note 1.
14 As to the meaning of 'opted-out shop worker' see PARA 323.
15 As to the meaning of 'protected betting worker' see PARA 321; and as to the meaning of 'betting worker' see PARA 321 note 2.
16 As to the meaning of 'opted-out betting worker' see PARA 323.
17 Ie the reason specified in the Employment Rights Act 1996 s 101(1), read with s 101(2): see PARA 787.
18 Employment Rights Act 1996 s 105(4)(a). See also s 105(8) (cited in note 3).
19 Ie the reason specified in the Employment Rights Act 1996 s 101(3): see PARA 787.
20 Employment Rights Act 1996 s 105(4)(b). See also s 105(8) (cited in note 3).

21 Ie the reasons specified in the Employment Rights Act 1996 s 101A: see PARA 788.

22 Employment Rights Act 1996 s 105(4A) (added by SI 1998/1833).

23 As from a day to be appointed under the Education and Skills Act 2008 s 173(4), the Employment Rights Act 1996 s 105(4B) is prospectively added by the Education and Skills Act 2008 s 39(1), (3). However, at the date at which this volume states the law, no such day had been appointed.

24 Ie the reason specified in the Employment Rights Act 1996 s 101B: see PARA 789.

25 Employment Rights Act 1996 s 105(4B) (prospectively added: see note 23).

26 Ie the reason specified in the Employment Rights Act 1996 s 102(1): see PARA 790.

27 Employment Rights Act 1996 s 105(5).

28 Ie the reason specified in the Employment Rights Act 1996 s 103: see PARA 791.

29 Employment Rights Act 1996 s 105(6).

30 Ie the reason specified in the Employment Rights Act 1996 s 103A: see PARA 792.

31 Employment Rights Act 1996 s 105(6A) (added by the Public Interest Disclosure Act 1998 ss 6, 18(2)). Where the Employment Rights Act 1996 s 105(6A) applies, there is no statutory limit on the compensatory award: see s 124(1A); and PARA 823 note 6.

32 Ie the reason specified in the Employment Rights Act 1996 s 104(1), read with s 104(2), (3): see PARA 793.

33 Employment Rights Act 1996 s 105(7).

34 Ie the reason specified in the Employment Rights Act 1996 s 104A(1), read with s 104A(2): see PARA 794.

35 Employment Rights Act 1996 s 105(7A) (added by the National Minimum Wage Act 1998 s 25(2)).

36 Ie the reason specified in the Employment Rights Act 1996 s 104B(1), read with s 104B(2): see PARA 795.

37 Employment Rights Act 1996 s 105(7B) (added by the Tax Credits Act 2002 s 27, Sch 1 para 3(3)).

38 Ie the reason specified in the Employment Rights Act 1996 s 104C: see PARA 796.

39 Employment Rights Act 1996 s 105(7BA) (added by the Employment Relations Act 2004 s 41(4)).

40 Ie the reason specified in the Employment Rights Act 1996 s 104E: see PARA 798.

41 Employment Rights Act 1996 s 105(7BB) (added by the Apprenticeships, Skills, Children and Learning Act 2009 s 40(5), Sch 1 paras 1, 3).

   At the date at which this volume states the law, the Apprenticeships, Skills, Children and Learning Act 2009 s 40 has come into force for all purposes except in relation to small employers and their employees: see the Apprenticeships, Skills, Children and Learning Act 2009 (Commencement No 2 and Transitional and Saving Provisions) Order 2010, SI 2010/303, art 4, Sch 3. As to the meaning of 'small employer' for these purposes see PARA 328 note 1.

42 Ie the reason specified in the Trade Union and Labour Relations (Consolidation) Act 1992 s 238A(2), with s 238A(3)–(5) applying to the dismissal: see PARA 1352.

43 Employment Rights Act 1996 s 105(7C) (added by the Employment Relations Act 1999 Sch 5 para 5(1), (3)).

44 Ie the reasons specified in the Transnational Information and Consultation of Employees Regulations 1999, SI 1999/3323, reg 28(3) or (6), read with reg 28(4), (7): see PARA 1277.

45 Employment Rights Act 1996 s 105(7D) (added by SI 1999/3323).

46 Ie one of the reasons specified in the Part-time Workers (Prevention of Less Favourable Treatment) Regulations 2000, SI 2000/1551, reg 7(3), unless the case is one to which reg 7(4) applies: see PARA 78.

47 Employment Rights Act 1996 s 105(7E) (added by SI 2000/1551).

48 Ie one of the reasons specified in the Fixed-term Employees (Prevention of Less Favourable Treatment) Regulations 2002, SI 2002/2034, reg 6(3), unless the case is one to which reg 6(4) applies: see PARA 90.

49 Employment Rights Act 1996 s 105(7F) (added by SI 2002/2034).

50 Ie one of the reasons specified in the European Public Limited-Liability Company (Employee Involvement) (Great Britain) Regulations 2009, SI 2009/2401, reg 29(3) or (6), unless the case is one to which reg 29(4) applies: see PARA 1333.

51 Employment Rights Act 1996 s 105(7G) (added by SI 2004/2326); Interpretation Act 1978 s 17(2).

52 Ie one of the reasons specified in the Information and Consultation of Employees Regulations 2004, SI 2004/3426, reg 30(3) or (6), read with reg 30(4), (7): see PARA 1312.

53 Employment Rights Act 1996 s 105(7H) (added by SI 2004/3426).

54 Ie one of the reasons specified in the Occupational and Personal Pension Schemes (Consultation by Employers and Miscellaneous Amendment) Regulations 2006, SI 2006/349, Schedule para 5(3) or 5(5), read with Schedule para 5(6): see PERSONAL AND OCCUPATIONAL PENSIONS vol 80 (2013) PARA 486.
55 Employment Rights Act 1996 s 105(7I) (added by SI 2006/349).
56 Ie one of the reasons specified in the European Co-operative Society (Involvement of Employees) Regulations 2006, SI 2006/2059, reg 31(3) or 31(6), read with reg 30(4), (7): see PARA 1338.
57 Employment Rights Act 1996 s 105(7J) (added by SI 2006/2059).
58 Ie the reason specified in the Employment Rights Act 1996 s 104D(1), read with s 104D(2): see PARA 797.
59 Employment Rights Act 1996 s 105(7JA) (added by the Pensions Act 2008 s 57(1), (4)).
60 Ie one of the reasons specified in the Companies (Cross-Border Mergers) Regulations 2007, SI 2007/2974, reg 46, read with reg 46(3), (4), or in reg 47, read with reg 47(3): see COMPANIES vol 15 (2009) PARA 1451.
61 Employment Rights Act 1996 s 105(7K) (added by SI 2007/2974).
62 Ie one of the reasons specified in the European Public Limited-Liability Company (Employee Involvement) (Great Britain) Regulations 2009, SI 2009/2401, reg 29(3) or (6), read with reg 29(4), (7): see COMPANIES vol 14 (2009) PARA 5.
63 Employment Rights Act 1996 s 105(7L) (added by SI 2009/2401).
64 Ie the reason (or, if more than one, the principal reason) specified in the opening words of the Employment Rights Act 1996 s 104F(1), and the condition in s 104F(1)(a) or (b) was met : see PARA 799.
65 Employment Rights Act 1996 s 105(7M) (added by SI 2010/493).
66 Ie one of the reasons specified in the Agency Workers Regulations 2010, SI 2010/93, reg 17(3), unless the case is one to which reg 17(4) applies: see PARA 103.
67 Employment Rights Act 1996 s 105(7N) (added by SI 2010/93).

782.   Redundancy dismissals unfair on general principles. In addition to the statutory grounds[1], a dismissal for redundancy may be unfair on general principles[2]. It has been held that reasonable employers should seek to act in accordance with the following principles[3]:

(1)   the employer should seek to give as much warning as possible of impending redundancies so as to enable any employees who may be affected (and, where appropriate, their trade union) to take early steps to inform themselves of the relevant facts, consider possible alternative solutions and, if necessary, find alternative employment in the undertaking or elsewhere[4];

(2)   the employer should consult the employees and, where appropriate, their trade union[5] as to the best means by which the desired management result can be achieved fairly and with as little hardship to the employees as possible; in particular, the employer should seek to agree with the union the criteria to be applied in selecting the employees to be made redundant and, when a selection has been made, the employer should consider with the employees or their union whether the selection has been made in accordance with those criteria[6];

(3)   whether or not an agreement as to the criteria to be adopted has been agreed with a trade union, the employer should seek to establish criteria for selection which as far as possible do not depend solely on the opinion of the person making the selection but can be objectively checked against such things as attendance record, efficiency at the job, experience, or length of service[7];

(4)   the employer should seek to ensure that the selection is made fairly in accordance with these criteria and should consider any representations the employees and their trade union may make as to such selection[8];

(5)   the employer should seek to see whether, instead of dismissing an employee, he could offer him alternative employment[9].

In deciding on the fairness of a redundancy dismissal, it is important that the employment tribunal applies the correct 'range of reasonable responses' test[10].

1 See PARA 781.

2 See PARA 780. The guidelines set out in the text are now so well established that they should be considered by an employment tribunal, even if not specifically raised by the parties: *Langston v Cranfield University* [1998] IRLR 172, EAT. There are particularly useful summaries of the guidance in *Langston v Cranfield University* and in *Mugford v Midland Bank plc* [1997] ICR 399, [1997] IRLR 208, EAT.

3 *Williams v Compair Maxam Ltd* [1982] ICR 156, [1982] IRLR 83, EAT (approved and applied in *Grundy (Teddington) Ltd v Plummer* [1983] ICR 367, [1983] IRLR 98, EAT; *Robinson v Carrickfergus Borough Council* [1983] IRLR 122, NI CA; *Holden v Bradville Ltd* [1985] IRLR 483, EAT; *Dyke v Hereford and Worcester County Council* [1989] ICR 800, EAT; not followed in *Meikle v McPhail (Charleston Arms)* [1983] IRLR 351, EAT; *A Simpson & Son (Motors) v Reid and Findlater* [1983] IRLR 401, EAT; *Buchanan v Tilcon Ltd* [1983] IRLR 417, Ct of Sess; *Gray v Shetland Norse Preserving Co Ltd* [1985] IRLR 53, EAT; *F Lafferty Construction Ltd v Duthie* [1985] IRLR 487, EAT (all Scottish cases and most decisions involving small or non-unionised employers)). The decision in *Williams v Compair Maxam Ltd* was not specifically approved in *Polkey v AE Dayton Services Ltd* [1988] AC 344, [1988] ICR 142, HL, but both decisions were subsequently applied by the Court of Appeal in *Walls Meat Co Ltd v Selby* [1989] ICR 601, CA.

4 Consultation, as opposed to unilateral action by the employer, is one of the foundation stones of modern industrial relations practice: *Freud v Bentalls Ltd* [1983] ICR 77 at 82, [1982] IRLR 443 at 446, EAT, per Browne-Wilkinson P. It is envisaged with individual employees, not just with their union, which may in an appropriate case require a two-stage procedure: *Huddersfield Parcels Ltd v Sykes* [1981] IRLR 115, EAT; *Pink v White and White & Co (Earls Barton) Ltd* [1985] IRLR 489, EAT (lack of individual consultation immaterial on the facts); *Walls Meat Co v Selby* [1989] ICR 601, CA; *Rolls Royce Motor Cars Ltd v Price* [1993] IRLR 203, EAT. Consultation does not have to take place until the particular employee is identified as a candidate for redundancy; it may be sufficient for the employer then to give an opportunity for the employee to make representations: *Mugford v Midland Bank plc* [1997] ICR 399, [1997] IRLR 208, EAT. Consultation is separate from a mere warning of impending redundancies, and must be fair and genuine (*Rowell v Hubbard Group Services Ltd* [1995] IRLR 195, EAT); its importance at each significant stage of a redundancy cannot be over-emphasised (*Dyke v Hereford and Worcester County Council* [1989] ICR 800 at 807, EAT, per Wood P). The more nebulous the selection criteria, the greater the need for consultation: *Graham v ABF Ltd* [1986] IRLR 90, EAT. It is no defence for an employer to argue that lack of consultation would in fact have made no difference, unless a positive decision was taken to that effect at the time for some specific, reasonable reason (*Polkey v AE Dayton Services Ltd* [1988] AC 344, [1988] ICR 142, HL), though the scope of this exception is uncertain (contrast *Spink v Express Foods Group Ltd* [1990] IRLR 320, EAT, with *Duffy v Yeomans & Partners Ltd* [1995] ICR 1, [1994] IRLR 642, CA). If the employee would have been dismissed even after consultation, compensation may be limited to loss of wages during what should have been the consultation period: *Polkey v AE Dayton Services Ltd*; *Mining Supplies (Longwall) Ltd v Baker* [1988] ICR 676, [1988] IRLR 417, EAT; *Abbotts and Standley v Wesson-Glynwed Steels Ltd* [1982] IRLR 51, EAT; *Red Bank Manufacturing Co Ltd v Meadows* [1992] ICR 204, [1992] IRLR 209, EAT (*Red Bank Manufacturing Co Ltd v Meadows* applied in *Davies v J & R Farragher (t/a Potens)*[2009] All ER (D) 103 (Jan), EAT). There is, however, no rigid rule that compensation falls to be calculated only by assessing how long the consultation process should have taken, it being more accurate to say that the appropriate measure of loss is calculated according to the usual just and equitable principles: *Elkouil v Coney Island Ltd* [2002] IRLR 174, [2001] All ER (D) 181 (Nov), EAT (appropriate measure of compensation was ten weeks' pay, representing the employee's lost opportunity to look for another job, attributable to the employer's failure to warn him of impending redundancy at the time when the decision to dismiss him had been taken).

5 There is a statutory obligation to do so in the case of collective redundancies where 20 or more employees are to be made redundant at one establishment within a period of 90 days and consultation is required with a recognised trade union or, if there is none, with elected employee representatives: see the Trade Union and Labour Relations (Consolidation) Act 1992 s 188; and PARA 1185.

6 *Grundy (Teddington) Ltd v Plummer* [1983] ICR 367, [1983] IRLR 98, EAT; *Kelly v Upholstery and Cabinet Works (Amesbury) Ltd* [1977] IRLR 91, EAT; *North East Midlands Co-operative Society Ltd v Allen* [1977] IRLR 212, EAT. Undue weight should not be placed on

this factor (*Hollister v National Farmers' Union* [1979] ICR 542, [1979] IRLR 238, CA); but cf *Walls Meat Co Ltd v Selby* [1989] ICR 601, CA (reaffirming the approach in *Williams v Compair Maxam Ltd* [1982] ICR 156, [1982] IRLR 83, EAT, including this factor).

7   The question of how the pool should be defined is primarily a matter for the employer to determine: *Taymech Ltd v Ryan* EAT/663/94, approved in *Samels v University of Creative Arts* [2012] EWCA Civ 1152, [2012] All ER (D) 213 (Jun). There is no legal requirement that a pool should be limited to employees doing the same or similar work: *Taymech Ltd v Ryan* (as so approved).

However, objective and fair selection criteria are central: see *BL Cars Ltd v Lewis* [1983] IRLR 58, EAT. Lack of objectivity in the criteria adopted (retaining those 'who, in the opinion of the managers concerned, would be able to keep the company viable') was one of the reasons for the finding of unfairness in *Williams v Compair Maxam Ltd* [1982] ICR 156, [1982] IRLR 83, EAT (see note 6). The employer must be able to show how, by whom and on what basis the selection has been made (*Bristol Channel Ship Repairers Ltd v O'Keefe* [1977] 2 All ER 258, [1977] IRLR 13, EAT) and the personal circumstances of the employee may have to be taken into consideration (*Forman Construction Ltd v Kelly* [1977] IRLR 468, EAT). Last-in-first-out ('LIFO') is usually fair (*Bessenden Properties Ltd v Corness* [1977] ICR 821n, [1974] IRLR 338, CA; *NC Watling & Co Ltd v Richardson* [1978] ICR 1049, [1978] IRLR 255, EAT); and it should not normally be open to attack as sexually discriminatory since it will usually be justified (*Eley (IMI) Kynoch Ltd v Powell, Clarke v Eley (IMI) Kynoch Ltd* [1983] ICR 165, [1982] IRLR 482, EAT; *Brook v London Borough of Haringey* [1992] IRLR 478, EAT), but any justification that may bring personal characteristics into play must now be considered in the light of the Equality Act 2010 (see PARA 780 note 15). Other criteria may be fairly considered, provided that they are capable of objective assessment, such as:

(1)   efficiency (*Farthing v Midland Household Stores Ltd* [1974] IRLR 354 (dismissal unfair on the facts));
(2)   experience (*Abbotts and Standley v Wesson-Glynwed Steels Ltd* [1982] IRLR 51, EAT);
(3)   attendance record (*Paine and Moore v Grundy (Teddington) Ltd* [1981] IRLR 267, EAT; *Buchanan v Tilcon Ltd* [1983] IRLR 417, Ct of Sess);
(4)   participation in industrial action (*Cruickshank v Hobbs* [1977] ICR 725, EAT).

An employee's domestic arrangements may be relevant: see *Jowett v Earl of Bradford (No 2)* [1978] ICR 431, sub nom *Earl of Bradford v Jowett* [1978] IRLR 16, EAT. Where an employer selects on merit, rather than just length of service, a measure of objectivity may be achieved by use of a 'points' system, but this raises problems as to confidentiality, whether the points of other employees should be disclosed to an employee challenging his selection, and how closely a tribunal should scrutinise the points awarded; initially it was held that a tribunal should only look at the overall fairness of the system and should not order disclosure of the points awarded to non-selected employees (*Eaton Ltd v King* [1995] IRLR 75, EAT; *British Aerospace plc v Green* [1995] ICR 1006, [1995] IRLR 433, CA), but subsequently the Employment Appeal Tribunal has ordered disclosure (at least where there was prima facie evidence of unfair selection), holding that failure to divulge scores could make a dismissal unfair on the facts (*FDR Ltd v Holloway* [1995] IRLR 400, EAT; *John Brown Engineering Ltd v Brown* [1997] IRLR 90, EAT). As to a tribunal's considerations see also the text and note 10. An employer may act reasonably by widening the area of selection, even if that means moving a longer-serving employee into the job of a shorter-serving employee and making the latter redundant instead ('bumping'): see *Thomas & Betts Manufacturing Ltd v Harding* [1980] IRLR 255, CA; *Babar Indian Restaurant v Rawat* [1985] IRLR 57, EAT (dismissal unfair on the facts); cf *Green v A & I Fraser (Wholesale Fish Merchants) Ltd* [1985] IRLR 55, EAT. This approach to 'bumping' is consistent with that taken in relation to it when applying the statutory definition of 'redundancy' in the Employment Rights Act 1996 s 139 (see PARA 870): *Murray v Foyle Meats Ltd* [1999] ICR 827, [1999] IRLR 562, HL.

8   In applying objective criteria, the particular circumstances of an employee may have to be considered, e g where attendance record is a criterion, there may be particular reasons for an employee's absence that should be taken into consideration: see *Paine and Moore v Grundy (Teddington) Ltd* [1981] IRLR 267, EAT.

9   *Williams v Compair Maxam Ltd* [1982] ICR 156 at 162, [1982] IRLR 83 at 87, EAT. These principles are, however, only guidelines: *Rolls Royce Motors Ltd v Dewhurst* [1985] ICR 869, [1985] IRLR 184, EAT; and see PARA 772. In applying them, the tribunal should consider the circumstances existing at the termination of the employment, which in a case of dismissal by notice means at the expiry of the notice (*Stacey v Babcock Power Ltd (Construction Division)* [1986] ICR 221, [1986] IRLR 3, EAT; *Dyke v Hereford and Worcester County Council* [1989] ICR 800, EAT), and in a case of summary dismissal means at the time of the dismissal (*Octavius Atkinson & Sons Ltd v Morris* [1989] ICR 431, [1989] IRLR 158, CA).

Efforts by the employer to seek alternative employment may be an important factor: *Vokes Ltd v Bear* [1974] ICR 1, [1973] IRLR 363, NIRC; *Thomas & Betts Manufacturing Ltd v Harding* [1980] IRLR 255, CA. Reasonable steps may be expected (*Quinton Hazell Ltd v Earl* [1976] IRLR 296, EAT; *British United Shoe Machinery Co Ltd v Clarke* [1978] ICR 70, [1977] IRLR 297, EAT), though this may not be relevant on the expiry of a temporary contract (*Dixon v BBC, Throsby v Imperial College of Science and Technology, Gwent County Council v Lane* [1978] QB 438, [1978] ICR 357, EAT; affd on other grounds sub nom *Dixon v BBC* [1979] QB 546, [1979] ICR 281, CA). Suggestions that an employer may be expected to look for alternative work elsewhere within a group of companies have been doubted: see *Barratt Construction Ltd v Dalrymple* [1984] IRLR 385, EAT; *MDH Ltd v Sussex* [1986] IRLR 123, EAT. Offering alternative work on unreasonable terms may make a dismissal unfair (*Elliot v Richard Stump Ltd* [1987] ICR 579, [1987] IRLR 215, EAT), but failure to offer work available after dismissal (even very shortly afterwards) does not (*Octavius Atkinson & Sons Ltd v Morris*). The employee should be given adequate information about the work offered: *Modern Injection Moulds Ltd v Price* [1976] ICR 370, [1976] IRLR 172, EAT. The Employment Rights Act 1996 s 138 (trial periods on renewal of contract or re-engagement) (see PARA 865) does not apply to an unfair dismissal claim: *Hempell v WH Smith & Sons Ltd* [1986] ICR 365, [1986] IRLR 95, EAT. A job of lower status or remuneration may reasonably be expected to be offered to (or, at least, discussed with) the employee, leaving it to him to decide whether to accept it: see *Avonmouth Construction Co Ltd v Shipway* [1979] IRLR 14, EAT; *Huddersfield Parcels Ltd v Sykes* [1981] IRLR 115, EAT; *Abbotts and Standley v Wesson-Glynwed Steels Ltd* [1982] IRLR 51, EAT; cf *Barratt Construction Ltd v Dalrymple*. Where there are one or more possibilities of suitable alternative employment, the employer should normally inform the employee of the financial prospects of those positions: *Fisher v Hoopoe Finance Ltd* [2005] All ER (D) 51 (Jun), EAT.

10 See *NC Watling & Co Ltd v Richardson* [1978] ICR 1049, [1978] IRLR 255, EAT; and PARA 767. With regard to procedure, an internal appeal against redundancy selection is not a requirement for a fair dismissal (*Robinson v Ulster Carpet Mills Ltd* [1991] IRLR 348, NI CA); but, where one exists, the normal rule applies that a fair appeal can cure an unfair initial decision (*Lloyd v Taylor Woodrow Construction* [1999] IRLR 782, EAT).

The courts have emphasised particularly that tribunals must not substitute their own view about how an employer defines the pool, although at the same time there are no established rules to guide the employer in this process (see note 7): *Samels v University of Creative Arts* [2012] EWCA Civ 1152, [2012] All ER (D) 213 (Jun). It would be difficult for the employee to challenge how a pool has been defined where the employer has genuinely applied his mind to the problem: *Taymech Ltd v Ryan* EAT/663/94, approved in *Samels v University of Creative Arts*. See also *Halpin v Sandpiper Books Ltd* [2012] All ER (D) 59 (Apr), EAT (selection of employee for redundancy from pool of one, there being no other similarly qualified persons, had been fair); and *Byard v Capita Hartshead Ltd* [2012] ICR 1256, [2012] IRLR 814, EAT (pool of one to be considered for redundancy was unfair because, although question of how the pool should be defined is primarily a matter for the employer to determine, employer had not genuinely applied its mind to the issue of who should have been in the pool).

E. CONTRAVENTION OF A STATUTORY DUTY

783.   Fairness of dismissal for reason related to contravention of a statutory duty or restriction. A dismissal[1] is not unfair if it is shown by the employer[2] that it was imposed for the reason that the employee[3] could not continue to work in the position[4] which he held without contravention, either on his part or on that of his employer, of a duty or restriction imposed by or under an enactment, and if it was reasonable in the circumstances[5].

1 As to the meaning of 'dismissal' see PARA 762.
2 As to the meaning of 'employer' see PARA 2.
3 As to the meaning of 'employee' see PARA 2.
4 As to the meaning of 'position' see PARA 765 note 13.
5 See the Employment Rights Act 1996 s 98(1)(b), (2)(d), (4); and PARA 765. To fall within this head, the potential statutory restriction must exist in fact; it is not enough that the employer genuinely but mistakenly believes it to exist (though in such a case the dismissal may be held to be for 'some other substantial reason': see PARA 766): *Bouchaala v Trusthouse Forte Hotels Ltd* [1980] ICR 721, [1980] IRLR 382, EAT. See also *Kelly v University of Southampton* [2008] ICR

357, [2007] All ER (D) 243 (Dec), EAT (employee's leave to remain in the UK had expired and employer believed erroneously that it would have been committing a criminal offence if it had continued to employ her; employment tribunal's decision that dismissal had been fair on this basis had been set aside and remitted to current tribunal to address remedies). Even where the statutory restriction clearly exists, the dismissal is not automatically fair and the normal test of unfairness (see the Employment Rights Act 1996 s 98(4); and PARA 765) must still be applied: *Sandhu v Department of Education and Science and Hillingdon London Borough* [1978] IRLR 208, EAT. In applying this test, it may be relevant to consider whether work patterns could be changed or the employee offered alternative work, but such matters must be considered realistically: see *Appleyard v Smith (Hull) Ltd* [1972] IRLR 19; *Fearn v Tayford Motor Co Ltd* [1975] IRLR 336 (both cases concerning loss of a driving licence). Statutory professional or trade regulations may be relevant: see *Sutcliffe and Eaton Ltd v Pinney* [1977] IRLR 349, EAT; *Alidair Ltd v Taylor* [1978] ICR 445, sub nom *Taylor v Alidair Ltd* [1978] IRLR 82, CA.

F. FAMILY REASONS

784. Fairness of dismissal for reason related to employee's leave for family reasons. An employee[1] who is dismissed[2] is to be regarded[3] as unfairly dismissed if[4]:

(1) the reason or principal reason for the dismissal is of a prescribed[5] kind relating to leave for family reasons[6]; or

(2) the reason or principal reason for the dismissal is that the employee is redundant, and the provisions concerning redundancy during either maternity leave[7] or adoption leave[8] (as the case may be) have not been complied with[9].

For the purposes of head (1) above, the specified kinds of reasons are reasons connected with[10]:

(a) the pregnancy of the employee[11];

(b) the fact that the employee has given birth to a child[12];

(c) the application of a relevant[13] requirement, or a relevant[14] recommendation[15];

(d) the fact that the employee took, sought to take or availed herself of the benefits of, ordinary maternity leave or additional maternity leave[16];

(e) the fact that the employee took or sought to take parental leave or time off for dependants[17];

(f) the fact that the employee failed to return after a period of ordinary or additional maternity leave in a case where either the employer[18] did not notify her of the date on which the period in question would end, and she reasonably believed that that period had not ended, or where the employer gave her less than 28 days' notice of the date on which the period in question would end, and it was not reasonably practicable for her to return on that date[19];

(g) the fact that the employee undertook, considered undertaking or refused to undertake work during the maternity leave period[20];

(h) the fact that the employee declined to sign[21] a workforce agreement[22]; or

(i) the fact that the employee, being a representative of members of the workforce[23] or a candidate in an election in which any person elected will, on being elected, become such a representative, performed, or proposed to perform, any functions or activities as such a representative or candidate[24];

(j) the fact that the employee took or sought to take time off work to accompany a woman to ante-natal appointments or to attend adoption appointments (or the employer so believed that this was likely) or took, or sought to take, paternity or adoption leave[25];

(k)   the fact that the employer believed that the employee was likely to take ordinary or additional adoption leave[26];

(l)   the fact that the employee undertook, considered undertaking or refused to undertake work during the adoption leave period[27]; or

(m)   the fact that the employee failed to return after a period of additional adoption leave in a case where either the employer did not notify him[28] of the date on which that period would end, and he reasonably believed that the period had not ended, or where the employer gave him less than 28 days' notice of the date on which the period would end, and it was not reasonably practicable for him to return on that date[29].

The provisions described above[30] do not apply in relation to an employee if:

(i)   it is not reasonably practicable for a reason other than redundancy for the employer (who may be the same employer or a successor[31] of his) to permit the employee to return to a job which is both suitable for the employee and appropriate for the employee to do in the circumstances[32];

(ii)   an associated employer offers the employee a job of that kind[33]; and

(iii) the employee accepts or unreasonably refuses that offer[34].

An employee who is dismissed is also to be regarded[35] as unfairly dismissed if: (A) the reason (or, if more than one, the principal reason) for the dismissal is that the employee was redundant[36]; (B) it is shown that the circumstances constituting the redundancy applied equally to one or more employees in the same undertaking[37] who held positions[38] similar to that held by the employee and who have not been dismissed by the employer[39]; and (C) it is shown that the reason (or, if more than one, the principal reason) for which the employee was selected for dismissal was of a kind specified in heads (a) to (i)[40] or in heads (j) to (m)[41] above[42].

1   As to the meaning of 'employee' see PARA 2.

2   As to the meaning of 'dismissal' see PARA 762.

3   Ie for the purposes of the Employment Rights Act 1996 Pt X (ss 94–134A) (unfair dismissal: see also PARAS 757 et seq, 785 et seq). As to the modification of Pt X in relation to governing bodies of schools having a right to a delegated budget, acting in the exercise of their employment powers, see EDUCATION vol 35 (2011) PARA 355 et seq; and as to the modification of Pt X in relation to persons holding ecclesiastical office under common tenure see the Ecclesiastical Offices (Terms of Service) Regulations 2009, SI 2009/2108, reg 33; and ECCLESIASTICAL LAW vol 34 (2011) PARA 407.

        The provisions of the Employment Rights Act 1996 replaced the pre-existing law on dismissal for pregnancy or maternity-related reasons, as part of the general reform of maternity and related rights by the Employment Relations Act 1999; and it is submitted that they should be construed de novo.

4   See the Employment Rights Act 1996 s 99(1) (s 99 substituted by the Employment Relations Act 1999 s 9, Sch 4 Pt III paras 5, 16);Maternity and Parental Leave etc Regulations 1999, SI 1999/3312, reg 20(1); Paternity and Adoption Leave Regulations 2002, SI 2002/2788, reg 29(1).

        Where a dismissal is unfair under the Employment Rights Act 1996 s 99, the qualifying period for unfair dismissal does not apply: see s 108(3)(b); and PARA 758 note 9. As to the right to make a complaint of unfair dismissal before an employment tribunal see PARA 804 et seq; and as to remedies see PARA 810 et seq.

5   For these purposes, 'prescribed' means prescribed by regulations made by the Secretary of State: see the Employment Rights Act 1996 s 99(2) (as substituted: see note 4). As to the Secretary of State see PARA 5 note 21. As to the making of regulations under the Employment Rights Act 1996 generally see PARA 162. Such regulations may make different provision for different cases or circumstances, and may apply any enactment, in such circumstances as may be specified

and subject to any conditions specified, in relation to persons regarded as unfairly dismissed by reason of s 99: see s 99(5) (as so substituted). A reason or set of circumstances prescribed under s 99 must relate to:

(1) pregnancy, childbirth or maternity (s 99(3)(a) (as so substituted));

(2) time off under s 57ZE (time off work to accompany woman to ante-natal appointments: see PARA 335) (s 99(3)(aa) (s 99 as so substituted; s 99(3)(aa) added by the Children and Families Act 2014 s 127(2)(b)));

(3) time off under the Employment Rights Act 1996 s 57ZJ (paid time off work to attend adoption appointments: see PARA 341) or s 57ZL (unpaid time off work to attend adoption appointments: see PARA 342) (s 99(3)(ab) (s 99 as so substituted; s 99(3)(ab) added by the Children and Families Act 2014 s 128(2)(c)));

(4) ordinary, compulsory or additional maternity leave (Employment Rights Act 1996 s 99(3)(b));

(5) ordinary or additional adoption leave (s 99(3)(ba) (s 99 as so substituted; s 99(3)(ba) added by the Employment Act 2002 s 53, Sch 7 paras 24, 33(1), (2)));

(6) shared parental leave (Employment Rights Act 1996 s 99(3)(bb) (s 99 as so substituted; s 99(3)(bb) added by the Children and Families Act 2014 s 126(1), Sch 7 paras 29, 39(a));

(7) parental leave (Employment Rights Act 1996 s 99(3)(c));

(8) paternity leave (s 99(3)(ca) (s 99 as so substituted; s 99(3)(ca) added by the Employment Act 2002 Sch 7 paras 24, 33(1), (3); substituted by the Work and families Act 2006 s 11(1), Sch 1 para 41; and amended by the Children and Families Act 2014 Sch 7 paras 29, 39(b)); or

(9) time off under the Employment Rights Act 1996 s 57A (time off for dependants: see PARA 347) (s 99(3)(d)).

A reason or set of circumstances so prescribed may also relate to redundancy or other factors: see s 99(3) (as so substituted). As to the meaning of 'redundancy' see PARA 870. A reason or set of circumstances prescribed under s 99(1) satisfies s 99(3)(c) (see head (7) above) or s 99(3)(d) (see head (9) above) if it relates to action which an employee takes, agrees to take, or refuses to take, under or in respect of a collective or workforce agreement which deals with parental leave: see s 99(4) (as so substituted). As to the meaning of 'collective agreement' see PARA 119 note 21; and as to the meaning of 'workforce agreement' see PARA 393. In exercise of the power conferred under s 99, the Secretary of State has made the Maternity and Parental Leave etc Regulations 1999, SI 1999/3312, reg 20, and the Paternity and Adoption Leave Regulations 2002, SI 2002/2788, reg 29: see also the text and notes 1–4, 6–42. As to the meanings of 'ordinary maternity leave' and 'additional maternity leave' see PARA 356 note 2; as to the meaning of 'childbirth' see PARA 356 note 4; as to the meaning of 'additional adoption leave' see PARA 373 note 5; and as to the meaning of 'ordinary adoption leave' see PARA 378 note 2. As to ordinary maternity leave and additional maternity leave see PARA 356 et seq; as to compulsory maternity leave see PARA 363; as to paternity leave see PARA 370 et seq; as to ordinary adoption leave see PARA 378 et seq; as to additional adoption leave see PARA 379 et seq; as to shared parental leave see PARA 398 et seq; and as to parental leave see PARA 391 et seq.

6   Employment Rights Act 1996 s 99(1)(a) (as substituted: see note 4); Maternity and Parental Leave etc Regulations 1999, SI 1999/3312, reg 20(1)(a); Paternity and Adoption Leave Regulations 2002, SI 2002/2788, reg 29(1)(a).

7   Ie in the Maternity and Parental Leave etc Regulations 1999, SI 1999/3312, reg 10: see PARA 364.

8   Ie in the Paternity and Adoption Leave Regulations 2002, SI 2002/2788, reg 23: see PARA 386.

9   Employment Rights Act 1996 s 99(1)(b) (as substituted: see note 4); Maternity and Parental Leave etc Regulations 1999, SI 1999/3312, reg 20(1)(b); Paternity and Adoption Leave Regulations 2002, SI 2002/2788, reg 29(1)(b). The Maternity and Parental Leave etc Regulations 1999, SI 1999/3312, reg 20(1)(b) only applies where the dismissal ends the employee's ordinary or additional maternity leave period: see reg 20(4).

10 As to 'connected with' see *Atkins v Coyle Personnel plc* [2008] IRLR 420, [2008] All ER (D) 108 (Feb), EAT (where no a causal connection between the dismissal and the prohibited ground was held to have been demonstrated as was required by the regulation).

11 Maternity and Parental Leave etc Regulations 1999, SI 1999/3312, reg 20(3)(a). The tribunal must be satisfied that the employer knew of, or believed in, the existence of the pregnancy: see *Sharkey v Eildon Ltd* [2004] All ER (D) 161 (Aug), EAT (Sc); *Ramdoolar v Bycity Ltd* [2005] ICR 368, EAT (it is not enough that symptoms of pregnancy existed which arguably, or in fact, ought to have meant that the employer realised that the employee was pregnant).

12 Maternity and Parental Leave etc Regulations 1999, SI 1999/3312, reg 20(3)(b). Regulation 20(3)(b) only applies where the dismissal ends the employee's ordinary or additional

maternity leave period: see reg 20(4). As to the ordinary maternity leave period see PARA 357; and as to the additional maternity leave period see PARA 358.

13 Ie as defined by the Employment Rights Act 1996 s 66(2): see PARA 598 note 7.

14 Ie as defined by the Employment Rights Act 1996 s 66(2): see PARA 598 note 8.

15 Maternity and Parental Leave etc Regulations 1999, SI 1999/3312, reg 20(3)(c).

16 Maternity and Parental Leave etc Regulations 1999, SI 1999/3312, reg 20(3)(d) (amended by SI 2008/1966). The Maternity and Parental Leave etc Regulations 1999, SI 1999/3312, reg 19(3), (3A) applies for the purposes of reg 20(3)(d) as it applies for the purposes of reg 19(2)(d) (see PARA 620): reg 20(5) (substituted by SI 2008/1966).

17 See the Maternity and Parental Leave etc Regulations 1999, SI 1999/3312, reg 20(3)(e) (amended by SI 2008/1966). As to taking time off for dependants see the Employment Rights Act 1996 s 57A; and PARA 347.

18 Ie in accordance with the Maternity and Parental Leave etc Regulations 1999, SI 1999/3312, reg 7(6), (7) (see PARAS 357, 358), or otherwise. As to the meaning of 'employer' see PARA 2.

19 See the Maternity and Parental Leave etc Regulations 1999, SI 1999/3312, reg 20(3)(ee) (added by SI 2002/2789).

20 Maternity and Parental Leave etc Regulations 1999, SI 1999/3312, reg 20(3)(eee) (added by SI 2006/2014). The reference is to work in accordance with the Maternity and Parental Leave etc Regulations 1999, SI 1999/3312, reg 12A: see PARA 366.

21 Ie for the purposes of the Maternity and Parental Leave etc Regulations 1999, SI 1999/3312: see PARA 393.

22 Maternity and Parental Leave etc Regulations 1999, SI 1999/3312, reg 20(3)(f).

23 Ie for the purposes of the Maternity and Parental Leave etc Regulations 1999, SI 1999/3312, reg 2(1), Sch 1: see PARA 393.

24 See the Maternity and Parental Leave etc Regulations 1999, SI 1999/3312, reg 20(3)(g).

25 Paternity and Adoption Leave Regulations 2002, SI 2002/2788, reg 29(3)(za)–(zd), (a) (reg 29(3)(za)–(zd) added by SI 2014/2112). The text refers to an employee's right to take time off under the Employment Rights Act 1996 s 57ZE (time off work to accompany woman to ante-natal appointments: see PARA 335), s 57ZJ (employee's right to paid time off work to attend adoption appointments: see PARA 341) or s 57ZL (employee's right to unpaid time off work to attend adoption appointments: see PARA 342): see the Paternity and Adoption Leave Regulations 2002, SI 2002/2788, reg 29(3)(za)–(zd) (as so added). The references to the Employment Rights Act 1996 s 57ZJ and s 57ZL have effect only from 5 April 2015, however: see the Paternity and Adoption Leave (Amendment) Regulations 2014, SI 2014/2112, regs 1(4), 14(4).

26 Paternity and Adoption Leave Regulations 2002, SI 2002/2788, reg 29(3)(b) (amended by SI 2006/2014).

27 Paternity and Adoption Leave Regulations 2002, SI 2002/2788, reg 29(3)(bb) (added by SI 2006/2014). The reference is to work in accordance with the Paternity and Adoption Leave Regulations 2002, SI 2002/2788, reg 21A: see PARA 388.

28 Ie in accordance with the Paternity and Adoption Leave Regulations 2002, SI 2002/2788, reg 17(7), (8) (see PARA 378), or otherwise.

29 Paternity and Adoption Leave Regulations 2002, SI 2002/2788, reg 29(3)(c).

30 Ie the Maternity and Parental Leave etc Regulations 1999, SI 1999/3312, reg 20(1) or the Paternity and Adoption Leave Regulations 2002, SI 2002/2788, reg 29(1): see heads (1), (2) in the text. Where on a complaint of unfair dismissal any question arises as to whether the operation of the Maternity and Parental Leave etc Regulations 1999, SI 1999/3312, reg 20(1) is excluded by the provisions of reg 20(7) (see the text and notes 31–34), or whether the operation of the Paternity and Adoption Leave Regulations 2002, SI 2002/2788, reg 29(1) is excluded by the provisions of reg 29(5) (see the text and notes 31–34), it is for the employer to show that the provisions in question were satisfied in relation to the complainant: Maternity and Parental Leave etc Regulations 1999, SI 1999/3312, reg 20(8) (amended by SI 2006/2014); Paternity and Adoption Leave Regulations 2002, SI 2002/2788, reg 29(6) (amended by SI 2006/2014).

31 As to the meaning of 'successor' see PARA 133 note 10.

32 Maternity and Parental Leave etc Regulations 1999, SI 1999/3312, reg 20(7)(a); Paternity and Adoption Leave Regulations 2002, SI 2002/2788, reg 29(5)(a). See also note 30.

33 Maternity and Parental Leave etc Regulations 1999, SI 1999/3312, reg 20(7)(b); Paternity and Adoption Leave Regulations 2002, SI 2002/2788, reg 29(5)(b). See also note 30. As to the meaning of 'associated employer' see PARA 3.

34 Maternity and Parental Leave etc Regulations 1999, SI 1999/3312, reg 20(7)(c); Paternity and Adoption Leave Regulations 2002, SI 2002/2788, reg 29(5)(c). See also note 30.

35 See note 3.

36 Maternity and Parental Leave etc Regulations 1999, SI 1999/3312, reg 20(2)(a); Paternity and
    Adoption Leave Regulations 2002, SI 2002/2788, reg 29(2)(a).
37 There is no statutory definition of 'undertaking' for these purposes: see PARA 781 note 5.
38 As to the meaning of 'position' see PARA 765 note 13.
39 Maternity and Parental Leave etc Regulations 1999, SI 1999/3312, reg 20(2)(b); Paternity and
    Adoption Leave Regulations 2002, SI 2002/2788, reg 29(2)(b).
40 Ie specified in the Maternity and Parental Leave etc Regulations 1999, SI 1999/3312, reg 20(3)
    (if in relation to maternity leave).
41 Ie specified in the Paternity and Adoption Leave Regulations 2002, SI 2002/2788, reg 29(3) (if
    in relation to paternity leave or adoption leave).
42 Maternity and Parental Leave etc Regulations 1999, SI 1999/3312, reg 20(2)(c); Paternity and
    Adoption Leave Regulations 2002, SI 2002/2788, reg 29(2)(c).

G. OTHER SPECIAL OR AUTOMATICALLY UNFAIR DISMISSALS

785.   Fairness of dismissal for reason related to employee's jury service. An
employee[1] who is dismissed[2] is to be regarded[3] as unfairly dismissed if the reason
(or, if more than one, the principal reason) for the dismissal is that[4]:

(1)   he has been summoned[5] to attend for service as a juror[6]; or
(2)   he has been absent from work because he attended at any place in
        pursuance of being so summoned[7].

These provisions do not apply, however, in relation to an employee who is
dismissed if the employer shows[8]:

(a)   that the circumstances were such that the employee's absence in
        pursuance of being so summoned was likely to cause substantial injury
        to the employer's undertaking[9];
(b)   that the employer brought those circumstances to the attention of the
        employee[10];
(c)   that the employee refused or failed to apply to the appropriate officer[11]
        for excusal from or a deferral of the obligation to attend in pursuance of
        being so summoned[12]; and
(d)   that the refusal or failure was not reasonable[13].

1   As to the meaning of 'employee' see PARA 2.
2   As to the meaning of 'dismissal' see PARA 762.
3   Ie for the purposes of the Employment Rights Act 1996 Pt X (ss 94–134A) (unfair dismissal: see
    also PARAS 757 et seq, 786 et seq). As to the modification of Pt X in relation to governing bodies
    of schools having a right to a delegated budget, acting in the exercise of their employment
    powers, see EDUCATION vol 35 (2011) PARA 355 et seq; and as to the modification of Pt X in
    relation to persons holding ecclesiastical office under common tenure see the Ecclesiastical
    Offices (Terms of Service) Regulations 2009, SI 2009/2108, reg 33; and ECCLESIASTICAL LAW
    vol 34 (2011) PARA 407.
4   See the Employment Rights Act 1996 s 98B(1) (s 98B added by the Employment Relations
    Act 2004 s 40(3)).
        Where a dismissal is unfair under the Employment Rights Act 1996 s 98B, the normal
    qualifying period for unfair dismissal does not apply: see s 108(3)(aa); and PARA 758 note 9. As
    to the right to make a complaint of unfair dismissal before an employment tribunal see
    PARA 804 et seq; and as to remedies see PARA 810 et seq.
5   Ie under the Juries Act 1974 (see JURIES vol 61 (2010) PARA 812 et seq) or the Coroners and
    Justice Act 2009 Pt 1 (ss 1–50) (see CORONERS vol 24 (2010) PARA 138 et seq).
6   Employment Rights Act 1996 s 98B(1)(a) (s 98B as added (see note 4); s 98B(1)(a) amended by
    the Coroners and Justice Act 2009 s 177(1), Sch 21 para 36(1), (3)).
7   Employment Rights Act 1996 s 98B(1)(b) (as added: see note4).
8   See the Employment Rights Act 1996 s 98B(2) (as added: see note4). As to the meaning of
    'employer' see PARA 2.
9   Employment Rights Act 1996 s 98B(2)(a) (as added: see note 4). There is no statutory definition
    of 'undertaking' for these purposes: see PARA 781 note 5.
10 Employment Rights Act 1996 s 98B(2)(b) (as added: see note 4).

11 For these purposes, 'appropriate officer' means, in the case of a person who has been summoned under the Juries Act 1974, the officer designated for the purposes of s 8 (excusal for previous jury service: see JURIES vol 61 (2010) PARA 806), s 9 (other excusals: see JURIES vol 61 (2010) PARA 808) or, as the case may be, s 9A (discretionary deferral: see JURIES vol 61 (2010) PARAS 807, 808): Employment Rights Act 1996 s 98B(3)(a) (as added: see note 4).
12 Employment Rights Act 1996 s 98B(2)(c) (as added: see note 4).
13 Employment Rights Act 1996 s 98B(2)(d) (as added: see note 4).

786. Fairness of dismissal for reason related to health and safety cases. An employee[1] who is dismissed[2] is to be regarded[3] as unfairly dismissed if the reason (or, if more than one, the principal reason) for the dismissal is that[4]:

(1)   having been designated by the employer[5] to carry out activities in connection with preventing or reducing risks to health and safety at work, the employee carried out, or proposed to carry out, any such activities[6];

(2)   being a representative of workers on matters of health and safety at work or member of a safety committee[7]:
    (a)   in accordance with arrangements established under or by virtue of any enactment[8]; or
    (b)   by reason of being acknowledged as such by the employer[9],
    the employee performed, or proposed to perform, any functions as such a representative or a member of such a committee[10];

(3)   the employee took part, or proposed to take part, in consultation with the employer[11] or in an election of representatives of employee safety, whether as a candidate or otherwise[12];

(4)   being an employee at a place where:
    (a)   there was no such representative or safety committee[13]; or
    (b)   there was such a representative or safety committee but it was not reasonably practicable for the employee to raise the matter by those means[14],
    he brought to his employer's attention, by reasonable means, circumstances connected with his work which he reasonably believed were harmful or potentially harmful to health or safety[15];

(5)   in circumstances of danger which the employee reasonably believed to be serious and imminent and which he could not reasonably have been expected to avert, he left, or proposed to leave, or, while the danger persisted, refused to return to his place of work or any dangerous part of his place of work[16]; or

(6)   in circumstances of danger which the employee reasonably believed to be serious and imminent, he took, or proposed to take, appropriate steps to protect himself or other persons from the danger[17].

The right not to be unfairly dismissed in such cases is extended to the police by providing that[18] the holding, otherwise than under a contract of employment[19], of the office of constable or an appointment as police cadet is to be treated as employment by the relevant officer[20] under a contract of employment[21].

1   As to the meaning of 'employee' see PARA 2.
2   As to the meaning of 'dismissal' see PARA 762.
3   Ie for the purposes of the Employment Rights Act 1996 Pt X (ss 94–134A) (unfair dismissal: see also PARAS 757 et seq, 787 et seq). As to the modification of Pt X in relation to governing bodies of schools having a right to a delegated budget, acting in the exercise of their employment powers, see EDUCATION vol 35 (2011) PARA 355 et seq; and as to the modification of Pt X in relation to persons holding ecclesiastical office under common tenure see the Ecclesiastical Offices (Terms of Service) Regulations 2009, SI 2009/2108, reg 33; and ECCLESIASTICAL LAW vol 34 (2011) PARA 407.

4 See the Employment Rights Act 1996 s 100(1).
5 As to the meaning of 'employer' see PARA 2.
6 Employment Rights Act 1996 s 100(1)(a). Where a dismissal is unfair under s 100(1)(a) or s 100(1)(b) (see head (2) in the text), there is a minimum for the basic award (see s 120(1); and PARA 816); and interim relief is available (see s 128(1); and PARA 805). As to the right to make a complaint of unfair dismissal before an employment tribunal see PARA 804 et seq; and as to remedies see PARA 810 et seq.
   An employer must appoint one or more competent persons to assist him in complying with health and safety requirements: see the Management of Health and Safety at Work Regulations 1999, SI 1999/3242, reg 7; PARA 38; and HEALTH AND SAFETY AT WORK vol 52 (2014) PARA 400.
7 See the Employment Rights Act 1996 s 100(1)(b). See note 6. Where a trade union is recognised, a system of safety representatives and safety committees may be required by law: see the Safety Representatives and Safety Committees Regulations 1977, SI 1977/500; PARAS 37, 1075; and HEALTH AND SAFETY AT WORK vol 52 (2014) PARA 414. Where there is no such recognised union, there must be consultation with, and/or the provision of information to, the workforce, either directly or through elected employee representatives: see the Health and Safety (Consultation with Employees) Regulations 1996, SI 1996/1513; PARA 38; and HEALTH AND SAFETY AT WORK vol 52 (2014) PARA 415.
8 Employment Rights Act 1996 s 100(1)(b)(i). See note 6.
9 Employment Rights Act 1996 s 100(1)(b)(ii). See note 6.
10 See the Employment Rights Act 1996 s 100(1)(b). See note 6. The protection for a safety representative only applies to acts within his jurisdiction or appointment: *Shillito v Van Leer (UK) Ltd* [1997] IRLR 495, EAT (a case on detriment short of dismissal under the Employment Rights Act 1996 s 44: see PARA 614). Once acts are covered, however, the protection applies not just to carrying them out but also to the way in which they are done: *Goodwin v Cabletel UK Ltd* [1998] ICR 112, [1997] IRLR 665, EAT.
11 Ie pursuant to the Health and Safety (Consultation with Employees) Regulations 1996, SI 1996/1513: see note 7.
12 Employment Rights Act 1996 s 100(1)(ba) (added by SI 1996/1513).
13 Employment Rights Act 1996 s 100(1)(c)(i).
14 Employment Rights Act 1996 s 100(1)(c)(ii).
15 Employment Rights Act 1996 s 100(1)(c).
16 Employment Rights Act 1996 s 100(1)(d). 'Danger' is to be construed widely, and has been held to apply to threats from a fellow employee (not just to danger from machines, chemicals, etc): *Harvest Press Ltd v McCaffrey* [1999] IRLR 778, EAT.
17 Employment Rights Act 1996 s 100(1)(e). The reference to protecting 'other persons' from danger is wide enough to cover members of the public: *Masiak v City Restaurants (UK) Ltd* [1999] IRLR 780, EAT (the Employment Rights Act 1996 s 100(1)(e) was held to cover dismissal of a chef for refusing to cook and serve suspect meat in a restaurant).
   For the purposes of head (6) in the text, whether steps which an employee took, or proposed to take, were appropriate is to be judged by reference to all the circumstances including, in particular, his knowledge and the facilities and advice available to him at the time: Employment Rights Act 1996 s 100(2). Where, however, the reason (or, if more than one, the principal reason) is that specified in head (6) in the text, the employee is not to be regarded as unfairly dismissed if the employer shows that it was, or would have been, so negligent for the employee to take the steps which he took, or proposed to take, that a reasonable employer might have dismissed him for taking, or proposing to take, them: s 100(3). See *Oudahar v Esporta Group Ltd* [2011] ICR 1406, [2011] IRLR 730, EAT (in construing the Employment Rights Act 1996 s 100(1)(e), the mere fact that an employer disagreed with an employee as to whether there were circumstances of danger was irrelevant; the intention of Parliament was that an employee should be protected from dismissal if he took or proposed to take steps falling within s 100). Where a dismissal is unfair under the Employment Rights Act 1996 s 100(1), read with s 100(2), (3), the normal qualifying period for unfair dismissal does not apply: see s 108(3)(c); and PARA 758 note 9. Also, there is no statutory limit on the compensatory award: see s 124(1A); and PARA 823 note 6.
18 Ie for the purposes of the Employment Rights Act 1996 s 100 and of the other provisions of Pt X (unfair dismissal: see also PARAS 757 et seq, 787 et seq), so far relating to the right not to be unfairly dismissed in a case where the dismissal is unfair by virtue of s 100: see s 134A(1) (s 134A added by the Police (Health and Safety) Act 1997 s 4).
19 As to the meaning of 'contract of employment' see PARA 2.
20 'Relevant officer', in relation to a person holding the office of constable, or a person holding an appointment as a police cadet, means the person who under the Health and Safety at Work etc

Act 1974 s 51A (see HEALTH AND SAFETY AT WORK vol 52 (2014) PARA 302) is to be treated as his employer for the purposes of Pt 1 (ss 1–54): see the Employment Rights Act 1996 s 134A(2) (s 134A as added (see note 18); s 134A(2) substituted by the Serious Organised Crime and Police Act 2005 s 158(2)(b), (3)).

21 Employment Rights Act 1996 s 134A(1) (as added: see note 18). The provision made by s 134A(1) does not apply to the holding of the office of constable by a member of a police force on secondment to the National Crime Agency: s 134A(3) (s 134A as so added; s 134A(3) added by the Serious Organised Crime and Police Act 2005 Sch 4 para 87; and amended by the Crime and Courts Act 2013 s 15(3), Sch 8 paras 49, 51). As to the National Crime Agency see POLICE AND INVESTIGATORY POWERS vol 84 (2013) PARA 424.

787. Fairness of dismissal related to shop workers and betting workers who refuse Sunday work. Where an employee[1] who is:

(1)   a protected shop worker[2] or an opted-out shop worker[3]; or
(2)   a protected betting worker[4] or an opted-out betting worker[5],

is dismissed[6], he is to be regarded[7] as unfairly dismissed if the reason (or, if more than one, the principal reason) for the dismissal is that he refused, or proposed to refuse, to do shop work[8], or betting work[9], on Sunday or on a particular Sunday[10].

These provisions do not, however, apply in relation to an opted-out shop worker or an opted-out betting worker where the reason, or principal reason, for the dismissal is that he refused, or proposed to refuse, to do shop work, or betting work, on any Sunday or Sundays falling before the end of the notice period[11].

A shop worker or betting worker who is dismissed is to be regarded as unfairly dismissed if the reason (or, if more than one, the principal reason) for the dismissal is that the shop worker or betting worker gave, or proposed to give, an opting-out notice[12] to the employer[13].

1   As to the meaning of 'employee' see PARA 2.
2   As to the meaning of 'protected shop worker' see PARA 321; and as to the meaning of 'shop worker' see PARA 321 note 1.
3   Employment Rights Act 1996 s 101(1)(a). As to the meaning of 'opted-out shop worker' see PARA 323.
4   As to the meaning of 'protected betting worker' see PARA 321; and as to the meaning of 'betting worker' see PARA 321 note 2.
5   Employment Rights Act 1996 s 101(1)(b). As to the meaning of 'opted-out betting worker' see PARA 323.
6   As to the meaning of 'dismissal' see PARA 762.
7   Ie for the purposes of the Employment Rights Act 1996 Pt X (ss 94–134A) (unfair dismissal: see also PARAS 757 et seq, 788 et seq). As to the modification of Pt X in relation to governing bodies of schools having a right to a delegated budget, acting in the exercise of their employment powers, see EDUCATION vol 35 (2011) PARA 355 et seq; and as to the modification of Pt X in relation to persons holding ecclesiastical office under common tenure see the Ecclesiastical Offices (Terms of Service) Regulations 2009, SI 2009/2108, reg 33; and ECCLESIASTICAL LAW vol 34 (2011) PARA 407.
8   As to the meaning of 'shop work' see PARA 321 note 1.
9   As to the meaning of 'betting work' see PARA 321 note 2.
10 See the Employment Rights Act 1996 s 101(1). For the purposes of s 36(2)(b) (employment as a shop worker or a betting worker: see PARA 321) or s 41(1)(b) (opted-out shop worker or betting worker: see PARA 323), the appropriate date in relation to s 101 is the effective date of termination: s 101(4). As to the meaning of 'effective date of termination' see PARA 764.
11 Employment Rights Act 1996 s 101(2). As to the meaning of 'notice period' see PARA 323 note 22.
      Where a dismissal is unfair under s 101(1), when read with s 101(2), or is unfair under s 101(3) (see the text and notes 12–13), the normal qualifying period for unfair dismissal does not apply: see s 108(3)(d); and PARA 758 note 9. As to the right to make a complaint of unfair dismissal before an employment tribunal see PARA 804 et seq; and as to remedies see PARA 810 et seq.

12 As to the meaning of 'opting-out notice' see PARA 323 note 9.
13 Employment Rights Act 1996 s 101(3). See also note 10. As to the meaning of 'employer' see PARA 2.

788. Fairness of dismissal related to working time cases. An employee[1] who is dismissed[2] is to be regarded[3] as unfairly dismissed if the reason (or, if more than one, the principal reason) for the dismissal is that the employee[4]:

(1)   refused, or proposed to refuse, to comply with a requirement which the employer imposed, or proposed to impose, in contravention of the statutory provisions[5] relating to working time[6];

(2)   refused, or proposed to refuse, to forgo a right conferred on him by those provisions[7];

(3)   failed to sign a workforce agreement[8] for the purposes of those provisions, or to enter into, or agree to vary or extend, any other agreement with his employer[9] which is provided for in those provisions[10]; or

(4)   being a representative of members of the workforce[11], or a candidate in an election in which any person elected will, on being elected, be such a representative, performed, or proposed to perform, any functions or activities as such a representative or candidate[12].

1 As to the meaning of 'employee' see PARA 2.
2 As to the meaning of 'dismissal' see PARA 762.
3 Ie for the purposes of the Employment Rights Act 1996 Pt X (ss 94–134A) (unfair dismissal: see also PARAS 757 et seq, 789 et seq). As to the modification of Pt X in relation to governing bodies of schools having a right to a delegated budget, acting in the exercise of their employment powers, see EDUCATION vol 35 (2011) PARA 355 et seq; and as to the modification of Pt X in relation to persons holding ecclesiastical office under common tenure see the Ecclesiastical Offices (Terms of Service) Regulations 2009, SI 2009/2108, reg 33; and ECCLESIASTICAL LAW vol 34 (2011) PARA 407.
4 See the Employment Rights Act 1996 s 101A(1) (s 101A added by SI 1998/1833; the Employment Rights Act 1996 s 101A(1) renumbered by SI 2003/3049).
     Where a dismissal is unfair under the Employment Rights Act 1996 s 101A (see heads (1)–(4) in the text), the normal qualifying period for unfair dismissal does not apply (see s 108(3)(dd); and PARA 758 note 9); and where a dismissal is unfair under s 101A(1)(d) (see head (4) in the text), there is a minimum for the basic award (see s 120(1); and PARA 816) and interim relief is available (see s 128(1); and PARA 805). As to the right to make a complaint of unfair dismissal before an employment tribunal see PARA 804 et seq; and as to remedies see PARA 810 et seq.
5 Ie the Working Time Regulations 1998, SI 1998/1833: see PARA 268 et seq. A reference in the Employment Rights Act 1996 s 101A to the Working Time Regulations 1998, SI 1998/1833, includes a reference to (see the Employment Rights Act 1996 s 101A(2) (s 101A as added (see note 4); s 101A(2) added by SI 2003/3049)):
     (1)   the Merchant Shipping (Working Time: Inland Waterways) Regulations 2003, SI 2003/3049 (see SHIPPING AND MARITIME LAW vol 94 (2008) PARA 625) (Employment Rights Act 1996 s 101A(2)(a) (s 101A(2) as so added; s 101A(2)(a) renumbered, s 101A(2)(b) added, by SI 2004/1713));
     (2)   the Fishing Vessels (Working Time: Sea-fishermen) Regulations 2004, SI 2004/1713 (see SHIPPING AND MARITIME LAW vol 94 (2008) PARA 626) (Employment Rights Act 1996 s 101A(2)(b) (s 101A(2) as so added, s 101A(2)(b) as so added));
     (3)   the Cross-border Railway Services (Working Time) Regulations 2008, SI 2008/1660 (see RAILWAYS AND TRAMWAYS vol 86 (2013) PARAS 33, 328) (Employment Rights Act 1996 s 101A(2)(c) (s 101A(2) as so added; s 101A(2)(c) added by SI 2008/1660));
     (4)   the Merchant Shipping (Hours of Work) Regulations 2002, SI 2002/2125 (see SHIPPING AND MARITIME LAW vol 94 (2008) PARA 625) (Employment Rights Act 1996 s 101A(2)(d) (s 101A(2) as so added; s 101A(2)(d) added by SI 2014/308)).
An employee's right, conferred by the Working Time Regulations 1998, SI 1998/1833, or by any of the provisions listed under heads (1) to (4) above, is also a 'relevant statutory right' for the purposes of the Employment Rights Act 1996 s 104: see PARA 793.

6 Employment Rights Act 1996 s 101A(1)(a) (s 101A as added, s 101A(1) as renumbered: see note 4). There is conflicting authority at the EAT level as to what constitutes 'refusal' for these purposes:

    (1)   on the one hand, see eg *McLean v Rainbow Homeloans Ltd* [2007] IRLR 14, EAT (all that is necessary is that the employee refused to accede to a requirement that would in fact have breached the Working Time Regulations 1998, SI 1998/1833, and that he was dismissed because of it; there is no requirement that he positively asserted his rights under the Regulations as part of his refusal);

    (2)   on the other hand, where care workers were dismissed for sleeping on a night shift and later claimed that they had not had proper rest breaks (during which they could lawfully have slept), it was held that the protection of the Employment Rights Act 1996 s 101A did not apply because there had been no express invocation of working time rights and no communicated 'refusal' (it not being enough that objectively there was a breach of working time law which might have been used by the claimant): *Ajayi v Aitch Care Homes (London) Ltd* [2012] All ER (D) 73 (Jun), EAT (*McLean v Rainbow Homeloans Ltd* not cited).

Pursuant to head (2) above, a refusal had to be explicit for the following reasons: (a) on a common-sense and natural reading of the Employment Rights Act 1996 s 101A, a refusal consisted of more than simply not doing something; (b) the word used in s 101A was 'refusal' and if simply non-compliance had been sufficient, Parliament would have used an expression such as 'failed' or 'did not comply'; and (c) reading 'refusal' as including non-compliance would be to create practical difficulties in the practical application of s 101A that Parliament could not have intended: *Ajayi v Aitch Care Homes (London) Ltd* (by being asleep, the employees were implicitly refusing the instruction issued to them in contravention of the Working Time Regulations 1998, SI 1998/1833).

7 Employment Rights Act 1996 s 101A(1)(b) (s 101A as added, s 101A(1) as renumbered: see note 4).

8 As to the meaning of 'workforce agreement' see PARA 272.

9 As to the meaning of 'employer' see PARA 2.

10 Employment Rights Act 1996 s 101A(1)(c) (s 101A as added, s 101A(1) as renumbered: see note 4).

11 Ie for the purposes of the Working Time Regulations 1998, SI 1998/1833, reg 2(1), Sch 1: see PARA 272.

12 See the Employment Rights Act 1996 s 101A(1)(d) (s 101A as added, s 101A(1) as renumbered: see note 4).

789. Fairness of dismissal for reason related to employee's participation in education and training. As from a day to be appointed[1], an employee[2] who is dismissed[3] is to be regarded[4] as unfairly dismissed if the reason (or, if more than one, the principal reason) for the dismissal is that, being a person entitled to be permitted to participate in education or training[5], the employee exercised, or proposed to exercise, that right[6].

1 As from a day to be appointed under the Education and Skills Act 2008 s 173(4), the Employment Rights Act 1996 s 101B is added by the Education and Skills Act 2008 s 38. However, at the date at which this volume states the law, no such day had been appointed.

2 As to the meaning of 'employee' see PARA 2.

3 As to the meaning of 'dismissal' see PARA 762.

4 Ie for the purposes of the Employment Rights Act 1996 Pt X (ss 94–134A) (unfair dismissal: see also PARAS 757 et seq, 790 et seq). As to the modification of Pt X in relation to governing bodies of schools having a right to a delegated budget, acting in the exercise of their employment powers, see EDUCATION vol 35 (2011) PARA 355 et seq; and as to the modification of Pt X in relation to persons holding ecclesiastical office under common tenure see the Ecclesiastical Offices (Terms of Service) Regulations 2009, SI 2009/2108, reg 33; and ECCLESIASTICAL LAW vol 34 (2011) PARA 407.

5 Ie by the Education and Skills Act 2008 s 27 or s 28: see PARAS 649, 650.

6 Employment Rights Act 1996 s 101B (prospectively added: see note 1).

    Where a dismissal is unfair under s 101B, the normal qualifying period for unfair dismissal does not apply: see s 108(3)(de) (not yet in force); and PARA 758 note 9. As to the right to make a complaint of unfair dismissal before an employment tribunal see PARA 804 et seq; and as to remedies see PARA 810 et seq.

790. Fairness of dismissal for reason related to employee's status as trustee of occupational pension scheme. An employee[1] who is dismissed[2] is to be regarded[3] as unfairly dismissed if the reason (or, if more than one, the principal reason) for the dismissal is that, being a trustee of a relevant occupational pension scheme[4] which relates to his employment[5], the employee performed, or proposed to perform, any functions as such a trustee[6].

1   As to the meaning of 'employee' see PARA 2.
2   As to the meaning of 'dismissal' see PARA 762.
3   Ie for the purposes of the Employment Rights Act 1996 Pt X (ss 94–134A) (unfair dismissal: see also PARAS 757 et seq, 791 et seq). As to the modification of Pt X in relation to governing bodies of schools having a right to a delegated budget, acting in the exercise of their employment powers, see EDUCATION vol 35 (2011) PARA 355 et seq; and as to the modification of Pt X in relation to persons holding ecclesiastical office under common tenure see the Ecclesiastical Offices (Terms of Service) Regulations 2009, SI 2009/2108, reg 33; and ECCLESIASTICAL LAW vol 34 (2011) PARA 407.
4   For these purposes, 'relevant occupational pension scheme' means an occupational pension scheme (as defined in the Pension Schemes Act 1993 s 1: see PERSONAL AND OCCUPATIONAL PENSIONS vol 80 (2013) PARA 208) established under a trust: Employment Rights Act 1996 s 102(2).
5   As to the meaning of 'employment' see PARA 2.
6   Employment Rights Act 1996 s 102(1). The provision made by s 102 applies to an employee who is a director of a company which is a trustee of a relevant occupational pension scheme as it applies to an employee who is a trustee of such a scheme, references to such a trustee being read for this purpose as references to such a director: s 102(1A) (added by the Welfare Reform and Pensions Act 1999 Sch 2 para 19(1), (4)).
    Where a dismissal is unfair under the Employment Rights Act 1996 s 102(1), the normal qualifying period for unfair dismissal does not apply (see s 108(3)(e); and PARA 758 note 9), there is a minimum for the basic award (see s 120(1); and PARA 816) and interim relief is available (see s 128(1); and PARA 805). As to the right to make a complaint of unfair dismissal before an employment tribunal see PARA 804 et seq; and as to remedies see PARA 810 et seq.

791. Fairness of dismissal for reason related to employee's representative status. An employee[1] who is dismissed[2] is to be regarded[3] as unfairly dismissed if the reason (or, if more than one, the principal reason) for the dismissal is[4]:

(1)   that the employee, being:

    (a)   an employee representative for the purposes of the statutory provisions that relate to collective redundancies[5] or to transfers of undertakings[6]; or

    (b)   a candidate in an election in which any person elected will, on being elected, be such an employee representative[7],

    performed, or proposed to perform, any functions or activities as such an employee representative or candidate[8];

(2)   that the employee took part in an election of employee representatives for the purposes of the law relating to collective redundancies[9] or transfers of undertakings[10].

1   As to the meaning of 'employee' see PARA 2.
2   As to the meaning of 'dismissal' see PARA 762.
3   Ie for the purposes of the Employment Rights Act 1996 Pt X (ss 94–134A) (unfair dismissal: see also PARAS 757 et seq, 792 et seq). As to the modification of Pt X in relation to governing bodies of schools having a right to a delegated budget, acting in the exercise of their employment powers, see EDUCATION vol 35 (2011) PARA 355 et seq; and as to the modification of Pt X in relation to persons holding ecclesiastical office under common tenure see the Ecclesiastical Offices (Terms of Service) Regulations 2009, SI 2009/2108, reg 33; and ECCLESIASTICAL LAW vol 34 (2011) PARA 407.
4   See the Employment Rights Act 1996 s 103(1) (renumbered by SI 1999/1925).
    Where a dismissal is unfair under the Employment Rights Act 1996 s 103, the normal qualifying period for unfair dismissal does not apply (see s 108(3)(f); and PARA 758 note 9),

there is a minimum for the basic award (see s 120(1); and PARA 816) and interim relief is available (see s 128(1); and PARA 805).As to the right to make a complaint of unfair dismissal before an employment tribunal see PARA 804 et seq; and as to remedies see PARA 810 et seq.

5 Ie for the purposes of the Trade Union and Labour Relations (Consolidation) Act 1992 Pt IV Ch II (ss 188–198B): see PARA 1185 et seq.

6 Employment Rights Act 1996 s 103(1)(a) (s 103(1) as renumbered (see note 4); s 103(1)(a) amended by SI 2006/246). The text refers to the statutory provisions that relate to transfers of undertakings contained in the Transfer of Undertakings (Protection of Employment) Regulations 2006, SI 2006/246, regs 9, 13, 15: see PARA 1196 et seq.

7 Employment Rights Act 1996 s 103(1)(b) (s 103(1) as renumbered: see note 4).

8 See the Employment Rights Act 1996 s 103(1) (s 103(1) as renumbered: see note 4).

9 See note 5.

10 Employment Rights Act 1996 s 103(2) (added by SI 1999/1925; and amended by SI 2006/246). As to the relevant statutory provisions that relate to transfers of undertakings see note 6.

792. Fairness of dismissal for reason related to employee who has made protected disclosures. An employee[1] who is dismissed[2] is to be regarded[3] as unfairly dismissed if the reason (or, if more than one, the principal reason) for the dismissal[4] is that the employee made a protected disclosure[5].

1 As to the meaning of 'employee' see PARA 2.

2 As to the meaning of 'dismissal' see PARA 762.

3 Ie for the purposes of the Employment Rights Act 1996 Pt X (ss 94–134A) (unfair dismissal: see also PARAS 757 et seq, 793 et seq). As to the modification of Pt X in relation to governing bodies of schools having a right to a delegated budget, acting in the exercise of their employment powers, see EDUCATION vol 35 (2011) PARA 355 et seq; and as to the modification of Pt X in relation to persons holding ecclesiastical office under common tenure see the Ecclesiastical Offices (Terms of Service) Regulations 2009, SI 2009/2108, reg 33; and ECCLESIASTICAL LAW vol 34 (2011) PARA 407.

4 The question of the principal reason for dismissal is a question of fact for the employment tribunal with which, in the absence of perversity, the EAT should not interfere: *El-Megrisi v Azad University (IR) In Oxford* [2009] All ER (D) 293 (Jul), EAT (tribunal had specifically excluded from its consideration any of the protected disclosures except the last one and had not only misdirected itself but, on its own findings of fact, would have had to conclude that the principal reason for the employee's dismissal was that she had made a protected disclosure). There is an evidential burden on the employee to show a prima facie case under the Employment Rights Act 1996 s 103A but, when he positively asserts that there was a different and inadmissible reason for his dismissal, it is sufficient for him to challenge the evidence produced by the employer to show the reason advanced by him for the dismissal and to produce some evidence of a different reason; the proper approach to the burden of proof in such a claim is as follows:
(1) has the claimant shown that there is a real issue as to whether the reason put forward by the respondent was not the true reason?;
(2) if so, has the employer proved his reason for dismissal?;
(3) if not, has the employer disproved the s 103A reason advanced by the claimant?;
(4) if not, dismissal is for the s 103A reason:
Kuzel v Roche Products Ltd [2008] EWCA Civ 380, [2008] ICR 799, [2008] IRLR 530 (following *Maund v Penwith District Council* [1984] ICR 143, [1984] IRLR 24, CA (see PARA 769)). See also *Nunn v Royal Mail Group Ltd* [2011] ICR 162, EAT.

5 Employment Rights Act 1996 s 103A (added by the Public Interest Disclosure Act 1998 ss 5, 18(2)). As to the meaning of 'protected disclosure' see PARA 69. Where a dismissal is unfair under the Employment Rights Act 1996 s 103A, the normal qualifying period for unfair dismissal does not apply (see s 108(3)(ff); and PARA 758 note 9), there is no statutory limit on the compensatory award (see s 124(1A); and PARA 823 note 6) and interim relief is available (see s 128(1); and PARA 805). As to the right to make a complaint of unfair dismissal before an employment tribunal see PARA 804 et seq; and as to remedies see PARA 810 et seq.

793. Fairness of dismissal for reason related to employee's assertion of relevant statutory right. An employee[1] who is dismissed[2] is to be regarded[3] as unfairly dismissed if the reason (or, if more than one, the principal reason) for the dismissal is that the employee[4]:

(1)   brought proceedings against the employer[5] to enforce a right of his which is a relevant statutory right[6]; or

(2)   alleged[7] that the employer had infringed a right of his which is a relevant statutory right[8].

For these purposes, it is immaterial whether or not the employee has the right[9], or whether or not the right has been infringed[10]. However, for the unfair dismissal provisions described above[11] to apply: (a) the claim to the right, and the claim that it has been infringed, must be made in good faith[12]; and (b) it is sufficient that the employee, without specifying the right, made it reasonably clear to the employer what the right claimed to have been infringed was[13].

1   As to the meaning of 'employee' see PARA 2.
2   As to the meaning of 'dismissal' see PARA 762.
3   Ie for the purposes of the Employment Rights Act 1996 Pt X (ss 94–134A) (unfair dismissal: see also PARAS 757 et seq, 794 et seq). As to the modification of Pt X in relation to governing bodies of schools having a right to a delegated budget, acting in the exercise of their employment powers, see EDUCATION vol 35 (2011) PARA 355 et seq; and as to the modification of Pt X in relation to persons holding ecclesiastical office under common tenure see the Ecclesiastical Offices (Terms of Service) Regulations 2009, SI 2009/2108, reg 33; and ECCLESIASTICAL LAW vol 34 (2011) PARA 407.
4   See the Employment Rights Act 1996 s 104(1).
5   As to the meaning of 'employer' see PARA 2. For these purposes, any reference to an employer includes, where the right in question is conferred by the Employment Rights Act 1996 s 63A (right to time off for study or training: see PARA 331), the principal, within the meaning of s 63A(3) (see PARA 331): s 104(5) (added by the Teaching and Higher Education Act 1998 Sch 3 para 13).
6   Employment Rights Act 1996 s 104(1)(a). For these purposes, the following are relevant statutory rights:
    (1)   any right conferred by the Employment Rights Act 1996 for which the remedy for its infringement is by way of a complaint or reference to an employment tribunal (s 104(4)(a) (amended by the Employment Rights (Dispute Resolution) Act 1998 s 1(2)(a)));
    (2)   the right conferred by the Employment Rights Act 1996 s 86 (rights of employer and employee to minimum notice: see PARA 736) (s 104(4)(b) (amended by SI 1998/1833));
    (3)   the rights conferred by the Trade Union and Labour Relations (Consolidation) Act 1992 s 68 (see PARA 1034), s 86 (see PARA 989), ss 145A, 145B (see PARAS 1051, 1052), s 146 (see PARA 1048), s 168 (see PARA 1065), s 168A (see PARA 1065), s 169 (see PARA 1065) and s 170 (see PARA 1066) (Employment Rights Act 1996 s 104(4)(c) (amended by the Employment Act 2002 Sch 7 paras 24, 34; and the Employment Relations Act 2004 Sch 1 para 31; and SI 1998/1833; SI 2006/246));
    (4)   the rights conferred by the Working Time Regulations 1998, SI 1998/1833 (see PARA 268 et seq), the Merchant Shipping (Hours of Work) Regulations 2002, SI 2002/2125 (see SHIPPING AND MARITIME LAW vol 94 (2008) PARA 625), the Merchant Shipping (Working Time: Inland Waterways) Regulations 2003, SI 2003/3049 (see SHIPPING AND MARITIME LAW vol 94 (2008) PARA 625), the Fishing Vessels (Working Time: Sea-fishermen) Regulations 2004, SI 2004/1713 (see SHIPPING AND MARITIME LAW vol 94 (2008) PARA 626) or the Cross-border Railway Services (Working Time) Regulations 2008, SI 2008/1660 (see RAILWAYS AND TRAMWAYS vol 86 (2013) PARAS 33, 328) (Employment Rights Act 1996 s 104(4)(d) (added by SI 1998/1833; substituted by SI 2004/1713; and amended by SI 2006/246; SI 2008/1660; SI 2014/308)); and
    (5)   the rights conferred by the Transfer of Undertakings (Protection of Employment) Regulations 2006, SI 2006/246 (see PARAS 137–141, 803) (Employment Rights Act 1996 s 104(4)(e) (added by SI 2006/246)).
    See *Elizabeth Claire Care Management Ltd v Francis* [2005] IRLR 858, EAT (complaint that salary had not been received on time was an assertion of the relevant statutory right as it constituted unlawful deduction from wages under the Employment Rights Act 1996 s 13(1) (see PARA 255)). The Part-time Workers (Prevention of Less Favourable Treatment) Regulations 2000, SI 2000/1551 (see PARA 78) and the Fixed-term Employees (Prevention of Less Favourable Treatment) Regulations 2002, SI 2002/2034 (see PARA 89) confer similar rights in relation to unfair dismissal that are conferred by the Employment Rights Act 1996 s 104. See

also note 13. As to the right to make a complaint of unfair dismissal before an employment tribunal see PARA 804 et seq; and as to remedies see PARA 810 et seq.

7 The complainant must have actually brought the complaint or made a substantive allegation; it is not enough that the employer's conduct could have given rise to a complaint or allegation: *Mennell v Newell and Wright (Transport Contractors) Ltd* [1997] ICR 1039, [1997] IRLR 519, CA. See also *Elizabeth Claire Care Management Ltd v Francis* [2005] IRLR 858, EAT; and note 6.

8 Employment Rights Act 1996 s 104(1)(b).

9 Employment Rights Act 1996 s 104(2)(a).

10 Employment Rights Act 1996 s 104(2)(b).

11 Ie the Employment Rights Act 1996 s 104(1): see the text and notes 1–8.

12 See the Employment Rights Act 1996 s 104(2). Where a dismissal is unfair under s 104(1), read with s 104(2), and s 104(3) (see head (b) in the text), the normal qualifying period for unfair dismissal does not apply: see s 108(3)(g); and PARA 758 note 9.

13 Employment Rights Act 1996 s 104(3). See note 12.

As to the approach that is required where an employer dismisses an employee who alleges specifically that he has refused to comply with a requirement which the employer imposed in contravention of the Working Time Regulations 1998, SI 1998/1833, see the Employment Rights Act 1996 s 101A; and PARA 788.

794. Fairness of dismissal for reason related to employee's enforcement of rights conferred under the National Minimum Wage Act 1998. An employee[1] who is dismissed[2] is to be regarded[3] as unfairly dismissed if the reason (or, if more than one, the principal reason) for the dismissal is that[4]:

(1)   any action was taken, or was proposed to be taken, by or on behalf of the employee with a view to enforcing, or otherwise securing the benefit of, a right of the employee conferred by the National Minimum Wage Act 1998[5]; or

(2)   the employer[6] was prosecuted for an offence under the National Minimum Wage Act 1998[7] as a result of action taken by or on behalf of the employee for the purpose of enforcing, or otherwise securing the benefit of, a right of the employee so conferred[8]; or

(3)   the employee qualifies, or will or might qualify, for the national minimum wage or for a particular rate of national minimum wage[9].

For the purposes of heads (1) and (2) above, it is immaterial whether or not the employee has the right[10], or whether or not the right has been infringed[11]. However, for either head (1) or head (2) above to apply, the claim to the right, and, if applicable, the claim that it has been infringed, must be made in good faith[12].

1 As to the meaning of 'employee' see PARA 2.

2 As to the meaning of 'dismissal' see PARA 762.

3 Ie for the purposes of the Employment Rights Act 1996 Pt X (ss 94–134A) (unfair dismissal: see also PARAS 757 et seq, 795 et seq). As to the modification of Pt X in relation to governing bodies of schools having a right to a delegated budget, acting in the exercise of their employment powers, see EDUCATION vol 35 (2011) PARA 355 et seq; and as to the modification of Pt X in relation to persons holding ecclesiastical office under common tenure see the Ecclesiastical Offices (Terms of Service) Regulations 2009, SI 2009/2108, reg 33; and ECCLESIASTICAL LAW vol 34 (2011) PARA 407.

4 See the Employment Rights Act 1996 s 104A(1) (s 104A added by the National Minimum Wage Act 1998 s 25(1)).

5 Employment Rights Act 1996 s 104A(1)(a) (as added: see note 4). For these purposes, the rights to which s 104A applies are:

(1)   any right conferred by, or by virtue of, any provision of the National Minimum Wage Act 1998 (see PARA 169 et seq) for which the remedy for its infringement is by way of a complaint to an employment tribunal (Employment Rights Act 1996 s 104A(3)(a) (as so added)); and

(2)   any right conferred by the National Minimum Wage Act 1998 s 17 (see PARA 242),

entitling a worker receiving less than the national minimum wage to additional remuneration (Employment Rights Act 1996 s 104A(3)(b) (as so added)).
As to the right to make a complaint of unfair dismissal before an employment tribunal see PARA 804 et seq; and as to remedies see PARA 810 et seq.

6   As to the meaning of 'employer' see PARA 2.
7   Ie under the National Minimum Wage Act 1998 s 31: see PARA 251.
8   Employment Rights Act 1996 s 104A(1)(b) (as added: see note 4). As to the rights to which s 104A applies see note 5.
9   Employment Rights Act 1996 s 104A(1)(c) (as added: see note 4).
10 Employment Rights Act 1996 s 104A(2)(a) (as added: see note 4).
11 Employment Rights Act 1996 s 104A(2)(b) (as added: see note 4).
12 See the Employment Rights Act 1996 s 104A(2) (as added: see note 4). Where a dismissal is unfair under s 104A(1), read with s 104A(2), the normal qualifying period for unfair dismissal does not apply: see s 108(3)(gg); and PARA 758 note 9.

795.   Fairness of dismissal for reason related to employee's enforcement of rights conferred under the Tax Credits Act 2002.   An employee[1] who is dismissed[2] is to be regarded[3] as unfairly dismissed if the reason (or, if more than one, the principal reason) for the dismissal is that[4]:

(1)   any action was taken, or was proposed to be taken, by or on behalf of the employee with a view to enforcing, or otherwise securing the benefit of, a right conferred on the employee by regulations under the Tax Credits Act 2002[5];

(2)   a penalty was imposed on the employer[6], or proceedings for a penalty were brought against him, under the Tax Credits Act 2002, as a result of action taken by or on behalf of the employee for the purpose of enforcing, or otherwise securing the benefit of, such a right[7]; or

(3)   the employee is entitled, or will or may be entitled, to working tax credit[8].

For the purposes of heads (1) and (2) above, it is immaterial whether or not the employee has the right[9], or whether or not the right has been infringed[10]. However, for either head (1) or head (2) above to apply, the claim to the right, and, if applicable, the claim that it has been infringed, must be made in good faith[11].

1   As to the meaning of 'employee' see PARA 2.
2   As to the meaning of 'dismissal' see PARA 762.
3   Ie for the purposes of the Employment Rights Act 1996 Pt X (ss 94–134A) (unfair dismissal: see also PARAS 757 et seq, 796 et seq). As to the modification of Pt X in relation to governing bodies of schools having a right to a delegated budget, acting in the exercise of their employment powers, see EDUCATION vol 35 (2011) PARA 355 et seq; and as to the modification of Pt X in relation to persons holding ecclesiastical office under common tenure see the Ecclesiastical Offices (Terms of Service) Regulations 2009, SI 2009/2108, reg 33; and ECCLESIASTICAL LAW vol 34 (2011) PARA 407.
4   See the Employment Rights Act 1996 s 104B(1) (s 104B added by the Tax Credits Act 1999 Sch 3 para 3(1); and substituted by the Tax Credits Act 2002 Sch 1 para 3(1), (2)).
5   Employment Rights Act 1996 s 104B(1)(a) (as added and substituted: see note 4). Head (1) in the text refers to regulations under the Tax Credits Act 2002 s 25: see WELFARE BENEFITS AND STATE PENSIONS vol 104 (2014) PARA 358.
6   As to the meaning of 'employer' see PARA 2.
7   Employment Rights Act 1996 s 104B(1)(b) (as added and substituted: see note 4).
8   Employment Rights Act 1996 s 104B(1)(c) (as added and substituted: see note 4). As to working tax credit see WELFARE BENEFITS AND STATE PENSIONS vol 104 (2014) PARA 335 et seq.
9   Employment Rights Act 1996 s 104B(2)(a) (as added and substituted: see note 4).
10 Employment Rights Act 1996 s 104B(2)(b) (as added and substituted: see note 4).
11 See the Employment Rights Act 1996 s 104B(2) (as added and substituted: see note 4). Where a dismissal is unfair under s 104B(1), read with s 104B(2), the normal qualifying period for unfair

dismissal does not apply: see s 108(3)(gh); and PARA 758 note 9. As to the right to make a complaint of unfair dismissal before an employment tribunal see PARA 804 et seq; and as to remedies see PARA 810 et seq.

796. Fairness of dismissal related to flexible working cases. An employee[1] who is dismissed[2] is to be regarded[3] as unfairly dismissed if the reason (or, if more than one, the principal reason) for the dismissal is that the employee[4]:

(1) made, or proposed to make, an application[5] for a change in his terms and conditions to allow for flexible working[6];

(2) brought proceedings against his employer[7] alleging that the employer had failed to comply with his statutory duties in relation to such an application or that a decision by his employer to reject the application was based on incorrect facts[8]; or

(3) alleged the existence of any circumstance which would constitute a ground for bringing such proceedings[9].

1 As to the meaning of 'employee' see PARA 2.
2 As to the meaning of 'dismissal' see PARA 762.
3 Ie for the purposes of the Employment Rights Act 1996 Pt X (ss 94–134A) (unfair dismissal: see also PARAS 757 et seq, 797 et seq). As to the modification of Pt X in relation to governing bodies of schools having a right to a delegated budget, acting in the exercise of their employment powers, see EDUCATION vol 35 (2011) PARA 355 et seq; and as to the modification of Pt X in relation to persons holding ecclesiastical office under common tenure see the Ecclesiastical Offices (Terms of Service) Regulations 2009, SI 2009/2108, reg 33; and ECCLESIASTICAL LAW vol 34 (2011) PARA 407.
4 See the Employment Rights Act 1996 s 104C(1) (s 104C added by the Employment Act 2002 s 47(1), (4)).
   Where a dismissal is unfair under the Employment Rights Act 1996 s 104C, the normal qualifying period for unfair dismissal does not apply: see s 108(3)(gi): and PARA 758 note 9. As to the right to make a complaint of unfair dismissal before an employment tribunal see PARA 804 et seq; and as to remedies see PARA 810 et seq.
5 Ie under the Employment Rights Act 1996 s 80F: see PARA 108.
6 Employment Rights Act 1996 s 104C(1)(a) (as added: see note 4).
7 Ie under the Employment Rights Act 1996 s 80H: see PARA 111. As to the meaning of 'employer' see PARA 2.
8 Employment Rights Act 1996 s 104C(1)(c) (as added: see note 4).
9 Employment Rights Act 1996 s 104C(1)(d) (as added: see note 4).

797. Fairness of dismissal for reason related to employee's enforcement of requirement imposed on employer under the Pensions Act 2008. An employee[1] who is dismissed[2] is to be regarded[3] as unfairly dismissed if the reason (or, if more than one, the principal reason) for the dismissal is that[4]:

(1) any action was taken, or was proposed to be taken, with a view to enforcing in favour of the employee a requirement imposed on the employer under the Pensions Act 2008[5] to enrol eligible jobholders into automatic enrolment schemes and to contribute to those arrangements[6];

(2) the employer[7] was prosecuted for an offence under the Pensions Act 2008[8], as a result of action taken for the purpose of enforcing in favour of the employee a requirement so imposed[9]; or

(3) any provision of Chapter 1 of Part 1 of the Pensions Act 2008[10] applies to the employee, or will or might apply[11].

For the purposes of heads (1) and (2) above, it is immaterial whether or not the requirement applies in favour of the employee[12], or whether or not the requirement has been contravened[13]. However, for either head (1) or head (2) above to apply, the claim that the requirement applies, and, if applicable, the claim that it has been contravened, must be made in good faith[14].

1   As to the meaning of 'employee' see PARA 2.
2   As to the meaning of 'dismissal' see PARA 762.
3   Ie for the purposes of the Employment Rights Act 1996 Pt X (ss 94–134A) (unfair dismissal: see
    also PARAS 757 et seq, 798 et seq). As to the modification of Pt X in relation to governing bodies
    of schools having a right to a delegated budget, acting in the exercise of their employment
    powers, see EDUCATION vol 35 (2011) PARA 355 et seq; and as to the modification of Pt X in
    relation to persons holding ecclesiastical office under common tenure see the Ecclesiastical
    Offices (Terms of Service) Regulations 2009, SI 2009/2108, reg 33; and ECCLESIASTICAL LAW
    vol 34 (2011) PARA 407.
4   See the Employment Rights Act 1996 s 104D(1) (s 104D added by the Pensions Act 2008
    s 57(1), (2)).
5   Ie a requirement to which the Employment Rights Act 1996 s 104D applies. The requirement to
    which s 104D applies is any requirement imposed on the employer by or under any provision of
    the Pensions Act 2008 Pt 1 Ch 1 (ss 1–33) (pension scheme membership for jobholders
    (employers' duties): see PERSONAL AND OCCUPATIONAL PENSIONS vol 80 (2013) PARA 737 et
    seq): Employment Rights Act 1996 s 104D(3) (as added: see note 4). For the purposes of
    s 104D, references to enforcing a requirement include references to securing its benefit in any
    way: s 104D(4) (as so added).
6   Employment Rights Act 1996 s 104D(1)(a) (as added: see note 4).
7   As to the meaning of 'employer' see PARA 2.
8   Ie under the Pensions Act 2008 s 45: see PERSONAL AND OCCUPATIONAL PENSIONS vol 80 (2013)
    PARA 761.
9   Employment Rights Act 1996 s 104D(1)(b) (as added: see note 4).
10 Ie any provision of the Pensions Act 2008 Pt 1 Ch 1 (pension scheme membership for jobholders
    (employers' duties)): see PERSONAL AND OCCUPATIONAL PENSIONS vol 80 (2013) PARA 737 et
    seq.
11 Employment Rights Act 1996 s 104D(1)(c) (as added: see note 4).
12 Employment Rights Act 1996 s 104D(2)(a) (as added: see note 4).
13 Employment Rights Act 1996 s 104D(2)(b) (as added: see note 4).
14 See the Employment Rights Act 1996 s 104D(2) (as added: see note 4). Where a dismissal is
    unfair under s 104D(1), read with s 104D(2), the normal qualifying period for unfair dismissal
    does not apply: see s 108(3)(gj); and PARA 758 note 9. As to the right to make a complaint of
    unfair dismissal before an employment tribunal see PARA 804 et seq; and as to remedies see
    PARA 810 et seq.

**798.   Fairness of dismissal for reason related to applications for employer
support for employee study and training.**   An employee[1] who is dismissed[2] is to
be regarded[3] as unfairly dismissed if the reason (or, if more than one, the
principal reason) for the dismissal is that[4]:

(1)   made, or proposed to make, an application[5] pursuant to his right to
      request study or training[6];

(2)   exercised, or proposed to exercise, a right conferred on him[7] in relation
      to such an application[8];

(3)   brought proceedings[9] against the employer alleging that the employer
      has failed to comply with his statutory duties in relation to such an
      application or that a decision by his employer to reject the application
      was based on incorrect facts[10]; or

(4)   alleged the existence of any circumstance which would constitute a
      ground for bringing such proceedings[11].

1   As to the meaning of 'employee' see PARA 2.
2   As to the meaning of 'dismissal' see PARA 762.
3   Ie for the purposes of the Employment Rights Act 1996 Pt X (ss 94–134A) (unfair dismissal: see
    also PARAS 757 et seq, 799 et seq). As to the modification of Pt X in relation to governing bodies
    of schools having a right to a delegated budget, acting in the exercise of their employment
    powers, see EDUCATION vol 35 (2011) PARA 355 et seq; and as to the modification of Pt X in
    relation to persons holding ecclesiastical office under common tenure see the Ecclesiastical
    Offices (Terms of Service) Regulations 2009, SI 2009/2108, reg 33; and ECCLESIASTICAL LAW
    vol 34 (2011) PARA 407.

4   See the Employment Rights Act 1996 s 104E(1) (s 104E added by the Apprenticeships, Skills,
     Children and Learning Act 2009 s 40(1), (4)). At the date at which this volume states the law,
     the Apprenticeships, Skills, Children and Learning Act 2009 s 40 has come into force for all
     purposes except in relation to small employers and their employees: see the Apprenticeships,
     Skills, Children and Learning Act 2009 (Commencement No 2 and Transitional and Saving
     Provisions) Order 2010, SI 2010/303, art 4, Sch 3. As to the meaning of 'small employer' for
     these purposes see PARA 328 note 1.
         Where a dismissal is unfair under the Employment Rights Act 1996 s 104E, the normal
     qualifying period for unfair dismissal does not apply: see s 108(3)(gk); and PARA 758 note 9. As
     to the right to make a complaint of unfair dismissal before an employment tribunal see
     PARA 804 et seq; and as to remedies see PARA 810 et seq.
5   Ie under the Employment Rights Act 1996 s 63D: see PARA 328.
6   Employment Rights Act 1996 s 104E(1)(a) (as added: see note 4).
7   Ie under the Employment Rights Act 1996 s 63F: see PARA 328.
8   Employment Rights Act 1996 s 104E(1)(b) (as added: see note 4).
9   Ie under the Employment Rights Act 1996 s 63I: see PARA 330.
10   Employment Rights Act 1996 s 104E(1)(c) (as added: see note 4).
11   Employment Rights Act 1996 s 104E(1)(d) (as added: see note 4).

**799.   Fairness of dismissal for reason related to blacklists of trade union
members.**   An employee[1] who is dismissed[2] is to be regarded[3] as unfairly
dismissed if the reason (or, if more than one, the principal reason) for the
dismissal relates to a prohibited list[4], and either:

(1)   in relation to that prohibited list, the employer contravenes the general
       prohibition[5] on compiling, using, selling or supplying such a list[6]; or
(2)   the employer: (a) relies on information supplied by a person who
       contravenes the general prohibition[7]; and (b) knows or ought to
       reasonably know that the information relied on is supplied in
       contravention of that prohibition[8].

If there are facts from which the tribunal can conclude, in the absence of any
other explanation, that the employer: (i) contravened the general prohibition[9]; or
(ii) relied on information supplied in contravention of that prohibition[10], the
tribunal must find that such a contravention or reliance on information
occurred, unless the employer shows that it did not[11].

1   As to the meaning of 'employee' see PARA 2.
2   As to the meaning of 'dismissal' see PARA 762.
3   Ie for the purposes of the Employment Rights Act 1996 Pt X (ss 94–134A) (unfair dismissal: see
     also PARAS 757 et seq, 800 et seq). As to the modification of Pt X in relation to governing bodies
     of schools having a right to a delegated budget, acting in the exercise of their employment
     powers, see EDUCATION vol 35 (2011) PARA 355 et seq; and as to the modification of Pt X in
     relation to persons holding ecclesiastical office under common tenure see the Ecclesiastical
     Offices (Terms of Service) Regulations 2009, SI 2009/2108, reg 33; and ECCLESIASTICAL LAW
     vol 34 (2011) PARA 407.
4   See the Employment Rights Act 1996 s 104F(1) (s 104F added by SI 2010/493). As to the
     meaning of 'prohibited list' for these purposes see PARA 1037 note 12; definition applied by the
     Employment Rights Act 1996 s 104F(3) (as so added).
5   Ie the employer contravenes the Employment Relations Act 1999 (Blacklists) Regulations 2010,
     SI 2010/493, reg 3: see PARA 1037. As to the meaning of 'employer' see PARA 2.
6   Employment Rights Act 1996 s 104F(1)(a) (as added: see note 4).
7   Employment Rights Act 1996 s 104F(1)(b)(i) (as added: see note 4). The text refers to
     information supplied by a person who contravenes the Employment Relations Act 1999
     (Blacklists) Regulations 2010, SI 2010/493, reg 3: see PARA 1037.
8   Employment Rights Act 1996 s 104F(1)(b)(ii) (as added: see note 4). The text refers to
     information supplied in contravention of the Employment Relations Act 1999 (Blacklists)
     Regulations 2010, SI 2010/493, reg 3: see PARA 1037.
9   Employment Rights Act 1996 s 104F(2)(a) (as added: see note 4). The text refers to an employer
     who contravened the Employment Relations Act 1999 (Blacklists) Regulations 2010,
     SI 2010/493, reg 3: see PARA 1037.

10 Employment Rights Act 1996 s 104F(2)(b) (as added: see note 4). The text refers to information
    supplied in contravention of the Employment Relations Act 1999 (Blacklists) Regulations 2010,
    SI 2010/493, reg 3: see PARA 1037.
11 See the Employment Rights Act 1996 s 104F(2) (as added: see note 4). Where a dismissal is
    unfair under s 104F(1), read with s 104F(2), the normal qualifying period for unfair dismissal
    does not apply: see s 108(3)(gl); and PARA 758 note 9. As to the right to make a complaint of
    unfair dismissal before an employment tribunal see PARA 804 et seq; and as to remedies see
    PARA 810 et seq.

800.   Fairness of dismissal for reason related to employee's shareholder status.
An employee[1] who is dismissed[2] is to be regarded[3] as unfairly dismissed if the
reason (or, if more than one, the principal reason) for the dismissal is that the
employee refused to accept an offer by the employer[4] to become an employee
shareholder[5].

1 As to the meaning of 'employee' see PARA 2.
2 As to the meaning of 'dismissal' see PARA 762.
3 Ie for the purposes of the Employment Rights Act 1996 Pt X (ss 94–134A) (unfair dismissal: see
   also PARAS 757 et seq, 801 et seq). As to the modification of Pt X in relation to governing bodies
   of schools having a right to a delegated budget, acting in the exercise of their employment
   powers, see EDUCATION vol 35 (2011) PARA 355 et seq; and as to the modification of Pt X in
   relation to persons holding ecclesiastical office under common tenure see the Ecclesiastical
   Offices (Terms of Service) Regulations 2009, SI 2009/2108, reg 33; and ECCLESIASTICAL LAW
   vol 34 (2011) PARA 407.
4 As to the meaning of 'employer' see PARA 2.
5 See the Employment Rights Act 1996 s 104G (added by the Growth and Infrastructure Act 2013
   s 31(4)). The text refers to an employee shareholder within the meaning of the Employment
   Rights Act 1996 s 205A (see PARA 154): see s 104G (as so added).
       Where a dismissal is unfair under s 104G, the normal qualifying period for unfair dismissal
   does not apply: see s 108(3)(gm); and PARA 758 note 9. As to the right to make a complaint of
   unfair dismissal before an employment tribunal see PARA 804 et seq; and as to remedies see
   PARA 810 et seq.

801.   Fairness of dismissal of replacements.   Where an employer[1]:
   (1)   on engaging an employee[2], informs the employee in writing that his
         employment[3] will be terminated on the resumption of work by another
         employee who is, or will be, absent wholly or partly because of
         pregnancy or childbirth[4], or on adoption leave[5], or shared parental
         leave[6], and dismisses[7] the first-mentioned employee in order to make it
         possible to give work to the other employee[8]; or
   (2)   on engaging an employee, informs the employee in writing that his
         employment will be terminated on the end of a suspension of another
         employee from work on medical grounds[9] or maternity grounds[10], and
         dismisses the first-mentioned employee in order to make it possible to
         allow the resumption of work by the other employee[11],
the employee is to be regarded[12] as having been dismissed for a substantial
reason of a kind such as to justify the dismissal of an employee holding the
position[13] which the employee held[14].

1 As to the meaning of 'employer' see PARA 2.
2 As to the meaning of 'employee' see PARA 2.
3 As to the meaning of 'employment' see PARA 2.
4 As to the meaning of 'childbirth' see PARA 356 note 4. As to ordinary maternity leave and
   additional maternity leave see PARA 356 et seq; and as to compulsory maternity leave see
   PARA 363.
5 As to adoption leave see PARA 377 et seq. As to ordinary adoption leave see PARA 378 et seq; and
   as to additional adoption leave see PARA 379 et seq.
6 Employment Rights Act 1996 s 106(2)(a) (amended by the Employment Act 2002 Sch 7
   paras 24, 35; the Work and Families Act 2006 Sch 1 para 42; and the Children and Families

Act 2014 Sch 7 paras 29, 40). As to shared parental leave see PARA 398 et seq. The Employment Rights Act 1996 s 106(2)(a) envisages a clear notice being given at the outset, so as to leave no doubt on the part of the employee as to the circumstances in which the contract would end: *Victoria and Albert Museum v Durrant* [2011] IRLR 290, EAT (longstanding employee already under threat of termination for incapability or redundancy was given a final extension of employment to cover for a maternity absence but employer's letter not sufficiently unambiguous to meet requirements of the Employment Rights Act 1996 s 106(2)(a)).

7   As to the meaning of 'dismissal' see PARA 762.

8   Employment Rights Act 1996 s 106(2)(b) See *Victoria and Albert Museum v Durrant* [2011] IRLR 290, EAT (where an employer had not shown clearly enough that an employee's termination of employment after the fixed term had expired was on account of another employee's return from maternity leave, the requirements of the Employment Rights Act 1996 s 106(2)(b) had not been complied with).

9   Ie within the meaning of the Employment Rights Act 1996 Pt VII (ss 64–70A) (suspension from work): see PARA 596.

10   Employment Rights Act 1996 s 106(3)(a). The text refers to maternity grounds within the meaning of Pt VII: see PARA 598 note 2.

11   Employment Rights Act 1996 s 106(3)(b).

12   Ie for the purposes of the Employment Rights Act 1996 s 98(1)(b) (see PARA 765).

13   As to the meaning of 'position' see PARA 765 note 13.

14   See the Employment Rights Act 1996 s 106(1). The provision made by s 106(1) is without prejudice to the application of s 98(4) (see PARA 765) in a case to which s 106 applies: s 106(4). As to the right to make a complaint of unfair dismissal before an employment tribunal see PARA 804 et seq; and as to remedies see PARA 810 et seq. As to the modification of Pt X (ss 94–134A) (unfair dismissal: see also PARAS 757 et seq, 802 et seq) in relation to governing bodies of schools having a right to a delegated budget, acting in the exercise of their employment powers, see EDUCATION vol 35 (2011) PARA 355 et seq; and as to the modification of Pt X in relation to persons holding ecclesiastical office under common tenure see the Ecclesiastical Offices (Terms of Service) Regulations 2009, SI 2009/2108, reg 33; and ECCLESIASTICAL LAW vol 34 (2011) PARA 407.

H. CHANGING BUSINESS NEEDS AND REORGANISATION

802. Possibility of fair dismissal on grounds of changing business needs and reorganisation. Where an employer considers that he needs to change an employee's work or terms and conditions, this can lead to one of three consequences:

(1)   if the changes lie within the contractual rights of the employer, he may insist on them and an employee refusing to accept them may be dismissed for disobedience of lawful orders[1];

(2)   the changes may affect the nature of the job itself to such an extent that the employee's old work decreases or disappears, in which case there is a redundancy[2], with a right to a redundancy payment if the employee is dismissed[3], but no claim for unfair dismissal unless the redundancy is conducted in such a way as to make it unfair[4];

(3)   the changes may involve a unilateral change to the employee's contractual terms and conditions of employment without producing a redundancy, as, for example, where the work remains the same but the employer decides it is necessary to alter the hours of work or the system or amount of payment in order to retain the economic viability of the firm.

If, in a case falling within head (3) above, one or more of the employees refuse to agree to the changes, the employer may ultimately decide to dismiss them for that reason, and in order to carry through the changes. A dismissal in breach of the employee's contractual rights would normally be unfair[5] but, in these circumstances, it has been held that the dismissal may be for 'some other substantial reason'[6] if the employer shows[7] that there are sound business reasons for insisting on the changes[8], and, if properly handled[9], the dismissal may be fair[10].

1   This applies particularly where the employer is insisting on new methods of performing the same work, eg by the introduction of new technology: *Cresswell v Board of Inland Revenue* [1984] 2 All ER 713, [1984] ICR 508. See also *George Wimpey & Co Ltd v Cooper* [1977] IRLR 205, EAT; *Glitz v Watford Electric Co Ltd* [1979] IRLR 89, EAT (flexibility, within a job description, particularly important in a small firm); and see PARA 64.

2   See eg *Wilson v Underhill House School Ltd* [1977] IRLR 475, EAT; *Robinson v British Island Airways Ltd* [1978] ICR 304, [1977] IRLR 477, EAT; *Murphy v Epsom College* [1985] ICR 80, [1984] IRLR 271, CA.

3   See PARA 835 et seq.

4   See PARAS 780–782.

5   The employee may also be able to bring a common law claim for wages (under the original terms of the contract) as a way of effectively enforcing the contract: *Rigby v Ferodo Ltd* [1988] ICR 29, [1987] IRLR 516, HL; and see PARA 833. However, in these circumstances the fact that the changes would be in breach of contract if not assented to does not necessarily make the dismissal unfair: *Farrant v Woodroffe School* [1998] ICR 184, [1998] IRLR 176, EAT.

6   Ie within the Employment Rights Act 1996 s 98(1)(b): see PARAS 765–766.

7   The employer must adduce evidence showing why he thought change necessary and how he reached the relevant decisions: *Banerjee v City and East London Area Health Authority* [1979] IRLR 147, EAT; *Ladbroke Courage Holidays Ltd v Asten* [1981] IRLR 59, EAT; *Orr v Vaughan* [1981] IRLR 63, EAT. See also *Slingsby v Griffith Smith Solicitors* [2008] All ER (D) 158 (Aug), EAT. A tribunal may decide on the facts that the reorganisation was a pretext for dismissing someone the employer wished to be without: *Labour Party v Oakley* [1988] ICR 403, sub nom *Oakley v Labour Party* [1988] IRLR 34, CA.

8   See eg *Hollister v National Farmers' Union* [1979] ICR 542, [1979] IRLR 238, CA; *Bowater Containers Ltd v McCormack* [1980] IRLR 50, EAT; *Genower v Ealing, Hammersmith and Hounslow Area Health Authority* [1980] IRLR 297, EAT; *Catamaran Cruisers Ltd v Williams* [1994] IRLR 386, EAT; *Garside and Laycock Ltd v Booth* [2011] IRLR 735, EAT. Earlier cases had assumed that, in order to succeed, the employer had to show that the changes were so vital that without them the business would come to a standstill (*Ellis v Brighton Co-operative Society* [1976] IRLR 419, EAT), but in *Hollister v National Farmers' Union* that was held to be too stringent a test.

9   Consultation with the employee or employees and consideration of any counter-proposals may be important: *Ellis v Brighton Co-operative Society* [1976] IRLR 419, EAT; *Martin v Automobile Pty Ltd* [1979] IRLR 64, EAT. The fact of agreement over the changes with the relevant trade union and/or the majority of the employees affected is significant: see *Robinson v Flitwick Frames Ltd* [1975] IRLR 261; *Ellis v Brighton Co-operative Society*; *Sycamore v H Myer & Co Ltd* [1976] IRLR 84; *Bowater Containers Ltd v McCormack* [1980] IRLR 50, EAT; *Catamaran Cruisers Ltd v Williams* [1994] IRLR 386, EAT.

  Where the employee is the only one, or one of only a few, to hold out against the changes, the employer may be expected at least to consider whether it is possible to make an exception in the case of an individual and not force him into a collective agreement: *Martin v Automobile Pty Ltd*. In *Hollister v National Farmers' Union* [1979] ICR 542, [1979] IRLR 238, CA, the emphasis on consultation was doubted.

10 *RS Components v Irwin* [1974] 1 All ER 41, [1973] ICR 535, NIRC; *Ellis v Brighton Co-operative Society* [1976] IRLR 419, EAT. When applying the general test of fairness and the range of reasonable responses test (see the Employment Rights Act 1996 s 98(4); and PARAS 765, 767), the correct approach is to consider the reasonableness of the decision to dismiss the employee for refusal to accept, not the reasonableness of the employer's offer: *St John of God (Care Services) Ltd v Brooks* [1992] ICR 715, [1992] IRLR 546, EAT. There is no distinction between dismissal for failure to sign a contract which, if imposed, would contain unreasonable terms and one which, if imposed, would contain terms which were unreasonably in restraint of trade; the question of the reasonableness of the covenant falls to be looked at the stage of fairness, and as part of the whole context, and in all the circumstances, as provided for in the Employment Rights Act 1996 s 98(4): *Silverwood v Willow Oak Developments Ltd (t/a Windsor Recruitment)* [2006] EWCA Civ 660, [2006] ICR 1552, [2006] IRLR 607. *Forshaw v Archcraft Ltd* [2006] ICR 70, [2005] IRLR 600, EAT (refusal by an employee to sign up to a restraint which was unreasonably wide cannot amount to a potentially fair reason for dismissal) was not followed in *Silverwood v Willow Oak Developments Ltd (t/a Windsor Recruitment)*.

It may be appropriate to consider whether the advantages to the employer outweighed the disadvantages to the employee from the changes, but this is only one factor: *Richmond Precision Engineering Ltd v Pearce* [1985] IRLR 179, EAT, considering *Chubb Fire Security Ltd v Harper* [1983] IRLR 311, EAT; cf *Evans v Elemeta Holdings Ltd* [1982] ICR 323, [1982] IRLR 143, EAT (emphasis on whether employee acted reasonably in refusing proposed terms). Ultimately, the application of the general test of unfairness (here or elsewhere) is a question of fact for the tribunal, with restricted scope for a challenge to its decision on appeal: see *Gilham v Kent County Council (No 2)* [1985] ICR 233, sub nom *Kent County Council v Gilham* [1985] IRLR 18, CA.

I. TRANSFERS OF UNDERTAKINGS

803.   Fairness of dismissal for reason related to relevant transfer. Where, either before or after a relevant transfer[1], any employee[2] of the transferor[3] or transferee[4] is dismissed, that employee is to be treated[5] as unfairly dismissed if the sole or principal reason for his dismissal is the transfer itself[6]. This provision does not apply, however, where the sole or principal reason for the dismissal is an economic, technical or organisational reason entailing changes in the workforce[7] of either the transferor or the transferee before or after a relevant transfer[8].

These provisions[9] apply irrespective of whether the employee in question is assigned to the organised grouping of resources or employees that is, or will, be transferred[10].

1   As to the meaning of 'relevant transfer' see PARA 137.
2   As to the meaning of 'employee' see PARA 137 note 8.
3   As to the meaning of 'transferor' see PARA 137.
4   As to the meaning of 'transferee' see PARA 137.
5   Ie for the purposes of the Employment Rights Act 1996 Pt X (ss 94–134A) (unfair dismissal: see also PARAS 757 et seq, 804 et seq). As to the modification of Pt X in relation to governing bodies of schools having a right to a delegated budget, acting in the exercise of their employment powers, see EDUCATION vol 35 (2011) PARA 355 et seq; and as to the modification of Pt X in relation to persons holding ecclesiastical office under common tenure see the Ecclesiastical Offices (Terms of Service) Regulations 2009, SI 2009/2108, reg 33; and ECCLESIASTICAL LAW vol 34 (2011) PARA 407.
6   Transfer of Undertakings (Protection of Employment) Regulations 2006, SI 2006/246, reg 7(1) (reg 7(1)–(3) substituted, reg 7(3A) added, by SI 2014/16). See also the text and notes 7–8. The Transfer of Undertakings (Protection of Employment) Regulations 2006, SI 2006/246, reg 7(1) does not apply:
    (1)   in relation to the dismissal of any employee which was required by reason of the application of the Aliens Restriction (Amendment) Act 1919 s 5 to his employment (Transfer of Undertakings (Protection of Employment) Regulations 2006, SI 2006/246, reg 7(5)); or
    (2)   in relation to a dismissal of an employee if the application of the Employment Rights Act 1996 s 94 (right not to be unfairly dismissed: see PARA 757) to the dismissal of the employee is excluded by or under any provision of the Employment Rights Act 1996, the Employment Tribunals Act 1996, or the Trade Union and Labour Relations (Consolidation) Act 1992 (Transfer of Undertakings (Protection of Employment) Regulations 2006, SI 2006/246, reg 7(6)).
    The Aliens Restriction (Amendment) Act 1919 s 5 (see head (1) above) is repealed by the Merchant Shipping Act 1995 Sch 12 as from such day as the Secretary of State may by order appoint: see s 314(3), Sch 14 para 5(1), (2). However, at the date at which this volume states the law, no such day had been appointed. As to the Secretary of State see PARA 5 note 21.
    The predecessor to the Transfer of Undertakings (Protection of Employment) Regulations 2006, SI 2006/246, reg 7(1) (ie the Transfer of Undertakings (Protection of Employment) Regulations 1981, SI 1981/1794, reg 8(1)) was held to be applicable to the dismissal of an employee in advance of a possible transfer, even though it has not been concluded: see *Morris v John Grose Group Ltd* [1998] ICR 655, [1998] IRLR 499, EAT (preferring the wide view in *Harrison Bowden Ltd v Bowden* [1994] ICR 186, EAT, to the narrower view in *Ibex Trading Co Ltd (in administration) v Walton* [1994] ICR 907, [1994] IRLR 564, EAT, that the actual transfer must be in contemplation). The decision in *Michael*

Peters Ltd v Farnfield and Michael Peters Group plc [1995] IRLR 190, EAT, was indecisive on the point but the Court of Appeal has applied *Harrison Bowden Ltd v Bowden* and *Morris v John Grose Group Ltd* in preference to *Ibex Trading v Walton*: see *Spaceright Europe Ltd v Baillavoine* [2011] EWCA Civ 1565, [2012] 2 All ER 812, [2012] IRLR 111, [2012] ICR 520 (in order for a dismissal to be automatically unfair under the Transfer of Undertakings (Protection of Employment) Regulations 2006, SI 2006/246, reg 7(1), it is not necessary for a particular transfer or transferee to be in existence or in contemplation at the time of the dismissal). Shedding labour as a direct condition of obtaining a contract may qualify as an 'economic, technical or organisational reason' (see the text and notes 7–8): *Whitehouse v Chas A Blatchford & Sons Ltd* [1999] IRLR 492, CA.

7   For these purposes, the expression 'changes in the workforce' includes a change to the place where employees are employed by the employer to carry on the business of the employer or to carry out work of a particular kind for the employer (and the reference to such a place has the same meaning as in the Employment Rights Act 1996 s 139 (redundancy: see PARA 870)): Transfer of Undertakings (Protection of Employment) Regulations 2006, SI 2006/246, reg 7(3A) (as added: see note 6). This provision amplifies the meaning of 'changes in the workforce' specifically by adding the concept of a change in the location of the employees' workplace to the list of 'economic, technical or organisational' reasons that was not available before 2014: see *Besagni v RR Donnelley Global Document Solutions Group Ltd* [2014] All ER (D) 115 (Jun), EAT.

What must be shown are changes in the number of the workforce, or possibly changes in the job descriptions of the constituent elements of the workforce, which, although involving no overall reduction in numbers, involves a change in the individual employees which together make up the workforce: *Berriman v Delabole Slate Ltd* [1985] ICR 546, [1985] IRLR 305, CA. It must be an objective of the employer's plan to achieve changes in the workforce, not just a possible consequence of it; nor could it be held that the dismissal of one employee followed by the engagement of another in his place constitutes a change in the 'workforce', since changes in the identity of the individuals who make up the workforce do not constitute changes in the workforce itself so long as the overall numbers and functions of the employees looked at as a whole remain unchanged: *Berriman v Delabole Slate Ltd* (the 'workforce' connotes the whole body of employees as an entity and corresponds to the 'strength' or the 'establishment'); and see *Nationwide Building Society v Benn* [2010] IRLR 922, EAT (it is not required for the organisational reason to entail changes in the entirety of the workforce, since the Transfer of Undertakings (Protection of Employment) Regulations 2006, SI 2006/246, apply not only to a transfer of an undertaking but also to a transfer of part of an undertaking). See also *Meter U Ltd v Ackroyd, Meter U Ltd v Hardy* [2012] IRLR 367, EAT (where transferee employer carries on business but engages staff on contract basis rather than as direct employees, that change in status qualifies as an 'economic, technical or organisational' reason, so that any transferring employees who do not accept that change are not automatically dismissed unfairly unless it can be shown that the whole change in set-up was a 'sham'); and *Manchester College v Hazel* [2014] EWCA Civ 72, [2014] IRLR 392 (where the principal reason for a particular dismissal was the refusal of a change of terms, the 'economic, technical or organisational' reason does not apply because new terms were not a 'change in the workforce').

The dismissal of an employee prior to sale of the employer's undertaking as a going concern, necessitating a reduction in the workforce, is for an economic, technical or organisational reason: *Thompson v SCS Consulting Ltd* [2001] IRLR 801, EAT. However, the 'economic, technical or organisational' defence in the Transfer of Undertakings (Protection of Employment) Regulations 2006, SI 2006/246, reg 7(2), is not available where an employee is dismissed to enable administrators to make the business of the company a more attractive proposition to prospective transferees of a going concern: *Spaceright Europe Ltd v Baillavoine* [2011] EWCA Civ 1565, [2012] 2 All ER 812, [2012] ICR 520, [2012] IRLR 111. *Spaceright Europe Ltd v Baillavoine* posits two alternative positions: (1) where the reason for a dismissal was the intention to change the workforce and to continue to conduct the business, there could be a dismissal for an 'economic, technical or organisational' reason; and (2) where the dismissal was part and parcel of a process with the purpose of selling the business, the reason does not apply: *Kavanagh v Crystal Palace FC (2000) Ltd* [2013] IRLR 291, EAT (dismissals had been for the purpose of selling the business, albeit it was not at that stage certain that there would have been a sale, nor necessarily to whom the sale would have been). Where it was clear that the dismissal of the employees by an administrator was due to the fact that the company had no money to pay them, that was an 'economic' reason: *Dynamex Friction Ltd v Amicus* [2008] EWCA Civ 381, [2008] IRLR 515.

8   See the Transfer of Undertakings (Protection of Employment) Regulations 2006, SI 2006/246, reg 7(2), (3)(a) (as substituted: see note 6). Where the circumstances set out in the text apply,

and without prejudice to the application of the Employment Rights Act 1996 s 98(4) (test of fair dismissal: see PARA 765), the dismissal must, for the purposes of ss 98(1), 135 (reason for dismissal: see PARAS 765, 836), be regarded as having been for redundancy where s 98(2)(c) (reason for dismissal is that the employee is redundant: see PARA 765) applies, or otherwise as having been for a substantial reason of a kind such as to justify the dismissal of an employee holding the position which that employee held: Transfer of Undertakings (Protection of Employment) Regulations 2006, SI 2006/246, reg 7(3)(b) (as so substituted). See generally *McGrath v Rank Leisure Ltd* [1985] ICR 527, [1985] IRLR 323, EAT (but note that the case is in the context of the Transfer of Undertakings (Protection of Employment) Regulations 1981, SI 1981/1794, reg 8(2)). Whether the dismissal is fair or unfair in such a case has been compared with the question whether a dismissal on the grounds of redundancy is fair or unfair (see PARAS 780–782): see *Meikle v McPhail (Charleston Arms)* [1983] IRLR 351, EAT.

Although the economic, technical or organisational reason may be that of the transferor or the transferee (Case C-319/94 *Jules Dethier Équipement SA v Dassy* [1998] ECR I-1061, [1998] ICR 541, ECJ), it may be the transferee, depending on the timing of the transfer, who has to defend the transferor's reason (*BSG Property Services v Tuck* [1996] IRLR 134, EAT; but see *Hynd v Armstrong* [2007] CSIH 16, [2007] IRLR 338). There have been suggestions that the two main elements of the regulation (ie the Transfer of Undertakings (Protection of Employment) Regulations 2006, SI 2006/246, reg 7(1) on the one hand (see the text and notes 1–6) and reg 7(2), (3) on the other; formerly the Transfer of Undertakings (Protection of Employment) Regulations 1981, SI 1981/1794, reg 8(1) and reg 8(2) respectively) operate disjunctively, or are mutually exclusive, so that a dismissal must be either transfer-related or for a 'reason' (so that, if it is the former on the facts, the defence under the second element cannot be raised): see *Whitehouse v Chas A Blatchford & Sons Ltd* [1999] IRLR 492, CA; *Kerry Foods Ltd v Creber* [2000] IRLR 10, EAT); but see the doubt cast on this in *Warner v Adnet Ltd* [1998] ICR 1056 at 1064, [1998] IRLR 394 at 397, CA, per Mummery LJ; and see also *Collins v John Ansell & Partners Ltd* [2000] Emp LR 555, EAT; *Thompson v SCS Consulting Ltd* [2001] IRLR 801, EAT (all cases in the context of the earlier regulations). In deciding if the reason for dismissal was an economic one or a transfer-related one, it is necessary to ascertain the reasons behind the employer's actions and, in an administration case, there must be consideration of the administrator's 'economic, technical or organisational reason': *Dynamex Friction Ltd v Amicus* [2008] EWCA Civ 381, [2008] IRLR 515. Where there is a case of constructive dismissal following a transfer, the tribunal must identify the principal reason for the conduct of the employer which entitled the employee to terminate the contract and then determine whether that reason is an economic, technical or organisational one entailing changes in the workforce: *Crawford v Swinton Insurance Brokers Ltd* [1990] ICR 85, [1990] IRLR 42, EAT.

The fact that the transferee (the purchaser of the business) has made it a condition of the purchase that the transferor must dismiss the workforce prior to the transfer is not for an 'economic, technical or organisational' reason, since 'economic' is to be construed *eiusdem generis* with 'technical' and 'organisational' and so must be given a limited meaning relating to the conduct of the business and does not include broad economic reasons for the dismissal such as the achievement of an agreement for the sale: *Wheeler v Patel* [1987] ICR 631, [1987] IRLR 211, EAT; *Gateway Hotels Ltd v Stewart* [1988] IRLR 287, EAT (not following *Anderson v Dalkeith Engineering Ltd* [1985] ICR 66, [1984] IRLR 429, EAT); *Ibex Trading Co Ltd (in administration) v Walton* [1994] ICR 907, [1994] IRLR 564, EAT (note these cases were in the context of the Transfer of Undertakings (Protection of Employment) Regulations 1981, SI 1981/1794, reg 8). The tactic of dismissing the workforce prior to the transfer does not avoid the general application of the regulations, since a dismissal contrary to the Transfer of Undertakings (Protection of Employment) Regulations 2006, SI 2006/246, reg 7 (formerly the Transfer of Undertakings (Protection of Employment) Regulations 1981, SI 1981/1794, reg 8) has the effect that the employee or employees affected is or are considered still in employment immediately before the transfer, and so automatically transferred to the employment of the transferee: see *Litster v Forth Dry Dock and Engineering Co Ltd (in receivership)* [1990] 1 AC 546, [1989] ICR 341, HL (again in the context of the earlier regulations); and PARA 139 note 4.

9 Ie the provisions of the Transfer of Undertakings (Protection of Employment) Regulations 2006, SI 2006/246, reg 7: see the text and notes 1–8.

10 Transfer of Undertakings (Protection of Employment) Regulations 2006, SI 2006/246, reg 7(4). As to the meaning of 'organised grouping of employees' see PARA 137 note 8. As to the general provisions and application of these regulations, and their effect on continuity of employment, see PARA 137; as to their effect on contracts of employment see PARA 139; and as to their effect on industrial relations see PARA 1196 et seq.

(3) REMEDIES FOR UNFAIR DISMISSAL

(i) Complaint to Employment Tribunal

804. Right to bring complaint of unfair dismissal before employment tribunal; time limits. A complaint may be presented to an employment tribunal[1] against an employer[2] by any person (the 'complainant') that he was unfairly dismissed[3] by the employer[4].

An employment tribunal must not consider such a complaint, however, unless it is presented to the tribunal[5]:

(1) before the end of the period of three months beginning with the effective date of termination[6]; or

(2) within such further period as the tribunal considers reasonable in a case where it is satisfied that it was not reasonably practicable for the complaint to be presented before the end of that period of three months[7].

However, where a dismissal is with notice[8], an employment tribunal must consider such a complaint if it is presented after the notice is given but before the effective date of termination[9].

If, on such a complaint, it is shown that the action complained of was taken for the purpose of safeguarding national security, the employment tribunal must dismiss the complaint[10].

1   As to employment tribunals see PARA 1399 et seq; as to the procedure on a complaint to an employment tribunal see PARA 1453 et seq; and as to appeals see PARA 1495 et seq.
2   As to the meaning of 'employer' see PARA 2.
3   As to the meaning of 'dismissal' see PARA 762.
4   See the Employment Rights Act 1996 s 111(1) (amended by the Employment Rights (Dispute Resolution) Act 1998 s 1(2)(a)).

     Evidence of pre-termination negotiations is inadmissible in any proceedings on a complaint under the Employment Rights Act 1996 s 111: see s 111A(1) (s 111A added by the Enterprise and Regulatory Reform Act 2013 s 14). For these purposes, 'pre-termination negotiations' means any offer made or discussions held, before the termination of the employment in question, with a view to it being terminated on terms agreed between the employer and the employee: Employment Rights Act 1996 s 111A(2) (as so added). The provision made by s 111A(1) is subject to s 111A(3)–(5): see s 111A(1) (as so added). Accordingly, s 111A(1) does not apply where, according to the complainant's case, the circumstances are such that a provision (whenever made) contained in, or made under, the Employment Rights Act 1996 or any other Act requires the complainant to be regarded for the purposes of Pt X (ss 94–134A) (unfair dismissal: see also PARAS 757 et seq, 805 et seq) as unfairly dismissed: s 111A(3) (as so added). As to the meanings of 'employee' and 'employment' see PARA 2. As to the modification of Pt X in relation to governing bodies of schools having a right to a delegated budget, acting in the exercise of their employment powers, see EDUCATION vol 35 (2011) PARA 355 et seq; and as to the modification of Pt X in relation to persons holding ecclesiastical office under common tenure see the Ecclesiastical Offices (Terms of Service) Regulations 2009, SI 2009/2108, reg 33; and ECCLESIASTICAL LAW vol 34 (2011) PARA 407.

     In relation to anything said or done which in the tribunal's opinion was improper, or was connected with improper behaviour, the Employment Rights Act 1996 s 111A(4) applies only to the extent that the tribunal considers just (s 111A(4) (as so added)); and s 111A(1) does not affect the admissibility, on any question as to costs or expenses, of evidence relating to an offer made on the basis that the right to refer to it on any such question is reserved (s 111A(5) (as so added)). The provision made by s 111A does not apply to an offer made or discussions held before 29 July 2013 (ie the commencement of the Enterprise and Regulatory Reform Act 2013 s 14): see s 24(4); and the Enterprise and Regulatory Reform Act 2013 (Commencement No 2) Order 2013, SI 2013/1648. The Employment Code of Practice (Settlement Agreements) Order 2013, SI 2013/1665 appointed 29 July 2013 as the day on which the Code of Practice on Settlement Agreements came into effect. See ACAS Code of Practice 4: Settlement Agreements (under section 111A of the Employment Rights Act 1996) (July 2013), which states that the

Employment Rights Act 1996 s 111A had been introduced to allow greater flexibility in the use of confidential discussions as a means of ending the employment relationship.

5   See the Employment Rights Act 1996 s 111(2) (amended by the Employment Rights (Dispute Resolution) Act 1998 s 1(2)(a); and SI 2010/493). The provision made by the Employment Rights Act 1996 s 111(2) is subject to s 111(2A)–(5) (see the text and notes 6–9): see s 111(2) (as so amended).

      Where, in accordance with regulations under the Employment Tribunals Act 1996 s 7 (see PARA 1410), an employment tribunal determines in the same proceedings (see the Employment Tribunals Act 1996 s 7(6) (amended by the Employment Rights (Dispute Resolution) Act 1998 s 1(2)(a))):

      (1)   a complaint presented under the Employment Rights Act 1996 s 111 (Employment Tribunals Act 1996 s 7(6)(a)); and

      (2)   a question referred to it under the Employment Rights Act 1996 s 163 (see PARA 886) (Employment Tribunals Act 1996 s 7(6)(b)),

      the presumption of redundancy in the Employment Rights Act 1996 s 163(2) (see PARA 886) has no effect for the purposes of the proceedings, in so far as they relate to the complaint under s 111 (see the Employment Tribunals Act 1996 s 7(6) (as so amended)).

6   Employment Rights Act 1996 s 111(2)(a). As to the meaning of 'effective date of termination' see PARA 764. For the purposes of head (1) in the text, s 207A(3) (extension because mediation in certain European cross-border disputes starts before the time limit expires: see PARA 1454) and s 207B (extension of time limits to facilitate conciliation before institution of proceedings: see PARA 1455) apply: s 111(2A) (added by SI 2011/1133; and amended by the Enterprise and Regulatory Reform Act 2013 s 8, Sch 2 paras 15, 33). The time limits applicable to unfair dismissal claims go to jurisdiction, and jurisdiction cannot be conferred on a tribunal by agreement or waiver: *Radakovits v Abbey National plc* [2009] EWCA Civ 1346, [2010] IRLR 307 (employer's acceptance that tribunal had jurisdiction not sufficient to confer jurisdiction on tribunal). A tribunal is entitled to re-open the question of jurisdiction as a preliminary issue except where it has already issued a declaration that the claim was in time: *Radakovits v Abbey National plc*. As to the correct approach of the court when considering whether a complaint has been presented to the tribunal within the three-month time limit see *Sealy v Consignia plc* [2002] EWCA Civ 878, [2002] 3 All ER 801, sub nom *Consignia plc (formerly the Post Office) v Sealy* [2002] ICR 1193; *Rai v Somerfield Stores Ltd* [2004] ICR 656, [2004] IRLR 124, EAT. See also *Tyne and Wear Autistic Society v Smith* [2005] ICR 663, [2005] IRLR 336, EAT (receipt by commercial email service, which hosted Employment Tribunals Service website, constituted receipt by tribunal); *Coldridge v Prison Service* [2005] All ER (D) 204 (Jun), EAT (complaint posted first class deemed to have been presented two posting days later; Sundays and bank holidays, when no post delivered, excluded); *Initial Electronic Security Systems Ltd v Avdic* [2005] ICR 1598, [2005] IRLR 671, EAT (sending of email eight hours before expiry of time limit allowed sufficient period within which sender reasonably entitled to expect it would be delivered). As to time limits generally see PARA 1453. See also *Thompson v Northumberland County Council* [2007] All ER (D) 95 (Sep), EAT; *Averns v Stagecoach in Warwickshire* [2008] All ER (D) 23 (Sep), EAT; *Bevan v Royal Bank of Scotland plc* [2008] ICR 682, [2007] All ER (D) 389 (Nov), EAT.

7   Employment Rights Act 1996 s 111(2)(b). Where the dismissal is alleged to be unfair by virtue of s 104F (dismissal for reason related to blacklists of trade union members: see PARA 799), s 111(2)(b) does not apply, and an employment tribunal may consider a complaint that is otherwise out of time if, in all the circumstances of the case, it considers that it is just and equitable to do so: see s 111(5) (added by SI 2010/493). As to time limits see PARA 1453.

      The Employment Rights Act 1996 s 111(2)(b) should be given a liberal construction in favour of the employee: it has consistently been held to be not reasonably practicable for an employee to present a claim within the primary time limit if he was, reasonably, in ignorance of that time limit; and, in a case where a claimant has consulted skilled advisers, the question of reasonable practicability is to be judged by what he could have done if he had been given such advice as the advisers should reasonably in all the circumstances have given him: *Northamptonshire County Council v Entwhistle* [2010] IRLR 740, EAT (the test under the Employment Rights Act 1996 s 111 was not one of causation as such, but of whether it was reasonably practicable for the claimant, at the material time, to present his claim within the time limit).

8   The delivery by an employer of an ultimatum or conditional notice and an employee's failure to return to work by the date specified does not constitute a dismissal with notice for these purposes: *Rai v Somerfield Stores Ltd* [2004] ICR 656, [2004] IRLR 124, EAT.

9   Employment Rights Act 1996 s 111(3) (amended by the Employment Rights (Dispute Resolution) Act 1998 s 1(2)(a)). In relation to a complaint which is presented as mentioned in

the Employment Rights Act 1996 s 111(3) the provisions of the Employment Rights Act 1996, so far as they relate to unfair dismissal, have effect as if:

(1)   references to a complaint by a person that he was unfairly dismissed by his employer included references to a complaint by a person that his employer has given him notice in such circumstances that he will be unfairly dismissed when the notice expires (s 111(4)(a));

(2)   references to reinstatement included references to the withdrawal of the notice by the employer (s 111(4)(b));

(3)   references to the effective date of termination included references to the date which would be the effective date of termination on the expiry of the notice (s 111(4)(c)); and

(4)   references to an employee ceasing to be employed included references to an employee having been given notice of dismissal (s 111(4)(d)).

Section 111(4) applies whether the notice is given by the employer or employee: *Presley v Llanelli Borough Council* [1979] ICR 419, [1979] IRLR 381, EAT. When an employee brings a claim under the Employment Rights Act 1996 s 111(3), (4), it remains good even if the employer then dismisses summarily during the currency of the notice: *Patel v Nagesan* [1995] ICR 988, [1995] IRLR 370, CA. The purpose of the Employment Rights Act 1996 s 111(3) is to enable employees to commence claims of unfair dismissal once an unequivocal decision to dismiss has been made and communicated, without them having to wait for the expiry of the notice period; it is however possible for a notice of dismissal to express the lodging of an appeal to be effective to keep the employment alive, even if the dismissal date could be or had been deferred by the lodging of an appeal, and even though the dismissal might, if the appeal were successful, be rescinded altogether: *Governing Body of Wishmorecross School v Balado* [2011] ICR D31, EAT.

10   See the Employment Tribunals Act 1996 s 10(1); and PARA 1448. See also *B v BAA plc* [2005] ICR 1530, [2005] IRLR 927, EAT; and PARA 1448 note 4.

(ii) Interim Relief

805.   Application for interim relief on complaint of unfair dismissal.   An employee[1] who presents a complaint[2] to an employment tribunal that[3]:

(1)   he has been unfairly dismissed[4] by his employer[5]; and

(2)   the reason (or, if more than one, the principal reason) for the dismissal: (a) is related to a health and safety case[6], or a working time case associated with his role as an employee representative (or candidate)[7], or a case where the employee performs functions as trustee of an occupational pension scheme[8], or as an employee representative (or candidate)[9], or because[10] the employee has made a protected disclosure[11]; or (b) is specified[12] in the provisions relating to the recognition of trade unions for collective bargaining purposes[13]; or

(3)   the reason (or, if more than one, the principal reason) for which the employee was selected for dismissal relates to a prohibited list and the required condition[14] was met[15];

may apply to the tribunal for interim relief[16].

The tribunal must not entertain such an application, however, unless it is presented to the tribunal before the end of the period of seven days immediately following the effective date of termination[17], whether before, on or after that date[18].

An employment tribunal must give to the employer, not later than seven days before the date of the hearing, a copy of the application together with notice of the date, time and place of the hearing[19]; and the tribunal must determine the application as soon as practicable after receiving the application[20]. An employment tribunal must not exercise any power it has of postponing the hearing of such an application except where it is satisfied that special circumstances exist which justify it in doing so[21].

1   As to the meaning of 'employee' see PARA 2.

2 Ie under the Employment Rights Act 1996 s 111: see PARA 804.
3 As to employment tribunals see PARA 1399 et seq; as to the procedure on a complaint to an employment tribunal see PARA 1453 et seq; and as to appeals see PARA 1495 et seq.
4 As to the meaning of 'dismissal' see PARA 762.
5 See the Employment Rights Act 1996 s 128(1) (substituted by SI 2010/493). As to the meaning of 'employer' see PARA 2.
   As to the modification of the Employment Rights Act 1996 Pt X (ss 94–134A) (unfair dismissal: see also PARAS 757 et seq, 806 et seq) in relation to governing bodies of schools having a right to a delegated budget, acting in the exercise of their employment powers, see EDUCATION vol 35 (2011) PARA 355 et seq; and as to the modification of Pt X in relation to persons holding ecclesiastical office under common tenure see the Ecclesiastical Offices (Terms of Service) Regulations 2009, SI 2009/2108, reg 33; and ECCLESIASTICAL LAW vol 34 (2011) PARA 407.
6 Ie the reason (or, if more than one, the principal reason) for the dismissal is specified in the Employment Rights Act 1996 s 100(1)(a), (b): see PARA 786.
7 Ie the reason (or, if more than one, the principal reason) for the dismissal is specified in the Employment Rights Act 1996 s 101A(1)(d): see PARA 788.
8 Ie the reason (or, if more than one, the principal reason) for the dismissal is specified in the Employment Rights Act 1996 s 102(1): see PARA 790.
9 Ie the reason (or, if more than one, the principal reason) for the dismissal is specified in the Employment Rights Act 1996 s 103: see PARA 791.
10 Ie the reason (or, if more than one, the principal reason) for the dismissal is specified in the Employment Rights Act 1996 s 103A: see PARA 792.
11 Employment Rights Act 1996 s 128(1)(a)(i) (as substituted: see note 5).
12 Ie the reason (or, if more than one, the principal reason) for the dismissal is specified in the Trade Union and Labour Relations (Consolidation) Act 1992 s 70A, Sch A1 para 161(2): see PARA 1171.
13 Employment Rights Act 1996 s 128(1)(a)(ii) (as substituted: see note 5).
14 Ie the reason (or, if more than one, the principal reason) for which the employee was selected for dismissal was the one specified in the opening words of the Employment Rights Act 1996 s 104F(1), and the condition in s 104F(1)(a) or (b) was met : see PARA 799. As to the meaning of 'prohibited list' for these purposes see PARA 799 note 4.
15 Employment Rights Act 1996 s 128(1)(b) (as substituted: see note 5).
16 See the Employment Rights Act 1996 s 128(1) (as substituted: see note 5). There is a separate power to apply for and grant interim relief in the Trade Union and Labour Relations (Consolidation) Act 1992 s 161 where dismissal is by reason of trade union membership or activities: see PARA 1058.
17 As to the meaning of 'effective date of termination' see PARA 764.
18 Employment Rights Act 1996 s 128(2).
19 Employment Rights Act 1996 s 128(4).
20 Employment Rights Act 1996 s 128(3).
21 Employment Rights Act 1996 s 128(5).

806. Interim relief on complaint of unfair dismissal; in general. Where, on hearing an employee's[1] application for interim relief[2], it appears to an employment tribunal[3] that it is likely[4] that, on determining the complaint to which the application relates, the tribunal will find that[5]:

(1) the reason (or, if more than one, the principal reason) for the dismissal[6]: (a) is related to a health and safety case[7], or a working time case associated with his role as an employee representative (or candidate)[8], or a case where the employee performs functions as trustee of an occupational pension scheme[9], or as an employee representative (or candidate)[10], or because[11] the employee has made a protected disclosure[12]; or (b) is specified[13] in the provisions relating to the recognition of trade unions for collective bargaining purposes[14]; or

(2) the reason (or, if more than one, the principal reason) for which the employee was selected for dismissal relates to a prohibited list and the required condition[15] was met[16],

the tribunal must announce its findings and explain to both parties, if present, what powers the tribunal may exercise on the application, and in what circumstances it may exercise them[17]. The tribunal must ask the employer[18], if present, whether he is willing, pending the determination or settlement of the complaint[19]:

(i)   to reinstate the employee (that is to say, to treat him in all respects as if he had not been dismissed)[20]; or

(ii)   if not, to re-engage him in another job[21] on terms and conditions not less favourable[22] than those which would have been applicable to him if he had not been dismissed[23].

If the employer:

(A)   states that he is willing to reinstate the employee, the tribunal must make an order to that effect[24];

(B)   states that he is willing to re-engage the employee in another job[25], and specifies the terms and conditions on which he is willing to do so[26], the tribunal must ask the employee whether he is willing to accept the job on those terms and conditions[27], and: (aa) if the employee is willing to accept the job on those terms and conditions, the tribunal must make an order to that effect[28], but (bb) if he is not willing to accept the job on those terms and conditions, then, where the tribunal is of the opinion that the refusal is reasonable, the tribunal must make an order for the continuation of his contract of employment[29], but otherwise the tribunal must make no order[30];

(C)   fails to attend before the tribunal on the hearing of such an application[31], or states that he is unwilling either to reinstate the employee in accordance with head (i) above, or to re-engage him in accordance with head (ii) above[32], the tribunal must make an order for the continuation of the employee's contract of employment[33].

1   As to the meaning of 'employee' see PARA 2.

2   Ie under the Employment Rights Act 1996 s 128: see PARA 805.

3   As to employment tribunals see PARA 1399 et seq; as to the procedure on a complaint to an employment tribunal see PARA 1453 et seq; and as to appeals see PARA 1495 et seq.

4   The employee must show a greater likelihood of success in the main complaint than either proving a reasonable prospect or a 51% probability of success: *Taplin v C Shippam Ltd* [1978] ICR 1068, [1978] IRLR 450, EAT; *Ministry of Justice v Sarfraz* [2011] IRLR 562, EAT ('likely' connotes something nearer to certainty than mere probability).

5   See the Employment Rights Act 1996 s 129(1) (substituted by SI 2010/493). As to the meaning of 'employer' see PARA 2.

     As to the modification of the Employment Rights Act 1996 Pt X (ss 94–134A) (unfair dismissal: see also PARAS 757 et seq, 807 et seq) in relation to governing bodies of schools having a right to a delegated budget, acting in the exercise of their employment powers, see EDUCATION vol 35 (2011) PARA 355 et seq; and as to the modification of Pt X in relation to persons holding ecclesiastical office under common tenure see the Ecclesiastical Offices (Terms of Service) Regulations 2009, SI 2009/2108, reg 33; and ECCLESIASTICAL LAW vol 34 (2011) PARA 407.

6   As to the meaning of 'dismissal' see PARA 762.

7   Ie the reason (or, if more than one, the principal reason) for the dismissal is specified in the Employment Rights Act 1996 s 100(1)(a), (b): see PARA 786.

8   Ie the reason (or, if more than one, the principal reason) for the dismissal is specified in the Employment Rights Act 1996 s 101A(1)(d): see PARA 788.

9   Ie the reason (or, if more than one, the principal reason) for the dismissal is specified in the Employment Rights Act 1996 s 102(1): see PARA 790.

10   Ie the reason (or, if more than one, the principal reason) for the dismissal is specified in the Employment Rights Act 1996 s 103: see PARA 791.

11   Ie the reason (or, if more than one, the principal reason) for the dismissal is specified in the Employment Rights Act 1996 s 103A: see PARA 792.

12   Employment Rights Act 1996 s 129(1)(a)(i) (as substituted: see note 5).

13 Ie the reason (or, if more than one, the principal reason) for the dismissal is specified in the Trade Union and Labour Relations (Consolidation) Act 1992 s 70A, Sch A1 para 161(2): see PARA 1171.

14 Employment Rights Act 1996 s 129(1)(a)(ii) (as substituted: see note 5).

15 Ie the reason (or, if more than one, the principal reason) for which the employee was selected for dismissal was the one specified in the opening words of the Employment Rights Act 1996 s 104F(1), and the condition in s 104F(1)(a) or (b) was met : see PARA 799. As to the meaning of 'prohibited list' for these purposes see PARA 799 note 4.

16 Employment Rights Act 1996 s 129(1)(b) (as substituted: see note 5).

17 See the Employment Rights Act 1996 s 129(2).

18 As to the meaning of 'employer' see PARA 2.

19 See the Employment Rights Act 1996 s 129(3).

20 Employment Rights Act 1996 s 129(3)(a).

21 As to the meaning of 'job' see PARA 119 note 17.

22 For these purposes, 'terms and conditions not less favourable than those which would have been applicable to him if he had not been dismissed' means, as regards seniority, pension rights and other similar rights, that the period prior to the dismissal is to be regarded as continuous with his employment following the dismissal: Employment Rights Act 1996 s 129(4).

23 Employment Rights Act 1996 s 129(3)(b).

24 Employment Rights Act 1996 s 129(5). As to revocation or variation of orders made under s 129 and non-compliance with such orders see PARA 808; and as to the application of s 129 to applications for orders under s 131 see PARA 808 note 6.

25 Employment Rights Act 1996 s 129(6)(a).

26 Employment Rights Act 1996 s 129(6)(b).

27 Employment Rights Act 1996 s 129(6).

28 Employment Rights Act 1996 s 129(7). See note 24.

29 Employment Rights Act 1996 s 129(8)(a). See note 24. As to orders for the continuation of a contract of employment see PARA 807; and as to the meaning of 'contract of employment' see PARA 2.

30 Employment Rights Act 1996 s 129(8)(b).

31 Employment Rights Act 1996 s 129(9)(a).

32 Employment Rights Act 1996 s 129(9)(b).

33 Employment Rights Act 1996 s 129(9). See notes 24, 29.

807. Order for continuation of contract of employment. An order for the continuation of a contract of employment[1] is an order that the contract of employment is to continue in force for the purposes of pay or any other benefit derived from the employment, seniority, pension rights and other similar matters, and for the purposes of determining for any purpose the period for which the employee has been continuously employed, from the date of its termination, whether before or after the making of the order, until the determination or settlement of the complaint[2].

Where the employment tribunal[3] makes such an order, it must specify in the order the amount which is to be paid by the employer[4] to the employee[5] by way of pay in respect of each normal pay period[6], or part of any such period[7], falling between the date of dismissal[8] and the determination or settlement of the complaint[9]. The amount so specified must[10] be that which the employee could reasonably have been expected to earn[11] during that period, or part, and must be paid, in the case of a payment for any such period falling wholly or partly after the making of the order, on the normal pay day[12] for that period and, in the case of a payment for any past period, within such time as may be specified in the order[13].

Any payment made to an employee by an employer under his contract of employment, or by way of damages for breach of that contract, in respect of a normal pay period, or part of any such period, goes towards discharging the employer's liability[14] in respect of that period; and, conversely, any payment[15] in respect of any period goes towards discharging any liability of the employer under, or in respect of breach of, the contract of employment in respect of that period[16].

1   Ie under the Employment Rights Act 1996 s 129: see PARA 806. As to the meanings of 'contract of employment' and 'employment' see PARA 2.
2   See the Employment Rights Act 1996 s 130(1). As to continuity of employment see PARA 130 et seq.
       As to the modification of Pt X (ss 94–134A) (unfair dismissal: see also PARAS 757 et seq, 808 et seq) in relation to governing bodies of schools having a right to a delegated budget, acting in the exercise of their employment powers, see EDUCATION vol 35 (2011) PARA 355 et seq; and as to the modification of Pt X in relation to persons holding ecclesiastical office under common tenure see the Ecclesiastical Offices (Terms of Service) Regulations 2009, SI 2009/2108, reg 33; and ECCLESIASTICAL LAW vol 34 (2011) PARA 407.
3   As to employment tribunals see PARA 1399 et seq; as to the procedure on a complaint to an employment tribunal see PARA 1453 et seq; and as to appeals see PARA 1495 et seq.
4   As to the meaning of 'employer' see PARA 2.
5   As to the meaning of 'employee' see PARA 2.
6   For these purposes, an employee's normal pay period is to be determined as if he had not been dismissed: see the Employment Rights Act 1996 s 130(7).
7   If an amount is payable in respect only of part of a normal pay period, the amount must be calculated by reference to the whole period and must be reduced proportionately: Employment Rights Act 1996 s 130(4).
8   As to the meaning of 'dismissal' see PARA 762.
9   Employment Rights Act 1996 s 130(2).
10 Ie subject to the Employment Rights Act 1996 s 130(4)–(7) (see also the text and notes 6, 7, 14–16). If an employee, on or after being dismissed by his employer, receives a lump sum which, or part of which, is in lieu of wages but is not referable to any normal pay period, the tribunal must take the payment into account in determining the amount of pay to be payable in pursuance of any such order: s 130(6).
11 For these purposes, the amount which an employee could reasonably have been expected to earn is to be determined as if he had not been dismissed: see the Employment Rights Act 1996 s 130(7).
12 For these purposes, an employee's normal pay day for each such period is to be determined as if he had not been dismissed: see the Employment Rights Act 1996 s 130(7).
13 See the Employment Rights Act 1996 s 130(3).
14 Ie under the Employment Rights Act 1996 s 130(2): see the text and notes 3–9.
15 See note 14.
16 Employment Rights Act 1996 s 130(5). As to the application of s 130 to orders made under s 132 see PARA 808 note 8.

808.   Revocation of, variation of, or non-compliance with, an order on application for interim relief.   At any time between the making of an order by an employment tribunal[1] on an application for interim relief[2], and the determination or settlement of the complaint to which it relates, the employer[3] or the employee[4] may apply to the tribunal[5] for the revocation or variation of the order on the ground of a relevant change of circumstances since the making of the order[6].

If, on the application of an employee, an employment tribunal is satisfied that the employer has not complied with the terms of an order for the reinstatement or re-engagement of the employee[7], the tribunal must:

(1)   make an order for the continuation of the employee's contract of employment[8]; and

(2)   order the employer to pay the employee compensation of such amount as the tribunal considers just and equitable in all the circumstances, having regard to the infringement of the employee's right to be reinstated or re-engaged in pursuance of the order and to any loss suffered by the employee in consequence of the non-compliance[9].

If, on the application of an employee, an employment tribunal is satisfied that the employer has not complied with the terms of an order for the continuation of a contract of employment[10], then:

(a) where the non-compliance consists of a failure to pay an amount by way of pay specified in the order, the tribunal must determine the amount owed by the employer on the date of the determination and, if on that date the tribunal also determines the employee's complaint that he has been unfairly dismissed[11], the tribunal must specify that amount separately from any other sum awarded to the employee[12]; and

(b) in any other case, the tribunal must order the employer to pay the employee such compensation as the tribunal considers just and equitable in all the circumstances having regard to any loss suffered by the employee in consequence of the non-compliance[13].

1 As to employment tribunals see PARA 1399 et seq; as to the procedure on a complaint to an employment tribunal see PARA 1453 et seq; and as to appeals see PARA 1495 et seq.
2 Ie under the Employment Rights Act 1996 s 129: see PARA 806.
3 As to the meaning of 'employer' see PARA 2.
4 As to the meaning of 'employee' see PARA 2.
5 The application may be to any tribunal having jurisdiction; it does not have to be to the same tribunal that made the order: *British Coal Corpn v McGinty* [1987] ICR 912, [1988] IRLR 7, EAT.
6 See the Employment Rights Act 1996 s 131(1) (amended by the Employment Rights (Dispute Resolution) Act 1998 s 1(2)(a)). The Employment Rights Act 1996 s 128 (see PARA 805) and s 129 (see PARA 806) apply in relation to such an application as they apply to an original application for interim relief, except that, in the case of an application by the employer, s 128(4) (see PARA 805) has effect with the substitution of a reference to the employee for the reference to the employer: s 131(2).
   As to the modification of Pt X (ss 94–134A) (unfair dismissal: see also PARAS 757 et seq, 810 et seq) in relation to governing bodies of schools having a right to a delegated budget, acting in the exercise of their employment powers, see EDUCATION vol 35 (2011) PARA 355 et seq; and as to the modification of Pt X in relation to persons holding ecclesiastical office under common tenure see the Ecclesiastical Offices (Terms of Service) Regulations 2009, SI 2009/2108, reg 33; and ECCLESIASTICAL LAW vol 34 (2011) PARA 407.
7 Ie under the Employment Rights Act 1996 s 129(5) or (7): see PARA 806.
8 Employment Rights Act 1996 s 132(1)(a). Section 130 (see PARA 807) applies to an order under s 132(1)(a) as in relation to an order under s 129 (see PARA 806): s 132(3).
9 See the Employment Rights Act 1996 s 132(1)(b), (2).
10 See the Employment Rights Act 1996 s 132(4) (amended by the Employment Rights (Dispute Resolution) Act 1998 s 1(2)(a)). As to orders for the continuation of a contract of employment see PARA 807. As to the meaning of 'contract of employment' see PARA 2.
11 As to the meaning of 'dismissal' see PARA 762.
12 See the Employment Rights Act 1996 s 132(5).
13 See the Employment Rights Act 1996 s 132(6).

(iii) Conciliation

809. Effect of a conciliated settlement of complaint of unfair dismissal. The general statutory restrictions on contracting out of employment protection rights[1] apply to the right to complain of unfair dismissal[2]. However, the longstanding principal exception[3] to those restrictions arises in the case of an agreement to refrain from presenting or proceeding with a complaint where a conciliation officer has taken[4] action[5]. Once such an agreement has been reached[6] after action by a conciliation officer[7], it is generally binding on the parties[8].

1 Ie the Employment Rights Act 1996 s 203(1): see PARA 150.
2 *Courage Take Home Trade Ltd v Keys* [1986] ICR 874, [1986] IRLR 427, EAT.

3   Binding effect can now also be achieved by the use of a compromise agreement: see the Employment Rights Act 1996 s 203(2)(f), (3)–(4); and PARAS 150, 151.
4   Ie under the Employment Tribunals Act 1996 ss 18, 18A–18C: see PARAS 152, 153.
5   See the Employment Rights Act 1996 s 203(2)(e); and PARA 150.
6   The resulting settlement is usually recorded on a form COT 3, such settlements often being referred to as 'COT 3 settlements', but it is not necessary that it be in any prescribed form; an oral agreement is, therefore, sufficient: *Gilbert v Kembridge Fibres Ltd* [1984] ICR 188, [1984] IRLR 52, EAT.
    The ostensible or implied authority for a citizens' advice bureau worker acting on behalf of a claimant before an employment tribunal to negotiate a settlement with the aid of a conciliation officer is wider than the strict common law position and includes all actual and potential issues between the parties arising out of the employment relationship which are known to the parties at the time: *Freeman v Sovereign Chicken Ltd* [1991] ICR 853, [1991] IRLR 408, EAT.
7   Ie even if that action is confined to recording a settlement already reached by the parties: *Moore v Duport Furniture Products Ltd* [1982] ICR 84, [1982] IRLR 31, HL.
    There is no legal obligation on the conciliation officer to explain the law to a party or to ensure that a settlement is fair: *Slack v Greenham (Plant Hire) Ltd* [1983] ICR 617, [1983] IRLR 271, EAT. Thus although, as a matter of practice, ACAS officers usually seek to ensure that the parties (particularly the complainant) understand their legal position and rights, there is no legal duty to do so; therefore there is nothing legally improper about a conciliation officer merely recording a settlement that has already been reached between the parties themselves: *Moore v Duport Furniture Products Ltd* [1982] ICR 84, [1982] IRLR 31, HL. These principles were reaffirmed in *Clarke v Redcar and Cleveland Borough Council, Wilson v Stockton-on-Tees Borough Council* [2006] ICR 897, [2006] IRLR 324, EAT.
8   It is no ground for setting aside the agreement that the conciliation officer did not advise a party as to his right, since there is no legal duty on the officer to do so: see note 7. An agreement to settle may, however, be attacked on common law grounds: see *Hennessy v Craigmyle & Co Ltd* [1986] ICR 461, [1986] IRLR 300, CA (economic duress a possible ground for avoidance, though unlikely to succeed in practice); *Larkfield of Chepstow Ltd v Milne* [1988] ICR 1, EAT (plea of joint mistake of fact not accepted).
    A conciliated ('COT 3') agreement (see note 6) may validly be cast in terms that it applies to 'all or any claims that exist or may exist', and to be 'in full and final settlement'; however, where the employee had no knowledge of a particular claim at the time of signing the COT 3, there is a general equitable power for a court or tribunal to allow the claim to proceed where it would be unconscionable not to do so: *Bank of Credit and Commerce International SA (in liquidation) v Ali* [2000] 3 All ER 51, [2000] IRLR 398, CA; affd [2001] UKHL 8, [2002] 1 AC 251, [2001] 1 All ER 961. See also *Clarke v Redcar and Cleveland Borough Council, Wilson v Stockton-on-Tees Borough Council* [2006] ICR 897, [2006] IRLR 324, EAT (employees not allowed to reopen a COT 3 agreement in an equal pay case because, they alleged, ACAS had not given them enough advice).

(iv) Remedies on Hearing of Complaint of Unfair Dismissal

A. IN GENERAL

810.   Remedies available on a complaint of unfair dismissal.   Where, on a complaint of unfair dismissal[1], an employment tribunal[2] finds that the grounds of the complaint are well-founded[3], it must:

(1)   explain to the complainant[4] what orders for reinstatement or re-engagement may be made[5], and in what circumstances they may be made[6]; and

(2)   ask him whether he wishes the tribunal to make such an order[7].

If the complainant does express such a wish, the tribunal may make such an order[8]. If, however, no such order is made, the tribunal must make an award of compensation for unfair dismissal[9] to be paid by the employer[10] to the employee[11].

1   Ie under the Employment Rights Act 1996 s 111: see PARA 804. As to the meaning of 'dismissal' see PARA 762.

2   As to employment tribunals see PARA 1399 et seq; as to the procedure on a complaint to an employment tribunal see PARA 1453 et seq; and as to appeals see PARA 1495 et seq.

3   See the Employment Rights Act 1996 s 112(1) (amended by the Employment Rights (Dispute Resolution) Act 1998 s 1(2)(a)).

As to the modification of the Employment Rights Act 1996 Pt X (ss 94–134A) (unfair dismissal: see also PARAS 757 et seq, 811 et seq) in relation to governing bodies of schools having a right to a delegated budget, acting in the exercise of their employment powers, see EDUCATION vol 35 (2011) PARA 355 et seq; and as to the modification of Pt X in relation to persons holding ecclesiastical office under common tenure see the Ecclesiastical Offices (Terms of Service) Regulations 2009, SI 2009/2108, reg 33; and ECCLESIASTICAL LAW vol 34 (2011) PARA 407.

4   As to the meaning of 'complainant' see PARA 804.

5   Ie under the Employment Rights Act 1996 s 113: see PARA 811.

6   Employment Rights Act 1996 s 112(2)(a). This imposes a mandatory duty on the tribunal, even where the complainant is professionally represented (*Pirelli General Cable Works Ltd v Murray* [1979] IRLR 190, EAT); failure to do so does not make the tribunal's decision automatically invalid (*Cowley v Manson Timber Ltd* [1995] ICR 367, [1995] IRLR 153, CA), but a decision reached without compliance with the requirement may be vulnerable to an appeal resulting in a remission to the tribunal to reconsider (*Constantine v McGregor Cory Ltd* [2000] ICR 938, EAT). See also *King v Royal Bank of Canada Europe Ltd* [2012] IRLR 280, EAT (tribunal had erred in law in failing properly to consider re-engagement).

7   Employment Rights Act 1996 s 112(2)(b). See note 6.

8   Employment Rights Act 1996 s 112(3). The text refers to making an order under s 113: see PARA 811.

9   Ie calculated in accordance with the Employment Rights Act 1996 ss 118–126: see PARA 814 et seq.

10 As to the meaning of 'employer' see PARA 2.

11 Employment Rights Act 1996 s 112(4) (amended by the Public Interest Disclosure Act 1998 ss 8(1), 18(2); the Employment Relations Act 1999 Sch 9; and the Employment Act 2002 Sch 7 paras 24, 36). As to the meaning of 'employee' see PARA 2.

As to whether an offer to meet the monetary part of a claim prevents an employee from maintaining a claim to the tribunal for the purposes of obtaining a finding that the dismissal was unfair see *Telephone Information Services Ltd v Wilkinson* [1991] IRLR 148, EAT (not vexatious to maintain claim on that basis); and *Nicolson Highlandwear Ltd v Nicolson* [2010] IRLR 859, EAT (Sc) (unlike a discrimination allegation, there is no provision in an unfair dismissal case for a declaration to be made as a remedy, so it is not open to an employee to pursue an unfair dismissal claim purely for the purpose of obtaining a declaration that he was unfairly dismissed).

B.   REINSTATEMENT OR RE-ENGAGEMENT

811.   Order for reinstatement or re-engagement. Where, on a complaint of unfair dismissal[1], an employment tribunal[2] finds that the grounds of the complaint are well-founded[3], it may make an order[4] which may be an order for reinstatement[5], or an order for re-engagement[6], as it may decide[7].

An order for reinstatement is an order that the employer[8] is to treat the complainant[9] in all respects as if he had not been dismissed[10]. On making such an order, the tribunal must specify[11]:

(1)   any amount payable by the employer in respect of any benefit which the complainant might reasonably be expected to have had but for the dismissal, including arrears of pay, for the period between the date of termination of employment and the date of reinstatement[12];

(2)   any rights and privileges, including seniority and pension rights, which must be restored to the employee[13]; and

(3)   the date by which the order must be complied with[14].

An order for re-engagement is an order, on such terms as the tribunal may decide, that the complainant be engaged by the employer, or by a successor[15] of the employer or by an associated employer[16], in employment comparable to that from which he was dismissed or other suitable employment[17]. On making such an order, the tribunal must specify the terms on which the re-engagement is to take place including:

(a)   the identity of the employer[18];

(b)   the nature of the employment[19];

(c)   the remuneration for the employment[20];

(d)   any amount payable by the employer in respect of any benefit which the complainant might reasonably be expected to have had but for the dismissal, including arrears of pay[21], for the period between the date of termination of employment and the date of re-engagement[22];

(e)   any rights and privileges, including seniority and pension rights, which must be restored to the employee[23]; and

(f)   the date by which the order must be complied with[24].

1   Ie under the Employment Rights Act 1996 s 111: see PARA 804. As to the meaning of 'dismissal' see PARA 762.

2   As to employment tribunals see PARA 1399 et seq; as to the procedure on a complaint to an employment tribunal see PARA 1453 et seq; and as to appeals see PARA 1495 et seq.

3   Ie under the Employment Rights Act 1996 s 112: see PARA 810.

4   Ie under the Employment Rights Act 1996 s 113: see the text and notes 1, 3, 5–7. As to the power to make such orders see PARA 810; as to the exercise of the tribunal's discretion in making such orders see PARA 812; and as to enforcement of such orders see PARA 813.

5   Ie in accordance with the Employment Rights Act 1996 s 114: see the text and notes 8–14. It is not sufficient for the tribunal to order the employer to make an offer of re-employment: *Lilley Construction Ltd v Dunn* [1984] IRLR 483, EAT.

6   Ie in accordance with the Employment Rights Act 1996 s 115: see the text and notes 15–24. See note 5.

7   See the Employment Rights Act 1996 s 113. Because the principal remedy in a claim for unfair dismissal is personal rather than proprietary, such a claim is not a 'thing in action' such as to vest in a trustee in bankruptcy: *Grady v Prison Service* [2003] EWCA Civ 527, [2003] 3 All ER 745, [2003] ICR 753, [2003] IRLR 474. Where an employee has died, the Employment Rights Act 1996 s 113, and ss 114–115 (see the text and notes 8–24), and s 116 (see PARA 812), do not apply; and accordingly, if the employment tribunal finds that the grounds of the complaint are well-founded, the case is to be treated as falling within s 112(4) (see PARA 810) as a case in which no order is made under s 113: s 133(3) (amended by the Employment Rights (Dispute Resolution) Act 1998 s 1(2)(a)). The Employment Rights Act 1996 s 133(3) does not, however, prejudice an order for reinstatement or re-engagement made before the employer's death: s 133(4). As to the meaning of 'employee' see PARA 2.

    As to the modification of Pt X (ss 94–134A) (unfair dismissal: see also PARAS 757 et seq, 812 et seq) in relation to governing bodies of schools having a right to a delegated budget, acting in the exercise of their employment powers, see EDUCATION vol 35 (2011) PARA 355 et seq; and as to the modification of Pt X in relation to persons holding ecclesiastical office under common tenure see the Ecclesiastical Offices (Terms of Service) Regulations 2009, SI 2009/2108, reg 33; and ECCLESIASTICAL LAW vol 34 (2011) PARA 407.

8   As to the meaning of 'employer' see PARA 2.

9   As to the meaning of 'complainant' see PARA 804.

10   Employment Rights Act 1996 s 114(1). See also notes 5, 7.

11   See the Employment Rights Act 1996 s 114(2). See also notes 5, 7.

12   Employment Rights Act 1996 s 114(2)(a). In calculating, for the purpose of s 114(2)(a), any amount payable by the employer, the tribunal must take into account, so as to reduce the employer's liability, any sums received by the complainant in respect of the period between the date of termination of employment and the date of reinstatement by way of:

    (1)   wages in lieu of notice or ex gratia payments paid by the employer (s 114(4)(a));

    (2)   remuneration paid in respect of employment with another employer (s 114(4)(b)),

    and such other benefits as the tribunal thinks appropriate in the circumstances (see s 114(4)). See also notes 5, 7. Otherwise, however, the ordinary doctrine of mitigation (see PARA 822) does not apply: *City and Hackney Health Authority v Crisp* [1990] ICR 95, [1990] IRLR 47, EAT (amount not reduced because of slowness in bringing complaint).

13   Employment Rights Act 1996 s 114(2)(b). See also notes 5, 7.

14 Employment Rights Act 1996 s 114(2)(c). If the complainant would have benefited from an improvement in his terms and conditions of employment had he not been dismissed, an order for reinstatement must require him to be treated as if he had benefited from that improvement from the date on which he would have done so but for being dismissed: s 114(3). See also notes 5, 7.
15 As to the meaning of 'successor' see PARA 133 note 10.
16 As to the meaning of 'associated employer' see PARA 3.
17 Employment Rights Act 1996 s 115(1). The statutory scheme does not allow a tribunal to order reinstatement under the guise of a re-engagement order: *Valencia v British Airways plc* [2014] IRLR 683, EAT (having concluded that an order for reinstatement was unjust because of the high level of contributory conduct in the claimant's case, the tribunal nevertheless made an order for reinstatement to the role the employee held before dismissal on precisely the same terms and conditions he had previously been employed on, but called it a re-engagement order). See also notes 6, 7.
18 Employment Rights Act 1996 s 115(2)(a). See also notes 6, 7.
19 Employment Rights Act 1996 s 115(2)(b). See also notes 6, 7.
20 Employment Rights Act 1996 s 115(2)(c). See also notes 6, 7.
21 If the pay for the new employment differs from that for the old employment, back pay is to be awarded at the latter rate: *Electronic Data Processing Ltd v Wright* [1986] ICR 76, [1986] IRLR 8, EAT.
22 Employment Rights Act 1996 s 115(2)(d). In calculating, for the purpose of s 115(2)(d), any amount payable by the employer, the tribunal must take into account, so as to reduce the employer's liability, any sums received by the complainant in respect of the period between the date of termination of employment and the date of re-engagement by way of:
   (1) wages in lieu of notice or ex gratia payments paid by the employer (s 115(3)(a));
   (2) remuneration paid in respect of employment with another employer (s 115(3)(b)), and such other benefits as the tribunal thinks appropriate in the circumstances (see s 115(3)). See also notes 6, 7.
23 Employment Rights Act 1996 s 115(2)(e). See also notes 6, 7.
24 Employment Rights Act 1996 s 115(2)(f). See also notes 6, 7.

812. Tribunal's exercise of discretion to make order. In exercising its discretion[1], the employment tribunal[2] must first consider whether to make an order for reinstatement[3] and, in so doing, must take into account:

(1) whether the complainant[4] wishes to be reinstated[5];

(2) whether it is practicable for the employer[6] to comply with an order for reinstatement[7]; and

(3) where the complainant caused or contributed to some extent to the dismissal[8], whether it would be just to order his reinstatement[9].

If the tribunal decides not to make an order for reinstatement, it must then consider whether to make an order for re-engagement[10] and, if so, on what terms[11]. In so doing, the tribunal must take into account:

(a) any wish expressed by the complainant as to the nature of the order to be made[12];

(b) whether it is practicable for the employer or a successor[13] or associated employer[14] to comply with an order for re-engagement[15]; and

(c) where the complainant caused or contributed to some extent to the dismissal, whether it would be just to order his re-engagement and, if so, on what terms[16].

Except in a case where the tribunal takes into account contributory fault under head (c) above, it must, if it orders re-engagement, do so on terms which are, so far as is reasonably practicable, as favourable as an order for reinstatement[17].

Where in any case an employer has engaged a permanent replacement for a dismissed employee[18], the tribunal is not to take that fact into account in determining[19] whether it is practicable to comply with an order for reinstatement or re-engagement[20] unless the employer shows:

(i)   that it was not practicable for him to arrange for the dismissed employee's work to be done without engaging a permanent replacement[21]; or

(ii)   that he engaged the replacement after the lapse of a reasonable period, without having heard from the dismissed employee that he wished to be reinstated or re-engaged[22], and that, when the employer engaged the replacement, it was no longer reasonable for him to arrange for the dismissed employee's work to be done except by a permanent replacement[23].

1   Ie under the Employment Rights Act 1996 s 113: see PARA 811.
2   As to employment tribunals see PARA 1399 et seq; as to the procedure on a complaint to an employment tribunal see PARA 1453 et seq; and as to appeals see PARA 1495 et seq.
3   As to orders for reinstatement see PARA 811.
4   As to the meaning of 'complainant' see PARA 804.

5   Employment Rights Act 1996 s 116(1)(a). Where an employee has died, ss 113–116 (see also PARA 811) do not apply; and accordingly, if the employment tribunal finds that the grounds of the complaint are well-founded, the case must be treated as falling within s 112(4) (see PARA 810) as a case in which no order is made under s 113 (see PARA 811): s 133(3) (amended by the Employment Rights (Dispute Resolution) Act 1998 s 1(2)(a)). The Employment Rights Act 1996 s 133(3) does not prejudice an order for reinstatement or re-engagement made before the employee's death: s 133(4).
    As to the modification of Pt X (ss 94–134A) (unfair dismissal: see also PARAS 757 et seq, 813 et seq) in relation to governing bodies of schools having a right to a delegated budget, acting in the exercise of their employment powers, see EDUCATION vol 35 (2011) PARA 355 et seq; and as to the modification of Pt X in relation to persons holding ecclesiastical office under common tenure see the Ecclesiastical Offices (Terms of Service) Regulations 2009, SI 2009/2108, reg 33; and ECCLESIASTICAL LAW vol 34 (2011) PARA 407.
6   As to the meaning of 'employer' see PARA 2.

7   Employment Rights Act 1996 s 116(1)(b). See also note 5. The test is practicability, not expediency: *Qualcast (Wolverhampton) Ltd v Ross* [1979] ICR 386, [1979] IRLR 98, EAT. As the employer has a second chance to argue impracticability under the Employment Rights Act 1996 s 117(3), (4)(a) (see PARA 813), a tribunal may make an order even where it is not convinced it would be practicable, provided that it 'has regard' to matters of practicability at this stage: *Timex Corpn v Thomson* [1981] IRLR 522, EAT; *Boots Co plc v Lees-Collier* [1986] ICR 728, [1986] IRLR 485, EAT. In *Port of London Authority v Payne* [1994] ICR 555, [1994] IRLR 9, CA, the Court of Appeal placed more emphasis on a substantive decision on practicability at this first stage, though in the knowledge that the existence of the second stage makes it effectively provisional. In practice, the incidence of orders for reinstatement or re-engagement is low; apart from the fact that it has to be requested by the employee, there are also many reasons of impracticability for not making an order, including:
    (1)   possible adverse reaction of the rest of the workforce (*Bateman v British Leyland UK Ltd* [1974] ICR 403, [1974] IRLR 101, NIRC; *Coleman v Magnet Joinery Ltd* [1975] ICR 46, [1974] IRLR 343, CA);
    (2)   'poisoned' atmosphere in the workplace (*Meridian Ltd v Gomersall* [1977] ICR 597, [1977] IRLR 425, EAT);
    (3)   distrust by employee of employer (*Nothman v London Borough of Barnet (No 2)* [1980] IRLR 65, CA); whilst a continuing belief by a superior in the employee's guilt may not generally be sufficient to prevent an order (*Boots Co plc v Lees-Collier*), a continuing breakdown in trust and respect may be enough (*Wood Group Heavy Industrial Turbines Ltd v Crossan* [1998] IRLR 680, EAT);
    (4)   failure of a genuine search for other employment (*Freemans plc v Flynn* [1984] ICR 874, [1984] IRLR 486, EAT);
    (5)   change of employment policy inconsistent with employee's return (*Redbridge London Borough Council v Fishman* [1978] ICR 569, [1978] IRLR 69, EAT);
    (6)   employee would be insufficiently employed (*Tayside Regional Council v McIntosh* [1982] IRLR 272, EAT) or his return would lead to a redundancy situation (*Cold Drawn Tubes Ltd v Middleton* [1992] ICR 318, [1992] IRLR 160, EAT);
    (7)   parties would be in a close personal relationship at work (*Enessy Co SA (t/a Tulchan Estate) v Minoprio and Minoprio* [1978] IRLR 489, EAT (obiter)); and

(8)   allegation of sexual misconduct not proved, but employers still responsible for safety of children (*ILEA v Gravett* [1988] IRLR 497, EAT).
Practicability is not simply a matter of possibility and has to include consideration of whether and how reinstatement would work: *Scottish Police Services Authority v McBride* [2010] All ER (D) 217 (May), EAT. The duty of an employer to make reasonable adjustments pursuant to the Disability Discrimination Act 1995 s 4A (see now the Equality Act 2010 s 29; and DISCRIMINATION vol 33 (2013) PARA 84) is relevant when considering the question of practicability under the Employment Rights Act 1996 s 116: *Patel v Great Ormond Street Hospital for Children NHS Trust* [2007] All ER (D) 263 (Jun), EAT.

8   For these purposes, the test for contributory fault is the same as that for contributory fault in relation to an order for compensation (see PARA 821) and should be applied consistently: *Boots Co plc v Lees-Collier* [1986] ICR 728, [1986] IRLR 485, EAT; *Morganite Electrical Carbon Ltd v Donne* [1988] ICR 18, [1987] IRLR 363, EAT. As to the meaning of 'dismissal' see PARA 762.

9   Employment Rights Act 1996 s 116(1)(c). See also note 5.

10   As to orders for re-engagement see PARA 811.

11   Employment Rights Act 1996 s 116(2). See also note 5.

12   Employment Rights Act 1996 s 116(3)(a). See also note 5.

13   As to the meaning of 'successor' see PARA 133 note 10.

14   As to the meaning of 'associated employer' see PARA 3.

15   Employment Rights Act 1996 s 116(3)(b). See note 5.

16   Employment Rights Act 1996 s 116(3)(c). Where a re-engagement order is made, s 116(3)(c) permits the tribunal some discretion as to the terms of such an order, where it finds that an employee contributed to his dismissal to a high degree, but it also requires the tribunal to consider, in light of such a finding, whether it would be just to order re-engagement, and if so, the terms of such an order: *Valencia v British Airways plc* [2014] IRLR 683, EAT (since the tribunal was in effect ordering reinstatement, it is impossible to see how a proper application of the statute could lead to any other conclusion than that it was not just to order re-engagement for the same reason that it was not just to order reinstatement). See also note 5.

17   Employment Rights Act 1996 s 116(4). See also note 5.

18   As to the meaning of 'employee' see PARA 2.

19   Ie for the purposes of the Employment Rights Act 1996 s 116(1)(b) (see head (2) in the text) or s 116(3)(b) (see head (b) in the text).

20   See the Employment Rights Act 1996 s 116(5). See also note 5.

21   Employment Rights Act 1996 s 116(6)(a). See also note 5.

22   Employment Rights Act 1996 s 116(6)(b)(i). See also note 5.

23   Employment Rights Act 1996 s 116(6)(b)(ii). See also note 5.

813.   Enforcement of order; compensation.   If an order for reinstatement or re-engagement[1] is made and the complainant[2] is reinstated or re-engaged[3], but the terms of the order are not fully complied with[4], an employment tribunal[5] must make an award of compensation, to be paid by the employer[6] to the employee[7], of such amount[8] as the tribunal thinks fit, having regard to the loss sustained by the complainant in consequence of the failure to comply fully with the terms of the order[9].

If an order for reinstatement or re-engagement[10] is made but the complainant is not reinstated or re-engaged in accordance with the order, the tribunal must make[11]:

(1)   an award of compensation for unfair dismissal[12] to be paid by the employer to the employee[13]; and

(2)   except in a case in which the employer satisfies the tribunal that it was not practicable to comply with the order[14], an additional award of compensation[15] of an amount not less than 26 and not more than 52 weeks' pay[16],

to be paid by the employer to the employee[17].

1   Ie under the Employment Rights Act 1996 s 113: see PARA 811.

2   As to the meaning of 'complainant' see PARA 804.

3   Employment Rights Act 1996 s 117(1)(a).

4 Employment Rights Act 1996 s 117(1)(b). This may be the case where the employer purports to reinstate but in fact does so on less favourable terms: *Artisan Press Ltd v Srawley* [1986] ICR 328, [1986] IRLR 126, EAT.

5 As to employment tribunals see PARA 1399 et seq; as to the procedure on a complaint to an employment tribunal see PARA 1453 et seq; and as to appeals see PARA 1495 et seq.

6 As to the meaning of 'employer' see PARA 2.

7 See the Employment Rights Act 1996 s 117(1) (amended by the Employment Rights (Dispute Resolution) Act 1998 s 1(2)(a)). As to the meaning of 'employee' see PARA 2.

8 Ie subject to the Employment Rights Act 1996 s 124 (maximum amount of compensatory award: see PARA 823).

9 See the Employment Rights Act 1996 s 117(2) (amended by the Public Interest Disclosure Act 1998 ss 8(2)(a), 18(2); and the Employment Relations Act 1999 Sch 9). There must be deducted from any such award the amount of any award made under the Employment Rights Act 1996 s 112(5) (see PARA 810) at the time of the order under s 113 (see PARA 811): s 117(2A) (added by the Employment Act 2002 s 34(1), (4)). Where an order for reinstatement or re-engagement has been made and the employee dies before the order is complied with:

    (1)   if the employer has before the death refused to reinstate or re-engage the employee in accordance with the order, the provisions of the Employment Rights Act 1996 s 117(3), (4)(a) (see head (2) in the text) apply, and an award must be made under s 117(3)(b) (see head (2) in the text), unless the employer satisfies the tribunal that it was not practicable at the time of the refusal to comply with the order (s 133(5)(a));

    (2)   if there has been no such refusal, the provisions of s 117(1) (see the text and notes 1–7) and s 117(2) apply if the employer fails to comply with any ancillary terms of the order which remain capable of fulfilment after the employee's death as they would apply to such a failure to comply fully with the terms of an order where the employee had been reinstated or re-engaged (s 133(5)(b)).

As to the modification of Pt X (ss 94–134A) (unfair dismissal: see also PARAS 757 et seq, 814 et seq) in relation to governing bodies of schools having a right to a delegated budget, acting in the exercise of their employment powers, see EDUCATION vol 35 (2011) PARA 355 et seq; and as to the modification of Pt X in relation to persons holding ecclesiastical office under common tenure see the Ecclesiastical Offices (Terms of Service) Regulations 2009, SI 2009/2108, reg 33; and ECCLESIASTICAL LAW vol 34 (2011) PARA 407.

10 See note 1.

11 See the Employment Rights Act 1996 s 117(3) (amended by the Public Interest Disclosure Act 1998 ss 8(2)(b), 18(2); and the Employment Relations Act 1999 Sch 9).

12 Ie calculated in accordance with the Employment Rights Act 1996 ss 118–126: see PARA 814 et seq. Where in any case an employment tribunal finds that the complainant has unreasonably prevented an order under s 113 (see PARA 811) from being complied with, it must, in making an award of compensation for unfair dismissal, take that conduct into account as a failure on the part of the complainant to mitigate his loss: s 117(8) (amended by the Employment Rights (Dispute Resolution) Act 1998 s 1(2)(a); and the Employment Rights (Dispute Resolution) Act 1998 Sch 2).

13 Employment Rights Act 1996 s 117(3)(a) (amended by the Employment Act 2002 Sch 7 paras 24, 37). Where the amount of a compensatory award falls to be calculated for the purposes of the Employment Rights Act 1996 s 117(3)(a), there must be deducted from any such award any award made under s 112(5) (see PARA 810) at the time of the order under s 113 (see PARA 811): s 123(8) (added by the Employment Act 2002 s 34(1), (5)). An employment tribunal is entitled to reconsider the amount of compensation awarded by way of the Employment Rights Act 1996 s 117(3)(a), irrespective of the sum awarded under s 114(2) (see PARA 811), even the amount between the date of dismissal and proposed reinstatement: *Awotona v South Tyneside Healthcare NHS Trust* [2005] EWCA Civ 217, [2005] ICR 958, [2005] All ER (D) 221 (Feb).

14 Ie except where the Employment Rights Act 1996 s 117(3)(b) does not apply: see s 117(3)(b) (amended by the Employment Relations Act 1999 s 33(2)). The Employment Rights Act 1996 s 117(3)(b) does not apply where the employer satisfies the tribunal that it was not practicable to comply with the order: s 117(4)(a) (amended by the Employment Relations Act 1999 s 33(1), Sch 9 Table 10). This gives the employer a second chance to argue impracticability, having failed to prevent an order being made in the first place on grounds of impracticability under the Employment Rights Act 1996 s 116(1)(b) (see PARA 812) or s 116(3)(b) (see PARA 812). On this second occasion the employer is not restricted to arguments based on facts arising since the order was made: *Timex Corpn v Thomson* [1981] IRLR 522, EAT; *Freemans plc v Flynn* [1984] ICR 874, [1984] IRLR 486, EAT. Where in any case an employer has engaged a permanent replacement for a dismissed employee, the tribunal is not to take that fact into account in determining, for the purposes of the Employment Rights Act 1996 s 117(4)(a), whether it was

practicable to comply with the order for reinstatement or re-engagement unless the employer shows that it was not practicable for him to arrange for the dismissed employee's work to be done without engaging a permanent replacement: s 117(7). As to the modification of s 117(4) where a teacher in a foundation, voluntary aided or foundation special school is dismissed by the governing body of the school in pursuance of a requirement of the local education authority see PARA 757 note 9.

15 Although the tribunal has a wide discretion when making an additional award, it must exercise that discretion judicially: *Morganite Electrical Carbon Ltd v Donne* [1988] ICR 18, [1987] IRLR 363, EAT. In fixing the award, the tribunal may take into account as factors one or both of: (1) the employer's conduct in not complying with the order; and (2) the employee's loss, including where that loss has been reduced by the application of the statutory maximum for the compensatory award: *Morganite Electrical Carbon Ltd v Donne*; *Motherwell Railway Club v McQueen* [1989] ICR 418, EAT; *George v Beecham Group Ltd* [1977] IRLR 43.

16 See the Employment Rights Act 1996 s 117(3)(b) (as amended: see note 14), s 117(4)(a) (as amended: see note 14). Where a compensatory award is an award under s 117(3)(a) (see head (1) in the text), and where an additional award falls to be made under s 117(3)(b), the limit imposed by s 124 (see PARA 823) on the compensatory award may be exceeded to the extent necessary to enable the aggregate of the compensatory award and additional award fully to reflect the amount specified in s 114(2)(a) (see PARA 811) or s 115(2)(d) (see PARA 811): see s 124(4). The provision made by 124(4) was enacted to deal with the possible problem of under-compensation (one benefit to an employer in refusing to reinstate or re-engage) encountered in *O'Laoire v Jackel International Ltd* [1990] ICR 197, [1990] IRLR 70, CA, and *Mabirizi v National Hospital for Nervous Diseases* [1990] ICR 281, [1990] IRLR 133, EAT. The statutory provisions may operate so as to impose a statutory maximum on the award for compensation and to prohibit a separate order for arrears of pay and benefits for the period between dismissal and reinstatement where reinstatement had not in fact occurred: *Parry v National Westminster Bank plc* [2004] EWCA Civ 1563, [2005] ICR 396, [2005] IRLR 193.

17 See the Employment Rights Act 1996 s 117(3) (as amended: see note 11).

C. COMPENSATION

814.   In general. Where an employment tribunal[1] makes an award of compensation for unfair dismissal[2], the award consists of[3]: (1) a basic[4] award[5]; and (2) a compensatory[6] award[7].

1   As to employment tribunals see PARA 1399 et seq; as to the procedure on a complaint to an employment tribunal see PARA 1453 et seq; and as to appeals see PARA 1495 et seq.

2   Ie under the Employment Rights Act 1996 s 112(4) (see PARA 810) or s 117(3)(a) (see PARA 813). As to the meaning of 'dismissal' see PARA 762.

3   See the Employment Rights Act 1996 s 118(1) (amended by the Public Interest Disclosure Act 1998 ss 8(3), 18(2); and the Employment Relations Act 1999 Sch 9).
      As to the modification of the Employment Rights Act 1996 Pt X (ss 94–134A) (unfair dismissal: see also PARAS 757 et seq, 815 et seq) in relation to governing bodies of schools having a right to a delegated budget, acting in the exercise of their employment powers, see EDUCATION vol 35 (2011) PARA 355 et seq; and as to the modification of Pt X in relation to persons holding ecclesiastical office under common tenure see the Ecclesiastical Offices (Terms of Service) Regulations 2009, SI 2009/2108, reg 33; and ECCLESIASTICAL LAW vol 34 (2011) PARA 407.

4   Ie calculated in accordance with the Employment Rights Act 1996 ss 119–122, 126: see PARAS 815–817, 821.

5   Employment Rights Act 1996 s 118(1)(a).

6   Ie calculated in accordance with the Employment Rights Act 1996 ss 123, 124, 124A, 126: see PARAS 818, 820–823.

7   Employment Rights Act 1996 s 118(1)(b) (amended by the Employment Rights (Dispute Resolution) Act 1998 Sch 1 para 21(1), (2); the Employment Relations Act 1999 Sch 4 Pt III paras 5, 22, Sch 9; and the Employment Act 2002 Sch 7 paras 24, 38).

815.   Calculation of the basic award of compensation for unfair dismissal. Where an employment tribunal[1] makes an award of compensation for unfair dismissal[2], the amount of the basic award[3] is to be calculated[4] by:

(1)   determining the period, ending with the effective date of termination[5], during which the employee[6] has been continuously employed[7];

(2)   reckoning backwards from the end of that period the numbers of years of employment falling within that period[8]; and

(3)   allowing the appropriate amount for each of those years of employment[9], the 'appropriate amount' for these purposes being:

    (a)   one and a half weeks' pay[10] for a year of employment in which the employee was not below the age of 41[11];

    (b)   one week's pay for each year of employment not falling within head (3)(a) above in which the employee was not below the age of 22[12]; and

    (c)   half a week's pay for each such year not falling within head (3)(a) or head (3)(b) above[13].

However, where 20 years of employment have been so reckoned, no account is to be taken of any year of employment earlier than those 20 years[14].

1   As to employment tribunals see PARA 1399 et seq; as to the procedure on a complaint to an employment tribunal see PARA 1453 et seq; and as to appeals see PARA 1495 et seq.

2   Ie under the Employment Rights Act 1996 s 112(4) (see PARA 810) or s 117(3)(a) (see PARA 813).

    As to the modification of Pt X (ss 94–134A) (unfair dismissal: see also PARAS 757 et seq, 816 et seq) in relation to governing bodies of schools having a right to a delegated budget, acting in the exercise of their employment powers, see EDUCATION vol 35 (2011) PARA 355 et seq; and as to the modification of Pt X in relation to persons holding ecclesiastical office under common tenure see the Ecclesiastical Offices (Terms of Service) Regulations 2009, SI 2009/2108, reg 33; and ECCLESIASTICAL LAW vol 34 (2011) PARA 407.

3   As to the basic award see PARA 815.

4   Ie subject to the Employment Rights Act 1996 s 120 (minimum basic award in certain cases) (see PARA 816), s 121 (basic award of two weeks' pay in certain cases) (see PARA 816), s 122 (reductions) (see PARAS 817, 821) and s 126 (acts which are both unfair dismissal and discrimination) (see PARA 820).

5   As to the meaning of 'effective date of termination' see PARA 764. See also PARA 764 note 17.

6   As to the meaning of 'employee' see PARA 2.

7   Employment Rights Act 1996 s 119(1)(a). As to continuity of employment see PARA 130 et seq.

8   Employment Rights Act 1996 s 119(1)(b). As to the meaning of 'year' for these purposes see PARA 130 note 11.

9   Employment Rights Act 1996 s 119(1)(c).

10   As to the meaning of 'week' for these purposes see PARA 126 note 13. As to the calculation of a week's pay see PARA 143 et seq. As to the maximum amount of a week's pay for these purposes see the Employment Rights Act 1996 s 227(1); and PARA 147.

11   Employment Rights Act 1996 s 119(2)(a).

12   Employment Rights Act 1996 s 119(2)(b).

13   Employment Rights Act 1996 s 119(2)(c).

14   Employment Rights Act 1996 s 119(3).

816.   Minimum amounts: basic award of compensation for unfair dismissal.

Where an employment tribunal[1] makes an award of compensation for unfair dismissal[2], the amount[3] of the basic award[4] is to be not less than £5,676 where the reason (or, if more than one, the principal reason)[5]:

(1)   in a redundancy case[6], for selecting the employee[7] for dismissal[8]; or

(2)   otherwise, for the dismissal[9],

is one of those specified[10] in relation to health and safety representatives, or specified[11] in relation to workforce representatives (in working time cases), or specified[12] in relation to trustees of occupational pension schemes, or specified[13] in relation to employee representatives[14]. Where an employee is regarded as unfairly dismissed for a reason that is related to the acquisition or use of blacklists of trade union members[15], whether or not the dismissal is unfair or regarded as unfair for any other reason, the amount of the basic award of compensation[16] must not be less than £5,000[17].

Where the tribunal finds that the reason (or, where there is more than one, the principal reason) for the dismissal of the employee is that he is redundant, and the employee[18]:

(a)   is not regarded[19] as dismissed for the purposes of the statutory provisions[20] that govern redundancy payments[21]; or

(b)   is not, or (if he were otherwise entitled) would not be, entitled[22] to a redundancy payment[23],

the amount of the basic award is two weeks' pay[24].

1   As to employment tribunals see PARA 1399 et seq; as to the procedure on a complaint to an employment tribunal see PARA 1453 et seq; and as to appeals see PARA 1495 et seq.
2   Ie under the Employment Rights Act 1996 s 112(4) (see PARA 810) or s 117(3)(a) (see PARA 813).
        As to the modification of Pt X (ss 94–134A) (unfair dismissal: see also PARAS 757 et seq, 817 et seq) in relation to governing bodies of schools having a right to a delegated budget, acting in the exercise of their employment powers, see EDUCATION vol 35 (2011) PARA 355 et seq; and as to the modification of Pt X in relation to persons holding ecclesiastical office under common tenure see the Ecclesiastical Offices (Terms of Service) Regulations 2009, SI 2009/2108, reg 33; and ECCLESIASTICAL LAW vol 34 (2011) PARA 407.
3   Ie before any reduction under the Employment Rights Act 1996 s 122: see PARA 821.
4   As to the calculation of the basic award see PARA 815.
5   See the Employment Rights Act 1996 s 120(1) (amended by SI 1998/1833; and SI 2014/382). As to the Secretary of State's duty to increase or decrease the amount in the Employment Rights Act 1996 s 120(1) in line with the retail prices index see the Employment Relations Act 1999 s 34(1)(b), (2), (3)(b); and PARA 160.
6   As to the meaning of 'redundancy case' for these purposes see the Employment Rights Act 1996 s 105(9); and PARA 781 note 4. As to the meaning of 'redundancy' see PARA 870.
7   As to the meaning of 'employee' see PARA 2.
8   Employment Rights Act 1996 s 120(1)(a). As to the meaning of 'dismissal' see PARA 762.
9   Employment Rights Act 1996 s 120(1)(b).
10 Ie in the Employment Rights Act 1996 s 100(1)(a) and s 100(1)(b) (see PARA 786).
11 Ie in the Employment Rights Act 1996 s 101A(1)(d): see PARA 788.
12 Ie in the Employment Rights Act 1996 s 102(1): see PARA 790.
13 Ie in the Employment Rights Act 1996 s 103: see PARA 791.
14 See the Employment Rights Act 1996 s 120(1) (amended: see note 5).
15 Ie by virtue of the Employment Rights Act 1996 s 104F (dismissal for reason related to blacklists of trade union members: see PARA 799).
16 See note 3.
17 Employment Rights Act 1996 s 120(1C) (added by SI 2010/493).
18 See the Employment Rights Act 1996 s 121.
19 Ie by virtue of the Employment Rights Act 1996 s 138 (no dismissal in cases of renewal of contract or re-engagement: see PARA 865).
20 Ie for the purposes of the Employment Rights Act 1996 Pt XI (ss 135–181): see PARA 835 et seq.
21 Employment Rights Act 1996 s 121(a).
22 Ie by virtue of the Employment Rights Act 1996 s 141 (renewal of contract or re-engagement): see PARA 874.
23 Employment Rights Act 1996 s 121(b).
24 See the Employment Rights Act 1996 s 121.

817.   Reduction in amount of basic award of compensation for unfair dismissal.   Where an employment tribunal[1] makes an award of compensation for unfair dismissal[2], and where the tribunal finds that the complainant[3] has unreasonably refused an offer by the employer[4] which, if accepted, would have the effect of reinstating the complainant in his employment[5] in all respects as if he had not been dismissed[6], the tribunal must reduce or further reduce the amount of the basic award[7] to such extent as it considers just and equitable having regard to that finding[8].

The amount of the basic award must be reduced or further reduced by the amount of any redundancy payment[9] awarded by the tribunal[10] in respect of the same dismissal, or by the amount of any payment made by the employer to the employee[11] on the ground that the dismissal was by reason of redundancy, whether in pursuance of the statutory provisions that govern redundancy payments[12] or otherwise[13].

The basic award must also be reduced where there is contributory fault on the part of the employee[14].

Where a dismissal is regarded as unfair for a reason that is related to the acquisition or use of blacklists of trade union members[15], the amount of the basic award of compensation must be reduced or further reduced by the amount of any basic award in respect of the same dismissal made under the Trade Union and Labour Relations (Consolidation) Act 1992[16] in respect fo a dismissal made on grounds related to trade union membership or activities[17].

1 As to employment tribunals see PARA 1399 et seq; as to the procedure on a complaint to an employment tribunal see PARA 1453 et seq; and as to appeals see PARA 1495 et seq.
2 Ie under the Employment Rights Act 1996 s 112(4) (see PARA 810) or s 117(3)(a) (see PARA 813).
   As to the modification of Pt X (ss 94–134A) (unfair dismissal: see also PARAS 757 et seq, 818 et seq) in relation to governing bodies of schools having a right to a delegated budget, acting in the exercise of their employment powers, see EDUCATION vol 35 (2011) PARA 355 et seq; and as to the modification of Pt X in relation to persons holding ecclesiastical office under common tenure see the Ecclesiastical Offices (Terms of Service) Regulations 2009, SI 2009/2108, reg 33; and ECCLESIASTICAL LAW vol 34 (2011) PARA 407.
3 As to the meaning of 'complainant' see PARA 804.
4 As to the meaning of 'employer' see PARA 2.
5 As to the meaning of 'employment' see PARA 2.
6 As to the meaning of 'dismissal' see PARA 762.
7 As to the basic award see PARA 815.
8 Employment Rights Act 1996 s 122(1). See *King v Royal Bank of Canada Europe Ltd* [2012] IRLR 280, EAT (tribunal ought to have considered the chance of a vacancy having arisen over the period during which the bank ought to have consulted).
9 As to the meaning of 'redundancy payment' see PARA 836.
10 Ie under the Employment Rights Act 1996 Pt XI (ss 135–181): see PARA 835 et seq.
11 As to the meaning of 'employee' see PARA 2.
12 Ie the Employment Rights Act 1996 Pt XI: see PARA 835 et seq.
13 See the Employment Rights Act 1996 s 122(4). Where the complainant has been awarded any amount in respect of the dismissal under a designated dismissal procedures agreement, the tribunal must reduce or further reduce the amount of the basic award to such extent as it considers just and equitable having regard to that award: s 122(3A) (added by the Employment Rights (Dispute Resolution) Act 1998 Sch 1 para 22). As to the meaning of 'dismissal procedures agreement' see PARA 150 note 9. Where an ex gratia payment is made by the employer, ostensibly including an amount in respect of a redundancy payment, the Employment Rights Act 1996 s 122(4) can only apply if the dismissal was in fact by reason of redundancy: *Boorman v Allmakes Ltd* [1995] ICR 842, [1995] IRLR 553, CA.
14 See the Employment Rights Act 1996 s 122(2); and PARA 821.
15 Ie by virtue of the Employment Rights Act 1996 s 104F (dismissal for reason related to blacklists of trade union members: see PARA 799).
16 Ie under the Trade Union and Labour Relations (Consolidation) Act 1992 s 156 (see PARA 1057).
17 Employment Rights Act 1996 s 122(5) (added by SI 2010/493).

818. Calculation of the compensatory award for unfair dismissal; in general.
The amount of the compensatory award is[1] to be such amount as the tribunal considers just and equitable[2] in all the circumstances having regard to the loss[3] sustained by the complainant[4] in consequence of the dismissal[5], in so far as that loss is attributable to action[6] taken by the employer[7].

The breadth of the tribunal's discretion is particularly important in two cases:
   (1)   misconduct discovered after the date of dismissal cannot make the dismissal fair[8] or constitute contributory fault[9]; but where such

misconduct is discovered by the time of the tribunal hearing, it may be taken into account in deciding what is just and equitable compensation, in a particularly serious case leading to a nominal or nil award[10];

(2)   whilst injustice, or lack of it, to the employee may not affect the issue of whether the dismissal was fair or not[11], it is highly relevant to the question of the appropriate remedy and, in particular, what, if any, compensation should be awarded, based on what the employee has actually lost, particularly by limiting it to the period during which the employment would probably have lasted[12].

In determining[13] how far any loss sustained by the complainant was attributable to action taken by the employer, no account is to be taken of any pressure which, by calling, organising, procuring or financing a strike or other industrial action[14], or threatening to do so, was exercised on the employer to dismiss the employee; and that question must be determined as if no such pressure had been exercised[15].

1   Ie subject to the Employment Rights Act 1996 s 123(2)–(7) (see also PARAS 821, 822), s 124 (see PARA 823), s 124A (see note 7), and s 126 (see PARA 820). As to the modification of Pt X (ss 94–134A) (unfair dismissal: see also PARAS 757 et seq, 820 et seq) in relation to governing bodies of schools having a right to a delegated budget, acting in the exercise of their employment powers, see EDUCATION vol 35 (2011) PARA 355 et seq; and as to the modification of Pt X in relation to persons holding ecclesiastical office under common tenure see the Ecclesiastical Offices (Terms of Service) Regulations 2009, SI 2009/2108, reg 33; and ECCLESIASTICAL LAW vol 34 (2011) PARA 407.

2   This is the essential element of the discretion to make a compensatory award: *W Devis & Sons Ltd v Atkins* [1977] AC 931 at 955, [1977] ICR 662 at 679, HL, per Viscount Dilhorne. Thus although the starting point should be financial loss and not the degree of unfairness involved in the dismissal (*Morris v Acco Co Ltd* [1985] ICR 306, EAT, explaining *Townson v Northgate Group Ltd* [1981] IRLR 382, EAT), the power to take into account that which is just and equitable (particularly to reduce compensation where the complainant is unmeritorious or the actual loss small) is of considerable importance. See also *Courage Take Home Trade Ltd v Keys* [1986] ICR 874, [1986] IRLR 427, EAT (not just or equitable to give compensation where the employee had apparently agreed to settle, taken the sum offered, and then carried on with the claim); *Dignity Funerals v Bruce* [2005] IRLR 189, 2004 SLT 1223, Ct of Sess (any application of the just and equitable test must be underpinned by findings in fact). The width of this discretion means that, although the tribunal must act judicially, it is not bound by common law concepts of foreseeability or remoteness of damage: *Leonard v Strathclyde Buses Ltd* [1998] IRLR 693, Ct of Sess (applied in *Balmoral Group Ltd v Rae* (2000) Times, 25 January, EAT, in preference to the stricter view of causation in *Simrad Ltd v Scott* [1997] IRLR 147, EAT).

3   The word 'loss' in the Employment Rights Act 1996 s 123(1) has a plain meaning which is limited to pecuniary loss: *Dunnachie v Kingston-upon-Hull City Council* [2004] UKHL 36, [2005] 1 AC 226, [2004] 3 All ER 1011 (legislature expressly did not provide for compensation for injury to feelings arising out of dismissal or the manner of dismissal, as contrasted with discrimination cases). See also PARA 819. The loss referred to in the Employment Rights Act 1996 s 123(1) is to be taken to include:
      (1)   any expenses reasonably incurred by the complainant in consequence of the dismissal (s 123(2)(a)); and
      (2)   loss of any benefit which he might reasonably be expected to have had but for the dismissal (s 123(2)(b)).
   As to the meaning of 'complainant' see PARA 804. However, in respect of any loss of:
      (a)   any entitlement or potential entitlement to a payment on account of dismissal by reason of redundancy, whether in pursuance of Pt XI (ss 135–181) (see PARA 835 et seq) or otherwise (s 123(3)(a)); or
      (b)   any expectation of such a payment (s 123(3)(b)),
   such loss is to be taken to include only the loss referable to the amount, if any, by which the amount of that payment would have exceeded the amount of a basic award, apart from any reduction under s 122 (see PARAS 817, 821) in respect of the same dismissal (see s 123(3)). See *Burlo v Langley* [2006] EWCA Civ 1778, [2007] 2 All ER 462, [2007] IRLR 145; and PARA 819 note 5. See also *Fox v British Airways plc* [2013] EWCA Civ 972, [2013] ICR 1257, [2013] IRLR 812 (estate of unfairly dismissed employee, who died shortly after dismissal and before he

could reasonably be expected to obtain alternative cover, was entitled in unfair dismissal proceedings to recover compensation in sum equivalent to full amount of death in service benefit which would have been payable under employer's pension scheme if employee had remained in employment at date of death; loss of the chance of death in service benefit being paid is to be regarded as a pecuniary loss suffered by the employee for which he could have claimed in proceedings brought prior to his death, and he—or his estate—can only be put in the position that he would have been in but for his dismissal by an award of compensation in the full amount of the payment that would have been made had he died in service less any payments already received by the estate, eg any repayment of contributions).

4   Loss by the employee is central to an award; the compensatory award should not be used to penalise a bad employer or to give a gratuitous benefit to an employee for whom the tribunal feels sympathy: see *Clarkson International Tools Ltd v Short* [1973] ICR 191, [1973] IRLR 90, NIRC; *Lifeguard Assurance Ltd v Zadrozny* [1977] IRLR 56, EAT; and see *Morgans v Alpha Plus Security Ltd* [2005] ICR 525, [2005] IRLR 234, EAT (if there is no loss, no compensation can be recovered even for the most unfair of unfair dismissals); *Optimum Group Services plc v Muir* [2013] IRLR 339, EAT (compensatory award should not exceed loss actually suffered; where claimant brought action for same loss against two defendants and reached settlement with one defendant, tribunal should deduct sum paid under that settlement from compensatory award against second defendant).

5   As to the meaning of 'dismissal' see PARA 762. An employment tribunal must be careful to distinguish losses in consequence of the dismissal from losses which flow from the employer's breach of the contract of employment: *GAB Robins (UK) Ltd v Triggs* [2008] EWCA Civ 17, [2007] ICR 1424, [2008] IRLR 317. See also *Chagger v Abbey National plc* [2009] EWCA Civ 1202, [2010] ICR 397, [2010] IRLR 47 (employer liable for losses resulting from fact that employee unlawfully stigmatised by future employers who were unwilling to employ him because he had taken legal action against employer).

6   As to the meaning of 'action' for these purposes see PARA 614 note 3.

7   Employment Rights Act 1996 s 123(1) (amended by the Employment Act 2002 Sch 7 paras 24, 39). The amount of such an award is subject to a statutory maximum: see PARA 823. If the amount of any payment made by the employer to the employee on the ground that the dismissal was by reason of redundancy, whether in pursuance of the Employment Rights Act 1996 Pt XI (see PARA 835 et seq) or otherwise, exceeds the amount of the basic award which would be payable but for s 122(4) (see PARA 817), that excess goes to reduce the amount of the compensatory award: s 123(7). Where an award of compensation for unfair dismissal falls to be (see s 124A (added by the Employment Act 2002 s 39)):

   (1)   reduced or increased under the Trade Union and Labour Relations (Consolidation) Act 1992 s 207A (effect of failure to comply with Code: adjustment of awards: see PARA 1234) (Employment Rights Act 1996 s 124A(a) (s 124A as so added; s 124A(a) amended by the Employment Act 2008 s 3(1), (4))); or

   (2)   increased under the Employment Act 2002 s 38 (failure to give statement of employment particulars: see PARA 127) (Employment Rights Act 1996 s 124A(b) (as so added)),

   the adjustment must be in the amount awarded under s 118(1)(b) (see PARA 814) and must be applied immediately before any reduction under s 123(7) (see s 124A (as so added)). As to the meaning of 'employer' see PARA 2; and as to the meaning of 'employee' see PARA 2.

8   *W Devis & Sons Ltd v Atkins* [1977] AC 931, [1977] ICR 662, HL; and see PARA 770.

9   See the Employment Rights Act 1996 s 123(6); and PARA 821.

10   *W Devis & Sons Ltd v Atkins* [1977] AC 931, [1977] ICR 662, HL; *Tele-Trading Ltd v Jenkins* [1990] IRLR 430, CA; *Soros v Davison* [1994] ICR 590, [1994] IRLR 264, EAT.

11   See *Polkey v AE Dayton Services Ltd* [1988] AC 344, [1988] ICR 142, HL; and PARA 767. As to unfairness due only to a breach of proper procedure see PARA 768.

12   *Polkey v AE Dayton Services Ltd* [1988] AC 344, [1988] ICR 142, HL; *Mining Supplies (Longwall) Ltd v Baker* [1988] ICR 676, [1988] IRLR 417, EAT; *James W Cook & Co (Wivenhoe) Ltd v Tipper* [1990] ICR 716, [1990] IRLR 386, CA; *Slaughter v C Brewer & Sons Ltd* [1990] ICR 730, [1990] IRLR 426, EAT; *Chaplin v HJ Rawlinson Ltd* [1991] ICR 553, EAT; *Red Bank Manufacturing Co Ltd v Meadows* [1992] ICR 204, [1992] IRLR 209, EAT; *Rao v Civil Aviation Authority* [1994] ICR 495, [1994] IRLR 240, CA; *Abbey National plc v Chagger* [2009] IRLR 86, [2008] All ER (D) 157 (Oct), EAT; *Davies v J & R Farragher (t/a Potens)* [2009] All ER (D) 103 (Jan), EAT. A tribunal may not, however, decrease compensation on the ground that the employer could have dismissed fairly on an entirely different ground, had he chosen to do so: *Devonshire v Trico-Folberth Ltd* [1989] ICR 747, sub nom *Trico-Folberth Ltd v Devonshire* [1989] IRLR 396, CA. If the evidence only shows that the employee might have been dismissed properly in any event, the tribunal is to make a percentage

assessment of that possibility (applying its own assessment) and apply that when assessing the compensation: *Dunlop Ltd v Farrell* [1993] ICR 885, EAT; *Wolesley Centers Ltd v Simmons* [1994] ICR 503, EAT; *Fisher v California Cake and Cookie Ltd* [1997] IRLR 212, EAT.

13 Ie for the purposes of the Employment Rights Act 1996 s 123(1): see the text and notes 1–7.

14 There is no statutory definition of 'strike' and 'other industrial action' for these purposes; but as to their meaning for the purposes of the Trade Union and Labour Relations (Consolidation) Act 1992 s 238 (dismissal in connection with a lockout, strike or other industrial action) see PARA 1351.

15 See the Employment Rights Act 1996 s 123(5); and see *Morris v Gestetner Ltd* [1973] 3 All ER 1168, [1973] ICR 587, NIRC. In a case falling within the Employment Rights Act 1996 s 123(5), there may still be a finding of contributory fault by the employee, eg by creating the situation leading to the industrial action or obstructing the employer's attempts to resolve the problem: *Hazells Offset Ltd v Luckett* [1977] IRLR 430, EAT; *Ford Motor Co Ltd v Hudson* [1978] ICR 482, [1978] IRLR 66, EAT (obiter); *Sulemanji v Toughened Glass Ltd* [1979] ICR 799, EAT; *Colwyn Borough Council v Dutton* [1980] IRLR 420, EAT. As to the modification of the Employment Rights Act 1996 s 123(5) where a teacher in a foundation, voluntary aided or foundation special school is dismissed by the governing body of the school in pursuance of a requirement of the local education authority see PARA 757 note 9.

819. Calculation of the compensatory award for unfair dismissal; heads of compensation. Although a tribunal is given a wide discretion to award such an amount as is just and equitable as a compensatory award for unfair dismissal[1], as a matter of practice there are certain well-established heads of compensation[2]:

(1) loss between the date of dismissal and the date of the hearing: loss of pay[3] during this period[4] is amenable to calculation; and payments from the employer, whether in lieu of notice or ex gratia, are to be taken into account[5], as are amounts earned by the employee in other employment[6];

(2) future loss: the tribunal must consider a series of imponderables, in the light of the facts of the case[7]; although a multiplier may be used[8], this is not an area for precise calculations[9];

(3) loss of accrued rights: loss of accrued rights generally may be dealt with on a conventional sum basis[10], although, if the employee in fact enjoyed greater than normal rights by contract, for example under an enhanced redundancy scheme, that may be reflected in the award[11];

(4) manner of dismissal: as at common law[12], distress etc caused by the dismissal is not normally compensated; loss may be claimed under this head only if there are financial implications, particularly if the employee will find it more difficult to find new employment because of the manner of his dismissal[13];

(5) loss of pension rights: because of the importance and difficulty of this head of compensation[14] the Government Actuary's Department has issued guidance[15] on the calculation of pension loss in an unfair dismissal claim, which a tribunal may be expected to adopt[16].

In its judgment on a compensatory award, a tribunal should set out its reasoning in sufficient detail to show the principles on which it has proceeded and the amounts awarded under the relevant heads of compensation[17].

1 See PARA 818.

2 See *Norton Tool Co Ltd v Tewson* [1973] 1 All ER 183, [1972] ICR 501, NIRC.

3 For these purposes, 'pay' means realistic, net pay and can include matters such as overtime which cannot be included in the more technical calculation of a week's pay for the purposes of fixing the basic award (see PARA 815): *Brownson v Hire Service Shops Ltd* [1978] ICR 517, [1978] IRLR 73, EAT; *Palmanor Ltd v Cedron* [1978] ICR 1008, [1978] IRLR 303, EAT. If there is a dispute as to what was properly payable under the contract, that must be resolved by the tribunal: *Kinzley v Minories Finance Ltd* [1988] ICR 113, [1987] IRLR 490, EAT. Tax matters need not be dealt with in detail unless significant sums are involved: *MBS Ltd v Calo*

[1983] ICR 459, [1983] IRLR 189, EAT; *Lucas v Laurence Scott and Electromotors Ltd* [1983] ICR 309, [1983] IRLR 61, EAT. As to the inclusion of fringe benefits see note 7.

4   The whole period must be considered (*Ging v Ellward Lancs Ltd* [1991] ICR 222n, 13 ITR 265, EAT), except possibly where either:
  (1)   the employee gains new employment but then loses it, still within the period, in which case the original employer is liable only for the period up to the gaining of the new employment (*Courtaulds Northern Spinning Ltd v Moosa* [1984] ICR 218, [1984] IRLR 43, EAT); or
  (2)   it would not be just and equitable to take the whole period into account, in particular where either there is substantial delay between the date of dismissal and the date of hearing, or the employee has obtained new permanent employment at a higher rate of pay, in which case it may be fair to consider only the period up to entering the new employment (*Lytlarch Ltd v Reid* [1991] ICR 216, EAT; *Fentiman v Fluid Engineering Products Ltd* [1991] IRLR 150, EAT).
However, these are ultimately matters for the tribunal, and not rules of law: *Dench v Flynn & Partners* [1998] IRLR 653, CA (disapproving on this point *Whelan (t/a Cheers Off Licence) v Richardson* [1998] ICR 318, [1998] IRLR 114, EAT). See also *Bentwood Bros (Manchester) Ltd v Shepherd* [2003] EWCA Civ 380, [2003] ICR 1000, [2003] IRLR 364; *Cowen v Rentokil Initial Facility Services (UK) Ltd* [2008] All ER (D) 70 (Apr), EAT; *Aegon UK Corporate Services Ltd v Roberts* [2009] EWCA Civ 932, [2010] ICR 596, [2009] IRLR 1042. The element of arrears of pay and benefits for the period between dismissal and reinstatement where there is a failure to comply with the reinstatement order is not a free-standing head of loss and must form part of the award which is subject to the statutory maximum under the Employment Rights Act 1996 s 124 (see PARA 823) where the circumstances do not fall within any other statutory exception: *Parry v National Westminster Bank plc* [2004] EWCA Civ 1563, [2005] ICR 396, [2005] IRLR 193.

Social security benefits which are not subject to recovery by the state from unfair dismissal compensation (ie under the Employment Protection (Recoupment of Jobseeker's Allowance and Income Support) Regulations 1996, SI 1996/2349: see PARA 1478), such as sickness benefit, are to be deducted: *Sun and Sand Ltd v Fitzjohn* [1979] ICR 268, [1979] IRLR 154, EAT; *Puglia v C James & Sons* [1996] ICR 301, [1996] IRLR 70, EAT (doubting on this point *Hilton International Hotels (UK) Ltd v Faraji* [1994] ICR 259, [1994] IRLR 267, EAT, and *Rubenstein and Roskin (t/a McGuffies Dispensing Chemists) v McGloughlin* [1997] ICR 318, [1996] IRLR 557, EAT); *Morgans v Alpha Plus Security Ltd* [2005] ICR 525, [2005] IRLR 234, EAT (incapacity benefit). Housing benefit payable to the employee after dismissal is not to be deducted: *Savage v Saxena* [1998] ICR 357, [1998] IRLR 182, EAT. Early pension payments are not to be deducted: *Knapton v ECC Card Clothing Ltd* [2006] ICR 1084, [2006] IRLR 756, EAT.

5   In the law of unfair dismissal, there is a special rule to the effect that amounts earned in other employment during what is, or should have been, the employee's notice period are not deducted from the compensatory award for future loss of income: *TBA Industrial Products Ltd v Locke* [1984] ICR 228, [1984] IRLR 48, EAT (approved in *Addison v Babcock FATA Ltd* [1988] QB 280, [1987] ICR 805, CA (disapproving *Finnie v Top Hat Frozen Foods* [1985] ICR 433, [1985] IRLR 365, EAT)); *Horizon Holidays Ltd v Grassi* [1987] ICR 851, [1987] IRLR 371, EAT; cf *Roadchef Ltd v Hastings* [1988] IRLR 142, EAT (where a payment which would have been made to the employee anyway was not taken into account). There is no principle that an employee should receive full pay for the notice period as unfair dismissal compensation, however, where that amount exceeds the loss resulting from the dismissal: *Addison v Babcock FATA Ltd*; *Burlo v Langley* [2006] EWCA Civ 1778, [2007] 2 All ER 462, [2007] IRLR 145, applying the principle in *Norton Tool Co Ltd v Tewson* [1973] 1 All ER 183, [1972] ICR 501, NIRC, for calculating compensation (ie that an employee is to be treated as having suffered a loss in so far as he recovers less than he would have received in accordance with good industrial practice which would require, in the absence of gross misconduct, that an employee who is summarily dismissed should at the time of his dismissal be paid a payment in lieu of notice covering the notice period). This rule, which provides a narrow exception to the rule of mitigation in unfair dismissal cases, is not to be applied in a case of constructive dismissal (see PARA 763): *Stuart Peters Ltd v Bell* [2009] EWCA Civ 938, [2010] 1 All ER 775, [2009] ICR 453 (dominant factor was felt to be the need to keep the exception to its narrowest, because of its breach of normal considerations of justice and logic). As to ex gratia payments see PARA 823.

It is unclear whether or not damages from a wrongful dismissal claim should be deducted from compensation for unfair dismissal in proceedings arising from the same dismissal: see *O'Laoire v Jackel International Ltd (No 2)* [1991] ICR 718, sub nom *O'Laoire v Jackel*

International Ltd [1991] IRLR 170, CA (compensation for unfair dismissal not to be deducted from later damages for wrongful dismissal); and PARA 831 note 19.

6 *Ging v Ellward Lancs Ltd* [1991] ICR 222n, 13 ITR 265, EAT; *Lee v IPC Business Press Ltd* [1984] ICR 306, EAT (earnings from self-employment). This includes amounts earned during what was or should have been the employee's notice period: *Hardy v Polk (Leeds) Ltd* [2005] ICR 557, [2004] IRLR 420, EAT, following *Cerberus Software Ltd v Rowley* [2001] EWCA Civ 78, [2001] ICR 376, [2001] IRLR 160, and not following in this respect *Norton Tool Co Ltd v Tewson* [1973] 1 All ER 183, [1972] ICR 501, NIRC, and *Addison v Babcock FATA Ltd* [1988] QB 280, [1987] ICR 805, CA, as neither made any reference to the duty to mitigate. As to mitigation see PARA 822.

7 There is no particular conventional sum (*Morganite Electrical Carbon Ltd v Donne* [1988] ICR 18, [1987] IRLR 363, EAT) and the basis of the correct approach is to consider how long it is likely to be before the employee obtains equivalent permanent employment (*Courtaulds Northern Spinning Ltd v Moosa* [1984] ICR 218, [1984] IRLR 43, EAT; *Gilham v Kent County Council (No 3)* [1986] ICR 52, [1986] IRLR 56, EAT). The fact that employment with the employer would have terminated soon may be relevant: see PARA 818. There may be a discount for accelerated receipt of capital, but this is not mandatory: *Les Ambassadeurs Club v Bainda* [1982] IRLR 5, EAT. Loss of fringe benefits may be taken into account: *Butler v J Wendon & Son* [1972] IRLR 15 (tied cottage); *Nohar v Granitstone (Galloway) Ltd* [1974] ICR 273, NIRC (company car); *Hedger v Davy & Co Ltd* [1974] IRLR 138 (free accommodation); *Lee v IPC Business Press Ltd* [1984] ICR 306, EAT (enhanced redundancy rights). Expenses in looking for a new job, or in setting up a new business, may be included, but not the cost of legal proceedings: *Co-operative Wholesale Society v Squirrell* (1974) 9 ITR 191, NIRC; *Nohar v Granitstone (Galloway) Ltd*; *Gardiner-Hill v Roland Berger Technics Ltd* [1982] IRLR 498, EAT. The tribunal should consider evidence, where it exists, that employment will not be indefinite in its calculations and clearly state the reasons for its conclusions: *Thornett v Scope* [2006] EWCA Civ 1600, [2007] ICR 236, sub nom *Scope v Thornett* [2007] IRLR 155. An intended cessation of employment by resignation was capable of stopping what otherwise would have been a continuing loss following an unfair dismissal: *Fanstone v Ros (t/a Cherry Tree Day Nursery)* [2008] All ER (D) 46 (Jan), EAT. See also *Chagger v Abbey National plc* [2009] EWCA Civ 1202, [2010] ICR 397, [2010] IRLR 47 ('stigma'); and PARA 818.

8 See *Qualcast (Wolverhampton) Ltd v Ross* [1979] ICR 386, [1979] IRLR 98, EAT. For guidelines on the 'Ogden Tables', issued from time to time by the Government Actuary's Department for use in personal injury and fatal accident cases (see CIVIL PROCEDURE vol 11 (2009) PARA 818), in the context of assessing a claimant's loss of future earnings, see *Kingston upon Hull City Council v Dunnachie (No 3)* [2004] ICR 227, [2003] IRLR 843, EAT; and *Abbey National plc v Chagger* [2009] IRLR 86, [2008] All ER (D) 157 (Oct), EAT. As to the Government Actuary see CONSTITUTIONAL AND ADMINISTRATIVE LAW vol 20 (2014) PARA 233.

9 See *Brown's Cycles Ltd v Brindley* [1978] ICR 467, EAT. See also *Wardle v Crédit Agricole Corporate and Investment Bank* [2011] EWCA Civ 545, [2011] ICR 1290, [2011] IRLR 604 (if an employee suffered career loss, it was incumbent on the tribunal to do its best to calculate the loss, notwithstanding that a considerable degree of speculation is required; exceptionally, a tribunal would be entitled to take the view on the evidence before it that there was no real prospect of the employee ever obtaining an equivalent job and, in such a case, the tribunal necessarily had to assess the loss on the basis that it would continue for the course of the claimant's working life).

10 *SH Muffett Ltd v Head* [1987] ICR 1, [1986] IRLR 488, EAT, considering *Daley v AE Dorsett (Almar Dolls Ltd)* [1982] ICR 1, [1981] IRLR 385, EAT.

11 *Lee v IPC Business Press Ltd* [1984] ICR 306, EAT.

12 See PARAS 829, 830.

13 *Vaughan v Weighpack Ltd* [1974] ICR 261, [1974] IRLR 105, NIRC. If, however, the dismissal had a direct effect on the employee's health, that may affect the period of future loss: *Devine v Designer Flowers Wholesale Florist Sundries Ltd* [1993] IRLR 517, EAT.

14 See eg *Copson v Eversure Accessories Ltd* [1974] ICR 636, [1974] IRLR 247, NIRC; *Powrmatic Ltd v Bull* [1977] ICR 469, [1977] IRLR 144, EAT. A precise calculation is not always appropriate: *Manpower Ltd v Hearne* [1983] ICR 567, [1983] IRLR 281, EAT.

15 See *Compensation for Loss of Pension Rights* (3rd Edn, 2003) (TSO), produced by a committee of tribunal chairmen in consultation with the Government Actuary's Department. These guidelines were revised following *Clancy v Cannock Chase Technical College* [2001] IRLR 331, [2001] All ER (D) 36 (Mar), EAT (the guidelines provided no yardstick for the computation of loss of pension rights under a scheme which yields not only an income benefit but also a lump sum arising as of right rather than by commutation). As to the current application of the guidance see *Griffin v Plymouth Hospital NHS Trust* [2014] EWCA Civ 1240 at [81], [2014]

All ER (D) 150 (Sep) at [81] per Underhill LJ (the extent to which [the guidance's] recommendations on particular points remain valid will increasingly need to be carefully considered in the light of important changes in pension law and practice that have occurred since the current edition of the Guidance was published in 2003).

16   *Tradewinds Airways Ltd v Fletcher* [1981] IRLR 272, EAT; *Manpower Ltd v Hearne* [1983] ICR 567, [1983] IRLR 281, EAT; *Mono Pumps Ltd v Froggatt and Radford* [1987] IRLR 368, EAT. There is, however, no absolute obligation to use it: *Bingham v Hobourn Engineering Ltd* [1992] IRLR 298, EAT; *Port of Tilbury (London) Ltd v Birch* [2005] IRLR 92, EAT (guidance may assist an employment tribunal when there is little forthcoming from the parties; but the first duty of the tribunal is to consider any credible evidence and submissions put forward by the parties). See also *Greenhoff v Barnsley Metropolitan Borough Council* [2006] ICR 1514, [2006] All ER (D) 300 (Jun), EAT; *Bone v Mayor and Burgess of the London Borough of Newham* [2009] All ER (D) 192 (Feb), EAT.

17   *Norton Tool Co Ltd v Tewson* [1973] 1 All ER 183, [1972] ICR 501, NIRC; *Adda International Ltd v Curcio* [1976] ICR 407, [1976] IRLR 425, EAT. As to the right to know the tribunal's reasoning as regard loss of promotion, loss of bonus and loss of future postgraduate study see *Bone v Mayor and Burgess of the London Borough of Newham* [2009] All ER (D) 192 (Feb), EAT. See also *Meek v City of Birmingham District Council* [1987] IRLR 250, CA; and *Aegon UK Corporate Services Ltd v Roberts* [2009] EWCA Civ 932, [2010] ICR 596, [2009] IRLR 1042 (employment tribunal cannot carve out pensions for special treatment; they are simply part of overall remuneration package and, even taking account of the pension loss, the overall package at the employee's new employment was more favourable than it had been with the employer).

820. Compensation for act which is both unlawful discrimination and unfair dismissal. Where compensation falls to be awarded in respect of any act[1] both under the provisions of the Employment Rights Act 1996 relating to unfair dismissal[2] and the Equality Act 2010[3], an employment tribunal[4] must not award compensation under either of those Acts in respect of any loss or other matter which is or has been taken into account under the other of them by the tribunal or another employment tribunal in awarding compensation on the same or another complaint in respect of that act[5].

1   As to the meaning of 'act' for these purposes see PARA 614 note 3.
2   Ie the Employment Rights Act 1996 Pt X (ss 94–134A) (unfair dismissal: see also PARAS 757 et seq, 821 et seq). As to the meaning of 'dismissal' see PARA 762. As to the modification of Pt X (ss 94–134A) in relation to governing bodies of schools having a right to a delegated budget, acting in the exercise of their employment powers, see EDUCATION vol 35 (2011) PARA 355 et seq; and as to the modification of Pt X in relation to persons holding ecclesiastical office under common tenure see the Ecclesiastical Offices (Terms of Service) Regulations 2009, SI 2009/2108, reg 33; and ECCLESIASTICAL LAW vol 34 (2011) PARA 407.
3   See the Employment Rights Act 1996 s 126(1) (amended by the Equality Act 2010 Sch 26 para 33(1), (2) (added by SI 2010/2279)). As to the Equality Act 2010 see DISCRIMINATION vol 33 (2013) PARA 1 et seq.
4   As to employment tribunals see PARA 1399 et seq; and as to the procedure on a complaint to an employment tribunal see PARA 1453 et seq.
5   See the Employment Rights Act 1996 s 126(2) (amended by the Employment Rights (Dispute Resolution) Act 1998 s 1(2)(a); and by the Equality Act 2010 Sch 26 para 33(1), (3) (added by SI 2010/2279)).

821. Effect of contributory fault on amount of compensation awarded for dismissal. Where a dismissal[1] is unfair but there is also fault[2] on the part of the employee[3], a tribunal may take that into account by reducing the amount of compensation that is awarded to the employee[4]. Where the tribunal finds that the dismissal was to any extent caused or contributed to by any action[5] of the complainant[6], it must reduce the amount of the compensatory award[7] by such proportion as it considers just and equitable having regard to that finding[8]. Where the reason (or principal reason) for the dismissal is that the complainant made a protected disclosure[9], and it appears to the tribunal that the disclosure was not made in good faith[10], the tribunal may, if it considers it just and equitable in all the circumstances to do so, reduce any award it makes to the complainant by no more than 25 per cent[11].

The basic award[12] may also be reduced, but on a wider basis[13]. Where the tribunal considers that any conduct of the complainant before the dismissal (or, where the dismissal was with notice, before the notice was given) was such that it would be just and equitable to reduce or further reduce the amount of the basic award to any extent, the tribunal must reduce or further reduce that amount accordingly[14].

In order to constitute contributory fault, the conduct of the complainant must be in some way blameworthy[15]. The general approach is for the tribunal to deal with the matter in a broad, commonsense manner[16]. Contributory fault is particularly likely to be found in a case of misconduct, but in the nature of the matter is unlikely to be found in a case of incapability[17]; it may apply in a case where the employee was constructively dismissed[18].

There are no limitations on the tribunal's discretion to fix the amount of a reduction, which might in an extreme case be of 100 per cent, if it considers that to be just and equitable[19]. It is a question of fact; and the tribunal's decision is unlikely to be upset on appeal[20].

1   As to the meaning of 'dismissal' see PARA 762.
2   Contributory fault by the employee is one of the factors to be taken into account when deciding whether or not to make an order for reinstatement or re-engagement: see the Employment Rights Act 1996 s 116(1)(c) (see PARA 812), s 116(3)(c) (see PARA 812). As to the modification of Pt X (ss 94–134A) (unfair dismissal: see also PARAS 757 et seq, 822 et seq) in relation to governing bodies of schools having a right to a delegated budget, acting in the exercise of their employment powers, see EDUCATION vol 35 (2011) PARA 355 et seq; and as to the modification of Pt X in relation to persons holding ecclesiastical office under common tenure see the Ecclesiastical Offices (Terms of Service) Regulations 2009, SI 2009/2108, reg 33; and ECCLESIASTICAL LAW vol 34 (2011) PARA 407.
3   As to the meaning of 'employee' see PARA 2.
4   Contributory fault is a separate element in an unfair dismissal action (*Nudds v W & JB Eastwood Ltd* [1978] ICR 171, EAT) and must be properly considered (*Mercia Rubber Mouldings Ltd v Lingwood* [1974] ICR 256, [1974] IRLR 82, NIRC). Whether it is dealt with at the same stage of the hearing as the question of fairness or by a 'split' hearing, it is desirable for the tribunal to make the intended procedure clear at the outset: *Iggesund Converters Ltd v Lewis* [1984] ICR 544 at 553, [1984] IRLR 431 at 435, EAT, per Waite P (obiter); *Ferguson v Gateway Training Centre Ltd* [1991] ICR 658, EAT. There can be a reduction in compensation to reflect contributory fault both where the employers have discharged the onus of showing what was the reason for the dismissal and where they have failed to do so: *Polentarutti v Autokraft Ltd* [1991] ICR 757, [1991] IRLR 457, EAT.
5   As to the meaning of 'action' for these purposes see PARA 614 note 3. The phrase 'caused or contributed to by' imposes a causal requirement (*Hutchinson v Enfield Rolling Mills Ltd* [1981] IRLR 318, EAT), although the reference to 'contributed' means that the employee's conduct need only be a factor and need not refer to the principal reason for dismissal (*Robert Whiting Designs Ltd v Lamb* [1978] ICR 89, EAT; *Polentarutti v Autokraft Ltd* [1991] ICR 757, [1991] IRLR 457, EAT). This means that contributory fault cannot be based on misconduct by the employee unknown to the employer at the time of the dismissal; but in such a case the compensatory award may be reduced instead under the tribunal's discretion in the Employment Rights Act 1996 s 123(1) to award 'just and equitable' compensation: see PARA 818. A failure to appeal against dismissal could not properly be said to be contributory conduct in the unfair dismissal itself, although it might be something which in an appropriate case could be raised and argued on the question of failure to mitigate (see PARA 822): *Ceesay v Securicor Security Ltd* [2005] All ER (D) 215 (Jan), EAT. See also *Millicent v Swallow Security Services Ltd* [2009] All ER (D) 299 (Mar), EAT; and note 8.
6   As to the meaning of 'complainant' see PARA 804.
7   As to the compensatory award see PARAS 818, 819.
8   Employment Rights Act 1996 s 123(6). Where an award of compensation for unfair dismissal falls to be (see s 124A (added by the Employment Act 2002 s 39)):

(1) reduced or increased under the Trade Union and Labour Relations (Consolidation) Act 1992 s 207A (effect of failure to comply with Code: adjustment of awards: see PARA 1234) (Employment Rights Act 1996 s 124A(a) (s 124A as so added; s 124A(a) amended by the Employment Act 2008 s 3(1), (4))); or

(2) increased under the Employment Act 2002 s 38 (failure to give statement of employment particulars: see PARA 127) (Employment Rights Act 1996 s 124A(b) (as so added)),

the adjustment must be in the amount awarded under s 118(1)(b) (see PARA 814) and must be applied immediately before any reduction under s 123(6) (see s 124A (as so added)).

The application of s 123(6) by a tribunal is a two-stage process: (a) whether to order a reduction (a question of causation); and (b) if so, by how much (a question of what is just and equitable): see *Warrilow v Robert Walker Ltd* [1984] IRLR 304, EAT. See also *Parker Foundry Ltd v Slack* [1992] ICR 302, [1992] IRLR 11, CA (in considering whether a compensation award for a finding of unfair dismissal should be reduced, the tribunal is required only to consider whether that dismissal was caused or contributed to by the action of the complainant and to make a reduction that is just and equitable to that finding). Thus once a finding of contributory fault is made, the tribunal must go on to make a reduction (of the amount thought just and equitable): *Optikinetics Ltd v Whooley* [1999] ICR 984, EAT. The proper approach was to decide, first, what was the real reason for dismissal and then to see whether the employee's conduct played any part at all in the history of events leading to dismissal and there was in the Employment Rights Act 1996 s 123(6) an express obligation on the tribunal, if it found that the dismissal was to any extent caused or contributed to by any action of the employee, to make a reduction in compensation to the extent that it considered just and equitable to do so: *Millicent v Swallow Security Services Ltd* [2009] All ER (D) 299 (Mar), EAT. The discretion under the Employment Rights Act 1996 s 123(6) lay in assessing the proportion of the reduction, and did not give the tribunal scope for the differential treatment of different elements of a compensatory award; once it had made that decision, however, it was bound to apply that reduction to the compensatory award as a whole, since s 123(6) does not talk in terms of proportions or elements of the award, but envisaged one reduction being applied to the whole award: *Audsley v Riverside Industrial Equipment Ltd* [2014] All ER (D) 109 (Apr), EAT (tribunal had either applied the wrong test or had reached a perverse decision, especially set against its finding that the employee had been 50% at fault; the language used was that of probability and not chance).

The Employment Rights Act 1996 s 123(6) differs from s 122(2) (see the text and notes 12–14) in requiring the tribunal to also find that the conduct complained of, in respect of which it may go on to think it just and equitable to reduce the award, caused or contributed to the dismissal 'to any extent', which emphasises that what is looked for need not be the principal or sole cause, or even a main cause, of the dismissal: *Frith Accountants v Law* [2014] IRLR 510, [2014] ICR 805, EAT (the words 'to any extent' are obviously and intentionally broad but they follow words of causation).

9 See PARAS 69, 70.

10 See note 9.

11 See the Employment Rights Act 1996 s 123(6A) (added by the Enterprise and Regulatory Reform Act 2013 s 18(5)).

12 As to the basic award see PARA 815.

13 Unlike the Employment Rights Act 1996 s 123(6) (see the text and notes 5–8), s 122(2) does not require the tribunal to find a causative element to the employee conduct that is being complained of (its deliberation being basically a question of what was just and equitable): *Steen v ASP Packaging Ltd* [2014] ICR 56, EAT; and see *Frith Accountants v Law* [2014] IRLR 510, [2014] ICR 805, EAT (cited in note 8).

The basic award is calculated mathematically, and, therefore, cannot be reduced or eliminated at the calculation stage on grounds that it would be just and equitable to do so. As to the possibility of an employee whose misconduct only came to light after the dismissal being entitled to a basic award, no matter how serious the misconduct, if a causal requirement applied, see *W Devis & Sons Ltd v Atkins* [1977] AC 931, [1977] ICR 662, HL (decided before the enactment of the Employment Rights Act 1996 s 122(2) in its present form).

14 Employment Rights Act 1996 s 122(2). Section 122(2) does not apply in a redundancy case, unless the reason for selection was one specified in s 100(1)(a) (health and safety activities: see PARA 786), s 100(1)(b) (health and safety representatives: see PARA 786), s 101A(1)(d) (working time cases (workforce representatives): see PARA 788), s 102(1) (trustees of occupational pension schemes: see PARA 790) or s 103 (employee representatives: see PARA 791); and in such a case s 122(2) applies only to so much of the basic award as is payable because of s 120 (see PARA 816): s 122(3) (amended by SI 1998/1833). As to the meaning of 'redundancy case' for

these purposes see the Employment Rights Act 1996 s 105(9); and PARA 781 note 4. As to the meaning of 'redundancy' see PARA 870. There is no power to reduce a basic award to reflect the percentage chance that the employee would have been dismissed anyway (ie a reduction which is possible in relation to the compensatory award on the principle enunciated in *Polkey v AE Dayton Services Ltd* [1988] AC 344, [1988] ICR 142, HL: see PARA 818): *Taylor v John Webster, Buildings Civil Engineering* [1999] ICR 561, EAT.

Although the contributory fault provisions in relation to the basic and compensatory awards are separate, a tribunal finding contributory fault should normally reduce both awards by the same amount: *G McFall & Co Ltd v Curran* [1981] IRLR 455, NI CA; *RSPCA v Cruden* [1986] ICR 205, [1986] IRLR 83, EAT; *Chaplin v HJ Rawlinson Ltd* [1991] ICR 553, EAT. However, there may be exceptional cases where different reductions may be justified: *Les Ambassadeurs Club v Bainda* [1982] IRLR 5, EAT; *Rao v Civil Aviation Authority* [1994] ICR 495, [1994] IRLR 240, CA; *Charles Robertson (Developments) Ltd v White* [1995] ICR 349, EAT. In *Optikinetics Ltd v Whooley* [1999] ICR 984, EAT, the Employment Appeal Tribunal accepted the possibility of different reductions by stressing the different wording and tests in the Employment Rights Act 1996 s 122(2) and s 123(6).

15 *Nelson v BBC (No 2)* [1980] ICR 110, [1979] IRLR 346, CA; *Slaughter v C Brewer & Sons Ltd* [1990] ICR 730, [1990] IRLR 426, EAT. Thus if the employee's actions were proper, eg refusing an unlawful order, the compensation should not be reduced: *Morrish v Henlys (Folkestone) Ltd* [1973] 2 All ER 137, [1973] ICR 482, NIRC. Fault by the employee's agent, eg a solicitor, may count: *Allen v Hammett* [1982] ICR 227, [1982] IRLR 89, EAT. If the dismissal is automatically unfair, the employee's conduct relating to the specially protected reason in question cannot be blameworthy: *Property Guards Ltd v Taylor and Kershaw* [1982] IRLR 175, EAT. As to failure to disclose a spent conviction see *Property Guards Ltd v Taylor and Kershaw*; and PARA 779.

16 *Maris v Rotherham Corpn* [1974] 2 All ER 776, [1974] ICR 435, NIRC; *Brown v Rolls Royce (1971) Ltd* (1977) 12 ITR 382, EAT; *Hollier v Plysu Ltd* [1983] IRLR 260, CA.

17 *Slaughter v C Brewer & Sons Ltd* [1990] ICR 730, [1990] IRLR 426, EAT, applying *Nelson v BBC (No 2)* [1980] ICR 110, [1979] IRLR 346, CA. It has been suggested that there could never be a finding of contributory fault in an incapability case, except where there was blame involved on the employee's part eg through laziness or unwillingness to improve (*Kraft Foods Ltd v Fox* [1978] ICR 311, [1977] IRLR 431, EAT; *Sutton and Gates (Luton) Ltd v Boxall* [1979] ICR 67, [1978] IRLR 486, EAT); but this has been doubted as a principle (*Moncur v International Paint Co Ltd* [1978] IRLR 223, EAT; *Finnie v Top Hat Frozen Foods* [1985] ICR 433, [1985] IRLR 365, EAT (disapproved on other grounds in *Addison v Babcock FATA Ltd* [1988] QB 280, [1987] ICR 805, CA)).

18 *Garner v Grange Furnishing Ltd* [1977] IRLR 206, EAT; *Associated Tyre Specialists (Eastern) Ltd v Waterhouse* [1977] ICR 218, [1976] IRLR 386, EAT; *Morrison v Amalgamated Transport and General Workers' Union* [1989] IRLR 361, NI CA (disapproving dicta to the contrary in *Holroyd v Gravure Cylinders Ltd* [1984] IRLR 259, EAT); *Polentarutti v Autokraft Ltd* [1991] ICR 757, [1991] IRLR 457, EAT.

19 *W Devis & Sons Ltd v Atkins* [1977] AC 931, [1977] IRLR 314, [1977] ICR 662, HL; *Thompson v Woodland Designs Ltd* [1980] IRLR 423, EAT; *Allders International Ltd v Parkins* [1981] IRLR 68, EAT; *Chaplin v H J Rawlinson Ltd* [1991] ICR 553, EAT. To justify such a finding, the employee's conduct must have been the sole cause of the dismissal: *Gibson v British Transport Docks Board* [1982] IRLR 228, EAT (EAT adjusted reduction of 100% to 90% as the employee's conduct was not the sole cause of dismissal). The power to reduce by 100% was reaffirmed in *Lemonious v Church Comrs* [2013] All ER (D) 199 (Jun), EAT. However as to the need for reasons see *Lemonious v Church Comrs* (applied in *Steen v ASP Packaging Ltd* [2014] ICR 56, EAT; and *Worrell v Hootenanny Brixton Ltd* [2014] All ER (D) 137 (Apr), EAT); and see PARA 1476.

20 See *Hollier v Plysu Ltd* [1983] IRLR 260, CA; *Associated Tyre Specialists (Eastern) Ltd v Waterhouse* [1977] ICR 218, [1976] IRLR 386, EAT; *Warrilow v Robert Walker Ltd* [1984] IRLR 304, EAT; *Parker Foundry Ltd v Slack* [1989] ICR 686, EAT (affd [1992] ICR 302, [1992] IRLR 11, CA); cf *Gibson v British Transport Docks Board* [1982] IRLR 228, EAT; *Nairne v Highland and Islands Fire Brigade* [1989] IRLR 366, Ct of Sess. As to the application of contributory fault to a case involving an ex gratia payment by the employer see PARA 823.

822. Mitigation of loss for the purpose of assessing the compensatory award.
In ascertaining the loss sustained by the complainant[1] for the purpose of assessing the compensatory award[2], the tribunal must apply the same rule concerning the duty of a person to mitigate his loss as applies to damages

recoverable under the common law[3] of England and Wales[4]. Whether there has been a failure to mitigate is a question of fact for the tribunal[5]; and the burden of proof is on the employer to show that there has been such a failure[6]. In considering an employee's ability to mitigate his loss by finding new employment[7], the tribunal must take into account the personal circumstances and characteristics of the employee[8].

1 As to the meaning of 'complainant' see PARA 804.
2 Ie in ascertaining the loss referred to in the Employment Rights Act 1996 s 123(1) (see PARAS 818, 819). The duty to mitigate does not apply to the basic award (see PARA 815), except in relation to refusal of an offer of re-employment where a similar rule applies: see s 122(1); and PARA 817. A person unreasonably preventing an order for reinstatement or re-engagement from being complied with is deemed to have failed to mitigate his loss: see s 117(8); and PARA 813 note 12. As to the modification of Pt X (ss 94–134A) (unfair dismissal: see also PARAS 757 et seq, 823 et seq) in relation to governing bodies of schools having a right to a delegated budget, acting in the exercise of their employment powers, see EDUCATION vol 35 (2011) PARA 355 et seq; and as to the modification of Pt X in relation to persons holding ecclesiastical office under common tenure see the Ecclesiastical Offices (Terms of Service) Regulations 2009, SI 2009/2108, reg 33; and ECCLESIASTICAL LAW vol 34 (2011) PARA 407.
3 As to the general rule see *British Westinghouse Electric and Manufacturing Co Ltd v Underground Electric Rlys Co of London Ltd* [1912] AC 673 at 689, HL, per Lord Haldane; and DAMAGES vol 12(1) (Reissue) PARA 1041 et seq. As to its application in a common law employment case see *Yetton v Eastwoods Froy Ltd* [1966] 3 All ER 353, [1967] 1 WLR 104; and PARA 831.
   There is a special rule, based on good industrial relations practice, in the law of unfair dismissal that amounts earned in other employment during what is, or should have been, the employee's notice period are not deducted from the compensatory award for future loss of income in an unfair dismissal case: *TBA Industrial Products Ltd v Locke* [1984] ICR 228, [1984] IRLR 48, EAT (approved in *Addison v Babcock FATA Ltd* [1988] QB 280, [1987] ICR 805, CA; and *Burlo v Langley* [2006] EWCA Civ 1778, [2007] 2 All ER 462, [2007] IRLR 145 ('good IR practice' approach of not deducting earnings during what should have been the notice period from the compensatory award for future loss of income in unfair dismissal case: see PARA 819 note 5), applying the principle in *Norton Tool Co Ltd v Tewson* [1973] 1 All ER 183, [1972] ICR 501, NIRC, for calculating compensation (see PARA 819), is not to be applied in a case of constructive dismissal (see PARA 763): *Stuart Peters Ltd v Bell* [2009] EWCA Civ 938, [2010] 1 All ER 775, [2009] ICR 453 (dominant factor was felt to be the need to keep the exception to its narrowest, because of its breach of normal considerations of justice and logic).
4 Employment Rights Act 1996 s 123(4); and see *Bessenden Properties Ltd v Corness* [1977] ICR 821n, [1974] IRLR 338, CA. As to the meanings of 'England' and 'Wales' see PARA 2 note 12. The obligation to consider mitigation when assessing loss applies both to loss up to the time of the hearing and loss into the future: *Morganite Electrical Carbon Ltd v Donne* [1988] ICR 18, [1987] IRLR 363, EAT. A tribunal might, if it was just and equitable, look at all the actual and probable losses and deduct all the mitigation; on the other hand, it might, permissibly, decide to draw a line between past and future losses and apply different tests and it would be committing no error of law if it were to do so: *Ridley v Islam Channel Ltd* [2009] All ER (D) 89 (Aug), EAT. Events before the time of dismissal, eg refusal of an offer of alternative work, are, however, not relevant: *Savoia v Chiltern Herb Farms Ltd* [1981] IRLR 65, EAT (affd [1982] IRLR 166, CA); *Prestwick Circuits Ltd v McAndrew* [1990] IRLR 191, Ct of Sess. See also *Konczak v BAE Systems (Operations) Ltd* [2012] All ER (D) 83 (Jun), EAT (refusal to accept offer of settlement from employer had not been so unreasonable as to terminate the loss otherwise flowing from the employer's act of dismissal).
5 *Bessenden Properties Ltd v Corness* [1977] ICR 821n, [1974] IRLR 338, CA. Where there is a finding of failure to mitigate, this should be applied by deciding when it would have been reasonable to expect the employee to have found work and taking into account the notional income, not by applying a percentage reduction of compensation: *Peara v Enderlin Ltd* [1979] ICR 804, EAT; *Gardiner-Hill v Roland Berger Technics Ltd* [1982] IRLR 498, EAT. See also *Dore v Aon Training Ltd* [2005] IRLR 891, [2005] All ER (D) 328 (Mar), CA (where an employee attempted to mitigate his loss by setting up his own business, an employment tribunal should first calculate what sums represented the employee's loss of remuneration; then consider the costs incurred in mitigating his loss; such a sum if reasonably incurred should be added to the figure for loss; finally, the earnings from new work should be deducted).

6   *Bessenden Properties Ltd v Corness* [1977] ICR 821n, [1974] IRLR 338, CA; *Sturdy
    Finance Ltd v Bardsley* [1979] ICR 249, [1979] IRLR 65, EAT; *Fyfe v Scientific Furnishings Ltd*
    [1989] ICR 648, [1989] IRLR 331, EAT (disapproving *Scottish and Newcastle Breweries plc v
    Halliday* [1986] ICR 577, [1986] IRLR 291, EAT, and *Morganite Electrical Carbon Ltd v
    Donne* [1988] ICR 18, [1987] IRLR 363, EAT); *Morris v Chrome Clothing Ltd* [2004] All ER
    (D) 243 (Nov), EAT (whilst it was open to a tribunal to raise the issue of failing to mitigate loss,
    the burden of showing that there had been such failure then falls on the employer).
7   As to the principles that may apply to determine whether a dismissed employee who has refused
    an offer of re-employment has failed in his duty to mitigate his loss see *Wilding v British
    Telecommunications plc* [2002] EWCA Civ 349, [2002] ICR 1079, [2002] IRLR 524. The
    refusal to accept an alternative offer of employment from the same employer, made after
    dismissal, does not necessarily constitute a failure to mitigate: *F & G Cleaners Ltd v Saddington*
    [2012] IRLR 892, EAT.
8   See e g *Fougère v Phoenix Motor Co Ltd* [1976] ICR 495, [1976] IRLR 259, EAT (age and poor
    health); *Brittains Arborfield Ltd v Van Uden* [1977] ICR 211, EAT (injury).

**823.   Maximum amounts of compensation awarded for unfair dismissal; ex
gratia payments.**   Statutory maxima are imposed on the compensation that may
be awarded for unfair dismissal[1]. In the case of basic awards[2] this is achieved by
setting a ceiling on the amount that may be counted when calculating the
employee's week's pay, by which those awards are themselves calculated[3].

The amount of any compensation awarded to a person under the statutory
provisions relating to enforcement of an order for reinstatement or
re-engagement[4], or of a compensatory award[5], must not exceed a specified
amount[6].

The maximum set for the compensatory award must be applied with care in a
case where there is either an ex gratia payment by the employer[7] or a finding of
contributory fault[8]. The limit mentioned above[9] applies to the amount which the
employment tribunal would otherwise[10] award in respect of the subject matter of
the complaint, after taking into account any payment made by the respondent to
the complainant[11] in respect of that matter, and any reduction in the amount of
the award required by any enactment or rule of law[12]. Thus in a case where an
ex gratia payment has been made, that payment should be deducted from the
prima facie measure of loss, and then the statutory limit applied[13]. Similarly, in a
case where the employee is guilty of contributory fault, the prima facie measure
of loss should first be reduced by the relevant fraction for contributory fault, and
then the statutory limit applied[14].

1   As to the remedy of compensation for unfair dismissal see PARA 814 et seq. As to the meaning of
    'dismissal' see PARA 762.
2   See PARA 815.
3   See PARAS 815, 816.
4   Ie under the Employment Rights Act 1996 s 117(1), (2) (failure fully to comply with an order
    for reinstatement or re-engagement: see PARA 813). In the case of compensation awarded to a
    person under s 117(1), (2), the limit imposed by s 124 may be exceeded to the extent necessary
    to enable the award fully to reflect the amount specified or payable under s 114(2)(a) (see
    PARA 811) or s 115(2)(d) (see PARA 811): s 124(3).
        As to the modification of Pt X (ss 94–134A) (unfair dismissal: see also PARA 757 et seq) in
    relation to governing bodies of schools having a right to a delegated budget, acting in the
    exercise of their employment powers, see EDUCATION vol 35 (2011) PARA 355 et seq; and as to
    the modification of Pt X in relation to persons holding ecclesiastical office under common tenure
    see the Ecclesiastical Offices (Terms of Service) Regulations 2009, SI 2009/2108, reg 33; and
    ECCLESIASTICAL LAW vol 34 (2011) PARA 407.
5   Ie an award calculated in accordance with the Employment Rights Act 1996 s 123: see PARAS
    818, 819.
6   Employment Rights Act 1996 s 124(1) (s 124(1) amended, s 124(1ZA) added, by
    SI 2013/1949). The amount mentioned in the text is that specified in the Employment Rights
    Act 1996 s 124(1ZA): see s 124(1) (as so amended). Accordingly, the amount is the lower of:

(1) £76,574 (s 124(1ZA)(a) (s 124(1ZA) as so added; s 124(1ZA)(a) amended by virtue of SI 2014/382)); and

(2) 52 multiplied by a week's pay of the person concerned (Employment Rights Act 1996 s 124(1ZA)(b) (as so added)).

The Secretary of State may by order made by statutory instrument amend s 124 so as to vary the limit imposed for the time being by s 124(1): Enterprise and Regulatory Reform Act 2013 s 15(1). A statutory instrument containing an order under s 15 is not to be made unless a draft of the instrument has been laid before each House of Parliament and approved by a resolution of each House (s 15(8)); and such an order may make consequential, supplemental, transitional, transitory or saving provision, including provision inserting a reference to the Employment Rights Act 1996 s 124 in s 226(3) (week's pay (calculation date in unfair dismissal cases): see PARA 146) (Enterprise and Regulatory Reform Act 2013 s 15(6), (7)). The limit as varied by s 15(1) may be:

(a) a specified amount (s 15(2)(a)); or

(b) the lower of a specified amount (s 15(2)(b)(i)), and a specified number (not being less than 52) multiplied by a week's pay of the individual concerned (see s 15(2)(b)(ii), (5)).

Different amounts may be specified under head (a) or head (b) above in relation to employers of different descriptions (s 15(3)); and any amount so specified may not be less than median annual earnings and may not be more than three times median annual earnings (s 15(4)). For these purposes, 'median annual earnings' means the latest figure for median gross annual earnings of full-time employees in the United Kingdom published by the Statistics Board (disregarding any provisional figures), or (if that figure was published by the Statistics Board more than two years before the laying of the draft of the statutory instrument in question) an estimate of the current amount of such earnings worked out in whatever way the Secretary of State thinks fit: see s 15(9). In exercise of the powers conferred by s 15, the Secretary of State has made the Unfair Dismissal (Variation of the Limit of Compensatory Award) Order 2013, SI 2013/1949. As to the Secretary of State see PARA 5 note 21. As to the Statistics Board see REGISTRATION CONCERNING THE INDIVIDUAL vol 88 (2012) PARA 353.

The Employment Rights Act 1996 s 124(1) does not apply to compensation awarded, or a compensatory award made, to a person in a case where he is regarded as unfairly dismissed by virtue of s 100 (see PARA 786), s 103A (see PARA 792), s 105(3) (see PARA 781) or s 105(6A) (see PARA 781): s 124(1A) (added by the Employment Relations Act 1999 s 37(1)).

7 Such an ex gratia payment is normally deducted from any later award of compensation for unfair dismissal: see PARA 819 note 5. As to the meaning of 'employer' see PARA 2.

8 See PARA 821.

9 Ie the limit imposed by the Employment Rights Act 1996 s 124(1): see the text and notes 4–6.

10 Ie apart from the Employment Rights Act 1996 s 124.

11 As to the meaning of 'complainant' see PARA 804.

12 See the Employment Rights Act 1996 s 124(5) (amended by the Employment Rights (Dispute Resolution) Act 1998 s 1(2)(a)).

13 *UBAF Bank Ltd v Davis* [1978] IRLR 442, EAT; *McCarthy v British Insulated Callenders Cables plc* [1985] IRLR 94, EAT; *Digital Equipment Co Ltd v Clements (No 2)* [1998] ICR 258, [1998] IRLR 134, CA; *Leonard v Strathclyde Buses Ltd* [1998] IRLR 693, Ct of Sess.

14 *Walter Braund (London) Ltd v Murray* [1991] ICR 327, [1991] IRLR 100, EAT. Where the statutory limit is not involved, but there is both an ex gratia payment and a finding of contributory fault, it has been held that the ex gratia sum should be deducted first and then the remainder reduced by contributory fault: see *UBAF Bank Ltd v Davis* [1978] IRLR 442, EAT; *Parker & Farr Ltd v Shelvey* [1979] ICR 896, [1979] IRLR 434, EAT; *Digital Equipment Co Ltd v Clements (No 2)* [1997] ICR 237, [1997] IRLR 140, EAT (revsd on other grounds [1998] ICR 258, [1998] IRLR 134, CA) (disapproving *Derwent Coachworks v Kirby* [1995] ICR 48, [1994] IRLR 639, EAT); *Heggie v Uniroyal Englebert Tyres Ltd* [1999] IRLR 802, Ct of Sess. Exceptionally, however, where the ex gratia payment is in fact a non-statutory redundancy payment, to be set off first against the basic award (see the Employment Rights Act 1996 s 122(4); and PARA 817) and then, to the extent of any excess, against the compensatory award (see s 123(7); and PARA 818 note 7), the ex gratia payment is to be deducted after the contributory fault, to allow the employer the full benefit of the payment: *Digital Equipment Co Ltd v Clements (No 2)* [1998] ICR 258, [1998] IRLR 134, CA (a case concerning an ex gratia redundancy payment and the reduction for the likelihood of being dismissed anyway; but it is submitted that the principle is equally good in the case of a reduction for contributory fault).

D. ALTERNATIVE DISPUTE RESOLUTION

824. Arbitration scheme for unfair dismissal cases. In an attempt to provide a simpler and quicker alternative method for resolving unfair dismissal cases than by application to an employment tribunal[1], the Advisory, Conciliation and Arbitration Service (ACAS)[2] may prepare a scheme providing for arbitration in the case of disputes involving proceedings, or claims which could be the subject of proceedings, before an employment tribunal[3] under, or arising out of a contravention or alleged contravention[4] of:

(1) the study and training provisions[5] of the Employment Rights Act 1996[6];

(2) the flexible working provisions[7] of the Employment Rights Act 1996[8];

(3) the unfair dismissal provisions[9] of the Employment Rights Act 1996[10]; or

(4) any enactment specified in an order made by the Secretary of State[11].

When ACAS has prepared such a scheme, it must submit a draft of the scheme to the Secretary of State who, if he approves it, must make an order setting out the scheme and making provision for it to come into effect[12]. ACAS may take any steps appropriate for promoting awareness of a scheme so prepared[13].

ACAS may from time to time prepare a revised version of such a scheme and, when it has done so, it must submit a draft of the revised scheme to the Secretary of State who, if he approves it, must make an order setting out the revised scheme, and making provision for it to come into effect[14].

Where the parties to any dispute that is subject to arbitration in this way[15] agree in writing to submit the dispute to arbitration in accordance with such a scheme[16], ACAS must refer the dispute to the arbitration of a person appointed by ACAS for the purpose, not being an officer or employee of ACAS[17].

1 See the Green Paper *Resolving employment rights disputes: options for reform* (Cm 2707).
2 As to the constitution and powers of ACAS see PARA 1213 et seq.
3 As to employment tribunals see PARA 1399 et seq; and as to the procedure on a complaint to an employment tribunal see PARA 1453 et seq.
4 See the Trade Union and Labour Relations (Consolidation) Act 1992 s 212A(1) (s 212A added by the Employment Rights (Dispute Resolution) Act 1998 s 7; the Trade Union and Labour Relations (Consolidation) Act 1992 s 212A(1) amended by the Employment Act 2002 Sch 7 paras 18, 22(a)).
5 Ie the Employment Rights Act 1996 s 63F(4), (5) or (6) (see PARA 328) or s 63I(1)(b) (see PARA 330).
6 Trade Union and Labour Relations (Consolidation) Act 1992 s 212A(1)(zza) (s 212A as added (see note 4); s 212A(1)(zza) added by the Apprenticeships, Skills, Children and Learning Act 2009 s 40(5), Sch 1 paras 12, 13(a)).
7 Ie the Employment Rights Act 1996 s 80G(1) (see PARA 109) or s 80H(1)(b) (see PARA 111).
8 Trade Union and Labour Relations (Consolidation) Act 1992 s 212A(1)(za) (s 212A as added (see note 4); s 212A(1)(za) added by the Employment Act 2002 Sch 7 paras 18, 22(b) and amended by the Apprenticeships, Skills, Children and Learning Act 2009 Sch 1, paras 12, 13(b)).
9 Ie the Employment Rights Act 1996 Pt X (ss 94–134A) (unfair dismissal: see PARA 757 et seq).
10 Trade Union and Labour Relations (Consolidation) Act 1992 s 212A(1)(a) (as added (see note 4); and amended by the Employment Act 2002 Sch 7 paras 18, 22(c)). See note 12.
11 Trade Union and Labour Relations (Consolidation) Act 1992 s 212A(1)(b) (as added: see note 4). See note 12.
12 Trade Union and Labour Relations (Consolidation) Act 1992 s 212A(2) (as added: see note 4). An order under s 212A must be made by statutory instrument: s 212A(10) (as so added). Where a scheme set out in an order under s 212A includes provision for the making of re-employment orders in arbitrations conducted in accordance with the scheme, the order setting out the scheme may require employment tribunals to enforce such orders:
   (1) in accordance with the Employment Rights Act 1996 s 117 (see PARA 813) (Trade Union and Labour Relations (Consolidation) Act 1992 s 212A(8)(a) (as so added)); or

(2)   in accordance with the Employment Rights Act 1996 s 117 as modified by the order (s 212A(8)(b) (as so added)).

For this purpose, 're-employment orders' means orders requiring that persons found to have been unfairly dismissed be reinstated, re-engaged or otherwise re-employed: see s 212A(8) (as so added). An order under s 212A setting out a scheme may provide that, in the case of disputes within s 212A(1)(a) (see head (3) in the text), such part of an award made in accordance with the scheme as is specified by the order is to be treated as a basic award of compensation for unfair dismissal for the purposes of the Employment Rights Act 1996 s 184(1)(d) (see PARA 628): Trade Union and Labour Relations (Consolidation) Act 1992 s 212A(9) (as so added). No order is to be made under s 212A(1)(b) (see head (4) in the text) unless a draft of the statutory instrument containing it has been laid before Parliament and approved by a resolution of each House: s 212A(11) (as so added). A statutory instrument containing an order under s 212A, other than one of which a draft has been approved by resolution of each House of Parliament, is subject to annulment in pursuance of a resolution of either House of Parliament: s 212A(12) (as so added). In exercise of the powers conferred by s 212A(1), (3), (6)–(9), the Secretary of State has made the ACAS Arbitration Scheme (Great Britain) Order 2004, SI 2004/753 (amended by SI 2006/2405; SI 2013/1956; SI 2014/386); and in exercise of the powers conferred by the Trade Union and Labour Relations (Consolidation) Act 1992 s 212A(3), (6), (7), the Secretary of State has made the ACAS (Flexible Working) Arbitration Scheme (Great Britain) Order 2004, SI 2004/2333 (amended by SI 2013/1956; SI 2014/386) (see PARA 111).

13 Trade Union and Labour Relations (Consolidation) Act 1992 s 212A(4) (as added: see note 4).
14 See the Trade Union and Labour Relations (Consolidation) Act 1992 s 212A(3) (as added: see note 4). See note 12.
15 Ie any dispute within the Trade Union and Labour Relations (Consolidation) Act 1992 s 212A(1): see the text and notes 1–11.
16 Ie a scheme having effect by virtue of an order under the Trade Union and Labour Relations (Consolidation) Act 1992 s 212A.
17 Trade Union and Labour Relations (Consolidation) Act 1992 s 212A(5) (as added: see note 4). Nothing in the Arbitration Act 1996 (see ARBITRATION) applies to an arbitration conducted in accordance with a scheme having effect by virtue of an order under the Trade Union and Labour Relations (Consolidation) Act 1992 s 212A, except to the extent that the order provides for any provision of the Arbitration Act 1996 Pt I (ss 1–84) (see ARBITRATION vol 2 (2008) PARA 1209 et seq) so to apply; and the order may provide for any such provision to apply subject to modifications: Trade Union and Labour Relations (Consolidation) Act 1992 s 212A(6) (as so added). See note 12.

(4)   WRONGFUL DISMISSAL

(i) In general

825.   Meaning of 'wrongful dismissal'.   A wrongful dismissal is a dismissal in breach of the relevant provision in the contract of employment relating to the expiration of the term for which the employee is engaged[1]. To entitle the employee to sue for damages, two conditions must normally be fulfilled[2], namely:

(1)   the employee must have been engaged for a fixed period[3], or for a period terminable by notice[4], and dismissed either before the expiration of that fixed period or without the requisite notice, as the case may be[5]; and

(2)   his dismissal must have been without sufficient cause to permit his employer to dismiss him summarily[6].

In addition, there may be cases where the contract of employment limits the grounds on which the employee may be dismissed[7], or makes dismissal subject to a contractual condition of observing a particular procedure[8], in which case it may be argued that, on a proper construction of the contract, a dismissal for an extraneous reason or without observance of the procedure is a wrongful dismissal on that ground[9].

The common law claim for wrongful dismissal must be considered entirely separately from the statutory claim for unfair dismissal[10]. The existence of the latter does not, however, abrogate the common law claim, which may still be particularly appropriate in two cases:

(a) where the employee is not entitled to bring a claim for unfair dismissal[11];

(b) where the damages for wrongful dismissal are likely to exceed the statutory maxima placed on compensation for unfair dismissal (as, for example, in the case of a well-remunerated employee on long notice or a fixed-term contract)[12].

When an employee is wrongfully dismissed, he is released, by the employer's repudiation, from the contract's provisions, in particular from a restraint of trade clause[13].

1   As to the contract of employment see PARA 1 et seq; and as to the duration of contracts of employment see PARA 723. As to the wrongful dismissal of apprentices see PARA 834. It is axiomatic that in order to found a claim for wrongful dismissal an employee has to show that he was employed under a contract of employment that was enforceable: see eg *Soteriou v Ultrachem Ltd* [2004] EWHC 983 (QB), [2004] IRLR 870 (contract found to be tainted with illegality; finding of illegality necessarily defeated claim). As to illegality in contracts of employment see PARA 18. As to whether a claim for breach of contract may be regarded as a 'possession' for the purposes of the Convention for the Protection of Human Rights and Fundamental Freedoms (Rome, 25 March 1957; TS 1 (1973); Cmnd 5179), First Protocol (1952), art 1 (right to the peaceful enjoyment of possessions: see RIGHTS AND FREEDOMS vol 88A (2013) PARA 534 et seq) (as incorporated into English law by the Human Rights Act 1998 s 1(3), Sch I Pt II) see *Soteriou v Ultrachem Ltd*.

2   These conditions are in addition to any special terms that may have been agreed on: *Hopkins v Wanostrocht* (1861) 2 F & F 368. See also the text and notes 7–9.

3   *Holcroft v Barber and Watson* (1843) 1 Car & Kir 4; *Peters v Staveley* (1866) 15 LT 275; *Down v Pinto* (1854) 9 Exch 327; cf *Baxter v Nurse* (1844) 6 Man & G 935; *Cook v Grubb* 1961 SLT 405. As to fixed-term contracts see PARA 725.

4   *Creen v Wright* (1876) 1 CPD 591; *Vibert v Eastern Telegraph Co* (1883) Cab & El 17; *Clarke v Lewisham Borough Council* (1902) 67 JP 195. As to dismissal by notice see PARA 733.

5   *Williams v Byrne* (1837) 7 Ad & El 177; *Emmens v Elderton* (1853) 4 HL Cas 624; *McKean v Cowley* (1863) 7 LT 828; *Whitehaven Colliery Co v M'Court* (1893) 57 JP 422, DC.

6   *Baillie v Kell* (1838) 4 Bing NC 638; *Edwards v Levy* (1860) 2 F & F 94; *Fletcher v Krell* (1872) 42 LJQB 55; cf *Cussons v Skinner* (1843) 11 M & W 161; *Hutton v Ras Steam Shipping Co Ltd* [1907] 1 KB 834, CA; *W Dennis & Sons Ltd v Tunnard Bros and Moore* (1911) 56 Sol Jo 162; *Acklam v Sentinel Insurance Co Ltd* [1959] 2 Lloyd's Rep 683. As to summary dismissal see PARAS 743–746. A Crown employee cannot bring a claim for wrongful dismissal: see PARA 6.

7   *McClelland v Northern Ireland General Health Services Board* [1957] 2 All ER 129, [1957] 1 WLR 594, HL; *Dietmann v Brent London Borough Council* [1988] ICR 842, sub nom *Dietman v Brent London Borough Council* [1988] IRLR 299, CA. The existence of valuable rights under a permanent health insurance scheme has been held to limit the ability of the employer to dismiss even by notice: see the cases cited in PARA 733 note 1.

8   *Jones v Lee and Guilding* [1980] ICR 310, [1980] IRLR 67, CA; *Gunton v Richmond-upon-Thames London Borough Council* [1981] Ch 448, [1980] ICR 755, CA; *Dietmann v Brent London Borough Council* [1988] ICR 842, sub nom *Dietman v Brent London Borough Council* [1988] IRLR 299, CA. See also the cases cited in PARAS 826 note 9, 829 note 7.

9   This does not mean, however, that the employee will be able to have the contract enforced by a court; that is a separate matter (see PARA 826) and in most cases the employee will have to seek a remedy in damages only (see PARAS 828–832).

10   See PARA 743. See also *Soteriou v Ultrachem Ltd* [2004] EWHC 983 (QB), [2004] IRLR 870 (when pursuing a claim for unfair dismissal before an employment tribunal, the claimant expressly reserved the right to make a claim for wrongful dismissal; however, the same factual issue lay at the heart of both claims and the findings of the tribunal constituted issue estoppel or

res judicata for the purpose of proceedings in the High Court for wrongful dismissal). See also *Fraser v HLMAD Ltd* [2006] EWCA Civ 738, [2006] ICR 1395, [2006] IRLR 687 where *Soteriou v Ultrachem Ltd* was approved.

11 Ie, in particular, where the employee has not served the necessary two-year qualifying period: see PARA 758.

12 As to the statutory maxima see PARA 823. However, this does not provide an avenue for suing in common law (for wrongful dismissal) for what otherwise the employee might have received under statute (for unfair dismissal): see PARA 828.

13 *General Billposting Co Ltd v Atkinson* [1909] AC 118, HL; *Measures Bros Ltd v Measures* [1910] 2 Ch 248, CA; *Briggs v Oates* [1991] 1 All ER 407, [1990] ICR 473; and see PARAS 826 note 2, 828 note 2. In *Rock Refrigeration Ltd v Jones* [1997] 1 All ER 1, [1997] ICR 938, CA, the Court of Appeal expressed some reservations about the continued acceptability of the rule in *General Billposting Co Ltd v Atkinson*, but felt obliged to apply it; cf *Lonmar Global Risks Ltd (formerly SBJ Global Risks Ltd) v West* [2010] EWHC 2878 (QB), [2011] IRLR 138 (unfair dismissal); and PARAS 19, 67, 776 note 28.

(ii) Remedies

A. ENFORCEMENT OF THE CONTRACT

826. Normal rule against enforcement of a contract of employment. There is a normal rule of practice that a court will not enforce a contract of employment[1], either by way of specific performance or by the granting of an injunction that would have a similar effect[2]. At common law, a dismissal to be effective has to be accepted by the employee[3], even if in practice an employee who has been wrongfully dismissed is normally obliged to accept the repudiation[4], and sue the employer for damages[5]. As an exception to this rule, there may be cases where a court will grant an injunction to a wrongfully dismissed employee to restrain the employer from acting on that dismissal where there remains a strong element of continuing mutual confidence between the parties[6], but this exception has been restrictively construed[7]; it cannot be considered a serious remedy for wrongful dismissal, in the sense of retaining the employment for the employee for any significant length of time[8], though there have been interesting examples of its use in obliging an employer to use properly a contractually-binding disciplinary procedure before dismissing[9].

1 See *Whitwood Chemical Co v Hardman* [1891] 2 Ch 416, CA; and CIVIL PROCEDURE vol 11 (2009) PARA 448; SPECIFIC PERFORMANCE vol 95 (2013) PARA 303.

2 This is partly on the grounds of the difficulty of policing any such court order and partly on the grounds of the personal nature of a contract of employment: *De Francesco v Barnum* (1890) 45 ChD 430; *CH Giles & Co Ltd v Morris* [1972] 1 All ER 960, [1972] 1 WLR 307 (where, however, specific performance of execution of a contract for personal services was ordered despite the possibility that that contract itself might not be specifically enforceable). Nor will an action be allowed that seeks a declaration that a contract still subsists: *Francis v Municipal Councillors of Kuala Lumpur* [1962] 3 All ER 633, [1962] 1 WLR 1411, PC. See also *Alexander v Standard Telephones and Cables plc* [1990] ICR 291, [1990] IRLR 55; *Jakeman v South West Thames Regional Health Authority and London Ambulance Service* [1990] IRLR 62; *Wishart v National Association of Citizens Advice Bureaux Ltd* [1990] ICR 794, [1990] IRLR 393, CA; and the cases cited in note 3. See generally CIVIL PROCEDURE vol 11 (2009) PARA 448 et seq; SPECIFIC PERFORMANCE vol 95 (2013) PARA 301 et seq.

A longstanding exception lies in the law relating to restraint of trade (see COMPETITION vol 18 (2009) PARA 377 et seq), in that a court may grant an injunction to enforce a valid negative restraint clause in a contract of employment, provided that it does not have the effect in practice of forcing the employee to work for the employer in question or starve: *Lumley v Wagner* (1852) 1 De GM & G 604 (distinguished in *Davis v Foreman* [1894] 3 Ch 654); *Warner Bros Pictures Inc v Nelson* [1937] 1 KB 209, [1936] 3 All ER 160; *Page One Records Ltd v Britton (t/a 'The Troggs')* [1967] 3 All ER 822, [1968] 1 WLR 157. See also the Trade Union and Labour Relations (Consolidation) Act 1992 s 236 (court has no power to compel an employee to do any work or attend at any place for the doing of any work); and PARAS 734 note 2, 1348.

3   *Geys v Société Générale, London Branch* [2012] UKSC 63, [2013] 1 AC 523, [2013] 1 All ER 1061, [2013] IRLR 122. The proposition set out in the text is known as the 'elective' theory, in contradistinction to the 'automatic' theory (which holds that, at common law, a dismissal automatically terminates the contract); there had been doubt about which theory provided the basis for the termination of an employment contract at common law until this was resolved by *Geys v Société Générale, London Branch* (common law claim for damages for breach of contract): see PARA 733 note 12.

As to the 'acceptance' or 'elective' theory, that a contract of employment is subject to the normal contractual rule that repudiation is not formally effective unless and until the innocent party accepts it ('an unaccepted repudiation is a thing writ in water and of no value to anybody': see *Howard v Pickford Tool Co* [1951] 1 KB 417 at 421, CA, per Asquith LJ; and CONTRACT vol 22 (2012) PARA 565 et seq), and the rule against enforcement remains one of frequent practice not one of law (thus leaving open the possibility of some form of enforcement, or at least continuation of the contract of employment in exceptional cases) see *Hill v CA Parsons & Co Ltd* [1972] Ch 305, [1971] 3 All ER 1345, CA (Stamp LJ dissenting); *Thomas Marshall (Exports) Ltd v Guinle* [1979] Ch 227, [1978] ICR 905; *Gunton v Richmond-upon-Thames London Borough Council* [1981] Ch 448, [1980] ICR 755 per Buckley LJ and Brightman LJ (doubted in *R v East Berkshire Health Authority, ex p Walsh* [1985] QB 152 at 161, [1984] ICR 743 at 748 per Sir John Donaldson MR); *Dietman v Brent London Borough Council* [1987] ICR 737, [1987] IRLR 259 (affd sub nom *Dietmann v Brent London Borough Council* [1988] ICR 842, [1988] IRLR 299, CA); *Boyo v Lambeth London Borough Council* [1994] ICR 727, [1995] IRLR 50, CA; and see *CH Giles & Co Ltd v Morris* [1972] 1 All ER 960, [1972] 1 WLR 307 (cited in note 2).

As to the 'automatic' or 'unilateral' theory, according to which a contract of employment provides an exception to the normal contractual rule, and repudiation automatically terminates it, so that an employee's *only* remedy in law then becomes one of damages (as to which see PARA 828 et seq), see *Vine v National Dock Labour Board* [1957] AC 488 at 500, [1956] 3 All ER 939 at 944, HL, per Viscount Kilmuir LC (obiter); *Denmark Productions Ltd v Boscobel Productions Ltd* [1969] 1 QB 699 at 726, [1968] 3 All ER 513 at 524, CA, per Salmon LJ; *Sanders v Ernest A Neale Ltd* [1974] 3 All ER 327, [1974] ICR 565, NIRC; *Ivory v Palmer* [1975] ICR 340 at 354–355, CA, per Browne LJ; *Gunton v Richmond-upon-Thames London Borough Council* at 460, 762–763 per Shaw LJ (dissenting); *R v East Berkshire Health Authority, ex p Walsh* at 168–169, 756–757 per May LJ.

The controversy was always considered to be a technical one because the application of either theory in most common law claims produces a similar result (ie immediate termination and no legal enforcement of the contract): see eg *Delaney v Staples (t/a De Montfort Recruitment)* [1992] 1 AC 687 at 692, [1992] ICR 483 at 489, HL, per Lord Browne-Wilkinson, to the effect that an unequivocal instant dismissal ends the employment relationship, whether or not it unilaterally discharges the contract of employment; and *Marsh v National Autistic Society* [1993] ICR 453, to the effect that, even if the elective theory is applied, the wrongfully dismissed employee's remedy still only lies in damages, not in debt under a continuing contract. It is important, however, for the sake of certainty, that the 'automatic' theory is applied when ascertaining the effective date of termination under the Employment Rights Act 1996 s 97 (ie summary termination by the employer does not require acceptance by the employee before the contract is terminated for the purposes of s 111: see PARA 764) (*Brown v Southall and Knight* [1980] ICR 617, [1980] IRLR 130, EAT; *Robert Cort & Son Ltd v Charman* [1981] ICR 816, [1981] IRLR 437, EAT; *Batchelor v British Railways Board* [1987] IRLR 136, CA; *Duniec v Travis Perkins Trading Co Ltd* [2014] All ER (D) 136 (Aug), EAT; and see PARA 764), whereas it is important to apply the 'acceptance theory' to the definition of dismissal under the Employment Rights Act 1996 s 95 (see PARA 762) in order to avoid 'self-dismissal' (see *London Transport Executive v Clarke* [1981] ICR 355, [1981] IRLR 166, CA (it would be manifestly unjust to allow a wrongdoer to determine a contract by repudiatory breach if the innocent party wished to affirm the contract for good reason); and PARA 762). See also *Adcock Coors Brewers Ltd* [2007] EWCA Civ 19, [2007] ICR 983, sub nom *Coors Brewers Ltd v Adcock* [2007] IRLR 440; *Small v Boots Co plc* [2009] IRLR 328, [2009] All ER (D) 200 (Jan), EAT.

4   Ie giving rise, technically, to a constructive dismissal (see PARA 763). Such acceptance will be readily found in any event: *Gunton v Richmond-upon-Thames London Borough Council* [1981] Ch 448 at 469, [1980] ICR 755 at 772, CA, per Buckley LJ.

5   As to such damages see PARAS 828–831. If the employee could keep the contract alive and claim to provide his side of the consideration, he could sue for wages due to him in a claim for debt, the advantage of this over a claim for damages for breach of contract being that the requirement of mitigation does not apply: see PARA 831. However see the authority against this in *Marsh v National Autistic Society* [1993] ICR 453.

6   *Hill v CA Parsons & Co Ltd* [1972] Ch 305, [1971] 3 All ER 1345, CA; *Irani v Southampton and South West Hampshire Health Authority* [1985] ICR 590, [1985] IRLR 203; *Powell v Brent London Borough Council* [1988] ICR 176, [1987] IRLR 466, CA; *Hughes v London Borough of Southwark* [1988] IRLR 55; *Wadcock v London Borough of Brent* [1990] IRLR 223. Alternatively, in a non-dismissal case, a court may be prepared to enforce a particular contractual right for the employee where there is a prospect of timely and effective court intervention (*Anderson v Pringle of Scotland Ltd* [1998] IRLR 64, Ct of Sess (where a contractual redundancy selection provision was enforced)) and/or the parties have not lost trust and clearly intend the employment to continue (*Peace v City of Edinburgh Council* [1999] IRLR 417, Ct of Sess (where the use of a new disciplinary procedure to which the employee had not agreed was restrained)).

7   *GKN (Cwmbran) Ltd v Lloyd* [1972] ICR 214, NIRC; *Sanders v Ernest A Neale Ltd* [1974] 3 All ER 327, [1974] ICR 565, NIRC; *Chappell v Times Newspapers Ltd* [1975] 2 All ER 233, [1975] ICR 145, CA; *City and Hackney Authority v National Union of Public Employees* [1985] IRLR 252, CA; *Ali v Southwark London Borough Council* [1988] ICR 567, [1988] IRLR 100; *Alexander v Standard Telephones and Cables plc* [1990] ICR 291, [1990] IRLR 55.

8   Few of the cases concern an ordinary wrongful dismissal claim, used by the employee to try to keep his job and his livelihood. Normally, the desire of the claimant is to keep the contract alive for some indirect reason or tactical advantage (even in *Hill v CA Parsons Ltd* [1972] Ch 305, [1971] 3 All ER 1345, CA, itself, the leading case, the aim was to keep the contract in existence notionally for six months, to allow the provisions of the Industrial Relations Act 1971 to come into force); and this distinction was utilised in *Robb v London Borough of Hammersmith and Fulham* [1991] ICR 514, [1991] IRLR 72, where Morland J held that, in cases where the employee is trying to keep the contract alive for collateral purposes only, the continued existence of mutual confidence is less important, the overall test being whether an injunction would be workable (injunction granted). Similarly, in cases where it is the employer seeking to keep the contract alive, it is not in order to retain the employee as a valued member of staff, but rather to be able to enforce certain contractual obligations against him for a little longer, particularly those relating to confidential information or competition during employment: *Thomas Marshall (Exports) Ltd v Guinle* [1979] Ch 227, [1978] ICR 905; *Evening Standard Co Ltd v Henderson* [1987] ICR 588, [1987] IRLR 64, CA. See also PARA 734.

9   *Irani v Southampton and South West Hampshire Health Authority* [1985] ICR 590, [1985] IRLR 203; *Gunton v Richmond-upon-Thames London Borough Council* [1981] Ch 448, [1980] ICR 755, CA; and see *Jones v Lee* [1980] ICR 310, [1980] IRLR 67, CA; *Dietmann v Brent London Borough Council* [1988] ICR 842, sub nom *Dietman v Brent London Borough Council* [1988] IRLR 299, CA; *Robb v London Borough of Hammersmith and Fulham* [1991] ICR 514, [1991] IRLR 72; *Boyo v Lambeth London Borough Council* [1994] ICR 727, [1995] IRLR 50, CA. As to a successful challenge to a suspension (and injunction granted) in perhaps atypical circumstances see *Mezey v South West London and St George's Mental Health NHS Trust* [2010] EWCA Civ 293, [2010] IRLR 512 (it is not permissible to enforce disciplinary proceedings against a doctor where lack of knowledge or ability has not been shown; it is possible to obtain an injunction so as to prevent the employer from bringing disciplinary proceedings in such a case).

827.   Public law remedies.   It may be possible to enforce a contract of employment by the use of public law remedies if it can be established that the employment in question has features over and above ordinary employment, so that a dismissal must not only be subject to contractual rules, but must also satisfy criteria imposed by public law, particularly in relation to the rules of natural justice[1], in the absence of which the dismissal may be a nullity and either declared[2] so or restrained as such by injunction[3].

Before the procedural reforms which introduced a single application for judicial review[4], the emphasis was on the status of the employee, and public law remedies might be available:

(1)   where the employment was in the nature of an office warranting legal protection[5]; or

(2)   more generally, where there was an element of public employment or service, support by statute or something in the nature of an office or status capable of protection[6].

However, this extra 'status' element remains elusive and the case law is confusing[7].

In applications for judicial review the approach of the courts has been generally restrictive[8]; the emphasis is now on the nature of the employee's complaint[9]. Judicial review may succeed only if the employee's complaint is of a public law nature, not if the complaint remains primarily a contractual one; and thus if the employee is merely complaining of the fact that the employer has broken his contract, judicial review will not lie, even though the employment is in the public sector and subject to statutory control or influence of sorts[10].

The court may order a claim to continue as if it had not been started under Part 54 of the Civil Procedure Rules so that proceedings may continue as proceedings brought under Part 7 of the Civil Procedure Rules[11], in which case the applicant may still seek a declaration or injunction on private law grounds under the older case law[12]; but in both areas there is a strong desire by the courts not to allow the use of essentially public law remedies to circumvent the jurisdiction of an employment tribunal which is the proper forum for all but the most exceptional dismissal cases[13].

1   As to procedural fairness and the rules of natural justice see JUDICIAL REVIEW vol 61 (2010) PARA 625 et seq. In the context of employment, it has been held that the rules of natural justice must be applied realistically, given that an employing organisation cannot necessarily function in as detached a manner as a court: *R v Chief Constable of South Wales, ex p Thornhill* [1987] IRLR 313, CA. (There is a similar approach in the analogous context of expulsion from a trade union: see *MacLean v Workers' Union* [1929] 1 Ch 602; and PARAS 1023–1024). Moreover, an applicant must be able to show not just that there was a breach of natural justice in the procedure adopted, but also that that breach actually affected the outcome: *R v Chief Constable of the Thames Valley Police, ex p Cotton* [1990] IRLR 344, CA.
        In addition to natural justice, there may be a challenge on the ground that the dismissal was *ultra vires*; normally this will mean *ultra vires* some statutory requirement (*Vine v National Dock Labour Board* [1957] AC 488, [1956] 3 All ER 939, HL) but it has also been applied to a dismissal falling outside particularly stringent restrictions on permissible grounds for dismissal in the contract itself (*McClelland v Northern Ireland General Health Services Board* [1957] 2 All ER 129, [1957] 1 WLR 594, HL). It is also possible, though factually unlikely to succeed, that there could be a challenge on the grounds of perversity: see *R v Hertfordshire County Council, ex p National Union of Public Employees* [1985] IRLR 258, CA.

2   A declaration will not normally be granted since the effect would be akin to enforcing the contract: *Barber v Manchester Regional Hospital Board* [1958] 1 All ER 322, [1958] 1 WLR 181; *Francis v Municipal Councillors of Kuala Lumpur* [1962] 3 All ER 633, [1962] 1 WLR 1411, PC. There must, therefore, be exceptional circumstances: see the text and notes 11–13.

3   See JUDICIAL REVIEW vol 61 (2010) PARA 716 et seq. One reason for increased interest in such remedies is that normally a former employee will not be reinstated by a tribunal, whereas an order that the dismissal was a nullity means that the employee remains in the employment. As to reinstatement in unfair dismissal cases see PARAS 811–813.

4   See JUDICIAL REVIEW vol 61 (2010) PARA 661.

5   *Ridge v Baldwin* [1964] AC 40, [1963] 2 All ER 66, HL (chief constable entitled to have the rules of natural justice observed). As to when an employment is regarded as an 'office' see *102 Social Club and Institute Ltd v Bickerton* [1977] ICR 911, EAT; *R v Hertfordshire County Council, ex p National Union of Public Employees* [1985] IRLR 258, CA.

6   *Malloch v Aberdeen Corpn* [1971] 2 All ER 1278 at 1294, [1971] 1 WLR 1578 at 1596, HL, per Lord Wilberforce. The word 'or' cannot be entirely disjunctive because it is clear that merely being in public employment is not enough to justify public law remedies: see the text and notes 8–10. The Dock Labour Scheme (now repealed) gave the necessary statutory element in *Vine v*

National Dock Labour Board [1957] AC 488, [1956] 3 All ER 939, HL. See also *Barnard v National Dock Labour Board* [1953] 2 QB 18, [1953] 1 All ER 1113, CA; *Taylor v Furness, Withy & Co Ltd* [1969] 1 Lloyd's Rep 324.

Public law remedies were thus not available in ordinary 'master and servant' cases: *Vine v National Dock Labour Board* at 500 and 944, HL, per Viscount Kilmuir LC. Theoretically, the extra status element could exist in non-statutory employment (see eg *Fisher v Jackson* [1891] 2 Ch 84) but in practice this is less likely to be the case, unless perhaps the employment involves other rights capable of protection, such as an employed trade union official's right to take part in his union's activities: *Stevenson v United Road Transport Union* [1977] 2 All ER 941, [1977] ICR 893, CA; cf *Taylor v National Union of Seamen* [1967] 1 All ER 767, [1967] 1 WLR 532. Even a 'strong statutory flavour' to the employment was, however, not sufficient in the case of a surgeon in *Barber v Manchester Regional Hospital Board* [1958] 1 All ER 322, [1958] 1 WLR 181.

7 'A comparative list in which persons have been held entitled or not entitled to a hearing, or to observance of rules of natural justice, according to the master and servant test, looks illogical and even bizarre. A specialist surgeon is denied protection which is given to a hospital doctor; a university professor, as a servant, has been denied the right to be heard, a dock labourer and an undergraduate have been granted it': *Malloch v Aberdeen Corpn* [1971] 2 All ER 1278 at 1294, [1971] 1 WLR 1578 at 1595, HL, per Lord Wilberforce. The cases to which he refers are *Barber v Manchester Regional Hospital Board* [1958] 1 All ER 322, [1958] 1 WLR 181; *Palmer v Inverness Hospitals Board* 1963 SC 311; *Vidyodaya University of Ceylon v Silva* [1964] 3 All ER 865, [1965] 1 WLR 77, PC; *Vine v National Dock Labour Board* [1957] AC 488, [1956] 3 All ER 939, HL; *Glynn v Keele University* [1971] 2 All ER 89, [1971] 1 WLR 487.

8 Ie in the light of the leading decision in *R v East Berkshire Health Authority, ex p Walsh* [1985] QB 152, [1984] ICR 743, CA; and see *R v Civil Service Appeal Board, ex p Bruce* [1988] 3 All ER 686, [1988] ICR 649 (affd [1989] 2 All ER 907, [1989] ICR 171, CA); *R v Derbyshire County Council, ex p Noble* [1990] ICR 808, [1990] IRLR 332, CA.

9 See *O'Reilly v Mackman* [1983] 2 AC 237, [1982] 3 All ER 1124, HL; *Cocks v Thanet District Council* [1983] 2 AC 286. [1982] 3 All ER 1135, HL; *Davy v Spelthorne Borough Council* [1984] AC 262, [1983] 3 All ER 278, HL; *Wandsworth London Borough Council v Winder* [1985] AC 461, [1984] 3 All ER 976, HL; and see JUDICIAL REVIEW vol 61 (2010) PARAS 607–609.

10 *R v East Berkshire Health Authority, ex p Walsh* [1985] QB 152, [1984] ICR 743, CA. Judicial review has been permitted in cases involving the police (*Calveley v Chief Constable of the Merseyside Police* [1989] QB 136, [1988] 3 All ER 385, CA (affd [1989] AC 1228, [1989] 1 All ER 1025, HL); *R v Chief Constable of the Thames Valley Police, ex p Cotton* [1990] IRLR 344, CA; *R v Deputy Chief Constable of the North Wales Constabulary, ex p Hughes* [1991] ICR 180, CA (the latter two applications being unsuccessful on the facts)), a police probationer (*Chief Constable of the North Wales Police v Evans* [1982] 3 All ER 141, [1982] 1 WLR 1155, HL) and a prison officer (*R v Secretary of State for the Home Department, ex p Benwell* [1985] QB 554, [1984] ICR 723; *R v Civil Service Appeal Board, ex p Cunningham* [1991] 4 All ER 310, [1991] IRLR 297, CA), but even in this case a prison officer's particular complaint may be categorised as contractual and so not amenable to judicial review (*McClaren v Home Office* [1990] ICR 824, [1990] IRLR 338, CA (applicant sought declarations as to the terms of his employment and a sum due for services rendered)). See also *Haigh v Department for Work and Pensions* [2004] EWHC 3015 (QB), [2004] All ER (D) 367 (Dec) (operation of performance related pay did not have the status of a contractual term, forming part of the administrative or regulatory element of the employee-employer relationship, and fell to be regarded as policy).

Judicial review has been refused to a police surgeon (*R v Derbyshire County Council, ex p Noble* [1990] ICR 808, [1990] IRLR 332, CA) and an Inland Revenue officer (*R v Civil Service Appeal Board, ex p Bruce* [1988] 3 All ER 686, [1988] ICR 649 (affd [1989] 2 All ER 907, [1989] ICR 171, CA)). See further *McClaren v Home Office* at 836–837 and 342 per Woolf LJ (the relevant principles being: (1) in relation to his personal claims against an employer, an employee of a public body is normally in exactly the same situation as other employees and can bring proceedings in the ordinary way for damages, a declaration or an injunction (except in relation to the Crown); (2) an employee of a public body can seek judicial review and obtain a remedy which would not be available to an employee in the private sector where there exists some disciplinary or other body established under the prerogative or by statute to which the employer or the employee is entitled or required to refer disputes affecting their relationship; (3) in addition, if an employee of the Crown or other public body is adversely affected by a decision of general application by his employer, he may be entitled to challenge that decision by way of judicial review on grounds that it is flawed; (4) judicial review will not be available where disciplinary procedures are of a purely domestic nature, albeit that their decisions might affect the public). As to the principle given under head (4) above see also *R v Lord Chancellor's Department, ex p Nangle* [1992] 1 All ER 897, [1991] ICR 743, DC.

11 See CPR 54.20; and JUDICIAL REVIEW vol 61 (2010) PARAS 660, 662. In *R v East Berkshire Health Authority, ex p Walsh* [1985] QB 152, [1984] ICR 743, CA, the Court of Appeal refused to exercise its discretion in the applicant's favour under the predecessor rule RSC Ord 53 r 9(5) (now revoked).

12 In *R v BBC, ex p Lavelle* [1983] 1 All ER 241, [1983] ICR 99, Woolf J applied RSC Ord 53 r 9(5) (now revoked: see note 11) and considered the matter as if brought by a writ seeking a declaration or injunction; the claim was rejected on the facts, but in the course of his judgment Woolf J suggested that in modern conditions an employee specifically protected by procedural requirements, either by contract or under the modern employment protection legislation, might be considered analogous to an office-holder under the older case law, and so able to enforce his contractual rights by declaration or injunction. This potentially expansive view has, however, not been followed subsequently (see e g the narrower view of office-holding in *R v Hertfordshire County Council, ex p National Union of Public Employees* [1985] IRLR 258, CA) and is inconsistent with the generally restrictive approach in *R v East Berkshire Health Authority, ex p Walsh* [1985] QB 152, [1984] ICR 743, CA, and subsequent decisions.

13 *R v East Berkshire Health Authority, ex p Walsh* [1985] QB 152, [1984] ICR 743, CA; *R v Civil Service Appeal Board, ex p Bruce* [1988] 3 All ER 686, [1988] ICR 649 (affd [1989] 2 All ER 907, [1989] ICR 171, CA).

B. DAMAGES

828. Employee's remedies. An employee who has been wrongfully dismissed[1] may accept the employer's repudiation and sue for damages for breach of contract[2]; but, where it is more appropriate, he may elect[3] to sue on the basis of an implied contractual term for him to be paid a reasonable sum for the value of the work that he has actually performed and for which he has not been paid[4]. The employee is bound by his election and may not pursue both claims[5].

Where, prior to and independently of a subsequent unfair dismissal[6], an employee has acquired a cause of action at common law which arises from treatment at the hands of his employer such that he sustains direct financial loss, his common law claim (which may be either in contract or in negligence) is not barred by the existence of the statutory unfair dismissal claim and is not subject to the statutory cap on the level of recovery[7]. An employee whose employment excludes him from the statutory right to complain of unfair dismissal[8] but who is entitled to compensation assessed by a public law body may seek judicial review of the amount of compensation awarded for his dismissal[9].

1 As to the meaning of 'wrongful dismissal' see PARA 825.

2 *General Billposting Co Ltd v Atkinson* [1909] AC 118, HL; *Denmark Productions Ltd v Boscobel Productions Ltd* [1969] 1 QB 699, [1968] 3 All ER 513, CA; *Ridge v Baldwin* [1964] AC 40 at 65, [1963] 2 All ER 66 at 71, HL, per Lord Reid (obiter). For exceptional cases where an employee may seek to keep the contract alive and sue for any continuing wages due in debt see PARA 826. The advantage of suing in debt is that the employee is not under a duty to mitigate (see PARA 831). However, an advantage of accepting the repudiation is that the employee may thereby claim to be released from obligations on himself under the contract, in particular a restraint of trade clause: *General Billposting Co Ltd v Atkinson*; *Measures Bros Ltd v Measures* [1910] 2 Ch 248, CA; *Briggs v Oates* [1991] 1 All ER 407, [1990] ICR 473. It has, however, been held that: (1) a dismissal with wages in lieu is not a wrongful dismissal such as to relieve the employee of a restraint clause (*W Dennis & Sons Ltd v Tunnard Bros and Moore* (1911) 56 Sol Jo 162; *Konski v Peet* [1915] 1 Ch 530; *Rex Stewart Jeffries Parker Ginsberg Ltd v Parker* [1988] IRLR 483, CA); and (2) a provision in a contract of employment for arbitration of disputes may be enforced in a claim by the employee for wrongful dismissal (*Renshaw v Queen Anne Residential Mansions Co Ltd* [1897] 1 QB 662, CA, distinguishing *Davis v Starr* (1889) 41 ChD 242, CA). See also PARAS 67, 776 note 28, 825 note 13.

3 *Goodman v Pocock* (1850) 15 QB 576.

4   *Cutter v Powell* (1795) 6 Term Rep 320; *Emmens v Elderton* (1853) 4 HL Cas 624; *Prickett v Badger* (1856) 1 CBNS 296; *Cook v Sherwood* (1863) 11 WR 595; cf *Planché v Colburn* (1831) 8 Bing 14; and see PARA 832.

5   *Lilley v Elwin* (1848) 11 QB 742; *Goodman v Pocock* (1850) 15 QB 576; cf *Dunn v Murray* (1829) 9 B & C 780; *Lush v Russell* (1849) 4 Exch 637. This form of claim cannot be used on the assumption that the contract still exists: *Planché v Colburn* (1831) 8 Bing 14 at 16 per Tindal CJ. See further CONTRACT vol 22 (2012) PARA 586 et seq.

6   As to unfair dismissal see PARA 762 et seq.

7   *Eastwood v Magnox Electric plc, McCabe v Cornwall County Council* [2004] UKHL 35, [2005] 1 AC 503, [2004] 3 All ER 991 (dismissed employee allowed to sue for loss flowing from stress-induced injury caused by course of conduct by employer leading up to dismissal, in spite of already having received the maximum remedy for unfair dismissal). *Eastwood v Magnox Electric plc, McCabe v Cornwall County Council* was applied in *Lakshmi v Mid-Cheshire Hospitals NHS Trust* [2008] EWHC 878 (QB), [2008] IRLR 956. See also PARA 829.

8   As to such employees see PARA 168.

9   *R v Civil Service Appeal Board, ex p Cunningham* [1991] 4 All ER 310, [1991] IRLR 297, CA. As to judicial review see also PARA 827.

829. Damages in claim for breach of contract. Where the employee elects to treat the contract as repudiated and sues for damages for its breach[1], he is entitled to recover estimated pecuniary loss resulting from the premature determination of his service[2]. The loss will include any amount of wages earned but not paid at the time of his dismissal[3] and (according to case law which departs from earlier authority) may include anticipated salary increases and bonuses which are at the discretion of the employer, if it can be established that the employer was in breach of contract by exercising that discretion in a manner which no reasonable employer would have done[4].

In cases where the contract includes an essential element of training, damages may be recovered for the loss of training or diminution of future prospects that result from the breach of contract[5]. Similarly, in certain cases where publicity or actually performing the work is an essential element of the employment, especially in the theatre, damages may be awarded for loss of publicity or loss of opportunity to enhance a reputation[6]. However, as a claim for breach of contract, damages are usually restricted to definable pecuniary loss, meaning in this context losses caused by breaches of the employment contract during employment and not upon termination, so no amounts may be recovered representing the manner of dismissal or prejudice to reputation or chances of other employment[7]. This rests on the basis that the common law right cannot co-exist with the statutory right not to be unfairly dismissed[8], although, exceptionally, a right of action in common law may still lie in respect of an employer's treatment of the employee prior to and independently of a subsequent unfair dismissal[9].

1   See PARA 828.

2   *Richardson v Mellish* (1824) 2 Bing 229; *French v Brookes* (1830) 6 Bing 354; *Lake v Campbell* (1862) 5 LT 582; *Burton v Pinkerton* (1867) LR 2 Exch 340; *Ross v Pender* (1874) 1 R 352. As to the measure of damages see PARA 830. General damages are, therefore, rarely awarded, one possible exception to this being where the wrongful dismissal deprives the employee of a valuable right specifically envisaged under the contract, as e g where the contract is terminated in order to deprive the employee of valuable rights under a permanent health insurance or redundancy scheme (see PARA 733 note 1). Whether any wider principle will evolve from the case law remains to be seen.

3   *Hartley v Harman* (1840) 11 Ad & El 798; *Goodman v Pocock* (1850) 15 QB 576; *Hochster v De la Tour* (1853) 2 E & B 678; *Frost v Knight* (1872) LR 7 Exch 111; *Brace v Calder* [1895] 2 QB 253, CA; and see PARA 833.

4   *Clark v BET plc* [1997] IRLR 348; *Clark v Nomura International plc* [2000] IRLR 766; *Mallone v BPB Industries plc* [2002] EWCA Civ 126, [2002] ICR 1045, [2002] IRLR 452. The traditional view holds that discretionary amounts cannot be recovered even if the employee was

in fact likely to have received them, an approach which limits losses to those amounts which an employee was contractually entitled to receive rather than those which he probably would in fact have received: *Lavarack v Woods of Colchester Ltd* [1967] 1 QB 278, [1966] 3 All ER 683, CA; *Micklefield v SAC Technology Ltd* [1990] 1 WLR 1002, [1990] IRLR 218 (loss of share option not recoverable). Note, however, the restrictive view of *Lavarack v Woods of Colchester Ltd* taken in *Horkulak v Cantor Fitzgerald International* [2004] EWCA Civ 1287, [2005] ICR 402, [2004] IRLR 942 (revsg in part [2003] EWHC 1918 (QB), [2004] ICR 697, [2003] IRLR 756). See also *Small v Boots Co plc* [2009] IRLR 328, [2009] All ER (D) 200 (Jan), EAT; *Czarnecki v Choice Textiles Ltd* [2013] All ER (D) 77 (Sep), EAT.

5   Eg in the case of wrongful termination of a contract of apprenticeship: see *Dunk v George Waller & Son Ltd* [1970] 2 QB 163, [1970] 2 All ER 630, CA; and PARA 834.

6   *Marbé v George Edwardes (Daly's Theatre) Ltd* [1928] 1 KB 269, CA; *Herbert Clayton and Jack Waller Ltd v Oliver* [1930] AC 209, HL; *Re Golomb and William Porter & Co Ltd's Arbitration* (1931) 144 LT 583, CA; *Withers v General Theatre Corpn Ltd* [1933] 2 KB 536, CA; *Tolnay v Criterion Film Productions Ltd* [1936] 2 All ER 1625; *Miller v Cecil Film Ltd* [1937] 2 All ER 464. See further DAMAGES vol 12(1) (Reissue) PARA 1113.

7   *Addis v Gramophone Co Ltd* [1909] AC 488, HL; *Shove v Downs Surgical plc* [1984] 1 All ER 7, [1984] ICR 532; *Bliss v South East Thames Regional Health Authority* [1987] ICR 700, [1985] IRLR 308, CA (overruling *Cox v Philips Industries Ltd* [1976] 3 All ER 161, [1976] ICR 138); *Johnson v Unisys Ltd* [2001] UKHL 13, [2003] 1 AC 518, [2001] 2 All ER 801. *Shove v Downs Surgical plc* was applied in *Jones v Global Crossing (UK) Telecommunications Ltd* [2008] All ER (D) 19 (Sep), EAT; and *Johnson v Unisys Ltd* was applied in *Lakshmi v Mid-Cheshire Hospitals NHS Trust* [2008] EWHC 878 (QB), [2008] IRLR 956, [2008] All ER (D) 353 (Apr). While contractual damages for dismissal in breach of a contractual procedure would fall foul of the exclusion zone established by *Johnson v Unisys Ltd*, there may still be contractual liability with open ended damages if an employee complains that reputational damage was caused by being suspended in breach of a contractual procedure, with no supervening dismissal, although the remedy for unjustified stigma lay, short of circumstances establishing a claim for defamation, in the restoration of reputation which might in the ordinary course be expected to result from a claim for wrongful or unfair dismissal: *Edwards v Chesterfield Royal Hospital NHS Foundation Trust, Botham v Ministry of Defence* [2011] UKSC 58, [2012] 2 AC 22, [2012] 2 All ER 278, [2012] IRLR 129 (decision by a majority, with differences in reasoning). In *Malik v Bank of Credit and Commerce International SA (in liquidation), Mahmud v Bank of Credit and Commerce International SA (in liquidation)* [1998] AC 20, [1997] 3 All ER 1, HL (a case concerning contractual breaches during employment), it was held that in principle there could be an award of 'stigma damages', at least where the employee had suffered financial loss (eg through unemployability). However, the claim in this case eventually foundered on the failure to prove that such stigma had caused the claimants actual, rather than hypothetical, past loss or would cause them loss in the future: *Bank of Credit and Commerce International SA (in compulsory liquidation) v Ali (No 2)* [1999] 4 All ER 83, sub nom *Bank of Credit and Commerce International SA (in compulsory liquidation) v Ali (No 3)* [1999] IRLR 508; affd sub nom *Bank of Credit and Commerce International SA (in liquidation) v Ali (No 2)* [2002] EWCA Civ 82, [2002] 3 All ER 750, [2002] ICR 1258. See also *Gogay v Hertfordshire County Council* [2000] IRLR 703, CA (damages for psychiatric illness could be recovered as the breach of the implied term of mutual trust and confidence was in the form of suspension rather than dismissal from employment). However, dicta in *Johnson v Unisys Ltd* at [55] per Lord Hoffmann, to the effect that an employment tribunal may award compensation for distress, humiliation, damage to reputation in the community or to family life and for the financial loss flowing from psychiatric injury which is said to be a consequence of the unfair manner of his dismissal, were obiter: see *Dunnachie v Kingston-Upon-Hull City Council* [2004] UKHL 36, [2005] 1 AC 226, [2004] 3 All ER 1011.

8   *Johnson v Unisys Ltd* [2001] UKHL 13, [2003] 1 AC 518, [2001] 2 All ER 801. This decision has been criticised for allowing 'legalism' to prevail: *Eastwood v Magnox Electric plc, McCabe v Cornwall County Council* [2004] UKHL 35 at [39], [2005] 1 AC 503 at [39], [2004] 3 All ER 991 at [39] per Lord Steyn. *Johnson v Unisys Ltd* and *Eastwood v Magnox Electric plc, McCabe v Cornwall County Council* were applied in *Lakshmi v Mid-Cheshire Hospitals NHS Trust* [2008] EWHC 878 (QB), [2008] IRLR 956, [2008] All ER (D) 353 (Apr). See also the text and note 9. As to unfair dismissal see PARA 762 et seq.

9   *Eastwood v Magnox Electric plc, McCabe v Cornwall County Council* [2004] UKHL 35, [2005] 1 AC 503, [2004] 3 All ER 991 (exceptionally, financial loss might flow directly from the employer's failure to act fairly when taking steps leading to dismissal, eg where an employee suffers financial loss from illness caused by unfair treatment pre-dating the dismissal). See note 8. See also PARA 828 note 7.

830. Measure of damages. Since a wrongfully dismissed employee must normally accept the repudiation and sue the employer for damages[1], the employee cannot simply wait until the termination of the period for which he was engaged and sue in debt for the whole of the remuneration which would have been due[2]. Exceptionally, an employee dismissed in breach of a contractually binding procedure may be able to refuse to accept the repudiation[3], but even in such a case the right to sue for continuing wages lasts only for the period it would have taken for the employer to have dismissed lawfully[4]. If the contract of employment specifies a particular sum to be payable as liquidated damages in the event of a breach, that too may be sued for directly[5]. However, in a more usual case where the employee is suing for breach of contract, the rule is that the wrongfully dismissed employee should, so far as money can do so, be placed in the same position as if the contract had been performed[6]. This is to be done by awarding as damages the amount of remuneration that the employee has been prevented from earning by the wrongful dismissal[7]; if necessary, it must be assumed for this purpose that the employer would have ended the contract in the way most beneficial to him (that is to say, to minimise the possible damages), not necessarily in the way the employee may have hoped or even expected[8].

In the case of a fixed-term contract, this means that the starting point is the remuneration for the remainder of the fixed term; but most contracts of employment are terminable by notice[9] so that the employee is entitled to recover only the amount of remuneration during the notice period[10]. That remuneration includes wages or salary, including a reasonable amount of any variable such as commission[11], loss of a vehicle and other fringe benefits[12], and any loss of pension rights[13]. Any additional sums, such as extra payments, bonuses or tips and gratuities, are recoverable if contractually binding[14], and, although the traditional view was that discretionary amounts could not be recovered even if the employee was in fact likely to have received them[15], it seems now that a capricious or perverse decision not to award a discretionary bonus or commission can be challenged[16]. Damages may not be awarded for humiliation, loss of reputation or similar non-pecuniary losses[17]. If the employee has been deprived of statutory rights by a wrongful dismissal[18], he cannot claim for statutory purposes that the employment should be notionally extended by the contractual notice he should have received, in order to qualify[19]; nor can he claim loss of statutory rights as a head of damage in a claim for wrongful dismissal[20].

As the claim is for breach of contract, not debt, the employee is under a duty to mitigate his loss; and certain amounts must also be deducted from the prima facie measure of damages[21], and adjustment made to reflect the incidents of taxation[22].

1   See PARA 826.
2   *Fewings v Tisdal* (1847) 1 Exch 295; *Emmens v Elderton* (1853) 4 HL Cas 624; *Goodman v Pocock* (1850) 15 QB 576; *Denmark Productions Ltd v Boscobel Productions Ltd* [1969] 1 QB 699, [1968] 3 All ER 513, CA.
3   See PARA 826.
4   *Gunton v Richmond-upon-Thames London Borough Council* [1981] Ch 448, [1980] ICR 755, CA; *Dietmann v Brent London Borough Council* [1988] ICR 842, sub nom *Dietman v Brent London Borough Council* [1988] IRLR 299, CA. The employee cannot go further and sue for future loss on the basis of the chance that he might have retained the job if the proper procedure had been used: *Focsa Services (UK) Ltd v Birkett* [1996] IRLR 325, EAT; *Janciuk v Winerite Ltd* [1998] IRLR 63, EAT. In *Gunton v Richmond-upon-Thames London Borough Council* at 459 and 763 per Buckley LJ, any advantage to the employee seemed to be nullified by the analysis that he cannot claim wages for services he is not given the opportunity of rendering;

sed quaere. Normally the employee's consideration is being ready and willing to work, not necessarily actually working: see e g *Henthorn and Taylor v Central Electricity Generating Board* [1980] IRLR 361, CA.

5   *Beckham v Drake* (1849) 2 HL Cas 579. This is, however, subject to the normal contractual rule against the enforcement of a penalty clause, which requires the drawing of the distinction between such a clause and liquidated damages: see DAMAGES vol 12(1) (Reissue) PARAS 1065–1066. In *Giraud UK Ltd v Smith* [2000] IRLR 763, EAT, a clause entitling the employer to recover a minimum amount from the employee in the event of the employee's breach but not providing a maximum amount recoverable was held to be a penalty clause rather than a legitimate liquidated damages clause and as such it was unenforceable. However, a clause may be more likely to be validated if negotiated at arm's length, for sound commercial reasons: see the upholding of a 'golden parachute' clause for a chief executive in *Murray v Leisureplay plc* [2005] EWCA Civ 963, [2005] IRLR 946 and a 'no-show' clause (reimbursing the employer if a key appointee did not take up the employment) in *Tullett Prebon Group Ltd v El-Hajjali* [2008] EWHC 1924 (QB), [2008] IRLR 760. The decisions in *Giraud UK Ltd v Smith*, in *Murray v Leisureplay plc*, and in *Tullet Prebon Group Ltd v El-Hajjali*, were applied in *Li v First Marine Solutions Ltd* [2014] All ER (D) 03 (Sep), EAT (employee failed to show that clause complained of was a penalty clause and not a genuine pre-estimate of loss). However, Langstaff P observed (obiter) that any tribunal who should consider such a clause in future are recommended to think carefully, in the light of the evidence before them in the particular case, whether the parties actually intended a clause such as this to operate as a penalty clause, liquidated damages clause, or simply as a provision that entitled the employer to withhold pay for the period of time not worked during notice (or in recognition of any period of short notice not given): see *Li v First Marine Solutions Ltd* at [42]–[48] per Langstaff P.

6   Ie in accordance with the normal rule in the law of contract: see e g *Robinson v Harman* (1848) 1 Exch 850; *Radford v De Froberville* [1978] 1 All ER 33, [1977] 1 WLR 1262.

7   *Smith v Thompson* (1849) 8 CB 44; *Inchbald v Western Neilgherry Coffee, Tea and Cinchona Plantation Co Ltd* (1864) 34 LJCP 15.

8   *Lavarack v Woods of Colchester Ltd* [1967] 1 QB 278, [1966] 3 All ER 683, CA; *Janciuk v Winerite Ltd* [1998] IRLR 63, EAT; *Morran v Glasgow Council of Tenants Associations* [1998] IRLR 67, Ct of Sess; *Gregory v Wallace* [1998] IRLR 387, CA.

9   See PARA 733.

10   *Addis v Gramophone Co Ltd* [1909] AC 488, HL; and see PARA 829.

11   *Addis v Gramophone Co Ltd* [1909] AC 488, HL; *Re Patent Floor Cloth Co, Dean and Gilbert's Claim* (1872) 41 LJ Ch 476; *Hartland v General Exchange Bank Ltd* (1866) 14 LT 863; *Re English and Scottish Marine Insurance Co, ex p Maclure* (1870) 5 Ch App 737, CA; *Turner v Goldsmith* [1891] 1 QB 544, CA; *Re RS Newman Ltd, Raphael's Claim* [1916] 2 Ch 309, CA.

12   *Lindsay v Queens Hotel Co Ltd* [1919] 1 KB 212; *British Guyana Credit Corpn v Da Silva* [1965] 1 WLR 248, PC; *Shove v Downs Surgical plc* [1984] 1 All ER 7, [1984] ICR 532. *Shove v Downs Surgical plc* was applied in *Jones v Global Crossing (UK) Telecommunications Ltd* [2008] All ER (D) 19 (Sep), EAT.

13   *Acklam v Sentinel Insurance Co Ltd* [1959] 2 Lloyd's Rep 683; *Bold v Brough, Nicholson and Hall Ltd* [1963] 3 All ER 849, [1964] 1 WLR 201. See also *Silvey v Pendragon plc* [2001] EWCA Civ 784, [2001] IRLR 685 (no difference in principle between lost pension rights and lost pay; employee entitled to the extra pension he would have received if the employment had continued for another 12 weeks).

14   *Manubens v Leon* [1919] 1 KB 208.

15   *Lavarack v Woods of Colchester Ltd* [1967] 1 QB 278, [1966] 3 All ER 683, CA.

16   *Clark v BET plc* [1997] IRLR 348 (which established the exception: see PARAS 113, 829 note 4); *Clark v Nomura International plc* [2000] IRLR 766; *Mallone v BPB Industries plc* [2002] EWCA Civ 126, [2002] ICR 1045, [2002] IRLR 452. See also *Horkulak v Cantor Fitzgerald International* [2004] EWCA Civ 1287, [2005] ICR 402, [2004] IRLR 942 (revsg in part [2003] EWHC 1918 (QB), [2004] ICR 697, [2003] IRLR 756) (payment of discretionary bonus provided for in a contract of employment was necessarily to be read as a contractual benefit to the employee as opposed to being a mere declaration of the employer's right to pay a bonus if he wished).

17   See PARA 829.

18   Eg if he has been dismissed summarily shortly before serving the two-year qualifying period for unfair dismissal.

19   *Dixon v Stenor Ltd* [1973] ICR 157, [1973] IRLR 28, NIRC; *Robert Cort & Son Ltd v Charman* [1981] ICR 816, [1981] IRLR 437, EAT; *Stapp v Shaftesbury Society* [1982] IRLR 326, CA; *Batchelor v British Railways Board* [1987] IRLR 136, CA.

20 *Harper v Virgin Net Ltd* [2004] EWCA Civ 271, [2005] ICR 921, [2004] IRLR 390 (disapproving *Raspin v United News Shops Ltd* [1999] IRLR 9, EAT). This decision closed off the avenue of suing in common law (for wrongful dismissal) for what otherwise the employee might have received under statute (for unfair dismissal) following the decision in *Johnson v Unisys Ltd* [2001] UKHL 13, [2003] 1 AC 518, [2001] 2 All ER 801, in which it was held that the common law right cannot co-exist with the statutory right not to be unfairly dismissed (see PARA 829). One consequence of the finding is that an employer who arranges his affairs (and who does so in full awareness of their likely consequences) so that it summarily dismisses an employee in breach of contract, in the employee's eleventh month of service, could properly be regarded as benefiting from its own breach of contract at the expense of the employee as it would be likely to suffer a more modest claim for compensation than had it given the same employee a proper contractual notice of dismissal taking effect in the thirteenth month of service: see *Wise Group v Mitchell* [2005] ICR 896, EAT (where *Harper v Virgin Net Ltd* was applied).

21 See PARA 831. The general principle is that, in assessing damages, the court may take into consideration all that has happened, or is likely to happen, to increase or mitigate the employee's loss down to the date of trial: *Hochster v De la Tour* (1853) 2 E & B 678; *Chaplin v Hicks* [1911] 2 KB 786, CA. References to increases in the loss may, however, have little application in this context where the court is primarily concerned with contractual losses only, not with compensating the employee more widely for general damages: see PARA 829.

22 See PARA 831.

831. Deductions from damages for wrongful dismissal. Since an employee's claim for wrongful dismissal is for breach of contract, not debt, there is an obligation on him to take reasonable steps to mitigate his loss[1]. If he obtains employment during the period by which damages are being calculated, amounts earned must be deducted from the damages[2]; and, if he is paid the same or a higher wage, his loss could be nominal[3]. If the period by which damages are being calculated is still running at the time of trial, the court may make a deduction for possible future mitigation[4]. If it can be shown that the employee could with reasonable diligence have avoided a loss, his damages may be reduced accordingly[5]; in this context, mitigation will normally be by finding other employment, so that, if it can be shown that he could reasonably have obtained suitable employment at similar wages soon after his dismissal, he may recover only nominal damages from the employer[6]. The question of what are reasonable steps to take to mitigate loss is, however, one of fact in all the circumstances of the case and must be considered realistically. In particular:

(1)   the dismissed employee may reasonably spend time looking for other employment at a comparable level before being prepared to take employment at a lower level[7];

(2)   it may well be reasonable not to accept an offer of re-employment by the same employer, depending on the circumstances of the dismissal[8];

(3)   some matters other than finding other employment may tend to reduce the employee's overall loss, but might be considered too remote to be brought into account[9].

Apart from mitigation, other amounts may have to be offset against damages[10]. If damages are continuing into the future, as, for example, in the case of breach of a long fixed-term contract or a long notice provision, certain vicissitudes of life may be taken into account[11] and an amount may be deducted for accelerated receipt of damages[12]. In a more usual case, where the contractual period which is the subject of the damages has expired, questions of offsetting normally involve other amounts received by the employee in consequence of the dismissal. Amounts received from the employer, by way of any payment in lieu of notice or ex gratia payment[13] or sick pay[14], must be deducted; and, similarly, amounts earned elsewhere must be taken into account[15]. Jobseeker's allowance received by the employee must be deducted[16], as must income support[17]. A redundancy payment is deductible[18], but compensation for unfair dismissal may not be, if it is not possible to show that that compensation was directly attributable to the same period as that for which damages are claimed[19]. Other miscellaneous amounts may arise on the particular facts of the case; and their deductibility or otherwise may depend on the application of rules evolved in the context of damages for personal injury, although these rules are not always clear[20].

The aim of damages being to compensate the claimant for actual loss, no more and no less[21], where a head of damage is based on an estimate of lost earnings, and those damages are not subject to tax in the claimant's hands, the court must take into account the tax that would have been paid, and so award the lost earnings net of tax[22]. Amounts received after the termination of employment, including damages for wrongful dismissal, are subject to income tax, but only to the extent that they exceed the prescribed threshold of £30,000[23].

1 Ie in accordance with the normal rule in the law of contract: see eg *British Westinghouse Electric and Manufacturing Co Ltd v Underground Electric Rlys Co of London Ltd* [1912] AC 673, HL; and DAMAGES vol 12(1) (Reissue) PARA 1041 et seq. A compensatory award for unfair dismissal is expressly made subject to the common law doctrine of mitigation: see the Employment Rights Act 1996 s 123(4); and PARA 822. Most of the modern case law has arisen in this statutory context but it could also be applied to a claim for wrongful dismissal. In both contexts, the burden of proof is on the defendant employer to show unreasonable failure to mitigate: see *Brace v Calder* [1895] 2 QB 253, CA; *Fyfe v Scientific Furnishings Ltd* [1989] ICR 648, [1989] IRLR 331, EAT. If, untypically, the claim can be brought in debt, there is no obligation to mitigate: *Hutchings v Coinseed Ltd* [1998] IRLR 190, CA.

2 *Re Imperial Wine Co, Shirreff's Case* (1872) LR 14 Eq 417; *Walton v Tucker* (1880) 45 JP 23; *Reid v Explosives Co* (1887) 19 QBD 264, CA.

3 *Reid v Explosives Co* (1887) 19 QBD 264, CA; *Secretary of State for Employment v Wilson* [1978] 3 All ER 137, [1978] ICR 200, EAT. There is, however, a special rule in the law of unfair dismissal, based on good industrial relations practice, that amounts earned in other employment during what is, or should have been, the employee's notice period are not deducted from the compensatory award for future loss of income: see *TBA Industrial Products Ltd v Locke* [1984] ICR 228, [1984] IRLR 48, EAT (approved in *Addison v Babcock FATA Ltd* [1988] QB 280, [1987] ICR 805, CA); and PARA 819 note 5.

4 *Edwards v Society of Graphical and Allied Trades* [1971] Ch 354, [1970] 3 All ER 689, CA.

5 *Beckham v Drake and Surgey* (1849) 2 HL Cas 579. As to the duty to mitigate damages generally see DAMAGES vol 12(1) (Reissue) PARA 1041 et seq.

6 *Brace v Calder* [1895] 2 QB 253, CA; *Macdonnell v Marston* (1884) Cab & El 281; *Re Gramophone Records Ltd* [1930] WN 42.

7 *Yetton v Eastwoods Froy Ltd* [1966] 3 All ER 353, [1967] 1 WLR 104; *Edwards v Society of Graphical and Allied Trades* [1971] Ch 354, [1970] 3 All ER 689, CA.

8 *Shindler v Northern Raincoat Co Ltd* [1960] 2 All ER 239, [1960] 1 WLR 1038. For the case law on this point in relation to unfair dismissal law see PARA 822.

9 *Lavarack v Woods of Colchester Ltd* [1967] 1 QB 278, [1966] 3 All ER 683, CA (termination of contract permitted employee to become employed by and purchase stock in company A, and to invest in company B; profits from shares in company A held liable to be taken into consideration, but profits from shares in company B too remote and so not taken into consideration).

10 The text and notes 11–20 is subject to the caveat that some of the cases cited are personal injury cases and the assumption is made that the same principles apply in a wrongful dismissal action. This has not been seriously challenged, nor has it been specifically affirmed. See further DAMAGES vol 12(1) (Reissue) PARA 903 et seq.

11 *Salt v Power Plant Co Ltd* [1936] 3 All ER 322, CA (employer may have terminated contract lawfully before expiry); *Bold v Brough, Nicholson & Hall Ltd* [1963] 3 All ER 849, [1964] 1 WLR 201 (possibility of early lawful termination for illness).

12 *Shove v Downs Surgical plc* [1984] 1 All ER 7, [1984] ICR 532. *Shove v Downs Surgical plc* was applied in *Jones v Global Crossing (UK) Telecommunications Ltd* [2008] All ER (D) 19 (Sep), EAT.

13 In contrast with wages from other employment (see note 3), the position in this context is the same as in unfair dismissal law: *Addison v Babcock FATA Ltd* [1988] QB 280, [1987] ICR 805, CA; and see PARAS 818, 823.

14 Ie whether or not provided under an insurance policy maintained by the employer: *Hussain v New Taplow Paper Mills Ltd* [1988] AC 514, [1988] ICR 259, HL (a personal injury case: see note 10).

15 See note 3.

16 *Parsons v BNM Laboratories Ltd* [1964] 1 QB 95, [1963] 2 All ER 658, CA; *Westwood v Secretary of State for Employment* [1985] AC 20, [1985] ICR 209, HL. See also *Foxley v Olton* [1965] 2 QB 306, [1964] 3 All ER 248n; *Cheeseman v Bowaters United Kingdom Paper Mills Ltd* [1971] 3 All ER 513, [1971] 1 WLR 1773, CA; *Nabi v British Leyland (UK) Ltd* [1980] 1 All ER 667, [1980] 1 WLR 529, CA (personal injury cases: see note 10). As to jobseeker's allowance see WELFARE BENEFITS AND STATE PENSIONS vol 104 (2014) PARA 419 et seq.

17 *Lincoln v Hayman* [1982] 2 All ER 819, [1982] 1 WLR 488, CA. If the employee takes new employment with earnings low enough to qualify him for what is now working families' tax credit, the amount of that benefit will presumably also be deductible: *Gaskill v Preston* [1981] 3 All ER 427; approved (in relation to deduction of supplementary benefit, now income support) in *Lincoln v Hayman* (both personal injury cases: see note 10).

18 *Colledge v Bass Mitchells & Butlers Ltd* [1988] 1 All ER 536, [1988] ICR 125, CA; *Stocks v Magna Merchants Ltd* [1973] 2 All ER 329, [1973] ICR 530, NIRC; *Wilson v National Coal Board* 1981 SLT 67, HL. The decisions on this point in *Yorkshire Engineering and Welding Co Ltd v Burnham* [1973] 3 All ER 1176, [1974] ICR 77, NIRC, *Millington v TH Goodwin & Sons Ltd* [1975] ICR 104, [1974] IRLR 379, and *Basnett v J and A Jackson Ltd* [1976] ICR 63, [1976] IRLR 154, must now be considered wrong.

19 *O'Laoire v Jackel International Ltd (No 2)* [1991] ICR 718, sub nom *O'Laoire v Jackel International Ltd* [1991] IRLR 170, CA; cf *Berry v Aynsley Trust Ltd* (1976) 127 NLJ 1052; and see *Shove v Downs Surgical plc* [1984] 1 All ER 7, [1984] ICR 532 (a basic award for unfair dismissal was not deducted on the ground that it would have been payable anyway). *Shove v Downs Surgical plc* was applied in *Jones v Global Crossing (UK) Telecommunications Ltd* [2008] All ER (D) 19 (Sep), EAT. Quaere whether *O'Laoire v Jackel International Ltd (No 2)* is confined to its own peculiar facts, ie where the unfair dismissal compensation was at the (then) maximum of £8,000 against a background of total wrongful dismissal damages of £100,700, so that it was impossible to say for what period the £8,000 was notionally payable; in a more mundane wrongful dismissal case it may be easier to show that unfair dismissal compensation was referable to the same period as that in respect of which damages are sought.

20 See DAMAGES vol 12(1) (Reissue) PARA 900 et seq. Two relatively clear rules are that no deduction will be made in respect of:
    (1)   amounts provided under the claimant's own insurance arrangements (*Bradburn v Great Western Rly Co* (1874) LR 10 Exch 1; *Smoker v London Fire and Civil Defence Authority, Wood v British Coal Corpn* [1991] 2 AC 502, [1991] ICR 449, HL); or
    (2)   amounts received from third parties by way of charity or sympathy (*Redpath v Belfast and County Down Rly* [1947] NI 167).
    Outside those rules, the decision in *Parry v Cleaver* [1970] AC 1, [1969] 1 All ER 555, HL (contributory police disablement fund payment not deducted) (applied to an incapacity pension in *Longden v British Coal Corpn* [1998] AC 653, [1998] ICR 26, HL) showed an emphasis against deduction, largely on grounds of policy, but more recent decisions have tended in the opposite direction, with more emphasis on factual compensation and the prevention of double recovery: see *Dews v National Coal Board* [1988] AC 1, [1987] ICR 602, HL; *Hussain v New Taplow Paper Mills Ltd* [1988] AC 514, [1988] ICR 259, HL; *Hodgson v Trapp* [1989] AC 807, [1988] 3 All ER 870, HL.

21 See PARA 830.

22 *British Transport Commission v Gourley* [1956] AC 185, [1955] 3 All ER 796, HL, the leading case on damages for personal injury, applied to damages for wrongful dismissal in *Beach v Reed Corrugated Cases Ltd* [1956] 2 All ER 652, [1956] 1 WLR 807; *Parsons v BNM Laboratories Ltd* [1964] 1 QB 95, [1963] 2 All ER 658, CA; *Stewart v Glentaggart Ltd* 1963 SLT 119, [1963] TR 345; *Bold v Brough, Nicholson and Hall Ltd* [1963] 3 All ER 849, [1964] 1 WLR 201; *Shove v Downs Surgical plc* [1984] 1 All ER 7, [1984] ICR 532. *Shove v Downs Surgical plc* was applied in *Jones v Global Crossing (UK) Telecommunications Ltd* [2008] All ER (D) 19 (Sep), EAT.

23 See the Income Tax (Earnings and Pensions) Act 2003 Pt VI Ch III (ss 400–414A); and INCOME TAXATION vol 58 (2014) PARA 881 et seq. See also *Dale (Inspector of Taxes) v de Soissons*

[1950] 2 All ER 460, 32 TC 118, CA; and the cases cited in note 22. In *Gothard v Mirror Group Newspapers Ltd* [1988] ICR 729, [1988] IRLR 396, CA, a voluntary severance scheme's reference to 'tax-free payments for unexpired notice' was construed literally, so that the employee was entitled to gross wages, but that was on the particular facts of the case which was not treated as one of wrongful dismissal.

832. Amount recoverable for value of the work actually performed but not fully remunerated. Where an employee elects to sue for the value of the work that he has actually performed and for which he has not been paid[1], the amount recoverable is a reasonable sum for his services up to the date of his dismissal[2]. He is not entitled to recover such sum or wages earned and remaining unpaid at that date[3], and he cannot recover anything further, either in respect of wages for the remainder of the period for which he was engaged[4] or by way of damages for wrongful dismissal[5].

Where an employee has been taking part in industrial action in the form of a work-to-rule or go-slow, it is possible that he may be able to recover a portion of his wages, but the point has not yet been decided[6].

1 See PARA 828.
2 *Prickett v Badger* (1856) 1 CBNS 296; and see CONTRACT vol 22 (2012) PARA 536.
3 *Lilley v Elwin* (1848) 11 QB 742; *Archard v Hornor* (1828) 3 C & P 349; cf *Keys v Harwood* (1846) 2 CB 905 (services to be paid for in goods). If he is to be paid a lump sum for his services, he is entitled to recover the whole: *O'Neil v Armstrong, Mitchell & Co* [1895] 2 QB 418, CA; followed in *Lloyd v Sheen* (1905) 93 LT 174; cf *Re London and Scottish Bank, ex p Logan* (1870) LR 9 Eq 149.
4 *Archard v Hornor* (1828) 3 C & P 349; *Smith v Hayward* (1837) 7 Ad & El 544; *Goodman v Pocock* (1850) 15 QB 576; *Emmens v Elderton* (1853) 4 HL Cas 624.
5 *Fewings v Tisdal* (1847) 1 Exch 295. A remedy in this context is not dependent on the original contract and is an alternative to a claim for wrongful dismissal: *Planché v Colburn* (1831) 8 Bing 14; *De Bernardy v Harding* (1853) 8 Exch 822. The characterisation of such a remedy as a species of quasi-contract is no longer supported by modern authority which views it rather as restitutionary: see *Benedetti v Sawiris* [2013] UKSC 50, [2013] 4 All ER 253, [2013] 3 WLR 351; and *Ajar-Tec Ltd v Stack* [2012] EWCA Civ 543, [2012] All ER (D) 136 (Apr). See also RESTITUTION vol 88 (2012) PARA 410 et seq.
6 *Miles v Wakefield Metropolitan District Council* [1987] AC 539, [1987] ICR 368, HL, per Lord Brightman and Lord Templeman (obiter); Lord Bridge of Harwich thought that it would not be possible to sue in such a case, and Lord Oliver of Aylmerton and Lord Brandon of Oakbrook deliberately expressed no opinion on the matter. As to wages during industrial action see PARA 29.

833. Damages for breach by employer short of termination. If an employer acts in breach of the contract of employment in such a way as to repudiate it in some way short of wrongfully dismissing the employee, the employee may accept that repudiation, terminate the contract and sue the employer for damages[1]. Alternatively, he may refuse to accept the repudiation[2], keep the contract alive and sue for wages[3]. If the employee is able still to perform his part of the contract, he may sue in debt for wages earned and due; and, if that is not possible, he may sue for the wages that should have been paid in a claim for breach of contract[4]. Such a claim may be of particular use to an employee in a case where his employer seeks to force through a unilateral change to his terms and conditions of employment, to which the employee objects; provided that he makes his objection clear[5], the employee may work to the new term or condition, and, if appropriate, hold himself ready and willing to work under the old term or condition, and then sue the employer for wages due under the original contract[6]. In this way, an employee has been able to stand on his contractual rights where the employer has sought unilaterally, without contractual authority, to cut his hours[7], reduce his pay[8], put him on short-time working[9] and withdraw a contractual benefit[10].

If the contract is for employment to be performed in the future but the employer informs the employee that he will not in fact be required, that too is a breach of contract and the employee may elect either to treat the contract as subsisting or to treat the breach as final and institute proceedings immediately[11].

1 See CONTRACT vol 22 (2012) PARA 565. In such a case, the employee may also claim to have been constructively dismissed and bring a claim for unfair dismissal: see PARA 763. In a common law claim for breach of contract during employment (as opposed to an claim for wrongful dismissal) the employee may be able to sue for 'stigma' damages, i e for financial loss caused by the employer's conduct (*Malik v Bank of Credit and Commerce International SA (in liquidation), Mahmud v Bank of Credit and Commerce International SA (in liquidation)* [1998] AC 20, [1997] 3 All ER 1, HL (allegations of breach of the terms of trust and respect through fraudulent trading, having an adverse effect on the employee's future employability)); but in such a case causation and damage must be proved by the employee which may be difficult, and the eventual decision in the case was that these had not been proved (*Bank of Credit and Commerce International SA (in compulsory liquidation) v Ali (No 2)* [1999] 4 All ER 83, sub nom *Bank of Credit and Commerce International SA (in compulsory liquidation) v Ali (No 3)* [1999] IRLR 508; affd sub nom *Bank of Credit and Commerce International SA (in liquidation) v Ali (No 2)* [2002] EWCA Civ 82, [2002] 3 All ER 750, [2002] ICR 1258). See also *Johnson v Unisys* [2001] UKHL 13, [2003] 1 AC 518, [2001] 2 All ER 801 (damages for manner of dismissal restricted to claims for breach of employment contract during employment not upon termination); *Eastwood v Magnox Electric plc, McCabe v Cornwall County Council* [2004] UKHL 35, [2005] 1 AC 503, [2004] 3 All ER 991 (exceptionally, a claim might be allowed for personal injury caused by stress arising from employer's actions leading up to dismissal); and see PARA 829 note 7. *Johnson v Unisys* and *Eastwood v Magnox Electric plc, McCabe v Cornwall County Council* were applied in *Lakshmi v Mid-Cheshire Hospitals NHS Trust* [2008] EWHC 878 (QB), [2008] IRLR 956. See *Robinson v Tescom Corpn* [2008] IRLR 408, [2008] All ER (D) 10 (Mar) (where an employee agreed under protest to work under varied terms, a subsequent failure to observe those varied terms might amount to misconduct justifying dismissal; and the employee could have claimed constructive dismissal but chose not to and continued to work under protest and without prejudice treating his contract as breached, himself as dismissed and retaining the right to claim damages). See also *O'Dowd v Adey-Jones* [2008] All ER (D) 68 (Oct), EAT.

2 See, however PARA 826 note 4.

3 *Rigby v Ferodo Ltd* [1988] ICR 29, [1987] IRLR 516, HL (where it was argued that any claim for wages is restricted to wages during what would have been the notice period if the employee had been dismissed, on the basis that the employer could have dismissed lawfully by giving that notice, but this was disapproved and so the employee can potentially recover wages on a continuing basis).

4 See *Rigby v Ferodo Ltd* [1988] ICR 29 at 36, [1987] IRLR 516 at 519, HL, per Lord Oliver of Aylmerton (distinction between debt and damages of no assistance in this case; immaterial on the facts whether the claim was treated as one for agreed remuneration for services rendered or as one for damages for breach of an agreement to pay such remuneration).

5 If he does not do so, it could be argued by the employer that the employee has impliedly assented to the employer's proposed variation of the term or condition in question; but continuing to work under protest, at least for a reasonable period, will not constitute acceptance of the variation: *Rigby v Ferodo Ltd* [1988] ICR 29, [1987] IRLR 516, HL. If the employee adopts the option of working under the new terms under protest ('stand and sue'), he must however abide by those terms: *Robinson v Tescom Corporation* [2008] IRLR 408, [2008] All ER (D) 10 (Mar), EAT.

6 *Rigby v Ferodo Ltd* [1988] ICR 29, [1987] IRLR 516, HL; *Robinson v Tescom Corpn* [2008] IRLR 408, [2008] All ER (D) 10 (Mar), EAT.

7 *Burdett-Coutts v Hertfordshire County Council* [1984] IRLR 91 (this entailed a decrease in pay: see the text and note 8).

8 *Gibbons v Associated British Ports* [1985] IRLR 376; *Rigby v Ferodo Ltd* [1988] ICR 29, [1987] IRLR 516, HL.

9 *Miller v Hamworthy Engineering Ltd* [1986] ICR 846, [1986] IRLR 461, CA.

10 *Keir and Williams v Hereford and Worcester County Council* [1985] IRLR 505.

11 *Hochster v De la Tour* (1853) 2 E & B 678; *Bracegirdle v Heald* (1818) 1 B & Ald 722; *Richardson v Mellish* (1824) 2 Bing 229; *Blogg v Kent* (1830) 6 Bing 614; *Wallis v Warren* (1849) 4 Exch 361; *Chaplin v Hicks* [1911] 2 KB 786, CA; *Denmark Productions Ltd v Boscobel Productions Ltd* [1969] 1 QB 699, [1968] 3 All ER 513, CA; *MS Rose (Heating) Ltd v Edgington* [1977] ICR 844, EAT.

834. Damages for wrongful dismissal of apprentice. An apprentice[1] who has been wrongfully dismissed is entitled to damages for:

(1)   loss of earnings and training during the remainder of the agreement;

(2)   diminution of his future prospects; and

(3)   the expenses incurred in trying to obtain other work[2].

1 As to the position of apprentices and youth trainees at common law see PARAS 112, 128–129, 636, 747–754. As to the statutory law on apprenticeships see EDUCATION vol 35 (2011) PARA 682 et seq.

2 *Dunk v George Waller & Son Ltd* [1970] 2 QB 163, [1970] 2 All ER 630, CA.

7. REDUNDANCY PAYMENTS

(1) RIGHT TO REDUNDANCY PAYMENT

(i) In general

835. In general. Part XI of the Employment Rights Act 1996[1] imposes on employers the obligation to make payments to their employees who have been dismissed by reason of redundancy[2].

Employers were formerly entitled to claim from the Secretary of State partial reimbursement for such payments by way of redundancy rebates out of the Redundancy Fund[3]. Such rebates were, however, phased out and finally abolished on 16 January 1990[4]; and on 1 February 1991 the assets and liabilities of the Redundancy Fund became assets and liabilities of the National Insurance Fund and the Redundancy Fund ceased to exist[5].

An employer proposing to dismiss as redundant 20 or more employees at one establishment within a period of 90 days or less must consult trade union representatives if there is a recognised trade union or, if not, employee representatives about the dismissal[6].

1   Ie the Employment Rights Act 1996 Pt XI (ss 135–181): see PARA 836 et seq. As to the restrictions on contracting out from those provisions see PARA 150; as to Her Majesty's power by Order in Council to extend those provisions see PARA 155; and as to the application of those provisions to Northern Ireland see PARA 157.

     If an Act of Tynwald is passed for purposes similar to the purposes of the Employment Rights Act 1996 Pt XI, the Secretary of State may, with the consent of the Treasury, make reciprocal arrangements with the appropriate Isle of Man authority for co-ordinating the provisions of Pt XI with the corresponding provisions of the Act of Tynwald so as to secure that they operate, to such extent as may be provided by the arrangements, as a single system: Employment Rights Act 1996 s 239(1). For the purposes of giving effect to any arrangements so made, the Secretary of State may, in conjunction with the appropriate Isle of Man authority, make any necessary financial adjustments between the National Insurance Fund and any fund established under the Act of Tynwald: Employment Rights Act 1996 s 239(2). The Secretary of State may make regulations for giving effect to any such arrangements (s 239(3)); and such regulations may provide that Pt XI is to have effect in relation to persons affected by the arrangements subject to such modifications and adaptations as may be specified in the regulations, including provision: (1) for securing that acts, omissions and events having any effect for the purposes of the Act of Tynwald have a corresponding effect for the purposes of the Employment Rights Act 1996 Pt XI, but not so as to confer a right to double payment in respect of the same act, omission or event; and (2) for determining, in cases where rights accrue both under the Employment Rights Act 1996 and under the Act of Tynwald, which of those rights are to be available to the person concerned: Employment Rights Act 1996 s 239(4). For these purposes, 'appropriate Isle of Man authority' means such authority as may be specified in that behalf in an Act of Tynwald: Employment Rights Act 1996 s 239(5). As to the Secretary of State see PARA 5 note 21. As to the making of regulations under the Employment Rights Act 1996 generally see PARA 162. At the date at which this volume states the law, no such regulations had been made. As to the National Insurance Fund see WELFARE BENEFITS AND STATE PENSIONS vol 104 (2014) PARA 18; and as to the constitutional status and government of the Isle of Man see COMMONWEALTH vol 13 (2009) PARA 799.

2   The overall purpose of the redundancy payments scheme has been variously expressed. It is clear that the scheme is not meant to be merely a form of anticipatory unemployment benefit, with the result that, if the redundant employee obtains other employment immediately, he may still receive the redundancy payment if he fulfils the qualifying provisions: see *Lloyd v Brassey* [1969] 2 QB 98 at 102–103, [1969] 1 All ER 382 at 383–384, CA, per Lord Denning MR. Since the essence of a redundancy payment is an accruing right in the employment and compensation for past service, its receipt, unlike that of a payment in lieu of notice, does not disentitle the employee to anticipatory unemployment benefit (now jobseeker's allowance: see WELFARE BENEFITS AND STATE PENSIONS vol 104 (2014) PARA 419 et seq), even where the employee

receives an amount over and above his statutory entitlement but still referable to past service on the same principle as a statutory redundancy payment: *R v National Insurance Comr, ex p Stratton* [1979] QB 361, [1979] ICR 290, CA.

3   See the Employment Protection (Consolidation) Act 1978 s 104, Sch 6 (repealed).

4   See the Employment Act 1989 ss 17, 30(3)(f) (repealed).

5   Employment Act 1990 s 13(1) (repealed); Employment Act 1990 (Commencement and Transitional Provisions) Order 1990, SI 1990/2378, art 3(a). References to the Redundancy Fund in subordinate legislation, within the meaning of the Interpretation Act 1978 (see STATUTES AND LEGISLATIVE PROCESS vol 96 (2012) PARA 609), are to be construed as references to the National Insurance Fund: Employment Act 1990 s 13(3). There must be paid out of the National Insurance Fund into the Consolidated Fund sums equal to the amount of any expenses incurred by the Secretary of State in consequence of the Employment Rights Act 1996 Pt XI: s 237(a). As to the National Insurance Fund see WELFARE BENEFITS AND STATE PENSIONS vol 104 (2014) PARA 15 et seq. As to the Consolidated Fund see CONSTITUTIONAL AND ADMINISTRATIVE LAW vol 20 (2014) PARA 480; PARLIAMENT vol 78 (2010) PARAS 1028–1031.

6   See the Trade Union and Labour Relations (Consolidation) Act 1992 ss 188–198; and PARA 1185 et seq. As to the circumstances in which a dismissal for redundancy may constitute unfair dismissal see PARAS 780–782.

836.   Right to payment.   Where an employee[1] who has been continuously employed[2] for the requisite period, that is to say, a period of not less than two years ending with the relevant date[3]:

(1)   is dismissed[4] by his employer[5] by reason of redundancy[6]; or

(2)   is eligible for a redundancy payment[7] by reason of being laid off or kept on short time[8] and complies with the specified requirements[9],

the employer is liable[10] to pay him a sum (a 'redundancy payment') calculated[11] in accordance with the prescribed conditions[12].

Any provision in an agreement, whether a contract of employment or not, is void in so far as it purports to exclude or limit the provisions of the Employment Rights Act 1996, including those provisions whereby an employee is entitled to a redundancy payment[13].

1   As to the meaning of 'employee' see PARA 2; and as to excluded classes of employment see PARA 854 et seq.

2   As to continuity of employment see PARAS 130 et seq, 861–863; and as to when an employee's period of continuous employment is treated as beginning for these purposes see PARA 130.

3   As to the meaning of 'relevant date' see PARA 871.

4   As to the meaning of 'dismissal' see PARA 864.

5   As to the meaning of 'employer' generally see PARA 2. For the purposes of the operation of the provisions of the Employment Rights Act 1996 Pt XI (ss 135–181) and Pt XIV Ch I (ss 210–219) (continuous employment) (see PARAS 130 et seq, 861–863) in relation to any employee whose remuneration is, by virtue of any statutory provision, payable to him by a person other than his employer, references to the employer in s 135(1) (first reference) (see head (1) in the text) must be construed as references to the person by whom the remuneration is payable: see s 173(1), (2). As to the meaning of 'statutory provision' see PARA 163 note 2. As to the application of s 179(1) (statutory provisions relating to notices) where an employee is paid by a person other than his employer see s 179(6); and PARA 837 note 6.

6   As to the meaning of 'dismissed by reason of redundancy' see PARA 870.

7   For the purposes of the Employment Rights Act 1996, 'redundancy payment' has the meaning given by Pt XI: s 235(1). As to the exclusion of s 235 where an exemption order is in force see s 157(1); and PARA 857. As to the limited exemptions for statutory redundancy payments from income tax see the Income Tax (Earnings and Pensions) Act 2003 s 309; and INCOME TAXATION vol 58 (2014) PARA 830.

8   Ie to the extent specified in the Employment Rights Act 1996 s 148: see PARA 876.

9   Ie the requirements of the Employment Rights Act 1996 s 148: see PARA 876.

10   Ie subject to the Employment Rights Act 1996 ss 140–144 (see PARAS 866, 868, 872–874), ss 149–152 (see PARAS 877–879), ss 155–161 (see PARA 854 et seq), s 164 (see PARA 880).

11   Ie calculated in accordance with the Employment Rights Act 1996 s 162: see PARA 881.

12   Employment Rights Act 1996 ss 135(1), (2), 155. See also *Foster v Bon Groundwork Ltd* [2012] EWCA Civ 252, [2012] ICR 1027, [2012] IRLR 517. As to the modification of the

Employment Rights Act 1996 s 155 in relation to any person to whom the Redundancy
Payments (Continuity of Employment in Local Government, etc) (Modification) Order 1999,
SI 1999/2277, applies see PARA 855 note 4; and as to the application of the Redundancy
Payments (Continuity of Employment in Local Government, etc) (Modification) Order 1999,
SI 1999/2277, see PARA 839.
13 See the Employment Rights Act 1996 s 203(1) (general restriction on contracting out); and
PARA 150. See also *Jenvey v Australian Broadcasting Corpn* [2002] EWHC 927 (QB), [2003]
ICR 79, [2002] IRLR 520 (term implied into a contract of employment so that an employer
cannot lawfully exclude or limit an employee's right to contractual benefits which accrue by
reason of redundancy by dismissing him for a reason other than redundancy, notwithstanding a
decision to make him redundant).

837.   Notices.   Any notice which is required or authorised to be given[1] by an
employer[2] to an employee[3] may be given by being delivered[4] to the employee, or
left[5] for him at his usual or last-known place of residence, or sent by post
addressed to him at that place[6].
Any notice which is required or authorised to be given[7] by an employee to an
employer may be given either by the employee himself or by a person authorised
by him to act on his behalf, and, whether given by or on behalf of the employee:

(1)   may be given by being delivered to the employer, or sent by post[8]
       addressed to him at the place where the employee is or was employed by
       him; or

(2)   if arrangements in that behalf have been made by the employer, may be
       given by being delivered to a person designated by the employer in
       pursuance of the arrangements, or left for such a person at a place so
       designated, or sent by post to such a person at an address so
       designated[9].

1   Ie under the Employment Rights Act 1996 Pt XI (ss 135–181).
2   As to the meaning of 'employer' see PARA 2.
3   As to the meaning of 'employee' see PARA 2; and as to excluded classes of employment see
    PARA 854 et seq.
4   For these purposes, any reference to the delivery of a notice includes, in relation to a notice
    which is not required by the Employment Rights Act 1996 Pt XI to be in writing, a reference to
    the oral communication of the notice: s 179(3). As to the meaning of 'writing' see PARA 2 note 8.
5   Any notice which, in accordance with any provision of the Employment Rights Act 1996 s 179,
    is left for a person at a place referred to in that provision is to be presumed, unless the contrary
    is proved, to have been received by him on the day on which it was left there: s 179(4).
6   Employment Rights Act 1996 s 179(1). Nothing in s 179(1) or (2) (see the text and notes 7–9)
    affects the capacity of an employer to act by a servant or agent for the purposes of any provision
    of Pt XI, including s 179(1) or (2): s 179(5). In relation to an employee to whom s 173 (see PARA
    836 note 5) applies, s 179 has effect as if: (1) any reference in s 179(1) or (2) to a notice required
    or authorised to be given by or to an employer included a reference to a notice which, by virtue
    of s 173, is required or authorised to be given by or to the person by whom the remuneration is
    payable; (2) in relation to a notice required or authorised to be given to that person, any
    reference to the employer in s 179(2)(a) or (b) (see heads (1), (2) in the text) were a reference to
    that person; and (3) the reference to the employer in s 179(5) included a reference to that
    person: s 179(6).
7   See note 1.
8   As to the service of documents by post see the Interpretation Act 1978 s 7; and STATUTES AND
    LEGISLATIVE PROCESS vol 96 (2012) PARA 1219.
9   Employment Rights Act 1996 s 179(2). See also note 6.

(ii) Special Cases

A. EMPLOYMENT NOT UNDER CONTRACT OF EMPLOYMENT

838.   Employment not under contract of employment.   In relation to
employment[1] of any description which:

(1)   is employment in the case of which secondary Class 1 contributions are payable[2] in respect of persons engaged in it; but

(2)   is not employment under a contract of service[3] or of apprenticeship[4] or employment of any excepted description[5],

the Secretary of State may by regulations[6] provide that, subject to such exceptions and modifications as may be prescribed by the regulations, Part XI of the Employment Rights Act 1996[7] and the provisions of that Act supplementary to that Part have effect as may be so prescribed as if:

(a)   it were employment under a contract of employment[8]; and

(b)   any person engaged in employment of that description were an employee[9]; and

(c)   such person as may be determined by or under the regulations were his employer[10].

The employments so prescribed are:

(i)   clerk of the peace or deputy clerk of the peace[11];

(ii)   justices' clerk[12];

(iii)   superintendent registrar or deputy superintendent registrar, registrar or deputy registrar of births and deaths[13];

(iv)   rent officer or deputy rent officer appointed under the Rent Act 1977[14];

(v)   certain[15] medical inspectors[16].

1   For these purposes, the definition of 'employment' in the Employment Rights Act 1996 s 230 (see PARA 2) does not apply: s 230(5)(a).

2   Ie under the Social Security Contributions and Benefits Act 1992 Pt I (ss 1–19A): see WELFARE BENEFITS AND STATE PENSIONS vol 104 (2014) PARA 384 et seq.

3   As to the meaning of 'contract of service' see PARA 1 note 1.

4   As to contracts of apprenticeship see PARA 112.

5   The descriptions so excepted are: (1) any employment mentioned in the Employment Rights Act 1996 s 159 (public offices etc) (see PARA 854), whether as originally enacted or as modified by an order under s 209(1) (see PARA 158); (2) any employment remunerated out of the revenue of the Duchy of Lancaster or the Duchy of Cornwall; (3) any employment remunerated out of the Sovereign Grant; and (4) any employment remunerated out of Her Majesty's Privy Purse: s 171(3) (amended by the Sovereign Grant Act 2011 Sch 1 para 31). As to the Duchy of Lancaster see CROWN PROPERTY vol 12(1) (Reissue) PARA 300 et seq; as to the Duchy of Cornwall see CROWN PROPERTY vol 12(1) (Reissue) PARA 318 et seq; as to the Civil List arrangements see CROWN AND ROYAL FAMILY vol 12(1) (Reissue) PARA 70 et seq; and as to the Privy Purse see CROWN AND ROYAL FAMILY vol 12(1) (Reissue) PARA 68. As to references to an employment tribunal made by persons employed under any of heads (1)–(4) above see PARA 888.

6   As to the making of regulations under the Employment Rights Act 1996 generally see PARA 162. As to the Secretary of State see PARA 5 note 21.

7   Ie the Employment Rights Act 1996 Pt XI (ss 135–181): see also PARAS 835 et seq, 854 et seq.

8   As to the meaning of 'contract of employment' see PARA 2.

9   As to the meaning of 'employee' see PARA 2.

10   Employment Rights Act 1996 s 171(1), (2). As to the meaning of 'employer' see PARA 2. At the date at which this volume states the law no such regulations had been made but, by virtue of s 241, Sch 2 para 2(1) (see PARA 162), the Redundancy Payments Office Holders Regulations 1965, SI 1965/2007 (see the text and notes 11–16) have effect as if so made.

11   The offices of clerk and deputy clerk of the peace have been abolished: see the Courts Act 1971 s 44(1)(a).

12   As to justices' clerks see MAGISTRATES vol 71 (2013) PARA 498 et seq.

13   See REGISTRATION CONCERNING THE INDIVIDUAL vol 88 (2012) PARA 337 et seq.

14   Ie under the Rent Act 1977 Pt IV (ss 62–75): see LANDLORD AND TENANT vol 63 (2012) PARA 1011 et seq.

15   Ie a medical inspector of aliens appointed under the Aliens Order 1953, SI 1953/1671 (now lapsed) or a medical inspector appointed under the Commonwealth Immigrants Act 1962 s 16 (repealed: see now the Immigration Act 1971 s 4(2), Sch 2 para 1(2)). See IMMIGRATION AND ASYLUM vol 57 (2012) PARA 152.

16 Redundancy Payments Office Holders Regulations 1965, SI 1965/2007, reg 3(3). The reference in reg 3(3) to a constable of the British Airports Authority constabulary is no longer applicable consequent on the dissolution of that Authority by the Airports Act 1986 s 2 (repealed): see AIR LAW vol 2 (2008) PARA 182.

The provisions of the Employment Rights Act 1996 have effect in relation to each of the employments specified, other than an employment of a description falling within s 171(3) (see note 5) or employment such that National Insurance Fund contributions are not payable under the Social Security Contributions and Benefits Act 1992 Pt I in respect of persons engaged therein, as if:

(1) it were employment within the meaning of the Employment Rights Act 1996 s 230 (see PARA 2);

(2) any person engaged in such employment were an employee within the meaning of s 230 (see PARA 2); and

(3) the person who is, or is treated as, his employer for the purposes of the Social Security Contributions and Benefits Act 1992 were his employer within the meaning of the Employment Rights Act 1996 s 230 (see PARA 2),

and any reference to 'employment', 'employee', or 'employer' in any provision of the Employment Rights Act 1996 is to be construed accordingly: Redundancy Payments Office Holders Regulations 1965, SI 1965/2007, reg 3(1). However, for the purposes of the application, by virtue of reg 3, of the Employment Rights Act 1996 to a person who is not employed under a contract of employment, any reference in that Act: (a) to a contract of employment is to be construed as a reference to the terms and conditions under which he is employed; (b) to a notice given by the employer terminating the contract of employment is to be construed as including a notice terminating the employment given by any person empowered to give such a notice: Redundancy Payments Office Holders Regulations 1965, SI 1965/2007, reg 3(2).

B. LOCAL GOVERNMENT EMPLOYMENT

839. Local government employment. The Redundancy Payments (Continuity of Employment in Local Government, etc) (Modification) Order 1999[1] applies to any person who, immediately before the occurrence of a relevant event[2], is employed by a specified employer[3], for the purpose of determining that person's entitlement to a redundancy payment[4] and the amount of such payment[5].

1 Ie the Redundancy Payments (Continuity of Employment in Local Government, etc) (Modification) Order 1999, SI 1999/2277, which came into force on 1 September 1999 (see art 1(1)).

2 For these purposes, 'relevant event', in relation to a person, means any event occurring on or after 1 September 1999, on the happening of which that person may become entitled to a redundancy payment in accordance with the Employment Rights Act 1996: Redundancy Payments (Continuity of Employment in Local Government, etc) (Modification) Order 1999, SI 1999/2277, art 1(1), (2)(i), (3). Where, however, an event has occurred on or after 21 June 1998 but before 1 September 1999, on the happening of which a person employed immediately before that event by the English Sports Council (now known as Sport England: see SPORTS LAW vol 96 (2012) PARA 20) may have become entitled to a redundancy payment in accordance with the Employment Rights Act 1996, 'relevant event' includes that event in relation to that person: Redundancy Payments (Continuity of Employment in Local Government, etc) (Modification) Order 1999, SI 1999/2277, art 1(1), (2)(i), (4).

In London, a relevant employee who was employed by an employer specified in art 2(1), Sch 1 (see PARA 840 et seq) immediately before the happening of a relevant event is to be treated as having been employed throughout the relevant period by an employer specified in Sch 1: London Government (Continuity of Employment) Order 2000, SI 2000/1042, art 3(1). 'Relevant employee' means a person who: (1) has been employed by the Secretary of State in exercise of the Secretary of State's power under the Greater London Authority Act 1999 s 407 (see LONDON GOVERNMENT vol 71 (2013) PARAS 97, 100); (2) immediately before he was so employed, was employed by an employer specified in the Redundancy Payments (Continuity of Employment in Local Government, etc) (Modification) Order 1999, SI 1999/2277, Sch 1; and (3) immediately after ceasing to be employed by the Secretary of State became an employee of the Greater London Authority or a functional body: London Government (Continuity of Employment) Order 2000, SI 2000/1042, art 2. 'Relevant period', in relation to a relevant employee, means the period during which the employee was employed by the Secretary of State:

art 2. A person for the time being employed by the Secretary of State under the Greater London Authority Act 1999 s 407 who, immediately before being so employed, was employed by an employer specified in the Redundancy Payments (Continuity of Employment in Local Government, etc) (Modification) Order 1999, SI 1999/2277, Sch 1 is to be treated, on the happening of an event which would, if employment by the Secretary of State were employment to which the Employment Rights Act 1996 Pt XI (ss 135–181) (see PARAS 835 et seq, 854 et seq) applied, be a relevant event, for the purposes of Pt XI, as if employment by the Secretary of State were employment to which Pt XI applied and as if the Secretary of State were an employer specified in the Redundancy Payments (Continuity of Employment in Local Government, etc) (Modification) Order 1999, SI 1999/2277, Sch 1: London Government (Continuity of Employment) Order 2000, SI 2000/1042, arts 2, 3(2). As to the Secretary of State see PARA 5 note 21. As to the Greater London Authority see LONDON GOVERNMENT vol 71 (2013) PARA 67 et seq; and as to the functional bodies see LONDON GOVERNMENT vol 71 (2013) PARA 148.

3   Ie an employer specified in the Redundancy Payments (Continuity of Employment in Local Government, etc) (Modification) Order 1999, SI 1999/2277, Sch 1: see PARA 840 et seq. Where a person commenced employment with a Further Education Funding Council established by the Further and Higher Education Act 1992 s 1 (repealed) before 1 April 1996 and left that employment either before that date or, by reason of a relevant event, after 1 September 1999, the Redundancy Payments (Continuity of Employment in Local Government, etc) (Modification) Order 1999, SI 1999/2277, applies to that person as if that Council were specified in Sch 1: arts 1(1), 2(2). As to the dissolution of further education corporations, and the subsequent provision made separately in relation to England and Wales, see EDUCATION vol 36 (2011) PARA 751 et seq.

4   Ie under the Employment Rights Act 1996: see PARAS 835 et seq, 854 et seq.

5   Redundancy Payments (Continuity of Employment in Local Government, etc) (Modification) Order 1999, SI 1999/2277, arts 1(2)(i), 2(1), 3. In relation to any person to whom the Redundancy Payments (Continuity of Employment in Local Government, etc) (Modification) Order 1999, SI 1999/2277, applies, certain provisions of the Employment Rights Act 1996 have effect subject to modifications: see the Redundancy Payments (Continuity of Employment in Local Government, etc) (Modification) Order 1999, SI 1999/2277, art 3, Sch 2 Pt I; and PARAS 855 note 4, 865 note 4, 881 note 4.

840.   Specified employers; local government.   In relation to local government, the specified employers[1] include:

(1)   in relation to England[2], a county council[3], a district council, a London borough council[4], the Common Council of the City of London[5], or the Council of the Isles of Scilly[6] and, in relation to Wales[7], a county council or a county borough council[8];

(2)   a council in Scotland[9];

(3)   in relation to England, a parish council, a common parish council, or a parish meeting[10] and, in relation to Wales, a community council or a common community council[11];

(4)   an authority established to discharge the functions of two or more other authorities[12];

(5)   a joint board or joint body[13] constituted by or under any enactment for the purposes of exercising the functions of two or more bodies described in any of heads (1) to (4) above;

(6)   any other authority or body, not specified in any of heads (1) to (4) above, established by or under any enactment for the purpose of exercising the functions of, or advising, one or more of the bodies specified in heads (1) to (4) above;

(7)   the Greater London Authority[14];

(8)   Transport for London[15];

(9)   a functional body[16];

(10)   the London Transport Users' Committee[17];

(11)   the Cultural Strategy Group for London[18];

(12)   any committee, including a joint committee, established by or under any

enactment for the purpose of exercising the functions of, or advising, one or more of the bodies specified in heads (1) to (6) above;

(13)   any two or more bodies described in any of heads (1) to (12) above acting jointly or as a combined authority;

(14)   any association which is representative of any two or more authorities described in any of heads (1) to (4) above;

(15)   any committee established by one or more of the associations described in head (14) above for the purpose of exercising the functions of, or advising, one or more of such associations;

(16)   an association which is representative of one or more of the associations described in head (14) above and of another body or other bodies, and included in whose objects is the assembling and dissemination of information and advising with regard to conditions of service in local government service and generally;

(17)   an organisation which is representative of an association or associations described in head (14) above and employees' organisations among whose objects is the negotiation of pay and conditions of service in local government service;

(18)   a national park authority[19];

(19)   a residuary body[20];

(20)   the Residuary Body for Wales (Corff Gweddilliol Cymru)[21];

(21)   Audit Scotland;

(22)   the Commission for Local Administration in England[22];

(23)   the Commission for Local Administration in Wales[23];

(24)   the Commission for Local Administration in Scotland;

(25)   the Local Government Management Board (now Local Government Employers)[24];

(26)   the Employers' Organisation for local government (now Local Government Employers)[25];

(27)   the Improvement and Development Agency for local government[26];

(28)   the Improvement Service Company[27].

1   Ie for the purposes of the Redundancy Payments (Continuity of Employment in Local Government, etc) (Modification) Order 1999, SI 1999/2277: see PARA 839.
2   As to the meaning of 'England' see PARA 2 note 12.
3   As to local government areas and authorities in England see LOCAL GOVERNMENT vol 69 (2009) PARA 22 et seq.
4   As to the London boroughs and their councils see LONDON GOVERNMENT vol 71 (2013) PARAS 15, 20–22, 55 et seq.
5   As to the Common Council of the City of London see LONDON GOVERNMENT vol 71 (2013) PARAS 34–38.
6   As to the Council of the Isles of Scilly see LOCAL GOVERNMENT vol 69 (2009) PARA 36.
7   As to the meaning of 'Wales' see PARA 2 note 12.
8   Ie established under the Local Government Act 1972 s 20. As to local government areas and authorities in Wales see LOCAL GOVERNMENT vol 69 (2009) PARA 37 et seq.
9   Ie a council established under the Local Government etc (Scotland) Act 1994 s 2.
10 As to parishes in England see LOCAL GOVERNMENT vol 69 (2009) PARA 27 et seq.
11 As to communities in Wales see LOCAL GOVERNMENT vol 69 (2009) PARA 41 et seq.
12 Ie any authority established under the Local Government Act 1985 s 10: see LOCAL GOVERNMENT vol 69 (2009) PARA 17.
13 As to joint boards see LOCAL GOVERNMENT vol 69 (2009) PARA 10. There is no general power to establish joint boards, which are the subject of special authorisation according to the legislation for the particular function concerned.
14 As to the Greater London Authority see LONDON GOVERNMENT vol 71 (2013) PARA 67 et seq.
15 As to Transport for London see LONDON GOVERNMENT vol 71 (2013) PARA 163 et seq.

16 Ie as defined in the Greater London Authority Act 1999 s 424 (see LONDON GOVERNMENT vol 71 (2013) PARA 148), but excluding Transport for London.

17 Ie established under the Greater London Authority Act 1999 s 247: see LONDON GOVERNMENT vol 71 (2013) PARA 192 et seq.

18 Ie established under the Greater London Authority Act 1999 s 375: see LONDON GOVERNMENT vol 71 (2013) PARA 285 et seq.

19 Ie established under the Environment Act 1995 s 63 or the National Parks (Scotland) Act 2000 ss 6–8: see OPEN SPACES AND COUNTRYSIDE vol 78 (2010) PARA 526 et seq.

20 Ie established under the Local Government Act 1985 s 57(1)(b) (repealed): see LOCAL GOVERNMENT vol 69 (2009) PARA 17.

21 The Residuary Body for Wales has now been wound up: see the Local Government (Wales) Act 1994 Sch 13 para 18; the Residuary Body for Wales (Winding Up) Order 1998, SI 1998/2859; and LOCAL GOVERNMENT vol 69 (2009) PARA 18.

22 See LOCAL GOVERNMENT vol 69 (2009) PARA 839.

23 See LOCAL GOVERNMENT vol 69 (2009) PARA 839.

24 The Local Government Management Board was one of the predecessor organisations of the Employers' Organisation for local government (see head (26) in the text).

25 See LOCAL GOVERNMENT vol 69 (2009) PARA 437.

26 See LOCAL GOVERNMENT vol 69 (2009) PARA 437.

27 Redundancy Payments (Continuity of Employment in Local Government, etc) (Modification) Order 1999, SI 1999/2277, art 2(1), Sch 1 Section 1 paras 1–23 (amended by SI 2000/1042; and SI 2010/903). The Improvement Service was set up in 2005 to help improve the efficiency, quality and accountability of local public services in Scotland and is a Company limited by guarantee.

841. Specified employers; planning and development. In relation to planning and development, the specified employers[1] include:

(1) One North East;

(2) Yorkshire Forward;

(3) North West Development Agency (NWDA);

(4) Advantage West Midlands;

(5) Dewsbury Partnership Limited;

(6) East Midlands Development Agency (EMDA);

(7) East of England Development Agency (EEDA);

(8) South East of England Development Agency (SEEDA);

(9) SEERA Limited;

(10) South West of England Development Agency (SWERDA);

(11) a development corporation[2];

(12) a Mayoral development corporation[3];

(13) an urban development corporation[4];

(14) a housing action trust[5];

(15) the Broads Authority[6];

(16) the Countryside Commission for Scotland;

(17) the Development Board for Rural Wales[7];

(18) the Edinburgh New Town Conservation Committee;

(19) the Regulator of Social Housing[8];

(20) Huddersfield Pride Limited;

(21) Scottish Enterprise[9];

(22) Scottish Homes[10];

(23) Springfield Horseshoe Housing Management Co-operative Limited;

(24) Housing for Wales (Tai Cymru) (whose functions were transferred to the National Assembly for Wales and are now exercised by the Welsh Ministers)[11];

(25) Batley Action Limited;

(26) Bethnal Green City Challenge Company Limited;

(27) the Blackburn City Challenge Partnership Board;

(28) Bolton City Challenge Partnership Limited;
(29) Bradford City Challenge Limited;
(30) Brixton Challenge Company Limited;
(31) Community North (Sunderland) Limited;
(32) Dalston City Partnership Limited;
(33) Deptford City Challenge Limited;
(34) Derby Pride Limited;
(35) Douglas Valley Partnership Limited;
(36) Harlesden City Challenge Limited;
(37) Hulme Regeneration Limited;
(38) Leicester City Challenge Limited;
(39) Manchester Investment and Development Agency Service Limited (MIDAS);
(40) Newcastle West End Partnership Limited;
(41) Newtown South Aston City Challenge Limited;
(42) North Kensington City Challenge Company Limited;
(43) North Tyneside City Challenge Partnership Limited;
(44) Stratford Development Partnership Limited;
(45) Wolverhampton City Challenge Limited;
(46) Pennine Housing 2000 Limited;
(47) Twin Valley Homes Limited;
(48) Urban Futures London Limited;
(49) Aire-Wharfe Community Housing Trust Limited;
(50) Bradford Building Services Limited;
(51) Bradford Community Housing Trust Limited;
(52) Bradford West City Community Housing Trust Limited;
(53) City Building (Glasgow) LLP.
(54) Coast and County Housing Limited;
(55) Dumfries and Galloway Housing Partnership Limited;
(56) East Bradford Community Housing Trust Limited;
(57) Knowsley Housing Trust;
(58) North Bradford Community Housing Trust Limited;
(59) Northern Housing Consortium Limited;
(60) Shipley Community Housing Trust Limited;
(61) South Bradford Community Housing Trust Limited;
(62) Sunderland Housing Group[12].

1   Ie for the purposes of the Redundancy Payments (Continuity of Employment in Local Government, etc) (Modification) Order 1999, SI 1999/2277: see PARA 839.
2   Ie within the meaning of the New Towns Act 1981: see PLANNING vol 83 (2010) PARA 1499.
3   Ie within the meaning of the Localism Act 2011 s 198: see LONDON GOVERNMENT vol 71 (2013) PARA 323.
4   Ie established under the Local Government, Planning and Land Act 1980 s 135: see PLANNING vol 83 (2010) PARA 1581.
5   Ie established under the Housing Act 1988 Pt III (ss 60–92): see HOUSING vol 56 (2011) PARA 326 et seq.
6   Ie established under the Norfolk and Suffolk Broads Act 1988: see WATER AND WATERWAYS vol 101 (2009) PARA 734.
7   As from 1 October 1998 the functions of the Development Board for Rural Wales ceased to exist (see the Government of Wales Act 1998 s 129(1)); and all property, rights and liabilities to which the Board was subject were transferred to the Welsh Development Agency (s 130(1)). The functions, property, rights and liabilities of the Welsh Development Agency from 1 April 2006 were transferred to the National Assembly for Wales (see the Welsh Development Agency (Transfer of Functions to the National Assembly for Wales and Abolition) Order 2005,

SI 2005/3226); and those functions of the National Assembly for Wales are now exercised by the Welsh Ministers (see the Government of Wales Act 2006 s 162(1), Sch 11 paras 30, 32).

8   As to the Regulator of Social Housing see HOUSING vol 56 (2011) PARA 34 et seq.
9   Ie established under the Enterprise and New Towns (Scotland) Act 1990.
10 Ie established under the Housing (Scotland) Act 1988.
11 See HOUSING vol 56 (2011) PARA 102.
12 Redundancy Payments (Continuity of Employment in Local Government, etc) (Modification) Order 1999, SI 1999/2277, art 2(1), Sch 1 Section 2 paras 1–60 (amended by SI 2001/866; SI 2002/532; SI 2004/1682; SI 2005/3226; SI 2008/2831; SI 2009/801; SI 2010/903; SI 2012/641; and SI 2012/666).

842. Specified employers; education. In relation to education, the specified employers[1] include:

(1) the governing body of a further education establishment for the time being mainly dependent for its maintenance on assistance from local authorities, or grants under the Education Act 1996[2] or on assistance and grants taken together;

(2) the governing body of an aided school[3];

(3) the governing body of a foundation school, voluntary aided school or foundation special school[4];

(4) the managers of a grant-aided school[5];

(5) the governing body of a central institution[6] other than a college of agriculture;

(6) the governing body of a college of education[7];

(7) the managers, other than a local authority, of a school which was[8] a school which was duly approved[9] if the employee was employed by those managers at the relevant date;

(8) a person carrying on a city technology college, a city college for the technology of the arts or an academy established under an agreement with the Secretary of State[10];

(9) a company formed to manage a college of further education[11];

(10) the board of management of a self-governing school[12];

(11) a further education corporation[13];

(12) the governing body of an institution which is duly designated[14] or, in the case of such an institution conducted by a company, that company;

(13) the board of management of a college of further education[15];

(14) the governing body of a designated institution[16];

(15) a higher education corporation[17];

(16) the governing body of an institution which is duly designated[18] or, in the case of such an institution conducted by a company, that company;

(17) an Education Action Forum[19];

(18) the governing body of a grant-maintained school[20];

(19) the governing body of a grant-maintained special school[21];

(20) the Central Council for Education and Training in Social Work[22];

(21) the Centre for Information on Language Teaching and Research;

(22) the Centre for Literacy in Primary Education;

(23) Connexions Lancashire Limited;

(24) Cwmni Cynnal;

(25) the General Teaching Council for Scotland[23];

(26) the National Institute of Adult Continuing Education (England and Wales);

(27) Newbattle Abbey College;

(28) the Scottish Community Education Council;

(29)   Scottish Consultative Council on the Curriculum;
(30)   the Scottish Council for Educational Technology;
(31)   the Scottish Council for Research in Education;
(32)   the Scottish Examination Board;
(33)   the Scottish Vocational Education Council;
(34)   Shetland Arts Development Agency;
(35)   VT Four S Limited[24].

1   Ie for the purposes of the Redundancy Payments (Continuity of Employment in Local Government, etc) (Modification) Order 1999, SI 1999/2277: see PARA 839.
2   Ie under the Education Act 1996 s 485: see EDUCATION vol 35 (2011) PARA 81.
3   Ie within the meaning of the Education Act 1996 s 32(1), (3) (repealed).
4   Ie within the meaning of the School Standards and Framework Act 1998: see EDUCATION vol 35 (2011) PARAS 106, 108.
5   Ie as defined in the Education (Scotland) Act 1980 s 135(1).
6   See note 5.
7   See note 5.
8   Ie before any direction made by the Secretary of State under the Social Work (Scotland) Act 1968 s 93, Sch 7 para 2(1).
9   Ie which, immediately before the commencement of the Social Work (Scotland) Act 1968 Pt III (ss 30–58) (repealed), was approved under the Children and Young Persons (Scotland) Act 1937 s 83 (repealed).
10   Ie under the Education Act 1996 s 482: see EDUCATION vol 35 (2011) PARA 510. As to the Secretary of State see PARA 5 note 21.
11   Ie by virtue of the Self-Governing Schools etc (Scotland) Act 1989 s 65(1).
12   Ie as defined in the Self-Governing Schools etc (Scotland) Act 1989 s 80(1).
13   Ie established under the Further and Higher Education Act 1992 s 15 (see EDUCATION vol 36 (2011) PARA 733) or s 16 (see EDUCATION vol 36 (2011) PARA 734), or in respect of which an order has been made under s 47 (see EDUCATION vol 36 (2011) PARA 730).
14   Ie established under the Further and Higher Education Act 1992 Pt I (ss 1–61A): see EDUCATION vol 36 (2011) PARA 733 et seq.
15   Ie established under the Further and Higher Education (Scotland) Act 1992 Pt I (ss 1–36).
16   Ie within the meaning of the Further and Higher Education (Scotland) Act 1992 s 44(2).
17   Ie established under the Education Reform Act 1988 s 121 (see EDUCATION vol 36 (2011) PARA 836) or s 122 (see EDUCATION vol 36 (2011) PARA 837), or in respect of which an order has been made under s 122A (see EDUCATION vol 36 (2011) PARA 731).
18   Ie designated under the Education Reform Act 1988 s 129: see EDUCATION vol 36 (2011) PARA 861.
19   Ie established under the School Standards and Framework Act 1998 ss 10–11: see EDUCATION vol 35 (2011) PARA 429.
20   See EDUCATION vol 35 (2011) PARA 106.
21   See note 20.
22   The functions of the Central Council for Training and Education in Social Work ('CCETSW') were abolished in relation to England and Wales by the Care Standards Act 2000 s 70 (repealed), in relation to Northern Ireland by the Health and Personal Social Services Act (Northern Ireland) 2001 s 17 and in relation to Scotland under the Regulation of Care (Scotland) Act 2001 s 67. See also the Abolition of the Central Council for Education and Training in Social Work Order 2002, SI 2002/797. CCETSW's assets and liabilities were transferred to the English Council (in relation to England) and to the Care Council for Wales (in relation to Wales) under the Central Council for Education and Training in Social Work (Transfer Scheme) Order 2001, SI 2001/2561, subject to certain savings. Those savings provisions are now revoked (see art 4) and any remaining assets and liabilities of CCETSW have been transferred either to the Secretary of State or to those successor bodies.
23   Ie established under the Public Services Reform (General Teaching Council for Scotland) Order 2011.
24   Redundancy Payments (Continuity of Employment in Local Government, etc) (Modification) Order 1999, SI 1999/2277, art 2(1), Sch 1 Section 3 paras 1–33 (amended by SI 2001/866; SI 2004/1682; SI 2010/903; SI 2010/1172; SSI 2011/215).

843. Specified employers; careers guidance. In relation to careers guidance, the specified employers[1] include:

(1)   Argyll and Bute Careers Partnership Limited;
(2)   Calderdale and Kirklees Careers Service Partnership Limited;
(3)   Cambridgeshire Careers Guidance Limited;
(4)   Capital Careers Limited;
(5)   Career Connections Limited;
(6)   Career Decisions Limited;
(7)   Career Development Edinburgh and Lothians;
(8)   Career Path (Northamptonshire) Limited;
(9)   Careerpaths (Cardiff and Vale) Limited;
(10)   Careers and Education Business Partnership;
(11)   Careers Central Limited;
(12)   Careers Enterprise (Futures) Limited;
(13)   Careers Partnership Limited;
(14)   Careers Service Lancashire Area West Limited;
(15)   Central Careers Limited;
(16)   Cornwall and Devon Careers Limited;
(17)   Coventry, Solihull and Warwickshire Partnership Limited;
(18)   Derbyshire Careers Service Limited;
(19)   East Lancashire Careers Services Limited;
(20)   Education Business Partnership (Wigan) Limited;
(21)   Essex Careers and Business Partnership Limited;
(22)   Future Steps Limited;
(23)   Futures Careers Limited;
(24)   Grampian Careers;
(25)   Guidance Enterprises Group Limited;
(26)   GuideLine Career Services Limited;
(27)   Gwent Careers Service Partnership Limited;
(28)   Hereford and Worcester Careers Service Limited;
(29)   Hertfordshire Careers Services Limited;
(30)   Highland Careers Services Limited;
(31)   the Humberside Partnership;
(32)   Learning Partnership West;
(33)   Leeds Careers Guidance;
(34)   Leicestershire Careers and Guidance Service Limited;
(35)   Lifetime Careers Barnsley, Doncaster and Rotherham Limited;
(36)   Lifetime Careers Bolton, Bury and Rochdale Limited;
(37)   Lifetime Careers Brent and Harrow Limited;
(38)   Lifetime Careers Stockport and High Peak Limited;
(39)   Lifetime Careers Wiltshire Limited;
(40)   Lincolnshire Careers and Guidance Services Limited;
(41)   London South Bank Careers;
(42)   Mid Glamorgan Careers Limited;
(43)   Norfolk Careers Services Limited;
(44)   North East Wales Careers Service Company Limited;
(45)   Oldham Education Business and Guidance Services;
(46)   Orkney Opportunities Centre;
(47)   Prospects Careers Services Limited;
(48)   Quality Careers Services Limited;
(49)   St Helens Careers Service Limited;
(50)   Sheffield Careers Guidance Services;
(51)   Shropshire Careers Service Limited;

(52) Suffolk Careers Limited;
(53) Tayside Careers Limited;
(54) West Glamorgan Careers and Education Business Centre Company Limited[2].

1 Ie for the purposes of the Redundancy Payments (Continuity of Employment in Local Government, etc) (Modification) Order 1999, SI 1999/2277: see PARA 839.
2 Redundancy Payments (Continuity of Employment in Local Government, etc) (Modification) Order 1999, SI 1999/2277, art 2(1), Sch 1 Section 4 paras 1–50 (amended by SI 2001/866; SI 2002/532; SI 2004/1682).

844. Specified employers; public transport. In relation to public transport, the specified employers[1] include:
(1) a passenger transport executive[2];
(2) a metropolitan county passenger transport authority[3];
(3) the Forth Road Bridge Joint Board;
(4) the Tay Road Bridge Joint Board[4].

1 Ie for the purposes of the Redundancy Payments (Continuity of Employment in Local Government, etc) (Modification) Order 1999, SI 1999/2277: see PARA 839.
2 Ie a passenger transport executive established under the Transport Act 1968 s 9(1): see ROAD TRAFFIC vol 89 (2011) PARA 47.
3 Ie a metropolitan county passenger transport authority established under the Local Government Act 1985 s 28: see LOCAL GOVERNMENT vol 69 (2009) PARA 49.
4 Redundancy Payments (Continuity of Employment in Local Government, etc) (Modification) Order 1999, SI 1999/2277, art 2(1), Sch 1 Section 5 paras 1–4.

845. Specified employers; police, fire and civil defence. In relation to the police, fire and civil defence, the specified employers[1] include:
(1) a fire authority[2];
(2) a fire and rescue authority[3];
(3) a police and crime commissioner[4];
(4) a chief constable[5];
(5) the Commissioner of Police of the Metropolis[6];
(6) a metropolitan county fire and rescue authority[7].
(7) a company the members of which comprise fire and rescue authorities in England and whose objects include the operation of a regional fire control centre[8].

1 Ie for the purposes of the Redundancy Payments (Continuity of Employment in Local Government, etc) (Modification) Order 1999, SI 1999/2277: see PARA 839.
2 Ie a fire authority constituted by a combination scheme made under the Fire Services Act 1947. A scheme approved under the Fire Services Act 1947 s 6 (repealed) (combination schemes made by the Secretary of State: see FIRE AND RESCUE SERVICES vol 51 (2013) PARA 18), which was in force immediately before the repeal of s 6 by the Fire and Rescue Services Act 2004 ss 52, 54, Sch 2, continues to have effect despite that repeal: see s 4; and FIRE AND RESCUE SERVICES vol 51 (2013) PARA 18.
3 Ie a fire and rescue authority constituted by a scheme under the Fire and Rescue Services Act 2004 s 2 or a scheme to which s 4 applies (see note 2): see FIRE AND RESCUE SERVICES vol 51 (2013) PARAS 18, 20.
4 Ie established under the Police Reform and Social Responsibility Act 2011 s 1: POLICE AND INVESTIGATORY POWERS vol 84 (2013) PARA 56.
5 Ie established under the Police Reform and Social Responsibility Act 2011 s 2: POLICE AND INVESTIGATORY POWERS vol 84 (2013) PARA 113.
6 Ie established under the Police Reform and Social Responsibility Act 2011 s 4: POLICE AND INVESTIGATORY POWERS vol 84 (2013) PARA 117.
7 Ie established by the Local Government Act 1985 s 26. As to metropolitan county fire and rescue authorities see FIRE AND RESCUE SERVICES, LOCAL GOVERNMENT vol 69 (2009) PARA 48.

8   Redundancy Payments (Continuity of Employment in Local Government, etc) (Modification) Order 1999, SI 1999/2277, art 2(1), Sch 1 Section 6 paras 1–4 (amended by the Civil Contingencies Act 2004 s 32(1), Sch 2 Pt 1 PARA 10(1), (2); and SI 2000/1042; SI 2004/3168; SI 2005/2929; SI 2010/903; and SI 2012/2733). As to fire and rescue authorities see FIRE AND RESCUE SERVICES vol 51 (2013) PARA 17.

846. Specified employers; sports councils. In relation to sports councils[1], the specified employers[2] include:

(1)   the English Sports Council[3];
(2)   the Scottish Sports Council;
(3)   the Sports Council for Wales;
(4)   the United Kingdom Sports Council[4].

1   As to the sport councils generally see NATIONAL CULTURAL HERITAGE vol 77 (2010) PARA 965.
2   Ie for the purposes of the Redundancy Payments (Continuity of Employment in Local Government, etc) (Modification) Order 1999, SI 1999/2277: see PARA 839.
3   The English Sports Council is now known as Sport England: see NATIONAL CULTURAL HERITAGE vol 77 (2010) PARA 965.
4   Redundancy Payments (Continuity of Employment in Local Government, etc) (Modification) Order 1999, SI 1999/2277, art 2(1), Sch 1 Section 7 paras 1–4. The United Kingdom Sports Council is now known as UK Sport: see NATIONAL CULTURAL HERITAGE vol 77 (2010) PARA 965.

847. Specified employers; social services. In relation to social services, the specified employers[1] include:

(1)   Coverage Care Limited;
(2)   Essex Cares Limited;
(3)   Essex Community Support Limited;
(4)   Essex Employment and Inclusion Limited;
(5)   Essex Equipment Services Limited;
(6)   Forfarshire Society for the Blind;
(7)   Harlow Welfare Rights and Advice;
(8)   the Humberside Independent Care Association;
(9)   New Charter Building Company Limited;
(10)   New Charter Housing Trust Limited;
(11)   Quantum Care Limited;
(12)   Sandwell Community Caring Trust Limited;
(13)   Social Care and Social Work Improvement Scotland;
(14)   the Scottish Social Services Council;
(15)   Shetland Council of Social Services;
(16)   Shetland Welfare Trust;
(17)   Tynedale Housing Company Limited;
(18)   Waltham Forest Specialist Housing Consortium Limited;
(19)   Wrekin Housing Trust Limited[2].

1   Ie for the purposes of the Redundancy Payments (Continuity of Employment in Local Government, etc) (Modification) Order 1999, SI 1999/2277: see PARA 839.
2   Redundancy Payments (Continuity of Employment in Local Government, etc) (Modification) Order 1999, SI 1999/2277, art 2(1), Sch 1 Section 8 paras 1–6 (amended by SI 2001/866; SI 2004/1682; SI 2010/903; SI 2011/2581).

848. Specified employers; museums. In relation to museums, the specified employers[1] include:

(1)   the Board of Governors of the Museum of London[2];
(2)   the Board of Trustees of the National Museums and Galleries on Merseyside[3];

(3)	Coventry Museum of British Road Transport;
(4)	the Geffrye Museum Trust;
(5)	the Horniman Public Museum and Public Park Trust;
(6)	National Coal Mining Museum for England Trust Limited;
(7)	the Scottish Museums Council;
(8)	Woodhorn Charitable Trust[4].

1	Ie for the purposes of the Redundancy Payments (Continuity of Employment in Local Government, etc) (Modification) Order 1999, SI 1999/2277: see PARA 839.
2	As to the Board of Governors see NATIONAL CULTURAL HERITAGE vol 77 (2010) PARA 857.
3	As to the Board of Trustees see NATIONAL CULTURAL HERITAGE vol 77 (2010) PARA 857.
4	Redundancy Payments (Continuity of Employment in Local Government, etc) (Modification) Order 1999, SI 1999/2277, art 2(1), Sch 1 Section 9 paras 1–8 (amended by SI 2010/903).

849. Specified employers; miscellaneous bodies. In relation to miscellaneous bodies, the specified employers[1] include:
(1)	a valuation tribunal[2];
(2)	an area tourist board[3];
(3)	a probation committee, a local probation board[4] or a probation trust;
(4)	a magistrates' court committee or the Committee of Magistrates for the Inner London Area[5];
(5)	a body designated as a care trust[6];
(6)	a community justice authority[7];
(7)	Active Stirling Limited;
(8)	Ardroy Outdoor Learning Trust;
(9)	Arts and Theatres Trust Fife Limited;
(10)	Blyth Valley Arts and Leisure Limited;
(11)	the Business Shop–Angus Limited;
(12)	the Care Quality Commission[8];
(13)	the Care Standards Inspectorate for Wales;
(14)	the Children and Family Court Advisory and Support Service[9];
(15)	City Markets (Glasgow) LLP;
(16)	City Parking (Glasgow) LLP;
(17)	City Property (Glasgow) LLP;
(18)	CIP (Hounslow) Limited;
(19)	Clackmannanshire Leisure;
(20)	Community Initiative Partnerships;
(21)	Cordia (Services) LLP;
(22)	Coventry Sports Trust Limited;
(23)	CV One Limited;
(24)	Culture and Sport Glasgow;
(25)	Culture and Sport Glasgow (Trading) CIC;
(26)	Derwentside Leisure Limited;
(27)	East End Partnership Limited;
(28)	Edinburgh Leisure;
(29)	Enfield Leisure Centres Limited;
(30)	Enjoy East Lothian Limited;
(31)	the Environment Agency[10];
(32)	Fife Coast and Countryside Trust;
(33)	Fife Sports and Leisure Trust Limited;
(34)	Forth Valley GIS Limited;
(35)	Glasgow Community and Safety Services Limited;
(36)	Greenwich Leisure Limited;

(37) Herefordshire Community Leisure Trust;
(38) Hounslow Cultural and Community Services;
(39) Hounslow Sports and Recreational Services;
(40) the Islesburgh Trust;
(41) Kirklees Active Leisure Trust;
(42) the Land Authority for Wales (now abolished)[11];
(43) Leisure Tynedale;
(44) the Lee Valley Regional Park Authority;
(45) the London Pensions Fund Authority[12];
(46) the National Care Standards Commission[13];
(47) National Mobility Services Trust Limited;
(49) New Park Village TMC Limited;
(50) North Lanarkshire Leisure Limited;
(51) Nuneaton and Bedworth Leisure Trust;
(52) Oldham Community Leisure Limited;
(53) Pendle Leisure Limited;
(54) Renfrewshire Leisure Limited;
(55) Salford Community Leisure Limited;
(56) Sandwell Arts Trust;
(57) Sandwell Sport and Leisure Trust;
(58) Scottish Children's Reporter Administration[14];
(59) Scottish Environment Protection Agency;
(60) Scottish Water;
(61) Shetland Recreational Trust;
(62) Somerset Leisure Limited;
(63) South Yorkshire Pensions Authority;
(64) Sport Aberdeen;
(65) Strathclyde European Partnerships Limited;
(66) Tameside Sports Trust;
(67) Tees Active Limited;
(68) Valuation Tribunal Service;
(69) Water Industry Commissioner for Scotland;
(70) West Lothian Leisure Limited;
(71) Wigan Leisure and Culture Trust[15].

1   Ie for the purposes of the Redundancy Payments (Continuity of Employment in Local Government, etc) (Modification) Order 1999, SI 1999/2277: see PARA 839.
2   Ie a valuation tribunal in Wales established under the Local Government Finance Act 1988 s 55(5), Sch 11: see LOCAL GOVERNMENT FINANCE vol 70 (2012) PARA 197 et seq.
3   Ie an area tourist board established by virtue of an order made under the Local Government etc (Scotland) Act 1994 s 172, s 173 or s 174.
4   Probation committees within the meaning of the Probation Service Act 1993 have been replaced by the National Probation Service and local probation boards within the meaning of the Criminal Justice and Court Services Act 2000 s 4 (prospectively repealed): see SENTENCING AND DISPOSITION OF OFFENDERS vol 92 (2010) PARA 737.
5   Magistrates' courts committees have been abolished as from 1 April 2005 and replaced by courts boards: see the Courts Act 2003 ss 4, 6; COURTS AND TRIBUNALS vol 24 (2010) PARA 829; and see MAGISTRATES vol 71 (2013) PARA 401 et seq.
6   Ie under the National Health Service Act 2006 s 77(1): see HEALTH SERVICES vol 54 (2008) PARA 235.
7   Ie under the Management of Offenders (Scotland) Act 2005 s 3.
8   As to the Care Quality Commission see SOCIAL SERVICES AND COMMUNITY CARE vol 95 (2013) PARA 217 et seq.
9   As to the Children and Family Court Advisory and Support Service (CAFCASS) see CHILDREN AND YOUNG PERSONS vol 9 (2012) PARA 213 et seq.

10 As to the Environment Agency see ENVIRONMENTAL QUALITY AND PUBLIC HEALTH vol 45 (2010) PARA 68 et seq.
11 See the Government of Wales Act 1998 ss 134–139; and the Land Authority for Wales (Abolition) Order 1999, SI 1999/372. Functions were transferred to the Welsh Development Agency accordingly and then subsequently to the Welsh Ministers: see TRADE AND INDUSTRY vol 97 (2010) PARA 954.
12 As to the London Pensions Fund Authority see LONDON GOVERNMENT vol 71 (2013) PARA 149.
13 The National Care Standards Commission was established under the Care Standards Act 2000 s 6 (repealed), whose functions were transferred to the Commission for Social Care Inspection established under the Health and Social Care (Community Health and Standards) Act 2003 s 42 (repealed) and then to the Care Quality Commission established under the Health and Social Care Act 2008 s 1 (see SOCIAL SERVICES AND COMMUNITY CARE vol 95 (2013) PARA 217 et seq).
14 Ie the Scottish Children's Reporter Administration established under the Local Government etc (Scotland) Act 1994 s 128 and continued by the Scottish Children's Reporter Administration) of the Children's Hearings (Scotland) Act 2011 s 15.
15 Redundancy Payments (Continuity of Employment in Local Government, etc) (Modification) Order 1999, SI 1999/2277, art 2(1), Sch 1 Section 10 paras 1–26 (amended by SI 2002/532; SI 2004/664; SI 2004/1682; SI 2008/912; SI 2008/2250; SI 2010/903; and SI 2013/195).

850. Employers with whom employment may constitute relevant local government service. The employers with whom employment may constitute relevant service[1] for local government purposes (many of whom no longer exist) are:

(1) any relevant employer[2], whether or not in existence at the time of the relevant event[3];

(2) the Greater London Council[4];

(3) the London Residuary Body[5];

(4) the council of an administrative county, county borough[6], metropolitan borough or county district[7];

(5) a regional council, islands council or district council[8];

(6) the council of a county, county of a city, large burgh, small burgh or district ceasing to exist after 15 May 1975;

(7) any joint board or joint body constituted by or under any enactment for the purpose of exercising the functions of two or more of the bodies described in heads (2) to (6) above and any special planning board[9];

(8) any other body, not specified in any of heads (2) to (7) above, established by or under any enactment for the purpose of exercising functions of, or advising, one or more of the bodies specified in any of heads (2) to (7) above;

(9) any committee, including a joint committee, established by or under any enactment for the purpose of exercising the functions of, or advising, one or more of the bodies described in any of heads (2) to (7) above;

(10) any two or more bodies described in heads (2) to (9) above acting jointly or as a combined authority;

(11) any association which was representative of any two or more bodies described in any of heads (2) to (6) above;

(12) any committee established by one or more of the associations described in head (11) above for the purpose of exercising the functions of, or advising, one or more such associations;

(13) an organisation which was representative of an association or associations described in head (11) above and employees' organisations among whose objects was to negotiate pay and conditions of service in local government service;

(14) the council of a county or district in Wales ceasing to exist after 31 March 1996;

(15) the Local Government Training Board;

(16) the Accounts Commission for Scotland;

(17) a development corporation[10];

(18) the Scottish Development Agency;

(19) the Scottish Special Housing Association;

(20) the English Industrial Estates Corporation[11];

(21) the governing body of an aided school[12];

(22) the governing body of a grant-maintained school[13];

(23) the governing body of a grant-maintained special school[14];

(24) the proprietor[15] of a school for the time being recognised as a grammar school[16];

(25) the proprietor[17] of a school not falling within head (21) above which throughout the period of employment was recognised as a grammar school or, as the case may be, a direct grant grammar school[18];

(26) the managers of a school which during the period of employment was duly approved[19];

(27) the managers of a school which during the period of employment was a grant-aided school[20];

(28) an institution within the PCFC funding sector[21];

(29) the Further Education Staff College;

(30) the Inner London Education Authority[22];

(31) the National Advisory Body for Public Sector Higher Education;

(32) the Polytechnics and College Funding Council[23];

(33) the Scottish Association for National Certificates and Diplomas;

(34) the Scottish Business Education Council;

(35) the Scottish Council for Commercial, Administrative and Professional Education;

(36) the Scottish Technical Education Council;

(37) the Secretary of State for Defence[24], in relation only to employees in schools administered by the Service Children's Education Authority;

(38) the Secretary of State for Education and Employment, the Secretary of State for Education and Skills[25] or the Secretary of State for Children, Schools and Families or the Secretary of State for Education, in relation only to teachers employed under contract in the European School[26] and in schools designated as European Schools[27];

(39) Shetland Arts Trust;

(40) a person who, during the period of employment, performed an education function of a local authority pursuant to a direction given by the Secretary of State[28];

(41) Black Country Careers Services Limited;

(42) Buckinghamshire Careers Service Limited;

(43) Kent Careers and Guidance Service Limited;

(44) a previous police authority[29];

(45) a police authority (now an elected police and crime commissioner)[30];

(46) the Metropolitan Police Authority (now The Mayor's Office for Policing and Crime)[31];

(47) the London Fire and Civil Defence Authority[32];

(48) the Sports Council[33];

(49) a person or body of persons responsible for the management of an assisted community home[34] or of an approved institution[35];

(50) a regional water board[36];

(51)   a river purification board[37];

(52)   a local valuation panel[38];

(53)   a valuation tribunal in England[39];

(54)   the Central Scotland Water Development Board;

(55)   the Scottish Industrial Estates Corporation (formerly the Industrial Estates Management Corporation for Scotland)[40];

(56)   the Small Industries Council for Rural Areas of Scotland[41];

(57)   the Traffic Director for London[42];

(58)   the Welsh Industrial Estates Corporation[43] (formerly the Industrial Estates Corporation for Wales)[44].

1   As to the meaning of 'relevant service' see PARA 855 note 4.
2   Ie any employer specified in the Redundancy Payments (Continuity of Employment in Local Government, etc) (Modification) Order 1999, SI 1999/2277, art 2(1), Sch 1: see PARAS 840–849.
3   As to the meaning of 'relevant event' see PARA 839 note 2.
4   As to the Greater London Council, and its abolition, see LONDON GOVERNMENT vol 71 (2013) PARAS 4–5, 18.
5   Ie established under the Local Government Act 1985 s 57(1)(a) (repealed). As to the London Residuary Body see LOCAL GOVERNMENT vol 69 (2009) PARA 17; LONDON GOVERNMENT vol 71 (2013) PARAS 5, 18.
6   Ie other than one established under the Local Government Act 1972 s 20: see LOCAL GOVERNMENT vol 69 (2009) PARA 39.
7   As to local government areas and authorities see LOCAL GOVERNMENT vol 69 (2009) PARA 22 et seq.
8   Ie established by or under the Local Government (Scotland) Act 1973.
9   Ie within the meaning of the Local Government Act 1972 s 184(6), Sch 17 para 3 (repealed). As to special planning boards see LOCAL GOVERNMENT vol 69 (2009) PARA 10.
10 Ie within the meaning of the New Towns Act 1946 or the New Towns Act 1965 or established under the New Towns (Scotland) Act 1968. As to development corporations see PLANNING vol 83 (2010) PARA 1499 et seq.
11 Ie established by the Local Employment Act 1960: see TRADE AND INDUSTRY vol 97 (2010) PARA 945.
12 Ie within the meaning of the Education Act 1996 s 32(1), (3) (repealed).
13 See EDUCATION vol 35 (2011) PARA 106.
14 See note 13.
15 Ie within the meaning of the Education Act 1996 s 579(1) (see EDUCATION vol 35 (2011) PARA 53).
16 Ie for the purposes of the Direct Grant Schools Regulations 1959, SI 1959/1182, reg 4(1) (revoked), being a school in relation to which, before 1 January 1976, the Secretary of State was satisfied as mentioned in the Direct Grant Grammar Schools (Cessation of Grant) Regulations 1975, SI 1975/1198, reg 3(1) (revoked).
17 Ie within the meaning of the Education Act 1944 s 114(1) (repealed).
18 Ie for the purposes of the Direct Grant Schools Regulations 1959, SI 1959/1182, reg 4(1) (revoked), the School Grant Regulations 1951, SI 1951/1743, Pt IV (regs 24–28) (revoked) or the Primary and Secondary Schools (Grant Conditions) Regulations 1945, SI 1945/636, Pt IV (regs 30–56) (revoked).
19 Ie a school approved under the Children and Young Persons (Scotland) Act 1937 s 83 (repealed) or a school which, immediately before the commencement of the Social Work (Scotland) Act 1968 Pt III (ss 30–58), was approved under the Children and Young Persons (Scotland) Act 1937 s 83 (repealed).
20 Ie within the meaning of the Education (Scotland) Act 1946 s 143(1) (repealed), the Education (Scotland) Act 1962 s 145(22) or the Education (Scotland) Act 1980 s 135(1).
21 Ie within the meaning of the Education Reform Act 1988 s 132(6) (repealed).
22 This body was known as the Inner London Interim Education Authority for a period prior to the abolition date as defined in the Local Government Act 1985 s 1(2) (namely 1 April 1986). The Inner London Education Authority was in fact abolished as from 1 April 1990: see the Education Reform Act 1988 s 162 (repealed).
23 Ie established by the Education Reform Act 1988 s 132.
24 As to the Secretary of State for Defence see ARMED FORCES vol 3 (2011) PARA 302.

25 The functions of the Secretary of State for Education and Employment have been divided between the Secretary of State for Education and Skills and the Secretary of State for Work and Pensions: see the Secretaries of State for Education and Skills and for Work and Pensions Order 2002, SI 2002/1397.

26 Ie established under the Statute of the European School (Luxembourg, 12 April 1957; TS 120 (1972); Cmnd 5145) art 1.

27 Ie designated under the Statute of the European School (Luxembourg, 12 April 1957; TS 120 (1972); Cmnd 5145) Protocol art 1.

28 Ie under the Education Act 1996 s 497A(4): see EDUCATION vol 35 (2011) PARA 64. For these purposes, 'education function' and 'local authority' have the meanings given by the Education Act 1996 see EDUCATION vol 35 (2011) PARAS 24, 43.

29 Ie a police authority in relation to which the Police Act 1964 s 64(5), Sch 11 (repealed) had effect or which was the police authority for an area or district which was before 1 April 1947 or after 31 March 1946 a separate police area or, in Scotland, a previous police authority for an area which was before 16 May 1975 a separate or combined police area.

30 See POLICE AND INVESTIGATORY POWERS vol 84 (2013) PARA 56 et seq.

31 See POLICE AND INVESTIGATORY POWERS vol 84 (2013) PARA 78 et seq.

32 The London Fire and Civil Defence Authority continues in being under the name of the London Fire and Emergency Planning Authority: see FIRE AND RESCUE SERVICES vol 51 (2013) PARA 17; LONDON GOVERNMENT vol 71 (2013) PARA 315.

33 As to the sport councils see NATIONAL CULTURAL HERITAGE vol 77 (2010) PARA 965.

34 Ie within the meaning of the Children and Young Persons Act 1969 s 36 (repealed): see CHILDREN AND YOUNG PERSONS vol 10 (2012) PARA 976.

35 Ie within the meaning of the Children and Young Persons Act 1969 s 46 (discontinuance of approved schools etc on establishment of community homes).

36 Ie established under the Water (Scotland) Act 1967 s 5.

37 Ie established under the Rivers (Prevention of Pollution) (Scotland) Act 1951 s 2 or the Local Government (Scotland) Act 1973 s 135.

38 Ie constituted under the Local Government Act 1948 or established under the General Rate Act 1967.

39 Ie established under the Local Government Finance Act 1988: see LOCAL GOVERNMENT FINANCE vol 70 (2012) PARA 197 et seq.

40 Ie established under the Local Employment Act 1960 s 8 (repealed).

41 Ie being a company which was dissolved by the Scottish Development Agency Act 1975 s 15(5) and was until then registered under the Companies Acts from time to time in force. As to the meaning of the 'Companies Acts' see COMPANIES vol 14 (2009) PARA 14.

42 The functions and responsibilities of the Traffic Director for London have now passed to Transport for London: see HIGHWAYS, STREETS AND BRIDGES vol 55 (2012) PARA 454.

43 Ie established by the Local Employment Act 1960 s 8 (repealed).

44 Redundancy Payments (Continuity of Employment in Local Government, etc) (Modification) Order 1999, SI 1999/2277, art 3, Sch 2 Pt II Sections 1–9 (amended by SI 2000/1042; SI 2001/866; SI 2002/1397; SI 2004/1682; SI 2007/3224; SI 2010/903; SI 2010/1836; SI 2012/666; SI 2013/1784).

C. NATIONAL HEALTH SERVICE EMPLOYMENT

851. National health service employment. The Redundancy Payments (National Health Service) (Modification) Order 1993[1] applies to any person who, immediately before the occurrence of the relevant event[2], is employed by a specified employer[3], for the purposes of determining that person's entitlement to a redundancy payment[4] and the amount of such payment[5].

1 Ie the Redundancy Payments (National Health Service) (Modification) Order 1993, SI 1993/3167, which came into force on 13 January 1994 (see art 1(1)). This order applies by virtue of the Employment Rights Act 1996 s 241, Sch 2 para 2(1) (see PARA 162).

2 For these purposes, 'relevant event' means any event occurring on or after 13 January 1994, on the happening of which an employee may become entitled to a redundancy payment in accordance with the provisions of the Employment Rights Act 1996: Redundancy Payments (National Health Service) (Modification) Order 1993, SI 1993/3167, art 1(1), (2).

3 Ie an employer specified in Employment Rights Act 1996: Redundancy Payments (National Health Service) (Modification) Order 1993, SI 1993/3167, art 2, Sch 1: see PARA 852.

4   Ie under the Employment Rights Act 1996: see PARAS 835 et seq, 854 et seq.
5   Redundancy Payments (National Health Service) (Modification) Order 1993, SI 1993/3167,
    arts 1(2)(b), 2. In relation to any person to whom the Redundancy Payments (National Health
    Service) (Modification) Order 1993, SI 1993/3167, applies, the provisions of the Employment
    Rights Act 1996 mentioned in the Redundancy Payments (National Health Service)
    (Modification) Order 1993, SI 1993/3167, art 3, Sch 2 have effect subject to modifications: see
    arts 1(2)(b), 3; and PARAS 855 note 4, 865 notes 4, 5, 881 note 4.

852.   Specified employers.   The employers with which employment may
constitute relevant service[1] for National Health Service purposes are:
  (1)   a strategic health authority[2];
  (2)   a special health authority[3];
  (3)   a National Health Service trust[4];
  (4)   an NHS foundation trust[5];
  (5)   a primary care trust[6];
  (6)   a clinical commissioning group[7];
  (7)   the National Health Service Commissioning Board[8];
  (8)   the National Institute for Health and Care Excellence[9];
  (9)   the Health and Social Care Information Centre[10].
  (10)   a Family Health Service authority[11];
  (11)   the Dental Practice Board[12];
  (12)   a health board[13] or a special health board[14];
  (13)   the Common Services Agency for the Scottish Health Service[15];
  (12)   the Scottish Dental Practice Board[16].

1   Ie for the purposes of the Redundancy Payments (National Health Service) (Modification)
    Order 1993, SI 1993/3167: see PARA 851.
2   Ie established under the National Health Service Act 2006 s 13: see HEALTH SERVICES vol 54
    (2008) PARA 94 et seq. Strategic health authorities continued in existence or established under
    National Health Service Act 2006 s 13 are abolished: see the Health and Social Care Act 2012
    s 33(1); and HEALTH SERVICES. See also local health boards established under the National
    Health Service (Wales) Act 2006 s 11: see HEALTH SERVICES vol 54 (2008) PARAS 17, 74.
3   Ie established under the National Health Service Act 2006 s 28 and the National Health Service
    (Wales) Act 2006 s 22: see HEALTH SERVICES vol 54 (2008) PARA 136 et seq.
4   Ie established by an order under the National Health Service Act 2006 s 25 and the National
    Health Service (Wales) Act 2006 s 18 (see HEALTH SERVICES vol 54 (2008) PARA 155 et seq) or
    under the National Health Service (Scotland) Act 1978 s 12A(1). The National Health Service
    Act 2006 s 25 is prospectively repealed by the Health and Social Care Act 2012 s 179(2).
5   Ie within the meaning of the National Health Service Act 2006 s 30(1): see HEALTH SERVICES
    vol 54 (2008) PARA 174.
6   Ie established under the National Health Service Act 2006 s 18: see HEALTH SERVICES vol 54
    (2008) PARA 111 et seq. The primary care trusts continued in existence or established under the
    National Health Service Act 2006 s 18 are abolished and Pt 2 Ch 2 (ss 18–24A) is repealed:
    Health and Social Care Act 2012 s 34.
7   Ie established under the National Health Service Act 2006 s 14D: see HEALTH SERVICES.
8   As to the National Health Service Commissioning Board see HEALTH SERVICES.
9   As to the National Institute for Health and Care Excellence see HEALTH SERVICES vol 54 (2008)
    PARA 149.
10 As to the Health and Social Care Information Centre see HEALTH SERVICES vol 54 (2008) PARA
    145.
11 Ie established by an order made under the National Health Service Act 1977 s 10(1) (repealed).
12 Ie constituted by regulations made under the National Health Service Act 1977 s 37(1)
    (repealed).
13 Ie constituted under the National Health Service (Scotland) Act 1978 s 2(1)(a).
14 Ie constituted under the National Health Service (Scotland) Act 1978 s 2(1)(b).
15 Ie established under the National Health Service (Scotland) Act 1978 s 10.
16 Redundancy Payments (National Health Service) (Modification) Order 1993, SI 1993/3167,
    art 2, Sch 1 paras 1–10 (amended by SI 2000/694; SI 2002/2469; SI 2004/696; SI 2005/1622;
    SI 2005/2078; and SI 2013/235); and see the Interpretation Act 1978 s 17(2)(a). The Scottish

Dental Practice Board was formerly called the Scottish Dental Estimates Board and is constituted under regulations made under the National Health Service (Scotland) Act 1978 s 4.

853. Employers with whom employment may constitute relevant health service. The employers with whom employment may constitute relevant health service[1] are any specified National Health Service employers[2], whether or not in existence at the time of the relevant event[3].

1 As to the meaning of 'relevant health service' see PARA 855 note 4.
2 Ie any employer described in the Redundancy Payments (National Health Service) (Modification) Order 1993, SI 1993/3167, art 2, Sch 1: see PARA 852.
3 Redundancy Payments (National Health Service) (Modification) Order 1993, SI 1993/3167, art 3, Sch 2, Appendix. As to the meaning of 'relevant event' see PARA 851 note 2.

(iii) Excluded Classes of Employment

854. In general. The following classes of employees are excluded from the statutory right to claim redundancy payments[1]:

(1) the master or members of the crew of a fishing vessel where the employee is remunerated only by a share in the profits or gross earnings of the vessel[2];

(2) any person in respect of:
   (a) any employment which is employment in a public office[3] or treated[4] for the purposes of pensions and other superannuation benefits as service in the civil service of the state[5];
   (b) his employment in any capacity under the government of an overseas territory[6].

1 Ie the right under the Employment Rights Act 1996 s 135: see PARA 836.
2 See the Employment Rights Act 1996 s 199(2); and PARA 167.
3 Ie for the purposes of the Superannuation Act 1965 s 39.
4 Ie whether by virtue of the Superannuation Act 1965 or otherwise.
5 Employment Rights Act 1996 s 159. Sections 159, 160 (see head (2)(b) in the text) are without prejudice to any exemptions or immunity of the Crown: s 191(6).
6 Employment Rights Act 1996 s 160(1). See also note 5. For these purposes, references to an overseas territory are references to any territory or country outside the United Kingdom (s 160(3)); and the reference to the government of an overseas territory includes a reference to a government constituted for two or more overseas territories and any authority established for the purpose of providing or administering services which are common to, or relate to matters of common interest to, two or more overseas territories (s 160(2)). As to the meaning of 'United Kingdom' see PARA 2 note 12.

855. Qualifying period of employment. An employee[1] does not have any right to a redundancy payment[2] unless he has been continuously employed[3] for a period of not less than two years ending with the relevant date[4].

1 As to the meaning of 'employee' see PARA 2.
2 As to the meaning of 'redundancy payment' see PARA 836.
3 As to continuity of employment see PARAS 130 et seq, 861–863.
4 Employment Rights Act 1996 s 155. As to the meaning of 'relevant date' see PARA 871. In relation to any person to whom the Redundancy Payments (Continuity of Employment in Local Government, etc) (Modification) Order 1999, SI 1999/2277 (see PARA 839 et seq) applies, the Employment Rights Act 1996 s 155 has effect as if: (1) for the words 'continuously employed' there were substituted the words 'employed in relevant service'; (2) the provisions of s 155 modified as provided in head (1) above were renumbered as s 155(1); and (3) there were added s 155(2), (3), providing that for the purposes of s 155(1), 'relevant service' means: (a) continuous employment by an employer specified in the Redundancy Payments (Continuity of Employment in Local Government, etc) (Modification) Order 1999, SI 1999/2277, Sch 2 Pt II; or (b) where immediately before the relevant event a person has been successively employed by two or more employers specified in Sch 2 Pt II, such aggregate period of service with such

employers as would be continuous employment if they were a single employer, and for these purposes 'relevant event' has the same meaning as in the Redundancy Payments (Continuity of Employment in Local Government, etc) (Modification) Order 1999, SI 1999/2277 (see PARA 839 note 2): arts 1(2)(i), 3, Sch 2 Pt I para 2.

In relation to any person to whom the Redundancy Payments (National Health Service) (Modification) Order 1993, SI 1993/3167 (see PARAS 851–853) applies, the Employment Rights Act 1996 s 155 has effect as if for the words 'has been continuously employed' there were substituted the words 'has been employed in relevant health service for the requisite period': Redundancy Payments (National Health Service) (Modification) Order 1993, SI 1993/3167, art 3, Sch 2 para 1(a); and see the Employment Rights Act 1996 s 241, Sch 2 para 2(1). For these purposes, 'relevant health service' means:

   (i)   continuous employment by an employer referred to in the Redundancy Payments (National Health Service) (Modification) Order 1993, SI 1993/3167, Sch 2, Appendix (see PARA 853); or

   (ii)   where immediately before the relevant event a person has been successively employed by two or more employers referred to in Sch 2, Appendix, such aggregate period of service with such employers as would be continuous employment if they were a single employer,

and 'relevant event' means any event occurring on or after 13 January 1994 on the happening of which an employee may become entitled to a redundancy payment in accordance with the Employment Rights Act 1996: Redundancy Payments (National Health Service) (Modification) Order 1993, SI 1993/3167, Sch 2 para 1(b); and see the Employment Rights Act 1996 Sch 2 para 2(1).

856. Domestic servants. A person does not have any right to a redundancy payment[1] in respect of employment[2] as a domestic servant in a private household, where the employer[3] is the parent or step-parent, grandparent, child or stepchild, grandchild or brother or sister, or half-brother or half-sister, of the employee[4].

Apart from this restriction[5], the statutory provisions relating to redundancy payments[6] apply to an employee who is employed as a domestic servant in a private household as if the household were a business[7] and the maintenance of the household were the carrying on of that business by the employer[8].

1   As to the meaning of 'redundancy payment' see PARA 836.
2   As to the meaning of 'employment' see PARA 2.
3   As to the meaning of 'employer' see PARA 2.
4   Employment Rights Act 1996 s 161(1). As to the meaning of 'employee' see PARA 2.
5   Ie subject to the Employment Rights Act 1996 s 161(1).
6   Ie the Employment Rights Act 1996 Pt XI (ss 135–181).
7   As to the meaning of 'business' see PARA 135 note 4.

8   Employment Rights Act 1996 s 161(2). For the purposes of the application, in accordance with s 161(2), of any provisions of Pt XI in relation to an employee who was employed as a domestic servant in a private household, references to a personal representative in s 175 (see PARA 876 note 8) and s 218(4), (5) (see PARA 135) include a person to whom, otherwise than in pursuance of a sale or other disposition for valuable consideration, the management of the household has passed in consequence of the death of the employer: s 174(6). In Pt XI, references to a personal representative include a person appointed under s 206(4) (see PARA 1456): s 206(5).

857. Exemption orders. Where there is in force an agreement between one or more employers[1] or organisations of employers and one or more trade unions[2] representing employees[3], under which employees to whom the agreement applies have a right in certain circumstances to payments on the termination of their contracts of employment[4], the Secretary of State[5] may, on the application of all the parties to the agreement, if he is satisfied, having regard to the provisions of the agreement, that the employees to whom the agreement applies should not have any right to a redundancy payment[6], make an order in respect of that agreement[7].

The Secretary of State is not, however, to make such an order in respect of an agreement unless the agreement indicates, in whatever terms, the willingness of the parties to it to submit to an employment tribunal[8] any question arising under the agreement as to the right of an employee to a payment on the termination of his employment or the amount of such a payment[9].

Where such an order is in force in respect of an agreement, an employee who, immediately before the relevant date[10], is an employee to whom the agreement applies does not have any right to a redundancy payment[11].

An order revoking an earlier order under these provisions may be made in pursuance of an application by all or any of the parties to the agreement in question or in the absence of any such application[12].

1   As to the meaning of 'employer' see PARA 2.
2   As to the meaning of 'trade union' see PARA 150 note 9.
3   As to the meaning of 'employee' see PARA 2.
4   As to the meaning of 'contract of employment' see PARA 2.
5   As to the Secretary of State see PARA 5 note 21.
6   As to the meaning of 'redundancy payment' see PARA 836.
7   Employment Rights Act 1996 s 157(2), (3). At the date at which this volume states the law no such orders had been made but, by virtue of s 241, Sch 2 para 2(1) (see PARA 162), the following orders have effect as if so made: the Redundancy Payments (Exemption) (No 1) Order 1969, SI 1969/207 (employees of the member companies of the Centrax Group); the Redundancy Payments (Exemption) (No 1) Order 1970, SI 1970/354 (amended by SI 1990/526) (employees of the Electricity Council, the North of Scotland Hydro-Electric Board, the South of Scotland Electricity Board, the Central Electricity Generating Board and Area Electricity Boards); and the Redundancy Payments (Exemption) Order 1980, SI 1980/1052 (employees of certain schools in Lancashire). As to the making of orders under the Employment Rights Act 1996 generally see PARA 162.
    The statutory restrictions on contracting out do not apply to any provision in an agreement if an order under the Employment Rights Act 1996 s 157 is for the time being in force in respect of it (see s 203(2)(c); and PARA 150) but may not otherwise be excluded by agreement (*Godridge v Yorkshire Imperial Metals Ltd* (1967) 3 ITR 30).
8   As to employment tribunals see PARAS 1399 et seq, 1453 et seq.
9   Employment Rights Act 1996 s 157(4) (amended by the Employment Rights (Dispute Resolution) Act 1998 s 1(2)(a)).
10 As to the meaning of 'relevant date' see PARA 871.
11 Employment Rights Act 1996 s 157(1).
12 Employment Rights Act 1996 s 157(5).

858. Exclusion or reduction of redundancy payments on account of pension rights. An employer[1] of a pensioned employee[2] may, by notice in writing[3] to that employee, claim:

(1)   to exclude the right of the employee to the redundancy payment to which he would otherwise be entitled; or

(2)   to reduce the amount thereof,

in accordance with or to the permitted extent[4]; and in such a case the employee is not entitled to a redundancy payment or, as the case may be, is entitled only to the reduced amount thereof[5].

These provisions are, however, without prejudice to the right of an employee to apply to a tribunal[6] to determine any question as to his right to a redundancy payment or as to the amount of such payment[7].

1   For these purposes, 'employer' has the meaning assigned to it in the Employment Rights Act 1996 s 230(4) (see PARA 2) and includes any person in respect of whom that Act has effect as if he were an employer within the meaning of s 230(4): Redundancy Payments Pensions Regulations 1965, SI 1965/1932, reg 2(2); and see the Employment Rights Act 1996 s 241, Sch 2 para 2(1).

In the case of any employee whose remuneration is, by virtue of any statutory provision, payable to him by a person other than his employer, then, for the purposes of the operation, in relation to any such employee, of the provisions specified in the Redundancy Payments Pensions Regulations 1965, SI 1965/1932, reg 6(2), Sch 2, any reference to the employer which is specified in Sch 2 is to be construed as a reference to the person responsible for paying the remuneration: reg 6(1), (2). The provisions so specified include: reg 4(1) (first reference to 'employer') (see note 2); and reg 5(1) (reference to 'employer') (see the text and notes 2–5): Sch 2. 'Employee' has the meaning assigned to it in the Employment Rights Act 1996 s 230(1) (see PARA 2) and includes any person in respect of whom that Act has effect as if he were an employee within the meaning of s 230(1): Redundancy Payments Pensions Regulations 1965, SI 1965/1932, reg 2(2); Employment Rights Act 1996 s 241, Sch 2 para 2(1).

2   For these purposes, 'pensioned employee' means an employee who is entitled, or would otherwise be entitled, to a redundancy payment from an employer and has a right or claim to a pension for himself which: (1) is to be paid by reference to the employee's last period of continuous employment with that employer; (2) if it is a lump sum, is to be paid, or, if it is a periodical payment, is to begin to accrue, at the time when the employee leaves the employment with that employer or within 90 weeks thereafter; and (3) in so far as it consists of periodical payments, satisfies the prescribed conditions: Redundancy Payments Pensions Regulations 1965, SI 1965/1932, regs 2(2), 4(1). 'Week' means a week ending with Saturday: reg 2(2). As to the meaning of 'period of continuous employment with that employer' in head (1) above see *Royal Ordnance plc v Pilkington* [1988] ICR 606, [1988] IRLR 466, EAT; revsd on another point [1989] ICR 737, [1989] IRLR 489, CA. References, in relation to a lump sum, to 'to be paid' or, in relation to periodical payments, to 'to begin to accrue' in head (2) above do not include payments which had accrued or been enjoyed prior to the termination of employment: *Royal Ordnance plc v Pilkington* [1989] ICR 737, [1989] IRLR 489, CA (disapproving *British Telecommunications plc v Burwell* [1986] ICR 35, EAT).

The conditions prescribed for the purposes of head (3) above are that the Secretary of State is satisfied that the pension is payable for life and is not capable of being terminated or suspended except for: (a) the operation of any provision for the termination or suspension of the pension: (i) on the commutation thereof; (ii) on assignment, charge or other alienation, whether by operation of law or otherwise, or any attempt thereat; or (iii) in case of mental disorder or inability to act, if there is provision enabling the pension in either of these circumstances to be paid or applied at discretion for the maintenance or support of the pensioner's spouse or of other persons dependent on him; (b) the operation of any provision for the suspension of the pension during imprisonment or detention in legal custody or on resumption of employment with the employer or of any other provision for the suspension of the pension during employment, being a provision contained in or made under any of the enactments specified in the National Insurance Act 1965 s 62(6), Sch 5 (repealed) or in s 62(6) (repealed), which relate to certain statutory superannuation schemes, or a provision of the Superannuation Acts 1934–1950 (repealed), and any Act amending those Acts, as applied by any enactment or other instrument having the force of law or by any instrument referred to in the Redundancy Payments Pensions Regulations 1965, SI 1965/1932, reg 3(1)(d) or (e) (see PARA 859 heads (4), (5)); (c) the operation of the Forfeiture Act 1870 s 2 (see CRIMINAL PROCEDURE vol 27 (2010) PARA 64): Redundancy Payments Pensions Regulations 1965, SI 1965/1932, reg 4(2). As to the meaning of 'pension' see PARA 859. As to the Secretary of State see PARA 5 note 21.

3   As to the meaning of 'writing' see PARA 2 note 8. Such a notice must contain a written statement explaining how the right of the pensioned employee to the redundancy payment has been excluded or, as the case may be, how the amount of the redundancy payment has been reduced by reason of the pension and specifying the amount of any redundancy payment so reduced: Redundancy Payments Pensions Regulations 1965, SI 1965/1932, reg 5(2). The notice must be served within a reasonable time: *Stowe-Woodward BTR Ltd v Beynon* [1978] ICR 609, EAT; *British Telecommunications plc v Burwell* [1986] ICR 35, EAT (no requirement that employers must serve notice by the effective date of termination).

4   Ie in accordance with, or to the extent permitted by, the Redundancy Payments Pensions Regulations 1965, SI 1965/1932, reg 5(1), Sch 1: see PARA 860.

5   Redundancy Payments Pensions Regulations 1965, SI 1965/1932, reg 5(1). See note 1.

6   For these purposes, 'tribunal' means a tribunal established under the Employment Tribunals Act 1996 s 1 (see PARA 1399): Redundancy Payments Pensions Regulations 1965, SI 1965/1932, reg 2(2); and see the Employment Rights Act 1996 Sch 2 para 2(1).

7   Redundancy Payments Pensions Regulations 1965, SI 1965/1932, reg 5(3).

859.   Meaning of 'pension'. 'Pension' means[1] a periodical payment or lump sum by way of pension, gratuity or superannuation allowance as respects which the Secretary of State[2] is satisfied that it is to be paid in accordance with any scheme or arrangement having for its object or one of its objects to make provision in respect of persons serving in particular employments for providing them with retirement benefits and, except in the case of such a lump sum which had been paid to the employee[3], that:

(1)   the scheme or arrangement is established by Act of Parliament or other instrument having the force of law; or

(2)   the benefits under the scheme or arrangement are secured by an irrevocable trust which is subject to the laws of any part of Great Britain[4]; or

(3)   the benefits under the scheme or arrangement are secured by a contract of assurance or an annuity contract which is made with:

    (a)   an insurance company to which the Financial Services and Markets Act 2000[5] applies; or

    (b)   a registered friendly society[6]; or

    (c)   an industrial and provident society registered under the Industrial and Provident Societies Act 1965[7]; or

(4)   the benefits under the scheme or arrangement are secured by any regulation or other instrument, not being a regulation or instrument having the force of law, made with the authority of a Minister of the Crown or with the consent of the Treasury for the purpose of authorising the payment to persons not employed in the civil service of the state of such pensions, gratuities or other like benefits as might have been granted to persons so employed; or

(5)   the scheme or arrangement is established by an enactment or other instrument having the force of law in any part of the Commonwealth outside the United Kingdom[8],

and that the provision made to enable benefits to be paid, taking into account any additional resources which could and would be provided by the employer[9], or any person connected with the employer, to meet any deficiency, is adequate to ensure payment in full of such benefits[10]. 'Pension' includes any part of a pension[11], but does not include:

(i)   a payment to an employee which consists solely of a return of his own contributions, with or without interest;

(ii)   that part of a payment to an employee which is attributable solely to additional voluntary contributions by that employee made in accordance with the scheme or arrangement;

(iii)   a periodical payment or lump sum, in so far as that payment or lump sum represents compensation under statutory compensation schemes[12] and is payable under a statutory provision, whether made or passed before, on or after 31 July 1978[13].

If in any case the Secretary of State is satisfied that benefits under the scheme or arrangement are wholly or mainly provided for the benefit of persons not resident in Great Britain, he may, if he thinks fit and subject to such conditions, if any, as he thinks proper, waive the requirement contained in head (2) above in respect of a scheme or arrangement the benefits under which are secured by an irrevocable trust or the requirements of heads (3)(a), (3)(b) or (3)(c) above in the case of a scheme or arrangement the benefits under which are secured by a contract of assurance or an annuity contract[14].

1 Ie for the purposes of the Redundancy Payments Pensions Regulations 1965, SI 1965/1932: see PARAS 858, 860.
2 As to the Secretary of State see PARA 5 note 21.
3 In the case of any employee whose remuneration is, by virtue of any statutory provision, payable to him by a person other than his employer, then, for the purposes of the operation, in relation to any such employee, of the provisions specified in the Redundancy Payments Pensions Regulations 1965, SI 1965/1932, reg 6(2), Sch 2, any reference to the employer which is specified in Sch 2 is to be construed as a reference to the person responsible for paying the remuneration: reg 6(1), (2). The provisions so specified include: reg 3(1) (references to 'employer'): Sch 2. 'Employee' has the meaning assigned to it in the Employment Rights Act 1996 s 230(1) (see PARA 2) and includes any person in respect of whom that Act has effect as if he were an employee within the meaning of s 230(1): Redundancy Payments Pensions Regulations 1965, SI 1965/1932, reg 2(2); Employment Rights Act 1996 s 241, Sch 2 para 2(1).
4 As to the meaning of 'Great Britain' see PARA 2 note 12.
5 As to insurance companies to which the Financial Services and Markets Act 2000 applies see FINANCIAL SERVICES AND INSTITUTIONS vol 48 (2008) PARA 348 et seq.
6 As to registered friendly societies see FINANCIAL SERVICES AND INSTITUTIONS vol 50 (2008) PARA 2081 et seq.
7 As to industrial and provident societies see FINANCIAL SERVICES AND INSTITUTIONS vol 50 (2008) PARA 2394 et seq.
8 As to the meaning of 'United Kingdom' see PARA 2 note 12.
9 As to the meaning of 'employer' see PARA 858 note 1.
10 Redundancy Payments Pensions Regulations 1965, SI 1965/1932, regs 2(2), 3(1); and see the Employment Rights Act 1996 s 241, Sch 2 para 2(1).
11 Redundancy Payments Pensions Regulations 1965, SI 1965/1932, reg 2(2).
12 Ie such compensation as is mentioned in the Employment Rights Act 1996 s 178(2): see PARA 883.
13 Redundancy Payments Pensions Regulations 1965, SI 1965/1932, regs 2(2), 3(3); and see the Employment Rights Act 1996 Sch 2 para 2(1).
14 Redundancy Payments Pensions Regulations 1965, SI 1965/1932, regs 2(2), 3(2).

860. Extent of exclusion of pensioned employees. An employer[1] of a pensioned employee[2] may exclude the right of that employee to the redundancy payment to which he would otherwise be entitled[3] by reason of his employment with the employer if the pension[4] to which he has a right or claim by reference to that employment amounts in the annual value[5] thereof to at least one-third of the employee's annual pay[6] and is one as respects which:

(1) in so far as it consists of periodical payments, the employee has a right or claim for the payments to begin to accrue; and

(2) in so far as it consists of a lump sum, the employee has a right or claim for it to be paid,

immediately the employee ceases to be employed by the employer[7].

An employer[8] of a pensioned employee may reduce by an amount, not exceeding the appropriate proportion[9], the amount of the redundancy payment to which that employee would otherwise be entitled by reason of his employment with the employer if the pension to which he has a right or claim by reference to that employment is one as respects which:

(a) in so far as it consists of periodical payments, the employee has a right or claim for the payments to begin to accrue; and

(b) in so far as it consists of a lump sum, the employee has a right or claim for it to be paid,

immediately the employee ceases to be employed by the employer[10].

In a case in which the provisions described above do not apply but in which a pensioned employee has a right or claim to a pension as respects which:

(i) in so far as it consists of periodical payments, the employee has a right or claim for the payments to begin to accrue; and

(ii)   in so far as it consists of a lump sum, the employee has a right or claim for it to be paid,

at some time, not exceeding 90 weeks[11], later than the time when the pensioned employee ceases to be employed by him, an employer[12] of that employee may reduce the amount of the redundancy payment by an amount not exceeding the appropriate proportion[13].

1   In the case of any employee whose remuneration is, by virtue of any statutory provision, payable to him by a person other than his employer, then, for the purposes of the operation, in relation to any such employee, of the provisions specified in the Redundancy Payments Pensions Regulations 1965, SI 1965/1932, reg 6(2), Sch 2, any reference to the employer which is specified in Sch 2 is to be construed as a reference to the person responsible for paying the remuneration: reg 6(1), (2). The provisions so specified include: Sch 1 para 1(1) (first reference to 'employer'); Sch 1 para 1(2) (first reference to 'employer') (see note 8); and Sch 1 para 2 (first reference to 'employer') (see note 12): Sch 2. 'Employee' has the meaning assigned to it in the Employment Rights Act 1996 s 230(1) (see PARA 2) and includes any person in respect of whom that Act has effect as if he were an employee within the meaning of s 230(1): Redundancy Payments Pensions Regulations 1965, SI 1965/1932, reg 2(2); Employment Rights Act 1996 s 241, Sch 2 para 2(1).

2   As to the meaning of 'pensioned employee' see PARA 858 note 2.

3   Ie under the Employment Rights Act 1996 s 135: see PARA 836.

4   As to the meaning of 'pension' see PARA 859.

5   For these purposes, 'annual value of the pension' means: (1) in the case of a pension to which the employee has a right or claim which consists of periodical payments: (a) where the pension is payable at intervals of seven days, the amount of the first payment multiplied by 52, any fraction of a pound in the product being disregarded if the pension consists wholly of periodical payments; (b) where the pension is payable at other than intervals of seven days, the amount which would accrue during the 12 calendar months beginning with the day on which the pension begins to accrue and assuming that the value of the pension does not change, any fraction of a pound being disregarded if the pension consists wholly of periodical payments; (2) in the case of a pension to which the employee has a right or claim which consists of a lump sum, one-tenth of the amount of such lump sum, any fraction of a pound being disregarded if the pension consists wholly of a lump sum; (3) in the case of a pension to which the employee has a right or claim which consists partly of periodical payments and partly of a lump sum, the total annual value ascertained in accordance with heads (1) and (2) above, any fraction of a pound in that total being disregarded: Redundancy Payments Pensions Regulations 1965, SI 1965/1932, reg 5(1), Sch 1 para 3.

6   For these purposes, 'annual pay' means the amount of a week's pay of the employee, calculated in accordance with the Employment Rights Act 1996 ss 225–227 (see PARAS 146, 147), multiplied by 52, any fraction of a pound in the product being disregarded: Redundancy Payments Pensions Regulations 1965, SI 1965/1932, Sch 1 para 3; and see the Employment Rights Act 1996 s 241, Sch 2 para 2(1).

7   Redundancy Payments Pensions Regulations 1965, SI 1965/1932, Sch 1 para 1(1); and see the Employment Rights Act 1996 Sch 2 para 2(1).

8   See note 1.

9   For these purposes, 'appropriate proportion' means the proportion which the annual value of the pension to the employee bears to one-third of that employee's annual pay: Redundancy Payments Pensions Regulations 1965, SI 1965/1932, Sch 1 para 3.

10 Redundancy Payments Pensions Regulations 1965, SI 1965/1932, Sch 1 para 1(2).

11 As to the meaning of 'week' for these purposes see PARA 858 note 2.

12 See note 1.

13 Redundancy Payments Pensions Regulations 1965, SI 1965/1932, Sch 1 para 2. To the reduced payment so ascertained there must be added the weekly value of the pension for each week that is to elapse between the cessation of the pensioned employee's employment with the employer and the time when the pensioned employee has a right or claim for the pension to begin to accrue or, as the case may be, to be paid; but the total payment due to the pensioned employee under Sch 1 para 2 is not to exceed the amount of the redundancy payment to which he would otherwise be entitled: Sch 1 para 2 proviso. For these purposes, 'weekly value of the pension' means the amount, not exceeding one-third of one week's pay of the employee, calculated in accordance with the Employment Rights Act 1996 ss 225–227 (see PARAS 146, 147) obtained by

dividing the annual value of the pension by 52: Redundancy Payments Pensions Regulations 1965, SI 1965/1932, Sch 1 para 3; and see the Employment Rights Act 1996 Sch 2 para 2(1).

(2) CONTINUITY OF EMPLOYMENT

861. In general. Unless the contrary is shown, a person's employment[1] during any period is presumed to have been continuous[2].

Where an employee[3] is regarded[4] as not having been dismissed by reason of a renewal[5] or re-engagement taking effect after an interval, then, in ascertaining[6] the period for which the employee has been continuously employed, the period of that interval counts as a period of employment, except so far as it is to be[7] disregarded[8].

Where the notice required to be given by an employer to terminate a contract of employment[9] would, if duly given when notice of termination was given by the employer, or, where no notice was given, when the contract of employment was terminated by the employer, expire on a date later than the relevant date[10], then, in ascertaining[11] the period for which the employee has been continuously employed, the period of the interval between those two dates counts as a period of employment, except in so far as it is to be[12] disregarded[13].

1 As to the meaning of 'employment' see PARA 2.
2 Employment Rights Act 1996 s 210(5). As to the computation of periods of continuous employment see also PARAS 130 et seq, 862, 863.
   The statutory presumption of continuity applies only in respect of the dismissing employer; and a tribunal which takes continuity into account with successive employers, in the absence of any statutory provision permitting it to do so, is acting outside its jurisdiction: *Secretary of State for Employment v Globe Elastic Thread Co Ltd* [1980] AC 506, [1979] ICR 706, HL (overruling *Evenden v Guildford City Association Football Club* [1975] QB 917, [1975] ICR 367, CA).
3 As to the meaning of 'employee' see PARA 2; and as to excluded classes of employment see PARA 854 et seq.
4 Ie by virtue of the Employment Rights Act 1996 s 138(1) (see PARA 865) and for the purposes of Pt XI (ss 135–181) (see PARAS 836 et seq, 864 et seq).
5 As to the meaning of 'renewal' see PARA 755 note 6.
6 Ie for the purposes of the Employment Rights Act 1996 s 155 (see PARA 855) or s 162(1) (see PARA 881).
7 Ie under the Employment Rights Act 1996 s 214 (see PARA 862) or s 215 (see PARA 863).
8 Employment Rights Act 1996 s 213(2).
9 Ie under the Employment Rights Act 1996 s 86: see PARAS 735, 736.
10 Ie where a date later than that which would be the relevant date under the Employment Rights Act 1996 s 145(2)–(4) is to be treated as the relevant date, by virtue of s 145(5): see PARA 871.
11 See note 6.
12 See note 7.
13 Employment Rights Act 1996 s 213(3).

862. Payment of previous redundancy payment. Where a period of continuous employment has to be determined for the purposes of the application of the provisions relating to the qualifying period of employment[1] for the right to a redundancy payment or the provisions relating to calculating the amount of a redundancy payment[2], the continuity of that period of employment is broken[3] where:

(1) a redundancy payment has previously been paid[4] to the employee, whether in respect of dismissal[5] or in respect of lay-off or short time[6]; and

(2) the contract of employment under which the employee was employed

was renewed[7], whether by the same or another employer, or the employee was re-engaged under a new contract of employment, whether by the same or another employer[8].

The continuity of a period of employment is also broken for these purposes where:

(a) a payment has been made to the employee, whether in respect of the termination of his employment or lay-off or short time, in accordance with a scheme under the Superannuation Act 1972[9] or arrangements in relation to equivalent payments[10]; and

(b) he commenced new, or renewed, employment[11].

The provisions described above do not apply where:

(i) in consequence of any specified action[12] a dismissed employee is reinstated or re-employed by his employer or by a successor[13] or associated employer[14] of the employer;

(ii) the terms on which he is so reinstated or re-engaged include provision for him to repay the amount of a redundancy payment or an equivalent payment paid[15] in respect of the relevant dismissal; and

(iii) that provision is complied with[16].

1 Ie under the Employment Rights Act 1996 s 155: see PARA 855.

2 Ie under the Employment Rights Act 1996 s 162(1): see PARA 881.

3 For these purposes, the date on which a person's continuity of employment is so broken: (1) if the employment was under a contract of employment, is the date which was the relevant date in relation to the payment mentioned in the Employment Rights Act 1996 s 214(2)(a) (see head (1) in the text) or s 214(3)(a) (see head (a) in the text); and (2) if the employment was otherwise than under a contract of employment, is the date which would have been the relevant date in relation to the payment mentioned in s 214(2)(a) or s 214(3)(a), had the employment been under a contract of employment: s 214(4). As to the meaning of 'contract of employment' see PARA 2.

4 For these purposes, a redundancy payment is to be treated as having been paid if: (1) the whole of the payment has been paid to the employee by the employer; (2) a tribunal has determined liability and found that the employer must pay part, but not all, of the redundancy payment and the employer has paid that part; or (3) the Secretary of State has paid a sum to the employee in respect of the redundancy payment under the Employment Rights Act 1996 s 167 (see PARA 884): s 214(5). For the purposes of the operation of the provisions of Pt XI (ss 135–181) and Pt XIV Ch I (ss 210–219) (continuous employment) (see PARAS 130 et seq, 861, 863) in relation to any employee whose remuneration is, by virtue of any statutory provision, payable to him by a person other than his employer, references to the employer in s 214(5) (any reference) must be construed as references to the person by whom the remuneration is payable: see s 173(1), (2). As to the meaning of 'statutory provision' see PARA 163 note 2. As to the meaning of 'employee' see PARA 2. As to employment tribunals see PARAS 1399 et seq, 1453 et seq. As to the Secretary of State see PARA 5 note 21.

Thus continuity is not broken if the payment has not actually been made (*Richards v S & HE Fielding Ltd (in liquidation)* (1966) 1 ITR 376) or if the payment is not made under the statutory scheme (*Rowan v Machinery Installations (South Wales) Ltd* [1981] ICR 386, [1981] IRLR 122, EAT; *Ross v Delrosa Caterers Ltd* [1981] ICR 393, EAT). Where, however, a redundancy payment was made on an assumption that the Transfer of Undertakings (Protection of Employment) Regulations 1981, SI 1981/1794 (now the Transfer of Undertakings (Protection of Employment) Regulations 2006, SI 2006/246) (see PARA 136 et seq) did not apply, but that assumption was then invalidated by later case law, it was held that the payment (ie under the Employment Rights Act 1996 s 214(5)(c): see head (3) above) remained valid for these purposes and so continuity was broken under s 214(2)(a) (see head (1) in the text): *Secretary of State for Trade and Industry v Lassman* [2000] ICR 1109, [2000] IRLR 411, CA.

5 As to the meaning of 'dismissal' see PARA 864.

6 As to the meanings of 'lay-off' and 'short time' see PARA 875. As to the special provisions relating to lay-off and short time see PARA 875 et seq.

7 As to the meaning of 'renewal' see PARA 755 note 6.

8 Employment Rights Act 1996 s 214(1), (2).

9 Ie under the Superannuation Act 1972 s 1: see CONSTITUTIONAL AND ADMINISTRATIVE LAW vol 20 (2014) PARA 218.

10 Ie under the Employment Rights Act 1996 s 177(3): see PARA 888 note 3. 'Equivalent payment'
    can only have this statutory meaning, which cannot be extended: *Rowan v Machinery
    Installations (South Wales) Ltd* [1981] ICR 386, [1981] IRLR 122, EAT.
11 Employment Rights Act 1996 s 214(3).
12 The action specified is any action taken in relation to the dismissal of an employee which
    consists of: (1) his making a claim in accordance with a dismissal procedures agreement
    designated by an order under the Employment Rights Act 1996 s 110 (see PARAS 759, 760); (2)
    the presentation by him of a relevant complaint of dismissal; (3) any action taken by a
    conciliation officer under the Employment Tribunals Act 1996 ss 18A–18C (see PARAS 152,
    153); (4) the making of a relevant settlement agreement (see PARA 151); (5) the making of an
    agreement to submit a dispute to arbitration in accordance with a scheme having effect by virtue
    of an order under the Trade Union and Labour Relations (Consolidation) Act 1992 s 212A (see
    PARA 824); (6) a decision taken arising out of the use of a statutory dispute resolution procedure
    contained in the Employment Act 2002 s 29, Sch 2 (repealed) in a case where, in accordance
    with the Employment Act 2002 (Dispute Resolution) Regulations 2004, SI 2004/752 (see PARA
    700), such a procedure applies (see also PARA 698); or (7) a decision taken arising out of the use
    of the statutory duty to consider procedure contained in the Employment Equality (Age)
    Regulations 2006, SI 2006/1031, Sch 6 (see DISCRIMINATION vol 33 (2013) PARA 1 et seq):
    Employment Protection (Continuity of Employment) Regulations 1996, SI 1996/3147, reg 2
    (amended by the Employment Rights (Dispute Resolution) Act 1998 s 1(2)(c); SI 2001/1188;
    SI 2004/752; SI 2006/1031; SI 2013/1856; SI 2014/386).
13 As to the meaning of 'successor' see PARA 133 note 10.
14 As to the meaning of 'associated employer' see PARA 3.
15 For these purposes, the cases in which a redundancy payment is to be treated as having been
    paid are the cases mentioned in the Employment Rights Act 1996 s 214(5) (see note 4):
    Employment Protection (Continuity of Employment) Regulations 1996, SI 1996/3147, reg 4(2).
16 Employment Protection (Continuity of Employment) Regulations 1996, SI 1996/3147, reg 4(1).

863.   Employment wholly or partly abroad.   A week[1] of employment[2] does
not count[3] if the employee:

(1)   was employed outside Great Britain[4] during the whole or part of that
      week; and

(2)   was not during that week an employed earner[5] in respect of whom a
      secondary Class 1 contribution was payable[6], whether or not the
      contribution was in fact paid[7].

Any question arising under these provisions whether a person was an
employed earner[8] and, if so, whether a secondary Class 1 contribution was
payable in respect of him, is to be determined by an officer of the Commissioners
for Revenue and Customs[9].

1 As to the meaning of 'week' for these purposes see PARA 130 note 3.
2 As to the meaning of 'employment' see PARA 2.
3 Ie in computing in relation to an employee the period specified in the Employment Rights
   Act 1996 s 155 (see PARAS 836, 855) or the period specified in s 162(1) (see PARA 881). As to the
   meaning of 'employee' see PARA 2.
4 As to the meaning of 'Great Britain' see PARA 2 note 12.
5 Ie under the Social Security Contributions and Benefits Act 1992: see s 2(1)(a), s 2(3); and
   WELFARE BENEFITS AND STATE PENSIONS vol 104 (2014) PARA 381.
6 Ie under the Social Security Contributions and Benefits Act 1992. As to secondary Class 1
   contributions see WELFARE BENEFITS AND STATE PENSIONS vol 104 (2014) PARA 385.
7 Employment Rights Act 1996 s 215(2). Section 215(2) does not, however, apply in relation to a
   person who is employed as a master or seaman in a British ship and is ordinarily resident in
   Great Britain: s 215(6). As to the meaning of 'British ship' see SHIPPING AND MARITIME LAW
   vol 93 (2008) PARA 230. As to ordinary residence see CONFLICT OF LAWS vol 19 (2011) PARA
   359; and see IMMIGRATION AND ASYLUM vol 57 (2012) PARA 140.
      Where, by virtue of s 215(2), a week of employment does not count in computing a period of
   employment, the continuity of that period is not broken by reason only that the week does not
   count in computing that period; and the number of days which, for the purposes of s 211(3) (see
   PARA 130), fall within the intervening period is seven for each week within this provision:
   s 215(3).

8 See note 5.
9 Employment Rights Act 1996 s 215(4) (amended by the Social Security Contributions (Transfer of Functions, etc) Act 1999 Sch 7 para 21(1), (2)). The Social Security Contributions (Transfer of Functions, etc) Act 1999 Pt II (ss 8–19) (decisions and appeals) (see WELFARE BENEFITS AND STATE PENSIONS vol 104 (2014) PARA 574) applies in relation to the determination of any issue by the Revenue and Customs under the Employment Rights Act 1996 s 215(4) as if it were a decision falling with the Social Security Contributions (Transfer of Functions, etc) Act 1999 s 8(1): Employment Rights Act 1996 s 215(5) (substituted by the Social Security Contributions (Transfer of Functions, etc) Act 1999 Sch 7 para 21(1), (3)). As to Her Majesty's Revenue and Customs see INCOME TAXATION vol 58 (2014) PARAS 33–34.

(3) MEANING OF 'DISMISSAL'

864. Dismissal by employer. An employee[1] is dismissed[2] by his employer[3] if, and only if:

(1) the contract under which he is employed by the employer is terminated by the employer, whether with notice or without notice[4];

(2) he is employed under a limited-term contract[5] and that contract terminates by virtue of the limiting event[6] without being renewed[7] under the same contract[8]; or

(3) the employee terminates the contract under which he is employed, with or without notice, in circumstances in which he is entitled to terminate it without notice by reason of the employer's conduct[9].

1 As to the meaning of 'employee' see PARA 2.
2 Ie subject to the provisions of the Employment Rights Act 1996 s 136 (see also PARA 866) and s 138 (see PARA 865) and for the purposes of Pt XI (ss 135–181) (see PARAS 836 et seq, 865 et seq).
3 As to the meaning of 'employer' see PARA 2.
4 Employment Rights Act 1996 ss 136(1)(a), 181(1). This applies where the employer dishonestly persuades the employee to resign: *Caledonian Mining Co Ltd v Bassett* [1987] ICR 425, [1987] IRLR 165, EAT.
   A notice of dismissal must specify a date or at least contain facts from which that date is ascertainable: *Morton Sundour Fabrics Ltd v Shaw* (1966) 2 ITR 84, DC; *Burton Group Ltd v Smith* [1977] IRLR 351, EAT; *Pritchard-Rhodes Ltd v Boon and Milton* [1979] IRLR 19, EAT; *International Computers Ltd v Kennedy* [1981] IRLR 28, EAT; *Doble v Firestone Tyre and Rubber Co Ltd* [1981] IRLR 300, EAT; *Griffiths v Buckinghamshire County Council, Arthur v Buckingham County Council* [1994] ICR 265. This does not, however, preclude a mutual agreement between an employer and his employee to postpone the date of expiry of a notice of dismissal for redundancy until the happening of a particular event: *Mowlem Northern Ltd v Watson* [1990] ICR 751, [1990] IRLR 500, EAT.
   The fact that the employee is willing and agrees to accept redundancy is not a ground for holding that he has not been dismissed: *Burton Allton & Johnson Ltd v Peck* [1975] ICR 193, [1975] IRLR 87; *Morley v CT Morley Ltd* [1985] ICR 499, EAT. Termination as a result of an agreement for voluntary retirement on agreed terms, however, has been held not to constitute a dismissal: *Birch v University of Liverpool* [1985] ICR 470, [1985] IRLR 165, CA; *Scott v Coalite Fuels and Chemicals Ltd* [1988] ICR 355, [1988] IRLR 131, EAT. However generally the fact that the redundancy was 'voluntary' does not prevent it being a 'dismissal': see *Optare Group Ltd v Transport and General Workers' Union* [2007] IRLR 931, [2007] All ER (D) 135 (Jul), EAT (a redundancy consultation case).
   Where there is a term in the employee's contract that it is subject to continuing external funding, the contract is terminable on the happening or non-happening of that future event: *Brown v Knowsley Borough Council* [1986] IRLR 102, EAT.
5 As to the meaning of 'limited-term contract' see PARA 755 note 5.
6 As to the meaning of 'limiting event' see PARA 755 note 5.
7 As to the meaning of 'renewal' see PARA 755 note 6.
8 Employment Rights Act 1996 s 136(1)(b) (substituted by SI 2002/2034); Employment Rights Act 1996 s 181(1).
9 Employment Rights Act 1996 ss 136(1)(c), 181(1). Section 136(1)(c) (see head (3) in the text) does not apply if the employee terminates the contract without notice in circumstances in which

he is entitled to do so by reason of a lockout by the employer: ss 136(2), 181(1). As to the meaning of 'lockout' see PARA 134 note 7. If the employer repudiates the contract and makes an offer of alternative employment, the employee has a common law right to a reasonable period in order to decide whether to treat himself as constructively dismissed or whether to take the alternative job: *Marriott v Oxford and District Co-operative Society Ltd (No 2)* [1970] 1 QB 186, [1969] 3 All ER 1126, CA; *Shields Furniture Ltd v Goff* [1973] 2 All ER 653, [1973] ICR 187, NIRC; *Sheet Metal Components Ltd v Plumridge* [1974] ICR 373, [1974] IRLR 86, NIRC. These common law rights apply irrespective of the statutory provisions relating to a trial period in the Employment Rights Act 1996 s 138 (see PARA 865): *East Suffolk Local Health Services NHS Trust v Palmer* [1997] ICR 425, EAT. However, an employee who resigns to get another job following an indefinite forecast of redundancy has no automatic entitlement to claim that his resignation was forced by the employer's conduct: *Devon County Council v Cook* [1977] IRLR 188, EAT. As to constructive dismissal in the context of unfair dismissal see PARA 763.

865. Renewal of contract or re-engagement. Where:

(1) an employee's[1] contract of employment[2] is renewed[3], or he is re-engaged[4] under a new contract of employment in pursuance of an offer[5], whether in writing[6] or not, made before the end of his employment under the previous contract; and

(2) the renewal or re-engagement takes effect either immediately on, or after an interval of not more than four weeks[7] after, the end of that employment,

the employee is not to be regarded[8] as having been dismissed[9] by his employer[10] by reason of the ending of his employment[11] under the previous contract[12].

These provisions do not apply if:

(a) the provisions of the contract as renewed, or of the new contract, as to:
    (i) the capacity and place in which the employee is employed; and
    (ii) the other terms and conditions of his employment,
    differ, wholly or in part, from the corresponding provisions of the previous contract; and

(b) during the trial period[13]:
    (i) the employee, for whatever reason, terminates the renewed or new contract, or gives notice to terminate it and it is in consequence terminated; or
    (ii) the employer, for a reason connected with or arising out of any difference between the renewed or new contract and the previous contract, terminates the renewed or new contract, or gives notice to terminate it and it is in consequence terminated[14].

Where there is such a termination during the trial period, then for the relevant purposes:

(A) the employee is to be regarded as dismissed on the date on which his employment under the previous contract (or, if there has been more than one trial period, the original contract) ended; and

(B) the reason for the dismissal is to be taken to be the reason for which the employee was then dismissed, or would have been dismissed had the offer (or original offer) of renewed or new employment not been made, or the reason which resulted in that offer being made[15].

1 As to the meaning of 'employee' see PARA 2.
2 As to the meaning of 'contract of employment' see PARA 2.
3 As to the meaning of 'renewal' see PARA 755 note 6.
4 For these purposes, references to re-engagement are references to re-engagement by the employer or by an associated employer: Employment Rights Act 1996 s 146(1)(a). This may include an associated employer who has no employees at the time of the offer of employment: *Lucas v Henry Johnson (Packers and Shippers) Ltd* [1986] ICR 384, EAT. As to the meaning of 'associated employer' see PARA 3. Where the contract of employment of an employee is taken for

the purposes of the Employment Rights Act 1996 Pt XI (ss 135–181) to be terminated by his employer by reason of the employer's death (see PARA 867), s 146(1) does not apply: s 174(5)(a).

In relation to any person to whom the Redundancy Payments (Continuity of Employment in Local Government, etc) (Modification) Order 1999, SI 1999/2277 (see PARA 839 et seq) applies, the Employment Rights Act 1996 s 146 has effect as if s 146(1A) were added, providing that the reference in s 146(1) to re-engagement by the employer is to include a reference to re-engagement by any employer specified in the Redundancy Payments (Continuity of Employment in Local Government, etc) (Modification) Order 1999, SI 1999/2277, Sch 2 Pt II and that the reference in the Employment Rights Act 1996 s 146(1) to an offer made by the employer is to include a reference to an offer made by any employer so specified: Redundancy Payments (Continuity of Employment in Local Government, etc) (Modification) Order 1999, SI 1999/2277, arts 1(2)(i), 3, Sch 2 Pt I para 1.

In relation to any person to whom the Redundancy Payments (National Health Service) (Modification) Order 1993, SI 1993/3167 (see PARAS 851–853) applies, the Employment Rights Act 1996 s 146(1)(a) has effect as if any reference to re-engagement by the employer were construed as including a reference to re-engagement by an employer referred to in the Redundancy Payments (National Health Service) (Modification) Order 1993, SI 1993/3167, reg 3, Sch 2, Appendix (see PARA 853): Sch 2 paras 2, 3; and see the Employment Rights Act 1996 s 241, Sch 2 para 2(1).

5   For these purposes, references to an offer are references to an offer made by the employer or an associated employer: Employment Rights Act 1996 s 146(1)(b). See also note 4. The onus is on the employer to show that such an offer was made: *Ubsdell v Paterson* [1973] 1 All ER 685, [1973] ICR 86, NIRC. See further PARA 874. See also *SI (Systems and Instrumentation) Ltd v Grist* [1983] ICR 788 at 798, sub nom *SI (Systems and Instruments) Ltd v Grist and Riley* [1983] IRLR 391 at 395, EAT, per Tudor Evans J (obiter) (a distinction is to be drawn between cases of renewal and of re-engagement; in the former, the offer is not required to be made before termination of the contract of employment); sed quaere. Cf the Employment Rights Act 1996 s 141; and PARA 874.

In relation to any person to whom the Redundancy Payments (National Health Service) (Modification) Order 1993, SI 1993/3167 applies, the Employment Rights Act 1996 s 146(1)(b) has effect as if any reference to an offer were construed as including an offer made by an employer referred to in the Redundancy Payments (National Health Service) (Modification) Order 1993, SI 1993/3167, reg 3, Sch 2, Appendix: Sch 2 paras 2, 3; and see the Employment Rights Act 1996 Sch 2 para 2(1).

6   As to the meaning of 'writing' see PARA 2 note 8.

7   As to the meaning of 'week' for these purposes see PARA 126 note 13.

8   Ie for the purposes of the Employment Rights Act 1996 Pt XI.

9   As to the meaning of 'dismissal' see PARA 864.

10 As to the meaning of 'employer' see PARA 2.

11 For the purposes of the application of the Employment Rights Act 1996 s 138(1) to a contract under which the employment ends on a Friday, Saturday or Sunday: (1) the renewal or re-engagement is to be treated as taking effect immediately on the ending of the employment under the previous contract if it takes effect on or before the next Monday after that Friday, Saturday or Sunday; and (2) the interval of four weeks referred to in s 138(1) must be calculated as if the employment had ended on that next Monday: s 146(2). Where the contract of employment of an employee is taken for the purposes of Pt XI to be terminated by his employer by reason of the employer's death (see PARA 867), s 146(2) applies as if head (1) above were omitted and in head (2) above for the word 'four' there were substituted the word 'eight': s 174(5)(b).

12 Employment Rights Act 1996 ss 138(1), 181(1). Where the contract of employment of an employee is taken for the purposes of Pt XI to be terminated by his employer by reason of the employer's death (see PARA 867), s 138(1) applies as if: (1) in s 138(1)(a) (see head (1) in the text), for the words 'in pursuance' onwards there were substituted 'by a personal representative of the deceased employer'; and (2) in s 138(1)(b) (see head (2) in the text), for the words 'either immediately' onwards there were substituted 'not later than eight weeks after the death of the deceased employer': s 174(1), (2)(a), (b). As to the meaning of references to a personal representative see PARA 856 note 8. In the absence of an express agreement, some indication is required that the deceased employer's personal representative and the employee have acted in such a way that they must be taken to have agreed to continue the employment: *Ranger v Brown* [1978] 2 All ER 726, [1978] ICR 603, EAT. The provisions of the Employment Rights Act 1996 s 138(1) only apply for the purposes of redundancy law; they do not apply for the purposes of unfair dismissal law and so an employee could accept an offer under s 138(1) (and not be considered dismissed for redundancy purposes) but still claim to have been unfairly

dismissed, eg because of the handling of the termination of the original contract: *Jones v Governing Body of Burdett Coutts School* [1999] ICR 38, [1998] IRLR 521, CA (approving on this point *Hempell v WH Smith & Sons Ltd* [1986] ICR 365, [1986] IRLR 95, EAT, rather than *Ebac Ltd v Wymer* [1995] ICR 466, EAT).

13 The 'trial period' is the period beginning at the end of the employee's employment under the previous contract and ending with the period of four weeks (ie four calendar weeks, not four working weeks: *Benton v Sanderson Kayser Ltd* [1989] ICR 136, [1989] IRLR 19, CA) beginning with the date on which the employee starts work under the renewed or new contract or such longer period as may be agreed for the purpose of retraining the employee for employment under that contract: Employment Rights Act 1996 ss 138(3), 181(1). For these purposes, a period of retraining is agreed only if the agreement: (1) is made between the employer and the employee or his representatives before the employee starts work under the contract as renewed, or the new contract; (2) is in writing; (3) specifies the date on which the period of retraining ends; and (4) specifies the terms and conditions of employment which will apply in the employee's case after the end of that period: ss 138(6), 181(1). Where the contract of employment of an employee is taken to be terminated by his employer by reason of the employer's death (see PARA 867), s 138(6) applies as if in s 138(6)(a) (see head (1) above) for the word 'employer' there were substituted 'personal representative of the deceased employer': s 174(1), (2)(c). A unilateral document signed by the employer only is not sufficient; the employee must do something to indicate his acceptance and the agreement must embody important matters such as remuneration, status and job description: *McKindley v William Hill (Scotland) Ltd* [1985] IRLR 492, EAT. Where there is an extension of the trial period, it must be for the purpose of retraining: *Meek v J Allen Rubber Co Ltd and Secretary of State for Employment* [1980] IRLR 21, EAT. Where the statutory four-week trial period applies, its requirements must be complied with and there is no room for reliance on any further 'common law trial period': *Optical Express Ltd v Williams* [2008] ICR 1, [2007] IRLR 936, EAT.

14 Employment Rights Act 1996 ss 138(2), 181(1). Section 138(2) does not apply if the employee's contract of employment is again renewed, or he is again re-engaged under a new contract of employment in circumstances such that s 138(1) (see the text and notes 1–12) applies again: s 138(5). Where a contract of employment of an employee is taken to be terminated by his employer by reason of the employer's death (see PARA 867), s 138(2) applies as if in s 138(2)(a) (see head (a) in the text) for the word 'employer' there were substituted 'personal representative of the deceased employer': s 174(1), (2)(c).

The existence of the trial period does not negate the employee's normal right to leave and claim constructive dismissal under s 136(1)(c) (see PARA 864) where the employer has repudiated the contract: *Air Canada v Lee* [1978] ICR 1202, [1978] IRLR 392, EAT; *Turvey v CW Cheney & Son Ltd* [1979] ICR 341, sub nom *Turvey v CW Cheyney & Son Ltd* [1979] IRLR 105, EAT; *East Suffolk Local Health Services NHS Trust v Palmer* [1997] ICR 425, EAT.

15 Employment Rights Act 1996 ss 138(4), 181(1). Where an employee's contract of employment has been renewed, or he has been re-engaged under a new contract, then, if during the trial period he gives notice to terminate the contract but dies before the notice expires, s 138(2) (see the text and notes 13, 14) applies as if the notice had expired, and the contract had been terminated by its expiry, on the date of the employee's death: s 176(4)(b).

866. Employee anticipating expiry of employer's notice. If:

(1) an employer[1] gives notice to an employee[2] to terminate his contract of employment[3]; and

(2) at a time within the obligatory period of notice[4], the employee gives notice in writing[5] to his employer to terminate the contract of employment on a date earlier than the date on which the employer's notice is due to expire ('counter-notice')[6],

the employee is to be taken[7] to be dismissed[8] by his employer[9].

An employee is not entitled to a redundancy payment[10] where:

(a) he is taken to be dismissed by virtue of heads (1) and (2) above[11];

(b) before the employee's notice is due to expire, the employer gives him notice[12] in writing:

(i)   requiring him to withdraw his notice terminating the contract of employment and to continue in employment until the date on which the employer's notice terminating the contract expires[13]; and

    (ii)   stating that, unless he does so, the employer[14] will contest any liability to pay to him a redundancy payment in respect of the termination of his contract of employment[15];

(c)   the employee does not comply with the requirements of that notice[16].

An employment tribunal[17] may determine that the employer[18] is liable to make an appropriate payment[19] to the employee if, on a reference to the tribunal, it appears to the tribunal, having regard to the reasons for which the employee seeks to leave the employment, and the reasons for which the employer requires him to continue in it, to be just and equitable[20].

1   As to the meaning of 'employer' see PARA 2. For the purposes of the operation of the provisions of the Employment Rights Act 1996 Pt XI (ss 135–181) and Pt XIV Ch I (ss 210–219) (continuous employment) (see PARAS 130 et seq, 861–863) in relation to any employee whose remuneration is, by virtue of any statutory provision, payable to him by a person other than his employer, references to the employer in s 142(2)(b) (any reference) (see head (ii) in the text; and note 14), and in s 142(3) (first reference: see note 18) must be construed as references to the person by whom the remuneration is payable: see s 173(1), (2). As to the meaning of 'statutory provision' see PARA 163 note 2.

2   As to the meaning of 'employee' see PARA 2; and as to excluded classes of employment see PARA 854 et seq.

3   Employment Rights Act 1996 s 136(3)(a). As to the meaning of 'contract of employment' see PARA 2.

4   For these purposes, the 'obligatory period of notice', in relation to notice given by an employer to terminate an employee's contract of employment, means: (1) the actual period of the notice in a case where the period beginning at the time when the notice is given and ending at the time when it expires is equal to the minimum period which, by virtue of any enactment or otherwise, is required to be given by the employer to terminate the contract of employment; and (2), in any other case, the period which is equal to the minimum period referred to in head (1) above and ends at the time when the notice expires: Employment Rights Act 1996 ss 136(4), 181(1). As to the right of an employee to a minimum period of notice see PARAS 735, 736.

    Where the employee's decision to leave is taken outside the obligatory period, he will still have been dismissed if his leaving before the expiry of the employer's notice is by mutual consent, being deemed to be an agreed variation of that notice: *McAlwane v Boughton Estates Ltd* [1973] 2 All ER 299, [1973] ICR 470, NIRC; *Tunnel Holdings Ltd v Woolf* [1976] ICR 387; *CPS Recruitment Ltd (t/a Blackwood Associates) v Bowen* [1982] IRLR 54, EAT.

5   As to the meaning of 'writing' see PARA 2 note 8.

6   Employment Rights Act 1996 s 136(3)(b).

7   Ie for the purposes of the Employment Rights Act 1996 Pt XI (ss 135–181).

8   As to the meaning of 'dismissal' see PARA 864.

9   Employment Rights Act 1996 ss 136(3), 181(1). As to the period of the employee's notice see *Ready Case Ltd v Jackson* [1981] IRLR 312, EAT (unfair dismissal case) (cited in PARA 762 note 14). Where, in the circumstances specified in the Employment Rights Act 1996 s 136(3)(a), (b) (see heads (1), (2) in the text), the employee dies before the notice given by him under s 136(3)(b) expires: (1) if he dies before his employer has given him a notice such as is specified in s 142(2) (see heads (b)(i), (b)(ii) in the text), then s 142(3), (4) (see the text and notes 17–20) applies as if the employer had given him such a notice and he had not complied with it; and (2) if he dies after his employer has given him such a notice, then s 142 applies as if the employee had not died but did not comply with the notice: s 176(5).

10   Ie subject to the Employment Rights Act 1996 s 142(3) (see the text and notes 17–20). As to the meaning of 'redundancy payment' see PARA 836.

11   Employment Rights Act 1996 s 142(1)(a).

12   Employment Rights Act 1996 s 142(1)(b).

13   Employment Rights Act 1996 s 142(2)(a). See also note 9.

14   As to the meaning of 'employer' for the purpose of head (ii) in the text see PARA 836 note 5.

15   Employment Rights Act 1996 s 142(2)(b). See also note 9.

16   Employment Rights Act 1996 s 142(1)(c).

17   As to employment tribunals see PARAS 1399 et seq, 1453 et seq.

18 As to the meaning of this reference to 'employer' see note 1.

19 For these purposes, 'appropriate payment' means: (1) the whole of the redundancy payment to which the employee would have been entitled apart from the Employment Rights Act 1996 s 142(1) (see heads (a)–(c) in the text); or (2) such part of that redundancy payment as the tribunal thinks fit: s 142(4). See also note 9.

20 Employment Rights Act 1996 s 142(3) (amended by the Employment Rights (Dispute Resolution) Act 1998 s 1(2)(a)). See also note 9.

867. Implied or constructive termination of contract. Where, in accordance with any enactment or rule of law:

(1) an act[1] on the part of an employer[2]; or

(2) an event[3] affecting an employer, including, in the case of an individual, his death[4],

operates to terminate a contract under which an employee[5] is employed by him, the act or event is to be taken[6] as a termination of the contract by the employer[7]. Where:

(a) the contract under which a person is employed is so treated as terminated by his employer by reason of an act or event; and

(b) the employee's contract of employment[8] is not renewed[9], and he is not re-engaged under a new contract of employment[10],

he is to be taken[11] to be dismissed[12] by reason of redundancy if the circumstances in which his contract is not renewed, and he is not re-engaged, are wholly or mainly attributable to either of the facts[13] by reference to which redundancy is defined[14].

1 As to the meaning of 'act' see PARA 614 note 3.

2 As to the meaning of 'employer' see PARA 2.

3 Whether an event is one which operates to terminate a contract of employment for this purpose is determined by the purpose of the event in question: *Barnes v Leavesley* [2001] ICR 38, EAT (Law Society's intervention into solicitors' practice for purpose of protecting clients not 'an event'). Although an event terminating the contract of employment might affect an employee as well as the employer, it must so affect the employer that, as a result of its effect on him, the contract was terminated: *British Airports Authority v Fenerty* [1976] ICR 361. See also *Rose v Dodd* [2005] EWCA Civ 957, [2006] 1 All ER 464, [2005] ICR 1776 (intervention by the Law Society in a legal practitioner's firm on suspicion of dishonesty was not considered, on the facts, an 'event affecting' the practitioner which terminated the employee's contract of employment by operation of law, and was not to be taken as a dismissal by the practitioner of the employee within the Employment Rights Act 1996 s 136(5)).

4 As to the death of the employer generally see PARA 889.

5 As to the meaning of 'employee' see PARA 2; and as to excluded classes of employment see PARA 854 et seq.

6 Ie for the purposes of the Employment Rights Act 1996 Pt XI (ss 135–181).

7 Employment Rights Act 1996 ss 136(5), 181(1). This did not apply to the opting out of a school from local authority control where the legislation specifically provided for continuance of contracts: *Pickwell v Lincolnshire County Council* [1993] ICR 87, EAT. As to the position where, by virtue of the Employment Rights Act 1996 s 136(5), the death of the employer is to be treated for the purposes of Pt XI as a termination by him of the contract of employment see PARA 865 note 12.

8 As to the meaning of 'contract of employment' see PARA 2.

9 As to the meaning of 'renewal' see PARA 755 note 6.

10 As to renewal and re-engagement see PARA 865.

11 Ie for the purposes of the Employment Rights Act 1996.

12 As to the meaning of 'dismissal' see PARA 864.

13 Ie either of the facts specified in the Employment Rights Act 1996 s 139(1)(a) (see PARA 870 head (1)) or in s 139(1)(b) (see PARA 870 head (2)). In its application to a case within s 139(4), s 139(1)(a)(i) (see PARA 870 head (1)(a)) has effect as if the reference therein to the employer

included a reference to any person to whom, in consequence of the act or event in question, power to dispose of the business has passed: s 139(5). As to the meaning of 'business' see PARA 135 note 4.

14 Employment Rights Act 1996 s 139(4).

868. Strike during currency of employer's notice to terminate contract; notice of extension. Where an employer[1] has given notice to an employee[2] to terminate his contract of employment[3] (a 'notice of termination') and, after the notice is given, the employee begins to take part in a strike[4] of employees of the employer, the employer may serve on him a notice in writing[5] (a 'notice of extension') which:

(1) requests the employee to agree to extend the contract of employment beyond the time of expiry[6] by an additional period comprising as many available days[7] as the number of working days lost by striking[8] (the 'proposed period of extension')[9];

(2) indicates the reasons for which the employer makes that request[10]; and

(3) states that unless either the employee complies with the request[11], or the employer is satisfied that, in consequence of sickness or injury or otherwise, he is unable to comply with it, or that, even though that he is able to comply with it, it is reasonable in the circumstances for him not to do so, the employer[12] will contest any liability to pay the employee a redundancy payment[13] in respect of the dismissal[14] effected by the notice of termination[15].

If an employee:

(a) complies with the request contained in the notice of extension; or

(b) does not comply with it, but attends at his proper or usual place of work and is ready and willing to work on one or more, but not all, of the available days within the proposed period of extension,

the notice of termination has effect, and is deemed at all material times to have had effect, as if the period specified in it had, in a case within head (a) above, been extended beyond the time of expiry by an additional period equal to the proposed period of extension or, in a case within head (b) above, been extended beyond the time of expiry up to the end of the day or, if more than one, the last of the days, on which he attends at his proper or usual place of work and is ready and willing to work[16].

If an employee does not comply with the request contained in the notice of extension, he is not entitled to a redundancy payment by reason of the dismissal effected by the notice of termination[17], unless the employer[18] agrees to pay a redundancy payment to the employee in respect of the dismissal effected by the notice of termination, even though he has not complied with the request contained in the notice of extension[19].

An employment tribunal[20] may determine that the employer is to be liable to make an appropriate payment[21] to the employee if, on a reference to the tribunal, it appears to the tribunal that:

(i) the employee has not complied with the request contained in the notice of extension and the employer has not agreed to pay a redundancy payment in respect of the dismissal effected by the notice of termination; but

(ii) either the employee was unable to comply with the request or it was reasonable in the circumstances for him not to comply with it[22].

1 As to the meaning of 'employer' see PARA 2. For the purposes of the operation of the provisions of the Employment Rights Act 1996 Pt XI (ss 135–181) and Pt XIV Ch I (ss 210–219)

(continuous employment) (see PARAS 130 et seq, 861–863) in relation to any employee whose remuneration is, by virtue of any statutory provision, payable to him by a person other than his employer, references to the employer in s 143(2)(c) (first reference) (see note 12), and in s 143(4), (5) (any reference) (see note 18) must be construed as references to the person by whom the remuneration is payable: see s 173(1), (2). As to the meaning of 'statutory provision' see PARA 163 note 2.

2 As to the meaning of 'employee' see PARA 2; and as to excluded classes of employment see PARA 854 et seq.

3 As to the meaning of 'contract of employment' see PARA 2.

4 As to the meaning of 'strike' see PARA 134 note 4.

5 As to the meaning of 'writing' see PARA 2 note 8.

6 For these purposes, 'time of expiry', in relation to a notice of termination, means the time at which the notice would expire apart from the Employment Rights Act 1996 s 143: s 144(3).

7 For these purposes, 'available day', in relation to an employee, means a working day beginning at or after the time of expiry which is a day on which he is not taking part in a strike of employees of the employer; and 'working day', in relation to an employee, means a day on which, in accordance with his contract of employment, he is normally required to work: Employment Rights Act 1996 s 144(3).

8 For these purposes, the reference to the number of working days lost by striking is a reference to the number of working days in the period beginning with the date of service of the notice of termination and ending with the time of expiry which are days on which the employee in question takes part in a strike of employees of the employer: Employment Rights Act 1996 s 144(2).

9 Employment Rights Act 1996 s 143(1), (2)(a). As to the giving of notices see PARA 837.

10 Employment Rights Act 1996 s 143(2)(b).

11 For these purposes, an employee complies with the request contained in a notice of extension if, but only if, on each available day within the proposed period of extension, he attends at his proper or usual place of work and is ready and willing to work, whether or not he has signified his agreement to the request in any other way: Employment Rights Act 1996 s 144(1). 'Available day within the proposed period of extension' means an available day which begins before the end of the proposed period of extension: s 144(3).

12 As to the meaning of this reference to 'employer' see note 1.

13 As to the meaning of 'redundancy payment' see PARA 836.

14 As to the meaning of 'dismissal' see PARA 864.

15 Employment Rights Act 1996 s 143(2)(c).

16 Employment Rights Act 1996 s 143(7), (8). Section 87 (see PARA 737), s 88 (see PARA 738), s 89 (see PARA 739), s 90 (see PARA 740) and s 91 (see PARAS 736, 737, 741, 742) apply accordingly as if the period of notice required by s 86 (see PARA 736) were extended to a corresponding extent: s 143(7).

Neither the service of a notice of extension nor any extension by virtue of s 143(7) of the period specified in a notice of termination affects: (1) any right either of the employer or of the employee to terminate the contract of employment, whether before, at or after the time of expiry, by a further notice or without notice; and (2) the operation of Pt XI (ss 135–181) in relation to any such termination of the contract of employment: s 144(4).

17 Employment Rights Act 1996 s 143(3).

18 As to the meaning of references to 'employer' in the Employment Rights Act 1996 s 143(4), (5) (see also the text and notes 20–22) see note 1.

19 Employment Rights Act 1996 s 143(4).

20 As to employment tribunals see PARAS 1399 et seq, 1453 et seq.

21 For these purposes, 'appropriate payment' means: (1) the whole of the redundancy payment to which the employee would have been entitled apart from the Employment Rights Act 1996 s 143(3) (see the text and note 17); or (2) such part of that redundancy payment as the tribunal thinks fit: s 143(6).

22 Employment Rights Act 1996 s 143(5) (amended by the Employment Rights (Dispute Resolution) Act 1998 s 1(2)(a)).

869. Termination of employment by statute. The Secretary of State[1] may by regulations[2] provide that, subject to such exceptions and modifications as may be prescribed by the regulations, the statutory provisions relating to redundancy payments[3] have effect in relation to any person who, by virtue of any statutory provisions[4]:

(1) is transferred to, and becomes a member of, a body specified in those provisions; but

(2) at a time so specified ceases to be a member of that body unless before that time certain conditions so specified have been fulfilled,

as if the cessation of his membership of that body by virtue of those provisions were dismissal[5] by his employer[6] by reason of redundancy[7].

The statutory provisions relating to redundancy payments accordingly have effect[8] in relation to the chief constable of a police force who is transferred[9] to, and becomes a member of, another police force, or the chief officer or assistant chief officer of a fire brigade maintained by a fire authority[10] who is transferred[11] to, and becomes a member of, another fire brigade, but who, not having accepted a fresh appointment in that force or brigade, ceases at the specified time[12] to be a member of that force or brigade, as if the cessation of his membership of that force or brigade were dismissal by his employer by reason of redundancy[13].

1 As to the Secretary of State see PARA 5 note 21.
2 As to the making of regulations under the Employment Rights Act 1996 generally see PARA 162.
3 Ie the Employment Rights Act 1996 Pt XI (ss 135–181).
4 As to the meaning of 'statutory provision' see PARA 163 note 2.
5 As to the meaning of 'dismissal' see PARA 864.
6 As to the meaning of 'employer' see PARA 2.
7 Employment Rights Act 1996 s 172(1). At the date at which this volume states the law no such regulations had been made but, by virtue of s 241, Sch 2 para 2(1) (see PARA 162), the Redundancy Payments Termination of Employment Regulations 1965, SI 1965/2022 (see the text and notes 8–13) have effect as if so made.
   The power conferred by the Employment Rights Act 1996 s 172(1) is exercisable whether or not membership of the body in question constitutes employment within the meaning of s 230(5) (see PARA 2); and, where that membership does not constitute such employment, that power may be exercised in addition to any power exercisable under s 171 (see PARA 838): s 172(2).
8 Ie subject to the provisions of the Redundancy Payments Termination of Employment Regulations 1965, SI 1965/2022, reg 3(2): see note 13.
9 Ie by virtue of the Police Act 1996 s 100 (chief constables affected by amalgamation or local government reorganisation): see POLICE AND INVESTIGATORY POWERS vol 84 (2013) PARA 112.
10 Ie now a fire and rescue authority under the Fire and Rescue Services Act 2004: see s 1; and FIRE AND RESCUE SERVICES vol 51 (2013) PARA 17 et seq.
11 Ie by virtue of an order under the Fire Services Act 1947 s 5 (repealed) or s 6 (repealed) or under the Local Government Act 1958 Pt II (ss 19–45) (repealed) (review of local government areas) (see now LOCAL GOVERNMENT vol 69 (2009) PARA 56 et seq). A scheme approved under the Fire Services Act 1947 s 5 (repealed) or s 6 (repealed) (combination schemes made by the Secretary of State) (see FIRE AND RESCUE SERVICES vol 51 (2013) PARA 18), which was in force immediately before the repeal of s 5 or s 6 by the Fire and Rescue Services Act 2004 ss 52, 54, Sch 2, continues to have effect despite that repeal: see s 4; and FIRE AND RESCUE SERVICES vol 51 (2013) PARA 18.
12 Ie a time specified in the Police Act 1996 s 100 or an order under the Fire Services Act 1947 s 5 (repealed) or s 6 (repealed) or under the Local Government Act 1958 Pt II (ss 19–45) (repealed). See note 11.
13 Redundancy Payments Termination of Employment Regulations 1965, SI 1965/2022, reg 3(1); and see the Employment Rights Act 1996 Sch 2 para 2(1). For the purposes of the application, by virtue of the Redundancy Payments Termination of Employment Regulations 1965, SI 1965/2022, reg 3, of the Employment Rights Act 1996 Pt XI to the chief constable of a police force: (1) Pt XI and the Redundancy Payments Termination of Employment Regulations 1965, SI 1965/2022, reg 3 have effect as if he were an employee, and the police authority of that police force were his employer, and his office were employment within the meaning of the Employment Rights Act 1996 s 230 (see PARA 2), and any reference to 'employment', 'employee' or 'employer' in any provision of the Act is to be construed accordingly; (2) any reference in the Employment Rights Act 1996 to a contract of employment is to be construed as a reference to the terms and conditions under which he is employed; (3) where a police authority is not a body

corporate, s 218(3) (see PARA 135) applies as if it were a body corporate: Redundancy Payments Termination of Employment Regulations 1965, SI 1965/2022, reg 3(2); and see the Employment Rights Act 1996 Sch 2 para 2(1).

(4) MEANINGS OF 'REDUNDANCY' AND 'RELEVANT DATE'

870. Meaning of 'redundancy'. An employee[1] who is dismissed[2] is to be taken to be dismissed by reason of redundancy[3] if the dismissal is wholly or mainly attributable to:

(1) the fact that his employer[4] has ceased[5], or intends to cease:

    (a) to carry on the business[6] for the purposes of which the employee was employed by him[7]; or

    (b) to carry on that business in the place where the employee was so employed[8]; or

(2) the fact that the requirements of that business for employees to carry out work of a particular kind[9], or for employees to carry out work of a particular kind in the place where he was so employed by the employer, have ceased or diminished[10] or are expected to cease or diminish[11].

1   As to the meaning of 'employee' see PARA 2; and as to excluded classes of employment see PARA 854 et seq.

2   As to the meaning of 'dismissal' see PARA 864.

3   The words of the statute must be followed closely and the expression 'redundancy situation' avoided in making a decision: *Ranson v GW Collins* [1978] ICR 765, EAT. The tribunal must examine the evidence to see whether the reason for dismissal is genuine and not just used as a pretext for getting rid of someone (*Timex Corpn v Thomson* [1981] IRLR 522, EAT). See further, in the context of unfair dismissal, PARAS 780–782. It is irrelevant, however, whether the ground for dismissal, once established, is unwise or based on a mistaken view of facts (*Hindle v Percival Boats Ltd* [1969] 1 All ER 836, [1969] 1 WLR 174, CA); and it is not the function of a tribunal to assess the rights and wrongs of the employer's decision to make the redundancy (*Moon v Homeworthy Furniture (Northern) Ltd* [1977] ICR 117, [1976] IRLR 298, EAT). It is the 'fact of redundancy' not the 'reason for redundancy' that is the material matter: *Association of University Teachers v University of Newcastle-upon-Tyne* [1987] ICR 317, [1988] IRLR 10, EAT.

    An employee may be made redundant where he is displaced by the transfer of another redundant employee in the employer's business (sometimes known as 'bumping'): *W Gimber & Sons Ltd v Spurrett* (1967) 2 ITR 308, DC; *Elliott Turbomachinery Ltd v Bates* [1981] ICR 218, EAT; and see *Babar Indian Restaurant v Rawat* [1985] IRLR 57, EAT; *Safeway Stores plc v Burrell* [1997] ICR 523, [1997] IRLR 200, EAT; *Murray v Foyle Meats Ltd* [1999] 3 All ER 769, [1999] ICR 827, HL (in the light of which, *Church v West Lancashire NHS Trust* [1998] ICR 423, [1998] IRLR 4, EAT, must be considered wrong on this point). Such an agreement may not, however, be used to exclude or limit an employee's statutory rights: *Tocher v General Motors Scotland Ltd* [1981] IRLR 55, EAT.

    An employee is entitled to a redundancy payment by virtue of the Employment Rights Act 1996 s 139(1), notwithstanding that it was foreseen that his temporary appointment might not be renewed: *Nottinghamshire County Council v Lee* [1980] ICR 635, sub nom *Lee v Nottinghamshire County Council* [1980] IRLR 284, CA. A person may be redundant even if he has done no work for a lengthy period due to sickness: *Marshall v Harland & Wolff Ltd* [1972] ICR 101, [1972] IRLR 90, NIRC; *Hebden v Forsey & Son* [1973] ICR 607, [1973] IRLR 344, NIRC.

    Where the reduction in staff is effected by the tactic of dismissing all and rehiring some, that can still constitute a statutory redundancy but there has been disagreement as to whether it is unfair to do so: in *Harris v Ralph Martindale & Co Ltd* [2007] All ER (D) 347 (Dec), EAT, it was suggested that there could be a finding of unfair dismissal, but this was restrictively construed later in *Morgan v Welsh Rugby Union* [2011] IRLR 376, EAT (*Harris v Ralph Martindale & Co Ltd* should not be treated as laying down any principle of law which a subsequent tribunal is bound to follow, except that the tribunal must apply the Employment Rights Act 1996 s 98(4) (see PARA 765)); and in *Samsung Electronics (UK) Ltd v Monte-D'Cruz* (2012) UKEAT/0039/11/DM.

4   As to the meaning of 'employer' see PARA 2.

5   For these purposes, 'cease' means cease either permanently or temporarily and for whatever reason: Employment Rights Act 1996 s 139(6).

6   As to the meaning of 'business' see PARA 135 note 4; and as to households in which domestic servants are employed see PARA 856. For these purposes, the business of the employer, together with the business or businesses of his associated employers, is to be treated as one, unless either of the conditions specified in the Employment Rights Act 1996 s 139(1)(a), (b) (see heads (1), (2) in the text) would be satisfied without so treating them: s 139(2). As to the meaning of 'associated employer' see PARA 3. Similarly, the activities carried on by a local authority with respect to the schools maintained by it, and the activities carried on by the governing bodies of those schools, are to be treated as one business unless either of the conditions specified in s 139(1)(a), (b) would be satisfied without so treating them: s 139(3) (amended by the Education Act 2002 Sch 21 para 31; and SI 2010/1158). 'Local authority' has the meaning given by the Education Act 1996 s 579(1) (see EDUCATION vol 35 (2011) PARA 24): Employment Rights Act 1996 s 139(7) (added by SI 2010/1158).

7   Employment Rights Act 1996 s 139(1)(a)(i). The employer does not have to be the owner of the business, only in control of it: *Thomas v Jones* [1978] ICR 274, EAT.

8   Employment Rights Act 1996 s 139(1)(a)(ii). The traditional view was that it was necessary to look not just at where geographically the employee was actually working, but where he could be required to work under the contract: *Sutcliffe v Hawker Siddeley Aviation Ltd* [1973] ICR 560, [1973] IRLR 304, NIRC; *Maher v Fram Gerrard Ltd* [1974] 1 All ER 449, [1974] ICR 31, NIRC; *United Kingdom Atomic Energy Authority v Claydon* [1974] ICR 128, [1974] IRLR 6, NIRC; *Rowbotham v Arthur Lee & Sons Ltd* [1975] ICR 109, [1974] IRLR 377; *Rank Xerox Ltd v Churchill* [1988] IRLR 280, EAT. Such a contractual test could require consideration of whether the contract contained an express or implied mobility clause; as to whether an implied term should be read into the contract in the absence of any express provision see *O'Brien v Associated Fire Alarms Ltd* [1969] 1 All ER 93, [1968] 1 WLR 1916, CA; *Mumford v Boulton and Paul (Steel Construction) Ltd* (1970) 5 ITR 222; cf *Stevenson v Teesside Bridge and Engineering Ltd* [1971] 1 All ER 296 (travel from site to site integral part of trade). A term may be implied so that an employee may be required to work within reasonable daily travelling distance of home: *Managers (Holborn) Ltd v Hohne* [1977] IRLR 230, EAT; *Jones v Associated Tunnelling Co Ltd* [1981] IRLR 477, EAT (approved in *Courtaulds Northern Spinning Ltd v Sibson* [1988] ICR 451, [1988] IRLR 305, CA). As to mobility clauses in the context of unfair dismissal see PARA 763 head (5).

     This case law in favour of a contractual test must now be approached with care because: (1) the Employment Appeal Tribunal subsequently held it only persuasive and preferred a factual, geographical test (*Bass Leisure Ltd v Thomas* [1994] IRLR 104, EAT); and (2) when the matter was reconsidered by the Court of Appeal, it was held that the factual, geographical test will normally be the correct one, with the contractual provisions on location and mobility only taking on more significance where the work itself has in fact required considerable mobility (thus making a purely geographical test more difficult to apply) (*High Table Ltd v Horst* [1998] ICR 409, [1997] IRLR 513, CA). The reasoning in *High Table Ltd v Horst* was applied in *Pitman v Foreign and Commonwealth Office* [2003] ICR 699, EAT (case remitted to tribunal to determine for the purposes of the Employment Rights Act 1996 s 139 where a security officer was employed when his contract suggested a potential requirement to work in the United Kingdom but he had worked almost exclusively overseas).

9   It is a question of fact for the tribunal whether changes in the work are sufficiently fundamental to constitute work of a different kind: see *Vaux and Associated Breweries Ltd v Ward* (1968) 3 ITR 385, DC (different attributes required for barmaids but function remained the same); *Hindle v Percival Boats Ltd* [1969] 1 All ER 836, [1969] 1 WLR 174, CA (change from wooden to fibreglass boats but function of 'boatbuilder' remained the same); *European Chefs (Catering) Ltd v Currell* (1970) 6 ITR 37, DC (redundancy where requirements for pastrycook's speciality ceased); *Pillinger v Manchester Area Health Authority* [1979] IRLR 430, EAT (no redundancy where position was to be downgraded but work remained the same); *Murphy v Epsom College* [1985] ICR 80, [1984] IRLR 271, CA (redundancy where plumber replaced by more highly skilled heating technician); *Macfisheries Ltd v Findlay* [1985] ICR 160, EAT (change from night to day shifts).

     If the change is great enough to turn it into work of a different kind, then an employee considered unable to perform the new function may claim for redundancy: *Robinson v British Island Airways Ltd* [1978] ICR 304, [1977] IRLR 477, EAT (unfair dismissal claim). Where, however, the work function remains the same and the employee is unable or unwilling to perform new tasks, his inability will not constitute dismissal for redundancy where the overall requirements of the business have not changed: *North Riding Garages Ltd v Butterwick* [1967] 2 QB 56, [1967] 1 All ER 644; *Arnold v Thomas Harrington Ltd* [1969] 1 QB 312, [1967] 2 All ER 866, DC; *Hindle v Percival Boats Ltd* above. An employer may have considerable scope to alter the way the work is done without there being a redundancy, especially where such reorganisation is introduced to bring about greater efficiency: *Chapman v Goonvean and Rostowrack China Clay Co Ltd* [1973] 2 All ER 1063, [1973] ICR 310, CA (withdrawal of free transport); *Johnson v Nottinghamshire Combined Police Authority* [1974] 1 All ER 1082, [1974] ICR 170, CA (change in working hours); *Lesney Products & Co Ltd v Nolan* [1977] ICR 235, [1977] IRLR 77, CA (reduction in overtime). There may be a redundancy where the employee's function disappears notwithstanding that the amount of work remains constant: *Bromby & Hoare Ltd v Evans* [1972] ICR 113, NIRC (contracting out work); *Amos v Max-Arc Ltd* [1973] ICR 46, [1973] IRLR 285, NIRC; *Sutton v Revlon Overseas Corpn* [1973] IRLR 173, NIRC (work done by two amalgamated for one); *Carry All Motors Ltd v Pennington* [1980] ICR 806, [1980] IRLR 455, EAT; *McCrea v Cullen & Davison Ltd* [1988] IRLR 30, NI CA.

10   For these purposes, 'diminish' means diminish either permanently or temporarily and for whatever reason: Employment Rights Act 1996 s 139(6).

11   Employment Rights Act 1996 s 139(1)(b). In the past there has been disagreement as to whether the issue under s 139(1)(b) ought to be determined by applying a functional test (ie whether the actual function being performed by the employee has ceased or diminished) or by a contractual test (whether all the work that the employee could be required to do under his contract has ceased or diminished); the balance of authority seemed to favour the latter: *O'Neill v Merseyside Plumbing Co Ltd* [1973] ICR 96, NIRC; *Nelson v BBC* [1977] ICR 649, [1977] IRLR 148, CA; *Nelson v BBC (No 2)* [1980] ICR 110, [1979] IRLR 346, CA; *Cowen v Haden Ltd* [1983] ICR 1, sub nom *Haden Ltd v Cowen* [1983] ICR 1, [1982] IRLR 314, CA; *Pink v White and White & Co (Earls Barton) Ltd* [1985] IRLR 489, EAT; *Johnson v Peabody Trust* [1996] IRLR 387, EAT. However, several of these authorities were ambiguous, and, when the matter was tested in *Safeway Stores plc v Burrell* [1997] ICR 523, [1997] IRLR 200, EAT, it was held that: (1) both tests are unnecessary glosses on the statute; (2) it is the plain wording of the Employment Rights Act 1996 s 139(1)(b) which must be applied; and (3) it is necessary to pose three questions: (a) was the employee dismissed?; (b) if so, had the employer's requirements for employees to carry out work of a particular kind ceased or diminished?; (c) if so, was the dismissal of the employee caused wholly or mainly by that state of affairs?. This restatement by Judge Peter Clark was then fully accepted and applied by the House of Lords in *Murray v Foyle Meats Ltd* [2000] 1 AC 51, [1999] 3 All ER 769, [1999] ICR 827, [1999] IRLR 562, HL. See also *Shawkat v Nottingham City Hospital NHS Trust (No 2)* [2001] EWCA Civ 954, [2002] ICR 7, [2001] IRLR 555 (no redundancy found where reorganisation in medical unit required employees to carry out cardiac work because requirement for employees to carry out thoracic surgery had not ceased or diminished); *Victoria and Albert Museum v Durrant* [2011] IRLR 290, EAT (question posed by the Employment Rights Act 1996 s 139(1)(b) is whether the need of the employer to carry out work of a particular kind had ceased or diminished – the issue was not whether the need to employ persons on certain terms and conditions, eg those on a civil service grade, to carry out work had ceased or diminished); *Packman (t/a Packman Lucas Associates v Fauchon)* [2012] ICR 1362, [2012] IRLR 721, EAT (there can be redundancy under the Employment Rights Act 1996 s 139 without a reduction in headcount); and see also *Swainston v TNS UK Ltd*, [2014] All ER (D) 252 (Jan), EAT.

871.   Meaning of 'relevant date'.   For the purposes of the provisions of the Employment Rights Act 1996, so far as they relate to redundancy payments[1], the 'relevant date', in relation to the dismissal[2] of an employee[3]:

(1)   in relation to an employee whose contract of employment[4] is terminated by notice, whether given by his employer[5] or by the employee, means the date on which the notice expires[6];

(2)   in relation to an employee whose contract of employment is terminated without notice, means the date on which the termination takes effect[7];

(3)   in relation to an employee who is employed under a limited-term

contract[8] which terminates by virtue of the limiting event[9] without being renewed[10] under the same contract, means the date on which the termination takes effect[11]; or

(4) where the employee is regarded[12] as having been dismissed on the date on which his employment under an earlier contract ended, means:

    (a) for the purposes of the statutory provisions relating to claims for redundancy payments[13], the date which is the relevant date[14] in relation to the renewed, or new, contract or, where there has been more than one trial period[15], the last such contract; and

    (b) for the purposes of any other provision, the date which is the relevant date[16] in relation to the previous contract or, where there has been more than one such trial period[17], the original contract[18]; and

(5) where the employee is taken to be dismissed by virtue of the statutory provisions relating to employees anticipating the expiry of employers' notices[19], means the date on which the employee's notice to terminate his contract of employment expires[20].

The 'relevant date', in relation to a notice of intention to claim[21] or a right to a redundancy payment in pursuance of such a notice:

(i) means[22] the date on which the last of the four or more consecutive weeks[23] before the service of the notice came to an end; or

(ii) means[24] the date on which the last of the series of six or more weeks before the service of the notice came to an end[25].

1 As to the meaning of 'redundancy payment' see PARA 836.
2 As to the meaning of 'dismissal' see PARA 864.
3 As to the meaning of 'employee' see PARA 2; and as to excluded classes of employment see PARA 854 et seq.
4 As to the meaning of 'contract of employment' see PARA 2.
5 As to the meaning of 'employer' see PARA 2.
6 Employment Rights Act 1996 ss 145(1), (2)(a), 235(1).
7 Employment Rights Act 1996 ss 145(1), (2)(b), 235(1).
8 As to the meaning of 'limited-term contract' see PARA 755 note 5.
9 As to the meaning of 'limiting event' see PARA 755 note 5.
10 As to the meaning of 'renewal' see PARA 755 note 6.
11 Employment Rights Act 1996 ss 145(1), (2)(c), 235(1) (s 145(2)(c) substituted by SI 2002/2034).
12 Ie by virtue of the Employment Rights Act 1996 s 138(4): see PARA 865.
13 Ie the Employment Rights Act 1996 s 164(1): see PARA 880.
14 Ie as defined in the Employment Rights Act 1996 s 145(2): see heads (1)–(3) in the text.
15 Ie under the Employment Rights Act 1996 s 138: see PARA 865.
16 See note 14.
17 See note 15.
18 Employment Rights Act 1996 ss 145(1), (4), 235(1).
19 Ie the Employment Rights Act 1996 s 136(3): see PARA 866.
20 Employment Rights Act 1996 ss 145(1), (3), 235(1). Where the contract of employment is terminated by the employer and the notice required by s 86 (see PARA 736) to be given by an employer would, if duly given on the date when notice of termination was given by the employer or, where no notice was given, the date when the contract of employment was terminated by the employer, expire on a date later than the relevant date as defined by s 145(1)–(4), then, for the purposes of s 155 (see PARA 855) and s 162(1) (see PARA 881), that later date is the relevant date: s 145(5), (6). This does not, however, apply to all the provisions of s 162 (see PARA 881); in particular, it does not apply for the purposes of s 162(4), (5): *Slater v John Swain & Son Ltd* [1981] ICR 554, [1981] IRLR 303, EAT; distinguished in *Staffordshire County Council v Secretary of State for Employment, Secretary of State for Employment v Cameron Iron Works Ltd* [1989] ICR 664, [1989] IRLR 117, CA.

    Where: (1) an employee's contract of employment has been terminated by the employer; (2) by virtue of the Employment Rights Act 1996 s 145(5), a date later than the relevant date as defined by s 145(1)–(4) is to be treated as the relevant date for the purposes of certain provisions of the Employment Rights Act 1996; and (3) the employee dies before that date, s 145(5) has effect as if the notice to which it refers would have expired on the employee's death: s 176(2).

21 As to the meaning of 'notice of intention to claim' see PARA 876.

22 Ie in a case falling within the Employment Rights Act 1996 s 148(2)(a): see PARA 876 head (1).

23 As to the meaning of 'week' for these purposes see PARA 126 note 13.

24 Ie in a case falling within the Employment Rights Act 1996 s 148(2)(b): see PARA 876 head (2).

25 Employment Rights Act 1996 ss 153, 235(1).

(5) LOSS OF RIGHT TO REDUNDANCY PAYMENT

872. Employee's conduct. An employee[1] is not entitled[2] to a redundancy payment[3] by reason of dismissal[4] where his employer[5], being entitled to terminate his contract of employment[6] without notice by reason of the employee's conduct[7], terminates it:

(1)   without notice[8]; or

(2)   by giving shorter notice[9] than that which, in the absence of conduct entitling the employer to terminate the contract without notice, the employer would be required to give to terminate the contract; or

(3)   by giving notice which includes, or is accompanied by, a statement in writing[10] that the employer would, by reason of the employee's conduct, be entitled to terminate the contract without notice[11].

1   As to the meaning of 'employee' see PARA 2; and as to excluded classes of employment see PARA 854 et seq.

2   Ie subject to the Employment Rights Act 1996 s 140(2), (3): see PARA 873.

3   As to the meaning of 'redundancy payment' see PARA 836.

4   As to the meaning of 'dismissal' see PARA 864.

5   As to the meaning of 'employer' see PARA 2.

6   As to the meaning of 'contract of employment' see PARA 2.

7   The action of an employee in taking part in a strike constitutes 'employee's conduct': *Simmons v Hoover Ltd* [1977] QB 284, [1977] ICR 61, EAT. The burden is on the employer to show that the employee was guilty of conduct which was a significant breach going to the root of the contract or which showed that the employee no longer intended to be bound by one or more of the essential terms of the contract: *Bonner v H Gilbert Ltd* [1989] IRLR 475, EAT.

8   As to the employer's right to dismiss without notice see PARAS 743–746.

9   As to the statutory minimum periods of notice see PARA 736.

10   As to the meaning of 'writing' see PARA 2 note 8.

11   Employment Rights Act 1996 s 140(1). This may apply: (1) where the employee is dismissed for redundancy in circumstances where the employer could have dismissed for cause; or (2) to add the procedural requirement that the employer must have given no, short or special notice if he is to rely on 'cause' to rebut the presumption of redundancy: *Sanders v Ernest A Neale Ltd* [1974] 3 All ER 327, [1974] ICR 565, NIRC; *Simmons v Hoover Ltd* [1977] 1 All ER 775, [1977] ICR 61, EAT. See also *Essen v Vanden Plas (England) 1923 Ltd* (1966) 1 ITR 186; *Fleming v Ritchies Ltd* (1966) 1 ITR 304; *Hindle v Percival Boats Ltd* [1969] 1 All ER 836, [1969] 1 WLR 174, CA; *Malton v Crystal of Scarborough Ltd* (1971) 6 ITR 106, DC; *Bonner v H Gilbert Ltd* [1989] IRLR 475, EAT.

873. Misconduct or industrial disputes. Where an employee[1] who:

(1)   has been given notice by his employer[2] to terminate his contract of employment[3]; or

(2)   has given notice[4] to his employer indicating his intention to claim a redundancy payment[5] in respect of lay-off or short time[6],

takes part in a strike[7] at any relevant time[8] in circumstances which entitle the employer to treat the contract of employment as terminable without notice, the statutory exclusion from the right to a redundancy payment[9] does not apply if the employer terminates the contract by reason of the employee's taking part in the strike[10].

Where an employee terminates his contract of employment without notice, being entitled to do so by reason of a lockout[11] by his employer, the statutory provision whereby an employee is treated as dismissed by his employer[12] does not apply to that termination of the contract[13].

Where the contract of employment of an employee who has been given notice by his employer to terminate his contract of employment or has given notice to his employer[14] indicating his intention to claim a redundancy payment in respect of lay-off or short time is terminated by his employer[15] at any relevant time otherwise than by reason of the employee's taking part in a strike, an employment tribunal[16] may determine that the employer[17] is liable to make an appropriate payment[18] to the employee if on a reference to the tribunal it appears to the tribunal, in the circumstances of the case, to be just and equitable that the employee should receive it[19].

1   As to the meaning of 'employee' see PARA 2; and as to excluded classes of employment see PARA 854 et seq.

2   As to the meaning of 'employer' see PARA 2. For the purposes of the operation of the provisions of the Employment Rights Act 1996 Pt XI (ss 135–181) and Pt XIV Ch I (ss 210–219) (continuous employment) (see PARAS 130 et seq, 861–863) in relation to any employee whose remuneration is, by virtue of any statutory provision, payable to him by a person other than his employer, references to the employer in s 140(3) (third reference) (see note 17) must be construed as references to the person by whom the remuneration is payable: see s 173(1), (2). As to the meaning of 'statutory provision' see PARA 163 note 2.

3   As to the meaning of 'contract of employment' see PARA 2.

4   Ie under the Employment Rights Act 1996 s 148(1): see PARA 876.

5   As to the meanings of 'lay-off' and 'short time' see PARA 875.

6   As to the meaning of 'redundancy payment' see PARA 836.

7   As to the meaning of 'strike' see PARA 134 note 4. As to notices of extension see PARA 868.

8   For these purposes, 'relevant time' means: (1) in the case of an employee who has been given notice by his employer to terminate his contract of employment, any time within the obligatory period of notice; (2) in the case of an employee who has given notice to his employer under the Employment Rights Act 1996 s 148(1) (see PARA 876), any time after the service of the notice: s 140(5). As to the meaning of 'obligatory period of notice' see PARA 866 note 4.

9   Ie the Employment Rights Act 1996 s 140(1): see PARA 872.

10   Employment Rights Act 1996 s 140(2). Section 140(2) applies only to negative the effect of s 140(1) (see PARA 872), in a case where an employee who has already been given notice of dismissal subsequently takes part in a strike in such circumstances as to justify dismissal without notice; it has no application to an employee who takes part in a strike in circumstances such as to justify dismissal without notice, but is not dismissed for that reason, but who, whilst still on strike, is given notice to terminate his contract by reason of redundancy: *Simmons v Hoover Ltd* [1977] QB 284, [1977] ICR 61, EAT.

11   As to the meaning of 'lockout' see PARA 134 note 7.

12   Ie the Employment Rights Act 1996 s 136(1)(c): see PARA 864.

13   See the Employment Rights Act 1996 s 136(2); and PARA 864.

14   Ie under the Employment Rights Act 1996 s 148(1): see PARA 876.

15   Ie as mentioned in the Employment Rights Act 1996 s 140(1): see PARA 872.

16   As to employment tribunals see PARAS 1399 et seq, 1453 et seq.

17   As to the meaning of 'employer' for these purposes see note 1.

18   For these purposes, 'appropriate payment' means: (1) the whole of the redundancy payment to which the employee would have been entitled apart from the Employment Rights Act 1996 s 140(1) (see PARA 872); or (2) such part of that redundancy payment as the tribunal thinks fit: s 140(4).

19   Employment Rights Act 1996 s 140(3) (amended by the Employment Rights (Dispute Resolution) Act 1998 s 1(2)(a)). The tribunal must guide itself according to the facts and circumstances; and its decision may be reversed on appeal only where it can be shown there was some error in principle: *Lignacite Products Ltd v Krollman* [1979] IRLR 22, EAT. See e g *Cairns v Burnside Shoe Repairs Ltd* (1966) 2 ITR 75; *Jarmain v E Pollard & Co Ltd* (1967) 2 ITR 406; *X v Y Ltd* (1969) 4 ITR 204.

874. Offer of renewal or re-engagement. Where an offer[1], whether in writing[2] or not, is made to an employee[3] before the end of his employment[4] to renew[5] his contract of employment[6], or to re-engage[7] him under a new contract of employment, with renewal or re-engagement to take effect either immediately on, or after an interval of not more than four weeks[8] after, the end of his employment[9], the employee is not entitled to a redundancy payment[10] if he unreasonably refuses[11] the offer[12] in circumstances where:

(1) the provisions of the contract as renewed, or of the new contract, as to the capacity and place in which he would be employed, and as to the other terms and conditions of his employment, would not differ from the corresponding provisions of the previous contract; or

(2) those provisions of the contract as renewed, or of the new contract, would differ from the corresponding provisions of the previous contract, but the offer constitutes an offer of suitable employment[13] in relation to the employee[14].

If:

(a) an employee's contract of employment is renewed, or he is re-engaged under a new contract of employment, in pursuance of the offer;

(b) the provisions of the contract as renewed or the new contract as to the capacity or place in which he is employed or the other terms and conditions of his employment differ, wholly or in part, from the corresponding provisions of the previous contract;

(c) the employment is suitable in relation to him; and

(d) during the trial period[15] he unreasonably terminates the contract, or unreasonably gives notice to terminate it and it is in consequence terminated,

he is not entitled to a redundancy payment[16].

1 As to the meaning of references to an offer see PARA 865 note 5. A written offer of re-engagement should show the material differences between the terms of the previous and new contracts: *Havenhand v Thomas Black Ltd* [1968] 2 All ER 1037, [1968] 1 WLR 1241, DC. Where the new employment follows on immediately from the previous employment, the offer does not have to specify the precise date when it is to take effect; and a written offer is not invalidated by a term made orally: *Kaye v Cooke's (Finsbury) Ltd* [1973] 3 All ER 434, [1974] ICR 65, NIRC. The onus is on the employer to prove an offer was made: *Simpson v Dickinson* [1972] ICR 474, NIRC. An offer posted on a notice board may suffice if it is in writing, brought to the notice of the employee, capable of being understood by him and in fact read by him: *McCreadie v Thomson and MacIntyre (Patternmakers) Ltd* [1971] 2 All ER 1135, [1971] 1 WLR 1193, HL; *Lonmet Engineering Ltd v Green* (1971) 7 ITR 86, NIRC; *Maxwell v Walter Howard Designs Ltd* [1975] IRLR 77. The suitability of any offer must, however, be considered on an individual, and not collective, basis: *E & J Davis Transport Ltd v Chattaway* [1972] ICR 267, NIRC; *John Fowler (Don Foundry) Ltd v Parkin* [1975] IRLR 89.

2 As to the meaning of 'writing' see PARA 2 note 8.

3 As to the meaning of 'employee' see PARA 2; and as to excluded classes of employment see PARA 854 et seq.

4 As to the meaning of 'employment' see PARA 2.

5 As to the meaning of 'renewal' see PARA 755 note 6.

6 As to the meaning of 'contract of employment' see PARA 2.

7 As to the meaning of references to re-engagement see PARA 865 note 4.

8 As to the meaning of 'week' for these purposes see PARA 126 note 13. For the purposes of the application of the Employment Rights Act 1996 s 141(1) to a contract under which the employment ends on a Friday, Saturday or Sunday: (1) the renewal or re-engagement is to be treated as taking effect immediately on the ending of the employment under the previous contract if it takes effect on or before the next Monday after that Friday, Saturday or Sunday; and (2) the interval of four weeks is to be calculated as if the employment had ended on that next Monday: s 146(2). Where the contract of employment of an employee is taken for the purposes of Pt XI (ss 135–181) to be terminated by his employer by reason of the employer's

death (see PARA 867), s 146(2) applies as if head (1) above were omitted and in head (2) above for the word 'four' there were substituted the word 'eight': s 174(5)(b).

9 Employment Rights Act 1996 s 141(1). See also *Lucas v Henry Johnson (Packers and Shippers) Ltd* [1986] ICR 384, EAT; and PARA 865 note 4. Where the contract of employment of an employee is taken for the purposes of the Employment Rights Act 1996 Pt XI to be terminated by his employer by reason of the employer's death, s 141(1) applies as if for the words 'before the end of his employment' there were substituted 'by a personal representative of the deceased employer' and for the words 'either immediately' onwards there were substituted 'not later than eight weeks after the death of the deceased employer': s 174(1), (3). As to the meaning of 'employer' see PARA 2; and as to the meaning of references to a personal representative see PARA 856 note 8.

   Where the contract of employment of an employee is taken for the purposes of Pt XI to be terminated by his employer by reason of the employer's death, then, for the purposes of s 141: (1) provisions of the contract as renewed, or of the new contract, do not differ from the corresponding provisions of the contract in force immediately before the death of the deceased employer by reason only that the personal representative would be substituted as the employer for the deceased employer; and (2) no account is to be taken of that substitution in determining whether the refusal of the offer was unreasonable or whether the employee acted reasonably in terminating or giving notice to terminate the new or renewed employment: s 174(1), (4).

10 As to the meaning of 'redundancy payment' see PARA 836.

11 As with the suitability test (see note 13), the question of reasonableness is a matter of fact for the tribunal in each case (*Spencer and Griffin v Gloucestershire County Council* [1985] IRLR 393, CA (lowered standards of work)); and its decision must not be interfered with unless it has misdirected itself (*Collier v Smith's Dock Co Ltd* (1969) 4 ITR 338). The onus of proof in both tests is on the employer: *Kitching v Ward* (1967) 2 ITR 464, DC; *Jones v Aston Cabinet Co Ltd* [1973] ICR 292, NIRC. The test is not the attitude of the reasonable person but whether the objections of the particular applicant are reasonable: *Fuller v Stephanie Bowman (Sales) Ltd* [1977] IRLR 87; *Executors of JF Everest v Cox* [1980] ICR 415, EAT; *Spencer and Griffin v Gloucestershire County Council* above. For this reason, the test is not equivalent to the 'band of reasonable responses' test under the Employment Rights Act 1996 s 98(4) (see PARA 765): *Hudson v George Harrison Ltd* (2003) Times, 15 January, [2003] All ER (D) 381 (Mar), EAT. An employee may have personal objections to the job itself, even if objectively it would be suitable: *Cambridge and District Co-operative Society Ltd v Ruse* [1993] IRLR 156, EAT. The reasons of each individual employee must be separately considered where a collective offer is made: *John Fowler (Don Foundry) Ltd v Parkin* [1975] IRLR 89. The circumstances relevant for consideration are those at the time the offer was refused either expressly or otherwise: *Williamson v National Coal Board* (1969) 5 ITR 43 at 47, Ct of Sess, per Lord Migdale.

   As to the relevant factors see eg: *Bryan v George Wimpey & Co Ltd* (1967) 3 ITR 28; *Scott v Salisbury and Chandler* (1970) 5 ITR 22; *Barratt v Thomas Glover & Co Ltd* (1970) 5 ITR 95 (cf *McNulty v T Bridges & Co Ltd* (1966) 1 ITR 367); *Thomas Wragg & Sons Ltd v Wood* [1976] ICR 313, [1976] IRLR 145, EAT (late offer); *Roberts v Essoldo Circuit (Control) Ltd* (1967) 2 ITR 351 (vague offer); *Douce v F Bond & Sons (Woodturners) Ltd* (1966) 1 ITR 365 (insufficient consideration of offer); *Bainbridge v Westinghouse Brake and Signal Co Ltd* (1966) 1 ITR 55 (housing; schooling); *Rose v Shelley & Partners Ltd* (1966) 1 ITR 169 (domestic problems); *Universal Fisher Engineering Ltd v Stratton* (1971) 7 ITR 66, NIRC (leisure); *Williamson v National Coal Board* above (medical grounds); *Hawkins v Thomas Forman & Sons Ltd* (1967) 2 ITR 59; cf *Spencer and Griffin v Gloucestershire County Council* above (underemployment); *Paton Calvert & Co Ltd v Westerside* [1979] IRLR 108, EAT (alternative employment; future prospects); *Belle v Fielding & Johnson Ltd* (1966) 1 ITR 167; *Ireland v Fairfield-Rowan Ltd* (1966) 1 ITR 191; *Pilkington v Pickstone* (1966) 1 ITR 363; *James & Jones v National Coal Board* (1969) 4 ITR 70; *Morganite Crucible Co Ltd v Street* [1972] 2 All ER 411, [1972] ICR 110, NIRC; *Devonald v JD Insulating Co Ltd* [1972] ICR 209, NIRC.

   As to the relationship between 'suitability' (see note 13) and 'reasonableness of refusal' see also *Ward v Commission for Healthcare Audit and Inspection* [2008] All ER (D) 107 (Jun), EAT (usually the issues are separate but there can be a connection, in particular, where an offer is 'overwhelmingly suitable' that may make it easier for the employer to show unreasonable refusal, and conversely, where the offered post was only marginally suitable, that may operate in the opposite direction).

   As to possible disqualification from jobseeker's allowance see WELFARE BENEFITS AND STATE PENSIONS vol 104 (2014) PARA 419 et seq.

12 Employment Rights Act 1996 s 141(2). The requirement in s 141(3)(a) (see head (1) in the text) that the offer is of identical employment is subject to the de minimis rule: *Allman v Rowland* [1977] ICR 201.

Where: (1) an employer has given notice to an employee to terminate his contract of employment and has offered to renew his contract of employment or to re-engage him under a new contract; and (2) the employee dies without having accepted or refused the offer and without the offer having been withdrawn, the Employment Rights Act 1996 s 141(2) applies as if, for the words 'he unreasonably refuses', there were substituted 'it would have been unreasonable on his part to refuse': s 176(3).

13 The suitability of the offer must usually be considered separately from the reasonableness of the refusal (see note 11); and, if the offer is deemed to be unsuitable, there is no need to go on and consider the reasonableness test: see *Carron Co v Robertson* (1967) 2 ITR 484, Ct of Sess; *Taylor v Kent County Council* [1969] 2 QB 560, [1969] 2 All ER 1080, DC; *Hindes v Supersine Ltd* [1979] ICR 517, [1979] IRLR 343, EAT; *Standard Telephones and Cables Ltd v Yates* [1981] IRLR 21, EAT. As to the relationship between 'suitability' and 'reasonableness of refusal' see also *Ward v Commission for Healthcare Audit and Inspection* [2008] All ER (D) 107 (Jun), EAT; and note 11. 'Suitable employment' means that 'which is substantially equivalent to the employment which has ceased' (*Taylor v Kent County Council* above at 566 and 1084 per Lord Parker CJ); but it has been said that such judicial gloss should not impose on the strict application of the wording of the statute (*Collier v Smith's Dock Co Ltd* (1969) 4 ITR 338 at 341 per Bridge J; *Standard Telephones and Cables Ltd v Yates* above). Suitability is almost entirely a matter of degree and fact for the tribunal: *Taylor v Kent County Council* above. As to some of the interrelating factors which might be taken into account see eg: *Gay v Commander, US Naval Activities, United Kingdom* (1966) 1 ITR 347; *Souter v Henry Balfour & Co Ltd* (1966) 1 ITR 383; *Collier v Smith's Dock Co Ltd* above; *Harris v E Turner & Sons (Joinery) Ltd* [1973] ICR 31, NIRC; *Standard Telephones and Cables Ltd v Yates* above (task); *Kennedy v Werneth Ring Mills Ltd* [1977] ICR 206, EAT; *Hindes v Supersine Ltd* above (working conditions); *Tocher v General Motors Scotland Ltd* [1981] IRLR 55, EAT (pay and status); *Morrison and Poole v Cramic Engineering Co Ltd* (1966) 1 ITR 404; *Kykot v Smith Hartley Ltd* [1975] IRLR 372; *Archibald v Rossleigh Commercials Ltd* [1975] IRLR 231; *O'Connor v Montrose Canned Foods Ltd* (1966) 1 ITR 171; *Bainbridge v Westinghouse Brake and Signal Co Ltd* (1966) 1 ITR 55 (location) (c f *Sheppard v National Coal Board* (1966) 1 ITR 177) (hours)); *Carron Co v Robertson* above ('perks'); *Gotch & Partners v Guest* (1966) 1 ITR 65; *Douce v F Bond & Sons (Woodturners) Ltd* (1966) 1 ITR 365; *McIntosh v British Rail (Scottish Region)* (1967) 3 ITR 26 (travelling); *Miller v Nettle Accessories Ltd* (1966) 1 ITR 328; *Taylor v Kent County Council* above; *Lee v British Wagon Co Ltd* (1970) 5 ITR 192, DC (c f *Eltringham v Sunderland Co-operative Society Ltd* (1971) 6 ITR 121, DC); *Kane v Raine & Co Ltd* [1974] ICR 300, NIRC (status); *Goode & Cooper Ltd v Thompson* [1974] IRLR 111, NIRC; *Samways v Swan Hunter Shipbuilders Ltd* [1975] IRLR 190; *Morganite Crucible Co Ltd v Street* [1972] 2 All ER 411, [1972] ICR 110, NIRC (temporary employment not necessarily unsuitable); *Dutton v Hawker Siddeley Aviation Ltd* [1978] ICR 1057, [1978] IRLR 390, EAT (temporary work). See also *Devon Primary Care Trust v Readman* [2013] EWCA Civ 1110, [2013] IRLR 878 (tribunal failing to address employee's core reason for refusing offer).

14 Employment Rights Act 1996 s 141(3).

15 As to the meaning of 'trial period' see PARA 865 note 13.

16 Employment Rights Act 1996 s 141(4). Where an employee's contract of employment has been renewed, or he has been re-engaged under a new contract: (1) if he dies during the trial period without having terminated, or given notice to terminate, the contract, s 141(4) applies as if the condition in s 141(4)(d) (see head (d) in the text) were that it would have been unreasonable for the employee during the trial period to terminate or give notice to terminate the contract; and (2) if during the trial period he gives notice to terminate the contract but dies before the notice expires, s 141(4) applies as if the notice had expired, and the contract had been terminated by its expiry, on the date of the employee's death: s 176(4)(a), (b).

(6) LAY-OFF AND SHORT TIME

875. **Lay-off and short time.** Where an employee[1] is employed under a contract on terms and conditions such that his remuneration under the contract depends on his being provided by the employer[2] with work of the kind which he

is employed to do but he is not entitled to any remuneration under the contract because the employer does not provide such work for him, he is taken[3] to be laid off for a week[4].

If, by reason of a diminution in the work provided[5] for an employee by his employer, being work of a kind which under his contract the employee is employed to do, the employee's remuneration for any week is less than half a week's pay[6], he is[7] to be taken to be kept on short time for that week[8].

1 As to the meaning of 'employee' see PARA 2; and as to excluded classes of employment see PARA 854 et seq.
2 As to the meaning of 'employer' see PARA 2.
3 Ie for the purposes of the Employment Rights Act 1996 Pt XI (ss 135–181).
4 Employment Rights Act 1996 ss 147(1), 181(2)(a). As to the meaning of 'week' for these purposes see PARA 126 note 13.
   There is no general right to lay off at common law (*Devonald v Rosser & Sons* [1906] 2 KB 728, CA; *Hanley v Pease & Partners Ltd* [1915] 1 KB 698; *Bond v CAV Ltd, Neads v CAV Ltd* [1983] IRLR 360); and such a right must be contained expressly or impliedly in the contract (*Browning v Crumlin Valley Collieries Ltd* [1926] 1 KB 522; *Puttick v John Wright & Sons (Blackwall) Ltd* [1972] ICR 457, NIRC). Where the employer has no right to lay off, any attempt to do so will constitute a repudiation of the contract and dismissal: *Powell Duffryn Wagon Co Ltd v House* [1974] ICR 123, NIRC; *Jewell v Neptune Concrete Ltd* [1975] IRLR 147; *Waine v R Oliver (Plant Hire) Ltd* [1977] IRLR 434, EAT; *Kenneth MacRae & Co Ltd v Dawson* [1984] IRLR 5, EAT. It has been held that, even where there is such a right, an employee may claim constructive dismissal after a reasonable period: *A Dakri & Co Ltd v Tiffen* [1981] ICR 256, [1981] IRLR 57, EAT (disapproved in *Kenneth MacRae & Co Ltd v Dawson* above; but cf *McLory v Post Office* [1992] ICR 758, sub nom *McClory v Post Office* [1993] IRLR 159). As to the application of what is now the Employment Rights Act 1996 s 147 see *Powell Duffryn Wagon Co Ltd v House* above; *Hulse v Perry* [1975] IRLR 181; cf *Hanson v Wood (Abington Process Engravers)* (1967) 3 ITR 46, DC; *Jewell v Neptune Concrete Ltd* above. As to constructive dismissal in the context of unfair dismissal see PARA 763.
5 It is not necessary for there to be an agreement on rate of pay in order for work to be 'provided'; an offer of work by the employer may be sufficient: *Spinpress Ltd v Turner* [1986] ICR 433, EAT.
6 As to the calculation of a week's pay see PARA 143 et seq; and as to the calculation date for these purposes see PARA 146 head (11).
7 See note 3.
8 Employment Rights Act 1996 ss 147(2), 181(2)(b). There is no inherent right to put an employee on short time; it can occur only where there is an agreed contractual term binding on the employee: *Miller v Hamworthy Engineering Ltd* [1986] ICR 846, [1986] IRLR 461, CA.

876. Notice of intention to claim. An employee[1] is eligible for a redundancy payment[2] by reason of being laid off[3] or kept on short time[4] if he gives notice in writing to his employer[5] indicating, in whatever terms, his intention to claim a redundancy payment in respect of lay-off or short time ('notice of intention to claim') and, before the service of the notice, he has been laid off or kept on short time:

(1) for four or more consecutive weeks[6] of which the last before the service of the notice ended on, or not more than four weeks before, the date of service of the notice[7]; or

(2) for a series of six or more weeks, of which not more than three were consecutive, within a period of 13 weeks, where the last week of the series before the service of the notice ended on, or not more than four weeks before, the date of service of the notice[8].

1 As to the meaning of 'employee' see PARA 2; and as to excluded classes of employment see PARA 854 et seq.
2 Ie subject to the Employment Rights Act 1996 ss 149–181 (see PARAS 836 et seq, 877 et seq) and for the purposes of Pt XI (ss 135–181) (see also PARAS 836 et seq, 877 et seq). As to the meaning of 'redundancy payment' see PARA 836.

3 As to the meaning of 'lay-off' see PARA 875.

4 As to the meaning of 'short time' see PARA 875.

5 As to the meaning of 'employer' see PARA 2. As to the meaning of 'writing' see PARA 2 note 8.

6 As to the meaning of 'week' for these purposes see PARA 126 note 13. For these purposes, it is immaterial whether a series of weeks consists wholly of weeks for which the employee is laid off or wholly of weeks for which he is kept on short time or partly of the one and partly of the other; and no account is to be taken of any week for which an employee is laid off or kept on short time where the lay-off or short time is wholly or mainly attributable to a strike or a lockout, whether or not in the trade or industry in which the employee is employed and whether in Great Britain or elsewhere: Employment Rights Act 1996 s 154. As to the meaning of 'strike' see PARA 134 note 4; and as to the meaning of 'lockout' see PARA 134 note 7. As to the meaning of 'Great Britain' see PARA 2 note 12.

7 An employee must be laid off or kept on short-time work for four or more consecutive weeks before the service of the notice of intention to claim a redundancy payment; the giving of a premature notice does not comply with the statutory requirement: *Allinson v Drew Simmons Engineering Ltd* [1985] ICR 488, EAT.

8 Employment Rights Act 1996 ss 148(1), (2), 181(1), (2)(a), (b). No particular terms of art are required to indicate notice of termination of employment: *Walmsley v C & R Ferguson Ltd* [1989] IRLR 112, Ct of Sess. As to the giving of notices see PARA 837.

   Where an employee, who has given notice of intention to claim, dies within the period of seven days after the service of that notice, and before the employer has given a counter-notice, the Employment Rights Act 1996 Pt XI Ch III (ss 147–154) (see also PARAS 875, 877–879) applies as if the employer had given a counter-notice within that period of seven days: s 176(6)(b). As to the meaning of 'counter-notice' see PARA 879.

   Where an employee is laid off or kept on short time and his employer dies, then, where the employee: (1) has been laid off or kept on short time for one or more weeks before the death of the employer; (2) has not given the deceased employer notice of intention to claim before the employer's death; (3) after the employer's death has his contract of employment renewed, or is re-engaged under a new contract, by a personal representative of the deceased employer; and (4) after renewal or re-engagement is laid off or kept on short time for one or more weeks by the personal representative, the week in which the employer died and the first week of the employee's employment by the personal representative are to be treated for the purposes of Pt XI Ch III as consecutive weeks; and references to four weeks or 13 weeks are to be construed accordingly: s 175(1), (2). As to the meaning of 'renewal' see PARA 755 note 6; and as to the meaning of references to a personal representative see PARA 856 note 8.

   Where: (a) an employee is laid off or kept on short time and his employer dies; (b) the employee has given the deceased employer notice of intention to claim before the employer's death; (c) the employer's death occurred before the end of the period of four weeks after the service of the notice; and (d) the employee has not terminated the contract of employment by notice expiring before the employer's death, then, if the contract of employment is not renewed, and the employee is not re-engaged under a new contract, by a personal representative of the deceased employer before the end of the period of four weeks after the service of the notice to claim, s 149 (see PARA 879) and s 152 (see PARA 878) do not apply, but, subject to that, Pt XI Ch III applies as if the employer had not died and the employee had terminated the contract of employment by a week's notice, or by the minimum notice which he is required to give to terminate the contract, if longer than a week, expiring at the end of that period: s 175(1), (3), (4).

   Where an employee is laid off or kept on short time and his employer dies, then if: (i) the contract of employment is renewed, or the employee is re-engaged under a new contract, by a personal representative of the deceased employer before the end of the period of four weeks after the service of the notice of intention to claim; and (ii) the employee was laid off or kept on short time by the deceased employer for one or more of those weeks and is laid off or kept on short time by the personal representative for the week, or for the next two or more weeks, following the renewal or re-engagement, Pt XI Ch III applies as if all the weeks for which the employee was laid off or kept on short time were consecutive weeks during which the employee was employed, but laid off or kept on short time, by the same employer, and the periods specified by s 150(3)(a), (b) (see PARA 877 note 7 heads (1), (2)) as the relevant period were extended by any week or weeks any part of which was after the death of the employer and before the date on which the renewal or re-engagement took effect: s 175(1), (5), (6).

877. Employee's notice terminating contract. An employee[1] is not entitled to a redundancy payment[2] by reason of being laid off[3] or kept on short time[4] unless he terminates his contract of employment[5] by giving the following period of notice[6] before the end of the relevant period[7]:

(1) where the employee is required by his contract of employment to give more than one week's[8] notice to terminate the contract, the minimum period which he is required to give; and

(2) otherwise, one week[9].

1 As to the meaning of 'employee' see PARA 2; and as to excluded classes of employment see PARA 854 et seq.

2 As to the meaning of 'redundancy payment' see PARA 836.

3 As to the meaning of 'lay-off' see PARA 875.

4 As to the meaning of 'short time' see PARA 875.

5 As to the meaning of 'contract of employment' see PARA 2.

6 Such notice may be oral or in writing and does not have to be in formal terms: *Fabar Construction Ltd v Race* [1979] ICR 529, [1979] IRLR 232, EAT; and see *Walmsley v C & R Ferguson Ltd* [1989] IRLR 112, Ct of Sess. As to the giving of notices see PARA 837.

7 For these purposes, the 'relevant period' is: (1) if the employer does not give a counter-notice within seven days after the service of the notice of intention to claim, three weeks after the end of those seven days; (2) if the employer gives a counter-notice within that period of seven days, but withdraws it by a subsequent notice in writing, three weeks after the service of the notice of withdrawal; (3) if the employer gives a counter-notice within that period of seven days and does not so withdraw it, and a question as to the right of the employee to a redundancy payment in pursuance of the notice of intention to claim is referred to an employment tribunal, three weeks after the tribunal has notified to the employee its decision on that reference: Employment Rights Act 1996 s 150(3) (amended by the Employment Rights (Dispute Resolution) Act 1998 s 1(2)(a)). However, for the purposes of head (3) above, no account is to be taken of any appeal against the decision of the tribunal or any proceedings or decision in consequence of any such appeal: Employment Rights Act 1996 s 150(4). See also PARA 876 notes 6, 8. For the purposes of the operation of Pt XI (ss 135–181) and Pt XIV Ch I (ss 210–219) (continuous employment) (see PARAS 130 et seq, 861–863) in relation to any employee whose remuneration is, by virtue of any statutory provision, payable to him by a person other than his employer, references to the employer in s 150(3) (any reference) must be construed as references to the person by whom the remuneration is payable: see s 173(1), (2). As to the meaning of 'statutory provision' see PARA 163 note 2. As to the meaning of 'writing' see PARA 2 note 8. As to employment tribunals see PARAS 1399 et seq, 1453 et seq.

8 As to the meaning of 'week' for these purposes see PARA 126 note 13.

9 Employment Rights Act 1996 s 150(1), (2). See also PARA 876 notes 6, 8. Where an employee has given notice of intention to claim and dies before he has given notice to terminate his contract of employment and before the relevant period has expired, s 150 does not apply: s 176(6)(a).

878. Exclusion of right to redundancy payment. An employee[1] is not entitled to a redundancy payment[2] by reason of being laid off[3] or kept on short time[4] if he is dismissed[5] by his employer[6], but this is without prejudice to any right to a redundancy payment by reason of the dismissal[7].

An employee is not entitled to a redundancy payment in pursuance of a notice of intention to claim[8] if:

(1) on the date of service of the notice, it was reasonably to be expected that the employee, if he continued to be employed by the same employer, would, not later than four weeks[9] after that date, enter on a period of employment[10] of not less than 13 weeks during which he would not be laid off or kept on short time for any week; and

(2) the employer[11] gives a counter-notice[12] to the employee within seven days after the service of the intention to claim[13].

However, this does not apply where the employee:

(a) continues or has continued, during the next four weeks after the date of service of the notice of intention to claim, to be employed by the same employer; and

(b)   is or has been laid off or kept on short time for each of those weeks[14].

1   As to the meaning of 'employee' see PARA 2; and as to excluded classes of employment see PARA 854 et seq.
2   As to the meaning of 'redundancy payment' see PARA 836.
3   As to the meaning of 'lay-off' see PARA 875.
4   As to the meaning of 'short time' see PARA 875.
5   As to the meaning of 'dismissal' see PARA 864.
6   As to the meaning of 'employer' see PARA 2; and see note 11.
7   Employment Rights Act 1996 s 151(1), (2).
8   As to the meaning of 'notice of intention to claim' see PARA 876.
9   As to the meaning of 'week' for these purposes see PARA 126 note 13. See also PARA 876 notes 6, 8.
10 For these purposes, 'period of employment' refers to employment under the contract of employment in relation to which the employee had been laid off, and not alternative employment, whether suitable or not: *Neepsend Steel and Tool Corpn Ltd v Vaughan* [1972] 3 All ER 725, [1972] ICR 278, NIRC.
11 For the purposes of the operation of the provisions of the Employment Rights Act 1996 Pt XI (ss 135–181) and Pt XIV Ch I (ss 210–219) (continuous employment) (see PARAS 130 et seq, 861–863) in relation to any employee whose remuneration is, by virtue of any statutory provision, payable to him by a person other than his employer, references to the employer in s 152(1)(b) (any reference) (see head (2) in the text) must be construed as references to the person by whom the remuneration is payable: see s 173(1), (2). As to the meaning of 'statutory provision' see PARA 163 note 2.
12 As to the meaning of 'counter-notice' see PARA 879.
13 Employment Rights Act 1996 s 152(1); and see *Taylor v Dunbar (Builders) Ltd* (1966) 1 ITR 249. See also PARA 876 notes 6, 8.
14 Employment Rights Act 1996 s 152(2). For these purposes, it is immaterial whether a series of weeks consists wholly of weeks for which the employee is laid off or wholly of weeks for which he is kept on short time or partly of the one and partly of the other; and no account is to be taken of any week for which an employee is laid off or kept on short time where the lay-off or short time is wholly or mainly attributable to a strike or a lockout, whether or not in the trade or industry in which the employee is employed and whether in Great Britain or elsewhere: s 154. As to the meaning of 'strike' see PARA 134 note 4; and as to the meaning of 'lockout' see PARA 134 note 7. As to the meaning of 'Great Britain' see PARA 2 note 12.

879.   Employer's counter-notice.   Where an employee[1] gives to his employer[2] notice of intention to claim[3] but:

(1)   the employer[4] gives to the employee, within seven days after the service of that notice, notice in writing[5] (a 'counter-notice') that he will contest any liability to pay to the employee a redundancy payment in pursuance of the employee's notice; and

(2)   the employer[6] does not withdraw the counter-notice by a subsequent notice in writing,

the employee is not entitled to a redundancy payment[7] in pursuance of his notice of intention to claim except in accordance with a decision of an employment tribunal[8].

1   As to the meaning of 'employee' see PARA 2. As to excluded classes of employment see PARA 854 et seq.
2   For the purposes of the operation of the provisions of the Employment Rights Act 1996 Pt XI (ss 135–181) and Pt XIV Ch I (ss 210–219) (continuous employment) (see PARAS 130 et seq, 861–863) in relation to any employee whose remuneration is, by virtue of any statutory provision, payable to him by a person other than his employer, references to the employer in s 149(a), (b) (any reference) (see heads (1), (2) in the text; and notes 4, 6) must be construed as references to the person by whom the remuneration is payable: see s 173(1), (2). As to the meaning of 'statutory provision' see PARA 163 note 2.
3   As to the meaning of 'notice of intention to claim' see PARA 876.
4   As to the meaning of 'employer' for this purpose see note 2.
5   As to the meaning of 'writing' see PARA 2 note 8.

6 As to the meaning of 'employer' for this purpose see note 2.
7 As to the meaning of 'redundancy payment' see PARA 836.
8 Employment Rights Act 1996 s 149 (amended by the Employment Rights (Dispute Resolution) Act 1998 s 1(2)(a)); Employment Rights Act 1996 s 181(1). See also *Fabar Construction Ltd v Race* [1979] ICR 529, [1979] IRLR 232, EAT. As to the giving of notices see PARA 837. As to employment tribunals see PARAS 1399 et seq, 1453 et seq.

(7) CLAIM FOR, AND CALCULATION OF, REDUNDANCY PAYMENT

880. Time for making claim. An employee[1] does not have any right to a redundancy payment[2] unless, before the end of the period of six months[3] beginning with the relevant date:

(1) the payment has been agreed and paid[4]; or

(2) the employee has made a claim for the payment by notice in writing[5] given to the employer[6]; or

(3) a question as to the employee's right to, or the amount of, the payment has been referred to an employment tribunal[7]; or

(4) a complaint of unfair dismissal has been presented[8] by the employee[9].

However, an employee is not so deprived of his right to a redundancy payment if, during the period of six months[10] immediately following the period of six months beginning with the relevant date[11], the employee:

(a) makes a claim for the payment by notice in writing given to the employer[12];

(b) refers to an employment tribunal a question as to his right to, or the amount of, the payment; or

(c) presents a complaint of unfair dismissal[13],

and it appears to the tribunal to be just and equitable that the employee should receive a redundancy payment[14]. In so determining whether it is just and equitable that an employee should receive a redundancy payment, an employment tribunal must have regard to:

(i) the reason shown by the employee for his failure to take any such step as is referred to in head (a), (b) or (c) above within the period of six months beginning with the relevant date[15]; and

(ii) all the other relevant circumstances[16].

1 As to the meaning of 'employee' see PARA 2; and as to excluded classes of employment see PARA 854 et seq.

2 As to the meaning of 'redundancy payment' see PARA 836.

3 Where a claim for a redundancy payment is made by a personal representative of a deceased employee who died before the end of the period of six months beginning with the relevant date, the Employment Rights Act 1996 s 164(1) applies as if for the words 'six months' there were substituted 'one year': s 176(7)(a). As to the meaning of references to a personal representative see PARA 856 note 8; and as to the meaning of 'relevant date' see PARA 871.

4 Employment Rights Act 1996 s 164(1)(a). Section 164 is a substantive provision barring a right which cannot be waived so that a failure to claim within six months absolves the employer from any legal liability: *Secretary of State for Employment v Atkins Auto Laundries Ltd* [1972] 1 All ER 987, [1972] ICR 76, NIRC. An action under head (1), (2) or (3) in the text will be invalid if performed before dismissal takes effect: *Watts v Rubery Owen Conveyancer Ltd* [1977] 2 All ER 1, [1977] ICR 429, EAT; *Pritchard-Rhodes Ltd v Boon and Milton* [1979] IRLR 19, EAT; sed quaere. Cf *North Western Electricity Board v Secretary of State for Employment* (1973) 8 ITR 209. Provided that such action is taken within the six-month period, the amount of payment may be decided at a later date: *Bentley Engineering Co Ltd v Miller* [1976] ICR 225 at 233–236, [1976] IRLR 146 at 150–151 per Phillips J; *Price v Smithfield & Zwanenberg Group Ltd* [1978] ICR 93, [1978] IRLR 80, EAT.

5　As to the meaning of 'writing' see PARA 2 note 8. Such a notice should be construed liberally in the employee's favour: *Hetherington v Dependable Products Ltd* (1970) 6 ITR 1, CA; *North Western Electricity Board v Secretary of State for Employment* (1973) 8 ITR 209; *Price v Smithfield & Zwanenberg Group Ltd* [1978] ICR 93, [1978] IRLR 80, EAT.

6　Employment Rights Act 1996 s 164(1)(b). For the purposes of the operation of the provisions of Pt XI (ss 135–181) and Pt XIV Ch I (ss 210–219) (continuous employment) (see PARAS 130 et seq, 861–863) in relation to any employee whose remuneration is, by virtue of any statutory provision, payable to him by a person other than his employer, references to the employer in s 164 (see also note 12) must be construed as references to the person by whom the remuneration is payable: see s 173(1), (2). As to the meaning of 'statutory provision' see PARA 163 note 2. See also note 4. As to the giving of notices see PARA 837.

7　Employment Rights Act 1996 s 164(1)(c) (amended by the Employment Rights (Dispute Resolution) Act 1998 s 1(2)(a)). See also note 4. Such an application is referred when it is received by the tribunal office and not on the date that it was sent by the employee: *Secretary of State for Employment v Banks* [1983] ICR 48, EAT (distinguishing *Nash v Ryan Plant International Ltd* [1978] 1 All ER 492, [1977] ICR 560, EAT). See further the Employment Tribunals (Constitution and Rules of Procedure) Regulations 2013, SI 2013/1237, reg 13(1), Sch 1 r 8–14; and PARA 1461. As to employment tribunals see PARAS 1399 et seq, 1453 et seq.

　　The Employment Rights Act 1996 s 164(1)(c) and s 164(2) (see text and notes 10–13) are subject to s 207A (extension because of mediation in certain European cross-border disputes: see PARA 1454): s 164(4) (added by SI 2011/1133). The Employment Rights Act 1996 s 207B (extension of time limits to facilitate conciliation before institution of proceedings: see PARA 1455) applies for the purposes of s 164(1)(c) and s 164(2) (see text and notes 10–13): s 164(5) (added by the Enterprise and Regulatory Reform Act 2013 Sch 2 para 34).

8　Ie under the Employment Rights Act 1996 s 111: see PARA 804. As to the meaning of 'dismissal' see PARA 762.

9　Employment Rights Act 1996 s 164(1)(d). See also note 4. A complaint of dismissal may involve consideration of whether a redundancy payment or compensation for unfair dismissal, or both, is due: *Coates v CJ Crispin Ltd* [1973] ICR 413, [1973] IRLR 211, NIRC. A complaint of unfair dismissal is valid for these purposes even if made after the three-month period laid down for that action: *Duffin v Secretary of State for Employment* [1983] ICR 766, EAT.

10　Where a claim for a redundancy payment is made by a personal representative of a deceased employee who died after the end of the period of six months beginning with the relevant date but before the end of the following period of six months, the Employment Rights Act 1996 s 164(2) applies as if for the words 'six months' there were substituted 'one year': s 176(7)(b).

11　Ie the period mentioned in the Employment Rights Act 1996 s 164(1): see the text and notes 1–9.

12　As to the meaning of 'employer' for this purpose see note 6.

13　See note 8.

14　Employment Rights Act 1996 s 164(2) (amended by the Employment Rights (Dispute Resolution) Act 1998 s 1(2)(a)). See also note 4. Where there is uncertainty whether there has been a transfer of undertaking (see PARA 136 et seq), the employee should still make a timeous claim, because failure to do so on erroneous official advice has been held not to be a good reason to extend the time limit under the Employment Rights Act 1996 s 164(2): *Crawford v Secretary of State for Employment and Colmore Depot* [1995] IRLR 523, EAT.

15　See note 11.

16　Employment Rights Act 1996 s 164(3) (amended by the Employment Rights (Dispute Resolution) Act 1998 s 1(2)(a)). See also note 4.

881.　Calculation of amount of payment. The amount of a redundancy payment[1] to which an employee[2] is entitled in any case is to be calculated by first determining the period, ending with the relevant date[3], during which he has been continuously employed[4].

The amount of the redundancy payment is then to be calculated by reference to that period by starting at the end of that period and reckoning backwards the number of years of employment[5] falling within that period[6] and allowing the appropriate amount for each of those years of employment, the appropriate amount being:

(1)　one and a half weeks' pay[7] for each such year of employment in which the employee was not below the age of 41;

(2)   one week's pay for each such year of employment, not within head (1) above, in which the employee was not below the age of 22; and

(3)   half a week's pay for each such year of employment not within either head (1) or head (2) above[8].

Where 20 years of employment have been so reckoned, no account is to be taken of any year of employment earlier than those 20 years[9].

For the purposes of any of the statutory provisions relating to redundancy payments[10] by virtue of which an employment tribunal[11] may determine that an employer[12] is liable to pay to an employee:

(a)   the whole of the redundancy payment to which the employee would have had a right apart from some other provision therein mentioned; or

(b)   such part of the redundancy payment to which the employee would have had a right apart from some other provision therein mentioned as the tribunal thinks fit,

the above provisions apply as if in those provisions any reference to the amount of a redundancy payment were a reference to the amount of the redundancy payment to which the employee would have otherwise been so entitled[13].

1   As to the meaning of 'redundancy payment' see PARA 836.

2   As to the meaning of 'employee' see PARA 2; and as to excluded classes of employment see PARA 854 et seq.

3   As to the meaning of 'relevant date' see PARA 871.

4   Employment Rights Act 1996 s 162(1)(a). As to when an employee's period of continuous employment is treated as beginning for these purposes see PARA 130 et seq. See also PARAS 861–863.

    In relation to any person to whom the Redundancy Payments (Continuity of Employment in Local Government, etc) (Modification) Order 1999, SI 1999/2277 (see PARA 839 et seq) applies, the Employment Rights Act 1996 s 162 has effect as if: (1) in s 162(1)(a) for the words 'continuously employed' there were substituted the words 'employed in relevant service'; (2) there were added s 162(1A), providing that for the purposes of s 162(1)(a) 'relevant service' means: (a) continuous employment by an employer specified in the Redundancy Payments (Continuity of Employment in Local Government, etc) (Modification) Order 1999, SI 1999/2277, Sch 2 Pt II; or (b) where immediately before the relevant event a person has been successively employed by two or more employers specified in Sch 2 Pt II, such aggregate period of service with such employers as would be continuous employment if they were a single employer, and for these purposes 'relevant event' has the same meaning as in the Redundancy Payments (Continuity of Employment in Local Government, etc) (Modification) Order 1999, SI 1999/2277 (see PARA 839 note 2): arts 1(2)(i), 3, Sch 2 Pt I para 3. See also *Allsop v North Tyneside Metropolitan Borough Council* (1991) 156 LG Rev 1007, [1991] RVR 209, DC (local authority acted unlawfully when it made redundancy payments which were for amounts in excess of those it was either specifically liable for or empowered to make).

    In relation to any person to whom the Redundancy Payments (National Health Service) (Modification) Order 1993, SI 1993/3167 (see PARAS 851–853) applies:

(i)   the Employment Rights Act 1996 s 162(1) applies subject to the modification that the amount of a redundancy payment to which an employee is entitled in any case to which the Redundancy Payments (National Health Service) (Modification) Order 1993, SI 1993/3167, applies is to be calculated by reference to the period ending with the relevant date during which he has been employed in relevant health service (art 3, Sch 2 para 4; and see the Employment Rights Act 1996 s 241, Sch 2 para 2(1));

(ii)   the Employment Rights Act 1996 s 162(1) has effect as if for the words 'has been continuously employed' there were substituted the words 'has been employed in relevant health service for the requisite period' (Redundancy Payments (National Health Service) (Modification) Order 1993, SI 1993/3167, Sch 2 para 1(a); and see the Employment Rights Act 1996 Sch 2 para 2(1)).

    As to the meaning of 'relevant health service' see PARA 855 note 4.

5   As to the meaning of 'employment' see PARA 2.

6   Employment Rights Act 1996 s 162(1)(b).

7   As to the calculation of a week's pay see PARA 143 et seq.

8   Employment Rights Act 1996 s 162(1)(c), (2).

9 Employment Rights Act 1996 s 162(3).
10 Ie the Employment Rights Act 1996 Pt XI (ss 135–181).
11 As to employment tribunals see PARAS 1399 et seq, 1453 et seq.
12 For the purposes of the operation of the provisions of the Employment Rights Act 1996 Pt XI
   (ss 135–181) and Pt XIV Ch I (ss 210–219) (continuous employment) (see PARAS 130 et seq,
   861–863) in relation to any employee whose remuneration is, by virtue of any statutory
   provision, payable to him by a person other than his employer, references to the employer in
   s 162(6) (any reference) must be construed as references to the person by whom the
   remuneration is payable: see s 173(1), (2). As to the meaning of 'statutory provision' see PARA
   163 note 2.
13 Employment Rights Act 1996 s 162(6) (amended by the Employment Rights (Dispute
   Resolution) Act 1998 s 1(2)(a); and SI 2006/1031).

882. Written particulars of redundancy payment. On making any redundancy payment[1], otherwise than in pursuance of a decision of a tribunal[2] which specifies the amount of the payment to be made, the employer[3] must give to the employee[4] a written[5] statement indicating how the amount of the payment has been calculated[6]. An employer who without reasonable excuse fails to give such a statement is guilty of an offence and liable on summary conviction to a fine[7].

If an employer fails to comply with the requirements to give such a statement, the employee may, by notice in writing to the employer, require him to give to the employee a written statement complying with those requirements within such period, not being less than one week beginning with the day on which the notice is given, as may be specified in the notice[8]; and, if the employer without reasonable excuse fails to comply with the notice, he is guilty of an offence and liable on summary conviction to a fine[9].

Where any such offence committed by a body corporate is proved to have been committed with the consent or connivance of, or to be attributable to any neglect on the part of, any director[10], manager[11], secretary or other similar officer of the body corporate or any person who was purporting to act in any such capacity, he, as well as the body corporate, is guilty of that offence and is liable to be proceeded against and punished accordingly[12].

1 As to the meaning of 'redundancy payment' see PARA 836.
2 As to employment tribunals see PARAS 1399 et seq, 1453 et seq.
3 For the purposes of the operation of the provisions of the Employment Rights Act 1996 Pt XI
   (ss 135–181) and Pt XIV Ch I (ss 210–219) (continuous employment) (see PARAS 130 et seq,
   861–863) in relation to any employee whose remuneration is, by virtue of any statutory
   provision, payable to him by a person other than his employer, references to the employer in
   s 165 (see also the text and notes 7–9) must be construed as references to the person by whom
   the remuneration is payable: see s 173(1), (2). As to the meaning of 'statutory provision' see
   PARA 163 note 2.
4 As to the meaning of 'employee' see PARA 2; and as to excluded classes of employment see
   PARA 854 et seq.
5 As to the meaning of 'writing' see PARA 2 note 8.
6 Employment Rights Act 1996 s 165(1). Where a payment without a written statement is found
   not to be a redundancy payment, the employee may still claim for one: *Collin v Flexiform Ltd*
   (1966) 1 ITR 253 (payment in lieu of notice); *Galloway v Export Packing Services Ltd* [1975]
   IRLR 306 (ex gratia payment). The absence of a written statement does not, however, of itself
   prevent a payment from being a redundancy payment; it is still necessary to look objectively at
   the intention of the parties: *Barnsley Metropolitan Borough Council v Prest* [1996] ICR
   85, EAT.
7 Employment Rights Act 1996 s 165(2). As to the meaning of 'employer' for this purpose see
   note 3. The penalty is a fine not exceeding level 1 on the standard scale: see s 165(2). As to the
   standard scale see SENTENCING AND DISPOSITION OF OFFENDERS vol 92 (2010) PARA 142.
8 Employment Rights Act 1996 s 165(3). As to the meaning of 'employer' for this purpose see
   note 3. As to the giving of notices see PARA 837.
9 Employment Rights Act 1996 s 165(4). As to the meaning of 'employer' for this purpose see
   note 3. The penalty is a fine not exceeding level 3 on the standard scale: see s 165(4).

10 For these purposes, 'director', in relation to a body corporate established by or under any enactment for the purpose of carrying on under national ownership any industry or part of an industry or undertaking, being a body corporate whose affairs are managed by its members, means a member of that body corporate: Employment Rights Act 1996 s 180(2).

11 As to the meaning of 'manager' see PARA 40 note 11.

12 Employment Rights Act 1996 s 180(1).

883. Statutory compensation schemes. The Secretary of State[1] may make provision by regulations[2] for securing that:

(1) where a person is otherwise entitled to compensation under any statutory provision[3] which was in force immediately before 6 December 1965 and under which the holders of such situations, places or employments as are specified in that provision are, or may become, entitled to compensation for loss of employment, or for loss or diminution of emoluments or of pension rights, in consequence of the operation of any other statutory provision referred to in that provision; and

(2) the circumstances are such that he is also entitled to a redundancy payment[4],

the amount of the redundancy payment is to be set off against the compensation to which he would otherwise be entitled[5]; and any statutory provision to which any such regulations apply has effect subject to the regulations[6].

The amount of the statutory compensation[7] which would otherwise become due to the employee[8] must be reduced[9] by the amount of the redundancy payment which is to be paid to the employee; and, in so far as the statutory compensation consists of more than one payment, the payments of such compensation as they become due are subject to such abatement or reduction as is necessary to reduce the amount of the statutory compensation by the amount of the redundancy payment[10].

1 As to the Secretary of State see PARA 5 note 21.

2 As to the making of regulations under the Employment Rights Act 1996 generally see PARA 162.

3 Ie apart from the Employment Rights Act 1996 s 178. As to the meaning of 'statutory provision' see PARA 163 note 2.

4 As to the meaning of 'redundancy payment' see PARA 836.

5 See note 3.

6 Employment Rights Act 1996 s 178(1), (2). At the date at which this volume states the law no such regulations had been so made but, by virtue of s 241, Sch 2 para 2(1) (see PARA 162), the Redundancy Payments Statutory Compensation Regulations 1965, SI 1965/1988 (see the text and notes 7–10) have effect as if so made.

7 For these purposes, 'statutory compensation' means compensation, whether it consists of one or more payments, under any of the statutory provisions specified in Redundancy Payments Statutory Compensation Regulations 1965, SI 1965/1988, reg 2, Schedule, being a statutory provision in force immediately before 6 December 1965, for loss of employment, or for loss or diminution of emoluments or of pension rights in consequence of the operation of any other statutory provision referred to in the statutory provision so specified; and 'statutory provision' means a provision, whether of a general or a special nature, contained in, or in any document made or issued under, any Act, whether of a general or a special nature: reg 2(2).

The statutory provisions specified in the Schedule are:

(1) the Railways Act 1921 ss 3, 5, 14, Sch 3 (repealed);

(2) the London Passenger Transport Act 1933 Pt VII (ss 73–80) (repealed);

(3) an order or scheme under the Local Government Act 1933 ss 43–45, Pt VI (ss 129–155) (repealed);

(4) any statutory provision (whether or not specifically included in the Redundancy Payments Statutory Compensation Regulations 1965, SI 1965/1988, Schedule) which applies or extends any of the provisions of the Local Government Act 1933 s 150 or Sch 4 (repealed);

(5) the Education Act 1944 s 98 (repealed);

(6)   the Water Act 1945 s 44 (repealed);
(7)   the Education Act 1946 s 12 (repealed);
(8)   regulations under the Coal Industry Nationalisation Act 1946 s 37 (prospectively repealed) (see MINES, MINERALS AND QUARRIES vol 76 (2013) PARA 83);
(9)   the Local Government (Scotland) Act 1947 s 318, Sch 11;
(10)   regulations under the Transport Act 1947 s 101 (repealed);
(11)   regulations under the Electricity Act 1947 s 55 (repealed);
(12)   regulations under the Local Government Act 1948 s 140 and such regulations as applied by any local Act (see LOCAL GOVERNMENT vol 69 (2009) PARA 1 et seq);
(13)   regulations under the Gas Act 1948 s 60 (repealed);
(14)   regulations under the Prevention of Damage by Pests Act 1949 s 25 (repealed);
(15)   regulations under the Justice of the Peace Act 1949 s 42 (repealed);
(16)   regulations under the Transport Act 1953 s 28 (repealed);
(17)   regulations under the Iron and Steel Act 1953 s 24 (repealed);
(18)   regulations under the Electricity Reorganisation (Scotland) Act 1954 s 12 (repealed);
(19)   regulations under the Electricity Act 1957 s 27 (repealed);
(20)   regulations under the Local Government Act 1958 s 60 (see the Local Government (Compensation) Regulations 1963, SI 1963/999; the Local Government (Executive Councils) (Compensation) Regulations 1964, SI 1964/1177; the Clerks of the Peace and Justices' Clerks (Compensation) Regulations 1965, SI 1965/517; the Fire Services (Compensation) Regulations 1965, SI 1965/563; the Police (Compensation) Regulations 1965, SI 1965/564; the Coroners (Compensation) Regulations 1965, SI 1965/576; and the Probation (Compensation) Regulations 1965, SI 1965/620);
(21)   regulations under the Water Officers Compensation Act 1960 s 1 (see the Water Officers (Compensation) Regulations 1964, SI 1964/26; and the Passenger Transport (Compensation to Officers) Regulations 1970, SI 1970/749);
(22)   regulations under the Land Drainage Act 1961 s 18(6) (repealed);
(23)   regulations under the Transport Act 1962 s 81 (see the British Transport Reorganisation (Compensation to Employees) Regulations 1962, SI 1962/2834; and RAILWAYS AND TRAMWAYS vol 86 (2013) PARA 6);
(24)   regulations under the London Government Act 1963 s 85 (see the Local Government (Executive Councils) (Compensation) Regulations 1964, SI 1964/1177; the London Government (Compensation) Regulations 1964, SI 1964/1953; the London Authorities (Registration Service) Order 1964, SI 1964/2066; the London Authorities (Staff) Order 1965, SI 1965/96; the London Government (Grants and Rates etc) Order 1965, SI 1965/97; the Clerks of the Peace and Justices' Clerks (Compensation) Regulations 1965, SI 1965/517; the Fire Services (Compensation) Regulations 1965, SI 1965/563; the Coroners (Compensation) Regulations 1965, SI 1965/576; the Probation (Compensation) Regulations 1965, SI 1965/620; the London Government (Probation Staff and Property) Order 1965, SI 1965/623; the London Courts (Transfer of Staff) Order 1965, SI 1965/624; the Alexandra Park and Palace Order 1966, SI 1966/199; the London Authorities (Staff) Order 1966, SI 1966/1216; the London Authorities (Parks and Open Spaces) (Staff) Order 1971, SI 1971/229; the London Authorities (Transfer of Housing Estates etc) (No 1) Order 1972, SI 1972/171; the London Authorities (Transfer of Housing Estates etc) Order 1973, SI 1973/417; the Greater London Council Housing (Staff Transfer and Protection) Order 1979, SI 1979/1737; and LONDON GOVERNMENT vol 71 (2013) PARA 9);
(25)   regulations under the Water Resources Act 1963 s 106 (repealed).
    Each of the statutory provisions so specified, being a statutory provision in force immediately before 6 December 1965, has effect subject to the Redundancy Payments Statutory Compensation Regulations 1965, SI 1965/1988: reg 4(2).

8   For these purposes, 'employee' has the meaning assigned to it in the Employment Rights Act 1996 s 230 (see PARA 2) and includes any person in respect of whom that Act has effect as if he were an employee within the meaning of s 230: Redundancy Payments Statutory Compensation Regulations 1965, SI 1965/1988, reg 2(2); and see the Employment Rights Act 1996 s 241, Sch 2 para 2(1).

9   Ie in any case in which an employee on or after 6 December 1965 becomes entitled to statutory compensation and the circumstances are such that he is also entitled to a redundancy payment under the Employment Rights Act 1996 from his employer. For these purposes, 'employer' has the meaning assigned to it in s 230 (see PARA 2) and includes any person in respect of whom that Act has effect as if he were an employer within the meaning of s 230: Redundancy Payments Statutory Compensation Regulations 1965, SI 1965/1988, reg 2(2); Interpretation Act 1978 s 17(2)(a). In a case where an employee's remuneration is, by virtue of any statutory provision,

payable to him by a person other than his employer, 'employer' means that other person: Redundancy Payments Statutory Compensation Regulations 1965, SI 1965/1988, reg 2(2).

10	Redundancy Payments Statutory Compensation Regulations 1965, SI 1965/1988, regs 2(2), 3, 4(1); and see the Employment Rights Act 1996 Sch 2 para 2(1).

**884.	Payment to employee by Secretary of State; calculation of amount.** Where an employee[1] claims that his employer[2] is liable to pay to him an employer's payment[3], and either:

(1)	that the employee has taken all reasonable steps[4], other than legal proceedings[5], to recover the payment from the employer and the employer has refused or failed to pay it, or has paid part of it and has refused or failed to pay the balance; or

(2)	that the employer is insolvent[6] and that the whole or part of the payment remains unpaid,

the employee may apply to the Secretary of State for a payment[7].

If, on such an application, the Secretary of State is satisfied that:

(a)	the employee is entitled to the employer's payment;

(b)	one of the conditions specified in heads (1) and (2) above is fulfilled; and

(c)	in a case[8] where the employer is liable, under an agreement in respect of which an exemption order is in force[9], to make a payment on the termination of an employee's contract of employment, the employee's right to the payment arises by virtue of a period of continuous employment[10], computed in accordance with the provisions of the agreement in question, which is not less than two years,

the Secretary of State must pay to the employee out of the National Insurance Fund[11] a sum calculated in accordance with the statutory provisions[12] reduced by so much, if any, of the employer's payment as has already been paid[13].

Where the Secretary of State pays a sum to an employee in respect of an employer's payment:

(i)	all rights and remedies of the employee with respect to the employer's payment, or, if the Secretary of State has paid only part of it, all the rights and remedies of the employee with respect to that part of the employer's payment, are transferred to and vest in the Secretary of State; and

(ii)	any decision of an employment tribunal requiring the employer's payment to be paid to the employee has effect as if it required that payment, or that part of it which the Secretary of State has paid, to be paid to the Secretary of State[14].

Any moneys recovered under these provisions by the Secretary of State must be paid into the National Insurance Fund[15].

1	As to the meaning of 'employee' see PARA 2; and as to excluded classes of employment see PARA 854 et seq. See also note 7.

2	For the purposes of the operation of the provisions of the Employment Rights Act 1996 Pt XI (ss 135–181) and Pt XIV Ch I (ss 210–219) (continuous employment) (see PARAS 130 et seq, 861–863) in relation to any employee whose remuneration is, by virtue of any statutory provision, payable to him by a person other than his employer, references to the employer in ss 166–168 must be construed as references to the person by whom the remuneration is payable: see s 173(1), (2). As to the meaning of 'statutory provision' see PARA 163 note 2.

3	For these purposes, 'employer's payment', in relation to an employee, means: (1) a redundancy payment which his employer is liable to pay to him under the Employment Rights Act 1996 Pt XI (ss 135–181) (see PARA 836 et seq); (2) a payment which his employer is liable to make to him under an agreement to refrain from instituting or continuing proceedings for a contravention or alleged contravention of s 135 (see PARA 836), which has effect by virtue of s 203(2)(e) or s 203(2)(f) (restrictions on contracting out) (see PARA 150); or (3) a payment which his employer is, under an agreement in respect of which an order is in force under s 157 (see PARA 857), liable to make to him on the termination of his contract of employment: s 166(2) (amended by the Employment Rights (Dispute Resolution) Act 1998 s 11(2) Sch 2); Employment Rights Act 1996 s 181(1). As to the meaning of 'contract of employment' see PARA 2. As to the meaning of 'redundancy payment' see PARA 836. In relation to any case where, in accordance with any provision of Pt XI, an employment tribunal determines that an employer is liable to pay only part, but not the whole, of a redundancy payment, the reference in head (1) above to a redundancy payment is a reference to the part of the redundancy payment: s 166(3) (amended by the Employment Rights (Dispute Resolution) Act 1998 s 1(2)(a)); Employment Rights Act 1996 s 181(1). As to employment tribunals see PARAS 1399 et seq, 1453 et seq.

4   See *Jeffrey v Grey* (1967) 2 ITR 335 (application to tribunal).
5   For these purposes, 'legal proceedings' does not include any proceedings before an employment tribunal, but includes any proceedings to enforce a decision or award of an employment tribunal: Employment Rights Act 1996 s 166(4) (amended by the Employment Rights (Dispute Resolution) Act 1998 s 1(2)(a)).
6   For these purposes, an employer is to be taken to be insolvent if, and only if: (1) where he is an individual: (a) he has been adjudged bankrupt or has made a composition or arrangement with his creditors; or (b) he has died and his estate falls to be administered in accordance with an order under the Insolvency Act 1986 s 421 (see BANKRUPTCY AND INDIVIDUAL INSOLVENCY vol 5 (2013) PARA 830 et seq); (2) where the employer is a company: (a) a winding-up order has been made or a resolution for voluntary winding up has been passed with respect to the company; (b) the company enters administration for the purposes of the Insolvency Act 1986 (see COMPANY AND PARTNERSHIP INSOLVENCY vol 16 (2011) PARA 1 et seq); (c) a receiver or manager of the company's undertaking has been duly appointed, or possession has been taken, by or on behalf of the holders of any debentures secured by a floating charge, of any property of the company comprised in or subject to the charge; or (d) a voluntary arrangement proposed for the purposes of Pt I (ss 1–7B) (see COMPANY AND PARTNERSHIP INSOLVENCY vol 16 (2011) PARA 83 et seq) has been approved thereunder; or (3) where the employer is a limited liability partnership: (a) a winding-up order, an administration order or a determination for a voluntary winding up has been made with respect to it; or (b) a receiver or manager of the undertaking has been duly appointed, or possession has been taken, by or on behalf of the holders of any debentures secured by a floating charge, of any property of the limited liability partnership comprised in or subject to the charge; or (c) a voluntary arrangement proposed for the purposes of Pt I is approved thereunder: Employment Rights Act 1996 s 166(5)(a)–(c) (amended by SI 2001/1090); Employment Rights Act 1996 s 166(6)(a), s 166(7)(a)–(c) (amended by the Enterprise Act 2002 Sch 17 para 49(1), (2), Sch 26); Employment Rights Act 1996 s 166(8)(a)–(c) (added by SI 2001/1090); Employment Rights Act 1996 181(1).

       For these purposes, references to a company are to be read as including references to a charitable incorporated organisation, and any reference to the Insolvency Act 1986 in relation to a company is to be read as including a reference to Insolvency Act 1986 as it applies to charitable incorporated organisations: Employment Rights Act 1996 s 166(9) (added by SI 2012/3014).
7   Employment Rights Act 1996 ss 166(1), 181(1). As to the meaning of 'employer' for this purpose see note 2. As to the Secretary of State see PARA 5 note 21. A managing director and/or majority shareholder of an insolvent company may still be found to be an employee for these purposes and therefore entitled to a redundancy payment: see *Secretary of State for Business, Innovation and Skills v Knight* [2014] IRLR 605, EAT; and *Crawford v Department for Employment and Learning* [2014] NICA 26, [2014] IRLR 626, NICA. As to when a director and shareholder of a company falls to be treated as an 'employee' of the company see PARAS 8, 9.
8   Ie in a case where the employer's payment is such a payment as is mentioned in the Employment Rights Act 1996 s 166(2)(b): see note 3 head (3). As to the meaning of 'employer' for this purpose see note 2.
9   Ie under the Employment Rights Act 1996 s 157: see PARA 857.
10   As to continuity of employment see PARAS 130 et seq, 861–863.
11   As to the National Insurance Fund see WELFARE BENEFITS AND STATE PENSIONS vol 104 (2014) PARA 15.
12   Ie calculated in accordance with the Employment Rights Act 1996 s 168. Where the employer's payment to which the employee's application under s 166 relates is a redundancy payment or a part of a redundancy payment, the sum referred to in s 167(1) is a sum equal to the amount of the redundancy payment or part: s 168(1)(a) (amended by the Employment Rights (Dispute Resolution) Act 1998 Sch 2).

Where the employer's payment to which the employee's application under the Employment Rights Act 1996 s 166 relates is a payment which his employer is liable to make to him under an agreement having effect by virtue of s 203(2)(e) or s 203(2)(f) (restrictions on contracting out) (see PARA 150), it is a sum equal to the amount of the employer's payment or of any redundancy payment which the employer would have been liable to pay to the employee but for the agreement, whichever is less: s 168(1)(aa) (added by the Employment Rights (Dispute Resolution) Act 1998 s 11(3)).

Where the employer's payment to which the employee's application under the Employment Rights Act 1996 s 166 relates is a payment which the employer is liable to make under an agreement in respect of which an order is in force under s 157 (see PARA 857), it is a sum equal to the amount of the employer's payment or of the relevant redundancy payment, whichever is less: s 168(1)(b). The reference in s 168(1)(b) to the amount of the relevant redundancy payment is a reference to the amount of the redundancy payment which the employer would have been liable to pay to the employee on the following assumptions, namely that: (1) the order in force in respect of the agreement had not been made; (2) the circumstances in which the employer's payment is payable had been such that the employer was liable to pay a redundancy payment to the employee in those circumstances; (3) the relevant date, in relation to any such redundancy payment, had been the date on which the termination of the employee's contract of employment is treated as having taken effect for the purposes of the agreement; and (4) in so far as the provisions of the agreement relating to the circumstances in which the continuity of an employee's period of employment is to be treated as broken, and the weeks which are to count in computing a period of employment, are inconsistent with the provisions of Pt XIV Ch I (ss 210–219) (see PARA 130 et seq), the provisions of the agreement were substituted for those provisions: s 168(2), (3). As to the meaning of 'employer' for this purpose see note 2.

13 Employment Rights Act 1996 s 167(1), (2). As to the meaning of 'employer' for this purpose see note 2. Where a tribunal has ordered the Secretary of State to pay a redundancy payment that the employer has failed to pay, it may not award interest from the date of the employer's default: *Secretary of State for Employment v Reeves* [1993] ICR 508, EAT.

14 Employment Rights Act 1996 s 167(3) (amended by the Employment Rights (Dispute Resolution) Act 1998 s 1(2)(a)). As to the meaning of 'employer' for this purpose see note 2.

15 Employment Rights Act 1996 s 167(4).

885. Payment to employee by Secretary of State; provision of information.
Where an employee[1] makes an application to the Secretary of State[2] for a sum in respect of an employer's payment[3], the Secretary of State may, by notice in writing[4] given to the employer[5], require the employer to provide the Secretary of State with such information, and to produce for examination on behalf of the Secretary of State documents in his custody or under his control of such description, as the Secretary of State may reasonably require for the purpose of determining whether the application is well-founded[6].

Where any person on whom a notice is so served fails without reasonable excuse to comply with a requirement imposed by the notice, he is guilty of an offence and liable on summary conviction to a fine[7].

If a person:

(1) in providing any information required by such a notice, makes a statement which he knows to be false in a material particular, or recklessly makes a statement which is false in a material particular; or

(2) produces for examination, in accordance with such a notice, a document which to his knowledge has been wilfully falsified,

he is guilty of an offence and liable on conviction to a penalty[8].

Where any such offence committed by a body corporate is proved to have been committed with the consent or connivance of, or to be attributable to any neglect on the part of, any director[9], manager[10], secretary or other similar officer of the body corporate or any person who was purporting to act in any such capacity, he, as well as the body corporate, is guilty of that offence and is liable to be proceeded against and punished accordingly[11].

1   As to the meaning of 'employee' see PARA 2; and as to excluded classes of employment see
    PARA 854 et seq.
2   As to the Secretary of State see PARA 5 note 21.
3   Ie under the Employment Rights Act 1996 s 166: see PARA 884. For the purposes of the
    operation of the provisions of Pt XI (ss 135–181) and Pt XIV Ch I (ss 210–219) (continuous
    employment) (see PARAS 130 et seq, 861–863) in relation to any employee whose remuneration
    is, by virtue of any statutory provision, payable to him by a person other than his employer,
    references to the employer in s 169 (see also note 5) must be construed as references to the
    person by whom the remuneration is payable: see s 173(1), (2). As to the meaning of 'statutory
    provision' see PARA 163 note 2.
4   As to the meaning of 'writing' see PARA 2 note 8.
5   As to the meaning of 'employer' for these purposes see note 3.
6   Employment Rights Act 1996 s 169(1). As to the giving of notices see PARA 837.
7   Employment Rights Act 1996 s 169(2). The penalty is a fine not exceeding level 3 on the
    standard scale: see s 169(2). As to the standard scale see SENTENCING AND DISPOSITION OF
    OFFENDERS vol 92 (2010) PARA 142.
8   Employment Rights Act 1996 s 169(3). The penalty on conviction on indictment is a fine or
    imprisonment for a term not exceeding two years, or both, and the penalty on summary
    conviction is a fine not exceeding the statutory maximum or imprisonment for a term not
    exceeding three months, or both: see s 169(4). As to the statutory maximum see SENTENCING
    AND DISPOSITION OF OFFENDERS vol 92 (2010) PARA 140.
9   As to the meaning of 'director' for these purposes see PARA 882 note 10.
10 As to the meaning of 'manager' see PARA 40 note 11.
11 Employment Rights Act 1996 s 180(1).

(8) DETERMINATION OF QUESTIONS

886.   Redundancy payments. Any question[1] as to the right of an employee[2] to
a redundancy payment[3], or as to the amount of a redundancy payment, must be
referred to and determined by an employment tribunal[4].

For the purposes of any such reference, an employee who has been dismissed[5]
by his employer[6] is to be presumed, unless the contrary is proved, to have been
so dismissed by reason of redundancy[7].

In relation to lay-off or short time[8], the questions which may be so referred to
and determined by an employment tribunal include any question whether an
employee will become entitled to a redundancy payment if he is not dismissed by
his employer and he terminates his contract of employment[9]; and any such
question is taken[10] to be a question as to the right of the employee to a
redundancy payment[11].

1   Ie arising under the Employment Rights Act 1996 Pt XI (ss 135–181): see PARA 835 et seq.
2   As to the meaning of 'employee' see PARA 2; and as to excluded classes of employment see
    PARA 854 et seq.
3   As to the meaning of 'redundancy payment' see PARA 836.
4   Employment Rights Act 1996 s 163(1). Where an exemption order under s 157 (see PARA 857)
    is in force in respect of an agreement, s 163 has effect in relation to any question arising under
    the agreement as to the right of an employee to a payment on the termination of his
    employment, or as to the amount of such a payment, as if the payment were a redundancy
    payment and the question arose under Pt XI: s 163(4). As to employment tribunals see PARA
    1399 et seq; and as to proceedings before employment tribunals see PARA 1453 et seq.
        Where a tribunal determines under s 163(1) that an employee has a right to a redundancy
    payment it may order the employer to pay to the worker such amount as the tribunal considers
    appropriate in all the circumstances to compensate the worker for any financial loss sustained
    by him which is attributable to the non-payment of the redundancy payment: s 163(5) (added by
    the Employment Act 2008 s 7(2)).
5   As to the meaning of 'dismissal' see PARA 864.
6   As to the meaning of 'employer' see PARA 2.
7   Employment Rights Act 1996 s 163(2). The test is the standard one of balance of probabilities
    and is discharged if the tribunal is satisfied that the ground put forward by the employer is

genuine and the one to which the dismissal is mainly attributable, even though it may be unwise or based on a mistaken view of the facts: *Hindle v Percival Boats Ltd* [1969] 1 All ER 836, [1969] 1 WLR 174, CA; *Wagstaff v Trade and Industrial Press Ltd* (1967) 3 ITR 1, DC. See also *Willcox v Hastings* [1987] IRLR 298, CA (one redundant position, but two employees dismissed for indistinguishable reasons; presumption not rebutted). The presumption does not apply in unfair dismissal proceedings: *Midland Foot Comfort Centre Ltd v Richmond* [1973] 2 All ER 294, sub nom *Midland Foot Comfort Centre Ltd v Moppett* [1973] ICR 219, NIRC. See also the Employment Tribunals Act 1996 s 7(6); and PARA 804 note 5.

8   As to lay-off and short time see PARA 875.
9   Ie as mentioned in the Employment Rights Act 1996 s 150(1): see PARA 877. As to the meaning of 'contract of employment' see PARA 2.
10 Ie for the purposes of the Employment Rights Act 1996 Pt XI.
11 Employment Rights Act 1996 s 163(3).

887. Payments by the Secretary of State.   Where, on an application made to the Secretary of State[1] for a payment out of the National Insurance Fund[2], it is claimed that an employer[3] is liable to pay an employer's payment[4], there must be referred to an employment tribunal[5]:

(1)   any question as to the liability of the employer to pay the employer's payment; and

(2)   any question as to the amount of the sum payable[6] in accordance with the statutory provisions[7].

For the purposes of any such reference, an employee[8] who has been dismissed[9] by his employer is to be presumed, unless the contrary is proved, to have been so dismissed by reason of redundancy[10].

1   As to the Secretary of State see PARA 5 note 21.
2   Ie under the Employment Rights Act 1996 s 166: see PARA 884.
3   For the purposes of the operation of the provisions of the Employment Rights Act 1996 Pt XI (ss 135–181) and Pt XIV Ch I (ss 210–219) (continuous employment) (see PARAS 130 et seq, 861–863) in relation to any employee whose remuneration is, by virtue of any statutory provision, payable to him by a person other than his employer, references to the employer in s 170(1) (any reference) must be construed as references to the person by whom the remuneration is payable: see s 173(1), (2). As to the meaning of 'statutory provision' see PARA 163 note 2.
4   As to the meaning of 'employer's payment' see PARA 884 note 3.
5   As to employment tribunals see PARA 1399 et seq; and as to proceedings before employment tribunals see PARA 1453 et seq.
6   Ie payable in accordance with the Employment Rights Act 1996 s 168: see PARA 884 note 12.
7   Employment Rights Act 1996 s 170(1) (amended by the Employment Rights (Dispute Resolution) Act 1998 s 1(2)(a)). As to the meaning of 'employer' for these purposes see note 3. Where a claim under the Employment Rights Act 1996 s 168 is disputed, the employee may make an application under s 170 joining the Secretary of State without the employer being joined as a party to the proceedings: *Jones v Secretary of State for Employment* [1982] ICR 389, EAT.
8   As to the meaning of 'employee' see PARA 2; and as to excluded classes of employment see PARA 854 et seq.
9   As to the meaning of 'dismissal' see PARA 864.
10 Employment Rights Act 1996 s 170(2). As to the meaning of 'employer' for these purposes see note 3.

888. Equivalent payments.   Where the terms and conditions, whether or not they constitute a contract of employment[1], on which a person is employed in certain employments[2] include provision:

(1)   for the making of a payment equivalent to a redundancy payment[3]; and

(2)   for referring to an employment tribunal[4] any question as to the right of any person to such a payment in respect of that employment, or as to the amount of such a payment,

the question must be referred to and determined by an employment tribunal[5].

1 As to the meaning of 'contract of employment' see PARA 2. For these purposes, the definition of 'employment' in the Employment Rights Act 1996 s 230 (see PARA 2) does not apply: s 230(5)(a).

2 Ie any such employment as is mentioned in the Employment Rights Act 1996 s 171(3) (eg public offices, offices remunerated out of the Sovereign Grant, etc): see PARA 838 note 5.

3 Ie any payment by way of compensation for loss of employment of any description mentioned in the Employment Rights Act 1996 s 171(3), which is payable in accordance with arrangements made with the approval of the Treasury (see PARA 838 note 5) (or, in the case of persons whose service is for the purposes of pensions and other superannuation benefits treated as service in the civil service of the state, of the Minister for the Civil Service) for securing that a payment will be made: (1) in circumstances which, in the opinion of the Treasury (or minister), correspond, subject to the appropriate modifications, to those in which a right to a redundancy payment would have accrued if the provisions of Pt XI (ss 135–181), apart from s 159 (see PARA 854) and s 177, applied; and (2) on a scale which, in the opinion of the Treasury (or minister), taking into account any sums payable in accordance with a scheme made under the Superannuation Act 1972 s 1 (see CONSTITUTIONAL AND ADMINISTRATIVE LAW vol 20 (2014) PARA 298) or the Superannuation Act 1965, as it continues to have effect by virtue of the Superannuation Act 1972 s 23(1) (repealed), to or in respect of the person losing the employment in question, corresponds, subject to the appropriate modifications, to that on which a redundancy payment would have been payable if those provisions applied: Employment Rights Act 1996 s 177(2), (3).

4 As to employment tribunals see PARA 1399 et seq; and as to proceedings before employment tribunals see PARA 1453 et seq.

5 Employment Rights Act 1996 s 177(1) (amended by the Employment Rights (Dispute Resolution) Act 1998 s 1(2)(a)). The 'equivalent payment' provisions (formerly contained in the Employment Protection (Consolidation) Act 1978 s 111(2), (4)–(6) (repealed), and not re-enacted in the Employment Rights Act 1996) were discontinued, in that no such payment may be made by the Secretary of State in respect of any termination of employment occurring after 31 July 1986: see the Wages Act 1986 s 28(6) (repealed).

The time limit of six months in the Employment Rights Act 1996 s 164 (see PARA 880) does not apply to references under s 177, which are governed by the general six-year limitation period under the Limitation Act 1980 (see LIMITATION PERIODS vol 68 (2008) PARA 911): *Greenwich Health Authority v Skinner, Greenwich Health Authority v Ward* [1989] ICR 220, [1989] IRLR 238, EAT; *Stevens v Bexley Health Authority* [1989] ICR 224, [1989] IRLR 240, EAT.

(9) DEATH OF EMPLOYER OR EMPLOYEE

(i) Death of Employer

889. In general. In relation to an employee[1] whose employer[2] dies, the statutory provisions relating to redundancy payments[3] have effect subject to certain modifications[4].

1 As to the meaning of 'employee' see PARA 2; and as to excluded classes of employment see PARA 854 et seq.

2 As to the meaning of 'employer' see PARA 2.

3 Ie the Employment Rights Act 1996 Pt XI (ss 135–181): see PARA 835 et seq.

4 See the Employment Rights Act 1996 ss 174–175. For the modifications see PARAS 135 note 12, 856 note 8, 865 notes 4, 11–14, 874 notes 8, 9, 876 note 8.

(ii) Death of Employee

890. In general. In relation to an employee[1] who dies, the statutory provisions relating to redundancy payments[2] have effect subject to certain modifications[3].

Where an employee whose employer[4] has given him notice to terminate his contract of employment[5] dies before the notice expires, the statutory provisions relating to redundancy payments apply as if the contract had been duly terminated by the employer by notice expiring on the date of the employee's death[6].

1 As to the meaning of 'employee' see PARA 2; and as to excluded classes of employment see PARA 854 et seq.
2 Ie the Employment Rights Act 1996 Pt XI (ss 135–181): see PARA 835 et seq.
3 See the Employment Rights Act 1996 s 176. For the modifications see PARAS 865 note 15, 866 note 9, 871 note 20, 874 notes 12, 16, 876 note 8, 877 note 9, 880 notes 3, 10.
4 As to the meaning of 'employer' see PARA 2.
5 As to the meaning of 'contract of employment' see PARA 2.
6 Employment Rights Act 1996 s 176(1).

8. TRADE UNIONS

(1) DEFINITION AND LEGAL STATUS OF TRADE UNIONS

(i) Definitions relating to Trade Unions

891. Meanings of 'trade union' and 'federated trade union'. 'Trade union' means[1] an organisation[2], whether temporary or permanent, which either:

(1) consists wholly or mainly of workers[3] of one or more descriptions and whose principal purposes[4] include the regulation of relations between workers of that description or those descriptions and employers[5] or employers' associations[6]; or

(2) consists wholly or mainly of constituent or affiliated organisations which fulfil the conditions in head (1) above or themselves consist wholly or mainly of constituent or affiliated organisations which fulfil those conditions, or of representatives of such constituent or affiliated organisations, and whose principal purposes include the regulation of relations between workers and employers or between workers and employers' associations, or the regulation of relations between its constituent or affiliated organisations[7].

'Federated trade union' means[8] a trade union which consists wholly or mainly of constituent or affiliated organisations, or representatives of such organisations, as described in head (2) above[9].

1 Ie in the Trade Union and Labour Relations (Consolidation) Act 1992: see PARA 892 et seq. The repeal and re-enactment of provisions in the Trade Union and Labour Relations (Consolidation) Act 1992 does not affect the continuity of the law: Sch 3 para 1(1). Anything done (including subordinate legislation made), or having effect as done, under a provision reproduced in the Trade Union and Labour Relations (Consolidation) Act 1992 has effect as if done under the corresponding provision of that Act: Sch 3 para 1(2). References, express or implied, in the Trade Union and Labour Relations (Consolidation) Act 1992 or any other enactment, instrument or document to a provision of that Act are to be construed, so far as the context permits, as including, in relation to times, circumstances and purposes before the commencement of the Trade Union and Labour Relations (Consolidation) Act 1992, a reference to corresponding earlier provisions: Sch 3 para 1(3). A reference, express or implied, in any enactment, instrument or other document to a provision reproduced in the Trade Union and Labour Relations (Consolidation) Act 1992 is to be construed, so far as is required for continuing its effect, and subject to any express amendment made by that Act, as being, or as the case may require including, a reference to the corresponding provision of that Act: Sch 3 para 1(4).

2 There must be some degree of formal structure as opposed to a casual grouping of workers: see *Midland Cold Storage Ltd v Turner* [1972] 3 All ER 773, [1972] ICR 230, NIRC.

3 As to the meaning of 'worker' see PARA 892.

4 A committee of shop stewards which had not entered into negotiations with employers or sought recognition by them was held not to satisfy this requirement: *Midland Cold Storage Ltd v Turner* [1972] 3 All ER 773, [1972] ICR 230, NIRC. It may be sufficient if the relevant purposes are included in the objects clause of the organisation's constitution: see *British Association of Advisers and Lecturers in Physical Education v National Union of Teachers* [1986] IRLR 497, CA.

5 As to the meaning of 'employer' see PARA 892.

6 As to the meaning of 'employers' association' see PARA 1079.

7 Trade Union and Labour Relations (Consolidation) Act 1992 s 1(a), (b). Any reference in an enactment passed, or instrument made under an enactment, before 16 September 1974, to a trade union registered under the Trade Union Acts 1871–1964 (repealed) or the Industrial Relations Act 1971 (repealed), or to an organisation of workers within the meaning of the Industrial Relations Act 1971, is to be construed as a reference to a trade union within the meaning of the Trade Union and Labour Relations (Consolidation) Act 1992; but this does not apply to any enactment relating to income tax or corporation tax: Sch 3 para 4(1), (2).

The question of whether an organisation fits the description in the Trade Union and Labour Relations (Consolidation) Act 1992 s 1(a) (see head (1) in the text) is a question of fact; in any case in which as a matter of fact the certification officer decides the purposes do not include the regulation of relations between workers and employers, he cannot certify the organisation as a trade union: *Akinosun (on behalf of General & Health Workers Union) v Certification Officer* [2013] IRLR 937. As to certification see PARA 904 et seq.

8 See note 1.
9 Trade Union and Labour Relations (Consolidation) Act 1992 s 118(1). The provisions of Pt I (ss 1–121) apply to federated trade unions subject to the following exceptions and adaptations (s 118(2)):

  (1) for the purposes of s 22 (limit on amount of damages) (see PARA 1390) as it applies to a federated trade union, the members of such of its constituent or affiliated organisations as have their head or main office in Great Britain are to be treated as members of the union (s 118(3));

  (2) s 27 (duty to supply copy of rules) (see PARA 912), s 28 (duty to keep accounting records) (see PARA 940), ss 32–37 (annual return, statement for members, accounts and audit) (see PARA 943 et seq), ss 37A–37E (investigation of financial affairs) (see PARA 949 et seq) and ss 38–42 (members' superannuation schemes) (see PARA 953 et seq) do not apply to a federated trade union which consists wholly or mainly of representatives of constituent or affiliated organisations (s 118(4) (amended by the Trade Union Reform and Employment Rights Act 1993 Sch 8 para 62, Sch 10));

  (3) the Trade Union and Labour Relations (Consolidation) Act 1992 ss 29–31 (right of member to access to accounting records) (see PARAS 941–942) do not apply to a federated trade union which has no members other than constituent or affiliated organisations or representatives of such organisations (s 118(5));

  (4) ss 24–26 (register of members' names and addresses) (see PARA 930 et seq) and Pt I Ch IV (ss 46–61) (elections for certain trade union positions) (see PARA 959 et seq) do not apply to a federated trade union if it has no individual members other than representatives of constituent or affiliated organisations, or if its individual members, other than such representatives, are all merchant seamen and a majority of them are ordinarily resident outside the United Kingdom; and for this purpose 'merchant seaman' means a person whose employment, or the greater part of it, is carried out on board sea-going ships (s 118(6));

  (5) the provisions of Pt I Ch VI (ss 71–96) (application of funds for political objects) (see PARA 974 et seq) apply to a trade union which is in whole or part an association or combination of other unions as if the individual members of the component unions were members of that union and not of the component unions; but nothing in Pt I Ch VI prevents a component union from collecting contributions on behalf of the association or combination from such of its members as are not exempt from the obligation to contribute to the political fund of the association or combination (s 118(7)); and

  (6) in the application of s 116A (see PARA 929) to a federated trade union, s 116A(2) is omitted (s 118(8) (added by the Employment Relations Act 2004 s 55(2))).

  As from a day to be appointed under the Transparency of Lobbying, Non-party Campaigning and Trade Union Administration Act 2014 s 45(1)(c), it is further provided that, in the case of a federated trade union which, by virtue of head (2) above, is not required to send an annual return to the Certification Officer under the Trade Union and Labour Relations (Consolidation) Act 1992 s 32 (see PARA 943), then s 24ZA (duty to provide membership audit certificate: see PARA 931) applies as if s 32 does apply to the union: see s 118(4A) (prospectively added by the Transparency of Lobbying, Non-party Campaigning and Trade Union Administration Act 2014 s 40(1), (4)). However, at the date at which this volume states the law, no such day had been appointed.

892. Meanings of 'worker', 'employee', 'employer' and 'contract of employment'.

'Worker' means[1] an individual who works, or normally works or seeks to work[2]:

(1) under a contract of employment; or

(2) under any other contract whereby he undertakes to do or perform personally any work or services for another party to the contract who is not a professional client of his[3]; or

(3) in employment under or for the purposes of a government department,

otherwise than as a member of the naval, military or air forces of the Crown[4], in so far as such employment does not fall within head (1) or head (2) above[5].

'Worker' includes an individual regarded in his capacity as one who works or normally works or seeks to work as a person performing personal dental services or providing general dental services, general ophthalmic services or pharmaceutical services in accordance with certain arrangements[6]. 'Worker' also includes an individual regarded in his capacity as one who works or normally works or seeks to work as a person performing primary medical services, primary dental services or, as from a day to be appointed[7], primary ophthalmic services, (a) in accordance with arrangements made by the National Health Service Commissioning Board or a local health board[8]; or (b) under a contract[9] entered into by him with the National Health Service Commissioning Board or a local health board[10]. 'Worker' does not, however, include a person in police service[11].

'Employee' means[12] an individual who has entered into or works under, or, where the employment has ceased, worked under, a contract of employment[13], but does not include a person in police service[14]; 'employer', in relation to an employee, means[15] the person by whom the employee is, or, where the employment has ceased, was, employed[16], and in relation to a worker, means a person for whom one or more workers work, or have worked or normally work or seek to work[17]; and 'contract of employment' means[18] a contract of service or of apprenticeship[19].

It is immaterial[20] whether the law which otherwise[21] governs any person's employment is the law of the United Kingdom, or of a part of the United Kingdom, or not[26].

1 Ie for the purposes of the Trade Union and Labour Relations (Consolidation) Act 1992: see PARAS 891, 893 et seq.

2 A person dismissed while on strike but seeking re-engagement is a worker within this definition: *Grunwick Processing Laboratories Ltd v Advisory, Conciliation and Arbitration Service* [1978] AC 655, [1978] ICR 231, HL.

3 A person who is an independent contractor can be a worker within this part of the definition: *Broadbent v Crisp* [1974] 1 All ER 1052, [1974] ICR 248, NIRC. Authors whose contracts do not require them to perform work or services are not workers: *Writers' Guild of Great Britain v BBC* [1974] 1 All ER 574, [1974] ICR 234, NIRC. Contracts with professional clients are excluded: *Carter v Law Society* [1973] ICR 113, NIRC.

4 As to employment as a member of the naval, military or air forces of the Crown see generally ARMED FORCES vol 3 (2011) PARA 304 et seq.

5 Trade Union and Labour Relations (Consolidation) Act 1992 s 296(1). Section 296 has effect subject to s 68(4) (see PARA 1034), s 145F(3) (see PARA 1051), and s 151(1B) (see PARA 1048): s 296(3) (added by the Trade Union Reform and Employment Rights Act 1993 Sch 8 para 88; amended by the Employment Relations Act 2004 Sch 1 para 21).

6 See the Trade Union and Labour Relations (Consolidation) Act 1992 s 279(1) numbered as such by the Health and Social Care (Community Health and Standards) Act 2003 Sch 11 para 59(1), (3); amended by the National Health Service (Primary Care) Act 1997 Sch 2 para 67; the Health and Social Care Act 2001 Sch 5 Pt 1 para 9; the National Health Service Reform and Health Care Professions Act 2002 s 2(5), Sch 2 Pt 2 para 60; the Health and Social Care (Community Health and Standards) Act 2003 Sch 11 para 59(1), (2), Sch 14 Pt 4; the National Health Service (Consequential Provisions) Act 2006 Sch 1 paras 153, 154; the Health and Social Care Act 2012 Sch 5 para 66; and by SI 2004/957; SI 2006/1056; SI 2007/961). The arrangements referred to in the text are arrangements made (1) by the National Health Service Commissioning Board under the National Health Service Act 2006 s 126 (see HEALTH SERVICES vol 54 (2008) PARA 339 et seq) or a local health board under the National Health Service (Wales) Act 2006 s 71 or s 80 (see HEALTH SERVICES vol 54 (2008) PARAS 338, 339); or (2) by a Health Board under the National Health Service (Scotland) Act 1978 s 17C, s 25 or s 26 or as a person providing local pharmaceutical services under a pilot scheme established under the

National Health Service Act 2006 s 134 or the National Health Service (Wales) Act 2006 s 92 (see HEALTH SERVICES vol 54 (2008) PARA 419), or under an LPS scheme established under the National Health Service Act 2006 Sch 12 or the National Health Service (Wales) Act 2006 Sch 7 (see HEALTH SERVICES vol 54 (2008) PARA 431): see the Trade Union and Labour Relations (Consolidation) Act 1992 s 279(1) (as so amended). 'Employer', in relation to such an individual, regarded in that capacity, means that board: s 279(1) (as so amended). For specific provisions on the definition of 'worker' in Scotland see also s 279(3), (4) (respectively added by SI 2004/957; SI 2006/1056).

7   Ie as from a day to be appointed under the Health Act 2006 s 83(7).
8   Ie under the National Health Service Act 2006 s 92 or s 107 or the National Health Service (Wales) Act 2006 s 50 or s 64: see HEALTH SERVICES vol 54 (2008) PARAS 267, 288.
9   Ie a contract under National Health Service Act 2006 s 84 or s 100 or the National Health Service (Wales) Act 2006 s 42 or s 57 entered into by him with the National Health Service Commissioning Board or a local health board (see HEALTH SERVICES vol 54 (2008) PARAS 242, 278) or a contract under the National Health Service Act 2006 s 117 entered into by him with the National Health Service Commissioning Board (see HEALTH SERVICES vol 54 (2008) PARA 330).
10 Trade Union and Labour Relations (Consolidation) Act 1992 s 279(2) (added by the Health and Social Care (Community Health and Standards) Act 2003 Sch 11 para 59(1), (4); amended by the National Health Service (Consequential Provisions) Act 2006 Sch 1 paras 153, 155; the Health and Social Care Act 2012 Sch 5, para 66; prospectively amended by the Health Act 2006 Sch 8 para 30, as from a day to be appointed (see note 7); at the date at which this volume states the law, no such day had been appointed). 'Employer' in relation to such an individual, regarded in that capacity, means the board referred to in note 9: see the Trade Union and Labour Relations (Consolidation) Act 1992 s 279(2) (as so added and amended).
11 Trade Union and Labour Relations (Consolidation) Act 1992 s 280(1). For these purposes, 'police service' means service as a member of any constabulary maintained by virtue of an enactment, or in any other capacity by virtue of which a person has the powers or privileges of a constable (see POLICE AND INVESTIGATORY POWERS vol 84 (2013) PARA 1 et seq): Trade Union and Labour Relations (Consolidation) Act 1992 s 280(2). In *Home Office v Evans* (18 November 1993, unreported), cited in *Boddington v Lawton* [1994] ICR 478 at 481–482, the court held that a prison officer was to be treated as a person in police service for these purposes, and was not, therefore, a 'worker'. However, the Trade Union and Labour Relations (Consolidation) Act 1992 and the Employment Rights Act 1996 now have effect as if an individual who as a member of the prison service acts in a capacity in which he has the powers and privileges of a constable were not, by virtue of his so having those powers or privileges, to be regarded as in police service for the purposes of any provision of the Trade Union and Labour Relations (Consolidation) Act 1992 or the Employment Rights Act 1996: Criminal Justice and Public Order Act 1994 s 126(1), (2)(a) (s 126(2)(a) substituted by the Employment Rights Act 1996 Sch 1 para 65). As to Crown employment generally see PARA 893.
    The Trade Union and Labour Relations (Consolidation) Act 1992 ss 137, 138 (rights in relation to trade union membership; access to employment) (see PARAS 1042–1043) do not apply in relation to police service: s 280(1).
12 See note 1.
13 Trade Union and Labour Relations (Consolidation) Act 1992 s 295(1). As to the meaning of 'employee' in the Employment Rights Act 1996 see s 230(1); and PARA 2.
14 Trade Union and Labour Relations (Consolidation) Act 1992 s 280(1). See also note 11.
15 Ie for the purposes of the Trade Union and Labour Relations (Consolidation) Act 1992 except s 68 (see s 68(4); and PARA 1034), s 68A (see s 68(4); and PARA 1034) and ss 226–234A (see s 235; and PARA 1370).
16 Trade Union and Labour Relations (Consolidation) Act 1992 s 295(1), (2). As to the meaning of 'employer' in the Employment Rights Act 1996 see s 230(4); and PARA 2. As to the meaning of 'employer' in relation to certain health service practitioners see notes 6, 10.
17 Trade Union and Labour Relations (Consolidation) Act 1992 s 296(2).
18 Ie for the purposes of the Trade Union and Labour Relations (Consolidation) Act 1992 except s 224 (see s 224(6); and PARA 1367) and ss 226–234A (see s 235; and PARA 1370).
19 Trade Union and Labour Relations (Consolidation) Act 1992 s 295(1), (2). As to the meaning of 'contract of employment' in the Employment Rights Act 1996 see s 230(2) and PARA 2; and as to the meaning of 'apprenticeship' see PARA 112.
20 See note 1.
21 Ie apart from the Trade Union and Labour Relations (Consolidation) Act 1992.
23 Trade Union and Labour Relations (Consolidation) Act 1992 s 289. As to the meaning of 'United Kingdom' see PARA 2 note 12.

893. Crown employment. The statutory provisions relating to trade unions and industrial relations[1] have effect[2] in relation to Crown employment[3] and persons in Crown employment as in relation to other employment and other workers[4] or employees[5].

The above provisions[6] do not, however, apply to:

(1)   service as a member of the naval, military or air forces of the Crown[7], although they do apply to employment by a territorial, auxiliary or reserve forces association[8] as they apply to employment for the purposes of a government department[9];

(2)   employment in respect of which there is in force a certificate[10] issued by or on behalf of a Minister of the Crown certifying that employment of a description specified in the certificate, or the employment of a particular person so specified, is, or, at a time specified in the certificate, was, required to be excepted for the purpose of safeguarding national security[11].

1   Ie the Trade Union and Labour Relations (Consolidation) Act 1992: see PARAS 891–892, 894 et seq.

2   Ie except as mentioned in the Trade Union and Labour Relations (Consolidation) Act 1992 s 273(2). The provisions excepted from s 273(1) are: (1) s 87(4)(b) (power of tribunal to make order in respect of failure to comply with duties as to union contributions) (see PARA 990 head (b)); (2) ss 184, 185 (remedy for failure to comply with declaration as to disclosure of information) (see PARA 1182); and (3) Pt IV Ch II (ss 188–198B) (procedure for handling redundancies) (see PARA 1185 et seq): s 273(2) (amended by the Employment Rights (Dispute Resolution) Act 1998 Sch 1 para 8).

3   For these purposes, 'Crown employment' means employment under or for the purposes of a government department or any officer or body exercising on behalf of the Crown functions conferred by an enactment: Trade Union and Labour Relations (Consolidation) Act 1992 s 273(3). For the purposes of the provisions of the Trade Union and Labour Relations (Consolidation) Act 1992, as they apply in relation to Crown employment or persons in Crown employment: (1) 'employee' and 'contract of employment' mean a person in Crown employment and the terms of employment of such a person, but subject to s 273(5) (see note 5); (2) 'dismissal' means the termination of Crown employment; (3) the reference in s 182(1)(e) (disclosure of information for collective bargaining; restrictions on general duty) (see PARA 1181 head (5)) to the employer's undertaking is to be construed as a reference to the national interest; and (4) any other reference to an undertaking is to be construed, in relation to a Minister of the Crown, as a reference to his functions or, as the context may require, to the department of which he is in charge, and, in relation to a government department, officer or body, is to be construed as a reference to the functions of the department, officer or body or, as the context may require, to the department, officer or body: s 273(4) (amended by the Trade Union Reform and Employment Rights Act 1993 Sch 10).

4   As to the meaning of 'worker' see PARA 892.

5   Trade Union and Labour Relations (Consolidation) Act 1992 s 273(1). Section 273 has effect subject to ss 274, s 275 (see the text and notes 6–11): s 273(6). Sections 137–143 (rights in relation to trade union membership; access to employment) (see PARA 1042 et seq) apply in relation to Crown employment otherwise than under a contract only where the terms of employment correspond to those of a contract of employment: s 273(5). As to the meaning of 'employee' see PARA 892.

6   Ie the Trade Union and Labour Relations (Consolidation) Act 1992 s 273.

7   Trade Union and Labour Relations (Consolidation) Act 1992 s 274(1). As to such service see generally ARMED FORCES.

8   Ie an association established for the purposes of the Reserve Forces Act 1996 Pt XI (ss 110–119): see ARMED FORCES vol 3 (2011) PARA 473.

9   Trade Union and Labour Relations (Consolidation) Act 1992 s 274(2) (amended by the Reserve Forces Act 1996 Sch 10 para 24).

10   A document purporting to be such a certificate is to be deemed to be such a certificate unless the contrary is proved: Trade Union and Labour Relations (Consolidation) Act 1992 s 275(2).

11   Trade Union and Labour Relations (Consolidation) Act 1992 s 275(1).

894. House of Lords staff. The statutory provisions relating to trade unions and industrial relations[1] apply[2] in relation to employment as a relevant member of the House of Lords staff[3] as in relation to other employment[4].

Nothing in any rule of law or the law or practice of Parliament prevents a person from bringing a civil employment claim[5] before the court[6] or from bringing before an employment tribunal proceedings of any description which could be brought before such a tribunal in relation to other employment[7].

1 Ie the Trade Union and Labour Relations (Consolidation) Act 1992: see PARAS 891–893, 895 et seq.
2 Ie except as mentioned in the Trade Union and Labour Relations (Consolidation) Act 1992 s 277(1A). The provisions excepted from s 277(1) are: (1) ss 184, 185 (remedy for failure to comply with declaration as to disclosure of information) (see PARA 1182); and (2) Pt IV Ch II (ss 188–198B) (procedure for handling redundancies) (see PARA 1185 et seq): s 277(1A) (added by the Trade Union Reform and Employment Rights Act 1993 Sch 7 para 12(b)).
3 For these purposes, 'relevant member of the House of Lords staff' means any person who is employed under a contract of employment with the Corporate Officer of the House of Lords: Trade Union and Labour Relations (Consolidation) Act 1992 s 277(3) (substituted by the Trade Union Reform and Employment Rights Act 1993 Sch 7 para 12(e)). As to the Corporate Officer of the House of Lords see PARLIAMENT vol 78 (2010) PARA 990 et seq.
4 Trade Union and Labour Relations (Consolidation) Act 1992 s 277(1) (amended by the Trade Union Reform and Employment Rights Act 1993 Sch 7 para 12(a)). For the purpose of the application of the other provisions of the Trade Union and Labour Relations (Consolidation) Act 1992, as they apply by virtue of s 277: (1) the reference in s 182(1)(e) (disclosure of information for collective bargaining; restrictions on general duty) (see PARA 1181 head (5)) to the employer's undertaking is to be construed as a reference to the national interest or, if the case so requires, the interests of the House of Lords; and (2) any other reference to an undertaking is to be construed as a reference to the House of Lords: s 277(2A) (added by the Trade Union Reform and Employment Rights Act 1993 Sch 7 para 12(d)).
5 For these purposes, 'civil employment claim' means a claim arising out of or relating to a contract of employment or any other contract connected with employment, or a claim in tort arising in connection with a person's employment: Trade Union and Labour Relations (Consolidation) Act 1992 s 277(3) (as substituted: see note 3).
6 For these purposes, the 'court' means the High Court or the County Court: Trade Union and Labour Relations (Consolidation) Act 1992 s 277(3) (as substituted (see note 3); amended by the Crime and Courts Act 2013 Sch 9 Pt 3 para 52(1)(b), (2)).
7 Trade Union and Labour Relations (Consolidation) Act 1992 s 277(2) (amended by the Trade Union Reform and Employment Rights Act 1993 Sch 7 para 12(c), Sch 10; the Employment Rights (Dispute Resolution) Act 1998 s 1(2)(a)).

895. House of Commons staff. The statutory provisions relating to trade unions and industrial relations[1] apply[2] in relation to employment as a relevant member of the House of Commons staff[3] as in relation to other employment[4].

Nothing in any rule of law or the law or practice of Parliament prevents a relevant member of the House of Commons staff from bringing a civil employment claim[5] before the court[6] or from bringing before an employment tribunal proceedings of any description which could be brought before such a tribunal by any person who is not such a member[7].

1 Ie the Trade Union and Labour Relations (Consolidation) Act 1992: see PARAS 891–894, 896 et seq.
2 Ie except as mentioned in the Trade Union and Labour Relations (Consolidation) Act 1992 s 278(2). The provisions excepted from s 278(1) are: (1) ss 184, 185 (remedy for failure to comply with declaration as to disclosure of information) (see PARA 1182); and (2) Pt IV Ch II (ss 188–198B) (procedure for handling redundancies) (see PARA 1185 et seq): s 278(2).
3 For these purposes, 'relevant member of the House of Commons staff' has the same meaning as in the Employment Rights Act 1996 s 195(5) (see PARA 165): Trade Union and Labour Relations (Consolidation) Act 1992 s 278(3); Interpretation Act 1978 s 17(2)(a).
4 Trade Union and Labour Relations (Consolidation) Act 1992 s 278(1). For the purpose of the other provisions of the Trade Union and Labour Relations (Consolidation) Act 1992, as they

apply by virtue of s 278: (1) 'employee' and 'contract of employment' include a relevant member of the House of Commons staff and the terms of employment of any such member, but subject to s 278(5) (see below); (2) 'dismissal' includes the termination of any such member's employment; (3) the reference in s 182(1)(e) (disclosure of information for collective bargaining; restrictions on general duty) (see PARA 1181 head (5)) to the employer's undertaking is to be construed as a reference to the national interest or, if the case so requires, the interests of the House of Commons; and (4) any other reference to an undertaking is to be construed as a reference to the House of Commons: s 278(4) (amended by the Trade Union Reform and Employment Rights Act 1993 Sch 7 para 27).

The Trade Union and Labour Relations (Consolidation) Act 1992 ss 137–143 (access to employment) (see PARA 1042 et seq) apply by virtue of s 278 in relation to employment otherwise than under a contract only where the terms of employment correspond to those of a contract of employment: s 278(5).

The Employment Rights Act 1996 s 195(6)–(12) (person to be treated as employer of House of Commons staff) (see PARA 165) applies, with any necessary modifications, for the purposes of the Trade Union and Labour Relations (Consolidation) Act 1992 s 278: s 278(6) (amended by the Employment Rights Act 1996 Sch 1 para 56(1), (17)).

5   For these purposes, 'civil employment claim' means a claim arising out of or relating to a contract of employment or any other contract connected with employment, or a claim in tort arising in connection with a person's employment: Trade Union and Labour Relations (Consolidation) Act 1992 s 278(3) (definition added by the Trade Union Reform and Employment Rights Act 1993 Sch 8 para 85(b)).

6   For these purposes, the 'court' means the High Court or a County Court: Trade Union and Labour Relations (Consolidation) Act 1992 s 278(3) (definition as added: see note 5).

7   Trade Union and Labour Relations (Consolidation) Act 1992 s 278(2A) (added by the Trade Union Reform and Employment Rights Act 1993 Sch 8 para 85(a); amended by the Employment Rights (Dispute Resolution) Act 1998 s 1(2)(a)).

(ii) Legal Status of Trade Unions

896.   Trade unions at common law.   At common law the agreement of association contained in the rules of a trade union may be unenforceable[1] or valid according to whether the main objects[2] of the association do or do not violate the general principles of law, in particular those as to unreasonable restraint of trade[3]. However, in so far as the purposes of trade unions are in unreasonable restraint of trade so that they are void or voidable at common law, they are made lawful by statute[4].

1   The making of an agreement or combination in unreasonable restraint of trade is not an offence at common law, and a combination based on such an agreement is not unlawful at common law, but the parties are at liberty to act on the agreement if they wish; to make a combination unlawful it must amount to a criminal conspiracy: *Mogul Steamship Co Ltd v McGregor, Gow & Co* [1892] AC 25, HL; *A-G of Commonwealth of Australia v Adelaide Steamship Co Ltd* [1913] AC 781 at 797, PC. See also *Swaine v Wilson* (1889) 24 QBD 252 at 260, CA.

2   An association whose main objects are not illegal is not an illegal association merely because certain of its rules are in unlawful restraint of trade: *Swaine v Wilson* (1889) 24 QBD 252, CA. Where, however, the main object of an association is unlawful as being in unreasonable restraint of trade and other rules are ancillary to, and inseparable from, the main object, the association is illegal: *Cullen v Elwin* (1904) 90 LT 840, CA.

3   *Gozney v Bristol Trade and Provident Society* [1909] 1 KB 901 at 915, CA per Cozens-Hardy MR; *Russell v Amalgamated Society of Carpenters and Joiners* [1912] AC 421 at 429, HL per Lord Macnaghten, at 432 per Lord Shaw of Dunfermline and at 439 per Lord Robson. As to restraint of trade generally see COMPETITION vol 18 (2009) PARA 377 et seq.

4   See the Trade Union and Labour Relations (Consolidation) Act 1992 s 11; and PARA 898.

897.   Quasi-corporate status of trade unions.   A trade union[1], other than a special register body[2], is not a body corporate[3]; and it is not to be treated[4] as if it were a body corporate[5]. However, legislation gives a trade union, other than a special register body, some of the most important attributes of corporate personality. Thus:

(1)   it is capable of making contracts;

(2)   it is capable of suing and being sued in its own name, whether in proceedings relating to property or founded on contract or tort or any other cause of action[6]; and

(3)   proceedings for an offence alleged to have been committed by it or on its behalf may be brought against it in its own name[7].

A trade union, other than a special register body, may not be registered as a company under (a) the Companies Act 2006[8]; (b) the Friendly Societies Act 1974[9]; or (c) the Co-operative and Community Benefit Societies Act 2014; and any such registration, whenever effected, is void[10].

1   As to the meaning of 'trade union' see PARA 891.
2   As to the meaning of 'special register body' see PARA 899.
3   Trade Union and Labour Relations (Consolidation) Act 1992 ss 10(1), 117(3)(a)(i).
4   Ie except to the extent authorised by the provisions of the Trade Union and Labour Relations (Consolidation) Act 1992 Pt I (ss 1–121): see PARAS 891–896, 898 et seq.
5   Trade Union and Labour Relations (Consolidation) Act 1992 ss 10(2), 117(3)(a)(i). In *London Underground Ltd v National Union of Rail, Maritime and Transport Workers* [2001] EWCA Civ 211, [2001] ICR 647, sub nom *National Union of Rail, Maritime and Transport Workers v London Underground Ltd* [2001] IRLR 228, it was held that the Trade Union and Labour Relations (Consolidation) Act 1992 s 10(2) could not inhibit the court, in determining what information the union possessed for the purposes of s 226A (see PARA 1372) and s 234A (see PARA 1382), from looking for guidance to the rules of attribution applicable to bodies corporate.
6   In *Electrical, Electronic, Telecommunication and Plumbing Union v Times Newspapers Ltd* [1980] QB 585, [1980] 1 All ER 1097, it was held that a trade union may not sue in its own name for defamation as it does not possess the necessary personality which it could protect by an action in defamation. Cf, however, *National Union of General and Municipal Workers v Gillian* [1946] KB 81, [1945] 2 All ER 593, CA, and *Derbyshire County Council v Times Newspapers Ltd* [1993] AC 534, [1993] 1 All ER 1011, HL (where it was assumed that a trade union can sue for defamation).
7   Trade Union and Labour Relations (Consolidation) Act 1992 s 10(1)(a)–(c). See also the Corporate Manslaughter and Corporate Homicide Act 2007 s 1(1), (2)(d); and CRIMINAL LAW vol 25 (2010) PARA 108 et seq.
8   As to registration under the Companies Act 2006 see COMPANIES vol 14 (2009) PARA 131 et seq.
9   As to registration under the Friendly Societies Act 1974 see FINANCIAL SERVICES AND INSTITUTIONS vol 50 (2008) PARA 2149 et seq.
10 Trade Union and Labour Relations (Consolidation) Act 1992 s 10(3) (amended by the Co-operative and Community Benefit Societies Act 2014 Sch 4 para 54).

898.   Exclusion of common law rules as to restraint of trade.   The purposes of a trade union[1] are not, by reason only that they are in restraint of trade[2], unlawful so as:

(1)   to make any member of the trade union liable to criminal proceedings for conspiracy or otherwise; or

(2)   to make any agreement[3] or trust void or voidable[4].

No rule[5] of a trade union is unlawful or unenforceable by reason only that it is in restraint of trade[6].

1   As to the meaning of 'trade union' see PARA 891. The purposes and rules of a trade union which is a special register body have only limited protection from the common law rules as to restraint of trade: see the Trade Union and Labour Relations (Consolidation) Act 1992 s 117(3)(b); and PARA 899 note 8 head (1). As to the meaning of 'special register body' see PARA 899.
2   As to restraint of trade generally see COMPETITION vol 18 (2009) PARA 377 et seq.
3   A payment made under any such agreement is made for valuable consideration and cannot be recovered, being neither ultra vires nor a breach of trust: *Osborne v Amalgamated Society of Railway Servants* [1911] 1 Ch 540 at 558, CA, per Fletcher Moulton LJ.
4   Trade Union and Labour Relations (Consolidation) Act 1992 s 11(1).
5   In relation to a trade union, 'rules', except where the context otherwise requires, includes the rules of any branch or section of the union; and 'branch or section', except where the context

otherwise requires, includes a branch or section which is itself a trade union: Trade Union and Labour Relations (Consolidation) Act 1992 s 119.

6 Trade Union and Labour Relations (Consolidation) Act 1992 s 11(2). It is submitted that the enactment of this provision has the result that the reasoning in *Edwards v Society of Graphical and Allied Trades* [1971] Ch 354, [1970] 3 All ER 689, CA, that a rule was in restraint of trade and, therefore, void, can no longer be followed. See also *Boddington v Lawton* [1994] ICR 478 (the rules of the Prison Officers' Association, which does not enjoy trade union status, nevertheless permit trustees acting in accordance with those rules to finance the defence of members involved in legal proceedings without intervention by the court to prevent their doing so by giving a remedy in damages to other members who might object to such a course).

899. Special register bodies. A 'special register body' means an organisation whose name appeared, immediately before 16 September 1974[1], in the special register[2], and which is a company registered under the Companies Act 2006 or is incorporated by charter or letters patent[3]. The statutory prohibitions on a trade union being incorporated[4] and on registration as a company under the Companies Act 2006[5] do not, therefore, apply to a special register body[6]. The statutory provisions relating to trade unions[7] otherwise apply to special register bodies as to other trade unions, subject to certain exceptions and adaptations[8].

1 Ie the date of the coming into force of the Trade Union and Labour Relations Act 1974 s 1, Sch 1, which repealed the Industrial Relations Act 1971 and re-enacted it with certain modifications.

2 Ie the register maintained under the Industrial Relations Act 1971 s 84 (repealed).

3 Trade Union and Labour Relations (Consolidation) Act 1992 s 117(1) (amended by SI 2009/1941). As to registration under the Companies Act 2006 see COMPANIES vol 14 (2009) PARA 131 et seq.

4 Ie the Trade Union and Labour Relations (Consolidation) Act 1992 s 10(1), (2): see PARA 897.

5 Ie the Trade Union and Labour Relations (Consolidation) Act 1992 s 10(3)(a): see PARA 897.

6 Trade Union and Labour Relations (Consolidation) Act 1992 s 117(3)(a) (amended by SI 2009/1941).

7 Ie the Trade Union and Labour Relations (Consolidation) Act 1992 Pt I (ss 1–121): see PARAS 891 et seq, 900 et seq. As to the meaning of 'trade union' see PARA 891.

8 Trade Union and Labour Relations (Consolidation) Act 1992 s 117(2). Those exceptions and adaptations are:
    (1) s 11 (exclusion of common law rules as to restraint of trade) (see PARA 898) applies to the purposes or rules of a special register body only so far as they relate to the regulation of relations between employers or employers' associations and workers (s 117(3)(b));
    (2) ss 12–14 (vesting of property in trustees; transfer of securities) (see PARAS 919–921) do not apply (s 117(3)(c));
    (3) in s 20 (liability of trade union in certain proceedings in tort) (see PARA 1388), the reference in s 20(7) to the contract between a member and the other members is to be construed as a reference to the contract between a member and the body (s 117(3)(d));
    (4) ss 33–35 (appointment and removal of auditors) (see PARAS 945–946) do not apply to a special register body which is registered as a company under the Companies Act 2006; and the Trade Union and Labour Relations (Consolidation) Act 1992 ss 36, 37 (rights and duties of auditors) (see PARAS 947–948) apply to the auditors appointed by such a body under the Companies Act 2006 Pt 16 Ch 2 (ss 485–494) (Trade Union and Labour Relations (Consolidation) Act 1992 s 117(4) (amended by SI 2009/1941)); and
    (5) the Trade Union and Labour Relations (Consolidation) Act 1992 ss 45B, 45C (disqualification) (see PARA 958) and Pt I Ch IV (ss 46–61) (elections for certain union positions) (see PARA 959 et seq) apply only to the position of voting member of the executive and any position by virtue of which a person is a voting member of the executive; and, for these purposes, 'voting member of the executive' has the meaning given by s 46(5) (see PARA 960 note 8) (s 117(5) (amended by the Trade Union Reform and Employment Rights Act 1993 Sch 8 para 61)).

(iii) Listing of Trade Unions

900.   The list of trade unions.   The certification officer[1] must keep a list of trade unions[2] containing the names of the organisations entitled[3] to be entered in that list[4]. He must keep copies of the list of trade unions, as for the time being in force, available for public inspection at all reasonable hours free of charge[5]; and a copy of the list must be included in the certification officer's annual report[6]. The fact that the name of an organisation is included in the list of trade unions is evidence that the organisation is a trade union[7]; and, on the application of an organisation whose name is so included, the certification officer must issue it with a certificate to that effect[8]. A document purporting to be such a certificate is evidence that the name of the organisation is entered in the list[9].

1   As to the certification officer see PARA 1443. The certification officer is also required to keep a list of employers' associations: see PARA 1083. The function of listing trade unions and employers' associations was formerly performed by the Chief Registrar of Friendly Societies: see PARA 1443 note 1.
2   As to the meaning of 'trade union' see PARA 891.
3   Ie in accordance with the Trade Union and Labour Relations (Consolidation) Act 1992 Pt I (ss 1–121): see PARAS 891 et seq, 901 et seq.
4   Trade Union and Labour Relations (Consolidation) Act 1992 s 2(1)(b). The list must also contain the names of those organisations whose names were, immediately before 16 October 1992 (ie the date on which the Trade Union and Labour Relations (Consolidation) Act 1992 came into force: see s 302), duly entered in the list kept by the certification officer under the Trade Union and Labour Relations Act 1974 s 8 (repealed): Trade Union and Labour Relations (Consolidation) Act 1992 s 2(1)(a).
5   Trade Union and Labour Relations (Consolidation) Act 1992 s 2(2).
6   Trade Union and Labour Relations (Consolidation) Act 1992 s 2(3). As to the certification officer's annual report see PARA 1443.
7   Trade Union and Labour Relations (Consolidation) Act 1992 s 2(4).
8   Trade Union and Labour Relations (Consolidation) Act 1992 s 2(5).
9   Trade Union and Labour Relations (Consolidation) Act 1992 s 2(6).

901.   The significance of trade union listing.   Entry on the list[1] of trade unions[2] carries a number of advantages. Only a listed trade union is entitled to apply for a certificate of independence[3]. A listed trade union which is precluded by statute or by its rules from assuring to any person a sum exceeding certain limits prescribed by statute by way of gross sum or annuity is entitled to certain tax reliefs on income and chargeable gains applied for the purpose of provident benefits[4]. Further, a listed union enjoys certain procedural advantages concerning the vesting of property in new trustees[5] and the transfer of securities[6]; and entry in the list is evidence that the organisation is in fact a trade union[7].

1   As to the list of trade unions see PARA 900.
2   As to the meaning of 'trade union' see PARA 891.
3   See the Trade Union and Labour Relations (Consolidation) Act 1992 s 6(1); and PARA 905.
4   See the Corporation Tax Act 2010 ss 981–983; PARA 927; and INCOME TAXATION vol 58A (2014) PARA 1724.
5   See the Trade Union and Labour Relations (Consolidation) Act 1992 s 13; and PARA 920.
6   See the Trade Union and Labour Relations (Consolidation) Act 1992 s 14; and PARA 921.
7   See the Trade Union and Labour Relations (Consolidation) Act 1992 s 2(4); and PARA 900.

902.   Entry in the list of trade unions.   An organisation of workers[1], whenever formed, whose name is not entered in the list[2] of trade unions[3] may apply to the certification officer[4] to have its name entered in the list[5]. The application must be made in such form and manner as the certification officer may require and must be accompanied by:

(1) a copy of the rules[6] of the organisation;
(2) a list of its officers[7];
(3) the address of its head office or main office; and
(4) the name under which it is or is to be known,
and by the prescribed fee[8].
If the certification officer is satisfied:
(a) that the organisation is a trade union;
(b) that the above conditions[9] have been complied with; and
(c) that entry of the name in the list is not prohibited by statute[10],
he must enter the name of the organisation in the list of trade unions[11].

An organisation aggrieved by the refusal of the certification officer to enter its name in the list of trade unions may appeal on any appealable question[12] to the Employment Appeal Tribunal[13].

1   As to the meaning of 'worker' see PARA 892.
2   As to the list of trade unions see PARA 900.
3   As to the meaning of 'trade union' see PARA 891.
4   As to the certification officer see PARA 1443.
5   Trade Union and Labour Relations (Consolidation) Act 1992 s 3(1).
6   As to the meaning of 'rules', in relation to a trade union, see PARA 898 note 5.
7   For these purposes, 'officer', in relation to a trade union, includes any member of the governing body of the union and any trustee of any fund applicable for the purposes of the union: Trade Union and Labour Relations (Consolidation) Act 1992 s 119.
8   Trade Union and Labour Relations (Consolidation) Act 1992 s 3(2). The fee so prescribed is £150: Certification Officer (Amendment of Fees) Regulations 2005, SI 2005/713, reg 5. The fee for the entry of an amalgamated trade union in the list of trade unions maintained by the certification officer where each of the amalgamating trade unions is already entered in the list is, however, £41: Trade Unions and Employers' Associations (Amalgamations, etc) Regulations 1975, SI 1975/536, reg 12 (substituted by SI 1978/1344; amended by SI 2005/713).
       The Secretary of State may by regulations prescribe anything authorised or required to be prescribed for the purposes of the Trade Union and Labour Relations (Consolidation) Act 1992: s 293(1). The regulations may contain such incidental, supplementary or transitional provisions as appear to the Secretary of State to be necessary or expedient: s 293(2). Regulations so made must be made by statutory instrument which is subject to annulment in pursuance of a resolution of either House of Parliament: s 293(3). Partly in the exercise of the power so conferred, the Secretary of State made the Certification Officer (Amendment of Fees) Regulations 2005, SI 2005/713, which came into force on 6 April 2005: reg 1(1).
9   Ie the Trade Union and Labour Relations (Consolidation) Act 1992 s 3(2): see the text and notes 6–8.
10 Ie by the Trade Union and Labour Relations (Consolidation) Act 1992 s 3(4). The certification officer must not enter the name of an organisation in the list of trade unions if the name is the same as that under which another organisation: (1) was registered as a trade union on 30 September 1971 (ie the day before the relevant provisions of the Industrial Relations Act 1971 were brought into force by the Industrial Relations Act 1971 (Commencement No 1) Order 1971, SI 1971/1522, art 2, Schedule) under the Trade Union Acts 1871 to 1964 (repealed); (2) was at any time registered as a trade union or employers' association under the Industrial Relations Act 1971 (repealed); or (3) is for the time being entered in the list of trade unions or in the list of employers' associations kept under the Trade Union and Labour Relations (Consolidation) Act 1992 Pt II (ss 122–136) (see PARA 1079 et seq); or if the name is one so nearly resembling any such name as to be likely to deceive the public: s 3(4).
11 Trade Union and Labour Relations (Consolidation) Act 1992 s 3(3). The organisation must satisfy the definition of a 'trade union' in s 1 (see PARA 891) at the time when certification is sought; it is not enough that the organisation may satisfy that definition at some future date: *Akinosun (on behalf of General & Health Workers Union) v Certification Officer* [2013] IRLR 937, EAT.
12 For these purposes, an appealable question is any question of law arising in the proceedings before, or arising from the decision of, the certification officer: Trade Union and Labour Relations (Consolidation) Act 1992 s 9(4) (amended by the Employment Relations Act 2004 s 51(1)(c)).

13 Trade Union and Labour Relations (Consolidation) Act 1992 s 9(1) (amended by the Employment Relations Act 2004 s 51(1)(a)). As to the Employment Appeal Tribunal see PARA 1422 et seq.

903. Removal from the list of trade unions. If it appears to the certification officer[1], on application made to him or otherwise, that an organisation whose name is entered in the list[2] of trade unions[3] is not a trade union, he may remove its name from the list[4]. He must not do so without giving the organisation notice of his intention and considering any representations made to him by the organisation within such period, of not less than 28 days beginning with the date of the notice, as may be specified in the notice[5]. He must remove the name of an organisation from the list of trade unions if he is requested by the organisation to do so or he is satisfied that the organisation has ceased to exist[6]. An organisation aggrieved by a decision of the certification officer to remove its name from the list of trade unions may appeal on any appealable question[7] to the Employment Appeal Tribunal[8].

1   As to the certification officer see PARA 1443.
2   As to the list of trade unions see PARA 900.
3   As to the meaning of 'trade union' see PARA 891.
4   Trade Union and Labour Relations (Consolidation) Act 1992 s 4(1).
5   Trade Union and Labour Relations (Consolidation) Act 1992 s 4(2).
6   Trade Union and Labour Relations (Consolidation) Act 1992 s 4(3).
7   For these purposes, an appealable question is any question of law arising in the proceedings before, or arising from the decision of, the certification officer: Trade Union and Labour Relations (Consolidation) Act 1992 s 9(4) (amended by the Employment Relations Act 2004 s 51(1)(c)).
8   Trade Union and Labour Relations (Consolidation) Act 1992 s 9(1) (amended by the Employment Relations Act 2004 s 51(1)(a)). As to the Employment Appeal Tribunal see PARA 1422 et seq.

(iv) Certification as an Independent Trade Union

904. Meaning of 'independent trade union'. An 'independent trade union' means[1] a trade union[2] which:

(1)   is not under the domination or control[3] of an employer[4] or group of employers or of one or more employers' associations[5]; and

(2)   is not liable to interference[6] by an employer or any such group or association, arising out of the provision of financial or material support or by any other means whatsoever, tending towards such control;

and references to 'independence', in relation to a trade union, are to be construed accordingly[7].

1   Ie for the purposes of the Trade Union and Labour Relations (Consolidation) Act 1992: see PARAS 891 et seq, 905 et seq.
2   As to the meaning of 'trade union' see PARA 891.
3   For the criteria applied by the certification officer in considering an application for a certificate of independence see *Blue Circle Staff Association v Certification Officer* [1977] 2 All ER 145, [1977] ICR 224, EAT (where the association was refused a certificate of independence because it had not proved that it was free from domination by the single employer by whom its members were employed).
4   As to the meaning of 'employer' see PARA 892.
5   As to the meaning of 'employers' association' see PARA 1079.
6   'Liable to interference' means vulnerable to interference or exposed to the risk of interference; the degree of likelihood of such interference occurring in practice is irrelevant, provided that it is not insignificant: *HSD (Hatfield) Employees Association v Certification Officer* [1978] ICR 21, [1977] IRLR 261, EAT (where a certificate was granted because the association was not dominated or liable to domination); *Squibb UK Staff Association v Certification Officer* [1979]

2 All ER 452, [1979] ICR 235, CA; *A Monk & Co Staff Association v Certification Officer* [1980] IRLR 431, EAT; *Government Communications Staff Federation v Certification Officer* [1993] ICR 163, EAT.

7   Trade Union and Labour Relations (Consolidation) Act 1992 s 5.

905.   Application for certificate of independence.   A trade union[1] whose name is entered on the list[2] of trade unions may apply to the certification officer[3] for a certificate that it is independent[4]; and the application must be made in such form and manner as the certification officer may require and must be accompanied by the prescribed fee[5]. The certification officer must maintain a record showing details of all applications for certificates of independence made to him and keep it available for public inspection, free of charge, at all reasonable hours[6].

If an application is made by a trade union whose name is not entered on the list of trade unions, the certification officer must refuse a certificate of independence and must enter that refusal on the record[7]. In any other case, he must not come to a decision on the application before the end of the period of one month after it has been entered on the record; and, before coming to his decision, he must make such inquiries as he thinks fit and must take into account any relevant information submitted to him by any person[8]. He must then decide whether the applicant trade union is independent and must enter his decision, and the date of his decision, on the record[9]. If he decides that the trade union is independent, he must issue a certificate accordingly; and, if he decides that it is not, he must give reasons for his decision[10].

An organisation aggrieved by the refusal of the certification officer to issue it with a certificate of independence may appeal on any appealable question[11] to the Employment Appeal Tribunal[12].

1   As to the meaning of 'trade union' see PARA 891.
2   As to the list of trade unions see PARA 900.
3   As to the certification officer see PARA 1443.
4   As to the meaning of 'independent' see PARA 904.
5   Trade Union and Labour Relations (Consolidation) Act 1992 s 6(1). The fee so prescribed is £4,066: Certification Officer (Amendment of Fees) Regulations 2005, SI 2005/713, reg 7. As to the Secretary of State's power to make regulations prescribing certain matters under the Trade Union and Labour Relations (Consolidation) Act 1992 see s 293; and PARA 902 note 8.
6   Trade Union and Labour Relations (Consolidation) Act 1992 s 6(2).
7   Trade Union and Labour Relations (Consolidation) Act 1992 s 6(3).
8   Trade Union and Labour Relations (Consolidation) Act 1992 s 6(4).
9   Trade Union and Labour Relations (Consolidation) Act 1992 s 6(5). The burden of proof is on the applicant trade union to satisfy the certification officer that it is independent: *HSD (Hatfield) Employees Association v Certification Officer* [1978] ICR 21, [1977] IRLR 261, EAT. The Trade Union and Labour Relations (Consolidation) Act 1992 s 6 must be construed in such a way that, when necessary, the certification officer can determine the historic status of a trade union: *Bone v North Essex Partnership NHS Foundation Trust* [2014] EWCA Civ 652 at [69], [2014] 3 All ER 964 at [69], [2014] IRLR 635 at [69].
10 Trade Union and Labour Relations (Consolidation) Act 1992 s 6(6).
11 For these purposes, an appealable question is any question of law arising in the proceedings before, or arising from the decision of, the certification officer: Trade Union and Labour Relations (Consolidation) Act 1992 s 9(4) (amended by the Employment Relations Act 2004 s 51(1)(c)).
12 Trade Union and Labour Relations (Consolidation) Act 1992 s 9(2) (amended by the Employment Relations Act 2004 s 51(1)(a)). The appeal takes the form of a rehearing: *Blue Circle Staff Association v Certification Officer* [1977] 2 All ER 145, [1977] ICR 224, EAT. There is no appeal against the grant of a certificate: *General and Municipal Workers' Union v Certification Officer* [1977] 1 All ER 771, [1977] ICR 183, EAT. The appeal will be heard on the basis of the available evidence at that time: *A Monk & Co Staff Association v Certification Officer* [1980] IRLR 431, EAT. As to the Employment Appeal Tribunal see PARA 1422 et seq.

906.   **Withdrawal or cancellation of certificate of independence.**   The certification officer[1] may withdraw the certificate of independence[2] of a trade union[3] if he is of the opinion that the union is no longer independent[4]. Where he proposes to do so, he must notify the trade union and enter notice of the proposal in the record[5]. However, he must not come to a decision on the proposal before the end of the period of one month after notice of it was entered on the record; and, before coming to his decision, he must make such inquiries as he thinks fit and must take into account any relevant information submitted to him by any person[6]. He must then decide whether the trade union is independent and must enter his decision, and the date of the decision, on the record[7]. He must confirm or withdraw the certificate accordingly; and, if he decides to withdraw it, he must give reasons for his decision[8].

Where the name of an organisation is removed from the list of trade unions, the certification officer must cancel any certificate of independence in force in respect of that organisation by entering on the record the fact that the organisation's name has been removed from the list and that the certificate is accordingly cancelled[9].

An organisation aggrieved by a decision of the certification officer to withdraw its certificate of independence may appeal on any appealable question[10] to the Employment Appeal Tribunal[11].

1   As to the certification officer see PARA 1443.
2   As to a certificate of independence see PARA 905. As to the meaning of 'independent' see PARA 904.
3   As to the meaning of 'trade union' see PARA 891.
4   Trade Union and Labour Relations (Consolidation) Act 1992 s 7(1).
5   Trade Union and Labour Relations (Consolidation) Act 1992 s 7(2).
6   Trade Union and Labour Relations (Consolidation) Act 1992 s 7(3).
7   Trade Union and Labour Relations (Consolidation) Act 1992 s 7(4).
8   Trade Union and Labour Relations (Consolidation) Act 1992 s 7(5).
9   Trade Union and Labour Relations (Consolidation) Act 1992 s 7(6). As to removal from the list see PARA 903.
10 For these purposes, an appealable question is any question of law arising in the proceedings before, or arising from the decision of, the certification officer: Trade Union and Labour Relations (Consolidation) Act 1992 s 9(4) (amended by the Employment Relations Act 2004 s 51(1)(c)).
11 Trade Union and Labour Relations (Consolidation) Act 1992 s 9(2) (amended by the Employment Relations Act 2004 s 51(1)(a)). As to the Employment Appeal Tribunal see PARA 1422 et seq.

907.   **Conclusive effect of certification officer's decision.**   A certificate of independence[1] which is in force is conclusive evidence for all purposes that a trade union[2] is independent[3]; and a refusal[4], withdrawal or cancellation[5] of a certificate of independence, entered on the record[6], is conclusive evidence for all purposes that a trade union is not independent[7].

If in any proceedings before a court, the Employment Appeal Tribunal[8], the Central Arbitration Committee[9], the Advisory, Conciliation and Arbitration Service[10] (ACAS) or an employment tribunal[11], a question arises whether a trade union is independent and there is no certificate of independence in force and no refusal, withdrawal or cancellation of a certificate recorded in relation to that trade union:

(1)   that question must not be decided in those proceedings; and

(2)   the proceedings must be stayed until a certificate has been issued or refused by the certification officer[12].

The body before which proceedings are stayed may refer the question of the independence of the trade union to the certification officer, who must proceed[13] as if the reference were an application by that trade union for a certificate[14].

1 As to a certificate of independence see PARA 905. A document purporting to be a certificate of independence and to be signed by the certification officer, or by a person authorised to act on his behalf, is to be taken to be such a certificate unless the contrary is proved: Trade Union and Labour Relations (Consolidation) Act 1992 s 8(2). As to the certification officer see PARA 1443.
2 As to the meaning of 'trade union' see PARA 891.
3 As to the meaning of 'independent' see PARA 904.
4 As to the refusal of a certificate of independence see PARA 905.
5 As to the withdrawal or cancellation of a certificate of independence see PARA 906.
6 Ie the record maintained by the certification officer under the Trade Union and Labour Relations (Consolidation) Act 1992 s 6(2): see PARA 905. A document purporting to be a certified copy of an entry on the record and to be signed by the certification officer or by a person authorised to act on his behalf is to be taken to be a true copy of such an entry unless the contrary is proved: s 8(3).
7 Trade Union and Labour Relations (Consolidation) Act 1992 s 8(1).
8 As to the Employment Appeal Tribunal see PARA 1422 et seq.
9 As to the Central Arbitration Committee see PARA 1226 et seq.
10 As to ACAS see PARA 1213 et seq.
11 As to employment tribunals see PARA 1399 et seq.
12 Trade Union and Labour Relations (Consolidation) Act 1992 s 8(4) (amended by the Employment Rights (Dispute Resolution) Act 1998 s 1(2)(a)).
13 Ie in accordance with the Trade Union and Labour Relations (Consolidation) Act 1992 s 6: see PARA 905.
14 Trade Union and Labour Relations (Consolidation) Act 1992 s 8(5). Section 8(5) is to be construed broadly, so as to enable a court or tribunal to refer a historic question to the certification officer: *Bone v North Essex Partnership NHS Foundation Trust* [2014] EWCA Civ 652 at [64], [69], [2014] 3 All ER 964 at [64], [69], [2014] IRLR 635 at [64], [69].

908. Consequences of being an independent trade union. If a trade union[1] is independent[2], certain benefits are conferred on it, its members and officials[3]. Thus:

(1) an employee[4] has the right not to be subjected to any detriment as an individual by any act, or any deliberate failure to act, by his employer[5] if the act or failure takes place for the purpose of preventing or deterring him from, or penalising him for, being or seeking to become a member of an independent trade union, or taking part in the activities of an independent trade union at an appropriate time[6];

(2) the dismissal of an employee is an unfair dismissal if the reason (or, if more than one, the principal reason) was that the employee was, or proposed to become, a member of an independent trade union, or had taken part, or proposed to take part, in the activities of an independent trade union at an appropriate time[7];

(3) if the reason or principal reason for the dismissal of an employee is that he is redundant, but it is shown that the circumstances constituting the redundancy applied equally to other employees who have not been dismissed and the reason or principal reason why he was selected for dismissal was because he was, or proposed to become, a member of an independent trade union, or had taken part, or proposed to take part, in the activities of an independent trade union at an appropriate time, the dismissal will be regarded as unfair[8];

(4) an employee who is an official of an independent trade union which is recognised by his employer is entitled to a reasonable amount of paid time off during working hours for the purpose of carrying out certain

trade union duties as such an official, and to undergo training in aspects of industrial relations relevant to those duties which is approved by the Trades Union Congress or by his union[9];

(5) an employee who is a member of an independent trade union which is recognised by his employer in respect of that description of employees is entitled to a reasonable amount of time off during working hours for the purpose of taking part in certain activities of his union[10];

(6) a collective agreement which prohibits or restricts the right of workers to engage in a strike or other industrial action, or has the effect of prohibiting or restricting that right, may not form part of any contract between a worker[11] and the person for whom he works unless each trade union which is a party to the agreement is an independent trade union[12];

(7) an employer who recognises an independent trade union has the duty to disclose certain information relating to his undertaking to representatives of the union for the purposes of collective bargaining[13];

(8) an employer proposing to dismiss as redundant 20 or more employees at one establishment within a period of 90 days or less must consult representatives of an independent trade union about the dismissals where any of the employees who may be affected by the proposed dismissals or by measures taken in connection with those dismissals are of a description in respect of which that union is recognised by the employer[14];

(9) a dismissal procedures agreement may not be designated so that its provisions relating to dismissal have effect in substitution for the statutory right not to be unfairly dismissed unless every trade union which is a party to that agreement is an independent trade union[15];

(10) where an undertaking or part of an undertaking is transferred, only an independent trade union recognised by the transferor employer will be deemed to be recognised by the transferee employer in respect of those employees who, in consequence of the transfer, become employees of the transferee[16];

(11) an employer must inform the representatives of an independent trade union recognised by him in respect of employees affected by the transfer, long enough before a transfer of an undertaking or part of an undertaking to enable consultation to take place, of various facts about the transfer, and must enter into consultations with the representatives of that union with a view to seeking their agreement to measures to be taken in relation to those employees[17];

(12) an employer must consult safety representatives appointed by an independent trade union with regard to certain specified matters concerning health and safety at work[18];

(13) an employer who proposes to establish a contracted-out occupational pension scheme must inform and consult with an independent trade union recognised by him in relation to the affected employees[19];

(14) the trustees of an occupational pension scheme must disclose certain information to an independent trade union recognised in relation to members and prospective members of the scheme[20];

(15) only a trade union with a certificate of independence may make a request for recognition to an employer[21].

1 As to the meaning of 'trade union' see PARA 891.

2   As to the meaning of 'independent' see PARA 904.
3   As to the meaning of 'official', in relation to a trade union, see PARA 1018.
4   As to the meaning of 'employee' see PARA 892.
5   As to the meaning of 'employer' see PARA 892.
6   See the Trade Union and Labour Relations (Consolidation) Act 1992 s 146; and PARA 1048 et seq.
7   See the Trade Union and Labour Relations (Consolidation) Act 1992 s 152; and PARA 1056 et seq. With regard to inducements against trade union membership and activities see also the Trade Union and Labour Relations (Consolidation) Act 1992 ss 145A–145F; and PARA 1051 et seq.
8   See the Trade Union and Labour Relations (Consolidation) Act 1992 s 153; and PARA 1056.
9   See the Trade Union and Labour Relations (Consolidation) Act 1992 s 168; and PARA 1065.
10   See the Trade Union and Labour Relations (Consolidation) Act 1992 s 170; and PARA 1066 et seq.
11   As to the meaning of 'worker' see PARA 892.
12   See the Trade Union and Labour Relations (Consolidation) Act 1992 s 180; and PARA 1177.
13   See the Trade Union and Labour Relations (Consolidation) Act 1992 s 181; and PARA 1179 et seq.
14   See the Trade Union and Labour Relations (Consolidation) Act 1992 s 188; and PARA 1185.
15   See the Employment Rights Act 1996 s 110; and PARAS 759, 760.
16   See the Transfer of Undertakings (Protection of Employment) Regulations 2006, SI 2006/246, reg 6; and PARA 1095.
17   See the Transfer of Undertakings (Protection of Employment) Regulations 2006, SI 2006/246, regs 13–18; and PARA 1196 et seq.
18   See the Safety Representatives and Safety Committees Regulations 1977, SI 1977/500; and PARA 1201. The employer's duty to consult with representatives of an independent trade union is imposed by the Health and Safety at Work etc Act 1974 s 2(6): see PARA 1201.
19   See the Occupational Pension Schemes (Contracting-out) Regulations 1996, SI 1996/1172; and PARA 1205.
20   See the Occupational Pension Schemes (Disclosure of Information) Regulations 2013, SI 2013/2734; and PARA 1206.
21   See the Trade Union and Labour Relations (Consolidation) Act 1992 Sch A1 para 6; and PARA 1104.

(2)   TRADE UNION RULES

(i)   Trade Union Rules; in general

909.   Nature and interpretation of trade union rules. The rules of a trade union represent both the constitution of the union, defining and delimiting the powers of the union, its officers and officials, and a contract between each member and the union[1] and between the members of the union inter se. The rules of a trade union are not always to be found in the rule book of the union alone; custom and practice may establish the existence of an implied rule[2]. With certain limited exceptions[3], the content of union rules is a matter for the union itself.

The rules of a trade union are not to be construed as if they were drafted by parliamentary draftsmen, but so as to give a reasonable interpretation which accords with what in the court's view they must have been intended to mean[4].

1   *Bonsor v Musicians' Union* [1954] Ch 479, [1954] 1 All ER 822, CA (revsd on another point [1956] AC 104, [1955] 3 All ER 518, HL); *Cheall v Association of Professional, Executive, Clerical and Computer Staff* [1983] 2 AC 180, [1983] ICR 398, HL. As to the capacity of a trade union to make a contract see the Trade Union and Labour Relations (Consolidation) Act 1992 s 10(1)(a); and PARA 897 head (1).
2   *Heatons Transport (St Helens) Ltd v Transport and General Workers' Union* [1973] AC 15, [1972] 3 All ER 101, HL; *General Aviation Services (UK) Ltd v Transport and General Workers' Union* [1985] ICR 615, [1976] IRLR 224, HL. The suggestion in *Heatons Transport (St Helens) Ltd v Transport and General Workers' Union* [1973] AC 15, [1972] 3 All ER

101, HL that custom and practice may operate by modifying a union's rules is not to be taken to mean that custom and practice may override an express rule: see *Taylor v National Union of Mineworkers (Derbyshire Area)* [1985] IRLR 99, [1985] BCLC 237.

3   See PARA 911.

4   *Heatons Transport (St Helens) Ltd v Transport and General Workers' Union* [1973] AC 15, [1972] 3 All ER 101, HL; *British Actors' Equity Association v Goring* [1978] ICR 791, HL; *Porter v National Union of Journalists* [1979] IRLR 404, CA (affd [1980] IRLR 404, HL); *Taylor v National Union of Mineworkers (Derbyshire Area)* [1985] IRLR 99; *Hamlet v General Municipal Boilermakers and Allied Trades Union* [1987] 1 All ER 631, [1987] ICR 150; *Jacques v Amalgamated Union of Engineering Workers (Engineering Section)* [1987] 1 All ER 621, [1986] ICR 683; *Douglas v Graphical Paper and Media Union* [1995] IRLR 426. See also *UNISON v Street* (2013) UKEAT/0256/13/LA (term to be implied into UNISON's rulebook (by UNISON's custom and practice) that many of the rules relating to branches have to be suspended in the process of putting a county branch that has descended into serious dysfunction through factionalism under 'regional supervision' and to enable effective supervision to take place, so long as suspension is seen as both necessary and a proportionate way of achieving the ends which regional supervision intended to achieve, having regard to the assault which that would make on the right of the rank and file members of the branch to participate in the democratic processes of the branch; applying *Heatons Transport (St Helens) Ltd v Transport and General Workers' Union* [1973] AC 15, [1972] 3 All ER 101, HL).

910.   Alteration of trade union rules.   Amendment of the rules of a trade union must be made in accordance with its rules[1]. A member of the union may seek an injunction restraining the union from giving effect to a purported alteration made otherwise than in accordance with the rules[2], although the court may refuse to intervene if there has been no more than a minor procedural irregularity[3]. A valid amendment of the rules is binding on all members of the union[4]. As a trade union has no inherent power to alter its rules[5], then, in the absence of a provision in the rules allowing for such an amendment, the rules may be amended only by the unanimous consent of all the members[6].

1   Thus, if an amendment may be made only if recommended by the executive committee as urgently required, there must be a resolution of the committee to that effect: *Osborne v Amalgamated Society of Railway Servants* [1909] 1 Ch 163, CA (affd sub nom *Amalgamated Society of Railway Servants v Osborne* [1910] AC 87, HL); *Edwards v Halliwell* [1950] 2 All ER 1064, CA. A claim that the rules have been impliedly altered otherwise than in accordance with the rule book procedures is unlikely to be accepted: *Goring v British Actors' Equity Association* [1987] IRLR 122.

2   *Clarke v Chadburn* [1985] 1 All ER 211, [1985] 1 WLR 78 (where a purported rule change made in defiance of an interim injunction restraining the union from changing its rules was declared void for illegality).

3   *Amalgamated Society of Engineers v Jones* (1913) 29 TLR 484 (where the rules provided that a delegate meeting should not have the power to alter any rule unless notice of the proposed alteration had been given; it was held that mere notice of intention to alter the rules was sufficient). See also *Edwards v Halliwell* [1950] 2 All ER 1064, CA.

4   *McEllistrim v Ballymacelligott Co-operative Agricultural and Dairy Society Ltd* [1919] AC 548, HL; *Burke v Amalgamated Society of Dyers* [1906] 2 KB 583, DC.

5   See *Dawkins v Antrobus* (1881) 17 ChD 615, CA; *Edwards v Halliwell* [1950] 2 All ER 1064, CA.

6   *Re Tobacco Trade Benevolent Association* [1958] 3 All ER 353, [1958] 1 WLR 1113; and see *Reel v Holder* [1979] 3 All ER 1041, [1979] 1 WLR 1252; affd [1981] 3 All ER 321, [1981] 1 WLR 1226, CA.

911.   Statutory constraints on trade union rules.   Subject to the following exceptions, the content of the rules[1] of a trade union[2] is a matter for the union itself:

(1)   the rules of every[3] trade union must contain provision for the appointment and removal of auditors[4];

(2) a trade union which wishes to apply funds in furtherance of certain political objects[5] must adopt certain rules as to the political ballot[6] and the political fund[7]; and

(3) a term conferring a right on a member to terminate his membership, on giving reasonable notice and complying with any reasonable conditions, is to be implied in every contract of membership of a trade union[8];

(4) as an organisation of workers for the purposes of the Equality Act 2010, a trade union may not discriminate against or victimise a person as to the terms on which it is prepared to admit him as a member[9]; and a rule of a trade union is unenforceable against a person in so far as it constitutes, promotes or provides for treatment of the person that is of a description prohibited by that Act[10];

(5) as from a day to be appointed[11], the rules of every trade union to which the duty to appoint an assurer[12] applies must contain provision for the appointment and removal of an assurer[13].

1   As to the meaning of 'rules', in relation to a trade union, see PARA 898 note 5.
2   As to the meaning of 'trade union' see PARA 891.
3   Ie other than certain newly formed trade unions, federated trade unions and special register bodies: see PARAS 899 note 8 head (4), 943 note 1.
4   Trade Union and Labour Relations (Consolidation) Act 1992 s 35(1). Section 35(2)–(8) (see PARA 946) has effect, however, notwithstanding anything in the rules: s 35(1).
5   Ie the political objects set out in the Trade Union and Labour Relations (Consolidation) Act 1992 s 72: see PARA 975.
6   As to the political ballot rules see PARA 978.
7   As to the political fund rules see PARA 985.
8   See the Trade Union and Labour Relations (Consolidation) Act 1992 s 69; and PARA 1033.
9   See the Equality Act 2010 s 57; PARA 1036; and DISCRIMINATION vol 33 (2013) PARA 125.
10 See the Equality Act 2010 s 145(2); and DISCRIMINATION vol 33 (2013) PARA 5. Section 145(2) refers to a rule of an 'undertaking', ie a rule made by a trade organisation or a qualifications body (see s 148(5), (6)) and 'trade organisation' includes an organisation of workers (see s 57(7); PARA 1036; and DISCRIMINATION vol 33 (2013) PARA 125.
11 Ie as from a day to be appointed under the Transparency of Lobbying, Non-Party Campaigning and Trade Union Administration Act 2014 s 45(1)(c).
12 Ie the duty imposed by the Trade Union and Labour Relations (Consolidation) Act 1992 s 24ZB: see PARA 932.
13 See the Trade Union and Labour Relations (Consolidation) Act 1992 s 24ZC(1); and PARA 932.

912.   Trade union's duty to supply copy of rules. A trade union[1] must, at the request of any person, supply him with a copy of its rules[2] either free of charge or on payment of a reasonable charge[3].

1   As to the meaning of 'trade union' see PARA 891.
2   As to the meaning of 'rules', in relation to a trade union, see PARA 898 note 5.
3   Trade Union and Labour Relations (Consolidation) Act 1992 s 27. If a trade union refuses or wilfully neglects to perform the duty imposed on it by or under s 27, it commits an offence: see s 45(1); and PARA 956.
    The duty imposed by s 27 does not apply to a trade union which has been in existence for less than 12 months (s 43(1)(a)) or to a federated trade union which consists wholly or mainly of representatives of constituent or affiliated organisations (see s 118(4); and PARA 891 note 9 head (2)). As to the meaning of 'federated trade union' see PARA 891.

(ii)   Enforcement of Trade Union Rules

913.   The court's jurisdiction to grant relief in respect of breach of trade union rules. The jurisdiction of the court[1] to grant relief to a member of a trade union in respect of a breach of the rules[2] is founded on the contractual rights of the member contained in the rules[3]. Accordingly, a member has the right to restrain the union from acting outside the powers contained in its rules and otherwise than in accordance with the procedures required by its rules[4]. Where, however, it is alleged by a member of a trade union that the union has acted in breach of its rules, the rule that in matters of internal management members of a company may not sue on their own behalf[5] applies to trade unions[6] and may operate to deny the member a remedy where the irregularity was minor or insignificant and not a matter of substance[7].

1 Trade union members are now entitled to complain to the certification officer about certain alleged breaches of the rules of their trade unions: see the Trade Union and Labour Relations (Consolidation) Act 1992 Pt I Ch VIIA (ss 108A–108C); and PARAS 916–918.

2 As to the rules of a trade union see PARA 909 et seq.

3 *Amalgamated Society of Carpenters, Cabinet Makers and Joiners v Braithwaite* [1922] 2 AC 440, HL; *Edwards v Halliwell* [1950] 2 All ER 1064; *Bonsor v Musicians' Union* [1956] AC 104 at 127, [1955] 3 All ER 518 at 524, HL, per Lord Morton of Henryton; *Cheall v Association of Professional, Executive, Clerical and Computer Staff* [1983] 2 AC 180, [1983] ICR 398, HL.

4 *Porter v National Union of Journalists* [1979] IRLR 404, CA (affd [1980] IRLR 404, HL); *Taylor v National Union of Mineworkers (Derbyshire Area)* [1984] IRLR 440; *Taylor and Foulstone v National Union of Mineworkers (Yorkshire Area) and National Union of Mineworkers* [1984] IRLR 445; *Wise v Union of Shop, Distributive and Allied Workers* [1996] ICR 691, [1996] IRLR 609.

5 Ie the rule in *Foss v Harbottle* (1843) 2 Hare 461: see COMPANIES vol 14 (2009) PARA 462.

6 *Cotter v National Union of Seamen* [1929] 2 Ch 58, CA; *Taylor v National Union of Mineworkers (Derbyshire Area)* [1985] IRLR 99.

7 *Cotter v National Union of Seamen* [1929] 2 Ch 58, CA (where it was held that the irregularity was insufficient to warrant the intervention of the court); *Hodgson v National and Local Government Officers Association* [1972] 1 All ER 15, [1972] 1 WLR 130. Cf *Hamlet v General Municipal Boilermakers and Allied Trades Union* [1987] 1 All ER 631, [1987] ICR 150. In *Wise v Union of Shop, Distributive and Allied Workers* [1996] ICR 691, [1996] IRLR 609, a challenge by two union members to a decision of the union's executive relating to the election of union officers was rejected by the court on the grounds that, as the source of the union executive's powers was the contract between all of the members embodied in the rules of the union, each union member had a contractual right to complain of a breach of the rules which was individual to that member, and so the rule in *Foss v Harbottle* (1843) 2 Hare 461 (see note 5) had no application.

914. Exhaustion of internal procedures of trade union. The rules of a trade union cannot prevent a member from seeking a remedy from the court on any point of law[1]. Where the rules seek to prevent members from pursuing a remedy in the court until internal procedures have been exhausted, the court is not bound by such a rule but the member may have to show cause why the court should interfere with the contractual position[2]. In the absence of a provision in the rules requiring the exhaustion of internal procedures, the court may choose to intervene before the internal procedures have been exhausted, if they do not provide all the relief which the court might provide[3] or the position of the member would otherwise be prejudiced[4]. In certain circumstances[5] the court's power to stay proceedings pending the completion of internal procedures is restricted by certain statutory provisions[6] giving union members a right not to be denied access to the courts[7]. Exceptionally, the court may restrain a trade union from beginning or continuing internal procedures[8], but only where the court is satisfied that no reasonable tribunal, acting bona fide, could uphold the complaint[9].

1 *Lee v Showmen's Guild of Great Britain* [1952] 2 QB 329, [1952] 1 All ER 1175, CA; *Lawlor v Union of Post Office Workers* [1965] Ch 712, [1965] 1 All ER 353; *Leigh v National Union of Railwaymen* [1970] Ch 326, [1969] 3 All ER 1249. The court will not construe a rule which purports to oust the jurisdiction of the court as a requirement to exhaust internal remedies first:

Leigh v National Union of Railwaymen [1970] Ch 326, [1969] 3 All ER 1249. See generally
JUDICIAL REVIEW vol 61 (2010) PARAS 630, 645.
2   *White v Kuzych* [1951] AC 585, [1951] 2 All ER 435, PC; *Leigh v National Union of
    Railwaymen* [1970] Ch 326, [1969] 3 All ER 1249.
3   *Lawlor v Union of Post Office Workers* [1965] Ch 712, [1965] 1 All ER 353; *Leigh v National
    Union of Railwaymen* [1970] Ch 326, [1969] 3 All ER 1249. The court will not imply a term
    requiring the exhaustion of internal remedies: *Lawlor v Union of Post Office Workers* [1965]
    Ch 712, [1965] 1 All ER 353.
4   *Hiles v Amalgamated Society of Woodworkers* [1968] Ch 440, [1967] 3 All ER 70; *Leigh v
    National Union of Railwaymen* [1970] Ch 326, [1969] 3 All ER 1249.
5   Ie those set out in the Trade Union and Labour Relations (Consolidation) Act 1992 s 63(1), (2):
    see PARA 915.
6   Ie the Trade Union and Labour Relations (Consolidation) Act 1992 s 63: see PARA 915.
7   As to the right not to be denied access to the courts see PARA 915.
8   *Esterman v National and Local Government Officers' Association* [1974] ICR 625; *Partington
    v National and Local Government Officers' Association* [1981] IRLR 537.
9   *Longley v National Union of Journalists* [1987] IRLR 109, CA.

915.   Right not to be denied access to the courts. If a member[1] or former
member of a trade union[2] begins proceedings in a court with respect to a matter
to which certain statutory provisions[3] apply[4], then, notwithstanding anything in
the rules[5] of the union or the practice of any court, if:

(1)   he has previously made a valid[6] application to the union for the matter
       to be submitted for determination or conciliation in accordance with the
       union's rules; and

(2)   the court proceedings are begun after the end of the period of six
       months[7] beginning with the day on which the union received the
       application,

the rules requiring or allowing the matter to be so submitted, and the fact that
any relevant steps[8] remain to be taken under the rules, are to be regarded for all
purposes as irrelevant to any question whether the court proceedings should be
dismissed, stayed or adjourned[9].

1   For the purposes of the Trade Union and Labour Relations (Consolidation) Act 1992 Pt I Ch V
    (ss 62–70) (rights of trade union members) (see also PARA 1025 et seq), 'member', in relation to
    a trade union consisting wholly or partly of, or of representatives of, constituent or affiliated
    organisations, includes a member of any of the constituent or affiliated organisations: s 70.
2   As to the meaning of 'trade union' see PARA 891.
3   Ie the Trade Union and Labour Relations (Consolidation) Act 1992 s 63: see the text and notes
    4–9.
4   The provisions of the Trade Union and Labour Relations (Consolidation) Act 1992 s 63 apply
    where a matter is required or allowed, under the rules of a trade union, to be submitted for
    determination or conciliation in accordance with the rules of the union, but a provision of the
    rules purporting to provide for that to be a person's only remedy has no effect, or would have no
    effect if there were one: s 63(1). As to the meaning of 'rules' for these purposes see note 5; and
    as to the meaning of 'rules' in in relation to a trade union generally see PARA 898 note 5.
5   For these purposes, references to the rules of a trade union include any arbitration or other
    agreement entered into in pursuance of a requirement imposed by or under the rules: Trade
    Union and Labour Relations (Consolidation) Act 1992 s 63(5)(a).
6   An application is deemed to be valid for these purposes unless the union informed the applicant,
    before the end of the period of 28 days beginning with the date on which the union received the
    application, of the respects in which the application contravened the requirements of the rules:
    Trade Union and Labour Relations (Consolidation) Act 1992 s 63(3). Unless the context
    otherwise requires, 'contravention' includes a failure to comply; and cognate expressions are to
    be construed accordingly: s 298.
7   The court may treat this period as extended by such further period as it considers appropriate if
    satisfied that any delay in the taking of relevant steps under the rules is attributable to
    unreasonable conduct of the person who commenced the proceedings: Trade Union and Labour
    Relations (Consolidation) Act 1992 s 63(4).

8   For these purposes, references to the relevant steps under the rules, in relation to any matter, include any steps falling to be taken in accordance with the rules for the purposes of, or in connection with, the determination or conciliation of the matter, or any appeal, review or reconsideration of any determination or award: Trade Union and Labour Relations (Consolidation) Act 1992 s 63(5)(b).

9   Trade Union and Labour Relations (Consolidation) Act 1992 s 63(2). Section 63 does not affect any enactment or rule of law by virtue of which a court would otherwise disregard any such rules or any such fact as is mentioned in s 63(2): s 63(6).

916.   Right to apply to the certification officer.   A person who claims that there has been a breach or threatened breach of the rules[1] of a trade union[2] relating to any of the following matters:

(1)   the appointment or election of a person to, or the removal of a person from, any office;

(2)   disciplinary proceedings by the union[3], including expulsion;

(3)   the balloting of members on any issue other than industrial action[4];

(4)   the constitution or proceedings of any executive committee[5] or of any decision-making meeting[6];

(5)   such other matters as may be specified in an order made by the Secretary of State[7],

may apply[8] to the certification officer[9] for a declaration to that effect[10]; but no application may be made regarding the dismissal of an employee of the union or disciplinary proceedings against an employee of the union[11].

The applicant must be a member of the union, or have been one at the time of the alleged breach or threatened breach[12].

An application must be made:

(a)   within the period of six months starting with the day on which the breach or threatened breach is alleged to have taken place; or

(b)   if, within that period, any internal complaints procedure of the union is invoked to resolve the claim, within the period of six months starting with the earlier of the day on which the procedure is concluded and the last day of the period of one year beginning with the day on which the procedure is invoked[13].

If a person applies to the certification officer under the above provisions in relation to an alleged breach or threatened breach, he may not apply to the court in relation to the breach or threatened breach; but such a person is not thereby prevented from exercising any right to appeal against or challenge the certification officer's decision on the application to him[14]. If a person applies to the court in relation to an alleged breach or threatened breach, and the breach or threatened breach is one in relation to which he could have made an application to the certification officer under the above provisions, he may not apply to the certification officer under those provisions in relation to the breach or threatened breach[15].

1   For these purposes, the reference to the rules of a union includes references to the rules of any branch or section of the union: Trade Union and Labour Relations (Consolidation) Act 1992 s 108A(8) (s 108A added by the Employment Relations Act 1999 Sch 6 paras 1, 19). As to the meaning of 'rules' generally, in relation to a trade union, see PARA 898 note 5; and as to the meaning of 'branch or section', in relation to a trade union, see PARA 898 note 5.

2   As to the meaning of 'trade union' see PARA 891.

3   As to the meaning of 'disciplinary proceedings' see *Irving v GMB* [2008] IRLR 202, [2007] All ER (D) 192 (Oct), EAT (the restriction to disciplinary proceedings is deliberate (as is the decision not to include grievances) and the essential requirement for something to qualify as a disciplinary procedure is that it must confer on one party a power to impose a sanction on the other party: if that is missing, it is not a disciplinary procedure, even if there is the possibility that disciplinary proceedings might follow determination of the grievance).

4   For these purposes, 'industrial action' means a strike or other industrial action by persons employed under contracts of employment: Trade Union and Labour Relations (Consolidation) Act 1992 s 108A(9) (as added: see note 1). As to the meaning of 'contract of employment' see PARA 892.

5   For these purposes, a committee is an executive committee if: (1) it is a committee of the union concerned and has power to make executive decisions on behalf of the union or on behalf of a constituent body; (2) it is a committee of a major constituent body and has power to make executive decisions on behalf of that body; or (3) it is a sub-committee of a committee falling within head (1) or head (2) above: Trade Union and Labour Relations (Consolidation) Act 1992 s 108A(10) (as added: see note 1). In relation to the trade union concerned: (a) a constituent body is any body which forms part of the union, including a branch, group, section or region; (b) a major constituent body is such a body which has more than 1,000 members: s 108A(12) (as so added).

6   For these purposes, a decision-making meeting is: (1) a meeting of members of the union concerned, or the representatives of such members, which has power to make a decision on any matter which, under the rules of the union, is final as regards the union or which, under the rules of the union or a constituent body, is final as regards that body; or (2) a meeting of members of a major constituent body, or the representatives of such members, which has power to make a decision on any matter which, under the rules of the union or the body, is final as regards that body: Trade Union and Labour Relations (Consolidation) Act 1992 s 108A(11) (as added: see note 1). See also note 5.

7   Any such order must be made by statutory instrument; and no such order is to be made unless a draft of it has been laid before and approved by resolution of each House of Parliament: Trade Union and Labour Relations (Consolidation) Act 1992 s 108A(13) (as added: see note 1). At the date at which this volume states the law, no such order had been made and none had effect as if so made.

8   Ie subject to the Trade Union and Labour Relations (Consolidation) Act 1992 s 108A(3)–(7): see the text and notes 11–13.

9   As to the certification officer see PARA 1443.

10 Trade Union and Labour Relations (Consolidation) Act 1992 s 108A(1), (2) (as added: see note 1). A person may not apply under s 108A(1) in relation to a claim if he is entitled to apply under s 80 (see PARA 983) in relation to the claim: s 108A(4) (as so added). As to appeals from the certification officer see PARA 918.

11 Trade Union and Labour Relations (Consolidation) Act 1992 s 108A(5) (as added: see note 1).

12 Trade Union and Labour Relations (Consolidation) Act 1992 s 108A(3) (as added: see note 1).

13 Trade Union and Labour Relations (Consolidation) Act 1992 s 108A(6), (7) (as added: see note 1). Informal correspondence following a suspension did not constitute the invocation of an internal complaints procedure within the meaning of s 108A(6); there had to be specific dates at which it could be said that the procedure was being invoked and at which it was concluded: *Bakhsh v Unison* [2009] IRLR 418, [2009] All ER (D) 169 (Apr), EAT.

14 Trade Union and Labour Relations (Consolidation) Act 1992 s 108A(14) (as added: see note 1).

15 Trade Union and Labour Relations (Consolidation) Act 1992 s 108A(15) (as added: see note 1).

917.   Declaration and orders by the certification officer. The certification officer[1] may refuse to accept an application relating to a breach or threatened breach of the rules of a trade union[2] unless he is satisfied that the applicant has taken all reasonable steps to resolve the claim by the use of any internal complaints procedure of the union[3]. If he accepts such an application, the certification officer:

(1)   must make such inquiries as he thinks fit;

(2)   must give the applicant and the union an opportunity to be heard;

(3)   must ensure that, so far as is reasonably practicable, the application is determined within six months of being made;

(4)   may make or refuse the declaration asked for; and

(5)   must, whether he makes or refuses the declaration, give reasons for his decision in writing[4].

Where the certification officer makes a declaration, he must also, unless he considers that to do so would be inappropriate, make an order (an 'enforcement order') imposing on the union one or both of the following requirements:

(a)   to take such steps to remedy the breach, or withdraw the threat of a breach, as may be specified in the order;

(b)   to abstain from such acts as may be so specified with a view to securing that a breach or threat of the same or a similar kind does not occur in future[5];

and the certification officer must, in an order imposing any such requirement as is mentioned in head (a) above, specify the period within which the union is to comply with the requirement[6].

Where the certification officer requests a person to furnish information to him in connection with inquiries made by him under the above provisions, he must specify the date by which that information is to be furnished and, unless he considers that it would be inappropriate to do so, must proceed with his determination of the application notwithstanding that the information has not been furnished to him by the specified date[7].

A declaration made by the certification officer under the above provisions may be relied on as if it were a declaration made by the court[8]. Where an enforcement order has been made, any person who is a member of the union and was a member at the time it was made is entitled to enforce obedience to the order as if he had made the application on which the order was made[9]. An enforcement order made by the certification officer may be enforced in the same way as an order of the court[10].

1   As to the certification officer see PARA 1443.
2   Ie under the Trade Union and Labour Relations (Consolidation) Act 1992 s 108A: see PARA 916. As to the meaning of 'trade union' see PARA 891; as to the meaning of 'rules' for the purposes of s 108A see PARA 916 note 1; and as to the meaning of 'rules' in relation to a trade union generally see PARA 898 note 5.
3   Trade Union and Labour Relations (Consolidation) Act 1992 s 108B(1) (s 108B added by the Employment Relations Act 1999 Sch 6 paras 1, 19). This provision provides the certification officer with a discretion; it does not oblige him to refuse to accept an application where he is not satisfied as described in the text: *Clarke v National Union of Mineworkers* [2002] All ER (D) 104 (Aug), EAT. As to appeals from the certification officer see PARA 918.
4   Trade Union and Labour Relations (Consolidation) Act 1992 s 108B(2) (as added: see note 3). An order under s 108A(2)(e) (see PARA 916) may provide that, in relation to an application under s 108A with regard to a prescribed matter, s 108B(1)–(8) is to apply with such omissions or modifications as may be specified in the order; and a prescribed matter is such matter specified under s 108A(2)(e) as is prescribed under this provision: s 108B(9) (as so added). 'Prescribed' means prescribed by regulations made by the Secretary of state: s 293(1). As to the power to make regulations see s 293; and PARA 902 note 8. At the date at which this volume states the law, no such matters had been prescribed.
5   Trade Union and Labour Relations (Consolidation) Act 1992 s 108B(3) (as added: see note 3).
6   Trade Union and Labour Relations (Consolidation) Act 1992 s 108B(4) (as added: see note 3).
7   Trade Union and Labour Relations (Consolidation) Act 1992 s 108B(5) (as added: see note 3).
8   Trade Union and Labour Relations (Consolidation) Act 1992 s 108B(6) (as added: see note 3).
9   Trade Union and Labour Relations (Consolidation) Act 1992 s 108B(7) (as added: see note 3).
10 Trade Union and Labour Relations (Consolidation) Act 1992 s 108B(8) (as added: see note 3).

918.   Appeals from certification officer.   An appeal lies to the Employment Appeal Tribunal[1] on any question of law arising in proceedings before or arising from any decision of the certification officer[2] in respect of an application[3] relating to a breach or threatened breach of the rules of a trade union[4].

1   As to the Employment Appeal Tribunal see PARA 1422 et seq.
2   As to the certification officer see PARA 1443.
3   Ie under the Trade Union and Labour Relations (Consolidation) Act 1992 Pt II Ch VIIA (ss 108A–108C): see also PARAS 916, 917.
4   Trade Union and Labour Relations (Consolidation) Act 1992 s 108C (added by the Employment Relations Act 1999 Sch 6 paras 1, 19).

(3) TRADE UNION PROPERTY

919. Trade union property must be vested in trustees. All property belonging to a trade union[1], other than a special register body[2], must be vested in trustees in trust for it[3]; and a judgment, order or award made in proceedings of any description brought against a trade union is enforceable[4], by way of execution, punishment for contempt or otherwise, against any property held in trust for it to the same extent and in the same manner as if it were a body corporate[5].

1   As to the meaning of 'trade union' see PARA 891.
2   As to special register bodies see PARA 899.
3   Trade Union and Labour Relations (Consolidation) Act 1992 ss 12(1), 117(2), (3)(c). The union, not the individual members, is the beneficial owner of the property: *Taff Vale Rly Co v Amalgamated Society of Railway Servants* [1901] AC 426, HL; *Cotter v National Union of Seamen* [1929] 2 Ch 58, CA.
4   Ie subject to the Trade Union and Labour Relations (Consolidation) Act 1992 s 23 (restriction on the enforcement of awards against certain property): see PARA 928.
5   Trade Union and Labour Relations (Consolidation) Act 1992 s 12(2), (3). As to the power of the Secretary of State to provide money to trade unions for the purposes of modernisation see s 116A; and PARA 929.
    The repeal of the Trade Union and Labour Relations Act 1974 s 19 (transitional provisions for trade unions ceasing to be incorporated) does not affect: (1) the title to property which by virtue of s 19 (repealed) vested on 16 September 1974 in the 'appropriate trustees' as defined by s 19 (repealed) (Trade Union and Labour Relations (Consolidation) Act 1992 Sch 3 para 6(1)); or (2) any liability, obligation or right affecting such property which, by virtue of the Trade Union and Labour Relations Act 1974 s 19 (repealed) became a liability, obligation or right of those trustees; and a certificate given by the persons who on that date were the president and general secretary of a trade union, or occupied positions equivalent thereto, that the persons named in the certificate are the appropriate trustees of the union for the purposes of s 19(2) (repealed) is conclusive evidence that those persons were the appropriate trustees for those purposes (Trade Union and Labour Relations (Consolidation) Act 1992 Sch 3 para 6((2)). A document which purports to be such a certificate is to be taken to be such a certificate unless the contrary is proved: Sch 3 para 6(3).

920. Change of trustee and vesting of trade union property in new trustees. On the death of a trustee in whom property is vested[1] in trust for a trade union[2] the general law of trusts applies to vest the trust property in the surviving trustees or the personal representative of the last surviving trustee[3].

Where, however, a trustee of a trade union wishes to be discharged from the trust and no new trustee is to replace him, the general statutory provisions which require the discharge to be by deed[4] are modified in relation to the trustee of a trade union, other than a special register body[5], whose name is entered in the list of trade unions[6], so as to permit the discharge to be by instrument in writing[7]. Subject to any express provision in it to the contrary, such an instrument in writing discharging the trustee operates to vest the trust property[8] automatically in the continuing trustees of the union without any conveyance or assignment of the property[9]. Similarly, the appointment of a new trustee by such an instrument in writing is sufficient to vest the trust property[10] in the new or continuing trustees without any conveyance or assignment of the property[11].

1   As to the vesting of property in trustees see PARA 919.
2   As to the meaning of 'trade union' see PARA 891.
3   As to the general law on the vesting of trust property on the death of a trustee see TRUSTS AND POWERS vol 98 (2013) PARA 157 et seq. As to the power of the Secretary of State to provide money to trade unions for the purposes of modernisation see the Trade Union and Labour Relations (Consolidation) Act 1992 s 116A; and PARA 929.
4   Ie the Trustee Act 1925 s 39(1): see TRUSTS AND POWERS vol 98 (2013) PARA 331.
5   As to the meaning of 'special register body' see PARA 899.

6   Ie the list of trade unions maintained by the certification officer under the Trade Union and Labour Relations (Consolidation) Act 1992 s 2: see PARA 900 et seq.

7   Trade Union and Labour Relations (Consolidation) Act 1992 ss 13(1), (2)(a), 117(2), (3)(c). Where a trustee is appointed or discharged by a resolution taken by or on behalf of the union, the written record of the resolution is to be treated as an instrument in writing appointing or discharging the trustee: s 13(3). As to the application of these provisions to Northern Ireland see PARA 1078.

8   Ie except land held under a lease which contains a covenant against assignment where consent to assign has not been obtained or where the instrument would operate as a breach of covenant or give rise to a forfeiture: see TRUSTS AND POWERS vol 98 (2013) PARA 307.

9   Trustee Act 1925 s 40(2) (amended by the Trusts of Land and Appointment of Trustees Act 1996 Sch 3 para 3(1), (14); modified by the Trade Union and Labour Relations (Consolidation) Act 1992 s 13(1), (2)(b)); Trustee Act 1925 s 40(4)(b) (applied by the Trade Union and Labour Relations (Consolidation) Act 1992 s 13(1), (4)). This is in contrast to the application of the Trustee Act 1925 to other trusts, where the discharge must be by deed to effect vesting without conveyance or assignment (see s 40(2); and TRUSTS AND POWERS vol 98 (2013) PARA 306), and where land held by way of mortgage for securing money subject to the trust (see s 40(4)(a); and TRUSTS AND POWERS vol 98 (2013) PARA 307) and shares, stocks, annuities and property transferable only in books kept by a company or other body or in manner directed by or under an Act of Parliament (see s 40(4)(c); and TRUSTS AND POWERS vol 98 (2013) PARA 307), as well as land held under a lease which contains a covenant against assignment where consent to assign has not been obtained or where the instrument would operate as a breach of covenant or give rise to a forfeiture (see s 40(4)(b); and TRUSTS AND POWERS vol 98 (2013) PARA 307), must be specifically conveyed or assigned. As to the special provisions facilitating the transfer of registered securities see PARA 921.

10   See note 8.

11   Trustee Act 1925 s 40(1) (modified by the Trade Union and Labour Relations (Consolidation) Act 1992 s 13(1), (2)(b)); Trustee Act 1925 s 40(4)(b) (applied by the Trade Union and Labour Relations (Consolidation) Act 1992 s 13(1), (4)). See also note 9.

921.   Transfer of securities held in trust for trade union. Where, by any enactment or instrument, the transfer of securities of any description is required to be effected or recorded by means of entries in a register, the person authorised or required to keep the register is required, notwithstanding anything in any enactment or instrument regulating the keeping of the register, to make such entries as may be necessary to give effect to an instrument of appointment[1] or discharge[2], if there is produced to that person a copy of such an instrument which contains or has attached to it a list identifying the securities of the relevant description held in trust for the union at the date of the appointment or discharge[3], and it appears to that person that any of the securities so identified are included in the register kept by him[4].

1   For these purposes, 'instrument of appointment' means an instrument in writing appointing a new trustee of a trade union whose name is entered in the list of trade unions: Trade Union and Labour Relations (Consolidation) Act 1992 s 14(1). As to the meaning of 'trade union' see PARA 891; and as to the list of trade unions see PARA 900. Section 14 does not apply to special register bodies: see PARA 899 note 8 head (2). As to the meaning of 'special register body' see PARA 899.

2   For these purposes, 'instrument of discharge' means an instrument in writing discharging a trustee of a trade union whose name is entered in the list of trade unions: Trade Union and Labour Relations (Consolidation) Act 1992 s 14(1). See also note 1.

3   A document purporting to be a copy of an instrument of appointment or discharge containing or having attached to it such a list, and to be certified in accordance with the Trade Union and Labour Relations (Consolidation) Act 1992 s 14(4) to be a copy of such an instrument, is to be taken to be a copy of such an instrument unless the contrary is proved: s 14(3). The certificate must be given by the president and general secretary of the union and, in the case of an instrument to which a list of securities is attached, must appear both on the instrument and on the list: s 14(4). For these purposes, 'president' and 'general secretary', in relation to a trade union, mean the officials of the union who hold the offices of president or general secretary, as the case may be, or, where there are no such offices, hold offices which are equivalent to those of president or general secretary respectively: s 119. Except for the purposes of s 14(4) (and, in the

case of the president), Pt I Ch IV (ss 46–61) (see PARA 960 et seq) those officials may also hold offices which are the nearest equivalent to those of president or general secretary respectively: s 119. An acting general secretary may come within the definition in s 119 where he exercises the relevant functions for a period of time and there is no reason not to hold an election for the position: *Corrigan v GMB Union, GMB Union v Corrigan* [2008] ICR 197, [2007] All ER (D) 288 (Oct), EAT.

4 Trade Union and Labour Relations (Consolidation) Act 1992 s 14(2). Nothing done for the purposes of or in pursuance of s 14 is to be taken to affect any person with notice of any trust or to impose on any person a duty to inquire into any matter: s 14(5). Where a trustee is appointed or discharged by a resolution taken by or on behalf of a trade union whose name is entered in the list of trade unions, the written record of the resolution is to be treated as an instrument in writing appointing or discharging the trustee: s 14(1). See also note 1. As to the application of these provisions to Northern Ireland see PARA 1078. As to the power of the Secretary of State to provide money to trade unions for the purposes of modernisation see s 116A; and PARA 929.

922. Prohibition on use of trade union funds to indemnify unlawful conduct.

It is unlawful for property of a trade union[1] to be applied in or towards:

(1) the payment for an individual of a penalty[2] which has been or may be imposed on him for an offence[3] or for contempt of court;

(2) the securing of any such payment; or

(3) the provision of anything for indemnifying an individual in respect of such a penalty[4].

Where any property of a trade union is so applied for the benefit of an individual on whom a penalty has been or may be imposed, then, in the case of a payment, an amount equal to the payment is recoverable by the union from him, and, in any other case, he is liable to account to the union for the value of the property applied[5]. If a trade union fails to bring or continue proceedings which it is so entitled to bring, a member[6] of the union who claims that the failure is unreasonable may apply to the High Court on that ground for an order authorising him to bring or continue the proceedings on the union's behalf and at the union's expense[7].

The above provisions do not affect any other enactment, rule of law or any provision of the rules[8] of a trade union which makes it unlawful for the property of a trade union to be applied in a particular way, or any other remedy available to a trade union, the trustees of its property or any of its members in respect of an unlawful application of the union's property[9].

1 As to the meaning of 'trade union' see PARA 891.

2 For these purposes, 'penalty', in relation to an offence, includes an order to pay compensation and an order for the forfeiture of any property; and references to the imposition of a penalty for an offence are to be construed accordingly: Trade Union and Labour Relations (Consolidation) Act 1992 s 15(4).

3 The Secretary of State may by order designate offences in relation to which these prohibitions do not apply; and any such order must be made by statutory instrument which is subject to annulment in pursuance of a resolution of either House of Parliament: Trade Union and Labour Relations (Consolidation) Act 1992 s 15(5). At the date at which this volume states the law, no such order had been made and none had effect as if so made. As to the Secretary of State see PARA 5 note 21.

4 Trade Union and Labour Relations (Consolidation) Act 1992 s 15(1). As to the power of the Secretary of State to provide money to trade unions for the purposes of modernisation see s 116A; and PARA 929.

5 Trade Union and Labour Relations (Consolidation) Act 1992 s 15(2).

6 For these purposes, 'member', in relation to a trade union consisting wholly or partly of, or of representatives of, constituent or affiliated organisations, includes a member of any of the constituent or affiliated organisations: Trade Union and Labour Relations (Consolidation) Act 1992 s 15(7).

7 Trade Union and Labour Relations (Consolidation) Act 1992 ss 15(3), 121.

8   As to the meaning of 'rules', in relation to a trade union, see PARA 898 note 5.
9   Trade Union and Labour Relations (Consolidation) Act 1992 s 15(6).

923.   Unlawful use of trade union property by trustees. A member[1] of a trade union who claims that the trustees of the union's property[2] have so carried out, or are proposing so to carry out, their functions as to cause or permit an unlawful application of the union's property, or have complied, or are proposing to comply, with an unlawful direction which has been or may be given to them under the rules[3] of the union, may apply[4] to the High Court for an order[5]. Without prejudice to any other power of the court, on such an application the court may grant such interim relief as it considers appropriate[6].

Where the court is satisfied that the complaint is well-founded, it must make such order as it considers appropriate; and it may, in particular:

(1)   require the trustees, if necessary, on behalf of the union, to take all such steps as may be specified in the order for protecting or recovering the property of the union;

(2)   appoint a receiver of the property of the union;

(3)   remove one or more of the trustees[7].

Where the court makes such an order in a case in which property of the union has been applied in contravention[8] of an order of any court, or in compliance with a direction given in contravention of such an order, or the trustees were proposing to apply property in contravention of such an order or to comply with any such direction, the court must by its order remove all the trustees except any trustee who satisfies the court that there is a good reason for allowing him to remain a trustee[9].

The above provisions do not affect any other remedy available in respect of a breach of trust by the trustees of a trade union's property[10].

1   For these purposes, 'member', in relation to a trade union consisting wholly or partly of, or of representatives of, constituent or affiliated organisations, includes a member of any of the constituent or affiliated organisations: Trade Union and Labour Relations (Consolidation) Act 1992 s 16(7). As to the meaning of 'trade union' see PARA 891.
2   As to the vesting of property in trustees see PARA 919.
3   As to the meaning of 'rules', in relation to a trade union, see PARA 898 note 5.
4   In a case relating to property which has already been unlawfully applied or to an unlawful direction that has already been complied with, an application may be made only by a person who was a member of the union at the time when the property was applied or the direction complied with: Trade Union and Labour Relations (Consolidation) Act 1992 s 16(2).
5   Trade Union and Labour Relations (Consolidation) Act 1992 ss 16(1), 121. As to the power of the Secretary of State to provide money to trade unions for the purposes of modernisation see s 116A; and PARA 929.
6   See the Trade Union and Labour Relations (Consolidation) Act 1992 s 16(5). The statutory wording is 'interlocutory' relief but interlocutory remedies have now been replaced by interim remedies: see generally CIVIL PROCEDURE vol 11 (2009) PARA 315 et seq.
7   Trade Union and Labour Relations (Consolidation) Act 1992 s 16(3).
8   As to the meaning of 'contravention' and cognate expressions see PARA 915 note 6.
9   Trade Union and Labour Relations (Consolidation) Act 1992 s 16(4).
10   Trade Union and Labour Relations (Consolidation) Act 1992 s 16(6). As to the remedies available against trustees under the general law see PARA 919.

924.   Nominations by members of trade unions. The Secretary of State may make provision by regulations for enabling members of trade unions[1] who are not under 16 years of age to nominate a person or persons to become entitled, on the death of the person making the nomination, to the whole or part of any money payable on his death out of the funds of the trade union[2]. The regulations may:

(1)   include provision as to the manner in which nominations may be made and as to the manner in which nominations may be varied or revoked[3];

(2)   provide that, subject to such exceptions as may be prescribed, no nomination made by a member of a trade union is to be valid if at the date of the nomination the person nominated is an officer[4] or employee[5] of the trade union or is otherwise connected with the trade union in such manner as may be prescribed by the regulations[6];

(3)   include such incidental, transitional or supplementary provisions as the Secretary of State may consider appropriate[7].

Accordingly, a member of a trade union who has attained the age of 16 years may nominate any person to receive the whole or part of any money not exceeding £5,000 payable on his death out of any funds of the trade union of which he is a member[8]. A nomination may be in favour of one person or of several persons[9], who must be clearly designated in the nomination; and, where there is more than one nominee, the nomination may direct that specific sums be paid to one or more of them or that they are to take the money nominated in specified shares, or the nomination may give directions to both effects[10].

A nomination must be made in writing in a form approved by the trade union, and must be signed by the nominator[11]. A nomination is of no effect unless it is delivered at, or sent to, the principal office of the trade union during the lifetime of the nominator[12]. The trade union must register every nomination and notify the nominator of the registration[13]. A nomination is not revoked by any will or by any act or means other than those prescribed[14]. On the death of the nominator[15] the trade union must pay to the nominee the amount due to him according to the directions of the nomination[16].

1   As to the meaning of 'trade union' see PARA 891. As to the Secretary of State see PARA 5 note 21.

2   Trade Union and Labour Relations (Consolidation) Act 1992 s 17(1). As to the power of the Secretary of State to provide money to trade unions for the purposes of modernisation see s 116A; and PARA 929.

3   Trade Union and Labour Relations (Consolidation) Act 1992 s 17(2).

4   As to the meaning of 'officer', in relation to a trade union, see PARA 902 note 7.

5   As to the meaning of 'employee' see PARA 892.

6   Trade Union and Labour Relations (Consolidation) Act 1992 s 17(3).

7   Trade Union and Labour Relations (Consolidation) Act 1992 s 17(4). The regulations may, in particular, include provision for securing, to such extent and subject to such conditions as may be prescribed in the regulations, that nominations made under the Trade Union Act 1871 Amendment Act 1876 (repealed) have effect as if made under the regulations and may be varied or revoked accordingly: Trade Union and Labour Relations (Consolidation) Act 1992 s 17(5). Such regulations must be made by statutory instrument which is subject to annulment in pursuance of a resolution of either House of Parliament: s 17(6). At the date at which this volume states the law, no such regulations had been made but, by virtue of Sch 3 para 1(2) (see PARA 891 note 1) and the Interpretation Act 1978 s 17(2)(b), the Trade Union (Nominations) Regulations 1977, SI 1977/789, have effect as if so made. Nominations made under earlier enactments are to be treated as having been validly made under the Trade Union (Nominations) Regulations 1977, SI 1977/789, and may be varied or revoked accordingly: see reg 10(2).

8   Trade Union (Nominations) Regulations 1977, SI 1977/789, reg 2(1) (amended by SI 1984/1290). Subject to the provisions of the Trade Union (Nominations) Regulations 1977, SI 1977/789, a nomination is deemed to extend to all sums to which a nominator is entitled at the time of his death, unless a contrary intention appears from the nomination: reg 4.

9   A nomination is not valid in respect of any nominee who at the date of the nomination is an officer or employee of the trade union, unless that person is the spouse or civil partner, father, mother, child, brother, sister, nephew or niece of the nominator: Trade Union (Nominations) Regulations 1977, SI 1977/789, reg 2(6) (amended by SI 2005/2114).

10   Trade Union (Nominations) Regulations 1977, SI 1977/789, reg 2(5).

11　Trade Union (Nominations) Regulations 1977, SI 1977/789, reg 2(2). If a person from whom a signature is required is unable to write, it is sufficient if the document is marked by that person in the presence of a witness: reg 7.

12　Trade Union (Nominations) Regulations 1977, SI 1977/789, reg 2(3).

13　Trade Union (Nominations) Regulations 1977, SI 1977/789, reg 2(4).

14　Trade Union (Nominations) Regulations 1977, SI 1977/789, reg 3(1). A nomination is revoked: (1) by the death of the nominee or, where there is more than one, by the death of all the nominees, in the lifetime of the nominator; (2) so far as relates to the interest thereunder of any nominee, being one of two or more nominees, by the death of that nominee in the nominator's lifetime, unless that nominee's interest is disposed of by the nomination; (3) by the formation of a subsequent marriage or civil partnership by the nominator; (4) by written notice of revocation signed by the nominator and delivered at, or sent to, the principal office of the trade union during the nominator's lifetime; (5) by a subsequent nomination duly made by the same nominator disposing of either the whole or any part of the money disposed of by the earlier nomination, but only so far as respects that money or that part of it, as the case may be: reg 3(1)(a)–(e) (amended by SI 2005/2114). Where the trade union has paid the money to the nominee in ignorance of the formation of a subsequent marriage or civil partnership by the nominator, then, notwithstanding that the nomination has been revoked by that marriage or civil partnership, the payment is valid as if the nomination had not been so revoked by that marriage or civil partnership: Trade Union (Nominations) Regulations 1977, SI 1977/789, reg 3(2) (amended by SI 2005/2114).

Marriage of same sex couples is lawful in the law of England and Wales, and such marriages have the same effect as marriages of opposite sex couples: see the Marriage (Same Sex Couples) Act 2013 s 1(1), 11(1); and MATRIMONIAL AND CIVIL PARTNERSHIP LAW vol 72 (2009) PARA 1 et seq.

15　The trade union may accept as conclusive proof of the death of a member any evidence which it considers satisfactory: Trade Union (Nominations) Regulations 1977, SI 1977/789, reg 9.

16　Trade Union (Nominations) Regulations 1977, SI 1977/789, reg 5. If, however, any nominee is under the age of 16, the trade union must not make any payment to him until he attains that age, but may pay the sum due or any part thereof to any person who satisfies the trade union that he will apply it for the maintenance or benefit of that nominee: reg 5 proviso.

The receipt of any person aged 16 years or over for any money paid to him in accordance with a nomination is a good discharge to the trade union for any money so paid: reg 8.

925.　Payments out of union funds on the death of a member. The Secretary of State may make provision by regulations for enabling money payable out of the funds of a trade union[1] on the death of a member, to an amount not exceeding £5,000[2], to be paid or distributed on his death without letters of administration, probate of any will or confirmation[3]. The regulations may include such incidental, transitional and supplementary provisions as the Secretary of State may consider appropriate[4].

Accordingly, where any money is payable out of the funds of a trade union on the death of a member[5], the trade union may, without letters of administration, or probate of any will or confirmation, pay out or distribute, otherwise than in accordance with a nomination[6], an amount not exceeding £5,000 to the person or persons the trade union considers to be entitled by law to receive it[7]. Where, however, any person to whom a payment may be so made is under the age of 16 years, the trade union may make the payment to any person who satisfies it that he will apply the money for the maintenance or benefit of the first-mentioned person[8].

1　As to the meaning of 'trade union' see PARA 891. As to the Secretary of State see PARA 5 note 21.

2　The Treasury may direct, by order under the Administration of Estates (Small Payments) Act 1965 s 6(1) (see WILLS AND INTESTACY vol 103 (2010) PARA 661), that the Trade Union and Labour Relations (Consolidation) Act 1992 s 18(1) is to have effect with the substitution for the reference to £5,000 of a reference to such higher amount as may be specified in the order: s 18(4). At the date at which this volume states the law, no such order had been made and none had effect as if so made. As to the Treasury see CONSTITUTIONAL AND ADMINISTRATIVE LAW vol 20 (2014) PARA 262 et seq.

3 Trade Union and Labour Relations (Consolidation) Act 1992 s 18(1). As to the power of the Secretary of State to provide money to trade unions for the purposes of modernisation see s 116A; and PARA 929.

4 Trade Union and Labour Relations (Consolidation) Act 1992 s 18(2). Such regulations must be made by statutory instrument which is subject to annulment in pursuance of a resolution of either House of Parliament: s 18(3). At the date at which this volume states the law no such regulations had been made but, by virtue of Sch 3 para 1(2) (see PARA 891 note 1) and the Interpretation Act 1978 s 17(2)(b), the Trade Union (Nominations) Regulations 1977, SI 1977/789, have effect as if so made.

5 As to proof of death see PARA 924 note 15.

6 As to nominations by members of trade unions see PARA 924.

7 Trade Union (Nominations) Regulations 1977, SI 1977/789, reg 6(1) (amended by SI 1984/1290).

8 Trade Union (Nominations) Regulations 1977, SI 1977/789, reg 6(2). The receipt of any person aged 16 or over for any money paid to him in accordance with a payment or distribution is a good discharge to the trade union for any money so paid: reg 8.

926. Application to trade unions of the law relating to insurance companies, industrial assurance or friendly societies. A trade union[1] is exempt from the general prohibition under the Financial Services and Markets Act 2000 from carrying on regulated activities in the United Kingdom[2] in respect of any specified regulated activity[3] of effecting and carrying out contracts of insurance[4] which it carries on in order to provide provident benefits or strike benefits for its members[5].

If a trade union enters into a contract of insurance under which benefit in excess of £800 is payable on the death of any person, and that person dies under the age of ten, then, without prejudice to any person's right to recover part of the premiums paid, the union's obligation is limited to the payment of £800 in benefit, except where the benefit is payable to a person who has an interest in the life of the person on whose death it is payable[6].

The statutory provisions relating to charitable subscriptions and contributions to other registered societies[7] extend to a trade union, or branch of a trade union, as regards contributing to the funds and taking part in the government of a medical society[8]; and a trade union or branch of a trade union must not withdraw from contributing to the funds of such a society except on three months' notice to the society and on payment of all contributions accrued or accruing due to the date of the expiry of the notice[9].

1 As to the meaning of 'trade union' see PARA 891.

2 As to the general prohibition see FINANCIAL SERVICES AND INSTITUTIONS vol 48 (2008) PARA 80.

3 As to regulated activities under the Financial Services and Markets Act 2000 see FINANCIAL SERVICES AND INSTITUTIONS vol 48 (2008) PARA 84 et seq.

4 Ie any regulated activity of the kind specified by the Financial Services and Markets Act 2000 (Regulated Activities) Order 2001, SI 2001/544, art 10: see FINANCIAL SERVICES AND INSTITUTIONS vol 48 (2008) PARA 100. As to the meaning of 'contract of insurance' see FINANCIAL SERVICES AND INSTITUTIONS vol 48 (2008) PARA 90.

5 See the Financial Services and Markets Act 2000 (Exemption) Order 2001, SI 2001/1201, para 43; and FINANCIAL SERVICES AND INSTITUTIONS vol 48 (2008) PARA 338.

6 Friendly Societies Act 1992 s 99(1), (2) (applied by the Trade Union and Labour Relations (Consolidation) Act 1992 s 19(1) (substituted by SI 1993/3084; amended by SI 2001/3649)). The Treasury may by order substitute some other sum for the sum for the time being specified in the Friendly Societies Act 1992 s 99(1): s 99(3) (amended by SI 2001/2617). At the date at which this volume states the law, no such order had been made. As to the Treasury see CONSTITUTIONAL AND ADMINISTRATIVE LAW vol 20 (2014) PARA 262 et seq.

7 Ie the Friendly Societies Act 1974 s 52: see FINANCIAL SERVICES AND INSTITUTIONS vol 50 (2008) PARAS 2200–2201.

8   For these purposes, 'medical society' means a society for the purpose of relief in sickness by providing medical attendance and medicine: Trade Union and Labour Relations (Consolidation) Act 1992 s 19(3).

9   Trade Union and Labour Relations (Consolidation) Act 1992 s 19(3).

927.   Tax exemption for trade unions.   A trade union[1] which is precluded by Act of Parliament or by its rules from assuring to any person a sum exceeding £4,000 by way of gross sum or £825[2] by way of annuity[3] is, on making a claim, entitled to exemption from corporation tax in respect of its income which is not trading income and which is applicable and applied for the purpose of provident benefits, and in respect of chargeable gains[4] which are applicable and applied for the purpose of provident benefits[5].

For these purposes, 'provident benefits' include:

(1)   a payment expressly authorised by the rules of the trade union which is made:

  (a)   to a member during sickness or incapacity from personal injury or while out of work;

  (b)   to a member by way of superannuation by reason of age, sickness or incapacity from personal injury;

  (c)   to a member who has met with an accident; or

  (d)   to a member who has lost tools by fire or theft;

(2)   a payment in discharge or aid of funeral expenses on the death of a member or the spouse or civil partner of a member; and

(3)   a payment as provision for the children of a deceased member[6].

1   For these purposes, 'trade union' means (1) an organisation the name of which is entered in the list maintained by the certification officer under the Trade Union and Labour Relations (Consolidation) Act 1992 s 2 (list of trade unions: see PARA 900); (2) the Police Federation for England and Wales, the Police Federation for Scotland, the Police Federation for Northern Ireland and any other organisation of persons in police service which has similar functions: Corporation Tax Act 2010 s 983(1), (2)(a), (c).

2   The amounts of £4,000 and £825 may be increased by order of the Treasury, which may also make provision about the income or gains in relation to which such an amendment has effect: see the Corporation Tax Act 2010 s 981(5). As to the Treasury see CONSTITUTIONAL AND ADMINISTRATIVE LAW vol 20 (2014) PARA 262 et seq.

3   In determining for this purpose whether a trade union is by Act of Parliament or its rules precluded from assuring to any person a sum exceeding £825 by way of annuity, there must be disregarded any annuity contract which constitutes a registered pension scheme or is issued or held in connection with a registered pension scheme other than an occupational pension scheme (within the meaning of the Finance Act 2004 s 150(5)) (see PERSONAL AND OCCUPATIONAL PENSIONS vol 80 (2013) PARA 442): Corporation Tax Act 2010 s 981(4).

4   As to the meaning of 'chargeable gain' see CAPITAL GAINS TAXATION vol 6 (2011) PARA 608; INCOME TAXATION vol 58 (2014) PARA 6.

5   Corporation Tax Act 2010 ss 981(1)–(3), 982(1).Payments from a union's general funds, e g for legal assistance on personal injuries claims, are not included: *R v Income Tax Special Comrs, ex p National Union of Railwaymen* [1966] 2 All ER 759, [1967] 1 WLR 263, DC.

6   Corporation Tax Act 2010 s 982(2).

928.   Restriction on enforcement of awards against trade unions.   Where in any proceedings an amount is awarded by way of damages, costs or expenses:

(1)   against a trade union[1];

(2)   against trustees in whom property is vested[2] in trust for a trade union, in their capacity as such, and otherwise than in respect of a breach of trust on their part; or

(3)   against members or officials[3] of a trade union on behalf of themselves and all of the members of the union,

no part of that amount is recoverable by enforcement against any protected property[4]. The following is protected property:

(a)   property belonging to the trustees otherwise than in their capacity as such;

(b)   property belonging to any member of the union otherwise than jointly or in common with the other members;

(c)   property belonging to an official of the union who is neither a member nor a trustee;

(d)   property comprised in a political fund[5] of the union, where that fund:

    (i)   is subject to rules[6] of the union which prevent property which is or has been comprised in the fund from being used for financing strikes or other industrial action; and

    (ii)   was so subject at the time when the act in respect of which the proceedings are brought was done; or

(e)   property comprised in a separate fund maintained in accordance with the rules of the union for the purpose only of providing provident benefits[7].

1   As to the meaning of 'trade union' see PARA 891.
2   As to the vesting of property in trustees see PARA 919.
3   As to the meaning of 'official', in relation to a trade union, see PARA 1018.
4   Trade Union and Labour Relations (Consolidation) Act 1992 s 23(1).
5   As to the political fund see PARA 977 et seq.
6   As to the meaning of 'rules', in relation to a trade union, see PARA 898 note 5.
7   Trade Union and Labour Relations (Consolidation) Act 1992 s 23(2). For these purposes, 'provident benefits' includes: (1) any payment expressly authorised by the rules of the union which is made: (a) to a member during sickness or incapacity from personal injury or while out of work; or (b) to an aged member by way of superannuation, or to a member who has met with an accident or has lost his tools by fire or theft; and (2) a payment in discharge or aid of funeral expenses on the death of a member or the spouse or civil partner of a member or as provision for the children of a deceased member: s 23(3) (amended by the Civil Partnership Act 2004 Sch 27 para 144).

929.   Provision of money for union modernisation.   The Secretary of State[1] may provide money to a trade union[2] to enable or assist it to do any or all of the following:

(1)   improve the carrying out of any of its existing functions[3];

(2)   prepare to carry out any new function[4];

(3)   increase the range of services it offers to persons who are or may become members of it[5];

(4)   prepare for an amalgamation or the transfer of any or all of its engagements[6];

(5)   ballot its members, whether as a result of an imposed requirement[7] or otherwise[8].

If money is provided to a trade union[9], the terms on which it is so provided are deemed to include a prohibition on any of it being added to the political fund of the union (a 'political fund prohibition')[10]. If a political fund prohibition is contravened, the Secretary of State is entitled to recover from the trade union as a debt due to him an amount equal to the amount of money added to the union's political fund in contravention of the prohibition, whether or not that money continues to form part of the political fund[11], and must take such steps as are reasonably practicable to recover that amount[12].

1   As to the Secretary of State see PARA 5 note 21.

2   No such money may be provided to a trade union unless at the time when the money is provided
     the union has a certificate of independence: Trade Union and Labour Relations (Consolidation)
     Act 1992 s 116A(2) (s 116A added by the Employment Relations Act 2004 s 55(1)). As to the
     meaning of 'trade union' see PARA 891. As to the meaning of 'certificate of independence' see
     PARA 1008 note 6. In the application of the Trade Union and Labour Relations (Consolidation)
     Act 1992 s 116A to federated trade unions s 116A(2) is omitted: s 118(8) (added by the
     Employment Relations Act 2004 s 55(2)). As to the meaning of 'federated trade union' see PARA
     891. Money may be provided in such a way as the Secretary of State thinks fit, whether as
     grants or otherwise, and on such terms as he thinks fit, whether as to repayment or otherwise:
     Trade Union and Labour Relations (Consolidation) Act 1992 s 116A(3) (as so added).
3   Trade Union and Labour Relations (Consolidation) Act 1992 s 116A(1)(a) (as added: see
     note 2).
4   Trade Union and Labour Relations (Consolidation) Act 1992 s 116A(1)(b) (as added: see
     note 2).
5   Trade Union and Labour Relations (Consolidation) Act 1992 s 116A(1)(c) (as added: see
     note 2).
6   Trade Union and Labour Relations (Consolidation) Act 1992 s 116A(1)(d) (as added: see
     note 2).
7   Ie a requirement imposed by the Trade Union and Labour Relations (Consolidation) Act 1992.
8   Trade Union and Labour Relations (Consolidation) Act 1992 s 116A(1)(e) (as added: see
     note 2).
9   Ie under the Trade Union and Labour Relations (Consolidation) Act 1992 s 116A.
10   Trade Union and Labour Relations (Consolidation) Act 1992 s 116A(4) (as added: see note 2).
11   Trade Union and Labour Relations (Consolidation) Act 1992 s 116A(5)(a) (as added: see
     note 2). An amount recoverable under s 116A(5) is a liability of the trade union's political fund:
     s 116A(6) (as so added). Section 116A(5) does not prevent money provided to a trade union
     under s 116A from being provided on terms containing further sanctions for a contravention of
     the political fund prohibition: s 116A(7) (as so added).
12   Trade Union and Labour Relations (Consolidation) Act 1992 s 116A(5)(b) (as added: see
     note 2). See also note 11.

(4) TRADE UNION ADMINISTRATION

(i) Register of Members' Names and Addresses

930.   Trade union's duty to maintain register. A trade union[1] must compile
and maintain a register[2] of the names and addresses[3] of its members, and must
secure, so far as is reasonably practicable, that the entries in the register are
accurate and are kept up-to-date[4]. A trade union must allow any member, on
reasonable notice, to ascertain from the register, free of charge and at any
reasonable time, whether there is an entry on it relating to him; and, if requested
to do so by any member, it must supply him as soon as reasonably practicable
with a copy of any entry on the register relating to him, either free of charge or
on payment of a reasonable fee[5]. The remedy for failure to comply with these
requirements is by way of application to the certification officer[6] or to the High
Court[7].

Where a trade union is required to appoint an independent scrutineer[8] to
carry out certain functions[9] in relation to union ballots for certain purposes[10],
the union must supply to the scrutineer a copy of the register of members' names
and addresses[11] as soon as is reasonably practicable after the relevant date[12], and
comply with any request made by the scrutineer to inspect the register[13]. The
scrutineer's appointment must require him to inspect the register or to examine
the copy of the register supplied to him whenever it appears to him appropriate
to do so[14], and, in particular, when requested to do so during the appropriate
period[15] by a member of the union[16] who suspects that the register is not
accurate or up-to-date[17], unless the scrutineer considers that the suspicion is
ill-founded[18]. The scrutineer's report[19] on the election or ballot must state:

(1) whether he has inspected the register or examined the copy of the register supplied to him;

(2) if he has, whether he was acting on a request by a member of the union or at his own instance;

(3) whether he declined to act on any such request; and

(4) whether any such inspection or examination has revealed any matter which he considers should be drawn to the attention of the trade union in order to assist it in securing that the register is accurate and up-to-date[20].

1 As to the meaning of 'trade union' see PARA 891. The Trade Union and Labour Relations (Consolidation) Act 1992 ss 24–26 (see the text and notes 2–20; and PARA 931 et seq) do not apply to a trade union until more than one year has elapsed since its formation, whether by amalgamation or otherwise: s 43(2). For this purpose, the date of formation of a trade union formed otherwise than by amalgamation is to be taken to be the date on which the first members of the executive of the union are first appointed or elected: s 43(2). Further, ss 24–26 do not apply to a federated trade union: (1) if it has no individual members other than representatives of constituent or affiliated organisations; or (2) if its individual members, other than such representatives, are all merchant seamen and a majority of them are ordinarily resident outside the United Kingdom: see s 118(6); and PARA 891 note 9 head (5). Where a trade union consists of or includes branches or sections, any duty falling on a branch or section under s 24 or, as from a day to be appointed, under 24ZA (duty to provide membership audit certificate: see PARA 931), or ss 24ZB, 24ZC (duty to appoint an assurer etc: see PARA 932), by reason of its being a trade union is to be treated as discharged to the extent to which the union of which it is a branch or section discharges the duty instead of it: s 44(1), (4) (s 44(4) prospectively amended by the Transparency of Lobbying, Non-Party Campaigning and Trade Union Administration Act 2014 ss 40(1), (3), 41(1), (4), as from a day to be appointed under s 45(1)(c); at the date at which this volume states the law, no such day had been appointed and those amendments were not yet in force). As to the meaning of 'federated trade union' see PARA 891; and as to the meaning of 'branch or section', in relation to a trade union, see PARA 898 note 5.

2 The register may be kept by means of a computer: Trade Union and Labour Relations (Consolidation) Act 1992 s 24(2).

3 For these purposes, a member's address means either his home address or another address which he has requested the union in writing to treat as his postal address: Trade Union and Labour Relations (Consolidation) Act 1992 s 24(5).

4 Trade Union and Labour Relations (Consolidation) Act 1992 s 24(1).

5 Trade Union and Labour Relations (Consolidation) Act 1992 s 24(3).

6 Ie under the Trade Union and Labour Relations (Consolidation) Act 1992 s 25: see PARA 938. As to the certification officer see PARA 1443.

7 Trade Union and Labour Relations (Consolidation) Act 1992 ss 24(6), 121. As from a day to be appointed, the certification officer also has power under s 24B (see PARA 935) to make a declaration and an enforcement order: see s 24(6) (prospectively amended by the Transparency of Lobbying, Non-Party Campaigning and Trade Union Administration Act 2014 s 43(3), as from a day to be appointed under s 45(1)(c); at the date at which this volume states the law, no such day had been appointed and that amendment was not yet in force).

As to the making of an application to the court see PARA 939. Formerly, the making of an application to the certification officer did not prevent the applicant, or any other person, from making an application to the court in respect of the same matter (see s 24(6) (as originally enacted)), but this is no longer the case (see s 24(6); and PARA 938).

8 As to the appointment of an independent scrutineer see PARA 966.

9 As to the functions of the scrutineer see PARAS 966, 967.

10 Ie in a ballot on: (1) certain union elections, in accordance with the Trade Union and Labour Relations (Consolidation) Act 1992 ss 46–61 (see PARA 960 et seq); (2) a political resolution, in accordance with ss 73–81 (see PARA 977 et seq); and (3) a resolution to approve an instrument of amalgamation or transfer, in accordance with ss 100–100E (see PARA 1003 et seq). The duty to supply a copy of the register and to allow inspection of the register does not apply in an industrial action ballot: see PARA 1370 et seq.

11 See the Trade Union and Labour Relations (Consolidation) Act 1992 s 49(5A)(a) (union elections) (see PARA 966); s 75(5A)(a) (political fund ballots) (see PARA 979); and s 100A(9)(a) (ballots for union amalgamations and transfers of engagements) (see PARA 1004). Where the

register is kept by means of a computer, the duty is either to supply a legible printed copy or, if the scrutineer prefers, to supply a copy of the computer data and allow the scrutineer use of the computer to read it at any time during the period when he is required to retain custody of the copy: see s 49(5B) and PARA 966 note 18; s 75(5B) and PARA 979 note 18; and s 100A(10) and PARA 1004 note 16.

12 For these purposes, 'relevant date' means: (1) where the union has rules determining who is entitled to vote in the election or ballot by reference to membership on a particular date, that date; and (2) otherwise the date, or the last date, on which voting papers are distributed for the purposes of the election or ballot: see the Trade Union and Labour Relations (Consolidation) Act 1992 s 49(8) and PARA 966 note 12; s 75(8) and PARA 979 note 12; and s 100A(13) and PARA 1004 note 11.

13 See the Trade Union and Labour Relations (Consolidation) Act 1992 s 49(5A)(a) and PARA 966; s 75(5A)(a) and PARA 979; and s 100A(9)(a) and PARA 1004.

14 See the Trade Union and Labour Relations (Consolidation) Act 1992 s 49(3)(aa) and PARA 966; s 75(3)(aa) and PARA 979; and s 100A(3)(b) and PARA 1004.

15 Ie the period beginning with the day on which the scrutineer is appointed (or alternatively in the case of union elections, the first day on which a person may become a candidate in the election) and ending with the day before the day on which the scrutineer makes his report to the union: see the Trade Union and Labour Relations (Consolidation) Act 1992 s 49(3B) and PARA 966 note 12; s 75(3B) and PARA 979 note 12; and s 100A(5) and PARA 1004 note 11.

16 Or a candidate in the case of an election: see the Trade Union and Labour Relations (Consolidation) Act 1992 s 49(3A); and PARA 966 note 12.

17 See the Trade Union and Labour Relations (Consolidation) Act 1992 s 49(3A)(a) and PARA 966 note 12; s 75(3A)(a) and PARA 979 note 12; and s 100A(4)(a) and PARA 1004 note 11.

18 See the Trade Union and Labour Relations (Consolidation) Act 1992 s 49(3A)(b) and PARA 966 note 12; s 75(3A)(b) and PARA 979 note 12; and s 100A(4)(b) and PARA 1004 note 11.

19 As to the scrutineer's report see PARA 967.

20 See the Trade Union and Labour Relations (Consolidation) Act 1992 s 52(2A) and PARA 967; s 78(2A) and PARA 981; and s 100E(3) and PARA 1006. The scrutineer's report must not state the name of any member who has requested such an examination or inspection: see ss 52(2A), 78(2A), 100E(3); and PARAS 967, 981, 1006.

931. Trade union's duty to provide membership audit certificate. As from a day to be appointed[1], the following provisions have effect.

A trade union[2] required to maintain a register of the names and addresses of its members[3] must send to the certification officer[4] a membership audit certificate in relation to each reporting period[5]. The union must send the membership audit certificate in relation to a reporting period to the certification officer at the same time as it sends to him its annual return[6] in relation to that period[7].

In the case of a trade union required[8] to appoint an assurer in relation to a reporting period, the 'membership audit certificate' in relation to that period is the certificate which the assurer is required to provide to the union in relation to that period pursuant to that appointment[9]. In any other case, the 'membership audit certificate' in relation to a reporting period is a certificate which:

(1)   must be signed by an officer[10] of the trade union who is authorised to sign on its behalf;

(2)   must state the officer's name; and

(3)   must state whether, to the best of the officer's knowledge and belief, the union has complied with its duties to maintain the register[11] throughout the reporting period[12].

A trade union must, at a person's request, supply the person with a copy of its most recent membership audit certificate either free of charge or on payment of a reasonable charge[13]; and the certification officer must at all reasonable hours keep available for public inspection, either free of charge or on payment of a reasonable charge, copies of all membership audit certificates sent to him under the above provisions[14].

1 Ie as from a day to be appointed under the Transparency of Lobbying, Non-Party Campaigning and Trade Union Administration Act 2014 s 45(1)(c). At the date at which this volume states the law, no such day had been appointed.

2 As to the meaning of 'trade union' see PARA 891. See also PARA 930 note 1.

3 Ie required by the Trade Union and Labour Relations (Consolidation) Act 1992 s 24: see PARA 930.

4 As to the certification officer see PARA 1443.

5 Trade Union and Labour Relations (Consolidation) Act 1992 s 24ZA(1) (s 24ZA prospectively added by the Transparency of Lobbying, Non-Party Campaigning and Trade Union Administration Act 2014 s 40(1), (2), as from a day to be appointed (see note 1); not yet in force). For these purposes, and the purposes of the Trade Union and Labour Relations (Consolidation) Act 1992 ss 24ZB–24ZF (see PARA 932), a 'reporting period' means a period in relation to which the union is required by s 32 (see PARA 943) to send an annual return to the certification officer: s 24ZA(2) (as so added).

Where a trade union consists of or includes branches or sections, any duty falling upon a branch or section by reason of its being a trade union under s 24ZA is to be treated as discharged to the extent to which the union of which it is a branch or section discharges the duty instead of it: s 44(1), (4) (s 44(4) prospectively amended by the Transparency of Lobbying, Non-Party Campaigning and Trade Union Administration Act 2014 s 40(1), (3), as from a day to be so appointed). As to the meaning of 'branch or section', in relation to a trade union, see PARA 898 note 5.

6 Ie under the Trade Union and Labour Relations (Consolidation) Act 1992 s 32: see PARA 943. In the case of a federated trade union which, by virtue of s 118(4) (see PARA 891 note 9 head (2)) is not required to send an annual return to the certification officer under s 32, s 24ZA applies as if s 32 does apply to the union: s 118(4A) (prospectively added by the Transparency of Lobbying, Non-Party Campaigning and Trade Union Administration Act 2014 s 40(1), (4), as from a day to be appointed (see note 1); not yet in force).

7 Trade Union and Labour Relations (Consolidation) Act 1992 s 24ZA(3) (as added: see note 5).

8 Ie required by the Trade Union and Labour Relations (Consolidation) Act 1992 s 24ZB: see PARA 932.

9 Trade Union and Labour Relations (Consolidation) Act 1992 s 24ZA(4) (as added: see note 5).

10 As to the meaning of 'officer' in relation to a trade union see PARA 902 note 7.

11 Ie its duties under the Trade Union and Labour Relations (Consolidation) Act 1992 24(1): see PARA 930.

12 Trade Union and Labour Relations (Consolidation) Act 1992 s 24ZA(5) (as added: see note 5).

13 Trade Union and Labour Relations (Consolidation) Act 1992 s 24ZA(6) (as added: see note 5).

14 Trade Union and Labour Relations (Consolidation) Act 1992 s 24ZA(7) (as added: see note 5).

932. Trade union's duty to appoint an assurer; assurer's duties in relation to membership audit certificate. Partly as from a day to be appointed[1], the following provisions have effect.

A trade union[2] required to maintain a register of the names and addresses of its members[3] must, in relation to each reporting period[4], appoint a qualified independent person[5] to be an assurer in relation to that period[6], unless the number of its members at the end of the preceding reporting period did not exceed 10,000[7]. There is incorporated in the assurer's appointment a duty which the assurer owes to the trade union (1) to provide to the union a membership audit certificate[8] in relation to the reporting period which accords with the statutory requirements[9]; and (2) to carry out such inquiries as the assurer considers necessary to enable the assurer to provide that certificate[10]. The duty of confidentiality as respects the register is also incorporated in an assurer's appointment by a trade union under the above provisions[11]. That duty is a duty which the assurer owes to the union not to disclose any name or address in the register of the names and addresses of the union's members except in permitted circumstances[12], and to take all reasonable steps to secure that there is no disclosure of any such name or address by another person except in permitted circumstances[13].

None of the following may act as an assurer:

(a)   an officer[14] or employee[15] of the trade union or of any of its branches or sections[16];

(b)   a person who is a partner of, or in the employment of, or who employs, such an officer or employee[17].

The rules[18] of every trade union to which the above duty to appoint an assurer applies must contain provision for the appointment and removal of an assurer; but the following provisions have effect notwithstanding anything in the rules[19]. An assurer must not be removed from office except by resolution passed at a general meeting of the members of the union or of delegates of its members[20]. A person duly appointed as an assurer in relation to a reporting period must be re-appointed as assurer in relation to the following reporting period, unless:

(i)   a resolution has been passed at a general meeting of the trade union appointing somebody else instead or providing expressly that the person is not to be re-appointed;

(ii)   the person has given notice to the union in writing of the person's unwillingness to be re-appointed,

(iii) the person is not qualified for the appointment[21];

(iv)   the person has ceased to act as assurer by reason of incapacity[22].

A person need not, however, automatically be re-appointed where:

(A)   the person is retiring;

(B)   notice has been given of an intended resolution to appoint somebody else instead; and

(C)   that resolution cannot be proceeded with at the meeting because of the death or incapacity of the proposed replacement[23].

An assurer appointed by a trade union under the above provisions[24] has a right of access at all reasonable times to the register of the names and addresses of the union's members and to all other documents[25] which the assurer considers may be relevant to whether the union has complied with any of the requirements[26] relating to the maintenance of the register[27]. He is also entitled to require from the union's officers, or the officers of any of its branches or sections, such information and explanations as he considers necessary for the performance of the assurer's functions[28].

If an assurer provides a membership audit certificate in relation to a reporting period to a trade union which states that, in the assurer's opinion:

(*aa*) the union's system for compiling and maintaining the register was not satisfactory for the purposes of complying with the union's duties relating to the maintenance of the register[29] throughout that period; or

(*bb*) the assurer has failed to obtain the information and explanations which the assurer considers necessary for the performance of the assurer's functions,

the assurer must send a copy of the certificate to the certification officer[30] as soon as is reasonably practicable after it is provided to the union[31].

1   Ie partly as from a day to be appointed under the Transparency of Lobbying, Non-Party Campaigning and Trade Union Administration Act 2014 s 45(1)(c).

2   As to the meaning of 'trade union' see PARA 891. See also PARA 930 note 1.

3   Ie required by the Trade Union and Labour Relations (Consolidation) Act 1992 s 24: see PARA 930.

4   As to the meaning of 'reporting period' see PARA 931 note 5.

5   A person is a 'qualified independent person' if (1) the person either satisfies such conditions as may be specified for these purposes by order of the Secretary of State or is specified by name in such an order; and (2) the trade union has no grounds for believing that (a) the person will carry out an assurer's functions otherwise than competently; or (b) the person's independence in relation to the union might reasonably be called into question: Trade Union and Labour

Relations (Consolidation) Act 1992 s 24ZB(3) (ss 24ZB–24ZG added by the Transparency of Lobbying, Non-Party Campaigning and Trade Union Administration Act 2014 s 41(1), (2), partly as from a day to be appointed (see note 1); at the date at which this volume states the law, s 41 was in force for the purpose of exercising the powers to make subordinate legislation under the Trade Union and Labour Relations (Consolidation) Act 1992 s 24ZB(3) (see the Transparency of Lobbying, Non-Party Campaigning and Trade Union Administration Act 2014 s 45(3)(c)), but the Trade Union and Labour Relations (Consolidation) Act 1992 ss 24ZB–24ZG were otherwise not yet in force). Any order under s 24ZB is to be made by statutory instrument and is to be subject to annulment in pursuance of a resolution of either House of Parliament: s 24ZB(6) (as so added).

6   Trade Union and Labour Relations (Consolidation) Act 1992 s 24ZB(1) (as added (see note 5); not yet in force).
    Where a trade union consists of or includes branches or sections, any duty falling upon a branch or section by reason of its being a trade union under s 24ZB, 24ZC is to be treated as discharged to the extent to which the union of which it is a branch or section discharges the duty instead of it: s 44(1), (4) (s 44(4) prospectively amended by the Transparency of Lobbying, Non-Party Campaigning and Trade Union Administration Act 2014 s 40(1), (3), as from a day to be so appointed). As to the meaning of 'branch or section', in relation to a trade union, see PARA 898 note 5.

7   Trade Union and Labour Relations (Consolidation) Act 1992 s 24ZB(5) (as added (see note 5); not yet in force).

8   As to the meaning of 'membership audit certificate' see PARA 931.

9   Ie the requirements of the Trade Union and Labour Relations (Consolidation) Act 1992 s 24ZD. For these purposes, the requirements of a membership audit certificate in relation to a reporting period provided by an assurer are as follows (Trade Union and Labour Relations (Consolidation) Act 1992 s 24ZD(1) (as added (see note 5); not yet in force):
    (1)   the certificate must state the name of, and be signed by, the assurer (s 24ZD(2) (as so added); not yet in force);
    (2)   the certificate must state whether, in the assurer's opinion, the trade union's system for compiling and maintaining the register of the names and addresses of its members was satisfactory for the purposes of complying with the union's duties under s 24(1) (see PARA 930) throughout the reporting period; and (b) whether, in the assurer's opinion, the assurer has obtained the information and explanations which the assurer considers necessary for the performance of the assurer's functions (s 24ZD(3) (as so added); not yet in force);
    (3)   if the certificate states that (a) in the assurer's opinion, the trade union's system for compiling and maintaining the register was not satisfactory for the purposes of complying with the union's duties under s 24(1) throughout the reporting period; or (b) in the assurer's opinion, the assurer has failed to obtain the information and explanations which the assurer considers necessary for the performance of the assurer's functions, the certificate must state the assurer's reasons for making that statement (s 24ZD(4) (as so added); not yet in force);
    (4)   In the case of a failure to obtain information or explanations as described in head (3)(b) above, the certificate must also (a) provide a description of the information or explanations requested or required which have not been obtained; and (b) state whether the assurer required that information or those explanations from the union's officers, or officers of any of its branches or sections, under s 24ZE (see the text and notes 24–28) (s 24ZD(5) (as so added); not yet in force).
    The reference in s 24ZD(2) (see head (1) above) to signature by the assurer is, where that office is held by a body corporate or partnership, to signature in the name of the body corporate or partnership by an individual authorised to sign on its behalf: s 24ZD(6) (as so added); not yet in force).

10 Trade Union and Labour Relations (Consolidation) Act 1992 s 24ZB(2) (as added (see note 5); not yet in force).

11 Trade Union and Labour Relations (Consolidation) Act 1992 s 24ZG(1) (as added (see note 5); not yet in force).

12 Trade Union and Labour Relations (Consolidation) Act 1992 s 24ZG(2)(a) (as added (see note 5); not yet in force). The circumstances in which disclosure of a member's name or address is permitted are (1) where the member consents; (2) where it is required or requested by the certification officer for the purposes of the discharge of any of the officer's functions; (3) where it is required for the purposes of the discharge of any of the functions of an inspector appointed by the officer; (4) where it is required for the purposes of the discharge of any of the functions of

the assurer; or (5) where it is required for the purposes of the investigation of crime or criminal proceedings: s 24G(3) (as so added: not yet in force).

13 Trade Union and Labour Relations (Consolidation) Act 1992 s 24ZG(2)(b) (as added (see note 5); not yet in force).
14 As to the meaning of 'officer' in relation to a trade union see PARA 902 note 7.
15 As to the meaning of 'employee' see PARA 892.
16 As to the meaning of 'branch or section', in relation to a trade union, see PARA 898 note 5.
17 Trade Union and Labour Relations (Consolidation) Act 1992 s 24ZB(4) (as added (see note 5); not yet in force).
18 As to the meaning of 'rules', in relation to a trade union, see PARA 898 note 5.
19 Trade Union and Labour Relations (Consolidation) Act 1992 s 24ZC(1) (as added (see note 5); not yet in force). See also note 6.
20 Trade Union and Labour Relations (Consolidation) Act 1992 s 24ZC(2) (as added (see note 5); not yet in force).
21 Ie he is not qualified in accordance with the Trade Union and Labour Relations (Consolidation) Act 1992 s 24ZB: see the text and notes 2–10, 14–17.
22 Trade Union and Labour Relations (Consolidation) Act 1992 s 24ZC(3) (as added (see note 5); not yet in force).
23 Trade Union and Labour Relations (Consolidation) Act 1992 s 24ZC(4) (as added (see note 5); not yet in force).
24 Ie under the Trade Union and Labour Relations (Consolidation) Act 1992 s 24ZB: see the text and notes 1–7.
25 For this purpose, references to documents include information recorded in any form: Trade Union and Labour Relations (Consolidation) Act 1992 s 24ZE(2) (as added (see note 5); not yet in force).
26 Ie the requirements of the Trade Union and Labour Relations (Consolidation) Act 1992 s 24(1): see PARA 930.
27 Trade Union and Labour Relations (Consolidation) Act 1992 s 24ZE(1)(a) (as added (see note 5); not yet in force).
28 Trade Union and Labour Relations (Consolidation) Act 1992 s 24ZE(1)(b) (as added (see note 5); not yet in force).
29 Ie its duties under the Trade Union and Labour Relations (Consolidation) Act 1992 s 24(1): see PARA 930.
30 As to the certification officer see PARA 1443.
31 Trade Union and Labour Relations (Consolidation) Act 1992 s 24ZF (as added (see note 5); not yet in force).

933.   Certification officer's power to require production of register of members and other documents etc.   As from a day to be appointed[1], the following provisions have effect.

If the certification officer[2] thinks there is good reason to do so, he may:

(1)   may give directions to a trade union[3], or a branch or section[4] of a trade union, requiring it to produce such relevant documents[5] as are specified in the directions[6];

(2)   authorise a member of the officer's staff or any other person ('an authorised person'), on producing (if so required) evidence of that authority, to require a trade union, or a branch or section of a trade union, to produce immediately to the authorised person such relevant documents as that person specifies[7].

Where the certification officer, or an authorised person, has power to require the production of documents by virtue of heads (1) and (2) above, the officer or authorised person has the like power to require production of those documents from any person who appears to the officer or authorised person to be in possession of them[8].

The power under these provisions to require the production of documents includes the power:

(a)   if the documents are produced:

(i)   to take copies of them or extracts from them;

  (ii)   to require the person by whom they are produced to provide an explanation of any of them;

  (iii) to require any person who is or has been an official[9] or agent[10] of the trade union to provide an explanation of any of them[11];

(b) if the documents are not produced, to require the person who was required to produce them to state, to the best of the person's knowledge and belief, where they are[12].

Nothing in the above provisions, however, requires or authorises anyone to require the disclosure by a person of information which the person would in an action in the High Court be entitled to refuse to disclose on grounds of legal professional privilege, or the production by a person of a document which the person would in such an action be entitled to refuse to produce on such grounds[13]; but a lawyer may be required to disclose the name and address of the lawyer's client[14].

1   Ie as from a day to be appointed under the Transparency of Lobbying, Non-Party Campaigning and Trade Union Administration Act 2014 s 45(1)(c). At the date at which this volume states the law, no such day had been appointed.
2   As to the certification officer see PARA 1443.
3   As to the meaning of 'trade union' see PARA 891. See also PARA 930 note 1.
4   As to the meaning of 'branch or section', in relation to a trade union, see PARA 898 note 5.
5   'Relevant documents', in relation to a trade union or a branch or section of a trade union, means (1) the register of the names and addresses of the trade union's members; and (2) documents of any other description which the certification officer or authorised person considers may be relevant to whether the union has failed to comply with any of the requirements of the Trade Union and Labour Relations (Consolidation) Act 1992 s 24(1) (duties regarding the register of members: see PARA 930): s 24ZH(2) (ss 24ZH, 24ZK added by the Transparency of Lobbying, Non-Party Campaigning and Trade Union Administration Act 2014 s 42(1), (2), as from a day to be appointed (see note 1); not yet in force). For these purposes, and the purposes of the Trade Union and Labour Relations (Consolidation) Act 1992 s 24ZI (see PARA 934), references to documents include information recorded in any form, and in relation to information recorded otherwise than in legible form, references to its production are to the production of a copy of the information in legible form: ss 24ZH(7), 24ZK(5) (as so added; not yet in force). As to the meaning of 'authorised person' see head (2) in the text.
6   Trade Union and Labour Relations (Consolidation) Act 1992 s 24ZH(1)(a) (as added (see note 5); not yet in force). Directions under s 24ZH(1)(a) must specify the time and place at which the documents are to be produced: s 24ZH(3) (as so added; not yet in force).
7   Trade Union and Labour Relations (Consolidation) Act 1992 s 24ZH(1)(b) (as added (see note 5); not yet in force).
8   Trade Union and Labour Relations (Consolidation) Act 1992 s 24ZH(4) (as added (see note 5); not yet in force).
9   As to the meaning of 'official', in relation to a trade union, see PARA 1018.
10 For these purposes, 'agent' includes an assurer appointed by the trade union under the Trade Union and Labour Relations (Consolidation) Act 1992 s 24ZB (see PARA 932): Trade Union and Labour Relations (Consolidation) Act 1992 s 24ZH(6) (as added (see note 5); not yet in force).
11 Trade Union and Labour Relations (Consolidation) Act 1992 s 24ZH(5)(a) (as added (see note 5); not yet in force). A person is not excused from providing an explanation or making a statement in compliance with a requirement imposed under s 24ZH(5) on the ground that to do so would tend to expose the person to proceedings for an offence; but an explanation so provided or a statement so made may only be used in evidence against the person by whom it is provided or made on a prosecution for an offence where, in giving evidence, the person makes a statement inconsistent with it: s 24K(3), (4) (as so added; not yet in force).
12 Trade Union and Labour Relations (Consolidation) Act 1992 s 24ZH(5)(b) (as added (see note 5); not yet in force). See also note 11.
13 Trade Union and Labour Relations (Consolidation) Act 1992 s 24ZK(1) (as added (see note 5); not yet in force); s 121. As to legal professional privilege see LEGAL PROFESSIONS vol 65 (2008) PARA 511.
14 Trade Union and Labour Relations (Consolidation) Act 1992 s 24ZK(2) (as added (see note 5); not yet in force).

934. Investigations and reports by inspectors relating to union's duties regarding register of members. As from a day to be appointed[1], the following provisions have effect.

The certification officer[2] may appoint one or more members of his staff or other persons as an inspector or inspectors to investigate whether a trade union[3] has failed to comply with any of the statutory requirements as to its duties regarding the register of members[4], and to report to the officer in such manner as he may direct[5]. The certification officer may, however, only make such an appointment if it appears to him that there are circumstances suggesting that the union has failed to comply with a relevant statutory requirement[6]. Where a person who is not a member of the certification officer's staff is appointed as an inspector under these provisions, there is incorporated in the appointment the duty of confidentiality as respects the register[7] of the names and addresses of the trade union's members[8].

Where any person appears to the inspector or inspectors to be in possession of information relating to a matter considered by the inspector or inspectors to be relevant to the investigation, the inspector or inspectors may require the person:

(1) to produce to the inspector or inspectors any relevant documents[9] relating to that matter;

(2) to attend before the inspector or inspectors, and

(3) otherwise to give the inspector or inspectors all assistance in connection with the investigation which the person is reasonably able to give[10].

Nothing in the above provisions, however, requires or authorises anyone to require the disclosure by a person of information which the person would in an action in the High Court be entitled to refuse to disclose on grounds of legal professional privilege, or the production by a person of a document which the person would in such an action be entitled to refuse to produce on such grounds[11]; but a lawyer may be required to disclose the name and address of the lawyer's client[12].

An inspector or inspectors appointed under the above provisions:

(a) may make interim reports to the certification officer;

(b) must make such reports if so directed by the officer; and

(c) on the conclusion of the investigation, must make a final report to the officer[13].

A report under heads (a) to (c) above must be in writing[14].

An inspector or inspectors may at any time inform the certification officer of any matters coming to their knowledge as a result of the investigation, and must do so if the officer so directs[15].

The certification officer may direct an inspector or inspectors to take no further steps in the investigation, or to take only such further steps as are specified in the direction[16]; and where such a direction is made, the inspector or inspectors are not required under head (c) above to make a final report to the certification officer unless the officer so directs[17].

1 Ie as from a day to be appointed under the Transparency of Lobbying, Non-Party Campaigning and Trade Union Administration Act 2014 s 45(1)(c). At the date at which this volume states the law, no such day had been appointed.
2 As to the certification officer see PARA 1443.
3 As to the meaning of 'trade union' see PARA 891. See also PARA 930 note 1.
4 Ie any of the requirements of the Trade Union and Labour Relations (Consolidation) Act 1992 s 24(1): see PARA 930.
5 Trade Union and Labour Relations (Consolidation) Act 1992 s 24ZI(1) (ss 24ZI–24ZK added by the Transparency of Lobbying, Non-Party Campaigning and Trade Union Administration Act 2014 s 42(1), (2), as from a day to be appointed (see note 1); not yet in force).

6 See the Trade Union and Labour Relations (Consolidation) Act 1992 s 24ZI(2) (as added (see note 5); not yet in force). The statutory requirements referred to in the text are the requirements of s 24(1), s 24ZA or s 24ZB (duties etc relating to the register of members: see PARAS 930–932): see s 24ZI(2) (as so added).

7 The duty of confidentiality as respects that register is a duty which the inspector owes to the certification officer (1) not to disclose any name or address in the register of the names and addresses of the union's members except in permitted circumstances; and (2) to take all reasonable steps to secure that there is no disclosure of any such name or address by another person except in permitted circumstances: Trade Union and Labour Relations (Consolidation) Act 1992 s 24ZI(6) (as added (see note 5); not yet in force). The circumstances in which disclosure of a member's name or address is permitted are (a) where the member consents; (b) where it is required or requested by the certification officer for the purposes of the discharge of any of the officer's functions; (c) where it is required for the purposes of the discharge of any of the functions of the inspector or any other inspector appointed by the officer; (d) where it is required for the purposes of the discharge of any of the functions of an assurer appointed under s 24ZB (see PARA 932); or (e) where it is required for the purposes of the investigation of crime or criminal proceedings: s 24ZI(7) (as so added; not yet in force).

8 Trade Union and Labour Relations (Consolidation) Act 1992 s 24ZI(5) (as added (see note 5); not yet in force).

9 'Relevant documents' means (1) the register of the names and addresses of the trade union's members; and (2) documents of any other description which the inspector or inspectors consider may be relevant to whether the union has failed to comply with any of the requirements of the Trade Union and Labour Relations (Consolidation) Act 1992 s 24(1): s 24ZI(4) (as added (see note 5); not yet in force). As to the meaning of references to 'documents' see PARA 933 note 5.

10 Trade Union and Labour Relations (Consolidation) Act 1992 s 24ZI(3) (as added (see note 5); not yet in force). A person is not excused from providing an explanation or making a statement in compliance with a requirement imposed under s 24ZI(3) on the ground that to do so would tend to expose the person to proceedings for an offence; but an explanation so provided or a statement so made may only be used in evidence against the person by whom it is provided or made on a prosecution for an offence where, in giving evidence, the person makes a statement inconsistent with it: s 24K(3), (4) (as so added; not yet in force).

11 Trade Union and Labour Relations (Consolidation) Act 1992 s 24ZK(1) (as added (see note 5); not yet in force); s 121. As to legal professional privilege see LEGAL PROFESSIONS vol 65 (2008) PARA 511.

12 Trade Union and Labour Relations (Consolidation) Act 1992 s 24ZK(2) (as added (see note 5); not yet in force).

13 Trade Union and Labour Relations (Consolidation) Act 1992 s 24ZJ(1) (as added (see note 5); not yet in force).

14 Trade Union and Labour Relations (Consolidation) Act 1992 s 24ZJ(2) (as added (see note 5); not yet in force).

15 Trade Union and Labour Relations (Consolidation) Act 1992 s 24ZJ(3) (as added (see note 5); not yet in force).

16 Trade Union and Labour Relations (Consolidation) Act 1992 s 24ZJ(4) (as added (see note 5); not yet in force).

17 Trade Union and Labour Relations (Consolidation) Act 1992 s 24ZJ(5) (as added (see note 5); not yet in force).

935. Enforcement by the certification officer of union's duties etc relating to the register of members. As from a day to be appointed[1], the following provisions have effect.

Where the certification officer[2] is satisfied that a trade union[3] has failed to comply with any of the requirements of the statutory provisions imposing duties etc relating to the register of members[4], the officer may make a declaration to that effect[5]. Before making such a declaration, the certification officer:

(1) may make such inquiries as he thinks fit[6];

(2) must give the union an opportunity to make written representations; and

(3) may give the union an opportunity to make oral representations[7].

Where, having given the union an opportunity to make written representations under head (2) above, the certification officer determines not to make a declaration as described above he must give the union notice in writing of that determination[8].

If the certification officer makes a declaration it must specify the provisions with which the union has failed to comply[9]. Where the certification officer makes a declaration and is satisfied:

(a)   that steps have been taken by the union with a view to remedying the declared failure or securing that a failure of the same or any similar kind does not occur in future; or

(b)   that the union has agreed to take such steps,

the officer must specify those steps in the declaration[10].

Where a declaration is made:

(i)   the certification officer must give reasons in writing for making the declaration[11];

(ii)   he must also make an enforcement order unless he considers that to do so would be inappropriate[12].

For these purposes, an 'enforcement order' is an order imposing on the union one or both of the following requirements:

(A)   to take such steps to remedy the declared failure, within such period, as may be specified in the order;

(B)   to abstain from such acts as may be so specified with a view to securing that a failure of the same or a similar kind does not occur in future[13].

A declaration made by the certification officer under these provisions may be relied on as if it were a declaration made by the High Court[14]; and an enforcement order so made by him may be enforced in the same way as an order of the court[15]. Where an enforcement order has been made, a person who is a member of the union and was a member at the time it was made is entitled to enforce obedience to the order as if the order had been made on an application by that person[16].

1   Ie as from a day to be appointed under the Transparency of Lobbying, Non-Party Campaigning and Trade Union Administration Act 2014 s 45(1)(c). At the date at which this volume states the law, no such day had been appointed.

2   As to the certification officer see PARA 1443.

3   As to the meaning of 'trade union' see PARA 891. See also PARA 930 note 1.

4   Ie the provisions of the Trade Union and Labour Relations (Consolidation) Act 1992 s 24, s 24ZA, s 24ZB or s 24ZC: see PARAS 930–932.

5   Trade Union and Labour Relations (Consolidation) Act 1992 s 24B(1) (s 24B added by the Transparency of Lobbying, Non-Party Campaigning and Trade Union Administration Act 2014 s 43(1), (2), as from a day to be appointed (see note 1); not yet in force). An appeal lies to the Employment Appeal Tribunal on any question of law arising in proceedings before or arising from any decision of the certification officer under the Trade Union and Labour Relations (Consolidation) Act 1992 s 24B: s 45D (added by the Employment Relations Act 1999 Sch 6 paras 1, 8; prospectively amended by the Transparency of Lobbying, Non-Party Campaigning and Trade Union Administration Act 2014 s 43(1), (6) (not yet in force)). As to the Employment Appeal Tribunal see PARA 1422 et seq.

6   Where the certification officer requests a person to provide information to him in connection with inquiries under the Trade Union and Labour Relations (Consolidation) Act 1992 s 24B, the officer must specify the date by which that information is to be provided: s 24B(9) (as added (see note 5); not yet in force). Where the information is not provided by the specified date, the certification officer must proceed with determining whether to make a declaration under s 24B(1) (see the text and notes 1–5) unless he considers that it would be inappropriate to do so: s 24B(10) (as so added; not yet in force).

7   Trade Union and Labour Relations (Consolidation) Act 1992 s 24B(2) (as added (see note 5); not yet in force).

8	Trade Union and Labour Relations (Consolidation) Act 1992 s 24B(8) (as added (see note 5); not yet in force).
9	Trade Union and Labour Relations (Consolidation) Act 1992 s 24B(3) (as added (see note 5); not yet in force).
10	Trade Union and Labour Relations (Consolidation) Act 1992 s 24B(4) (as added (see note 5); not yet in force).
11	Trade Union and Labour Relations (Consolidation) Act 1992 s 24B(5) (as added (see note 5); not yet in force).
12	Trade Union and Labour Relations (Consolidation) Act 1992 s 24B(6) (as added (see note 5); not yet in force).
13	Trade Union and Labour Relations (Consolidation) Act 1992 s 24B(7) (as added (see note 5); not yet in force).
14	Trade Union and Labour Relations (Consolidation) Act 1992 s 24B(11) (as added (see note 5); not yet in force); s 121.
15	Trade Union and Labour Relations (Consolidation) Act 1992 s 24B(12) (as added (see note 5); not yet in force).
16	Trade Union and Labour Relations (Consolidation) Act 1992 s 24B(13) (as added (see note 5); not yet in force).

**936.	Enforcement by the certification officer of provisions relating to the production of the register and other documents and provisions relating to investigations by inspectors.**	As from a day to be appointed[1], the following provisions have effect.

Where the certification officer[2] is satisfied that a trade union[3] or any other person has failed to comply with any relevant statutory requirement[4], the officer may make an order requiring the trade union or person to comply with the requirement[5]. Before making such an order, the certification officer must give the trade union or person an opportunity to be heard[6].

In the case of a failure to comply with a requirement to produce a document[7], the certification officer may make an order only if he is satisfied that the document is in the possession of the union or person, and it is reasonably practicable for the union or person to comply with the requirement[8]. In the case of a failure to comply with any other relevant requirement[9], the certification officer may make an order only if he is satisfied that it is reasonably practicable for the union or person to comply with the requirement[10].

The order must specify the requirement with which the trade union or person has failed to comply, and the date by which the trade union or person must comply[11].

An order made by the certification officer under the above provisions may be enforced in the same way as an order of the High Court[12].

1	Ie as from a day to be appointed under the Transparency of Lobbying, Non-Party Campaigning and Trade Union Administration Act 2014 s 45(1)(c). At the date at which this volume states the law, no such day had been appointed.
2	As to the certification officer see PARA 1443.
3	As to the meaning of 'trade union' see PARA 891. See also PARA 930 note 1.
4	Ie any requirement imposed under (1) the Trade Union and Labour Relations (Consolidation) Act 1992 s 24ZH (power of certification officer to require production of documents etc: see PARA 933); or (2) s 24ZI (investigations by inspectors: see PARA 934).
5	Trade Union and Labour Relations (Consolidation) Act 1992 s 24C(1) (s 24C added by the Transparency of Lobbying, Non-Party Campaigning and Trade Union Administration Act 2014 s 43(1), (2), as from a day to be appointed (see note 1); not yet in force). An appeal lies to the Employment Appeal Tribunal on any question of law arising in proceedings before or arising from any decision of the certification officer under the Trade Union and Labour Relations (Consolidation) Act 1992 s 24C: s 45D (added by the Employment Relations Act 1999 Sch 6 paras 1, 8; prospectively amended by the Transparency of Lobbying, Non-Party Campaigning and Trade Union Administration Act 2014 s 43(1), (6) (not yet in force)). As to the Employment Appeal Tribunal see PARA 1422 et seq.

6 Trade Union and Labour Relations (Consolidation) Act 1992 s 24C(2) (as added (see note 5); not yet in force).

7 Ie a requirement imposed under the Trade Union and Labour Relations (Consolidation) Act 1992 s 24ZH or s 24ZI to produce a document: see PARAS 933, 934.

8 Trade Union and Labour Relations (Consolidation) Act 1992 s 24C(3) (as added (see note 5); not yet in force).

9 Ie any other requirement imposed under the Trade Union and Labour Relations (Consolidation) Act 1992 s 24ZH or s 24ZI: see PARAS 933, 934.

10 Trade Union and Labour Relations (Consolidation) Act 1992 s 24C(4) (as added (see note 5); not yet in force).

11 Trade Union and Labour Relations (Consolidation) Act 1992 s 24C(5) (as added (see note 5); not yet in force).

12 Trade Union and Labour Relations (Consolidation) Act 1992 s 24C(6) (as added (see note 5); not yet in force); s 121.

937. Securing confidentiality of register during ballots. A trade union[1] must impose a duty of confidentiality in relation to the register[2] of members' names and addresses on the scrutineer[3] appointed by the union for the purposes of certain ballots[4] and on any person appointed by the union as the independent person[5] for the purposes of any such ballot[6]. The duty of confidentiality as respects the register[7] must be incorporated in the appointment of the scrutineer[8] and of any independent person[9], and the duty thereby imposed on the scrutineer or independent person is a duty owed by him to the trade union[10].

The remedy for failure by a trade union to comply with this requirement is by way of application to the certification officer[11] or to the High Court[12].

1 As to the meaning of 'trade union' see PARA 891. As to the exemption from the Trade Union and Labour Relations (Consolidation) Act 1992 s 24A of newly formed trade unions and certain federated trade unions see PARA 930 note 1.

2 As to the register of members' names and addresses see PARA 930.

3 As to the appointment of an independent scrutineer see PARA 966.

4 Ie in a ballot on: (1) an election under the Trade Union and Labour Relations (Consolidation) Act 1992 Pt I Ch IV (ss 46–61) (see PARA 960 et seq) for a position to which Pt I Ch IV applies; (2) a political resolution under Pt I Ch VI (ss 71–96) (see PARA 977 et seq); and (3) a resolution to approve an instrument of amalgamation or transfer under Pt I Ch VII (ss 97–108) (see PARA 1003 et seq).

5 Ie a person appointed by the union to undertake the storage and distribution of the voting papers for the purposes of the ballot, and the counting of the votes cast in the ballot: see the Trade Union and Labour Relations (Consolidation) Act 1992 s 51A(1) and PARA 962; s 77A(1) and PARA 980; and s 100D(1) and PARA 1005.

6 Trade Union and Labour Relations (Consolidation) Act 1992 s 24A(1), (2) (s 24A added by the Trade Union Reform and Employment Rights Act 1993 s 6).

7 For these purposes, the duty of confidentiality, in the context of a scrutineer or independent person, in relation to the register of members' names and addresses is, when imposed on a scrutineer or on an independent person, a duty not to disclose any name or address in the register except in permitted circumstances, and to take all reasonable steps to secure that there is no disclosure of any such name or address by any other person except in permitted circumstances: Trade Union and Labour Relations (Consolidation) Act 1992 s 24A(3) (as added (see note 6); prospectively amended by the Transparency of Lobbying, Non-Party Campaigning and Trade Union Administration Act 2014 s 41(1), (3), as from a day to be appointed under s 45(1)(c); at the date at which this volume states the law, that amendment was not yet in force and the words 'in the context of a scrutineer or independent person' were to be omitted). Any reference in the Trade Union and Labour Relations (Consolidation) Act 1992 to 'the duty of confidentiality' is a reference to the duty so prescribed: s 24A(3) (as so added). The circumstances in which disclosure of a member's name and address is permitted are: (1) where the member consents; (2) where it is required or requested by the certification officer for the purposes of the discharge of any of his functions or it is required for the purposes of the discharge of any of the functions of an inspector appointed by him; (3) where it is required for the purposes of the discharge of any of the functions of the scrutineer or independent person, as the case may be, under the terms of his appointment; or (4) where it is required for the purposes of the investigation of crime or of criminal proceedings: s 24A(4) (as so added; prospectively

amended by the Transparency of Lobbying, Non-Party Campaigning and Trade Union Administration Act 2014 s 42(1), (3), as from a day to be appointed under s 45(1)(c); at the date at which this volume states the law, that amendment was not yet in force and the words 'required or' in head (2) above were to be omitted). As to the certification officer see PARA 1443. As to the appointment of an inspector see PARA 950.

8 See the Trade Union and Labour Relations (Consolidation) Act 1992 s 49(3C) and PARA 966 note 10; s 75(3C) and PARA 979 note 10; and s 100A(6) and PARA 1004 note 9.

9 See the Trade Union and Labour Relations (Consolidation) Act 1992 s 51A(4) and PARA 962 note 15; s 77A(4) and PARA 980 note 13; and s 100D(4) and PARA 1005 note 13.

10 Trade Union and Labour Relations (Consolidation) Act 1992 s 24A(5) (as added: see note 6).

11 Ie under the Trade Union and Labour Relations (Consolidation) Act 1992 s 25: see PARA 938.

12 Trade Union and Labour Relations (Consolidation) Act 1992 s 24A(6) (as added (see note 6); amended by the Employment Relations Act 1999 Sch 6 paras 1, 3, Sch 9 Table 7); Trade Union and Labour Relations (Consolidation) Act 1992 s 121. As to the making of an application to the court see PARA 939.

938. Remedy for failure to comply with the statutory requirements relating to the register; application to certification officer. A member of a trade union[1] who claims that the union has failed to comply with any of the statutory requirements[2] relating to the register[3] of members' names and addresses may apply to the certification officer[4] for a declaration to that effect[5].

On an application being made to him, the certification officer must make such inquiries as he thinks fit[6], and give the applicant and the trade union an opportunity to be heard[7]. The certification officer may make or refuse the declaration asked for; and, whether he makes or refuses a declaration, he must give reasons for his decision in writing and the reasons may be accompanied by written observations on any matter arising from, or connected with, the proceedings[8]. If he makes a declaration, he must specify in it the provisions with which the trade union has failed to comply[9]. Where he makes a declaration and is satisfied that steps have been taken by the union with a view to remedying the declared failure or securing that a failure of the same or any similar kind does not occur in future, or that the union has agreed to take such steps, he must specify those steps in the declaration[10].

Where the certification officer makes a declaration, he must also, unless he considers that to do so would be inappropriate, make an order (an 'enforcement order') imposing on the union one or both of the following requirements:

(1) to take such steps to remedy the declared failure, within such period, as may be specified in the order;

(2) to abstain from such acts as may be so specified with a view to securing that a failure of the same or a similar kind does not occur in future[11].

Where an enforcement order has been made, any person who is a member of the union and was a member at the time it was made is entitled to enforce obedience to the order as if he had made the application on which the order was made[12]. An enforcement order so made by the certification officer may be enforced in the same way as an order of the court[13].

If a person applies to the court[14] in relation to an alleged failure:

(a) that person may not apply to the certification officer[15] in relation to that failure;

(b) on an application to the certification officer by a different person in relation to that failure, the certification officer must have due regard to any declaration, order, observations or reasons made or given by the court regarding that failure and brought to the certification officer's notice[16].

1   As to the meaning of 'trade union' see PARA 891. As to the exemption from the Trade Union and
     Labour Relations (Consolidation) Act 1992 s 25 (see the text and notes 2–16) of newly formed
     trade unions and certain federated trade unions see PARA 930 note 1.
2   Ie under the Trade Union and Labour Relations (Consolidation) Act 1992 s 24 (see PARA 930) or
     s 24A (see PARA 937).
3   As to the register of members' names and addresses see PARA 930.
4   As to the certification officer see PARA 1443.
5   Trade Union and Labour Relations (Consolidation) Act 1992 s 25(1) (amended by the Trade
     Union Reform and Employment Rights Act 1993 Sch 8 para 40(a)). The certification officer
     must not entertain an application for a declaration as respects an alleged failure to comply with
     the requirements of the Trade Union and Labour Relations (Consolidation) Act 1992 s 24A (see
     PARA 937) in relation to a ballot to which s 24A applies unless the application is made before the
     end of the period of one year beginning with the last day on which votes could be cast in the
     ballot: s 25(8) (added by the Trade Union Reform and Employment Rights Act 1993 Sch 8
     para 40(b)).
        In exercising his functions under the Trade Union and Labour Relations (Consolidation)
     Act 1992 s 25, the certification officer must ensure that, so far as is reasonably practicable, an
     application to him is determined within six months of being made: s 25(6). As from a day to be
     appointed, for these purposes the circumstances in which it is not reasonably practicable to
     determine an application within that time frame may include, in particular, where delay is
     caused by the exercise of the powers under s 24ZH or s 24ZI (powers to require production of
     documents etc and to appoint inspectors: see PARAS 933, 934): s 25(6A) (prospectively added by
     the Transparency of Lobbying, Non-Party Campaigning and Trade Union Administration
     Act 2014 s 43(1), (4), as from a day to be appointed under s 45(1)(c); not yet in force).
        An appeal lies to the Employment Appeal Tribunal on any question of law arising in
     proceedings before or arising from any decision of the certification officer under the Trade
     Union and Labour Relations (Consolidation) Act 1992 s 25: s 45D (added by the Employment
     Relations Act 1999 Sch 6 paras 1, 8). As to the Employment Appeal Tribunal see PARA 1422 et
     seq.
6   Where the certification officer requests a person to furnish information to him in connection
     with his inquiries, he must specify the date by which that information is to be furnished, and he
     must proceed with his determination of the application notwithstanding that the information
     has not been furnished to him by the specified date, unless he considers that it would be
     inappropriate to do so: Trade Union and Labour Relations (Consolidation) Act 1992 s 25(7).
7   Trade Union and Labour Relations (Consolidation) Act 1992 s 25(2) (amended by the
     Employment Relations Act 1999 Sch 6 paras 1, 4(1), (2), Sch 9). A declaration made by the
     certification officer under the Trade Union and Labour Relations (Consolidation) Act 1992 s 25
     may be relied on as if it were a declaration made by the court: s 25(9) (s 25(9)–(11) added by the
     Employment Relations Act 1999 Sch 6 para 4(1), (4)).
8   Trade Union and Labour Relations (Consolidation) Act 1992 s 25(5).
9   Trade Union and Labour Relations (Consolidation) Act 1992 s 25(3).
10   Trade Union and Labour Relations (Consolidation) Act 1992 s 25(4).
11   Trade Union and Labour Relations (Consolidation) Act 1992 s 25(5A) (s 25(5A), (5B) added by
     the Employment Relations Act 1999 Sch 6 para 4(1), (3)).
12   Trade Union and Labour Relations (Consolidation) Act 1992 s 25(5B) (as added: see note 11).
13   Trade Union and Labour Relations (Consolidation) Act 1992 s 25(10) (as added: see note 7).
14   Ie under the Trade Union and Labour Relations (Consolidation) Act 1992 s 26: see PARA 939.
15   Ie under the Trade Union and Labour Relations (Consolidation) Act 1992 s 25.
16   Trade Union and Labour Relations (Consolidation) Act 1992 s 25(11) (as added: see note 7).

939.   Remedy for failure to comply with the statutory requirements; application to the court.   A member of a trade union[1] who claims that the union has failed to comply with any of the statutory requirements[2] relating to the register[3] of members' names and addresses may apply to the High Court for a declaration to that effect[4]. Without prejudice to any other power of the court, the court may on such an application grant such interim relief as it considers appropriate[5].

If the court makes a declaration, it must specify in it the provisions with which the union has failed to comply[6]. If the court makes a declaration, it must also, unless it considers that to do so would be inappropriate, make an order (an 'enforcement order') imposing on the union one or both of the following requirements:

(1)   to take such steps to remedy the declared failure, within such period, as may be specified in the order;

(2)   to abstain from such acts as may be so specified with a view to securing that a failure of the same or a similar kind does not occur in future[7].

Where an enforcement order has been made, any person who is a member of the union and was a member at the time it was made is entitled to enforce obedience to the order as if he had made the application on which the order was made[8].

If a person applies to the certification officer[9] in relation to an alleged failure:

(a)   that person may not apply to the court[10] in relation to that failure;

(b)   on an application to the court by a different person in relation to that failure, the court must have due regard to any declaration, order, observations or reasons made or given by the certification officer regarding that failure and brought to the court's notice[11].

1   As to the meaning of 'trade union' see PARA 891. As to the exemption from the Trade Union and Labour Relations (Consolidation) Act 1992 s 26 (see the text and notes 2–11) of newly formed trade unions and certain federated trade unions see PARA 930 note 1.

2   Ie under the Trade Union and Labour Relations (Consolidation) Act 1992 s 24 (see PARA 930) or s 24A (see PARA 937).

3   As to the register of members' names and addresses see PARA 930.

4   Trade Union and Labour Relations (Consolidation) Act 1992 s 26(1) (amended by the Trade Union Reform and Employment Rights Act 1993 Sch 8 para 41(a)). The court must not entertain an application for a declaration as respects an alleged failure to comply with the requirements of the Trade Union and Labour Relations (Consolidation) Act 1992 s 24A in relation to a ballot to which s 24A applies unless the application is made before the end of the period of one year beginning with the last day on which votes could be cast in the ballot: s 26(7) (added by the Trade Union Reform and Employment Rights Act 1993 Sch 8 para 41(b)).

5   See the Trade Union and Labour Relations (Consolidation) Act 1992 s 26(6).

6   Trade Union and Labour Relations (Consolidation) Act 1992 s 26(3). As from a day to be appointed, where a person applies under s 26 in relation to an alleged failure and the certification officer has made a declaration regarding that failure under s 24B (see PARA 935), the court must have due regard to the declaration and any order, observations or reasons made or given by the officer under s 24B regarding that failure and brought to the court's notice: s 26(9) (prospectively added by the Transparency of Lobbying, Non-Party Campaigning and Trade Union Administration Act 2014 s 43(1), (5), as from a day to be appointed under s 45(1)(c); not yet in force).

7   Trade Union and Labour Relations (Consolidation) Act 1992 s 26(4).

8   Trade Union and Labour Relations (Consolidation) Act 1992 s 26(5).

9   Ie under the Trade Union and Labour Relations (Consolidation) Act 1992 s 25: see PARA 938.

10 Ie under the Trade Union and Labour Relations (Consolidation) Act 1992 s 26.

11 Trade Union and Labour Relations (Consolidation) Act 1992 s 26(8) (added by the Employment Relations Act 1999 s 29, Sch 6 paras 1, 5(1), (3)).

(ii) Trade Union's Accounting Records

940.   Trade union's duty to keep accounting records.   A trade union[1] must:

(1)   cause to be kept proper accounting records with respect to its transactions and its assets and liabilities; and

(2)   establish and maintain a satisfactory system of control of its accounting records, its cash holdings and all its receipts and remittances[2];

but proper accounting records are not to be taken to be kept with respect to the matters mentioned in head (1) above unless there are kept such records as are necessary to give a true and fair view of the state of its affairs and to explain its transactions[3].

A trade union must keep available for inspection such of the records of the union, or of any branch or section[4] of the union, as are or purport to be records required to be kept by the union in accordance with the above requirements[5]. Those records must be kept available for inspection from their creation until the end of the period of six years beginning with 1 January following the end of the period to which they relate[6].

1   As to the meaning of 'trade union' see PARA 891. The duty to keep accounting records does not apply to a federated trade union which consists wholly or mainly of representatives of constituent or affiliated organisations: see the Trade Union and Labour Relations (Consolidation) Act 1992 s 118(4)(b); and PARA 891 note 9 head (2). As to the meaning of 'federated trade union' see PARA 891. Where a trade union consists of or includes branches or sections, any duty falling on the union in relation to a branch or section under the provisions of s 28 (see the text and notes 2–6) is to be treated as discharged to the extent to which the duty is discharged by the branch or section (s 44(1), (2)); and any such duty falling on a branch or section by reason of its being a trade union is to be treated as discharged to the extent to which the union of which it is a branch or section discharges the duty instead of it (s 44(4)). As to the meaning of 'branch or section', in relation to a trade union, see PARA 898 note 5.

2   Trade Union and Labour Relations (Consolidation) Act 1992 s 28(1). If a trade union refuses or wilfully neglects to comply with the duty imposed on it by or under s 28, it commits an offence: see s 45(1); and PARA 956.

3   Trade Union and Labour Relations (Consolidation) Act 1992 s 28(2).

4   For the purposes of the Trade Union and Labour Relations (Consolidation) Act 1992 ss 29–31 (see the text and notes 5–6; and PARAS 940–942), references to a branch or section do not include a branch or section which is itself a trade union: s 44(3).

5   Trade Union and Labour Relations (Consolidation) Act 1992 s 29(1). The duty does not apply to records relating to periods before 1 January 1988 (s 29(1)); nor to a federated trade union which has no members other than constituent or affiliated organisations or representatives of such organisations (s 118(5)).

6   Trade Union and Labour Relations (Consolidation) Act 1992 s 29(1). If a trade union refuses or wilfully neglects to comply with the duty imposed on it by or under s 29, it commits an offence: see s 45(1); and PARA 956. The expiry of the six-year period mentioned in s 29(1) does not affect the duty of a trade union to comply with a request for access made under s 30 (see PARA 941) before the end of that period: s 29(3).

941.   Union member's right of access to accounting records.   A member[1] of a trade union[2] has a right to request access to any accounting records[3] of the union which are available for inspection[4] and relate to periods including a time when he was a member of the union[5].

Where such access is requested, the union must:

(1)   make arrangements[6] with the member for him to be allowed to inspect the records requested before the end of the period of 28 days beginning with the day the request was made;

(2)   allow him and any accountant[7] accompanying him to inspect the records at the time and place arranged; and

(3)   secure that at the time of inspection he is allowed to take, or is supplied with, any copies of records, or of extracts from records, inspected by him which he requires[8].

A person who claims that a trade union has failed in any respect to comply with a request for access so made by him may apply to the High Court[9].

1   For these purposes, 'member', in relation to a trade union consisting wholly or partly of, or of representatives of, constituent or affiliated organisations, includes a member of any of the constituent or affiliated organisations: Trade Union and Labour Relations (Consolidation) Act 1992 s 30(7).

2   As to the meaning of 'trade union' see PARA 891. The duty to allow a member access to accounting records does not apply to a federated trade union which has no members other than constituent or affiliated organisations or representatives of such organisations: see the Trade Union and Labour Relations (Consolidation) Act 1992 s 118(5); and PARA 891 note 9 head (4). As to the meaning of 'federated trade union' see PARA 891.

3   For these purposes, references to a union's accounting records are to any such records as are mentioned in the Trade Union and Labour Relations (Consolidation) Act 1992 s 29(1) (see PARA 940): s 29(2)(a). As to the meaning of references to a branch or section for these purposes see PARA 940 note 4.

4   For these purposes, references to records available for inspection are to records which the union is required by the Trade Union and Labour Relations (Consolidation) Act 1992 s 29(1) to keep available for inspection: s 29(2)(b). See also PARA 940.

5   Trade Union and Labour Relations (Consolidation) Act 1992 s 30(1). In the case of records relating to a branch or section of the union it is immaterial whether he was a member of that branch or section: s 30(1). See, however, note 3.

6   The inspection must be at a reasonable hour and at the place where the records are normally kept, unless the parties to the arrangements agree otherwise: Trade Union and Labour Relations (Consolidation) Act 1992 s 30(3). Where a member who makes a request for access to a union's accounting records is informed by the union, before any arrangements are made in pursuance of the request: (1) of the union's intention to charge for allowing him to inspect the records to which the request relates, for allowing him to take copies of, or extracts from, those records, or for supplying any such copies; and (2) of the principles in accordance with which its charges will be determined, then, where the union complies with the request, he is liable to pay the union on demand such amount, not exceeding the reasonable administrative expenses incurred by the union in complying with the request, as is determined in accordance with those principles: s 30(6).

7   For these purposes, an 'accountant' means a person who is eligible for appointment as a statutory auditor under the Companies Act 2006 Pt 42 (ss 1209–1264) (see COMPANIES vol 15 (2009) PARA 905 et seq): Trade Union and Labour Relations (Consolidation) Act 1992 s 30(4) (amended by SI 2008/948). The union need not allow the member to be accompanied by an accountant if the accountant fails to enter into such agreement as the union may reasonably require for protecting the confidentiality of the records: Trade Union and Labour Relations (Consolidation) Act 1992 s 30(5).

8   Trade Union and Labour Relations (Consolidation) Act 1992 s 30(2).

9   Ie under the Trade Union and Labour Relations (Consolidation) Act 1992 s 31: see PARA 942. If a trade union refuses or wilfully neglects to perform the duty imposed on it by or under s 30, it commits an offence: see s 45(1); and PARA 956.

942.   Remedy for failure to comply with request for access to union's accounting records. A person who claims that a trade union[1] has failed in any respect to comply with a request for access to accounting records made by him[2] may apply to the High Court or to the certification officer[3].

Where, on an application to it, the court is satisfied that the claim is well-founded, it must make such order as it considers appropriate for ensuring that the applicant:

(1)   is allowed to inspect the records requested;

(2)   is allowed to be accompanied by an accountant when inspecting those records[4]; and

(3)   is allowed to take, or is supplied with, such copies of, or of extracts from, the records as he may require[5].

On an application to him, the certification officer must make such inquiries as he thinks fit[6] and give the applicant and the trade union an opportunity to be heard[7]. Where the certification officer is satisfied that the claim is well-founded, he must make such order as he considers appropriate[8] for ensuring that the applicant:

(a)   is allowed to inspect the records requested;
(b)   is allowed to be accompanied by an accountant when making the inspection of those records; and
(c)   is allowed to take, or is supplied with, such copies of, or of extracts from, the records as he may require[9].

1   As to the meaning of 'trade union' see PARA 891. The Trade Union and Labour Relations (Consolidation) Act 1992 s 31 (see the text and notes 2–9) does not apply to certain federated trade unions: see PARA 891 note 9 head (4).
2   Ie under the Trade Union and Labour Relations (Consolidation) Act 1992 s 30: see PARA 941.
3   Trade Union and Labour Relations (Consolidation) Act 1992 s 31(1) (amended by the Employment Relations Act 1999 Sch 6 paras 1, 6(1), (2)); Trade Union and Labour Relations (Consolidation) Act 1992 s 121. As to the certification officer see PARA 1443. If a person applies to the court under s 31 in relation to an alleged failure, he may not apply to the certification officer under s 31 in relation to that failure: s 31(6) (s 31(4)–(7) added by Employment Relations Act 1999 Sch 6 paras 1, 6(1), (6)). If a person applies to the certification officer under the Trade Union and Labour Relations (Consolidation) Act 1992 s 31 in relation to an alleged failure, he may not apply to the court under s 31 in relation to that failure: s 31(7) (as so added).
4   The accountant must agree to protect the confidentiality of the records: see the Trade Union and Labour Relations (Consolidation) Act 1992 s 30(5); and PARA 941 note 7.
5   Trade Union and Labour Relations (Consolidation) Act 1992 s 31(2) (amended by the Employment Relations Act 1999 Sch 6 paras 1, 6(1), (3)). Without prejudice to any other power of the court, the court may on an application to it under the Trade Union and Labour Relations (Consolidation) Act 1992 s 31 grant such interim relief as it considers appropriate: see s 31(3) (amended by the Employment Relations Act 1999 Sch 6 paras 1, 6(1), (5).
6   Where the certification officer requests a person to furnish information to him in connection with inquiries made by him under the Trade Union and Labour Relations (Consolidation) Act 1992 s 31, he must specify the date by which that information is to be furnished and, unless he considers that it would be inappropriate to do so, must proceed with his determination of the application notwithstanding that the information has not been furnished to him by the specified date: s 31(4) (as added: see note 3).
7   Trade Union and Labour Relations (Consolidation) Act 1992 s 31(2A) (s 31(2A)–(2C) added by the Employment Relations Act 1999 Sch 6 paras 1, 6(1), (4)). In exercising his functions under the Trade Union and Labour Relations (Consolidation) Act 1992 s 31, the certification officer must ensure that, so far as is reasonably practicable, an application made to him is determined within six months of being made: s 31(2C) (as so added).
8   An order made by the certification officer under the Trade Union and Labour Relations (Consolidation) Act 1992 s 31 may be enforced in the same way as an order of the court: s 31(5) (as added: see note 3). An appeal lies to the Employment Appeal Tribunal on any question of law arising in proceedings before or arising from any decision of the certification officer under s 31: s 45D (added by Employment Relations Act 1999 Sch 6 paras 1, 8). As to the Employment Appeal Tribunal see PARA 1422 et seq.
9   Trade Union and Labour Relations (Consolidation) Act 1992 s 31(2B) (as added: see note 7).

(iii)   Trade Union's Annual Return and Auditors

943.   Annual return of trade union. A trade union[1] must send to the certification officer[2] as respects each calendar year[3] a return relating to its affairs[4]. The annual return must be in such form and be signed by such persons as the certification officer may require, and must be sent to him before 1 June in the calendar year following that to which it relates[5]. The certification officer must at all reasonable hours keep available for public inspection copies of all annual returns sent to him under these provisions, either free of charge or on payment of a reasonable charge[6]; and a trade union must at the request of any person supply him with a copy of its most recent annual return, either free of charge or on payment of a reasonable charge[7].

The annual return must contain:
(1)   revenue accounts indicating the income and expenditure of the trade union for the period to which the return relates, a balance sheet as at the

end of that period and such other accounts as the certification officer may require, each of which must give a true and fair view of the matters to which it relates[8];

(2) details of the salary paid to and other benefits provided to or in respect of each member of the executive[9], the president[10] and the general secretary[11] by the trade union during the period to which the return relates[12];

(3) a copy of the report made by the auditor or auditors of the trade union on those accounts[13], and such other documents relating to those accounts and such further particulars as the certification officer may require[14];

(4) a copy of the rules of the union as in force at the end of the period to which the return relates[15]; and

(5) in the case of a trade union required to maintain a register[16] of members' names and addresses, a statement of the number of names on the register as at the end of the period to which the return relates and the number of those names which were not accompanied by an address which is a member's address for the statutory purposes[17].

The annual return must also have attached to it a note of all the changes in the officers[18] of the union and of any change in the address of the head or main office of the union during the period to which the return relates[19].

1   As to the meaning of 'trade union' see PARA 891. The provisions of the Trade Union and Labour Relations (Consolidation) Act 1992 ss 32–37 (annual return, statement for members, accounts and audit (see the text and notes; and PARA 944 et seq) do not apply to a trade union which has been in existence for less than 12 months (s 43(1)(b) (amended by the Trade Union Reform and Employment Rights Act 1993 Sch 8 para 43(a), Sch 10), or to a federated trade union which consists wholly or mainly of representatives of constituent or affiliated organisations (see the Trade Union and Labour Relations (Consolidation) Act 1992 s 118(4)(c); and PARA 891 note 9 head (2); but see also PARA 931 note 6). As to the meaning of 'federated trade union' see PARA 891. Where a trade union consists of or includes branches or sections, any duty falling on the union in relation to a branch or section under the provisions of s 32 and ss 33–37 (annual return, accounts and audit) is to be treated as discharged to the extent to which the duty is discharged by the branch or section; and any such duty falling on a branch or section by reason of its being a trade union is to be treated as discharged to the extent to which the union of which it is a branch or section discharges the duty instead of it: s 44(1), (2), (4) (s 44(2), (4) amended by the Trade Union Reform and Employment Rights Act 1993 Sch 8 para 44(a)). See also PARA 944 note 1. As to the meaning of 'branch or section', in relation to a trade union, see PARA 898 note 5.

2   As to the certification officer see PARA 1443.

3   If in any particular case he considers it appropriate to do so, the certification officer may direct that the period for which a return is to be sent to him is to be a period other than the calendar year last preceding the date on which the return is sent: Trade Union and Labour Relations (Consolidation) Act 1992 s 32(4)(a).

4   Trade Union and Labour Relations (Consolidation) Act 1992 s 32(1). If a trade union refuses or wilfully neglects to perform a duty imposed on it by or under s 32, it commits an offence: see s 45(1); and PARA 956.

5   Trade Union and Labour Relations (Consolidation) Act 1992 s 32(2). If in any particular case he considers it appropriate to do so, the certification officer may direct that the date before which a return is to be sent to him is to be such date, whether before or after 1 June, as may be specified in the direction: s 32(4)(b).

6   Trade Union and Labour Relations (Consolidation) Act 1992 s 32(6).

7   Trade Union and Labour Relations (Consolidation) Act 1992 s 32(5).

8   Trade Union and Labour Relations (Consolidation) Act 1992 s 32(3)(a).

9   'Executive', in relation to a trade union, means the principal committee of the union exercising executive functions, by whatever name it is called: Trade Union and Labour Relations (Consolidation) Act 1992 s 119. For these purposes, and the purposes of s 32A (see PARA 944), 'member of the executive' includes any person who, under the rules or practice of the union,

may attend and speak at some or all of the meetings of the executive, otherwise than for the purpose of providing the committee with factual information or with technical or professional advice with respect to matters taken into account by the executive in carrying out its functions: s 32(7) (added by the Trade Union Reform and Employment Rights Act 1993 Sch 8 para 42). As to the meaning of 'rules', in relation to a trade union, see PARA 898 note 5.

10 As to the meaning of 'president', in relation to a trade union, see PARA 921 note 3; and as to the meaning of 'official', in relation to a trade union, see PARA 1018.

11 As to the meaning of 'general secretary', in relation to a trade union, see PARA 921 note 3. See also PARA 960 note 7.

12 Trade Union and Labour Relations (Consolidation) Act 1992 s 32(3)(aa) (added by the Trade Union Reform and Employment Rights Act 1993 s 8(a)).

13 Ie the report made under the Trade Union and Labour Relations (Consolidation) Act 1992 s 36: see PARA 947.

14 Trade Union and Labour Relations (Consolidation) Act 1992 s 32(3)(b) (amended by the Trade Union Reform and Employment Rights Act 1993 Sch 10).

15 Trade Union and Labour Relations (Consolidation) Act 1992 s 32(3)(c).

16 Ie required by the Trade Union and Labour Relations (Consolidation) Act 1992 s 24: see PARA 930.

17 Trade Union and Labour Relations (Consolidation) Act 1992 s 32(3)(d) (added by the Trade Union Reform and Employment Rights Act 1993 s 8(b)). For these purposes, 'member's address' means the address which is a member's address for the purposes of the Trade Union and Labour Relations (Consolidation) Act 1992 s 24: see PARA 930 note 3.

18 As to the meaning of 'officer', in relation to a trade union, see PARA 902 note 7.

19 Trade Union and Labour Relations (Consolidation) Act 1992 s 32(3).

944.   Statement to members following union's annual return. A trade union[1] must take all reasonable steps to secure that, not later than the end of the period of eight weeks beginning with the day on which the annual return[2] of the union is sent to the certification officer[3], all members of the union are provided with the required[4] statement[5] specifying:

(1) the total income and expenditure of the trade union for the period to which the return relates;

(2) how much of the income of the union for that period consisted of payments in respect of membership;

(3) the total income and expenditure for that period of any political fund of the union[6]; and

(4) the salary paid to and other benefits provided to or in respect of each member of the executive[7], the president[8] and the general secretary[9] by the trade union during that period[10].

The statement:

(a) must also set out in full the report made by the auditor or auditors of the union on the accounts contained in the return[11] and state the name and address of that auditor or of each of the auditors; and

(b) may include any other matter which the union considers may give a member significant assistance in making an informed judgment about the financial activities of the union in the period to which the return relates[12];

(c) must also include the statutory statement[13] as to possible irregularity in the conduct of the union's financial affairs[14];

(d) may also include such other details of the steps which a member may take for the purpose mentioned in the statement as the trade union considers appropriate[15].

The union may provide members with the statement by sending them individual copies of the statement, or by any other means, whether by including the statement in a publication of the union or otherwise, which it is the practice of the union to use when information of general interest needs to be provided to them[16]; but, if at any time during the period of two years beginning with the day on which the annual return of the union is sent to the certification officer any member of the union requests a copy of the statement, the union must, as soon as reasonably practicable, furnish him with such a copy free of charge[17].

The requirements imposed by the above provisions are not satisfied if the statement specifies anything inconsistent with the contents of the return[18].

1   As to the meaning of 'trade union' see PARA 891. As to the application of these provisions to newly formed trade unions and federated trade unions see PARA 943 note 1. Where the duty falling on a trade union to send an annual return to the certification officer is treated as discharged by the union in accordance with the Trade Union and Labour Relations (Consolidation) Act 1992 s 44(2) or (4) (discharge of duties in case of union having branches or sections) (see PARA 943 note 1), the duties imposed in relation to the return by s 32A (see the text and notes 2–18) are to be treated as duties of the branch or section of the union, or the trade union of which it is a branch or section, by which that duty is in fact discharged: s 44(5) (added by the Trade Union Reform and Employment Rights Act 1993 Sch 8 para 44(b)). As to the meaning of 'branch or section', in relation to a trade union, see PARA 898 note 5.

2   As to the annual return see PARA 943.

3   As to the certification officer see PARA 1443.

4   Ie required by the Trade Union and Labour Relations (Consolidation) Act 1992 s 32A.

5   Trade Union and Labour Relations (Consolidation) Act 1992 s 32A(1) (s 32A added by the Trade Union Reform and Employment Rights Act 1993 s 9).

6   As to the political fund see PARA 977 et seq.

7   As to the meaning of 'executive', and as to the meaning of 'member of the executive' for these purposes, see PARA 943 note 9.

8   As to the meaning of 'president' see PARA 921 note 3.

9   As to the meaning of 'general secretary' see PARA 921 note 3.

10   Trade Union and Labour Relations (Consolidation) Act 1992 s 32A(3) (as added: see note 5).

11   As to the report of the auditors under the Trade Union and Labour Relations (Consolidation) Act 1992 s 36 see PARA 947.

12   Trade Union and Labour Relations (Consolidation) Act 1992 s 32A(5) (as added: see note 5).

13   The wording of that statement is as follows: 'A member who is concerned that some irregularity may be occurring, or have occurred, in the conduct of the financial affairs of the union may take steps with a view to investigating further, obtaining clarification and, if necessary, securing regularisation of that conduct. The member may raise any such concern with such one or more of the following as it seems appropriate to raise it with: the officials of the union, the trustees of the property of the union, the auditor or auditors of the union, the certification officer (who is an independent officer appointed by the Secretary of State) and the police. Where a member believes that the financial affairs of the union have been or are being conducted in breach of the law or in breach of rules of the union and contemplates bringing civil proceedings against the union or responsible officials or trustees, he should consider taking legal advice.'

14   See the Trade Union and Labour Relations (Consolidation) Act 1992 s 32A(6)(a) (as added (see note 5); amended by the Employment Relations Act 1999 s 28(3)). For these purposes, 'financial affairs', in relation to a trade union, means affairs of the union relating to any fund which is applicable for the purposes of the union, including any fund of a branch or section of the union which is so applicable: Trade Union and Labour Relations (Consolidation) Act 1992 s 119 (definition added by the Trade Union Reform and Employment Rights Act 1993 Sch 8 para 63(b)).

15   Trade Union and Labour Relations (Consolidation) Act 1992 s 32A(6)(b) (as added: see note 5). As to officials of the union see PARA 1018; and as to trustees of the union see PARA 919. As to the meaning of 'rules', in relation to a trade union, see PARA 898 note 5.

16   Trade Union and Labour Relations (Consolidation) Act 1992 s 32A(1), (2) (as added: see note 5).

17   Trade Union and Labour Relations (Consolidation) Act 1992 s 32A(9) (as added: see note 5). The union must also send a copy of the statement which is provided to members to the certification officer as soon as is reasonably practicable after it is so provided: s 32A(7) (as so added). Where the same form of statement is not provided to all members, the union must send to the certification officer a copy of each form of statement provided to any of them: s 32A(8) (as so added).

18   Trade Union and Labour Relations (Consolidation) Act 1992 s 32A(4) (as added: see note 5). If a trade union refuses or wilfully neglects to perform a duty imposed on it by or under s 32A, it commits an offence: see s 45(1); and PARA 956.

945. Trade union's duty to appoint auditors; eligibility for appointment. A trade union[1] must, in respect of each accounting period[2], appoint an auditor or auditors[3] to audit the accounts contained in its annual return[4].

A person is not qualified to be the auditor or one of the auditors of a trade union unless he is eligible for appointment[5] as a statutory auditor[6]. Two or more persons who are not so qualified may, however, act as auditors of a trade union in respect of an accounting period if the receipts and payments in respect of the union's last preceding accounting period did not in the aggregate exceed £5,000, the number of its members at the end of that period did not exceed 500, and the value of its assets at the end of that period did not in the aggregate exceed £5,000[7]. None of the following is to act as auditor of a trade union:

(1)   an officer[8] or employee[9] of the trade union or of any of its branches or sections[10]; or

(2)   a person who is a partner of, or in the employment of, or who employs, such an officer or employee[11].

1   As to the meaning of 'trade union' see PARA 891. As to the application of these provisions to newly formed trade unions, federated trade unions and unions which consist of branches or sections see PARA 943 note 1. The duty to appoint auditors and the eligibility provisions do not apply to a special register body which is registered as a company under the Companies Act 2006: see the Trade Union and Labour Relations (Consolidation) Act 1992 s 117(4); and PARA 899 note 8 head (4). As to the meaning of 'special register body' see PARA 899.

2   For these purposes, 'accounting period' means any period in relation to which a trade union is required to send a return to the certification officer: Trade Union and Labour Relations (Consolidation) Act 1992 s 33(2). As to the certification officer see PARA 1443.

3   As to the appointment of auditors see PARA 946.

4   Trade Union and Labour Relations (Consolidation) Act 1992 s 33(1). As to the annual return see PARA 943. If a trade union refuses or wilfully neglects to perform a duty imposed on it by or under s 33 or s 34, it commits an offence: see s 45(1); and PARA 956.

5   Ie under the Companies Act 2006 Pt 42 (ss 1209–1264): see COMPANIES vol 15 (2009) PARA 957 et seq.

6   Trade Union and Labour Relations (Consolidation) Act 1992 s 34(1) (amended by SI 2008/948). A person who is not qualified as mentioned in the Trade Union and Labour Relations (Consolidation) Act 1992 s 34(1) may, however, act as auditor of a trade union in respect of an accounting period if: (1) the union was registered under the Trade Union Acts 1871 to 1964 (repealed) on 30 September 1971; (2) he acted as its auditor in respect of the last period in relation to which it was required to make an annual return under the Trade Union Act 1871 s 16 (repealed); (3) he has acted as its auditor in respect of every accounting period since that period; and (4) he retains an authorisation formerly granted by the Board of Trade or the Secretary of State under the Companies Act 1948 s 16(1)(b) (repealed) (adequate knowledge and experience, or pre-1947 practice): Trade Union and Labour Relations (Consolidation) Act 1992 Sch 3 para 11(2). Nothing in s 34 affects the validity of any appointment as auditor of a trade union or employers' association made before 1 October 1991 (when the Companies Act 1985 s 389 was repealed and replaced by the provisions of the Companies Act 1989 Pt II (ss 24–54) (see now the Companies Act 2006 Pt 42) (see COMPANIES vol 15 (2009) PARA 957 et seq)): Trade Union and Labour Relations (Consolidation) Act 1992 Sch 3 para 11(1). As to employers' associations see PARA 1079 et seq.

7   Trade Union and Labour Relations (Consolidation) Act 1992 s 34(2). The Secretary of State may by regulations substitute for any sum or number specified in s 34(2) such sum or number as may be specified in the regulations, and may prescribe what receipts and payments are to be taken into account for those purposes; and any such regulations must be made by statutory instrument which is subject to annulment in pursuance of a resolution of either House of Parliament: s 34(4). At the date at which this volume states the law, no such regulations had been made and none had effect as if so made.

    Where, by virtue of s 34(2), persons who are not qualified act as auditors of a trade union in respect of an accounting period, the certification officer may, during that period or after it comes to an end, direct the union to appoint a person who is qualified to audit its accounts for that period: s 34(3).

8   As to the meaning of 'officer', in relation to a trade union, see PARA 902 note 7.

9   As to the meaning of 'employee' see PARA 892.

10   As to the meaning of 'branch or section', in relation to a trade union, see PARA 898 note 5.
11   Trade Union and Labour Relations (Consolidation) Act 1992 s 34(5) (amended by the Trade
     Union Reform and Employment Rights Act 1993 Sch 7 para 18, Sch 10; the Employment
     Relations Act 2004 Sch 2).

946.   Appointment and removal of trade union's auditors.   The rules[1] of every
trade union[2] must contain provision for the appointment and removal of
auditors[3], but, notwithstanding anything in the rules, an auditor of a trade union
may not be removed from office except by resolution passed at a general meeting
of its members or of delegates of its members[4]; and an auditor duly appointed to
audit the accounts must be reappointed as auditor for the following accounting
period unless:

(1)   a resolution has been passed at a general meeting of the trade union
      appointing someone instead of him or providing expressly that he is not
      to be reappointed; or

(2)   he has given notice to the trade union in writing of his unwillingness to
      be reappointed; or

(3)   he is ineligible[5] for reappointment; or

(4)   he has ceased to act as auditor by reason of incapacity[6].

Where notice has been given of an intended resolution to appoint somebody
in place of a retiring auditor but the resolution cannot be proceeded with at the
meeting because of the death or incapacity of the person, or because he is
ineligible for the appointment, the retiring auditor need not automatically be
reappointed[7].

The Secretary of State may make provision by regulations as to the procedure
to be followed when it is intended to move a resolution appointing another
auditor in place of a retiring auditor, or providing expressly that a retiring
auditor is not to be reappointed, and as to the rights of auditors and members of
the trade union in relation to such a motion[8]. Where such regulations require
copies of any representations made by a retiring auditor to be sent out, or require
any such representations to be read out at a meeting, the High Court may
dispense with the requirement, on the application of the trade union or of any
other person, if the court is satisfied that the rights conferred on the retiring
auditor by the regulations are being abused to secure needless publicity for
defamatory matter[9].

1   As to the meaning of 'rules', in relation to a trade union, see PARA 898 note 5.
2   As to the meaning of 'trade union' see PARA 891. As to the application of these provisions to
    newly formed trade unions, federated trade unions and unions which consist of branches or
    sections see PARA 943 note 1. These provisions do not apply to a special register body which is
    registered as a company under the Companies Act 1985: see the Trade Union and Labour
    Relations (Consolidation) Act 1992 s 117(4); and PARA 899 note 8 head (4). As to the meaning
    of 'special register body' see PARA 899.
3   Trade Union and Labour Relations (Consolidation) Act 1992 s 35(1).
4   Trade Union and Labour Relations (Consolidation) Act 1992 s 35(1), (2).
5   For these purposes, the references to a person being ineligible for appointment as auditor of a
    trade union are to his not being qualified for the appointment in accordance with the Trade
    Union and Labour Relations (Consolidation) Act 1992 s 34(1)–(4) (see PARA 945) or being
    precluded by s 34(5) (see PARA 945) from acting as its auditor: s 35(5) (amended by the Trade
    Union Reform and Employment Rights Act 1993 Sch 7 para 19).
6   Trade Union and Labour Relations (Consolidation) Act 1992 s 35(1), (3). If a trade union
    refuses or wilfully neglects to perform a duty imposed on it by or under s 35, it commits an
    offence: see s 45(1); and PARA 956.
7   Trade Union and Labour Relations (Consolidation) Act 1992 s 35(1), (4).
8   Trade Union and Labour Relations (Consolidation) Act 1992 s 35(1), (6). Any such regulations
    must be made by statutory instrument which is subject to annulment in pursuance of a

resolution of either House of Parliament: s 35(6). At the date at which this volume states the law, no such regulations had been made and none had effect as if so made.

9   Trade Union and Labour Relations (Consolidation) Act 1992 ss 35(1), (7), 121. On such an application the court may order the costs or expenses of the trade union to be paid, in whole or in part, by the retiring auditor, whether he is a party to the application or not: s 35(1), (8).

947. Auditors' report on trade union's accounts. The auditor or auditors of a trade union[1] must make a report to it on the accounts audited by him or them and contained in its annual return[2]. The report must state the names of, and be signed[3] by, the auditor or auditors[4]. The report must state whether, in the opinion of the auditor or auditors, the accounts give a true and fair view of the matters to which they relate[5]. In preparing his or their report, it is the duty of the auditor or auditors to carry out such investigations as will enable him or them to form an opinion as to:

(1)   whether the trade union has kept proper accounting records in accordance with the statutory requirements[6];

(2)   whether it has maintained a satisfactory system of control over its transactions in accordance with those requirements; and

(3)   whether the accounts to which the report relates agree with the accounting records[7].

If, in the opinion of the auditor or auditors, the trade union has failed to comply with its statutory duty to keep proper accounting records[8], or if the accounts do not agree with the accounting records, the auditor or auditors must state that fact in the report[9].

1   As to the meaning of 'trade union' see PARA 891. As to the application of these provisions to newly formed trade unions, federated trade unions and unions which consist of branches or sections see PARA 943 note 1. These provisions apply to the auditors appointed by a special register body under the Companies Act 1985 Pt XI Ch V (ss 384–394A) (repealed) or the Companies Act 2006 Pt 16 Ch 2 (ss 485–494): see the Trade Union and Labour Relations (Consolidation) Act 1992 s 117(4); and PARA 899 note 8 head (4). As to the meaning of 'special register body' see PARA 899.

2   Trade Union and Labour Relations (Consolidation) Act 1992 s 36(1). As to the annual return see PARA 943.

3   Any reference to signature by an auditor is, where the office of auditor is held by a body corporate or partnership, to signature in the name of the body corporate or partnership by an individual authorised to sign on its behalf: Trade Union and Labour Relations (Consolidation) Act 1992 s 36(5) (added by the Employment Relations Act 2004 s 53(3)).

4   Trade Union and Labour Relations (Consolidation) Act 1992 s 36(1A) (added by the Employment Relations Act 2004 s 53(2)).

5   Trade Union and Labour Relations (Consolidation) Act 1992 s 36(2).

6   Ie in accordance with the Trade Union and Labour Relations (Consolidation) Act 1992 s 28: see PARA 940.

7   Trade Union and Labour Relations (Consolidation) Act 1992 s 36(3).

8   Ie under the Trade Union and Labour Relations (Consolidation) Act 1992 s 28.

9   Trade Union and Labour Relations (Consolidation) Act 1992 s 36(4).

948. Rights of auditors of a trade union. Every auditor of a trade union[1]:

(1)   has a right of access at all times to its accounting records and to all other documents relating to its affairs; and

(2)   is entitled to require from its officers[2], or the officers of any of its branches or sections[3], such information and explanations as he thinks necessary for the performance of his duties as auditor[4].

Every auditor of a trade union is also entitled:

(a)   to attend any general meeting of its members, or of delegates of its members, and to receive all notices of, and other communications relating to, any general meeting which any such member or delegate is entitled to receive; and

(b)   to be heard at any meeting which he attends on any part of the business of the meeting which concerns him as auditor[5].

In the case of an auditor which is a body corporate or partnership, its right to attend or be heard at a meeting is exercisable by an individual authorised by it to act as its representative at the meeting[6].

If an auditor fails to obtain all the information and explanations which, to the best of his knowledge and belief, are necessary for the purposes of an audit, he must state that fact in his report[7].

1   As to the meaning of 'trade union' see PARA 891. As to the application of these provisions to newly formed trade unions, federated trade unions and unions which consist of branches or sections see PARA 943 note 1. These provisions apply to the auditors appointed by a special register body under the Companies Act 1985 Pt XI Ch V (ss 384–394A) (repealed) or the Companies Act 2006 Pt 16 Ch 2 (ss 485–494): see the Trade Union and Labour Relations (Consolidation) Act 1992 s 117(4); and PARA 899 note 8 head (4). As to the meaning of 'special register body' see PARA 899.
2   As to the meaning of 'officer', in relation to a trade union, see PARA 902 note 7.
3   As to the meaning of 'branch or section', in relation to a trade union, see PARA 898 note 5.
4   Trade Union and Labour Relations (Consolidation) Act 1992 s 37(1).
5   Trade Union and Labour Relations (Consolidation) Act 1992 s 37(3).
6   Trade Union and Labour Relations (Consolidation) Act 1992 s 37(4) (added by the Employment Relations Act 2004 s 53(4)).
7   Trade Union and Labour Relations (Consolidation) Act 1992 s 37(2). If a trade union refuses or wilfully neglects to perform a duty imposed under or by virtue of any of the provisions of s 37, it commits an offence: see s 45(1); and PARA 956.

(iv) Investigation of Trade Union's Financial Affairs

949.   Power of certification officer to require production of accounting and other relevant documents.   The certification officer[1] may at any time, if he thinks there is good reason to do so[2]:

(1)   give directions to a trade union[3], or a branch or section[4] of a trade union, requiring it to produce such relevant documents[5] as may be specified in the directions[6]; and

(2)   authorise a member of his staff or any other person, on producing evidence of his authority if so required, to require a trade union, or a branch or section of a trade union, to produce forthwith to the member of staff or other person such relevant documents as that person may specify[7].

The power to require the production of documents includes power:

(a)   if the documents are produced, to take copies of them or extracts from them and to require the person by whom they are produced, or any person who is or has been an official[8] or agent[9] of the trade union, to provide an explanation of any of them; and

(b)   if the documents are not produced, to require the person who was required to produce them to state where they are, to the best of his knowledge and belief[10].

A person is not to be excused from providing an explanation or making a statement in compliance with a requirement so imposed on the ground that to do so would tend to expose him to proceedings for an offence; but an explanation so provided or a statement so made may only be used in evidence against the person by whom it is provided or made on a prosecution for the offence of providing or making a false explanation or statement[11], or on a prosecution for some other offence where, in giving evidence, the person makes a statement inconsistent with it[12].

Nothing in the above provisions requires or authorises anyone:

(i)   to require the disclosure by a person of information which he would be entitled to refuse to disclose in an action in the High Court on the grounds of legal professional privilege except, if he is a lawyer, the name and address of his client[13];

(ii)   to require the production by a person of a document which he would in such an action be entitled to refuse on such grounds[14];

(iii)   to require the disclosure of information or the production of documents in respect of which the person to whom the requirement would relate owes an obligation of confidence by virtue of carrying on the business of banking, unless the person to whom the obligation is owed is the trade union, or any branch or section of the trade union, concerned or a trustee of any fund concerned, or the person to whom the obligation of confidence is owed consents to the disclosure or production[15].

The certification officer must consider whether it is appropriate for him to exercise any of the powers conferred on him by the above provisions where:

(A)   a report[16] of the auditor or auditors[17] of a trade union, or a branch or section of a trade union, on the accounts audited by him or them and contained in the annual return[18] of the union, or branch or section, does not state without qualification that the accounts give a true and fair view of the matters to which they relate, or includes a statement in compliance with the statutory requirements[19] that, in the opinion of the auditor or auditors, the union has failed to comply with its statutory duty to keep proper accounting records[20] or that the accounts do not agree with the accounting records[21]; or

(B)   a member of a trade union has complained to the certification officer that there are circumstances suggesting the existence of certain specified[22] states of affairs[23].

1   As to the certification officer see PARA 1443.
2   As to the circumstances where the certification officer is required to consider whether to exercise any of these powers see text and notes 3–23.
3   As to the meaning of 'trade union' see PARA 891. The Trade Union and Labour Relations (Consolidation) Act 1992 ss 37A–37E (see the text and notes 1–2, 4–23; and PARA 950 et seq) do not apply to a trade union which has been in existence for less than 12 months (s 43(1)(ba) (added by the Trade Union Reform and Employment Rights Act 1993 Sch 8 para 43(b))), or to a federated trade union which consists wholly or mainly of representatives of constituent or affiliated organisations (see the Trade Union and Labour Relations (Consolidation) Act 1992 s 118(4); and PARA 891 note 9 head (2)). As to the meaning of 'federated trade union' see PARA 891.
4   As to the meaning of 'branch or section', in relation to a trade union, see PARA 898 note 5.
5   For these purposes, 'relevant documents', in relation to a trade union or a branch or section of a trade union, means accounting documents, and documents of any other description, which may be relevant in considering the financial affairs of the trade union: Trade Union and Labour Relations (Consolidation) Act 1992 s 37A(6) (ss 37A, 37E added by the Trade Union Reform and Employment Rights Act 1993 s 10). As to the meaning of 'financial affairs', in relation to a trade union, see PARA 944 note 14. References to documents in the Trade Union and Labour Relations (Consolidation) Act 1992 ss 37A, 37B, 37E (see the text and notes 1–4, 6–23; and PARAS 950, 951) include information recorded in any form, and, in relation to information recorded otherwise than in legible form, references to its production are to the production of a copy of the information in legible form: s 37E(5) (as so added).
6   Trade Union and Labour Relations (Consolidation) Act 1992 s 37A(1) (as added: see note 5). The documents must be produced at such time and place as may be specified: s 37A(1) (as so

added). Where the certification officer, or a member of his staff or any other person, has power to require the production of documents by virtue of s 37A(1) or s 37A(2), the certification officer, member of staff or other person has the like power to require production of those documents from any person who appears to him to be in possession of them: s 37A(3) (as so added). Where such a person claims a lien on documents produced by him, the production is without prejudice to the lien: s 37A(4) (as so added).

7　Trade Union and Labour Relations (Consolidation) Act 1992 s 37A(2) (as added: see note 5). See also note 6.

8　As to the meaning of 'official', in relation to a trade union, see PARA 1018.

9　For these purposes, 'agent', in relation to a trade union, means a banker or solicitor of, or any person employed as an auditor by, the union or any branch or section of the union: Trade Union and Labour Relations (Consolidation) Act 1992 s 119 (definition added by the Trade Union Reform and Employment Rights Act 1993 Sch 8 para 63(a)).

10　Trade Union and Labour Relations (Consolidation) Act 1992 s 37A(5) (as added: see note 5).

11　Ie under the Trade Union and Labour Relations (Consolidation) Act 1992 s 45(9): see PARA 957.

12　Trade Union and Labour Relations (Consolidation) Act 1992 s 37A(7) (as added: see note 5).

13　Trade Union and Labour Relations (Consolidation) Act 1992 s 37E(3)(a) (as added: see note 5).

14　Trade Union and Labour Relations (Consolidation) Act 1992 s 37E(3)(b) (as added: see note 5).

15　Trade Union and Labour Relations (Consolidation) Act 1992 s 37E(4) (as added: see note 5).

16　As to the auditors' report see PARA 947.

17　As to the appointment of auditors see PARA 946.

18　As to the annual return see PARA 943.

19　Ie under the Trade Union and Labour Relations (Consolidation) Act 1992 s 36(4): see PARA 947.

20　Ie under the Trade Union and Labour Relations (Consolidation) Act 1992 s 28: see PARA 940.

21　Trade Union and Labour Relations (Consolidation) Act 1992 s 37E(1)(a) (as added: see note 5).

22　Ie any of the states of affairs specified in the Trade Union and Labour Relations (Consolidation) Act 1992 s 37B(2)(a)–(d): see PARA 950 heads (1)–(4).

23　Trade Union and Labour Relations (Consolidation) Act 1992 s 37E(1)(b) (as added: see note 5). If, in a case where a member of a trade union has so complained, the certification officer decides not to exercise any of the powers so conferred on him, he must, as soon as reasonably practicable after making a decision not to do so, notify the member of his decision and, if he thinks fit, of the reasons for it: s 37E(2) (as so added).

950. Appointment of inspectors to investigate financial affairs of trade union.

The certification officer[1] may appoint one or more members of his staff or other persons as an inspector or inspectors to investigate the financial affairs[2] of a trade union[3] and to report on them in such a manner as he may direct[4]. The certification officer may only make such an appointment if it appears to him that there are circumstances suggesting:

(1)　that the financial affairs of the trade union are being or have been conducted for a fraudulent or unlawful purpose;

(2)　that persons concerned with the management of those financial affairs have, in connection with that management, been guilty of fraud, misfeasance or other misconduct;

(3)　that the trade union has failed to comply with any duty imposed on it[5] in relation to its financial affairs; or

(4)　that a rule[6] of the union relating to its financial affairs has not been complied with[7].

The certification officer must consider whether it is appropriate for him to exercise any of the powers conferred on him by the above provisions where:

(a)　a report[8] of the auditor or auditors[9] of a trade union, or a branch or section of a trade union, on the accounts audited by him or them and contained in the annual return[10] of the union, or branch or section[11], does not state without qualification that the accounts give a true and fair view of the matters to which they relate, or includes a statement in compliance with the statutory requirements[12] that, in the opinion of the auditor or auditors, the union has failed to comply with its statutory duty to keep proper accounting records[13] or that the accounts do not agree with the accounting records[14]; or

(b) a member of a trade union has complained to the certification officer that there are circumstances suggesting the existence of any of the states of affairs specified in heads (1) to (4) above[15].

1 As to the certification officer see PARA 1443.
2 As to the meaning of 'financial affairs', in relation to a trade union, see PARA 944 note 14.
3 As to the meaning of 'trade union' see PARA 891. As to the application of the Trade Union and Labour Relations (Consolidation) Act 1992 ss 37B–37E (see the text and notes 1–2, 4–15; and PARAS 951, 952) to newly formed trade unions and federated trade unions see PARA 949 note 3.
4 Trade Union and Labour Relations (Consolidation) Act 1992 s 37B(1) (ss 37B, 37D, 37E added by the Trade Union Reform and Employment Rights Act 1993 s 10). The expenses of such an investigation, which may include such reasonable sums as the certification officer may determine in respect of general staff costs and overheads, must be defrayed in the first instance by the certification officer; but a person who is convicted on a prosecution instituted as a result of the investigation may in the same proceedings be ordered to pay the expenses of the investigation to such extent as may be specified in the order: Trade Union and Labour Relations (Consolidation) Act 1992 s 37D(1)–(3) (as so added). As to the investigation see further PARA 951; and as to the inspectors' reports see PARA 952.
5 Ie a duty imposed on it by the Trade Union and Labour Relations (Consolidation) Act 1992.
6 As to the meaning of 'rules', in relation to a trade union, see PARA 898 note 5.
7 Trade Union and Labour Relations (Consolidation) Act 1992 s 37B(2) (as added: see note 4).
8 As to the auditors' report see PARA 947.
9 As to the appointment of auditors see PARA 946.
10 As to the annual return see PARA 943.
11 As to the meaning of 'branch or section', in relation to a trade union, see PARA 898 note 5.
12 Ie under the Trade Union and Labour Relations (Consolidation) Act 1992 s 36(4): see PARA 947.
13 Ie under the Trade Union and Labour Relations (Consolidation) Act 1992 s 28: see PARA 940.
14 Trade Union and Labour Relations (Consolidation) Act 1992 s 37E(1)(a) (as added: see note 4).
15 Trade Union and Labour Relations (Consolidation) Act 1992 s 37E(1)(b) (as added: see note 4). If, in a case where a member of a trade union has so complained, the certification officer decides not to exercise any of the powers so conferred on him, he must, as soon as reasonably practicable after making a decision not to do so, notify the member of his decision and, if he thinks fit, of the reasons for it: s 37E(2) (as so added).

951. Investigations of trade union's financial affairs by inspectors. Where an inspector is, or inspectors are, appointed to investigate the affairs of a trade union[1] and to report on them[2], it is the duty of all persons who are or have been officials[3] or agents[4] of the trade union:

(1) to produce to the inspector or inspectors all relevant documents[5] which are in their possession;

(2) to attend before the inspector or inspectors when required to do so; and

(3) otherwise to give the inspector or inspectors all assistance in connection with the investigation which they are reasonably able to give[6].

Where any person[7] appears to the inspector or inspectors to be in possession of information relating to a matter which he considers, or they consider, to be relevant to the investigation, he or they may require that person:

(a) to produce to the inspector or inspectors any relevant documents relating to that matter;

(b) to attend before the inspector or inspectors; and

(c) otherwise to give all assistance in connection with the investigation which he is reasonably able to give;

and it is the duty of that person to comply with the requirement[8].

A person is not excused from providing such an explanation or making such a statement on the ground that to do so would tend to expose him to proceedings for an offence; but such an explanation or statement may only be used in evidence against the person by whom it is provided or made on a prosecution for the offence of providing or making a false explanation or statement[9], or on a prosecution for some other offence where, in giving evidence, the person makes a statement inconsistent with it[10].

Nothing in the above provisions requires or authorises anyone:

(i)   to require the disclosure by a person of information which he would be entitled to refuse to disclose in an action in the High Court on the grounds of legal professional privilege except, if he is a lawyer, the name and address of his client[11];

(ii)   to require the production by a person of a document which he would in such an action be entitled to refuse on such grounds[12];

(iii)   to require the disclosure of information or the production of documents in respect of which the person to whom the requirement would relate owes an obligation of confidence by virtue of carrying on the business of banking, unless the person to whom the obligation is owed is the trade union, or any branch or section[13] of the trade union, concerned or a trustee of any fund concerned, or the person to whom the obligation of confidence is owed consents to the disclosure or production[14].

1   As to the meaning of 'trade union' see PARA 891. As to the application of the Trade Union and Labour Relations (Consolidation) Act 1992 ss 37B–37E to newly formed trade unions and federated trade unions see PARA 949 note 3.

2   Ie under the Trade Union and Labour Relations (Consolidation) Act 1992 s 37B: see PARA 950.

3   As to the meaning of 'official', in relation to a trade union, see PARA 1018.

4   As to the meaning of 'agent', in relation to a trade union, see PARA 949 note 9.

5   For these purposes, 'relevant documents', in relation to an investigation of the financial affairs of a trade union, means accounting documents, and documents of any other description, which may be relevant to the investigation: Trade Union and Labour Relations (Consolidation) Act 1992 s 37B(5) (ss 37B, 37E added by the Trade Union Reform and Employment Rights Act 1993 s 10). See also PARA 949 note 5. As to the meaning of 'financial affairs', in relation to a trade union, see PARA 944 note 14.

6   Trade Union and Labour Relations (Consolidation) Act 1992 s 37B(3) (as added: see note 5).

7   Ie whether or not an officer or agent of the union within the Trade Union and Labour Relations (Consolidation) Act 1992 s 37B(3).

8   Trade Union and Labour Relations (Consolidation) Act 1992 s 37B(4) (as added: see note 5).

9   Ie under Trade Union and Labour Relations (Consolidation) Act 1992 s 45(9): see PARA 957.

10   Trade Union and Labour Relations (Consolidation) Act 1992 s 37B(6) (as added: see note 5).

11   Trade Union and Labour Relations (Consolidation) Act 1992 s 37E(3)(a) (as added: see note 5).

12   Trade Union and Labour Relations (Consolidation) Act 1992 s 37E(3)(b) (as added: see note 5).

13   As to the meaning of 'branch or section', in relation to a trade union, see PARA 898 note 5.

14   Trade Union and Labour Relations (Consolidation) Act 1992 s 37E(4) (as added: see note 5).

952. Inspectors' reports on trade union's financial affairs. An inspector or inspectors appointed to investigate the affairs of a trade union[1] and to report on them[2] may, and if so directed by the certification officer[3] must, make interim reports, and, on the conclusion of his or their investigation, must make a final report, to the certification officer[4].

An inspector or inspectors so appointed may at any time, and if so directed by the certification officer must, inform the certification officer of any matters coming to his or their knowledge as a result of the investigation[5]. The certification officer may direct an inspector or inspectors so appointed to take no further steps in the investigation, or to take only those further steps as are specified in the direction, if:

(1)   it appears to the certification officer that matters have come to light in

the course of the investigation which suggest that a criminal offence has been committed and those matters have been referred to the appropriate prosecuting authority; or

(2)   it appears to him appropriate to do so in any other circumstances[6];

but, where an investigation is the subject of such a direction, the inspector or inspectors must make a final report to the certification officer only where the certification officer directs him or them to do so at the time of such a direction or subsequently[7].

The certification officer must publish a final report so made to him[8]; and he must furnish a copy of that report free of charge to:

(a)   the trade union which is the subject of the report;

(b)   any auditor[9] of that trade union or of any branch or section[10] of the union, if he requests a copy before the end of the period of three years beginning with the day on which the report is published; and

(c)   any member of the trade union if:

  (i)   he has complained to the certification officer that there are circumstances suggesting the existence of certain specified states of affairs[11];

  (ii)   the certification officer considers that the report contains findings which are relevant to the complaint; and

  (iii)   the member requests a copy before the end of the period of three years beginning with the day on which the report is published[12].

A copy of any such report, certified by the certification officer to be a true copy[13], is admissible in any legal proceedings as evidence of the opinion of the inspector or inspectors in relation to any matter contained in the report[14].

1   As to the meaning of 'trade union' see PARA 891. As to the application of these provisions to newly formed trade unions and federated trade unions see PARA 949 note 3.
2   Ie under the Trade Union and Labour Relations (Consolidation) Act 1992 s 37B: see PARA 950. As to their investigations see PARA 951.
3   As to the certification officer see PARA 1443.
4   Trade Union and Labour Relations (Consolidation) Act 1992 s 37C(1) (s 37C added by the Trade Union Reform and Employment Rights Act 1993 s 10). Any such report must be written or printed, as the certification officer directs: Trade Union and Labour Relations (Consolidation) Act 1992 s 37C(2) (as so added).
5   Trade Union and Labour Relations (Consolidation) Act 1992 s 37C(3) (as added: see note 4).
6   Trade Union and Labour Relations (Consolidation) Act 1992 s 37C(4) (as added: see note 4).
7   Trade Union and Labour Relations (Consolidation) Act 1992 s 37C(5) (as added: see note 4).
8   Trade Union and Labour Relations (Consolidation) Act 1992 s 37C(6) (as added: see note 4).
9   As to the appointment of auditors see PARA 946.
10   As to the meaning of 'branch or section', in relation to a trade union, see PARA 898 note 5.
11   Ie any of the states of affairs specified in the Trade Union and Labour Relations (Consolidation) Act 1992 s 37B(2)(a)–(d): see PARA 950 heads (1)–(4).
12   Trade Union and Labour Relations (Consolidation) Act 1992 s 37C(7) (as added: see note 4).
13   A document purporting to be such a certificate of the certification officer is to be received in evidence and is deemed to be such a certificate unless the contrary is proved: Trade Union and Labour Relations (Consolidation) Act 1992 s 37C(8) (as added: see note 4).
14   Trade Union and Labour Relations (Consolidation) Act 1992 s 37C(8) (as added: see note 4).

(v) Members' Superannuation Schemes

953.   Maintenance of separate funds. A 'members' superannuation scheme' means any scheme or arrangement made by or on behalf of a trade union[1], including a scheme or arrangement shown in the rules[2] of the union, in so far as it provides:

(1)   for benefits to be paid by way of pension, including any widows' or

children's pensions or dependants' pensions, to or in respect of members or former members of the trade union; and

(2)   for those benefits to be so paid either out of the funds of the union or under an insurance scheme maintained out of those funds[3].

A trade union may not maintain a members' superannuation scheme unless it maintains a separate fund[4] for the payment of benefits in accordance with the scheme[5].

1   As to the meaning of 'trade union' see PARA 891. The provisions of the Trade Union and Labour Relations (Consolidation) Act 1992 ss 38–42 (see the text and notes 2–5; and PARAS 954, 955) do not apply to a trade union which has been in existence for less than 12 months (s 43(1)(c)); or to a federated trade union which consists wholly or mainly of representatives of constituent or affiliated organisations (see s 118(4)(d); and PARA 891 note 9 head (2)). As to the meaning of 'federated trade union' see PARA 891.
    Where a trade union consists of or includes branches or sections: (1) any duty falling on the union in relation to a branch or section under the provisions of ss 38–42 is to be treated as discharged to the extent to which a branch or section discharges it instead of the union (s 44(1), (2)); and (2) any such duty falling on a branch or section by reason of its being a trade union under ss 38–42 is to be treated as discharged to the extent to which the union of which it is a branch or section discharges the duty instead of it (s 44(4)). As to the meaning of 'branch or section', in relation to a trade union, see PARA 898 note 5.
2   As to the meaning of 'rules', in relation to a trade union, see PARA 898 note 5.
3   Trade Union and Labour Relations (Consolidation) Act 1992 s 38(1).
4   For these purposes, a 'separate fund' means a fund separate from the general funds of the trade union: Trade Union and Labour Relations (Consolidation) Act 1992 s 38(2).
5   Trade Union and Labour Relations (Consolidation) Act 1992 s 38(2). If a trade union refuses or wilfully neglects to perform a duty imposed on it by or under s 38, it commits an offence: see s 45(1); and PARA 956.

954.   Examination of proposals for new scheme.   A trade union[1] may not begin to maintain a members' superannuation scheme[2] unless, before the date on which the scheme begins to be maintained:

(1)   the proposals for the scheme have been examined by an appropriately qualified actuary[3]; and

(2)   a copy of a report made to the trade union by the actuary on the results of his examination of the proposals, signed by the actuary, has been sent to the certification officer[4];

and a copy of the actuary's report must, on the application of any of the union's members, be supplied to him free of charge[5].

The actuary's report must state:

(a)   whether, in his opinion, the premium or contribution rates will be adequate;

(b)   whether the accounting or funding arrangements are suitable; and

(c)   whether, in his opinion, the fund for the payment of benefits will be adequate[6].

On the application of a trade union, the certification officer may exempt a members' superannuation scheme which the union proposes to maintain from the requirement for examination of a new scheme[7] if he is satisfied that, by reason of the small number of members to which the scheme is applicable or for any other special reasons, it is unnecessary for the scheme to be so examined[8]. An exemption may be revoked if it appears to the certification officer that the circumstances by reason of which it was granted have ceased to exist[9].

1   As to the meaning of 'trade union' see PARA 891. As to the application of these provisions to newly formed trade unions, federated trade unions and unions which consist of branches or sections see PARA 953 note 1.
2   As to the meaning of 'members' superannuation scheme' see PARA 953.

3   For these purposes, and for the purposes of the Trade Union and Labour Relations (Consolidation) Act 1992 s 40 (see PARA 955), 'appropriately qualified actuary' means a person who is either a Fellow of the Institute of Actuaries or a Fellow of the Faculty of Actuaries, or is approved by the certification officer on the application of the trade union as a person having actuarial knowledge: s 42. As to the certification officer see PARA 1443.

4   Trade Union and Labour Relations (Consolidation) Act 1992 s 39(1). If a trade union refuses or wilfully neglects to perform a duty imposed on it by or under s 39, it commits an offence: see s 45(1); and PARA 956.

5   Trade Union and Labour Relations (Consolidation) Act 1992 s 39(3).

6   Trade Union and Labour Relations (Consolidation) Act 1992 s 39(2).

7   Ie pursuant to the Trade Union and Labour Relations (Consolidation) Act 1992 s 39.

8   Trade Union and Labour Relations (Consolidation) Act 1992 s 41(1)(a).

9   Trade Union and Labour Relations (Consolidation) Act 1992 s 41(2).

955.   Periodical re-examination of existing schemes.   Where a trade union[1] maintains a members' superannuation scheme[2], it must arrange for the scheme to be examined periodically by an appropriately qualified actuary[3] and for a report to be made to it by the actuary on the results of his examination[4]. The examination must:

(1)   be of the scheme as it has effect at such date as the trade union may determine, not being more than five years[5] after the date by reference to which the last examination, or, as the case may be, the examination of the proposals for the scheme, was carried out[6];

(2)   include a valuation, as at the date by reference to which the examination is carried out, of the assets comprised in the fund maintained for the payment of benefits and of the liabilities falling to be discharged out of it[7];

and the actuary's report must state:

(a)   whether in his opinion the premium or contribution rates are adequate;

(b)   whether the accounting or funding arrangements are suitable; and

(c)   whether in his opinion the fund for the payment of benefits is adequate[8].

A copy of the report, signed by the actuary, must be sent to the certification officer[9]; and the trade union must make such arrangements as will enable the report to be sent to the certification officer within a year of the date by reference to which the examination was carried out[10]. A copy of the actuary's report must also be supplied free of charge to any member of the union, on his application[11].

On the application of a trade union, the certification officer may exempt a members' superannuation scheme which the union maintains from the requirement for periodical re-examination[12] if he is satisfied that, by reason of the small number of members to which the scheme is applicable or for any other special reasons, it is unnecessary for the scheme to be so examined[13]. An exemption may be revoked if it appears to the certification officer that the circumstances by reason of which it was granted have ceased to exist[14], in which case the date as at which the next periodical re-examination must be carried out is such date as he may direct[15].

1   As to the meaning of 'trade union' see PARA 891. As to the application of these provisions to newly formed trade unions, federated trade unions and unions which consist of branches or sections see PARA 953 note 1.

2   As to the meaning of 'members' superannuation scheme' see PARA 953.

3   As to the meaning of 'appropriately qualified actuary' see PARA 954 note 3.

4   Trade Union and Labour Relations (Consolidation) Act 1992 s 40(1). If a trade union refuses or wilfully neglects to perform a duty imposed on it by or under s 40, it commits an offence: see s 45(1); and PARA 956.

5 The certification officer may in any case direct that the Trade Union and Labour Relations (Consolidation) Act 1992 s 40 is to apply to a trade union with the substitution for the reference to five years of a reference to such shorter period as may be specified in the direction: s 41(4). As to the certification officer see PARA 1443.
6 Trade Union and Labour Relations (Consolidation) Act 1992 s 40(2).
7 Trade Union and Labour Relations (Consolidation) Act 1992 s 40(3).
8 Trade Union and Labour Relations (Consolidation) Act 1992 s 40(4).
9 Trade Union and Labour Relations (Consolidation) Act 1992 s 40(5).
10 Trade Union and Labour Relations (Consolidation) Act 1992 s 40(6).
11 Trade Union and Labour Relations (Consolidation) Act 1992 s 40(7).
12 Ie pursuant to the Trade Union and Labour Relations (Consolidation) Act 1992 s 40.
13 Trade Union and Labour Relations (Consolidation) Act 1992 s 41(1)(b).
14 Trade Union and Labour Relations (Consolidation) Act 1992 s 41(2).
15 Trade Union and Labour Relations (Consolidation) Act 1992 s 41(3) (amended by the Employment Relations Act 2004 Sch 1 para 4).

(vi) Offences and Penalties with regard to Administration

956. Breaches of certain administrative duties. If a trade union[1] refuses or wilfully neglects to perform a duty imposed on it by or under certain statutory provisions relating to:
(1) the duty to supply a copy of the rules[2];
(2) accounting records[3];
(3) the annual return, statement for members, accounts and audit[4]; and
(4) members' superannuation schemes[5],
it commits an offence[6] and is liable on summary conviction to a fine not exceeding level 5 on the standard scale[7].

Any such offence is deemed to have been also committed by:
(a) every officer[8] of the trade union who is bound by the rules of the union to discharge on its behalf the relevant duty breach of which constitutes the offence; or
(b) if there is no such officer, every member of the general committee of management of the union[9];
and, in any proceedings so brought against such an officer or member in respect of a breach of duty, it is a defence for him to prove that he had reasonable cause to believe, and did believe, that some other person who was competent to discharge that duty was authorised to discharge it instead of him and had discharged it or would do so[10].

A person who wilfully alters or causes to be altered a document which is required for the purposes of any of the statutory provisions mentioned in heads (1) to (4) above with intent to falsify the document or to enable a trade union to evade any of those provisions commits an offence[11] and is liable on summary conviction to imprisonment for a term not exceeding six months or a fine not exceeding level 5 on the standard scale, or to both[12].

1 As to the meaning of 'trade union' see PARA 891.
2 Ie the Trade Union and Labour Relations (Consolidation) Act 1992 s 27: see PARA 912. As to the meaning of 'rules', in relation to a trade union, see PARA 898 note 5.
3 Ie under the Trade Union and Labour Relations (Consolidation) Act 1992 ss 28–30: see PARAS 940–941.
4 Ie under the Trade Union and Labour Relations (Consolidation) Act 1992 ss 32–37: see PARA 943 et seq.
5 Ie under the Trade Union and Labour Relations (Consolidation) Act 1992 ss 38–42: see PARAS 953–955.
6 Trade Union and Labour Relations (Consolidation) Act 1992 s 45(1) (amended by the Trade Union Reform and Employment Rights Act 1993 Sch 8 para 45). Proceedings for an offence under the Trade Union and Labour Relations (Consolidation) Act 1992 s 45(1) relating to the

duty to send an annual return to the certification officer under s 32 (see PARA 943) may be commenced at any time before the end of the period of three years beginning with the date when the offence was committed: s 45A(2) (s 45A added by the Trade Union Reform and Employment Rights Act 1993 s 11(2)). Proceedings for any other offence under the Trade Union and Labour Relations (Consolidation) Act 1992 s 45(1) may be commenced: (1) at any time before the end of the period of six months beginning with the date when the offence was committed; or (2) at any time after the end of that period but before the end of the period of 12 months beginning with the date when evidence sufficient in the opinion of the certification officer to justify the proceedings came to his knowledge; but no proceedings may be commenced by virtue of head (2) above after the end of the period of three years beginning with the date when the offence was committed: s 45A(3) (as so added). For the purposes of head (2) above, a certificate signed by or on behalf of the certification officer which states the date on which evidence sufficient in his opinion to justify the proceedings came to his knowledge is conclusive evidence of that fact (s 45A(4) (as so added)); and a certificate stating that matter and purporting to be so signed is deemed to be so signed unless the contrary is proved (s 45A(5) (as so added)). Proceedings are commenced for these purposes when an information is laid: s 45A(6)(a) (as so added).

7 Trade Union and Labour Relations (Consolidation) Act 1992 s 45A(1)(a) (as added: see note 6). As to the standard scale see SENTENCING AND DISPOSITION OF OFFENDERS vol 92 (2010) PARA 142.
8 As to the meaning of 'officer', in relation to a trade union, see PARA 902 note 7.
9 Trade Union and Labour Relations (Consolidation) Act 1992 s 45(2).
10 Trade Union and Labour Relations (Consolidation) Act 1992 s 45(3).
11 Trade Union and Labour Relations (Consolidation) Act 1992 s 45(4).
12 Trade Union and Labour Relations (Consolidation) Act 1992 s 45A(1)(b) (as added: see note 6).

957. Offences relating to financial investigations. If a person contravenes any duty or requirement imposed under the statutory provisions relating to the production of documents[1] or investigations by inspectors[2], he commits an offence[3] and is liable on summary conviction to a fine not exceeding level 5 on the standard scale[4].

Further, if a person, in purported compliance with a duty or requirement so imposed[5] to provide an explanation or make a statement:

(1) provides or makes an explanation or statement which he knows to be false in a material particular; or

(2) recklessly provides or makes an explanation or statement which is false in a material particular,

he commits an offence[6] and is liable on summary conviction to imprisonment for a term not exceeding six months or a fine not exceeding level 5 on the standard scale, or to both[7].

In any proceedings brought against a person in respect of a contravention of a requirement imposed[8] to produce documents it is, however, a defence for him to prove that the documents were not in his possession and that it was not reasonably practicable for him to comply with the requirement[9].

If an official[10] or agent[11] of a trade union[12]:

(a) destroys, mutilates or falsifies, or is privy to the destruction, mutilation or falsification of, a document relating to the financial affairs[13] of the trade union, or makes, or is privy to the making of, a false entry in any such document, he commits an offence unless he proves that he had no intention to conceal the financial affairs of the trade union or to defeat the law[14];

(b) fraudulently parts with, alters or deletes anything in any such document, or is privy to the fraudulent parting with, fraudulent alteration of or fraudulent deletion in, any such document, he commits an offence[15];

and, in either case, he is liable on summary conviction to imprisonment for a term not exceeding six months or a fine not exceeding level 5 on the standard scale, or to both[16].

1   Ie under the Trade Union and Labour Relations (Consolidation) Act 1992 s 37A: see PARA 949.
    As to the meaning of 'contravention' and cognate expressions see PARA 915 note 6.
2   Ie under the Trade Union and Labour Relations (Consolidation) Act 1992 s 37B: see PARAS 950,
    951.
3   Trade Union and Labour Relations (Consolidation) Act 1992 s 45(5) (s 45(5) substituted and
    s 45(6)–(9) added by the Trade Union Reform and Employment Rights Act 1993 s 11(1)).
4   Trade Union and Labour Relations (Consolidation) Act 1992 s 45A(1)(a) (s 45A added by the
    Trade Union Reform and Employment Rights Act 1993 s 11(2)). As to the standard scale see
    SENTENCING AND DISPOSITION OF OFFENDERS vol 92 (2010) PARA 142.
5   Ie under the Trade Union and Labour Relations (Consolidation) Act 1992 s 37A or s 37B.
6   Trade Union and Labour Relations (Consolidation) Act 1992 s 45(9) (as added: see note 3).
7   Trade Union and Labour Relations (Consolidation) Act 1992 s 45A(1)(b) (as added: see note 4).
8   Ie under the Trade Union and Labour Relations (Consolidation) Act 1992 s 37A(3) (see PARA
    949 note 6) or s 37B(4) (see PARA 951).
9   Trade Union and Labour Relations (Consolidation) Act 1992 s 45(6) (as added: see note 3).
10 As to the meaning of 'official', in relation to a trade union, see PARA 1018.
11 As to the meaning of 'agent', in relation to a trade union, see PARA 949 note 9.
12 As to the meaning of 'trade union' see PARA 891.
13 As to the meaning of 'financial affairs', in relation to a trade union, see PARA 944 note 14.
14 Trade Union and Labour Relations (Consolidation) Act 1992 s 45(7) (as added: see note 3).
15 Trade Union and Labour Relations (Consolidation) Act 1992 s 45(8) (as added: see note 3).
16 Trade Union and Labour Relations (Consolidation) Act 1992 s 45A(1)(b) (as added: see note 4).

958. Disqualification of offenders. A trade union[1] must secure that a person does not at any time hold one of the following positions[2] in the union if, within a specified period[3] immediately preceding that time, he has been convicted of an offence[4] under certain statutory provisions[5]. The positions are:

(1)   member of the executive[6];
(2)   any position by virtue of which a person is a member of the executive;
(3)   president[7]; and
(4)   general secretary[8].

The statutory disqualification does not, however, apply to the position of president or general secretary if the holder of that position is not, in respect of that position, either a voting member of the executive[9] or an employee[10] of the union, holds that position for a period which under the rules of the union cannot end more than 13 months after he took it up and has not held either position at any time in the period of 12 months ending with the day before he took up that position[11].

A member of a trade union who claims that the union has failed to comply with the above requirements in relation to the disqualification of offenders may apply to the certification officer[12] or to the High Court for a declaration to that effect[13]. On an application being made to him, the certification officer:

(a)   must make such inquiries as he thinks fit[14];
(b)   must give the applicant and the trade union an opportunity to be heard[15];
(c)   must ensure that, so far as is reasonably practicable, the application is determined within six months of being made[16];
(d)   may make or refuse the declaration asked for[17]; and
(e)   must give reasons for his decision in writing, whether he makes or refuses the declaration[18].

Where the certification officer makes a declaration, he must also, unless he considers that it would be inappropriate, make an order imposing on the trade union a requirement to take within such period as may be specified in the order such steps to remedy the declared failure as may be so specified[19]. If a person applies to the certification officer[20] in relation to an alleged failure:

(i)   that person may not apply to the court in relation to that failure;
(ii)   on an application by a different person to the court in relation to that failure, the court must have due regard to any declaration, order, observations or reasons made or given by the certification officer regarding that failure and brought to the court's notice[21].

Where the court makes a declaration, it must also, unless it considers that it would be inappropriate to do so, make an order imposing on the trade union a requirement to take within any specified period such steps to remedy the declared failure as may be specified in the order[22]. If a person applies to the court in relation to an alleged failure[23]:

(A)   that person may not apply to the certification officer in relation to that failure;
(B)   on an application by a different person to the certification officer in relation to that failure, the certification officer must have due regard to any declaration, order, observations or reasons made or given by the court regarding that failure and brought to the certification officer's notice[24].

Where an order has been made by the court or the certification officer[25], any person who is a member of the trade union and was a member at the time the order was made is entitled to enforce the order as if he had made the application on which the order was made[26].

1   As to the meaning of 'trade union' see PARA 891.
2   Ie a position to which the Trade Union and Labour Relations (Consolidation) Act 1992 s 45B applies: see the text and notes. As to the application of ss 45B, 45C to special register bodies see PARA 899 note 8 head (5).
3   Ie within the period of five years in the case of a conviction for an offence under the Trade Union and Labour Relations (Consolidation) Act 1992 s 45(1) (see PARA 956) or s 45(5) (see PARA 957), or within the period of ten years in the case of a conviction for an offence under s 45(4) (see PARA 956) or s 45(7), (8) or (9) (see PARA 957).
4   Ie under the Trade Union and Labour Relations (Consolidation) Act 1992 s 45: see PARAS 956, 957.
5   Trade Union and Labour Relations (Consolidation) Act 1992 s 45B(1) (ss 45B, 45C added by the Trade Union Reform and Employment Rights Act 1993 s 12).
6   As to the meaning of 'executive', in relation to a trade union, see PARA 943 note 9. For these purposes, 'member of the executive' includes any person who, under the rules or practice of the union, may attend and speak at some or all of the meetings of the executive, otherwise than for the purpose of providing the committee with practical information or with technical or professional advice with respect to matters taken into account by the executive in carrying out its functions: Trade Union and Labour Relations (Consolidation) Act 1992 s 45B(3) (as added: see note 5). As to the meaning of 'rules', in relation to a trade union, see PARA 898 note 5.
7   As to the meaning of 'president', in relation to a trade union, see PARA 921 note 3.
8   Trade Union and Labour Relations (Consolidation) Act 1992 s 45B(2) (as added: see note 5). As to the meaning of 'general secretary', in relation to a trade union, see PARA 921 note 3.
9   For these purposes, a 'voting member of the executive' means a person entitled in his own right to attend meetings of the executive and to vote on matters on which votes are taken by the executive, whether or not he is entitled to attend all such meetings or to vote on all such matters or in all circumstances: Trade Union and Labour Relations (Consolidation) Act 1992 s 45B(5) (as added: see note 5).
10 As to the meaning of 'employee' see PARA 892.
11 Trade Union and Labour Relations (Consolidation) Act 1992 s 45B(4) (as added: see note 5).
12 As to the certification officer see PARA 1443. An appeal lies to the Employment Appeal Tribunal on any question of law arising in proceedings before or arising from any decision of the certification officer under the Trade Union and Labour Relations (Consolidation) Act 1992 s 45C: s 45D (added by Employment Relations Act 1999 Sch 6 paras 1, 8). As to the Employment Appeal Tribunal see PARA 1422 et seq.
13 Trade Union and Labour Relations (Consolidation) Act 1992 s 45C(1) (as added: see note 5); Trade Union and Labour Relations (Consolidation) Act 1992 s 121.

14 Trade Union and Labour Relations (Consolidation) Act 1992 s 45C(2)(aa) (added by the Employment Relations Act 1999 Sch 6 paras 1, 7(1), (2)). Where the certification officer requests a person to furnish information to him in connection with inquiries made by him under the Trade Union and Labour Relations (Consolidation) Act 1992 s 45C, he must specify the date by which that information is to be furnished and, unless he considers that it would be inappropriate to do so, must proceed with his determination of the application notwithstanding that the information has not been furnished to him by the specified date: s 45C(7) (s 45C(7)–(9) added by Employment Relations Act 1999 Sch 6 paras 1, 7(1), (7)).

15 Trade Union and Labour Relations (Consolidation) Act 1992 s 45C(2)(a) (as added (see note 5); amended by the Employment Relations Act 1999 Sch 6 paras 1, 7, Sch 9).

16 Trade Union and Labour Relations (Consolidation) Act 1992 s 45C(2)(b) (as added: see note 5).

17 Trade Union and Labour Relations (Consolidation) Act 1992 s 45C(2)(c) (as added: see note 5). A declaration made by the certification officer under s 45C may be relied on as if it were a declaration made by the court: s 45C(8) (as added: see note 14).

18 Trade Union and Labour Relations (Consolidation) Act 1992 s 45C(2)(d) (as added: see note 5).

19 Trade Union and Labour Relations (Consolidation) Act 1992 s 45C(5A) (s 45C(5A)–(5C) added by the Employment Relations Act 1999 Sch 6 paras 1, 7(1), (5)). An order made by the certification officer under the Trade Union and Labour Relations (Consolidation) Act 1992 s 45C may be enforced in the same way as an order of the court: s 45C(9) (as added: see note 14).

20 Ie under the Trade Union and Labour Relations (Consolidation) Act 1992 s 45C.

21 Trade Union and Labour Relations (Consolidation) Act 1992 s 45C(5B) (as added: see note 19).

22 Trade Union and Labour Relations (Consolidation) Act 1992 s 45C(5) (as added: see note 5).

23 See note 20.

24 Trade Union and Labour Relations (Consolidation) Act 1992 s 45C(5C) (as added: see note 19).

25 Ie under Trade Union and Labour Relations (Consolidation) Act 1992 s 45C(5) or (5A).

26 Trade Union and Labour Relations (Consolidation) Act 1992 s 45C(6) (as added (see note 5); amended by the Employment Relations Act 1999 Sch 6 paras 1, 7(1), (6)).

(5) TRADE UNION ELECTIONS

(i) Duty to Hold Trade Union Elections

959. Trade union elections in general. A trade union which wishes to hold an election for union office must comply with the rules of the union concerning the holding of such elections[1], although the court has a discretion not to declare an election invalid because of a minor irregularity[2]. Once the election is completed[3], a trade union has no power to cancel the election and order a fresh ballot, unless such a power is expressly conferred under its rules[4], or the whole election process is shown to be a nullity because it was not conducted in accordance with the rules[5]. A member of a trade union has no inherent right of access to union records to obtain information about the result of an election, save to the extent that such a right is conferred by the rules of the union[6].

1 *Burn v National Amalgamated Labourers' Union of Great Britain and Ireland* [1920] 2 Ch 364; *Leigh v National Union of Railwaymen* [1970] Ch 326, [1969] 3 All ER 1249. Cf *Breen v Amalgamated Engineering Union* [1971] 2 QB 175, [1971] 1 All ER 1148, CA. A rule may be incorporated by implication where necessary to give efficacy to the union's election rules: *AB v CD* [2001] IRLR 808, [2001] All ER (D) 354 (May). As to the appointment or election of union officials generally see PARA 1018; and as to the statutory duty to hold elections for certain positions see PARA 960 et seq.

2 *Brown v Amalgamated Union of Engineering Workers* [1976] ICR 147; *Hamlet v General Municipal Boilermakers and Allied Trades Union* [1987] 1 All ER 631, [1987] ICR 150.

3 See *Wise v Union of Shop, Distributive and Allied Workers* [1996] ICR 691, [1996] IRLR 609.

4 *Brown v Amalgamated Union of Engineering Workers* [1976] ICR 147 at 159; *Veness v National Union of Public Employees* [1992] ICR 193, [1991] IRLR 76; *Douglas v Graphical Paper and Media Union* [1995] IRLR 426; *Wise v Union of Shop, Distributive and Allied Workers* [1996] ICR 691, [1996] IRLR 609.

5   Douglas v Graphical Paper and Media Union [1995] IRLR 426; AB v CD [2001] IRLR 808, [2001] All ER (D) 354 (May).
6   Hughes v Transport and General Workers' Union [1985] IRLR 382.

960. Statutory duty to hold elections for certain positions. A trade union[1] must secure that every person who holds one of the specified positions[2] in the union does so by virtue of having been elected to it at an election satisfying specified statutory requirements[3], and that no person continues to hold such a position for more than five years without being re-elected at such an election[4]. The specified positions are:

(1)   member of the executive[5];

(2)   any position by virtue of which a person is a member of the executive;

(3)   president[6]; and

(4)   general secretary[7].

The statutory duty to hold elections for certain positions does not, however, apply to the position of president or general secretary if the holder of that position:

(a)   is not, in respect of that position, either a voting member of the executive[8] or an employee[9] of the union;

(b)   holds that position for a period which under the rules of the union cannot end more than 13 months after he took it up; and

(c)   has not held either position at any time in the period of 12 months ending with the day before he took up that position[10].

The statutory duty to hold elections for certain positions also does not apply to the position of president if:

(i)   the holder of that position was elected or appointed to it in accordance with the rules of the union;

(ii)   at the time of his election or appointment as president he held a position mentioned in head (1), head (2) or head (4) above by virtue of having been elected to it at a qualifying election[11];

(iii) it is no more than five years since he was elected, or re-elected, to that position, which he held at the time of his election or appointment as president; or he was elected to another position of the kind mentioned in head (ii) above at a qualifying election held after his election or appointment as president of the union; and

(iv)   he has, at all times since his election or appointment as president, held a position mentioned in head (1), head (2) or head (4) above by virtue of having been elected to it at a qualifying election[12].

The requirement of re-election does not apply to a person holding a position to which the statutory requirements apply and who is nearing retirement if certain conditions are satisfied[13]. The conditions are that:

(A)   he holds the position by virtue of having been elected at an election in relation to which the statutory requirements[14] were satisfied;

(B)   he is a full-time employee of the union by virtue of the position;

(C)   he will reach retirement age[15] within five years;

(D)   he is entitled under the rules of the union to continue as the holder of the position until retirement age without standing for re-election;

(E)   he has been a full-time employee of the union for a period, which need not be continuous, of at least ten years; and

(F)   the period between the day on which his election took place and the day immediately preceding that on which he is within five years of reaching retirement age does not exceed five years[16].

The statutory requirements apply notwithstanding anything in the rules or practice of the union; and the terms and conditions on which a person is employed by the union are to be disregarded, in so far as they would prevent the union from complying with the statutory requirements[17]. Nothing in those requirements is, however, to be taken to require a ballot to be held at an uncontested election[18], or affects the validity of anything done by a person holding a position to which they apply[19].

1 As to the meaning of 'trade union' see PARA 891. As to the application of these provisions to newly formed trade unions and federated trade unions see PARA 968; and as to their application to special register bodies see PARA 899 note 8 head (5).

2 Ie a position to which the Trade Union and Labour Relations (Consolidation) Act 1992 Pt I Ch IV (ss 46–61) applies: see the text and notes 3–19; and PARA 961 et seq.

3 Ie the requirements of the Trade Union and Labour Relations (Consolidation) Act 1992 ss 47–52: see s 46(5B) (s 46(5A), (5B) added by the Employment Relations Act 2004 s 52(1), (5)). The statutory duty to hold trade union elections was introduced by the Trade Union Act 1984 s 8 (repealed), with effect from 1 October 1985, and initially applied only to voting members of the union's national executive committee. The Employment Act 1988 s 12 (repealed) extended the scope of the statutory requirements to cover non-voting members of the executive and also the position of president and general secretary, with effect from 26 July 1989; and that Act also introduced, with effect from 26 July 1988, a requirement to circulate election addresses and to hold a fully postal ballot (see ss 13, 14 (repealed)) and, with effect from 1 February 1989, a requirement of independent scrutiny (see s 15 (repealed)). The Employment Act 1990 required the ballot paper, with effect from 1 January 1991, to state the name of the independent scrutineer and the union to take steps to notify members of the name of the scrutineer (see s 5 (repealed)); and the Trade Union Reform and Employment Rights Act 1993 required the scrutineer to check the union's register of members, introduced a requirement for votes to be counted by an independent person, and made provision for the confidentiality of the register: see ss 1, 2, 5. Unless otherwise stated, an election will be valid for present purposes if it satisfied the statutory balloting requirements in force at the date of the election: see the Trade Union and Labour Relations (Consolidation) Act 1992 Sch 3 para 9. However, whilst the transitional provisions state that the statutory election requirements do not apply to a person who was, within the period of five years ending with 25 July 1989, elected to a position to which the election requirements were extended by the Employment Act 1988 (see the Trade Union and Labour Relations (Consolidation) Act 1992 Sch 3 para 9(1)), this does not apply if the only persons entitled to vote in the election were themselves members of the executive (see Sch 3 para 9(2)).

4 Trade Union and Labour Relations (Consolidation) Act 1992 s 46(1). As to the exemption of those nearing retirement see the text and notes 13–16.

Section 46 establishes the duty to hold elections for the positions specified in s 46(2) (see the text and notes 5–7, and the following provisions of Pt I Ch IV are by way of amplification of that duty. The provisions of Pt I Ch IV apply, and apply only, to the process of election that arises once candidates have been nominated for election, and they do not apply to the processes which precede nomination, even if those processes may involve a vote. That conclusion follows from the structure of the group of sections as a whole but is reinforced by consideration of the detailed provisions and, moreover, by authority: *Scargill v National Union of Mineworkers* (2010) UKEAT/0407/09/RN at [35]–[37].

5 As to the meaning of 'executive', in relation to a trade union, see PARA 943 note 9. For the purposes of the Trade Union and Labour Relations (Consolidation) Act 1992 Pt I Ch IV, 'member of the executive' includes any person who, under the rules or practice of the union, may attend and speak at some or all of the meetings of the executive, otherwise than for the purpose of providing the committee with factual information or with technical or professional advice with respect to matters taken into account by the executive in carrying out its functions: s 46(3). As to the meaning of 'rules', in relation to a trade union, see PARA 898 note 5.

6 For the purposes of the Trade Union and Labour Relations (Consolidation) Act 1992 Pt I Ch IV, 'president' means the official of the union who holds the office of president or, where there is no such office, who holds an office which is equivalent to that of president: s 119. As to the meaning of 'official', in relation to a trade union, see PARA 1018.

7 Trade Union and Labour Relations (Consolidation) Act 1992 s 46(2) (amended by the Employment Relations Act 2004 s 52(1), (2), Sch 2). As to the meaning of 'general secretary', in relation to a trade union, see PARA 921 note 3. There can be a temporary gap if there is a good

explanation: see *Corrigan v GMB Union, GMB Union v Corrigan* [2008] ICR 197, [2007] All ER (D) 288 (Oct), EAT (postponement of election for general secretary was legitimate where inquiry was pending into allegations of electoral malpractice).

8   For the purposes of the Trade Union and Labour Relations (Consolidation) Act 1992 s 46(4), a 'voting member of the executive' means a person entitled in his own right to attend meetings of the executive and to vote on matters on which votes are taken by the executive, whether or not he is entitled to attend all such meetings or to vote on all such matters or in all circumstances: s 46(5) (amended by the Employment Relations Act 2004 s 52(1), (4)).

9   As to the meaning of 'employee' see PARA 892.

10 Trade Union and Labour Relations (Consolidation) Act 1992 s 46(4).

11 For these purposes, 'qualifying election' means an election satisfying the requirements of the Trade Union and Labour Relations (Consolidation) Act 1992 Pt I Ch IV; and the requirements referred to are those set out in ss 47–52: s 46(5A), (5B) (as added: see note 3).

12 Trade Union and Labour Relations (Consolidation) Act 1992 s 46(4A) (added by the Employment Relations Act 2004 s 52(1), (3)).

13 Trade Union and Labour Relations (Consolidation) Act 1992 s 58(1).

14 Ie the requirements contained in the Trade Union and Labour Relations (Consolidation) Act 1992 Pt I Ch IV. Where the election took place before 26 July 1989, the reference to satisfying the requirements of Pt I Ch IV is not to be construed as requiring compliance with any provision concerning election addresses or independent scrutiny which was not then in force; and, where the election took place before the coming into force of the requirement of postal ballots on 26 July 1988, that reference is to be construed as requiring compliance with the provisions of the Trade Union Act 1984 s 3 (repealed), which allowed for non-postal ballots in certain circumstances: see the Trade Union and Labour Relations (Consolidation) Act 1992 Sch 3 para 10.

15 For these purposes, 'retirement age', in relation to any person, means the earlier of: (1) the age fixed by, or in accordance with, the rules of the union for him to retire from the position in question; or (2) the age which is for the time being pensionable age within the meaning given by the rules in the Pensions Act 1995 Sch 4 para 1 (see WELFARE BENEFITS AND STATE PENSIONS vol 104 (2014) PARA 488): Trade Union and Labour Relations (Consolidation) Act 1992 s 58(3) (amended by the Pensions Act 1995 Sch 4 para 15).

16 Trade Union and Labour Relations (Consolidation) Act 1992 s 58(2). For the purposes of Pt I Ch IV, the date on which a contested election is held is to be taken, in the case of an election in which votes may be cast on more than one day, to be the last of those days: s 61(1).

17 Trade Union and Labour Relations (Consolidation) Act 1992 s 46(6).

18 Trade Union and Labour Relations (Consolidation) Act 1992 s 53.

19 Trade Union and Labour Relations (Consolidation) Act 1992 s 61(2).

(ii) Statutory Requirements with respect to Trade Union Elections

961.   Entitlement to vote in a trade union election. Entitlement to vote in an election to which the statutory provisions apply[1] must be accorded equally to all members of the trade union[2], save that the union may exclude or restrict the entitlement to vote in certain specified circumstances[3]. The rules[4] of the union may exclude entitlement to vote in the case of all members belonging to one of the following classes, or to a class falling within one of the following:

(1)   members who are not in employment;

(2)   members who are in arrears in respect of any subscription or contribution due to the union; and

(3)   members who are apprentices, trainees or students or new members of the union[5].

The rules of the union may restrict entitlement to vote to members who fall within:

(a)   a class determined by reference to a trade or occupation;

(b)   a class determined by reference to a geographical area;

(c)   a class which is, by virtue of the rules of the union, treated as a separate section within the union[6], or to members who fall within a class determined by reference to any combination of the factors mentioned in heads (a) to (c) above[7]; but entitlement may not be so restricted if the effect is that any member of the union is denied entitlement to vote at all elections held for the purposes of the statutory requirements[8] otherwise than by virtue of belonging to a class excluded in accordance with heads (1) to (3) above[9].

1   As to the scope of the statutory election requirements see PARA 960.
2   Trade Union and Labour Relations (Consolidation) Act 1992 s 50(1). As to the meaning of 'trade union' see PARA 891. As to the application of these provisions to newly formed trade unions and federated trade unions see PARA 968; and as to their application to special register bodies see PARA 899 note 8 head (5).
3   Ie the circumstances specified in the Trade Union and Labour Relations (Consolidation) Act 1992 s 50(2)–(4): see the text and notes 4–9. A union which has overseas members may choose whether or not to accord any of those members entitlement to vote: see PARA 970.
4   As to the meaning of 'rules', in relation to a trade union, see PARA 898 note 5.
5   Trade Union and Labour Relations (Consolidation) Act 1992 s 50(2).
6   The reference in the text to a section of the union includes a part of the union which is itself a trade union: Trade Union and Labour Relations (Consolidation) Act 1992 s 50(4).
7   Trade Union and Labour Relations (Consolidation) Act 1992 s 50(3).
8   Ie the requirements of the Trade Union and Labour Relations (Consolidation) Act 1992 Pt I Ch IV (ss 46–61): see PARAS 960, 962 et seq.
9   Trade Union and Labour Relations (Consolidation) Act 1992 s 50(4).

962. Conduct of the ballot in a trade union election. The method of voting in an election to which the statutory provisions apply[1] must be by the marking of a voting paper by the person voting[2]; and each voting paper must:

(1)   state the name of the independent scrutineer[3] and clearly specify the address to which, and the date by which, it is to be returned;

(2)   be given one of a series of consecutive whole numbers, every one of which is used in giving a different number in that series to each voting paper printed or otherwise produced for the purposes of the election; and

(3)   be marked with its number[4].

Every person who is entitled to vote at the election[5] must be allowed to do so without interference[6] from, or constraint imposed by, the union or any of its members, officials[7] or employees[8] and, so far as is reasonably practicable, must be enabled to do so without incurring any direct cost to himself[9]. So far as is reasonably practicable, every person who is entitled to vote at the election must:

(a)   have a voting paper sent to him by post[10] at his home address or another address which he has requested the trade union[11] in writing to treat as his postal address; and

(b)   must be given a convenient opportunity to vote by post[12].

The voting paper must either list the candidates at the election or be accompanied by a separate list of those candidates[13].

The trade union must ensure that the storage and distribution of the voting papers for the purposes of the election, and the counting of the votes cast in the election, are undertaken by one or more independent persons[14] appointed by the union[15]; and the ballot must be conducted so as to secure that, so far as is reasonably practicable, those voting do so in secret, and the votes given at the election are fairly and accurately counted[16].

The ballot must be so conducted as to secure that the result of the election is determined solely[17] by counting the number of votes cast directly for each candidate[18]; but nothing in that requirement is to be taken to prevent the system of voting used for the election being the single transferable vote[19].

1 As to the scope of the statutory election requirements see PARA 960.
2 Trade Union and Labour Relations (Consolidation) Act 1992 s 51(1). For an account of the amendments to the statutory balloting requirements since their introduction in the Trade Union Act 1984 (repealed) see PARA 960 note 3.
3 As to the independent scrutineer see PARA 966.
4 Trade Union and Labour Relations (Consolidation) Act 1992 s 51(2).
5 As to entitlement to vote see PARA 961.
6 This relates to intimidation or other physical interference rather than mere persuasion: *Paul v National and Local Government Officers' Association* [1987] IRLR 43 (no interference by including on the ballot paper a list of union branches supporting each candidate).
7 As to the meaning of 'official', in relation to a trade union, see PARA 1018.
8 As to the meaning of 'employee' see PARA 892.
9 Trade Union and Labour Relations (Consolidation) Act 1992 s 51(3). 'Cost' includes postage costs incurred in returning the ballot paper by post: *Paul v National and Local Government Officers' Association* [1987] IRLR 43.
10 Any enactment which requires or authorises a document or other thing to be sent by post, whether or not it makes any other provision in that respect, is not to be construed as limited to requiring or, as the case may be, authorising that thing to be sent by the postal system of the Post Office company: Postal Services Act 2000 Sch 8 para 1(1).
11 As to the meaning of 'trade union' see PARA 891. As to the application of these provisions to newly formed trade unions and federated trade unions see PARA 968; and as to their application to special register bodies see PARA 899 note 8 head (5).
12 Trade Union and Labour Relations (Consolidation) Act 1992 s 51(4).
13 Trade Union and Labour Relations (Consolidation) Act 1992 s 51(4)(a).
14 For these purposes, a person is an 'independent person' in relation to an election if: (1) he is the scrutineer; or (2) he is a person other than the scrutineer and the trade union has no grounds for believing either that he will carry out any functions conferred on him in relation to the election otherwise than competently or that his independence in relation to the union, or in relation to the election, might reasonably be called into question: Trade Union and Labour Relations (Consolidation) Act 1992 s 51A(2) (s 51A added by the Trade Union Reform and Employment Rights Act 1993 s 2(1)).
15 Trade Union and Labour Relations (Consolidation) Act 1992 s 51A(1) (as added: see note 14). An appointment of an independent person under these provisions must require the person appointed to carry out his functions so as to minimise the risk of any contravention of the requirements imposed by or under any enactment or the occurrence of any unfairness or malpractice: s 51A(3) (as so added). Further, the trade union must: (1) ensure that nothing in the terms of such an appointment is such as to make it reasonable for any person to call into question the independence of the person appointed in relation to the union; (2) ensure that a person so appointed duly carries out his functions and that there is no interference with his carrying out of those functions which would make it reasonable for any person to call into question his independence in relation to the union; and (3) comply with all reasonable requests made by a person so appointed for the purposes of, or in connection with, the carrying out of his functions: s 51A(6) (as so added). The duty of confidentiality as respects the register of members' names and addresses (see PARA 937) is incorporated in the appointment of an independent person under these provisions: s 51A(4) (as so added). Where the person appointed to undertake the counting of votes is not the scrutineer, his appointment must require him to send the voting papers back to the scrutineer as soon as reasonably practicable after the counting has been completed: s 51A(5) (as so added). As to the meaning of 'contravention' and cognate expressions see PARA 915 note 6.
16 Trade Union and Labour Relations (Consolidation) Act 1992 s 51(5). For these purposes, an inaccuracy in counting is to be disregarded if it is accidental and on a scale which could not affect the result of the election: s 51(5).
17 It seems that this requirement is not infringed by an electoral rule of the union interpreting the result of an election, as long as the only votes determining the outcome of the election are those directly cast by the individual members voting, and not those cast through any system of weighted voting, block voting or voting through the medium of an electoral college: *R v Certification Officer for Trade Unions and Employers' Associations, ex p Electrical Power Engineers' Association* [1990] ICR 682, [1990] IRLR 398, HL (decided under the scheme for state funding of ballots established under the Trade Union and Labour Relations (Consolidation) Act 1992 s 115 (repealed), which contained a similar requirement).
18 Trade Union and Labour Relations (Consolidation) Act 1992 s 51(6).
19 Trade Union and Labour Relations (Consolidation) Act 1992 s 51(7). For these purposes, 'single transferable vote' means a vote capable of being given so as to indicate the voter's order of

preference for the candidates and of being transferred to the next choice: (1) when it is not required to give a prior choice the necessary quota of votes; or (2) when, owing to the deficiency in the number of votes given for a prior choice, that choice is eliminated from the list of candidates: s 51(7).

963.   Means of voting in trade union ballots and elections.   The Secretary of State[1] may by order provide, in relation to any description of ballot or election authorised or required[2], that any ballot or election of that description is to be conducted by such one or more permissible means[3] as the responsible person[4] determines[5].

Such an order may:

(1)   include provision about the determinations that may be made by the responsible person, including provision requiring specified[6] factors to be taken into account, or specific criteria to be applied, in making a determination[7];

(2)   allow the determination of different means of voting for voters in different circumstances[8];

(3)   allow a determination to be such that voters have a choice of means of voting[9];

(4)   include supplemental, incidental and consequential provisions[10]; and

(5)   make different provision for different cases or circumstances[11].

The Secretary of State may not make an order[12] which provides that a means of voting is permissible for a description of ballot or election unless he considers:

(a)   that a ballot or election of that description conducted by that means could, if particular conditions were satisfied, meet the required standard[13]; and

(b)   that, in relation to any ballot or election of that description held after the order comes into force, the responsible person will not be permitted to determine that that means must or may be used by any voters unless he has taken specified factors into account or applied specified criteria[14].

1   As to the Secretary of State see PARA 5 note 21.
2   Ie authorised or required by the Trade Union and Labour Relations (Consolidation) Act 1992.
3   A 'permissible means' is a means of voting that the order provides is permissible for that description of ballot or election: Employment Relations Act 2004 s 54(2). The means that an order specifies as permissible means must, in the case of any description of ballot or election, include or consist of postal voting: s 54(5).
4   'Responsible person' means a person specified, or of a description specified, by the order: Employment Relations Act 2004 s 54(3).
5   Employment Relations Act 2004 s 54(1). The power to make such an order is exercisable by statutory instrument: s 54(8). No such order may be made unless a draft of the order has been laid before Parliament and approved by a resolution of each House: s 54(9). At the date at which this volume states the law, no such order had been made.
6   'Specified' means specified in an order under the Employment Relations Act 2004 s 54: s 54(13).
7   Employment Relations Act 2004 s 54(4)(a). In specifying in an order factors to be taken into account or criteria to be applied by the responsible person, the Secretary of State must have regard to the need for ballots and elections to meet the required standard: s 54(11). For the purposes of s 54(10), (11) a ballot or election meets the required standard if it is such that those entitled to vote have an opportunity to do so, votes are cast in secret, and the risk of any unfairness or malpractice is minimised: s 54(12).
8   Employment Relations Act 2004 s 54(4)(b).
9   Employment Relations Act 2004 s 54(4)(c).
10   Employment Relations Act 2004 s 54(6)(a).
11   Employment Relations Act 2004 s 54(6)(b). Such an order may also (1) modify the provisions of the Trade Union and Labour Relations (Consolidation) Act 1992; (2) exclude or apply, with or without modifications, any provision of the Trade Union and Labour Relations (Consolidation)

Act 1992; and (3) make provision as respects any ballot or election conducted by specified means which is similar to any provision of the Trade Union and Labour Relations (Consolidation) Act 1992 relating to ballots or elections: Employment Relations Act 2004 s 54(7).

12 Ie an order under the Employment Relations Act 2004 s 54.

13 Employment Relations Act 2004 s 54(10)(a).

14 Employment Relations Act 2004 s 54(10)(b).

964. Candidacy in trade union elections. No member of a trade union[1] may be unreasonably excluded from standing as a candidate in an election to which the statutory provisions apply[2]. A member is not to be taken to be unreasonably excluded from standing as a candidate if he is excluded on the ground that he belongs to a class of which all members are excluded by the rules of the union[3]; but a rule which provides for such a class to be determined by reference to whom the union chooses to exclude must be disregarded[4]. No candidate may be required, directly or indirectly, to be a member of a political party[5].

1 As to the meaning of 'trade union' see PARA 891. As to the application of these provisions to newly formed trade unions and federated trade unions see PARA 968; and as to their application to special register bodies see PARA 899 note 8 head (5).

2 Trade Union and Labour Relations (Consolidation) Act 1992 s 47(1). As to the scope of the statutory election requirements see PARA 960. This requirement was infringed by a procedure whereby an ordinary member had to be nominated by the central union council or a district council (*Paul v National and Local Government Officers' Association* [1987] IRLR 43); by a requirement that a person must have the confidence of the union's executive in order to stand as a candidate (*Ecclestone v National Union of Journalists* [1999] IRLR 166); and by the exclusion of a person under a precautionary suspension from standing (*Unison v Bakhsh and Staunton* (2009) UKEAT/0375/08/RN, UKEAT/0376/08/RN). It seems that this requirement cannot be evaded by declaring the election void under the rules of the union after the election has been held: *R v Certification Officer for Trade Unions and Employers' Associations, ex p Electrical Power Engineers' Association* [1990] ICR 682, [1990] IRLR 398, HL, per Lord Bridge of Harwich (cited in PARA 962 note 17). A union which fails to send information about the election and nomination process directly to all members may be held to have excluded a member from standing as a candidate: *Read v Musicians Union* [2001] 1 CL 208.

3 Trade Union and Labour Relations (Consolidation) Act 1992 s 47(3). As to the meaning of 'rules', in relation to a trade union, see PARA 898 note 5.

4 Trade Union and Labour Relations (Consolidation) Act 1992 s 47(3) proviso.

5 Trade Union and Labour Relations (Consolidation) Act 1992 s 47(2).

965. Election addresses. The trade union[1] must:

(1) provide every candidate[2] with an opportunity of preparing an election address in his own words and of submitting it to the union to be distributed to the persons accorded entitlement to vote in the election[3]; and

(2) secure that, so far as reasonably practicable, copies of every election address submitted to it in time[4] are distributed to each of those persons by post[5] along with the voting papers for the election[6].

The trade union may provide that election addresses submitted to it for distribution must not exceed such length, not being less than 100 words, as may be determined by the union, and may, as regards photographs and other matter not in words, incorporate only such matter as the union may determine[7].

The trade union must secure that:

(a) no modification of an election address submitted to it is made by any person in any copy of the address to be distributed except:
    (i) at the request or with the consent of the candidate; or
    (ii) where the modification is necessarily incidental to the method adopted for producing that copy[8];

(b)   the same method of producing copies is applied in the same way to every election address submitted and, so far as reasonably practicable, no such facility or information as would enable a candidate to gain any benefit from the method by which copies of the election addresses are produced, or the modifications which are necessarily incidental to that method, is provided to any candidate without being provided equally to all the others[9]; and

(c)   so far as reasonably practicable, the same facilities and restrictions with respect to the preparation, submission, length or modification of an election address, and with respect to the incorporation of photographs or other matter not in words, are provided or applied equally to each of the candidates[10].

The arrangements made by the trade union for the production of the copies to be so distributed must be such as to secure that none of the candidates is required to bear any of the expense of producing the copies[11]. No one other than the candidate himself incurs any civil or criminal liability in respect of the publication of a candidate's election address or of any copy required[12] to be made[13].

1   As to the meaning of 'trade union' see PARA 891. As to the application of these provisions to newly formed trade unions and federated trade unions see PARA 968; and as to their application to special register bodies see PARA 899 note 8 head (5).
2   Ie every candidate in an election to which the Trade Union and Labour Relations (Consolidation) Act 1992 Pt I Ch IV (ss 46–61) applies: see PARAS 960 et seq, 966 et seq. As to the scope of the statutory election requirements see PARA 960; and as to candidacy see PARA 964.
3   As to entitlement to vote in the election see PARA 961.
4   The trade union may determine the time by which an election address must be submitted to it for distribution, but that time must not be earlier than the latest time at which a person may become a candidate in the election: Trade Union and Labour Relations (Consolidation) Act 1992 s 48(2).
5   As to the construction of references to requiring or authorising a document or other thing to be sent by post see PARA 962 note 10.
6   Trade Union and Labour Relations (Consolidation) Act 1992 s 48(1).
7   Trade Union and Labour Relations (Consolidation) Act 1992 s 48(3).
8   Trade Union and Labour Relations (Consolidation) Act 1992 s 48(4).
9   Trade Union and Labour Relations (Consolidation) Act 1992 s 48(5).
10 Trade Union and Labour Relations (Consolidation) Act 1992 s 48(6).
11 Trade Union and Labour Relations (Consolidation) Act 1992 s 48(7).
12 Ie required by the Trade Union and Labour Relations (Consolidation) Act 1992 s 48.
13 Trade Union and Labour Relations (Consolidation) Act 1992 s 48(8).

966.   Appointment of independent scrutineer of trade union election.   Before the election is held[1], the trade union[2] must appoint a qualified independent person (the 'scrutineer') to carry out certain functions in relation to the election which are required[3] to be contained in his appointment, and such additional functions in relation to the election as may be specified in his appointment[4].

A person is a qualified independent person in relation to an election if:

(1)   he satisfies such conditions as may be specified for these purposes by order[5] of the Secretary of State or is himself so specified[6]; and

(2)   the trade union has no grounds for believing either that he will carry out his functions in relation to the election otherwise than competently or that his independence in relation to the union, or in relation to the election, might reasonably be called into question[7].

The scrutineer's appointment must require him:

(a)   to be the person who supervises the production of the voting papers and, unless he is appointed[8] to undertake the distribution of the voting papers, their distribution, and to whom the voting papers are returned by those voting[9];

(b) to inspect the register of names and addresses of the members of the trade union[10], or to examine the copy of the register which is supplied to him[11], whenever it appears to him appropriate to do so and, in particular, when certain conditions are satisfied[12];

(c) to take such steps as appear to him to be appropriate for the purpose of enabling him to make his report[13];

(d) to make his report to the union as soon as reasonably practicable after the last date for the return of voting papers[14]; and

(e) to retain custody of all voting papers returned for the purposes of the election, and the copy of the register supplied to him, until the end of the period of one year beginning with the announcement by the union of the result of the election[15].

The trade union must ensure that nothing in the terms of the scrutineer's appointment, including any additional functions specified in it, is such as to make it reasonable for any person to call his independence in relation to the union into question[16].

Before the scrutineer begins to carry out his functions, the trade union must either:

(i) send a notice stating the name of the scrutineer to every member of the union to whom it is reasonably practicable to send such a notice; or

(ii) take all such other steps for notifying members of the name of the scrutineer as it is the practice of the union to take when matters of general interest to all its members need to be brought to their attention[17].

The trade union must also (A) supply to the scrutineer, as soon as is reasonably practicable after the relevant date, a copy of the register of members' names and addresses as at that date; and (B) comply with any request made by the scrutineer to inspect the register[18].

The trade union must ensure that the scrutineer duly carries out his functions and that there is no interference with his carrying out of those functions which would make it reasonable for any person to call his independence in relation to the union into question[19]; and the trade union must comply with all reasonable requests made by the scrutineer for the purposes of, or in connection with, the carrying out of his functions[20].

1 Ie an election to which the Trade Union and Labour Relations (Consolidation) Act 1992 Pt I Ch IV (ss 46–61) applies: see PARA 960 et seq.

2 As to the meaning of 'trade union' see PARA 891. As to the application of these provisions to newly formed trade unions and federated trade unions see PARA 968; and as to their application to special register bodies see PARA 899 note 8 head (5).

3 Ie under the Trade Union and Labour Relations (Consolidation) Act 1992 s 49: see the text and notes 1–2, 4–20.

4 Trade Union and Labour Relations (Consolidation) Act 1992 s 49(1). The appointment must be a specific event and relate to a specific election: *Read v Musicians Union* [2001] 1 CL 208.

5 Such an order must be made by statutory instrument which is subject to annulment in pursuance of a resolution of either House of Parliament: Trade Union and Labour Relations (Consolidation) Act 1992 s 49(2). Partly in exercise of the power so conferred, the Secretary of State made the Trade Union Ballots and Elections (Independent Scrutineer Qualifications) Order 1993, SI 1993/1909, which came into force on 30 August 1993: art 1(1).

An individual satisfies the condition specified for the purposes of the Trade Union and Labour Relations (Consolidation) Act 1992 s 49(2)(a), s 75(2)(a) (see PARA 979), s 100A(2)(a) (see PARA 1004) and s 226B(2)(a) (see PARA 1373) in relation to an election if: (1) he has in force a practising certificate issued by the Law Society of England and Wales or the Law Society of Scotland and he is not disqualified from satisfying the condition by virtue of the Trade Union Ballots and Elections (Independent Scrutineer Qualifications) Order 1993, SI 1993/1909, art 5 (arts 1(2), 2, 3); or (2) he is qualified to be an auditor of a trade union by virtue of the Trade Union and Labour Relations (Consolidation) Act 1992 s 34(1) (see PARA 945) and he is not disqualified by virtue of the Trade Union Ballots and Elections (Independent Scrutineer Qualifications) Order 1993, SI 1993/1909, art 5 (arts 1(2), 2, 4); and a partnership satisfies the specified condition if every member of the partnership is an individual potentially qualified to be a scrutineer and no member of the partnership is disqualified from being a scrutineer by virtue of art 5 (art 6). An individual potentially so qualified to be a scrutineer does not, however, satisfy the condition specified in head (1) or head (2) above if he or any existing partner of his: (a) has during the preceding 12 months been a member, an officer or an employee of the trade union proposing to hold the election (art 5(1)(a)); or (b) in acting at any time as a scrutineer for any trade union, has knowingly permitted any member, officer or employee of the union to assist him in carrying out any of the functions referred to in the Trade Union and Labour Relations (Consolidation) Act 1992 s 49(3) (see the heads (a)–(e) in the text), s 75(3) (see PARA 979), s 100A(3) (see PARA 1004) and s 226B(1) (see PARA 1373) (Trade Union Ballots and Elections (Independent Scrutineer Qualifications) Order 1993, SI 1993/1909, art 5(1)(b)). For these purposes, references to an officer are to be construed as not including an auditor: art 5(2).

6   The persons so specified for these purposes are Association of Electoral Administrators; DRS Data Services Limited; Electoral Reform Services Limited; Involvement and Participation Association; Opt2Vote Limited; and Popularis Limited: Trade Union Ballots and Elections (Independent Scrutineer Qualifications) Order 1993, SI 1993/1909, art 7 (substituted by SI 2010/436).

7   Trade Union and Labour Relations (Consolidation) Act 1992 s 49(2).

8   Ie under the Trade Union and Labour Relations (Consolidation) Act 1992 s 51A: see PARA 962.

9   Trade Union and Labour Relations (Consolidation) Act 1992 s 49(3)(a) (amended by the Trade Union Reform and Employment Rights Act 1993 Sch 8 para 46).

10 As to the register of members' names and addresses see PARA 930. The duty of confidentiality as respects the register (see PARA 937) is incorporated in the scrutineer's appointment: Trade Union and Labour Relations (Consolidation) Act 1992 s 49(3C) (s 49(3A)–(3C) added by the Trade Union Reform and Employment Rights Act 1993 s 1(1)(c)).

11 Ie in accordance with the Trade Union and Labour Relations (Consolidation) Act 1992 s 49(5A)(a): see head (A) in the text.

12 Trade Union and Labour Relations (Consolidation) Act 1992 s 49(3)(aa) (added by the Trade Union Reform and Employment Rights Act 1993 s 1(1)(a)). The conditions so referred to are: (1) that a request that the scrutineer inspect the register or examine the copy is made to him during the appropriate period by a member of the trade union or candidate who suspects that the register is not, or at the relevant date was not, accurate and up-to-date; and (2) that the scrutineer does not consider that the suspicion of the member or candidate is ill-founded: Trade Union and Labour Relations (Consolidation) Act 1992 s 49(3A) (as added: see note 10). For these purposes, 'appropriate period' means the period: (a) beginning with the first day on which a person may become a candidate in the election or, if later, the day on which the scrutineer is appointed; and (b) ending with the day before the day on which the scrutineer makes his report to the trade union (s 49(3B) (as so added)); and 'relevant date' means: (i) where the trade union has rules determining who is entitled to vote in the election by reference to membership on a particular date, that date; and (ii) otherwise, the date, or the last date, on which voting papers are distributed for the purposes of the election: s 49(8) (added by the Trade Union Reform and Employment Rights Act 1993 s 1(1)(e)). As to the meaning of 'rules', in relation to a trade union, see PARA 898 note 5.

13 Trade Union and Labour Relations (Consolidation) Act 1992 s 49(3)(b).

14 Trade Union and Labour Relations (Consolidation) Act 1992 s 49(3)(c). As to the scrutineer's report see PARA 967.

15 Trade Union and Labour Relations (Consolidation) Act 1992 s 49(3)(d)(i) (s 49(3)(d)(i), (ii) amended by the Trade Union Reform and Employment Rights Act 1993 s 1(1)(b)). If within that period an application is made under the Trade Union and Labour Relations (Consolidation) Act 1992 s 54 (see PARA 971) complaining of a failure to comply with the statutory election requirements, the scrutineer must retain custody of the voting papers and the copy of the register until the certification officer or the High Court authorises him to dispose of them: s 49(3)(d)(ii) (as so amended); Trade Union and Labour Relations (Consolidation) Act 1992 s 121.

16 Trade Union and Labour Relations (Consolidation) Act 1992 s 49(4).

17 Trade Union and Labour Relations (Consolidation) Act 1992 s 49(5).

18 Trade Union and Labour Relations (Consolidation) Act 1992 s 49(5A) (s 49(5A), (5B) added by
    the Trade Union Reform and Employment Rights Act 1993 s 1(1)(d)). As to the duty to supply
    a copy of the register and to comply with a request to inspect the register generally see PARA
    930. Where the register is kept by means of a computer, the duty so imposed on the trade union
    is either to supply a legible printed copy or, if the scrutineer prefers, to supply a copy of the
    computer data and allow the scrutineer use of the computer to read it at any time during the
    period when he is required to retain custody of the copy: Trade Union and Labour Relations
    (Consolidation) Act 1992 s 49(5B) (as so added).
19 Trade Union and Labour Relations (Consolidation) Act 1992 s 49(6).
20 Trade Union and Labour Relations (Consolidation) Act 1992 s 49(7).

967.   Scrutineer's report. The scrutineer[1] must make a report to the trade
union[2] as soon as reasonably practicable after the last date for the return of the
voting papers[3]. The scrutineer's report on the election must state:

(1)   the number of voting papers distributed for the purposes of the election;
(2)   the number of voting papers returned to the scrutineer;
(3)   the number of valid votes cast in the election for each candidate;
(4)   the number of spoiled or otherwise invalid voting papers returned; and
(5)   the name of any independent person or persons appointed by the union[4]
       to perform certain functions in relation to the election or, if no such
       person was so appointed, that fact[5].

The report must also state whether the scrutineer is satisfied:

(a)   that there are no reasonable grounds for believing that there was any
       contravention[6] of a requirement imposed by or under any enactment in
       relation to the election;
(b)   that the arrangements made, whether by the scrutineer or by any other
       person, with respect to the production, storage, distribution, return or
       other handling of the voting papers used in the election, and the
       arrangements for the counting of the votes, included all such security
       arrangements as were reasonably practicable for the purpose of
       minimising the risk that any unfairness or malpractice might occur; and
(c)   that he has been able to carry out his functions without such
       interference as would make it reasonable for any person to call his
       independence in relation to the union into question;

and, if he is not satisfied as to any of these matters, the report must give
particulars of his reasons for not being satisfied as to that matter[7].

The report must also state:

(i)   whether the scrutineer has inspected the register of names and addresses
       of the members of the trade union[8] or has examined the copy of the
       register supplied to him[9];
(ii)   if he has, whether in the case of each inspection or examination he was
       acting on a request by a member of the trade union or a candidate or at
       his own instance;
(iii) whether he declined to act on any such request; and
(iv)   whether any inspection of the register, or any examination of the copy
       of the register, has revealed any matter which he considers should be
       drawn to the attention of the trade union in order to assist it in securing
       that its register is accurate and up-to-date;

but the report must not state the name of any member or candidate who has
requested such an inspection or examination[10].

The trade union must not publish the result of the election until it has received
the scrutineer's report[11]; and it must, within three months after it receives the
report, either:

(A) send a copy of it to every member of the union to whom it is reasonably practicable to send such a copy; or

(B) take all such other steps for notifying the contents of the report to the members of the union, whether by publishing the report or otherwise, as it is the practice of the union to take when matters of general interest to all its members need to be brought to their attention[12].

Any such copy or notification must be accompanied by a statement that the union will, on request, supply any member with a copy of the report, either free of charge or on payment of such reasonable fee as may be specified in the notification[13]; and the trade union must so supply any member of the union who makes such a request and pays the fee, if any, notified to him[14].

1 Ie the person appointed under the Trade Union and Labour Relations (Consolidation) Act 1992 s 49: see PARA 966.
2 As to the meaning of 'trade union' see PARA 891. As to the application of these provisions to newly formed trade unions and federated trade unions see PARA 968; and as to their application to special register bodies see PARA 899 note 8 head (5).
3 Trade Union and Labour Relations (Consolidation) Act 1992 s 49(3)(c).
4 Ie under the Trade Union and Labour Relations (Consolidation) Act 1992 s 51A: see PARA 962. Where one or more independent persons other than the scrutineer is or are so appointed, the statement included in the scrutineer's report in accordance with s 52(2)(b) (see head (b) in the text) must also indicate: (1) whether he is satisfied with the performance of the person, or each of the persons, so appointed; and (2) if he is not satisfied with the performance of the person, or any of them, particulars of his reasons for not being so satisfied: s 52(2B) (s 52(2A), (2B) added by the Trade Union Reform and Employment Rights Act 1993 s 2(2)(c)).
5 Trade Union and Labour Relations (Consolidation) Act 1992 s 52(1) (amended by the Trade Union Reform and Employment Rights Act 1993 s 2(2)(a), Sch 10).
6 As to the meaning of 'contravention' and cognate expressions see PARA 915 note 6.
7 Trade Union and Labour Relations (Consolidation) Act 1992 s 52(2) (amended by the Trade Union Reform and Employment Rights Act 1993 s 2(2)(b)).
8 As to the register of members' names and addresses see PARA 930.
9 Ie the copy of the register as at the relevant date which is supplied to him in accordance with the Trade Union and Labour Relations (Consolidation) Act 1992 s 49(5A)(a): see PARA 966 head (A).
10 Trade Union and Labour Relations (Consolidation) Act 1992 s 52(2A) (as added: see note 4).
11 Trade Union and Labour Relations (Consolidation) Act 1992 s 52(3). Where a candidate is declared elected following a favourable report, a trade union has no power to cancel the election and order a new election unless such a power is expressly given in its rules or the whole election process is shown to be a nullity: *Douglas v Graphical Paper and Media Union* [1995] IRLR 426.
12 Trade Union and Labour Relations (Consolidation) Act 1992 s 52(4).
13 Trade Union and Labour Relations (Consolidation) Act 1992 s 52(5).
14 Trade Union and Labour Relations (Consolidation) Act 1992 s 52(6).

968. Trade unions exempted from election requirements. The statutory requirements relating to elections to certain positions[1] do not apply to a trade union[2] until more than one year has elapsed since its formation[3], whether by amalgamation or otherwise[4]. Furthermore, where a trade union is formed by amalgamation[5], the statutory requirements relating to elections to certain positions do not apply in relation to a person who, by virtue of an election, held a position to which those requirements apply in one of the amalgamating unions immediately before the amalgamation, and who becomes the holder of a position to which those requirements apply in the amalgamated union in accordance with the appropriate instrument[6], until after the end of the period for which he would have been entitled[7] to continue to hold the first position without being re-elected[8].

Where a trade union transfers its engagements[9] to another trade union, the statutory requirements relating to elections to certain positions do not apply to a person who held a position to which those requirements apply in the transferring union immediately before the transfer, and who becomes the holder of a position to which those requirements apply in the transferee union in accordance with the instrument of transfer, until after the end of the period of one year beginning with the date of the transfer[10] or, if he held the first-mentioned position by virtue of an election, any longer period for which he would have been entitled[11] to continue to hold that position without being re-elected[12].

The statutory requirements relating to elections to certain positions do not apply to a federated trade union[13] if it has no individual members other than representatives of constituent or affiliated organisations, or if its individual members, other than such representatives, are all merchant seamen and a majority of them are ordinarily resident outside the United Kingdom[14]; and, in relation to special register bodies, those requirements apply only to the position of voting member of the executive and any position by virtue of which a person is such a voting member[15].

1 Ie the requirements contained in the Trade Union and Labour Relations (Consolidation) Act 1992 Pt I Ch IV (ss 46–61): see PARA 960 et seq.
2 As to the meaning of 'trade union' see PARA 891.
3 For these purposes, the date of formation of a trade union formed otherwise than by amalgamation is to be taken to be the date on which the first members of the executive of the union are first appointed or elected: Trade Union and Labour Relations (Consolidation) Act 1992 s 57(1). An instrument of amalgamation does not take effect until it has been registered by the certification officer: see PARA 1007. As to the meaning of 'executive', in relation to a trade union, see PARA 943 note 9.
4 Trade Union and Labour Relations (Consolidation) Act 1992 s 57(1).
5 As to union amalgamations see PARA 998 et seq.
6 The Trade Union and Labour Relations (Consolidation) Act 1992 s 57(2)(b) refers to 'the instrument of transfer' (sic), but it is submitted that this is a drafting error and that the reference should be to the instrument of amalgamation.
7 Ie in accordance with the Trade Union and Labour Relations (Consolidation) Act 1992 Pt I Ch IV.
8 Trade Union and Labour Relations (Consolidation) Act 1992 s 57(2).
9 As to transfers of engagements see PARA 999 et seq.
10 An instrument of transfer does not take effect until it has been registered by the certification officer: see PARA 1007.
11 See note 7.
12 Trade Union and Labour Relations (Consolidation) Act 1992 s 57(3).
13 As to the meaning of 'federated trade union' see PARA 891.
14 See the Trade Union and Labour Relations (Consolidation) Act 1992 s 118(6); and PARA 891 note 9 head (5).
15 See the Trade Union and Labour Relations (Consolidation) Act 1992 s 117(5); and PARA 899 note 8 head (5).

969. Period for giving effect to election. Where a person holds a position to which the statutory requirements relating to elections to certain positions[1] apply immediately before an election at which he is not re-elected to that position, nothing in those requirements is to be taken to require the trade union[2] to prevent him from continuing to hold that position for such period, not exceeding six months, as may reasonably be required for effect to be given to the result of the election[3].

1 Ie the requirements contained in the Trade Union and Labour Relations (Consolidation) Act 1992 Pt I Ch IV (ss 46–61): see PARA 960 et seq.

2   As to the meaning of 'trade union' see PARA 891. As to the application of these provisions to
     newly formed trade unions and federated trade unions see PARA 968; and as to their application
     to special register bodies see PARA 899 note 8 head (5).
3   Trade Union and Labour Relations (Consolidation) Act 1992 s 59.

970.   Overseas members.   A trade union[1] which has overseas members may
choose whether or not to accord any of those members entitlement to vote at an
election for a position to which the statutory requirements relating to elections to
certain positions[2] apply[3]. For these purposes, an 'overseas member' means a
member of the union, other than a merchant seaman[4] or offshore worker[5], who
is outside Great Britain throughout the period during which votes may be cast[6].

1   As to the meaning of 'trade union' see PARA 891. As to the application of these provisions to
     newly formed trade unions and federated trade unions see PARA 968; and as to their application
     to special register bodies see PARA 899 note 8 head (5).
2   Ie the requirements contained in the Trade Union and Labour Relations (Consolidation)
     Act 1992 Pt I Ch IV (ss 46–61): see PARA 960 et seq.
3   Trade Union and Labour Relations (Consolidation) Act 1992 s 60(1). Where the union chooses
     to accord an overseas member entitlement to vote, s 51 (requirements as to voting) (see PARA
     962) applies in relation to him; but nothing in s 47 (candidates) (see PARA 964) or s 50
     (entitlement to vote) (see PARA 961) applies in relation to an overseas member or in relation to a
     vote cast by such a member: s 60(3).
4   For these purposes, 'merchant seaman' means a person whose employment, or the greater part
     of it, is carried out on board sea-going ships: Trade Union and Labour Relations (Consolidation)
     Act 1992 s 60(2).
5   For these purposes, 'offshore worker' means a person in offshore employment, other than one
     who is in such employment in an area where the law of Northern Ireland applies: Trade Union
     and Labour Relations (Consolidation) Act 1992 s 60(2). 'Offshore employment' means
     employment for the purposes of activities: (1) in the territorial waters of the United Kingdom; or
     (2) connected with the exploration of the sea bed or subsoil, or the exploitation of their natural
     resources, in the United Kingdom sector of the continental shelf; or (3) connected with the
     exploration or exploitation, in a foreign sector of the continental shelf, of a cross-boundary
     petroleum field: s 287(1). 'Cross-boundary petroleum field' means a petroleum field that extends
     across the boundary between the United Kingdom sector of the continental shelf and a foreign
     sector; 'foreign sector of the continental shelf' means an area outside the territorial waters of any
     state, within which rights with respect to the sea bed and subsoil and their natural resources are
     exercisable by a state other than the United Kingdom; 'petroleum field' means a geological
     structure identified as an oil or gas field by the Order in Council concerned; and 'United
     Kingdom sector of the continental shelf' means the areas designated under the Continental Shelf
     Act 1964 s 1(7) (see ENERGY AND CLIMATE CHANGE vol 44 (2011) PARA 1040): Trade Union
     and Labour Relations (Consolidation) Act 1992 s 287(5). Section 287(1) is prospectively
     substituted, and s 287(5) is prospectively repealed, by the Petroleum Act 1998 Sch 4
     para 34(2), (3), Sch 5 Pt I, as from a day to be appointed. At the date at which this volume states
     the law, no such day had been appointed. As to the application of these provisions to Northern
     Ireland see PARA 1078. As to the extent of the territorial sea (or waters) of the United Kingdom
     see the Territorial Sea Act 1987 s 1; and INTERNATIONAL RELATIONS LAW vol 61 (2010) PARA
     123 et seq.
         Her Majesty may by Order in Council provide that the provisions of the Trade Union and
     Labour Relations (Consolidation) Act 1992, and any Northern Ireland legislation making
     provisions for any corresponding purposes, apply, to such extent and for such purposes as may
     be specified in the Order and with or without modification, to or in relation to a person in
     offshore employment or, in relation to ss 137–143 (access to employment) (see PARA 1042 et
     seq), a person seeking such employment: s 287(2). Such an Order in Council may: (a) make
     different provision for different cases; (b) provide that the enactments to which s 287 applies, as
     applied, apply to individuals whether or not they are British subjects and to bodies corporate
     whether or not they are incorporated under the law of a part of the United Kingdom, and apply
     notwithstanding that the application may affect the activities of such an individual or body
     outside the United Kingdom; (c) make provision for conferring jurisdiction on any court or class
     of court specified therein, or on employment tribunals, in respect of offences, causes of action or
     other matters arising in connection with offshore employment; (d) provide that the enactments
     to which s 287 applies apply in relation to a person in offshore employment in a part of the
     areas referred to in s 287(1)(a), (b) (see heads (1)–(2) above); (e) exclude from the operation of

the Territorial Waters Jurisdiction Act 1878 s 3 (consents required for prosecutions: see CRIMINAL PROCEDURE vol 27 (2010) PARA 12) proceedings for offences under the enactments to which the Trade Union and Labour Relations (Consolidation) Act 1992 s 287 applies in connection with offshore employment; (f) provide that such proceedings are not to be brought without such consent as may be required by the Order; and (g) modify or exclude any of ss 281–285 (excluded classes of employment) (see PARAS 1071, 1072, 1194) or any corresponding provision of Northern Ireland legislation: s 287(3) (amended by the Employment Rights (Dispute Resolution) Act 1998 s 1(2)(a)). An Order in Council under the Trade Union and Labour Relations (Consolidation) Act 1992 s 287 is subject to annulment in pursuance of a resolution of either House of Parliament: s 287(3A) (added by the Employment Relations Act 1999 s 32(2)). Any jurisdiction so conferred on a court or tribunal is without prejudice to jurisdiction exercisable apart from the Trade Union and Labour Relations (Consolidation) Act 1992 s 287, by that or any other court or tribunal: s 287(4). As to the meaning of 'British subject' see BRITISH NATIONALITY vol 4 (2011) PARA 407. The use of the term 'British subject' in s 287(3) seems strange and appears to have been copied by the draftsman from the Employment Protection Act 1975 s 127(3)(b) (repealed), when it would have had a different and less restrictive meaning than that term now has in the British Nationality Act 1981. It is not clear whether 'British subject' is really what is meant, in which case the British Nationality Act 1981 s 51(2) (see BRITISH NATIONALITY vol 4 (2011) PARAS 407, 409) applies, or whether the Trade Union and Labour Relations (Consolidation) Act 1992 s 287(3) should be construed in the same way as the Employment Protection Act 1975 s 127(3) would have been, in which case the British Nationality Act 1981 s 51(1) (see BRITISH NATIONALITY vol 4 (2011) PARAS 407, 409) would apply despite the fact that the 1992 Act does not predate the 1981 Act.

In exercise of the power so conferred the Secretary of State made the Employment Relations (Offshore Employment) Order 2000, SI 2000/1828 (extending certain provisions of the Trade Union and Labour Relations (Consolidation) Act 1992 to employment for the purposes of activities in the territorial waters of the United Kingdom and specified areas of the continental shelf) (see PARA 156), and, by virtue of Sch 3 para 1(2) (see PARA 891 note 1) and the Interpretation Act 1978 s 17(2)(b), the Employment Protection (Offshore Employment) Order 1976, SI 1976/766, has effect as if so made (see PARA 156).

'Northern Ireland legislation' means: (i) Acts of the Parliament of Ireland; (ii) Acts of the Parliament of Northern Ireland; (iii) Orders in Council under the Northern Ireland (Temporary Provisions) Act 1972 s 1(3) (repealed); (iv) Measures of the Northern Ireland Assembly established under the Northern Ireland Assembly Act 1973 s 1 (repealed); (v) Orders in Council under the Northern Ireland Act 1974 s 1(3), Sch 1 (repealed); (vi) Acts of the Northern Ireland Assembly; and (vii) Orders in Council under the Northern Ireland Act 1998 s 85 (reserved matters): Interpretation Act 1978 s 24(5) (amended by the Northern Ireland Act 1998 Sch 13 para 3).

6   Trade Union and Labour Relations (Consolidation) Act 1992 s 60(2).

(iii) Remedy for Trade Union's Failure to Comply with Election Requirements

971.   Remedy for trade union's failure to comply with election requirements; in general.   The remedy for a failure on the part of a trade union[1] to comply with the statutory requirements relating to elections to certain positions[2] is by way of application to the certification officer[3] or to the High Court[4]. An application may be so made by a person having a sufficient interest, namely:

(1)   a person who is a member of the trade union, provided, where the election has been held, that he was also a member at the time when it was held; or

(2)   a person who is or was a candidate at the election[5];

but where an election has been held, no such application with respect to that election may be made after the end of the period of one year beginning with the day on which the union announced the result of the election[6].

1   As to the meaning of 'trade union' see PARA 891. As to the application of these provisions to newly formed trade unions and federated trade unions see PARA 968; and as to their application to special register bodies see PARA 899 note 8 head (5).

2   Ie the Trade Union and Labour Relations (Consolidation) Act 1992 Pt I Ch IV (ss 46–61): see PARA 960 et seq.

3   Ie under the Trade Union and Labour Relations (Consolidation) Act 1992 s 55: see PARA 972. As to the certification officer see PARA 1443.
4   Trade Union and Labour Relations (Consolidation) Act 1992 s 54(1) (amended by the Employment Relations Act 1999 Sch 6 paras 1, 9, Sch 9); Trade Union and Labour Relations (Consolidation) Act 1992 s 121. Application to the court is under s 56: see PARA 973.
5   Trade Union and Labour Relations (Consolidation) Act 1992 s 54(2).
6   Trade Union and Labour Relations (Consolidation) Act 1992 s 54(3) (amended by the Employment Relations Act 2004 Sch 1 para 5).

972.   Application to the certification officer for a declaration of non-compliance by a trade union. A person having a sufficient interest[1] who claims that a trade union[2] has failed to comply with any of the statutory requirements relating to elections to certain positions[3] may apply to the certification officer for a declaration to that effect[4]. On such an application being made to him, the certification officer must make such inquiries as he thinks fit[5] and must give the applicant and the trade union an opportunity to be heard; and he may make or refuse the declaration asked for[6]. Whether he makes or refuses a declaration, he must give reasons for his decision in writing; and the reasons may be accompanied by written observations on any matter arising from, or connected with, the proceedings[7]. If he makes a declaration, he must specify in it the provisions with which the trade union has failed to comply[8]; and, where he makes a declaration and is satisfied that steps have been taken by the union with a view to remedying the declared failure, or securing that a failure of the same or any similar kind does not occur in future, or that the union has agreed to take such steps, he must specify those steps in the declaration[9].

Where the certification officer makes a declaration, he must, unless he considers that to do so would be inappropriate, make an order (an 'enforcement order') imposing on the union one or more of the following requirements:

(1)   to secure the holding of an election in accordance with the order;
(2)   to take such other steps to remedy the declared failure as may be specified in the order;
(3)   to abstain from such acts as may be so specified with a view to securing that a failure of the same or a similar kind does not occur in future[10].

Where the certification officer makes an order requiring the union to hold a fresh election, he must require the election to be conducted in accordance with the statutory requirements[11] and such other provisions as may be made by the order, unless he considers that it would be inappropriate to do so in the particular circumstances of the case[12].

Where an enforcement order has been made, any person who is a member of the union and was a member at the time the order was made, or any person who is or was a candidate in the election in question, is entitled to enforce obedience to the order as if he had made the application on which the order was made[13].

If a person applies to the court[14] in relation to an alleged failure:

(a)   that person may not apply to the certification officer[15] in relation to that failure;
(b)   on an application by a different person to the certification officer in relation to that failure, the certification officer must have due regard to any declaration, order, observations or reasons made or given by the court regarding that failure and brought to the certification officer's notice[16].

1   Ie a person to whom the Trade Union and Labour Relations (Consolidation) Act 1992 s 54(2) applies: see PARA 971.

2   As to the meaning of 'trade union' see PARA 891. As to the application of these provisions to newly formed and federated trade unions see PARA 968; and as to their application to special register bodies see PARA 899 note 8 head (5).

3   Ie the requirements contained in the Trade Union and Labour Relations (Consolidation) Act 1992 Pt I Ch IV (ss 46–61): see PARA 960 et seq.

4   Trade Union and Labour Relations (Consolidation) Act 1992 s 55(1). As to when the application may be made see PARA 971; and as to the certification officer see PARA 1443. An appeal lies to the Employment Appeal Tribunal on any question of law arising in proceedings before or arising from any decision of the certification officer under s 55: s 56A (added by the Employment Relations Act 1999 Sch 6 paras 1, 12). As to the Employment Appeal Tribunal see PARA 1422 et seq.

5   Where the certification officer requests a person to furnish information to him in connection with his inquiries, he must specify the date by which it is to be furnished; and he must proceed with his determination of the application notwithstanding that the information has not been furnished to him by the specified date, unless he considers that it would be inappropriate to do so: Trade Union and Labour Relations (Consolidation) Act 1992 s 55(7).

6   Trade Union and Labour Relations (Consolidation) Act 1992 s 55(2) (amended by the Employment Relations Act 1999 Sch 6 paras 1, 10). In exercising his functions under the Trade Union and Labour Relations (Consolidation) Act 1992 s 55, the certification officer must ensure that, so far as is reasonably practicable, an application made to him is determined within six months of being made: s 55(6).

7   Trade Union and Labour Relations (Consolidation) Act 1992 s 55(5).

8   Trade Union and Labour Relations (Consolidation) Act 1992 s 55(3).

9   Trade Union and Labour Relations (Consolidation) Act 1992 s 55(4). A declaration made by the certification officer under s 55 may be relied on as if it were a declaration made by the court: s 55(8) (s 55(8)–(10) added by the Employment Relations Act 1999 Sch 6 paras 1, 10(1), (4)).

10 Trade Union and Labour Relations (Consolidation) Act 1992 s 55(5A) (s 55(5A)–(5C) added by the Employment Relations Act 1999 Sch 6 paras 1, 10(1), (3)). The certification officer must in an order imposing any such requirement as is mentioned in the Trade Union and Labour Relations (Consolidation) Act 1992 s 55(5A)(a) or (b) (see heads (1)–(2) in the text) specify the period within which the union is to comply with the requirements of the order: s 55(5A) (as so added).

11 See note 3.

12 Trade Union and Labour Relations (Consolidation) Act 1992 s 55(5B) (as added: see note 10).

13 Trade Union and Labour Relations (Consolidation) Act 1992 s 55(5C) (as added: see note 10). An enforcement order made by the certification officer under s 55 may be enforced in the same way as an order of the court: s 55(9) (as added: see note 9).

14 Ie under the Trade Union and Labour Relations (Consolidation) Act 1992 s 56: see PARA 973.

15 Ie under the Trade Union and Labour Relations (Consolidation) Act 1992 s 55.

16 Trade Union and Labour Relations (Consolidation) Act 1992 s 55(10) (as added: see note 9).

973.   Application to the court for a declaration of non-compliance by a trade union. A person having a sufficient interest[1] who claims that a trade union[2] has failed to comply with any of the statutory requirements relating to elections to certain positions[3] may apply to the High Court for a declaration to that effect[4]. If the court makes the declaration asked for, it must specify in it the provisions with which the trade union has failed to comply[5]; and it must, unless it considers that to do so would be inappropriate, also make an order (an 'enforcement order') imposing on the union one or more of the following requirements:

(1)   to secure the holding of an election in accordance with the order[6];

(2)   to take such other steps to remedy the declared failure as may be specified in the order;

(3)   to abstain from such acts as may be so specified with a view to securing that a failure of the same or of a similar kind does not occur in future[7].

Where the court makes an order requiring the union to hold a fresh election, the court must require the election to be conducted in accordance with the statutory requirements and such other provisions as may be made by the order, unless the court considers that it would be inappropriate to do so in the particular circumstances of the case[8].

Where an enforcement order has been made, any person who is a member of the union and was a member at the time the order was made, or any person who is or was a candidate in the election in question, is entitled to enforce obedience to the order as if he had made the application on which the order was made[9].

If a person applies to the certification officer[10] in relation to an alleged failure:

(a) that person may not apply to the court[11] in relation to that failure;

(b) on an application by a different person to the court in relation to that failure, the court must have due regard to any declaration, order, observations or reasons made or given by the certification officer regarding that failure and brought to the court's notice[12].

1 Ie a person to whom the Trade Union and Labour Relations (Consolidation) Act 1992 s 54(2) applies: see PARA 971.
2 As to the meaning of 'trade union' see PARA 891. As to the application of these provisions to newly formed and federated trade unions see PARA 968; and as to their application to special register bodies see PARA 899 note 8 head (5).
3 Ie the requirements contained in the Trade Union and Labour Relations (Consolidation) Act 1992 Pt I Ch IV (ss 46–61): see PARA 960 et seq.
4 Trade Union and Labour Relations (Consolidation) Act 1992 ss 56(1), 121. As to when the application may be made see PARA 971. Without prejudice to any other power of the court, the court may, on such an application, grant such interim relief as it considers appropriate: see s 56(7).
5 Trade Union and Labour Relations (Consolidation) Act 1992 s 56(3).
6 The court must specify the period within which the union must comply with the requirements of the order: Trade Union and Labour Relations (Consolidation) Act 1992 s 56(4).
7 Trade Union and Labour Relations (Consolidation) Act 1992 s 56(4).
8 Trade Union and Labour Relations (Consolidation) Act 1992 s 56(5).
9 Trade Union and Labour Relations (Consolidation) Act 1992 s 56(6).
10 Ie under the Trade Union and Labour Relations (Consolidation) Act 1992 s 55: see PARA 972.
11 Ie under the Trade Union and Labour Relations (Consolidation) Act 1992 s 56.
12 Trade Union and Labour Relations (Consolidation) Act 1992 s 56(8) (added by the Employment Relations Act 1999 Sch 6 paras 1, 11(1), (3)).

(6) APPLICATION OF FUNDS FOR POLITICAL OBJECTS

(i) Restriction on the Use of Funds for Certain Political Objects

974. Restriction on the use of funds for political objects. The funds of a trade union[1] may not be applied in the furtherance of certain political objects[2] unless:

(1) there is in force in accordance with the statutory requirements[3] a resolution (a 'political resolution'[4]) approving the furtherance of those objects as an object of the union; and

(2) there are in force rules[5] of the union as to:

(a) the making of payments in furtherance of those objects out of a separate fund[6]; and

(b) the exemption of any member of the union objecting to contribute to that fund[7],

which comply with the statutory requirements[8] and have been approved by the certification officer[9].

This restriction applies whether the funds are so applied directly, or in conjunction with another trade union, association or body, or otherwise indirectly[10].

1 As to the meaning of 'trade union' see PARA 891. As to the application of the statutory provisions concerning the use of funds for political objects to federated trade unions see PARA 891 note 9 head (6).

2   Ie the political objects set out in the Trade Union and Labour Relations (Consolidation) Act 1992 s 72: see PARA 975.
3   Ie the Trade Union and Labour Relations (Consolidation) Act 1992 Pt I Ch VI (ss 71–96): see the text and notes 1–2, 4–10; and PARA 975 et seq. As to the application of these provisions to Northern Ireland see PARA 1078.
4   As to the passing and effect of a political resolution see PARA 977.
5   As to the meaning of 'rules', in relation to a trade union, see PARA 898 note 5.
6   See further PARA 985 et seq. As to the restrictions on the enforcement of awards against property comprised in the political fund see PARA 928.
7   See further PARA 987 et seq.
8   See note 3.
9   Trade Union and Labour Relations (Consolidation) Act 1992 s 71(1). As to the certification officer see PARA 1443; and as to the application of funds in breach of s 71 see s 72A; and PARA 976.
10 Trade Union and Labour Relations (Consolidation) Act 1992 s 71(2).

975.   Political objects to which the restriction applies.   The political objects to which the statutory restrictions[1] apply are the expenditure of money[2]:

(1)   on any contribution[3] to the funds of, or on the payment of expenses incurred directly or indirectly by, a political party;

(2)   on the provision of any service or property for use by or on behalf of any political party;

(3)   in connection with the registration of electors[4], the candidature of any person, the selection of any candidate[5] or the holding of any ballot by the union in connection with any election to a political office;

(4)   on the maintenance of any holder of a political office;

(5)   on the holding of any conference or meeting by or on behalf of a political party or of any other meeting the main purpose of which is the transaction of business in connection with a political party[6];

(6)   on the production, publication or distribution of any literature, document, film[7], sound recording or advertisement the main purpose of which is to persuade people to vote for a political party or candidate or to persuade them not to vote for a political party or candidate[8].

1   Ie the restrictions contained in the Trade Union and Labour Relations (Consolidation) Act 1992 Pt I Ch VI (ss 71–96): see PARAS 974, 976 et seq.
2   In determining for these purposes whether a trade union has incurred expenditure of a kind mentioned in the Trade Union and Labour Relations (Consolidation) Act 1992 s 72(1) (see heads (1)–(6) in the text), no account is to be taken of the ordinary administrative expenses of the union: s 72(3). As to the meaning of 'trade union' see PARA 891. As to the application of the statutory provisions concerning the use of funds for political objects to federated trade unions see PARA 891 note 9 head (6).
3   For these purposes, 'contribution' in relation to the funds of a political party, includes any fee payable for affiliation to, or membership of, the party and any loan made to the party: Trade Union and Labour Relations (Consolidation) Act 1992 s 72(4).
4   For these purposes, 'electors' means electors at an election to a political office; 'political office' means the office of member of Parliament, member of the European Parliament or member of a local authority or any position within a political party; and 'local authority' means a local authority within the meaning of the Local Government Act 1972 s 270 (see LOCAL GOVERNMENT vol 69 (2009) PARA 23): Trade Union and Labour Relations (Consolidation) Act 1992 s 72(4).
5   For these purposes, 'candidate' means a candidate for election to a political office and includes a prospective candidate: Trade Union and Labour Relations (Consolidation) Act 1992 s 72(4).
6   Where a person attends a conference or meeting as a delegate or otherwise as a participator in the proceedings, any expenditure incurred in connection with his attendance as such is to be taken to be expenditure incurred on the holding of the conference or meeting: Trade Union and Labour Relations (Consolidation) Act 1992 s 72(2).

7 For these purposes, 'film' includes any record, however made, of a sequence of visual images, which is capable of being used as a means of showing that sequence as a moving picture: Trade Union and Labour Relations (Consolidation) Act 1992 s 72(4).

8 Trade Union and Labour Relations (Consolidation) Act 1992 s 72(1). See *Paul and Fraser v National and Local Government Officers' Association* [1987] IRLR 413 (where it was held that the main purpose of a campaign mounted by the union at election time against government spending cuts in the public services was to persuade people not to vote for the Conservative party, despite the inclusion in the relevant leaflets of a disclaimer stating that the union was not affiliated to any political party). Such a campaign would not, however, necessarily fall within the statutory restrictions if undertaken at any other time: *Paul and Fraser v National and Local Government Officers' Association* [1987] IRLR 413 at 421 obiter.

A resolution under the Trade Union Act 1913 s 3 (repealed), or rules made for the purposes thereof, in relation to which the Trade Union Act 1984 s 17(2) applied immediately before 16 October 1992 (ie the date on which the Trade Union and Labour Relations (Consolidation) Act 1992 came into force: see s 302) continues to have effect as if for any reference to the political objects to which the Trade Union Act 1913 s 3 (repealed) formerly applied there were substituted a reference to the objects to which it applied as amended by the Trade Union Act 1984: Trade Union and Labour Relations (Consolidation) Act 1992 Sch 3 para 8.

976. Application of funds in breach of statutory restrictions. A person who is a member of a trade union[1] and who claims that it has applied its funds in breach of the statutory restrictions[2] may apply to the certification officer[3] for a declaration that it has done so[4]. On such an application, the certification officer:

(1) must make such inquiries as he thinks fit;

(2) must give the applicant and the union an opportunity to be heard;

(3) must ensure that, so far as is reasonably practicable, the application is determined within six months of being made;

(4) may make or refuse the declaration asked for;

(5) must, whether he makes or refuses the declaration, give reasons for his decision in writing; and

(6) may make written observations on any matter arising from, or connected with, the proceedings[5].

If he makes a declaration, he must specify in it the provisions breached[6] and the amount of the funds applied in breach[7]. If he makes a declaration and is satisfied that the union has taken or agreed to take steps with a view to remedying the declared breach or securing that a breach of the same or any similar kind does not occur in future, he must specify those steps in making the declaration[8]. If he makes a declaration, he may make such order for remedying the breach as he thinks just under the circumstances[9]. A declaration made by the certification officer may be relied on as if it were a declaration made by the court[10].

Where the certification officer requests a person to furnish information to him in connection with inquiries made by him under these provisions, he must specify the date by which that information is to be furnished and, unless he considers that it would be inappropriate to do so, must proceed with his determination of the application, notwithstanding that the information has not been furnished to him by the specified date[11].

Where an order has been so made, any person who is a member of the union and was a member at the time it was made is entitled to enforce obedience to the order as if he had made the application on which the order was made[12]. An order made by the certification officer may be enforced in the same way as an order of the court[13].

If a person applies to the certification officer under the above provisions in relation to an alleged breach, he may not apply to the High Court in relation to the breach; but nothing in that prohibition prevents such a person from exercising any right to appeal against or challenge the certification officer's decision on the application to him[14]. If a person applies to the court in relation to an alleged breach and the breach is one in relation to which he could have made an application to the certification officer under the above provisions, he may not apply to the certification officer under the above provisions in relation to the breach[15].

1 As to the meaning of 'trade union' see PARA 891. As to the application of the statutory provisions concerning the use of funds for political objects to federated trade unions see PARA 891 note 9 head (6).
2 Ie in breach of the Trade Union and Labour Relations (Consolidation) Act 1992 s 71: see PARA 974.
3 As to the certification officer see PARA 1443. An appeal lies to the Employment Appeal Tribunal on any question of law arising in proceedings before or arising from any decision of the certification officer under the Trade Union and Labour Relations (Consolidation) Act 1992 s 72A: see PARA 997. As to the Employment Appeal Tribunal see PARA 1422 et seq.
4 Trade Union and Labour Relations (Consolidation) Act 1992 s 72A(1) (s 72A added by Employment Relations Act 1999 Sch 6 paras 1, 13).
5 Trade Union and Labour Relations (Consolidation) Act 1992 s 72A(2) (as added: see note 4).
6 Ie the provisions of the Trade Union and Labour Relations (Consolidation) Act 1992 s 71 which have been breached.
7 Trade Union and Labour Relations (Consolidation) Act 1992 s 72A(3) (as added: see note 4).
8 Trade Union and Labour Relations (Consolidation) Act 1992 s 72A(4) (as added: see note 4).
9 Trade Union and Labour Relations (Consolidation) Act 1992 s 72A(5) (as added: see note 4).
10 Trade Union and Labour Relations (Consolidation) Act 1992 s 72A(7) (as added: see note 4).
11 Trade Union and Labour Relations (Consolidation) Act 1992 s 72A(6) (as added: see note 4).
12 Trade Union and Labour Relations (Consolidation) Act 1992 s 72A(8) (as added: see note 4).
13 Trade Union and Labour Relations (Consolidation) Act 1992 s 72A(9) (as added: see note 4).
14 Trade Union and Labour Relations (Consolidation) Act 1992 s 72A(10) (as added: see note 4); s 121.
15 Trade Union and Labour Relations (Consolidation) Act 1992 s 72A(11) (as added: see note 4).

(ii) Establishing a Political Fund

977. Passing and effect of a political resolution. A political resolution[1] must be passed by a majority of those voting on a ballot of the members of the trade union[2] held in accordance with the statutory requirements[3]. A political resolution so passed takes effect as if it were a rule of the union and may be rescinded in the same manner and subject to the same provisions as such a rule[4]. If not previously rescinded, a political resolution ceases to have effect at the end of the period of ten years beginning with the date of the ballot[5] on which it was passed[6]. Where, before the end of that period, a ballot is held on a new political resolution, then:

(1) if the new resolution is passed, the old resolution is to be treated as rescinded; and

(2) if it is not passed, the old resolution ceases to have effect at the end of the period of two weeks beginning with the date of the ballot[7].

1 As to the meaning of 'political resolution' see PARA 974.
2 As to the meaning of 'trade union' see PARA 891. As to the application of these provisions to federated trade unions see PARA 891 note 9 head (6).
3 Trade Union and Labour Relations (Consolidation) Act 1992 s 73(1). The statutory requirements referred to are those contained in Pt I Ch VI (ss 71–96): see PARAS 974–976, 978 et seq. As to the conduct of the ballot see PARA 980.
4 Trade Union and Labour Relations (Consolidation) Act 1992 s 73(2). A union may not make payments in pursuance of a political resolution unless the union's political fund rules have been approved by the certification officer in accordance with ss 71(1)(b), 82: see PARA 985. As to the meaning of 'rules', in relation to a trade union, see PARA 898 note 5. For transitional provisions see PARA 975 note 8.

5   For these purposes, the 'date of the ballot' means, in the case of a ballot in which votes may be cast on more than one day, the last of those days: Trade Union and Labour Relations (Consolidation) Act 1992 s 96.
6   Trade Union and Labour Relations (Consolidation) Act 1992 s 73(3).
7   Trade Union and Labour Relations (Consolidation) Act 1992 s 73(4). As to the position where a political resolution expires see PARA 991 et seq.

978. Approval of political ballot rules. A ballot on a political resolution[1] must be held in accordance with rules of the trade union[2] (its 'political ballot rules') approved by the certification officer[3]. Fresh approval is required for the purposes of each ballot which it is proposed to hold, notwithstanding that the rules have been approved for the purposes of an earlier ballot[4]. The certification officer must not approve a union's political ballot rules unless he is satisfied that the statutory requirements relating to the appointment of the independent scrutineer[5], entitlement to vote[6], the method of voting[7], the counting of votes by an independent person[8] and the scrutineer's report[9] would be satisfied in relation to a ballot held by the union in accordance with the rules[10].

1   As to the meaning of 'political resolution' see PARA 974.
2   As to the meaning of 'trade union' see PARA 891; and as to the meaning of 'rules', in relation to a trade union, see PARA 898 note 5. As to the application of the statutory provisions concerning the use of funds for political objects to federated trade unions see PARA 891 note 9 head (6).
3   Trade Union and Labour Relations (Consolidation) Act 1992 s 74(1). As to the certification officer see PARA 1443. The remedy for a failure by a trade union to comply with its political ballot rules is by way of application to the certification officer under s 80 (see PARA 983) or to the High Court under s 81 (see PARA 984): see s 79(1); and PARA 982. As to the special method for the adoption of political ballot rules see PARA 994. An appeal lies to the Employment Appeal Tribunal on any question of law arising in proceedings before or arising from any decision of the certification officer under s 74: see PARA 997. As to the Employment Appeal Tribunal see PARA 1422 et seq.
4   Trade Union and Labour Relations (Consolidation) Act 1992 s 74(2).
5   Ie the Trade Union and Labour Relations (Consolidation) Act 1992 s 75: see PARA 979.
6   Ie the Trade Union and Labour Relations (Consolidation) Act 1992 s 76: see PARA 980.
7   Ie the Trade Union and Labour Relations (Consolidation) Act 1992 s 77: see PARA 980.
8   Ie the Trade Union and Labour Relations (Consolidation) Act 1992 s 77A: see PARA 980.
9   Ie the Trade Union and Labour Relations (Consolidation) Act 1992 s 78: see PARA 981.
10 Trade Union and Labour Relations (Consolidation) Act 1992 s 74(3) (amended by the Trade Union Reform and Employment Rights Act 1993 Sch 1 para 1, Sch 10).

979. Appointment of independent scrutineer of political ballot. Before the ballot on a political resolution is held[1], the trade union[2] must appoint a qualified independent person (the 'scrutineer') to carry out the functions in relation to the ballot which are required[3] to be contained in his appointment, and such additional functions in relation to the ballot as may be specified in his appointment[4].

A person is a qualified independent person in relation to a ballot if:

(1)   he satisfies such conditions as may be specified by order of the Secretary of State[5] or is himself so specified[6]; and

(2)   the trade union has no grounds for believing either that he will carry out his functions in relation to the ballot otherwise than competently or that his independence in relation to the union, or in relation to the ballot, might reasonably be called into question[7].

The scrutineer's appointment must require him:

(a)   to be the person who supervises the production of the voting papers and, unless he is appointed[8] to undertake the distribution of the voting papers, their distribution, and to whom the voting papers are returned by those voting[9];

(b)   to inspect the register of names and addresses of the members of the trade union[10] or examine the copy of the register which is supplied to him[11], whenever it appears to him appropriate to do so and, in particular, when certain conditions are satisfied[12];

(c)   to take such steps as appear to him to be appropriate for the purpose of enabling him to make his report[13];

(d)   to make his report to the union as soon as reasonably practicable after the last date for the return of voting papers[14]; and

(e)   to retain custody of all voting papers returned for the purposes of the ballot, and the copy of the register supplied to him, until the end of the period of one year beginning with the announcement by the union of the result of the ballot[15].

The trade union must ensure that nothing in the terms of the scrutineer's appointment, including any additional functions specified in it, is such as to make it reasonable for any person to call his independence in relation to the union into question[16].

Before the scrutineer begins to carry out his functions, the trade union must either send a notice stating the name of the scrutineer to every member of the union to whom it is reasonably practicable to send such a notice, or take all such other steps for notifying members of the name of the scrutineer as it is the practice of the union to take when matters of general interest to all its members need to be brought to their attention[17]. The trade union must also:

(i)   supply to the scrutineer a copy of the register of members' names and addresses, as soon as is reasonably practicable after the relevant date; and

(ii)   comply with any request made by the scrutineer to inspect the register[18].

The trade union must ensure that the scrutineer duly carries out his functions and that there is no interference with his carrying out of those functions which would make it reasonable for any person to call his independence in relation to the union into question[19]; and it must comply with all reasonable requests made by the scrutineer for the purposes of, or in connection with, the carrying out of his functions[20].

1   As to the requirement to hold a ballot on a political resolution see PARA 977.
2   As to the meaning of 'trade union' see PARA 891. As to the application of the statutory provisions concerning the use of funds for political objects to federated trade unions see PARA 891 note 9 head (6).
3   Ie required under the Trade Union and Labour Relations (Consolidation) Act 1992 s 75: see the text and notes.
4   Trade Union and Labour Relations (Consolidation) Act 1992 s 75(1).
5   An order so made must be made by statutory instrument which is subject to annulment in pursuance of a resolution of either House of Parliament: Trade Union and Labour Relations (Consolidation) Act 1992 s 75(2). Partly in exercise of the power so conferred, the Secretary of State made the Trade Union Ballots and Elections (Independent Scrutineer Qualifications) Order 1993, SI 1993/1909, which came into force on 30 August 1993: art 1(1). As to the conditions to be satisfied by individuals and partnerships see arts 1(2), 3–6; and PARA 966 note 5.
6   As to the persons so specified see the Trade Union Ballots and Elections (Independent Scrutineer Qualifications) Order 1993, SI 1993/1909, art 7; and PARA 966 note 6.
7   Trade Union and Labour Relations (Consolidation) Act 1992 s 75(2).
8   Ie under the Trade Union and Labour Relations (Consolidation) Act 1992 s 77A: see PARA 980.
9   Trade Union and Labour Relations (Consolidation) Act 1992 s 75(3)(a) (amended by the Trade Union Reform and Employment Rights Act 1993 Sch 1 para 2(a)).
10 As to the register of members' names and addresses see PARA 930. The duty of confidentiality as respects the register (see PARA 937) is incorporated in the scrutineer's appointment: Trade Union

and Labour Relations (Consolidation) Act 1992 s 75(3C) (s 75(3A)–(3C) added by the Trade Union Reform and Employment Rights Act 1993 Sch 1 para 2(d)).

11 Ie in accordance with the Trade Union and Labour Relations (Consolidation) Act 1992 s 75(5A)(a): see head (i) in the text.

12 Trade Union and Labour Relations (Consolidation) Act 1992 s 75(3)(aa) (added by Trade Union Reform and Employment Rights Act 1993 Sch 1 para 2(b)). The conditions referred to in the text are: (1) that a request that the scrutineer inspect the register or examine the copy is made to him during the appropriate period by a member of the trade union who suspects that the register is not, or at the relevant date was not, accurate and up-to-date; and (2) that the scrutineer does not consider that the member's suspicion is ill-founded: Trade Union and Labour Relations (Consolidation) Act 1992 s 75(3A) (as added: see note 10). For these purposes, 'the appropriate period' means the period beginning with the day on which the scrutineer is appointed and ending with the day before the day on which the scrutineer makes his report to the trade union (s 75(3B) (as so added)); and 'the relevant date' means: (a) where the trade union has rules determining who is entitled to vote in the ballot by reference to membership on a particular date, that date; and (b) otherwise, the date, or the last date, on which voting papers are distributed for the purposes of the ballot (s 75(8) (added by the Trade Union Reform and Employment Rights Act 1993 Sch 1 para 2(f))). As to the duty of the scrutineer to inspect the register see PARA 930. As to the meaning of 'rules', in relation to a trade union, see PARA 898 note 5.

13 Trade Union and Labour Relations (Consolidation) Act 1992 s 75(3)(b). As to the scrutineer's report see PARA 981.

14 Trade Union and Labour Relations (Consolidation) Act 1992 s 75(3)(c).

15 Trade Union and Labour Relations (Consolidation) Act 1992 s 75(3)(d)(i) (s 75(3)(d)(i), (ii) amended by the Trade Union Reform and Employment Rights Act 1993 Sch 1 para 2(c)). If within that period an application is made to the certification officer or the court under the Trade Union and Labour Relations (Consolidation) Act 1992 s 79 (complaint of failure to comply with the ballot rules) (see PARA 982), the scrutineer must retain custody of the voting papers and the copy of the register until the certification officer or the court authorises him to dispose of them: s 75(3)(d)(ii) (as so amended).

16 Trade Union and Labour Relations (Consolidation) Act 1992 s 75(4).

17 Trade Union and Labour Relations (Consolidation) Act 1992 s 75(5).

18 Trade Union and Labour Relations (Consolidation) Act 1992 s 75(5A) (s 75(5A), (5B) added by the Trade Union Reform and Employment Rights Act 1993 Sch 1 para 2(e)). Where the register is kept by means of a computer, the duty so imposed on the trade union is either to supply a legible printed copy or, if the scrutineer prefers, to supply a copy of the computer data and allow the scrutineer use of the computer to read it at any time during the period when he is required to retain custody of the copy: Trade Union and Labour Relations (Consolidation) Act 1992 s 75(5B) (as so added). As to the duty to supply a copy of, and to comply with a request to inspect, the register generally see PARA 930.

19 Trade Union and Labour Relations (Consolidation) Act 1992 s 75(6).

20 Trade Union and Labour Relations (Consolidation) Act 1992 s 75(7).

980. Conduct of the political ballot. Entitlement to vote in a ballot on a political resolution[1] must be accorded equally to all members[2] of the trade union[3]. The method of voting must be by the marking of a voting paper by the person voting[4]; and each voting paper must:

(1) state the name of the independent scrutineer[5] and clearly specify the address to which, and the date by which, it is to be returned;

(2) be given one of a series of consecutive whole numbers every one of which is used in giving a different number in that series to each voting paper printed or otherwise produced for the purposes of the ballot; and

(3) be marked with its number[6].

Every person who is entitled to vote in the ballot must be allowed to do so without interference from, or constraint imposed by, the union or any of its members, officials[7] or employees[8] and, so far as is reasonably practicable, must be enabled to do so without incurring any direct cost to himself[9].

So far as is reasonably practicable, every person who is entitled to vote in the ballot must:

(a)   have a voting paper sent to him by post[10] at his home address or another address which he has requested the union in writing to treat as his postal address; and

(b)   be given a convenient opportunity to vote by post[11].

The trade union must ensure that the storage and distribution of the voting papers for the purposes of the ballot, and the counting of the votes cast in the ballot, are undertaken by one or more independent persons[12] appointed by the union[13]; and the ballot must be conducted so as to secure that, so far as is reasonably practicable, those voting do so in secret, and the votes given in the ballot are fairly and accurately counted[14].

1   As to the meaning of 'political resolution' see PARA 974.
2   As to the entitlement of overseas members to vote see PARA 996.
3   Trade Union and Labour Relations (Consolidation) Act 1992 s 76. As to the meaning of 'trade union' see PARA 891. As to the application of the statutory provisions concerning the use of funds for political objects to federated trade unions see PARA 891 note 9 head (6).
4   Trade Union and Labour Relations (Consolidation) Act 1992 s 77(1).
5   As to the independent scrutineer see PARA 979; and as to the scrutineer's report see PARA 981.
6   Trade Union and Labour Relations (Consolidation) Act 1992 s 77(2).
7   As to the meaning of 'official', in relation to a trade union, see PARA 1018.
8   As to the interpretation of the equivalent provisions relating to elections for union office see PARA 962. As to the meaning of 'employee' see PARA 892.
9   Trade Union and Labour Relations (Consolidation) Act 1992 s 77(3). As to the interpretation of the equivalent provisions relating to elections for union office see PARA 962.
10 As to the construction of references to requiring or authorising a document or other thing to be sent by post see PARA 962 note 10.
11 Trade Union and Labour Relations (Consolidation) Act 1992 s 77(4).
12 For these purposes, a person is an independent person in relation to a ballot if he is the scrutineer, or he is a person other than the scrutineer and the trade union has no grounds for believing either that he will carry out any functions conferred on him in relation to the ballot otherwise than competently or that his independence in relation to the union, or in relation to the ballot, might reasonably be called into question: Trade Union and Labour Relations (Consolidation) Act 1992 s 77A(2) (s 77A added by the Trade Union Reform and Employment Rights Act 1993 Sch 1 para 3).
13 Trade Union and Labour Relations (Consolidation) Act 1992 s 77A(1) (as added: see note 12). An appointment of an independent person under these provisions must require the person appointed to carry out his functions so as to minimise the risk of any contravention of requirements imposed by or under any enactment or the occurrence of any unfairness or malpractice: s 77A(3) (as so added). Further, the trade union must: (1) ensure that nothing in the terms of such an appointment is such as to make it reasonable for any person to call into question the independence of the person appointed in relation to the union; (2) ensure that a person so appointed duly carries out his functions and that there is no interference with his carrying out of those functions which would make it reasonable for any person to call into question his independence in relation to the union; and (3) comply with all reasonable requests made by a person so appointed for the purposes of, or in connection with, the carrying out of his functions: s 77A(6) (as so added). The duty of confidentiality as respects the register of members' names and addresses (see PARA 937) is incorporated in the appointment of an independent person: s 77A(4) (as so added). Where the person appointed to undertake the counting of votes is not the scrutineer, his appointment must require him to send the voting papers back to the scrutineer as soon as reasonably practicable after the counting has been completed: s 77A(5) (as so added). As to the meaning of 'contravention' and cognate expressions see PARA 915 note 6.
14 Trade Union and Labour Relations (Consolidation) Act 1992 s 77(5). An inaccuracy in counting is to be disregarded if it is accidental and on a scale which could not affect the result of the ballot: s 77(5).

981.   Scrutineer's report on political ballot.   The scrutineer[1] must make a report to the trade union[2] as soon as reasonably practicable after the last date for the return of the voting papers[3]. The scrutineer's report must state:

(1)   the number of voting papers distributed for the purposes of the ballot;

(2)   the number of voting papers returned to the scrutineer;
(3)   the number of valid votes cast in the ballot for and against the resolution;
(4)   the number of spoiled or otherwise invalid voting papers returned; and
(5)   the name of any independent person or persons appointed by the union[4] to perform certain functions in relation to the ballot or, if no person was so appointed, that fact[5].

The report must also state whether the scrutineer is satisfied:

(a)   that there are no reasonable grounds for believing that there was any contravention[6] of a requirement imposed by or under any enactment in relation to the ballot;
(b)   that the arrangements made, whether by the scrutineer or by any other person, with respect to the production, storage, distribution, return or other handling of the voting papers used in the ballot, and the arrangements for the counting of the votes, included all such security arrangements as were reasonably practicable for the purpose of minimising the risk that any unfairness or malpractice might occur; and
(c)   that he has been able to carry out his functions without such interference as would make it reasonable for any person to call his independence in relation to the union into question;

and, if he is not satisfied as to any of those matters, the report must give particulars of his reasons for not being satisfied as to that matter[7].

The report must also state:

(i)   whether the scrutineer has inspected the register of names and addresses of the members of the trade union[8] or has examined the copy of the register supplied to him[9];
(ii)   if so, whether in each case he was acting on a request by a member of the trade union or at his own instance;
(iii) whether he declined to act on any such request; and
(iv)   whether any such inspection or examination has revealed any matter which he considers should be drawn to the attention of the trade union in order to assist it in securing that the register is accurate and up-to-date;

but the report must not state the name of any member who has requested such an inspection or examination[10].

The trade union must not publish the result of the ballot until it has received the scrutineer's report[11]; and the trade union must, within the period of three months after it receives the report, either:

(A)   send a copy of it to every member of the union to whom it is reasonably practicable to send such a copy; or
(B)   take all such other steps for notifying the contents of the report to the members of the union, whether by publishing the report or otherwise, as it is the practice of the union to take when matters of general interest to all its members need to be brought to their attention[12].

Any such copy or notification must be accompanied by a statement that the union will, on request, supply any member of the union with a copy of the report, either free of charge or on payment of such reasonable fee as may be specified in the notification[13]; and the trade union must so supply any member of the union who makes such a request and pays the fee, if any, notified to him[14].

1   Ie the person appointed under the Trade Union and Labour Relations (Consolidation) Act 1992 s 75: see PARA 979.

2   As to the meaning of 'trade union' see PARA 891. As to the application of the statutory
    provisions concerning the use of funds for political objects to federated trade unions see PARA
    891 note 9 head (6).
3   Trade Union and Labour Relations (Consolidation) Act 1992 s 75(3)(c).
4   Ie under the Trade Union and Labour Relations (Consolidation) Act 1992 s 77A: see PARA 980.
    Where one or more persons other than the scrutineer is or are so appointed, the statement
    included in the scrutineer's report in accordance with s 78(2)(b) (see head (b) in the text) must
    also indicate whether he is satisfied with the performance of the person, or each of the persons,
    so appointed, and, if he is not satisfied, the report must indicate particulars of his reasons for
    not being so satisfied: s 78(2B) (s 78(2A), (2B) added by the Trade Union Reform and
    Employment Rights Act 1993 Sch 1 para 4(c)).
5   Trade Union and Labour Relations (Consolidation) Act 1992 s 78(1) (amended by the Trade
    Union Reform and Employment Rights Act 1993 Sch 1 para 4(a), Sch 10).
6   As to the meaning of 'contravention' and cognate expressions see PARA 915 note 6.
7   Trade Union and Labour Relations (Consolidation) Act 1992 s 78(2) (amended by the Trade
    Union Reform and Employment Rights Act 1993 Sch 1 para 4(b)).
8   As to the register of members' names and addresses see PARA 930.
9   Ie the copy of the register as at the relevant date which is supplied to him in accordance with the
    Trade Union and Labour Relations (Consolidation) Act 1992 s 75(5A)(a): see PARA 979 head (i).
10 Trade Union and Labour Relations (Consolidation) Act 1992 s 78(2A) (as added: see note 4).
11 Trade Union and Labour Relations (Consolidation) Act 1992 s 78(3).
12 Trade Union and Labour Relations (Consolidation) Act 1992 s 78(4).
13 Trade Union and Labour Relations (Consolidation) Act 1992 s 78(5).
14 Trade Union and Labour Relations (Consolidation) Act 1992 s 78(6).

982.   Remedy for failure to comply with political ballot rules; in general.   The
remedy for:
  (1)   the taking by a trade union[1] of a ballot on a political resolution[2]
        otherwise than in accordance with political ballot rules approved by the
        certification officer[3]; or
  (2)   the failure of a trade union to comply with the political ballot rules so
        approved, in relation to a proposed ballot on a political resolution,
is by way of application to the certification officer[4] or to the High Court[5].
   An application may be so made only by a person having a sufficient interest,
namely a person who is a member of the trade union and who, where the ballot
has been held, was a member at the time when it was held[6]; but no such
application may be made after the end of the period of one year beginning with
the day on which the union announced the result of the ballot[7].

1   As to the meaning of 'trade union' see PARA 891. As to the application of the statutory
    provisions concerning the use of funds for political objects to federated trade unions see PARA
    891 note 9 head (6).
2   As to the meaning of 'political resolution' see PARA 974.
3   As to approval of political ballot rules see PARA 978; and as to the certification officer see PARA
    1443. As to the meaning of 'rules', in relation to a trade union, see PARA 898 note 5.
4   Ie under the Trade Union and Labour Relations (Consolidation) Act 1992 s 80: see PARA 983.
    An appeal lies to the Employment Appeal Tribunal on any question of law arising in
    proceedings before or arising from any decision of the certification officer under s 80: see s 95;
    and PARA 997. As to the Employment Appeal Tribunal see PARA 1422 et seq.
5   Trade Union and Labour Relations (Consolidation) Act 1992 ss 79(1), 121. Application to the
    High Court is under s 81: see PARA 984.
6   See the Trade Union and Labour Relations (Consolidation) Act 1992 s 79(2).
7   Trade Union and Labour Relations (Consolidation) Act 1992 s 79(3).

**983.   Application to the certification officer for a declaration relating to a
political ballot.**   A person having a sufficient interest[1] who claims that a trade
union[2]:
  (1)   has held a ballot on a political resolution[3] otherwise than in accordance
        with political ballot rules approved by the certification officer[4]; or

(2)   has failed in relation to a proposed ballot on a political resolution to comply with political ballot rules so approved,

may apply to the certification officer for a declaration to that effect[5].

On such an application being made to him, the certification officer must make such inquiries as he thinks fit[6] and must give the applicant and the trade union an opportunity to be heard; and he may make or refuse the declaration asked for[7]. Whether he makes or refuses a declaration, he must give reasons for his decision in writing; and the reasons may be accompanied by written observations on any matter arising from, or connected with, the proceedings[8]. If he makes a declaration, he must specify in it the provisions with which the trade union has failed to comply[9]; and, where he makes a declaration and is satisfied that steps have been taken by the union with a view to remedying the declared failure, or securing that a failure of the same or any similar kind does not occur in future, or that the union has agreed to take such steps, he must, in making the declaration, specify those steps[10].

Where the certification officer makes a declaration, he must, unless he considers that to do so would be inappropriate, make an order (an 'enforcement order') imposing on the union one or more of the following requirements:

(a)   to secure the holding of a ballot in accordance with the order;

(b)   to take such other steps to remedy the declared failure as may be specified in the order;

(c)   to abstain from such acts as may be so specified with a view to securing that a failure of the same or a similar kind does not occur in future[11].

Where the certification officer makes an order requiring the union to hold a fresh ballot, he must require the ballot to be conducted in accordance with the union's political ballot rules and such other provisions as may be made by the order, unless he considers that it would be inappropriate to do so in the particular circumstances of the case[12].

Where an enforcement order has been made, any person who is a member of the union and was a member at the time the order was made is entitled to enforce obedience to the order as if he had made the application on which the order was made[13].

If a person applies to the court[14] in relation to a matter:

(i)   that person may not apply to the certification officer[15] in relation to that matter;

(ii)   on an application by a different person to the certification officer in relation to that matter, the certification officer must have due regard to any declaration, order, observations or reasons made or given by the court regarding that matter and brought to the certification officer's notice[16].

1   Ie a person to whom the Trade Union and Labour Relations (Consolidation) Act 1992 s 79(2) applies: see PARA 982.

2   As to the meaning of 'trade union' see PARA 891. As to the application of the statutory provisions concerning the use of funds for political objects to federated trade unions see PARA 891 note 9 head (6).

3   As to the meaning of 'political resolution' see PARA 974; and as to ballots see PARA 977 et seq.

4   As to the approval of political ballot rules see PARA 978; and as to the certification officer see PARA 1443. As to the meaning of 'rules', in relation to a trade union, see PARA 898 note 5.

5   Trade Union and Labour Relations (Consolidation) Act 1992 s 80(1). As to when the application may be made see PARA 982. A declaration made by the certification officer under s 80 may be relied on as if it were a declaration made by the court: s 80(8) (s 80(8)–(10) added by the Employment Relations Act 1999 Sch 6 paras 1, 15(1), (4)). An appeal lies to the Employment Appeal Tribunal on any question of law arising in proceedings before or arising

from any decision of the certification officer under the Trade Union and Labour Relations (Consolidation) Act 1992 s 80: see s 95; and PARA 997. As to the Employment Appeal Tribunal see PARA 1422 et seq.

6 Where the certification officer requests a person to furnish information to him in connection with his inquiries, he must specify the date by which it is to be furnished, and he must proceed with his determination of the application notwithstanding that the information has not been furnished to him by the specified date, unless he considers that it would be inappropriate to do so: Trade Union and Labour Relations (Consolidation) Act 1992 s 80(7).

7 Trade Union and Labour Relations (Consolidation) Act 1992 s 80(2) (amended by the Employment Relations Act 1999 Sch 6 paras 1, 15, Sch 9). In exercising his functions under the Trade Union and Labour Relations (Consolidation) Act 1992 s 80, the certification officer must ensure that, so far as is reasonably practicable, the application is determined within six months of being made: s 80(6).

8 Trade Union and Labour Relations (Consolidation) Act 1992 s 80(5).

9 Trade Union and Labour Relations (Consolidation) Act 1992 s 80(3).

10 Trade Union and Labour Relations (Consolidation) Act 1992 s 80(4).

11 Trade Union and Labour Relations (Consolidation) Act 1992 s 80(5A) (s 80(5A)–(5C) added by the Employment Relations Act 1999 Sch 6 paras 1, 15(1), (3)). The certification officer must in an order imposing any such requirement as is mentioned in the Trade Union and Labour Relations (Consolidation) Act 1992 s 80(5A)(a) or (b) (see heads (a)–(b) in the text) specify the period within which the union is to comply with the requirements of the order: s 80(5A) (as so added).

12 Trade Union and Labour Relations (Consolidation) Act 1992 s 80(5B) (as added: see note 11).

13 Trade Union and Labour Relations (Consolidation) Act 1992 s 80(5C) (as added: see note 11). An enforcement order made by the certification officer under s 80 may be enforced in the same way as an order of the court: s 80(9) (as added: see note 5).

14 Ie under the Trade Union and Labour Relations (Consolidation) Act 1992 s 81: see PARA 984.

15 Ie under the Trade Union and Labour Relations (Consolidation) Act 1992 s 80.

16 Trade Union and Labour Relations (Consolidation) Act 1992 s 80(10) (as added: see note 5).

984. Application to the court for a declaration relating to a political ballot. A person having a sufficient interest[1] who claims that a trade union[2]:

(1) has held a ballot on a political resolution[3] otherwise than in accordance with political ballot rules approved by the certification officer[4]; or

(2) has failed in relation to a proposed ballot on a political resolution to comply with political ballot rules so approved,

may apply to the High Court for a declaration to that effect[5].

If the court makes the declaration asked for, it must specify in it the provisions with which the union has failed to comply[6]. Where the court makes a declaration, it must also, unless it considers that to do so would be inappropriate, make an order (an 'enforcement order') imposing on the union one or more of the following requirements:

(a) to secure the holding of a ballot in accordance with the order[7];

(b) to take such other steps to remedy the declared failure as may be specified in the order;

(c) to abstain from such acts as may be so specified with a view to securing that a failure of the same or a similar kind does not occur in future[8].

Where the court makes an order requiring the union to hold a fresh ballot, the court must require the ballot to be conducted in accordance with the union's political ballot rules and such other provisions as may be made by the order, unless the court considers that it would be inappropriate to do so in the particular circumstances of the case[9].

Where an enforcement order has been made, any person who is a member of the union and was a member at the time the order was made is entitled to enforce obedience to the order as if he had made the application on which the order was made[10].

If a person applies to the certification officer[11] in relation to a matter:

(i)   that person may not apply to the court[12] in relation to that matter;
(ii)   on an application by a different person to the court in relation to that matter, the court must have due regard to any declaration, order, observations or reasons made or given by the certification officer regarding that matter and brought to the court's notice[13].

1   Ie a person to whom the Trade Union and Labour Relations (Consolidation) Act 1992 s 79(2) applies: see PARA 982.
2   As to the meaning of 'trade union' see PARA 891. As to the application of the statutory provisions concerning the use of funds for political objects to federated trade unions see PARA 891 note 9 head (6).
3   As to the meaning of 'political resolution' see PARA 974; and as to ballots see PARA 977 et seq.
4   As to the approval of political ballot rules see PARA 978; and as to the certification officer see PARA 1443. As to the meaning of 'rules', in relation to a trade union, see PARA 898 note 5.
5   Trade Union and Labour Relations (Consolidation) Act 1992 ss 81(1), 121. As to when the application may be made see PARA 982. Without prejudice to any other power of the court, the court may, on such an application, grant such interlocutory relief as it considers appropriate: s 81(7).
6   Trade Union and Labour Relations (Consolidation) Act 1992 s 81(3).
7   The court must specify the period within which the union must comply with the requirements of the order: Trade Union and Labour Relations (Consolidation) Act 1992 s 81(4).
8   Trade Union and Labour Relations (Consolidation) Act 1992 s 81(4).
9   Trade Union and Labour Relations (Consolidation) Act 1992 s 81(5).
10 Trade Union and Labour Relations (Consolidation) Act 1992 s 81(6).
11 Ie under the Trade Union and Labour Relations (Consolidation) Act 1992 s 80: see PARA 983.
12 Ie under the Trade Union and Labour Relations (Consolidation) Act 1992 s 81.
13 Trade Union and Labour Relations (Consolidation) Act 1992 s 81(8) (added by Employment Relations Act 1999 Sch 6 paras 1, 16(1), (3)).

(iii)   The Political Fund

985.   Rules as to the political fund.   The funds of a trade union[1] may not be applied in the furtherance of certain political objects[2] unless there are in force rules[3] of the union which have been approved by the certification officer[4] and which provide:
(1)   that payments in the furtherance of those political objects must be made out of a separate fund (the 'political fund' of the union);
(2)   that a member who gives notice[5] that he objects to contributing to the political fund is to be exempt from any obligation to contribute to it;
(3)   that a member is not, by reason of being so exempt, to be excluded from any benefits of the union, or to be placed in any respect, either directly or indirectly, under a disability or at a disadvantage[6] as compared with other members of the union, except in relation to the control or management of the political fund[7]; and
(4)   that contribution to the political fund is not to be made a condition for admission to the union[8].
A member of a trade union who claims that he is aggrieved by a breach of any rule made in pursuance of the above requirements may complain to the certification officer[9]. On a complaint being made to him, the certification officer must make such inquiries as he thinks fit[10].
Where, after giving the member and a representative of the union an opportunity of being heard, the certification officer considers that a breach has been committed, he may make such order for remedying the breach as he thinks just under the circumstances[11]. Where such an order has been made, any person who is a member of the union and was a member at the time it was made is entitled to enforce obedience to the order as if he had made the complaint on

which it was made[12]. Such an order made by the certification officer may be enforced in the same way as an order of the County Court[13].

1 As to the meaning of 'trade union' see PARA 891. As to the application of the statutory provisions concerning the use of funds for political objects to federated trade unions see PARA 891 note 9 head (6).
2 Ie the political objects set out in the Trade Union and Labour Relations (Consolidation) Act 1992 s 72: see PARA 975.
3 As to the meaning of 'rules', in relation to a trade union, see PARA 898 note 5.
4 See the Trade Union and Labour Relations (Consolidation) Act 1992 s 71(1)(b); and PARA 974 head (2). As to the special method for the adoption of political fund rules see PARA 994; and as to the certification officer see PARA 1443.
5 Ie in accordance with the Trade Union and Labour Relations (Consolidation) Act 1992 s 84: see PARA 987.
6 The disadvantage must be material and substantial, and not merely technical: *Reeves v Transport and General Workers' Union* [1980] ICR 728, [1980] IRLR 307, EAT; cf *Elliott v SOGAT 1975* [1983] IRLR 3.
7 The protection of exempt members continues after the union's political fund rules cease to have effect: see the Trade Union and Labour Relations (Consolidation) Act 1992 s 91(4); and PARA 993.
8 Trade Union and Labour Relations (Consolidation) Act 1992 s 82(1).
9 Trade Union and Labour Relations (Consolidation) Act 1992 s 82(2). Where a rule ceases to have effect, s 82(2) continues to operate in relation to a breach of that rule occurring before that date: see s 91(3); and PARA 993. An appeal lies to the Employment Appeal Tribunal on any question of law arising in proceedings before or arising from any decision of the certification officer under s 82: see s 95; and PARA 997. As to the Employment Appeal Tribunal see PARA 1422 et seq.
10 Trade Union and Labour Relations (Consolidation) Act 1992 s 82(2A) (added by the Employment Relations Act 1999 Sch 6 paras 1, 17(1), (2)). Where the certification officer requests a person to furnish information to him in connection with inquiries made by him under the Trade Union and Labour Relations (Consolidation) Act 1992 s 82, he must specify the date by which that information is to be furnished; and, unless he considers that it would be inappropriate to do so, he must proceed with his determination of the application notwithstanding that the information has not been furnished to him by the specified date: s 82(3A) (added by the Employment Relations Act 1999 Sch 6 paras 1, 17(1), (3)).
11 Trade Union and Labour Relations (Consolidation) Act 1992 s 82(3).
12 Trade Union and Labour Relations (Consolidation) Act 1992 s 82(4A) (s 82(4A), (4B) respectively substituted and added by the Employment Relations Act 2004 Sch 1 para 6).
13 Trade Union and Labour Relations (Consolidation) Act 1992 s 82(4B) (as added: see note 12). As to enforcement of County Court judgments see CIVIL PROCEDURE vol 12 (2009) PARA 1223 et seq.

986. Assets and liabilities of the political fund. There may be added to the political fund[1] of a trade union[2] only:

(1) sums representing contributions made to the fund by members of the union or by any person other than the union itself; and

(2) property which accrues to the fund in the course of administering its assets[3].

The rules[4] of the union are not to be taken to require any member to contribute to the political fund at a time when there is no political resolution[5] in force in relation to the union[6].

No liability of a union's political fund may be discharged out of any other fund of the union, notwithstanding any term or condition on which the liability was incurred or that an asset of the other fund has been charged in connection with the liability[7].

The political fund is protected property for the purposes of the statutory provisions[8] restricting the enforcement of certain awards of damages[9].

1 As to the political fund see PARA 985.

2   As to the meaning of 'trade union' see PARA 891. As to the application of the statutory
    provisions concerning the use of funds for political objects to federated trade unions see PARA
    891 note 9 head (6).
3   Trade Union and Labour Relations (Consolidation) Act 1992 s 83(1).
4   As to the meaning of 'rules', in relation to a trade union, see PARA 898 note 5.
5   As to the meaning of 'political resolution' see PARA 974.
6   Trade Union and Labour Relations (Consolidation) Act 1992 s 83(2). As to the position where
    a political resolution expires see PARA 991 et seq.
7   Trade Union and Labour Relations (Consolidation) Act 1992 s 83(3).
8   Ie the Trade Union and Labour Relations (Consolidation) Act 1992 s 23: see PARA 928.
9   See the Trade Union and Labour Relations (Consolidation) Act 1992 s 23(2)(d); and PARA 928
    head (d).

987.   Notice of objection to contributing to the political fund.   On the
adoption of a political resolution[1], notice must be given to the members of the
trade union[2] acquainting them:

(1)   that each member has the right to be exempted from contributing to the
      union's political fund[3]; and

(2)   that a form of exemption notice can be obtained by or on behalf of a
      member either by application at or by post[4] from the head office or any
      branch office of the union or the office of the certification officer[5].

The notice to members must be given in accordance with rules[6] of the union
approved for the purpose by the certification officer, who must have regard in
each case to the existing practice and character of the union[7].

A member of a trade union may give notice in the statutory form[8], or in a
form to the like effect, that he objects to contribute to the political fund of the
union[9]. On so giving an exemption notice, a member is exempt from
contributing to the union's political fund as from 1 January next after the
exemption notice is given, or, where the notice is given within one month of the
giving of notice to members following the passing of a political resolution on a
ballot held at a time when no such resolution is in force, as from the date on
which the exemption notice is given[10]. An exemption notice continues to have
effect until it is withdrawn[11].

1   As to the meaning of 'political resolution' see PARA 974.
2   As to the meaning of 'trade union' see PARA 891. As to the application of the statutory
     provisions concerning the use of funds for political objects to federated trade unions see PARA
     891 note 9 head (6).
3   As to the establishment of the political fund see PARA 977 et seq.
4   As to the construction of references to requiring or authorising a document or other thing to be
     sent by post see PARA 962 note 10.
5   Trade Union and Labour Relations (Consolidation) Act 1992 s 84(2). As to the certification
     officer see PARA 1443.
6   As to the meaning of 'rules', in relation to a trade union, see PARA 898 note 5.
7   Trade Union and Labour Relations (Consolidation) Act 1992 s 84(3).
8   Ie in the form set out in the Trade Union and Labour Relations (Consolidation) Act 1992
     s 84(1).
9   Trade Union and Labour Relations (Consolidation) Act 1992 s 84(1).
10   Trade Union and Labour Relations (Consolidation) Act 1992 s 84(4).
11   Trade Union and Labour Relations (Consolidation) Act 1992 s 84(5).

**988.   Manner of giving effect to exemption from contributing to the political
fund.**   Effect may be given to the exemption of members from contributing to
the political fund[1] of a trade union[2] either:

(1)   by a separate levy of contributions to that fund from the members who
      are not exempt; or

(2) by relieving members who are exempt from the payment of the whole or part of any periodical contribution required from members towards the expenses of the union[3].

In the latter case the rules[4] must provide:

(a) that the relief is to be given as far as possible to all members who are exempt on the occasion of the same periodical payment[5]; and

(b) for enabling each member of the union to know what portion, if any, of any periodical contribution payable by him is a contribution to the political fund[6].

1 As to the political fund see PARA 985; and as to the right to exemption from contributing to the political fund see PARA 987.
2 As to the meaning of 'trade union' see PARA 891. As to the application of the statutory provisions concerning the use of funds for political objects to federated trade unions see PARA 891 note 9 head (6).
3 Trade Union and Labour Relations (Consolidation) Act 1992 s 85(1).
4 As to the meaning of 'rules', in relation to a trade union, see PARA 898 note 5.
5 An employer's practice of deducting contributions to the political fund from the pay of both contributing and exempt members and refunding those contributions to exempt members in advance or, if not possible, as soon as possible thereafter, was held lawful in *Reeves v Transport and General Workers' Union* [1980] ICR 728, [1980] IRLR 307, EAT; but this would now be unlawful under the Trade Union and Labour Relations (Consolidation) Act 1992 s 86 (see PARA 989).
6 Trade Union and Labour Relations (Consolidation) Act 1992 s 85(2).

(iv) Protection against Unauthorised Deduction of Political Fund Contributions by Employer

989. Certificate of exemption or objection to contributing to the political fund. If a member of a trade union[1] which has a political fund[2] certifies in writing to his employer[3] that, or to the effect that:

(1) he is exempt from the obligation to contribute to the political fund; or

(2) he has notified the union in writing[4] of his objection to contributing to the fund,

the employer must ensure that no amount representing a contribution to the political fund is deducted by him from emoluments payable to the member[5].

An employer may not refuse to deduct any union dues from emoluments payable to a person who has given such a certificate if he continues to deduct union dues from emoluments payable to other members of the union, unless his refusal is not attributable to the giving of the certificate or otherwise connected with the duty imposed[6] as a result of the certificate[7].

1 As to the meaning of 'trade union' see PARA 891. As to the application of the statutory provisions concerning the use of funds for political objects to federated trade unions see PARA 891 note 9 head (6).
2 As to the political fund see PARA 985.
3 As to the meaning of 'employer' see PARA 892.
4 Ie in accordance with the Trade Union and Labour Relations (Consolidation) Act 1992 s 84: see PARA 987.
5 Trade Union and Labour Relations (Consolidation) Act 1992 s 86(1). The employer's duty under s 86(1) applies from the first day, following the giving of the certificate, on which it is reasonably practicable for him to comply with that duty, and continues until the certificate is withdrawn: s 86(2). As to a person's right to apply to an employment tribunal in respect of an employer's failure to comply with s 86 see PARA 990.
6 Ie the duty not to deduct political fund contributions imposed by the Trade Union and Labour Relations (Consolidation) Act 1992 s 86(1).
7 Trade Union and Labour Relations (Consolidation) Act 1992 s 86(3). Where, on a complaint under s 87(1) (see PARA 990) arising out of s 86(3), the question arises whether the employer's

refusal to deduct an amount was attributable to the giving of the certificate or was otherwise connected with the duty under s 86(1), it will be for the employer to satisfy the tribunal that it was not: see s 87(3); and PARA 990 note 3. If an employee is dismissed or selected for redundancy because he brought proceedings to enforce the right under s 86, his dismissal is automatically regarded as unfair: see PARAS 1063, 1064.

990.   Application to employment tribunal in respect of the employer's failure.
A person who claims that his employer[1] has failed to comply with his statutory duty[2] in deducting or refusing to deduct any amount from emoluments payable to him may present a complaint to an employment tribunal[3]. A tribunal must not consider such a complaint unless it is presented[4]:

(1)   within the period of three months beginning with the date of the payment of the emoluments or, if the complaint relates to more than one payment, the last of the payments[5], subject to an extension to facilitate conciliation before the institution of proceedings[6]; or

(2)   where the tribunal is satisfied that it was not reasonably practical for the complaint to be presented within that period, within such further period as the tribunal considers reasonable[7].

Where a tribunal finds that such a complaint is well-founded:

(a)   it must make a declaration to that effect and, where the complaint arises out of a deduction of union dues[8], order the employer to pay to the complainant the amount deducted in contravention of the statutory duty[9] less any part of that amount already paid to him by the employer; and

(b)   it may, if it considers it appropriate to do so in order to prevent a repetition of the failure, make an order requiring the employer to take, within a specified time, the steps specified in the order in relation to emoluments payable by him to the complainant[10].

A person who claims that his employer has failed to comply with an order made under head (b) above on a complaint presented by him may present a further complaint to an employment tribunal, but only one such further complaint may be presented in relation to any order[11]; but a tribunal must not consider such a complaint unless it is presented after the end of the period of four weeks beginning with the date of the order, but before the end of the period of six months beginning with that date[12]. Where, on such a complaint, a tribunal finds that an employer has, without reasonable excuse, failed to comply with an order under head (b) above, it must order the employer to pay to the complainant an amount equal to two weeks' pay[13].

1   As to the meaning of 'employer' see PARA 892.
2   Ie the duty imposed by the Trade Union and Labour Relations (Consolidation) Act 1992 s 86: see PARA 989.
3   Trade Union and Labour Relations (Consolidation) Act 1992 s 87(1) (s 87 substituted by the Employment Rights (Dispute Resolution) Act 1998 s 6). Where, on a complaint under the Trade Union and Labour Relations (Consolidation) Act 1992 s 87(1) arising out of s 86(3) (refusal to deduct union dues: see PARA 989), the question arises whether the employer's refusal to deduct an amount was attributable to the giving of the certificate or was otherwise connected with his duty under by s 86(1) (see PARA 989), it is for the employer to satisfy the tribunal that it was not: s 87(3) (as so substituted). If an employee is dismissed or selected for redundancy because he brought proceedings to enforce the right under s 86, his dismissal is automatically regarded as unfair: see PARAS 1063, 1064.
    The provisions of the Employment Tribunals Act 1996 ss 18A–18B (conciliation) (see PARA 152) apply in the case of matters which could be the subject of employment tribunal proceedings under the Trade Union and Labour Relations (Consolidation) Act 1992 s 87, and the Employment Tribunals Act 1996 s 18C applies in the case of such proceedings themselves: see

s 18(1)(a), (1A) (s 18(1)(a) substituted by SI 2014/431; the Employment Tribunals Act 1996 s 18(1A) added by the Enterprise and Regulatory Reform Act 2013 Sch 1 paras 2, 5(1), (7)).

4　As to when a complaint is presented see PARA 804. The expression 'beginning with' means that the day on which the complaint is presented must be counted in: *Trow v Ind Coope (West Midlands) Ltd* [1967] 2 QB 899, [1967] 2 All ER 900, CA, applied in *Hammond v Haigh Castle & Co Ltd* [1973] 2 All ER 289, [1973] ICR 148, NIRC. The proper method to calculate the final date for presentation is to go back one day from the date of the conduct and then to go forward three calendar months from that date; if there is no corresponding date in that month, the last day of the month is taken: *Pruden v Cunard Ellerman Ltd* [1993] IRLR 317, EAT (a decision in the context of unfair dismissal law).

5　Trade Union and Labour Relations (Consolidation) Act 1992 s 87(2)(a) (as substituted: see note 3).

6　The Trade Union and Labour Relations (Consolidation) Act 1992 s 292A (extension of time limits to facilitate conciliation before institution of proceedings: see PARA 1455) applies for the purposes of s 87(2)(a): s 87(2A) (added by the Enterprise and Regulatory Reform Act 2013 Sch 2 paras 1, 5).

7　Trade Union and Labour Relations (Consolidation) Act 1992 s 87(2)(b) (as substituted: see note 3). For the case law on the extension of time limits, especially in the context of the law of unfair dismissal, see PARAS 804, 1453.

8　Ie under the Trade Union and Labour Relations (Consolidation) Act 1992 s 86(1).

9　Ie the duty imposed by the Trade Union and Labour Relations (Consolidation) Act 1992 s 86(1).

10　Trade Union and Labour Relations (Consolidation) Act 1992 s 87(4) (as substituted: see note 3). Such an order may not be made in relation to Crown employment: see s 273(2); and PARA 893. As to the meaning of 'Crown employment' see PARA 893 note 3.

11　Trade Union and Labour Relations (Consolidation) Act 1992 s 87(5) (as substituted: see note 3).

12　Trade Union and Labour Relations (Consolidation) Act 1992 s 87(6) (as substituted: see note 3).

13　Trade Union and Labour Relations (Consolidation) Act 1992 s 87(7) (as substituted: see note 3). For these purposes, the Employment Rights Act 1996 Pt XIV Ch II (ss 220–229) (calculation of a week's pay) (see PARA 143 et seq) applies, except that, for the purposes of Pt XIV Ch II in its application to the Trade Union and Labour Relations (Consolidation) Act 1992 s 87(7), the calculation date is the date of the payment or, if more than one, the last of the payments, to which the complaint related: Employment Rights Act 1996 s 225 (substituted for these purposes by the Trade Union and Labour Relations (Consolidation) Act 1992 s 87(8) (as substituted: see note 3)). Where the making of a deduction contravenes both the Trade Union and Labour Relations (Consolidation) Act 1992 s 86(1) and s 68(1) (deduction of unauthorised subscriptions) (see PARA 1034), the aggregate amount which may be ordered to be paid in respect of the contraventions is not to exceed the amount, or the greatest amount, which may be ordered to be paid in respect of any one of them: see s 68A(3), (4)(c); and PARA 1035 note 9.

(v) Political Resolution ceasing to have Effect

991. Administration of the political fund where a political resolution is no longer in force. Where there ceases to be any political resolution[1] in force in relation to a trade union[2] as a consequence of the passage of time[3], no payments may be made out of the political fund[4] in furtherance of political objects after the political resolution ceases to have effect[5]. If the resolution ceases to have effect by reason of a ballot being held on which a new political resolution is not passed[6], the union may continue to make payments out of the fund as if the resolution had continued in force for six months beginning with the date of the ballot[7], but no payment is to be made which causes the fund to be in deficit or increases a deficit in it[8]. Where a political resolution ceases to have effect, there may be added to the political fund only contributions to the fund paid to the union, or to a person on its behalf, before the resolution ceased to have effect[9], and property which accrues to the fund in the course of administering the assets of the fund[10]; and the union may transfer the whole or part of the political fund to such other fund of the union as it thinks fit, notwithstanding any of its rules[11] or any trusts on which the fund is held[12]. If a new political resolution is subsequently passed, no property held immediately before the date of the ballot by or on behalf of the union otherwise than in its political fund, and no sums representing such property, may be added to the fund[13].

1 As to the meaning of 'political resolution' see PARA 974.
2 As to the meaning of 'trade union' see PARA 891. As to the application of the statutory provisions concerning the use of funds for political objects to federated trade unions see PARA 891 note 9 head (6).
3 Ie under the Trade Union and Labour Relations (Consolidation) Act 1992 s 73(3), which provides that a political resolution will cease to have effect at the end of the period of ten years beginning with the date of the ballot on which it was passed: see PARA 977.
4 As to the political fund see PARA 985.
5 See the Trade Union and Labour Relations (Consolidation) Act 1992 s 71(1); and PARA 974.
6 As to the passing and effect of a new political resolution see PARA 977.
7 As to the meaning of 'date of the ballot' see PARA 977 note 5.
8 Trade Union and Labour Relations (Consolidation) Act 1992 s 89(1), (2).
9 As to the duty of the union to discontinue the collection of contributions to the political fund where there ceases to be a political resolution in force see PARA 992.
10 Trade Union and Labour Relations (Consolidation) Act 1992 s 89(1), (3).
11 As to the meaning of 'rules', in relation to a trade union, see PARA 898 note 5.
12 Trade Union and Labour Relations (Consolidation) Act 1992 s 89(1), (4).
13 Trade Union and Labour Relations (Consolidation) Act 1992 s 89(1), (5).

992. Discontinuance of contributions to the political fund. Where there ceases to be any political resolution[1] in force in relation to a trade union[2], the union must take such steps as are necessary to ensure that the collection of subscriptions to its political fund is discontinued as soon as is reasonably practicable[3]. The union may, notwithstanding any of its rules[4], pay into any of its other funds any contribution to the political fund which is received by it after the resolution ceases to have effect[5]; but, if the union continues to collect contributions, it must refund to a member who applies for a refund the contribution made by him collected after the resolution ceased to have effect[6].

A member of a trade union who claims that the union has failed to comply with the duty to discontinue the collection of subscriptions may apply to the High Court for a declaration to that effect[7]; and, where the court is satisfied that the complaint is well-founded, it may make an order requiring the union to take, within such time as may be specified in the order, such steps as may be so specified, if the court considers it appropriate to do so in order to secure that the collection of contributions to the political fund is discontinued[8]. Such an order may be enforced by a person who is a member of the union and was a member at the time the order was made as if he had made the application[9].

1 As to the meaning of 'political resolution' see PARA 974. As to when a political resolution ceases to be in force see PARA 977.
2 As to the meaning of 'trade union' see PARA 891. As to the application of the statutory provisions concerning the use of funds for political objects to federated trade unions see PARA 891 note 9 head (6).
3 Trade Union and Labour Relations (Consolidation) Act 1992 s 90(1).
4 As to the meaning of 'rules', in relation to a trade union, see PARA 898 note 5.
5 Trade Union and Labour Relations (Consolidation) Act 1992 s 90(2).
6 Trade Union and Labour Relations (Consolidation) Act 1992 s 90(3).
7 Trade Union and Labour Relations (Consolidation) Act 1992 ss 90(4), 121.
8 Trade Union and Labour Relations (Consolidation) Act 1992 s 90(5). The remedy for failure to comply with s 90(1) is in accordance with s 90(4), (5) and not otherwise; but this does not affect any right to recover sums payable to a person under s 90(3) (see the text and note 6): s 90(6). Where the making of a deduction contravenes both s 90(1) and s 68 (deduction of unauthorised subscriptions) (see PARA 1034), the aggregate amount which may be ordered to be paid in respect of the contraventions is not to exceed the amount, or the greatest amount, which may be ordered to be paid in respect of any one of them: see s 68A(3), (4)(c); and PARA 1035 note 9.
9 Trade Union and Labour Relations (Consolidation) Act 1992 s 90(5).

993. Effect of expiry of political resolution on political fund rules. If there ceases to be any political resolution in force[1] in relation to a trade union[2], the rules[3] of the union made for the purpose of complying with the statutory requirements[4] also cease to have effect, except so far as they are required to enable the political fund to be administered at a time when there is no such resolution in force[5]. If the resolution ceases to have effect by reason of a ballot being held on which a new political resolution is not passed, the rules cease to have effect at the end of the period of six months beginning with the date of the ballot[6], but in any other case the rules cease to have effect when the resolution ceases to have effect[7].

No member of a trade union who has at any time been exempt from the obligation to contribute to its political fund[8] is, by reason of his having been so exempt, to be excluded from any benefits of the union or be placed in any respect either directly or indirectly under a disability or at a disadvantage[9] as compared with other members of the union, except in relation to the control or management of the political fund[10].

Nothing in the above provisions affects the right of an aggrieved member of a union to make a complaint to the certification officer[11] in relation to a breach of a rule occurring before the rule in question ceased to have effect[12].

1 As to when a political resolution ceases to be in force see PARA 977.
2 As to the meaning of 'trade union' see PARA 891. As to the application of the statutory provisions concerning the use of funds for political objects to federated trade unions see PARA 891 note 9 head (6).
3 As to the meaning of 'rules', in relation to a trade union, see PARA 898 note 5.
4 Ie the requirements of the Trade Union and Labour Relations (Consolidation) Act 1992 Pt I Ch VI (ss 71–96): see PARAS 974 et seq, 994 et seq.
5 Trade Union and Labour Relations (Consolidation) Act 1992 s 91(1).
6 Trade Union and Labour Relations (Consolidation) Act 1992 s 91(2). As to the meaning of 'date of the ballot' see PARA 977 note 5. In such a case the union may continue to make payments out of the fund for six months beginning with the date of the ballot: see PARA 991.
7 Trade Union and Labour Relations (Consolidation) Act 1992 s 91(2).
8 As to the right to exemption from contributing to the political fund see PARA 987.
9 As to the meaning of 'disadvantage' see PARA 985 note 6.
10 Trade Union and Labour Relations (Consolidation) Act 1992 s 91(4). This provision is necessary because the union's political fund rules (which give protection to exempt members in similar terms: see s 82(1)(c); and PARA 985 head (3)) cease to have effect when the political resolution expires.
11 Ie nothing in the Trade Union and Labour Relations (Consolidation) Act 1992 s 91 affects the operation of s 82(2): see PARA 985. As to the certification officer see PARA 1443.
12 Trade Union and Labour Relations (Consolidation) Act 1992 s 91(3).

(vi) Application of Funds for Political Objects; Supplementary Provisions

994. Special method for adoption of political fund and political ballot rules. A trade union[1] is required[2] to obtain the approval of the certification officer[3] for its political fund rules[4] and its political ballot rules[5]. Any such rules may be adopted in accordance with the provisions as to the alteration of rules or the making of new rules contained in the rules of the union[6]. If, however, the certification officer is satisfied and certifies that such rules have been approved by a majority of the members of the union voting for the purpose, or by a majority of delegates of the union at a meeting called for the purpose, those rules have effect as rules of the union notwithstanding that the rules of the union as to the alteration of rules or the making of new rules have not been complied with[7].

1   As to the meaning of 'trade union' see PARA 891. As to the application of the statutory
    provisions concerning the use of funds for political objects to federated trade unions see PARA
    891 note 9 head (6).
2   Ie under the Trade Union and Labour Relations (Consolidation) Act 1992 s 71(1)(b) (political
    fund rules) (see PARA 974 head (2)) and s 74(1) (political ballot rules) (see PARA 978).
3   As to the certification officer see PARA 1443.
4   See PARA 985.
5   See PARA 978.
6   As to the making and alteration of union rules see PARA 910. As to the meaning of 'rules', in
    relation to a trade union, see PARA 898 note 5.
7   Trade Union and Labour Relations (Consolidation) Act 1992 s 92. An appeal lies to the
    Employment Appeal Tribunal on any question of law arising in proceedings before or arising
    from any decision of the certification officer under s 92: see s 95; and PARA 997. As to the
    Employment Appeal Tribunal see PARA 1422 et seq.

995.   Effect of an amalgamation of trade unions. Where, on an
amalgamation[1] of two or more trade unions[2], there is in force in relation to each
of them a political resolution[3] and such rules[4] as are required by the statutory
provisions relating to the application of funds for political objects[5], and the rules
of the amalgamated union in force immediately after the amalgamation include
such rules, the amalgamated union is to be treated for the purposes of the
statutory provisions as having passed a political resolution[6].

1   As to union amalgamations see PARA 998 et seq.
2   As to the meaning of 'trade union' see PARA 891. As to the application of the statutory
    provisions concerning the use of funds for political objects to federated trade unions see PARA
    891 note 9 head (6).
3   As to the meaning of 'political resolution' see PARA 974. As to the passing and effect of a
    political resolution see PARA 977.
4   As to the meaning of 'rules', in relation to a trade union, see PARA 898 note 5.
5   Ie the political fund and political ballot rules required for the purposes of the Trade Union and
    Labour Relations (Consolidation) Act 1992 Pt I Ch VI (ss 71–96): see PARAS 978, 985. Where
    one of the amalgamating unions is a Northern Ireland union, the references to the requirements
    of Pt I Ch VI (ss 71–96) are to be construed as references to the requirements of the
    corresponding provisions of the law of Northern Ireland: s 93(3). For these purposes, a
    'Northern Ireland union' means a trade union whose principal office is situated in Northern
    Ireland: s 120.
6   Trade Union and Labour Relations (Consolidation) Act 1992 s 93(1). The resolution is to be
    treated as having been passed on the date of the earliest of the ballots on which the resolutions
    in force immediately before the amalgamation with respect to the amalgamating unions were
    passed: s 93(2). As to the meaning of 'date of the ballot' see PARA 977 note 5.

996.   Effect of political resolution on overseas members of a trade union.
Where a political resolution is in force[1] in relation to a trade union[2], the union's
political ballot rules[3] in relation to a proposed ballot may provide for overseas
members of the union not to be accorded entitlement to vote in the ballot[4]; and
the rules providing for notice to be given to members of their right to object to
contribute to the political fund[5] may provide for notice not to be given by the
union to its overseas members[6]. 'Overseas member' means a member of the trade
union, other than a merchant seaman[7] or offshore worker[8], who is outside Great
Britain throughout the period during which votes may be cast[9].

1   As to the meaning of 'political resolution' see PARA 974. As to the passing and effect of a
    political resolution see PARA 977. The special rules concerning overseas members apply only
    where a political resolution is in force in relation to the union: see the Trade Union and Labour
    Relations (Consolidation) Act 1992 s 94(1).
2   As to the meaning of 'trade union' see PARA 891. As to the application of the statutory
    provisions concerning the use of funds for political objects to federated trade unions see PARA
    891 note 9 head (6).

3 Ie the rules made by the union for the purpose of complying with the Trade Union and Labour Relations (Consolidation) Act 1992 s 74: see PARA 978. As to the meaning of 'rules' generally, in relation to a trade union, see PARA 898 note 5.

4 Trade Union and Labour Relations (Consolidation) Act 1992 s 94(1)(a). Where provision is made in accordance with s 94(1)(a), the certification officer is not on that ground to withhold his approval of the rules: s 94(2). As to the certification officer see PARA 1443.

5 Ie the rules made by the union for the purpose of complying with the Trade Union and Labour Relations (Consolidation) Act 1992 s 84: see PARA 987.

6 Trade Union and Labour Relations (Consolidation) Act 1992 s 94(1)(b). Where provision is made in accordance with s 94(1)(b), the provisions of s 84(2) requiring notice to be given to members is not to be taken to require notice to be given to overseas members: s 94(2).

7 For these purposes, 'merchant seaman' means a person whose employment, or the greater part of it, is carried out on board sea-going ships: Trade Union and Labour Relations (Consolidation) Act 1992 s 94(3). As to the meaning of 'employment' see PARA 1042 note 2.

8 For these purposes, 'offshore worker' means a person in offshore employment, other than one who is in such employment in an area where the law of Northern Ireland applies: Trade Union and Labour Relations (Consolidation) Act 1992 s 94(3). As to the meaning of 'offshore employment' see PARA 970 note 5.

9 Trade Union and Labour Relations (Consolidation) Act 1992 s 94(3).

997. Appeals from certification officer's decisions as to the application of funds for political objects. An appeal lies to the Employment Appeal Tribunal[1] on any question of law arising in proceedings before or arising from any decision of the certification officer[2] under any of the statutory provisions[3] relating to the application of funds for political objects[4].

1 As to the Employment Appeal Tribunal see PARA 1422 et seq.
2 As to the certification officer see PARA 1443.
3 Ie the provisions of the Trade Union and Labour Relations (Consolidation) Act 1992 Pt I Ch VI (ss 71–96): see PARA 974 et seq.
4 Trade Union and Labour Relations (Consolidation) Act 1992 s 95.

(7) MERGER, SECESSION AND DISSOLUTION OF TRADE UNIONS

(i) Amalgamations and Transfers of Engagements

998. Amalgamation of trade unions. Two or more trade unions[1] may amalgamate and become one trade union, with or without a division or dissolution of the funds of any one or more of the amalgamating unions[2], but may not do so unless the instrument of amalgamation is approved by the certification officer[3] and certain statutory requirements relating to the giving of notice to members[4] and the passing by the required majority of a resolution approving the instrument of amalgamation[5] are complied with in respect of each of the amalgamating unions[6].

An amalgamation does not prejudice any right of any creditor of any trade union party to the amalgamation[7].

1 As to the meaning of 'trade union' see PARA 891. As to the application of these provisions to Northern Ireland unions see PARA 1013.
2 As to the effect of an amalgamation on the political fund see PARA 995.
3 Ie in accordance with the Trade Union and Labour Relations (Consolidation) Act 1992 s 98: see PARA 1001. As to the certification officer see PARA 1443.
4 Ie under the Trade Union and Labour Relations (Consolidation) Act 1992 s 99: see PARA 1002.
5 Ie under the Trade Union and Labour Relations (Consolidation) Act 1992 s 100: see PARA 1003 et seq.
6 Trade Union and Labour Relations (Consolidation) Act 1992 s 97(1) (amended by the Trade Union Reform and Employment Rights Act 1993 Sch 8 para 52). The statutory provisions apply

to every amalgamation notwithstanding anything in the rules of any of the trade unions concerned: Trade Union and Labour Relations (Consolidation) Act 1992 s 97(4). As to the meaning of 'rules', in relation to a trade union, see PARA 898 note 5. The statutory provisions do not apply to de-amalgamations, or the secession of a group of workers from a trade union, the legality of which depends on the union's rules: see *Burnley Nelson Rossendale and District Textile Workers' Union v Amalgamated Textile Workers' Union* [1986] 1 All ER 885, [1987] ICR 69; and PARA 1014.

7 Trade Union and Labour Relations (Consolidation) Act 1992 s 97(3).

999. Transfer of engagements to another trade union. A trade union[1] may transfer its engagements to another trade union which undertakes to fulfil those engagements, but may not do so unless the instrument of transfer is approved by the certification officer[2] and certain statutory requirements relating to the giving of notice to members[3] and the passing by the required majority of a resolution approving the instrument of transfer[4] are complied with in respect of the transferor union[5].

A transfer of engagements does not prejudice any right of any creditor of any trade union party to the transfer[6].

1 As to the meaning of 'trade union' see PARA 891. As to the application of these provisions to Northern Ireland unions see PARA 1013.
2 Ie in accordance with the Trade Union and Labour Relations (Consolidation) Act 1992 s 98: see PARA 1001. As to the certification officer see PARA 1443.
3 Ie under the Trade Union and Labour Relations (Consolidation) Act 1992 s 99: see PARA 1002.
4 Ie under the Trade Union and Labour Relations (Consolidation) Act 1992 s 100: see PARA 1003 et seq.
5 Trade Union and Labour Relations (Consolidation) Act 1992 s 97(2) (amended by the Trade Union Reform and Employment Rights Act 1993 Sch 8 para 52). The statutory provisions apply to every transfer of engagements notwithstanding anything in the rules of any of the trade unions concerned: Trade Union and Labour Relations (Consolidation) Act 1992 s 97(4). As to the meaning of 'rules', in relation to a trade union, see PARA 898 note 5.
6 Trade Union and Labour Relations (Consolidation) Act 1992 s 97(3).

1000. Power to make regulations with regard to amalgamations etc. The Secretary of State may make regulations[1] as respects:
(1) applications to the certification officer[2] under the statutory provisions relating to amalgamations and similar matters[3];
(2) the registration thereunder of any document or matter;
(3) the inspection of documents kept by the certification officer thereunder;
(4) the charging of fees in respect of such matters, and of such amounts, as may, with the approval of the Treasury, be prescribed by the regulations, and generally for carrying those provisions into effect[4].

Provision may, in particular, be made:
(a) requiring an application for the registration of an instrument of amalgamation or transfer[5], or of a change of name[6], to be accompanied by such statutory declarations or other documents as may be specified in the regulations[7];
(b) as to the form or content of any document required[8] to be sent or submitted to the certification officer and as to the manner in which any such document is to be signed or authenticated[9]; and
(c) authorising the certification officer to require notice to be given or published in such manner as he may direct of the fact that an application for registration of an instrument of amalgamation or transfer has been or is to be made to him[10].

Regulations so made may make different provision for different circumstances[11].

1 Such regulations must be made by statutory instrument which is subject to annulment in pursuance of a resolution of either House of Parliament: Trade Union and Labour Relations (Consolidation) Act 1992 s 108(4). In exercise of the power so conferred the Secretary of State made the Certification Officer (Amendment of Fees) Regulations 2005, SI 2005/713, and, by virtue of the Trade Union and Labour Relations (Consolidation) Act 1992 Sch 3 para 1(2) (see PARA 891 note 1) and the Interpretation Act 1978 s 17(2)(b), the Trade Unions and Employers' Associations (Amalgamations etc) Regulations 1975, SI 1975/536, have effect as if made under that power: see PARA 1001 et seq. As to the Secretary of State see PARA 5 note 21.

2 As to the certification officer see PARA 1443.

3 Ie under the Trade Union and Labour Relations (Consolidation) Act 1992 Pt I Ch VII (ss 97–108): see PARAS 998, 999, 1001 et seq.

4 Trade Union and Labour Relations (Consolidation) Act 1992 s 108(1). As to the Treasury see CONSTITUTIONAL AND ADMINISTRATIVE LAW vol 20 (2014) PARA 262 et seq.

5 See PARA 1007.

6 See PARA 1016.

7 See eg the Trade Unions and Employers' Associations (Amalgamations etc) Regulations 1975, SI 1975/536, reg 3(1); and PARA 1001 note 3.

8 Ie required by the Trade Union and Labour Relations (Consolidation) Act 1992 Pt I Ch VII (ss 97–108) or by the Trade Unions and Employers' Associations (Amalgamations etc) Regulations 1975, SI 1975/536.

9 See eg the Trade Unions and Employers' Associations (Amalgamations etc) Regulations 1975, SI 1975/536, regs 4(1), (2), Schs 1, 2; and PARA 1001.

10 Trade Union and Labour Relations (Consolidation) Act 1992 s 108(2). See eg the Trade Unions and Employers' Associations (Amalgamations etc) Regulations 1975, SI 1975/536, reg 3(2); and PARA 1002 note 9.

11 Trade Union and Labour Relations (Consolidation) Act 1992 s 108(3).

1001. Approval of the instrument of amalgamation or transfer. Before a ballot[1] of the members of any amalgamating union or, as the case may be, of the transferor union is held on a resolution to approve an instrument of amalgamation or transfer[2], as the case may be, that instrument must be submitted[3] to the certification officer for approval[4]. If the certification officer is satisfied that an instrument of amalgamation complies with the regulations in force[5], and that he is not prevented from approving the instrument of amalgamation, he must approve the instrument[6].

However, the certification officer must not approve an instrument of amalgamation if it appears to him that the proposed name of the amalgamated union is the same as the name under which another organisation (1) was on 30 September 1971 registered[7] as a trade union[8]; (2) was at any time registered[9] as a trade union or employers' association[10]; or (3) is for the time being entered in the list of trade unions[11] or in the list of employers' associations[12], or if the proposed name is one so nearly resembling any name under heads (1) to (3) above as to be likely to deceive the public[13]. This does not apply if the proposed name is the name of one of the amalgamating unions[14].

If the certification officer is satisfied that an instrument of transfer complies with the requirements of any regulations in force[15], he must approve the instrument[16].

The instrument must state that it is an instrument of amalgamation or transfer, as the case may be, and that, on its coming into operation, the members of the amalgamating organisations or the transferor organisation, as the case may be, will become members of the amalgamated organisation or the transferee organisation, as the case may be, and subject to that organisation's rules[17]. The instrument must[18] state the date on which it is to take effect[19]; and it must be signed by three members of the committee of management or other governing body and the secretary of each of the organisations concerned[20]. The instrument must specify any property held for the benefit of any of the amalgamating organisations or of the transferor organisation[21] which is not to be vested in the appropriate trustees[22]; and it must state the proposed disposition of any such property[23]. An instrument of amalgamation must either set out the proposed rules of the amalgamated organisation or state who are the persons authorised to draw up those rules[24]; and, if it does not set out the proposed rules, it must contain a summary of what those rules will provide with regard to specified matters[25]. An instrument of transfer must set out specified matters relating to the effect of the transfer on members of the transferor organisation[26].

1 Ie under the Trade Union and Labour Relations (Consolidation) Act 1992 ss 100–100E: see PARA 1003 et seq. As to the application of these provisions to Northern Ireland unions see PARA 1013.

2 As to such resolutions see PARAS 998, 999.

3 An application for approval of a proposed instrument of amalgamation or transfer must be submitted to the certification officer: (1) in the case of a proposed instrument of amalgamation, by one of the amalgamating organisations; and (2) in the case of a proposed instrument of transfer, by the transferor organisation; and the application must be accompanied by two signed copies of the proposed instrument, by copies of the current rules of the organisations which are parties to the instrument, and by the prescribed fee: Trade Unions and Employers' Associations (Amalgamations etc) Regulations 1975, SI 1975/536, reg 3(1) (amended by SI 1978/1344; SI 1997/677); Trade Union and Labour Relations (Consolidation) Act 1992 Sch 3 para 1(4). The fee so prescribed is £1,850: Trade Unions and Employers' Associations (Amalgamations etc) Regulations 1975, SI 1975/536, reg 11(1) (substituted by SI 1988/310; amended by SI 2005/713). The Trade Unions and Employers' Associations (Amalgamations etc) Regulations 1975, SI 1975/536, reg 3 does not, however, apply to a Northern Ireland union where it is a party to an amalgamation or transfer of engagements: reg 10(a). For these purposes, 'certification officer' means the officer appointed under the Trade Union and Labour Relations (Consolidation) Act 1992 s 254(1), (2) (see PARA 1443) or any assistant certification officer appointed under s 254(3) (see PARA 1443) to whom functions have been delegated in accordance with s 254(4) (see PARA 1443) in relation to any matter authorised or required to be dealt with under the Trade Unions and Employers' Associations (Amalgamations etc) Regulations 1975, SI 1975/536: reg 2(2) (definition substituted by SI 1978/1344; amended by virtue of the Trade Union and Labour Relations (Consolidation) Act 1992 Sch 3 para 1(4)). 'Organisation' means any trade union as defined in the Trade Union and Labour Relations (Consolidation) Act 1992 s 1 (see PARA 891) or, in the context of the application of these provisions to employers' associations (see PARA 1091), means any employers' association as defined in s 122 (see PARA 1079) which is not a corporate body: Trade Unions and Employers' Associations (Amalgamations etc) Regulations 1975, SI 1975/536, reg 2(2); Trade Union and Labour Relations (Consolidation) Act 1992 Sch 3 para 1(4). As to the meaning of 'Northern Ireland union' see PARA 995 note 5.

4 Trade Union and Labour Relations (Consolidation) Act 1992 s 98(1) (amended by the Trade Union Reform and Employment Rights Act 1993 Sch 8 para 53). The certification officer may not refuse to approve the instrument of amalgamation or transfer on the grounds that it is inconsistent with the rules of the amalgamated or the transferee union, although such inconsistency may subsequently be grounds for a refusal to register the instrument: *R v Certification Officer, ex p Amalgamated Union of Engineering Workers (Engineering Section)* [1983] ICR 125, [1983] IRLR 113, CA. As to the registration of an instrument of amalgamation or transfer see PARA 1007.

5 Ie regulations in force under the Trade Union and Labour Relations (Consolidation) Act 1992 Pt I Ch VII (ss 97–108): see PARA 1000. The requirements referred to are those of the Trade Unions and Employers' Associations (Amalgamations etc) Regulations 1975, SI 1975/536, reg 4(1), (2), Schs 1, 2.

6 Trade Union and Labour Relations (Consolidation) Act 1992 s 98(2) (s 98(2) substituted and s 98(3)–(5) added by the Employment Relations Act 2004 s 50(1)). The certification officer must signify his approval of the instrument by returning one of the copies to the applicant organisation indorsed with the word 'Approved' and duly authenticated: Trade Unions and Employers' Associations (Amalgamations etc) Regulations 1975, SI 1975/536, reg 3(3) (amended by SI 1978/1344). The Trade Unions and Employers' Associations (Amalgamations etc) Regulations 1975, SI 1975/536, reg 3(3) does not apply to a Northern Ireland union: see note 3.

7 Ie under the Trade Union Acts 1871–1964 (repealed).

8 As to the meaning of 'trade union' see PARA 891.
9 Ie under the Industrial Relations Act 1971 (repealed).
10 As to the meaning of 'employers' association' see PARA 1079.
11 As to the list of trade unions see PARA 900.
12 As to the list of employers' associations see PARA 1083.
13 Trade Union and Labour Relations (Consolidation) Act 1992 s 98(3) (as added: see note 6).
14 Trade Union and Labour Relations (Consolidation) Act 1992 s 98(4) (as added: see note 6).
15 See note 5.
16 Trade Union and Labour Relations (Consolidation) Act 1992 s 98(5) (as added: see note 6).
17 Trade Unions and Employers' Associations (Amalgamations etc) Regulations 1975, SI 1975/536, reg 4(1), (2), Sch 1 para 1, Sch 2 para 1. Regulation 4(2) does not apply to an instrument of transfer if the transferor organisation is a Northern Ireland union (reg 10(b)); and reg 4 does not apply to any instrument of amalgamation or instrument of transfer which had been duly approved before 12 May 1975 (regs 1(1), 5 (reg 5 amended by SI 1978/1344)).
18 Ie without prejudice to the Trade Union and Labour Relations (Consolidation) Act 1992 s 101: see PARA 1007.
19 Trade Unions and Employers' Associations (Amalgamations etc) Regulations 1975, SI 1975/536, Sch 1 para 5, Sch 2 para 2(iv); Trade Union and Labour Relations (Consolidation) Act 1992 Sch 3 para 1(4).
20 Trade Unions and Employers' Associations (Amalgamations etc) Regulations 1975, SI 1975/536, Sch 1 para 6, Sch 2 para 4.
21 Ie or for the benefit of a branch of any such organisation. As to the vesting of property when an instrument of amalgamation or transfer takes effect see PARA 1012.
22 Ie as defined in the Trade Union and Labour Relations (Consolidation) Act 1992 s 105(2), (3): see PARA 1012 note 3.
23 Trade Unions and Employers' Associations (Amalgamations etc) Regulations 1975, SI 1975/536, Sch 1 para 4, Sch 2 para 3; Trade Union and Labour Relations (Consolidation) Act 1992 Sch 3 para 1(4).
24 Trade Unions and Employers' Associations (Amalgamations etc) Regulations 1975, SI 1975/536, Sch 1 para 2.
25 Trade Unions and Employers' Associations (Amalgamations etc) Regulations 1975, SI 1975/536, Sch 1 para 3. The matters so specified are: (1) the name and principal purposes of the amalgamated organisation; (2) the conditions of admission to membership; (3) the structure of the amalgamated organisation; (4) the method of appointing and removing its governing body and principal officials and of altering its rules; and (5) the contributions and benefits applicable to members of the amalgamating organisations: Sch 1 para 3(i)–(v).
26 Trade Unions and Employers' Associations (Amalgamations etc) Regulations 1975, SI 1975/536, Sch 2 para 2. The instrument must: (1) state what contributions and benefits will be applicable to members of the transferor organisation under the transferee organisation's rules; (2) if members of the transferor organisation are to be allocated to a branch or section or to branches or sections of the transferee organisation, give particulars of the allocation or the method by which it is to be decided; and (3) state whether before registration of the instrument the transferee organisation's rules are to be altered in their application to members of the transferor organisation and, if so, the effect of any alterations: Sch 2 para 2(i)–(iii).

1002. Notice to members regarding proposed amalgamation or transfer. The trade union[1] must take all reasonable steps to secure that every voting paper which is supplied[2] for voting in the ballot[3] on the resolution to approve the instrument of amalgamation or transfer[4] is accompanied by a notice in writing approved for the purpose[5] by the certification officer[6]. A notice to members must be in writing and must either:

(1) set out in full the instrument of amalgamation or transfer to which the resolution relates; or

(2) give an account of it sufficient to enable those receiving the notice to form a reasonable judgment of the main effects of the proposed amalgamation or transfer[7];

and the notice must comply with the requirements of any relevant[8] regulations[9].

The notice must not contain any statement making a recommendation or expressing an opinion about the proposed amalgamation or transfer[10].

1   As to the meaning of 'trade union' see PARA 891. As to the application of these provisions to
    Northern Ireland unions see PARA 1013.
2   As to the requirements concerning the supply of voting papers see PARA 1004 et seq.
3   As to such ballots see the Trade Union and Labour Relations (Consolidation) Act 1992
    ss 100–100E; and PARA 1003 et seq.
4   As to such resolutions see PARAS 998, 999.
5   The notice proposed to be supplied to members of the union must be submitted to the
    certification officer for approval; and he must approve it if he is satisfied that it meets the
    requirements of the Trade Union and Labour Relations (Consolidation) Act 1992 s 99: s 99(5).
    As to the certification officer see PARA 1443.
6   Trade Union and Labour Relations (Consolidation) Act 1992 s 99(1) (amended by the Trade
    Union Reform and Employment Rights Act 1993 Sch 8 para 54).
7   Trade Union and Labour Relations (Consolidation) Act 1992 s 99(2). If the notice does not set
    out the instrument in full, it must state where copies of the instrument may be inspected by those
    receiving the notice: s 99(3).
8   Ie any regulations in force under the Trade Union and Labour Relations (Consolidation)
    Act 1992 Pt I Ch VII (ss 97–108): see PARA 1000. The relevant regulations are the Trade Unions
    and Employers' Associations (Amalgamations etc) Regulations 1975, SI 1975/536: see note 9.
9   Trade Union and Labour Relations (Consolidation) Act 1992 s 99(4). An application for
    approval of a proposed notice to be supplied to members must be accompanied by two copies of
    the proposed notice: Trade Unions and Employers' Associations (Amalgamations etc)
    Regulations 1975, SI 1975/536, reg 3(2) (amended by SI 1978/1344); Trade Union and Labour
    Relations (Consolidation) Act 1992 s 300(3), Sch 3 para 1(4). The certification officer must
    signify his approval of the notice by returning one of the copies to the applicant organisation
    indorsed with the word 'Approved' and duly authenticated: Trade Unions and Employers'
    Associations (Amalgamations etc) Regulations 1975, SI 1975/536, reg 3(3) (amended by
    SI 1978/1344). The Trade Unions and Employers' Associations (Amalgamations etc)
    Regulations 1975, SI 1975/536, reg 3 does not apply to a Northern Ireland union where it is a
    party to an amalgamation or transfer of engagements: reg 10(a). As to the meaning of
    'certification officer' and 'organisation' for these purposes see PARA 1001 note 3; and as to the
    meaning of 'Northern Ireland union' see PARA 995 note 5.
10 Trade Union and Labour Relations (Consolidation) Act 1992 s 99(3A) (added by the Trade
    Union Reform and Employment Rights Act 1993 s 5).

**1003.   Requirement of a ballot on a resolution approving an instrument of
amalgamation or transfer.**   A resolution approving an instrument of
amalgamation or transfer[1] must be passed on a ballot of the members of the
trade union[2] held in accordance with certain statutory requirements[3]. A simple
majority of those voting is sufficient to pass such a resolution unless the rules[4] of
the union expressly require it to be approved by a greater majority or by a
specified proportion of the members of the union[5].

1   As to such resolutions see PARAS 998, 999.
2   As to the meaning of 'trade union' see PARA 891. As to the application of these provisions to
    Northern Ireland unions see PARA 1013.
3   Trade Union and Labour Relations (Consolidation) Act 1992 s 100(1) (s 100 substituted by the
    Trade Union Reform and Employment Rights Act 1993 s 4). The statutory requirements
    referred to are those of the Trade Union and Labour Relations (Consolidation) Act 1992
    ss 100A–100E (see PARAS 1004–1006): s 100(1) (as so substituted).
4   As to the meaning of 'rules', in relation to a trade union, see PARA 898 note 5.
5   Trade Union and Labour Relations (Consolidation) Act 1992 s 100(2) (as substituted: see
    note 3).

**1004.   Appointment of independent scrutineer for ballot on a resolution
approving an instrument of amalgamation or transfer.**   Before the ballot on a
resolution approving an instrument of amalgamation or transfer[1] is held, the
trade union[2] must appoint a qualified independent person (the 'scrutineer') to
carry out certain functions in relation to the ballot which are required[3] to be
contained in his appointment, and such additional functions in relation to the
ballot as may be specified in his appointment[4].

A person is a qualified independent person in relation to a ballot if:

(1)   he satisfies such conditions as may be specified for these purposes by order of the Secretary of State[5] or is himself so specified[6]; and

(2)   the trade union has no grounds for believing either that he will carry out his functions in relation to the ballot otherwise than competently or that his independence in relation to the union, or in relation to the ballot, might reasonably be called into question[7].

The scrutineer's appointment must require him:

(a)   to be the person who supervises the production of the voting papers and, unless he is appointed[8] to undertake the distribution of the voting papers, their distribution, and to whom the voting papers are returned by those voting;

(b)   to inspect the register of names and addresses of the members of the trade union[9], or to examine the copy of the register which is supplied to him[10], whenever it appears to him appropriate to do so and, in particular, when specified conditions are satisfied[11];

(c)   to take such steps as appear to him to be appropriate for the purpose of enabling him to make his report[12];

(d)   to make his report to the trade union as soon as reasonably practicable after the last date for the return of the voting papers; and

(e)   to retain custody of all voting papers returned for the purposes of the ballot, and the copy of the register supplied to him, until the end of the period of one year beginning with the announcement by the union of the result of the ballot[13].

The trade union must ensure that nothing in the terms of the scrutineer's appointment, including any additional functions specified in it, is such as to make it reasonable for any person to call his independence in relation to the union into question[14].

Before the scrutineer begins to carry out his functions, the trade union must either send a notice stating the name of the scrutineer to every member of the union to whom it is reasonably practicable to send such a notice, or take all such other steps for notifying members of the name of the scrutineer as it is the practice of the union to take when matters of general interest to all its members need to be brought to their attention[15]. The trade union must also:

(i)   supply to the scrutineer, as soon as is reasonably practicable after the relevant date, a copy of the register of members' names and addresses as at that date; and

(ii)   comply with any request made by the scrutineer to inspect the register[16].

The trade union must ensure that the scrutineer duly carries out his functions and that there is no interference with his carrying out of those functions which would make it reasonable for any person to call his independence in relation to the union into question[17]; and the trade union must comply with all reasonable requests made by the scrutineer for the purposes of, or in connection with, the carrying out of his functions[18].

1   As to such resolutions see PARAS 998, 999.

2   As to the meaning of 'trade union' see PARA 891. As to the application of these provisions to Northern Ireland unions see PARA 1013.

3   Ie under the Trade Union and Labour Relations (Consolidation) Act 1992 s 100A: see the text and notes 1–2, 4–18.

4   Trade Union and Labour Relations (Consolidation) Act 1992 s 100A(1) (s 100A added by the Trade Union Reform and Employment Rights Act 1993 s 4).

5   Any such order must be made by statutory instrument which is subject to annulment in pursuance of a resolution of either House of Parliament: Trade Union and Labour Relations (Consolidation) Act 1992 s 100A(2) (as added: see note 4). In exercise of the power so conferred the Secretary of State made the Trade Union Ballots and Elections (Independent Scrutineer Qualifications) Order 1993, SI 1993/1909, which came into force on 30 August 1993: art 1(1). As to the conditions to be satisfied by individuals and partnerships see arts 1(2), 3–6; and PARA 966 note 5.

6   As to the persons so specified see the Trade Union Ballots and Elections (Independent Scrutineer Qualifications) Order 1993, SI 1993/1909, art 7; and PARA 966 note 6.

7   Trade Union and Labour Relations (Consolidation) Act 1992 s 100A(2) (as added: see note 4).

8   Ie under the Trade Union and Labour Relations (Consolidation) Act 1992 s 100D: see PARA 1005.

9   As to the register of members' names and addresses see PARA 930. The duty of confidentiality as respects the register (see PARA 937) is incorporated in the scrutineer's appointment: Trade Union and Labour Relations (Consolidation) Act 1992 s 100A(6) (as added: see note 4).

10   Ie in accordance with the Trade Union and Labour Relations (Consolidation) Act 1992 s 100A(9)(a): see head (i) in the text.

11   The conditions so specified are: (1) that a request that the scrutineer inspect the register or examine the copy is made to him during the appropriate period by a member of the trade union who suspects that the register is not, or at the relevant date was not, accurate and up-to-date; and (2) that the scrutineer does not consider that the member's suspicion is ill-founded: Trade Union and Labour Relations (Consolidation) Act 1992 s 100A(4) (as added: see note 4). For these purposes, 'appropriate period' means the period: (a) beginning with the day on which the scrutineer is appointed; and (b) ending with the day before the day on which the scrutineer makes his report to the trade union (s 100A(5) (as so added)); and 'relevant date' means: (i) where the trade union has rules determining who is entitled to vote in the ballot by reference to membership on a particular date, that date; and (ii) otherwise, the date, or the last date, on which voting papers are distributed for the purposes of the ballot (s 100A(13) (as so added)). As to the duty of the scrutineer to inspect the register see PARA 930. As to the meaning of 'rules', in relation to a trade union, see PARA 898 note 5.

12   As to the scrutineer's report see PARA 1006.

13   Trade Union and Labour Relations (Consolidation) Act 1992 s 100A(3) (as added: see note 4). If, within the period so specified, an application is made under s 103 (complaint as regards passing of resolution) (see PARAS 1010, 1011), the scrutineer must retain custody of the voting papers and the copy of the register until the certification officer or the Employment Appeal Tribunal authorises him to dispose of them: s 100A(3)(e)(ii) (as added: see note 4). As to the Employment Appeal Tribunal see PARA 1422 et seq.

14   Trade Union and Labour Relations (Consolidation) Act 1992 s 100A(7) (as added: see note 4).

15   Trade Union and Labour Relations (Consolidation) Act 1992 s 100A(8) (as added: see note 4).

16   Trade Union and Labour Relations (Consolidation) Act 1992 s 100A(9) (as added: see note 4). Where the register is kept by means of a computer, the duty so imposed on the trade union is either to supply a legible printed copy or, if the scrutineer prefers, to supply a copy of the computer data and allow the scrutineer use of the computer to read it at any time during the period when he is required to retain custody of the copy: s 100A(10) (as so added). As to the duty to supply a copy of the register and to comply with a request to inspect the register generally see PARA 930.

17   Trade Union and Labour Relations (Consolidation) Act 1992 s 100A(11) (as added: see note 4).

18   Trade Union and Labour Relations (Consolidation) Act 1992 s 100A(12) (as added: see note 4).

1005.   Conduct of the ballot on a resolution approving an instrument of amalgamation or transfer. Entitlement to vote in the ballot on a resolution approving an instrument of amalgamation or transfer[1] must be accorded equally to all members[2] of the trade union[3]. The method of voting must be by the marking of a voting paper by the person voting[4]; and each voting paper must:

  (1)   state the name of the independent scrutineer[5] and clearly specify the address to which, and the date by which, it is to be returned;

  (2)   be given one of a series of consecutive whole numbers every one of which is used in giving a different number in that series to each voting paper printed or otherwise produced for the purposes of the ballot; and

  (3)   be marked with its number[6].

Every person who is entitled to vote in the ballot must be allowed to do so without interference or constraint and, so far as is reasonably practicable, must be enabled to do so without incurring any direct cost to himself[7].

So far as is reasonably practicable, every person who is entitled to vote in the ballot must have a voting paper sent to him by post[8] at his home address or another address which he has requested the union in writing to treat as his postal address, and must be given a convenient opportunity to vote by post[9]. No voting paper which is sent to a person for voting must have any other document enclosed with it except:

(a)   the notice to members[10];
(b)   an addressed envelope; and
(c)   a document containing instructions for the return of the voting paper, without any other statement[11].

The trade union must ensure that the storage and distribution of the voting papers for the purposes of the ballot, and the counting of the votes cast in the ballot, are undertaken by one or more independent persons[12] appointed by the trade union[13]; and the ballot must be conducted so as to secure that, so far as is reasonably practicable, those voting do so in secret, and the votes given in the ballot are fairly and accurately counted[14].

1   As to such resolutions see PARAS 998, 999.
2   As to the meaning of 'member' see *National Union of Mineworkers (Yorkshire Area) v Millward* [1995] ICR 482, [1995] IRLR 411, EAT ('limited members' paying a reduced subscription and having only limited membership rights are not 'members of the trade union' for the purposes of the Trade Union and Labour Relations (Consolidation) Act 1992 s 100B).
3   Trade Union and Labour Relations (Consolidation) Act 1992 s 100B (ss 100B, 100C, 100D added by the Trade Union Reform and Employment Rights Act 1993 s 4). As to the meaning of 'trade union' see PARA 891. As to the application of these provisions to Northern Ireland unions see PARA 1013.
4   Trade Union and Labour Relations (Consolidation) Act 1992 s 100C(1) (as added: see note 3).
5   As to the independent scrutineer see PARA 1004.
6   Trade Union and Labour Relations (Consolidation) Act 1992 s 100C(2) (as added: see note 3).
7   Trade Union and Labour Relations (Consolidation) Act 1992 s 100C(3) (as added: see note 3). As to the interpretation of the equivalent provisions relating to elections for union office see PARA 962.
8   As to the construction of references to requiring or authorising a document or other thing to be sent by post see PARA 962 note 10.
9   Trade Union and Labour Relations (Consolidation) Act 1992 s 100C(4) (as added: see note 3).
10 Ie the notice which is to accompany the voting paper under the Trade Union and Labour Relations (Consolidation) Act 1992 s 99(1): see PARA 1002.
11 Trade Union and Labour Relations (Consolidation) Act 1992 s 100C(5) (as added: see note 3).
12 A person is an independent person in relation to a ballot if: (1) he is the scrutineer; or (2) he is a person other than the scrutineer and the trade union has no grounds for believing either that he will carry out any functions conferred on him in relation to a ballot otherwise than competently or that his independence in relation to the union, or in relation to the ballot, might reasonably be called into question: Trade Union and Labour Relations (Consolidation) Act 1992 s 100D(2) (as added: see note 3).
13 Trade Union and Labour Relations (Consolidation) Act 1992 s 100D(1) (as added: see note 3). An appointment of an independent person under these provisions must require the person appointed to carry out his functions so as to minimise the risk of any contravention of the statutory requirements or the occurrence of any unfairness or malpractice: s 100D(3) (as so added). Further, the trade union must: (1) ensure that nothing in the terms of the appointment of an independent person is such as to make it reasonable for any person to call into question his independence in relation to the union; (2) ensure that a person so appointed duly carries out his functions and that there is no interference with his carrying out of those functions which would make it reasonable for any person to call into question his independence in relation to the union; and (3) comply with all reasonable requests made by him for the purposes of, or in connection with, the carrying out of his functions: s 100D(6) (as so added). The duty of confidentiality as respects the register of members' names and addresses (see PARA 937) is incorporated in the

appointment: s 100D(4) (as so added). Where the person appointed to undertake the counting of votes is not the scrutineer, his appointment must require him to send the voting papers back to the scrutineer as soon as reasonably practicable after the counting has been completed: s 100D(5) (as so added). Section s 100D(4) refers to the scrutineer's appointment, but it is submitted that this is a drafting error and the reference should be to the appointment of the independent person: c f s 77A(4) (similar provision relating to a ballot on a political resolution); and PARA 980 note 13. As to the meaning of 'contravention' and cognate expressions see PARA 915 note 6.

14 Trade Union and Labour Relations (Consolidation) Act 1992 s 100C(6) (as added: see note 3). An inaccuracy in counting is to be disregarded if it is accidental and on a scale which could not affect the result of the ballot: s 100C(6) (as so added).

1006. Scrutineer's report after ballot on a resolution approving an instrument of amalgamation or transfer. The scrutineer[1] must make a report to the trade union[2] as soon as reasonably practicable after the last date for the return of the voting papers in the ballot on a resolution approving an instrument of amalgamation or transfer[3].

The scrutineer's report must state:

(1) the number of voting papers distributed for the purposes of the ballot;

(2) the number of voting papers returned to the scrutineer;

(3) the number of valid votes cast in the ballot for and against the resolution;

(4) the number of spoiled or otherwise invalid voting papers returned; and

(5) the name of any independent person or persons appointed by the union[4] to perform certain functions in relation to the ballot or, if no person was so appointed, that fact[5].

The report must also state whether the scrutineer is satisfied:

(a) that there are no reasonable grounds for believing that there was any contravention[6] of a requirement imposed by or under any enactment in relation to the ballot;

(b) that the arrangements made, whether by him or any other person, with respect to the production, storage, distribution, return or other handling of the voting papers used in the ballot, and the arrangements for the counting of the votes, included all such security arrangements as were reasonably practicable for the purpose of minimising the risk that any unfairness or malpractice might occur; and

(c) that he has been able to carry out his functions without such interference as would make it reasonable for any person to call his independence in relation to the union into question;

and, if the scrutineer is not satisfied as to any of those matters, the report must give particulars of his reasons for not being satisfied as to that matter[7].

The report must also state:

(i) whether the scrutineer has inspected the register of names and addresses of the members of the trade union[8] or has examined the copy of the register supplied to him[9];

(ii) if so, whether in each case he was acting on a request by a member of the trade union or at his own instance;

(iii) whether he declined to act on any such request; and

(iv) whether any such inspection or examination has revealed any matter which he considers should be brought to the attention of the trade union in order to assist it in securing that its register is accurate and up-to-date;

but the report must not state the name of any member who has requested such an inspection or examination[10].

The trade union must not publish the result of the ballot until after it has received the scrutineer's report[11]; and it must, within the period of three months after it receives the report, either send a copy of it to every member of the union to whom it is reasonably practicable to send such a copy, or take all such other steps for notifying the contents of the report to the members of the union, whether by publishing the report or otherwise, as it is the practice of the union to take when matters of general interest to all its members need to be brought to their attention[12]. Any such copy or notification must be accompanied by a statement that the union will, on request, supply any member of the union with a copy of the report, either free of charge or on payment of such reasonable fee as may be specified in the notification[13]; and the trade union must so supply any member of the union who makes such a request and pays the fee, if any, notified to him[14].

1   Ie the person appointed under the Trade Union and Labour Relations (Consolidation) Act 1992 s 100A: see PARA 1004.
2   As to the meaning of 'trade union' see PARA 891. As to the application of these provisions to Northern Ireland unions see PARA 1013.
3   Trade Union and Labour Relations (Consolidation) Act 1992 s 100A(3)(d) (ss 100A, 100E added by the Trade Union Reform and Employment Rights Act 1993 s 4). As to such resolutions see PARAS 998, 999.
4   Ie under the Trade Union and Labour Relations (Consolidation) Act 1992 s 100D: see PARA 1005. Where one or more persons other than the scrutineer is or are so appointed, the statement included in the scrutineer's report in accordance with s 100E(2)(b) (see head (b) in the text) must also indicate whether he is satisfied with the performance of the person, or each of the persons, so appointed, and, if he is not satisfied, the report must indicate particulars of his reasons for not being so satisfied: s 100E(4) (as added: see note 3).
5   Trade Union and Labour Relations (Consolidation) Act 1992 s 100E(1) (as added: see note 3).
6   As to the meaning of 'contravention' and cognate expressions see PARA 915 note 6.
7   Trade Union and Labour Relations (Consolidation) Act 1992 s 100E(2) (as added: see note 3).
8   As to the register of members' names and addresses see PARA 930.
9   Ie the copy of the register as at the relevant date which is supplied to him in accordance with the Trade Union and Labour Relations (Consolidation) Act 1992 s 100A(9)(a): see PARA 1004 head (i).
10 Trade Union and Labour Relations (Consolidation) Act 1992 s 100E(3) (as added: see note 3).
11 Trade Union and Labour Relations (Consolidation) Act 1992 s 100E(5) (as added: see note 3).
12 Trade Union and Labour Relations (Consolidation) Act 1992 s 100E(6) (as added: see note 3).
13 Trade Union and Labour Relations (Consolidation) Act 1992 s 100E(7) (as added: see note 3).
14 Trade Union and Labour Relations (Consolidation) Act 1992 s 100E(8) (as added: see note 3).

1007.   Registration of the instrument of amalgamation or transfer.   An instrument of amalgamation or transfer does not take effect before it has been registered by the certification officer[1] in accordance with regulations made for that purpose[2]. An application for registration of an instrument of amalgamation or transfer must be signed by three members of the committee of management or other governing body and the secretary of each of the amalgamating organisations[3] or each of the organisations concerned in the transfer, and must be submitted to the certification officer in a form to be provided by him for that purpose[4]. Such an application must not be sent to the certification officer until certain statutory requirements[5] in relation to the scrutineer's report on the ballot[6] have been complied with[7]. In certain circumstances[8] the certification officer may require notice to be given or published of the fact that the application for registration has been or is to be made to him[9]. Before registering an instrument of amalgamation or transfer, the certification officer must satisfy himself that the proposed rules of the amalgamated or transferee organisation are in no way inconsistent with the terms of the instrument[10].

The instrument of amalgamation or transfer must not be registered[11] by the certification officer before the end of the period of six weeks beginning with the date on which an application for its registration is sent to him[12].

1 Trade Union and Labour Relations (Consolidation) Act 1992 s 101(1). As to the certification officer see PARA 1443. As to the listing, certification and supply of information after amalgamation, see ss 101A, 101B; and PARA 1008.

2 Ie in accordance with the Trade Unions and Employers' Associations (Amalgamations etc) Regulations 1975, SI 1975/536, regs 6–8: see the text and notes 3–12. As to the power to make regulations see PARA 1000.

3 As to the meaning of 'organisation' see PARA 1001 note 3. As to the application of these provisions to Northern Ireland unions see PARA 1013.

4 See the Trade Unions and Employers' Associations (Amalgamations etc) Regulations 1975, SI 1975/536, reg 6(1), (2) (amended by SI 1978/1344). In the case of an instrument of transfer, the application must be submitted by the transferee organisation unless that is a Northern Ireland union, in which case it must be submitted by the transferor: Trade Unions and Employers' Associations (Amalgamations etc) Regulations 1975, SI 1975/536, regs 6(2), 10(d) (reg 6(2) as so amended). The application must be accompanied by two copies of the instrument and, except in the case of a Northern Ireland union which is a party to the amalgamation or transfer, by statutory declarations from each of the organisations in the form to be provided by the certification officer for that purpose: regs 6(1), (2) (as so amended), 10(c). An application for registration of an instrument of amalgamation must also be accompanied by two copies of the proposed rules of the amalgamated organisation, signed by the secretary of each of the amalgamating organisations: reg 6(1) (as so amended). An application for registration of an instrument of transfer must be accompanied by two copies of any amendments to the rules of the transferee organisation made since the date of the application for approval of the proposed instrument of transfer under reg 3(1) (see PARA 1001): reg 6(2) (as so amended).

5 Ie the requirement to take steps to notify members of the contents of the scrutineer's report under the Trade Union and Labour Relations (Consolidation) Act 1992 s 100E(6): see PARA 1006.

6 Ie the ballot held on the resolution to approve the instrument of amalgamation or transfer: see PARA 1003 et seq.

7 Trade Union and Labour Relations (Consolidation) Act 1992 s 101(3) (added by the Trade Union Reform and Employment Rights Act 1993 Sch 8 para 55).

8 Ie where he considers it desirable with a view to ensuring that adequate publicity is given to the date by which complaints must be made to him under the Trade Union and Labour Relations (Consolidation) Act 1992 s 103 (see PARAS 1010, 1011) and not later than seven days after the date on which he receives the application for registration of the instrument.

9 Trade Unions and Employers' Associations (Amalgamations etc) Regulations 1975, SI 1975/536, reg 6(3) (amended by SI 1978/1344); Trade Union and Labour Relations (Consolidation) Act 1992 Sch 3 para 1(4). The certification officer may require the notice to be given or published in such manner, in such form, and on or before such date, as he may direct: Trade Unions and Employers' Associations (Amalgamations etc) Regulations 1975, SI 1975/536, reg 6(3) (as so amended). Regulation 6(3) does not, however, apply to a Northern Ireland union where it is a party to an amalgamation or transfer of engagements: reg 10(a).

10 Trade Unions and Employers' Associations (Amalgamations etc) Regulations 1975, SI 1975/536, regs 7(1), 8(1) (amended by SI 1978/1344). See *R v Certification Officer, ex p Amalgamated Union of Engineering Workers (Engineering Section)* [1983] ICR 125, [1983] IRLR 113, CA.

11 It is open to question whether an inadvertent premature registration is invalid: cf *Rothwell v Association of Professional, Executive, Clerical and Computer Staff* [1976] ICR 211, [1975] IRLR 375 (where it was held that the six-week period was directory and not mandatory so as not to invalidate an inadvertent premature registration).

12 Trade Union and Labour Relations (Consolidation) Act 1992 s 101(2). On registering the instrument, the certification officer must send one copy of the instrument, indorsed with the word 'Registered' and duly authenticated, to the address specified for that purpose on the form of application for registration in the case of an instrument of amalgamation and to the transferee organisation in the case of an instrument of transfer: Trade Unions and Employers' Associations (Amalgamations etc) Regulations 1975, SI 1975/536, regs 7(2), 8(2) (amended by SI 1978/1344).

1008. Listing, certification and supply of information after amalgamation. If, when an instrument of amalgamation is registered by the certification officer[1], each of the amalgamating unions is entered in the list of trade unions[2], the certification officer must enter, with effect from the amalgamation date[3], the name of the amalgamated union in the list of trade unions, and remove, with effect from that date, the names of the amalgamating unions from that list[4].

If, when an instrument of amalgamation is registered by the certification officer[5], each of the amalgamating unions has a certificate of independence[6] which is in force, the certification officer must issue to the amalgamated trade union, with effect from the amalgamation date, a certificate that the union is independent[7].

If an instrument of amalgamation is registered[8] by the certification officer and the amalgamated union is entered in the list of trade unions[9], that union must send to the certification officer, in such manner and form as he may require, a copy of the rules of the union, a list of its officers, and the address of its head or main office[10]. The information must be sent before the end of the period of six weeks beginning with the date on which the instrument of amalgamation takes effect or, if the certification officer considers that it is not reasonably practicable for the amalgamated union to send it in that period, before the end of such longer period, beginning with that date, as he may specify to the amalgamated union[11].

1   Ie under the Trade Union and Labour Relations (Consolidation) Act 1992 Pt I Ch VII (ss 97–108). As to the certification officer see PARA 1443.
2   As to the list of trade unions see PARA 900. As to the meaning of 'trade union' see PARA 891.
3   'Amalgamation date' means the date on which the instrument of amalgamation takes effect: Trade Union and Labour Relations (Consolidation) Act 1992 s 101A(5) (ss 101A, 101B added by the Employment Relations Act 2004 s 50(2)).
4   Trade Union and Labour Relations (Consolidation) Act 1992 s 101A(1), (2) (as added: see note 3).
5   See note 1.
6   'Certificate of independence' means a certificate issued under the Trade Union and Labour Relations (Consolidation) Act 1992 s 6(6) (see PARA 905) or s 101A(4): s 298 (definition added by the Employment Relations Act 2004 s 50(4)).
7   Trade Union and Labour Relations (Consolidation) Act 1992 s 101A(3), (4) (as added: see note 3).
8   See note 1.
9   Ie in accordance with the Trade Union and Labour Relations (Consolidation) Act 1992 s 101A: see the text and notes 1–4.
10 Trade Union and Labour Relations (Consolidation) Act 1992 s 101B(1) (as added: see note 3). The information required to be sent must be accompanied by any fee prescribed for the purpose under s 108 (see PARA 1000): s 101B(2) (as so added). The fee of £41 is prescribed for the purposes of s 101B(2) in circumstances where, at the time the instrument of amalgamation was registered by the certification officer, the condition in s 101A(3) was satisfied and the certification officer was, accordingly, under the duty in s 101A(4) to issue a certificate of independence to the amalgamated union: Certification Officer (Amendment of Fees) Regulations 2005, SI 2005/713, reg 8.
11 Trade Union and Labour Relations (Consolidation) Act 1992 s 101B(3) (as added: see note 3). If any of s 101B(1)–(3) is not complied with by the amalgamated union, the certification officer must remove its name from the list of trade unions: s 101B(4) (as so added).

1009. Power to alter rules of transferee union for purposes of transfer. Where a trade union[1] proposes to transfer its engagements[2] to another trade union and an alteration of the rules[3] of the transferee union is necessary to give effect to provisions in the instrument of transfer, the committee of management or other governing body of that union may, notwithstanding anything in the rules of the union[4], by memorandum in writing alter the rules of that union, so far as is necessary to give effect to those provisions[5], unless the rules of the union expressly provide that this statutory power[6] is not to apply to that union[7]. An alteration of the rules of a trade union so made does not take effect unless or until the instrument of transfer takes effect[8].

1   As to the meaning of 'trade union' see PARA 891. As to the application of these provisions to Northern Ireland unions see PARA 1013.
2   As to transfers of engagements see PARA 999.
3   As to the meaning of 'rules', in relation to a trade union, see PARA 898 note 5.
4   Trade Union and Labour Relations (Consolidation) Act 1992 s 102(3).
5   Trade Union and Labour Relations (Consolidation) Act 1992 s 102(1).
6   Ie the Trade Union and Labour Relations (Consolidation) Act 1992 s 102.
7   Trade Union and Labour Relations (Consolidation) Act 1992 s 102(1) proviso.
8   Trade Union and Labour Relations (Consolidation) Act 1992 s 102(2). The instrument of transfer does not take effect until it has been registered: see PARA 1007.

1010.   Complaints by members with regard to amalgamation or transfer.   A member of a trade union[1] who claims that the union:

(1)   has failed to comply with any of the statutory requirements relating to the notice to members[2] or the ballot[3] on a resolution approving an instrument of amalgamation or transfer[4]; or

(2)   has, in connection with any such resolution, failed to comply with any rule of the union relating to the passing of the resolution[5],

may complain to the certification officer[6].

Any complaint must be made before the end of the period of six weeks beginning with the date on which an application for registration of an instrument of amalgamation or transfer is sent to the certification officer; and, where a complaint is made, the certification officer must not register the instrument before the complaint is finally determined or is withdrawn[7].

On a complaint being made to him, the certification officer must make such inquiries as he thinks fit[8].

1   As to the meaning of 'trade union' see PARA 891. As to the application of these provisions to Northern Ireland unions see PARA 1013.
2   Ie under the Trade Union and Labour Relations (Consolidation) Act 1992 s 99: see PARA 1002.
3   Ie under the Trade Union and Labour Relations (Consolidation) Act 1992 ss 100–100E: see PARA 1003 et seq.
4   As to such resolutions see PARAS 998, 999.
5   There must be a direct link or relationship between the rule and the way the resolution is passed; a rule which relates to the constitution of the union, even if it indirectly affects the lawfulness of the resolution, is not a rule which relates to its passing by a ballot of the members: *Boxshall v PTC and CPSA, England v PTC* EAT/24/98, EAT/25/98. As to the meaning of 'rules', in relation to a trade union, see PARA 898 note 5.
6   Trade Union and Labour Relations (Consolidation) Act 1992 s 103(1) (substituted by the Trade Union Reform and Employment Rights Act 1993 Sch 8 para 56). As to the certification officer see PARA 1443; and as to the determination of complaints see PARA 1011.
7   Trade Union and Labour Relations (Consolidation) Act 1992 s 103(2).
8   Trade Union and Labour Relations (Consolidation) Act 1992 s 103(2A) (added by the Employment Relations Act 1999 Sch 6 paras 1, 18(1), (2)).

1011.   Determination of complaints by the certification officer.   Where a complaint is made in relation to the passing of a resolution approving an instrument of amalgamation or transfer[1], if the certification officer[2], after giving the complainant and the trade union[3] an opportunity to be heard, finds the complaint to be justified[4]:

(1)   he must make a declaration to that effect[5]; and

(2)   he may make an order specifying the steps which must be taken before he will entertain any application to register the instrument of amalgamation or transfer;

and, where he makes such an order, he may not entertain an application to register the instrument of amalgamation or transfer unless he is satisfied that the steps specified in the order have been taken. Such an order may be varied by the certification officer by a further order[6].

The certification officer must furnish a statement, orally or in writing, of the reasons for his decision on any such complaint[7].

Where an order has been made under the above provisions, any person who is a member of the union and was a member at the time it was made is entitled to enforce obedience to the order as if he had made the complaint on which the order was made[8].

The validity of a resolution approving an instrument of amalgamation or transfer may not be questioned in any legal proceedings whatsoever on any ground on which a complaint could be, or could have been, made to the certification officer, except by means of a complaint to him or in proceedings arising out of such a complaint[9]. An appeal lies to the Employment Appeal Tribunal[10] at the instance of the complainant or the trade union on any question of law arising in any proceedings before, or from any decision of, the certification officer on such a complaint[11].

1   As to the grounds of complaint see PARA 1010.
2   As to the certification officer see PARA 1443.
3   As to the meaning of 'trade union' see PARA 891. As to the application of these provisions to Northern Ireland unions see PARA 1013.
4   Where the certification officer requests a person to furnish information to him in connection with inquiries made by him under the Trade Union and Labour Relations (Consolidation) Act 1992 s 103, he must specify the date by which that information is to be furnished and, unless he considers that it would be inappropriate to do so, must proceed with his determination of the application notwithstanding that the information has not been furnished to him by the specified date: s 103(6) (s 103(6)–(9) added by the Employment Relations Act 1999 Sch 6 paras 1, 18(1), (3)).
5   A declaration so made by the certification officer may be relied on as if it were a declaration made by the court: Trade Union and Labour Relations (Consolidation) Act 1992 s 103(7) (as added: see note 4).
6   Trade Union and Labour Relations (Consolidation) Act 1992 s 103(3). An order made by the certification officer under s 103 may be enforced in the same way as an order of the court: s 103(9) (as added: see note 4). As to the registration of an instrument of amalgamation or transfer see PARA 1007.
7   Trade Union and Labour Relations (Consolidation) Act 1992 s 103(4).
8   Trade Union and Labour Relations (Consolidation) Act 1992 s 103(8) (as added (see note 4); amended by the Employment Relations Act 2004 Sch 1 para 7).
9   Trade Union and Labour Relations (Consolidation) Act 1992 s 103(5).
10   As to the Employment Appeal Tribunal see PARA 1422 et seq.
11   Trade Union and Labour Relations (Consolidation) Act 1992 s 104.

1012.   Vesting of property on an amalgamation or transfer.   Where an instrument of amalgamation or transfer takes effect[1], the property held:

(1)   for the benefit of any of the amalgamating trade unions[2], or for the benefit of a branch of any of those unions, by the trustees of the union or branch; or

(2)   for the benefit of the transferor union, or for the benefit of a branch of that union, by the trustees of the union or branch,

vests in the appropriate trustees[3], without any conveyance or assignment, on the instrument taking effect or on the appointment of the appropriate trustees, whichever is the later[4].

The above provisions do not, however, apply to property excepted from their operation by the instrument of amalgamation or transfer[5], or to stocks and securities in the public funds of the United Kingdom or Northern Ireland[6].

An amalgamation or transfer of engagements does not prejudice any right of any creditor of any trade union which is party to it[7].

1   As to when an instrument of amalgamation or transfer takes effect see PARA 1007. See also *UNISON v Allen* [2008] ICR 114, [2007] IRLR 975, EAT.

2   As to the meaning of 'trade union' see PARA 891. As to the application of these provisions to Northern Ireland unions see PARA 1013.

3   For these purposes, 'appropriate trustees' means: (1) in the case of property to be held for the benefit of a branch of the amalgamated union, or of the transferee union, the trustees of that branch, unless the rules of the amalgamated or transferee union provide that the property to be so held is to be held by the trustees of the union (Trade Union and Labour Relations (Consolidation) Act 1992 s 105(2)); and (2) in any other case, the trustees of the amalgamated or transferee union (s 105(3)). As to the meaning of 'rules', in relation to a trade union, see PARA 898 note 5. Contracts of employment cannot naturally be described as an aspect of the union's property held by its trustees, and do not transfer merely by virtue of the merger legislation itself, but rather pursuant to TUPE (as so which see PARA 136 et seq): *UNISON v Allen* [2008] ICR 114, [2007] IRLR 975, EAT.

4   Trade Union and Labour Relations (Consolidation) Act 1992 s 105(1).

5   The instrument must specify any property held for the benefit of any of the amalgamating organisations or of the transferor organisation (or for the benefit of a branch of any such organisation) which is not to be vested in the appropriate trustees, and must state the proposed disposition of any such property: see the Trade Unions and Employers' Associations (Amalgamations etc) Regulations 1975, SI 1975/536, regs 4(1), (2), Sch 1 para 4, Sch 2 para 3; and PARA 1001.

6   Trade Union and Labour Relations (Consolidation) Act 1992 s 105(4).

7   See the Trade Union and Labour Relations (Consolidation) Act 1992 s 97(3); and PARAS 998, 999.

1013. Amalgamations and transfers in the case of Northern Ireland unions.
In the case of an amalgamation[1] or transfer of engagements[2] to which a trade union[3] and a Northern Ireland union[4] are party, the statutory provisions[5] have effect subject to the following modifications[6]:

(1)   the requirements relating to approval of the instrument[7], notice to members[8] and the ballot on a resolution[9] do not apply in relation to the Northern Ireland union, but the certification officer[10] must not register the instrument[11] unless he is satisfied that it will be effective under the law of Northern Ireland[12];

(2)   the instrument of amalgamation or transfer submitted to the certification officer for his approval[13] must state which of the bodies concerned is a Northern Ireland union and, in the case of an amalgamation, whether the amalgamated body is to be a Northern Ireland union, and the certification officer must withhold his approval if the instrument does not contain that information[14]; and

(3)   nothing in the provisions relating to the alteration of rules[15] or complaints as to the passing of a resolution[16] applies in relation to the Northern Ireland union[17].

1   As to amalgamations see PARA 998.

2   As to transfers of engagements see PARA 999.

3   As to the meaning of 'trade union' see PARA 891.

4   As to the meaning of 'Northern Ireland union' see PARA 995 note 5.

5 Ie the Trade Union and Labour Relations (Consolidation) Act 1992 Pt I Ch VII (ss 97–108): see PARA 998 et seq. Subject to the exceptions specified in heads (1)–(3) in the text, the provisions of Pt I Ch VII as to amalgamations or transfers of engagements apply in relation to the Northern Ireland union: s 106(5).
6 Trade Union and Labour Relations (Consolidation) Act 1992 s 106(1).
7 Ie the Trade Union and Labour Relations (Consolidation) Act 1992 s 98: see PARA 1001.
8 Ie the Trade Union and Labour Relations (Consolidation) Act 1992 s 99: see PARA 1002.
9 Ie the Trade Union and Labour Relations (Consolidation) Act 1992 ss 100–100E (see PARA 1003 et seq) and s 101(3) (see PARA 1007).
10 As to the certification officer see PARA 1443.
11 Ie under the Trade Union and Labour Relations (Consolidation) Act 1992 s 101: see PARA 1007.
12 Trade Union and Labour Relations (Consolidation) Act 1992 s 106(2) (amended by the Trade Union Reform and Employment Rights Act 1993 Sch 8 para 57(a)). See also the Trade Unions and Employers' Associations (Amalgamations etc) Regulations 1975, SI 1975/536, reg 10 (cited in PARAS 1001 note 3, 1002 note 9, 1007 notes 4, 9).
13 Ie under the Trade Union and Labour Relations (Consolidation) Act 1992 s 98.
14 Trade Union and Labour Relations (Consolidation) Act 1992 s 106(3).
15 Ie the Trade Union and Labour Relations (Consolidation) Act 1992 s 102: see PARA 1009. As to the meaning of 'rules', in relation to a trade union, see PARA 898 note 5.
16 Ie the Trade Union and Labour Relations (Consolidation) Act 1992 s 103 (see PARAS 1010, 1011) and s 104 (see PARA 1011).
17 Trade Union and Labour Relations (Consolidation) Act 1992 s 106(4) (amended by the Trade Union Reform and Employment Rights Act 1993 Sch 8 para 57(b)).

(ii) Secession from, Dissolution of and Change of Name of Trade Unions

1014. Secession from trade union. The secession of one group of members from a trade union is a matter for the rules of the union, and in the absence of such rules the court will not infer rules governing the secession[1].

1 *Burnley Nelson Rossendale and District Textile Workers' Union v Amalgamated Textile Workers' Union* [1986] 1 All ER 885, [1987] ICR 69 (where the court refused to infer a rule entitling the seceding union to a proportion of the funds of the amalgamated union), distinguishing *Keys v Boulter (No 2)* [1972] 2 All ER 303, [1972] 1 WLR 642 (where the parties were able to reach agreement on the terms of the secession).

1015. Dissolution of a trade union. The dissolution of a trade union is primarily a matter for the rules of the union. On the dissolution[1] of a trade union which has no rules governing the manner of distribution of assets, it seems that the assets are to be distributed on a per capita basis and that there is no resulting trust in favour of the members[2].

1 As to the inherent jurisdiction of the High Court to dissolve an unincorporated association where the rules of the association are silent see *Keys v Boulter (No 2)* [1972] 2 All ER 303, [1972] 1 WLR 642. It is not certain whether a trade union is an 'unregistered company' within the meaning of the Insolvency Act 1986 s 220 and can be wound up as such by the court under s 221(5): see COMPANY AND PARTNERSHIP INSOLVENCY vol 17 (2011) PARA 1109 et seq.
2 *Re Sick and Funeral Society of St John's Sunday School, Golcar* [1973] Ch 51, [1972] 2 All ER 439 (where it was held that the assets of an unincorporated association should be distributed on a per capita basis but with a half-share only for child members having regard to the inequality in the rights and obligations of membership contained in the rules between child and other members; applied in *Re GKN Bolts and Nuts Ltd Sports and Social Club, Leek v Donkersley* [1982] 2 All ER 855, [1982] 1 WLR 774), not following *Re Printers and Transferrers Amalgamated Trades Protection Society* [1899] 2 Ch 184 (where it was held that there was a resulting trust of the net funds in favour of the members).

1016. Change of name of trade union. A trade union[1] may change its name by any method expressly provided for by its rules[2] or, if its rules do not expressly provide for a method of doing so, by adopting, in accordance with its rules, an alteration of the provision in them which gives the union its name[3]. Where, however, the name of a trade union is entered in the list of trade unions[4] maintained by the certification officer[5], a change of name does not take effect until approved by him[6]; and he must not approve a change of name if it appears to him that the proposed new name is the same as one entered in the list of trade unions or the list of employers associations[7], or is a name so nearly resembling such a name as to be likely to deceive the public[8].

A change of name by a trade union does not affect any right or obligation of the union or any of its members; and any pending legal proceedings may be continued by or against the union, the trustees of the union or any other officer[9] of the union who can sue or be sued on its behalf, notwithstanding its change of name[10].

1   As to the meaning of 'trade union' see PARA 891.
2   As to the meaning of 'rules', in relation to a trade union, see PARA 898 note 5.
3   Trade Union and Labour Relations (Consolidation) Act 1992 s 107(1).
4   As to the list of trade unions see PARA 900.
5   As to the certification officer see PARA 1443.
6   Trade Union and Labour Relations (Consolidation) Act 1992 s 107(2).
7   As to the list of employers' associations see PARA 1083.
8   Trade Union and Labour Relations (Consolidation) Act 1992 s 107(3). An application for an approval of a change of name must be signed by three members of the committee of management or other governing body and the secretary of the organisation and must be submitted to the certification officer in duplicate in the form to be provided by him for that purpose: Trade Unions and Employers' Associations (Amalgamations etc) Regulations 1975, SI 1975/536, reg 9(1) (reg 9 amended by SI 1978/1344). The application must be accompanied by a statutory declaration by the secretary of the union as to the manner in which the change of name was effected, in the form to be provided by the certification officer for the purpose: Trade Unions and Employers' Associations (Amalgamations etc) Regulations 1975, SI 1975/536, reg 9(2) (as so amended). On approving the change of name, the certification officer must return to the organisation one copy of the application indorsed with the word 'Approved' and duly authenticated: reg 9(3) (as so amended). The fee prescribed for an approval of a change of name is £96: reg 11(2) (substituted by SI 1988/310; amended by SI 2005/713). As to the meaning of 'organisation' see PARA 1001 note 3.
9   As to the meaning of 'officer', in relation to a trade union, see PARA 902 note 7.
10 Trade Union and Labour Relations (Consolidation) Act 1992 s 107(4).

(8) INTER-UNION DISPUTES

1017. Implementation of TUC's disputes committee awards. The Trades Union Congress ('TUC') has established a set of principles governing relations between unions which are set out in the 'TUC Disputes Principles and Procedures' based on the 'Bridlington Principles' as subsequently supplemented and amended[1]. Those principles are not intended to be a legally enforceable contract, but form a code of practice which is accepted by all affiliated organisations as a binding commitment for their continued affiliation to the TUC[2]. They are subject to internal enforcement by a disputes committee[3].

A trade union may not expel a member in order to comply with an award of the TUC's disputes committee unless the rules of the union make express provision for such an expulsion[4]. Expulsion of a member under such a rule is not contrary to public policy[5]; but an individual may not be expelled from a trade union unless the expulsion is permitted[6] by certain statutory provisions[7].

1   As to the history of the 'Bridlington Principles' and their amplification by the further recommendations adopted at Croydon in 1969 see the TUC Disputes Principles and Procedures (2007) pp 41–44. In 2007 the TUC published a simple guide to the Disputes Principles and Procedures called 'Working Together': see www.tuc.org.uk.
2   TUC Disputes Principles and Procedures (2007) p 4.

3   See TUC Disputes Principles and Procedures (2007) pp 18–26.
4   *Spring v National Amalgamated Stevedores and Dockers Society* [1956] 2 All ER 221, [1956] 1 WLR 585. Cf *Rothwell v Association of Professional, Executive, Clerical and Computer Staff* [1976] ICR 211, [1975] IRLR 375.
5   *Cheall v Association of Professional, Executive, Clerical and Computer Staff* [1983] 2 AC 180, [1983] ICR 398, HL.
6   Ie permitted by the Trade Union and Labour Relations (Consolidation) Act 1992 s 174: see PARA 1026.
7   Trade Union and Labour Relations (Consolidation) Act 1992 s 174(1) (substituted by the Trade Union Reform and Employment Rights Act 1993 s 14). As to the right not to be excluded or expelled from a trade union see PARA 1026 et seq.

(9) TRADE UNION OFFICIALS

1018.   Meaning of 'official'; appointment or election.   'Official', in relation to a trade union[1], means[2]:

(1)   an officer[3] of the union or of a branch or section[4] of the union; or
(2)   a person elected or appointed in accordance with the rules[5] of the union to be a representative of its members or of some of them,

and includes a person so elected or appointed who is an employee[6] of the same employer[7] as the members, or one or more of the members, whom he is to represent[8].

The status of a trade union official will depend on whether that official is an employee of the union, a member of the union, or both, or neither.

An official of a trade union who holds a position in the union to which the statutory requirements[9] on elections apply must be elected to that position at an election satisfying those requirements and may not continue to hold that position for more than five years without being re-elected at such an election[10]. No member of a trade union may be unreasonably excluded from standing as a candidate in such an election[11]; and as an organisation of workers for the purposes of the Equality Act 2010, a trade union must not discriminate against or victimise a member by subjecting that member to any detriment on the grounds of age, disability, gender reassignment, marriage and civil partnership, pregnancy and maternity, race, religion or belief, sex or sexual orientation[12]. Otherwise, the appointment or election of union officials must be in strict compliance with the union's rules[13], although the court has a discretion not to declare an election invalid because of a minor irregularity[14]. A member elected to a full-time post as a union official has no remedy over and above his common law rights to damages for breach of contract if the number of such posts is subsequently reduced for economic reasons, the union's rules are amended accordingly and he is not allowed to take up the appointment[15].

1   As to the meaning of 'trade union' see PARA 891.
2   Ie for the purposes of the Trade Union and Labour Relations (Consolidation) Act 1992 see PARAS 891 et seq, 1019 et seq.
3   As to the meaning of 'officer', in relation to a trade union, see PARA 902 note 7.
4   As to the meaning of 'branch or section', in relation to a trade union, see PARA 898 note 5.
5   As to the meaning of 'rules', in relation to a trade union, see PARA 898 note 5.
6   As to the meaning of 'employee' see PARA 892.
7   As to the meaning of 'employer' see PARA 892.
8   Trade Union and Labour Relations (Consolidation) Act 1992 s 119. See *Harris v Richard Lawson Autologistics Ltd* [2002] EWCA Civ 442, [2002] ICR 765, [2002] IRLR 476 (employees bound by contractual terms negotiated by shop steward on their behalf).
9   Ie the requirements of the Trade Union and Labour Relations (Consolidation) Act 1992 Pt I Ch IV (ss 46–61): see PARA 960 et seq.
10 See the Trade Union and Labour Relations (Consolidation) Act 1992 s 46(1); and PARA 960.

11   See the Trade Union and Labour Relations (Consolidation) Act 1992 s 47(1); and PARA 964.
12   See the Equality Act 2010 s 57; and DISCRIMINATION vol 33 (2013) PARA 125.
     Marriage of same sex couples is lawful in the law of England and Wales, and such marriages
have the same effect as marriages of opposite sex couples: see the Marriage (Same Sex Couples)
Act 2013 s 1(1), 11(1); and MATRIMONIAL AND CIVIL PARTNERSHIP LAW vol 72 (2009) PARA 1 et
seq.
13   *Leigh v National Union of Railwaymen* [1970] Ch 326, [1969] 3 All ER 1249.
14   *Brown v Amalgamated Union of Engineering Workers* [1976] ICR 147, 119 Sol Jo 709; *Hamlet
v General Municipal Boilermakers and Allied Trades Union* [1987] 1 All ER 631, [1987] ICR
150.
15   See *Meacham v Amalgamated Engineering and Electrical Union* [1994] IRLR 218.

1019.   Discipline or removal from office.   The principles which apply to the
discipline or removal from office of trade union officials are similar to those
which apply to the discipline or expulsion of a member[1]. Thus, there must be
strict compliance with the rules[2], and in certain circumstances the domestic body
of the union taking the decision to discipline an official or remove an official
from office must also comply with the rules of natural justice[3].

1   As to the discipline or expulsion of members see PARA 1023.
2   *Leary v National Union of Vehicle Builders* [1971] Ch 34, [1970] 2 All ER 713.
3   *Stevenson v United Road Transport Union* [1977] 2 All ER 941, [1977] ICR 893, CA; *Roebuck
v National Union of Mineworkers (Yorkshire Area), O'Brien v National Union of Mineworkers
(Yorkshire Area)* [1977] ICR 573; *Roebuck v National Union of Mineworkers (Yorkshire Area),
O'Brien v National Union of Mineworkers (Yorkshire Area) (No 2)* [1978] ICR 676. As to
natural justice see PARA 1024; and JUDICIAL REVIEW vol 61 (2010) PARA 629 et seq.

1020.   Time off work for trade union duties and industrial relations training.
An employer[1] must permit an employee[2] of his who is an official[3] of an
independent trade union[4] recognised[5] by the employer to take time off work with
pay during his working hours[6] for the purpose of carrying out any duties of his,
as such an official, concerned with:
   (1)   negotiations with the employer that are related to, or connected with,
         any matter which falls within the statutory meaning of collective
         bargaining[7] and in relation to which the trade union is recognised by the
         employer[8]; or
   (2)   the performance, on behalf of employees of the employer, of functions
         that are related to, or connected with, any such matters[9] which the
         employer has agreed may be so performed by the trade union[10]; or
   (3)   receipt of information from the employer and consultation by the
         employer in relation to redundancies[11] or the transfer[12] of an
         undertaking; or
   (4)   negotiations with a view to entering into an agreement under the
         specified provision of the Transfer of Undertakings (Protection of
         Employment) Regulations 2006[13] permitting certain variations in a
         contract of employment that applies to employees of the employer; or
   (5)   the performance on behalf of employees of the employer of functions
         related to or connected with the making of an agreement under that
         regulation[14].
The employer must also permit such an employee to take time off work with
pay during his working hours for the purpose of undergoing training in aspects
of industrial relations which is relevant to the carrying out of the above duties
and is approved by the Trades Union Congress or by the independent trade
union of which he is an official[15].

1   As to the meaning of 'employer' see PARA 892.

2 As to the meaning of 'employee' see PARA 892.
3 As to the meaning of 'official' see PARA 1018.
4 As to the meaning of 'independent trade union' see PARA 904.
5 As to the meaning of 'recognition', in relation to a trade union, see PARA 1094.
6 For these purposes, the working hours of an employee are to be taken to be any time when in accordance with his contract of employment he is required to be at work: Trade Union and Labour Relations (Consolidation) Act 1992 s 173(1). As to the meaning of 'contract of employment' see PARA 892. As to the contract of employment generally see PARA 1 et seq.
7 Ie matters falling within the Trade Union and Labour Relations (Consolidation) Act 1992 s 178(2): see PARA 1093 heads (1)–(7).
8 See further PARA 1065 et seq.
9 See note 7.
10 See note 8.
11 Ie under the Trade Union and Labour Relations (Consolidation) Act 1992 s 188: see PARA 1185.
12 Ie under the Transfer of Undertakings (Protection of Employment) Regulations 2006, SI 2006/246: see PARA 1196 et seq.
13 Ie under the Transfer of Undertakings (Protection of Employment) Regulations 2006, SI 2006/246, reg 9: see PARA 138.
14 Trade Union and Labour Relations (Consolidation) Act 1992 s 168(1) (amended by SI 1999/1925; SI 2006/246); Trade Union and Labour Relations (Consolidation) Act 1992 s 169(1). Where s 198A (see PARA 1186) applies and the transferee elects to carry out pre-transfer consultation (and has not cancelled the election), both before and after the transfer s 168(1)(c) (see head (3) in the text) applies as follows in relation to an official of an independent trade union who, as such an official, is an affected transferring individual's appropriate representative under s 188(1B)(a) (see PARA 1187): (1) in relation to the official's duties as such a representative, the reference in the opening words of s 168(1) to an independent trade union being recognised by the employer is to be read as a reference to an independent trade union being recognised by the transferor; (2) the references in s 168(1)(c) to the employer in relation to s 188 are to be read as references to the transferee: s 198B(2) (added by SI 2014/16). As to the meanings of 'transferor' and 'transferee' see PARA 1186 note 1; as to the meaning of 'affected transferring individual' see PARA 1186 note 8; and as to the meaning of 'pre-transfer consultation' see PARA 1186.

    The remedy of an employee for infringement of the right so conferred is by way of complaint to an employment tribunal and not otherwise: s 173(2) (amended by the Employment Rights (Dispute Resolution) Act 1998 s 1(2)(a)). See also PARAS 1065, 1068. An appeal lies to the Employment Appeal Tribunal on any question of law arising from any decision of, or arising in any proceedings before, an employment tribunal under or by virtue of the Trade Union and Labour Relations (Consolidation) Act 1992: see the Employment Tribunals Act 1996 s 21(1)(d); and PARA 1428. As to the Employment Appeal Tribunal see PARA 1422 et seq.
15 Trade Union and Labour Relations (Consolidation) Act 1992 ss 168(2), 169(1). See also note 14. As to time off work for trade union duties and activities see further PARA 1065 et seq. As to time off for union learning representatives see PARAS 1065, 1068.

1021. Responsibility of the union for its officials in contract and tort. A trade union[1] may be bound by contracts made in its name by an official or other agent of the union acting within the scope of his actual or ostensible authority, but will not be bound by a contract made by such a person acting outside the scope of such authority[2]. The union may, however, choose to ratify such unauthorised acts where they are not outside the powers of the union[3].

A trade union may be vicariously liable[4] for torts committed by its servants or agents[5]. Where, however, a trade union is sued for one of the industrial torts of inducing a breach of contract or interfering with the performance of a contract[6], intimidation[7] or conspiracy[8], the union may be liable for the act in question if, but only if, that act is taken to have been authorised or indorsed by the union in accordance with the relevant statutory provisions[9].

1 As to the meaning of 'trade union' see PARA 891.
2 See AGENCY vol 1 (2008) PARA 25.
3 See PARA 913.

4   See *Heatons Transport (St Helens) Ltd v Transport and General Workers' Union* [1973] AC 15, [1972] 3 All ER 101, HL; *General Aviation Services (UK) Ltd v Transport and General Workers' Union* [1985] ICR 615, [1976] IRLR 224, HL; *Thomas v National Union of Mineworkers (South Wales Area)* [1986] Ch 20, [1985] ICR 886.

5   See the Trade Union and Labour Relations (Consolidation) Act 1992 s 10(1)(b); and PARA 897 head (2).

6   See the Trade Union and Labour Relations (Consolidation) Act 1992 s 20(1)(a)(i); and PARA 1388 head (1)(a).

7   See the Trade Union and Labour Relations (Consolidation) Act 1992 s 20(1)(a)(ii); and PARA 1388 head (1)(b).

8   See the Trade Union and Labour Relations (Consolidation) Act 1992 s 20(1)(b); and PARA 1388 head (2).

9   As to the liability at a trade union for industrial torts see the Trade Union and Labour Relations (Consolidation) Act 1992 s 20; and PARA 1387 et seq.

(10) TRADE UNION MEMBERSHIP

(i) Membership Rights at Common Law

1022.   Admission to membership of a trade union.   A person becomes a member of a trade union on acceptance of his application for membership in accordance with the rules of the union[1]. The purported admission of a person to a class of membership not provided for in the rules is void[2]. Similarly, the purported admission of a person to membership in contravention of a qualification required in the rules is void[3]. At common law there is no general right in an individual to be admitted to a trade union which is unwilling to admit him[4].

1   *Luby v Warwickshire Miners' Association* [1912] 2 Ch 371.

2   *Martin v Scottish Transport and General Workers' Union* [1952] 1 All ER 691, HL (union officials purported to admit the plaintiff to temporary membership, for which there was no provision in the rules; it was held that the plaintiff had never been a member).

3   *Faramus v Film Artistes' Association* [1964] AC 925, [1964] 1 All ER 25, HL (rule provided that no person convicted of a criminal offence should be eligible for membership; it was held that a person who had been convicted of minor offences in a different country many years previously and had been admitted to membership had never been a member).

4   *Faramus v Film Artistes' Association* [1964] AC 925, [1964] 1 All ER 25, HL; *Cheall v Association of Professional, Executive, Clerical and Computer Staff* [1983] 2 AC 180, [1983] ICR 398, HL. It was formerly possible to put forward the argument for a right to be admitted to a trade union based on a 'right to work' (see *Nagle v Feilden* [1966] 2 QB 633, [1966] 1 All ER 689, CA; *Edwards v Society of Graphical and Allied Trades* [1971] Ch 354, [1970] 3 All ER 689, CA); but, if there were such a right, it could have applied only where membership of the trade union in question was a prerequisite for obtaining employment in a particular trade, profession or occupation, and that is now unlawful under the Trade Union and Labour Relations (Consolidation) Act 1992 s 137 (see PARA 1042). Cf the statutory right not to be excluded from a trade union: see ss 174–177; and PARA 1026 et seq.

1023.   Discipline and expulsion of trade union member.   A member of a trade union cannot be disciplined or expelled from the union unless there is a rule giving the union that power[1]. If the power exists, it must be exercised strictly in accordance with the rules[2]; and any penalty imposed must be in accordance with the rules[3].

A person will normally have no right of redress at common law if he is disciplined or expelled in accordance with the rules[4]; but in certain circumstances the domestic body of the union taking the decision to discipline or expel a member must also comply with the rules of natural justice[5].

If the rules give a right of appeal, deprivation of that right makes the original decision invalid, even if it was correct[6]. Conversely, a fair appeal will not always cure a defect in the original hearing[7].

1 *Luby v Warwickshire Miners' Association* [1912] 2 Ch 371. The court will not normally imply a power to discipline or expel (*Abbott v Sullivan* [1952] 1 KB 189, [1952] 1 All ER 226, CA; *Spring v National Amalgamated Stevedores and Dockers Society* [1956] 2 All ER 221, [1956] 1 WLR 585); but the court may imply a disciplinary power where there are 'compelling circumstances to justify it' (*McVitae v UNISON* [1996] IRLR 33 (rule implied empowering the union to discipline a member for conduct prior to an amalgamation)).

2 *Bonsor v Musicians' Union* [1954] Ch 479, [1954] 1 All ER 822, CA (revsd on another point [1956] AC 104, [1955] 3 All ER 518, HL); *Hiles v Amalgamated Society of Woodworkers* [1968] Ch 440, [1967] 3 All ER 70; *Santer v National Graphical Association* [1973] ICR 60.

3 *Annamunthodo v Oilfields Workers' Trade Union* [1961] AC 945, [1961] 3 All ER 621, PC; *Burn v National Amalgamated Labourers' Union of Great Britain and Ireland* [1920] 2 Ch 364; but cf *Santer v National Graphical Association* [1973] ICR 60.

4 *Maclean v Workers' Union* [1929] 1 Ch 602; *Cheall v Association of Professional, Executive, Clerical and Computer Staff* [1983] 2 AC 180, [1983] ICR 398, HL. As to the statutory right not to be expelled from a trade union see the Trade Union and Labour Relations (Consolidation) Act 1992 ss 174–177; and PARA 1026 et seq.

5 As to natural justice see PARA 1024; and JUDICIAL REVIEW vol 61 (2010) PARA 629 et seq.

6 *Braithwaite v Electrical Electronic and Telecommunication Union–Plumbing Trades Union* [1969] 2 All ER 859, CA.

7 *Annamunthodo v Oilfields Workers' Trade Union* [1961] AC 945, [1961] 3 All ER 621, PC; *Leary v National Union of Vehicle Builders* [1971] Ch 34, [1970] 2 All ER 713. The correct procedure in such a case is for there to be a rehearing: *Leary v National Union of Vehicle Builders* [1971] Ch 34, [1970] 2 All ER 713. Subject to any express provision to the contrary, there is an implied term in the rules of a trade union that the union has the power to reopen or rehear a disciplinary matter where justice requires it: *McKenzie v National Union of Public Employees* [1991] ICR 155.

1024. Trade union must comply with the rules of natural justice. A domestic body of a trade union purporting to discipline or expel a member for his conduct must comply with the rules of natural justice[1]. While the requirements of the rules of natural justice may vary according to the circumstances, in the case of a decision to discipline or expel a trade union member it is settled that he must be given notice of the charges against him[2] and have an opportunity to state his case[3], and that the domestic body taking the decision must act honestly and in good faith, and without bias[4]. Where a rule of the union requires expulsion if factual circumstances prescribed by the rule are fulfilled and the conduct of the member is not in issue, the rules of natural justice do not apply[5].

1 As to natural justice see further JUDICIAL REVIEW vol 61 (2010) PARA 629 et seq.

2 *Annamunthodo v Oilfields Workers' Trade Union* [1961] AC 945, [1961] 3 All ER 61, PC; *Radford v National Society of Operative Printers, Graphical and Media Personnel* [1972] ICR 484; *Stevenson v United Road Transport Union* [1977] 2 All ER 941, [1977] ICR 893, CA.

3 *Burn v National Amalgamated Labourers' Union of Great Britain and Ireland* [1920] 2 Ch 364; *Annamunthodo v Oilfields Workers' Trade Union* [1961] AC 945, [1961] 3 All ER 621, PC; *Breen v Amalgamated Engineering Union* [1971] 2 QB 175, [1971] 1 All ER 1148, CA.

4 *Maclean v Workers' Union* [1929] 1 Ch 602; *White v Kuzych* [1951] AC 585, [1951] 2 All ER 435, PC; *Taylor v National Union of Seamen* [1967] 1 All ER 767, [1967] 1 WLR 532; *Roebuck v National Union of Mineworkers (Yorkshire Area), O'Brien v National Union of Mineworkers (Yorkshire Area)* [1977] ICR 573; *Roebuck v National Union of Mineworkers (Yorkshire Area), O'Brien v National Union of Mineworkers (Yorkshire Area) (No 2)* [1978] ICR 676. The domestic body is not required to act impartially in a judicial sense, and the fact that its members have preconceived views on the issues for decision does not mean that the body is not acting honestly and in good faith: see *White v Kuzych* [1951] AC 585, [1951] 2 All ER 435, PC. Cf *Hamlet v General Municipal Boilermakers and Allied Trades Union* [1987] 1 All ER 631, [1987] ICR 150 (where it was held that there is no immutable rule of natural justice that a member of a body at first instance is thereby disabled from sitting on appeal).

5 *Cheall v Association of Professional, Executive, Clerical and Computer Staff* [1983] 2 AC 180
 at 190, [1983] ICR 398 at 404, HL per Lord Diplock. Cf *Edwards v Society of Graphical and
 Allied Trades* [1971] Ch 354, [1970] 3 All ER 689, CA (where it was stated, obiter, that a rule
 which provided for automatic lapse of membership after six weeks' arrears of subscriptions was
 void at common law as an unreasonable restraint on the plaintiff's right to work; but see now
 PARA 1022 note 4).

(ii) Statutory Rights in relation to Trade Union Membership

A. RIGHT TO AN INDUSTRIAL ACTION BALLOT

1025. The right to a ballot before industrial action. A member[1] of a trade
union[2] who claims that members of the union, including himself, are likely to be
or have been induced[3] by the union[4] to take part, or to continue to take part, in
industrial action[5] which does not have the support of a ballot[6] may apply to the
High Court for an order[7]. Where, on such an application, the court is satisfied
that the claim is well-founded, it must make such order[8] as it considers
appropriate for requiring the union to take steps for ensuring:
 (1)   that there is no, or no further, inducement of members of the union to
       take part, or to continue to take part, in the industrial action to which
       the application relates; and
 (2)   that no member engages in conduct after the making of the order by
       virtue of having been induced before the making of the order to take
       part, or to continue to take part, in the action[9].
For these purposes, industrial action is to be regarded as having the support of
a ballot only if:
 (a)   the union has held a ballot in respect of the action in relation to which
       certain statutory requirements[10] were satisfied, and in which the
       majority voting in the ballot answered 'yes' to the question applicable[11]
       to industrial action of the kind which the applicant has been or is likely
       to be induced to take part in;
 (b)   such of the statutory requirements[12] as have fallen to be satisfied at the
       relevant time[13] have been satisfied;
 (c)   the statutory provision relating to inducement of a member denied the
       entitlement to vote[14] does not prevent the industrial action from being
       regarded as having the support of the ballot; and
 (d)   the statutory requirements[15] relating to the calling of industrial action
       are satisfied[16].

1 As to the meaning of 'member' for these purposes see PARA 915 note 1.
2 As to the meaning of 'trade union' see PARA 891.
3 For these purposes, 'inducement' includes an inducement which is or would be ineffective,
 whether because of the member's unwillingness to be influenced by it or for any other reason:
 Trade Union and Labour Relations (Consolidation) Act 1992 s 62(6).
4 For these purposes, an act is to be taken to be done by a trade union if it is authorised or
 indorsed by the union, and the provisions of the Trade Union and Labour Relations
 (Consolidation) Act 1992 s 20(2)–(4) (see PARA 1388) apply for the purpose of determining
 whether an act is to be taken to be so authorised or indorsed: s 62(5).
5 For these purposes, 'industrial action' means a strike or other industrial action by persons
 employed under contracts of employment: Trade Union and Labour Relations (Consolidation)
 Act 1992 s 62(6). 'Strike' is not defined for the purposes of s 62, but for the purposes of the
 statutory balloting requirements, 'strike' is defined as 'any concerted stoppage of work': see
 s 246; and PARA 1340. For the purposes of the provisions in s 62 relating to the right to a ballot
 before industrial action: (1) where a person holds any office or employment under the Crown on
 terms which do not constitute a contract of employment between that person and the Crown,
 those terms are nevertheless to be deemed to constitute such a contract (s 62(7)); and

(2) references to a contract of employment include any contract under which one person personally does work or performs services for another, and related expressions are to be construed accordingly (s 62(8)). As to the meaning of 'contract of employment' generally see PARA 892.

6 Nothing in the Trade Union and Labour Relations (Consolidation) Act 1992 s 62 is to be construed as requiring a union to hold separate ballots for these purposes and for the purposes of ss 226–234 (see PARA 1370 et seq): s 62(9).

7 Trade Union and Labour Relations (Consolidation) Act 1992 ss 62(1), 121. As to the means of voting in ballots see the Employment Relations Act 2004 s 54; and PARA 963.

8 Without prejudice to any other power of the court, the court may grant such interim relief as it considers appropriate: see the Trade Union and Labour Relations (Consolidation) Act 1992 s 62(4). The provisions of s 20(2)–(4) (see PARA 1388) apply in relation to proceedings for failure to comply with such an order as they apply in relation to the original proceedings: s 62(5).

9 Trade Union and Labour Relations (Consolidation) Act 1992 s 62(3).

10 Ie the requirements of the Trade Union and Labour Relations (Consolidation) Act 1992 s 226B (see PARA 1373), so far as applicable before and during the holding of the ballot, and the requirements of ss 227–231 (see PARA 1374 et seq).

11 Ie in accordance with the Trade Union and Labour Relations (Consolidation) Act 1992 s 229(2): see PARA 1376.

12 Ie the requirements of the Trade Union and Labour Relations (Consolidation) Act 1992 s 226B, so far as applicable after the holding of the ballot, and the requirements of s 231B (see PARA 1373).

13 For these purposes, 'relevant time' means the time when the application is made: Trade Union and Labour Relations (Consolidation) Act 1992 s 62(1) (amended by the Trade Union Reform and Employment Rights Act 1993 Sch 8 para 47(a)).

14 Ie the Trade Union and Labour Relations (Consolidation) Act 1992 s 232A: see PARA 1374.

15 Ie the requirements of the Trade Union and Labour Relations (Consolidation) Act 1992 s 233: see PARA 1380.

16 Trade Union and Labour Relations (Consolidation) Act 1992 s 62(2) (amended by the Trade Union Reform and Employment Rights Act 1993 Sch 8 para 47(b); the Employment Relations Act 2004 s 24(2), Sch 2). Any reference in the Trade Union and Labour Relations (Consolidation) Act 1992 s 62(2) to the requirements of any provision which is disapplied or modified by s 232 (balloting of overseas members) (see PARA 1379) has effect subject to s 232: s 62(2) (as so amended).

B. RIGHT NOT TO BE EXCLUDED OR EXPELLED FROM UNION

1026. Right not to be excluded or expelled from trade union. An individual may not be excluded[1] or expelled[2] from a trade union[3] unless the exclusion or expulsion is permitted by the following provisions[4].

The exclusion or expulsion of an individual from a trade union is permitted if, and only if:

(1) he does not satisfy, or no longer satisfies, an enforceable membership requirement[5] contained in the rules of the union;

(2) he does not qualify, or no longer qualifies, for membership of the union by reason of the union operating only in a particular part or particular parts of Great Britain[6];

(3) in the case of a union whose purpose is the regulation of relations between its members and one particular employer[7], or a number of particular employers who are associated[8], he is not, or is no longer, employed by that employer or one of those employers; or

(4) the exclusion or expulsion is entirely attributable to conduct[9] of his (other than excluded conduct)[10] and the conduct to which it is wholly or mainly attributable is not protected conduct[11].

1 For these purposes, if an individual's application for membership of a trade union is neither granted nor rejected before the end of the period within which it might reasonably have been

expected to be granted if it was to be granted, he is to be treated as having been excluded from the union on the last day of that period: Trade Union and Labour Relations (Consolidation) Act 1992 s 177(2)(a) (s 177 substituted by the Trade Union Reform and Employment Rights Act 1993 s 14). 'Exclusion' from membership refers to a refusal to admit into membership, not to the suspension of the privileges of membership: *NACODS v Gluchowski* [1996] IRLR 252, EAT.

2   For these purposes, an individual who under the rules of a trade union ceases to be a member of the union on the happening of an event specified in the rules is to be treated as having been expelled from the union: Trade Union and Labour Relations (Consolidation) Act 1992 s 177(2)(b) (as substituted: see note 1). Under the predecessor of this provision, ie the Employment Act 1980 s 4 (repealed), it was held that there is no concept of 'constructive expulsion' whereby a union member can resign and claim that he was driven to do so by the union: *McGhee v Midlands British Road Services Ltd, McGhee v Transport and General Workers' Union* [1985] ICR 503, [1985] IRLR 198, EAT. As to the meaning of 'rules', in relation to a trade union, see PARA 898 note 5.

3   For these purposes, 'trade union' does not include an organisation falling within the Trade Union and Labour Relations (Consolidation) Act 1992 s 1(b) (see PARA 891 head (2)): s 177(1)(a) (as substituted: see note 1). As to the meaning of 'trade union' generally see PARA 891.

4   Trade Union and Labour Relations (Consolidation) Act 1992 s 174(1) (s 174 substituted by the Trade Union Reform and Employment Rights Act 1993 s 14). The rights conferred by the Trade Union and Labour Relations (Consolidation) Act 1992 s 174 are in addition to, and not in substitution for, any right which exists apart from that provision; and, subject to s 177(4) (see PARA 1027 note 4), nothing in any of ss 174–177 (see the text and notes 1–3, 5–11; and PARAS 1027, 1028) affects any remedy for infringement of any such right: s 177(5) (as substituted: see note 1). See also s 174(4C)–(4H); and note 11.

5   For these purposes, a requirement in relation to membership of a union is 'enforceable' if it restricts membership solely by reference to one or more of the following criteria: (1) employment in a specified trade, industry or profession; (2) occupational description, including grade, level or category of appointment; and (3) possession of specified trade, industrial or professional qualifications or work experience: Trade Union and Labour Relations (Consolidation) Act 1992 s 174(3) (as substituted: see note 4). 'Employment' includes any relationship whereby an individual personally does work or performs services for another person; and related expressions are to be construed accordingly: s 177(1)(c) (as substituted: see note 1).

6   As to the meaning of 'Great Britain' see PARA 2 note 12.

7   As to the meaning of 'employer' generally see PARA 892. See also note 5.

8   For these purposes, any two employers are to be treated as associated if one is a company of which the other, directly or indirectly, has control, or both are companies of which a third person, directly or indirectly, has control; and 'associated employer' is to be construed accordingly: Trade Union and Labour Relations (Consolidation) Act 1992 s 297. The definition of 'associated employer' in the Trade Union and Labour Relations (Consolidation) Act 1992 is the same as that in the Employment Rights Act 1996 s 231: see PARA 3.

9   For these purposes, 'conduct' includes statements, acts and omissions: Trade Union and Labour Relations (Consolidation) Act 1992 s 177(1)(b) (as substituted: see note 1).

10   'Excluded conduct', in relation to an individual, means (1) conduct which consists in his being or ceasing to be, or having been or ceased to be, a member of another trade union; (2) conduct which consists in his being or ceasing to be, or having been or ceased to be, employed by a particular employer or at a particular place; or (3) conduct to which s 65 (see PARA 1030) applies or would apply if the references in s 65 to the trade union which is relevant for the purposes of s 65 were references to any trade union: s 174(4) (s 174(4) substituted by the Employment Relations Act 2004 s 33(1), (3), (7)).

11   Trade Union and Labour Relations (Consolidation) Act 1992 s 174(2) (as substituted (see note 4); amended by the Employment Relations Act 2004 s 33(1), (2), (7)). 'Protected conduct' is conduct which consists in the individual's being or ceasing to be, or having been or ceased to be, a member of a political party: Trade Union and Labour Relations (Consolidation) Act 1992 s 174(4A) (s 174(4A), (4B) added by the Employment Relations Act 2004 s 33(1), (3), (7))). Conduct which consists of activities undertaken by an individual as a member of a political party is not conduct falling within the Trade Union and Labour Relations (Consolidation) Act 1992 s 174(4A): s 174(4B) (as so added). As to the right of complaint to an employment tribunal see PARA 1027.

Conduct which consists in an individual's being or having been a member of a political party is not conduct falling within s 174(4A) if membership of that political party is contrary to (1) a rule of the trade union; or (2) an objective of the trade union: s 174(4C) (s 174(4C)–(4H) added by the Employment Act 2008 s 19(1), (2)). For the purposes of the Trade Union and Labour Relations (Consolidation) Act 1992 s 174(4C)(b) (see head (2) above): (a) in the case of conduct consisting in an individual's being a member of a political party, an objective is to be disregarded (i) in relation to an exclusion, if it is not reasonably practicable for the objective to be ascertained by a person working in the same trade, industry or profession as the individual; (ii) in relation to an expulsion, if it is not reasonably practicable for the objective to be ascertained by a member of the union (s 174(4D) (as so added)); (b) in the case of conduct consisting in an individual's having been a member of a political party, an objective is to be disregarded (i) in relation to an exclusion, if at the time of the conduct it was not reasonably practicable for the objective to be ascertained by a person working in the same trade, industry or profession as the individual; (ii) in relation to an expulsion, if at the time of the conduct it was not reasonably practicable for the objective to be ascertained by a member of the union (s 174(4E) (as so added)).

Where the exclusion or expulsion of an individual from a trade union is wholly or mainly attributable to conduct which consists of an individual's being or having been a member of a political party but which by virtue of s 174(4C) is not conduct falling within s 174(4A) (ie it is not protected conduct), the exclusion or expulsion is not permitted by virtue of s 174(2)(d) (see head (4) in the text) if any one or more of the conditions in s 174(4G) apply: s 174(4F) (as so added). Those conditions are: (A) the decision to exclude or expel is taken otherwise than in accordance with the union's rules; (B) the decision to exclude or expel is taken unfairly; (C) the individual would lose his livelihood or suffer other exceptional hardship by reason of not being, or ceasing to be, a member of the union: s 174(4G) (as so added). For the purposes of s 174(4G)(b) (see head (B) above) a decision to exclude or expel an individual is taken unfairly if (and only if) (*aa*) before the decision is taken the individual is not given notice of the proposal to exclude or expel him and the reasons for that proposal, and a fair opportunity to make representations in respect of that proposal; or (*bb*) representations made by the individual in respect of that proposal are not considered fairly: s 174(4H) (as so added). See also the Employment Act 2008 (Commencement No 2, Transitional Provisions and Savings) Order 2009, SI 2009/603, art 3, Schedule. The Trade Union and Labour Relations (Consolidation) Act 1992 s 174(4C)–(4H) was added by the Employment Act 2008 s 19 in order to comply with Application 11002/05 *Associated Society of Locomotive Engineers and Firemen v United Kingdom* (2007) 45 EHRR 793, [2007] IRLR 361, ECtHR (violation of trade union's freedom of association established where expulsion had not caused member any particular detriment).

1027. Complaint to employment tribunal. An individual who claims that he has been excluded or expelled from a trade union[1] in contravention[2] of the statutory provisions[3] may present a complaint to an employment tribunal[4].

An employment tribunal must not entertain a complaint by an individual that he has been so excluded or expelled unless it is presented[5]:

(1) before the end of the period of six months beginning with the date of the exclusion or expulsion[6], subject to an extension to facilitate conciliation before the institution of proceedings[7]; or

(2) where the tribunal is satisfied that it was not reasonably practicable for the complaint to be presented before the end of that period, within such further period as the tribunal considers reasonable[8].

1 As to the meaning of 'trade union' see PARA 891. See also PARA 1026 note 3.
2 As to the meaning of 'contravention' and cognate expressions see PARA 915 note 6.
3 Ie in contravention of the Trade Union and Labour Relations (Consolidation) Act 1992 s 174: see PARA 1026.
4 Trade Union and Labour Relations (Consolidation) Act 1992 s 174(5) (substituted by the Trade Union Reform and Employment Rights Act 1993 s 14; amended by the Employment Rights (Dispute Resolution) Act 1998 s 1(2)(a)). As to employment tribunals see PARA 1399 et seq. The rights conferred by the Trade Union and Labour Relations (Consolidation) Act 1992 s 174 are in addition to, and not in substitution for, any right which exists apart from that provision; and, subject to s 177(4), nothing in any of ss 174–177 affects any remedy for infringement of any such right: s 177(5) (s 177 substituted by the Trade Union Reform and Employment Rights Act 1993 s 14).

The remedy of an individual for infringement of the rights conferred by the Trade Union and Labour Relations (Consolidation) Act 1992 s 174 is by way of complaint to an employment tribunal in accordance with ss 174–177 (see the text and notes 1–3, 5–6; and PARA 1028) and not otherwise: s 177(3) (as so substituted; amended by the Employment Rights (Dispute Resolution) Act 1998 s 1(2)(a)). Where a complaint relating to an expulsion which is presented under the Trade Union and Labour Relations (Consolidation) Act 1992 s 174 is declared to be well-founded, no complaint in respect of the expulsion is to be presented or proceeded with under s 66 (complaint of infringement of the right not to be unjustifiably disciplined: see PARA 1031): s 177(4) (as so substituted).

The provisions of the Employment Tribunals Act 1996 ss 18A–18B (conciliation) (see PARA 152) apply in the case of matters which could be the subject of employment tribunal proceedings under the Trade Union and Labour Relations (Consolidation) Act 1992 s 174, and the Employment Tribunals Act 1996 s 18C applies in the case of such proceedings themselves: see s 18(1)(a), (1A) (s 18(1)(a) substituted by SI 2014/431; the Employment Tribunals Act 1996 s 18(1A) added by the Enterprise and Regulatory Reform Act 2013 Sch 1 paras 2, 5(1), (7)). An appeal lies to the Employment Appeal Tribunal on any question of law arising from any decision of, or arising in any proceedings before, an employment tribunal under or by virtue of the Trade Union and Labour Relations (Consolidation) Act 1992: see the Employment Tribunals Act 1996 s 21(1)(d); and PARA 1428. As to the Employment Appeal Tribunal see PARA 1422 et seq.

5   As to when a complaint is presented see PARAS 804, 1461.

6   Trade Union and Labour Relations (Consolidation) Act 1992 s 175(1)(a) (substituted by the Trade Union Reform and Employment Rights Act 1993 s 14; amended by the Employment Rights (Dispute Resolution) Act 1998 s 1(2)(a); renumbered by the Enterprise and Regulatory Reform Act 2013 Sch 2 paras 1, 10).

7   The Trade Union and Labour Relations (Consolidation) Act 1992 s 292A (extension of time limits to facilitate conciliation before institution of proceedings: see PARA 1455) applies for the purposes of s 175(1)(a): s 175(2) added by the Enterprise and Regulatory Reform Act 2013 Sch 2 paras 1, 10).

8   Trade Union and Labour Relations (Consolidation) Act 1992 s 175(1)(b) (as amended and renumbered: see note 6). For the case law on the extension of time limits, especially in the context of the law of unfair dismissal, see PARAS 804, 1453. Cf *GMB v Hamm* [2000] All ER (D) 1830, EAT.

1028. Remedies for unlawful exclusion or expulsion, etc.

Where an employment tribunal[1] finds a complaint[2] of expulsion or exclusion from a trade union[3] well-founded, it must make a declaration to that effect[4], although this is subject to a qualification[5].

An individual whose complaint has been declared to be well-founded may make an application to an employment tribunal for an award of compensation to be paid to him by the union[6]. An application for compensation may not be entertained if made:

(1)   before the end of the period of four weeks beginning with the date of the declaration[7]; or

(2)   after the end of the period of six months beginning with that date[8].

The amount of compensation awarded is to be such as the employment tribunal considers just and equitable in all the circumstances[9], subject to certain statutory limitations[10]. Where the employment tribunal finds that the exclusion or expulsion complained of was to any extent caused or contributed to by the action[11] of the applicant, it must reduce the amount of the compensation by such proportion as it considers just and equitable having regard to that finding[12].

1   As to employment tribunals see PARA 1399 et seq.

2   Ie under the Trade Union and Labour Relations (Consolidation) Act 1992 s 174: see PARA 1026.

3   As to the meaning of 'trade union' see PARA 891. See also PARA 1026 note 3.

4   Trade Union and Labour Relations (Consolidation) Act 1992 s 176(1) (s 176 substituted by the Trade Union Reform and Employment Rights Act 1993 s 14; the Trade Union and Labour Relations (Consolidation) Act 1992 s 176(1) amended by the Employment Rights (Dispute Resolution) Act 1998 s 1(2)(a)). See further note 5.

5 If a tribunal makes a declaration under the Trade Union and Labour Relations (Consolidation) Act 1992 s 176(1) (see the text and notes 1–4) and it appears to the tribunal that the exclusion or expulsion was mainly attributable to conduct falling within s 174(4A) (see PARA 1026 note 11), it must make a declaration to that effect: s 176(1A) (s 176(1A)–(1D) added by the Employment Relations Act 2004 s 33(1), (4), (7)). If a tribunal makes such a declaration and it appears to the tribunal that the other conduct to which the exclusion or expulsion was attributable consisted wholly or mainly of conduct of the complainant which was contrary to a rule of the union or an objective of the union, it must make a declaration to that effect; and it is immaterial whether the complainant was a member of the union at the time of the conduct contrary to the rule or objective: Trade Union and Labour Relations (Consolidation) Act 1992 s 176(1B), (1C) (as so added). A declaration made in circumstances where it appears to the tribunal that the conduct in question was contrary to an objective of the union must not be made unless the union shows that, at the time of the conduct of the complainant which was contrary to the objective in question, it was reasonably practicable for that objective to be ascertained (1) if the complainant was not at that time a member of the union, by a person working in the same trade, industry or profession as the complainant; and (2) if he was at that time a member of the union, by a member of the union: s 176(1D) (as so added; amended by the Employment Act 2008 s 19(1), (3)). See also the Employment Act 2008 (Commencement No 2, Transitional Provisions and Savings) Order 2009, SI 2009/603, art 3, Schedule.

6 Trade Union and Labour Relations (Consolidation) Act 1992 s 176(2) (as substituted (see note 4); and amended by the Employment Rights (Dispute Resolution) Act 1998 s 1(2)(a); and the Employment Relations Act 2004 s 34(7), (8)). Every application under the Trade Union and Labour Relations (Consolidation) Act 1992 s 176 to the Appeal Tribunal must be made in writing in, or substantially in, accordance with the Employment Appeal Tribunal Rules 1993, SI 1993/2854, Schedule Form 4, and must be served on the Appeal Tribunal together with a copy of the decision or order declaring that the applicant's complaint against the trade union was well-founded: see r 8. As to applications under r 8 see further rr 9–12, 32, Schedule Form 5 (rr 9–11 amended by the Employment Rights (Dispute Resolution) Act 1998 s 1(2)(b)). As to the Employment Appeal Tribunal see PARA 1422 et seq.

7 Ie the declaration under the Trade Union and Labour Relations (Consolidation) Act 1992 s 176(1).

8 Trade Union and Labour Relations (Consolidation) Act 1992 s 176(3) (as substituted (see note 4); amended by the Employment Relations Act 2004 s 33(1), (5), (7)).

9 Trade Union and Labour Relations (Consolidation) Act 1992 s 176(4) (as substituted (see note 4); amended by the Employment Rights (Dispute Resolution) Act 1998 s 1(2)(a); and the Employment Relations Act 2004 s 34(7), (9), Sch 2). For the interpretation of this formula under an earlier version of this provision, ie the Employment Act 1980 s 5 (repealed), see *Day v SOGAT 1982* [1986] ICR 640, EAT.

10 The amount of compensation calculated in accordance with the Trade Union and Labour Relations (Consolidation) Act 1992 s 176(4), (5) must not exceed the aggregate of: (1) an amount equal to 30 times the limit for the time being imposed by the Employment Rights Act 1996 s 227(1)(a) (maximum amount of a week's pay for basic award in unfair dismissal cases) (see PARA 147); and (2) an amount equal to the limit for the time being imposed by s 124(1) (maximum compensatory award in such cases) (see PARA 823): Trade Union and Labour Relations (Consolidation) Act 1992 s 176(6) (as substituted (see note 4); amended by the Employment Rights Act 1996 Sch 1 para 56(1), (13); the Employment Relations Act 2004 s 34(7), (11), Sch 2). The maximum amount of compensation to be awarded under head (1) above is 30 times the weekly amount of £464 (see the Employment Rights Act 1996 s 227(1); and PARA 147); and the maximum amount of compensation payable under head (2) above is the lower of (a) £76,574, and (b) 52 multiplied by a week's pay of the person concerned (see the Employment Rights Act 1996 s 124(1), 124(1ZA); and PARA 823). See further the Work and Families Act 2006 s 14; and PARA 147 note 14. If on the date on which the application was made the applicant had not been admitted or re-admitted to the union, the award must not be less than £8,669: Trade Union and Labour Relations (Consolidation) Act 1992 s 176(6A) (s 176(6A), (6B) added by the Employment Relations Act 2004 s 33(1), (6), (7); the Trade Union and Labour Relations (Consolidation) Act 1992 s 176(6A) amended by SI 2014/382). The above sums have effect on or after 6 April 2014: Employment Rights (Increase of Limits) Order 2014, SI 2014/382, arts 1(1), 4(1). In a case where the appropriate date fell before 6 April 2014, the limits having effect immediately before that date continue to apply: see art 4(1). As to the meaning of 'appropriate date' see art 4(2). The Trade Union and Labour Relations (Consolidation) Act 1992 s 176(6A) does not apply in a case where the tribunal which made the declaration under s 176(1) also made declarations under s 176(1A), (1B) (see note 5): s 176(6B) (as so added). The sums specified in s 176(6A), and in the Employment Rights Act 1996

ss 124(1), 227(1), may be varied by the Secretary of State in accordance with the retail prices index: see the Employment Relations Act 1999 s 34; and PARA 160.

11 For these purposes, unless the context otherwise requires, 'act' and 'action' each includes omission; and references to doing an act or taking action are to be construed accordingly: Trade Union and Labour Relations (Consolidation) Act 1992 s 298.

12 Trade Union and Labour Relations (Consolidation) Act 1992 s 176(5) (as substituted (see note 4); amended by the Employment Rights (Dispute Resolution) Act 1998 s 1(2)(a); the Employment Relations Act 2004 s 34(7), (10), Sch 2). See also note 10. For the interpretation of contributory fault under an earlier version of this provision, ie the Employment Act 1980 s 5 (repealed), see *Howard v National Graphical Association* [1985] ICR 101, [1984] IRLR 489, EAT; *Day v SOGAT 1982* [1986] ICR 640, EAT.

C. RIGHT NOT TO BE UNJUSTIFIABLY DISCIPLINED

1029. Right not to be unjustifiably disciplined by a trade union. An individual who is or has been a member[1] of a trade union[2] has the right not to be unjustifiably disciplined by the union[3]. For these purposes, an individual is 'disciplined' by a trade union if a determination[4] is made, or purportedly made, under the rules[5] of the union or by an official[6] of the union or a number of persons including an official that:

(1) he should be expelled from the union or a branch or section[7] of the union;

(2) he should pay a sum to the union, to a branch or section of the union or to any other person;

(3) sums tendered by him in respect of an obligation to pay subscriptions or other sums to the union, or to a branch or section of the union, should be treated as unpaid or paid for a different purpose;

(4) he should be deprived to any extent of, or of access to, any benefits, services or facilities which would otherwise be provided or made available to him by virtue of his membership of the union, or of a branch or section of the union[8];

(5) another trade union, or a branch or section of it, should be encouraged or advised not to accept him as a member; or

(6) he should be subjected to some other detriment[9];

and whether an individual is 'unjustifiably disciplined' is to be determined[10] in accordance with the relevant statutory provisions[11].

The right not to be unjustifiably disciplined is in addition to, and not in substitution for, any right which exists apart from the statutory provisions[12]. The remedies for an infringement of the right not to be unjustifiably disciplined are by way of complaint to an employment tribunal[13] and not otherwise[14]; but, where a determination made in infringement of an individual's right not to be unjustifiably disciplined requires the payment of a sum or the performance of an obligation, no person is entitled in any proceedings to rely on that determination for the purpose of recovering the sum or enforcing the obligation[15].

1 As to the meaning of 'member' for these purposes see PARA 915 note 1.
2 As to the meaning of 'trade union' see PARA 891.
3 Trade Union and Labour Relations (Consolidation) Act 1992 s 64(1).
4 For a decision to constitute a 'determination' it must be one which achieves a disposal of the issue, and not one which contains within it a condition subsequent or gives rise to continuing uncertainty as to whether the member is to be disciplined: *Transport and General Workers' Union v Webber* [1990] ICR 711, [1990] IRLR 462, EAT; approved and applied in *Beaumont v Amicus* [2007] ICR 341, EAT.
5 As to the meaning of 'rules', in relation to a trade union, see PARA 898 note 5.
6 As to the meaning of 'official', in relation to a trade union, see PARA 1018.
7 As to the meaning of 'branch or section', in relation to a trade union, see PARA 898 note 5.

8 Suspension from membership of a trade union inevitably means being deprived of the benefits which accrue from membership: *National and Local Government Officers' Association v Killorn* [1991] ICR 1, [1990] IRLR 464, EAT.

9 Naming a person as a strike-breaker in a union publication may be a detriment: *National and Local Government Officers' Association v Killorn* [1991] ICR 1, [1990] IRLR 464, EAT.

10 Ie in accordance with the Trade Union and Labour Relations (Consolidation) Act 1992 s 65: see PARA 1030.

11 Trade Union and Labour Relations (Consolidation) Act 1992 s 64(2).

12 Trade Union and Labour Relations (Consolidation) Act 1992 s 64(5) (amended by the Trade Union Reform and Employment Rights Act 1993 Sch 8 para 48).

13 Ie under the Trade Union and Labour Relations (Consolidation) Act 1992 ss 66, 67: see PARAS 1031, 1032. Where a complaint relating to an expulsion which is presented under s 66 is declared to be well-founded, no complaint in respect of the expulsion is to be presented or proceeded with under s 174 (right not to be excluded or expelled from a trade union: see PARA 1026): s 66(4) (substituted by the Trade Union Reform and Employment Rights Act 1993 Sch 8 para 50). Subject to the Trade Union and Labour Relations (Consolidation) Act 1992 s 66(4), nothing in ss 64–67 affects any remedy for infringement of any right which exists apart from those provisions: s 64(5) (as amended: see note 12).

The provisions of the Employment Tribunals Act 1996 ss 18A–18B (conciliation) (see PARA 152) apply in the case of matters which could be the subject of employment tribunal proceedings under the Trade Union and Labour Relations (Consolidation) Act 1992 s 66, and the Employment Tribunals Act 1996 s 18C applies in the case of such proceedings themselves: see s 18(1)(a), (1A) (s 18(1)(a) substituted by SI 2014/431; the Employment Tribunals Act 1996 s 18(1A) added by the Enterprise and Regulatory Reform Act 2013 Sch 1 paras 2, 5(1), (7)). As to employment tribunals see PARA 1399 et seq. An appeal lies to the Employment Appeal Tribunal on any question of law arising from any decision of, or arising in any proceedings before, an employment tribunal under or by virtue of the Trade Union and Labour Relations (Consolidation) Act 1992: see the Employment Tribunals Act 1996 s 21(1)(d); and PARA 1428. As to the Employment Appeal Tribunal see PARA 1422 et seq.

14 Trade Union and Labour Relations (Consolidation) Act 1992 s 64(4).

15 Trade Union and Labour Relations (Consolidation) Act 1992 s 64(3).

1030. Meaning of 'unjustifiably disciplined'. An individual is unjustifiably disciplined by a trade union[1] if the actual or supposed conduct[2] which constitutes the reason, or one of the reasons, for disciplining him is conduct to which the following provisions apply, or something which is believed by the union to amount to such conduct[3]; but an individual is not unjustifiably disciplined if it is shown:

(1) that the reason for disciplining him, or one of them, is that he made such an assertion as is mentioned in head (c) below, or encouraged or assisted another person to make or attempt to vindicate such an assertion;

(2) that the assertion was false; and

(3) that he made the assertion, or encouraged or assisted another person to make or attempt to vindicate it, in the belief that it was false or otherwise in bad faith,

and that there was no other reason for disciplining him or that the only other reasons were reasons in respect of which he does not fall to be treated as unjustifiably disciplined[4].

These provisions apply to conduct which consists in:

(a) failing to participate in or support a strike or other industrial action[5], whether by members[6] of the union or by others, or indicating opposition to or a lack of support for such action[7];

(b) failing to contravene, for a purpose connected with such a strike or other industrial action, a requirement imposed on him by or under a contract of employment[8];

(c) asserting, whether by bringing proceedings or otherwise, that the union, any official[9] or representative[10] of it or a trustee[11] of its property has contravened, or is proposing to contravene, a requirement which is, or is thought to be, imposed by or under the rules[12] of the union or any other agreement or by or under any enactment, whenever passed, or any rule of law[13];

(d)   encouraging or assisting a person to perform an obligation imposed on him by a contract of employment, or to make or attempt to vindicate any such assertion as is mentioned in head (c) above[14];

(e)   contravening a requirement imposed by or in consequence of a determination which infringes the individual's or another individual's right not to be unjustifiably disciplined[15];

(f)   failing to agree, or withdrawing agreement, to the making from his wages[16], in accordance with arrangements between his employer[17] and the union, of deductions representing payments to the union in respect of his membership[18];

(g)   resigning or proposing to resign from the union or from another union, becoming or proposing to become a member of another union, refusing to become a member of another union, or being a member of another union[19];

(h)   working with, or proposing to work with, individuals who are not members of the union or who are or are not members of another union[20];

(i)   working for, or proposing to work for, an employer who employs or who has employed individuals who are not members of the union or who are or are not members of another union[21]; or

(j)   requiring[22] the union to do an act which it is required to do[23] on the requisition of a member[24].

These provisions also apply to:

(i)   conduct which involves the certification officer[25] being consulted or asked to provide advice or assistance with respect to any matter whatever, or which involves any person being consulted or asked to provide advice or assistance with respect to a matter which forms, or might form, the subject matter of any such assertion as is mentioned in head (c) above[26]; and

(ii)   conduct which consists in proposing to engage in, or doing anything preparatory or incidental to, conduct falling within any of heads (a) to (j) above[27].

These provisions do not, however, apply to an act, omission or statement comprised in the above conduct if it is shown that the act, omission or statement is one in respect of which individuals would be disciplined by the union irrespective of whether their acts, omissions or statements were in connection with such conduct as is mentioned in heads (a) to (j) above or conduct involving such consultation with the certification officer as is mentioned above[28].

1   As to the meaning of 'trade union' see PARA 891.
2   For these purposes, 'conduct' includes statements, acts and omissions: Trade Union and Labour Relations (Consolidation) Act 1992 s 65(7).
3   Trade Union and Labour Relations (Consolidation) Act 1992 s 65(1).
4   Trade Union and Labour Relations (Consolidation) Act 1992 s 65(1), (6). As to the meaning of 'disciplined' see PARA 1029.
5   'Industrial action' is not defined in the Trade Union and Labour Relations (Consolidation) Act 1992. The question what constitutes industrial action for these purposes is a mixed question of fact and law, to be judged in the context of the 1992 Act, and requires an examination of all

the circumstances, including the contracts of employment of the employees and whether any breach of or departure from the terms of the contract is involved, the effect on the employer of what is done or omitted and the object which the union or the employees seek to achieve: *Knowles v Fire Brigades Union* [1996] 4 All ER 653 at 662, [1997] ICR 595 at 604–605, CA. See further PARA 1340.

6 As to the meaning of 'member' for these purposes see PARA 915 note 1.

7 Trade Union and Labour Relations (Consolidation) Act 1992 s 65(2)(a).

8 Trade Union and Labour Relations (Consolidation) Act 1992 s 65(2)(b). For these purposes, 'contract of employment', in relation to an individual, includes any agreement between that individual and a person for whom he works or normally works; 'employer' includes such a person; and related expressions are to be construed accordingly: s 65(7) (amended by the Trade Union Reform and Employment Rights Act 1993 Sch 8 para 49(a)). Where a person holds any office or employment under the Crown on terms which do not constitute a contract of employment between him and the Crown, those terms are nevertheless to be deemed to constitute such a contract for these purposes: Trade Union and Labour Relations (Consolidation) Act 1992 s 65(8). As to the meaning of 'contravention' and cognate expressions see PARA 915 note 6.

9 As to the meaning of 'official', in relation to a trade union, see PARA 1018.

10 For these purposes, 'representative', in relation to a union, means a person acting, or purporting to act: (1) in his capacity as a member of the union; or (2) on the instructions or advice of a person acting or purporting to act in that capacity or in the capacity of an official of the union: Trade Union and Labour Relations (Consolidation) Act 1992 s 65(7).

11 As to the vesting of property in trustees see PARA 919.

12 As to the meaning of 'rules', in relation to a trade union, see PARA 898 note 5.

13 Trade Union and Labour Relations (Consolidation) Act 1992 s 65(2)(c). The restrictions on trade union discipline imposed by s 65(2)(c) do not contravene the right to freedom of association under the Convention for the Protection of Human Rights and Fundamental Freedoms (Rome, 4 November 1950; TS 71 (1953); Cmd 8969) (the 'European Convention on Human Rights') art 11 (now incorporated into domestic law by the Human Rights Act 1998 Sch 1 Pt I art 11: see RIGHTS AND FREEDOMS vol 88A (2013) PARA 461 et seq): *Unison v Kelly* [2012] IRLR 442, EAT (rather than threatening the right of trade unions generally to administer their own affairs, the Trade Union and Labour Relations (Consolidation) Act 1992 s 65(2)(c) protects against the maladministration of union affairs contrary to the union's own rules or the law). The Court of Appeal has granted leave to appeal against this decision, subject to a condition upon the appellant that it will not, if successful, seek any order for costs against the respondents or any of them and on the undertaking of the respondents not to pursue an application for costs against the appellant if the appellant is unsuccessful: see *Unison v Kelly* [2012] EWCA Civ 1148, [2012] IRLR 951.

14 Trade Union and Labour Relations (Consolidation) Act 1992 s 65(2)(d) (s 65(2)(d) amended by the Trade Union Reform and Employment Rights Act 1993 s 16(1), Sch 10).

15 Trade Union and Labour Relations (Consolidation) Act 1992 s 65(2)(e).

16 For these purposes, 'wages' is to be construed in accordance with the definitions of 'contract of employment', 'employer' and related expressions (see note 8): Trade Union and Labour Relations (Consolidation) Act 1992 s 65(7) (amended by the Trade Union Reform and Employment Rights Act 1993 Sch 8 para 49(b)).

17 As to the meaning of 'employer' for these purposes see note 8; and as to the meaning of 'employer' generally see PARA 892.

18 Trade Union and Labour Relations (Consolidation) Act 1992 s 65(2)(f) (s 65(2)(f)–(j) added by the Trade Union Reform and Employment Rights Act 1993 s 16(1), Sch 10).

19 Trade Union and Labour Relations (Consolidation) Act 1992 s 65(2)(g) (as added: see note 18).

20 Trade Union and Labour Relations (Consolidation) Act 1992 s 65(2)(h) (as added: see note 18).

21 Trade Union and Labour Relations (Consolidation) Act 1992 s 65(2)(i) (as added: see note 18).

22 For these purposes, 'require', on the part of an individual, includes request or apply for; and 'requisition' is to be construed accordingly: Trade Union and Labour Relations (Consolidation) Act 1992 s 65(7) (amended by the Trade Union Reform and Employment Rights Act 1993 s 16(2)).

23 Ie by any provision of the Trade Union and Labour Relations (Consolidation) Act 1992: see PARAS 891 et seq, 1031 et seq.

24 Trade Union and Labour Relations (Consolidation) Act 1992 s 65(2)(j) (as added: see note 18).

25 As to the certification officer see PARA 1443.

26 Trade Union and Labour Relations (Consolidation) Act 1992 s 65(3) (amended by the Employment Relations Act 1999 Sch 9).

27   Trade Union and Labour Relations (Consolidation) Act 1992 s 65(4).
28   Trade Union and Labour Relations (Consolidation) Act 1992 s 65(5).

1031. Complaint to employment tribunal that individual has been unjustifiably disciplined by union. An individual who claims that he has been unjustifiably disciplined[1] by a trade union[2] may present a complaint against the union to an employment tribunal[3]. The tribunal must not entertain such a complaint unless it is presented[4]:

(1)   before the end of the period of three months beginning with the date of the making of the determination claimed to infringe the right[5], subject to an extension to facilitate conciliation before the institution of proceedings[6]; or

(2)   where the tribunal is satisfied that it was not reasonably practicable for the complaint to be presented before the end of that period, or that any delay in making the complaint is wholly or partly attributable to a reasonable attempt to appeal[7] against the determination or to have it reconsidered or reviewed, within such further period as the tribunal considers reasonable[8].

1   As to the meaning of 'unjustifiably disciplined' see PARA 1030.
2   As to the meaning of 'trade union' see PARA 891.
3   Trade Union and Labour Relations (Consolidation) Act 1992 s 66(1) (amended by the Employment Rights (Dispute Resolution) Act 1998 s 1(2)(a)). As to employment tribunals see PARA 1399 et seq; and as to the right of appeal under these provisions see PARA 1029 note 13. Where a complaint relating to an expulsion which is presented under the Trade Union and Labour Relations (Consolidation) Act 1992 s 66 is declared to be well-founded, no complaint in respect of the expulsion is to be presented or proceeded with under s 174 (right not to be excluded or expelled from a trade union: see PARA 1026): s 66(4) (substituted by the Trade Union Reform and Employment Rights Act 1993 Sch 8 para 50). On quantum of compensation (especially for injury to feelings, applying the scale in *Vento v Chief Constable of West Yorkshire Police* [2002] EWCA Civ 1871, [2003] ICR 318, [2003] IRLR 102 for personal injury) see *Massey v UNIFI* [2007] EWCA Civ 800, [2008] ICR 62, [2007] IRLR 902.
4   As to when a complaint is presented see PARAS 804, 1461.
5   Trade Union and Labour Relations (Consolidation) Act 1992 s 66(2)(a).
6   The Trade Union and Labour Relations (Consolidation) Act 1992 s 292A (extension of time limits to facilitate conciliation before institution of proceedings: see PARA 1455) applies for the purposes of s 66(2)(a): s 66(2A) (added by the Enterprise and Regulatory Reform Act 2013 Sch 2 paras 1, 2).
7   As the statutory provisions do not lay down any specific method of stating an appeal, a letter to the union questioning the imposition of discipline may be held to constitute a 'reasonable attempt to appeal': *National and Local Government Officers' Association v Killorn* [1991] ICR 1, [1990] IRLR 464, EAT.
8   Trade Union and Labour Relations (Consolidation) Act 1992 s 66(2)(b). For the case law on the extension of time limits, especially in the context of the law of unfair dismissal, see PARAS 804, 1453.

1032. Remedies for an infringement of the right not to be unjustifiably disciplined. Where an employment tribunal[1] finds a complaint of unjustifiable discipline[2] against a trade union[3] well-founded, it must make a declaration to that effect[4]. An individual whose complaint has been declared to be well-founded may make an application to an employment tribunal for one or both of the following:

(1)   an award of compensation to be paid to him by the union;

(2)   an order that the union pay him an amount equal to any sum which he has paid in pursuance of a determination[5] under the rules[6] of the union

or by an official[7] of the union or a number of persons including an official that he should pay a sum to the union, to a branch or section[8] of the union or to any other person[9].

Such an application may not be entertained if made before the end of the period of four weeks beginning with the date of the declaration, or after the end of the period of six months beginning with that date[10].

The amount of compensation awarded must be such as the employment tribunal considers just and equitable in all the circumstances[11], subject to certain statutory limitations[12]. The applicant has a duty to mitigate his loss[13]; and, where the employment tribunal finds that the infringement complained of was to any extent caused or contributed to by the action[14] of the applicant, it must reduce the amount of the compensation by such proportion as it considers just and equitable having regard to that finding[15].

1 As to employment tribunals see PARA 1399 et seq.
2 Ie under the Trade Union and Labour Relations (Consolidation) Act 1992 s 66: see PARA 1031.
3 As to the meaning of 'trade union' see PARA 891.
4 Trade Union and Labour Relations (Consolidation) Act 1992 s 66(3).
5 Ie any such determination as is mentioned in the Trade Union and Labour Relations (Consolidation) Act 1992 s 64(2)(b): see PARA 1029 head (2). As to what constitutes a determination see PARA 1029 note 4.
6 As to the meaning of 'rules', in relation to a trade union, see PARA 898 note 5.
7 As to the meaning of 'official, in relation to a trade union, see PARA 1018.
8 As to the meaning of 'branch or section', in relation to a trade union, see PARA 898 note 5.
9 Trade Union and Labour Relations (Consolidation) Act 1992 s 67(1) (amended by the Employment Relations Act 2004 s 34(1), (2)). Every application under the Trade Union and Labour Relations (Consolidation) Act 1992 s 67 to the Appeal Tribunal must be made in writing in, or substantially in, accordance with the Employment Appeal Tribunal Rules 1993, SI 1993/2854, Schedule Form 4, and must be served on the Appeal Tribunal together with a copy of the decision or order declaring that the applicant's complaint against the trade union was well-founded: see r 8. As to applications under r 8 see further rr 9–12, 32, Schedule Form 5 (rr 9–11 amended by the Employment Rights (Dispute Resolution) Act 1998 s 1(2)(b)). As to the Employment Appeal Tribunal see PARA 1422 et seq.
10 Trade Union and Labour Relations (Consolidation) Act 1992 s 67(3).
11 Trade Union and Labour Relations (Consolidation) Act 1992 s 67(5) (amended by the Employment Rights (Dispute Resolution) Act 1998 s 1(2)(a); the Employment Relations Act 2004 s 34(1), (4), Sch 2). Compensation may be awarded for injury to feelings, provided that the cause arises solely from the disciplining complained of and not from other activities: *Bradley v National and Local Government Officers' Association* [1991] ICR 359, [1991] IRLR 159, EAT. See also *Massey v UNIFI* [2007] EWCA Civ 800, [2008] ICR 62, [2007] IRLR 902 (claimant suffered a stroke, but her medical condition meant she would have suffered a stroke at a later date in the absence of unjustifiable discipline; compensation discounted so that it reflected the fact that the stroke and its consequential effects were suffered at the earlier date) (see also PARA 1031 note 3).
12 The amount of compensation calculated in accordance with the Trade Union and Labour Relations (Consolidation) Act 1992 s 67(5)–(7) must not exceed the aggregate of: (1) an amount equal to 30 times the limit for the time being imposed by the Employment Rights Act 1996 s 227(1)(a) (maximum amount of a week's pay for basic award in unfair dismissal cases) (see PARA 147); and (2) an amount equal to the limit for the time being imposed by s 124(1) (maximum compensatory award in such cases) (see PARA 823): Trade Union and Labour Relations (Consolidation) Act 1992 s 67(8) (amended by the Trade Union Reform and Employment Rights Act 1993 Sch 8 para 51(a); the Employment Relations Act 2004 s 34(1), (5), Sch 2). The maximum amount of compensation to be awarded under head (1) above is 30 times the weekly amount of £464 (see the Employment Rights Act 1996 s 227(1); and PARA 147); and the maximum amount of compensation payable under head (2) above is the lower of (a) £76,574, and (b) 52 multiplied by a week's pay of the person concerned (see the Employment Rights Act 1996 s 124(1), 124(1ZA); and PARA 823). See further the Work and Families Act 2006 s 14; and PARA 147 note 14. The above sums have effect on or after 6 April 2014: Employment Rights (Increase of Limits) Order 2014, SI 2014/382, arts 1(1), 4(1). In a case where the appropriate date fell before 6 April 2014, the limits having effect immediately

before that date continue to apply: see art 4(1). As to the meaning of 'appropriate date' see art 4(2). If on the date on which the application was made the determination infringing the applicant's right not to be unjustifiably disciplined has not been revoked, or the union has failed to take all the steps necessary for securing the reversal of anything done for the purpose of giving effect to the determination, the amount of compensation must not be less than the amount specified in the Trade Union and Labour Relations (Consolidation) Act 1992 s 176(6A) (see PARA 1028 note 10): s 67(8A) (added by the Employment Relations Act 2004 s 34(1), (6)).

13   In determining the amount of compensation to be awarded, the same rule is to be applied concerning the duty of a person to mitigate his loss as applies to damages recoverable under the common law: Trade Union and Labour Relations (Consolidation) Act 1992 s 67(6). As to mitigation of damages generally see DAMAGES vol 12(1) (Reissue) PARA 1041 et seq; and as to the duty to mitigate in the context of unfair dismissal law see PARA 822.

14   As to the meaning of 'action' see PARA 1028 note 11.

15   Trade Union and Labour Relations (Consolidation) Act 1992 s 67(7) (amended by the Employment Rights (Dispute Resolution) Act 1998 s 1(2)(a); the Employment Relations Act 2004 s 34(1), (4), Sch 2).

D. RIGHT TO TERMINATE MEMBERSHIP OF THE UNION

1033. Right to terminate membership of the union. In every contract of membership of a trade union[1], whether made before, on or after 16 July 1992[2], there is to be implied a term conferring a right on the member[3], on giving reasonable notice and complying with any reasonable conditions, to terminate his membership of the union[4].

1   As to the meaning of 'trade union' see PARA 891.

2   Ie the date when the Trade Union and Labour Relations (Consolidation) Act 1992 was passed.

3   As to the meaning of 'member' for these purposes see PARA 915 note 1.

4   Trade Union and Labour Relations (Consolidation) Act 1992 s 69. As to what would amount to reasonable conditions see obiter dicta in *Ashford v Association of Scientific, Technical and Managerial Staffs* [1973] ICR 296, NIRC (decided under the similar provisions of the Industrial Relations Act 1971 (repealed)).

E. RIGHT NOT TO SUFFER DEDUCTION OF UNAUTHORISED SUBSCRIPTIONS

1034. Right not to suffer deduction of unauthorised union subscriptions. Where arrangements ('subscription deduction arrangements') exist between the employer[1] of a worker[2] and a trade union[3] relating to the making of subscription deductions[4] from workers' wages, the employer must ensure that no such deduction is made from wages payable to the worker on any day unless the worker has authorised in writing the making from his wages of subscription deductions and has not withdrawn the authorisation[5]. A worker withdraws an authorisation in relation to a subscription deduction which falls to be made from wages payable to him on any day, if a written notice withdrawing the authorisation has been received by the employer in time for it to be reasonably practicable for the employer to secure that no deduction is made[6]. A worker's authorisation of the making of subscription deductions from his wages does not give rise to any obligation on the part of the employer to the worker to maintain or continue subscription deduction arrangements[7].

1   For these purposes, 'employer', in relation to a worker, means the person by whom the worker is, or, where the employment has ceased, was, employed: Employment Rights Act 1996 s 230(4) (applied by the Trade Union and Labour Relations (Consolidation) Act 1992 s 68(4) (s 68 substituted by SI 1998/1529)). As to the meaning of 'worker' see note 2. See further PARA 5.

2   For these purposes, 'worker', except in the phrases 'shop worker' and 'betting worker', means an individual who has entered into or works under, or, where the employment has ceased, worked under: (1) a contract of employment; or (2) any other contract, whether express or implied and, if it is express, whether oral or in writing, whereby the individual undertakes to do

or perform personally any work or services for another party to the contract whose status is not, by virtue of the contract, that of a client or customer of any profession or business undertaking carried on by the individual: Employment Rights Act 1996 s 230(3) (applied by the Trade Union and Labour Relations (Consolidation) Act 1992 s 68(4) (as substituted: see note 1)). See further PARA 5.

3   As to the meaning of 'trade union' see PARA 891.
4   For these purposes, 'subscription deductions' means deductions from workers' wages representing payments to the union in respect of the workers' membership of the union: see the Trade Union and Labour Relations (Consolidation) Act 1992 s 68(1) (as substituted: see note 1). 'Wages' has the same meaning as in the Employment Rights Act 1996 s 27 (see PARA 254): Trade Union and Labour Relations (Consolidation) Act 1992 s 68(4) (as so substituted).
5   Trade Union and Labour Relations (Consolidation) Act 1992 s 68(1) (as substituted: see note 1). If an employee is dismissed or selected for redundancy because he brought proceedings to enforce the right under s 68, his dismissal is automatically regarded as unfair: see PARAS 1063, 1064.
6   Trade Union and Labour Relations (Consolidation) Act 1992 s 68(2) (as substituted: see note 1).
7   Trade Union and Labour Relations (Consolidation) Act 1992 s 68(3) (as substituted: see note 1).

1035. Complaint to employment tribunal regarding deduction of unauthorised union subscriptions. A worker[1] may present a complaint to an employment tribunal that his employer[2] has made a deduction from his wages[3] in contravention of the statutory requirements[4] concerning the deduction of unauthorised union subscriptions:

(1)   within the period of three months beginning with the date of payment of the wages from which the deduction, or, if the complaint relates to more than one deduction, the last of the deductions, was made[5], subject to an extension to facilitate conciliation before the institution of proceedings[6]; or

(2)   where the tribunal is satisfied that it was not reasonably practicable for the complaint to be presented[7] within that period, within such further period as the tribunal considers reasonable[8].

Where a tribunal finds that such a complaint is well-founded, it must make a declaration to that effect and must order the employer to pay to the worker the whole amount of the deduction, less any such part of the amount as has already been paid to the worker by the employer[9].

1   As to the meaning of 'worker' for these purposes see PARA 1034 note 2.
2   As to the meaning of 'employer' for these purposes see PARA 1034 note 1.
3   As to the meaning of 'wages' for these purposes see PARA 1034 note 4.
4   Ie the requirements of the Trade Union and Labour Relations (Consolidation) Act 1992 s 68: see PARA 1034.
5   Trade Union and Labour Relations (Consolidation) Act 1992 s 68A(1)(a) (s 68A added by the Trade Union Reform and Employment Rights Act 1993 s 15; the Trade Union and Labour Relations (Consolidation) Act 1992 s 68A(1) amended by the Employment Rights (Dispute Resolution) Act 1998 s 1(2)(a)).
6   The Trade Union and Labour Relations (Consolidation) Act 1992 s 292A (extension of time limits to facilitate conciliation before institution of proceedings: see PARA 1455) applies for the purposes of s 68A(1)(a): s 68A(1A) added by the Enterprise and Regulatory Reform Act 2013 Sch 2 paras 1, 3).
7   As to when a complaint is presented see PARAS 804, 1461.
8   Trade Union and Labour Relations (Consolidation) Act 1992 s 68A(1)(b) (as added and amended: see note 5). For the case law on the extension of time limits, especially in the context of the law of unfair dismissal, see PARAS 804, 1453. If an employee is dismissed or selected for redundancy because he brought proceedings to enforce the right under the Trade Union and Labour Relations (Consolidation) Act 1992 s 68, his dismissal is automatically regarded as unfair: see PARAS 1063, 1064.
    The provisions of the Employment Tribunals Act 1996 ss 18A–18B (conciliation) (see PARA 152) apply in the case of matters which could be the subject of employment tribunal proceedings under the Trade Union and Labour Relations (Consolidation) Act 1992 s 68A, and the

Employment Tribunals Act 1996 s 18C applies in the case of such proceedings themselves: see s 18(1)(a), (1A) (s 18(1)(a) substituted by SI 2014/431; the Employment Tribunals Act 1996 s 18(1A) added by the Enterprise and Regulatory Reform Act 2013 Sch 1 paras 2, 5(1), (7)). As to employment tribunals see PARA 1399 et seq. An appeal lies to the Employment Appeal Tribunal on any question of law arising from any decision of, or arising in any proceedings before, an employment tribunal under or by virtue of the Trade Union and Labour Relations (Consolidation) Act 1992: see the Employment Tribunals Act 1996 s 21(1)(d); and PARA 1428. As to the Employment Appeal Tribunal see PARA 1422 et seq.

9   Trade Union and Labour Relations (Consolidation) Act 1992 s 68A(2) (substituted by SI 1998/1529). Where the making of a deduction from the wages of a worker both contravenes the Trade Union and Labour Relations (Consolidation) Act 1992 s 68(1) and involves one or more specified contraventions of the statutory requirements, the aggregate amount which may be ordered by an employment tribunal or court, whether on the same occasion or on different occasions, to be paid in respect of the contraventions must not exceed the amount, or, where different amounts may be ordered to be paid in respect of different contraventions, the greatest amount, which may be ordered to be paid in respect of any one of them: s 68A(3) (as added (see note 5); amended by the Employment Rights (Dispute Resolution) Act 1998 s 1(2)(a)). The contraventions so specified are: (1) a contravention of the requirement not to make a deduction without having given the particulars required by the Employment Rights Act 1996 s 8 (itemised pay statements) (see PARA 124) or s 9(1) (standing statements of fixed deductions) (see PARA 124); (2) a contravention of s 13 (requirement not to make unauthorised deductions) (see PARA 255); (3) a contravention of the Trade Union and Labour Relations (Consolidation) Act 1992 s 86(1) or s 90(1) (requirements not to make deductions of political fund contributions in certain circumstances) (see PARAS 989, 992): s 68A(4) (as so added; amended by the Employment Rights Act 1996 Sch 1 para 56(1), (4)).

F. RIGHT NOT TO SUFFER DISCRIMINATION ETC

1036.   Prohibition on discrimination etc in membership. A trade union comes within the statutory definition of a 'trade organisation' for the purposes of the Equality Act 2010[1]. As such it must not discriminate[2] against or victimise[3] a person ('B'):

(1)   in the arrangements it makes for deciding to whom to offer membership of the organisation;

(2)   as to the terms on which it is prepared to admit B as a member;

(3)   by not accepting B's application for membership[4].

Nor must it discriminate against or victimise a member ('B'):

(a)   in the way it affords B access, or by not affording B access, to opportunities for receiving a benefit, facility or service[5];

(b)   by depriving B of membership;

(c)   by varying the terms on which B is a member;

(d)   by subjecting B to any other detriment[6].

A trade union, as such a trade organisation, must not, in relation to membership of it, harass[7] a member, or an applicant for membership[8].

A duty to make reasonable adjustments for disabled persons applies to a trade organisation such as a trade union[9].

1   See the Equality Act 2010 s 57(7)(a).
2   As to direct discrimination see DISCRIMINATION vol 33 (2013) PARA 65; and as to indirect discrimination see DISCRIMINATION vol 33 (2013) PARA 72.
3   As to victimisation see DISCRIMINATION vol 33 (2013) PARA 75.
4   Equality Act 2010 s 57(1), (4).
5   As to the meaning of 'benefit, facility or service' for these purposes see DISCRIMINATION vol 33 (2013) PARA 111 note 7. There are exceptions to this provision in connection with the provision of childcare: see Sch 9 para 15; and DISCRIMINATION vol 33 (2013) PARA 161.
6   Equality Act 2010 s 57(2), (5). As to the meaning of 'detriment' see DISCRIMINATION vol 33 (2013) PARA 75 note 1. Where a trade union's actions or policy in favouring one group of members over another (to promote the greater good overall) are indirectly sexually

discriminatory, the union my seek to establish the defence of justification, but to do so it must show not just a legitimate aim (which the 'greater good' may be) but also that it pursued that aim by proportionate means: *Allen v GMB* [2008] EWCA Civ 810, [2008] IRLR 690, [2008] All ER (D) 207 (Jul). In *Furniture, Timber and Allied Trades Union v Mogdill, Pel Ltd v Mogdill* [1980] IRLR 142, EAT, poor support, representation etc by a union of its Asian members was held not to be discriminatory because there was no evidence that union members of other racial groups were treated more favourably by the union. For a member to have been subjected to a 'detriment', the detriment must have been caused to the complainant while they were a member of the union, and not after their membership had ended: *Diakou v Islington UNISON 'A' Branch* [1997] ICR 121, EAT. All these authorities were decided under earlier legislation.

7 As to harassment see DISCRIMINATION vol 33 (2013) PARA 73.
8 Equality Act 2010 s 57(3).
9 See the Equality Act 2010 s 57(6). See further Sch 8 paras 1, 2, 4, 20; and DISCRIMINATION vol 33 (2013) PARA 247.

(11) RIGHTS AGAINST EMPLOYERS IN RELATION TO TRADE UNION MEMBERSHIP AND ACTIVITIES

(i) Access to Employment

A. BLACKLISTING OF TRADE UNION MEMBERS

1037. Prohibition of blacklists of trade union members. The Secretary of State may make regulations prohibiting the compilation of lists[1] which:

(1) contain details of members of trade unions[2] or persons who have taken part in the activities of trade unions; and

(2) are compiled with a view to being used by employers or employment agencies[3] for the purposes of discrimination in relation to recruitment or in relation to the treatment of workers[4];

and the Secretary of State may also make regulations prohibiting the use, sale or supply of such lists[5].

Such regulations may, in particular:

(a) confer jurisdiction, including exclusive jurisdiction, on employment tribunals[6] and on the Employment Appeal Tribunal[7];

(b) include provision for or about the grant and enforcement of specified remedies by courts and tribunals;

(c) include provision for the making of awards of compensation calculated in accordance with the regulations;

(d) include provision permitting proceedings to be brought by trade unions on behalf of members in specified circumstances;

(e) include provision about cases where an employee is dismissed by his employer and the reason or principal reason for the dismissal, or why the employee was selected for dismissal, relates to such a list;

(f) create criminal offences[8];

(g) in specified cases or circumstances, extend liability for a criminal offence created under head (f) above to a person who aids the commission of the offence or to a person who is an agent, principal, employee, employer or officer of a person who commits the offence;

(h) provide for specified obligations or offences not to apply in specified circumstances;

(i) include supplemental, incidental, consequential and transitional provision, including provision amending an enactment;

(j) make different provision for different cases or circumstances[9].

Subject to certain exceptions[10], no person is to compile, use[11], sell or supply a prohibited list[12]. A person does not contravene this prohibition in the following cases[13]:

(i)   where a person supplies a prohibited list, but does not know, and could not reasonably be expected to know, that he is supplying a prohibited list[14];

(ii)   where a person compiles, uses or supplies a prohibited list, but:

  (A)   in doing so, that person's sole or principal purpose is to make known a contravention of the prohibition or the possibility of such a contravention;

  (B)   no information in relation to a person whose details are included in the prohibited list is published without the consent of that person; and

  (C)   in all the circumstances compiling, using or supplying the prohibited list is justified in the public interest[15];

(iii)   where a person compiles, uses, sells or supplies a prohibited list, but in doing so that person's sole or principal purpose is to apply a requirement either:

  (A)   that a person may not be considered for appointment to an office[16] or for employment unless that person has experience or knowledge of trade union matters, and in all the circumstances it is reasonable to apply such a requirement; or

  (B)   that a person may not be considered for appointment or election to an office in a trade union unless he is a member of the union[17];

(iv)   where a person compiles, uses, sells or supplies a prohibited list, but the compilation, use, sale or supply of the prohibited list is required or authorised under an enactment, by any rule of law, or by an order of the court[18];

(v)   where a person uses or supplies a prohibited list for the purpose of, or in connection with, legal proceedings (including prospective legal proceedings), or for the purpose of giving or obtaining legal advice, where the use or supply is necessary in order to determine whether the relevant regulations[19] have been, are being or will be complied with[20].

A contravention of the above prohibition[21] is actionable as a breach of statutory duty[22]. If there are facts from which the court could conclude, in the absence of any other explanation, that the defendant has contravened, or is likely to contravene, that prohibition, the court must find that such a contravention occurred, or is likely to occur, unless the defendant shows that it did not, or is not likely to, occur[23]. In proceedings brought by virtue of this provision, the court may, without prejudice to any of its other powers, make such order as it considers appropriate for the purpose of restraining or preventing the defendant from contravening that prohibition, and may also award damages, which may include compensation for injured feelings[24].

1   For these purposes, 'list' includes any index or other set of items whether recorded electronically or by any other means: Employment Relations Act 1999 s 3(5). As to the Secretary of State see PARA 5 note 21.

2   Expressions used in the Employment Relations Act 1999 s 3 and in the Trade Union and Labour Relations (Consolidation) Act 1992 have the same meaning in the Employment Relations Act 1999 s 3 as in the Trade Union and Labour Relations (Consolidation) Act 1992: Employment Relations Act 1999 s 3(6). As to the meaning of 'trade union' see PARA 891.

3   As to the meaning of 'employment agency' see PARA 1042 note 12.

4   Employment Relations Act 1999 s 3(1). In the exercise of this power, the Secretary of State has made the Employment Relations Act 1999 (Blacklists) Regulations 2010, SI 2010/493, which

came into force on 2 March 2010: see reg 1(b). For these purposes, 'worker' has the meaning given to it by the Employment Relations Act 1999 s 13 (statutory right to be accompanied at disciplinary and grievance hearings) (see PARA 718): s 3(5).

5   Employment Relations Act 1999 s 3(2).

6   As to employment tribunals see PARA 1399 et seq.

7   As to the Employment Appeal Tribunal see PARA 1422 et seq.

8   Regulations creating an offence may not provide for it to be punishable by imprisonment, by a fine in excess of level 5 on the standard scale in the case of an offence triable only summarily or by a fine in excess of the statutory maximum in the case of summary conviction for an offence triable either way: Employment Relations Act 1999 s 3(4). As to the standard scale see SENTENCING AND DISPOSITION OF OFFENDERS vol 92 (2010) PARA 142; and as to the statutory maximum see SENTENCING AND DISPOSITION OF OFFENDERS vol 92 (2010) PARA 140.

9   Employment Relations Act 1999 s 3(3).

10 Ie subject to the Employment Relations Act 1999 (Blacklists) Regulations 2010, SI 2010/493, reg 4: see the text and notes 13–20.

11 'Use', in relation to a prohibited list (see note 12), includes use of information contained in the list: Employment Relations Act 1999 (Blacklists) Regulations 2010, SI 2010/493, reg 2(1).

12 Employment Relations Act 1999 (Blacklists) Regulations 2010, SI 2010/493, reg 3(1). A 'prohibited list' is a list which (1) contains details of persons who are or have been members of trade unions or persons who are taking part or have taken part in the activities of trade unions; and (2) is compiled with a view to being used by employers or employment agencies for the purposes of discrimination in relation to recruitment or in relation to the treatment of workers: regs 2(1), 3(2). 'Discrimination' means treating a person less favourably than another on grounds of trade union membership or trade union activities: reg 3(3). For these purposes, references to membership of a trade union include references to (a) membership of a particular branch or section of a trade union; and (b) membership of one of a number of particular branches or sections of a trade union; and references to taking part in the activities of a trade union have a corresponding meaning: reg 3(4).

13 Employment Relations Act 1999 (Blacklists) Regulations 2010, SI 2010/493, reg 4(1).

14 Employment Relations Act 1999 (Blacklists) Regulations 2010, SI 2010/493, reg 4(2).

15 Employment Relations Act 1999 (Blacklists) Regulations 2010, SI 2010/493, reg 4(3).

16 For these purposes, 'office', in relation to a trade union, means any position (1) by virtue of which the holder is an official of the trade union; (2) or to which Chapter 4 of Part 1 of the Trade Union and Labour Relations (Consolidation) Act 1992 Pt I Ch IV (ss 46–61) (duty to hold elections: see PARA 960 et seq) applies; and 'official' has the meaning given by s 119 (see PARA 1018): Employment Relations Act 1999 (Blacklists) Regulations 2010, SI 2010/493, reg 2(1).

17 Employment Relations Act 1999 (Blacklists) Regulations 2010, SI 2010/493, reg 4(4).

18 Employment Relations Act 1999 (Blacklists) Regulations 2010, SI 2010/493, reg 4(5).

19 Ie the Employment Relations Act 1999 (Blacklists) Regulations 2010, SI 2010/493: see the text and notes 10–18, 20; and PARA 1038 seq.

20 Employment Relations Act 1999 (Blacklists) Regulations 2010, SI 2010/493, reg 4(6).

21 Ie the Employment Relations Act 1999 (Blacklists) Regulations 2010, SI 2010/493, reg 3: see the text and notes 10–12.

22 Employment Relations Act 1999 (Blacklists) Regulations 2010, SI 2010/493, reg 13(1). A person may complain to an employment tribunal under reg 5, reg 6 or reg 9 (see PARAS 1038, 1040) or under the Employment Rights Act 1996 Pt X (ss 94–134A) (unfair dismissal: see PARA 757 et seq) as it applies by virtue of the Employment Relations Act 1999 (Blacklists) Regulations 2010, SI 2010/493, and bring a claim for breach of statutory duty in respect of the same conduct for the purpose of restraining or preventing the defendant from contravening reg 3: see reg 13(4). Except as mentioned in reg 13(4), a person may not bring a claim for breach of statutory duty and complain to an employment tribunal under the Employment Relations Act 1999 (Blacklists) Regulations 2010, SI 2010/493, reg 5, 6 or 9, or under the Employment Rights Act 1996 Pt X as it applies by virtue of the Employment Relations Act 1999 (Blacklists) Regulations 2010, SI 2010/493, in respect of the same conduct: see reg 13(5). As to the sanctions and remedies for breach of statutory duty see STATUTES AND LEGISLATIVE PROCESS vol 96 (2012) PARA 752 et seq; and as to claims for damages for breach of statutory duty see TORT vol 97 (2010) PARA 495 et seq.

23 Employment Relations Act 1999 (Blacklists) Regulations 2010, SI 2010/493, reg 13(2).

24 Employment Relations Act 1999 (Blacklists) Regulations 2010, SI 2010/493, reg 13(3).

1038. Refusal of employment or employment agency services for reason relating to a prohibited list. A person ('P') has a right of complaint to an employment tribunal[1] against another ('R') if R refuses to employ P[2] for a reason which relates to a prohibited list[3], and either:

(1) R contravenes the general prohibition on compiling, using, selling or supplying such a list[4] in relation to that list; or

(2) R relies on information supplied by a person who contravenes that prohibition[5] in relation to that list, and knows or ought reasonably to know that the information relied on is supplied in contravention of that prohibition[6].

If there are facts from which the tribunal could conclude, in the absence of any other explanation, that R contravened the prohibition referred to in head (1) above or relied on information supplied in contravention of that prohibition, the tribunal must find that such a contravention or reliance on information occurred unless R shows that it did not[7].

Similarly, a person ('P') has a right of complaint to an employment tribunal against an employment agency[8] ('E') if E refuses P any of its services[9] for a reason which relates to a prohibited list, and either:

(a) E contravenes the general prohibition on compiling, using, selling or supplying such a list[10] in relation to that list; or

(b) E relies on information supplied by a person who contravenes that prohibition in relation to that list, and knows or ought reasonably to know that information relied on is supplied in contravention of that prohibition[11].

If there are facts from which the tribunal could conclude, in the absence of any other explanation, that E contravened the prohibition referred to in head (a) above or relied on information supplied in contravention of that prohibition, the tribunal must find that such a contravention or reliance on information occurred unless E shows that it did not[12].

An employment tribunal may not consider a complaint under heads (1) and (2) or heads (a) and (b) above unless it is presented to the tribunal before the end of the period of three months beginning with the date of the conduct to which the complaint relates[13], subject to an extension to facilitate conciliation before the institution of proceedings[14]. Further, an employment tribunal may consider such a complaint that is otherwise out of time if, in all the circumstances of the case, it considers that it is just and equitable to do so[15].

Where an employment tribunal finds that a complaint under heads (1) and (2) or heads (a) and (b) above is well-founded, it must make a declaration to that effect and may make such of the following as it considers just and equitable:

(i) an order requiring the respondent to pay compensation;

(ii) a recommendation that the respondent take within a specified period action appearing to the tribunal to be practicable for the purpose of obviating or reducing the adverse effect on the complainant of any conduct to which the complaint relates[16].

Compensation must be assessed on the same basis as damages for breach of statutory duty[17] and may include compensation for injury to feelings[18]. If the respondent fails without reasonable justification to comply with a recommendation under head (ii) above, the tribunal may increase its award of compensation or, if it has not made such an award, make one[19]. Where the tribunal considers that any conduct of the complainant before the refusal to which the complaint[20] relates was such that it would be just and equitable to reduce the award of compensation, the tribunal must reduce that amount accordingly[21]. The amount of compensation must be reduced or further reduced by the amount of any compensation awarded by the tribunal under the Trade Union and Labour Relations (Consolidation) Act 1992[22] in respect of the same refusal[23]. Where an award of compensation is made, the amount of compensation before any increase or reduction is made under the above provisions[24] must not be less than £5,000[25]; and the total amount of compensation must not exceed £65,300[26].

1 As to employment tribunals see PARA 1399 et seq.

2 R is to be taken to refuse to employ P if P seeks employment of any description with R and R (1) refuses or deliberately omits to entertain and process P's application or inquiry; (2) causes P to withdraw or cease to pursue P's application or inquiry; (3) refuses or deliberately omits to offer P employment of that description; (4) makes P an offer of such employment the terms of which are such as no reasonable employer who wished to fill the post would offer and which is not accepted; or (4) makes P an offer of such employment but withdraws it or causes P not to accept it: Employment Relations Act 1999 (Blacklists) Regulations 2010, SI 2010/493, reg 5(2).

3 As to the meaning of 'prohibited list' see PARA 1037 note 12.

4 Ie contravenes the Employment Relations Act 1999 (Blacklists) Regulations 2010, SI 2010/493, reg 3: see PARA 1037.

5 For these purposes, references to information supplied by a person who contravenes the Employment Relations Act 1999 (Blacklists) Regulations 2010, SI 2010/493, reg 3 include information supplied by a person who would contravene reg 3 if that person's actions took place in Great Britain: reg 2(2).

6 Employment Relations Act 1999 (Blacklists) Regulations 2010, SI 2010/493, reg 5(1). The Trade Union and Labour Relations (Consolidation) Act 1992 s 288 (restriction on contracting out: see PARA 150) applies to the Employment Relations Act 1999 (Blacklists) Regulations 2010, SI 2010/493, reg 5 as if it were contained in the 1992 Act: Employment Relations Act 1999 (Blacklists) Regulations 2010, SI 2010/493, reg 16. A person may make a complaint under reg 5 and bring court proceedings for a claim for breach of statutory duty in respect of the same conduct for the purpose of restraining or preventing the defendant from contravening reg 3: see PARA 1037 note 22.

  For an example of an unsuccessful complaint under reg 5 see *Miller v Interserve Industrial Services Ltd* [2013] ICR 445, [2012] All ER (D) 121 (Dec), EAT.

  The provisions of the Employment Tribunals Act 1996 ss 18A–18B (conciliation) (see PARA 152) apply in the case of matters which could be the subject of employment tribunal proceedings under the Employment Relations Act 1999 (Blacklists) Regulations 2010, SI 2010/493, regs 5, 6, and the Employment Tribunals Act 1996 s 18C applies in the case of such proceedings themselves: see s 18(1)(z2), (1A) (s 18(1)(z2) substituted by SI 2014/431; the Employment Tribunals Act 1996 s 18(1A) added by the Enterprise and Regulatory Reform Act 2013 Sch 1 paras 2, 5(1), (7)).

7 Employment Relations Act 1999 (Blacklists) Regulations 2010, SI 2010/493, reg 5(3).

8 For these purposes, 'employment agency' means a person who, for profit or not, provides services for the purposes of finding employment for workers or supplying employers with workers, and does not include a trade union by reason only of the services a trade union provides only for and in relation to its members: Employment Relations Act 1999 (Blacklists) Regulations 2010, SI 2010/493, reg 2(1). 'Services', in relation to an employment agency, means services for the purposes of finding employment for workers or supplying employers with workers: reg 2(1).

9 E is to be taken to refuse P a service if P seeks to make use of the service and E (1) refuses or deliberately omits to make the service available to P; (2) causes P not to make use of the service or to cease to make use of it; or (3) does not provide P the same service, on the same terms, as is provided to others: Employment Relations Act 1999 (Blacklists) Regulations 2010, SI 2010/493, reg 6(2).

10 See note 4.

11 Employment Relations Act 1999 (Blacklists) Regulations 2010, SI 2010/493, reg 6(1). The Trade Union and Labour Relations (Consolidation) Act 1992 s 288 (restriction on contracting out: see PARA 150) applies to the Employment Relations Act 1999 (Blacklists) Regulations 2010, SI 2010/493, reg 6 as if it were contained in the 1992 Act: Employment Relations Act 1999 (Blacklists) Regulations 2010, SI 2010/493, reg 16. A person may make a complaint under reg 6

and bring court proceedings for a claim for breach of statutory duty in respect of the same conduct for the purpose of restraining or preventing the defendant from contravening reg 3: see PARA 1037 note 22.

As to conciliation see note 6.

12   Employment Relations Act 1999 (Blacklists) Regulations 2010, SI 2010/493, reg 6(3).
13   Employment Relations Act 1999 (Blacklists) Regulations 2010, SI 2010/493, reg 7(1). The date of the conduct to which a complaint under reg 5 relates is to be taken to be (1) in the case of an actual refusal, the date of the refusal; (2) in the case of a deliberate omission to entertain and process P's application or inquiry, or to offer employment, the end of the period within which it was reasonable to expect R to act; (3) in the case of conduct causing P to withdraw or cease to pursue P's application or inquiry, the date of that conduct; (4) in a case where R made but withdrew an offer, the date R withdrew the offer; (5) in any other case where R made an offer which was not accepted, the date on which R made the offer: reg 7(3). The date of the conduct to which a complaint under reg 6 relates is to be taken to be (a) in the case of an actual refusal, the date of the refusal;(b) in the case of a deliberate omission to make a service available, the end of the period within which it was reasonable to expect E to act; (c) in the case of conduct causing P not make use of a service or to cease to make use of it, the date of that conduct; (d) in the case of failure to provide the same service, on the same terms, as is provided to others, the date or last date on which the service in fact was provided: reg 7(4).
14   See the Employment Relations Act 1999 (Blacklists) Regulations 2010, SI 2010/493, regs 7(1A), 18 (both added by SI 2014/386).
15   Employment Relations Act 1999 (Blacklists) Regulations 2010, SI 2010/493, reg 7(2).
16   Employment Relations Act 1999 (Blacklists) Regulations 2010, SI 2010/493, reg 8(1).
17   As to the sanctions and remedies for breach of statutory duty see STATUTES AND LEGISLATIVE PROCESS vol 96 (2012) PARA 752 et seq; and as to claims for damages for breach of statutory duty see TORT vol 97 (2010) PARA 495 et seq.
18   Employment Relations Act 1999 (Blacklists) Regulations 2010, SI 2010/493, reg 8(2).
19   Employment Relations Act 1999 (Blacklists) Regulations 2010, SI 2010/493, reg 8(4).
20   Ie the complaint under the Employment Relations Act 1999 (Blacklists) Regulations 2010, SI 2010/493, reg 5 or reg 6: see heads (1)–(2), (a)–(b) in the text.
21   Employment Relations Act 1999 (Blacklists) Regulations 2010, SI 2010/493, reg 8(5).
22   Ie under the Trade Union and Labour Relations (Consolidation) Act 1992 s 140: see PARA 1045.
23   Employment Relations Act 1999 (Blacklists) Regulations 2010, SI 2010/493, reg 8(6).
24   Ie under the Employment Relations Act 1999 (Blacklists) Regulations 2010, SI 2010/493, reg 8(4), (5) or (6): see the text and notes 19–23.
25   Employment Relations Act 1999 (Blacklists) Regulations 2010, SI 2010/493, reg 8(3).
26   Employment Relations Act 1999 (Blacklists) Regulations 2010, SI 2010/493, reg 8(7).

1039. Complaint against employer and employment agency where employment or agency services refused for reason relating to a prohibited list. Where a person ('P') has a right of complaint against another ('R') and against an employment agency ('E') that he has been refused employment or employment agency services for a reason which relates to a prohibited list[1] and the complaint arises out of the same facts, P may present a complaint against either R or E or against R and E jointly[2]. If P presents a complaint against only one party, that party or P may request the employment tribunal[3] to join the other as a party to the proceedings[4]. The request must be granted if it is made before the hearing of the complaint begins, but may be refused if it is made after that time; and no such request may be made after the tribunal has made its decision as to whether the complaint is well-founded[5].

Where P brings a complaint against R and E jointly, or where P brings a complaint against one of them and the other is joined as a party to the proceedings, and the tribunal finds that the complaint is well-founded as against R and E, and awards compensation[6], the tribunal may order that the compensation must be paid by R, by E, or partly by R and partly by E, as the tribunal may consider just and equitable in all the circumstances[7].

1   Ie a right of complaint under the Employment Relations Act 1999 (Blacklists) Regulations 2010, SI 2010/493, reg 5 or reg 6: see PARA 1038.

2   See the Employment Relations Act 1999 (Blacklists) Regulations 2010, SI 2010/493, reg 14(1).
3   As to employment tribunals see PARA 1399 et seq.
4   See the Employment Relations Act 1999 (Blacklists) Regulations 2010, SI 2010/493, reg 14(2).
5   Employment Relations Act 1999 (Blacklists) Regulations 2010, SI 2010/493, reg 14(3).
6   As to awards of compensation see PARA 1038.
7   Employment Relations Act 1999 (Blacklists) Regulations 2010, SI 2010/493, reg 14(4).

1040. Victimisation for reason relating to a prohibited list. A person ('P') has a right of complaint to an employment tribunal[1] against P's employer ('D') if D, by any act or any deliberate failure to act, subjects P to a detriment (other than unfair dismissal)[2] for a reason which relates to a prohibited list[3], and either:

(1)   D contravenes the general prohibition on compiling, using, selling or supplying such a list[4] in relation to that list; or

(2)   D relies on information supplied by a person who contravenes that prohibition[5] in relation to that list, and knows or ought reasonably to know that information relied on is supplied in contravention of that prohibition[6].

If there are facts from which the tribunal could conclude, in the absence of any other explanation, that D contravened the prohibition referred to in head (1) above or relied on information supplied in contravention of that prohibition, the tribunal must find that such a contravention or reliance on information occurred unless D shows that it did not[7].

An employment tribunal may not consider such a complaint unless it is presented before the end of the period of three months beginning with the date of the act or failure to which the complaint relates or, where that act or failure is part of a series of similar acts or failures (or both) the last of them[8], subject to an extension to facilitate conciliation before the institution of proceedings[9]. Further, an employment tribunal may consider such a complaint that is otherwise out of time if, in all the circumstances of the case, it considers that it is just and equitable to do so[10].

Where the employment tribunal finds that a complaint under the above provisions is well-founded, it must make a declaration to that effect and may make an award of compensation to be paid by D to P in respect of the act or failure complained of[11]. Subject to the following provisions, the amount of the compensation awarded must be such as the tribunal considers just and equitable in all the circumstances having regard to the act or failure complained of and to any loss sustained by P which is attributable to D's act or failure[12]; and that loss is to be taken to include any expenses P reasonably incurred in consequence of the act or failure complained of and loss of any benefit which P might reasonably be expected to have had but for that act or failure[13]. In ascertaining the loss, the tribunal must apply the same rule concerning the duty of a person to mitigate his loss as applies to damages recoverable under the common law of England and Wales[14].

Where the conduct of P before the act or failure complained of was such that it would be just and equitable to reduce the amount of compensation, the tribunal must reduce that amount accordingly[15]; and where the tribunal finds that the act or failure complained of was to any extent caused or contributed to by action of P, it must reduce or further reduce the amount of the compensation by such proportion as it considers just and equitable having regard to that finding[16]. The amount of compensation must be reduced or further reduced by the amount of any compensation awarded by the tribunal under the Trade Union and Labour Relations (Consolidation) Act 1992[17] in respect of the same act or failure[18]. In determining the amount of compensation to be awarded no account must, however, be taken of any pressure exercised on D by calling, organising, procuring or financing a strike or other industrial action, or by threatening to do so; and that question must be determined as if no such pressure had been exercised[19]. Where an award of compensation is made, the amount of compensation before any increase or reduction is made under the above provisions[20], or under the statutory provision under which an award of damages may be increased if an employer has failed to comply with a code of practice[21], must not be less than £5,000[22]; and where P is a worker[23] and the detriment to which P is subjected is the termination of P's contract, and that contract is not a contract of employment[24], the compensation awarded to P under these provisions must not exceed £65,300[25].

1   As to employment tribunals see PARA 1399 et seq.
2   The Employment Relations Act 1999 (Blacklists) Regulations 2010, SI 2010/493, reg 9 (see the text and notes1, 3–7) does not apply where the detriment in question amounts to the dismissal of an employee within the meaning in the Employment Rights Act 1996 Pt X (ss 94–134A) (unfair dismissal: see PARA 757 et seq): Employment Relations Act 1999 (Blacklists) Regulations 2010, SI 2010/493, reg 9(3).
3   As to the meaning of 'prohibited list' see PARA 1037 note 12.
4   Ie D contravenes the Employment Relations Act 1999 (Blacklists) Regulations 2010, SI 2010/493, reg 3: see PARA 1037.
5   As to the meaning of references to information supplied by a person who contravenes the Employment Relations Act 1999 (Blacklists) Regulations 2010, SI 2010/493, reg 3 see PARA 1038 note 5.
6   See the Employment Relations Act 1999 (Blacklists) Regulations 2010, SI 2010/493, reg 9(1), (3). The Trade Union and Labour Relations (Consolidation) Act 1992 s 288 (restriction on contracting out: see PARA 150) applies to the Employment Relations Act 1999 (Blacklists) Regulations 2010, SI 2010/493, reg 9 as if it were contained in the 1992 Act: Employment Relations Act 1999 (Blacklists) Regulations 2010, SI 2010/493, reg 16. A person may make a complaint under reg 9 and bring court proceedings for a claim for breach of statutory duty in respect of the same conduct for the purpose of restraining or preventing the defendant from contravening reg 3: see PARA 1037 note 22.
    The provisions of the Employment Tribunals Act 1996 ss 18A–18B (conciliation) (see PARA 152) apply in the case of matters which could be the subject of employment tribunal proceedings under the Employment Relations Act 1999 (Blacklists) Regulations 2010, SI 2010/493, reg 9, and the Employment Tribunals Act 1996 s 18C applies in the case of such proceedings themselves: see s 18(1)(z2), (1A) (s 18(1)(z2) substituted by SI 2014/431; the Employment Tribunals Act 1996 s 18(1A) added by the Enterprise and Regulatory Reform Act 2013 Sch 1 paras 2, 5(1), (7)).
7   Employment Relations Act 1999 (Blacklists) Regulations 2010, SI 2010/493, reg 9(2).
8   Employment Relations Act 1999 (Blacklists) Regulations 2010, SI 2010/493, reg 10(1). For these purposes: (1) where an act extends over a period, the reference to the date of the act is a reference to the last day of the period; (2) a failure to act is to be treated as done when it was decided on: reg 10(3). For the purposes of reg 10(3), in the absence of evidence establishing the contrary D is to be taken to decide on a failure to act (a) when D does an act which is inconsistent with doing the failed act; or (b) if D has done no such inconsistent act, when the period expires within which D might reasonably have been expected to do the failed act if it was done: reg 10(4).
9   See the Employment Relations Act 1999 (Blacklists) Regulations 2010, SI 2010/493, regs 10(1A), 18 (both added by SI 2014/386).
10 Employment Relations Act 1999 (Blacklists) Regulations 2010, SI 2010/493, reg 10(2).
11 Employment Relations Act 1999 (Blacklists) Regulations 2010, SI 2010/493, reg 11(1).
12 Employment Relations Act 1999 (Blacklists) Regulations 2010, SI 2010/493, reg 11(2).
13 Employment Relations Act 1999 (Blacklists) Regulations 2010, SI 2010/493, reg 11(3).
14 Employment Relations Act 1999 (Blacklists) Regulations 2010, SI 2010/493, reg 11(4). As to the common law duty to mitigate loss generally see DAMAGES vol 12(1) (Reissue) PARA 1041 et seq.
15 Employment Relations Act 1999 (Blacklists) Regulations 2010, SI 2010/493, reg 11(6).
16 Employment Relations Act 1999 (Blacklists) Regulations 2010, SI 2010/493, reg 11(7).

17 Ie under the Trade Union and Labour Relations (Consolidation) Act 1992 s 149: see PARA 1050.
18 Employment Relations Act 1999 (Blacklists) Regulations 2010, SI 2010/493, reg 11(8).
19 Employment Relations Act 1999 (Blacklists) Regulations 2010, SI 2010/493, reg 11(9).
20 Ie under the Employment Relations Act 1999 (Blacklists) Regulations 2010, SI 2010/493, reg 11(6), (7) or (8): see the text and notes 15–18.
21 Ie under the Trade Union and Labour Relations (Consolidation) Act 1992 s 207A: see PARA 1234.
22 Employment Relations Act 1999 (Blacklists) Regulations 2010, SI 2010/493, reg 11(5).
23 As to the meaning of 'worker' see PARA 5.
24 As to the meaning of 'contract of employment' see PARA 2.
25 Employment Relations Act 1999 (Blacklists) Regulations 2010, SI 2010/493, reg 11(10).

1041. Awards against third parties in tribunal proceedings on complaint relating to a prohibited list. If in proceedings on a complaint relating to a prohibited list[1] either the respondent or complainant claims that another person contravened the general prohibition on compiling, using, selling or supplying a prohibited list[2] in respect of the prohibited list to which the complaint relates, the complainant or respondent may request the employment tribunal[3] to direct that other person be joined as a party to the proceedings[4]. The request must be granted if it is made before the hearing of the complaint begins, but may be refused if it is made after that time; and no such request may be made if it is made after the tribunal has made a decision as to whether the complaint is well-founded[5].

Where a person has been so joined as a party to the proceedings and the tribunal finds that the complaint is well-founded, awards compensation, and finds the claim with regard to the other person[6] is well-founded, the tribunal must make a declaration to that effect and may award such of the remedies mentioned in heads (1) and (2) below as it considers just and equitable[7]. The remedies the tribunal may award are:

(1) an order that compensation is to be paid by the person joined instead of by the respondent, or partly by that person and partly by the respondent;

(2) a recommendation that within a specified period the person joined takes action appearing to the tribunal to be practicable for the purpose of obviating or reducing the adverse effect on the complainant of any conduct to which the complaint relates[8].

If the person joined fails without reasonable justification to comply with a recommendation to take action, the tribunal may increase its award of compensation or, if it has not made such an award, make one[9].

Where there is more than one respondent[10], the above provisions apply to either or both of them[11].

1 Ie proceedings under the Employment Relations Act 1999 (Blacklists) Regulations 2010, SI 2010/493, reg 5, reg 6 or reg 9 (see PARAS 1038, 1040), or under the Employment Rights Act 1996 Pt X (ss 94–134A) (unfair dismissal: see PARA 757 et seq) as it applies by virtue of the Employment Relations Act 1999 (Blacklists) Regulations 2010, SI 2010/493.
2 Ie contravened the Employment Relations Act 1999 (Blacklists) Regulations 2010, SI 2010/493, reg 3: see PARA 1037.
3 As to employment tribunals see PARA 1399 et seq.
4 Employment Relations Act 1999 (Blacklists) Regulations 2010, SI 2010/493, reg 15(1).
5 Employment Relations Act 1999 (Blacklists) Regulations 2010, SI 2010/493, reg 15(2).
6 Ie the claim in the Employment Relations Act 1999 (Blacklists) Regulations 2010, SI 2010/493, reg 15(1): see the text and notes 1–4.
7 Employment Relations Act 1999 (Blacklists) Regulations 2010, SI 2010/493, reg 15(3).
8 Employment Relations Act 1999 (Blacklists) Regulations 2010, SI 2010/493, reg 15(4).
9 Employment Relations Act 1999 (Blacklists) Regulations 2010, SI 2010/493, reg 15(5).

10 Ie by virtue of the Employment Relations Act 1999 (Blacklists) Regulations 2010, SI 2010/493, reg 14 (complaint against employer and employment agency): see PARA 1039.
11 Employment Relations Act 1999 (Blacklists) Regulations 2010, SI 2010/493, reg 15(6).

B. PROHIBITION OF OTHER RESTRICTIONS ON UNION MEMBERS' ACCESS TO EMPLOYMENT

1042. Refusal of employment on grounds related to union membership. It is unlawful to refuse[1] a person employment[2]:

    (1)   because he is, or is not, a member of a trade union[3]; or

    (2)   because he is unwilling to accept a requirement:

        (a)   to take steps to become or cease to be, or to remain or not to become, a member of a trade union; or

        (b)   to make payments or suffer deductions in the event of his not being a member of a trade union[4].

Where a person is offered employment on terms which include a requirement that he is, or is not, a member of a trade union, or any such requirement as is mentioned in head (2) above, and he does not accept the offer because he does not satisfy or, as the case may be, is unwilling to accept that requirement, he is to be treated as having been refused employment for that reason[5].

A person is also to be taken to have been refused employment because he is not a member of the trade union where there is an arrangement or practice under which employment is offered only to persons put forward or approved by the trade union, and the trade union puts forward or approves only persons who are members of the union, if he is not a member of the union and is refused employment in pursuance of the arrangement or practice[6].

Where an advertisement[7] is published which indicates, or might reasonably be understood as indicating:

    (i)   that employment to which it relates is open only to a person who is, or is not, a member of a trade union; or

    (ii)   that any such requirement as is mentioned in head (2) above will be imposed in relation to employment to which the advertisement relates,

a person who does not satisfy that condition or, as the case may be, is unwilling to accept that requirement, and who seeks and is refused employment to which the advertisement relates, is conclusively presumed to have been refused employment for that reason[8].

Where, however, a person may not be considered for appointment or election to an office[9] in a trade union unless he is a member of the union, or of a particular branch or section of the union or of one of a number of particular branches or sections of the union, nothing in the above provisions applies to anything done for the purpose of securing compliance with that condition, although as holder of the office he would be employed by the union[10].

A person who is thus unlawfully refused employment has a right of complaint to an employment tribunal[11].

The above provisions apply in relation to an employment agency[12] acting, or purporting to act, on behalf of an employer as they apply in relation to an employer[13]; and, where a person has a right of complaint against both a prospective employer and an employment agency arising out of the same facts, he may present a complaint against either of them or against them jointly[14].

1 A person is to be taken to be refused employment if he seeks employment of any description with a person and that person: (1) refuses or deliberately omits to entertain or process his application or inquiry; or (2) causes him to withdraw or cease to pursue his application or inquiry; or (3) refuses or deliberately omits to offer him employment of that description; or

(4) makes him an offer of such employment the terms of which are such that no reasonable employer who wished to fill the post would offer and which is not accepted; or (5) makes him an offer of such employment but withdraws it or causes him not to accept it: Trade Union and Labour Relations (Consolidation) Act 1992 s 137(5). As to the meaning of 'employment' see note 2.

2 For these purposes, 'employment' means employment under a contract of employment, and related expressions are to be construed accordingly: Trade Union and Labour Relations (Consolidation) Act 1992 s 143(1). As to the meaning of 'contract of employment' see PARA 892. As to Crown employment etc see PARAS 893–895; and as to excluded classes of employment see PARA 1071.

3 For these purposes, references to being or not being a member of a trade union are to being or not being a member of any trade union, of a particular trade union or of one of a number of particular trade unions; and any such reference includes a reference to being or not being a member of a particular branch or section of a trade union or one of a number of particular branches or sections of a trade union: Trade Union and Labour Relations (Consolidation) Act 1992 s 143(3). As to the meaning of 'trade union' see PARA 891; and as to the meaning of 'branch or section', in relation to a trade union, see PARA 898 note 5.

4 Trade Union and Labour Relations (Consolidation) Act 1992 s 137(1). Section 137 does not apply in relation to police service: see s 280(1); and PARA 892. This provision, originally enacted in the Employment Act 1988, was introduced to deal with the pre-entry closed shop, and so its main purpose was to make illegal a refusal of employment on the grounds of non-membership of a trade union; but it is drafted to include also a refusal of employment on the grounds of membership of a trade union, which is of primary significance as no such protection existed before. The protection is, however, only against discrimination on the ground of union 'membership'; there is no mention of union 'activities', in contrast to the position in the protection of existing employees in the Trade Union and Labour Relations (Consolidation) Act 1992 ss 146, 152 (see PARAS 1048, 1056). Thus, although ss 146, 152 can apply to action taken against an employee because of his history of union militancy with previous employers (*Fitzpatrick v British Railways Board* [1992] ICR 221, [1991] IRLR 376, CA), it is uncertain whether the Trade Union and Labour Relations (Consolidation) Act 1992 s 137 could apply to refusal of employment on that ground, e g by an employer who maintains that he has no objection to membership as such, but objects to this individual trade unionist. In *Harrison v Kent County Council* [1995] ICR 434, EAT the tribunal adopted a wide interpretation that 'membership' may, on the facts, include activities or (as in that case) past activities when previously employed by the respondent employer (applying a similar approach in *Discount Tobacco & Confectionery Ltd v Armitage* [1995] ICR 431n, [1990] IRLR 15. EAT (decided under the Trade Union and Labour Relations (Consolidation) Act 1992 s 152: see PARA 1056)). Immediately subsequently, however, the distinction between membership and activities arose incidentally before the House of Lords in *Associated Newspapers Ltd v Wilson, Associated British Ports v Palmer* [1995] ICR 406, [1995] IRLR 258, HL (decided under the Trade Union and Labour Relations (Consolidation) Act 1992 s 152) and a majority (Lords Keith of Kinkel, Bridge of Harwich and Lloyd of Berwick) gave the opinion obiter that *Discount Tobacco and Confectionery Ltd v Armitage* [1995] ICR 431n, [1990] IRLR 15. EAT, though correct on its facts, did not establish any general principle that activities are to be included in membership. (For the decision of the European Court of Human Rights in *Associated Newspapers Ltd v Wilson, Associated British Ports v Palmer* above, see Application 30668/96 *Wilson v United Kingdom* (2002) 13 BHRC 39, [2002] IRLR 568, ECtHR.) It may be questioned whether these obiter dicta can be applied to access to employment under the Trade Union and Labour Relations (Consolidation) Act 1992 s 137, contrary to *Harrison v Kent County Council*[1995] ICR 434, EAT. Even in the context of the Trade Union and Labour Relations (Consolidation) Act 1992 s 152, the Employment Appeal Tribunal subsequently followed *Discount Tobacco & Confectionery Ltd v Armitage* [1995] ICR 431n, [1990] IRLR 15. EAT and did not feel bound to follow these obiter dicta: *Speciality Care plc v Pachela* [1996] ICR 633, [1996] IRLR 248, EAT.

5 Trade Union and Labour Relations (Consolidation) Act 1992 s 137(6).

6 Trade Union and Labour Relations (Consolidation) Act 1992 s 137(4).

7 For these purposes, 'advertisement' includes every form of advertisement or notice, whether to the public or not; and references to publishing an advertisement are to be construed accordingly: Trade Union and Labour Relations (Consolidation) Act 1992 s 143(1).

8 Trade Union and Labour Relations (Consolidation) Act 1992 s 137(3).

9 For these purposes, 'office' means any position: (1) by virtue of which the holder is an official of the union; or (2) to which the duty to hold elections under the Trade Union and Labour

Relations (Consolidation) Act 1992 Pt I Ch IV (ss 46–61) (see PARA 960 et seq) applies: s 137(7). As to the meaning of 'official', in relation to a trade union, see PARA 1018.

10 Trade Union and Labour Relations (Consolidation) Act 1992 s 137(7).

11 Trade Union and Labour Relations (Consolidation) Act 1992 s 137(2) (amended by the Employment Rights (Dispute Resolution) Act 1998 s 1(2)(a)). The remedy of a person for conduct which is unlawful by virtue of the Trade Union and Labour Relations (Consolidation) Act 1992 s 137 is by way of complaint to an employment tribunal and not otherwise, and no other legal liability arises by reason that conduct is unlawful by virtue of s 137: s 143(4) (amended by the Employment Rights (Dispute Resolution) Act 1998 s 1(2)(a)). As to the time limit for proceedings see PARA 1044.

The provisions of the Employment Tribunals Act 1996 ss 18A–18B (conciliation) (see PARA 152) apply in the case of matters which could be the subject of employment tribunal proceedings under the Trade Union and Labour Relations (Consolidation) Act 1992 s 137, and the Employment Tribunals Act 1996 s 18C applies in the case of such proceedings themselves: see s 18(1)(a), (1A) (s 18(1)(a) substituted by SI 2014/431; the Employment Tribunals Act 1996 s 18(1A) added by the Enterprise and Regulatory Reform Act 2013 Sch 1 paras 2, 5(1), (7)). As to employment tribunals see PARA 1399 et seq. An appeal lies to the Employment Appeal Tribunal on any question of law arising from any decision of, or arising in any proceedings before, an employment tribunal under or by virtue of the Trade Union and Labour Relations (Consolidation) Act 1992: see the Employment Tribunals Act 1996 s 21(1)(d); and PARA 1428. As to the Employment Appeal Tribunal see PARA 1422 et seq.

12 For these purposes, 'employment agency' means a person who, for profit or not, provides services for the purpose of finding employment for workers or supplying employers with workers; but services other than these are to be disregarded, and a trade union is not to be regarded as an employment agency by reason of services provided by it only for, or in relation to, its members: Trade Union and Labour Relations (Consolidation) Act 1992 s 143(1), (2). As to the meanings of 'employer' and 'worker' see PARA 892.

13 Trade Union and Labour Relations (Consolidation) Act 1992 s 137(8). As to the unlawful refusal of services by an employment agency see PARA 1043.

14 See the Trade Union and Labour Relations (Consolidation) Act 1992 s 141; and PARA 1046.

1043. Refusal of employment agency services on grounds related to union membership. It is unlawful for an employment agency[1] to refuse[2] a person any of its services[3]:

(1)   because he is, or is not, a member of a trade union[4]; or

(2)   because he is unwilling to accept a requirement to take steps to become or cease to be, or to remain or not to become, a member of a trade union[5].

Where a person is offered a service on terms which include a requirement that he is, or is not, a member of a trade union, or any such requirement as is mentioned in head (2) above, and he does not accept the offer because he does not satisfy or, as the case may be, is unwilling to accept that requirement, he is to be treated as having been refused the service for that reason[6].

Where an advertisement[7] is published which indicates, or might reasonably be understood as indicating:

(a)   that any service of an employment agency is available only to a person who is, or is not, a member of a trade union; or

(b)   that any such requirement as is mentioned in head (2) above will be imposed in relation to a service to which the advertisement relates,

a person who does not satisfy that condition or, as the case may be, is unwilling to accept that requirement, and who seeks to avail himself of and is refused that service, is to be conclusively presumed to have been refused it for that reason[8].

A person who is thus unlawfully refused any services of an employment agency has a right of complaint to an employment tribunal[9]; and, where a person has a right of complaint against both a prospective employer and an employment agency arising out of the same facts, he may present a complaint against either of them or against them jointly[10].

These provisions[11] bind the Crown so far as they relate to the activities of an employment agency in relation to employment to which they apply[12].

1   As to the meaning of 'employment agency' see PARA 1042 note 12.
2   A person is to be taken to be refused a service if he seeks to avail himself of it and the agency: (1) refuses or deliberately omits to make the service available to him; or (2) causes him not to avail himself of the service or to cease to avail himself of it; or (3) does not provide the same service, on the same terms, as is provided to others: Trade Union and Labour Relations (Consolidation) Act 1992 s 138(4).
3   As to the meaning of 'services' see PARA 1042 note 12.
4   As to the meaning of references to being, or not being, a member of a trade union for these purposes see PARA 1042 notes 3–4. As to the meaning of 'trade union' see PARA 891.
5   Trade Union and Labour Relations (Consolidation) Act 1992 s 138(1). Section 138 does not apply in relation to police service: see s 280(1); and PARA 892.
6   Trade Union and Labour Relations (Consolidation) Act 1992 s 138(5).
7   As to the meaning of 'advertisement' see PARA 1042 note 7.
8   Trade Union and Labour Relations (Consolidation) Act 1992 s 138(3).
9   Trade Union and Labour Relations (Consolidation) Act 1992 s 138(2) (amended by the Employment Rights (Dispute Resolution) Act 1998 s 1(2)(a)). The remedy of a person for conduct which is unlawful by virtue of the Trade Union and Labour Relations (Consolidation) Act 1992 s 138 is by way of complaint to an employment tribunal and not otherwise, and no other legal liability arises by reason that conduct is unlawful by virtue of s 138: s 143(4) (amended by the Employment Rights (Dispute Resolution) Act 1998 s 1(2)(a)). As to the time limit for proceedings see PARA 1044.
     The Employment Tribunals Act 1996 s 12A (financial penalties: see PARA 1477) applies in relation to a complaint under the Trade Union and Labour Relations (Consolidation) Act 1992 s 138 as it applies in relation to a claim involving an employer and a worker (reading references to an employer as references to the employment agency and references to a worker as references to the complainant): s 138(2A) (added by the Enterprise and Regulatory Reform Act 2013 Sch 3 para 1).
     The provisions of the Employment Tribunals Act 1996 ss 18A–18B (conciliation) (see PARA 152) apply in the case of matters which could be the subject of employment tribunal proceedings under the Trade Union and Labour Relations (Consolidation) Act 1992 s 138, and the Employment Tribunals Act 1996 s 18C applies in the case of such proceedings themselves: see s 18(1)(a), (1A) (s 18(1)(a) substituted by SI 2014/431; the Employment Tribunals Act 1996 s 18(1A) added by the Enterprise and Regulatory Reform Act 2013 Sch 1 paras 2, 5(1), (7)). As to employment tribunals see PARA 1399 et seq. An appeal lies to the Employment Appeal Tribunal on any question of law arising from any decision of, or arising in any proceedings before, an employment tribunal under the Trade Union and Labour Relations (Consolidation) Act 1992: see the Employment Tribunals Act 1996 s 21(1)(d); and PARA 1428. As to the Employment Appeal Tribunal see PARA 1422 et seq.
10 See the Trade Union and Labour Relations (Consolidation) Act 1992 s 141; and PARA 1046. An employment agency acting or purporting to act on behalf of an employer may also be subject to a complaint under s 137 (refusal of access to employment): see PARA 1042.
11 Ie the Trade Union and Labour Relations (Consolidation) Act 1992 s 138 and the other provisions of Pt III (ss 137–177) (see PARAS 1042, 1044 et seq) applying in relation to s 138.
12 Trade Union and Labour Relations (Consolidation) Act 1992 s 276(1). This does not, however, affect the operation of the provisions referred to in note 11 in relation to Crown employment by virtue of s 273 (see PARA 893): s 276(1) proviso. As to the meaning of 'employment' for these purposes see PARA 1042 note 2; and as to excluded classes of employment see PARA 1071.

1044.   Time limit for proceedings on complaint of refusal of employment or agency services on grounds related to union membership.   An employment tribunal must not consider a complaint of refusal of employment[1] or of refusal of employment agency services[2] unless it is presented[3] to the tribunal:

(1)   before the end of the period of three months beginning with the date of the conduct to which the complaint relates[4], subject to an extension to facilitate conciliation before the institution of proceedings[5]; or

(2)   where the tribunal is satisfied that it was not reasonably practicable for

the complaint to be presented before the end of that period, within such further period as the tribunal considers reasonable[6].

The date of the conduct to which a complaint of refusal of employment relates is to be taken to be:

(a) in the case of an actual refusal, the date of the refusal;

(b) in the case of a deliberate omission to entertain and process the complainant's application or inquiry, or to offer employment, the end of the period within which it was reasonable to expect the employer[7] to act;

(c) in the case of conduct causing the complainant to withdraw or cease to pursue his application or inquiry, the date of that conduct;

(d) in a case where an offer was made but withdrawn, the date when it was withdrawn; and

(e) in any other case where an offer was made but not accepted, the date on which it was made[8].

The date of the conduct to which a complaint of refusal of employment agency services relates is to be taken to be:

(i) in the case of an actual refusal, the date of the refusal;

(ii) in the case of a deliberate omission to make a service available, the end of the period within which it was reasonable to expect the employment agency to act;

(iii) in the case of conduct causing the complainant not to avail himself of a service or to cease to avail himself of it, the date of that conduct; and

(iv) in the case of failure to provide the same service, on the same terms, as is provided to others, the date or last date on which the service in fact provided was provided[9].

1 Ie a complaint under the Trade Union and Labour Relations (Consolidation) Act 1992 s 137: see PARA 1042. As to the meaning of 'employment' for these purposes see PARA 1042 note 2. As to employment tribunals see PARA 1399 et seq.

2 Ie a complaint under the Trade Union and Labour Relations (Consolidation) Act 1992 s 138: see PARA 1043. As to the meaning of 'employment agency' see PARA 1042 note 12.

3 As to when a complaint is presented see PARAS 804, 1461.

4 Trade Union and Labour Relations (Consolidation) Act 1992 s 139(1)(a) (amended by the Employment Rights (Dispute Resolution) Act 1998 s 1(2)(a)).

5 The Trade Union and Labour Relations (Consolidation) Act 1992 s 292A (extension of time limits to facilitate conciliation before institution of proceedings: see PARA 1455) applies for the purposes of s 139(1)(a): s 139(4) (added by the Enterprise and Regulatory Reform Act 2013 Sch 2 paras 1, 6).

6 Trade Union and Labour Relations (Consolidation) Act 1992 s 139(1)(b) (as amended: see note 4). For the case law on the extension of time limits, especially in the context of the law of unfair dismissal, see PARAS 804, 1453.

7 As to the meaning of 'employer' see PARA 892.

8 Trade Union and Labour Relations (Consolidation) Act 1992 s 139(2).

9 Trade Union and Labour Relations (Consolidation) Act 1992 s 139(3).

1045. Remedies for refusal of employment or agency services on grounds related to union membership. Where an employment tribunal finds that a complaint of refusal of employment[1] or refusal of employment agency services[2] is well-founded, it must make a declaration to that effect and may make such of the following as it considers just and equitable:

(1) an order requiring the respondent to pay compensation to the complainant of such amount as it determines; or

(2) a recommendation that the respondent take within a specified period action appearing to the tribunal to be practicable for the purpose of

obviating or reducing the adverse effect on the complainant of any conduct to which the complaint relates[3].

Compensation is to be assessed on the same basis as damages for breach of statutory duty[4] and may include compensation for injury to feelings[5]; but the total amount of compensation is not to exceed the limit for the time being imposed[6] on the compensatory award for unfair dismissal[7].

If the respondent fails without reasonable justification to comply with a recommendation to take action, the tribunal may increase its award of compensation or, if it has not made such an award, may make one[8].

Where a complaint is brought against an employer and an employment agency jointly[9], the tribunal may order that the compensation is to be paid by one or the other, or partly by one and partly by the other[10].

1 Ie a complaint under the Trade Union and Labour Relations (Consolidation) Act 1992 s 137: see PARA 1042. As to the meaning of 'employment' for these purposes see PARA 1042 note 2.
2 Ie a complaint under the Trade Union and Labour Relations (Consolidation) Act 1992 s 138: see PARA 1043. As to the meaning of 'employment agency' see PARA 1042 note 12.
3 Trade Union and Labour Relations (Consolidation) Act 1992 s 140(1) (amended by the Employment Rights (Dispute Resolution) Act 1998 s 1(2)(a)). An appeal lies to the Employment Appeal Tribunal on any question of law arising from any decision of, or arising in any proceedings before, an employment tribunal under or by virtue of the Trade Union and Labour Relations (Consolidation) Act 1992: see the Employment Tribunals Act 1996 s 21(1)(d); and PARA 1428. As to the Employment Appeal Tribunal see PARA 1422 et seq.
4 As to the sanctions and remedies for breach of statutory duty see STATUTES AND LEGISLATIVE PROCESS vol 96 (2012) PARA 752 et seq; and as to claims for damages for breach of statutory duty see TORT vol 97 (2010) PARA 495 et seq.
5 Trade Union and Labour Relations (Consolidation) Act 1992 s 140(2).
6 Ie the limit imposed by the Employment Rights Act 1996 s 124(1): see PARA 823. The maximum amount of compensation payable is the lower of (a) £76,574; and (b) 52 multiplied by a week's pay of the person concerned: see the Employment Rights Act 1996 s 124(1), 124(1ZA); and PARA 823. The sum so specified may be varied by the Secretary of State in accordance with the retail prices index: see the Employment Relations Act 1999 s 34; and PARA 160.
7 Trade Union and Labour Relations (Consolidation) Act 1992 s 140(4) (amended by the Employment Rights Act 1996 Sch 1 para 56).
8 Trade Union and Labour Relations (Consolidation) Act 1992 s 140(3).
9 See PARA 1046.
10 See the Trade Union and Labour Relations (Consolidation) Act 1992 s 141(3); and PARA 1046.

1046. Complaint against employer and employment agency on grounds related to union membership. Where a person has a right of complaint[1] against a prospective employer and against an employment agency[2] arising out of the same facts, he may present a complaint against either of them or against them jointly[3]. If a complaint is brought against one only, he or the complainant may request the tribunal to join the other as a party to the proceedings. The request must be granted if it is made before the hearing of the complaint begins but may be refused if it is made after that time; and no such request may be made after the tribunal has made its decision as to whether the complaint is well-founded[4].

Where a complaint is brought against an employer[5] and an employment agency jointly, or where it is brought against one and the other is joined as a party to the proceedings, and the tribunal finds that the complaint is well-founded as against the employer and the agency, and makes an award of compensation[6], it may order that the compensation is to be paid by the one or the other, or partly by one and partly by the other, as the tribunal may consider just and equitable in the circumstances[7].

1 Ie a complaint under the Trade Union and Labour Relations (Consolidation) Act 1992 s 137 (see PARA 1042) or s 138 (see PARA 1043).

2 As to the meaning of 'employment agency' see PARA 1042 note 12.
3 Trade Union and Labour Relations (Consolidation) Act 1992 s 141(1).
4 Trade Union and Labour Relations (Consolidation) Act 1992 s 141(2). As to the tribunal's duty to make a declaration, and as to its power to make an order or a recommendation, where it finds the complaint well-founded see PARA 1045.
5 As to the meaning of 'employer' see PARA 892.
6 As to the statutory limit on the amount of compensation see PARA 1045.
7 Trade Union and Labour Relations (Consolidation) Act 1992 s 141(3).

1047.   Awards against third parties on complaint of refusal of employment or agency services on grounds relating to union membership. If in proceedings on a complaint of refusal of employment[1] or refusal of employment agency services[2] either the complainant or the respondent[3] claims that the respondent was induced to act in the manner complained of by pressure which a trade union[4] or other person exercised on him by calling, organising, procuring or financing a strike or other industrial action[5], or by threatening to do so, the complainant or the respondent may request the employment tribunal to direct that the person who he claims exercised the pressure be joined as a party to the proceedings[6]. The request must be granted if it is made before the hearing of the complaint begins but may be refused if it is made after that time; and no such request may be made after the tribunal has made its decision as to whether the complaint is well-founded[7].

Where a person has been so joined as a party to the proceedings and the tribunal:

(1)   finds that the complaint is well-founded;
(2)   makes an award of compensation[8]; and
(3)   also finds that the claim against the joined party is well-founded,

it may order that the compensation is to be paid by the person joined instead of by the respondent, or partly by that person and partly by the respondent, as the tribunal may consider just and equitable in the circumstances[9].

1 Ie a complaint under the Trade Union and Labour Relations (Consolidation) Act 1992 s 137: see PARA 1042. As to the meaning of 'employment' for these purposes see PARA 1042 note 2.
2 Ie a complaint under the Trade Union and Labour Relations (Consolidation) Act 1992 s 138: see PARA 1043. As to the meaning of 'employment agency' see PARA 1042 note 12.
3 Where, by virtue of the Trade Union and Labour Relations (Consolidation) Act 1992 s 141 (complaint against employer and employment agency) (see PARA 1046), there is more than one respondent, these provisions apply to either or both of them: s 142(4).
4 As to the meaning of 'trade union' see PARA 891.
5 There is no statutory definition of 'strike' or 'other industrial action' for these purposes. For the case law on these terms as they apply in the context of unfair dismissal law etc see PARA 1340.
6 Trade Union and Labour Relations (Consolidation) Act 1992 s 142(1) (amended by the Employment Rights (Dispute Resolution) Act 1998 s 1(2)(a)).
7 Trade Union and Labour Relations (Consolidation) Act 1992 s 142(2).
8 As to the statutory limit on the amount of compensation see PARA 1045.
9 Trade Union and Labour Relations (Consolidation) Act 1992 s 142(3).

(ii) Victimisation for Trade Union Reasons

1048.   Detriment on grounds related to trade union membership or activities.
A worker[1] has the right not to be subjected to any detriment[2] as an individual[3] by any act, or any deliberate failure to act[4], by his employer[5] if the act or failure takes place for the sole or main purpose of:

(1)   preventing or deterring him from being or seeking to become a member[6] of an independent trade union[7], or penalising[8] him for doing so[9];

(2)   preventing or deterring him from taking part in the activities[10] of an independent trade union at an appropriate time[11], or penalising him for doing so[12];

(3)   preventing or deterring him from making use of trade union services at an appropriate time, or penalising him for doing so[13]; or

(4)   compelling him to be or become a member of any trade union or of a particular trade union or of one of a number of particular trade unions[14]; or

(5)   enforcing a requirement (whether or not imposed by a contract of employment or in writing) that, in the event of his not being a member of any trade union or of a particular trade union or of one of a number of particular trade unions, he must make one or more payments[15].

A worker also has the right not to be subjected to any detriment as an individual by any act, or any deliberate failure to act, by his employer if the act or failure takes place because of the worker's failure to accept an offer made in contravention of the provisions on inducements relating to union membership or activities, or inducements relating to collective bargaining[16].

A worker or former worker may present a complaint to an employment tribunal on the ground that he has been subjected to a detriment by his employer in contravention[17] of the above right[18]. An employment tribunal must not consider such a complaint unless it is presented[19]:

(a)   before the end of the period of three months beginning with the date of the act[20] or failure to act[21] to which the complaint relates or, where that act or failure is part of a series of similar acts or failures, or both, the last of them[22], subject to an extension to facilitate conciliation before the institution of proceedings[23]; or

(b)   where the tribunal is satisfied that it was not reasonably practicable for the complaint to be presented before the end of that period, within such further period as it considers reasonable[24].

1   For the purposes of the Trade Union and Labour Relations (Consolidation) Act 1992 ss 146–150, 'worker' means an individual who works, or normally works, as mentioned in s 296(1)(a)–(c) (see PARA 892): s 151(1B) (added by the Employment Relations Act 2004 s 30(8)). An agency worker who cannot establish a contract between himself and the end-user and who does not otherwise fall within the Trade Union and Labour Relations (Consolidation) Act 1992 s 296(1) cannot bring himself within the protection of s 146: see *Smith v Carillion (JM) Ltd* [2014] IRLR 344, [2014] All ER (D) 253 (Jan), EAT. As to excluded classes of employment see PARA 1071. See also note 2.

    As to inducements relating to trade union membership and activities see the Trade Union and Labour Relations (Consolidation) Act 1992 ss 145A–145F; and PARA 1051 et seq.

2   The Trade Union and Labour Relations (Consolidation) Act 1992 s 146 does not apply where the worker is an employee and the detriment in question amounts to dismissal: s 146(5A) (added by the Employment Relations Act 2004 s 30(6)). As to the meaning of 'employee' see PARA 892.

    Previously there was a provision indicating that 'detriment' means detriment short of dismissal: Trade Union and Labour Relations (Consolidation) Act 1992 s 146(6) (repealed) but see now s 146(5A) (see above). If the employer actually dismissed for the reasons set out in s 146(1) (as then previously enacted), that fell within s 152 (see PARA 1056) and, since much of the drafting was common between s 146 and s 152, cases decided under one provision could also be authoritative under the other: see *Fitzpatrick v British Railways Board* [1990] ICR 674 at 676, EAT per Wood P; revsd on other grounds [1992] ICR 221, [1991] IRLR 376, CA; *Johnstone v BBC Enterprises Ltd* [1994] ICR 180, EAT. The provisions of the Trade Union and Labour Relations (Consolidation) Act 1992 s 146 were intended to prevent discrimination during the currency of the employment and did not, therefore, apply to failure to renew a fixed term contract: *Johnstone v BBC Enterprises Ltd* [1994] ICR 180, EAT. Under the Trade Union and Labour Relations (Consolidation) Act 1992 s 146(1) (as originally enacted) the right was 'not to have action short of dismissal taken against him as an individual by his employer'; and that was held to apply to the taking of disciplinary proceedings against the employee (*British*

Airways Board v Clark and Havill [1982] IRLR 238, EAT) and a refusal of promotion
(*Department of Transport v Gallacher* [1994] ICR 967, sub nom *Gallacher v Department of
Transport* [1994] IRLR 231, CA).

3   The action must be taken against the complainant as an individual; purely collective action
against his union may not be sufficient per se, but, if that action also means that individual
members are made to suffer, that may be sufficient: *National Coal Board v Ridgeway* [1987]
3 All ER 582, [1987] ICR 641, CA. The effects of this decision were later negated by statute (see
PARA 1049) and it was eventually overruled by the House of Lords on other grounds (see
Associated Newspapers Ltd v Wilson, Associated British Ports v Palmer [1995] ICR 406, [1995]
IRLR 258, HL, cited in note 4); but it seems this particular aspect of the case is still good law. It
was relied on and applied in *FW Farnsworth Ltd v McCoid* [1999] ICR 1047, [1999] IRLR
626, CA to hold that derecognising an individual shop steward could be action taken against
him 'as an individual', not just action aimed at the union (even though it did not affect him as an
employee).

4   It was held in *Associated Newspapers Ltd v Wilson, Associated British Ports v Palmer* [1995]
ICR 406, [1995] IRLR 258, HL that under the wording of the Trade Union and Labour
Relations (Consolidation) Act 1992 s 146(1) (as originally enacted) (see note 2) the word
'action' was incapable of including an omission, as a matter of the legislative history of these
provisions. Thus, giving a 'sweetener payment' to employees who agreed to give up collective
bargaining and refusing it to those who would not agree could not constitute 'action' against the
latter. (For the decision of the European Court of Human Rights in *Associated Newspapers Ltd
v Wilson, Associated British Ports v Palmer* above, see Application 30668/96 *Wilson v United
Kingdom* (2002) 13 BHRC 39, [2002] IRLR 568, ECtHR.) The present wording, introduced by
the Employment Relations Act 1999 Sch 2 paras 1, 2, reverses that element of the decision.
However, it was argued that the case would still be decided the same way because the 1999 Act
did not repeal the Trade Union and Labour Relations (Consolidation) Act 1992 s 148(3)–(5)
which specifically legitimised such payments, provided that they were made for the proper
purpose but s 148(3)–(5) has now been repealed. Cf *Southwark London Borough Council v
Whillier* [2001] EWCA Civ 808, [2001] ICR 1016 (decided under the Trade Union and Labour
Relations (Consolidation) Act 1992 s 146(1) (as originally enacted)).

5   For the purposes of the Trade Union and Labour Relations (Consolidation) Act 1992
ss 146–150, 'employer' means, in relation to a worker, the person for whom he works and, in
relation to a former worker, the person for whom he worked: s 151(1B) (as added: see note 1).

6   For these purposes, references to being, becoming or ceasing to remain a member of a trade
union include references to being, becoming or ceasing to remain a member of a particular
branch or section of that union and to being, becoming or ceasing to remain a member of one of
a number of particular branches or sections of that union: Trade Union and Labour Relations
(Consolidation) Act 1992 s 151(1) (amended by the Employment Relations Act 2004 s 31(6),
Sch 2). References to taking part in the activities of a trade union, and to services made available
by a trade union by virtue of membership of the union are to be construed in accordance with
the Trade Union and Labour Relations (Consolidation) Act 1992 s 151(1): s 151(1A) (added by
the Employment Relations Act 2004 s 31(7)). As to the meaning of 'trade union' see PARA 891;
and as to the meaning of 'branch or section', in relation to a trade union, see PARA 898 note 5.
As to whether the reference to membership can include a reference to important effects and
incidents of membership see PARA 1056 note 5.

7   As to the meaning of 'independent trade union' see PARA 904.

8   'Penalising' means subjecting to a disadvantage; it is, therefore, not confined to the imposition of
a positive punishment or financial penalty: *Carlson v Post Office* [1981] ICR 343, [1981] IRLR
158, EAT.

9   Trade Union and Labour Relations (Consolidation) Act 1992 s 146(1)(a) (s 146(1) amended by
the Employment Relations Act 1999 Sch 2 paras 1, 2(1), (2); the Employment Relations
Act 2004 s 30(1), (2), Sch 1 para 8). As to where it is shown that the action complained of was
taken for the purpose of safeguarding national security see the Employment Tribunals Act 1996
s 10(1); and PARA 1448.

10   As to the meaning of 'activities of an independent trade union' see PARA 1056 note 6.

11   For the purposes of the Trade Union and Labour Relations (Consolidation) Act 1992 s 146(1),
an 'appropriate time' means: (1) a time outside the worker's working hours; or (2) a time within
his working hours at which, in accordance with arrangements agreed with or consent given by
his employer, it is permissible for him to take part in the activities of a trade union or (as the case
may be) make use of trade union services; and 'working hours', in relation to a worker, means
any time when, in accordance with his contract of employment (or other contract personally to
do work or perform services), he is required to be at work: Trade Union and Labour Relations
(Consolidation) Act 1992 s 146(2) (amended by the Employment Relations Act 2004

s 30(1), (2), (3)). See further PARA 1056 note 7. As to the meaning of 'contract of employment' see PARA 892. Where an employer consented to an employee conducting a union recruitment meeting during working hours, that consent was not subject to an implied condition that nothing critical of the employer would be said: *Bass Taverns Ltd v Burgess* [1995] IRLR 596, CA. 'Trade union services' means services made available to the worker by an independent trade union by virtue of his membership of the union, and references to a worker's 'making use' of trade union services include his consenting to the raising of a matter on his behalf by an independent trade union of which he is a member: Trade Union and Labour Relations (Consolidation) Act 1992 s 146(2A) (s 146(2A)–(2D) added by the Employment Relations Act 2004 s 31(1), (4)).

12 Trade Union and Labour Relations (Consolidation) Act 1992 s 146(1)(b) (amended by the Employment Relations Act 2004 s 31(1), (2), Sch 2). See *Gayle v Sandwell & West Birmingham Hospitals NHS Trust* [2011] EWCA Civ 924, [2011] IRLR 810, [2012] ICR D3 (final written warning imposed for employee's failure to comply with management instruction to discuss time off for union activities (and not for the purpose of penalising her for trade union activities) not a detriment within the Trade Union and Labour Relations (Consolidation) Act 1992 s 146(1)(b)). See also note 9.

Section 146(1)(b) does not make the existence of a certificate of independence a pre-condition for asserting a claim for breach of statutory rights pursuant to s 146. If the respondent does not dispute the independence of the union, then that issue drops out of the dispute which is being adjudicated. If the respondent denies that the union is independent and if no certificate has been given, refused or withdrawn, then the question of independence remains at large and has to be referred to the certification officer. In those circumstances, the question of independence is merely one of the matters in dispute in the proceedings. Consequently, the question whether a trade union is independent does not affect the jurisdiction of the employment tribunal in a claim under s 146 (see the text and notes 17–24); it is merely one of a number of issues upon which the claimant may or may not succeed: *Bone v North Essex Partnership NHS Foundation Trust* [2014] EWCA Civ 652 at [48]–[50], [2014] 3 All ER 964 at [48]–[50], [2014] IRLR 635 at [48]–[50]. Further, a certificate of independence is retrospective in its effect for a reasonable period before the date of the certificate; and historic questions of independence are to be referred to the certification officer: *Bone v North Essex Partnership NHS Foundation Trust* at [41], [66].

13 Trade Union and Labour Relations (Consolidation) Act 1992 s 146(1)(ba) (added by the Employment Relations Act 2004 s 31(1), (2)). If an independent trade union of which a worker is a member raises a matter on his behalf (with or without his consent), penalising the worker for that is to be treated as penalising him as mentioned in Trade Union and Labour Relations (Consolidation) Act 1992 s 146(1)(ba): s 146(2B) (as added: see note 11). See also note 9.

14 Trade Union and Labour Relations (Consolidation) Act 1992 s 146(1)(c) (amended by the Employment Relations Act 1999 Sch 2 paras 1, 2(1), (2)). See also note 9.

15 Trade Union and Labour Relations (Consolidation) Act 1992 s 146(3) (amended by the Employment Relations Act 1999 Sch 2 paras 1, 2(1), (3); the Employment Relations Act 2004 s 30(1), (2), (4), Sch 1 para 8). For these purposes, any deduction made by an employer from the remuneration payable to a worker in respect of his employment is to be treated, if it is attributable to his not being a member of any trade union or of a particular trade union or of one of a number of particular trade unions, as a detriment to which he has been subjected as an individual by an act of his employer taking place for the sole or main purpose of enforcing such a requirement: Trade Union and Labour Relations (Consolidation) Act 1992 s 146(4) (amended by the Employment Relations Act 1999 Sch 2 paras 1, 2(1), (4); the Employment Relations Act 2004 s 30(1), (2), Sch 1 para 8).

16 Trade Union and Labour Relations (Consolidation) Act 1992 s 146(2C) (as added: see note 11). The reference to provisions on inducements is a reference to s 145A or s 145B: see PARAS 1051–1052. For the purposes of s 146(2C), not conferring a benefit that, if the offer had been accepted by the worker, would have been conferred on him under the resulting agreement is taken to be subjecting him to a detriment as an individual (and to be a deliberate failure to act): s 146(2D) (as so added).

17 As to the meaning of 'contravention' and cognate expressions see PARA 915 note 6.

18 Trade Union and Labour Relations (Consolidation) Act 1992 s 146(5) (amended by the Employment Rights (Dispute Resolution) Act 1998 s 1(2)(a); the Employment Relations Act 1999 Sch 2 paras 1, 2(1), (5); the Employment Relations Act 2004 s 30(1), (5)). The remedy of a person for infringement of the right conferred on him by the Trade Union and Labour Relations (Consolidation) Act 1992 s 146 is by way of a complaint to an employment tribunal, and not otherwise: s 151(2) (amended by the Employment Rights (Dispute Resolution) Act 1998 s 1(2)(a); the Employment Relations Act 2004 s 30(9)). If an employee is dismissed or selected

for redundancy because he brought proceedings to enforce the right under the Trade Union and Labour Relations (Consolidation) Act 1992 s 146, his dismissal is automatically regarded as unfair: see PARAS 1063, 1064.

The provisions of the Employment Tribunals Act 1996 ss 18A–18B (conciliation) (see PARA 152) apply in the case of matters which could be the subject of employment tribunal proceedings under the Trade Union and Labour Relations (Consolidation) Act 1992, and the Employment Tribunals Act 1996 s 18C applies in the case of such proceedings themselves: see s 18(1)(a), (1A) (s 18(1)(a) substituted by SI 2014/431; the Employment Tribunals Act 1996 s 18(1A) added by the Enterprise and Regulatory Reform Act 2013 Sch 1 paras 2, 5(1), (7)). As to employment tribunals see PARA 1399 et seq. An appeal lies to the Employment Appeal Tribunal on any question of law arising from any decision of, or arising in any proceedings before, an employment tribunal under or by virtue of the Trade Union and Labour Relations (Consolidation) Act 1992: see the Employment Tribunals Act 1996 s 21(1)(d); and PARA 1428. As to the Employment Appeal Tribunal see PARA 1422 et seq.

19   As to when a complaint is presented see PARAS 804, 1461.
20   For these purposes, where an act extends over a period, the reference to the date of the act is a reference to the last day of that period: Trade Union and Labour Relations (Consolidation) Act 1992 s 147(2)(a) (s 147(2), (3) added by the Employment Relations Act 1999 Sch 2 paras 1, 3(1), (4)).
21   For these purposes, a failure to act is to be treated as done when it was decided on: Trade Union and Labour Relations (Consolidation) Act 1992 s 147(2)(b) (as added: see note 20). In the absence of evidence establishing the contrary, an employer is to be taken to decide on a failure to act: (1) when he does an act inconsistent with doing the failed act; or (2) if he has done no such inconsistent act, when the period expires within which he might reasonably have been expected to do the failed act if it was to be done: Trade Union and Labour Relations (Consolidation) Act 1992 s 147(3) (as so added).
22   Trade Union and Labour Relations (Consolidation) Act 1992 s 147(1)(a) (renumbered and amended by the Employment Relations Act 1999 Sch 2 paras 1, 3(1)–(3)). For the case law on the extension of time limits, especially in the context of the law of unfair dismissal, see PARAS 804, 1453.
23   The Trade Union and Labour Relations (Consolidation) Act 1992 s 292A (extension of time limits to facilitate conciliation before institution of proceedings: see PARA 1455) applies for the purposes of s 147(1)(a): s 147(4) (added by the Enterprise and Regulatory Reform Act 2013 Sch 2 paras 1, 8).
24   Trade Union and Labour Relations (Consolidation) Act 1992 s 147(1)(b) (as renumbered and amended: see note 22).

1049.   Consideration of complaint of victimisation for trade union reasons.

On a complaint of victimisation for trade union reasons[1], it is for the employer[2] to show what was the sole or main purpose for which he acted or failed to act[3].

In determining any question whether the employer acted or failed to act, or the purpose for which he did so, no account is to be taken of any pressure which was exercised on him by calling, organising, procuring or financing a strike or other industrial action[4], or by threatening to do so; and that question is to be determined as if no such pressure had been exercised[5].

1   Ie under the Trade Union and Labour Relations (Consolidation) Act 1992 s 146: see PARA 1048.
2   As to the meaning of 'employer' see PARA 892.
3   Trade Union and Labour Relations (Consolidation) Act 1992 s 148(1) (amended by the Employment Relations Act 1999 Sch 2 paras 1, 4(1), (2); the Employment Relations Act 2004 Sch 1 para 9).
    As to inducements relating to trade union membership and activities see the Trade Union and Labour Relations (Consolidation) Act 1992 ss 145A–145F; and PARA 1051 et seq.
4   There is no statutory definition of 'strike' or 'other industrial action' for these purposes. For the case law on these terms as they apply in the context of unfair dismissal law etc see PARA 1340.
5   Trade Union and Labour Relations (Consolidation) Act 1992 s 148(2) (amended by the Employment Relations Act 1999 Sch 2 paras 1, 4(1), (3)); and see *Colwyn Borough Council v Dutton* [1980] IRLR 420, EAT. If, however, in proceedings on a complaint under the Trade Union and Labour Relations (Consolidation) Act 1992 s 146 (see PARA 1048): (1) the complaint is made on the ground that the complainant has been subjected to detriment by an act or failure by his employer taking place for the sole or main purpose of compelling him to be or become a

member of any trade union or of a particular trade union or of one of a number of particular trade unions; and (2) either the complainant or the employer claims in proceedings before the tribunal that the employer was induced to act or fail to act in the way complained of by pressure which a trade union or other person exercised on him by calling, organising, procuring or financing a strike or other industrial action, or by threatening to do so, the complainant or the employer may request the tribunal to direct that the person who he claims exercised the pressure be joined as a party to the proceedings: s 150(1) (amended by the Employment Relations Act 1999 Sch 2 paras 1, 6; the Employment Relations Act 2004 Sch 1 para 10). The request must be granted if it is made before the hearing of the complaint begins, but may be refused if it is made after that time; and no such request may be made after the tribunal has made a declaration that the complaint is well-founded: Trade Union and Labour Relations (Consolidation) Act 1992 s 150(2). Where a person has been so joined as a party to proceedings and the tribunal makes an award of compensation and finds that the claim mentioned in head (2) above is well-founded, it may order that the compensation is to be paid by the person joined instead of by the employer, or partly by that person and partly by the employer, as the tribunal may consider just and equitable in the circumstances: s 150(3). As to the meaning of 'trade union' see PARA 891.

1050. Remedies for victimisation for trade union reasons. Where an employment tribunal finds that a complaint of victimisation for union reasons[1] is well-founded, it must make a declaration to that effect and may make an award of compensation to be paid by the employer[2] to the complainant in respect of the act or failure complained of[3]. The amount of the compensation to be awarded is such as the tribunal considers just and equitable in all the circumstances, having regard to the infringement complained of and to any loss sustained by the complainant which is attributable to the act or failure which infringed his right[4]. In particular, the loss is to be taken to include any expenses reasonably incurred by the complainant in consequence of the act or failure complained of, and loss of any benefit which he might reasonably be expected to have had but for that act or failure[5].

In determining the amount of compensation, no account is to be taken of any pressure which was exercised on the employer by calling, organising, procuring or financing a strike or other industrial action[6], or threatening to do so, and that question is to be determined as if no such pressure had been exercised[7].

Where the tribunal finds that the act or failure complained of was to any extent caused or contributed to by any action of the complainant, it must reduce the amount of the compensation by such proportion as it considers just and equitable having regard to that finding[8].

1 Ie a complaint under the Trade Union and Labour Relations (Consolidation) Act 1992 s 146: see PARA 1048. If an employee is dismissed or selected for redundancy because he brought proceedings to enforce the right under s 146, his dismissal is automatically regarded as unfair: see PARAS 1063, 1064.

2 As to the meaning of 'employer' see PARA 892.

3 Trade Union and Labour Relations (Consolidation) Act 1992 s 149(1) (amended by the Employment Rights (Dispute Resolution) Act 1998 s 1(2)(a); the Employment Relations Act 1999 Sch 2 paras 1, 5(a)).
    As to inducements relating to trade union membership and activities see the Trade Union and Labour Relations (Consolidation) Act 1992 ss 145A–145F; and PARA 1051 et seq.

4 Trade Union and Labour Relations (Consolidation) Act 1992 s 149(2) (amended by the Employment Relations Act 1999 Sch 2 paras 1, 5(a)). Although the basis for awarding compensation is compensatory not penal, that compensation may include not only pecuniary loss but also injury to reputation, feelings etc: *Brassington v Cauldon Wholesale Ltd* [1978] ICR 405, [1977] IRLR 479, EAT; *Cleveland Ambulance NHS Trust v Blane* [1997] ICR 851, [1997] IRLR 332, EAT. The employer's default may be considered in the context of its effect on the employee, e g in inducing stress: *Cheall v Vauxhall Motors Ltd* [1979] IRLR 253. In ascertaining the loss to the complainant, the tribunal must apply the same rule concerning the duty of a person to mitigate his loss as applies to damages recoverable under the common law: Trade Union and Labour Relations (Consolidation) Act 1992 s 149(4). As to mitigation of damages

generally see DAMAGES vol 12(1) (Reissue) PARA 1041 et seq; and as to the duty to mitigate in the context of unfair dismissal law see PARA 822.

The scale in *Vento v Chief Constable of West Yorkshire Police* [2002] EWCA Civ 1871, [2003] ICR 318, [2003] IRLR 102 on injury to feelings applies under the Trade Union and Labour Relations (Consolidation) Act 1992 s 149, although with possibly a higher burden of proof on the claimant than in discrimination claims: see *Hackney London Borough Council v Adams* [2003] IRLR 402, EAT.

5 Trade Union and Labour Relations (Consolidation) Act 1992 s 149(3) (amended by the Employment Relations Act 1999 Sch 2 paras 1, 5(a)).

6 There is no statutory definition of 'strike' or 'other industrial action' for these purposes. For the case law on these terms as they apply in the context of unfair dismissal law see PARA 1340.

7 Trade Union and Labour Relations (Consolidation) Act 1992 s 149(5). Cf PARA 1049 note 5.

8 Trade Union and Labour Relations (Consolidation) Act 1992 s 149(6) (amended by the Employment Relations Act 1999 Sch 2 paras 1, 5(b)). As to contributory fault in the context of unfair dismissal law see PARA 821.

(iii) Inducements relating to Union Membership etc

1051. Inducements relating to union membership or activities. A worker[1] has the right not to have an offer made to him by his employer[2] for the sole or main purpose of inducing the worker:

(1)   not to be or seek to become a member of an independent trade union[3];

(2)   not to take part, at an appropriate time[4], in the activities of an independent trade union[5];

(3)   not to make use, at an appropriate time, of trade union services[6]; or

(4)   to be or become a member of any trade union or of a particular trade union or one of a number of particular trade unions[7].

A worker or former worker may present a complaint to an employment tribunal on the ground that his employer has made him such an offer[8].

1 'Worker' means an individual who works, or normally works, as mentioned in the Trade Union and Labour Relations (Consolidation) Act 1992 s 296(1)(a)–(c) (see PARA 892): s 145F(3) (ss 145A, 145F added by the Employment Relations Act 2004 s 29).

2 'Employer' means, in relation to a worker, the person for whom he works, and, in relation to a former worker, the person for whom he worked: Trade Union and Labour Relations (Consolidation) Act 1992 s 145F(3) (as added: see note 1).

3 Trade Union and Labour Relations (Consolidation) Act 1992 s 145A(1)(a) (as added: see note 1). References in ss 145A–145E to being or becoming a member of a trade union include references to being or becoming a member of a particular branch or section of that union, and to being or becoming a member of one of a number of particular branches or sections of that union, and references to taking part in the activities of a trade union and to services made available by a trade union by virtue of membership of that union are to be construed accordingly: s 145F(1), (2) (as added: see note 1). As to the meaning of 'trade union' see PARA 891. As to where it is shown that the action complained of was taken for the purpose of safeguarding national security see the Employment Tribunals Act 1996 s 10(1); and PARA 1448.

4 'Appropriate time' means a time outside the worker's working hours, or a time within his working hours at which, in accordance with arrangements agreed with or consent given by his employer, it is permissible for him to take part in the activities of a trade union or, as the case may be, make use of trade union services: Trade Union and Labour Relations (Consolidation) Act 1992 s 145A(2) (as added: see note 1). 'Working hours', in relation to a worker, means any time when, in accordance with his contract of employment (see PARA 892), or other contract personally to do work or perform services, he is required to be at work: s 145A(3) (as so added). 'Trade union services' means services made available to the worker by an independent trade union by virtue of his membership of the union, and references to a worker's 'making use' of trade union services include his consenting to the raising of a matter on his behalf by an independent trade union of which he is a member: s 145A(4) (as so added). As to the meaning of 'independent trade union' see PARA 904.

5 Trade Union and Labour Relations (Consolidation) Act 1992 s 145A(1)(b) (as added: see note 1).

6   Trade Union and Labour Relations (Consolidation) Act 1992 s 145A(1)(c) (as added: see note 1).

7   Trade Union and Labour Relations (Consolidation) Act 1992 s 145A(1)(d) (as added: see note 1).

8   Trade Union and Labour Relations (Consolidation) Act 1992 s 145A(5) (as added: see note 1). The remedy of a person for infringement of a right conferred on him by s 145A is by way of a complaint to an employment tribunal in accordance with Pt III (ss 137–177), and not otherwise: s 145F(4) (as so added).

The provisions of the Employment Tribunals Act 1996 ss 18A–18B (conciliation) (see PARA 152) apply in the case of matters which could be the subject of employment tribunal proceedings under the Trade Union and Labour Relations (Consolidation) Act 1992 s 145A, and the Employment Tribunals Act 1996 s 18C applies in the case of such proceedings themselves: see s 18(1)(a), (1A) (s 18(1)(a) substituted by SI 2014/431; the Employment Tribunals Act 1996 s 18(1A) added by the Enterprise and Regulatory Reform Act 2013 Sch 1 paras 2, 5(1), (7)). As to employment tribunals see PARA 1399 et seq. An appeal lies to the Employment Appeal Tribunal on any question of law arising from any decision of, or arising in any proceedings before, an employment tribunal under or by virtue of the Trade Union and Labour Relations (Consolidation) Act 1992: see the Employment Tribunals Act 1996 s 21(1)(d); and PARA 1428. As to the Employment Appeal Tribunal see PARA 1422 et seq.

1052.   Inducements relating to collective bargaining. A worker[1] who is a member of an independent trade union which is recognised, or seeking to be recognised, by his employer[2] has the right not to have an offer made to him by his employer if acceptance of the offer, together with other workers' acceptance of offers which the employer also makes to them[3], would have the prohibited result[4], and the employer's sole or main purpose in making the offers is to achieve that result[5]. A worker or former worker may present a complaint to an employment tribunal on the ground that his employer has made him such an offer[6].

1   As to the meaning of 'worker' for these purposes see PARA 1051 note 1.
2   As to the meaning of 'employer' for these purposes see PARA 1051 note 2.
3   It is immaterial whether such offers are made to the workers simultaneously: Trade Union and Labour Relations (Consolidation) Act 1992 s 145B(3) (ss 145B, 145F added by the Employment Relations Act 2004 s 29).
4   Ie that the workers' terms of employment, or any of those terms, will not, or will no longer, be determined by collective agreement negotiated by or on behalf of the union: Trade Union and Labour Relations (Consolidation) Act 1992 s 145B(2) (as added: see note 3).
5   Trade Union and Labour Relations (Consolidation) Act 1992 s 145B(1) (as added: see note 3). Having terms of employment determined by collective agreement is not regarded for the purposes of s 145A (see PARA 1051), s 146 (see PARA 1048) or s 152 (see PARA 1056) as making use of a trade union service: s 145B(4) (as so added). As to where it is shown that the action complained of was taken for the purpose of safeguarding national security see the Employment Tribunals Act 1996 s 10(1); and PARA 1448.
6   Trade Union and Labour Relations (Consolidation) Act 1992 s 145B(5) (as added: see note 3). The remedy of a person for infringement of a right conferred on him by s 145B is by way of a complaint to an employment tribunal in accordance with Pt III (ss 137–177), and not otherwise: s 145F(4) (as so added).

The provisions of the Employment Tribunals Act 1996 ss 18A–18B (conciliation) (see PARA 152) apply in the case of matters which could be the subject of employment tribunal proceedings under the Trade Union and Labour Relations (Consolidation) Act 1992 s 145B, and the Employment Tribunals Act 1996 s 18C applies in the case of such proceedings themselves: see s 18(1)(a), (1A) (s 18(1)(a) substituted by SI 2014/431; the Employment Tribunals Act 1996 s 18(1A) added by the Enterprise and Regulatory Reform Act 2013 Sch 1 paras 2, 5(1), (7)). As to employment tribunals see PARA 1399 et seq. An appeal lies to the Employment Appeal Tribunal on any question of law arising from any decision of, or arising in any proceedings before, an employment tribunal under or by virtue of the Trade Union and Labour Relations (Consolidation) Act 1992: see the Employment Tribunals Act 1996 s 21(1)(d); and PARA 1428. As to the Employment Appeal Tribunal see PARA 1422 et seq.

1053.   Time limit for proceedings on complaint regarding inducements.   An employment tribunal[1] must not consider a complaint[2] unless it is presented:
  (1)   before the end of the period of three months beginning with the date when the offer was made or, where the offer is part of a series of similar offers to the complainant, the date when the last of the series of offers was made[3], subject to an extension to facilitate conciliation before the institution of proceedings[4]; or
  (2)   where the tribunal is satisfied that it was not reasonably practicable for the complaint to be presented before the end of that period, within such further period as it considers reasonable[5].

1   As to employment tribunals see PARA 1399 et seq.
2   Ie a complaint under the Trade Union and Labour Relations (Consolidation) Act 1992 s 145A or 145B: see PARAS 1051–1052.
3   Trade Union and Labour Relations (Consolidation) Act 1992 s 145C(1)(a) (added by the Employment Relations Act 2004 s 29; renumbered by the Enterprise and Regulatory Reform Act 2013 Sch 2 paras 1, 7).
4   The Trade Union and Labour Relations (Consolidation) Act 1992 s 292A (extension of time limits to facilitate conciliation before institution of proceedings: see PARA 1455) applies for the purposes of s 145C(1)(a): s 145C(2) (added by the Enterprise and Regulatory Reform Act 2013 Sch 2 paras 1, 7).
5   Trade Union and Labour Relations (Consolidation) Act 1992 s 145C(1)(b) (as added and renumbered: see note 3).

1054.   Consideration of complaint regarding inducements.   On a complaint[1] it is for the employer[2] to show what was his sole or main purpose in making the offer or offers[3]. In determining any question whether the employer made the offer or offers, or the purpose for which he did so, no account is to be taken of any pressure which was exercised on him by calling, organising, procuring or financing a strike or other industrial action, or by threatening to do so, and any such question must be determined as if no such pressure had been exercised[4].

1   Ie a complaint under the Trade Union and Labour Relations (Consolidation) Act 1992 s 145A or s 145B: see PARAS 1051–1052.
2   As to the meaning of 'employer' for these purposes see PARA 1051 note 2.
3   Trade Union and Labour Relations (Consolidation) Act 1992 s 145D(1), (2) (s 145D added by the Employment Relations Act 2004 s 29).
4   Trade Union and Labour Relations (Consolidation) Act 1992 s 145D(3) (as added: see note 3). In determining whether an employer's sole or main purpose in making offers was the purpose mentioned in s 145B(1) (see PARA 1052), the matters taken into account must include any evidence (1) that when the offers were made the employer had recently changed or sought to change, or did not wish to use, arrangements agreed with the union for collective bargaining; (2) that when the offers were made the employer did not wish to enter into arrangements proposed by the union for collective bargaining; or (3) that the offers were made only to particular workers, and were made with the sole or main purpose of rewarding those particular workers for their high level of performance or of retaining them because of their special value to the employer: s 145D(4) (as so added).

1055.   Remedies on a complaint regarding inducements.   Where the employment tribunal[1] finds that a complaint[2] is well-founded, it must make a declaration to that effect and must make an award[3] to be paid by the employer[4] to the complainant in respect of the offer complained of[5]. Where an offer made[6] is accepted (1) if the acceptance results in the worker's[7] agreeing to vary his terms of employment, the employer cannot enforce the agreement to vary, or recover any sum paid or other asset transferred by him under the agreement to vary[8]; and (2) if as a result of the acceptance the worker's terms of employment are varied, nothing[9] makes the variation unenforceable by either party[10].

In ascertaining any amount of compensation[11], no reduction may be made on the ground that the complainant caused or contributed to his loss, or to the act or failure complained of, by accepting or not accepting an offer[12], or that he has received or is entitled to an award[13].

1   As to employment tribunals see PARA 1399 et seq.
2   Ie a complaint under the Trade Union and Labour Relations (Consolidation) Act 1992 s 145A or s 145B: see PARAS 1051–1052.
3   The amount of the award is £3,715, subject to any adjustment of the award that may fall to be made under the Employment Act 2002 Pt 3 (ss 34–40): Trade Union and Labour Relations (Consolidation) Act 1992 s 145E(3) (s 145E added by the Employment Relations Act 2004 s 29; the Trade Union and Labour Relations (Consolidation) Act 1992 s 145E(3) amended by SI 2014/382). This amount has effect on or after 6 April 2014: Employment Rights (Increase of Limits) Order 2014, SI 2014/382, arts 1(1), 4(1). In a case where the appropriate date fell before 6 April 2014, the limit having effect immediately before that date continues to apply: see art 4(1). As to the meaning of 'appropriate date' see art 4(2).
4   As to the meaning of 'employer' for these purposes see PARA 1051 note 2.
5   Trade Union and Labour Relations (Consolidation) Act 1992 s 145E(1), (2) (as added: see note 3).
6   Ie made in contravention of the Trade Union and Labour Relations (Consolidation) Act 1992 s 145A or s 145B: see note 2.
7   As to the meaning of 'worker' for these purposes see PARA 1051 note 1.
8   Trade Union and Labour Relations (Consolidation) Act 1992 s 145E(4)(a) (as added: see note 3).
9   Ie nothing in the Trade Union and Labour Relations (Consolidation) Act 1992 s 145A or s 145B: see note 2.
10 Trade Union and Labour Relations (Consolidation) Act 1992 s 145E(4)(b) (as added: see note 3). Nothing in s 145A (see PARA 1051), s 145B (see PARA 1052) or s 145E prejudices any rights conferred by s 146 (see PARA 1048) or s 149 (see PARA 1050): s 145E(5) (as so added).
11 Ie under the Trade Union and Labour Relations (Consolidation) Act 1992 s 149: see PARA 1050.
12 Ie an offer made in contravention of the Trade Union and Labour Relations (Consolidation) Act 1992 s 145A or s 145B (see note 2): s 145E(6)(a) (as added: see note 3).
13 Ie an award under the Trade Union and Labour Relations (Consolidation) Act 1992 s 145E: s 145E(6)(b) (as added: see note 3).

(iv) Dismissal for Trade Union Reasons

1056. Dismissal or selection for redundancy on grounds related to trade union membership or activities. The dismissal[1] of an employee[2] is to be regarded as unfair[3] if the reason for it (or, if more than one, the principal reason[4]) was that the employee:

(1)   was, or proposed to become, a member of an independent trade union[5];

(2)   had taken part, or proposed to take part, in the activities[6] of an independent trade union at an appropriate time[7];

(3)   had made use, or proposed to make use, of trade union services at an appropriate time[8];

(4)   had failed to accept an offer made in contravention of the provisions on inducements relating to union membership or activities, or inducements relating to collective bargaining[9]; or

(5)   was not a member of any trade union, or of a particular trade union, or of one of a number of particular trade unions, or had refused, or proposed to refuse, to become or remain a member[10].

Where the reason or principal reason for the dismissal of an employee was that he was redundant[11], but it is shown:

(a)   that the circumstances constituting the redundancy applied equally to one or more other employees in the same undertaking who held positions similar to that held by him and who have not been dismissed by the employer; and

(b)   that the reason (or, if more than one, the principal reason) why he was selected for dismissal was one of those specified in heads (1) to (5) above,

the dismissal is also to be regarded[12] as unfair[13].

The qualifying period[14] does not apply to a dismissal which is regarded[15] as unfair[16].

1   For these purposes, 'dismiss' and 'dismissal' are to be construed in accordance with the Employment Rights Act 1996 Pt X (ss 94–134A) (see PARA 757 et seq): Trade Union and Labour Relations (Consolidation) Act 1992 s 298 (definition amended by the Employment Rights Act 1996 Sch 1 para 56(1), (19)).

2   As to the meaning of 'employee' see PARA 892.

3   Ie unfair for the purposes of the Employment Rights Act 1996 Pt X which contains the general law on unfair dismissal. Part X has effect subject to the provisions of the Trade Union and Labour Relations (Consolidation) Act 1992 ss 152–166 (see the text and notes 1–2, 4–16; and PARAS 1057–1062): s 167(1) (amended by the Employment Rights Act 1996 Sch 1 para 56(1), (12)(a)). The use of the phrase 'is to be regarded' shows that this head of dismissal is automatically unfair. The Trade Union and Labour Relations (Consolidation) Act 1992 ss 152–166 are to be construed as one with the Employment Rights Act 1996 Pt X but nothing therein is to be construed as conferring a right to complain of unfair dismissal from employment of a description to which Pt X does not otherwise apply: Trade Union and Labour Relations (Consolidation) Act 1992 s 167(2), (3) (amended by the Employment Rights Act 1996 Sch 1 para 56(1), (12)(b)). As to excluded classes of employment for these purposes see PARA 758 et seq.

4   As to the meaning of 'reason or principal reason' see PARA 769. One of the enumerated reasons must be shown; it is not enough to show simply that the employee would not have been dismissed had he not been a union member: *CGB Publishing v Killey* [1993] IRLR 520, EAT. In a redundancy case this may entail inquiring why this particular employee was not offered other work when others were: *Driver v Cleveland Structural Engineering Co Ltd* [1994] ICR 372, [1994] IRLR 636, EAT.

5   Trade Union and Labour Relations (Consolidation) Act 1992 s 152(1)(a) (amended by the Employment Rights Act 1996 Sch 1 para 56(1), (7)(a); the Employment Relations Act 2004 s 32(1), (2), Sch 2). For these purposes, references to being or becoming or ceasing to remain a member of a trade union include references to being, becoming or ceasing to remain a member of a particular branch or section of that union or of one of a number of particular branches or sections of that trade union: Trade Union and Labour Relations (Consolidation) Act 1992 s 152(4) (amended by the Employment Relations Act 2004 s 32(1), (5), Sch 2). References in the Trade Union and Labour Relations (Consolidation) Act 1992 s 152 to taking part in the activities of a trade union, and to services made available by a trade union by virtue of membership of the union are to be construed in accordance with s 152(4): s 152(5) (added by the Employment Relations Act 2004 s 32(6)). As to the meaning of 'branch or section', in relation to a trade union, see PARA 898 note 5; as to the meaning of 'trade union' see PARA 891; and as to the meaning of 'independent trade union' see PARA 904. It has been held that 'membership' can include important aspects and consequences of membership, eg having one's employment law rights protected by the union: *Discount Tobacco and Confectionery Ltd v Armitage* [1995] ICR 431n, [1990] IRLR 15, EAT. In *Associated Newspapers Ltd v Wilson, Associated British Ports v Palmer* [1995] ICR 406, [1995] IRLR 258, HL (decided under the Trade Union and Labour Relations (Consolidation) Act 1992 s 146: see PARA 1048) a majority stated obiter that, although *Discount Tobacco and Confectionery Ltd v Armitage* [1995] ICR 431n, [1990] IRLR 15, EAT was correct on its facts, it established no such general principles. (For the decision of the European Court of Human Rights in *Associated Newspapers Ltd v Wilson, Associated British Ports v Palmer* [1995] ICR 406, [1995] IRLR 258, HL see Application 30668/96 *Wilson v United Kingdom* (2002) 13 BHRC 39, [2002] IRLR 568, ECtHR.) Subsequently, however, the Employment Appeal Tribunal held that its own previous decision in that case can still be relied on in a case under the Trade Union and Labour Relations (Consolidation) Act 1992 s 152, where a robust approach is to be taken as to what really caused the dismissal: *Speciality Care plc v Pachela* [1996] ICR 633, [1996] IRLR 248, EAT.

6   In order to come within this protection, the activity in question must have a genuine trade union connection, and not merely be the actions of an individual trade unionist: *Chant v Aquaboats Ltd* [1978] 3 All ER 102, [1978] ICR 643, EAT; *Drew v St Edmundsbury Borough Council* [1980] ICR 513, [1980] IRLR 459, EAT. If that is the case, the approach to what constitutes a trade union activity should be broadly construed: *Dixon and Shaw v West Ella Developments Ltd* [1978] ICR 856, [1978] IRLR 151, EAT. If an activity is that of a trade union, it does not lose that quality merely because it involves criticism of union policy (*British Airways Engine Overhaul Ltd v Francis* [1981] ICR 278, [1981] IRLR 9, EAT) or because criticism of the employers is made in the course of a recruiting presentation to new employees (*Bass Taverns Ltd v Burgess* [1995] IRLR 596, CA). Not every such act is protected, however, because, eg wholly unreasonable, extraneous or malicious acts done in support of trade union activities might be a ground for a dismissal which would not be unfair: *Lyon and Scherk v St James Press Ltd* [1976] ICR 413, [1976] IRLR 215, EAT; *Bass Taverns Ltd v Burgess* [1995] IRLR 596, CA. A balance must be struck between, on the one hand, obstructing the right to take part in the affairs of the trade union by too easily finding acts done for the purpose to be a justification for dismissal and, on the other, using the protection afforded by the legislation as a cloak or an excuse for conduct which ordinarily would justify dismissal: *Lyon and Scherk v St James Press Ltd*. Unless trade union activity is carried out in a way involving acting in bad faith, dishonestly or for some extraneous cause or in any other way such as to take the actions in question outside the proper scope of trade union activities, the way in which trade union activities are carried out is not relevant for the purposes of the Trade Union and Labour Relations (Consolidation) Act 1992 s 152: *Mihaj v Sodexho Ltd* [2014] All ER (D) 63 (Jun), EAT.

    With regard to previous union activities (ie with a former employer, or in previous employment with the same employer) there is a difficult distinction to draw; if the employer's objections relate purely to those previous activities, this special protection does not apply (*Birmingham City District Council v Beyer* [1978] 1 All ER 910, [1977] IRLR 211, EAT), but, if the employer acts in order to prevent or deter an employee from acting in similar fashion in the current employment, that may come within the protection (*Fitzpatrick v British Railways Board* [1992] ICR 221, [1991] IRLR 376, CA). Fraud in obtaining employment remains a dismissible offence, even if the false name, particulars etc were given because of the employee's previous history of union activities: *Birmingham City District Council v Beyer* [1978] 1 All ER 910, [1977] IRLR 211, EAT.

7   Trade Union and Labour Relations (Consolidation) Act 1992 s 152(1)(b) (amended by the Employment Rights Act 1996 Sch 1 para 56(1), (7)(a); the Employment Relations Act 2004 s 32(1), (2), Sch 2). For the purposes of the Trade Union and Labour Relations (Consolidation) Act 1992 s 152(1), an 'appropriate time' means: (1) a time outside the employee's working hours; or (2) a time within his working hours at which, in accordance with arrangements agreed with or consent given by his employer, it is permissible for him to take part in the activities of a trade union or (as the case may be) make use of trade union services; and 'working hours', in relation to an employee, means any time when, in accordance with his contract of employment, he is required to be at work: Trade Union and Labour Relations (Consolidation) Act 1992 s 152(2) (amended by the Employment Relations Act 2004 s 32(1), (3)). As to the meanings of 'employer', 'employment' and 'contract of employment' see PARA 892. 'Trade union services' means services made available to the employee by an independent trade union by virtue of his membership of the union; and references to an employee's 'making use' of trade union services include his consenting to the raising of a matter on his behalf by an independent trade union of which he is a member: Trade Union and Labour Relations (Consolidation) Act 1992 s 152(2A) (s 152(2A), (2B) added by the Employment Relations Act 2004 s 32(4)). The employer's consent may be established by custom or implication (*Zucker v Astrid Jewels Ltd* [1978] ICR 1088, [1978] IRLR 385, EAT); but it is not to be inferred simply from silence (*Marley Tile Co Ltd v Shaw* [1980] ICR 72, [1980] IRLR 25, CA). If the employer in fact refuses, however unreasonably, there cannot be an 'appropriate time' and the employee's recourse lies for breach of the Trade Union and Labour Relations (Consolidation) Act 1992 s 170 (time off for trade union activities: see PARA 1066) if the union is recognised: *Robb v Leon Motor Services Ltd* [1978] ICR 506, [1978] IRLR 26, EAT. Time outside working hours can be an 'appropriate time', even though the employees are on the employer's premises: *Post Office v Union of Post Office Workers and Crouch* [1974] 1 All ER 229, [1974] ICR 378, HL (decided under similar provisions in the Industrial Relations Act 1971 (repealed)); *Carter v Wiltshire County Council* [1979] IRLR 331.

    If the employer does give consent, that is not to be construed as subject to an implied limitation that the employee will say or do nothing contrary to the employer's interests: *Bass Taverns Ltd v Burgess* [1995] IRLR 596, CA.

One gap in the protection of the Trade Union and Labour Relations (Consolidation) Act 1992 s 152(1)(b) arose where union members were dismissed as a reprisal for the actions of their union, not because of anything they had done as members: *Carrington v Therm-A-Stor Ltd* [1983] 1 All ER 796, [1983] ICR 208, CA. This may now be addressed in certain cases (such as *Carrington v Therm-A-Stor Ltd* [1983] 1 All ER 796, [1983] ICR 208, CA) by the inclusion of the Trade Union and Labour Relations (Consolidation) Act 1992 s 152(1)(ba) (see the text and note 8); if not, employees could seek to claim unfair dismissal on ordinary principles, but only if they have the necessary one year's qualifying service.

8 Trade Union and Labour Relations (Consolidation) Act 1992 s 152(1)(ba) (s 152(1)(ba), (bb) added by the Employment Relations Act 2004 s 32(1), (2), Sch 2). Where the reason or one of the reasons for dismissal was that an independent trade union, with or without the employee's consent, raised a matter on behalf of the employee as one of its members, the reason is to be treated as falling within the Trade Union and Labour Relations (Consolidation) Act 1992 s 152(1)(ba): s 152(2B) (as added: see note 7).

9 Trade Union and Labour Relations (Consolidation) Act 1992 s 152(1)(bb) (as added: see note 8). The reference to provisions on inducements relating to union membership or activities, or inducements relating to collective bargaining is a reference to s 145A or s 145B: see PARAS 1051–1052.

10 Trade Union and Labour Relations (Consolidation) Act 1992 s 152(1)(c) (amended by the Employment Rights Act 1996 Sch 1 para 56(1), (7)(a)). Where the reason, or one of the reasons, for the dismissal was: (1) the employee's refusal, or proposed refusal, to comply with a requirement, whether or not imposed by his contract of employment or in writing, that, in the event of his not being a member of any trade union, or of a particular trade union, or of one of a number of particular trade unions, he must make one or more payments; or (2) his objection, or proposed objection, however expressed, to the operation of a provision, whether or not forming part of his contract of employment or in writing, under which, in the event mentioned in head (1) above, his employer is entitled to deduct one or more sums from the remuneration payable to him in respect of his employment, the reason is to be treated as falling within the Trade Union and Labour Relations (Consolidation) Act 1992 s 152(1)(c): s 152(3).

11 As to redundancy generally see PARA 835 et seq.

12 Ie for the purposes of the Employment Rights Act 1996 Pt X: see PARA 757 et seq.

13 Trade Union and Labour Relations (Consolidation) Act 1992 s 153 (amended by the Employment Rights Act 1996 Sch 1 para 56(1), (7)(b)). As to the Trade Union and Labour Relations (Consolidation) Act 1992 ss 152, 153 see *Bombadier Aerospace/Short Brothers plc v McConnell* [2007] NICA 27, [2008] IRLR 51; and PARA 1057 note 7.

14 Ie the Employment Rights Act 1996 s 108: see PARA 758.

15 Ie by virtue of the Trade Union and Labour Relations (Consolidation) Act 1992 s 152 or s 153: see the text and notes 1–13.

16 Trade Union and Labour Relations (Consolidation) Act 1992 s 154 (substituted by the Employment Relations Act 2004 s 35). The reference is to being unfair for the purposes of the Employment Rights Act 1996 Pt X: see the Trade Union and Labour Relations (Consolidation) Act 1992 s 154 (as so substituted).

1057. Special provisions concerning compensation and other remedies where dismissal is for trade union reasons. Where a dismissal[1] is unfair because it is a dismissal, or selection for redundancy, on grounds related to union membership or activities[2], there is a minimum set for the basic award of compensation[3].

Where an employment tribunal makes an award of compensation in a case of unfair dismissal on grounds related to union membership or activities[4], the tribunal must disregard, in considering whether it would be just and equitable to reduce, or further reduce, the amount of any part of the award, certain conduct or action of the complainant[5].

An employee who presents a complaint of unfair dismissal[6] alleging that the dismissal is unfair on grounds relating to trade union membership or activities[7] may also apply to the tribunal for interim relief[8].

1 As to the meaning of 'dismissal' see PARA 1056 note 1.

2 Ie under the Trade Union and Labour Relations (Consolidation) Act 1992 s 152(1) or s 153: see PARA 1056. See also note 7.

3 Trade Union and Labour Relations (Consolidation) Act 1992 s 156(1). The minimum so set is £5,676: s 156(1) (amended by SI 2014/382). This minimum has effect on or after 6 April 2014: Employment Rights (Increase of Limits) Order 2014, SI 2014/382, arts 1(1), 4(1). In a case where the appropriate date fell before 6 April 2014, the limits having effect immediately before that date continue to apply: see art 4(1). As to the meaning of 'appropriate date' see art 4(2). This is the minimum amount of the award before any reduction is made in relation to unreasonable refusal of reinstatement, contributory fault or receipt of a redundancy payment under the Employment Rights Act 1996 s 122 (see PARA 817): Trade Union and Labour Relations (Consolidation) Act 1992 s 156(1) (amended by the Employment Rights Act 1996 Sch 1 para 56(1), (9)(a)). Where, however, the dismissal is unfair by reason of the Trade Union and Labour Relations (Consolidation) Act 1992 s 153 (see PARA 1056), the Employment Rights Act 1996 s 122(2) (reduction for contributory fault) applies in relation to so much of the basic award as is payable because of the Trade Union and Labour Relations (Consolidation) Act 1992 s 156(1): s 156(2) (amended by the Employment Rights Act 1996 Sch 1 para 56(1), (9)(b)).

4 Ie under the Trade Union and Labour Relations (Consolidation) Act 1992 s 152 or s 153: see PARA 1056.

5 Trade Union and Labour Relations (Consolidation) Act 1992 s 155(1) (amended by the Employment Rights (Dispute Resolution) Act 1998 s 1(2)(a)). The conduct in question is conduct or action of the complainant in so far as it constitutes a breach or proposed breach of a requirement: (1) to be or become a member of any trade union or a particular trade union or one of a number of particular trade unions; (2) to cease to be, or refrain from becoming, a member of any trade union or a particular trade union or one of a number of particular trade unions; (3) not to take part in the activities of any trade union or a particular trade union or one of a number of particular trade unions; or (4) not to make use of services made available by any trade union or by a particular trade union or by one of a number of particular trade unions: s 155(2) (amended by the Employment Relations Act 2004 Sch 1 para 11(1), (2), Sch 2). For these purposes, a requirement means a requirement imposed on the complainant by or under an arrangement or contract of employment or other agreement: Trade Union and Labour Relations (Consolidation) Act 1992 s 155(2). Conduct or action of the complainant is to be disregarded in so far as it constitutes acceptance of or failure to accept an offer made in contravention of s 145A (see PARA 1051) or s 145B (see PARA 1052): s 155(2A) (added by the Employment Relations Act 2004 Sch 1 para 11(1), (3)). Conduct or action of the complainant is also to be disregarded in so far as it constitutes a refusal, or proposed refusal, to comply with a requirement of a kind mentioned in the Trade Union and Labour Relations (Consolidation) Act 1992 s 152(3)(a) (payment in lieu of membership) (see PARA 1056 note 10 head (1)) or an objection, or proposed objection (however expressed) to the operation of a provision of a kind mentioned in s 152(3)(b) (deductions in lieu of membership) (see PARA 1056 note 10 head (2)): s 155(3). If, however, the complainant's conduct prior to the dismissal, eg in how he handled the dispute, is capable of criticism, that can be taken into account as contributory fault: *Transport and General Workers' Union v Howard* [1992] ICR 106, [1992] IRLR 170, EAT. As to the meaning of 'trade union' see PARA 891; and as to the meaning of 'contract of employment' see PARA 892.

6 For these purposes, 'complaint of unfair dismissal' means a complaint under the Employment Rights Act 1996 s 111 (see PARA 804): Trade Union and Labour Relations (Consolidation) Act 1992 s 167(2) (definition amended by the Employment Rights Act 1996 Sch 1 para 56(1), (12)(b)). See, however, the Trade Union and Labour Relations (Consolidation) Act 1992 s 167(1), (3); and PARA 1056 note 3.

7 Ie under the Trade Union and Labour Relations (Consolidation) Act 1992 s 152. On its face, s 152 does not apply interim relief in a case where the employee claims that he was made redundant for trade union reasons (because the case comes under s 153 rather than under s 152); however, the Northern Ireland Court of Appeal held that a 'fabricated' redundancy (ie one engineered to get rid of the claimant) can come within s 152, and so give rise to an application for interim relief: *Bombadier Aerospace/Short Brothers plc v McConnell* [2007] NICA 27, [2008] IRLR 51 (but cf *McConnell v Bombadier Aerospace/Short Brothers plc* [2009] IRLR 201, NICA where the claim finally failed because the tribunal found that there was actually a genuine redundancy, so that only the Trade Union and Labour Relations (Consolidation) Act 1992 s 153 was in issue).

8 Trade Union and Labour Relations (Consolidation) Act 1992 s 161(1). As to the procedure on such an application, the orders which may be made and the consequences of non-compliance see PARAS 1058–1061.

1058. Application for interim relief where dismissal is for trade union reasons. An employment tribunal must not entertain an application for interim relief[1] unless it is presented[2] to the tribunal before the end of the period of seven days immediately following the effective date of termination[3], whether before, on or after that date[4]. In a case where the employee alleges that the dismissal related to union membership or activities[5], the tribunal must not entertain an application for interim relief unless, before the end of that period, there is also so presented a certificate in writing signed by an authorised official[6] of the independent trade union[7] of which the employee was or proposed to become a member, stating:

(1)   that on the date of the dismissal[8] the employee was or proposed to become a member of the union; and

(2)   that there appear to be reasonable grounds for supposing that the reason for his dismissal (or, if more than one, the principal reason[9]) was one alleged in the complaint[10].

An employment tribunal must determine an application for interim relief as soon as practicable after receiving the application and, where appropriate, the requisite certificate[11]. It must not exercise any power it has of postponing the hearing of such an application, except where it is satisfied that special circumstances exist which justify it in doing so[12].

1   Ie under the Trade Union and Labour Relations (Consolidation) Act 1992 s 161(1): see PARA 1057. As to the hearing of such an application, and as to the making of an order for interim relief, see PARA 1059. As to employment tribunals see PARA 1399 et seq.

2   As to when an application is presented see PARAS 804, 1461.

3   For these purposes, 'effective date of termination', in relation to an employee, is to be construed in accordance with the Employment Rights Act 1996 Pt X (ss 94–134A) (see PARA 757 et seq): Trade Union and Labour Relations (Consolidation) Act 1992 s 298 (definition substituted by the Employment Rights Act 1996 s 240, Sch 1 para 56(1), (19)). The Employment Rights Act 1996 Pt X and the Trade Union and Labour Relations (Consolidation) Act 1992 ss 152–166 are to be construed as one: s 167(2) (amended by the Employment Rights Act 1996 Sch 1 para 56(1), (12)(b)). As to the meaning of 'employee' see PARA 892.

4   Trade Union and Labour Relations (Consolidation) Act 1992 s 161(2).

5   Ie where the employee relies on the Trade Union and Labour Relations (Consolidation) Act 1992 s 152(1)(a), (b) or (ba) (see PARA 1056 heads (1), (2), (3)) or on s 152(1)(bb) (see PARA 1056 head (4)) otherwise than in relation to an offer in contravention of s 145A(1)(d) (see PARA 1051). This category of 'unfair by reason of s 152' can potentially, it seems, cover a redundancy dismissal too if it is a sham: see *Bombardier Aerospace/Short Brothers plc v McConnell* [2007] NICA 27, [2008] IRLR 51 (a case relating to the equivalent Northern Ireland provisions).

6   For these purposes, an 'authorised official' means an official of the trade union authorised by it to act for these purposes: Trade Union and Labour Relations (Consolidation) Act 1992 s 161(4). A document purporting to be an authorisation of an official by a trade union to act for these purposes and to be signed on behalf of the union is to be taken to be such an authorisation unless the contrary is proved; and a document purporting to be a certificate signed by such an official is to be taken to be signed by him unless the contrary is proved: s 161(5). There is no need for the person signing to state expressly that he is the duly authorised official; such authority will be assumed unless challenged: *Sulemany v Habib Bank Ltd* [1983] ICR 60, EAT. See also *Stone v Charrington & Co Ltd* [1977] ICR 248, EAT.

7   As to the meaning of 'independent trade union' see PARA 904.

8   For these purposes, the date of dismissal is to be taken to be: (1) where the employee's contract of employment was terminated by notice, whether given by his employer or him, the date on which the employer's notice was given; and (2) in any other case, the effective date of termination: Trade Union and Labour Relations (Consolidation) Act 1992 s 161(6). As to the meaning of 'contract of employment' see PARA 892.

9   As to the meaning of 'reason or principal reason' see PARA 769.

10   Trade Union and Labour Relations (Consolidation) Act 1992 s 161(3) (amended by the Employment Relations Act 2004 Sch 1 para 12). The certificate need not be in any particular form, but must comply in substance with the Trade Union and Labour Relations

(Consolidation) Act 1992 s 161(3): *Stone v Charmington & Co Ltd* [1977] ICR 248, EAT; *Bradley v Edward Ryde & Sons* [1979] ICR 488, EAT; *Sulemany v Habib Bank Ltd* [1983] ICR 60, EAT.
11 Trade Union and Labour Relations (Consolidation) Act 1992 s 162(1) (amended by the Employment Rights (Dispute Resolution) Act 1998 s 1(2)(a)). The tribunal must give to the employer, not later than seven days before the hearing, a copy of the application and any certificate, together with notice of the date, time and place of the hearing: Trade Union and Labour Relations (Consolidation) Act 1992 s 162(2). If a request under s 160 (awards against third parties) (see PARA 1062) is made three days or more before the date of the hearing, the tribunal must also give to the person to whom the request relates, as soon as reasonably practicable, a copy of the application and of any certificate, together with notice of the date, time and place of the hearing: s 162(3). As to the procedure on such an application see PARAS 1059, 1473 text and notes 19–20.
12 Trade Union and Labour Relations (Consolidation) Act 1992 s 162(4).

1059. Procedure on hearing of application for interim relief where dismissal is for trade union reasons and making of order. If, on hearing an application for interim relief[1], it appears to the employment tribunal that it is likely that, on determining the complaint to which the application relates, it will find[2] that the complainant has been unfairly dismissed, the following provisions apply[3].

The tribunal must announce its findings and explain to both parties, if present, what powers the tribunal may exercise on the application and in what circumstances it will exercise them, and ask the employer[4], if present, whether he is willing, pending the determination or settlement of the complaint:

(1)   to reinstate the employee[5], that is to say, to treat him in all respects as if he had not been dismissed; or

(2)   if not, to re-engage him in another job on terms and conditions not less favourable[6] than those which would have been applicable to him if he had not been dismissed[7].

If the employer states that he is willing to reinstate the employee, the tribunal must make an order to that effect[8].

If the employer states that he is willing to re-engage the employee in another job, and specifies the terms and conditions on which he is willing to do so, the tribunal must ask the employee whether he is willing to accept the job on those terms and conditions; and:

(a)   if the employee is willing to accept the job on those terms and conditions, the tribunal must make an order to that effect; and

(b)   if he is not, then, if the tribunal is of the opinion that the refusal is reasonable, the tribunal must make an order for the continuation of his contract of employment[9], and otherwise the tribunal must make no order[10].

If, on the hearing of an application for interim relief, the employer fails to attend before the tribunal, or states that he is unwilling either so to reinstate the employee or re-engage him, the tribunal must make an order for the continuation of the employee's contract of employment[11].

1   As to applications for interim relief see PARA 1058.
2   Ie by virtue of the Trade Union and Labour Relations (Consolidation) Act 1992 s 152: see PARA 1056.
3   See the Trade Union and Labour Relations (Consolidation) Act 1992 s 163(1). As to employment tribunals see PARA 1399 et seq.
4   As to the meaning of 'employer' see PARA 892.
5   As to the meaning of 'employee' see PARA 892.
6   For these purposes, 'terms and conditions not less favourable than those which would have been applicable to him if he had not been dismissed' means, as regards seniority, pension rights and

other similar rights, that the period prior to the dismissal is to be regarded as continuous with his employment following the dismissal: Trade Union and Labour Relations (Consolidation) Act 1992 s 163(3).

7   Trade Union and Labour Relations (Consolidation) Act 1992 s 163(2).
8   Trade Union and Labour Relations (Consolidation) Act 1992 s 163(4).
9   As to the meaning of 'contract of employment' see PARA 892.
10   Trade Union and Labour Relations (Consolidation) Act 1992 s 163(5). As to orders for continuation of a contract of employment see PARA 1060.
11   Trade Union and Labour Relations (Consolidation) Act 1992 s 163(6).

1060. Order for continuation of the contract of employment. An order for the continuation of a contract of employment[1] is an order that the contract of employment continue in force:

(1)   for the purposes of pay or any other benefit derived from the employment, seniority, pension rights and other similar matters; and

(2)   for the purpose of determining for any purpose the period for which the employee[2] has been continuously employed,

from the date of its termination, whether before or after the making of the order, until the determination or settlement of the complaint[3].

Where the tribunal makes such an order, it must specify in the order the amount which is to be paid by the employer[4] to the employee by way of pay in respect of each normal pay period, or part of any such period, falling between the date of dismissal and the determination or settlement of the complaint[5].

The amount so specified is to be that which the employee could reasonably have been expected to earn during that period, or part, and must be paid:

(a)   in the case of payment for any such period falling wholly or partly after the making of the order, on the normal pay day for that period; and

(b)   in the case of a payment for any past period, within such time as may be specified in the order[6].

Any payment made to an employee by an employer under his contract of employment, or by way of damages for breach of that contract, in respect of a normal pay period or part of any such period is to go towards discharging the employer's liability in respect of that period[7]; and, conversely, any such payment in respect of a period is to go towards discharging any liability of the employer under, or in respect of the breach of, the contract of employment in respect of that period[8].

If an employee, on or after being dismissed by his employer, receives a lump sum which, or part of which, is in lieu of wages but is not referable to any normal pay period, the tribunal must take the payment into account in determining the amount of pay to be payable in pursuance of any such order[9].

At any time between the making of an order for the continuation of a contract of employment[10] and the determination or settlement of the complaint, the employer or the employee may apply to an employment tribunal for the revocation or variation of the order on the ground of a relevant change of circumstances since the making of the order[11].

1   Ie under the Trade Union and Labour Relations (Consolidation) Act 1992 s 163: see PARA 1059. As to the meaning of 'contract of employment' see PARA 892.
2   As to the meaning of 'employee' see PARA 892.
3   Trade Union and Labour Relations (Consolidation) Act 1992 s 164(1) (amended by the Trade Union Reform and Employment Rights Act 1993 Sch 8 para 69). The obligations of an employer under a continuation order are not capable of being transferred under what are now the Transfer of Undertakings (Protection of Employment) Regulations 2006, SI 2006/246 (see PARA 136 et seq): *Dowling v Ilic Haulage* [2004] ICR 1176, [2004] All ER (D) 87 (Apr), EAT.
4   As to the meaning of 'employer' see PARA 892.

5 Trade Union and Labour Relations (Consolidation) Act 1992 s 164(2). If an amount is payable in respect only of part of a normal pay period, the amount must be calculated by reference to the whole period and reduced proportionately: s 164(4).

6 Trade Union and Labour Relations (Consolidation) Act 1992 s 164(3). For these purposes, the amount which an employee could reasonably have been expected to earn, his normal pay period and the normal pay day for each such period are to be determined as if he had not been dismissed: s 164(7).

7 Ie under the Trade Union and Labour Relations (Consolidation) Act 1992 s 164(2).

8 Trade Union and Labour Relations (Consolidation) Act 1992 s 164(5).

9 Trade Union and Labour Relations (Consolidation) Act 1992 s 164(6).

10 See note 1.

11 Trade Union and Labour Relations (Consolidation) Act 1992 s 165(1) (amended by the Employment Rights (Dispute Resolution) Act 1998 s 1(2)(a)). An application may be to any tribunal having jurisdiction; it does not need to be to the same tribunal that made the order: *British Coal Corpn v McGinty* [1987] ICR 912, [1988] IRLR 7, EAT.

The Trade Union and Labour Relations (Consolidation) Act 1992 ss 161–163 (see PARAS 1057–1059) apply in relation to such an application as in relation to an original application for interim relief, except that: (1) no certificate need be presented to the tribunal under s 161(3) (see PARA 1058); and (2) in the case of an application by the employer, s 162(2) (service of copy of application and notice of hearing) (see PARA 1058 note 11) has effect with the substitution of a reference to the employee for the reference to the employer: s 165(2). As to the procedure on such an application see also PARA 1473 text and notes 19–20.

1061. Consequences of failure to comply with an order for reinstatement or re-engagement. If, on the application of an employee[1], an employment tribunal is satisfied that the employer[2] has not complied with the terms of an order for the reinstatement or re-engagement[3] of the employee[4], the tribunal must:

(1) make an order for the continuation of the employee's contract of employment[5]; and

(2) order the employer to pay the employee such compensation as the tribunal considers just and equitable in all the circumstances having regard:

(a) to the infringement of the employee's right to be reinstated or re-engaged in pursuance of the order; and

(b) to any loss suffered by the employee in consequence of the non-compliance[6].

If, on the application of an employee, an employment tribunal is satisfied that the employer has not complied with the terms of an order for the continuation of a contract of employment, the following provisions apply[7].

If the non-compliance consists of a failure to pay an amount by way of pay specified in the order, the tribunal must determine the amount owed by the employer on the date of the determination. If on that date the tribunal also determines the employee's complaint that he has been unfairly dismissed, it must specify that amount separately from any other sum awarded to the employee[8].

In any other case, the tribunal must order the employer to pay the employee such compensation as the tribunal considers just and equitable in all the circumstances, having regard to any loss suffered by the employee in consequence of the non-compliance[9].

1 As to the meaning of 'employee' see PARA 892.

2 As to the meaning of 'employer' see PARA 892.

3 For these purposes, 'order for reinstatement or re-engagement' means an order for reinstatement or re-engagement under the Employment Rights Act 1996 s 113 (see PARA 811): Trade Union and Labour Relations (Consolidation) Act 1992 s 167(2) (definition amended by the Employment Rights Act 1996 Sch 1 paras 56(1), (12)(b)).

4 Ie under the Trade Union and Labour Relations (Consolidation) Act 1992 s 163(4) or (5): see PARA 1059.

5   As to the meaning of 'contract of employment' see PARA 892.

6   Trade Union and Labour Relations (Consolidation) Act 1992 s 166(1) (amended by the Trade Union Reform and Employment Rights Act 1993 Sch 7 para 22; the Employment Rights (Dispute Resolution) Act 1998 s 1(2)(a)). The Trade Union and Labour Relations (Consolidation) Act 1992 s 164 (order for continuation of the contract of employment) (see PARA 1060) applies to an order under s 166(1)(a) (see head (1) in the text) as in relation to an order made in the first instance under s 163 (see PARA 1059): s 166(2). As to employment tribunals see PARA 1399 et seq.

7   Trade Union and Labour Relations (Consolidation) Act 1992 s 166(3) (amended by the Employment Rights (Dispute Resolution) Act 1998 s 1(2)(a)).

8   Trade Union and Labour Relations (Consolidation) Act 1992 s 166(4).

9   Trade Union and Labour Relations (Consolidation) Act 1992 s 166(5).

1062. Awards against third parties on complaint of unfair dismissal for trade union reasons. If, in proceedings before an employment tribunal on a complaint of unfair dismissal[1], either the employer[2] or the complainant claims:

(1)   that the employer was induced to dismiss the complainant by pressure which a trade union[3] or other person exercised on the employer by calling, organising, procuring or financing a strike or other industrial action[4], or by threatening to do so; and

(2)   that the pressure was exercised because the complainant was not a member of any trade union or of a particular trade union or of one of a number of particular trade unions,

the employer or the complainant may request the tribunal to direct that the person who he claims exercised the pressure be joined as a party to the proceedings[5].

The request must be granted if it is made before the hearing of the complaint begins, but may be refused after that time; and no such request may be made after the tribunal has made an award of compensation for unfair dismissal or an order for reinstatement or re-engagement[6].

Where a person has been so joined as a party to the proceedings and the tribunal:

(a)   makes an award of compensation for unfair dismissal; and

(b)   finds that the claim mentioned in heads (1) and (2) above is well-founded,

the tribunal may order that the compensation be paid by that person instead of by the employer, or partly by that person and partly by the employer, as the tribunal may consider just and equitable[7].

1   As to the meaning of 'complaint of unfair dismissal' see PARA 1057 note 6. As to employment tribunals see PARA 1399 et seq.

2   As to the meaning of 'employer' see PARA 892.

3   As to the meaning of 'trade union' see PARA 891.

4   There is no statutory definition of 'strike' or 'other industrial action' for these purposes. For the case law on these terms as they apply in the context of unfair dismissal law etc see PARA 1340.

5   Trade Union and Labour Relations (Consolidation) Act 1992 s 160(1) (amended by the Employment Rights (Dispute Resolution) Act 1998 s 1(2)(a)). For these purposes, 'award of compensation for unfair dismissal' means an award of compensation for unfair dismissal under the Employment Rights Act 1996 s 112(4) (see PARA 810) or s 117(3)(a) (see PARA 813): Trade Union and Labour Relations (Consolidation) Act 1992 s 167(2) (definition amended by the Employment Relations Act 1996 Sch 1 para 56(1), (12)(b)).

6   Trade Union and Labour Relations (Consolidation) Act 1992 s 160(2). As to the meaning of 'order for reinstatement or re-engagement' see PARA 1061 note 3.

7   Trade Union and Labour Relations (Consolidation) Act 1992 s 160(3). In addition, industrial action aimed at enforcing membership of a trade union is likely to be illegal and restrainable because the statutory immunities are withheld from such action by s 222: see PARA 1365.

(v) Dismissal for Asserting Statutory Rights

1063. Dismissal on grounds of assertion of a statutory right. The dismissal of an employee[1] by an employer[2] is to be regarded as having been unfair[3] if the reason for it (or, if more than one, the principal reason[4]) was that the employee:

(1) brought proceedings against the employer to enforce a right of his which is a relevant statutory right[5]; or

(2) alleged that the employer had infringed a right of his which is a relevant statutory right[6].

Likewise, the dismissal of an employee on the ground of redundancy is to be regarded as unfair if the reason or principal reason for the selection of that employee for dismissal was within head (1) or head (2) above[7].

The one-year qualifying period normally applying to unfair dismissal claims[8] does not apply to a dismissal, or selection for redundancy, on the above grounds[9].

1 As to the meaning of 'employee' for these purposes see PARA 2.
2 As to the meaning of 'employer' for these purposes see PARA 2.
3 Ie unfair for the purposes of the Employment Rights Act 1996 Pt X (ss 94–134A): see PARA 757 et seq. The use of the phrase 'is to be regarded' shows that dismissal on these grounds is automatically unfair.
4 As to the meaning of 'reason or principal reason' see PARA 769.
5 As to the relevant statutory rights see PARA 1064.
6 See the Employment Rights Act 1996 s 104(1); and PARA 793. It is immaterial for these purposes whether the employee has the right or not and whether it has been infringed or not, but, for s 104 to apply, the claim to the right and that it has been infringed must be made in good faith: see s 104(2); and PARA 793. It is sufficient for s 104 to apply that the employee, without specifying the right, made it reasonably clear to the employer what the right claimed to have been infringed was: see s 104(3); and PARA 793. For the purposes of s 104(1), it is necessary that the complainant has actually brought the relevant action or made a substantive allegation; it is not enough that he could have done so on the facts: *Mennell v Newell & Wright (Transport Contractors) Ltd* [1997] ICR 1039, [1997] IRLR 519, CA.
7 See the Employment Rights Act 1996 s 105(1), (7); and PARA 781.
8 Ie the Employment Rights Act 1996 s 108(1): see PARA 758.
9 See the Employment Rights Act 1996 s 108(3)(g); and PARA 758.

1064. Relevant statutory rights in relation to trade union membership. The relevant statutory rights[1] in relation to trade union membership are those relating to:

(1) the deduction of union subscriptions from wages[2];

(2) exemption from contributing to a political fund[3];

(3) inducements in regard to union membership or activities and collective bargaining[4];

(4) action short of dismissal for union reasons[5]; and

(5) time off work for union duties[6] or activities[7].

1 Ie those protected by the Employment Rights Act 1996 s 104: see PARA 1063. See also PARA 793.
2 Ie the rights conferred by the Trade Union and Labour Relations (Consolidation) Act 1992 s 68: see PARA 1034.
3 Ie the rights conferred by the Trade Union and Labour Relations (Consolidation) Act 1992 s 86: see PARA 989.
4 Ie the rights conferred by the Trade Union and Labour Relations (Consolidation) Act 1992 ss 145A, 145B: see PARAS 1051–1052.
5 Ie the rights conferred by the Trade Union and Labour Relations (Consolidation) Act 1992 s 146: see PARA 1048.
6 Ie the rights conferred by the Trade Union and Labour Relations (Consolidation) Act 1992 ss 168–170: see PARAS 1065, 1066.
7 See the Employment Rights Act 1996 s 104(4)(c); and PARA 793.

(vi) Time Off Work for Trade Union Duties and Activities

1065. Time off for carrying out trade union duties and for union learning representatives.   An employer[1] must permit an employee[2] of his who is an official[3] of an independent trade union[4] recognised[5] by him to take time off during the employee's working hours[6] for the purpose of:

(1)   carrying out any duties of his, as such an official, concerned with:

    (a)   negotiations with the employer related to, or connected with, matters falling within the statutory meaning of collective bargaining[7] in relation to which the trade union is recognised by the employer; or

    (b)   the performance, on behalf of employees of the employer, of functions related to, or connected with, such matters which the employer has agreed may be so performed by the trade union; or

    (c)   receipt of information from the employer and consultation by the employer under the provisions relating to collective redundancies[8] or transfers of undertakings[9]; or

    (d)   negotiations with a view to entering into an agreement under the provision on variations of contracts in a transfer where the transferors are subject to relevant insolvency proceedings[10] that applies to employees of the employer; or

    (e)   the performance on behalf of employees of the employer of functions related to or connected with the making of an agreement under that provision[11]; or

(2)   undergoing training in aspects of industrial relations relevant to the carrying out of the above duties and approved by the Trades Union Congress or by the independent trade union of which he is an official[12].

The amount of time off which an employee is to be permitted so to take[13] and the purposes for which, the occasions on which and any conditions subject to which time off may be so taken are those that are reasonable[14] in all the circumstances[15].

An employer must also permit an employee of his who is a member of an independent trade union recognised by the employer, and a learning representative[16] of the trade union, to take time off during his working hours for any of the following purposes[17]:

(i)   carrying on any of the following activities in relation to qualifying members of the trade union[18]: analysing learning or training needs, providing information and advice about learning or training matters, arranging learning or training, and promoting the value of learning or training;

(ii)   consulting the employer about carrying on any such activities in relation to such members of the trade union;

(iii)   preparing for any of the things mentioned in heads (i) and (ii) above[19].

The amount of time off which an employee is to be permitted so to take[20] and the purposes for which, the occasions on which and any conditions subject to which time off may be so taken are those that are reasonable[21] in all the circumstances[22].

An employer who permits an employee to take such time off[23] must pay him for the time taken off pursuant to the permission[24]:

(A)   where the employee's remuneration for the work he would ordinarily have been doing during that time does not vary with the amount of work done, as if he had worked at that work for the whole of that time[25];

(B) where the employee's remuneration for that work varies with the amount of work done, an amount calculated by reference to the average hourly earnings[26] for that work[27].

A right to be so paid any amount does not affect any right of an employee in relation to remuneration under his contract of employment ('contractual remuneration')[28].

1 As to the meaning of 'employer' see PARA 892.

2 As to the meaning of 'employee' see PARA 892. As to excluded classes of employment see PARA 1071.

3 As to the meaning of 'official', in relation to a trade union, see PARA 1018.

4 As to the meaning of 'independent trade union' see PARA 904.

5 As to the meaning of 'recognised' see PARA 1094 note 5.

6 For the purposes of the Trade Union and Labour Relations (Consolidation) Act 1992 ss 168, 168A, 170 (see also PARAS 1066, 1068), the working hours of an employee are to be taken to be any time when, in accordance with his contract of employment, he is required to be at work: s 173(1) (amended by the Employment Act 2002 Sch 7 para 21(a)). As to the meaning of 'contract of employment' see PARA 892.

7 Ie falling within the Trade Union and Labour Relations (Consolidation) Act 1992 s 178(2): see PARA 1093.

8 Ie under the Trade Union and Labour Relations (Consolidation) Act 1992 s 188: see PARA 1185.

9 Ie under the Transfer of Undertakings (Protection of Employment) Regulations 2006, SI 2006/246: see PARA 1196 et seq. See also PARA 136 et seq.

10 Ie an agreement under the Transfer of Undertakings (Protection of Employment) Regulations 2006, SI 2006/246, reg 9: see PARA 138.

11 Trade Union and Labour Relations (Consolidation) Act 1992 s 168(1) (amended by SI 1999/1925; SI 2006/246). The reference is to the Transfer of Undertakings (Protection of Employment) Regulations 2006, SI 2006/246, reg 9. See also the Trade Union and Labour Relations (Consolidation) Act 1992 s 198B(2), cited in PARA 1020 note 14.

12 Trade Union and Labour Relations (Consolidation) Act 1992 s 168(2). These provisions, as originally enacted in 1975, were subject to major amendment by the Employment Act 1989 with a view to restricting what had previously been a wider right. Case law under the corresponding statutory provisions before 1989 is thus of little value. The formulation (ie before the most recent amendments in 2006) has been held to apply to union meetings to prepare for negotiations, where the necessary nexus is shown with the relevant collective bargaining: *London Ambulance Service v Charlton* [1992] ICR 773, [1992] IRLR 510, EAT.

For the similar provisions concerning time off for safety representatives see PARA 1074; and for the separate provisions concerning time off for directly elected workforce representatives and representatives of employee safety see PARAS 1209, 1210.

13 Ie under the Trade Union and Labour Relations (Consolidation) Act 1992 s 168.

14 Ie having regard to any relevant provisions of a Code of Practice issued by ACAS under the Trade Union and Labour Relations (Consolidation) Act 1992 s 199: see PARA 1067. The question of reasonableness is one of fact, on which a tribunal's decision is unlikely to be reversed on appeal: *Thomas Scott & Sons (Bakers) Ltd v Allen* [1983] IRLR 329, CA. In deciding whether the time off allowed was reasonable, the tribunal should not impose its own views, but should decide whether the employer was within the band of reasonable conduct (see PARA 767): *Ministry of Defence v Crook and Irving* [1982] IRLR 488, EAT.

15 Trade Union and Labour Relations (Consolidation) Act 1992 s 168(3).

16 For the purposes of the Trade Union and Labour Relations (Consolidation) Act 1992 s 168A, a person is a learning representative of a trade union if he is appointed or elected as such in accordance with its rules: s 168A(11) (s 168A added by the Employment Act 2002 s 43(1), (2)).

The Secretary of State may by order made by statutory instrument amend the Trade Union and Labour Relations (Consolidation) Act 1992 s 168A for the purpose of changing the purposes for which an employee may take time off under s 168A: s 173(3) (s 173(3), (4) added by the Employment Act 2002 s 43(1), (6)). No order may be made under the Trade Union and Labour Relations (Consolidation) Act 1992 s 173(3) unless a draft of the order has been laid before and approved by resolution of each House of Parliament: s 173(4) (as so added). As to the Secretary of State see PARA 5 note 21.

17 Trade Union and Labour Relations (Consolidation) Act 1992 s 168A(1) (as added: see note 16). Section 168A(1) only applies if (1) the trade union has given the employer notice in writing that the employee is a learning representative of the trade union; and (2) the training condition is met in relation to him: s 168A(3) (as so added). The training condition is met if (a) the employee has undergone sufficient training to enable him to carry on the activities mentioned in s 168A(2) (see heads (i)–(iii) in the text), and the trade union has given the employer notice in writing of that fact; (b) the trade union has in the last six months given the employer notice in writing that the employee will be undergoing such training; or (c) within six months of the trade union giving the employer notice in writing that the employee will be undergoing such training, the employee has done so, and the trade union has given the employer notice of that fact: s 168A(4) (as so added). Only one notice under head (b) above may be given in respect of any one employee: s 168A(5) (as so added). References in s 168A(4) to sufficient training to carry out the activities mentioned in s 168A(2) (see heads (i)–(iii) in the text) are to training that is sufficient for those purposes having regard to any relevant provision of a Code of Practice issued by ACAS or the Secretary of State: s 168A(6) (as so added). As to the Code of Practice see PARA 1067.

If an employer is required to permit an employee to take time off under s 168A(1), he must also permit the employee to take time off during his working hours for the following purposes: (i) undergoing training which is relevant to his functions as a learning representative; and (ii) where the trade union has in the last six months given the employer notice under head (b) above in relation to the employee, undergoing such training as is mentioned in head (a) above: s 168A(7) (as so added).

18 For these purposes, the reference to qualifying members of the trade union is to members of the trade union (1) who are employees of the employer of a description in respect of which the union is recognised by the employer; and (2) in relation to whom it is the function of the union learning representative to act as such: Trade Union and Labour Relations (Consolidation) Act 1992 s 168A(10) (as added: see note 16).

19 Trade Union and Labour Relations (Consolidation) Act 1992 s 168A(2) (as added: see note 16).

20 Ie under the Trade Union and Labour Relations (Consolidation) Act 1992 s 168A.

21 Ie having regard to any relevant provision of a Code of Practice issued by ACAS or the Secretary of State: see note 14.

22 Trade Union and Labour Relations (Consolidation) Act 1992 s 168A(8) (as added: see note 16).

23 Ie under the Trade Union and Labour Relations (Consolidation) Act 1992 s 168 or s 168A.

24 Trade Union and Labour Relations (Consolidation) Act 1992 s 169(1) (amended by the Employment Act 2002 s 43(1), (3)).

25 Trade Union and Labour Relations (Consolidation) Act 1992 s 169(2).

26 For these purposes, the average hourly earnings are those of the employee concerned or, if no fair estimate can be made of those earnings, the average hourly earnings for work of that description of persons in comparable employment with the same employer or, if there are no such persons, a figure of average hourly earnings which is reasonable in the circumstances: Trade Union and Labour Relations (Consolidation) Act 1992 s 169(3). If only part of the time off was for matters falling within s 168, only that proportion need be paid: *RHP Bearings Ltd v Brookes* [1979] IRLR 452, EAT. Once it is established that there is a relevant duty and that the time off is reasonable, the right to payment arises automatically: *Beecham Group Ltd v Beal (No 2)* [1983] IRLR 317, EAT. If an employee attends a course outside working time and takes time off in lieu, no right to payment arises: *Hairsine v Kingston-upon-Hull City Council* [1992] ICR 212, [1992] IRLR 211, EAT.

27 Trade Union and Labour Relations (Consolidation) Act 1992 s 169(3). A problem may, however, arise in relation to part-time workers needing more time off, e g for a training course, than they would normally have worked. Under s 169(2) ('paid as if he has worked') they would only be entitled to be paid for their normal part-time hours, not for the full time of the training course. Such a provision under German law was held to discriminate against part-time workers and to constitute unlawful sex discrimination: Case C-360/90 *Arbeiterwohlfahrt der Stadt Berlin eV v Bötel* [1992] ECR I-3589, [1992] IRLR 423, ECJ; applied in *Davies v Neath Port Talbot County Borough Council* [1999] ICR 1132, [1999] IRLR 769, EAT (disapproving the earlier decision to the contrary in *Manor Bakeries Ltd v Nazir* [1996] IRLR 604, EAT), holding that the Trade Union and Labour Relations (Consolidation) Act 1992 s 169(2) is contrary to what is now the Treaty on the Functioning of the European Union (Rome, 25 March 1957; TS 1 (1973); Cmnd 5179) art 157 (equal pay) and so is to be disapplied in such a case.

28 Trade Union and Labour Relations (Consolidation) Act 1992 s 169(4). Any contractual remuneration paid to an employee in respect of a period of time off to which s 169 applies is to go towards discharging any liability of the employer under these provisions in respect of that period; and any payment under s 169 in respect of a period is to go towards discharging any liability of the employer to pay contractual remuneration in respect of that period: s 169(4)(a),

(b). As to the right of complaint to an employment tribunal see PARA 1068. If an employee is dismissed or selected for redundancy because he brought proceedings to enforce the rights under s 168, s 168A or s 169, his dismissal is automatically regarded as unfair: see PARAS 1063, 1064.

1066. Time off for trade union activities. An employer[1] must permit an employee[2] of his who is a member of an independent trade union[3] recognised[4] by the employer in respect of that description of employee to take time off during his working hours[5] for the purpose of taking part in any activities of the union, and any activities in relation to which the employee is acting as a representative of the union[6].

An employer must also permit an employee of his who is a member of an independent trade union recognised by the employer in respect of that description of employee to take time off during his working hours for the purpose of having access to services provided by a person in his capacity as a learning representative of the trade union[7].

The amount of time off which an employee is to be permitted so to take, and the purposes for which, the occasions on which and any conditions subject to which time off may be so taken are those that are reasonable[8] in all the circumstances[9].

1   As to the meaning of 'employer' see PARA 892.
2   As to the meaning of 'employee' see PARA 892. As to excluded classes of employment see PARA 1071.
3   As to the meaning of 'independent trade union' see PARA 904.
4   As to the meaning of 'recognised' see PARA 1094 note 5.
5   As to the meaning of 'working hours' for these purposes see PARA 1065 note 6.
6   Trade Union and Labour Relations (Consolidation) Act 1992 s 170(1). This right does not extend to activities which themselves consist of industrial action, whether or not in contemplation or furtherance of a trade dispute: s 170(2). There must be a genuine link between the activity in question and the employment relationship between the employer, the employee and the trade union: *Luce v Bexley London Borough Council* [1990] ICR 591, [1990] IRLR 422, EAT (teacher refused time off to attend TUC lobby of Parliament in connection with proposed legislation affecting the teaching profession; attending lobby of Parliament 'intended to convey only political or ideological objections to legislation' and held not to be within the right to time off).
     The right conferred by the Trade Union and Labour Relations (Consolidation) Act 1992 s 170(1) also does not extend to time off for the purpose of acting as, or having access to services provided by, a learning representative of a trade union: s 170(2A) (s 170(2A)–(2C) added by the Employment Act 2002 s 43(1), (4)). For the purposes of the Trade Union and Labour Relations (Consolidation) Act 1992 s 170: (1) a person is a learning representative of a trade union if he is appointed or elected as such in accordance with its rules; and (2) a person who is a learning representative of a trade union acts as such if he carries on the activities mentioned in s 168A(2) (see PARA 1065) in that capacity: s 170(5) (added by the Employment Act 2002 s 43(1), (5)).
7   Trade Union and Labour Relations (Consolidation) Act 1992 s 170(2B) (as added: see note 6). Section 170(2B) only applies if the learning representative would be entitled to time off under s 168A(1) (see PARA 1065) for the purpose of carrying on in relation to the employee activities of the kind mentioned in s 168A(2) (see PARA 1065): s 170(2C) (as so added).
8   Ie having regard to any relevant provisions of a Code of Practice issued by ACAS under the Trade Union and Labour Relations (Consolidation) Act 1992 s 199: see PARA 1067.
9   Trade Union and Labour Relations (Consolidation) Act 1992 s 170(3). In deciding what is a reasonable amount of time off, the employer may take into consideration not just the circumstances of the particular request by the employee, but also the amount of time off that has already been granted to him on other occasions: *Wignall v British Gas Corpn* [1984] ICR 716, [1984] IRLR 493, EAT. As to the right of complaint to an employment tribunal see PARA 1068. When deciding a case under the Trade Union and Labour Relations (Consolidation) Act 1992 s 170, a tribunal should decide the question of reasonableness under s 170(3) as well as the primary question whether the activity is appropriate under s 170(1): *Luce v Bexley London Borough Council* [1990] ICR 591, [1990] IRLR 422, EAT.

Unlike the right to time off for union duties (see PARA 1065) this right does not carry a statutory right to pay during the time taken. If an employee is dismissed or selected for redundancy because he brought proceedings to enforce the right under the Trade Union and Labour Relations (Consolidation) Act 1992 s 170, his dismissal is automatically regarded as unfair: see PARAS 1063, 1064.

1067. The Code of Practice on Time Off for Trade Union Duties and Activities. Pursuant to its statutory powers to issue Codes of Practice[1], the Advisory, Conciliation and Arbitration Service[2] (ACAS) has issued the Code of Practice on Time Off for Trade Union Duties and Activities[3]. The provisions of the Code are admissible in evidence and may be taken into account in determining any question arising during employment tribunal proceedings relating to time off work for trade union duties or activities; but failure to observe any provisions of the Code does not of itself render a person liable to any proceedings[4].

The general purpose of the statutory provisions[5] and the Code is to aid and improve the effectiveness of relationships between employers and trade unions, who have a joint responsibility to ensure that agreed arrangements work to mutual advantage by specifying how reasonable time off for union duties and activities and for training will work[6].

1 Ie under the Trade Union and Labour Relations (Consolidation) Act 1992 ss 199–202: see PARA 1223.
2 As to the constitution and powers of ACAS see PARA 1213 et seq.
3 The current Code was brought into force on 1 January 2010 by the Employment Protection Code of Practice (Time Off for Trade Union Duties and Activities) Order 2009, SI 2009/3223, art 2.
4 See the Trade Union and Labour Relations (Consolidation) Act 1992 s 207; and PARA 1224.
5 Ie the Trade Union and Labour Relations (Consolidation) Act 1992 ss 168–170: see PARAS 1065, 1066.
6 Code of Practice on Time Off for Trade Union Duties and Activities para 4.
    Section 1 of the Code provides guidance on time off for trade union duties. Section 2 deals with time off for training of trade union officials and offers guidance on sufficient training for union learning representatives. Section 3 considers time off for trade union activities: in each case the amount and frequency of time off, and the purposes for which and any conditions subject to which time off may be taken, are to be those that are reasonable in all the circumstances. Section 4 describes the responsibilities which employers and trade unions share in considering reasonable time off. Section 5 notes the advantages of reaching formal agreements on time off. Section 6 deals with industrial action and Section 7 with methods of appeal: see the Code of Practice on Time Off for Trade Union Duties and Activities para 5.

1068. Remedies where employer does not permit employee to take time off for trade union duties etc. An employee[1] who is an official[2] of an independent trade union[3] and, in the case of the provision on time off for union learning representatives[4] a member of such an independent trade union and such a representative, may present a complaint to an employment tribunal that his employer has failed to permit[5] him to take time off for trade union duties[6] or relevant purposes in the case of the provision on time off for union learning representatives[7] or has failed[8] to pay him for such time off[9]; and an employee who is a member of an independent trade union may present a complaint to an employment tribunal that his employer has failed to permit him to take time off[10] for trade union activities[11].

An employment tribunal must not consider any such complaint[12] unless it is presented[13] to the tribunal:

(1)   within three months of the date when the failure occurred[14], subject to an extension to facilitate conciliation before the institution of proceedings[15]; or

(2)	within such further period as the tribunal considers reasonable in a case where it is satisfied that it was not reasonably practicable for the complaint to be presented within the period of three months[16].

Where a tribunal finds any such complaint of failure to allow time off[17] well-founded, it must make a declaration to that effect and may make an award of compensation to be paid by the employer to the employee, the amount of such compensation to be such as the tribunal considers just and equitable in all the circumstances, having regard to the employer's default in failing to permit time off to be taken by the employee and to any loss sustained by the employee which is attributable to the matters complained of[18]. Where, on a complaint relating to paid time off for union duties[19], the tribunal finds that the employer has failed to pay the employee in accordance with the statutory requirements[20], it must order the employer to pay to the employee the amount which it finds to be due to him[21].

1	As to the meaning of 'employee' see PARA 892. As to excluded classes of employment see PARA 1071.

2	As to the meaning of 'official', in relation to a trade union, see PARA 1018.

3	Ie an independent trade union recognised by his employer. As to the meaning of 'independent trade union' see PARA 904; and as to the meaning of 'recognised' see PARA 1094 note 5.

4	Ie in the case of Trade Union and Labour Relations (Consolidation) Act 1992 s 168A: see PARA 1065.

5	The phrase 'failed to permit' imports knowledge on the employer's part; if the employer simply fails to respond and that knowledge cannot be shown, there is no failure to permit: *Ryford Ltd v Drinkwater* [1996] IRLR 16, EAT.

6	Ie as required by the Trade Union and Labour Relations (Consolidation) Act 1992 s 168: see PARA 1065.

7	Ie as required by the Trade Union and Labour Relations (Consolidation) Act 1992 s 168A: see PARA 1065.

8	Ie as required by the Trade Union and Labour Relations (Consolidation) Act 1992 s 169: see PARA 1065.

9	Trade Union and Labour Relations (Consolidation) Act 1992 ss 168(4), 168A(9), 169(5) (s 168(4) amended by the Employment Rights (Dispute Resolution) Act 1998 s 1(2)(a)); the Trade Union and Labour Relations (Consolidation) Act 1992 s 168A(9) added by the Employment Act 2002 s 43(1), (2); the Trade Union and Labour Relations (Consolidation) Act 1992 s 169(5) amended by the Employment Rights (Dispute Resolution) Act 1998 s 1(2)(a)). The remedy of an employee for infringement of the rights conferred on him by the Trade Union and Labour Relations (Consolidation) Act 1992 s 168, s 168A, s 169 or s 170 is by way of complaint to an employment tribunal, and not otherwise: s 173(2) (amended by the Employment Rights (Dispute Resolution) Act 1998 s 1(2)(a); the Employment Act 2002 Sch 7 paras 18, 21(b)).

	The provisions of the Employment Tribunals Act 1996 ss 18A–18B (conciliation) (see PARA 152) apply in the case of matters which could be the subject of employment tribunal proceedings under the Trade Union and Labour Relations (Consolidation) Act 1992 ss 168, 168A, 169, 170, and the Employment Tribunals Act 1996 s 18C applies in the case of such proceedings themselves: see s 18(1)(a), (1A) (s 18(1)(a) substituted by SI 2014/431; the Employment Tribunals Act 1996 s 18(1A) added by the Enterprise and Regulatory Reform Act 2013 Sch 1 paras 2, 5(1), (7)). As to employment tribunals see PARA 1399 et seq. An appeal lies to the Employment Appeal Tribunal on any question of law arising from any decision of, or arising in any proceedings before, an employment tribunal under or by virtue of the Trade Union and Labour Relations (Consolidation) Act 1992: see the Employment Tribunals Act 1996 s 21(1)(d); and PARA 1428. As to the Employment Appeal Tribunal see PARA 1422 et seq.

	If an employee is dismissed or selected for redundancy because he brought proceedings to enforce the rights under the Trade Union and Labour Relations (Consolidation) Act 1992 s 168, 168A, 169 or s 170, his dismissal is automatically regarded as unfair: see PARAS 1063, 1064.

10	Ie as required by Trade Union and Labour Relations (Consolidation) Act 1992 s 170: see PARA 1066.

11	Trade Union and Labour Relations (Consolidation) Act 1992 s 170(4) (amended by the Employment Rights (Dispute Resolution) Act 1998 s 1(2)(a)). See also note 9.

12 Ie under the Trade Union and Labour Relations (Consolidation) Act 1992 s 168, s 168A, s 169 or s 170.

13 As to when a complaint is presented see PARAS 804, 1461.

14 Trade Union and Labour Relations (Consolidation) Act 1992 s 171(1)(a) (s 171(1) amended by the Employment Rights (Dispute Resolution) Act 1998 s 1(2)(a); the Employment Act 2002 Sch 7 paras 18, 19; renumbered by the Enterprise and Regulatory Reform Act 2013 Sch 2 paras 1, 9). For the case law on the extension of time limits, especially in the context of the law of unfair dismissal, see PARAS 804, 1453.

15 The Trade Union and Labour Relations (Consolidation) Act 1992 s 292A (extension of time limits to facilitate conciliation before institution of proceedings: see PARA 1455) applies for the purposes of s 171(1)(a): s 171(2) (added by the Enterprise and Regulatory Reform Act 2013 Sch 2 paras 1, 9).

16 Trade Union and Labour Relations (Consolidation) Act 1992 s 171(1)(b) (as amended and renumbered: see note 14).

17 Ie under the Trade Union and Labour Relations (Consolidation) Act 1992 s 168, s 168A or s 170.

18 Trade Union and Labour Relations (Consolidation) Act 1992 s 172(1), (2) (s 172(1) amended by the Employment Act 2002 Sch 7 paras 18, 20). In adjudicating on a complaint, the tribunal must confine itself to the facts before it and not seek to impose conditions on the parties: see *Corner v Buckinghamshire County Council* [1978] ICR 836, [1978] IRLR 320, EAT. The reference to the employer's default and any loss to the employer means that an award can be made reflecting the wrong done, even if there was no actual loss to the employee: *Skiggs v South West Trains Ltd* [2005] IRLR 459, [2005] All ER (D) 96 (Mar), EAT.

19 Ie under the Trade Union and Labour Relations (Consolidation) Act 1992 s 169: see PARA 1065.

20 Ie in accordance with the Trade Union and Labour Relations (Consolidation) Act 1992 s 169.

21 Trade Union and Labour Relations (Consolidation) Act 1992 s 172(3). As to the similar provisions with regard to complaints by safety representatives see PARA 1074.

(vii) Avoidance of, and Prohibition on, Trade Union Membership Requirements

1069. Union membership requirement in contract is void. A term or condition of a contract for the supply of goods or services is void in so far as it purports to require that the whole, or some part, of the work done for the purposes of the contract is done only by persons who are, or are not, members of trade unions[1] or of a particular trade union[2].

The above provisions bind the Crown[3].

1 As to the meaning of 'trade union' see PARA 891.

2 Trade Union and Labour Relations (Consolidation) Act 1992 s 144. In addition, there are the following further provisions governing the practice of 'contract compliance': (1) s 145 renders unlawful any refusal to deal with a supplier on union membership grounds (see PARA 1070); (2) ss 186, 187 contain corresponding provisions applying to union recognition requirements (see PARAS 1183, 1184); and (3) ss 222, 225 remove the immunities from suit from any industrial action taken to induce a person to act contrary to the above provisions (see PARAS 1365, 1368).

3 Trade Union and Labour Relations (Consolidation) Act 1992 s 276(2).

1070. Refusal to deal on union membership grounds is prohibited. A person may not refuse to deal[1] with a supplier or prospective supplier of goods or services on union membership grounds[2]. The obligation to comply with this provision is a duty owed to the person with whom there is a refusal to deal and to any other person who may be adversely affected by its contravention[3]; and a breach of the duty is actionable accordingly, subject to the defences and other incidents applying to claims for breach of statutory duty[4].

A person refuses to deal with a person if:

   (1)   where he maintains, in whatever form, a list of approved suppliers of

goods or services, or of persons from whom tenders for the supply of goods or services may be invited, he fails to include the name of that person in that list[5];

(2)   in relation to a proposed contract for the supply of goods or services:

(a)   he excludes that person from the group of persons from whom tenders for the supply of goods or services are invited; or

(b)   he fails to permit that person to submit such a tender; or

(c)   he otherwise determines not to enter into a contract with that person for the supply of the goods or services[6]; or

(3)   he terminates a contract with him for the supply of goods or services[7].

He so refuses on union membership grounds:

(i)   in a case falling within head (1) above, if the ground, or one of the grounds, for failing to include the person's name is that, if that person were to enter into a contract with him for the supply of goods or services, work to be done for the purposes of the contract would, or would be likely to, be done by persons who were, or who were not, members of trade unions[8] or of a particular trade union[9];

(ii)   in a case falling within head (2) above, if the ground, or one of the grounds, on which he makes the exclusion, fails to give the permission, or makes the determination is that, if the proposed contract were entered into with that person, work to be done for the purposes of the contract would, or would be likely to, be done by persons who were, or were not, such members[10]; and

(iii)   in a case falling within head (3) above, if the ground, or one of the grounds, on which he terminates the contract is that work done, or to be done, for the purposes of the contract has been, or is likely to be, done by persons who are or are not such members[11].

The above provisions bind the Crown[12].

1   For these purposes, 'refuse to deal' is to be construed in accordance with the Trade Union and Labour Relations (Consolidation) Act 1992 s 145(2)–(4) (see heads (1)–(3) in the text): s 145(1).
2   Trade Union and Labour Relations (Consolidation) Act 1992 s 145(1). For these purposes, 'union membership grounds' is to be construed in accordance with s 145(2)–(4) (see heads (i)–(iii) in the text): s 145(1). The statutory immunities are withdrawn from any act which constitutes an inducement or attempted inducement of a person to contravene s 145: see s 222(3)(b); and PARA 1365.
3   As to the meaning of 'contravention' and cognate expressions see PARA 915 note 6.
4   See the Trade Union and Labour Relations (Consolidation) Act 1992 s 145(5). As to the sanctions and remedies for breach of statutory duty see STATUTES AND LEGISLATIVE PROCESS vol 96 (2012) PARA 752 et seq; and as to claims for damages for breach of statutory duty see TORT vol 97 (2010) PARA 495 et seq.
5   Trade Union and Labour Relations (Consolidation) Act 1992 s 145(2).
6   Trade Union and Labour Relations (Consolidation) Act 1992 s 145(3).
7   Trade Union and Labour Relations (Consolidation) Act 1992 s 145(4).
8   As to the meaning of 'trade union' see PARA 891.
9   Trade Union and Labour Relations (Consolidation) Act 1992 s 145(2).
10 Trade Union and Labour Relations (Consolidation) Act 1992 s 145(3).
11 Trade Union and Labour Relations (Consolidation) Act 1992 s 145(4).
12 Trade Union and Labour Relations (Consolidation) Act 1992 s 276(2).

(viii) Excluded Classes of Employment

1071.   Classes of employment excluded from certain rights relating to union membership and activities.   The statutory provisions relating to rights in relation to access to employment[1], inducements and detriment[2] and time off for trade union duties and activities[3] do not apply to employment:

(1)   as master or as a member of the crew of a fishing vessel where the employee[4] or worker[5] is remunerated only by a share in the profits or gross earnings of the vessel[6]; and

(2)   where under his contract of employment[7] an employee works, or in the case of a prospective employee would ordinarily work, outside Great Britain[8].

Certain rights relating to access to employment[9] do not apply in relation to police service[10].

1   Ie the Trade Union and Labour Relations (Consolidation) Act 1992 ss 137–143: see PARA 1042 et seq.

2   Ie the Trade Union and Labour Relations (Consolidation) Act 1992 ss 145A–151: see PARA 1048 et seq. See also note 8.

3   Ie the Trade Union and Labour Relations (Consolidation) Act 1992 ss 168–173: see PARA 1065 et seq.

4   As to the meaning of 'employee' see PARA 892. As to Crown employment etc see PARA 893 et seq; and as to the Secretary of State's power to make further provision as to excluded classes of employment see PARA 1072.

5   Ie in the case of the Trade Union and Labour Relations (Consolidation) Act 1992 ss 145A–151: see PARA 1048 et seq. See also note 8.

6   Trade Union and Labour Relations (Consolidation) Act 1992 s 284 (amended by the Employment Relations Act 2004 Sch 1 paras 16(1)–(3)).

7   As to the meaning of 'contract of employment' see PARA 892.

8   Trade Union and Labour Relations (Consolidation) Act 1992 s 285(1) (amended by the Employment Relations Act 2004 Sch 1 para 17(1), (2)). The Trade Union and Labour Relations (Consolidation) Act 1992 ss 145A–151 do not apply to employment where under his contract personally to do work or perform services a worker who is not an employee works outside Great Britain: s 285(1A) (added by the Employment Relations Act 2004 Sch 1 para 17(1), (3)). For the purposes of the Trade Union and Labour Relations (Consolidation) Act 1992 s 285(1), (1A), employment on board a ship registered in the United Kingdom is to be treated as employment where under his contract a person ordinarily works in Great Britain unless: (1) the ship is registered at a port outside Great Britain; or (2) the employment is wholly outside Great Britain; or (3) the employee or, as the case may be, the worker or the person seeking employment or seeking to avail himself of a service of an employment agency, is not ordinarily resident in Great Britain: s 285(2) (amended by the Employment Relations Act 2004 Sch 1 para 17(1), (4)). As to the meanings of 'Great Britain' and 'United Kingdom' see PARA 2 note 12. As to the meaning of 'employment agency' see PARA 1042 note 12.

9   Ie the Trade Union and Labour Relations (Consolidation) Act 1992 ss 137, 138: see PARAS 1042–1043.

10   See the Trade Union and Labour Relations (Consolidation) Act 1992 s 280(1); and PARA 892. As to the meaning of 'police service' see PARA 892 note 11.

1072.   Power to make further provision as to excluded classes of employment.
The Secretary of State[1] may by order made by statutory instrument provide that any of the statutory provisions relating to inducements and detriment[2], the procedure for handling redundancies[3] or the dismissal of those taking part in unofficial industrial action[4] are not to apply to persons or to employment of such classes as may be prescribed by the order, or are to apply to persons or employments of such classes as may be prescribed by the order subject to such exceptions and modifications as may be so prescribed[5]. He may also vary or revoke any of the statutory provisions relating to excluded classes of employment[6], so far as they relate to any such provision[7].

Any such order must be made by statutory instrument and may contain such incidental, supplementary or transitional provisions as appear to the Secretary of State to be necessary or expedient[8]; but no such order is to be made unless a draft of it has been laid before Parliament and approved by a resolution of each House of Parliament[9].

1 As to the Secretary of State see PARA 5 note 21.
2 Ie the Trade Union and Labour Relations (Consolidation) Act 1992 ss 145A–151: see PARA 1048 et seq.
3 Ie the Trade Union and Labour Relations (Consolidation) Act 1992 Pt IV Ch II (ss 188–198B): see PARA 1185 et seq.
4 Ie the Trade Union and Labour Relations (Consolidation) Act 1992 s 237: see PARA 1350.
5 Trade Union and Labour Relations (Consolidation) Act 1992 s 286(1), (2) (s 286(1) amended by the Employment Relations Act 2004 Sch 1 para 18).
6 Ie the Trade Union and Labour Relations (Consolidation) Act 1992 ss 281–285: see PARAS 1071, 1194.
7 Trade Union and Labour Relations (Consolidation) Act 1992 s 286(2).
8 Trade Union and Labour Relations (Consolidation) Act 1992 s 286(3).
9 Trade Union and Labour Relations (Consolidation) Act 1992 s 286(4). Partly in the exercise of this power, the Secretary of State has made the Trade Union and Labour Relations (Consolidation) Act 1992 (Amendment) Order 2013, SI 2013/763, which came into force on 6 April 2013: art 1. Amendments made by art 3(2), (3) affect the provisions referred to in note 3 above.

(ix) Safety Representatives and Safety Committees

1073. Appointment and functions of safety representatives. Regulations made by the Secretary of State may provide for the appointment in prescribed cases by recognised trade unions[1] of safety representatives from amongst the employees[2]; and those representatives are to represent the employees in consultations with the employers[3] and to have such other functions as may be prescribed[4].

A recognised trade union may appoint safety representatives from amongst the employees in all cases where one or more employees are employed by an employer by whom it is recognised[5]. A person so appointed must, so far as is reasonably practicable, either have been employed by his employer throughout the preceding two years or have had at least two years' experience in similar employment[6].

Where the employer has been notified in writing by or on behalf of a trade union of the names of the persons so appointed and the group or groups of employees they represent, each such representative has the following functions[7]:

(1) to represent the employees in consultations with the employer[8];

(2) to investigate potential hazards and dangerous occurrences at the workplace[9], whether or not they are drawn to his attention by the employees he represents, and to examine the causes of accidents at the workplace;

(3) to investigate complaints by any employee he represents relating to that employee's health, safety or welfare at work[10];

(4) to make representations to the employer on matters arising out of heads (2) and (3) above and on general matters affecting the health, safety or welfare at work of the employees at the workplace;

(5) to carry out inspections of the workplace or part of it[11], inspections following over three day injuries, notifiable accidents, dangerous occurrences and notifiable diseases[12] and inspections of documents[13];

(6) to represent the employees he was appointed to represent in consultations at the workplace with inspectors of the Health and Safety Executive[14] and of any other enforcing authority;

(7) to receive information from inspectors[15]; and

(8) to attend meetings of safety committees[16] where he attends in his capacity as a safety representative in connection with any of the above functions[17].

No function so given to a safety representative is, however, to be construed as imposing a duty on him[18]; and nothing in these provisions is to be construed as giving any person a right to inspect any place, article, substance or document which is the subject of restrictions on the grounds of national security, unless he satisfies any test or requirement imposed on those grounds by or on behalf of the Crown[19].

Every employer[20] must[21] provide such facilities and assistance as safety representatives may reasonably require for the purpose of carrying out their statutory functions[22]. The Health and Safety Executive may, however, grant exemptions from any requirement imposed by the statutory provisions[23]; and any such exemption may be unconditional or subject to such conditions as the Executive may impose and may be with or without a limit of time[24].

1   Ie within the meaning of the regulations. For these purposes, 'recognised trade union' means an independent trade union as defined in the Trade Union and Labour Relations (Consolidation) Act 1992 s 5 (see PARA 904) which the employer concerned recognises for the purpose of negotiations relating to or connected with one or more of the matters specified in s 178(1), (2) (see PARA 1093) in relation to persons employed by him: Safety Representatives and Safety Committees Regulations 1977, SI 1977/500, reg 2(1), (2) (definition amended by SI 1999/860; SI 2006/594); Trade Union and Labour Relations (Consolidation) Act 1992 Sch 3 para 1(4).

2   For these purposes, 'employee' has the meaning assigned by the Health and Safety at Work etc Act 1974 s 53(1) (see HEALTH AND SAFETY AT WORK vol 52 (2014) PARA 302): Safety Representatives and Safety Committees Regulations 1977, SI 1977/500, reg 2(1). Only an 'employee' as so defined may validly be appointed as a safety representative: *Costain Building & Civil Engineering Ltd v Smith* [2000] ICR 215, EAT.

3   Ie under the Health and Safety at Work etc Act 1974 s 2(6): see PARA 1201.

4   Health and Safety at Work etc Act 1974 s 2(4). In exercise of the power so conferred the Secretary of State made the Safety Representatives and Safety Committees Regulations 1977, SI 1977/500, which came into operation on 1 October 1978: reg 1.

5   Safety Representatives and Safety Committees Regulations 1977, SI 1977/500, reg 3(1) (amended by SI 1996/1513). Safety representatives appointed under the Safety Representatives and Safety Committees Regulations 1977, SI 1977/500, reg 3(1) need not be employees of the employer concerned in cases in which the employees in the group or groups they are appointed to represent are members of the British Actors' Equity Association or of the Musicians' Union: reg 8(1), (2).

6   Safety Representatives and Safety Committees Regulations 1977, SI 1977/500, reg 3(4). Regulation 3(4) does not apply to safety representatives appointed by virtue of reg 8 (see note 5): reg 8(3). A person ceases to be a safety representative when: (1) the trade union which appointed him notifies the employer in writing that his appointment has been terminated; or (2) he ceases, except in a case in which reg 8 applies, to be employed at the workplace, but, if he was appointed to represent employees at more than one workplace, he does not so cease to be a safety representative so long as he continues to be employed at any one of them; or (3) he resigns: regs 3(3), 8(3). As to the meaning of 'workplace' see note 9.

7   Safety Representatives and Safety Committees Regulations 1977, SI 1977/500, reg 3(2).

8   See note 3.

9   For these purposes, 'workplace', in relation to a safety representative, means any place or places where the group or groups of employees he is appointed to represent are likely to work or which they are likely to frequent in the course of their employment or incidentally to it: Safety Representatives and Safety Committees Regulations 1977, SI 1977/500, reg 2(1).

10 For these purposes, 'welfare at work' means those aspects of welfare at work which are the subject of health and safety regulations or of any of the existing statutory provisions within the meaning of the Health and Safety at Work etc Act 1974 s 53(1) (see HEALTH AND SAFETY AT WORK vol 52 (2014) PARA 302): Safety Representatives and Safety Committees Regulations 1977, SI 1977/500, reg 2(1).

11 Ie in accordance with the Safety Representatives and Safety Committees Regulations 1977, SI 1977/500, reg 5, which provides for inspections: (1) after reasonable notice to the employer and where no such inspection has been carried out in the previous three months, or for more frequent inspections by agreement with the employer (see reg 5(1)); (2) where there has been a substantial change in the conditions of work or new information has been published by the Health and Safety Executive relevant to the hazards of the workplace since the last inspection

(see reg 5(2) (amended by SI 2008/960)). Employers are under a duty to provide reasonable facilities and assistance for such inspections: see the Safety Representatives and Safety Committees Regulations 1977, SI 1977/500, reg 5(3).

12 Ie in accordance with the Safety Representatives and Safety Committees Regulations 1977, SI 1977/500, reg 6. For these purposes, 'notifiable accident or dangerous occurrence' and 'notifiable disease' mean any accident, dangerous occurrence or disease, as the case may be, notice of which is required to be given by virtue of any of the relevant statutory provisions within the meaning of the Health and Safety at Work etc Act 1974 s 53(1) (see HEALTH AND SAFETY AT WORK vol 52 (2014) PARA 302); and 'over three day injury' means an injury required to be recorded in accordance with the Reporting of Injuries, Diseases and Dangerous Occurrences Regulations 2013, SI 2013/1471, reg 12(1)(b) (see HEALTH AND SAFETY AT WORK vol 52 (2014) PARA 375): Safety Representatives and Safety Committees Regulations 1977, SI 1977/500, reg 6(3) (substituted by SI 2013/1471).

13 Ie in accordance with the Safety Representatives and Safety Committees Regulations 1977, SI 1977/500, reg 7: see PARA 1202.

14 As to the Health and Safety Executive see HEALTH AND SAFETY AT WORK vol 52 (2014) PARA 326 et seq.

15 Ie in accordance with the Health and Safety at Work etc Act 1974 s 28(8): see HEALTH AND SAFETY AT WORK vol 52 (2014) PARA 345.

16 As to safety committees see PARA 1075.

17 Safety Representatives and Safety Committees Regulations 1977, SI 1977/500, reg 4(1).

18 Safety Representatives and Safety Committees Regulations 1977, SI 1977/500, reg 4(1). Regulation 4(1) is without prejudice to the Health and Safety at Work etc Act 1974 ss 7, 8 (general duties of employees at work and others) (see HEALTH AND SAFETY AT WORK vol 52 (2014) PARA 410): Safety Representatives and Safety Committees Regulations 1977, SI 1977/500, reg 4(1).

19 Safety Representatives and Safety Committees Regulations 1977, SI 1977/500, reg 2(3).

20 For these purposes, 'employer' is to be construed in accordance with the meaning of 'employee' assigned by the Health and Safety at Work etc Act 1974 s 53(1) (see HEALTH AND SAFETY AT WORK vol 52 (2014) PARA 302): Safety Representatives and Safety Committees Regulations 1977, SI 1977/500, reg 2(1).

21 Ie without prejudice to the Safety Representatives and Safety Committees Regulations 1977, SI 1977/500, regs 5, 6.

22 Safety Representatives and Safety Committees Regulations 1977, SI 1977/500, reg 4A(2) (added by SI 1992/2051).

23 Ie any requirement imposed by the Safety Representatives and Safety Committees Regulations 1977, SI 1977/500.

24 Safety Representatives and Safety Committees Regulations 1977, SI 1977/500, reg 10 (amended by SI 2008/960).

1074. Safety representative's right to time off with pay. An employer[1] must permit a safety representative[2] to take such time off with pay[3] during the employee's[4] working hours as is necessary for the purposes of:

(1) performing his statutory functions[5]; and

(2) undergoing such training in aspects of those functions as may be reasonable in all the circumstances, having regard to any relevant provisions of a Code of Practice relating to time off for training and approved[6] for the time being by the Health and Safety Executive[7].

A safety representative may present a complaint to an employment tribunal that the employer has failed:

(a) so to permit him to take time off; or

(b) to pay him in accordance with the above provisions[8].

An employment tribunal must not consider such a complaint unless it is presented[9]:

(i) within three months of the date when the failure occurred; or

(ii) within such further period as the tribunal considers reasonable in a case where it is satisfied that it was not reasonably practicable for the complaint to be presented within the period of three months[10], subject to an extension to facilitate conciliation before the institution of proceedings[11].

Where an employment tribunal finds a complaint under head (a) above well-founded, it must make a declaration to that effect and may make an award of compensation to be paid by the employer to the employee, which must be of such amount as the tribunal considers just and equitable in all the circumstances, having regard to the employer's default in failing to permit time off to be taken by the employee and to any loss sustained by the employee which is attributable to the matters complained of[12].

Where, on a complaint under head (b) above, an employment tribunal finds that the employer has failed to pay the employee the whole or part of the amount required to be paid, the tribunal must order the employer to pay the employee the amount which it finds due to him[13].

1 As to meaning of 'employer' see PARA 1073 note 20.

2 As to the appointment and functions of safety representatives see PARA 1073.

3 As to meaning of 'employee' see PARA 1073 note 2.

4 Ie in accordance with the Safety Representatives and Safety Committees Regulations 1977, SI 1977/500, reg 4(2), Sch 2 (reg 4(2) amended by SI 2008/960). Where a safety representative is permitted so to take time off, his employer must pay him: (1) as if he had worked at the work he would ordinarily have been doing for the whole of that time; or (2) where his remuneration varies with the amount of work done, an amount calculated by reference to the average hourly earnings for that work: Safety Representatives and Safety Committees Regulations 1977, SI 1977/500, Sch 2 para 1 (Sch 2 renumbered by SI 1999/860). The average hourly earnings referred to in head (2) above are the average hourly earnings of the safety representative concerned or, if no fair estimate can be made of those earnings, the average hourly earnings for work of that description of persons in comparable employment with the same employer or, if there are no such persons, a figure of average hourly earnings which is reasonable in the circumstances: Safety Representatives and Safety Committees Regulations 1977, SI 1977/500, Sch 2 para 2 (as so renumbered). Any payment to a safety representative by an employer in respect of a period of time off which is a payment under a contractual obligation is to go towards discharging the employer's liability in respect of the same period under the Safety Representatives and Safety Committees Regulations 1977, SI 1977/500, reg 4(2), and vice versa: see Sch 2 para 3 (as so renumbered).

5 Ie under the Health and Safety at Work etc Act 1974 s 2(4) and the Safety Representatives and Safety Committees Regulations 1977, SI 1977/500, reg 4(1)(a)–(h): see PARA 1073 heads (1)–(8).

6 Ie under the Health and Safety at Work etc Act 1974 s 16: see HEALTH AND SAFETY AT WORK vol 52 (2014) PARA 390.

7 Safety Representatives and Safety Committees Regulations 1977, SI 1977/500, reg 4(2) (amended by SI 1999/860; SI 2008/960). The Safety Representatives and Safety Committees Regulations 1977, SI 1977/500, reg 4(2) does not apply to safety representatives appointed by virtue of reg 8 (see PARA 1073 note 5): reg 8(3). As to exemption from this requirement see reg 10 (cited in PARA 1073). As to the Health and Safety Executive see HEALTH AND SAFETY AT WORK vol 52 (2014) PARA 326 et seq. See *Duthie v Bath & North East Somerset Council* [2003] ICR 1405, EAT; *Walker v North Tees and Hartlepool NHS Trust* [2008] All ER (D) 55 (Oct), EAT.

8 Safety Representatives and Safety Committees Regulations 1977, SI 1977/500, reg 11(1) (amended by the Employment Rights (Dispute Resolution) Act 1998 s 1(2)(a)). As to employment tribunals see PARA 1399 et seq.

9 As to when a complaint is presented see PARAS 804, 1461.

10 Safety Representatives and Safety Committees Regulations 1977, SI 1977/500, reg 11(2) (amended by the Employment Rights (Dispute Resolution) Act 1998 s 1(2)(a)). For the case law on the extension of time limits, especially in the context of the law of unfair dismissal, see PARAS 804, 1453.

11 See the Safety Representatives and Safety Committees Regulations 1977, SI 1977/500, regs 11(2A), 12 (added by SI 2014/431).

12 Safety Representatives and Safety Committees Regulations 1977, SI 1977/500, reg 11(3) (amended by the Employment Rights (Dispute Resolution) Act 1998 s 1(2)(a)).

13 Safety Representatives and Safety Committees Regulations 1977, SI 1977/500, reg 11(4) (amended by the Employment Rights (Dispute Resolution) Act 1998 s 1(2)(a)). As to the similar

provisions regarding the right to paid time off for trade union duties under the Trade Union and Labour Relations (Consolidation) Act 1992 ss 168, 169 see PARAS 1065, 1068.

1075. Safety committees. In such cases as may be prescribed it is the duty of every employer, if requested to do so by the safety representatives appointed by recognised trade unions[1], to establish a safety committee in accordance with regulations made by the Secretary of State[2]. Such a committee has the function of keeping under review the measures taken to ensure the health and safety at work of his employees[3] and such other functions as may be prescribed[4].

Such a committee must be established in any case in which at least two safety representatives request the employer[5] in writing to do so[6]. Where an employer is so requested to establish a safety committee, he must:

(1) consult with the safety representatives who made the request and with the representatives of recognised trade unions whose members work in any workplace[7] in respect of which he proposes that the committee should function[8]; and

(2) post a notice stating the composition of the committee and the workplace or workplaces to be covered by it in a place where it may be easily read by the employees[9].

The committee must be established not later than three months after the request for it[10].

1 Ie the safety representatives mentioned in the Health and Safety at Work etc Act 1974 s 2(4): see PARA 1073. As to the meaning of 'recognised trade union' for these purposes see PARA 1073 note 1.

2 Health and Safety at Work etc Act 1974 s 2(7) (amended by the Employment Protection Act 1975 Sch 15 para 2). In exercise of the power so conferred the Secretary of State made the Safety Representatives and Safety Committees Regulations 1977, SI 1977/500, reg 9: see the text and notes 5–10.

3 As to the meaning of 'employee' for these purposes see PARA 1073 note 2.

4 Health and Safety at Work etc Act 1974 s 2(7).

5 As to the meaning of 'employer' for these purposes see PARA 1073 note 20.

6 Safety Representatives and Safety Committees Regulations 1977, SI 1977/500, reg 9(1).

7 As to the meaning of 'workplace' see PARA 1073 note 9.

8 Safety Representatives and Safety Committees Regulations 1977, SI 1977/500, reg 9(2)(a).

9 Safety Representatives and Safety Committees Regulations 1977, SI 1977/500, reg 9(2)(b).

10 Safety Representatives and Safety Committees Regulations 1977, SI 1977/500, reg 9(2)(c). As to exemption from the requirement to establish a safety committee see reg 10; and PARA 1073.

1076. Right not to suffer detriment in health and safety cases. An employee[1] has the right not to be subjected to any detriment[2] by any act, or any deliberate failure to act, by his employer[3] done on the ground that, being a representative of workers on matters of health and safety at work[4] or a member of a safety committee[5]:

(1) in accordance with arrangements established under or by virtue of any enactment; or

(2) by reason of being acknowledged as such by the employer,

he performed, or proposed to perform, any functions as such a representative or a member of such a committee in accordance with arrangements established under or by virtue of any enactment or by reason of being acknowledged as such by the employer[6]. An employee has no such right where the detriment in question amounts to dismissal[7].

An employee may present a complaint to an employment tribunal on the ground that he has been subjected to a detriment in contravention of the above provisions[8]. An employment tribunal must not consider such a complaint unless it is presented[9]:

(a)   before the end of the period of three months beginning with the date of the act[10] or failure to act[11] to which the complaint relates or, where that act or failure is part of a series of similar acts or failures, the last of them[12], subject to an extension because of mediation in certain European cross-border disputes or to facilitate conciliation before the institution of proceedings[13];

(b)   where the tribunal is satisfied that it was not reasonably practicable for the complaint to be presented before the end of that period, within such further period as it considers reasonable[14].

On such a complaint it is for the employer to show the ground on which any act, or deliberate failure to act, was done[15]; and, where the tribunal finds such a complaint well-founded, it must make a declaration to that effect and may make an award of compensation to be paid to the complainant in respect of the act or failure to act to which the complaint relates[16]. The amount of the compensation awarded must be such as the tribunal considers just and equitable in all the circumstances, having regard to the infringement complained of and to any loss[17] which is attributable to the act or failure which infringed his right[18]; but, where the tribunal finds that that act or failure was to any extent caused or contributed to by action of the complainant, it must reduce the amount of the compensation by such proportion as it considers just and equitable, having regard to that finding[19].

1   As to the meaning of 'employee' for the purposes of the Employment Rights Act 1996 see PARA 2.
2   As to the meaning of 'detriment' see PARA 1048 note 2; see also PARA 614.
3   As to the meaning of 'employer' for the purposes of the Employment Rights Act 1996 see PARA 2.
4   As to health and safety representatives see PARA 1073.
5   As to safety committees see PARA 1075.
6   See the Employment Rights Act 1996 s 44(1)(b); and PARA 614. This protection only applies to actions in the scope of the representatives authority: *Shillito v Van Leer (UK) Ltd* [1997] IRLR 495, EAT. As to the meaning of 'employer' for these purposes see PARA 2. As to the other circumstances in which an employee, not being a health and safety representative or a member of a safety committee, is not to suffer a detriment on health and safety grounds see the Employment Rights Act 1996 s 44(1)(a), (ba)–(e); and PARA 614.
7   Employment Rights Act 1996 s 44(4) (amended by the Employment Relations Act 1999 ss 18(1), (2), Sch 9). For these purposes, 'dismissal' has the meaning given in the Employment Rights Act 1996 Pt X (ss 94–134A) (see PARA 757 et seq: s 44(4) (as so amended). See also PARA 614.
8   Employment Rights Act 1996 s 48(1) (amended by the Employment Rights (Dispute Resolution) Act 1998 s 1(2)(a)). The reference in the text to 'the above provisions' is to the Employment Rights Act 1996 s 44. See also PARA 625. As to employment tribunals see PARA 1399 et seq.
9   As to when a complaint is presented see PARAS 804, 1461.
10   For these purposes, where an act extends over a period, the 'date of the act' means the last day of that period: Employment Rights Act 1996 s 48(4)(a). See also PARA 625.
11   For these purposes, a deliberate failure to act is to be treated as done when it was decided on; and, in the absence of evidence establishing the contrary, an employer is to be taken to decide on a failure to act when he does an act inconsistent with doing the failed act or, if he has done no such inconsistent act, when the period expires within which he might reasonably have been expected to do the failed act if it was to be done: Employment Rights Act 1996 s 48(4)(b). See also PARA 625.
12   Employment Rights Act 1996 s 48(3)(a) (amended by the Employment Rights (Dispute Resolution) Act 1998 s 1(2)(a)). See also PARA 625. For the case law on the extension of time limits, especially in the context of the law of unfair dismissal, see PARAS 804, 1453.

13 The Employment Rights Act 1996 s 207A(3) (extension because of mediation in certain European cross-border disputes: see PARA 1454) and s 207B (extension of time limits to facilitate conciliation before institution of proceedings: see PARA 1455) apply for the purposes of s 48(3)(a): s 48(4A) (added by SI 2011/1133; amended by the Enterprise and Regulatory Reform Act 2013 Sch 2 paras 15, 19).

14 Employment Rights Act 1996 s 48(3)(b) (amended by the Employment Rights (Dispute Resolution) Act 1998 s 1(2)(a)). See also note 12.

15 Employment Rights Act 1996 s 48(2). See also PARA 625.

16 Employment Rights Act 1996 s 49(1) (amended by the Employment Rights (Dispute Resolution) Act 1998 s 1(2)(a)). See also PARA 626.

17 The loss is to be taken to include: (1) any expenses reasonably incurred by the complainant in consequence of the act or failure complained of; and (2) loss of any benefit which he might reasonably be expected to have had but for that act or failure: Employment Rights Act 1996 s 49(3). In ascertaining the loss, the tribunal must apply the same rule concerning the duty of a person to mitigate his loss as applies to damages recoverable under the common law: s 49(4). See also PARA 626. As to the duty to mitigate loss in the context of law of unfair dismissal see PARA 822.

18 Employment Rights Act 1996 s 49(2). See also PARA 626.

19 Employment Rights Act 1996 s 49(5). See also PARA 626. As to contributory fault in the context of law of unfair dismissal see PARA 821.

1077. Dismissal or selection for redundancy in health and safety cases. The dismissal[1] of an employee[2] by an employer[3] is to be regarded as having been unfair[4] if the reason for it (or, if more than one, the principal reason[5]), was that the employee was a representative of workers on matters of health and safety at work[6], or a member of a safety committee[7], and performed, or proposed to perform, any functions as such a representative or a member of such a committee:

(1)   in accordance with arrangements established under or by virtue of any enactment; or

(2)   by reason of being acknowledged as such by the employer[8].

Such a reason for selection for redundancy is also deemed to be unfair[9], and the protection from unfair dismissal or selection for redundancy on these grounds is not lost if the employee was taking part in industrial action at the time of the dismissal[10].

1   As to the meaning of 'dismissal' for these purposes see PARA 762.
2   As to the meaning of 'employee' for these purposes see PARA 2.
3   As to the meaning of 'employer' for these purposes see PARA 2.
4   Ie for the purposes of the Employment Rights Act 1996 Pt X (ss 94–134A): see PARA 757 et seq.
5   As to the meaning of 'reason or principal reason' see PARA 769.
6   As to safety representatives see PARA 1073.
7   As to safety committees see PARA 1075.
8   See the Employment Rights Act 1996 s 100(1)(b); and PARA 786. This protection covers not just the exercise of the functions but also the manner of the exercise, and it will be lost only if the actions of the representative are so extreme or malicious that he is no longer pursuing the relevant functions: *Goodwin v Cabletel UK Ltd* [1998] ICR 112, [1997] IRLR 665, EAT. Where a dismissal is unfair on these grounds: (1) there is a minimum basic award of £5,676, subject to periodic review (see the Employment Rights Act 1996 s 120(1); and PARA 816); (2) the compensatory award is not subject to the normal statutory maximum (see s 124(1A); and PARA 823); and (3) interim relief is available (see s 128(1); and PARA 805). In addition, there is no need for the employee to have served the normal one-year qualifying period: see s 108(3)(c); and PARA 758.
      As to the other circumstances in which an employee, not being a health and safety representative or a member of a safety committee, is not to be unfairly dismissed or unfairly selected for redundancy on health and safety grounds see s 100(1)(a), (ba)–(e); and PARA 786.
9   See the Employment Rights Act 1996 s 105(1), (3); and PARA 781.
10 See the Trade Union and Labour Relations (Consolidation) Act 1992 ss 237(1A), 238(2A); and PARA 1351.

(12) RECIPROCAL ARRANGEMENTS WITH NORTHERN IRELAND

1078. Power to make reciprocal arrangements. If provision is made by Northern Ireland legislation[1] for purposes corresponding to the purposes of any provision of the Trade Union and Labour Relations (Consolidation) Act 1992 re-enacting a provision of the Employment Protection Act 1975 or the Employment Protection (Consolidation) Act 1978, the Secretary of State[2] may, with the consent of the Treasury[3], make reciprocal arrangements with the appropriate Northern Ireland authority[4] for co-ordinating the relevant provisions of the Trade Union and Labour Relations (Consolidation) Act 1992 with the corresponding Northern Ireland provisions so as to secure that they operate, to such extent as may be provided by the arrangements, as a single system[5]. The Secretary of State may make regulations for giving effect to any such arrangements[6]; and the regulations may provide that the relevant provisions of the Trade Union and Labour Relations (Consolidation) Act 1992 are to have effect in relation to persons affected by the arrangements subject to such modifications and adaptations as may be specified in the regulations, including provisions:

(1) for securing that acts, omissions and events having any effect for the purposes of the Northern Ireland legislation have a corresponding effect for the purposes of the relevant provisions of the Trade Union and Labour Relations (Consolidation) Act 1992, but not so as to confer a right to double payment in respect of the same act, omission or event; and

(2) for determining, in cases where rights accrue both under the relevant provisions of the Trade Union and Labour Relations (Consolidation) Act 1992 and under the Northern Ireland legislation, which of these rights is available to the person concerned[7].

Certain provisions[8] of the Trade Union and Labour Relations (Consolidation) Act 1992 extend to Northern Ireland, but that Act does not otherwise extend there[9].

1 As to the meaning of 'Northern Ireland legislation' see PARA 970 note 5.
2 As to the Secretary of State see PARA 5 note 21.
3 As to the Treasury see CONSTITUTIONAL AND ADMINISTRATIVE LAW vol 20 (2014) PARA 262 et seq.
4 For these purposes, 'appropriate Northern Ireland authority' means such authority as is specified in that behalf in the Northern Ireland legislation: Trade Union and Labour Relations (Consolidation) Act 1992 s 294(5).
5 Trade Union and Labour Relations (Consolidation) Act 1992 s 294(1).
6 Trade Union and Labour Relations (Consolidation) Act 1992 s 294(2). Such regulations must be made by statutory instrument which is subject to annulment in pursuance of a resolution of either House of Parliament (s 294(6)); and they may make different provision for different cases and may contain such supplementary, incidental and transitional provisions as appear to the Secretary of State to be necessary or expedient (s 294(3)). At the date at which this volume states the law no such regulations had been made and none have effect as if so made.
7 Trade Union and Labour Relations (Consolidation) Act 1992 s 294(4).
8 Ie the following provisions: (1) the Trade Union and Labour Relations (Consolidation) Act 1992 ss 13, 14 (provisions as to property held in trust for trade union) (see PARAS 920, 921) and s 129 (application of provisions to employers' associations) (see PARA 1086) so far as it applies ss 13, 14; (2) Pt I Ch VI (ss 71–96) (application of funds for political objects) (see PARA 974 et seq), except ss 86, 87 (duties of employer who deducts union contributions) (see PARAS 989, 990), for the purposes of the application of Pt I Ch VI to trade unions or unincorporated employers' associations having their head or main office outside Northern Ireland; (3) s 287 (offshore employment) (see PARA 970); (4) s 294 (see the text and notes 1–7); and (5) s 300, Schs 1–3

(repeals, consequential amendments, transitional provisions and savings), so far as they relate to enactments which extend to Northern Ireland, other than the Conspiracy and Protection of Property Act 1875: Trade Union and Labour Relations (Consolidation) Act 1992 s 301(2). Section 301(2)(b) (see head (2) above), does not, however, affect the operation of the Trade Union and Labour Relations (Northern Ireland) Order 1995, SI 1995/1980, art 71(2)–(4) (application of Northern Ireland law to contributions by members in Northern Ireland); and the closing words of the Trade Union and Labour Relations (Consolidation) Act 1992 s 301(2)(b) do not affect the operation in relation to persons or property in Northern Ireland of any provision of Pt I Ch VII (ss 97–108) (amalgamations and similar matters) (see PARA 998 et seq) which is capable of so applying as part of the law of England and Wales or Scotland: s 301(3) (amended by SI 1995/1980).

9   Trade Union and Labour Relations (Consolidation) Act 1992 s 301(2). The 1992 Act does, however, extend to Scotland, except for s 212A(6) (arbitration scheme for unfair dismissal etc) (see PARA 824): s 301(1) (amended by the Employment Rights (Dispute Resolution) Act 1998 Sch 1 para 10). However generally Scottish matters are beyond the scope of this work. As to the extension of certain of the amending provisions of the Trade Union Reform and Employment Rights Act 1993 to Northern Ireland see s 54(3).

9. EMPLOYERS' ASSOCIATIONS

(1) DEFINITION AND LEGAL STATUS OF EMPLOYERS' ASSOCIATIONS

(i) Meaning of 'Employers' Association'

1079. Meanings of 'employers' association' and 'federated employers' association'. An 'employers' association' means[1] an organisation, whether temporary or permanent, which either:

(1)   consists wholly or mainly of employers[2] or individual owners of undertakings of one or more descriptions and whose principal purposes include the regulation of relations between employers of that description or those descriptions and workers[3] or trade unions[4]; or

(2)   consists wholly or mainly of:

    (a)   constituent or affiliated organisations which fulfil the conditions in head (1) above or themselves consist wholly or mainly of constituent or affiliated organisations which fulfil those conditions; or

    (b)   representatives of such constituent or affiliated organisations,

and whose principal purposes include the regulation of relations between employers and workers or between employers and trade unions, or the regulation of relations between its constituent or affiliated organisations[5].

References[6] to employers' associations include combinations of employers and employers' associations[7].

A 'federated employers' association' means an employers' association which consists wholly or mainly of constituent or affiliated organisations, or representatives of such organisations, as described in head (2) above[8].

1   Ie in the Trade Union and Labour Relations (Consolidation) Act 1992: see PARAS 891 et seq, 1080 et seq.
2   As to the meaning of 'employer' see PARA 892.
3   As to the meaning of 'worker' see PARA 892.
4   As to the meaning of 'trade union' see PARA 891.
5   Trade Union and Labour Relations (Consolidation) Act 1992 s 122(1). Cf *National Federation of Self-Employed and Small Businesses Ltd v Philpott* [1997] ICR 518, [1997] IRLR 340, EAT (decided under the Sex Discrimination Act 1975 (repealed: see now the Equality Act 2010)).
6   See note 1.
7   Trade Union and Labour Relations (Consolidation) Act 1992 s 122(2). Any reference in an enactment passed, or instrument made under an enactment, before 16 September 1974, to an employers' association registered under the Trade Union Acts 1871 to 1964 (repealed) or the Industrial Relations Act 1971 (repealed), or to an organisation of employers within the meaning of the 1971 Act, is to be construed as a reference to an employers' association within the meaning of the Trade Union and Labour Relations (Consolidation) Act 1992; but this does not apply to any enactment relating to income tax or corporation tax: Sch 3 para 4.
8   Trade Union and Labour Relations (Consolidation) Act 1992 s 135(1). The provisions of Pt I (ss 1–121) (see PARA 891 et seq) applied by Pt II (ss 122–136) (see PARA 1083 et seq) to employers' associations apply to federated employers' associations, subject to the following exceptions and adaptations (s 135(2)):

    (1)   the following provisions of Pt I Ch III (ss 24–45D) (administration) (see PARA 930 et seq) do not apply to a federated employers' association which consists wholly or mainly of representatives of constituent or affiliated organisations: s 27 (duty to supply copy of rules) (see PARA 912); s 28 (duty to keep accounting records) (see PARA 940); s 32(1), (2), (3)(a), (b), (c), (4)–(6) and ss 33–37 (annual return, accounts and audit) (see PARA 943 et seq); ss 37A–37E (investigation of financial affairs) (see PARA 949 et

seq); and ss 38–42 (members' superannuation schemes) (see PARA 953 et seq) (s 135(3) (amended by the Trade Union Reform and Employment Rights Act 1993 Sch 8 para 66, Sch 10));

(2) the provisions of the Trade Union and Labour Relations (Consolidation) Act 1992 Pt I Ch VI (ss 71–96) (application of funds for political objects) (see PARA 974 et seq) apply to an employers' association which is in whole or part an association or combination of other associations as if the individual members of the component associations were members of the association and not of the component associations; but nothing in Pt I Ch VI prevents a component association from collecting contributions on behalf of the association or combination from such of its members as are not exempt from the obligation to contribute to the political fund of the association or combination (s 135(4)).

(ii) Legal Status of Employers' Associations

1080. Corporate or quasi-corporate status of employers' associations. An employers' association[1] may be either a body corporate or an unincorporated association[2]. However, legislation gives an unincorporated employers' association some of the most important attributes of corporate personality. Thus:

(1) it is capable of making contracts;

(2) it is capable of suing and being sued in its own name, whether in proceedings relating to property or founded on contract or tort or any other cause of action[3]; and

(3) proceedings for an offence alleged to have been committed by it or on its behalf may be brought against it in its own name[4].

1 As to the meaning of 'employers' association' see PARA 1079.
2 Trade Union and Labour Relations (Consolidation) Act 1992 s 127(1).
3 It is permissible for an employee to bring a claim against an employer who is the management committee of an unincorporated association by using the name of the association in employment tribunals (unlike the position in the civil courts): see *Asim v Nazir* [2010] ICR 1225, [2010] All ER (D) 113 (Aug), EAT (applying *Affleck v Newcastle MIND* [1999] ICR 852, [1999] IRLR 405, EAT: see PARA 2).
4 Trade Union and Labour Relations (Consolidation) Act 1992 s 127(2). See also the Corporate Manslaughter and Corporate Homicide Act 2007; and CRIMINAL LAW vol 25 (2010) PARA 108 et seq.

1081. Exclusion of common law rules as to restraint of trade. The purposes of an unincorporated employers' association[1] and, so far as they relate to the regulation of relations between employers[2] and workers[3] or trade unions[4], the purposes of an employers' association which is a body corporate, are not, by reason only that they are in restraint of trade[5], unlawful so as:

(1) to make any member of the association liable to criminal proceedings for conspiracy or otherwise; or

(2) to make any agreement or trust void or voidable[6].

No rule of an unincorporated employers' association or, so far as it relates to the regulation of relations between employers and workers or trade unions, of an employers' association which is a body corporate, is unlawful or unenforceable by reason only that it is in restraint of trade[7].

1 As to the meaning of 'employers' association' see PARA 1079.
2 As to the meaning of 'employer' see PARA 892.
3 As to the meaning of 'worker' see PARA 892.
4 As to the meaning of 'trade union' see PARA 891.
5 As to restraint of trade generally see COMPETITION vol 18 (2009) PARA 377 et seq.
6 Trade Union and Labour Relations (Consolidation) Act 1992 s 128(1).
7 Trade Union and Labour Relations (Consolidation) Act 1992 s 128(2).

1082. Prohibition on discrimination etc in membership. An employers' association comes within the statutory definition of a 'trade organisation' for the purposes of the Equality Act 2010[1]. As such it must not discriminate[2] against or victimise[3] a person ('B'):

(1) in the arrangements it makes for deciding to whom to offer membership of the organisation;

(2) as to the terms on which it is prepared to admit B as a member;

(3) by not accepting B's application for membership[4].

Nor must it discriminate against or victimise a member ('B'):

(a) in the way it affords B access, or by not affording B access, to opportunities for receiving a benefit, facility or service[5];

(b) by depriving B of membership;

(c) by varying the terms on which B is a member;

(d) by subjecting B to any other detriment[6].

An employers' association, as such a trade organisation, must not, in relation to membership of it, harass[7] a member, or an applicant for membership[8].

A duty to make reasonable adjustments for disabled persons applies to a trade organisation such as an employers' association[9].

A rule of an employers' association is unenforceable against a person in so far as it constitutes, promotes or provides for treatment of the person that is of a description prohibited by the 2010 Act[10].

1 See the Equality Act 2010 s 57(7)(b).
2 As to direct discrimination see DISCRIMINATION vol 33 (2013) PARA 65; and as to indirect discrimination see DISCRIMINATION vol 33 (2013) PARA 72.
3 As to victimisation see DISCRIMINATION vol 33 (2013) PARA 75.
4 Equality Act 2010 s 57(1), (4).
5 As to the meaning of 'benefit, facility or service' for these purposes see DISCRIMINATION vol 33 (2013) PARA 111 note 7. There are exceptions to this provision in connection with the provision of childcare: see Sch 9 para 15; and DISCRIMINATION vol 33 (2013) PARA 161.
6 Equality Act 2010 s 57(2), (5). As to the meaning of 'detriment' see DISCRIMINATION vol 33 (2013) PARA 75 note 1. Where a trade union's actions or policy in favouring one group of members over another (to promote the greater good overall) are indirectly sexually discriminatory, the union my seek to establish the defence of justification, but to do so it must show not just a legitimate aim (which the 'greater good' may be) but also that it pursued that aim by proportionate means: *Allen v GMB* [2008] EWCA Civ 810, [2008] IRLR 690, [2008] All ER (D) 207 (Jul). In *Furniture, Timber and Allied Trades Union v Mogdill, Pel Ltd v Mogdill* [1980] IRLR 142, EAT, poor support, representation etc by a union of its Asian members was held not to be discriminatory because there was no evidence that union members of other racial groups were treated more favourably by the union. For a member to have been subjected to a 'detriment', the detriment must have been caused to the complainant while they were a member of the union, and not after their membership had ended: *Diakou v Islington UNISON 'A' Branch* [1997] ICR 121, EAT. All these authorities were decided under earlier legislation.
7 As to harassment see DISCRIMINATION vol 33 (2013) PARA 73.
8 Equality Act 2010 s 57(3).
9 See the Equality Act 2010 s 57(6). See further Sch 8 paras 1, 2, 4, 20; and DISCRIMINATION vol 33 (2013) PARA 247.
10 See the Equality Act 2010 s 145(2); and DISCRIMINATION vol 33 (2013) PARA 5. Section 145(2) refers to a rule of an 'undertaking', ie a rule made by a trade organisation or a qualifications body (see s 148(5), (6)).

(iii) Listing of Employers' Associations

1083. The list of employers' associations. The certification officer[1] must keep a list of employers' associations[2] containing the names of the organisations entitled[3] to have their names entered in that list[4]. He must keep copies of the list of employers' associations, as for the time being in force, available for public inspection at all reasonable hours free of charge[5]; and a copy of the list must be included in his annual report[6]. The fact that the name of an organisation is included in the list of employers' associations is evidence that the organisation is an employers' association[7]; and, on the application of an organisation whose name is so entered, the certification officer must issue it with a certificate to that effect[8]. A document purporting to be such a certificate is evidence that the name of the organisation is entered in the list[9].

1 As to the certification officer see PARA 1443. The certification officer is also required to keep a list of trade unions: see PARA 900. The function of listing trade unions and employers' associations was formerly performed by the Chief Registrar of Friendly Societies: see PARA 1443 note 1.
2 As to the meaning of 'employers' association' see PARA 1079.
3 Ie in accordance with the Trade Union and Labour Relations (Consolidation) Act 1992 Pt II (ss 122–136).
4 Trade Union and Labour Relations (Consolidation) Act 1992 s 123(1)(b). The list must also contain the names of the organisations whose names were, immediately before 16 October 1992 (ie the commencement date of the Trade Union and Labour Relations (Consolidation) Act 1992: see s 302), duly entered in the list kept by the certification officer under the Trade Union and Labour Relations Act 1974 s 8 (repealed): Trade Union and Labour Relations (Consolidation) Act 1992 s 123(1)(a).
5 Trade Union and Labour Relations (Consolidation) Act 1992 s 123(2).
6 Trade Union and Labour Relations (Consolidation) Act 1992 s 123(3). As to the certification officer's annual report see PARA 1443.
7 Trade Union and Labour Relations (Consolidation) Act 1992 s 123(4).
8 Trade Union and Labour Relations (Consolidation) Act 1992 s 123(5).
9 Trade Union and Labour Relations (Consolidation) Act 1992 s 123(6).

1084. Entry in the list of employers' associations. An organisation of employers[1], whenever formed, whose name is not entered in the list[2] of employers' associations[3] may apply to the certification officer[4] to have its name entered in the list[5]. The application must be made in such form and manner as the certification officer may require and it must be accompanied by:

(1) a copy of the rules of the organisation;
(2) a list of its officers[6];
(3) the address of its head or main office;
(4) the name under which it is or is to be known,

and by the prescribed fee[7].

If the certification officer is satisfied that the organisation is an employers' association, that the above conditions[8] have been complied with, and that entry of the name in the list is not prohibited by statute[9], he must enter the name of the organisation in the list of employers' associations[10].

An organisation aggrieved by the refusal of the certification officer to enter its name in the list of employers' associations may appeal on any appealable question[11] to the Employment Appeal Tribunal[12].

1 As to the meaning of 'employer' see PARA 892.
2 As to the list of employers' associations see PARA 1083.
3 As to the meaning of 'employers' association' see PARA 1079.
4 As to the certification officer see PARA 1443.
5 Trade Union and Labour Relations (Consolidation) Act 1992 s 124(1).
6 For these purposes, 'officer', in relation to an employers' association, includes any member of the governing body of the association and any trustee of any fund applicable for the purposes of the association: Trade Union and Labour Relations (Consolidation) Act 1992 s 136.
7 Trade Union and Labour Relations (Consolidation) Act 1992 s 124(2). The fee so prescribed is £150: Certification Officer (Amendment of Fees) Regulations 2005, SI 2005/713, reg 6. The fee for the entry of an amalgamated employers' association in the list of employers' associations maintained by the certification officer where each of the amalgamating employers' associations

is already entered in the list is, however, £41: Trade Unions and Employers' Associations (Amalgamations etc) Regulations 1975, SI 1975/536, reg 12 (substituted by SI 1978/1344; amended by SI 2005/713). As to the Secretary of State's power to make regulations prescribing certain matters under the Trade Union and Labour Relations (Consolidation) Act 1992 see s 293; and PARA 902 note 8.

8   Ie the Trade Union and Labour Relations (Consolidation) Act 1992 s 124(2).

9   Ie by the Trade Union and Labour Relations (Consolidation) Act 1992 s 124(4). The certification officer must not enter the name of an organisation in the list of employers' associations if the name is the same as that under which another organisation: (1) was registered as a trade union on 30 September 1971 (ie the day before the relevant provisions of the Industrial Relations Act 1971 were brought into force by the Industrial Relations Act 1971 (Commencement No 1) Order 1971, SI 1971/1522, art 2, Schedule) under the Trade Union Acts 1871 to 1964 (repealed); (2) was at any time registered as an employers' association or trade union under the Industrial Relations Act 1971 (repealed); or (3) is for the time being entered in the list of employers' associations or in the list of trade unions kept under the Trade Union and Labour Relations (Consolidation) Act 1992 Pt I Ch I (ss 1–9) (see PARA 891 et seq); or if the name is one so nearly resembling any such name as to be likely to deceive the public: s 124(4).

10 Trade Union and Labour Relations (Consolidation) Act 1992 s 124(3).

11 For these purposes, an 'appealable question' is any question of law arising in the proceedings before, or arising from the decision of, the certification officer: Trade Union and Labour Relations (Consolidation) Act 1992 s 126(3) (amended by the Employment Relations Act 2004 s 51(2)(c)).

12 Trade Union and Labour Relations (Consolidation) Act 1992 s 126(1) (amended by the Employment Relations Act 2004 s 51(2)(a)). As to the Employment Appeal Tribunal see PARA 1422 et seq.

1085.   Removal from the list of employers' associations.   Where it appears to the certification officer[1], on application made to him or otherwise, that an organisation whose name is entered in the list[2] of employers' associations[3] is not an employers' association, he may remove its name from the list[4]; but he must not do so without giving the organisation notice of his intention and considering any representations made to him by the organisation within such period, of not less than 28 days beginning with the date of the notice, as may be specified in the notice[5]. The certification officer must remove the name of an organisation from the list if he is requested by the organisation to do so or if he is satisfied that the organisation has ceased to exist[6]. An organisation aggrieved by a decision of the certification officer to remove its name from the list of employers' associations may appeal on any appealable question[7] to the Employment Appeal Tribunal[8].

1   As to the certification officer see PARA 1443.
2   As to the list of employers' associations see PARA 1083.
3   As to the meaning of 'employers' association' see PARA 1079.
4   Trade Union and Labour Relations (Consolidation) Act 1992 s 125(1).
5   Trade Union and Labour Relations (Consolidation) Act 1992 s 125(2).
6   Trade Union and Labour Relations (Consolidation) Act 1992 s 125(3).
7   As to the meaning of 'appealable question' see PARA 1084 note 11.
8   Trade Union and Labour Relations (Consolidation) Act 1992 s 126(1) (amended by the Employment Relations Act 2004 s 51(2)(a)). As to the Employment Appeal Tribunal see PARA 1422 et seq.

(2) PROPERTY AND ADMINISTRATION OF EMPLOYERS' ASSOCIATIONS

1086.   Property of unincorporated employers' associations.   All property belonging to an unincorporated employers' association[1] must be vested in trustees in trust for it[2]; and a judgment, order or award made in proceedings of any description brought against such an association is enforceable, by way of execution, punishment for contempt or otherwise, against any property held in trust for it to the same extent and in the same manner as if it were a body corporate[3].

On the death of a trustee in whom property is vested in trust for an employers' association the general law of trusts applies to vest the trust property in the surviving trustees or the personal representative of the last surviving trustee[4]. Where, however, a trustee wishes to be discharged from the trust and no new trustee is to replace him, the general statutory provisions which require the discharge to be by deed[5] are modified in relation to the trustee of an unincorporated employers' association whose name is entered in the list of employers' associations[6], so as to permit the discharge to be by instrument in writing[7]. Subject to any express provision in it to the contrary, such an instrument in writing discharging the trustee operates to vest the trust property[8] automatically in the continuing trustees of the association without any conveyance or assignment of the property[9]. Similarly, the appointment of a new trustee by such an instrument in writing is sufficient to vest the trust property[10] in the new or continuing trustees without any conveyance or assignment of the property[11].

Where, by any enactment or instrument, the transfer of securities of any description is required to be effected or recorded by means of entries in a register, the person authorised or required to keep the register is required, notwithstanding anything in any enactment or instrument regulating the keeping of the register, to make such entries as may be necessary to give effect to an instrument of appointment[12] or discharge[13], if there is produced to that person a copy of such an instrument which contains or has attached to it a list identifying the securities of the relevant description held in trust for the association at the date of the appointment or discharge[14], and it appears to that person that any of the securities so identified are included in the register kept by him[15].

1   As to the meaning of 'employers' association' see PARA 1079.

2   Trade Union and Labour Relations (Consolidation) Act 1992 s 12(1) (applied by s 129(1)(a)). The repeal of the Trade Union and Labour Relations Act 1974 s 19 (transitional provisions for employers' associations ceasing to be incorporated) does not affect: (1) the title to property which by virtue of s 19 (repealed) vested on 16 September 1974 in the 'appropriate trustees' as defined by s 19 (repealed) (Trade Union and Labour Relations (Consolidation) Act 1992 Sch 3 para 6(1)); or (2) any liability, obligation or right affecting such property which, by virtue of the Trade Union and Labour Relations Act 1974 s 19 (repealed), became a liability, obligation or right of those trustees; and a certificate given by the persons who on that date were the president and general secretary of an employers' association, or occupied positions equivalent thereto, that the persons named in the certificate are the appropriate trustees of the association for the purposes of s 19(2) (repealed) is conclusive evidence that those persons were the appropriate trustees for those purposes (Trade Union and Labour Relations (Consolidation) Act 1992 Sch 3 para 6(2)). A document which purports to be such a certificate is to be taken to be such a certificate unless the contrary is proved: Sch 3 para 6(3).

3   Trade Union and Labour Relations (Consolidation) Act 1992 s 12(2) (applied by s 129(1)(a)). This is subject to the restrictions in s 130 on the enforcement of awards against certain property: see PARA 1088.

4   As to the general law on the vesting of trust property on the death of a trustee see TRUSTS AND POWERS vol 98 (2013) PARA 157 et seq.

5   Ie the Trustee Act 1925 s 39(1): see TRUSTS AND POWERS vol 98 (2013) PARA 331.

6   Ie the list of employers' associations maintained by the certification officer under the Trade Union and Labour Relations (Consolidation) Act 1992 s 123: see PARA 1083.

7   Trade Union and Labour Relations (Consolidation) Act 1992 s 13(1), (2)(a); applied by s 129(1)(b)). Where a trustee is appointed or discharged by a resolution taken by or on behalf of the association, the written record of the resolution is to be treated as an instrument in writing appointing or discharging the trustee: s 13(1), (3) (applied by s 129(1)(b)).

8 Ie except land held under a lease which contains a covenant against assignment where consent to assign has not been obtained or where the instrument would operate as a breach of covenant or give rise to a forfeiture: see TRUSTS AND POWERS vol 98 (2013) PARA 307.

9 Trustee Act 1925 s 40(2) (amended by the Trusts of Land and Appointment of Trustees Act 1996 Sch 3 para 3(1), (14); modified by the Trade Union and Labour Relations (Consolidation) Act 1992 s 13(1), (2)(b); applied by s 129(1)(b)); Trustee Act 1925 s 40(4)(b) (applied by the Trade Union and Labour Relations (Consolidation) Act 1992 ss 13(1), (4), 129(1)(b)). This is in contrast to the application of the Trustee Act 1925 to other trusts, where the discharge must be by deed to effect vesting without conveyance or assignment (see s 40(2); and TRUSTS AND POWERS vol 98 (2013) PARA 306), and where land held by way of mortgage for securing money subject to the trust (see s 40(4)(a); and TRUSTS AND POWERS vol 98 (2013) PARA 307) and shares, stocks, annuities and property transferable only in books kept by a company or other body or in a manner directed by or under an Act of Parliament (see s 40(4)(c); and TRUSTS AND POWERS vol 98 (2013) PARA 307), as well as land held under a lease which contains a covenant against assignment where consent to assign has not been obtained or where the instrument would operate as a breach of covenant or give rise to a forfeiture (see s 40(4)(b); and TRUSTS AND POWERS vol 98 (2013) PARA 307), must be specifically conveyed or assigned.

10 See note 8.

11 Trustee Act 1925 s 40(1) (modified by the Trade Union and Labour Relations (Consolidation) Act 1992 s 13(1), (2)(b); applied by s 129(1)(b)); Trustee Act 1925 s 40(4)(b) (applied by the Trade Union and Labour Relations (Consolidation) Act 1992 ss 13(1), (4), 129(1)(b)). See also note 9.

12 For these purposes, 'instrument of appointment' means an instrument in writing appointing a new trustee of an employers' association whose name is entered in the list of employers' associations: Trade Union and Labour Relations (Consolidation) Act 1992 s 14(1) (applied by s 129(1)(c); modified by s 129(2)).

13 For these purposes, 'instrument of discharge' means an instrument in writing discharging a trustee of such an employers' association: Trade Union and Labour Relations (Consolidation) Act 1992 s 14(1) (applied by s 129(1)(c)).

14 A document purporting to be a copy of an instrument of appointment or discharge containing or having attached to it such a list, and to be certified in accordance with the Trade Union and Labour Relations (Consolidation) Act 1992 s 14(4) to be a copy of such an instrument, is to be taken to be a copy of such an instrument unless the contrary is proved: s 14(3) (applied by s 129(1)(c)). The certificate must be given by the president and general secretary of the association and, in the case of an instrument to which a list of securities is attached, must appear both on the instrument and on the list: s 14(4) (applied by s 129(1)(c)).

15 Trade Union and Labour Relations (Consolidation) Act 1992 s 14(2) (applied by 129(1)(c)). Nothing done for the purpose of or in pursuance of s 14 (as so applied) is to be taken to affect any person with notice of any trust or to impose on any person a duty to inquire into any matter: s 14(5) (applied by s 129(1)(c)). Where a trustee is appointed or discharged by a resolution taken by or on behalf of such an association, the written record of the resolution is to be treated as an instrument in writing appointing or discharging the trustee: s 14(1) (applied by s 129(1)(c)). As to the application of these provisions to Northern Ireland see PARA 1078.

1087. Application to employers' associations of the law relating to insurance companies, etc. The statutory provisions applying to trade unions[1] the law relating to insurance companies, industrial assurance or friendly societies apply to any employers' association[2] as they apply in relation to a trade union[3].

1 Ie the Trade Union and Labour Relations (Consolidation) Act 1992 s 19: see PARA 926. As to the meaning of 'trade union' see PARA 891.

2 As to the meaning of 'employers' association' see PARA 1079.

3 Trade Union and Labour Relations (Consolidation) Act 1992 s 129(3) (amended by SI 2001/3649).

1088. Restriction on enforcement of awards against property of employers' associations. Where in any proceedings an amount is awarded by way of damages, costs or expenses:

(1) against an employers' association[1];

(2)   against trustees² in whom property is vested in trust for an employers' association, in their capacity as such, and otherwise than in respect of a breach of trust on their part; or

(3)   against members or officials of an employers' association on behalf of themselves and all of the members of the association,

no part of that amount is recoverable by enforcement against any protected property³.

The following is protected property:

(a)   property belonging to the trustees otherwise than in their capacity as such;

(b)   property belonging to any member of the association otherwise than jointly or in common with the other members; and

(c)   property belonging to an official of the association who is neither a member nor a trustee⁴.

1   As to the meaning of 'employers' association' see PARA 1079.
2   As to the vesting of property in trustees see PARA 1086.
3   Trade Union and Labour Relations (Consolidation) Act 1992 s 130(1).
4   Trade Union and Labour Relations (Consolidation) Act 1992 s 130(2).

1089. Administrative provisions applying to employers' associations. The following administrative provisions apply¹ to an employers' association² as they apply in relation to a trade union³:

(1)   the duty to supply a copy of the rules⁴;

(2)   the duty to keep accounting records⁵;

(3)   certain of the provisions concerning the annual return, accounts and audit⁶;

(4)   the provisions concerning the investigation of financial affairs⁷;

(5)   the provisions concerning members' superannuation schemes⁸;

(6)   the exemption for newly formed organisations⁹;

(7)   the provisions concerning the discharge of duties in the case of an organisation having branches or sections¹⁰; and

(8)   the provisions concerning offences¹¹.

1   Ie by virtue of the Trade Union and Labour Relations (Consolidation) Act 1992 s 131(1) (amended by the Trade Union Reform and Employment Rights Act 1993 Sch 8 para 64).
2   As to the meaning of 'employers' association' see PARA 1079. The provisions in heads (1)–(5) in the text do not apply to a federated employers' association which consists wholly or mainly of representatives of constituent or affiliated organisations: see the Trade Union and Labour Relations (Consolidation) Act 1992 s 135(3); and PARA 1079 note 8 head (1). As to the meaning of 'federated employers' association' see PARA 1079.
3   Trade Union and Labour Relations (Consolidation) Act 1992 s 131(1) (as amended: see note 1). As to the meaning of 'trade union' see PARA 891.
4   Ie the Trade Union and Labour Relations (Consolidation) Act 1992 s 27: see PARA 912.
5   Ie the Trade Union and Labour Relations (Consolidation) Act 1992 s 28: see PARA 940. Thus, the provisions in ss 29–31 (see PARAS 940–942) concerning access to accounting records do not apply to employers' associations.
6   Ie the Trade Union and Labour Relations (Consolidation) Act 1992 s 32(1), (2), (3)(a), (b), (c), (4)–(6), and ss 33–37: see PARA 943 et seq. Thus, the provisions in s 32(3)(aa) and (d) (additional information to be contained in the annual return) (see PARA 943), and in s 32A (statement to members following annual return) (see PARA 944), do not apply to employers' associations. The provisions in ss 33–35 (appointment and removal of auditors) (see PARAS 945, 946) do not apply to an employers' association which is registered as a company under the Companies Act 2006 (see COMPANIES vol 14 (2009) PARA 131 et seq); and the provisions in the Trade Union and Labour Relations (Consolidation) Act 1992 ss 36, 37 (rights and duties of auditors) (see PARAS 947, 948) apply to the auditors appointed by such an association under the

Companies Act 2006 Pt 16 Ch 2 (ss 485–494) (see COMPANIES vol 15 (2009) PARA 912 et seq): Trade Union and Labour Relations (Consolidation) Act 1992 s 131(2) (amended by SI 2007/2194; SI 2008/948; SI 2009/1941).

7 Ie the Trade Union and Labour Relations (Consolidation) Act 1992 ss 37A–37E: see PARA 949 et seq.

8 Ie the Trade Union and Labour Relations (Consolidation) Act 1992 ss 38–42: see PARA 953 et seq.

9 Ie the Trade Union and Labour Relations (Consolidation) Act 1992 s 43(1): see PARAS 912, 943, 949, 953. The effect is to exempt an employers' association which has been in existence for less than 12 months from the provisions in heads (1), (3)–(5) in the text: see s 131(1) (as amended: see note 1).

10 Ie the Trade Union and Labour Relations (Consolidation) Act 1992 s 44(1), (2), (4): see PARAS 940, 943, 953. The effect is that, where an employers' association consists of or includes branches or sections, any duty falling on the association in relation to a branch or section under the provisions in heads (2), (3), (5) in the text is to be treated as discharged to the extent to which a branch or section discharges it instead of the association; and, similarly, any duty falling on a branch or section by reason of its being an employers' association under those provisions is to be treated as discharged to the extent to which the association of which it is a branch or section discharges the duty instead of it: see s 131(1) (as amended: see note 1).

11 Ie the Trade Union and Labour Relations (Consolidation) Act 1992 ss 45, s 45A: see PARAS 956, 957.

1090. Application of employers' association funds for political objects. The statutory provisions[1] concerning the application of funds for political objects[2] apply to an unincorporated employers' association[3] as they apply in relation to a trade union[4], save that certain of those provisions are modified[5] in their application to employers' associations[6].

An incorporated employers' association must give details in its annual directors' report of political donations and expenditure where the aggregate amount of such donations and expenditure is more than £2,000 in the relevant financial year[7].

1 Ie the Trade Union and Labour Relations (Consolidation) Act 1992 Pt I Ch VI (ss 71–96): see PARA 974 et seq.

2 As to the meaning of 'political objects' see PARA 975.

3 As to the meaning of 'employers' association' see PARA 1079. As to the application of the Trade Union and Labour Relations (Consolidation) Act 1992 Pt I Ch VI (ss 71–96) to an employers' association which is in whole or part an association or combination of other associations see PARA 1079 note 8 head (2).

4 Trade Union and Labour Relations (Consolidation) Act 1992 s 132(1) (amended by the Employment Relations Act 1999 Sch 6 paras 1, 20). As to the meaning of 'trade union' see PARA 891.

5 Ie by the Trade Union and Labour Relations (Consolidation) Act 1992 s 132(2)–(5) (added by the Employment Relations Act 1999 Sch 6 paras 1, 20).

6 Thus:
  (1) the provisions in the Trade Union and Labour Relations (Consolidation) Act 1992 s 72A (application of funds in breach of the statutory restrictions) (see PARA 976), s 80(5A)–(5C), (8)–(10) (application to the certification officer) (see PARA 983) and s 81(8) (application to the court) (see PARA 984) do not apply to unincorporated employers' associations (s 132(2) (as added: see note 5));
  (2) in its application to an unincorporated employers' association, s 79 (remedy for failure to comply with ballot rules) (see PARA 982) is modified to provide that the making of an application to the certification officer does not prevent the applicant, or any other person, from making an application to the court in respect of the same matter (s 132(3) (as added: see note 5));
  (3) in its application to an unincorporated employers' association, s 80(2)(b) (application to the certification officer) (see PARA 983) is modified to provide that the certification officer must give the applicant and the employers' association an opportunity to be heard where he considers it appropriate (s 132(4) (as added: see note 5)); and
  (4) in its application to an unincorporated employers' association, s 81 (application to the court) (see PARA 984) is modified to provide that, if an application in respect of the

same matter has been made to the certification officer, the court must have due regard to any declaration, reasons or observations of his which are brought to its notice (s 132(5) (as added: see note 5)).

7   See the Companies Act 2006 s 415; the Small Companies and Groups (Accounts and Directors' Report) Regulations 2008, SI 2008/409, reg 7, Sch 5 paras 2, 3; the Large and Medium-sized Companies and Groups (Accounts and Reports) Regulations 2008, SI 2008/410, reg 10, Sch 7 paras 3, 4; and COMPANIES vol 15 (2009) PARA 821.

(3) MERGER AND CHANGE OF NAME OF EMPLOYERS' ASSOCIATIONS

1091.   Amalgamations of employers' associations and transfers of engagements.   The statutory provisions concerning amalgamations and similar matters[1] apply to unincorporated employers' associations[2] as they apply in relation to trade unions[3], save that certain of those provisions are modified[4] in their application to employers' associations[5].

1   Ie the Trade Union and Labour Relations (Consolidation) Act 1992 Pt I Ch VII (ss 97–108): see PARA 998 et seq.
2   As to the meaning of 'employers' association' see PARA 1079.
3   Trade Union and Labour Relations (Consolidation) Act 1992 s 133(1) (s 133 substituted by the Trade Union Reform and Employment Rights Act 1993 Sch 8 para 65). As to the meaning of 'trade union' see PARA 891.
4   Ie by the Trade Union and Labour Relations (Consolidation) Act 1992 s 133(2) (as substituted (see note 3); amended by the Employment Relations Act 1999 Sch 6 paras 1, 21; the Employment Relations Act 2004 s 50(3), Sch 2).
5   Thus:
    (1)   the provisions in the Trade Union and Labour Relations (Consolidation) Act 1992 s 99(1) (see PARA 1002) concerning the giving of notice to members are modified in their application to employers' associations so as to provide that the association must take all reasonable steps to secure that, not less than seven days before the ballot on the resolution to approve the instrument of amalgamation or transfer is held, every member is supplied with a notice in writing approved for the purpose by the certification officer (s 133(2)(a) (as substituted: see note 3));
    (2)   of the requirements imposed by ss 100A–100E (see PARAS 1004–1006), only those specified in s 100B (entitlement to vote in the ballot) (see PARA 1005), s 100C(1) (voting by the marking of a voting paper) (see PARA 1005) and s 100C(3)(a) (voting without interference or constraint) (see PARA 1005) are to apply to employers' associations, together with the requirement that every member of the association must, so far as is reasonably possible, be given a fair opportunity of voting (s 133(2)(b) (as substituted: see note 3));
    (3)   ss 101A, 101B (listing and certification after amalgamation) (see PARA 1008) apply as if the references to the list of trade unions were to the list of employers' associations (s 133(2)(ba) (as substituted and amended: see notes 3, 4)); and
    (4)   s 101(3) (scrutineer's report) (see PARA 1007), s 101A(3), (4) (certificate of independence) (see PARA 1008), s 103(2A), (6)–(9) (complaints as regards passing of resolution) (see PARAS 1010, 1011) and s 107 (change of name) (see PARA 1016) do not apply to employers' associations (s 133(2)(c) (as substituted and amended: see notes 3, 4)).
    As to the change of name of an employers' association see PARA 1092.

1092.   Change of name of employers' association.   An incorporated employers' association[1] may change its name by special resolution or by other means in accordance with the Companies Act 2006[2].

An unincorporated employers' association may change its name by any method expressly provided for by its rules or, if its rules make no such express provision, by adopting in accordance with its rules an alteration of the provision in them which gives the association its name[3]. If, however, the name of an employers' association, whether incorporated or unincorporated, is entered in the list of employers' associations[4] maintained by the certification officer[5], a change of name does not take effect until approved by him[6]; and he must not approve a change of name if it appears to him that the proposed new name is the same as one entered in the list as the name of another employers' association, or is the same as one entered in the list of trade unions[7], or is a name so nearly resembling such a name as to be likely to deceive the public[8].

A change of name by an unincorporated employers' association does not affect any right or obligation of the association or any of its members; and any pending legal proceedings may be continued by or against the association, the trustees of the association or any other officer[9] of the association who can sue or be sued on its behalf, notwithstanding its change of name[10].

The power to make regulations for carrying certain provisions into effect[11] applies[12] in relation to the above provisions[13].

1   As to the meaning of 'employers' association' see PARA 1079.
2   See the Companies Act 2006 ss 67, 68, 75, 77, 80, 81; and COMPANIES vol 14 (2009) PARAS 214, 215, 219.
3   Trade Union and Labour Relations (Consolidation) Act 1992 s 134(1).
4   As to the list of employers' associations see PARA 1083.
5   As to the certification officer see PARA 1443.
6   Trade Union and Labour Relations (Consolidation) Act 1992 s 134(2).
7   As to the list of trade unions see PARA 900 et seq. As to the meaning of 'trade union' see PARA 891.
8   Trade Union and Labour Relations (Consolidation) Act 1992 s 134(3). The application must be signed by three members of the committee of management or other governing body and the secretary of the association and must be submitted to the certification officer in duplicate in the form to be provided by him for that purpose: Trade Unions and Employers' Associations (Amalgamations etc) Regulations 1975, SI 1975/536, reg 9(1) (reg 9 amended by SI 1978/1344). It must be accompanied by a statutory declaration by the secretary of the association as to the manner in which the change of name was effected in the form to be provided by the certification officer for the purpose: Trade Unions and Employers' Associations (Amalgamations etc) Regulations 1975, SI 1975/536, reg 9(2) (as so amended). On approving the change of name, the certification officer must return to the association one copy of the application indorsed with the word 'Approved' and duly authenticated: reg 9(3) (as so amended). The fee so prescribed for an approval of a change of name is £96: reg 11(2) (substituted by SI 1988/310; amended by SI 2005/713).
9   As to the meaning of 'officer', in relation to an employers' association, see PARA 1084 note 6.
10   Trade Union and Labour Relations (Consolidation) Act 1992 s 134(4).
11   Ie the Trade Union and Labour Relations (Consolidation) Act 1992 s 108: see PARA 1000.
12   Ie as it applies in relation to a provision of the Trade Union and Labour Relations (Consolidation) Act 1992 Pt I Ch VII (ss 97–108): see PARA 998 et seq.
13   Trade Union and Labour Relations (Consolidation) Act 1992 s 134(5). In exercise of the power so conferred the Secretary of State made the Certification Officer (Amendment of Fees) Regulations 2005, SI 2005/713, which came into force on 6 April 2005: reg 1(1). In addition, by virtue of the Trade Union and Labour Relations (Consolidation) Act 1992 s 300(3), Sch 3 para 1(2) (see PARA 891 note 1) and the Interpretation Act 1978 s 17(2)(b), the Trade Unions and Employers' Associations (Amalgamations etc) Regulations 1975, SI 1975/536 (see note 8) have effect as if so made.

INDEX

Employment

ADVISORY, CONCILIATION AND
ARBITRATION SERVICE
(ACAS)—*continued*
Code of Practice on Disciplinary and
Grievance Procedures—*continued*
non-mandatory nature of, 701
common seal—
evidential value of documents
executed under, 1213
use of, 1213
conciliation officer—
designation as, 1214
duties, 152
privileged nature of communications
to, $152n^7$
constitution, 1213
Council—
appointment and vacation of office,
1213
membership, 1213
procedure, power to determine, 1213
remuneration etc, 1213
early conciliation to promote settlement,
requirement for—
meaning, $152n^4$
early conciliation certificate:
meaning, $152n^{12}$
early conciliation form: meaning,
$152n^4$
exemption from requirement, $152n^6$
generally, 152
more than one prospective claimant,
where, $152n^4$
settlement: meaning, $152n^{8, 16}$
employment tribunal advising parties of
ACAS services etc, 1468
European Company, jurisdiction as to
proceedings under regulations,
1335
fees for exercise of functions, 1225
funding, 1214
general duty, 1217
information and consultation of
employees regulations, reference of
complaint etc under, 1316
information held by, prohibition on
disclosure, 1215
inquiries, power to conduct, 1222
officers—
conciliation. *See* conciliation officers
above
power to appoint, 1214
offices, duty to maintain, 1214
prescribed information—
conciliation officer, duty to forward
to, 152

ADVISORY, CONCILIATION AND
ARBITRATION SERVICE
(ACAS)—*continued*
prescribed information—*continued*
prescribed: meaning, $152n^4$
prospective claimant's duty to
provide, 152
recognition dispute— 1219
meaning, $1219n^3$
ballot, power to arrange, 1219
information to help settle, power to
request, 1219
references to, 1281
secretary, power to appoint, 1214
settlement of disputes—
arbitration, power to arrange, 1220
power to assist with, 1218
staff, power to appoint, 1214
unfair dismissal cases. scheme to
resolve, 824

AGENCY WORKER
meaning, $94n^5$, 97
adoption appointment, time off for—
detriment, right not to suffer, 620
employment tribunal, complaint to,
346
paid time off to attend, 344
unpaid time off to attend, 345
ante-natal care, time off for—
accompaniment to ante-natal care—
employment tribunal, complaint
to, 340
qualifying relationship, $339n^1$
right to accompany woman, 339
detriment, right not to suffer, 620
employment tribunal, complaint to,
338
requirements to be met, 337
right to, 337
armed forces' member, 107
assignment—
meaning, $96n^3$, $99n^4$
contract providing for payment
between, 100
basic working and employment
conditions—
meaning, $96n^3$, 98
evidence to tribunal, admissibility, 98
night work: meaning, $98n^6$
pay: meaning, $98n^6$
pay reference period: meaning,
$100n^{22}$
permanent contract, effect where
person having, 100
qualifying period for right to, 99

AGENCY WORKER—*continued*
  basic working and employment
      conditions—*continued*
    relevant terms and conditions:
        meaning, 98n[6]
    right to, 98
    working time: meaning, 98n[6]
    written statement, right to, 98
  common law—
    legal position as question of, 11
    rights at, 95
  comparable employee, 98n[12]
  comparable worker, 101n[3, 6]
  Crown employment, 107
  detriment, right not to suffer—
    complaint to employment tribunal,
        625, 626
    generally, 620
  employers' and principals' liabilities
      under regulations, 106
  employment tribunal, complaint to, 105
  equal treatment of—
    basic working and employment
        conditions. *See* basic working
        and employment conditions
        above
    collective facilities etc, right to, 101
    detriment, right not to be subjected
        to, 104
    EU requirements, 96
    generally, 11, 96
    permanent contract, effect, 100
    permanent employment opportunities,
        right to, 101
    purpose of EU Directive, 96
    special classes of persons, treatment
        of, 107
  exclusion from meaning of, 97
  hirer—
    meaning, 97n[3]
    liabilities under regulations, 102
  House of Commons' staff, 107
  House of Lords' staff, 107
  legal position, as question of common
      law, 11, 95
  maternity grounds, supply ended on—
    meaning, 601
    alternative work, right to offer of,
        603
    employment tribunal, complaint to,
        607
    right to remuneration—
      calculation of remuneration, 605
      exclusion from, 602
      generally, 601

AGENCY WORKER—*continued*
  maternity grounds, supply ended
      on—*continued*
    right to remuneration—*continued*
      no duty beyond duration of
          assignment, 601n[3], 602n[4]
  national minimum wage, right to, 178
  regulations—
    dismissal for applying, 103
    employers' and principals' liability
        under, 106
    equal treatment under, right to. *See*
        equal treatment of *above*
    hirer's liabilities under, 102
    special classes of persons under, 107
  temporary agency worker—
    meaning, 96n[2]
    equal treatment. *See* equal treatment
        of *above*
  temporary work agency—
    meaning, 96n[2], 97
    liabilities under regulations, 102
  time off to study or train, 328n[1]
  unfair dismissal, 103
  working hours, 339n[3], 344n[4], 345n[7]
  working time protection, 273
AGENT
  meaning, 13
  employee, whether, 13
AGRICULTURAL WORK
  meaning, 12n[3]
  gangmasters, 12n[3]
AIRMAN
  meaning, 567n[1]
  statutory sick pay, treatment for, 567
ALIEN
  industrial action, promoting, 1395
ANNUAL LEAVE. *See under* WORKING
    TIME
ANTE-NATAL CARE
  time off work for. *See under* TIME OFF
    WORK
APPEAL
  improvement notice, against, 316
  notice of underpayment, against, 245
  prohibition notice, against, 316
APPRENTICESHIP
  agreement. *See* APPRENTICESHIP
      AGREEMENT
  common law position, 112
  corporation taking apprentice, 128
  modern legal context, 112
  national minimum wage, 199
  wrongful dismissal of apprentice,
      damages for, 834

APPRENTICESHIP AGREEMENT
breach by apprentice, 747
consent requirements, 128
covenants in, 129
employee under, person treated as, 494
form of, 128
injunction against breach, restriction on
right to, 747
justification for quitting service, 748
non-performance, excuses for, 748
outside UK, whether apprentice obliged
to serve outside, 748
parties to, 128
specific performance, no right to, 747
termination—
at will, prohibition on, 128n[1]
bankruptcy of master, on, 752
change in composition of firm or
business, on, 753
death of master or apprentice, on,
751
minimum period of notice,
apprentice's right to, 750
minor's power to dissolve, 749
misconduct by apprentice, on, 754
mutual consent, by, 750
woman treated as employee, for
maternity pay purposes, 406
writing, need for, 128

ARBITRATION
ACAS involvement. *See* ADVISORY,
CONCILIATION AND ARBITRATION
SERVICE

ARBITRATION CLAUSE
minor, binding on, 15

ARMED FORCES, MEMBER
agency worker regulations, and, 107
continuous employment, following
reinstatement with former
employer, 419, 461, 507
industrial action, statutory restriction
on, 1391
national minimum wage, not qualifying
for, 192
part-time workers regulations—
application of, 82
employment tribunal, complaint to,
82n[11]
substitute labour, use as, 1398
working time protection—
exclusion from provisions, 306
generally, 275

ATTENDANCE ALLOWANCE
wages, as part of, 255n[2]

AUDIT
industrial training board accounts, of,
672

BAILMENT
employment relationship distinguished,
13

BANKRUPTCY
apprenticeship agreement, effect on,
752
contract of employment, effect on, 727

BETTING WORKER
meaning, 321n[2]
betting transactions: meaning, 321n[2]
betting work: meaning, 321n[2]
protected: meaning, 321
Sunday work—
detriment—
date of the act: meaning, 615n[7]
examples of no detriment suffered,
615n[6]
opted-out worker, 615n[8]
right not to suffer, 615
enforceability of employment
contract, 322
explanatory statements, requirement
for, 324
opting-in notice, effect, 321, 322
opting-out notice, 323
protected betting worker: meaning,
321
protected shop worker: meaning, 321
statutory protection, 320
unfair dismissal, 320, 787

BODY CORPORATE
national minimum wage offence by,
252

CADET FORCE
national minimum wage, member not
qualifying for, 190

CAREERS GUIDANCE
providers of, application of redundancy
payments legislation, 843

CAREERS SERVICES
ancillary goods and services, provision
of, 642
Her Majesty's Chief Inspector of
Education, Children's Services and
Skills, inspection by, 641
inspection, 641
local authority—
meaning, 640n[4]
ancillary goods and services, provision
of, 642
arrangements with, 640
control by Secretary of State, 643
directions to, 640

CODE OF PRACTICE
ACAS. *See under* ADVISORY,
    ARBITRATION AND CONCILIATION
    SERVICE
admissibility in evidence, 1232
collective bargaining, disclosure of
    information, 1180
disciplinary procedures. *See*
    DISCIPLINARY PROCEDURES (ACAS
    code of practice)
failure to comply with, effect, 1232,
    1234
grievance procedures. *See* GRIEVANCE
    PROCEDURE (ACAS code of
    practice)
industrial action ballots, as to, 1371
part-time workers, as to, 83
picketing, on, 1386
trade union recognition and
    derecognition, unfair practices,
    1174

COLLECTIVE AGREEMENT
meaning, 88n[11], 116n[3], 1093
Acquired Rights Directive, protection
    afforded by, 139n[24]
binding, whether, 116
contract of employment, incorporation
    into, 1176
contracting out of statutory protection,
    150
discriminatory, 1178
no-strike clause in, 1177
prohibited terms in, 116, 1178
'static' approach to, 139n[32]
statutory provisions applicable, power
    to vary or adapt, 1195
terms of employment, provisions
    incorporated into, 116, 117
transfer of undertaking, effect, 139,
    1175n[7]
unenforceability, statutory presumption
    of, 1175
withdrawal from, 117
working time protection, exclusion from
    provisions, 303

COLLECTIVE BARGAINING
meaning, 1093
agreed method, failure to carry out,
    1124
ballot—
    cancellation, on failure of employer to
        fulfil duties, 1120
    conditions to be fulfilled prior to,
        1117
    conduct, 1118

COLLECTIVE BARGAINING—*continued*
ballot—*continued*
    costs, responsibility for payment of,
        1121
    employer's duties, 1120
    holding of, 1118
    notice as to holding of, 1117, 1118
    of no effect, on failure of employer to
        fulfil duties, 1120
    outcome-specific offer, party making,
        1119n[5]
    procedure following, 1122
    qualified independent person to
        conduct, 1118n[15]
    result, declaration following, 1122
    secret nature of, 1118
    special factors as to conduct, 1118n[18]
    unfair practices, 1119
bargaining unit—
    agreement of parties, 1105
    appropriate bargaining unit—
        agreement as to what constitutes,
            1110
        Central Arbitration Committee,
            application to, 1133
        no longer appropriate, belief that—
            application to CAC, 1133
            bargaining arrangements ceasing
                to apply, 1136
            parties agreeing new unit or
                units, 1134
            parties not agreeing new unit or
                units, 1135
    ballot. *See* ballot *above*
    ceasing to exist, employer believing—
        application for questions to be
            decided—
            acceptance, 1138
            admissibility of application, 1138
            nature of questions, 1138
            notice of receipt, 1138
            procedure following acceptance,
                1139
        notice as to, 1137
        parties agreeing different unit or
            units, 1140
        validation period: meaning, 1137n[8]
    changes affecting—
        admissibility of applications as to,
            1146
        application of provisions, 1132
        appropriateness of bargaining unit.
            See appropriate bargaining unit
            above
        new unit. *See* new unit *below*

References are to paragraph numbers; superior figures refer to notes

COLLECTIVE BARGAINING—*continued*
　bargaining unit—*continued*
　　changes affecting—*continued*
　　　unit ceasing to exist. *See* ceasing to
　　　　exist, employer believing *above*
　　　withdrawal of applications as to,
　　　　1147
　　demand to be recognised as, 1097
　　method of bargaining, negotiations as
　　　to, 1123
　　new unit—
　　　construction of references to
　　　　collective bargaining, 1132n[5]
　　　decision as to—
　　　　procedure generally, 1141
　　　　relevant bargaining arrangements:
　　　　　meaning, 1142n[5]
　　　　secret ballot, notice of, 1144
　　　　statutory outside unit, at least
　　　　　one worker within, 1142
　　　　voluntary or statutory outside
　　　　　unit, no worker within,
　　　　　1144
　　　　voluntary outside unit, at least
　　　　　one worker within, 1143
　　　guidance from Secretary of State,
　　　　1144n[17]
　　　method of bargaining in relation to,
　　　　effect, 1148
　　　parties agreeing, 1134
　　　residual workers, provisions as to,
　　　　1145
　　　secret ballot as to, 1144
　　residual workers, provisions as to,
　　　1145
　　specific performance for breach of
　　　arrangements, 1148
　　statutory outside bargaining unit:
　　　meaning, 1142n[4]
　　training for workers within—
　　　consultation provisions—
　　　　complaint to tribunal, 1173
　　　　employer's failure to consult,
　　　　　1173
　　　　generally, 1172
　　　　meeting. *See* meeting to discuss
　　　　　below
　　　meeting to discuss—
　　　　arrangements for, 1172
　　　　date for, 1172n[7]
　　　　subsequent meeting, employer
　　　　　wishing to convene, 1172n[9]
　　voluntary outside bargaining unit:
　　　meaning, 1143n[4]
　　'dynamic' interpretation of clauses,
　　　139n[32]

COLLECTIVE BARGAINING—*continued*
　information, disclosure of—
　　Central Arbitration Committee,
　　　complaint to—
　　　award, 1182
　　　claim in addition to—
　　　　expiry of right to present,
　　　　　1182n[16]
　　　　right to present, 1182
　　　further complaint, 1182
　　　hearing, 1182n[9, 12]
　　　procedure on receipt, 1182
　　　right to present, 1182
　　Code of Practice, 1180
　　employer's duty—
　　　generally, 1179
　　　restriction on, 1181
　　failure to disclose, complaint. *See*
　　　Central Arbitration Committee,
　　　complaint to *above*
　　restrictions on duty of, 1181
　method of—
　　application to Central Arbitration
　　　Committee to specify—
　　　admissibility of, 1130
　　　agreement, in absence of, 1129
　　　failure to carry out agreement,
　　　　where, 1129
　　　generally, 1129
　　　procedure where application
　　　　made, 1130
　　　response to application, 1131
　　　withdrawal, restriction on, 1131
　　failure to carry out, 1124, 1129
　　negotiations as to, 1123
　partnerships at work, encouraging,
　　1096
　trade union recognition. *See* TRADE
　　UNION RECOGNITION

COMMISSIONER OF POLICE OF THE
　METROPOLIS
redundancy payments legislation,
　application of, 845

CONFIDENTIAL INFORMATION
disclosure in public interest, 68
European Works Council—
　breach of duty not to disclose, 1273
　withholding of information by central
　　management, 1274
information and consultation
　representative—
　breach of duty not to disclose, 1273,
　　1309
　withholding of information by central
　　management, 1274

References are to paragraph numbers; superior figures refer to notes

CONTRACT OF
EMPLOYMENT—*continued*
employee's obligations—*continued*
disruption of business operation,
avoiding, 66
duty of care in the workplace, 65
fidelity, duty surviving termination of
employment, 71
good faith during employment, 67
intellectual property rights, as to, 72
invention or discovery, as trustee of,
72
new methods and techniques,
adaptation to, 64
no duty to volunteer information
about misdeeds, 67n[3]
obedience to lawful orders, 63
secret profits, avoiding, 67
employer's liabilities—
Equality Act 2010, under, 51
third parties, to, on contracts made.
See third parties, contractual
liability to *below*
vicarious liability for employees'
acts, 52
employer's obligations—
duty of care—
equal treatment, 21
health and safety, as to. *See* health
and safety, as to *below*
indemnification, implied duty of,
39
personal data, as to processing of,
21
remuneration, as to. *See*
remuneration under *below*
work, provision of. *See* work under,
provision of *below*
duty to insure. *See* EMPLOYERS'
LIABILITY INSURANCE
employee's losses and liabilities,
indemnification etc, 39
grievances, implied term to treat
seriously, 49
health and safety, as to—
common law duty, extent of, 33
consultation with employees, 38
employee with mischievous
tendencies, removal of, 33n[3]
implied duty of care, 32
level of duty, 32
plant and equipment, adequacy of,
33n[4]
safety committee, 37
safety representatives, 36

CONTRACT OF
EMPLOYMENT—*continued*
employer's obligations—*continued*
health and safety, as to—*continued*
statement of general policy, duty to
prepare, 35
statutory duties, 34
insurance against liabilities etc. *See*
EMPLOYERS' LIABILITY INSURANCE
suitable working environment,
implied term to provide, 50
trust and respect—
breach of, examples, 48
duty to maintain, 48
implied duty of, 48
employment tribunal's approach to
determining existence of, 14
form of, 14
garden leave clause, 19
illegality—
burden of proof, 18n[6]
effect, 18
severance of illegal element, 18
immoral, effect, 18
implied termination of, 867
importance, 1
inference as to—
conduct, from, 14
rebuttal, 14
injunction to enforce, not normally
granted, 1437
limited-term contract, 755n[5]
limiting event in, 755n[5]
mental disorder, employer suffering
from, 15
minor entering into, 15
mutuality of obligation, 16n[4]
non-solicitation of staff clause, 19n[4]
remuneration under—
accruing from day to day, 22
additional, 24
apportionable nature of, 22
common law claim to recover, 25n[1]
evidential value of contract, 22
fees or commission only, 22
fixed by agreement, where, 22
illness, employee's temporary
incapacity through, 27
irregular payment, 22
itemised pay statement, right to, 124
lay-off, payment during, 28
minimum rates of pay—
introduction of, 26
See further NATIONAL MINIMUM
WAGE
mode of payment, 25

References are to paragraph numbers; superior figures refer to notes

DATA PROTECTION
employees, information as to, 21
DATABASE
employee making, ownership, 72
DESIGN
employee creating, ownership, 72
DIRECTOR OF COMPANY
contract of service etc, company's duty
to keep, 8n[2]
employee, as, 8
employee involvement duties, 1235
office-holder, as, 8
one-man company, 8n[3]
DIRECTORS' REPORT
employee involvement, statement as to,
1235
DISABLED PERSON
sheltered employment. See SHELTERED
EMPLOYMENT
DISCIPLINARY PROCEDURE
ACAS code of practice—
generally, 698, 700
See also under revised system below
contractual basis for powers, 699
former dispute resolution procedures—
generally, 698
statutory—
ACAS code of practice, replacement
by, 700
application, 700
hearing, right to be accompanied at—
alternative time, where companion
not available, 717n[9]
detriment, right not to be subjected
to, 720
disciplinary hearing: meaning, 717n[3]
employment tribunal, complaint to,
719
generally, 717
participation of companion, 717n[7]
reasonable nature of request, 717n[5]
specified description of companion,
717n[6]
time off to accompany employee,
717n[11]
unfair dismissal, 721
worker: meaning, 718
powers—
contractual basis for, 699
examples, 699
revised system—
ACAS code of practice—
admissibility in evidence, 701
general principles, 702
guidance booklet, 701
helpline, 701

DISCIPLINARY
PROCEDURE—continued
revised system—continued
ACAS code of practice—continued
issue, 701
non-mandatory nature of, 701
appeal—
ad hoc procedure, arrangements
for, 708n[16]
generally, 708
internal, 708n[2]
no contractual right to, where,
708n[16]
time-limit for lodging, 708n[2]
appropriate action, decision on, 707
criminal offence involved, 709
disciplinary situations, examples of,
702n[2]
dismissal without notice, behaviour
warranting, 707
facts, establishing, 703
final written warning, 707
general principles, 702
generally, 698
hearing, right to be accompanied at.
See hearing, right to be
accompanied at above
informing employee of problem, 704
meeting—
companion accompanying employee
to, 706
inability or unwillingness to
attend, 707
procedure at, 705
time for holding, 705
special cases, 709
trade union representative action
against, 709
written warning, 707
written statement of, duty to provide,
120
DISCLOSURE OF INFORMATION
working time regulations, information
obtained by inspector, 313
DISCRIMINATION
employers' association, by, 1082
Equality Act 2010, under—
equal pay audit. See EQUAL PAY AUDIT
generally, 608
prohibited conduct, 51
protected characteristics, 51
sheltered employment. See SHELTERED
EMPLOYMENT
trade union, by, 1036
DISMISSAL
adoption leave, during, 386

EDUCATION—*continued*
  penalty notice—*continued*
    employer's duty to enable
      participation, breach of—
        appeal against, 656
        determination notice, 655
        notice of objection to, 655
        withdrawal or variation of notice,
          655, 657

EDUCATIONAL ESTABLISHMENT
  redundancy payments legislation,
    application of, 842

EMPLOYEE
  meaning. See under WORDS AND
    PHRASES *post*
  agent as alternative to, 13
  bailee as alternative to, 13
  common law test, 4
  database made by, ownership, 72
  death of—
    redundancy payment provisions, effect
      on, 890
    termination of employment on, 732
    unfair dismissal provisions,
      modification of, 761
  design created by, ownership, 72
  duty of care in the workplace, breach
    of, 65
  film made by, ownership, 72
  flexible working. *See* FLEXIBLE WORKING
  independent contractor as alternative
    to, 13
  intellectual property rights, ownership,
    72
  literary, dramatic, musical or artistic
    work, ownership, 72
  losses and liabilities, employer's duty to
    indemnify, 39
  majority shareholder as, 9
  obligations—
    competing with employer, restriction
      on, 67
    confidential information. *See*
      CONFIDENTIAL INFORMATION
      (misuse by employee)
    disruption of business operation,
      avoiding, 66
    duty of care in the workplace, 65
    fidelity, duty surviving termination of
      employment, 71
    good faith during employment, 67
    intellectual property rights, as to, 72
    invention or discovery, as trustee of,
      72
    new methods and techniques,
      adaptation to, 64

EMPLOYEE—*continued*
  obligations—*continued*
    no duty to volunteer information
      about misdeeds, 67n[3]
    obedience to lawful orders, 63
    secret profits, avoiding, 67
  partner as alternative to, 13
  profit sharing scheme, participation in,
    10
  share option scheme, participation in,
    10
  shareholder. *See* EMPLOYEE
    SHAREHOLDER

EMPLOYEE REPRESENTATIVE
  redundancy, consultation with. *See*
    REDUNDANCY (employees'
    representatives, consultation with)
  rights—
    detriment, right not to suffer, 1208
    employee safety, representative of,
      1210
    generally, 1207
    time off work, 1209
    transfer of undertaking, consultation as
      to. *See under* TRANSFER OF
      UNDERTAKING

EMPLOYEE SHAREHOLDER
  meaning, 154
  drag-along rights, 154n[7]
  employment rights, 154
  employment status of, 154
  refusing to become—
    right not to suffer detriment, 624
    unfair dismissal for, 800
  statement of status etc, contents of,
    154n[7]
  tag-along rights, 154n[7]
  unfair dismissal for refusing to become,
    800

EMPLOYER
  meaning. See under WORDS AND
    PHRASES *post*
  associated—
    meaning, 3
    foreign company as, 3n[5]
  death of—
    redundancy payment provisions, effect
      on, 889
    termination of contract of
      employment on, 732
    unfair dismissal provisions,
      modification of, 761
  disability, under, effect on contract of
    employment, 15
  flexible working application, duties
    following, 109

EMPLOYERS'
ASSOCIATION—*continued*
awards against, restriction on
    enforcement of, 1088
certification officer—
    list kept by, 1083
    power to make entry in list, 1084
    power to remove from list, 1085
discrimination by, prohibition on, 1082
federated: meaning, 1079
friendly societies, application of law
    relating to, 1087
legal status—
    corporate, 1080
    quasi-corporate, 1080
list—
    certification officer, kept by, 1083
    entry in, application for, 1084
    fee for entry, 1084n^7
    generally, 1083
    removal from, 1085
name, change of, 1092
political objects, application of funds
    for, 1090
property—
    awards against, restriction on
        enforcement of, 1088
    vesting of, 1086
restraint of trade, exclusion of common
    law rules as to, 1081
transfer of engagements, 1091
trustees—
    death, effect, 1086
    instrument of appointment, 1086n^{12}
    instrument of discharge, 1086n^{13}
    property vesting in, 1086

EMPLOYERS' LIABILITY INSURANCE
approved policy: meaning, 40n^3
certificate of insurance—
    duty to display, 46
    inspection, 47
    offence and penalty, 45
    offshore installation etc, employee on
        or from, 46
    power to issue, 45
    production, 47
    surrender, 45
employees covered by, 42
excluded employees, 42
exempted employers, 43
generally, 40
offence where not insured, 40
offshore installation, and, 41
prohibited conditions in, 44
regulations as to limits, 40

EMPLOYMENT
meaning, 2
civil courts' jurisdiction, 1436
continuity. *See* CONTINUITY OF
    EMPLOYMENT
discrimination, protection from—
    Equality Act 2010, under—
        equal pay audit. *See* EQUAL PAY
            AUDIT
        generally, 608
        prohibited conduct, 51
        protected characteristics, 51
        sheltered employment. *See* SHELTERED
            EMPLOYMENT
sheltered employment. *See* SHELTERED
    EMPLOYMENT
'subject to satisfactory references',
    construction of meaning, 724
suspension. *See* SUSPENSION FROM WORK
terms of. *See* TERMS OF EMPLOYMENT
trial period: meaning, 865n^{13}
tribunals. *See* EMPLOYMENT APPEAL
    TRIBUNAL; EMPLOYMENT TRIBUNAL

EMPLOYMENT AGENCY
meaning, 1038n^8
conduct of, 11
employment by, 11
trade union membership, refusal of
    services on grounds of, 1038

EMPLOYMENT APPEAL TRIBUNAL
    (EAT)
appeal from, 1530
appeal to—
    abandonment or withdrawal, 1503
    case management, 1501
    cross-appeal, notice of, 1499
    disposal of—
        consent, by, 1503
        notice of hearing, 1502
    documents. *See* document *below*
    employment tribunal hearing,
        complaint about conduct of,
        1497
    fee for making. *See* fees *below*
    institution of, 1495
    listing of appeals. *See* listing of
        appeals *below*
    national security proceedings—
        answer and cross-appeal, restriction
            as to contents, 1499
        notice, service of, 1498
    no merit in cross-appeal, where, 1499
    notice of—
        amendment or clarification—
            application to amend, 1501
            generally, 1495n^3

EMPLOYMENT RIGHTS—*continued*
detriment, right not to
suffer—*continued*
trade union membership,
from—*continued*
See also under TRADE UNION
RECOGNITION
working time cases, 616
employee shareholder. *See* EMPLOYEE
SHAREHOLDER
employment outside Great Britain, 166
employment protection legislation—
amendment powers, 158
Crown employment, application to,
163
employment outside Great Britain,
166
House of Commons staff, application
to, 165
House of Lords staff, application to,
164
mariners, disapplication of
provisions, 167
Northern Ireland, provision for, 157
offshore areas, extension to, 155, 156
orders, rules and regulations, 162
police officers, whether applicable
to, 168
power to extend, 155
excluded classes of employment—
mariners, 167
outside Great Britain, 166
police officers, 168
generally, 149
guarantee payments. *See* GUARANTEE
PAYMENT
House of Commons staff, of, 165
House of Lords staff, of, 164
independent adviser, 151n[15, 24]
individuals, power to confer rights on,
159
mariners, of, 167
monetary limits, review of, 160
Northern Ireland authority, reciprocal
arrangements with, 157
origin and nature of, 149
police officers, of, 168
settlement agreement, conditions
regulating, 151
shareholder. *See* employee shareholder
above
statutory payments for family leave—
development, 400
See also STATUTORY ADOPTION LEAVE;
STATUTORY MATERNITY LEAVE;
STATUTORY PATERNITY LEAVE

EMPLOYMENT RIGHTS—*continued*
Sunday working. *See* SUNDAY WORKING
time off work. *See* TIME OFF WORK
working time. *See* WORKING TIME

EMPLOYMENT TRIBUNAL
ACAS services, duty to encourage use
of, 1466
agency worker—
compensation, payment of, 105n[31]
complaint by, 105, 607
detriment, right not to suffer. *See*
under complaint to *below*
aggravated breach of worker's rights,
financial penalty, 1477
allowances for attendance at, 1405
assessor, remuneration etc paid to, 1405
award—
adjustment for failure to comply with
Code of Practice, 1234
allowances etc, no recoupment of,
1478
contributory fault, deduction for,
1478
death, enforcement in case of, 1485
interest on—
meaning, 1482n[4]
computation, 1482
order for, 1481
particulars to be included when
making, 1478
prescribed element, 1478
recovery, 1484
bankruptcy of either party before
proceedings completed, 1409
case management—
ACAS services, encouraging use of,
1466
compliance with rules, orders and
practice directions, tribunal's
response to, 1465
conciliation, provisions as to, 1468
Court of Justice of the European
Union, reference of question to,
1471
deposit, payment of, 1466
devolution issues, 1470
documents, delivery to and by
tribunal, 1467
more than one claim, where, 1466
order—
meaning, 1460n[4]
application for, 1466
power to make, 1466
response permitted to stand,
where, 1464
scope of, 1466

EMPLOYMENT TRIBUNAL—*continued*
costs order—*continued*
  power to make, 1480
  represented by a lay representative:
    meaning, 1480n[3]
Court of Justice of the European Union,
  reference of question to, 1471
death of employee or employer—
  absence of personal representative,
    proceedings in, 1456
  continuation of proceedings, 1456
  effect on complaint, 1409
  institution of proceedings, 1456
  personal representative's
    involvement, 1456
decision—
  communication, method of, 1476
  correction of error in, 1476
  decision day: meaning, 1483
  effective date of judgment or order,
    1476
  monetary award. *See* award *above*
  order or judgment by consent, 1476
  reasons for, 1476
  reconsideration of, 1479
  register of judgments and reasons,
    1476
  relevant decision day: meaning, 1483
  variation or revocation, 1479
devolution issues, 1470
disability cases, restriction of publicity
  in, 1417
documents, delivery to and by, 1467
employer's contract claim—
  meaning, 1457n[7]
  rejection, 1463
  response, as part of, 1463
  time limit for response to, 1463
employment judge—
  meaning, 1402n[3]
  alone, hearing by, 1403
  reference of claim to, 1461
  regional, appointment, 1401
  remuneration, 1405
equal value claim—
  meaning, 1491n[3]
  comparator, use of, 1492n[7]
  expert evidence, use of—
    generally, 1491
    stage 1 hearing, at, 1492
    stage 2 hearing, at, 1493
  final hearing, 1494
  procedure generally, 1491
  stage 1 hearing, 1492
  stage 2 hearing, 1493
establishment, 1399

EMPLOYMENT TRIBUNAL—*continued*
fees—
  claim: meaning, 1457n[2]
  exemption from, 1457
  fee group: meaning, 1457n[5]
  introduction of fees regime, 1457
  Lord Chancellor's power to
    prescribe, 1411
  non-payment, effect, 1457
  payment, 1457
  remission of—
    application for, 1459
    disposable capital test, need to
      satisfy, 1458n[6]
    generally, 1457, 1458
    gross monthly income test,
      application of, 1458n[8]
  type A claims, 1457
  type B claims, 1457
fixed-term work regulations, complaint
  under, 91
flexible working application, complaint
  as to, 111
guarantee payment, complaint as to,
  265
hearing—
  conduct of, 1472
  disclosure of information, restriction
    on, 1472
  electronic communication, by means
    of, 1472
  employment judge alone, by, 1403
  failure to attend, 1472
  final, 1474
  majority decision, 1472
  National Insurance Fund, proceedings
    as to, 1472
  national security proceedings, public
    nature of, 1472
  pre-hearing review, 1414
  preliminary, 1473
  preliminary issue, as to, 1414
  procedure, power to regulate, 1472
  reconsideration of judgment at, 1479
  rules common to all kinds of, 1472
  second or casting vote, 1472
  withdrawal of claim, 1475
  witness evidence, 1472
  written representations, consideration
    of, 1472
High Court, appeal to, 1436
improvement notice, appeal against,
  316, 1489
industrial tribunal, formerly known as,
  1399n[3]

References are to paragraph numbers; superior figures refer to notes

References are to paragraph numbers; superior figures refer to notes

References are to paragraph numbers; superior figures refer to notes

EUROPEAN WORKS
  COUNCIL—*continued*
members—*continued*
  unfair dismissal, 1277
national employee representation
  body—
    meaning, 1252n[9]
    links with, 1267
number of employees, calculating, 1241
regulations on information and
  consultation, 1237
special negotiating body—
  meaning, 1244n[13]
  ballot—
    arrangements, 1248
    conduct, 1249
    costs of, 1249
    defective arrangements, right to
      present complaint, 1248
    independent ballot supervisor:
      meaning, 1248n[10]
    ineffective ballot report, 1249
    requirements, 1248
  composition, 1247
  consultative committee—
    meaning, 1250n[1]
    information and consultation
      function: meaning, 1250n[1]
    nomination of UK members, 1250
  co-operative spirit, duty of, 1252
  expenses incurred by, payment, 1251
  experts, assistance of, 1251
  functions, 1246
  majority vote, decision-taking by,
    1251
  membership where consultative
    committee exists, 1250
  merchant navy, exclusion of member
    of, 1287
  time off work, 1275, 1276
  training, right to, 1265
  UK members—
    ballot. *See* ballot *above*
    nomination, 1250
  unfair dismissal of member, 1277
subsidiary requirements—
  application of, 1253
  continuing application, 1262
training, member's right to, 1265
Transnational Information and
  Consultation Directive—
  consultation: meaning, 1236n[3]
  contracting out of provisions,
    restrictions on, 1238
  implementation, 1237
  information: meaning, 1236n[2]

EUROPEAN WORKS
  COUNCIL—*continued*
Transnational Information and
  Consultation Directive—*continued*
  merchant navy crews, exemption for,
    1236
  purpose, 1236
  regulations implementing, 1237
  requirements, 1236
  UK members—
    appointment or election, 1255
    ballot—
      arrangements, 1256
      conduct, 1257
      costs, 1257
      defective arrangements, remedy,
        1256
      ineffective ballot report, 1257
      requirements to be satisfied, 1256
      supervisor, 1257
  unfair dismissal, 1277
FILM
  ownership, where made by employee,
    72
FINE
  discharging by unpaid work, no
    national minimum wage for, 191
  enforcement, where levied by
    Employment Appeal Tribunal,
    1529
FIRE AND RESCUE AUTHORITY
  redundancy payments legislation,
    application of, 845
FIRE AUTHORITY
  redundancy payments legislation,
    application of, 845
FISHING VESSEL
  master or crew—
    redundancy procedure, exclusion,
      1194
    trade union rights, exclusion of
      master and crew from, 1071
FIXED-TERM EMPLOYEE
  meaning, 86n[2]
  comparable permanent employee, 86
  detriment, right not to be subjected to,
    90
  employee: meaning, 85n[3]
  employment tribunal, complaint to, 91
  fixed-term contract, 86n[2], 1194n[2]
  less favourable treatment under
    regulations—
    detriment, right not to be subjected
      to, 90
    Employment Rights Act 1996 rights,
      and, 87

HOUSE OF LORDS STAFF—*continued*
national minimum wage, right to, 181
part-time workers regulations,
    application of, 82
redundancy procedure, exclusion, 1194
trade unions and industrial relations,
    application of provisions, 894
working time protection, 276

IMPROVEMENT NOTICE
Energy Act notice, appeal against, 1489
health and safety notice, appeal
    against, 1489
working time regulations, under. *See
    under* WORKING TIME

INCOME SUPPORT
industrial action, effect of, 1356

INDUSTRIAL ACTION
meaning, 1025n[5]
aliens promoting, offence by, 1395
armed forces—
    prohibition on taking part in, 1391
    substitute labour, use as, 1398
ballot—
    calling of action with support of,
      1380
    Code of Practice, 1371
    conduct, 1377
    economic torts, as protection
      against, 1370
    effective period of, 1381
    entitlement to vote in, 1374
    independent scrutiny—
      appointment and functions of
        scrutineer, 1373
      generally, 1373
      report by, right to, 1373
    industrial action not having support
      of, where certain conditions
      applying, 1374
    newly recruited members joining
      after, 1374n[5]
    notice of, 1372
    opening day of: meaning, 1372n[2]
    overseas members—
      meaning, 1379
      balloting of, 1379
      information as to result, 1378
    requirement before taking action,
      1370
    result, right to information as to,
      1378
    right to, 1025
    separate workplaces, in, 1375
    statutory provisions, failure to comply
      with, 1377

INDUSTRIAL ACTION—*continued*
ballot—*continued*
    voting paper—
      contents, 1376
      inadvertent failure to supply to
        some voters, 1377n[5]
      merchant seaman, provision to,
        1377n[6]
      sample, provision of, 1372
breach of contract, as—
    criminal action, whether, 1341
    factors to consider, 1342
    See also contract of employment,
      effect on *below*
conspiracy, as, 1341
contract of employment, effect on—
    court not compelling employee to
      work, 1348
    damages, liability for, 1346
    summary dismissal, 1345
    wages, withholding of, 1347
criminal liability, 1341
economic duress, consequences of
    unlawful, 1344
emergency powers—
    armed forces, use as substitute
      labour, 1398
    state of emergency, during, 1397
generally, 1339
immunity. *See under* TRADE DISPUTE
inducement to take part in, 1025n[3],
    1370n[3]
liability—
    contract, in, 1342
    criminal, 1341
    generally, 1344
    tort, in, 1343
lockout—
    meaning, 1340
    breach of contract, as, 1339
merchant seaman, offence by, 1393
National Crime Agency, offence by
    officer of, 1392
notice to employer, requirement of—
    appropriate period for receipt of,
      1382n[11]
    contents of notice, 1382
    discontinuous action, 1382n[15]
    generally, 1382
    notified category of employee:
      meaning, 1382n[12]
    relevant notice: meaning, 1382
other industrial action: meaning, 1340
picketing. *See* PICKETING
police officer, by, 1392

References are to paragraph numbers; superior figures refer to notes

INDUSTRIAL RELATIONS—*continued*
  trade union recognition. *See* TRADE
    UNION RECOGNITION

INDUSTRIAL TRAINING BOARD
  meaning, 658n[7]
  activities, transfer of establishment's—
    generally, 674
    orders made, 674n[9]
  body corporate, as, 658
  borrowing powers, 659
  chairman—
    compensation on cessation of office,
      661
    pension payment, 661
    remuneration etc, 661
  committees—
    establishment, 663
    person appointed to attend, 663
    remuneration, 663
  contracts of service or apprenticeship,
    entry into, 666
  control by Secretary of State, 664, 665
  establishment, 658
  grants etc to, 659
  industrial training order—
    meaning, 658n[6]
    consultation prior to making, 658
    revocation order, 677
    scope, 658
    transfer of assets on revocation or
      amendment, 675
  information from employers—
    disclosure, prohibition on, 671
    enterprise zone, establishment
      within, 670
    power to obtain from, 669
    publication, 673
  levies—
    employment tribunal, appeal to—
      determination of appeal, 1488
      notice of appeal, 1487
      rules of procedure, 1486
    enterprise zone, establishment in, 679
    exemption certificate—
      meaning, 681
      ceasing to have effect, 682
      effect, 682
      generally, 682
      proposals for, 681
      publication, 681
      references. *See* reference *below*
    hearing of reference—
      appearance at, 695
      evidence at, 696
      failure to appear at, 696
      procedure at, 696

INDUSTRIAL TRAINING
  BOARD—*continued*
  levies—*continued*
    hearing of reference—*continued*
      public nature of, 695
      representations, submission of, 695
      time and place, 693
    High Court, appeal to, 1531
    order. *See* levy order *below*
    proposals for—
      meaning, 678
      contents, 678
      levy periods in, 678n[4]
      submission of, 678
    referees—
      appeal from decision of, to High
        Court, 1531
      appointment and vacation of
        office, 685
      assignment to, 689
      determination of, 697
      divisions, sitting in, 685
      establishment, 685
      expenses, power to defray, 685
      numbers of, 685
      persons who may be, 685
      President unable to act, where, 685
      secretary to, 686
    reference—
      appeals, 697
      assessors, appointment of, 694
      assignment, 689
      decision, of, 687
      determinations, 697
      directions, 692
      errors, correction of, 697
      extension of time, 692
      further particulars, 691
      hearing. *See* hearing of reference
        above
      notices etc, 690
      referees. *See* referees *above*
      registration, 688
      regulations, 684
      right to make, 683
    levy order—
      meaning, 680
      contents, 680
      making of, 680
      power to make, 678
      statutory instrument, made by, 680n[9]
  loan to, 659
  meetings, person appointed to attend,
    662
  membership—
    allowances etc, payment of, 661

References are to paragraph numbers; superior figures refer to notes

References are to paragraph numbers; superior figures refer to notes

NATIONAL MINIMUM
WAGE—*continued*
records—*continued*
offence in connection with, 251
remuneration counting towards—
deductions to be subtracted from total
of remuneration, 222
living accommodation, provision of—
adjusted deductions and payments
for, 225
amount to be taken into account
where, 224
payments made by or due from
worker, subtraction, 223
payments taken into account—
list of, 220
reductions from, 221
revenue officials, supply of information
obtained by, 241
right to, 169, 176
salaried hours work—
meaning, 204
absence from work, effect, 204
contract to do, 204
determining hours of—
basic hours: meaning, $214n^5$,
$215n^3$
basic hours exceeded, where, 215
calculation year: meaning, $215n^1$
employment terminating, where,
216
method, 214
excluded time, 209
extension of scope of, 209
performance bonus, $204n^4$
travelling incidental to duties, $209n^{11}$
time work—
meaning, 203
determining hours of, 213
excluded time, 208
extension of scope of, 208
time spent on training treated as, 212
travelling as part of, $208n^7$
travelling incidental to duties, $208n^8$
underpayment—
additional remuneration, right to,
242
arrears—
payment of, 243
recovery of, 246
notice of. *See* notice of underpayment
above
unfair dismissal for attempting to secure
right to etc, 169, 794
unmeasured work—
meaning, 206

NATIONAL MINIMUM
WAGE—*continued*
unmeasured work—*continued*
ascertained hours: meaning, $218n^{10}$
determining hours of, 218
extension of scope of, 211
work: meaning, 172
worker: meaning, 171
workers not qualifying for—
armed forces, member of, 192
Cadet Forces, member of, 192
EU programmes, participation in, 198
generally, 186
government training scheme,
participation in, 194
homeless workers provide with shelter
and other benefits, 197
persons discharging fines by unpaid
work, 191
prisoners, 190
religious and other communities,
resident workers in, 189
share fishermen, 187
temporary work scheme, participation
in, 194
traineeship in England, participation
in, 195
voluntary workers, 188
work experience—
course in, attendance at, 196
participation in, 194
work-based learning programme,
participation in, 193
workers qualifying for—
agency workers, 178
Crown employees, 180
generally, 177
home workers, 179
House of Commons staff, 182
House of Lords staff, 181
individuals who are not otherwise
workers, 185
mariners, 183
offshore employment, in, 184
working time, determining—
output work, extension of scope of,
210
salaried hours work, extension of
scope of, 209
time work—
extension of scope of, 208
time spent on training treated as,
212
unmeasured work, extension of scope
of, 211
written statement, right to, 207

NATIONAL MINIMUM
   WAGE—*continued*
young persons, 199
NATIONAL SECURITY
   disclosure of information, restrictions
     on, 1446
   proceedings—
     meaning, 1447n[1]
     Employment Appeal Tribunal, before.
      See under EMPLOYMENT APPEAL
      TRIBUNAL
     employment tribunal, before. *See*
      under EMPLOYMENT TRIBUNAL
NORTHERN IRELAND
   employment rights, 157
   trade union reciprocal arrangements,
     1078
OCCUPATIONAL PENSION SCHEME
   contracted-out certificate, issue of—
     consultation prior to, 1205
     notice of intention prior to, 1205
   detriment, trustee's right not to suffer,
     617
   listed changes to, 1302
   transfer of undertaking, effect, 141n[21]
   trust and respect, implied term of,
     48n[24]
   trustee—
     detriment, right not to suffer, 617
     information, duty to disclose, 1206
     time off work—
      employment tribunal, complaint
       to, 353
      right to, 352
      unfair dismissal, 790
     unfair dismissal, 790
OFFICE-HOLDER
   categorisation as, 7
   company director as, 8
   determining, matters relevant to, 7n[1]
   wrongful deprivation of, 7
OFFSHORE AREA
   employment protection legislation,
     extension of, 155, 156
   Frigg Gas Field, 156n[4]
OFFSHORE EMPLOYMENT
   meaning, 155n[5], 184
   employment protection legislation,
     extension of, 155, 156
   national minimum wage, right to, 184
   working time provisions, exclusion of,
     308
OFFSHORE INSTALLATION
   meaning, 40n[8], 156n[8]
   associated structure, 40n[8], 41n[4]

OFFSHORE INSTALLATION—*continued*
   employers' liability insurance—
     certificate of insurance, production
      of, 46
     duty to insure, 41
     Frigg Gas Field, 156n[4]
PARENTAL LEAVE
   basic rights, 354
   default provisions—
     generally, 392
     workforce agreements used to
      replace, 393
   detriment, employee's right not to
     suffer, 620
   development of statutory rights, 354
   Directive, 354
   employment tribunal, complaint to, 397
   entitlement to, 391
   evidence of entitlement, 392n[9]
   maximum period, 392
   minimum period of, 390n[5]
   notification requirements, 392
   postponement, 392
   regulations as to, power to make, 390
   responsibility for child: meaning, 391n[5]
   restrictions on taking, 392
   return after, right to, 395
   shared. *See* SHARED PARENTAL LEAVE
   terms and conditions of employment,
     application during leave, 394
   unfair dismissal in connection with, 784
   week's pay, calculation of, 396
PARTNER
   change of, as wrongful dismissal, 726
   death of, whether dissolving
     partnership, 726
   employee or agent as, 13
   former, as employee, 13
   salaried, 13
PARTNERSHIP
   dissolution, termination of employment
     on, 726
PART-TIME WORK
   Framework Agreement—
     comparable full-time worker:
      meaning, 73n[4]
     generally, 73
     implementation, 73n[1]
     purpose, 73
   regulations—
     power to make, 74
     types of worker to be considered
      under, 75
   workers. *See* PART-TIME WORKER
PART-TIME WORKER
   meaning, 75

References are to paragraph numbers; superior figures refer to notes

References are to paragraph numbers; superior figures refer to notes

References are to paragraph numbers; superior figures refer to notes

References are to paragraph numbers; superior figures refer to notes

References are to paragraph numbers; superior figures refer to notes

References are to paragraph numbers; superior figures refer to notes

References are to paragraph numbers; superior figures refer to notes

TRADE UNION
  RECOGNITION—*continued*
bargaining unit—
  agreement of parties, 1105
  appropriate bargaining unit—
    agreement as to what constitutes,
      1110
    Central Arbitration Committee,
      application to, 1133
    no longer appropriate, belief that—
      application to CAC, 1133
      bargaining arrangements ceasing
        to apply, 1136
      parties agreeing new unit or
        units, 1134
      parties not agreeing new unit or
        units, 1135
  ballot. *See* ballot *above*
  ceasing to exist, employer believing—
    application for questions to be
      decided—
      acceptance, 1138
      admissibility of application, 1138
      nature of questions, 1138
      notice of receipt, 1138
      procedure following acceptance,
        1139
    notice as to, 1137
    parties agreeing different unit or
      units, 1140
    validation period: meaning, 1137n[8]
  changes affecting—
    admissibility of applications as to,
      1146
    application of provisions, 1132
    appropriateness of bargaining unit.
      See appropriate bargaining unit
      above
    new unit. *See* new unit *below*
    unit ceasing to exist. *See* ceasing to
      exist, employer believing *above*
    withdrawal of applications as to,
      1147
  demand to be recognised as, 1097
  method of bargaining, negotiations as
    to, 1123
  new unit—
    construction of references to
      collective bargaining, 1132n[5]
    decision as to—
      procedure generally, 1141
      relevant bargaining arrangements:
        meaning, 1142n[5]
      secret ballot, notice of, 1144
      statutory outside unit, at least
        one worker within, 1142

TRADE UNION
  RECOGNITION—*continued*
bargaining unit—*continued*
  new unit—*continued*
    decision as to—*continued*
      voluntary or statutory outside
        unit, no worker within,
        1144
      voluntary outside unit, at least
        one worker within, 1143
    guidance from Secretary of State,
      1144n[17]
    method of bargaining in relation to,
      effect, 1148
    parties agreeing, 1134
    residual workers, provisions as to,
      1145
    secret ballot as to, 1144
    residual workers, provisions as to,
      1145
    specific performance for breach of
      arrangements, 1148
    statutory outside bargaining unit:
      meaning, 1142n[4]
    training for workers within—
      consultation provisions—
        complaint to tribunal, 1173
        employer's failure to consult,
          1173
        generally, 1172
        meeting. *See* meeting to discuss
          below
      meeting to discuss—
        arrangements for, 1172
        date for, 1172n[7]
        subsequent meeting, employer
          wishing to convene, 1172n[9]
    voluntary outside bargaining unit:
      meaning, 1143n[4]
  Central Arbitration Committee—
    application, consideration of. *See*
      under application for *above*
    appropriate bargaining unit,
      determining—
      application to CAC, 1133
      bargaining arrangements ceasing to
        apply, 1136
      parties agreeing new unit or units,
        1134
      parties not agreeing new unit or
        units, 1135
    ballot, notice as to holding of, 1117,
      1118
    CAC case manager: meaning, 1102n[5]

TRADE UNION
  RECOGNITION—*continued*
Central Arbitration
  Committee—*continued*
  collective bargaining methods,
    assistance in negotiating—
    absence of agreement, in, 1129
    admissibility of application to
      specify method, 1130
    failure of agreement, on, 1129
    generally, 1123
    procedure where application
      made, 1130
    response to application to specify
      method, 1131
    withdrawal of application,
      restriction on, 1131
  declaration by—
    bargaining unit ceasing to have
      effect, as to, 1140
    correction of errors in, 1230
    employer's failure to comply with
      ballot duties, following, 1120
    new unit, as to, 1144
    recognition, as to, 1117, 1123
    result of ballot, following, 1122
    unfair ballot practice, as to, 1119
  errors in decision or declaration,
    correction of, 1230
  new unit, decision as to. *See under*
    bargaining unit (new unit) *above*
  panels, 1229
  procedure, 1229
  Secretary of State's guidance, $1117n^8$,
    $1144n^{17}$
  unfair ballot practice, complaint as
    to, 1119
  unit ceasing to exist, involvement
    where. *See* bargaining unit
    (ceasing to exist, employer
    believing) *above*
  voluntary agreement, application in
    respect of, 1127
  consequences, 1123
  declaration of, 1117, 1123
  derecognition—
    agreement to end bargaining
      arrangements, 1152
    application of provisions, 1149
    automatic recognition, where—
      application of provisions, 1160
      employer's request to end
        arrangements—
        acceptance period: meaning,
          $1161n^{23}$
        generally, 1161

TRADE UNION
  RECOGNITION—*continued*
  derecognition—*continued*
    automatic recognition,
      where—*continued*
      employer's request to end
        arrangements—*continued*
        negotiation period: meaning,
          $1161n^8$
    ballot on—
      arrangements for, 1155
      conduct—
        combination of methods,
          $1155n^{14}$
        general requirements, 1155
        qualified independent person,
          by, $1155n^{10}$
      costs of holding, payment of, 1158
      employer's duties, 1157
      general requirements, 1155
      procedure following, 1159
      result, 1159
      unfair practices in relation to—
        CAC declaration as to, 1156
        examples, 1156
        outcome-specific offer, making,
          $1156n^5$
        prohibition on use of, 1156
        remedies, 1156
      workplace, at, arrangements
        where, $1155n^{14}$
    employer's request to end bargaining
      arrangements—
      ACAS, involvement in
        negotiations, 1152
      agreement to end arrangements,
        1152
      application of provisions, 1151
      generally, 1151
      negotiations, 1152
      secret ballot, application to hold,
        1153
      validity of request, 1151
    fewer than 21 workers, employer
      with—
      admissibility of application, 1150
      average number of workers,
        determining, $1150n^{11}$
      CAC's response to notice, 1150
      notice for bargaining arrangements
        to cease, 1150
      validation period: meaning,
        $1150n^{14}$
    unfair practices, Secretary of State's
      power to prohibit, 1174

References are to paragraph numbers; superior figures refer to notes

TRAINING
  meaning, 634n[9]
  allowances etc, payment of, 637
  careers service. *See* CAREERS SERVICES
  detriment, employee's right not to
    suffer, 618, 623
  expenses etc, payment of, 637
  financial provisions, 637
  information, disclosure of, 635
  national minimum wages, exclusion
    from, 194
  non-employed trainee, working time
    protection, 279
  participation in—
    appropriate arrangements before
      commencement of employment—
      failure, financial penalty, 645
      penalty notice. *See under* penalty
        notice *below*
      relevant contract of employment:
        meaning, 644n[2]
      requirement for, 644
    employer's duty to enable—
      arrangements subsequently
        notified, 650
      contravention of duties, 652
      enforcement notice. *See*
        enforcement notice *below*
      initial arrangements, 649
      penalty notice. *See under* penalty
        notice *below*
      persons reaching 18, extension for,
        651
    enforcement notice—
      meaning, 652
      contents, 652
      non-compliance with, financial
        penalty, 653
      service, 652
      withdrawal, 654
    unfair dismissal for, 789
  penalty notice—
    appropriate arrangements, as to
      failure to have in place—
      appeal against, 647
      contents, 645
      determination notice, 646
      notice of objection to, 646
      power to give, 645
      variation or withdrawal, 646, 648
    employer's duty to enable
      participation, breach of—
      appeal against, 656
      determination notice, 655
      notice of objection to, 655

TRAINING—*continued*
  penalty notice—*continued*
    employer's duty to enable
      participation, breach
      of—*continued*
      withdrawal or variation of notice,
        655, 657
    refund of allowance, where contract
      terminated, 15
    Secretary of State—
      disabled persons, duties in connection
        with, 634n[7]
      expenses incurred by, payment of,
        637
      functions and powers, 634
      information, disclosure of, 635
      payments by—
        allowances, expenses etc, 637
        benefits, of, 637
        facility providers etc, to, 634n[12, 13]
    skills programme in England, worker's
      exclusion from national minimum
      wage, 195
    status of trainees etc, 636
    time off work to make arrangements
      for. *See* TIME OFF WORK (training,
      to make arrangements for)

TRAINING COMMISSION
  dissolution, 633
  transfer of property, rights and liabilities
    to Secretary of State, 633

TRANSFER OF UNDERTAKING
  Acquired Rights Directive,
    implementation, 136
  changes in the workforce: meaning,
    139n[20]
  collective agreement, effect on, 139,
    1175n[7]
  common sense approach, 137n[7]
  consultation—
    appropriate representatives—
      meaning, 1196
      duty to consult, 141, 1198
      election of, 1196
      requirements, restriction on
        contracting out of, 1196
    default provisions, 1199
    duty of, 141, 1198
    failure to consult, remedies, 1200
    special circumstances defence, 1199
  contract of employment, effect on—
    collective agreement provisions, 139
    employee's objection to transfer, 139
    employee's rights before and after
      transfer, 141
    generally, 139

References are to paragraph numbers; superior figures refer to notes

TRANSFER OF
  UNDERTAKING—*continued*
contract of employment, effect
  on—*continued*
  notification of employee liability
    information, 140
  pension rights, 141n21
  permitted variations, 139
  relevant transfer: meaning, 137
  substantial change causing material
    detriment, 141n12
  tort, employer's duty in, 141n28
debts, transfer of, 139n10
employee liability information—
  meaning, 140n3
  data protection guidance, 140n5
  duty to notify, 140
  remedy for failure to notify, 140
employees' representative—
  detriment, right not to suffer, 1208
  duty to consult with. *See* consultation
    above
  employment protection generally,
    1207
  time off work, 1209
employees' rights before and after
  transfer, 141
information, duty to provide—
  agency workers, suitable information
    relating to use of, 1197n9
  appropriate representatives—
    meaning, 1196
    duty to inform, 141, 1197
    election of, 1196
    requirements, restriction on
      contracting out of, 1196
  default provisions, 1199
  failure to inform, remedies, 1200
  generally, 141
  manner of delivery, 1197n8
  measures to be taken, as to, 1197n6
  special circumstances defence, 1199
interim relief order, non-transfer of,
  139n10
liabilities, transfer of, 139n10
material detriment, employee suffering,
  141n12
multi-factorial test, application of,
  137n7
objection to transfer, 139
occupational pension scheme, effect on,
  141n21
regulations, application of, 137
relevant insolvency proceedings—
  meaning, 138n3

TRANSFER OF
  UNDERTAKING—*continued*
relevant insolvency
  proceedings—*continued*
  appropriate representatives: meaning,
    138n13
  assigned employees: meaning, 138n13
  permitted variation to contract,
    138n13
  relevant employee: meaning, 138n5
  transferor subject to, 138
relevant transfers under regulations,
  137
restraint clause, attempt to add, 139n10
service provision change, 137n8
statutory protection, 632
substantial change causing material
  detriment, 141n12
tort, employer's duty in, 141n28
unfair dismissal on, 803

TRUSTEE
  employee's act, liability for, 62

UNFAIR DISMISSAL
  agency worker, 103
  arbitration scheme to resolve cases,
    824, 1220
  burden of proof, 769
  capability or qualifications, dismissal on
    grounds of—
    capability: meaning, 773
    general, 773
    ill health, for. *See* ill health, for *below*
    procedural fairness, need for, 774
    qualifications: meaning, 773
  changing business needs, whether
    justifying dismissal, 802
  compensation for—
    components of award, 814
    basic award—
      calculation, 815
      minimum amounts, 816
      reduction in amount, 817
    compensatory award—
      amounts earned elsewhere,
        non-deductibility, 819n5
      calculation, 818
      career loss, complainant suffering,
        819n9
      heads of compensation, 819
      Ogden Tables, use of, 819n8
      pay: meaning, 819n3
      social security benefits not
        recoverable by state, 819n4
    contributory fault, reduction for, 821
    ex gratia payments, 823
    generally, 814

WORKING TIME—*continued*
  exclusions—*continued*
    force majeure, and young worker,
      309
    generally, 297
    mobile worker, 305
    offshore work, employment in, 308
    seafarers, 297
    shift workers, 302
    special cases, 301
    specific exclusions, 298
    unmeasured working time, 300
    workforce agreement, provided for
      by, 303
    young workers, 309, 310
  improvement notice—
    meaning, 314
    appeal against, 316
    contents, 314
    directions in, 314
    power to serve, 314
    withdrawal, 314
  information and advice, publication,
    269
  inspector—
    appointment, 312
    claim against, 312
    improvement notice. *See* improvement
      notice *above*
    indemnification, 312
    information obtained by, restriction
      on disclosure, 313
    legal professional privilege, and, 312
    powers, 312
  maximum weekly—
    agreement to exclude, 283
    compliance with limit on, 280
    determining, 280
    excluded days: meaning, $280n^7$
    records, need to keep, 287
    worker living on site, $280n^4$
    young worker, 281
  mediation—
    meaning, $319n^{25}$
    end of, $319n^{29}$
    mediator: meaning, $319n^{26}$
    start of, $319n^{26}$
  mobile worker—
    meaning, $267n^{23}$, $305n^1$
    exclusion of provisions, 305
  night worker—
    meaning, $267n^{13}$, $284n^1$
    adult worker: meaning, $285n^2$
    day work, transfer to, 285
    health assessment, 285
    length of night work, 284

WORKING TIME—*continued*
  night worker—*continued*
    records, need to keep, 287
    rest periods, $284n^4$
    special hazards etc, having, $284n^7$
    young worker, 285
  offences—
    act or default of another party, due
      to, 317
    body corporate, by, 317
    failure to comply with requirements,
      317
    inspector's powers, hindering, 317
    remedying cause of, 318
  offshore work—
    meaning, $267n^{10}$, $301n^2$
    exclusion of provisions, 301, 308
  pattern of work, risks presented by, 286
  prohibition notice—
    meaning, 315
    appeal against, 316
    contents, 315
    directions in, 315
    power to serve, 315
    withdrawal, 315
  records, need to keep, 287
  regulations—
    contracting out, restrictions on, 282
    generally, 268
    information and advice as to,
      publication of, 269
  rest breaks, 290, 296
  rest period—
    meaning, $267n^5$
    daily, 288
    entitlement under other provisions,
      296
    night work, $284n^4$
    pattern of work determining need
      for, 286
    shift worker, 302
    weekly, 289
  seafarers, exclusion of provisions, 297
  shift worker—
    meaning, $302n^1$
    exclusion of provisions, 302
    rest periods, 302
    shift work: meaning, $267n^4$
  transport sector, exclusion of
    provisions, 298
  unfair dismissal in cases of, 788
  unmeasured, exclusion of provisions,
    300
  workers entitled to protection—
    meaning, 271
    agency worker, 273

Words and Phrases

Words in parentheses indicate the context in which the word or phrase is used

References are to paragraph numbers; superior figures refer to notes

References are to paragraph numbers; superior figures refer to notes

References are to paragraph numbers; superior figures refer to notes